University Casebook Series

March, 1991

ACCOUNTING AND THE LAW, Fourth Edition (1978), with Problems Pamphlet (Successor to Dohr, Phillips, Thompson & Warren)

George C. Thompson, Professor, Columbia University Graduate School of Business.
Robert Whitman, Professor of Law, University of Connecticut.
Ellis L. Phillips, Jr., Member of the New York Bar.
William C. Warren, Professor of Law Emeritus, Columbia University.

ACCOUNTING FOR LAWYERS, MATERIALS ON (1980)

David R. Herwitz, Professor of Law, Harvard University.

ADMINISTRATIVE LAW, Eighth Edition (1987), with 1989 Case Supplement and 1983 Problems Supplement (Supplement edited in association with Paul R. Verkuil, Dean and Professor of Law, Tulane University)

Walter Gellhorn, University Professor Emeritus, Columbia University.
Clark Byse, Professor of Law, Harvard University.
Peter L. Strauss, Professor of Law, Columbia University.
Todd D. Rakoff, Professor of Law, Harvard University.
Roy A. Schotland, Professor of Law, Georgetown University.

ADMIRALTY, Third Edition (1987), with Statute and Rule Supplement

Jo Desha Lucas, Professor of Law, University of Chicago.

ADVOCACY, see also Lawyering Process

AGENCY, see also Enterprise Organization

AGENCY—PARTNERSHIPS, Fourth Edition (1987)

Abridgement from Conard, Knauss & Siegel's Enterprise Organization, Fourth Edition.

AGENCY AND PARTNERSHIPS (1987)

Melvin A. Eisenberg, Professor of Law, University of California, Berkeley.

ANTITRUST: FREE ENTERPRISE AND ECONOMIC ORGANIZATION, Sixth Edition (1983), with 1983 Problems in Antitrust Supplement and 1990 Case Supplement

Louis B. Schwartz, Professor of Law, University of Pennsylvania.
John J. Flynn, Professor of Law, University of Utah.
Harry First, Professor of Law, New York University.

BANKRUPTCY, Second Edition (1989), with 1990 Case Supplement

Robert L. Jordan, Professor of Law, University of California, Los Angeles.
William D. Warren, Professor of Law, University of California, Los Angeles.

BANKRUPTCY AND DEBTOR–CREDITOR LAW, Second Edition (1988)

Theodore Eisenberg, Professor of Law, Cornell University.

BUSINESS CRIME (1990)

> Harry First, Professor of Law, New York University.

BUSINESS ORGANIZATION, see also Enterprise Organization

BUSINESS PLANNING, Temporary Second Edition (1984)

> David R. Herwitz, Professor of Law, Harvard University.

BUSINESS TORTS (1972)

> Milton Handler, Professor of Law Emeritus, Columbia University.

CHILDREN IN THE LEGAL SYSTEM (1983) with 1990 Supplement (Supplement edited in association with Elizabeth S. Scott, Professor of Law, University of Virginia)

> Walter Wadlington, Professor of Law, University of Virginia.
> Charles H. Whitebread, Professor of Law, University of Southern California.
> Samuel Davis, Professor of Law, University of Georgia.

CIVIL PROCEDURE, see Procedure

CIVIL RIGHTS ACTIONS (1988), with 1990 Supplement

> Peter W. Low, Professor of Law, University of Virginia.
> John C. Jeffries, Jr., Professor of Law, University of Virginia.

CLINIC, see also Lawyering Process

COMMERCIAL AND DEBTOR–CREDITOR LAW: SELECTED STATUTES, 1990 EDITION

COMMERCIAL LAW, Second Edition (1987)

> Robert L. Jordan, Professor of Law, University of California, Los Angeles.
> William D. Warren, Professor of Law, University of California, Los Angeles.

COMMERCIAL LAW, Fourth Edition (1985), with 1990 Case Supplement

> E. Allan Farnsworth, Professor of Law, Columbia University.
> John Honnold, Professor of Law, University of Pennsylvania.

COMMERCIAL PAPER, Third Edition (1984), with 1990 Case Supplement

> E. Allan Farnsworth, Professor of Law, Columbia University.

COMMERCIAL PAPER, Second Edition (1987) (Reprinted from COMMERCIAL LAW, Second Edition (1987))

> Robert L. Jordan, Professor of Law, University of California, Los Angeles.
> William D. Warren, Professor of Law, University of California, Los Angeles.

COMMERCIAL PAPER AND BANK DEPOSITS AND COLLECTIONS (1967), with Statutory Supplement

> William D. Hawkland, Professor of Law, University of Illinois.

COMMERCIAL TRANSACTIONS—Principles and Policies, Second Edition (1991)

> Alan Schwartz, Professor of Law, Yale University.
> Robert E. Scott, Professor of Law, University of Virginia.

COMPARATIVE LAW, Fifth Edition (1988)

> Rudolf B. Schlesinger, Professor of Law, Hastings College of the Law.
> Hans W. Baade, Professor of Law, University of Texas.
> Mirjan P. Damaska, Professor of Law, Yale Law School.
> Peter E. Herzog, Professor of Law, Syracuse University.

UNIVERSITY CASEBOOK SERIES—Continued

COMPETITIVE PROCESS, LEGAL REGULATION OF THE, Fourth Edition (1990), with 1989 Selected Statutes Supplement

Edmund W. Kitch, Professor of Law, University of Virginia.

Harvey S. Perlman, Dean of the Law School, University of Nebraska.

CONFLICT OF LAWS, Ninth Edition (1990)

Willis L. M. Reese, Professor of Law, Columbia University.

Maurice Rosenberg, Professor of Law, Columbia University.

Peter Hay, Professor of Law, University of Illinois.

CONSTITUTIONAL LAW, Eighth Edition (1989), with 1990 Case Supplement

Edward L. Barrett, Jr., Professor of Law, University of California, Davis.

William Cohen, Professor of Law, Stanford University.

Jonathan D. Varat, Professor of Law, University of California, Los Angeles.

CONSTITUTIONAL LAW, CIVIL LIBERTY AND INDIVIDUAL RIGHTS, Second Edition (1982), with 1989 Supplement

William Cohen, Professor of Law, Stanford University.

John Kaplan, Professor of Law, Stanford University.

CONSTITUTIONAL LAW, Eleventh Edition (1985), with 1990 Supplement (Supplement edited in association with Frederick F. Schauer, Professor, Harvard University)

Gerald Gunther, Professor of Law, Stanford University.

CONSTITUTIONAL LAW, INDIVIDUAL RIGHTS IN, Fourth Edition (1986), (Reprinted from CONSTITUTIONAL LAW, Eleventh Edition), with 1990 Supplement (Supplement edited in association with Frederick F. Schauer, Professor, Harvard University)

Gerald Gunther, Professor of Law, Stanford University.

CONSUMER TRANSACTIONS, Second Edition (1991), with Selected Statutes and Regulations Supplement

Michael M. Greenfield, Professor of Law, Washington University.

CONTRACT LAW AND ITS APPLICATION, Fourth Edition (1988)

Arthur Rosett, Professor of Law, University of California, Los Angeles.

CONTRACT LAW, STUDIES IN, Third Edition (1984)

Edward J. Murphy, Professor of Law, University of Notre Dame.

Richard E. Speidel, Professor of Law, Northwestern University.

CONTRACTS, Fifth Edition (1987)

John P. Dawson, late Professor of Law, Harvard University.

William Burnett Harvey, Professor of Law and Political Science, Boston University.

Stanley D. Henderson, Professor of Law, University of Virginia.

CONTRACTS, Fourth Edition (1988)

E. Allan Farnsworth, Professor of Law, Columbia University.

William F. Young, Professor of Law, Columbia University.

CONTRACTS, Selections on (statutory materials) (1988)

CONTRACTS, Second Edition (1978), with Statutory and Administrative Law Supplement (1978)

Ian R. Macneil, Professor of Law, Cornell University.

UNIVERSITY CASEBOOK SERIES—Continued

COPYRIGHT, PATENTS AND TRADEMARKS, see also Competitive Process; see also Selected Statutes and International Agreements

COPYRIGHT, PATENT, TRADEMARK AND RELATED STATE DOCTRINES, Third Edition (1990), with 1989 Selected Statutes Supplement and 1981 Problem Supplement

Paul Goldstein, Professor of Law, Stanford University.

COPYRIGHT, Unfair Competition, and Other Topics Bearing on the Protection of Literary, Musical, and Artistic Works, Fifth Edition (1990), with 1990 Statutory Supplement

Ralph S. Brown, Jr., Professor of Law, Yale University.
Robert C. Denicola, Professor of Law, University of Nebraska.

CORPORATE ACQUISITIONS, The Law and Finance of (1986), with 1990 Supplement

Ronald J. Gilson, Professor of Law, Stanford University.

CORPORATE FINANCE, Third Edition (1987)

Victor Brudney, Professor of Law, Harvard University.
Marvin A. Chirelstein, Professor of Law, Columbia University.

CORPORATION LAW, BASIC, Third Edition (1989), with Documentary Supplement

Detlev F. Vagts, Professor of Law, Harvard University.

CORPORATIONS, see also Enterprise Organization

CORPORATIONS, Sixth Edition—Concise (1988), with 1990 Case Supplement and 1990 Statutory Supplement

William L. Cary, late Professor of Law, Columbia University.
Melvin Aron Eisenberg, Professor of Law, University of California, Berkeley.

CORPORATIONS, Sixth Edition—Unabridged (1988), with 1990 Case Supplement and 1990 Statutory Supplement

William L. Cary, late Professor of Law, Columbia University.
Melvin Aron Eisenberg, Professor of Law, University of California, Berkeley.

CORPORATIONS AND BUSINESS ASSOCIATIONS—STATUTES, RULES, AND FORMS (1990)

CORRECTIONS, SEE SENTENCING

CREDITORS' RIGHTS, see also Debtor-Creditor Law

CRIMINAL JUSTICE ADMINISTRATION, Fourth Edition (1991)

Frank W. Miller, Professor of Law, Washington University.
Robert O. Dawson, Professor of Law, University of Texas.
George E. Dix, Professor of Law, University of Texas.
Raymond I. Parnas, Professor of Law, University of California, Davis.

CRIMINAL LAW, Fourth Edition (1987)

Fred E. Inbau, Professor of Law Emeritus, Northwestern University.
Andre A. Moenssens, Professor of Law, University of Richmond.
James R. Thompson, Professor of Law Emeritus, Northwestern University.

CRIMINAL LAW AND APPROACHES TO THE STUDY OF LAW, Second Edition (1991)

John M. Brumbaugh, Professor of Law, University of Maryland.

CRIMINAL LAW, Second Edition (1986)

Peter W. Low, Professor of Law, University of Virginia.
John C. Jeffries, Jr., Professor of Law, University of Virginia.
Richard C. Bonnie, Professor of Law, University of Virginia.

CRIMINAL LAW, Fourth Edition (1986)

Lloyd L. Weinreb, Professor of Law, Harvard University.

CRIMINAL LAW AND PROCEDURE, Seventh Edition (1989)

Ronald N. Boyce, Professor of Law, University of Utah.
Rollin M. Perkins, Professor of Law Emeritus, University of California, Hastings College of the Law.

CRIMINAL PROCEDURE, Third Edition (1987), with 1990 Supplement

James B. Haddad, Professor of Law, Northwestern University.
James B. Zagel, Chief, Criminal Justice Division, Office of Attorney General of Illinois.
Gary L. Starkman, Assistant U. S. Attorney, Northern District of Illinois.
William J. Bauer, Chief Judge of the U.S. Court of Appeals, Seventh Circuit.

CRIMINAL PROCESS, Fourth Edition (1987), with 1990 Supplement

Lloyd L. Weinreb, Professor of Law, Harvard University.

DAMAGES, Second Edition (1952)

Charles T. McCormick, late Professor of Law, University of Texas.
William F. Fritz, late Professor of Law, University of Texas.

DECEDENTS' ESTATES AND TRUSTS, Seventh Edition (1988)

John Ritchie, late Professor of Law, University of Virginia.
Neill H. Alford, Jr., Professor of Law, University of Virginia.
Richard W. Effland, late Professor of Law, Arizona State University.

DISPUTE RESOLUTION, Processes of (1989)

John S. Murray, President and Executive Director of The Conflict Clinic, Inc., George Mason University.
Alan Scott Rau, Professor of Law, University of Texas.
Edward F. Sherman, Professor of Law, University of Texas.

DOMESTIC RELATIONS, see also Family Law

DOMESTIC RELATIONS, Second Edition (1990)

Walter Wadlington, Professor of Law, University of Virginia.

EMPLOYMENT DISCRIMINATION, Second Edition (1987), with 1990 Supplement

Joel W. Friedman, Professor of Law, Tulane University.
George M. Strickler, Professor of Law, Tulane University.

EMPLOYMENT LAW, Second Edition (1991), with Statutory Supplement

Mark A. Rothstein, Professor of Law, University of Houston.
Andria S. Knapp, Visiting Professor of Law, Golden Gate University.
Lance Liebman, Professor of Law, Harvard University.

ENERGY LAW (1983) with 1986 Case Supplement

Donald N. Zillman, Professor of Law, University of Utah.
Laurence Lattman, Dean of Mines and Engineering, University of Utah.

UNIVERSITY CASEBOOK SERIES—Continued

ENTERPRISE ORGANIZATION, Fourth Edition (1987), with 1987 Corporation and Partnership Statutes, Rules and Forms Supplement

Alfred F. Conard, Professor of Law, University of Michigan.
Robert L. Knauss, Dean of the Law School, University of Houston.
Stanley Siegel, Professor of Law, University of California, Los Angeles.

ENVIRONMENTAL POLICY LAW 1985 Edition, with 1985 Problems Supplement (Supplement in association with Ronald H. Rosenberg, Professor of Law, College of William and Mary)

Thomas J. Schoenbaum, Professor of Law, University of Georgia.

EQUITY, see also Remedies

EQUITY, RESTITUTION AND DAMAGES, Second Edition (1974)

Robert Childres, late Professor of Law, Northwestern University.
William F. Johnson, Jr., Professor of Law, New York University.

ESTATE PLANNING, Second Edition (1982), with 1985 Case, Text and Documentary Supplement

David Westfall, Professor of Law, Harvard University.

ETHICS, see Legal Profession, Professional Responsibility, and Social Responsibilities

ETHICS OF LAWYERING, THE LAW AND (1990)

Geoffrey C. Hazard, Jr., Professor of Law, Yale University.
Susan P. Koniak, Professor of Law, University of Pittsburgh.

ETHICS AND PROFESSIONAL RESPONSIBILITY (1981) (Reprinted from THE LAWYERING PROCESS)

Gary Bellow, Professor of Law, Harvard University.
Bea Moulton, Legal Services Corporation.

EVIDENCE, Sixth Edition (1988 Reprint), with 1990 Case Supplement (Supplement edited in association with Roger C. Park, Professor of Law, University of Minnesota)

John Kaplan, Professor of Law, Stanford University.
Jon R. Waltz, Professor of Law, Northwestern University.

EVIDENCE, Eighth Edition (1988), with Rules, Statute and Case Supplement (1990)

Jack B. Weinstein, Chief Judge, United States District Court.
John H. Mansfield, Professor of Law, Harvard University.
Norman Abrams, Professor of Law, University of California, Los Angeles.
Margaret Berger, Professor of Law, Brooklyn Law School.

FAMILY LAW, see also Domestic Relations

FAMILY LAW Second Edition (1985), with 1991 Supplement

Judith C. Areen, Professor of Law, Georgetown University.

FAMILY LAW AND CHILDREN IN THE LEGAL SYSTEM, STATUTORY MATERIALS (1981)

Walter Wadlington, Professor of Law, University of Virginia.

FEDERAL COURTS, Eighth Edition (1988), with 1990 Supplement

Charles T. McCormick, late Professor of Law, University of Texas.
James H. Chadbourn, late Professor of Law, Harvard University.
Charles Alan Wright, Professor of Law, University of Texas, Austin.

UNIVERSITY CASEBOOK SERIES—Continued

FEDERAL COURTS AND THE FEDERAL SYSTEM, Hart and Wechsler's Third Edition (1988), with 1989 Case Supplement, and the Judicial Code and Rules of Procedure in the Federal Courts (1989)

Paul M. Bator, Professor of Law, University of Chicago.
Daniel J. Meltzer, Professor of Law, Harvard University.
Paul J. Mishkin, Professor of Law, University of California, Berkeley.
David L. Shapiro, Professor of Law, Harvard University.

FEDERAL COURTS AND THE LAW OF FEDERAL–STATE RELATIONS, Second Edition (1989), with 1990 Supplement

Peter W. Low, Professor of Law, University of Virginia.
John C. Jeffries, Jr., Professor of Law, University of Virginia.

FEDERAL PUBLIC LAND AND RESOURCES LAW, Second Edition (1987), with 1990 Case Supplement and 1990 Statutory Supplement

George C. Coggins, Professor of Law, University of Kansas.
Charles F. Wilkinson, Professor of Law, University of Oregon.

FEDERAL RULES OF CIVIL PROCEDURE and Selected Other Procedural Provisions, 1990 Edition

FEDERAL TAXATION, see Taxation

FOOD AND DRUG LAW (1980), with Statutory Supplement

Richard A. Merrill, Dean of the School of Law, University of Virginia.
Peter Barton Hutt, Esq.

FUTURE INTERESTS (1970)

Howard R. Williams, Professor of Law, Stanford University.

FUTURE INTERESTS AND ESTATE PLANNING (1961), with 1962 Supplement

W. Barton Leach, late Professor of Law, Harvard University.
James K. Logan, formerly Dean of the Law School, University of Kansas.

GOVERNMENT CONTRACTS, FEDERAL, Successor Edition (1985), with 1989 Supplement

John W. Whelan, Professor of Law, Hastings College of the Law.

GOVERNMENT REGULATION: FREE ENTERPRISE AND ECONOMIC ORGANIZATION, Sixth Edition (1985)

Louis B. Schwartz, Professor of Law, Hastings College of the Law.
John J. Flynn, Professor of Law, University of Utah.
Harry First, Professor of Law, New York University.

HEALTH CARE LAW AND POLICY (1988)

Clark C. Havighurst, Professor of Law, Duke University.

HINCKLEY, JOHN W., JR., TRIAL OF: A Case Study of the Insanity Defense (1986)

Peter W. Low, Professor of Law, University of Virginia.
John C. Jeffries, Jr., Professor of Law, University of Virginia.
Richard C. Bonnie, Professor of Law, University of Virginia.

INJUNCTIONS, Second Edition (1984)

Owen M. Fiss, Professor of Law, Yale University.
Doug Rendleman, Professor of Law, College of William and Mary.

INSTITUTIONAL INVESTORS, (1978)

David L. Ratner, Professor of Law, Cornell University.

UNIVERSITY CASEBOOK SERIES—Continued

INSURANCE, Second Edition (1985)

William F. Young, Professor of Law, Columbia University.
Eric M. Holmes, Professor of Law, University of Georgia.

INSURANCE LAW AND REGULATION (1990)

Kenneth S. Abraham, University of Virginia.

INTERNATIONAL LAW, see also Transnational Legal Problems, Transnational Business Problems, and United Nations Law

INTERNATIONAL LAW IN CONTEMPORARY PERSPECTIVE (1981), with Essay Supplement

Myres S. McDougal, Professor of Law, Yale University.
W. Michael Reisman, Professor of Law, Yale University.

INTERNATIONAL LEGAL SYSTEM, Third Edition (1988), with Documentary Supplement

Joseph Modeste Sweeney, Professor of Law, University of California, Hastings.
Covey T. Oliver, Professor of Law, University of Pennsylvania.
Noyes E. Leech, Professor of Law Emeritus, University of Pennsylvania.

INTRODUCTION TO LAW, see also Legal Method, On Law in Courts, and Dynamics of American Law

INTRODUCTION TO THE STUDY OF LAW (1970)

E. Wayne Thode, late Professor of Law, University of Utah.
Leon Lebowitz, Professor of Law, University of Texas.
Lester J. Mazor, Professor of Law, University of Utah.

JUDICIAL CODE and Rules of Procedure in the Federal Courts, Students' Edition, 1989 Revision

Daniel J. Meltzer, Professor of Law, Harvard University.
David L. Shapiro, Professor of Law, Harvard University.

JURISPRUDENCE (Temporary Edition Hardbound) (1949)

Lon L. Fuller, late Professor of Law, Harvard University.

JUVENILE, see also Children

JUVENILE JUSTICE PROCESS, Third Edition (1985)

Frank W. Miller, Professor of Law, Washington University.
Robert O. Dawson, Professor of Law, University of Texas.
George E. Dix, Professor of Law, University of Texas.
Raymond I. Parnas, Professor of Law, University of California, Davis.

LABOR LAW, Eleventh Edition (1991), with 1991 Statutory Supplement

Archibald Cox, Professor of Law, Harvard University.
Derek C. Bok, President, Harvard University.
Robert A. Gorman, Professor of Law, University of Pennsylvania.
Matthew W. Finkin, Professor of Law, University of Illinois.

LABOR LAW, Second Edition (1982), with Statutory Supplement

Clyde W. Summers, Professor of Law, University of Pennsylvania.
Harry H. Wellington, Dean of the Law School, Yale University.
Alan Hyde, Professor of Law, Rutgers University.

LAND FINANCING, Third Edition (1985)

The late Norman Penney, Professor of Law, Cornell University.
Richard F. Broude, Member of the California Bar.
Roger Cunningham, Professor of Law, University of Michigan.

LAW AND MEDICINE (1980)

Walter Wadlington, Professor of Law and Professor of Legal Medicine, University of Virginia.
Jon R. Waltz, Professor of Law, Northwestern University.
Roger B. Dworkin, Professor of Law, Indiana University, and Professor of Biomedical History, University of Washington.

LAW, LANGUAGE AND ETHICS (1972)

William R. Bishin, Professor of Law, University of Southern California.
Christopher D. Stone, Professor of Law, University of Southern California.

LAW, SCIENCE AND MEDICINE (1984), with 1989 Supplement

Judith C. Areen, Professor of Law, Georgetown University.
Patricia A. King, Professor of Law, Georgetown University.
Steven P. Goldberg, Professor of Law, Georgetown University.
Alexander M. Capron, Professor of Law, University of Southern California.

LAWYERING PROCESS (1978), with Civil Problem Supplement and Criminal Problem Supplement

Gary Bellow, Professor of Law, Harvard University.
Bea Moulton, Professor of Law, Arizona State University.

LEGAL METHOD (1980)

Harry W. Jones, Professor of Law Emeritus, Columbia University.
John M. Kernochan, Professor of Law, Columbia University.
Arthur W. Murphy, Professor of Law, Columbia University.

LEGAL METHODS (1969)

Robert N. Covington, Professor of Law, Vanderbilt University.
E. Blythe Stason, late Professor of Law, Vanderbilt University.
John W. Wade, Professor of Law, Vanderbilt University.
Elliott E. Cheatham, late Professor of Law, Vanderbilt University.
Theodore A. Smedley, Professor of Law, Vanderbilt University.

LEGAL PROFESSION, THE, Responsibility and Regulation, Second Edition (1988)

Geoffrey C. Hazard, Jr., Professor of Law, Yale University.
Deborah L. Rhode, Professor of Law, Stanford University.

LEGISLATION, Fourth Edition (1982) (by Fordham)

Horace E. Read, late Vice President, Dalhousie University.
John W. MacDonald, Professor of Law Emeritus, Cornell Law School.
Jefferson B. Fordham, Professor of Law, University of Utah.
William J. Pierce, Professor of Law, University of Michigan.

LEGISLATIVE AND ADMINISTRATIVE PROCESSES, Second Edition (1981)

Hans A. Linde, Judge, Supreme Court of Oregon.
George Bunn, Professor of Law, University of Wisconsin.
Fredericka Paff, Professor of Law, University of Wisconsin.
W. Lawrence Church, Professor of Law, University of Wisconsin.

LOCAL GOVERNMENT LAW, Second Revised Edition (1986)

Jefferson B. Fordham, Professor of Law, University of Utah.

MASS MEDIA LAW, Fourth Edition (1990)

Marc A. Franklin, Professor of Law, Stanford University.
David A. Anderson, Professor of Law, University of Texas.

MUNICIPAL CORPORATIONS, see Local Government Law

NEGOTIABLE INSTRUMENTS, see Commercial Paper

NEGOTIATION (1981) (Reprinted from THE LAWYERING PROCESS)

Gary Bellow, Professor of Law, Harvard Law School.
Bea Moulton, Legal Services Corporation.

NEW YORK PRACTICE, Fourth Edition (1978)

Herbert Peterfreund, Professor of Law, New York University.
Joseph M. McLaughlin, Dean of the Law School, Fordham University.

OIL AND GAS, Fifth Edition (1987)

Howard R. Williams, Professor of Law, Stanford University.
Richard C. Maxwell, Professor of Law, University of California, Los Angeles.
Charles J. Meyers, late Dean of the Law School, Stanford University.
Stephen F. Williams, Judge of the United States Court of Appeals.

ON LAW IN COURTS (1965)

Paul J. Mishkin, Professor of Law, University of California, Berkeley.
Clarence Morris, Professor of Law Emeritus, University of Pennsylvania.

PENSION AND EMPLOYEE BENEFIT LAW (1990)

John H. Langbein, Professor of Law, University of Chicago.
Bruce A. Wolk, Professor of Law, University of California, Davis.

PLEADING AND PROCEDURE, see Procedure, Civil

POLICE FUNCTION, Fifth Edition (1991)

Reprint of Chapters 1–10 of Miller, Dawson, Dix and Parnas's CRIMINAL JUSTICE ADMINISTRATION, Fourth Edition.

PREPARING AND PRESENTING THE CASE (1981) (Reprinted from THE LAW-YERING PROCESS)

Gary Bellow, Professor of Law, Harvard Law School.
Bea Moulton, Legal Services Corporation.

PROCEDURE (1988), with Procedure Supplement (1989)

Robert M. Cover, late Professor of Law, Yale Law School.
Owen M. Fiss, Professor of Law, Yale Law School.
Judith Resnik, Professor of Law, University of Southern California Law Center.

PROCEDURE—CIVIL PROCEDURE, Second Edition (1974), with 1979 Supplement

The late James H. Chadbourn, Professor of Law, Harvard University.
A. Leo Levin, Professor of Law, University of Pennsylvania.
Philip Shuchman, Professor of Law, Cornell University.

PROCEDURE—CIVIL PROCEDURE, Sixth Edition (1990)

Richard H. Field, late Professor of Law, Harvard University.
Benjamin Kaplan, Professor of Law Emeritus, Harvard University.
Kevin M. Clermont, Professor of Law, Cornell University.

UNIVERSITY CASEBOOK SERIES—Continued

PROCEDURE—CIVIL PROCEDURE, Fifth Edition (1990)

Maurice Rosenberg, Professor of Law, Columbia University.
Hans Smit, Professor of Law, Columbia University.
Rochelle C. Dreyfuss, Professor of Law, New York University.

PROCEDURE—PLEADING AND PROCEDURE: State and Federal, Sixth Edition (1989), with 1990 Case Supplement

David W. Louisell, late Professor of Law, University of California, Berkeley.
Geoffrey C. Hazard, Jr., Professor of Law, Yale University.
Colin C. Tait, Professor of Law, University of Connecticut.

PROCEDURE—FEDERAL RULES OF CIVIL PROCEDURE, 1990 Edition

PRODUCTS LIABILITY AND SAFETY, Second Edition, (1989), with 1989 Statutory Supplement

W. Page Keeton, Professor of Law, University of Texas.
David G. Owen, Professor of Law, University of South Carolina.
John E. Montgomery, Professor of Law, University of South Carolina.
Michael D. Green, Professor of Law, University of Iowa

PROFESSIONAL RESPONSIBILITY, Fifth Edition (1991), with 1991 Selected Standards on Professional Responsibility Supplement

Thomas D. Morgan, Professor of Law, George Washington University.
Ronald D. Rotunda, Professor of Law, University of Illinois.

PROPERTY, Sixth Edition (1990)

John E. Cribbet, Professor of Law, University of Illinois.
Corwin W. Johnson, Professor of Law, University of Texas.
Roger W. Findley, Professor of Law, University of Illinois.
Ernest E. Smith, Professor of Law, University of Texas.

PROPERTY—PERSONAL (1953)

S. Kenneth Skolfield, late Professor of Law Emeritus, Boston University.

PROPERTY—PERSONAL, Third Edition (1954)

Everett Fraser, late Dean of the Law School Emeritus, University of Minnesota.
Third Edition by Charles W. Taintor, late Professor of Law, University of Pittsburgh.

PROPERTY—INTRODUCTION, TO REAL PROPERTY, Third Edition (1954)

Everett Fraser, late Dean of the Law School Emeritus, University of Minnesota.

PROPERTY—FUNDAMENTALS OF MODERN REAL PROPERTY, Second Edition (1982), with 1985 Supplement

Edward H. Rabin, Professor of Law, University of California, Davis.

PROPERTY, REAL (1984), with 1988 Supplement

Paul Goldstein, Professor of Law, Stanford University.

PROSECUTION AND ADJUDICATION, Fourth Edition (1991)

Reprint of Chapters 11–26 of Miller, Dawson, Dix and Parnas's CRIMINAL JUSTICE ADMINISTRATION, Fourth Edition.

PSYCHIATRY AND LAW, see Mental Health, see also Hinckley, Trial of

PUBLIC UTILITY LAW, see Free Enterprise, also Regulated Industries

UNIVERSITY CASEBOOK SERIES—Continued

REAL ESTATE PLANNING, Third Edition (1989), with Revised Problem and Statutory Supplement (1991)

Norton L. Steuben, Professor of Law, University of Colorado.

REAL ESTATE TRANSACTIONS, Revised Second Edition (1988), with Statute, Form and Problem Supplement (1988)

Paul Goldstein, Professor of Law, Stanford University.

RECEIVERSHIP AND CORPORATE REORGANIZATION, see Creditors' Rights

REGULATED INDUSTRIES, Second Edition, (1976)

William K. Jones, Professor of Law, Columbia University.

REMEDIES, Second Edition (1987)

Edward D. Re, Chief Judge, U. S. Court of International Trade.

REMEDIES, (1989)

Elaine W. Shoben, Professor of Law, University of Illinois.
Wm. Murray Tabb, Professor of Law, Baylor University.

SALES, Second Edition (1986)

Marion W. Benfield, Jr., Professor of Law, University of Illinois.
William D. Hawkland, Chancellor, Louisiana State Law Center.

SALES AND SALES FINANCING, Fifth Edition (1984)

John Honnold, Professor of Law, University of Pennsylvania.

SALES LAW AND THE CONTRACTING PROCESS, Second Edition (1991)

(Reprinted from Commercial Transactions, Second Edition (1991)
Alan Schwartz, Professor of Law, Yale University.
Robert E. Scott, Professor of Law, University of Virginia.

SECURED TRANSACTIONS IN PERSONAL PROPERTY, Second Edition (1987) (Reprinted from COMMERCIAL LAW, Second Edition (1987))

Robert L. Jordan, Professor of Law, University of California, Los Angeles.
William D. Warren, Professor of Law, University of California, Los Angeles.

SECURITIES REGULATION, Sixth Edition (1987), with 1990 Selected Statutes, Rules and Forms Supplement and 1990 Cases and Releases Supplement

Richard W. Jennings, Professor of Law, University of California, Berkeley.
Harold Marsh, Jr., Member of California Bar.

SECURITIES REGULATION, Second Edition (1988), with Statute, Rule and Form Supplement (1988)

Larry D. Soderquist, Professor of Law, Vanderbilt University.

SECURITY INTERESTS IN PERSONAL PROPERTY, Second Edition (1987)

Douglas G. Baird, Professor of Law, University of Chicago.
Thomas H. Jackson, Dean of the Law School, University of Virginia.

SECURITY INTERESTS IN PERSONAL PROPERTY (1985) (Reprinted from Sales and Sales Financing, Fifth Edition)

John Honnold, Professor of Law, University of Pennsylvania.

SELECTED STANDARDS ON PROFESSIONAL RESPONSIBILITY, 1991 Edition

UNIVERSITY CASEBOOK SERIES—Continued

SELECTED STATUTES AND INTERNATIONAL AGREEMENTS ON UNFAIR COMPETITION, TRADEMARK, COPYRIGHT AND PATENT, 1989 Edition

SELECTED STATUTES ON TRUSTS AND ESTATES, 1991 Edition

SOCIAL RESPONSIBILITIES OF LAWYERS, Case Studies (1988)

Philip B. Heymann, Professor of Law, Harvard University.
Lance Liebman, Professor of Law, Harvard University.

SOCIAL SCIENCE IN LAW, Second Edition (1990)

John Monahan, Professor of Law, University of Virginia.
Laurens Walker, Professor of Law, University of Virginia.

TAXATION, FEDERAL INCOME (1989)

Stephen B. Cohen, Professor of Law, Georgetown University

TAXATION, FEDERAL INCOME, Second Edition (1988), with 1990 Supplement (Supplement edited in association with Deborah H. Schenk, Professor of Law, New York University)

Michael J. Graetz, Professor of Law, Yale University.

TAXATION, FEDERAL INCOME, Sixth Edition (1987)

James J. Freeland, Professor of Law, University of Florida.
Stephen A. Lind, Professor of Law, University of Florida and University of California, Hastings.
Richard B. Stephens, late Professor of Law Emeritus, University of Florida.

TAXATION, FEDERAL INCOME, Successor Edition (1986), with 1990 Legislative Supplement

Stanley S. Surrey, late Professor of Law, Harvard University.
Paul R. McDaniel, Professor of Law, Boston College.
Hugh J. Ault, Professor of Law, Boston College.
Stanley A. Koppelman, Professor of Law, Boston University.

TAXATION, FEDERAL INCOME, OF BUSINESS ORGANIZATIONS (1991)

Paul R. McDaniel, Professor of Law, Boston College.
Hugh J. Ault, Professor of Law, Boston College.
Martin J. McMahon, Jr., Professor of Law, University of Kentucky.
Daniel L. Simmons, Professor of Law, University of California, Davis.

TAXATION, FEDERAL INCOME, OF PARTNERSHIPS AND S CORPORATIONS (1991)

Paul R. McDaniel, Professor of Law, Boston College.
Hugh J. Ault, Professor of Law, Boston College.
Martin J. McMahon, Jr., Professor of Law, University of Kentucky.
Daniel L. Simmons, Professor of Law, University of California, Davis.

TAXATION, FEDERAL INCOME, OIL AND GAS, NATURAL RESOURCES TRANSACTIONS (1990)

Peter C. Maxfield, Professor of Law, University of Wyoming.
James L. Houghton, CPA, Partner, Ernst and Young.
James R. Gaar, CPA, Partner, Ernst and Young.

TAXATION, FEDERAL WEALTH TRANSFER, Successor Edition (1987)

Stanley S. Surrey, late Professor of Law, Harvard University.
Paul R. McDaniel, Professor of Law, Boston College.
Harry L. Gutman, Professor of Law, University of Pennsylvania.

TAXATION, FUNDAMENTALS OF CORPORATE, Second Edition (1987), with 1989 Supplement

Stephen A. Lind, Professor of Law, University of Florida and University of California, Hastings.
Stephen Schwarz, Professor of Law, University of California, Hastings.
Daniel J. Lathrope, Professor of Law, University of California, Hastings.
Joshua Rosenberg, Professor of Law, University of San Francisco.

TAXATION, FUNDAMENTALS OF PARTNERSHIP, Second Edition (1988)

Stephen A. Lind, Professor of Law, University of Florida and University of California, Hastings.
Stephen Schwarz, Professor of Law, University of California, Hastings.
Daniel J. Lathrope, Professor of Law, University of California, Hastings.
Joshua Rosenberg, Professor of Law, University of San Francisco.

TAXATION, PROBLEMS IN THE FEDERAL INCOME TAXATION OF PARTNERSHIPS AND CORPORATIONS, Second Edition (1986)

Norton L. Steuben, Professor of Law, University of Colorado.
William J. Turnier, Professor of Law, University of North Carolina.

TAXATION, PROBLEMS IN THE FUNDAMENTALS OF FEDERAL INCOME, Second Edition (1985)

Norton L. Steuben, Professor of Law, University of Colorado.
William J. Turnier, Professor of Law, University of North Carolina.

TORT LAW AND ALTERNATIVES, Fourth Edition (1987)

Marc A. Franklin, Professor of Law, Stanford University.
Robert L. Rabin, Professor of Law, Stanford University.

TORTS, Eighth Edition (1988)

William L. Prosser, late Professor of Law, University of California, Hastings.
John W. Wade, Professor of Law, Vanderbilt University.
Victor E. Schwartz, Adjunct Professor of Law, Georgetown University.

TORTS, Third Edition (1976)

Harry Shulman, late Dean of the Law School, Yale University.
Fleming James, Jr., Professor of Law Emeritus, Yale University.
Oscar S. Gray, Professor of Law, University of Maryland.

TRADE REGULATION, Third Edition (1990)

Milton Handler, Professor of Law Emeritus, Columbia University.
Harlan M. Blake, Professor of Law, Columbia University.
Robert Pitofsky, Professor of Law, Georgetown University.
Harvey J. Goldschmid, Professor of Law, Columbia University.

TRADE REGULATION, see Antitrust

TRANSNATIONAL BUSINESS PROBLEMS (1986)

Detlev F. Vagts, Professor of Law, Harvard University.

TRANSNATIONAL LEGAL PROBLEMS, Third Edition (1986) with 1991 Revised Edition of Documentary Supplement

Henry J. Steiner, Professor of Law, Harvard University.
Detlev F. Vagts, Professor of Law, Harvard University.

TRIAL, see also Evidence, Making the Record, Lawyering Process and Preparing and Presenting the Case

UNIVERSITY CASEBOOK SERIES—Continued

TRUSTS, Fifth Edition (1978)

George G. Bogert, late Professor of Law Emeritus, University of Chicago.
Dallin H. Oaks, President, Brigham Young University.

TRUSTS AND ESTATES, SELECTED STATUTES ON, 1991 Edition

TRUSTS AND SUCCESSION (Palmer's), Fourth Edition (1983)

Richard V. Wellman, Professor of Law, University of Georgia.
Lawrence W. Waggoner, Professor of Law, University of Michigan.
Olin L. Browder, Jr., Professor of Law, University of Michigan.

UNFAIR COMPETITION, see Competitive Process and Business Torts

WATER RESOURCE MANAGEMENT, Third Edition (1988)

The late Charles J. Meyers, formerly Dean, Stanford University Law School.
A. Dan Tarlock, Professor of Law, IIT Chicago-Kent College of Law.
James N. Corbridge, Jr., Chancellor, University of Colorado at Boulder, and
    Professor of Law, University of Colorado.
David H. Getches, Professor of Law, University of Colorado.

WILLS AND ADMINISTRATION, Fifth Edition (1961)

Philip Mechem, late Professor of Law, University of Pennsylvania.
Thomas E. Atkinson, late Professor of Law, New York University.

WRITING AND ANALYSIS IN THE LAW, Second Edition (1991)

Helene S. Shapo, Professor of Law, Northwestern University
Marilyn R. Walter, Professor of Law, Brooklyn Law School
Elizabeth Fajans, Writing Specialist, Brooklyn Law School

University Casebook Series

CASES AND MATERIALS

ON

FUNDAMENTALS

OF

CORPORATE TAXATION

By

STEPHEN A. LIND

Professor of Law, University of Florida
and
Hastings College of the Law

STEPHEN SCHWARZ

Professor of Law,
Hastings College of the Law

DANIEL J. LATHROPE

Professor of Law,
Hastings College of the Law

JOSHUA D. ROSENBERG

Professor of Law,
University of San Francisco School of Law

THIRD EDITION

Westbury, New York
THE FOUNDATION PRESS, INC.
1991

Library of Congress Cataloging-in-Publication Data

Cases and materials on fundamentals of corporate taxation / by Stephen
A. Lind . . . [et al.]. — 3rd ed.
p.   cm. — (University casebook series)
Includes index.
ISBN 0–88277–877–3
1. Corporations—Taxation—Law and legislation—United States—
Cases. I. Lind, Stephen A. II. Series.
KF6463.C37 1991
343.7306'7—dc20
[347.30367]
91–368

To our families

*

PREFACE TO THE THIRD EDITION

Since the second edition of *Fundamentals of Corporate Taxation* was published in June of 1987, the flow of corporate tax developments has slowed but not totally abated. Congress continues to tinker with the Code in its efforts to reduce the deficit, and the Supreme Court's recent docket has included several significant cases involving corporations and their shareholders. The Third Edition has been updated to incorporate all of the major cases, regulations, rulings and legislation since 1987, including the Revenue Act of 1987, the Technical and Miscellaneous Revenue Act of 1988 and the Revenue Reconciliation Acts of 1989 and 1990. The text is current through January, 1991.

More importantly, with the fifth anniversary of the Tax Reform Act of 1986 drawing near, the unsettled "transitional" regime that we described in our last preface has passed and the scene, though not entirely tranquil, is at least stabilizing for the near term. Although the spread has narrowed, the top rate applicable to C corporations remains higher than the maximum individual rate (even after all the new phase-outs). A small capital gains rate preference has reappeared almost by accident, but it is not significant enough to influence most taxpayer behavior. *General Utilities* is still dead. Despite predictions to the contrary, the disincorporation of America has not yet occurred. And at this writing, the Treasury's long-promised studies on Subchapter C and integration are still over the next horizon. In view of all these developments, it was time for a new edition that pares down coverage of "pre-1987" law and confronts the reality of Subchapters C and S, post-tax reform.

Although our yellowed notes on "old Section 337" and other obsolete topics have been sent to the archives, we are not ready to discard the Preface to the first edition. It follows in its entirety despite some changes in organization and coverage and continues to express our views as to pedagogy. We reaffirm here our allegiance to a problem-oriented approach to teaching corporate taxation, with an emphasis on the fundamentals, and adhere to the "cradle to grave" organization of earlier editions. We are confident that sticking to the basics will not deprive students of steady doses of complexity. Like its predecessors, this revision persists in avoiding an excess of casenotes, distracting rhetorical asides, and meanderings into specialized minutia.

Turning to specific organizational changes, the Third Edition includes a substantially revised introductory chapter, offering students perspective on the influential policies that have shaped Subchapter C, previewing the pervasive judicial doctrines such as substance over form, business purpose and step transactions, introducing the S corporation alternative, and hitting the highlights of the corporate alternative minimum tax.

Chapter 7 has been extensively revised, first providing an introduction to complete liquidations (including liquidation of a subsidiary) and then turning to a more tightly organized survey of taxable corporate acquisitions. Chapter 12, covering corporate divisions, has been reorganized in light of the 1989 final Section 355 regulations and the changing role of Section 355 in connection with acquisitions. The Third Edition also includes highly selective coverage of the consolidated return regulations, particularly their impact on carryover of net operating losses in the consolidated group setting. Finally, in recognition of the greater use of S corporations, Chapter 15 has been expanded and includes a discussion of the interaction of Subchapters C and S in liquidations, taxable acquisitions and reorganizations.

The Third Edition also reflects our decision to integrate corporate tax policy issues throughout the book rather than in a separate policy chapter. To that end, Chapter 1 addresses the prospect of integrating the corporate and individual income taxes. Chapter 3 introduces the increasing pressures to capitalize a C corporation with excessive debt, and Chapter 7 looks at the debt vs. equity problem in a transactional context with excerpts from the 1989 Congressional hearings on leveraged buyouts and other debt-financed transactions. The current acquisitions regime is critically evaluated in both Chapter 7, where we propose to "rethink" *General Utilities* repeal, and Chapter 11, which includes an overview of the American Law Institute's long pending elective carryover basis proposals.

The authors are grateful for the many constructive suggestions from colleagues and students who used earlier editions of this text. We extend special thanks to Ray Kawasaki, Terri Murray and Mitch Salamon, who provided invaluable research assistance on the Third Edition, and we continue to be indebted to the students who contributed to the Second Edition, including: Jim Potratz, Jeff Anthony, Garo Kalfayan, Steve Vogelsang and Julie Divola.

As always, timely publication would not have been possible without the support and cooperation of Jim Coates and the excellent production staff at Foundation Press.

STEPHEN A. LIND
STEPHEN SCHWARZ
DANIEL J. LATHROPE
JOSHUA D. ROSENBERG

San Francisco, California
March, 1991

PREFACE

It has become a tradition for students who encounter corporate tax to describe it as their hardest course in law school. With the expansion of the J.D. tax curriculum and the recent barrage of complex legislation, corporate tax no longer may deserve its reputation—and perhaps it never did. But the taxation of corporations and their shareholders remains a dynamic, highly technical and exceedingly challenging field. Fortunately, it also can be fascinating and fun. The provisions that make up Subchapter C of the Code enjoy a rich history—a veritable folklore, complete with famous taxpayers (what student will ever forget Evelyn Gregory, Frederick H. Foglesong and the Court Holding Company?), notorious tax avoidance schemes (e.g., the preferred stock bailout), historic judicial decisions and a marvelously intricate statutory scheme. The landscape of Subchapter C and its newer relative, Subchapter S, is a case study of competing social and economic forces and a window on the endless and entertaining struggle between human greed and the tax collector.

Over the years, academics have debated the objectives of the corporate tax course. Some instructors emphasize cases and doctrinal analysis. Others focus principally on tax and economic policy considerations. Still others concentrate on statutory details, sometimes to the exclusion of the bigger picture, through a problem-oriented methodology. Another camp approaches the subject matter through a transactional or planning context. The organization of the course also reflects competing pedagogical tastes. Some materials begin with a study of corporate reorganizations. Others embark by examining the problems created by the so-called "double tax," entering the fray with corporate distributions and deferring corporate formations, capital structure and reorganizations to later in the term. The most traditional approach is to follow a corporation through its life cycle, beginning with formations and ending with liquidations and reorganizations. Whatever the organization, Subchapter S often is relegated to the end of the course or only mentioned in passing.

There is much to be said for aspects of all these approaches. But in our collective experience, we have been troubled by a common denominator in the many fine corporate tax casebooks and texts: their sheer bulk. In this book and a previously published companion volume, *Fundamentals of Partnership Taxation*, we attempt to chart a different course by bringing the "fundamentals" philosophy to the teaching of taxation of the business enterprise. To reiterate what we said in the preface to the partnership tax book, the fundamentals approach involves selectivity of subject matter, emphasis on basic concepts, avoidance of esoteric detail and realistic depth of coverage. To those ends, this volume is the product of self restraint—although perhaps not enough. At times, we opted for over inclusion to accommodate the varied teaching biases and favorite cases and topics of experienced instructors (including ourselves). We have continued, however, to select and edit cases with care. Lengthy citations, obscure questions and meanderings into minutia have been avoided. Throughout the book, we have made an effort to remember what it was like when we studied corporate tax. This volume is designed as a teaching book, not the definitive treatise. And so, of course, we expect students to do the reading!

We also believe that the most effective way to teach and learn tax fundamentals is by the problem method. This book thus contains a comprehensive yet manageable set of problems to accompany every major topic. The problems are designed to help students decipher the statute and apply it in a wide variety of alternative fact situations. Some are "building block" problems with specific answers. We are mindful, however, of the tendency to become preoccupied with technical trivia and also have included some more sophisticated (and realistic) problems with a planning orientation.

The primary sources in any tax course are the Code and Regulations. But the statute frequently is unintelligible when read out of context. To provide a foundation of understanding, this book includes extensive explanatory text to accompany the problems and a selection of cases, rulings, legislative history and other materials. The goal of the text is not merely to paraphrase the Code. In addition to describing the *workings* of the statute, we have attempted to explain *why* it works the way it does. If presented as a purely mechanical exercise, the problem method can degenerate into a mindless series of computations, leaving one without insights into the function of the statute, the relationship between sections and the broad principles governing the taxation of corporations and shareholders. By first explaining the "why" as well as the "how," we hope that even the computational problems will serve as launching pads for the discussion of more important policy and planning issues.

Turning to organization, we decided to begin at the beginning. Part One (Chapter 1) introduces the corporate income tax and then covers classification issues, the problems and opportunities of corporate classification and some special problems of personal service corporations. This last topic is far less compelling than it used to be, but it continues to serve as a useful introduction to the concept of the corporation as a separate taxable entity and the pervasive themes of assignment of income, business purpose and timing.

Part Two examines the taxation of C corporations, beginning in Chapters 2 and 3 with the formation of a corporation and its capital structure. There is considerable room for disagreement over whether this "cradle to grave" organization is the most desirable. We concluded that it makes sense for students to get their feet wet by studying the familiar tax concept of nonrecognition and reviewing, in that context, the corollary basis rules and the impact of assumption of liabilities. Focusing first on formation and capital structure also gives students an early exposure to the distinction between debt and equity, and the different forms of each type of corporate interest.

Chapters 4 through 7 are the heart of the typical three or four unit class in corporate tax. It is there that we make a special effort to go beyond the mechanics. The rise and fall of the *General Utilities* doctrine and its relationship to the integrity of the corporate tax is a particularly pervasive theme in these chapters, which also explore planning considerations and common transactions. In Chapter 4, for example, students are introduced to the opportunities and pitfalls of the use of dividends in bootstrap sales. The basic principles of redemptions are followed in Chapter 5 by a closer look at buy-sell agreements, and combined sale and redemption techniques. Section 304—a particularly inscrutable provision—is introduced by a case that shows why tax lawyers need malpractice insurance. Chapter 7 goes beyond a mere survey of liquidations by comparing the methods of selling a corporate business.

Chapters 8 and 9, which cover collapsible corporations and the anti-avoidance penalty taxes, are overview chapters. It is unlikely that either of these topics can be considered in depth in a basic corporate tax course, but instructors who wish to alert students to these important areas can do so with selective assignments from the text and a few very basic problems.

Chapters 10 through 12 cover corporate reorganizations. Several of the authors admit to a teaching bias in this area, and it is here that our efforts at self restraint may have failed. Chapter 10, however, is easily adaptable to an efficient survey of the three basic types of acquisitive reorganizations. For those who prefer greater depth, it also includes coverage of triangular reorganization techniques, the operative provisions and carryover of tax attributes. Chapters 11 and 12 complete the reorganization alphabet and also can be adapted for selective coverage or omitted entirely.

After a brief overview of affiliated corporations in Chapter 13 [now Chapter 14. Ed.] the study of Subchapter C concludes with a look at its future. As this book goes to press, the corporate tax seems secure but its precise shape is uncertain. Chapter 14 [now integrated into the text. Ed.] acquaints students with the alternatives, exploring the pros and cons of total and partial integration. It also includes excerpts from the 1983 Senate Finance Committee proposals on Subchapter C and the 1984 Treasury report on tax simplification and reform. Although most instructors may not have the time to assign this entire chapter, we believed it was important to include policy materials for selective assignment at an appropriate point in the course. In our view, that point is not at the beginning, when students are not yet familiar with the current system.

Part Three (Chapter 15) is devoted exclusively to the S corporation. A similar chapter is included in our partnership book to permit comparative study of partnerships and S corporations. With the significant reforms in the Subchapter S Revision Act and the lowering of the top individual rates (and the future prospects for further reductions), S corporations have become far more prominent vehicles for conducting a closely held business enterprise. Our placement of S corporations at the end of the book is not intended as a value judgment. Unless it is covered elsewhere in the curriculum, we consider Subchapter S to be one of the least expendable topics in a basic corporate tax course.

As for matters of style, we have assumed that this book will be assigned with a recent edition of the Code and Regulations and have provided suggested assignments to these primary sources. We have freely deleted extraneous material from cases and other authorities and have indicated deletions with asterisks. Editorial additions are in brackets. Footnotes to our own text are numbered consecutively within each section. We have deleted many footnotes from cases and rulings without renumbering those that remain. In general, the materials and text are current through April of 1985 and include all changes made by the Tax Reform Act of 1984.

We salute the many law students who "experienced" the early drafts of this book. Their willingness to cart around large stacks of photocopied materials and their constructive suggestions are most appreciated. We also are indebted to the administrations of Hastings College of the Law, the University of San Francisco School of Law and the University of Florida College of Law for their support and tolerance during this two volume project. Our research assistants have made a valuable contribution to the accuracy and occasional coherence of the book. We wish to acknowledge the special contributions of Joe Bartlett, Marilyn Cleveland, Chris Detzel and Jeffrey Essner.

And last, but hardly least, we owe a continuing debt of gratitude to the capable word processing staff at Hastings College of the Law and the faculty secretaries at the University of San Francisco School of Law who assisted in the preparation of the manuscript. It would not have been possible without LaWanda Douglas, Stephen Lothrop and Peggie MacDonald of Hastings and the special contributions of Penelope Gwilliam of USF. We also thank Vera Costella for her many efforts on our behalf.

STEPHEN A. LIND
STEPHEN SCHWARZ
DANIEL J. LATHROPE
JOSHUA D. ROSENBERG

San Francisco, California
May 22, 1985

SUMMARY OF CONTENTS

	Page
PREFACE TO THE THIRD EDITION	xxi
PREFACE	xxiii
TABLE OF INTERNAL REVENUE CODE SECTIONS	xxxvii
TABLE OF TREASURY REGULATIONS	lvii
TABLE OF REVENUE RULINGS	lxiii
TABLE OF MISCELLANEOUS RULINGS	lxv
TABLE OF CASES	lxvii
TABLE OF AUTHORITIES	lxxi

PART ONE. INTRODUCTION

Chapter

1. An Overview of the Taxation of Corporations and Shareholders — 1
   - A. Introduction — 1
   - B. The Corporation as a Separate Taxable Entity — 11
   - C. Corporate Classification — 31
   - D. Recognition of the Corporate Entity — 50

PART TWO. TAXATION OF C CORPORATIONS

2. Formation of a Corporation — 57
   - A. Introduction to Section 351 — 57
   - B. Requirements for Nonrecognition of Gain or Loss Under Section 351 — 61
   - C. Treatment of Boot — 69
   - D. Assumption of Liabilities — 78
   - E. Incorporation of a Going Business — 95
   - F. Collateral Issues — 104
3. The Capital Structure of a Corporation — 119
   - A. Introduction — 119
   - B. Debt vs. Equity — 126
   - C. The Section 385 Regulations Saga — 135
   - D. Character of Loss on Corporate Investment — 139
4. Nonliquidating Distributions — 150
   - A. Dividends: In General — 150
   - B. Earnings and Profits — 153
   - C. Distributions of Cash — 156
   - D. Distributions of Property — 160
   - E. Constructive Distributions — 167
   - F. Anti–Avoidance Limitations on the Dividends Received Deduction — 172
   - G. Use of Dividends in Bootstrap Sales — 180
5. Redemptions and Partial Liquidations — 195
   - A. Introduction — 195

5. Redemptions and Partial Liquidations—Continued
   B.   Constructive Ownership of Stock _____ 197
   C.   Redemptions Tested at the Shareholder Level _____ 199
   D.   Redemptions Tested at the Corporate Level: Partial Liqui-
       dations _____ 238
   E.   Consequences to the Distributing Corporation _____ 243
   F.   Redemption Planning Techniques _____ 249
   G.   Redemptions Through Related Corporations _____ 279
   H.   Redemptions to Pay Death Taxes _____ 291
6. Stock Dividends and Section 306 Stock _____ 294
   A.   Introduction _____ 294
   B.   Taxation of Stock Dividends Under Section 305 _____ 296
   C.   Section 306 Stock _____ 305
7. Complete Liquidations and Taxable Corporate Acquisitions ____ 329
   A.   Introduction _____ 329
   B.   Complete Liquidations _____ 330
   C.   Taxable Corporate Acquisitions _____ 362
8. Collapsible Corporations _____ 434
   A.   Introduction _____ 434
   B.   Definition of a Collapsible Corporation _____ 437
   C.   Exceptions to Section 341(a) _____ 441
9. Preventing the Improper Retention of Corporate Earnings ____ 447
   A.   Introduction _____ 447
   B.   The Accumulated Earnings Tax _____ 449
   C.   The Personal Holding Company Tax _____ 467
10. Acquisitive Reorganizations _____ 484
   A.   Introduction _____ 484
   B.   Types of Acquisitive Reorganizations _____ 488
   C.   Treatment of the Parties to an Acquisitive Reorganization 558
   D.   Carryover of Tax Attributes _____ 581
   E.   Policy: An Elective Carryover Basis Regime _____ 590
11. Nonacquisitive, Nondivisive Reorganizations _____ 596
   A.   Type E: Recapitalizations _____ 596
   B.   Type D: Liquidation—Reincorporation _____ 608
   C.   Type F: Mere Change in Identity, Form, or Place of
       Organization _____ 620
   D.   Type G: Insolvency Reorganizations _____ 621
12. Corporate Divisions _____ 628
   A.   Introduction _____ 628
   B.   The Requirements for a Tax–Free Corporate Division _____ 630
   C.   Tax Treatment of the Parties to a Corporate Division ____ 668
   D.   Use of Section 355 in Corporate Acquisitions _____ 674
13. Limitations on Carryovers of Corporate Attributes _____ 696
   A.   Introduction _____ 696
   B.   Limitations on Net Operating Loss Carryforwards: Section
       382 _____ 697
   C.   Limitations on Other Tax Attributes: Section 383 _____ 713

Chapter   **Page**

13. Limitations on Carryovers of Corporate Attributes—Continued
    D. Other Loss Limitations _____ 713
14. Affiliated Corporations _____ 723
    A. Restrictions on Affiliated Corporations _____ 723
    B. Consolidated Returns _____ 742

PART THREE. TAXATION OF S CORPORATIONS

15. The S Corporation _____ 749
    A. Introduction _____ 749
    B. Eligibility for S Corporation Status _____ 751
    C. Election, Revocation and Termination_____ 756
    D. Treatment of the Shareholders _____ 761
    E. Distributions to Shareholders _____ 774
    F. Taxation of the S Corporation_____ 778
    G. Coordination With Subchapter C_____ 787
    H. Tax Planning With the S Corporation_____ 793

Index_____ 805

*

TABLE OF CONTENTS

	Page
PREFACE TO THE THIRD EDITION	xxi
PREFACE	xxiii
TABLE OF INTERNAL REVENUE CODE SECTIONS	xxxvii
TABLE OF TREASURY REGULATIONS	lvii
TABLE OF REVENUE RULINGS	lxiii
TABLE OF MISCELLANEOUS RULINGS	lxv
TABLE OF CASES	lxvii
TABLE OF AUTHORITIES	lxxi

PART ONE. INTRODUCTION

Chapter
1. An Overview of the Taxation of Corporations and Shareholders 1
   A.   Introduction 1
      1. Taxation of Business Entities 1
      2. Influential Policies 3
      3. The Common Law of Corporate Taxation 8
   B.   The Corporation as a Separate Taxable Entity 11
      1. The Corporate Income Tax 11
      2. The Alternative Minimum Tax 15
      3. Multiple Corporations 18
      4. The S Corporation Alternative 19
      5. The Integration Alternative 21
   C.   Corporate Classification 31
      1. In General 31
      2. Corporations vs. Partnerships 32
         a. Limited Partnerships 32
         b. Publicly Traded Partnerships 46
      3. Corporations vs. Trusts 47
   D.   Recognition of the Corporate Entity 50

PART TWO. TAXATION OF C CORPORATIONS

2. Formation of a Corporation 57
   A.   Introduction to Section 351 57
   B.   Requirements for Nonrecognition of Gain or Loss Under Section 351 61
      1. "Control" Immediately After the Exchange 61
      2. Transfers of "Property" and Services 66
      3. Solely for "Stock" 67
   C.   Treatment of Boot 68
      1. In General 69
      2. Timing of Section 351(b) Gain 75
   D.   Assumption of Liabilities 78

Chapter   **Page**

2. Formation of a Corporation—Continued
    E. Incorporation of a Going Business _____ 95
    F. Collateral Issues _____ 104
        1. Contributions to Capital _____ 104
        2. Intentional Avoidance of Section 351 _____ 115
        3. Organizational Expenses _____ 117
3. The Capital Structure of a Corporation _____ 119
    A. Introduction _____ 119
    B. Debt vs. Equity _____ 126
    C. The Section 385 Regulations Saga _____ 135
    D. Character of Loss on Corporate Investment _____ 139
4. Nonliquidating Distributions _____ 150
    A. Dividends: In General _____ 150
    B. Earnings and Profits _____ 153
    C. Distributions of Cash _____ 156
    D. Distributions of Property _____ 160
        1. Consequences to the Distributing Corporation _____ 160
            a. Background: The *General Utilities* Doctrine ____ 160
            b. Corporate Gain or Loss _____ 162
            c. Effect on the Distributing Corporation's Earnings and Profits _____ 163
        2. Consequences to the Shareholders _____ 164
        3. Distributions of a Corporation's Own Obligations ____ 165
    E. Constructive Distributions _____ 167
    F. Anti–Avoidance Limitations on the Dividends Received Deduction _____ 172
        1. In General _____ 172
        2. Special Holding Period Requirements _____ 173
        3. Extraordinary Dividends: Basis Reduction _____ 174
        4. Debt–Financed Portfolio Stock _____ 177
        5. Section 301(e) _____ 178
    G. Use of Dividends in Bootstrap Sales _____ 180
5. Redemptions and Partial Liquidations _____ 195
    A. Introduction _____ 195
    B. Constructive Ownership of Stock _____ 197
    C. Redemptions Tested at the Shareholder Level _____ 199
        1. Substantially Disproportionate Redemptions _____ 199
        2. Complete Termination of a Shareholder's Interest ____ 203
            a. Waiver of Family Attribution _____ 203
            b. Waiver of Attribution by Entities _____ 218
        3. Redemptions Not Essentially Equivalent to a Dividend 222
    D. Redemptions Tested at the Corporate Level: Partial Liquidations _____ 238
    E. Consequences to the Distributing Corporation _____ 243
        1. Distributions of Appreciated Property in Redemption 243
        2. Effect on Earnings and Profits _____ 244
        3. Stock Redemption Expenses _____ 247

Chapter				Page
5.	Redemptions and Partial Liquidations—Continued			
	F.	Redemption Planning Techniques		249
		1.	Bootstrap Sales	249
		2.	Buy–Sell Agreements	253
		3.	Charitable Contribution and Redemption	270
	G.	Redemptions Through Related Corporations		279
	H.	Redemptions to Pay Death Taxes		291
6.	Stock Dividends and Section 306 Stock			294
	A.	Introduction		294
	B.	Taxation of Stock Dividends Under Section 305		296
	C.	Section 306 Stock		305
		1.	The Preferred Stock Bailout	305
		2.	The Operation of Section 306	312
			a. Section 306 Stock Defined	312
			b. Dispositions of Section 306 Stock	317
			c. Dispositions Exempt From Section 306	318
7.	Complete Liquidations and Taxable Corporate Acquisitions			329
	A.	Introduction		329
	B.	Complete Liquidations		330
		1.	Consequences to the Shareholders	330
		2.	Consequences to the Liquidating Corporation	334
			a. Background	334
			b. Liquidating Distributions and Sales	342
			c. Limitations on Recognition of Loss	342
		3.	Liquidation of a Subsidiary	348
			a. Consequences to the Shareholders	348
			b. Consequences to the Liquidating Subsidiary	358
	C.	Taxable Corporate Acquisitions		362
		1.	Introduction	362
		2.	Asset Acquisitions	364
		3.	Stock Acquisitions	365
			a. Background	365
			b. Operation of Section 338	370
			c. Acquisition of Stock of a Subsidiary	377
			d. Stock Acquisitions With No Section 338 Election	380
		4.	Comparison of Acquisition Methods	380
		5.	Allocation of the Purchase Price	383
			a. Background	383
			b. Deemed Asset Acquisitions Under Section 338	385
			c. Actual Asset Acquisitions	386
		6.	Tax Treatment of Acquisition Expenses	388
		7.	Other Acquisition Issues: Planning and Policy	390
			a. Dispositions of Unwanted Assets	390
			b. Corporate Acquisitions and the Problem of Excessive Debt	396
			c. Rethinking *General Utilities* Repeal	417

Chapter   **Page**

8. Collapsible Corporations _____ 434
   - A. Introduction _____ 434
   - B. Definition of a Collapsible Corporation_____ 437
   - C. Exceptions to Section 341(a)_____ 441
     1. Section 341(d)_____ 441
     2. Section 341(e)_____ 443
     3. Section 341(f)_____ 444
9. Preventing the Improper Retention of Corporate Earnings ____ 447
   - A. Introduction _____ 447
   - B. The Accumulated Earnings Tax_____ 449
     1. The Proscribed Tax Avoidance Purpose _____ 449
     2. The Reasonable Needs of The Business_____ 452
     3. Calculation of Accumulated Taxable Income_____ 465
   - C. The Personal Holding Company Tax_____ 467
     1. Introduction _____ 467
     2. Definition of a Personal Holding Company _____ 469
        - a. Stock Ownership Requirement _____ 469
        - b. Income Test _____ 469
     3. Taxation of Personal Holding Companies _____ 479
        - a. Adjustments to Taxable Income_____ 479
        - b. Dividends Paid Deduction _____ 480
10. Acquisitive Reorganizations _____ 484
   - A. Introduction _____ 484
     1. Historical Background _____ 484
     2. Overview of Reorganizations_____ 485
   - B. Types of Acquisitive Reorganizations_____ 488
     1. Type A: Statutory Mergers and Consolidations _____ 488
        - a. Continuity of Interest _____ 489
        - b. Continuity of Business Enterprise_____ 513
     2. Type B: Acquisitions of Stock Solely for Voting Stock 520
     3. Type C: Acquisitions of Assets for Voting Stock____ 545
     4. Triangular Reorganizations _____ 554
   - C. Treatment of the Parties to an Acquisitive Reorganization 558
     1. Consequences to Shareholders and Security Holders 559
     2. Consequences to the Target Corporation_____ 574
     3. Consequences to the Acquiring Corporation _____ 577
   - D. Carryover of Tax Attributes _____ 581
     1. Introduction _____ 581
     2. Section 381 _____ 583
   - E. Policy: An Elective Carryover Basis Regime _____ 590
11. Nonacquisitive, Nondivisive Reorganizations_____ 596
   - A. Type E: Recapitalizations _____ 596
     1. Introduction _____ 596
     2. Types of Recapitalizations_____ 597
        - a. Bonds for Stock _____ 598
        - b. Bonds for Bonds _____ 598
        - c. Stock for Stock _____ 599

Chapter				Page
11.	Nonacquisitive, Nondivisive Reorganizations—Continued			
		d.	Stock for Bonds	604
	B.	Type D: Liquidation—Reincorporation		608
	C.	Type F: Mere Change in Identity, Form, or Place of Organization		620
	D.	Type G: Insolvency Reorganizations		621
12.	Corporate Divisions			628
	A.	Introduction		628
	B.	The Requirements for a Tax–Free Corporate Division		630
		1.	Historical Background	630
		2.	Overview of Requirements	634
		3.	The Active Trade or Business Requirement	636
		4.	Judicial and Statutory Limitations	651
			a. Business Purpose	651
			b. Continuity of Interest	660
			c. The "Device" Limitation	661
		5.	The Changing Role of Section 355	667
	C.	Tax Treatment of the Parties to a Corporate Division		668
	D.	Use of Section 355 in Corporate Acquisitions		674
		1.	Limitations on Use of Section 355 in Taxable Acquisitions	674
			a. Introduction	674
			b. Dispositions of Recently Acquired Businesses	674
			c. Corporate–Level Tax on Divisive Transactions in Connection With Certain Changes of Ownership	676
		2.	Dispositions of Unwanted Assets in Conjunction With Tax–Free Reorganizations	681
13.	Limitations on Carryovers of Corporate Attributes			696
	A.	Introduction		696
	B.	Limitations on Net Operating Loss Carryforwards: Section 382		697
		1.	Introduction	697
		2.	The Ownership Change Requirements	700
		3.	Results of an Ownership Change	706
	C.	Limitations on Other Tax Attributes: Section 383		713
	D.	Other Loss Limitations		713
		1.	Acquisitions Made to Evade Tax: Section 269	713
		2.	Limitations on Use of Preacquisition Losses to Offset Built-in Gains: Section 384	716
		3.	Consolidated Return Rules	720
			a. Introduction	720
			b. The "SRLY" Limitation	721
			c. The "CRCO" Limitation	721
14.	Affiliated Corporations			723
	A.	Restrictions on Affiliated Corporations		723
		1.	Limitations on Multiple Tax Benefits	723

Chapter   **Page**

14. Affiliated Corporations—Continued
    2. Section 482 _____ 731
    B. Consolidated Returns _____ 742

PART THREE. TAXATION OF S CORPORATIONS

15. The S Corporation _____ 749
    A. Introduction _____ 749
    B. Eligibility for S Corporation Status _____ 751
    C. Election, Revocation and Termination _____ 756
    D. Treatment of the Shareholders _____ 761
    E. Distributions to Shareholders _____ 774
    F. Taxation of the S Corporation _____ 778
    G. Coordination With Subchapter C _____ 787
    H. Tax Planning With the S Corporation _____ 793
       1. Compensation Issues _____ 793
       2. Family Income Splitting _____ 797

Index _____ 805

TABLE OF INTERNAL REVENUE CODE SECTIONS

Sec.	Page	Sec.	Page
1	21	56(g)	16
	278		365
	447	56(g)(1)	15
1(a)	751		16
1(e)	47	56(g)(2)	15
1(h)	6		16
1(h)(1)	436	56(g)(3)	15
1(i)	803	56(g)(4)(A)—(g)(4)(C)(ii)	15
1(i)(4)(A)(i)	803	56(g)(4)(A)(i)	17
11	11		21
	14	56(g)(4)(B)	21
	18	56(g)(4)(C)(i)	21
	21	56(g)(4)(C)(ii)	17
	47	56(g)(5)	15
	447	56(g)(6)	15
	467	57(a)	18
	468	57(a)(5)	15
	720	57(a)(6)	15
	749		278
11(b)	11	59(a)	18
	18	61	66
11(b)(1)	723		598
11(b)(2)	11	61(a)	604
27	15	61(a)(7)	151
38(c)	18		749
41	15	63(a)	11
46—48	15		12
51	15	63(c)(4)	803
53	15	63(c)(5)	803
53(a)	18	67	12
53(b)	18	68	6
53(c)	18		447
53(d)(1)(B)	18		751
55	15	79	21
55(a)	15	83	66
55(b)	15		69
55(b)(2)	15		754
55(b)(2)(A)	15	83(b)	69
55(d)(2)	15		754
55(d)(3)	15	101(a)	253
56	15	105(a)	21
	18	105(b)	21
	21	106	21
56(a)(1)	16	108	599
56(a)(1)(A)	15	108(e)(2)	80
	16	108(e)(8)	598
	17	108(e)(10)(A)	598
56(a)(1)(A)(ii)	21	108(e)(10)(B)	598
56(a)(4)	16	108(e)(11)	599
56(a)(6)	16	118(a)	104
56(c)	15	119	21
56(d)	16	151	803
56(f)	16	151(d)	6

Sec.	Page	Sec.	Page
151(d)(2)	803	172 (Cont'd)	697
151(d)(3)	447		706
	751		707
162	12	172(b)	697
	103	172(h)	416
	247	172(h)(2)	417
	389	172(h)(2)(D)	417
162(a)	389	172(h)(3)(B)	416
162(a)(2)	21	172(h)(3)(B)(ii)	416
162(k)	247	172(h)(3)(C)	417
	248	179	762
162(k)(1)	248	179(d)(8)	762
162(k)(2)	248	183(a)	12
162*l*(1)	797	212	12
162*l*(5)	797	212(3)	117
163	21	213	12
	248	215	12
163(a)	120	243	120
163(e)	599		154
	608		173
163(e)(5)	415		177
163(e)(5)(A)	416		178
163(e)(5)(B)	416		318
163(e)(5)(C)	416		348
163(h)	80		559
163(i)	138		573
	415		663
163(i)(2)	415		666
163(i)(3)(B)	416		788
163(j)	417	243(a)	11
163(j)(1)(B)	417		17
163(j)(2)(A)	417		150
163(j)(2)(B)	417		151
163(j)(2)(C)	417		365
163(j)(4)	417	243(a)(1)	172
165	147	243(a)(3)	172
	390		173
165(c)	12		675
165(g)(1)	139		742
165(g)(2)	139	243(b)	675
165(g)(2)(C)	146	243(b)(1)	150
166	146		151
166(a)	139		172
	146		176
166(d)	12	243(c)	151
	139		173
	146	246(a)(1)	172
166(e)	139	246(b)	172
168(a)	16	246(c)	172
	17		173
168(b)(3)	359	246(c)(1)	173
168(g)	16	246(c)(2)	173
	17	246(c)(3)	173
168(g)(2)	155	246(c)(4)	173
	164	246A	172
	165		177
170(b)(2)	13	246A(a)	177
170(e)(1)(A)	6		178
170(f)(2)	278	246A(c)(1)	177
170(f)(3)	278	246A(c)(2)	177
172	416	246A(c)(4)	177
	696		

Sec.	Page
246A(d)	177
	178
246A(d)(3)(A)	177
246A(d)(4)	177
246A(e)	177
248	117
	118
	389
	590
	762
	788
248(b)	117
263(a)	247
264(a)(1)	253
265	155
265(a)(2)	177
267	14
	21
	115
	155
	342
	343
	344
	417
	774
267(a)(1)	14
	70
	334
	342
267(a)(2)	14
267(b)	14
	334
	680
267(b)(2)	14
	343
267(c)	14
	197
	334
	343
267(e)	774
269	583
	696
	713
	714
	717
	720
269(a)	714
269(a)(2)	714
269(b)	369
	380
	714
269A(b)(1)	13
269A(b)(2)	13
274	155
280H	14
280H(a)	14
280H(b)	14
280H(c)	14
301	17
	196
	240
	244

Sec.	Page
301 (Cont'd)	279
	280
	281
	303
	304
	318
	331
	480
	559
	604
	608
	630
	668
	672
	673
	749
	775
	789
301—307	671
301–318	277
301(a)	150
	156
	158
	164
	774
301(b)	156
	164
	774
301(b)(1)(A)	480
301(b)(3)	164
301(c)	150
	156
	158
	164
	775
	789
301(c)(1)	150
	156
	775
301(c)(2)	151
	156
	179
	281
	318
301(c)(3)	151
	156
	179
	318
301(c)(3)(A)	435
301(d)	162
	164
	676
	774
301(d)(1)	776
301(e)	155
	179
	190
301(e)(1)	179
301(e)(2)	179
302	120
	195
	196

Sec.	Page	Sec.	Page
302 (Cont'd)	208	302(c)(1)	196
	236		197
	279	302(c)(2)	204
	280		216
	331		217
	608		218
	630		238
	668		291
	673	302(c)(2)(A)	204
	775	302(c)(2)(A)(ii)	216
302(a)	196		662
	221	302(c)(2)(A)(iii)	220
	247		662
	249	302(c)(2)(B)	204
	250	302(c)(2)(C)	219
	279	302(d)	196
	281		789
	435	302(e)	176
	662		196
302(b)	196		238
	197		239
	217		241
	238		664
	279	302(e)(1)	238
	280		241
	291	302(e)(2)	239
	560	302(e)(3)	239
	673	302(e)(4)	239
302(b)(1)	222	302(e)(5)	240
	234	303	291
	235		292
	236		293
	237		435
	238		461
	239		662
	249	303(a)	291
	250	303(b)(1)—(b)(3)	291
	251	303(b)(1)(A)	292
302(b)(1)—(b)(3)	196	303(b)(1)(B)	292
302(b)(2)	199	303(b)(1)(C)	292
	200	303(b)(2)	292
	203	303(b)(2)(B)	292
	204	303(b)(3)	292
302(b)(2)(B)	199	303(b)(4)	292
302(b)(2)(C)	199	303(c)	291
	200	304	279
302(b)(2)(D)	200		280
302(b)(3)	203		282
	204		290
	217		313
	220		395
	290		447
	318	304(a)	284
	391		395
302(b)(4)	196	304(a)(1)	279
	238		280
	318		313
	664	304(a)(2)	280
	673	304(b)(1)	280
302(c)	203	304(b)(2)	280
	236		281
		304(b)(3)	282

Sec.	Page	Sec.	Page
304(b)(3)(C)	279	306(b)(3)	319
304(b)(3)(D)	279	306(b)(4)	319
304(b)(4)	279	306(c)—(e)	312
	395	306(c)(1)(A)	296
304(c)(1)	279		312
	280	306(c)(1)(B)	600
304(c)(3)	279	306(c)(1)(C)	312
305	294	306(c)(2)	312
	295	306(c)(3)	313
	298	306(c)(3)(A)	313
	303	306(c)(4)	313
	304	307	296
	596	307(a)	303
	600		304
	775	307(b)	304
305(a)	295	307(b)(2)	304
	296	311	163
	303		243
	304		342
	312		671
305(b)	295	311(a)	162
	296		165
	304		196
	789		243
305(b)(4)	600		244
305(c)	296		334
	305		668
	600		776
305(d)	296	311(a)(1)	303
305(d)(1)	294	311(a)(2)	162
	304		163
306	6		673
	200	311(b)	162
	238		196
	294		244
	295		245
	296		293
	311		334
	313		668
	314		671
	317		673
	318		774
	319		776
	447		789
	596	311(b)(1)	165
	600	311(b)(1)(A)	165
	789	311(b)(2)	163
306(a)	317	311(c)	162
	318	311(d)	243
306(a)(1)	296		244
	311	311(d)(2)	243
306(a)(1)(A)	296	311(d)(2)(A)(i)	244
	317	311(d)(2)(B)	244
306(a)(1)(B)	318		508
306(a)(1)(C)	318	311(d)(2)(C)	244
306(a)(2)	312	311(e)(2)	244
	318	312	153
306(b)	318	312(a)	153
306(b)(1)	318		156
306(b)(1)(A)(iii)	318		245
306(b)(1)(B)	318		559
306(b)(2)	318		668

Sec.	Page	Sec.	Page
312(a)(2)	165	316(a) (Cont'd)	156
312(a)(3)	163		158
	164		481
312(b)	163	316(b)	480
	245		481
	668	316(b)(2)	480
312(b)(1)	163	316(b)(2)(B)	481
312(b)(2)	164	317(a)	150
312(c)	153		151
	163		279
	164		294
312(d)(1)(B)	296	317(b)	195
	304	318	179
312(e)	245		197
312(f)(1)	153		198
	154		199
	155		200
	163		279
312(f)(2)	296		280
312(h)	668		281
	669		313
	672		318
312(h)(2)	583		371
312(k)	178		388
	179		560
	190		700
	746		704
312(k)(1)—(k)(3)	153		705
312(k)(3)	165	318(a)(1)	197
312(k)(3)(A)	155	318(a)(2)	680
312(k)(3)(B)	155	318(a)(2)(A)	197
312(*l*)(1)	154	318(a)(2)(B)	198
312(n)	153	318(a)(2)(C)	198
	155		313
	178		704
	179	318(a)(3)(A)	198
	190	318(a)(3)(B)	198
	746	318(a)(3)(C)	198
312(n)(1)	155		313
312(n)(2)	155	318(a)(4)	198
312(n)(4)	155	318(a)(5)	198
312(n)(5)	155	318(a)(5)(A)	198
	178	318(a)(5)(B)	197
312(n)(6)	155		198
312(n)(7)	244	318(a)(5)(C)	198
	246	318(a)(5)(D)	198
	281	318(a)(5)(E)	198
312(o)	165	318(b)	197
316	17	331	239
	150		330
	151		481
	158		608
	159		620
	250		630
	331		778
	466		781
	471		784
	480		789
	775	331(a)	331
316(a)	150		333
	151		349
	153		365

Sec.	Page	Sec.	Page
331(a) (Cont'd)	434	336(a) (Cont'd)	342
	673		358
332	330		364
	348		673
	349	336(b)	163
	359		334
	360		342
	361	336(c)	334
	368		342
	369		485
	371		487
	377		545
	378		574
	391		668
	392		671
	445	336(d)	163
	552		334
	553	336(d)(1)	343
	675		347
	696	336(d)(1)(A)(i)	344
	698	336(d)(1)(A)(ii)	344
	717	336(d)(1)(B)	343
	719		344
	791	336(d)(2)	344
	792		345
332(b)	359		346
332(b)(1)	19		347
	349	336(d)(2)(A)	344
332(b)(2)	349	336(d)(2)(B)(ii)	344
332(b)(3)	349	336(d)(2)(C)	346
332(c)	358	336(d)(3)	359
334(a)	330	336(e)	342
	331		379
	332		675
	359	336(e)(1)	19
	364	337	339
	434		340
334(b)	378		342
	391		358
334(b)(1)	348		359
	359		360
	360		377
	368		392
	371		418
	380		435
334(b)(2)	367		575
	369		576
336	162		591
	243		791
	418	337(a)	358
	434		359
	591		360
	608	337(b)(1)	358
	619		360
	671	337(b)(2)	360
	778	337(b)(2)(B)(ii)	360
	784	337(c)	358
	789		359
	791		395
336(a)	163	337(c)(1)(A)	435
	243	337(d)	358
	334		392

Sec.	Page	Sec.	Page
337(d) (Cont'd)	677	338(e)(2)(A)	370
338	367		375
	369	338(e)(2)(B)	375
	370	338(e)(2)(D)	370
	371		376
	372	338(f)	376
	374	338(g)	370
	375	338(g)(1)	372
	376	338(g)(3)	372
	377	338(h)(1)	370
	378		371
	380		373
	381	338(h)(2)	370
	383		372
	385	338(h)(3)	371
	386	338(h)(3)(A)	370
	388	338(h)(4)(A)	370
	392		375
	416	338(h)(4)(B)	375
	591	338(h)(5)	370
	674	338(h)(6)(A)	376
	676	338(h)(9)	370
	706		372
	711	338(h)(10)	342
	714		372
	719		375
	790		377
	791		378
	792		379
338(a)	370		381
	371		388
	711		391
338(a)(1)	791		675
338(a)(2)	372		676
338(b)	370	338(h)(10)(A)	378
	371	338(h)(10)(B)	378
	378	338(h)(10)(C)	388
338(b)(1)	373	338(h)(11)	370
	374		372
	385	338(h)(15)	372
338(b)(1)(A)	373	338(i)(1)	377
338(b)(2)	374	341	435
	385		436
338(b)(3)	373		437
	374		438
338(b)(3)(A)	374		439
338(b)(3)(B)	374		440
338(b)(4)	373		442
338(b)(5)	375	341(a)	434
	385		435
	386		440
	388		441
338(b)(6)(A)	373		442
338(b)(6)(B)	373		443
338(d)	370	341(a)(2)(A)	436
338(d)(1)	371	341(b)	437
338(d)(3)	19		440
	371		441
338(e)	375		442
	376	341(b)(1)	437
338(e)(1)	370		438
	376		439

Sec.	Page	Sec.	Page
341(b)(2)	438	351 (Cont'd)	96
341(b)(2)(A)	438		101
	439		102
341(b)(2)(B)	439		104
341(b)(2)(C)	439		115
341(b)(3)	438		116
341(c)	437		121
	440		154
	441		160
341(d)	441		282
	442		313
	445		318
341(d)(1)	442		343
341(d)(2)	442		344
341(d)(3)	442		348
341(e)	437		371
	438		439
	441		443
	443		445
	445		484
341(e)(1)	443		560
	444		574
341(e)(1)(C)(i)	444		619
341(e)(5)	444		620
341(e)(5)(A)(i)	443		630
341(e)(5)(A)(ii)	443		672
341(e)(5)(A)(iii)	444		680
341(e)(5)(A)(iv)	444		698
341(e)(6)(A)	444		701
341(e)(6)(B)	443	351(a)	57
341(e)(6)(C)	443		61
341(e)(8)	197		67
341(e)(9)	443		69
	444		70
341(e)(10)	443		76
	444		788
341(e)(12)	443	351(b)	69
341(f)	441		70
	444		71
	445		75
	446		77
341(f)(3)	445		81
341(f)(4)(A)	444	351(c)	57
346(a)	330	351(d)(1)	66
	332	351(d)(1)—(d)(2)	57
346(b)	239	351(e)(1)	58
351	58	354	448
	59		485
	60		487
	61		596
	63		599
	66		600
	67		606
	69		618
	71		621
	74		635
	75	354(a)	488
	78		520
	79		545
	80		559
	93		598
	94		608

Sec.	Page	Sec.	Page
354(a) (Cont'd)	620	355(a)(2)(D)	674
354(a)(1)	559	355(a)(3)	668
354(a)(2)(A)	559		669
	599	355(a)(3)(A)	671
354(a)(2)(B)	598	355(a)(3)(A)(i)	636
	599	355(a)(3)(A)(ii)	636
354(a)(3)(A)	599	355(a)(3)(B)	636
354(a)(3)(B)	598		671
	599	355(a)(4)	669
354(b)	608	355(a)(4)(A)	636
	618	355(b)	635
	621		636
354(b)(1)	702	355(b)(2)	395
355	10	355(b)(2)(B)	638
	239	355(b)(2)(C)	635
	395	355(b)(2)(D)	635
	396		648
	485		674
	486		675
	598		676
	618		677
	621	355(b)(2)(D)(ii)	675
	628	355(c)	636
	629		668
	630		670
	633		671
	634		672
	635		676
	636	355(c)(1)	671
	645	355(c)(2)	671
	651		679
	660	355(c)(2)(A)	671
	662	355(c)(2)(B)	671
	663	355(c)(3)	671
	666	355(d)	396
	667		636
	668		668
	669		670
	670		672
	671		676
	672		677
	673		679
	674		680
	675		681
	677	355(d)(1)	679
	679	355(d)(2)	679
	681	355(d)(2)—(d)(4)	679
	792	355(d)(3)	679
355(a)(1)	635	355(d)(5)(A)	680
	669	355(d)(5)(B)	680
355(a)(1)(A)	634	355(d)(5)(C)	680
	668	355(d)(6)	681
355(a)(1)(B)	635	355(d)(7)(A)	680
	661	355(d)(7)(B)	680
	663	355(d)(8)(A)	680
355(a)(1)(C)	635	355(d)(8)(B)	680
	636	356	485
355(a)(1)(D)	635		487
355(a)(1)(D)(ii)	635		596
355(a)(2)	634		599
	635		600
355(a)(2)(C)	630		606

Sec.	Page	Sec.	Page
356 (Cont'd)	621	357(c)(3)(B)	80
	628	358	59
	636		60
	668		69
356(a)	488		71
	545		75
	559		80
	608		448
	620		485
	669		487
356(a)(1)	559		520
	599		560
	669		578
356(a)(2)	559		596
	560		598
	572		599
	573		608
	599		620
	600		628
	603		670
	607		672
	670		675
356(b)	669		788
	673	358(a)	57
356(c)	559		69
	670		344
356(d)	559		488
	599		545
	607		559
356(d)(2)(C)	636		574
	669		668
356(e)	559	358(a)—(c)	668
357	78	358(a)(1)	59
	79		81
	104		560
	487		576
	488		670
	545	358(a)(1)(B)(ii)	70
	628	358(a)(2)	71
	630		560
357(a)	78		575
	80		576
	82		580
	574		670
357(b)	79	358(b)	559
	82		669
	95	358(b)(1)	57
	574		69
357(b)(2)	79		574
357(c)	79	358(b)(2)	670
	80	358(c)	669
	81		670
	82	358(d)	78
	93		80
	94		81
	176		559
	574	358(d)(1)	81
	788	358(d)(2)	80
357(c)(1)	81	358(e)	559
	574	358(f)	574
357(c)(3)	80		575
	81		

Sec.	Page	Sec.	Page
361	485	368 (Cont'd)	558
	488		574
	545		604
	574		605
	575		606
	576	368(a)	604
	608		605
	620	368(a)(1)	485
	628	368(a)(1)(A)	486
	668		488
361(a)	487		552
	574	368(a)(1)(B)	486
	575		520
	577		554
	630	368(a)(1)(C)	545
	668		546
361(b)(1)	574		552
361(b)(2)	574		554
361(b)(3)	574	368(a)(1)(D)	608
	576		628
361(c)	575		630
	670		668
361(c)(1)	575		672
	671	368(a)(1)(E)	596
361(c)(2)	575		599
	671		604
	679		607
361(c)(2)(B)	671		608
361(c)(3)	575	368(a)(1)(F)	620
	576		621
361(c)(4)	671	368(a)(1)(G)	621
362	60	368(a)(2)(B)	545
	63		546
	69		574
	75	368(a)(2)(C)	488
	628		520
362(a)	57		545
	60		554
	69		555
	71	368(a)(2)(D)	554
	75		555
	281		557
	344		581
	576		590
	672	368(a)(2)(E)	554
	788		555
362(a)(1)	104		556
362(a)(2)	104		557
362(b)	485		577
	487		581
	488	368(a)(2)(E)(ii)	556
	520	368(a)(2)(G)	545
	545		547
	577		574
	630		576
	668	368(a)(2)(G)(ii)	545
	669	368(a)(2)(H)	608
	716	368(b)	485
362(c)	104		488
368	364		520
	448		545
	555		554

Sec.	Page	Sec.	Page
368(b) (Cont'd)	555	382 (Cont'd)	710
	559		711
	577		712
368(c)	57		713
	59		714
	61		716
	485		717
	520		718
	628		720
	634	382(a)	697
	635		699
368(c)(1)	556		711
381	380		714
	487	382(a)—(f)	706
	583	382(b)	699
	584	382(b)(1)	697
	590		699
	628		707
	669		709
	696	382(b)(2)	706
	703		708
	775	382(b)(3)(A)	708
	792	382(b)(3)(B)	708
381(a)	485	382(c)	699
	581		706
	583	382(c)(1)	706
	668	382(c)(2)	706
381(a)(1)	348	382(c)(3)(B)	718
	358	382(d)(2)	699
	698		707
381(a)(2)	488		711
	545	382(e)(1)	708
	547		709
	608	382(e)(2)	710
	698	382(f)	707
381(b)	583		708
	584	382(g)	699
	620		700
381(b)(3)	584		702
381(c)	581		703
	583	382(g)(1)	697
381(c)(1)	584		698
381(c)(1)—(c)(26)	583		700
381(c)(2)	358		701
	583	382(g)(1)(A)	701
381(c)(2)(B)	583	382(g)(2)	700
381(c)(3)	358	382(g)(3)	700
382	380	382(g)(3)(A)	701
	583	382(g)(3)(B)	702
	584	382(g)(4)(A)	701
	696	382(g)(4)(B)(i)	703
	698	382(h)	706
	699		711
	700	382(h)(1)	711
	701	382(h)(1)(A)(ii)	712
	702	382(h)(1)(B)	710
	703	382(h)(1)(B)(ii)	711
	704	382(h)(1)(C)	711
	705	382(h)(2)(A)	711
	706		718
	707	382(h)(2)(B)	711
	709	382(h)(2)(B)(i)	711

TABLE OF INTERNAL REVENUE CODE SECTIONS

Sec.	Page	Sec.	Page
382(h)(3)	718	384(b)	719
382(h)(3)(A)	710	384(b)(3)	719
	711	384(c)(1)(A)	718
382(h)(3)(B)	711	384(c)(1)(B)	718
	712	384(c)(1)(C)	718
	719	384(c)(2)	718
382(h)(3)(B)(i)	711	384(c)(3)(A)	718
382(h)(3)(B)(ii)	711	384(c)(4)	717
382(h)(7)	710	384(c)(5)	717
	717	384(c)(7)	717
382(i)	698	384(c)(8)	717
	699		718
	700		719
382(i)(1)	697	384(f)	719
	700	384(h)(1)(B)	718
382(i)(2)	700	385	135
382(i)(3)	700		137
382(j)	707		138
	708	385(a)	137
382(k)	700	441	13
	702		104
382(k)(2)	699	441(e)	13
382(k)(3)	699	441(i)(1)	13
	702	441(i)(2)	13
382(k)(6)(A)	709	444	13
382(k)(7)	699		14
	700		761
382(l)(1)	706	444(a)	756
	709		760
382(l)(1)(B)	709	444(b)	756
382(l)(3)	700	444(b)(1)	760
	704	444(b)(2)	13
382(l)(3)(A)(i)	705	444(b)(3)	760
382(l)(3)(A)(ii)	704	444(c)(1)	756
382(l)(3)(A)(ii)(I)	704	444(e)	756
382(l)(3)(A)(ii)(II)	704	448	104
382(l)(3)(A)(iii)	704	448(a)	14
382(l)(3)(B)	701	448(b)	14
	705	448(d)(2)	11
382(l)(3)(C)	701		12
382(l)(4)	700		14
	706	453	6
	709		75
382(l)(4)(A)	709		76
382(l)(4)(D)	709		155
383	583		332
	696		711
	713	453(b)(2)(A)	16
	714	453(c)	76
	720	453(d)	332
383(a)(2)(A)	713		333
383(a)(2)(B)	713		358
383(b)	713	453(d)(1)	359
383(c)	713	453(e)	116
384	583	453(f)(1)	116
	696	453(f)(6)	75
	716		573
	717	453(h)	789
	718	453(h)(1)(A)	333
	720	453(h)(1)(A)—(h)(1)(B)	330
384(a)	717	453(h)(1)(B)	333
	719	453(h)(2)	333

l

Sec.	Page	Sec.	Page
453(i)	6	533(a) (Cont'd)	464
	75	533(b)	450
	78	534	464
453(j)(2)	332		467
453(k)	333	534(a)	465
453(k)(2)	181	534(a)—(c)	452
	332	534(b)	465
	333	534(c)	465
	366	535	449
	573	535(a)	449
453(k)(2)(A)	217		465
	261		466
453(l)	16	535(b)	465
	75	535(b)(1)	465
453A	366	535(b)(2)	465
453B	162	535(b)(3)	465
453B(a)	60	535(b)(4)	465
453B(h)	789	535(b)(5)(A)	466
465	3	535(b)(5)(B)	466
	13	535(b)(5)(C)	466
	32	535(b)(6)	465
	763		466
465(a)(1)	13	535(b)(7)	465
465(a)(1)(A)	764	535(b)(8)	465
465(c)(2)(A)	764	535(c)	449
465(c)(2)(B)	764		465
465(c)(3)(B)	764		466
469	3		723
	13	535(c)(1)	452
	32		466
	47	535(c)(2)	466
	751	535(c)(2)(B)	449
	762	535(c)(4)	467
	764	537(a)	452
	797		458
469(a)(2)(A)	764	537(a)(2)	461
469(a)(2)(B)	13	537(a)(3)	461
469(b)	764	537(b)(1)	452
469(c)(1)	764		461
469(e)(1)	764	537(b)(2)	461
469(g)	764	541	467
469(h)(1)	764		468
469(j)(1)	13		479
469(k)	47		480
482	731		482
	732		483
	740	541 et seq.	5
	741		365
511 et seq.	360	542(a)	467
531	449		469
	467	542(a)(1)	469
	468	542(a)(2)	469
531 et seq.	5	542(c)	469
	120	543	469
532	449		470
532(a)	449		471
532(b)	450		474
532(b)(1)	448	543(a)	470
532(c)	450	543(a)(1)	471
533	464		474
533(a)	450	543(a)(1)(C)	474
	452	543(a)(3)	473

Sec.	Page	Sec.	Page
543(a)(4)	473	565 (Cont'd)	481
	474	565(a)—(d)	465
543(a)(5)	473	565(b)(1)	481
543(a)(6)	476	565(c)	466
543(a)(7)	476		481
543(a)(8)	476	565(f)	465
543(b)(1)	470	664	278
543(b)(1)(A)	469	671	756
543(b)(1)(B)	469	671 et seq.	753
543(b)(2)(A)	470	701	2
543(b)(2)(B)	470		32
543(b)(2)(C)	470	702	33
543(b)(3)	470	702(a)	749
543(d)(1)	474	702(b)	749
543(d)(2)—(d)(5)	474	704(b)(2)	751
544	197	704(d)	3
	469		32
544(a)	469	705	2
544(a)(1)	469	706(b)	760
544(a)(2)	469	707	3
544(a)(3)	469	707(b)	417
544(b)(1)	469		680
545	481	721	3
545(a)	479	722	774
545(b)	479	731(a)	749
545(b)(1)	479	736(a)	80
545(b)(2)	479	741	3
545(b)(3)	479	752	94
545(b)(4)	479	752(a)	751
545(b)(5)	479		774
545(b)(6)	479	801	33
547	480	904(c)	713
	482	1001	784
547(b)(1)	482	1001(a)	57
547(d)(1)	482		434
547(e)	482		778
561	248	1012	57
	465		247
	480		281
561(a)	466	1014	313
	480		448
562(a)	465		680
	466	1014(a)	59
	480		291
562(b)	465	1017	154
	480	1031	7
562(b)(1)	466		75
562(b)(2)	481		344
562(c)	465		348
	466		439
	480		444
563	480		780
563(a)	465		786
	466	1031(d)	780
	467	1032	60
563(b)	480		485
	481		487
563(d)	465		488
564	480		577
	481		596
565	466		598
	480		600

Sec.	Page	Sec.	Page
1032 (Cont'd)	608	1060(c)	386
	620	1060(e)	388
	668	1060(e)(2)(A)	388
	672	1201(a)	11
1032(a)	57	1211	13
	58	1211(a)	11
	520	1211(b)	436
	545	1212	13
	577	1212(a)(1)	11
	668	1221(3)	444
1033	154	1222(9)	782
	367	1223(1)	57
	444		59
	762		348
1036	596		560
	599		576
1041	746		596
1059	174		598
	175		599
	176		600
	191		628
	240		668
1059(a)	172		669
	191		670
	240	1223(2)	57
1059(a)(1)	174		60
1059(a)(2)	176		576
1059(b)	172		577
	176		668
	240		669
1059(c)	172	1223(5)	296
	191		303
1059(c)(1)	175	1231	60
1059(c)(2)	175		437
1059(c)(3)(A)	175		438
1059(c)(3)(B)	175		440
1059(c)(3)(C)	175		442
1059(c)(4)	175		443
1059(d)	172		469
1059(d)(1)(A)	176		471
1059(d)(1)(B)	176		482
1059(d)(5)	174		762
1059(d)(6)	174		763
1059(e)(1)	172	1231(a)(1)	438
	176	1231(b)	438
	240		443
1059(e)(1)(B)	573	1231(c)	438
1059(e)(2)	172	1239	70
	176		115
1059(e)(3)	172	1244	147
1059(e)(3)(A)	176		148
1059(e)(3)(A)(ii)	176	1244(a)	147
1059(e)(3)(B)	176	1244(a)—(c)	139
1059(e)(3)(C)(i)	176	1244(b)	148
1060	383	1244(c)(1)	147
	385	1244(c)(1)(C)	148
	386	1244(c)(2)(A)	148
	387	1244(c)(3)	147
	388		148
1060(a)	386	1245	359
	387		482
1060(b)	387	1245(a)(2)	359

Sec.	Page	Sec.	Page
1245(b)(3)	57	1361(c)(6)	752
	70	1361(d)	753
	358	1361(d)(1)	753
	359	1361(d)(2)	753
1250	359	1361(d)(3)	753
1250(b)(1)	359	1362	752
1250(b)(3)	359		756
1250(d)(3)	70	1362(a)	756
	358	1362(b)(1)	756
	359	1362(b)(2)	757
1271	120	1362(b)(2)(B)	757
1271(a)(1)	131	1362(b)(3)	792
1272—1273	415	1362(b)(4)	756
1272—1275	599	1362(c)	756
	608	1362(c)(3)(A)(ii)	757
1272(a)(1)	165	1362(c)(3)(A)(iii)(II)	757
1273(a)(1)	165	1362(d)	756
1274	755	1362(d)(1)(B)	757
1274(d)	708	1362(d)(1)(C)	757
	741	1362(d)(1)(D)	757
1348	447	1362(d)(2)	757
1361	19		790
	751	1362(d)(2)(B)	757
1361(a)	750	1362(d)(3)	365
1361(a)(1)	3		757
1361(a)(2)	2		781
1361(b)	751	1362(d)(3)(C)	758
	752		782
	791	1362(d)(3)(D)(i)	758
1361(b)(1)	752		782
1361(b)(1)(A)	19	1362(d)(3)(D)(ii)—(d)(3)(D)(iv)	782
	46	1362(d)(3)(D)(ii)—(d)(3)(D)(v)	758
	752	1362(e)	757
1361(b)(1)(A)—(b)(1)(D)	757	1362(e)(1)	758
1361(b)(1)(B)	19	1362(e)(1)(B)	758
	749		791
	752	1362(e)(3)	758
	790	1362(e)(5)(A)	758
	792	1362(e)(6)	758
1361(b)(1)(C)	19	1362(e)(6)(D)	758
	752	1362(f)	758
1361(b)(1)(D)	19	1362(g)	758
	46	1363	778
	754	1363(a)	21
1361(b)(2)	752		797
	792	1363(b)	761
1361(b)(2)(A)	19		762
	752	1363(b)(1)	762
	791	1363(b)(2)	762
1361(c)(1)	752	1363(b)(3)	762
1361(c)(2)(A)	753	1363(c)	761
1361(c)(2)(A)(i)	753	1363(c)(1)	762
1361(c)(2)(A)(ii)	753	1364(c)(1)	783
1361(c)(2)(A)(iii)	753	1366	94
1361(c)(2)(A)(iv)	753	1366(a)	20
1361(c)(2)(B)(i)	753		751
1361(c)(2)(B)(iii)	753	1366(a)—(e)	761
1361(c)(2)(B)(iv)	753	1366(a)(1)	21
1361(c)(3)	752		762
1361(c)(4)	754		763
1361(c)(5)	754	1366(a)(1)(A)	762
	788		

Sec.	Page	Sec.	Page
1366(b)	20	1374 (Cont'd)	783
	762		784
1366(c)	21		789
	762		790
1366(d)	763		792
	772	1374(a)	779
1366(d)(2)	763	1374(b)(1)	779
1366(e)	797	1374(b)(2)	779
	798	1374(c)(1)	779
	801	1374(c)(2)	780
	802	1374(d)(1)	780
	803	1374(d)(2)	779
1366(f)	761	1374(d)(2)(A)(ii)	779
1366(f)(2)	783	1374(d)(2)(B)	779
1366(f)(3)	783		780
1367	761	1374(d)(3)	779
	763	1374(d)(4)	779
	790		782
1367(a)	20		783
1367(a)(2)(A)	776	1374(d)(6)	780
1367(b)(2)(A)	763	1374(d)(7)	779
1367(b)(2)(B)	763	1374(d)(8)	780
1368	755		792
	774	1375	20
	775		365
	776		776
	789		778
1368(a)	20		781
1368(b)	20		782
	151		783
1368(b)(1)	774		784
1368(b)(2)	775		786
1368(c)	151		792
	775	1375(a)	750
1368(c)(1)	775	1375(b)(1)(A)	782
1368(c)(2)	776	1375(b)(1)(B)	779
1368(c)(3)	776		782
1368(e)(1)(A)	775	1375(b)(2)	782
1368(e)(3)	776	1375(b)(3)	782
1371	787	1375(b)(4)	783
1371(a)	776	1375(d)	750
1371(a)(1)	20		783
	774	1375(f)	750
	787	1377	761
1371(a)(2)	788	1377(a)	751
	791	1377(a)(1)	763
	792	1378	756
1371(b)	761		759
1371(c)	774	1378(b)	759
1371(c)(1)	775	1378(b)(2)	761
	783	1501	18
1371(e)	774		720
1371(e)(2)	776		742
1372	787	1501—1504	19
	796		391
1373	750	1502	18
1374	20		742
	750	1503	18
	778	1503(a)	742
	779	1503(e)	746
	780	1504	378
	781		

Sec.	Page	Sec.	Page
1504(a)	18	2522(c)(2)	278
	675	2701 et seq.	295
	742	2703(a)	265
	752	2703(b)	265
	791	3121(x)	793
1504(a)(1)	720	3201	793
1504(a)(2)	19	3221	793
	349	4943	461
	371	6166	291
	391		292
	717	6221—6233	762
	720	6241—6245	762
1504(a)(3)	745	6501(a)	292
1504(a)(4)	19	6742(d)	387
	349	7519	760
	709		761
	720	7519(a)	756
1504(b)	18	7519(a)(2)	760
	720	7519(b)	756
	742		760
	752	7519(b)(2)	760
1551	18	7519(c)	760
	723	7519(d)	760
1552	742	7519(d)(1)	756
1561	18	7519(e)(4)	756
1561(a)	723		760
1563	18	7701	31
	19		34
	719	7701(a)(3)	31
	723	7701(a)(42)—(a)(44)	59
2031	265	7701(a)(44)	59
2031(b)	265	7701(g)	342
2032	265	7704	3
2032A	291		46
2053	293	7704(b)	47
2054	293	7704(c)	47
2056(b)(5)	754	7872	80
2056(b)(7)	753		168
	756		741
2503(b)	754	7872(a)	167
2503(c)	754	7872(c)(1)(C)	167

TABLE OF TREASURY REGULATIONS

Temp.Reg.	Page
1.469–2T(c)(3)(i)(B)	764
1.469–5T	764
1.1502–20T	395

Prop.Reg.	Page
1.269–7	714
1.358–6	578
1.385–0(c)(2)	136
1.385–3(d)	136
1.385–3(e)	136
1.385–6	136
1.385–6(a)(3)	136
1.385–6(e)	136
1.385–6(f)(2)	137
1.385–6(g)	136
1.385–6(g)(3)	137
1.385–6(g)(4)	136
1.385–6(h)	137
1.453–1(f)(1)(i)	76
1.453–1(f)(1)(iii)	75
	76
1.453–1(f)(2)	573
1.453–1(f)(3)(i)	75
1.453–1(f)(3)(ii)	75
	76
	77
1.453–1(f)(3)(iii), Ex. (1)	75
	77
1.1032–2	577
	578
1.1361–1(b)(3)	754
1.1361–1(l)(2)(i)	754
1.1361–1(l)(3)(iii)(A)	754
1.1361–1(l)(3)(iii)(B)—(l)(3)(iii)(C)	754
1.1361–1(l)(4)(i)(B)	755
1.1361–1(l)(4)(ii)	755
1.1361–1(l)(4)(ii)(A)	755
1.1361–1(l)(4)(ii)(B)	755
1.1361–1(l)(4)(ii)(C)	755
1.1361–1(l)(4)(iii)	755
1.1361–1(l)(4)(v)	755
1.1361–1A(c)	752
1.1361–1A(d)(2)	752
1.1361–1A(e)(1)	752
1.1361–1A(e)(2)	752
1.1361–1A(i)(3)—(i)(6)	753
1.1362–1	756
1.1362–1(c)	756
1.1362–1(c)(1)	756
1.1362–1(c)(3)	756
1.1362–1(e)	756
1.1362–2	756
1.1362–2(b)(1)	756
1.1362–3	756
1.1362–3(b)	757
1.1362–3(b)(1)	756

Prop.Reg.	Page
1.1362–3(c)	756
	757
1.1362–3(d)	757
1.1362–5(b)	756
	759
1.7872–2(a)(2)(iii)	741

Reg.	Page
1.118–1	104
1.165–5(a)—(c)	139
1.166–5	139
1.248–1(a)	117
1.248–1(b)	117
1.248–1(b)(2)	117
1.248–1(b)(3)(i)	117
1.263(a)–2(c)	247
1.263(a)–2(e)	247
1.301–1(a)	156
1.301–1(b)	156
1.301–1(c)	150
1.301–1(d)(1)(ii)	165
	303
1.301–1(h)	303
1.301–1(h)(2)(i)	165
1.301–1(l)	596
	608
1.302–1(l)	604
1.302–2	222
1.302–2(a)	235
	281
1.302–2(b)	235
1.302–3	199
1.302–3(a)	200
	542
1.302–4	203
1.302–4(d)	217
1.302–4(e)	217
1.304–2(a)	279
	280
	281
1.304–2(c), Ex. (1)	279
	280
1.304–2(c), Ex. (2)	281
1.304–2(c), Ex. (3)	279
1.304–2(c), Ex. (4)	279
1.305–1	296
1.305–1(b)(1)	303
1.305–2	296
1.305–3(a)	296
1.305–3(b)	296
1.305–3(c)	296
1.305–3(e), Ex. (1)	296
1.305–3(e), Ex. (2)	296
1.305–3(e), Ex. (3)	296
1.305–3(e), Ex. (4)	296
1.305–3(e), Ex. (8)	296

Reg.	Page	Reg.	Page
1.305–3(e), Ex. (10)	296	1.332–2	348
1.305–3(e), Ex. (11)	296	1.332–2(c)	329
1.305–3(e), Ex. (12)	600	1.332–3	349
1.305–4	296	1.332–4	349
1.305–5(a)	296	1.332–5	348
1.305–5(d), Ex. (1)	600		350
1.305–5(d), Ex. (2)	600	1.332–7	358
1.305–5(d), Ex. (3)	600	1.338–4T(e)	375
1.305–5(d), Ex. (6)	600	1.338–4T(f)	375
1.305–6	296	1.338–4T(f)(6)	376
1.305–7(a)	296	1.338–4T(f)(6)(i)(A)	370
1.305–7(c)	596		377
	600	1.338–4T(f)(6)(ii)	376
1.305–8	303	1.338–4T(g)	375
1.306–1	317	1.338–4T(h)	372
1.306–1(b)(1)	317	1.338–4T(h)(1)	370
	318	1.338–4T(h)(3)	370
1.306–1(b)(2), Ex. (3)	318	1.338(b)–1T(a)	370
1.306–2	318	1.338(b)–1T(b)	370
1.306–3(a)—(c)	312	1.338(b)–1T(c)	370
1.306–3(d)	600	1.338(b)–1T(c)(1)	374
1.306–3(e)	312	1.338(b)–1T(d)(1)	370
1.307–1	296	1.338(b)–1T(e)	370
	303	1.338(b)–1T(f)(1)	370
1.307–1(a)	304		374
1.311–1(a)	162	1.338(b)–2T(a)	383
1.312–1(d)	303	1.338(b)–2T(b)	375
1.312–3	163		383
	164	1.338(b)–2T(b)(1)	385
1.312–6(a)	153	1.338(b)–2T(b)(2)(i)	386
	154	1.338(b)–2T(b)(2)(ii)	386
1.312–6(b)	153	1.338(b)–2T(b)(2)(iii)	386
	154	1.338(b)–2T(b)(2)(iv)	386
1.312–6(c)	154	1.338(b)–2T(c)	383
1.312–6(d)	153	1.338(b)–2T(c)(1)	386
1.312–7(b)(1)	153	1.338(b)–2T(c)(3)	386
1.312–10	668	1.338(b)–3T	386
1.312–10(a)	669	1.338(h)(10)–1T(d)(1)	378
	672	1.338(h)(10)–1T(e)(3)	378
1.312–10(b)	672	1.338(h)(10)–1T(e)(6)(C)	378
1.312–10(c)	669	1.338(h)(10)–1T(f)	378
	672	1.338(h)(10)–1T(g), Ex. (5)	378
1.312–11(a)	672	1.341–1	434
1.312–15(d)	165		435
1.316–1(a)(1)	151	1.341–2	437
1.316–1(a)(1)—(a)(2)	150	1.341–2(a)(2)	439
1.316–2(a)	158	1.341–2(a)(3)	439
1.316–2(a)—(c)	156	1.341–2(a)(4)	440
1.316–2(b)	157	1.341–3	437
	159	1.341–4	441
1.316–2(c), Ex.	157	1.341–4(c)(2)	442
1.318–1(a)	197	1.341–4(d)	443
1.318–1(b)	197	1.341–5	437
1.318–2	197	1.341–5(b)(5)	440
1.318–3(a)	197	1.341–5(c)(1)	440
1.318–3(b)	197	1.341–5(c)(2)	440
1.318–4	197	1.341–5(d), Ex. (2)	440
1.331–1(a)	330	1.341–5(d), Ex. (3)	439
1.331–1(b)	330	1.341–5(d), Ex. (4)	440
1.331–1(e)	330	1.351–1(a)	57
	332	1.351–1(a)(1)	61
1.332–1	348		66

Reg.	Page	Reg.	Page
1.351–1(a)(1) (Cont'd)	67	1.355–2(d)(3)(iv)	666
1.351–1(a)(1)(i)	66	1.355–2(d)(4), Ex. (2)	665
1.351–1(a)(1)(ii)	66	1.355–2(d)(4), Ex. (3)	665
	67	1.355–2(d)(5), Ex. (6)	659
1.351–1(a)(2)	66	1.355–2(d)(5)(i)	662
1.351–1(a)(2), Ex. (3)	66	1.355–2(d)(5)(ii)	662
1.351–1(b)	57	1.355–2(d)(5)(iii)	662
1.351–1(c)	58	1.355–2(d)(5)(iv)	662
1.351–2(a)	69	1.355–2(d)(5)(v), Ex. (2)	662
1.351–3(a)(6)	79	1.355–3	636
1.351–3(b)(7)	79	1.355–3(b)	239
1.354–1(a)	559	1.355–3(b)(1)—(b)(5)	646
1.354–1(b)	559	1.355–3(b)(2)(ii)	644
1.354–1(d), Ex. (3)	559	1.355–3(b)(2)(iii)	644
	608		645
1.354–1(e)	559	1.355–3(b)(2)(iv)	645
1.355–1(b)	634		647
	636	1.355–3(b)(3)(ii)	647
1.355–1(c)(3)	645	1.355–3(c)	239
1.355–2(b)	10	1.355–3(c), Ex. (2)	647
	635	1.355–3(c), Ex. (3)	647
	651	1.355–3(c), Ex. (4)	645
1.355–2(b)(1)	651	1.355–3(c), Ex. (5)	645
1.355–2(b)(2)	598	1.355–3(c), Ex. (7)	646
	659		647
1.355–2(b)(2)(B)—(b)(2)(D)	646	1.355–3(c), Ex. (8)	646
1.355–2(b)(3)	659	1.355–3(c), Ex. (9)	645
1.355–2(b)(4)	651	1.355–3(c), Ex. (10)	646
1.355–2(b)(5), Ex. (1)	659	1.355–3(c), Ex. (11)	646
1.355–2(b)(5), Ex. (2)	659		665
1.355–2(b)(5), Ex. (3)	659	1.355–3(c), Ex. (12)	647
1.355–2(b)(5), Ex. (4)	659	1.355–3(c), Ex. (13)	647
1.355–2(b)(5), Ex. (5)	659	1.356–1	559
1.355–2(c)	635	1.356–1(b)(2)	670
	660	1.356–3	559
1.355–2(c)(1)	660	1.356–4	559
1.355–2(c)(2), Ex. (2)	660	1.357–1	78
1.355–2(c)(2), Ex. (3)	660	1.357–1(a)	574
1.355–2(d)	661	1.357–1(c)	79
1.355–2(d)(1)	661	1.357–2	78
	662	1.357–2(a)	79
1.355–2(d)(2)	662	1.357–2(b)	95
1.355–2(d)(2)(i)	662	1.358–1	69
	663		559
1.355–2(d)(2)(ii)	663	1.358–1(a)	57
1.355–2(d)(2)(iii)(A)	663	1.358–2	69
1.355–2(d)(2)(iii)(B)	663		560
1.355–2(d)(2)(iii)(C)	663		668
1.355–2(d)(2)(iii)(D)	663		670
1.355–2(d)(2)(iii)(E)	664	1.358–2(a)(1)—(a)(4)	559
1.355–2(d)(2)(iv)	664	1.358–2(b)	559
1.355–2(d)(2)(iv)(A)	665	1.358–2(b)(2)	57
1.355–2(d)(2)(iv)(B)	665		69
1.355–2(d)(2)(iv)(C)	646	1.358–3	78
	647	1.362–1	69
	665	1.362–1(a)	57
1.355–2(d)(3)	651	1.368–1	488
	663	1.368–1(b)	484
1.355–2(d)(3)(i)	662		487
	663		495
1.355–2(d)(3)(ii)	666		597
1.355–2(d)(3)(iii)	666	1.368–1(c)	485

Reg.	Page
1.368–1(d)	706
1.368–2(a)	488
	495
1.368–2(b)(1)	488
1.368–2(b)(2)	554
	556
1.368–2(c)	520
1.368–2(d)	545
1.368–2(e)	596
1.368–2(e)(1)	598
1.368–2(e)(2)—(e)(4)	599
1.368–2(f)	554
	559
1.368–2(g)	487
	559
1.368–2(j)(1)	554
1.368–2(j)(3)—(j)(6)	554
1.368–2(j)(3)(ii)	556
1.381(a)–1(b)(2)	583
1.381(c)(2)–1(c)(2)	378
1.383–1T	713
1.453–9(c)(2)	60
1.482–1(a)	731
1.482–1(b)	731
1.482–1(b)(1)	741
1.482–1(c)	731
1.482–1(d)(2)	741
1.482–2(a)(1)—(a)(2)	731
1.482–2(a)(2)(iii)	741
1.533–1(a)(2)	450
1.533–1(b)	464
1.534–2(a)	465
1.534–2(b)	465
1.534–2(d)	465
1.537–1(a)	452
1.537–1(b)	452
1.537–1(b)(1)	459
1.537–1(b)(2)	459
1.537–1(c)	452
1.537–2	452
1.537–2(a)	458
1.537–2(b)	458
1.537–2(b)(3)	120
1.537–2(c)	458
1.537–2(c)(3)	467
1.537–3	452
1.537–3(a)	459
1.537–3(b)	459
	467
1.543–1(b)(3)	471
1.543–1(b)(8)	476
1.562–1(a)	466
	480
1.704–1(d)(2)	774
1.752–1T	751
1.1002–1(c)	484
1.1032–1	577
1.1032–1(a)	57
	58
1.1032–1(d)	57
1.1036–1(a)	599
1.1060–1T	386

Reg.	Page
1.1060–1T(b)(4)	386
1.1060–1T(h)	387
	388
1.1244(a)–1(a)	139
1.1244(a)–1(b)	139
	147
1.1244(a)–1(b)(2)	147
1.1244(b)–1(a)	148
1.1244(c)–1(d)	147
1.1244(c)–2(b)	148
1.1361–1A(e)	751
1.1362–3(d)(4)(ii)(B)	782
1.1502–1(e)	721
1.1502–1(f)	721
1.1502–1(g)(1)	721
1.1502–2	720
	746
	747
1.1502–11(a)(1)	720
1.1502–12	720
1.1502–13(a)(2)	747
1.1502–13(b)(1)	748
1.1502–13(b)(2)	748
1.1502–13(c)	747
1.1502–13(d)	747
	748
1.1502–13(f)	747
1.1502–14(a)	191
1.1502–14(a)(1)	151
	676
	747
1.1502–14(a)(2)	747
1.1502–14(b)	747
1.1502–14(c)	747
1.1502–15	721
1.1502–17(a)	746
1.1502–19(b)	747
1.1502–20	396
1.1502–21(c)	721
1.1502–21(d)	721
1.1502–21(d)(3)	721
1.1502–21(e)	720
1.1502–22(c)	721
1.1502–22(d)	721
1.1502–31(a)	747
1.1502–32	746
	747
1.1502–32(b)(2)	191
	676
1.1502–32(b)(2)(iii)	747
1.1502–32(e)(1)	747
1.1502–34	392
1.1502–75(d)(3)(i)	722
15A.453–1(c)	332
15A.453–1(d)	333
20.2031–2(f)(2)	265
20.2031–2(h)	265
301.7701–1(c)	31
301.7701–2(a)	31
301.7701–2(a)—(e)	31
301.7701–2(a)(1)	32
301.7701–2(a)(3)	33

TABLE OF TREASURY REGULATIONS

Reg.	Page	Reg.	Page
301.7701–2(b)	36	301.7701–2(e)	43
301.7701–2(c)(4)	39	301.7701–4	47
301.7701–2(d)	41		

*

L., S., L. & R. Corp. Tax. 3rd Ed. UCB—3

lxi

TABLE OF REVENUE RULINGS

Rulings with accompanying text are indicated by italic type

Rev.Rul.	Page	Rev.Rul.	Page
54–230	154	72–320	792
54–518	329	*72–327*	*578*
55–440	*540*	72–334	216
	542	72–380	216
56–345	542	73–54	542
56–373	672	73–427	366
56–451	647	73–496	791
56–556	216	73–552	547
56–655	647	73–580	390
57–114	542	74–5	661
57–276	620		675
57–278	577	*74–164*	*157*
57–328	317		*159*
57–518	*547*	74–515	560
59–119	*212*	74–516	670
	216	75–2	216
59–233	218	*75–67*	*476*
59–259	61	75–83	560
59–400	*648*	75–222	312
64–56	66	75–223	664
65–91	*784*	75–305	450
66–23	497	75–321	635
66–112	543	*75–406*	*692*
66–142	79	*75–447*	*251*
66–224	*491*	75–469	635
	496	*75–502*	*228*
66–365	542	*75–512*	*230*
67–274	*539*	75–561	621
	698	76–187	659
67–448	555	76–385	235
68–55	*72*	*76–386*	*314*
	74	77–22	659
68–285	542	77–108	313
68–348	332	77–238	599
68–388	218	77–245	240
68–601	198	*77–293*	*214*
69–6	364	77–426	235
69–330	388	77–467	218
69–357	66	78–197	277
69–566	791	78–280	102
69–608	*266*	78–401	235
70–225	*691*	*79–8*	*171*
70–359	388	*79–77*	*48*
70–360	388	79–106	46
70–496	281	79–155	598
70–609	154	*79–163*	*312*
71–326	349		316
71–383	661	*79–184*	*240*
71–426	216	79–250	487
71–427	599	79–273	366
72–71	304		660
72–265	598	79–376	245
	599	80–26	236

Rev.Rul.	Page	Rev.Rul.	Page
80–180	281	85–106	231
80–198	100	85–122	655
	101		659
	102	85–164	74
81–25	517	87–88	200
81–41	200	88–34	657
81–233	216	88–48	549
81–289	235	89–37	661
82–34	487	89–57	279
	596	89–63	319
84–114	600	89–64	198
84–131	763	90–95	366
84–137	477		369
85–14	201		377
85–48	332		

TABLE OF MISCELLANEOUS RULINGS

Rev.Proc.	Page	Rev.Proc.	Page
74–33	759	83–22	217
77–37	67	84–22	438
	488	84–42	543
	496	86–41, § 4.06	660
	543	87–3, § 3.01(22)	156
	546	87–3, § 4.02(1)	127
81–60, § 4.04	597	87–32	759
81–70	577	89–12	46
82–40	239	89–50	547

*

TABLE OF CASES

Principal cases are in italic type. Non-principal cases are in roman type. References are to Pages.

Abegg v. Commissioner, 104
Ambassador Apartments, Inc. v. Commissioner, 128
American Bantam Car Co. v. Commissioner, 62
American Potash & Chemical Corp. v. United States, 369
Anderson v. Commissioner, 92 T.C. 138, p. 162
Anderson v. Commissioner, 67 T.C. 522, p. 245
Aqualane Shores, Inc. v. Commissioner, 116
Ashby v. Commissioner, 167
Ashland Oil & Refining Co., Commissioner v., 62
Atlantic Commerce & Shipping Co., Inc. v. Commissioner, 460

Baan, Commissioner v., 636
Baker Commodities, Inc. v. Commissioner, 128
Bardahl Mfg. Corp. v. Commissioner, 459
Bashford, Helvering v., 555
Bauer v. Commissioner, 128
Bausch & Lomb Optical Co. v. Commissioner, 547, 551
Bazley v. Commissioner, 604, 607
Bedford's Estate, Commissioner v., 560
Benak v. Commissioner, 146
Bentsen v. Phinney, 513, 520
Bercy Industries, Inc. v. Commissioner, 584
Berger Machine Products, Inc. v. Commissioner, 620
B. Forman Co. v. Commissioner, 732, 741
Bhada v. Commissioner, 279
Blake v. Commissioner, 277
Bollinger, Commissioner v., 51
Bongiovanni v. Commissioner, 81
Bowers v. Commissioner, 146
Bradshaw v. United States, 116, 128
Broadview Lumber Co., Inc. v. United States, 281
Brown v. Commissioner, 772
Burnet v. Logan, 332
Burr Oaks Corp. v. Commissioner, 116
Bush Bros. and Co. v. Commissioner, 162

Camp Wolters Enterprises, Inc. v. Commissioner, 67
Carlberg v. United States, 543
Cerone v. Commissioner, 235

Chamberlin v. Commissioner, 296, 305, 311, 312
Chapman v. Commissioner, 520, 541
Charles McCandless Tile Service v. United States, 167
Charter Wire, Inc. v. United States, 129
Chrome Plate, Inc. v. United States, 369
Clark, Commissioner v., 560, 572, 573
Coady v. Commissioner, 645
Coates Trust v. Commissioner, 282
Commissioner v. ___ (see opposing party)
Court Holding Co., Commissioner v., 10, 161, 335, 339, 340
Crane v. Commissioner, 78, 81, 93, 332, 374
Crawford v. Commissioner, 218
Cumberland Public Service Co., United States v., 337, 339

D'Angelo Associates, Inc. v. Commissioner, 62
Danielson, Commissioner v., 384, 387
D'Arcy–Macmanus & Masius, Inc. v. Commissioner, 714
Davant v. Commissioner, 619, 620
Davis v. Commissioner, 797
Davis, United States v., 222, 236, 237
Day & Zimmermann, Inc, Commissioner v., 349
Donruss Co., United States v., 450, 451, 452
Drybrough v. Commissioner, 154
Dunn v. Commissioner, 217

Edna Louise Dunn Trust v. Commissioner, 636
E. I. Du Pont de Nemours & Co. v. United States, 66
Eisner v. Macomber, 297, 298
Elliotts, Inc. v. Commissioner, 167
Esmark, Inc. v. Commissioner, 10, 244, 507, 508, 677
Estate of (see name of party)

Farley Realty Corporation v. Commissioner, 138
FEC Liquidating Corp. v. United States, 575
Fellinger v. United States, 127
Fin Hay Realty Co. v. United States, 129
Fink, Commissioner v., 104, 105
Fireoved v. United States, 319

lxvii

First Nat. Bank of Altoona, Commissioner v., 456

First Sec. Bank of Utah, N. A., Commissioner v., 741

First State Bank of Stratford, Commissioner v., 150, 162

Five Star Mfg. Co. v. Commissioner, 247

Focht v. Commissioner, 81

Foster Lumber Co., Inc., United States v., 697

Fowler Hosiery Co. v. Commissioner, 240

Frank Lyon Co. v. United States, 9

Fulman v. United States, 466, 480

Gazette Pub. Co. v. Self, 461

General Geophysical Co., United States v., 9

General Housewares Corp. v. United States, 575

General Utilities & Operating Co. v. Helvering, 161, 162, 163, 243, 244, 334, 339, 340, 341, 370, 375, 380, 381, 390, 391, 392, 393, 395, 417, 418, 434, 437, 508, 591, 618, 668, 674, 677, 678, 778

Generes, United States v., 139, 146

George L. Riggs Inc. v. Commissioner, 349, 350

Gilbert v. Commissioner, 128

Godley's Estate, Commissioner v., 161

Golconda Min. Corp. v. Commissioner, 450

Golden Nugget, Inc. v. Commissioner, 487

Gooding Amusement Co. v. Commissioner, 236 F.2d 159, p. 128

Gooding Amusement Co., Inc. v. Commissioner, 23 T.C. 408, p. 128

Gordon v. Commissioner, 636

Gordon, Commissioner v., 636

Gowran, Helvering v., 297

GPD, Inc. v. Commissioner, 449

Gregory v. Commissioner, 633

Gregory v. Helvering, 630, *631,* 633, 651

Gregory, Helvering v., 10, 633

Grob, Inc. v. United States, 460

Groman v. Commissioner, 555

Grove v. Commissioner, 9, *270,* 274, 277, 278

Gunther v. Commissioner, 282

G. U. R. Co. v. Commissioner, 741

Haft Trust v. Commissioner, 510 F.2d 43, pp. 236, 237

Haft Trust v. Commissioner, 61 T.C. 398, p. 236

Hamrick v. Commissioner, 543

Harlan v. United States, 129

Harris v. United States, 765, *772*

Haserot v. Commissioner, 282

Haserot, Commissioner v., 282

Helvering v. —— (see opposing party)

Hempt Bros., Inc. v. United States, 96, 101, 102

Hendler, United States v., 78

Henricksen v. Braicks, 62

Henry T. Patterson Trust by Reeves Banking & Trust Co. v. United States, 237

Herbert v. Riddell, 435

Heverly v. Commissioner, 541

Hillsboro Nat. Bank v. Commissioner, 162, 334

Hilton Hotels Corp., United States v., 117, 247

Honigman v. Commissioner, 168

Howard v. Commissioner, 535

Idol v. Commissioner, 677

Imler v. Commissioner, 239

Intermountain Lumber Co. v. Commissioner, 62, 116

International Artists, Ltd. v. Commissioner, 167

Ivan Allen Co. v. United States, 458

Jackson v. Commissioner, 94

Jacobs v. Commissioner, 435

Jarvis v. Commissioner, 245

John A. Nelson Co. v. Helvering, 496

John B. Lambert & Associates v. United States, 461

John Lizak, Inc. v. Commissioner, 128

Johnson Trust v. Commissioner, 218

Joseph Radtke, S.C. v. United States, 794

Juden, Estate of v. Commissioner, 94

Kamborian, Estate of v. Commissioner, 67

Kass v. Commissioner, 491

Kelley, Commissioner v., 434, 439

Kimbell–Diamond Mill. Co. v. Commissioner, 366, 368, 369, 370, 372

Kintner, United States v., 34

Knetsch v. United States, 9

Koshland v. Helvering, 297, 298

Lamark Shipping Agency, Inc. v. Commissioner, 461

Larson v. Commissioner, 34, 46

Laughton, Commissioner v., 468

Leavitt, Estate of v. Commissioner, 875 F.2d 420, pp. 772, 773

Leavitt, Estate of v. Commissioner, 90 T.C. 206, p. 772

Lennard, Estate of v. Commissioner, 216, 217

Lessinger v. Commissioner, 82, 86, 87, 93, 94, 104

Lewis v. Commissioner, 47 T.C. 129, p. 216

Lewis v. Commissioner, 176 F.2d 646, p. 597

Libson Shops v. Koehler, 582

Lincoln Sav. & Loan Ass'n, Commissioner v., 389

Lisle v. Commissioner, 217

Litton Industries, Inc. v. Commissioner, 191, 192

Locke Mfg. Companies v. United States, 390

Lockwood's Estate v. Commissioner, 637, 644, 646, 647
Lynch v. Commissioner, 205, 216
Lynch v. Hornby, 152

Manassas Airport Industrial Park, Inc. v. Commissioner, 439
Marett, United States v., 645
Marr v. United States, 484
Matter of (see name of party)
McDonald's Restaurants of Illinois, Inc. v. Commissioner, 10, *497*, 507
Metropolitan Edison Co., Helvering v., 582
Metzger Trust v. Commissioner, 693 F.2d 459, p. 235
Metzger Trust v. Commissioner, 76 T.C. 42, pp. 218, 236
Microdot, Inc. v. United States, 487
Miller v. Commissioner, 496
Mills v. Commissioner, 542
Minnesota Tea Co., Helvering v., 496
Mixon, Estate of v. United States, 128
Morgenstern v. Commissioner, 664, 673
Morris Trust, Commissioner v., 659, *682*
Morrissey v. Commissioner, 34
Mountain State Steel Foundries, Inc. v. Commissioner, 461
Movielab, Inc. v. United States, 620
Munter, Commissioner v., 582
Murphy Logging Co. v. United States, 128
Myron's Enterprises v. United States, *452*, 457

Nash v. United States, 102
National Starch and Chemical Corp. v. Commissioner, 918 F.2d 426, pp. 389, 390
National Starch and Chemical Corp. v. Commissioner, 93 T.C. 67, p. 389
Neustadt's Trust, Commissioner v., 598
New Colonial Ice Co. v. Helvering, 582
Niedermeyer v. Commissioner, *283*, 290
Nye v. Commissioner, 128

O'Brien v. Commissioner, 435
Olson v. Commissioner, 659
O. P. P. Holding Corp., Commissioner v., 119
O'Sullivan Rubber Co. v. Commissioner, 471
Owen v. Commissioner, 94

P.A. Birren & Son v. Commissioner, 74
Paige v. United States, 754
Palmer v. Commissioner, 277
Parker v. Delaney, 93
Parshelsky's Estate v. Commissioner, 597, 659
Pelton Steel Casting Co. v. Commissioner, 461
Penrod v. Commissioner, 506, 507
Phellis, United States v., 484
Phipps, Commissioner v., 582

Pinellas Ice & Cold Storage Co. v. Commissioner, 496
Plantation Patterns, Inc. v. Commissioner, 128, 772
P. M. Finance Corp. v. Commissioner, 128, 129
Pollock v. Farmers' Loan & Trust Co., 1

Rafferty v. Commissioner, 598, *651*
R. C. Owen Co. v. Commissioner, 129
Redding v. Commissioner, 636
Rice's Toyota World, Inc. v. Commissioner, 9
Richmond, Fredericksburg and Potomac R. Co. v. Commissioner, 138
Rickey v. United States, 218
Rockefeller v. United States, 484
Romy Hammes, Inc. v. Commissioner, 621
Rooney v. United States, 741
Rosen v. Commissioner, 94
Rosenberg, Estate of v. Commissioner, 296
Russell v. Commissioner, 488

Sansome, Commissioner v., 581
Schnitzer v. Commissioner, 127
Seide v. Commissioner, 607
Selfe v. United States, 772
Slappey Drive Indus. Park v. United States, 128
Smith v. Commissioner, 94
Smoot Sand & Gravel Corp. v. Commissioner, 120
Smothers v. United States, *609*, 618, 620
Southwest Consol. Corp., Helvering v., 542
Southwest Natural Gas Co. v. Commissioner, *489*
Standard Linen Service, Inc. v. Commissioner, 677
Stanton v. United States, 62
Stauffer's Estate v. Commissioner, 620
Stinnett's Pontiac Service, Inc. v. Commissioner, *168*
St. Louis County Bank v. United States, 265
Strassburger v. Commissioner, 298, 298

T.C. Heyward & Co. v. United States, 452
Thatcher v. Commissioner, 81
Thompson Engineering Company, Inc. v. Commissioner, 460
Tomlinson v. 1661 Corp., 128
Towne v. Eisner, 297
Transport Mfg. & Equipment Co. v. Commissioner, 167
TSN Liquidating Corp., Inc. v. United States, *180*, 183, 190, 191, 192, 253
Tufts, Commissioner v., 93, 342
Tyler v. Tomlinson, 129

Ullman v. Commissioner, 384
Union Mut. Ins. Co. of Providence, Commissioner v., 127

United States v. ___ (see opposing party)

Vogel Fertilizer Co., United States v., 723

Waltham Netoco Theatres, Inc. v. Commissioner, 162
Waterman S. S. Corp. v. Commissioner, 9, 192
Webb v. Commissioner, 154
Wilcox Mfg. Co. Inc. v. Commissioner, 461
Williams v. Commissioner, 168

Williams v. McGowan, 383
Wood Preserving Corp. of Baltimore v. United States, 127
Woodward v. Commissioner, 117, 247
Wright v. United States, 234, 560
Wyman Bldg. Trust v. Commissioner, 49, 50

Zager v. Commissioner, 168
Zenz v. Quinlivan, 249
Zychinski v. Commissioner, 782

TABLE OF AUTHORITIES

American Law Institute, Federal Income Tax Project, Subchapter C (1986), 698

American Law Institute, Federal Income Tax Project—Subchapter C (1982), 4, 340

Andrews, "Comment: Estate Waiver of the Estate-Beneficiary Attribution Rules in Nonliquidating Redemptions Under Section 302 and Related Matters: The Rickey Case in the Fifth Circuit," 35 Tax L.Rev. 147 (1979), 218

Andrews, " 'Out of Its Earnings and Profits': Some Reflections on the Taxation of Dividends," 69 Harv.L.Rev. 1403 (1956), 153

Andrews, "Tax Neutrality Between Equity Capital and Debt," 30 Wayne L.Rev. 1057 (1984), 120

Bittker & Eustice, Federal Income Taxation of Corporations and Shareholders (5th ed. 1987), p. 168; ¶ 1.01 p. 1; ¶ 1.02 p. 447; ¶ 3.14 p. 116; ¶ 7.02 p. 151; ¶ 7.20 p. 161; ¶ 7.41 p. 297; ¶ 8.06 p. 459; ¶ 8.07 p. 121; ¶ 8.20 p. 468; ¶ 9.01 p. 196; ¶ 11.03 p. 332; ¶ 11.45 p. 369; ¶ 12.03 p. 438; ¶ 13.02 p. 633; ¶ 13.12 p. 670; ¶ 13.15 p. 673; ¶ 14.01 p. 485; ¶ 14.56 p. 543

Bittker & Eustice, Federal Income Taxation of Corporations and Shareholders (1990 Supp. to 5th ed., 1987), ¶ 9.35 p. 281

Bittker & Eustice, Federal Income Taxation of Corporations and Shareholders (4th ed. 1979), ¶ 4.04 p. 127; ¶ 9.24 p. 236

Bittker & Eustice, Federal Income Taxation of Corporations and Shareholders (3rd ed. 1971), ¶ 4.05 p. 135

Bittker & Lokken, Federal Taxation of Income, Estates and Gifts (2d ed. 1989) ¶ 1.1.2 p. 1; ¶ 4.3.1 p. 8; ¶ 5.7.1 p. 102; ¶ 4.3.1 p. 8; ¶ 25.11 p. 697

Block, "Liquidations Before and After Repeal of General Utilities," 21 Harv.J.Legis. 307 (1984), 162

Blum, "Behind the General Utilities Doctrine, or Why Does the General Have So Much Support from the Troops," 62 Taxes 292 (1984), 340

Blum, "Motive, Intent, and Purpose in Federal Income Taxation," 34 U.Chi.L.Rev. 485 (1967), 630

Blum, "Taxing Transfers of Incorporated Business: A Proposal for Improvement," 52 Taxes 516 (1974), 162

Blum, "The Earnings and Profits Limitations on Dividend Income: A Reappraisal," 53 Taxes 68 (1975), 153

Bogdanski, "Closely Held Corporations: Section 351 and Installment 'Boot' ", 11 J.Corp.Tax'n 268 (1984), 77

Bogdanski, "Of Debt, Discharge, and Discord: Jackson v. Com'r", 10 J.Corp. Tax'n 357 (1984), 94

Bogdanski, "Shareholder Debt, Corporate Debt: Lessons for Leavitt and Lessinger", 16 J.Corp.Tax'n 348, 352–53 (1990), 93

Bonovitz, "S Corporations and Section 332," Tax Notes 1545 (Sept. 17, 1990), 791

Bravenec, Federal Taxation of S Corporations and Shareholders (1988), 749

Bravenec & Gray, "Shareholder Agreements Can Preserve the S Election and Remedy Its Termination," 63 J.Tax'n 130 (1985), 757

Bravenec & Orbach, "Accumulated Adjustments Account of S Corporation Should Not Strictly Mirror Shareholders' Basis Adjustments," 39 Tax Notes 111 (April 4, 1988), 775

Break, "The Incidence and Economic Effects of Taxation," in The Economics of Public Finance (Brookings, 1974), 4

Burrough and Helyar, "Barbarians at the Gate," (Harper & Row, 1989), 396

Cain, "Taxation of Boot Notes in a 351/453 Transaction," 27 S.Texas L.Rev. 61 (1985), 75

Canellos, "Corporate Tax Integration: By Design or By Default?" in Corporate Tax Reform: A Report of the Invitational Conference on Subchapter C 129 (Am.Bar Ass'n Section on Taxation; N.Y. State Bar Ass'n Tax Section, 1988), 21

Canellos, "Tax Integration By Design or By Default?" Corporate Tax Reform: A Report of the Invitational Conference on Subchapter C 132–35 (American Bar Association, Section of Taxation; New York State Bar Association, Tax Section, 1988), 22

Cary & Eisenberg, Cases and Materials on Corporations (6th ed. 1988), 1, 488

Chirelstein, "Learned Hand's Contribution to the Law of Tax Avoidance," 77 Yale L.J. 440 (1968), 630

Citizens for Tax Justice, "Corporate Taxpayers and Corporate Freeloaders," 29 Tax Notes 947 (Dec. 2, 1985), 16

Clark, "The Morphogenesis of Subchapter C: An Essay in Statutory Evolution and Reform," 87 Yale L.J. 90 (1977), 1

Cohen, Surrey, Tarleau and Warren, "A Technical Revision of the Federal Income Tax Treatment of Corporate Distributions to Shareholders," 52 Colum. L.Rev. 1, 11–14 (1952), 311

Cooper, "Negative Basis," 75 Harv. L.Rev. 1352 (1962), 80

Cunningham, "More Than You Ever Wanted to Know About the Accumulated Earnings Tax," 6 J.Corp.Tax'n 187, 209 (1979), 449, 459

Del Cotto & Wolf, "The Proportionate Interest Test of Section 305 and the Supreme Court," 27 Tax L.Rev. 49 (1971), 294

Dentino & Walker, "Impact of the Installment Sales Revision Act of 1980 on Evidences of Indebtedness in a Section 351 Transaction," 9 J.Corp.Tax'n 330 (1983), 75

Doernberg, "The Accumulated Earnings Tax: The Relationship Between Earnings and Profits and Accumulated Taxable Income in a Redemption Transaction," 34 U.Fla.L.Rev. 715 (1982), 449

Dubroff & Daileader, "Kimbell-Diamond Revisited: A Critique of Judicial Analysis of the Exclusivity of Section 334(b)(2)," 43 Albany L.Rev. 739 (1979), 369

Eustice, "A Case Study in Technical Tax Reform: Section 361, or How Not to Revise a Statute," 35 Tax Notes 283 (April 20, 1987), 575

Eustice, "Alternatives for Limiting Loss Carryovers," 22 San Diego L.Rev. 149 (1985), 698

Eustice, "Section 361 Redux," 44 Tax Notes 443 (July 24, 1989), 575

Eustice and Kuntz, Federal Income Taxation of Subchapter S Corporations (rev. ed. 1985), 749; ¶ 6.03, p. 788; ¶ 11.02(2) p. 793

Eustice, The Tax Reform Act of 1984, 3–35, 36 (1984), 608

Eustice et al., The Tax Reform Act of 1986 (1987), 436, 449

Faber, "Business Purpose and Section 355," 43 Taxes 855 (1990), 651

Faber, "Capital Gains v. Dividends in Corporate Transactions: Is the Battle Still Worth Fighting?" 64 Taxes 865, 866 (1986), 449, 572, 619

Federal Income Tax Project, Subchapter C, American Law Institute (1982), 485

Feinberg & Robinson, "The Corporate Alternative Minimum Tax—Working With BURP While Waiting for ACE," 15 J.Corp.Tax'n 3 (1988), 16

Ferguson & Ginsburg, "Triangular Reorganizations," 28 Tax L.Rev. 159 (1973), 554

Fisher, "Classification Under Section 7701—The Past, Present and Prospects for the Future," 30 Tax Lawyer 627 (1977), 34

Gideon Holds Secret Meeting With CFOs to Discuss Corporate Integration Study," 46 Tax Notes 379 (Jan. 22, 1990), 8

Ginsburg, "Collapsible Corporations—Revisiting An Old Misfortune," 33 Tax L.Rev. 307 (1978), 434

Ginsburg, "Taxing Corporate Acquisitions," 38 Tax L.Rev. 171 (1983), 240

Ginsburg & Levin, Mergers, Acquisitions and Leveraged Buyouts (Vol. F1), ¶ 207, p. 379

Ginsburg & Levin, Mergers, Acquisitions and Leveraged Buyouts (Vol. F2), ¶ 704.021, p. 660; ¶ 1105, p. 791

Goode, The Corporate Income Tax (1951), 4

Harberger, "The Incidence of the Corporation Income Tax," 70 J.Pol.Econ. 215 (1962), 4

Hearings Before the Senate Finance Committee, Reform of Corporate Taxation, S.Hrg. 98–556, 98th Cong., 1st Sess. 150–70 (1983), 418

Henderson, "Federal Tax Techniques for Asset Redeployment Transactions," 37 Tax L.Rev. 325 (1982), 240, 244

Hutton, "Musings on Continuity of Interest—Recent Developments," 56 Taxes 904 (1978), 495

Jacobs, "Tax Treatment of Corporate Net Operating Losses and Other Tax Attribute Carryovers," 5 Va. Tax Rev. 701 (1986), 698

Johnson & Cochran, "Looking a Gift-Horse in the Mouth: Some Observations and Suggestions for Improving Internal Revenue Code Section 1244," 39 Sw.L.J. 975 (1986), 147

Joint Committee on Taxation, Federal Income Tax Aspects of Corporate Financial Structures, 101st Cong., 1st Sess. (JCS 1–89, Jan. 18, 1989), 121, 390, 397

Joint Committee on Taxation, Tax Shelter Proposals and Other Tax-Motivated Transactions, 98th Cong., 2d Sess. 39–40 (1984), 174

Jones, Patrick G., "Consolidated Tax Returns: Post Acquisition Losses", 27 Emory Law Journal 79 (1978), 742

Kaden & Wolfe, "Spin-offs, Split-offs, and Split-ups: A Detailed Analysis of Section 355," 44 Tax Notes 565 (July 31, 1989), 628, 661, 677

Kahn, "Closely Held Stocks—Deferral and Financing of Estate Tax Costs through Sections 303 and 6166," 35 Tax Lawyer 639, 676–681 (1982), 292

Klein, "The Incidence of the Corporation Income Tax: A Lawyer's View of a Problem in Economics," 65 Wisc.L.Rev. 576 (1965), 4

Klein & Coffee, Business Organization and Finance 306–338 (4th ed. 1990), 119

Kuntz, "Stock Redemptions Following Stock Transfers—An Expanding 'Safe Harbor,' Under Section 302(c)(2)(B)," 58 Taxes 29 (1980), 204

Kwall, "Subchapter G of the Internal Revenue Code: Crusade Without a Cause," 5 Va. Tax Rev. 223 (1985), 448

Lang, "Dividends Essentially Equivalent to Redemptions: The Taxation of Boot-strap Stock Acquisitions," 41 Tax L.Rev. 309 (1986), 249

Levin & Bowen, "The Section 385 Regulations Regarding Debt Versus Equity: Is the Cure Worse than the Malady?" 35 Tax Lawyer 1 (1981), 137

Lewis, "A Proposal for a Corporate Level Tax on Major Stock Sales," 37 Tax Notes 1041 (1987), 381

Lewis, "A Proposed New Treatment for Corporate Distributions and Sales in Liquidations," 86th Cong., 1st Sess., House Committee on Ways and Means, 3 Tax Revision Compendium 1643 (1959), 340

Limberg, "Master Limited Partnerships Offer Significant Benefits," 65 J.Tax'n 84 (1986), 46

Lind, Schwarz, Lathrope & Rosenberg, Cases and Materials on Fundamentals of Corporate Taxation 3–4 (1st ed. 1985), 7

Lind, Schwarz, Lathrope & Rosenberg, Cases and Materials on Fundamentals of Partnership Taxation (2d ed. 1988), 3, 749

Lowe, "Bailouts: Their Role in Corporate Planning," 30 Tax L.Rev. 357 (1975), 294, 314

McLure, "Integration of the Personal and Corporate Income Taxes: The Missing Element in Recent Tax Reform Proposals," 88 Harv.L.Rev. 532 (1975), 4, 21

McLure, "Must Corporate Income Be Taxed Twice?," (1979), 2

McNulty, "Reform of the Individual Income Tax By Integration of the Corporate Income Tax," 46 Tax Notes 1445 (Mar. 19, 1990), 8

Meale, "Eligibility, Election and Termination Under the Subchapter S Revision Act of 1982," 11 Fla.St.U.L.Rev. 93 (1983), 751

Mentz, Carlisle & Nevas, "Leveraged Buyouts: A Washington Perspective of 1989 Legislation and Prospects for 1990," 46 Tax Notes 1047 (Feb. 26, 1990), 396

Miller, "The Nominee Conundrum: The Live Dummy is Dead, But the Dead

Dummy Should Live," 34 Tax L.Rev. 213 (1979), 50

Morgan, "The Domestic Technology Base Company: The Dilemma of an Operating Company Which Might Be a Personal Holding Company," 33 Tax L.Rev. 233 (1978), 474

New York State Bar Association, Tax Section, "Report on Reverse Triangular Mergers and Basis-Nonrecognition Rules in Triangular Reorganizations," 36 Tax L.Rev. 395 (1981), 578

"News: Treasury Punts on Mirror Transactions," 33 Tax Notes 988 (Dec. 15, 1986), 392

Nolan, "Taxing Corporate Distributions of Appreciated Property: Repeal of the General Utilities Doctrine and Relief Measures," 22 San Diego L.Rev. 97 (1985), 340

Note, "Deductibility of Stock Redemption Expenses and the Corporate Survival Doctrine," 58 So.Cal.L.Rev. 895 (1985), 247

Nuzum, "Waiver of the Family Ownership Rules Under Section 302(c)(2)(A): Retention or Reacquisition of a Prohibited Interest," 11 J.Corp.Tax'n 19 (1984), 203

Paul, Studies in Federal Taxation 82 (3d ed. 1940), 620

Peel, "Definition of a Partnership: New Suggestions on an Old Issue," 1979 Wis.L.Rev. 989 (1979), 34

Plumb, "The Federal Income Tax Significance of Corporate Debt: A Critical Analysis and a Proposal," 26 Tax L.Rev. 369 (1971), 127

Posin, "Taxing Corporate Reorganizations: Purging Penelope's Web," 133 U.Penn.L.Rev. 1335 (1985), 557

Postlewaite & Finnerman, "Section 302(b)(1): The Expanding Minnow", 64 Va.L.Rev. 561 (1978), 222

Pugh, "The F Reorganization: Reveille for a Sleeping Giant?" 24 Tax L.Rev. 437 (1969), 620

Raum, "Dividends in Kind: Their Tax Aspects," 63 Harv.L.Rev. 593 (1950), 162

Recommendations as to Federal Tax Distinction between Corporate Stock and Indebtedness, N.Y. State Bar Association Tax Section Committee on Reorganization Problems, 25 Tax Lawyer 47 (1971), 135

"Reform of Corporate Taxation," Hearing before the Committee on Finance, United States Senate, 98th Cong., 1st Sess. 148, 151, 153–157, 174–176, 185, 268–270 (Oct. 24, 1983), 340

Report of Senate Finance Committee on Bankruptcy Tax Bill of 1980, S.Rep. No. 96–1035, 96th Cong., 2d Sess. 34–38, p. 622

Rose, "The Prohibited Interest of Section 302(c)(2)(A)," 36 Tax L.Rev. 131 (1981), 216

Rosenberg, "Tax Avoidance and Income Measurement," 87 Mich.L.Rev. 365 (1988), 10, 138

Rosenberg, K., "Toward Uniformity in Basis Terminology," 32 Tax Notes 1099 (Sept. 15, 1986), 59

Rudick, " 'Dividends' and 'Earnings or Profits' Under the Income Tax Law; Corporate Non-Liquidating Distributions," 89 U.Pa.L.Rev. 865 (1941), 153

Rudolph, "Stock Redemptions and the Accumulated Earnings Tax—an Update," 4 J.Corp.Tax 101 (1977), 461

Scallen, "Federal Income Taxation of Professional Associations and Corporations," 49 Minn.L.Rev. 603 (1965), 34

Schenk, Federal Taxation of S Corporations (1985), 749

Schlenger, J. and H. Nussenfeld, "Valuing Closely Held Business Interests and Planning the Buy-Sell Agreement," 44 N.Y.U.Inst. on Fed. Tax'n 52–1 (1986), 254

Schler, "Avoiding the Technical Requirements of New Section 355," 38 Tax Notes 417 (Jan. 25, 1988), 677

Senate Finance Committee Explanation of the Tax Reform Act of 1984, S.Rep. No. 98–169, 98th Cong., 2d Sess. 188–90 (1984), 166

Senate Finance Committee Report on Tax Reform Act of 1969, S.Rep. No. 91–552, 91st Cong., 1st Sess. 150–54 (1969), 299

Simmons, "Net Operating Losses and Section 382: Searching for a Limitation on Loss Carryovers," 63 Tul.L.Rev. 1045 (1989), 696

Simon & Simmons, "The Future of Section 355," 40 Tax Notes 291 (July 18, 1988), 668

Staff of Joint Committee on Taxation, 32 Tax Notes 1033 (Sept. 8, 1986), 393

Staff of Joint Committee on Taxation, Description of the Technical Corrections Bill of 1988, 100th Cong., 2d Sess. 421 (1988), 717

Staff of Joint Committee on Taxation, General Explanation of Tax Equity and Fiscal Responsibility Act of 1982, 97th Cong., 2d Sess. 125 (1982), 219, 244, 282

Staff of Joint Committee on Taxation, General Explanation of the Tax Reform Act of 1984, 98th Cong., 2d Sess. 181 (1984), 246

Staff of Joint Committee on Taxation, General Explanation of the Revenue Act of 1978, 96th Cong., 1st Sess. 219–220 (1979), 82

Staff of Joint Committee on Taxation, General Explanation of the Revenue Provisions of the Deficit Reduction Act of 1984, 98th Cong., 2d Sess. 183 (1984), 178

Staff of Joint Committee on Taxation, General Explanation of the Tax Reform Act of 1986, 100th Cong., 1st Sess. 343 (1987), 345, 384

Staff of the Senate Finance Committee, Preliminary Report on the Reform and Simplification of the Income Taxation of Corporations, 98th Cong., 1st Sess. (S.Prt. 98–95, 1983), 153, 340, 434, 448, 557

Staff of the Senate Finance Committee, The Subchapter C Revision Act of 1985: A Final Report Prepared by the Staff, 99th Cong., 1st Sess. (S.Prt. 99–47, 1985), 153, 341, 427, 437, 485, 557, 572, 591, 698

Steines, "Policy Considerations in the Taxation of B Reorganizations," 31 Hastings L.J. 993 (1980), 520

Stephan, "Disaggregation and Subchapter C: Rethinking Corporate Tax Reform," 76 Va.L.Rev. 655 (1990), 674

Stone, "Back to Fundamentals: Another Version of the Stock Dividend Saga," 79 Colum.L.Rev. 898 (1979), 294

Stone, "Debt-Equity Distinctions in the Tax Treatment of the Corporation and its Shareholders," 42 Tulane L.Rev. 251 (1968), 127

Stone & McGeehan, "Distinguishing Corporate Debt From Stock Under Section 385," 36 Tax L.Rev. 341 (1981), 137

Taggart, "Emerging Tax Issues in Corporate Acquisitions," 44 Tax L.Rev. 459, 481 (1989), 780

"Tax Officials Discuss Integration, Future Legislation at ABA Meeting," 46 Tax Notes 756 (Feb. 12, 1990), 8

Thompson, "An Analysis of the Proposal to Repeal General Utilities with an Escape Hatch," 31 Tax Notes 1121 (June 16, 1986), 163

U.S. Department of the Treasury, 2 Tax Reform for Fairness, Simplification and Economic Growth—General Explanation of the Treasury Department's Proposals 146–150 (1984), 34

U.S. Treasury Department, Technical Explanation of Treasury Tax Reform Proposals: Hearings Before the House Comm. on Ways and Means, 91st Cong., 1st Sess. 5228–5275 (April 22, 1969), 750

Walter, " 'Preferred Stock' and 'Common Stock': The Meaning of the Terms and the Importance of the Distinction for Tax Purposes," 5 J.Corp.Tax'n 211 (1978), 312

Walter, "Spin-Offs, Split-Offs and Split-Ups in Two Step Acquisitions and Dispositions," 66 Taxes 970, 980–986 (1988), 677

Warren, "The Relation and Integration of Individual and Corporate Income Taxes," 94 Harv.L.Rev. 719 (1981), 8

Wolfman, "Continuity of Interest and the American Law Institute Study," 57 Taxes 840 (1979), 495

Wolfman, "Subchapter C and the 100th Congress," 33 Tax Notes 669 (Nov. 17, 1986), 7, 436, 448, 572

Wolfman, "Whither C," 38 Tax Notes 1269 (Mar. 14, 1988), 8

Yin, "A Carryover Basis Regime? A Few Words of Caution," 37 Tax Notes 415 (1987), 381

Yin, "General Utilities Repeal: Is Tax Reform Really Going to Pass it By?",

31 Tax Notes 1111 (June 11, 1986), 163, 340

Yin, "Taxing Corporate Liquidations (and Related Matters) After the Tax Reform Act of 1986," 42 Tax L.Rev. 573 (1987), 334, 379

Zolt, "Corporate Taxation After the Tax Reform Act of 1986: A State of Disequilibrium," 66 N.C.L.Rev. 839 (1988), 4

Zolt, "The General Utilities Doctrine: Examining the Scope of Repeal," 65 Taxes 819 (1987), 381

CASES AND MATERIALS

ON

FUNDAMENTALS

OF

CORPORATE TAXATION

*

PART ONE: INTRODUCTION

CHAPTER 1. AN OVERVIEW OF THE TAXATION OF CORPORATIONS AND SHAREHOLDERS

A. INTRODUCTION *

1. TAXATION OF BUSINESS ENTITIES

Since the time when the British Crown begrudgingly recognized collective profit-seeking enterprises,[1] the artificial legal entity known as the "corporation" has served as a principal vehicle for conducting business in a capitalist economic system. Legal advisors to the earliest American corporations spent much of their time defining the relationship between the corporation and the state and developing hoary doctrines to regulate corporate governance and control. It was not until late in the 19th century that the genteel world of corporate law was jolted by the emergence of the income tax as a principal government revenue raising device. The life of the corporate lawyer would never be the same again. From the ill-fated Income Tax of 1894, which at the time was viewed as a Socialist plot because it imposed a two percent tax on individual and corporate net income,[2] to the Payne-Aldrich Tariff Act of 1909, which imposed a modest one percent tax on corporate net income over $5,000,[3] to the Sixteenth Amendment and beyond, the income tax gradually came to influence how corporations conducted their affairs. It is now well acknowledged, though often lamented, that the federal tax law has invaded virtually every aspect of American business life. It shapes and often twists management decisions and generally is an unpleasant distraction to those who would prefer to devote their full resources to the pursuit of profit. There is no reason to believe that this is any less true under the "simplified" Internal Revenue Code of 1986 than it was under the 1954 Code.

The decision to superimpose an income tax on a system that recognized artificial entities as separate from their owners raised a fundamental structural question. Simply put, the dilemma confronting the architects of the federal income tax was whether to treat corpora-

---

* See generally Clark, "The Morphogenesis of Subchapter C: An Essay in Statutory Evolution and Reform," 87 Yale L.J. 90 (1977).

1. See generally Cary & Eisenberg, Cases and Materials on Corporations 1 (6th ed. 1988).

2. See Bittker, Federal Income Taxation of Income, Estates and Gifts ¶ 1.1.2 (2d ed. 1989); See also Pollock v. Farmers' Loan & Trust Co., 157 U.S. 429, 15 S.Ct. 673 (1895).

3. See Bittker & Eustice, Federal Income Taxation of Corporations and Shareholders ¶ 1.01 (5th ed. 1987).

1

tions, partnerships, trusts and other vehicles for conducting business as separate taxable entities or as an aggregate of the underlying owners.

Since the earliest income tax acts, a corporation has been treated as a distinct taxable entity, separate and apart from its shareholders. Once that policy decision was made, a host of additional questions followed. What rates should be applied to corporate income? Should they resemble the graduated rates applicable to individuals or is a flat rate more appropriate? How should the tax system treat transactions between a corporation and its shareholders? If a corporation already has been taxed on its earnings, should those earnings be taxed again when they are distributed to the shareholders? If so, is it appropriate to give the corporation a deduction for the amount of the distribution? In short, as one prominent economist has asked, must corporate income be taxed twice—once when earned by the corporation and again, after distribution to the shareholders? [4]

The answers to these and many other questions will unfold throughout this course. But it serves no purpose to hide the ball on the most fundamental question. Congress, having decided to treat the corporation as a separate taxpaying entity, went on to adopt a double tax regime. A tax is imposed annually, at the rates set forth in Section 11, on the taxable income of a corporation. That income is effectively taxed again when distributed to the shareholders in the form of dividends, which are not deductible by the distributing corporation.[5] Because the corporation is treated as a separate taxable entity, transactions between corporations and their shareholders are taxable events. The tax consequences of these transactions and other major changes and adjustments in a corporation are governed by Subchapter C (Sections 301 to 385) of the Internal Revenue Code of 1986, a challenging and fascinating body of law that is the principal subject of this book. Corporations subject to the double tax regime also draw their identity (and monogram) from Subchapter C. Collectively, the Code refers to them as "C corporations." [6]

Congress made a markedly different decision in the case of partnerships, which are treated by Subchapter K of the Code as pass-through entities that do not pay federal income tax. Instead, partners include their respective shares of partnership income, deductions, losses and other items when determining their tax liability.[7] Ongoing adjustments to the basis of a partner's interest in the partnership ensure that income and losses are not taxed (or deducted) twice.[8] Partnerships are treated as entities, however, for purposes of selecting a taxable year, computing and characterizing partnership income, filing information

---

4. See McLure, Must Corporate Income Be Taxed Twice? (1979).

5. Prior to 1987, limited relief from the double tax was provided by allowing individuals to exclude the first $100 of dividends received. Congress repealed this exclusion in the Tax Reform Act of 1986. Corporate shareholders continue to qualify

for a 70, 80 or 100 percent dividends received deduction under Section 243. See Section B1 of this chapter, infra.

6. I.R.C. § 1361(a)(2).

7. I.R.C. § 701.

8. I.R.C. § 705.

returns, making elections, undergoing an audit by the Internal Revenue Service and in several substantive contexts, such as formation and termination, transactions between partners and partnerships, and sales of partnership interests.[9] The principal features of a pass-through tax regime are: (1) income generated by the business is taxed only once to the beneficial owners of the enterprise, whether or not they receive current distributions, and (2) losses pass through to the owners and, subject to various timing limitations,[10] may be deducted against income from other sources.

The double tax regime generally applicable to corporations and the pass-through system governing partnerships represent the Code's two fundamental alternatives for taxing business enterprises. To level the playing field and respond to the special problems of unique industries, Congress occasionally has deviated from these two basic models. Thus, to minimize the role of taxes on the choice of form for smaller businesses, certain closely held corporations may elect under Subchapter S to be treated as conduits.[11] Conversely, to preclude widely held businesses from disincorporating to escape the double tax regime of Subchapter C, "publicly traded" partnerships are treated as corporations for tax purposes.[12] Other types of hybrid entities qualify for pass-through treatment if they satisfy requirements designed to limit the nature of their business operations,[13] and corporations in certain discrete industries are governed by specialized taxing regimes.[14] Despite these departures from the norm, the central question remains—shall business profits be subjected to one or two levels of tax? The debate on this question is ongoing and will arise repeatedly throughout the text.

2.   INFLUENTIAL POLICIES

Four broad tax policy decisions have shaped the development of Subchapter C and contributed to its corpulent physique. The relationship of these policies to one another influences taxpayer behavior regarding the type of entity in which to conduct a business enterprise, capital structure and financing of corporate activities, dividend and compensation policy, estate planning and a myriad of other tax and business planning decisions. The 1980's were a decade of radical change in the tax world, and the corporate income tax was a particular focus of legislative attention. The interaction of the policies underlying

9. I.R.C. §§ 721; 707; 741. See generally, Lind, Schwarz, Lathrope & Rosenberg, Cases and Materials on Fundamentals of Partnership Taxation (2d ed. 1988).

10. See I.R.C. §§ 704(d); 465; 469.

11. These are known as "S corporations." I.R.C. § 1361(a)(1). The Code imposes no limit on the value of an S corporation, but eligibility for Subchapter S status is limited to corporations having not more than 35 shareholders or more than one

class of stock. See Section 1B4 of this chapter and Chapter 15, infra.

12. See I.R.C. § 7704 and Section C2b of this chapter, infra.

13. See e.g., Subchapter M, governing regulated investment companies (mutual funds) and real estate investment trusts.

14. See, e.g., Subchapter L (Insurance Companies), Subchapter H (banks and trust companies), and Subchapter F (tax-exempt organizations and cooperatives).

Subchapter C has been shifting and is in a state of disequilibrium.[1] An overview of the past and current synergy of these influential policies is appropriate before moving on.

The Double Tax. The concept at the heart of Subchapter C is the double taxation of corporate income. Earnings are taxed once at the corporate level when earned and again when distributed as dividends to shareholders.[2] This decision to treat corporations as separate taxable entities, distinct from their shareholders, has been controversial.[3] Some of the debate is over the incidence of the corporate tax—whether it is borne by shareholders, employees, corporate managers, consumers of the company's goods or services, or investors in general.[4] Critics also point to the adverse impact of the tax on the allocation of economic resources; its complexity; and a variety of other evils, including three distinct biases: (1) a bias against corporate as opposed to noncorporate investment (because only corporate capital is subject to a second tax); (2) a bias in favor of excessive debt financing; and (3) a bias in favor of retention of earnings at the corporate level as opposed to distribution of dividends.[5]

Once a double tax is accepted as the inevitable taxing model, much of the debate has shifted to the "integrity" of the corporate income tax. For example, should the corporate tax apply not only to operating income but also to distributions of appreciated property and sales in connection with corporate liquidations? The outcome of this controversy will unfold as these and other transactions are studied. For now, it is sufficient to observe that the defenders of the corporate income tax largely prevailed in the recent barrage of tax reform. The results are a significantly strengthened double tax regime, an increase in the tax costs of operating a business as a C corporation and greater pressure on techniques to reduce these costs.

Rate Structure on Ordinary Income. Before 1981, the maximum individual income tax rates on ordinary income peeked at 70 percent while the maximum corporate rate was only 46 percent. The combination of a steeply progressive rate structure for individuals with a lower,

---

1. See generally Zolt, "Corporate Taxation After the Tax Reform Act of 1986: A State of Disequilibrium," 66 N.C.L.Rev. 839 (1988).

2. Of course, many shareholders, such as pension funds and charitable organizations, generally do not pay taxes on the dividends they receive.

3. See generally Goode, The Corporate Income Tax (1951); McLure, "Integration of the Personal and Corporate Income Taxes: The Missing Element in Recent Tax Reform Proposals," 88 Harv.L.Rev. 532 (1975).

4. See e.g., Harberger, "The Incidence of the Corporation Income Tax," 70 J.Pol. Econ. 215 (1962); Klein, "The Incidence of the Corporation Income Tax: A Lawyer's View of a Problem in Economics," 65 Wisc. L.Rev. 576 (1965). Lest there be any suspense, economists have concluded that they are unable to ascertain who bears the burden of the corporate tax. See generally Break, "The Incidence and Economic Effects of Taxation," in The Economics of Public Finance (Brookings 1974).

5. See generally American Law Institute, Federal Income Tax Project—Subchapter C 341–355 (1982). Commentators also point to the "compensating biases" in the individual income tax, such as the rate structure, the capital gains preference and the ability of individuals to obtain a stepped-up basis in property held at death. See Zolt, supra note 1, at 845–846, and text accompanying notes 6–12, infra.

relatively flat rate for corporations encouraged taxpayers to use corporations to conduct profitable business and investment activities and to accumulate earnings within a corporation. Profits retained in a C corporation were subject to a lower rate of tax and could be left in corporate solution to compound at a tax preferred rate until needed by the shareholders for personal consumption. Retention of earnings also deferred imposition of the shareholder-level tax that would result from a dividend distribution.

Shareholders historically devised strategies to extract corporate earnings at the lowest tax cost. For example, owner-employees may withdraw business profits in the form of tax-deductible salary and fringe benefits. Shareholders also may attempt to disguise equity contributions as debt and withdraw earnings in the form of tax-deductible interest payments. Another strategy, known as a "bailout," is designed to extract profits in a transaction, such as a redemption of stock, which qualifies as an "exchange" so that the shareholder recovers all or part of her stock basis tax free and benefits from preferential capital gain treatment on any realized gain. Funds not needed for consumption are left in the corporation until the shareholder's death, when Section 1014 steps up the basis of the stock to fair market value and sets the stage for a tax-free bailout by the deceased shareholder's heirs.

To be sure, the Service has weapons to combat these strategies. Payments of salary or interest can be attacked as unreasonable compensation or disguised dividends. In addition, Congress long ago enacted two penalty taxes which augment the regular corporate tax in the case of certain corporations which do not distribute their profits. If a corporation is closely held and principally collects passive investment income, it is subject to the personal holding company tax.[6] Even if a corporation has substantial operating profits, it may be subject to the accumulated earnings tax if it retains earnings beyond the reasonable needs of its business.[7] With foresight and good planning, however, a corporation that could justify its accumulations of earnings on the basis of sound business judgment could avoid the corporate penalty taxes with relative ease.

When the top individual rate was lowered to 50 percent in 1981, the incentive to accumulate corporate profits diminished. The stakes changed even more dramatically in 1986, when for the first time in our tax history the top corporate rate (34 percent) exceeded the highest effective individual rate (then 28 percent). This rate "inversion" displaced the corporation from its role as a refuge from the steeply progressive individual rates and reduced the importance of the accumulated earnings and personal holding company taxes. More importantly, the current rate structure, coupled with a strengthened corporate tax, creates a major disincentive for conducting a business as a C corpora-

---

6. See I.R.C. § 541 et seq. and Chapter 9C, infra.

7. See I.R.C. § 531 et seq. and Chapter 9B, infra.

tion. Operating as a partnership or an S corporation produces a higher after-tax return than accumulating earnings in a C corporation and then selling the business. For those businesses, such as publicly traded companies, that must remain as C corporations, the current system places a premium on strategies to reduce the corporate-level tax.

Preferential Capital Gains Rates. As previewed above, the decision to tax long-term capital gains at substantially lower rates than ordinary income [8] historically motivated corporations and shareholders to avoid the sting of the double tax by devising methods to "bail out" earnings at capital gain rates. The history of Subchapter C is replete with shareholder attempts to convert ordinary income into capital gain, and Congress's efforts to curtail bailouts is chronicled throughout this text.[9]

The repeal of the capital gains rate preference in 1986 removed most of the incentive to engage in "bailout" transactions. But it was deja vu all over again when Congress reinstated a modest capital gains rate preference in 1991,[10] and the bailout battle may rage anew if the amounts at stake are large enough. Even in the absence of a significant rate preference, the dichotomy between ordinary income and capital gain still may be relevant. Individual capital losses are deductible against capital gains plus a maximum of $3,000 of ordinary income while ordinary losses generally may be deducted without limitation. Consequently, capital gains are preferable to ordinary income insofar as they may fully absorb capital losses.[11] Moreover, a corporate distribution that is treated as received in exchange for all or part of a shareholder's stock is preferable to a dividend distribution because the shareholder may recover the basis in the stock before recognizing any gain.[12] Calls for a more meaningful capital gains preference to stimulate economic growth continue to reverberate from both ends of Pennsylvania Avenue. For all these reasons, this edition continues to assume that characterization issues remain an important dynamic in the taxation of corporations and shareholders.

Nonrecognition. Under the realization principle, gains and losses are not taxable until they are realized in a sale, exchange or other

---

8. In 1981, for example, the maximum individual rate on ordinary income was 70 percent as compared to a maximum rate of 20 percent on long-term capital gains.

9. See, e.g., Chapter 5 (redemptions), Chapter 6 (Section 306 stock) and Chapter 12 (corporate divisions).

10. Beginning in 1991, the highest individual rate is 31 percent. An individual's top marginal rate between certain ranges of income may be slightly higher because of the phase-out of personal exemptions required by Section 151(d) and the reduction of itemized deductions for high-income taxpayers provided by Section 68. The maximum rate on long-term capital gains,

however, is 28 percent. I.R.C. § 1(h). No rate preference is provided for corporate capital gains.

11. Characterization also may be significant for other purposes—e.g., gain recaptured as ordinary income may not be reported on the installment method under Section 453 (see I.R.C. § 453(i)), and a donor may not deduct the full fair market value of certain "ordinary income property" contributed to a charity. (I.R.C. § 170(e)(1)(A)).

12. See, e.g., the treatment of distributions in redemption, discussed in Chapter 5, infra.

event that makes the gain or loss "real" and more easily measurable. The nonrecognition concept assumes that certain realization events should not be impeded by the imposition of a tax. Transactions that qualify for nonrecognition treatment may go forward on a tax-free basis on the theory that they are mere changes in form which result in a continuity of investment. To ensure that any realized gain or loss is merely deferred rather than eliminated, the typical nonrecognition provision includes corollary rules providing for transferred and exchanged bases and tacked holding periods.[13] The nonrecognition principle pervades Subchapter C, affecting transactions ranging from the simple corporate formation to complex mergers and acquisitions.

The opportunity to qualify a corporate transaction for nonrecognition has assumed even greater importance with the strengthening of the corporate tax. A corporation must pay tax on the appreciation in its assets on a sale or distribution in connection with a complete liquidation.[14] Standing in sharp contrast are acquisitions known as tax-free reorganizations, which ordinarily are free of tax to all the parties, albeit with the trade-off of transferred bases and a carryover of other tax attributes. Taxpayers are thus encouraged to structure sales of a corporate business to come within an applicable nonrecognition provision in order to avoid (or at least defer) tax at the corporate and shareholder levels.

Perspective. In the first edition of this book, published in 1985, we observed that "[t]he corporate tax system previewed here is not engraved in stone," and predicted that "change is in the air, and tax lawyers and students must be prepared, often at a moment's notice, to discard old concepts and master new ones."[15] And so it was that Congress enacted the historic Tax Reform Act of 1986. Subsequent developments have been less dramatic, but the continuing controversies over spending and taxes promise to contribute to an unstable environment for the immediate future.

And what of that future? In the conference agreement accompanying the Tax Reform Act of 1986, the conferees directed the Treasury Department to consider whether changes to the provisions of Subchapter C and related sections of the Code were desirable and to report to the tax-writing committees of the Congress. The extended due date for the report is now January 1, 1992.[16] In the meantime, the spirited debate over Subchapter C continues,[17] and more changes may be in the wind. At this writing, the Treasury is completing (yet another) study

---

13. See, e.g., I.R.C. § 1031, which provides for nonrecognition on certain like-kind exchanges.

14. See Chapter 7C, infra. Certain taxable acquisitions of stock will continue to trigger only shareholder-level gain but the bases of the acquired corporation's assets will transfer to the purchaser.

15. Lind, Schwarz, Lathrope & Rosenberg, Cases and Materials on Fundamen-

tals of Corporate Taxation 3–4 (1st ed. 1985).

16. After the original January 1, 1988 due date for the report passed, Congress extended the deadline in Section 11831 of the Revenue Reconciliation Act of 1990.

17. For an excellent discussion of the possible legislative agenda, see Wolfman, "Subchapter C and the 100th Congress," 33 Tax Notes 669 (Nov. 17, 1986) and

of options for integrating the corporate and personal taxes,[18] and the results of that work are eagerly anticipated.

As always, any more "reforms" will test the ability of tax teachers and students to adapt and reevaluate their environment. To assist in that process, policy readings have been interspersed throughout the text. Later in this chapter, for example, students are invited to consider the pros and cons of "integration" of the corporate and individual income taxes [19]—a policy long debated by economists. Other proposals emanating from Congress, the American Law Institute and commentators are considered in connection with the specific trouble spots to which they relate.

3. THE COMMON LAW OF CORPORATE TAXATION

Although the study of corporate taxation principally involves the application of a complex statute to particular transactions, the Code is not the only analytical tool. In scrutinizing taxpayer behavior, the courts at an early date went beyond the literal statutory language and began to formulate a set of doctrines that have become the "common law" of federal taxation. Some of these principles, such as the assignment of income doctrine, were encountered in the basic income tax course. Unlike the Code, which often provides bright-line rules for solving problems, the judicial doctrines are imprecise. The very vagueness of these pronouncements, however, has contributed to their influence. They loom large in the tax advisor's conscience and serve to thwart aggressive schemes that literally comply with the statute but are incompatible with its intended purpose.[1] This introductory survey is intended to preview some of the reasoning that lies at the heart of corporate tax jurisprudence.

Viewed most broadly, the judicial doctrines ask a simple question that is central to virtually every case in this text. Has the taxpayer actually done what it, and its documents, represent, or are the economic realities of the transaction—and the attendant tax consequences—other than what the taxpayer purports them to be? The tests used to resolve this question bear many labels which are often used interchangeably. What follows is a summary of the terminology that will soon become familiar.

Sham Transaction. If a transaction is a "sham," it will not be respected for tax purposes. A "sham" might be defined as a transac-

---

Wolfman, "Whither C," 38 Tax Notes 1269 (Mar. 14, 1988).

18. See "Gideon Holds Secret Meeting With CFOs to Discuss Corporate Integration Study," 46 Tax Notes 379 (Jan. 22, 1990); "Tax Officials Discuss Integration, Future Legislation at ABA Meeting," 46 Tax Notes 756 (Feb. 12, 1990).

19. See generally Warren, "The Relation and Integration of Individual and Cor-

porate Income Taxes," 94 Harv.L.Rev. 719 (1981); McNulty, "Reform of the Individual Income Tax By Integration of the Corporate Income Tax," 46 Tax Notes 1445 (Mar. 19, 1990).

1. See generally Bittker & Lokken, Federal Taxation of Income, Estates and Gifts ¶ 4.3.1 (2d ed. 1989).

tion that never actually occurred but is represented by the taxpayer to have transpired—with favorable tax consequences of course.[2]   One court has colorfully described a sham as an "attempt by a taxpayer to ward off tax blows with paper armor," [3] in a purported transaction that "gives off an unmistakeably hollow sound when it is tapped." [4]

Because a "sham" generally connotes fraudulent behavior, the courts tend to reserve this doctrine for the more egregious cases.   But the pejorative term might well be appropriate to describe the kinds of transactions that are challenged under the widely used doctrines discussed below.   In one typically overlapping formulation, a court offered the following definition of a sham: [5]

> To treat a transaction as a sham, the court must find that the taxpayer was motivated by no business purpose other than obtaining tax benefits in entering the transaction, and that the transaction has no economic substance because no reasonable possibility of a profit exists.

Substance Over Form.   The form of a transaction frequently is determinative of its tax consequences.   Since the early days of the income tax, however, the courts have been willing to go beyond the formal papers and evaluate the "substance" of a transaction.   A familiar example is the proper classification of a business arrangement as a sale or a lease.[6]   The documents used by the taxpayer may use one label, but the courts are not inhibited from examining the arrangement and restructuring it for tax purposes to comport with the economic realities.

The tension between form and substance will be evident throughout the chapters that follow.   Is a corporate instrument "debt," as the taxpayer contends, or "equity," as the Service usually will assert?   Is a payment to a shareholder-employee really "compensation" or is it a disguised dividend?   Was a distribution a dividend or really part of the purchase price for the business?   Who, in substance, made a sale of corporate assets—the corporation or its shareholders?   It is impossible to generalize as to when and how this doctrine will be applied.   Individual cases turn on unique fact pressures and the court's attitude toward tax avoidance.[7]

Despite the influence of this doctrine over time, the courts recently have exhibited some reluctance to accept attempts by the Service to restructure legitimate corporate transactions to reach a result that will

2. See, e.g., Knetsch v. United States, 364 U.S. 361, 81 S.Ct. 132 (1960).

3. Waterman Steamship Corp. v. Commissioner, 430 F.2d 1185 (5th Cir.1970), cert. denied 401 U.S. 939, 91 S.Ct. 936 (1971).

4. Id. at 1196, quoting United States v. General Geophysical Co., 296 F.2d 86, 89 (5th Cir.1961), cert. denied 369 U.S. 849, 82 S.Ct. 932 (1962).

5. Rice's Toyota World, Inc. v. Commissioner, 752 F.2d 89, 91 (4th Cir.1985).

6. See, e.g., Frank Lyon Co. v. United States, 435 U.S. 561, 98 S.Ct. 1291 (1978).

7. See, e.g., Grove v. Commissioner, infra p. 270, where the majority and dissenting opinions evidence a sharply conflicting philosophy about the use of the substance-versus-form doctrine in tax cases.

produce more revenue. The Tax Court, for example, is wary of extending the judicial doctrines where Congress has mandated that particular results shall flow from a given form and the taxpayers have carefully structured an otherwise legitimate transaction to comply with the statutory requirements.[8]

Business Purpose. The business purpose doctrine is conceptually linked to the sham and substance-versus-form tests. A transaction motivated by a business purpose usually is compared to one that has no substance, purpose or utility apart from tax avoidance. As originally formulated by Judge Learned Hand,[9] the business purpose doctrine was applied to deny tax-free status to a transaction that would not have been consummated but for the tax savings that would result if its form were respected. The doctrine took hold and has become an independent requirement for many transactions in Subchapter C that seek to qualify for nonrecognition treatment.[10]

Step Transaction Doctrine. When courts apply the step transaction doctrine, they combine (or "step") formally distinct transactions to determine the tax treatment of the single integrated series of events. The doctrine frequently is applied in conjunction with the other judicial tests and is particularly influential in Subchapter C.

The courts disagree on the standard to be employed in applying the step transaction doctrine. Some require a binding legal commitment to complete all the steps from the outset before combining them, while others require only a "mutual interdependence" of steps or a preconceived intent to reach a particular end result.[11]

The meaning and scope of all this common law corporate tax jurisprudence has befuddled (and yet challenged) tax advisors for decades. Our goal here is to identify the principal terminology and give fair warning that literal compliance with the Code may not be enough for a transaction to pass muster. Students should not expect to master a precise or consistent explanation of the judicial doctrines. It will be enough simply to develop a sense of smell for the kinds of cases in which the doctrines might be invoked.[12]

8. See, e.g., Esmark, Inc. v. Commissioner, 90 T.C. 171 (1988), affirmed 886 F.2d 1318 (7th Cir.1989).

9. See Helvering v. Gregory, 69 F.2d 809 (2d Cir.1934).

10. See, e.g., Reg. § 1.355–2(b), requiring a corporate business purpose to qualify as a tax-free corporate division under Section 355.

11. This doctrine is analyzed in some detail in connection with liquidations and corporate reorganizations. See, e.g., Commissioner v. Court Holding Co., infra p. 335 and McDonald's Restaurants of Illinois v. Commissioner, infra p. 497.

12. For a recent analysis of the current state of the judicial doctrines, see Rosenberg, "Tax Avoidance and Income Measurement," 87 Mich.L.Rev. 365 (1988).

B. THE CORPORATION AS A SEPARATE TAXABLE ENTITY

1. THE CORPORATE INCOME TAX

Code: §§ 11; 63(a).   Skim §§ 243(a); 1201(a); 1211(a); 1212(a)(1).

Students often are surprised to learn that a course in corporate taxation devotes very little time to the determination of a corporation's tax liability.   The reason is that the concepts used in making that determination already have been studied in the basic federal income tax course.   Those same broad principles—gross income, deductions, assignment of income, timing and characterization—apply in computing the taxable income of a C corporation, and we only need to pause briefly to discuss the rate structure and a few other special rules applicable to C corporations.

Rates.   A corporation, like an individual, is a separate taxable entity for federal income tax purposes.   The corporation selects its own taxable year and method of accounting, computes its taxable income under applicable principles of the tax law and otherwise is generally treated for tax purposes like any other person.   The special rates applicable to corporations are found in Section 11, which contains a three step graduated rate structure which is similar to the individual rates in that it provides a limited number of brackets for lower income corporations but becomes an essentially flat rate tax for more profitable companies.   The maximum corporate rate is 34 percent on a corporation's taxable income in excess of $75,000.[1]   For corporate income under $75,000, the rates currently are as follows: [2]

Taxable Income	Rate
0 to $50,000	15%
$50,000 to $75,000	25%

The rates are modified in one respect to prevent corporations with more than $100,000 of taxable income from benefiting from the lower graduated rates.   Section 11(b) imposes an additional five percent tax on taxable income in excess of $100,000 up to a maximum increase of $11,750, which is the amount of tax savings from the lower rates on the first $75,000 of taxable income.   This rate "bubble" in effect creates a 39 percent marginal bracket on taxable income between $100,000 and $335,000.   A corporation with taxable income of $335,000 or more will be subject to a flat rate of 34 percent on all of its taxable income.

To prevent doctors, lawyers, entertainers and other incorporated service providers from taking advantage of the lower rates on taxable income below $75,000, Section 11(b)(2) denies the benefit of those rates to any "qualified personal service corporation" as defined in Section 448(d)(2).   Incorporated service businesses are thus subject to a 34 percent flat rate tax on all their taxable income.   In general, a

---

1. I.R.C. § 11(b).   2. Id.

"qualified personal service corporation" is a corporation substantially engaged in the performance of services in the fields of health, law, engineering, architecture, accounting, actuarial science, performing arts, or consulting, if substantially all of the corporation's stock is held (directly or indirectly) by employees performing services for the corporation, retired employees, or the estates of employees or retirees.[3]

Determination of Taxable Income. Section 63(a) defines taxable income as "gross income minus the deductions allowed by this chapter." In the case of a corporation, this amount generally is determined by applying the same principles and Code sections applicable to individuals. A few differences, primarily attributable to the distinct status of the corporation as an artificial business entity, are worth mentioning.

First, because a corporation has no "personal" expenses, it is not entitled to any personal or dependency exemptions and, unlike an individual, it receives no standard deduction. Corporations thus are not concerned with distinguishing between "above-the-line" deductions allowable in reaching adjusted gross income and "below-the-line" itemized deductions or in applying the Section 67 two percent of adjusted gross income floor to "miscellaneous itemized deductions" or the Section 68 overall limitation on itemized deductions.

In addition, most of the personal deductions allowed to individuals may not be taken by corporations. For example, a corporation is not entitled to a medical expense deduction under Section 213 or a spousal support deduction under Section 215. Moreover, Section 212, which allows a deduction for certain expenses incurred for the production of income or maintenance of income-producing property or for tax advice, is expressly applicable only to individuals. Corporations need not worry however, because virtually all of their ordinary expenses in the pursuit of profit are deductible under Section 162.

On the other hand, certain *limitations* on the deductibility of personal expenses of individuals do not apply to corporations. For example, Section 165(c), which limits the deductibility of nonbusiness losses; Section 166(d), which characterizes nonbusiness bad debts as short-term capital losses; and Section 183(a), which limits deductions for activities not motivated by profit, are among a number of restrictive sections that do not apply to C corporations. This is because it is generally assumed that all of a corporation's activities are motivated by the pursuit of profit.[4]

By virtue of their unique status, corporations are entitled to one important deduction not available to individuals. To prevent multiple taxation as earnings wend their way through a chain of corporations, corporate shareholders generally are entitled to deduct 70 percent (or,

---

3. I.R.C. § 448(d)(2).

4. Certain payments made by a corporation to or on behalf of its shareholders may be nondeductible because they are in fact dividends, but their disallowance is the result of the classification of the payments as constructive dividends rather than the "personal" nature of the payments. See Chapter 4E, infra.

in some cases, 80 or 100 percent) of the dividends they receive from other corporations. The effect of the 70 percent dividends received deduction is that corporations are subject to tax at a maximum rate of 10.2 percent on dividends—an amount derived by applying the top 34 percent corporate rate to the 30 percent includable portion of the dividends.

The remaining differences in the treatment of corporations and individuals are the result of a conscious legislative choice to treat them differently. For example, the percentage limitation on corporate charitable deductions is 10 percent of taxable income as compared to an overall 50 percent limit on individual charitable contributions.[5] No doubt on the theory that corporations are normally ineffective tax shelter vehicles, most C corporations are immune from the at-risk limitations in Section 465 and the passive loss limitations in Section 469.[6]

Another significant difference relates to the treatment of corporate capital losses. Corporations may deduct capital losses only to the extent of capital gains during the year. Although the excess may not be applied against ordinary income for the taxable year, it may be carried back for three years and carried forward for five years. By contrast, individuals are permitted to deduct capital losses to the extent of capital gains, and up to $3,000 of excess losses may be deducted against ordinary income. Unused capital losses may be carried forward indefinitely by an individual taxpayer.[7]

Taxable Year and Accounting Method. Most C corporations have the flexibility to adopt either a calendar year or a fiscal year as their annual accounting period.[8] Certain "personal service corporations" must use a calendar year, however, unless they can show a business purpose for using a fiscal year.[9] For this purpose, a "personal service corporation" is one whose principal activity is the performance of personal services that are substantially performed by "employee-owners" who collectively own more than 10 percent (by value) of the corporation's stock.[10] This generally forces most personal service corporations to use a calendar year, subject to an exception in Section 444 which permits them to elect to adopt or change to a fiscal year with a "deferral period" of not more than three months.[11] As a result, a personal service corporation that otherwise would be required to use a

---

5. I.R.C. § 170(b)(2).

6. I.R.C. §§ 465(a)(1); 469(a)(2)(B), (j)(1).

7. I.R.C. §§ 1211, 1212.

8. See generally I.R.C. § 441. A fiscal year is any period of 12 months ending on the last day of any month other than December. I.R.C. § 441(e).

9. I.R.C. § 441(i)(1). Deferral of income to shareholders is not treated as a business purpose. Id.

10. I.R.C. §§ 269A(b)(1); 441(i)(2). An employee-owner is defined as any employee

who owns, on any day during the taxable year, any of the outstanding stock of the corporation after applying certain attribution rules. I.R.C. § 269A(b)(2), as modified by I.R.C. § 441(i)(2).

11. I.R.C. § 444(b)(2). The "deferral period" of a taxable year is the number of months between the beginning of the taxable year elected and the close of the required taxable year that ends within the taxable year elected.

calendar year may elect a taxable year ending September 30, October 31 or November 30. To prevent any tax savings that might result from the use of a fiscal year, personal service corporations making a Section 444 election must make certain minimum distributions (e.g., primarily of compensation) to employee-owners during the portion of the employee's fiscal year that ends on December 31.[12] If these minimum distribution requirements are not met, the electing corporation must defer certain otherwise currently deductible payments (e.g., compensation) to employee-owners.[13] A personal service corporation that establishes a business purpose for a fiscal year is not required to make a Section 444 election and is not subject to these distribution requirements and deduction limitations.[14]

In general, C corporations are required to use the accrual method of accounting.[15] Exemptions are provided for corporations engaged in the farming business, "qualified personal service corporations"[16] and any other corporation whose average annual gross receipts for a three-year measuring period preceding the taxable year do not exceed $5 million.[17]

In addition to these general accounting rules, Section 267 regulates certain transactions between corporations and their shareholders to prevent the acceleration of losses on related party transactions and to preclude timing advantages when the corporation and its owner-employees use different methods of accounting. For example, Section 267(a)(1) provides that losses from sales or exchanges of property between an individual shareholder and a 50 percent (or more) owned corporation may not be deducted.[18] The forced matching rules in Section 267(a)(2) prevent an accrual method corporation from accruing and deducting compensation paid to a cash method owner-employee in the year when the services are performed but deferring payment until the following taxable year to provide the employee with a timing advantage. When an owner-employee owns, directly or indirectly, 50 percent or more of the payor corporation, the corporation's deduction is deferred until such time as the owner-employee includes the amount in income.[19]

---

12. See generally I.R.C. § 280H.

13. I.R.C. § 280H(a), (b), (c).

14. I.R.S. Notice 88–10, 1988–1 C.B. 478.

15. I.R.C. § 448(a).

16. This is the same category of corporations that is deprived of the lower graduated rates in Section 11. Substantially all of the activities of the corporation must involve the performance of services in the fields of health, law, engineering, accounting, architecture, actuarial science, performing arts, or consulting, and substantially all of the stock must be held by employees, their estates or their heirs. I.R.C. § 448(d)(2).

17. I.R.C. § 448(b).

18. The loss disallowance applies to transactions between related parties as defined in Section 267(b). A corporation and its 50 percent or more (measured by value) shareholders are considered related. I.R.C. § 267(b)(2). Percentage ownership is determined after application of attribution rules in Section 267(c).

19. I.R.C. § 267(a)(2). This section also may apply to payments of interest and other deductible expenses. In the case of personal service corporations, the corporation and *any* owner-employee (regardless of the percentage ownership) are treated as related parties for purposes of the forced matching rules in Section 267. Id.

Credits. Like any taxpayer engaged in business or investment activities, a corporation is entitled to several valuable tax credits. The most significant is the foreign tax credit, which is available to corporations doing business abroad.[20] Others include the rehabilitation and energy credits,[21] targeted jobs credit,[22] and the credit for research expenditures.[23]

2. THE ALTERNATIVE MINIMUM TAX

Code: §§ 55, 56(a)(1)(A), (c), (g)(1), (2), (3), (4)(A)–(C)(ii), (5), (6); 57(a)(5), (6); Skim § 53.

Corporations also are potentially subject to the alternative minimum tax, which is designed "to ensure that no taxpayer with substantial economic income can avoid significant tax liability by using exclusions, deductions and credits."[1] In the Tax Reform Act of 1986, Congress strengthened the alternative minimum tax and extended it to corporations, which previously had been subject to an "add-on" tax on a short list of tax preference items.[2] The alternative minimum tax generally can be described as a flat rate tax which is imposed on a broader income base than the taxable income yardstick used for the regular corporate tax. But that deceptively simple description only begins to explain a complex statutory scheme that takes many twists and turns before reaching "alternative minimum taxable income," the base that Congress believed was a truer measure of a corporation's economic results.

The corporate alternative minimum tax ("AMT") is payable only to the extent that it exceeds a corporation's regular tax liability.[3] The tax generally equals 20 percent of the amount by which a corporation's alternative minimum taxable income, as defined in Section 55(b)(2), exceeds a $40,000 exemption amount.[4] "Alternative minimum taxable income" ("AMTI") is the corporation's taxable income, increased by various tax preference items and adjusted to eliminate certain timing benefits (e.g., accelerated cost recovery) that are available under the regular tax.[5]

Section 56 lists the principal adjustments made in arriving at a corporation's alternative minimum taxable income.[6] Many are narrow and well beyond the scope of this text, but a few adjustments will be familiar to students who have completed the basic income tax course.

20. I.R.C. § 27.

21. I.R.C. §§ 46–48.

22. I.R.C. § 51.

23. I.R.C. § 41.

1. S. Rep. No. 99–313, 99th Cong., 2d Sess. 518 (1986).

2. I.R.C. § 56 (pre-1987).

3. I.R.C. § 55(a).

4. I.R.C. § 55(b), (d)(2). The $40,000 exemption amount is phased out at the rate of 25 cents for each dollar that a corporation's alternative minimum taxable income exceeds $150,000. I.R.C. § 55(d)(3). The exemption is thus fully phased out when a corporation's alternative minimum taxable income reaches $310,000.

5. I.R.C. § 55(b)(2).

6. Certain specialized adjustments in Section 58 also must be made. I.R.C. § 55(b)(2)(A).

For example, in computing alternative minimum taxable income, a corporation that places tangible property in service after 1986 generally must use a modified version of the alternative depreciation system in Section 168(g) rather than the generally applicable accelerated cost recovery system ("ACRS") in Section 168(a).[7] Thus, machinery and equipment must be depreciated using the 150 percent declining balance method over longer recovery periods than those used under ACRS.[8] Real estate must be depreciated using the straight line method and a 40-year useful life.[9] Another adjustment affects corporations that are still eligible to use the installment method for reporting gain on dispositions of dealer property. For AMT purposes, all payments made on such dispositions are deemed received in the year of disposition.[10] Finally, a special net operating loss, known as the "alternative minimum tax net operating loss," must be used in computing alternative minimum taxable income.[11]

In extending the AMT concept to corporations, Congress was responding to several highly publicized cases of corporations which reported significant operating profits in their financial statements to shareholders but paid minimal amounts of corporate income tax.[12] In an effort to improve perceptions, Section 56(g) requires an upward AMTI adjustment equal to 75 percent of the amount by which "adjusted current earnings" ("ACE") exceed AMTI determined without regard to this adjustment or AMT net operating losses ("pre–ACE AMTI").[13] The purpose of the ACE adjustment is to reach an even more accurate measure of a corporation's economic performance. ACE is determined by starting with pre–ACE AMTI and making several additional adjustments.[14] One example of an ACE adjustment is depreciation. For property placed in service after 1989, depreciation for ACE purposes must be determined under the alternative depreciation system in Section 168(g)—i.e., the straight line method over longer recovery

---

7. I.R.C. § 56(a)(1).

8. I.R.C. §§ 56(a)(1)(A); 168(g).

9. Id.

10. I.R.C. § 56(a)(6). In most cases, dispositions of property by a dealer would not be eligible for installment sale reporting under the regular tax. See I.R.C. § 453(b) (2)(A), (l).

11. In general, the AMT net operating loss must be computed in a manner consistent with the adjustments and preferences in the alternative minimum tax scheme. The special net operating loss may not offset more than 90 percent of a corporation's alternative minimum taxable income, determined without the net operating loss deduction. I.R.C. § 56(a)(4), (d).

12. See, e.g., Citizens for Tax Justice, "Corporate Taxpayers and Corporate Free-

loaders," 29 Tax Notes 947 (Dec. 2, 1985). Congress's first response to this problem was to adjust alternative minimum taxable income by 50 percent of the difference between a corporation's taxable income and the "book income" reported on its financial statements. See I.R.C. § 56(f). Affectionately known as the "business untaxed reported profit," or "BURP" adjustment, this expired at the end of 1988, to be replaced by the "ACE" adjustment discussed in the text. See generally Feinberg & Robinson, "The Corporate Alternative Minimum Tax—Working With BURP While Waiting for ACE," 15 J.Corp.Tax'n 3 (1988).

13. A negative adjustment also is allowed—i.e., pre–ACE AMTI may be reduced by 75 percent of the excess of pre–ACE AMTI over ACE. I.R.C. § 56(g)(2).

14. I.R.C. § 56(g)(1).

periods than those generally available under ACRS.[15] To illustrate, assume that X Corporation purchases a $14,000 piece of equipment with a seven year "class life" that qualifies as 5–year property under the ACRS depreciation system used to compute the regular corporate tax.[16] X's first year depreciation deduction is computed using the 200 percent declining balance method with a half-year convention and is $2,800. In determining pre–ACE AMTI, X depreciates the equipment under the Section 168(g) alternative depreciation system, using a seven-year recovery period (the class life), a half-year convention and the 150 percent declining balance method. X's AMT depreciation is thus $1,500, and it must increase taxable income by the $1,300 difference between regular and AMT depreciation in determining pre–ACE AMTI. For ACE purposes, X also uses the alternative depreciation system but is limited to the straight line method over a seven-year life with a half-year convention. ACE depreciation is thus $1,000, and X must adjust pre–ACE AMTI by the $500 difference between regular AMTI and ACE depreciation.[17]

Understanding the final round of ACE adjustments requires a brief introduction to the concept of "earnings and profits." The principal function of earnings and profits is to determine whether distributions paid by C corporations to their shareholders are dividends or a return of capital.[18] The computation of earnings and profits begins with taxable income and requires a number of adjustments which are designed to provide a truer measure of the corporation's economic performance. Consequently, certain amounts that were excluded from gross income for purposes of computing pre–ACE AMTI but that are taken into account in determining a corporation's "earnings and profits" must be included in determining ACE. An example is tax-exempt municipal bond interest, which increases a corporation's wealth but (except for interest on certain private activity bonds) is not included in the AMT base. Similarly, items that are disallowed as deductions in computing earnings and profits are added back for ACE purposes. An example is the 70 percent dividends received deduction for corporate shareholders.[19]

Once ACE is determined, the final step is to increase pre–ACE AMTI by 75 percent of the excess of ACE over pre–ACE AMTI.[20] After this orgy of adjustments, one wonders why Congress did not simply

15. The basic AMT adjustment for depreciation in Section 56(a)(1)(A) also mandates the Section 168(g) alternative depreciation system but permits the 150 percent declining balance method for equipment and other tangible personal property. ACE depreciation is limited to straight line in all cases.

16. See I.R.C. § 168(a).

17. I.R.C. § 56(g)(4)(A)(i).

18. See I.R.C. §§ 301; 316; and Chapter 4, infra.

19. See I.R.C. § 243(a). An exception is provided for deductions that qualify for a 100 or 80 percent dividends received deduction, provided that the dividends are paid from earnings that were taxable to the payor. I.R.C. § 56(g)(4)(C)(ii).

20. As noted earlier, if pre–ACE AMTI exceeds ACE, then pre–ACE AMTI is decreased by the difference. See note 13, supra.

adopt ACE (or earnings and profits, for that matter) as the base for the corporate AMT. The answer presumably is political compromise, a force that has complicated the tax system in general and the alternative minimum tax in particular.

The determination of alternative minimum taxable income requires one more step. Once the required adjustments under Section 56 are made, a corporation must increase taxable income by the amount of certain tax preference items. Most of these preferences are highly specialized. Some of the more familiar preferences included in Section 57(a) are: (1) the excess of percentage depletion over cost depletion; (2) excess intangible drilling costs; (3) tax-exempt interest on certain private activity bonds issued after August 7, 1986; (4) the untaxed appreciation on charitable contributions of capital gain property; and (5) the excess of accelerated depreciation over straight line on certain property placed in service before 1987.

A limited number of credits are permitted to be applied against a corporation's alternative minimum tax liability.[21] In addition, a minimum tax credit is allowed against a corporation's *regular* tax liability. The minimum credit was enacted in recognition of the fact that many of the alternative minimum tax adjustments and items of tax preference reflect deferral of tax liability rather than permanent tax avoidance. An adjustment thus is required so that taxpayers do not lose these benefits altogether.[22] In general, Section 53(a) allows the alternative minimum tax attributable to certain adjustments and items of tax preference to be credited against regular tax liability (reduced by certain other credits) in later years.[23] The minimum tax credit may be carried over until it is fully used, but it cannot be used as a credit against the alternative minimum tax.[24]

3. MULTIPLE CORPORATIONS

Code: Skim §§ 1501; 1502; 1503; 1504(a), (b); 1551; 1561; 1563.

Because corporations are easier to create than individuals, multiple corporations might be used to save taxes. For example, if Sole Shareholder owns a corporation that generates $1,000,000 of net income annually, he might be tempted to divide the enterprise into 20 separate companies, each with an annual income of $50,000 and each therefore taxed at a maximum rate of only 15 percent. This income-splitting ploy is precluded by Section 1561, which denies certain multiple tax benefits to a "controlled group of corporations."[1] Generally speaking, corporations are a controlled group if they constitute either a "parent-

---

21. See I.R.C. § 38(c) (regular investment tax credit); § 59(a) (alternative minimum tax foreign tax credit).

22. S. Rep. No. 99–313, supra note 1, at 521.

23. I.R.C. § 53(a), (b), (d)(1)(B).

24. I.R.C. § 53(c).

1. Section 1551 limits controlled groups to one use of the lower rates in Section 11(b). The entire group's income must be combined for purposes of applying Section 11. See Chapter 14, infra.

subsidiary controlled group" or a "brother-sister controlled group" under ownership tests in Section 1563.

The Code also contains provisions which permit an "affiliated group of corporations" to elect to consolidate its results for purposes of tax reporting.[2]   In broad outline, the effect of a consolidated return election is to treat the affiliated group as a single corporate entity for tax purposes. The consolidated return rules are covered in more detail in Chapter 14, and selected issues involving consolidated returns are raised in the context of various transactions discussed later in this book. The ownership test applied to determine whether corporations are affiliated, however, is used in several provisions of Subchapter C[3] and is worth a brief glance at this early juncture. Section 1504(a)(2) employs an 80 percent of voting power and value standard to test corporate ownership of another corporation. That standard is met if a corporation possesses at least 80 percent of the total voting power of the stock in another corporation and has at least 80 percent of the total value of the stock of such corporation. For purposes of this test, certain nonconvertible, nonvoting preferred stock is disregarded.[4]

4. THE S CORPORATION ALTERNATIVE

The double tax on a C corporation's profits coupled with the present rate structure in which individuals pay tax at rates lower than corporations are two powerful incentives favoring a pass-through taxing mechanism as the entity of choice for a business enterprise. Subchapter S of the Code provides a simple method for qualifying closely held corporations to achieve this preferred pass-through treatment. Enacted to reduce the tax influences on the choice of entity decision, Subchapter S permits the shareholders of a "small business corporation" to elect to be taxed under a conduit approach similar to the taxation of partnerships. The emergence of Subchapter S as a desirable alternative to the two-tier system applicable to C corporations merits a brief introduction to its provisions.[1]

The principal obstacle to making an S election are the eligibility requirements found in the Code's definition of "small business corporation" in Section 1361. In general, a corporation may make an S election only if it has not more than 35 shareholders who must be individuals other than nonresident aliens, estates or certain trusts.[2]   In addition, an S corporation may not have more than one class of stock[3] and may not be a member of an affiliated group of corporations.[4]

2. I.R.C. §§ 1501–1504; see Chapter 14, infra.

3. See, e.g., I.R.C. §§ 332(b)(1), 336(e)(1), 338(d)(3).

4. I.R.C. § 1504(a)(4).

1. For detailed coverage of S corporations, see Chapter 15, infra.

2. I.R.C. § 1361(b)(1)(A), (B), (C).

3. I.R.C. § 1361(b)(1)(D).

4. I.R.C. § 1361(b)(2)(A). This means that an S corporation may not have a wholly owned subsidiary.

The income of an S corporation generally is subject to a single, shareholder-level tax.[5] The income, losses, deductions and credits of an S corporation pass through to its shareholders, but the character of those items is determined at the corporate level.[6] Basis and distribution rules are designed to assure that the shareholders may receive previously taxed income without paying additional tax.[7]

Even though S corporations and their shareholders are taxed under a special regime, S corporations remain "corporations" for purposes of Subchapter C.[8] Thus, the two corporate subchapters often operate in tandem when an S corporation engages in transactions, such as distributions of appreciated property, stock redemptions and liquidations, that are subject to Subchapter C.[9]

PROBLEM

Boots, Inc. is a "C" corporation engaged in the shoe manufacturing business. It also holds a small portfolio of marketable securities and is engaged in a passive equipment leasing activity. Boots is a calendar year, accrual method taxpayer with two equal shareholders, Emil and Betty, who are unrelated cash method taxpayers. Assume for convenience that Emil and Betty each are taxable at a 30% flat individual rate. During the current year, Boots has the following income and expense items and makes no distributions to its shareholders:

Income:

Gross profit—sale of inventory	$2,500,000
Dividends received	100,000
Capital gains	200,000
Municipal bond interest (not private activity bond)	10,000

Expenses and Losses:

Operating Expenses	600,000
ACRS depreciation (5–year property; 8–year class life; $4,000,000 cost; all placed in service in current year)	800,000
Net loss from passive leasing activity	130,000
Capital losses	220,000

(a) Determine Boots, Inc.'s taxable income and its regular tax liability for the current year.

(b) What result in (a), above, if Boots distributes $330,000 each to Emil and Betty as dividends?

(c) What result in (a), above, if instead of paying dividends Boots pays Emil and Betty salaries of $500,000 each? What other strategies could Emil and Betty employ to reduce the impact of the corporate "double tax"? In general, what are the risks of

---

5. But see I.R.C. §§ 1374 and 1375, which impose a corporate-level tax on certain S corporations that previously were C corporations.

6. I.R.C. § 1366(a), (b).

7. I.R.C. §§ 1367(a); 1368(a), (b).

8. I.R.C. § 1371(a)(1).

9. See Chapter 15G, infra.

these strategies.   See, e.g., §§ 79; 105(a), (b); 106; 119; 162(a)
(2); 163; 267; 1363(a); 1366(a)(1), (c).

(d)   Assume the highest corporate and individual tax rates in § 11
and § 1 are 34% and 50%, respectively, and that long-term
capital gains recognized by individuals are taxed at a 20%
rate?   What strategies could Emil and Betty employ to reduce
the overall tax liability on Boots' income in this tax regime?

(e)   Assume the same facts as in (a), above, except that the cost of
the equipment placed in service during the current year is
$8,000,000, and ACRS depreciation is $1,600,000.   Compute
Boots' regular tax and alternative minimum tax, if any, for the
current year.   [Hint: See § 56.   Depreciation under § 56(a)(1)
(A)(ii) is $750,000;   depreciation under § 56(g)(4)(A)(i) is
$500,000; in determining Boots' "earnings and profits," tax-
exempt interest is included but the dividends received deduction is not deductible (see § 56(g)(4)(B), (C)(i)).   Assume Boots
has no other alternative minimum tax preference items or
adjustments.]

(f)   Assume in (e), above, that Emil and Betty are contemplating
the acquisition of Sox, Inc., which expects to have annual
taxable income of $2,000,000 and no AMT preference items or
adjustments for the foreseeable future.   Based on these projections, could Emil and Betty or Boots, Inc. achieve any tax
benefits by acquiring Sox, Inc.?

5.   THE INTEGRATION ALTERNATIVE

The double tax on corporate profits has always been controversial.
Economists and corporate finance theorists have argued that taxing the
operating profits of C corporations more than businesses which qualify
for pass-through treatment creates economic distortions and is inequitable.   Calls frequently have been made for "integration" of the individual and corporate income taxes into a single comprehensive system.[1]
The Treasury has recently embarked on a study of this question and its
report is expected to be available during 1991.

The conventional wisdom is that an integrated system is not
realistic in the near term.   A separate tax on corporations is a political-
ly popular way to raise revenue.   Classic proponents of the double tax
system have argued that the concentration of economic power represented by the earnings of at least public companies is an appropriate
object of a tax system that purports to be built on principles of fairness
and ability to pay.   Many closely held businesses are able to avoid the
double tax by operating as partnerships or S corporations.   Even if they

1. See, e.g., McLure, "Integration of the
Personal and Corporate Income Taxes:
The Missing Element in Recent Tax Reform Proposals," 88 Harv.L.Rev. 532
(1975); Canellos, "Corporate Tax Integration: By Design or By Default?" in Corporate Tax Reform: A Report of the Invitational Conference on Subchapter C 129
(Am. Bar Ass'n Section on Taxation; N.Y.
State Bar Ass'n Tax Section, 1988).

do not qualify for pass-through treatment, closely held C corporations have engaged in many "self-help" integration techniques (such as payments of deductible compensation or interest) to avoid the sting of the corporate tax.

Despite these current political realities, the proponents of integration have been speaking out with renewed vigor, contending that the corporate tax is an indirect tax on shareholders rather than a cost of doing business that is passed on to consumers. So viewed, the tax is said to violate notions of vertical equity (by uniformly taxing income earned indirectly by dissimilarly situated shareholders) and horizontal equity (because income earned through a C corporation is taxed more heavily than the same item of income earned through a proprietorship, S corporation or partnership).[2] Free-market economists contend that integration would encourage corporate earnings to be more freely distributed to shareholders, who then could decide whether to reinvest in the business instead of leaving that reinvestment decision to corporate managers.

With the renewed interest in integration, it is worth pausing to consider how such a system might be implemented. The potential integration models fall into two broad categories. The first, referred to as "full" or "complete" integration, would eliminate the corporate income tax and apply a pass-through taxing system to C corporations and their shareholders. A leading alternative is "partial" integration, which typically contemplates different types of tax relief for dividends paid by a corporation. Variations include giving shareholders a tax credit equal to a percentage of dividends paid or allowing shareholders to exclude from gross income a portion of dividends received during the year. Alternatively, the corporation could be permitted to deduct some or all of the dividends it pays its shareholders. The first excerpt following this note surveys the alternative means for achieving integration. The second excerpt describes a 1977 Treasury proposal for a full integration model.

EXCERPT FROM CANELLOS, "TAX INTEGRATION BY DESIGN OR BY DEFAULT?"

Reprinted in Corporate Tax Reform: A Report of the Invitational Conference on Subchapter C 132–35 (American Bar Association, Section of Taxation; New York State Bar Association, Tax Section, 1988.) *

Formal Means for Achieving Integration

If it is determined that there should be some formal integration of corporate and shareholder taxation, the next issue is to choose among the range of techniques for achieving such integration. These techniques differ in terms of whether (1) double taxation is mitigated with

---

2. See Canellos, supra note 1, at 130–131.

* Reprinted by permission of Peter C. Canellos; American Bar Association; and New York State Bar Association. Copyright © American Bar Association, 1988. All Rights Reserved.

respect to both retained and distributed assets; and (2) the actual taxpayer on corporate earnings is the corporation or the shareholder.

The purest form of integration is referred to as full or complete integration, and in effect represents the system of tax applicable to partnerships and S corporations. Under full integration, corporate earnings are attributed on some basis to shareholders who pay tax on them whether or not distributed. In turn, corporate losses flow through to shareholders for deduction by them subject to applicable restrictions on such flow through (such as basis rules, at risk rules, and the new passive loss limitations). The mechanics of existing full integration schemes differ. Thus, in the case of S corporations, the "entity" nature of the corporation predominates more than in the case of partnerships, which under Subchapter K are more often viewed as aggregates. As an example, the basis of corporate assets is generally not affected by sales of the S corporation's stock, whereas Section 754 allows for such an adjustment in the case of sales of partnership interests.

A scheme of complete integration was recommended in the 1977 Treasury Department study entitled "Blueprints for Basic Tax Reform." Under that system, the holder of corporate shares on the first day of the corporation's taxable year would be attributed all the earnings of the corporation for the taxable year. His basis would be increased by any allocated earnings, and would be decreased by distributions and losses. Where shares were sold during the taxable year, the seller would not be taxed on the current year's income, nor would he have any basis increase in respect of such income. Given the premise of "Blueprints" that capital gain and ordinary income would be taxed alike, the exclusion of current year's income was fully offset by the failure to increase basis for current year's income.

"Blueprints" dealt at length with the administrative difficulties of a fully integrated scheme. Thus, the problem of taxing shareholders on amounts not received was to be ameliorated through a system of corporate remittance of a "withholding" tax. This tax was to be considered paid on behalf of shareholders. The audit adjustment problem was to be solved by having the adjustment treated as an income or deduction item attributed to those persons holding shares on the first day of the year in which the adjustment was made. Despite these efforts to grapple with the problems of full integration, "Blueprints" never got off the drawing board. In this respect, it shares the fate of all other schemes for applying a full integration system to corporations in general. In this connection, full integration systems were considered and rejected by Canada and Germany for reasons of theory as well as practicality.

A second system of integration provides for a deemed paid credit for shareholders receiving distributions. The corporation is the initial taxpayer. In essence, tax paid by the corporation on distributed earnings would be attributed to shareholders. Distributions would be "grossed up" and the shareholder would apply the attributed tax as a credit against his tax on the "grossed up" dividend. In effect, this system taxes the shareholder in much the same way in which United States domestic corporations are taxed on distributions from foreign subsidiaries. The credit system has been adopted in many foreign countries and represents the generally prevailing corporate integration system.

The credit system raises a number of serious issues. First, there is the issue whether credit should be allowed only for corporate taxes actually paid. If so, integration has the effect of cutting back on corporate tax preferences such as investment tax credits, as well as possibly eliminating the benefit of foreign tax credits. Second, there is the issue whether tax should be paid by the corporation in connection with distributions (the advance corporation tax in the United Kingdom being an example). Such a tax payment assures that the Treasury will receive tax equal to the credit claimed by shareholders and represents in effect a corporate minimum tax applicable even if preferences would otherwise reduce the effective rate of corporate "mainstream" tax below the rate of attributed credit. A third significant issue is whether the credit should be made available to foreign shareholders in domestic corporations. Such credit has generally not been provided to foreign shareholders in the absence of tax treaties. Indeed, a major advantage of the credit system is the leverage which it provides to the taxing jurisdiction in negotiating favorable treaties with other countries.

A third system of integration reduces the corporate tax on distributed profits. This can be achieved by either a dividends-paid deduction or a split-rate system which taxes distributed earnings at a lower rate than retained earnings. The split-rate system had been used in Germany prior to Germany's adoption of the credit system. A dividends-paid deduction had been recommended in the 1984 Treasury Department Tax Reform Proposals, as well as the House version of the 1986 Act. This system of integration relieves corporate tax on distributed earnings at the corporate level rather than offsetting the second tax otherwise payable by shareholders. It raises some of the same issues discussed above in the case of the credit system. In addition, it raises other serious concerns. First, unless measures are taken to alter this result, a dividends-paid deduction or split-rate system has the effect of allowing corporate earnings to pass untaxed to shareholders who are not taxpayers (e.g., tax-exempt organizations and foreign shareholders). The Treasury Department's tax reform proposals would have sought to recapture some of the tax lost as the result of distributions to foreign shareholders by imposing a special withholding tax on dividends qualifying for the dividends-paid deduction. It acknowledged, however, that such a withholding tax would violate most existing tax treaties.

A final system for achieving integration with respect to distributed earnings is to exclude such distributions from the recipient's income.* This system would permit a shareholder to exclude from income dividends paid from a "previously taxed income" account. Issues raised by this system of integration include whether a selling shareholder should receive a basis increase for undistributed, previously-taxed income allocated to his account; and the allocation of distributions among the categories of previously-taxed income, pre-integration earnings, and earnings accumulated after integration which had not been previously taxed (for example, because of corporate tax preferences).

As this short summary demonstrates, difficult issues must be considered and dealt with in determining which, if any, path to express integration should be taken. Typically, the integration scheme which is adopted is tailored to meet the needs of the particular taxing jurisdiction—its historic tax system, the nature of its capital markets, the role of inward and outward international investment, and other factors. Where integration was adopted, it followed a long period of scholarly analysis and political input. Much of that work has already been undertaken in the United States. Despite these efforts, however, we are no closer to formal integration than we were in the sixties. Indeed, the 1986 Act has gone in the opposite direction by increasing the relative burden of corporate as compared with individual income taxes.

EXCERPT FROM DEPARTMENT OF THE TREASURY, BLUEPRINTS FOR BASIC TAX REFORM 68–75 (JANUARY 17, 1977)

INTEGRATION OF THE INDIVIDUAL AND CORPORATION IN-COME TAXES

Strictly speaking, the uses concept of income—consumption plus change in net worth—is an attribute of individuals or families, not of business organizations. Corporations do not consume, nor do they have a "standard of living." The term "corporate income" is shorthand for the contribution of the corporate entity to the income of its stockholders.

The Corporation Income Tax

Under existing law, income earned in corporations is taxed differently from other income. All corporate earnings are subject to the corporate income tax, and dividend distributions are also taxed separately as income to shareholders. Undistributed earnings are taxed to shareholders only as they raise the value of the common stock and only when the shareholder sells his stock. The resulting gains upon sale are taxed under the special capital gains provisions of the individual

---

* An analysis of this approach is contained in Peel, A Proposal for Eliminating Double Taxation of Corporate Dividends, 39 Tax Lawyer 1 (1985).

income tax. Thus, the tax on retained earnings generally is not at all closely related to the shareholder's individual tax bracket.

Subchapter S Corporations. An exception to these general rules exists for corporations that are taxed under subchapter S of the Internal Revenue Code. If a corporation has 10 (in some cases 15) [now 35, Ed.] or fewer shareholders and meets certain other requirements, it may elect to be taxed in a manner similar to a partnership. The income of the entity is attributed directly to the owners, so that there is no corporate income tax and retained earnings are immediately and fully subject to the individual income tax. For earnings of these corporations, then, complete integration of the corporate and individual income taxes already exists.

Inefficiency of the Corporation Income Tax

The separate taxation of income earned in corporations is responsible for a number of serious economic distortions. It raises the overall rate of taxation on earnings from capital and so produces a bias against saving and investment. It inhibits the flow of saving to corporate equities relative to other forms of investment. Finally, the separate corporate tax encourages the use of debt, relative to equity, for corporate finance.

The existing differential treatment of dividends and undistributed earnings also results in distortions. Distribution of earnings is discouraged, thus keeping corporate investment decisions from the direct test of the capital market and discouraging lower-bracket taxpayers from ownership of stock.

Owners of closely held corporations are favored relative to those that are publicly held. Owner-managers may avoid the double taxation of dividends by accounting for earnings as salaries rather than as dividends, and they may avoid high personal tax rates by retention of earnings in the corporation with eventual realization as capital gains. Provisions of the law intended to minimize these types of tax avoidance add greatly to the complexity of the law and to costs of administration.

A Model Integration Plan

In the model tax system, the corporate income tax would be eliminated, and the effect of subchapter S corporation treatment would be extended to all corporations. There are alternative methods of approximating this result. Because the direct attribution of corporate income to shareholders most nearly matches the concept of an integrated tax, a particular set of rules for direct attribution is prescribed as the model tax plan. However, there are potential administrative problems with this approach. These problems will be noted and alternative approaches described.

The model tax treatment of corporate profits may be summarized by the following four rules:

1. The holder of each share of stock on the first day of the corporation's accounting year (the "tax record date") would be designated the "shareholder of record."

2. Each shareholder of record would add to his tax base his share of the corporation's income annually. If the corporation had a loss for the year, the shareholder would subtract his share of loss.

3. The basis of the shareholder of record in his stock would be increased by his share of income and decreased by his share of loss.

4. Any shareholder's basis in his stock would be reduced, but not to below zero, by cash dividends paid to him or by the fair market value of property distributed to him. Once the shareholder's basis had been reduced to zero, the value of any further distributions would be included in income. (A distribution after the basis had been reduced to zero would indicate the shareholder had, in the past, income that was not reported.)

Designation of a shareholder of record to whom to allocate income earned in the corporation is necessary for large corporations with publicly traded stock. This treatment is designed to avoid recordkeeping problems associated with transfers of stock ownership within the tax year and to avoid "trafficking" in losses between taxpayers with different marginal rates.

Importance of the Record Date. Suppose that the record date were at the end of the taxable year when reliable estimates of the amount of corporate earnings or losses would be known. Shortly before the record date, shareholders with high marginal rates could bid away shares from shareholders with relatively low marginal rates whose corporations are expected to show a loss.

The losses for the year then would be attributed to the new shareholders for whom the offset of losses against other income results in the greatest reduction in tax liability. Thus, a late-year record date would have the effect of reducing the intended progressivity of the income tax and would bring about stock trading that is solely tax motivated.

The earlier in the tax year that the record date were placed the more the shareholder's expected tax liability would become just another element in the prediction of future returns from ownership of stock in the corporation, as is now the case under the corporation income tax. If the record date were the first day of the tax year, the tax consequences of current or corporate earnings or losses already accrued in the corporation could not be transferred to another taxpayer.

Treatment of the Full-Year Shareholder. Under the model tax scheme, a shareholder who holds his stock for the entire taxable year would be taxed on the full amount of income for the year (or would deduct the full amount of loss). Any gain from sale of the stock in a future year would be calculated for tax purposes by subtracting from sale proceeds the amount of his original basis plus the undistributed earnings upon which he has been subject to tax. His corporation would provide him with a statement at the end of each taxable year that informed him of his share of corporate earnings. He then could increase his basis by that amount of earnings less the sum of distributions received during the year. For full-year stockholders, then, basis would be increased by their share of taxable earnings and reduced by the amount of any distributions.

It should be noted that, under this treatment, dividends would not be considered income to the shareholder, but would be just a partial liquidation of his portfolio. Income would accrue to him as the corporation earned it, rather than as the corporation distributed it. Hence, dividend distributions would merely reduce the shareholder's basis, so that subsequent gains (or losses) realized on the sale of his stock would be calculated correctly.

Treatment of a Shareholder Who Sells During the Year. A shareholder of record who sells his stock before the end of the tax year would not have to wait to receive an end-of-year statement in order to calculate his tax. He simply would calculate the difference between the sale proceeds and his basis as of the date of sale. The adjustment to basis of the shareholder's stock to which he would be entitled at the time of the corporation's annual accounting would always just offset the amount of corporate income or loss that he would normally have to report as the shareholder of record. Therefore, the income of a shareholder who sold his shares would be determined fully at the time of sale, and he would have no need for the end-of-year statement.

A numerical example may be useful in explaining the equivalence of treatment of whole-year and part-year stockholders. Suppose that, as of the record date (January 1), shareholder X has a basis of $100 in his one share of stock. By June 20, the corporation has earned $10 per share, and X sells his stock for $110 to Y. The shareholder would thus realize a gain of $10 on the sale, and this would be reported as income.

To illustrate that subsequent corporate earnings would be irrelevant to the former shareholder's calculation of income for taxes, suppose the corporation earns a further $15 after the date of sale, so that as the shareholder of record X receives a report attributing $25 of income to him, entitling him to a $25 basis increase (on shares he no longer owns). One might insist that X take into his tax base the full $25 and recalculate his gain from sale. In this event, the increase in basis from $100 to $125 would convert his gain of $10 from sale to a loss of $15 (adjusted basis = $125; sale price = $110). The $15 loss, netted against $25 of corporate income attributed to him as the shareholder of record, yields $10 as his income to be reported for tax, the same outcome as a simple calculation of his gain at the time of sale. The equivalence between these two approaches may not be complete, however, if the date of sale and the corporate accounting occur in different taxable years. Nonetheless, in the case cited, the model plan appears superior in the simplicity of its calculations, in allowing the taxpayer to know immediately the tax consequences of his transactions, and in its better approximation to taxing income as it is accrued.

In the event there had been a dividend distribution to X of the $10 of earnings before he sold, this distribution would be reflected in the value of the stock, which would now command a market price of $100 on June 20. The amount of the dividend also would reduce his basis to $90, so that his gain for tax purposes would be $10, just as before. The dividend per se has no tax consequences. At the end of the year he again would be allocated $25 of corporation income, but, as before, an offsetting increase in basis. Thus, he will not report any income other than his gain on the sale of the share on June 20.

Note that the same result would obtain in this case if the shareholder included the dividend in income but did not reduce his basis. There would then be $10 attributable to the dividend and no gain on the sale. This treatment of dividends in the income calculation gives correct results for the shareholder who disposes of his shares. However, it would attribute income to a purchaser receiving dividends before the next record date even though such distributions would represent merely a change in portfolio composition. This approach (all distributions are taken into the tax base with only retained earnings allocated to record date shareholders and giving rise to basis adjustments) might nevertheless be considered an alternative to the treatment of the model plan because it is more familiar and would involve fewer basis adjustments and hence a reduced recordkeeping burden. The substance of the full integration proposal would be preserved in this alternative treatment.

The proposed full integration system would make it possible to tax income according to the circumstances of families who earn it, regardless of whether income derives from labor or capital services, regardless of the legal form in which capital is employed, and regardless of whether income earned in corporations is retained or distributed. To the extent that retained earnings increase the value of corporate stock, this system would have the effect of taxing capital gains from ownership of corporate stock as they accrued, thereby eliminating a major source of controversy and complexity in the present law.

Administrative Problems of Model Tax Integration

The Liquidity Problem. Some problems of administration of the system just described would remain. One such problem is that income would be attributed to corporate shareholders whether or not it actually was distributed. To the extent the corporation retained its earnings, the shareholders would incur a current tax liability that must be paid in cash, even though their increases in net worth would not be immediately available to them in the form of cash. Taxpayers with relatively small current cash incomes might then be induced to trade for stocks that had higher rates of dividend payout to assure themselves sufficient cash flow to pay the tax.

Imposition of a withholding tax at the corporate level would help to reduce this liquidity problem and perhaps also reduce the cost of enforcement of timely collections of the tax.

One method of withholding that is compatible with the model tax method for assigning tax liabilities is to require corporations to remit an estimated flat-rate withholding tax at regular intervals during the tax year. This tax would be withheld on behalf of stockholders of record. Stockholders of record would report their total incomes, including all attributed earnings, but also would be allowed a credit for their share of taxes withheld. Taxpayers who hold a stock throughout the entire year would receive one additional piece of tax information from the corporation—the amount of their share of tax withheld throughout the year—and would subtract the tax withheld as a credit against their individual liability.

This withholding system would complicate somewhat the taxation of part-year stockholders. As explained above, the taxable income of the corporation attributed to stockholders could be determined fully at the time of sale as the sum of dividends received during the year and excess of sale price over basis that existed on the record date. However, if withholding were always attributed to the shareholder of record, he would be required to wait until corporate income for the year had been determined to know the amount of his tax credit for withholding during the full tax year. The selling price of the stock may be expected to reflect the estimated value of this prospective credit in the same way that share prices reflect estimates of future profits. But, in this case, the seller who was a stockholder of record would retain an interest in the future earnings of the corporation, because the earnings would determine tax credit entitlement to the end of the tax year. Despite this apparent drawback, such corporate-level withholding would insure sufficient liquidity to pay the tax, except in cases where the combination of distributions and withheld taxes is less than the amount of tax due from the shareholder of record.

Audit Adjustment Problem. Another administrative problem could arise because of audit adjustments to corporate income, which may extend well beyond the taxable year. This would appear to require reopening the returns of shareholders of earlier record dates, possibly long after shares have been sold. In the present system, changes in corporate income and tax liability arising from the audit process are borne by shareholders at the time of the adjustment. Precisely this principle would apply in the model plan. Changes in income discovered in audit, including possible interest or other penalties, would be treated like all other income and attributed to shareholders in the year the issue is resolved. Naturally, shares exchanged before such resolutions but after the matter is publicly known would reflect the anticipated outcome.

Deferral Problem. There are also some equity considerations. A deferral of tax on a portion of corporate income may occur in a year when shares are purchased. The buyer would not be required to report income earned after the date of purchase but before the end of the taxable year. All earnings in the year of sale that were not reflected in the purchase price would escape tax until the buyer sells the stock.

The 1975 Administration Proposal for Integration

In the context of a thorough revision of the income tax, integration of the corporate and personal tax takes on particular importance. The model tax plan has provisions designed to assure that the various forms of business income bear the same tax, as nearly as possible. If incomes from ownership of corporate equities are subject to greater, or lesser, tax relative to incomes from unincorporated business pension funds, or bonds, the economic distortions would be concentrated on the corporate sector. For this reason, a specific plan for attributing to stockholders the whole earnings of corporations has been presented here in some detail.

A significant movement in the direction of removing the distortions caused by the separate corporation income tax would be accomplished by the dividend integration plan proposed by the Administration in 1975. That proposal may be regarded as both an improvement in the present code, in the absence of comprehensive tax reform, and as a major step in the transition to a full integration of the income taxes, such as the model tax.

C. CORPORATE CLASSIFICATION

1. IN GENERAL

Code: § 7701(a)(3).

Regulations: §§ 301.7701–2(a)–(e).

Because the Internal Revenue Code imposes a separate corporate-level tax and otherwise distinguishes corporations from other types of business forms, it is necessary to determine what entities are considered to be corporations for federal tax purposes. The label used under state law is not determinative of an entity's status under the Internal Revenue Code.[1] Rather, Section 7701 defines a corporation as including "associations, joint-stock companies, and insurance companies." If an entity is an unincorporated "association" under the criteria set forth in the regulations, it will be classified as a corporation.[2]

The regulations do not define the term "association." Instead, they list six characteristics ordinarily found in a "pure" corporation: (1) associates (i.e., two or more persons joining together in shared control and ownership of the venture); (2) an objective to carry on business and divide the gains therefrom; (3) continuity of life (a corporation continues in existence despite the death or withdrawal of one or more

---

1. Reg. § 301.7701–1(c).   **2.** Reg. § 301.7701–2(a).

shareholders); (4) centralization of management (i.e., management responsibility is vested in directors who act on behalf of the owners; management responsibility is not exercised directly by the shareholders); (5) limited liability (shareholders are not personally liable for corporate debts); and (6) free transferability of interests (i.e., shareholders may dispose of their shares).[3] The regulations then explain that "an organization will be treated as an association if the corporate characteristics are such that the organization more nearly resembles a corporation than a partnership or trust."[4] The principal controversies thus involve distinguishing corporations from partnerships and trusts.

2.　CORPORATIONS vs. PARTNERSHIPS

a.　LIMITED PARTNERSHIPS

Unlike a corporation, a partnership is not a separate taxable entity. Instead, each partner takes into account his share of partnership income, deductions and other items in determining his individual tax liability.[1] This difference historically contributed to the use of partnerships as the primary vehicles for tax shelter investments. Subject to the passive loss limitations,[2] partnership losses offered more instant gratification because the pass-through scheme enabled partners to deduct their allocable share of partnership losses against income from other sources.[3] In contrast, losses of C corporations simply create a net operating loss under Section 172 which the corporation may carry back or forward but are not immediately available to the owners of the business.

Most investors who historically sought the tax benefits of partnership status also desired certain nontax advantages that were not available to partners in a general partnership. The nontax characteristics that appealed most to investors were: (1) limited liability;[4] (2) centralized management—i.e., representative management vested in a group smaller than all members so that passive investors are relieved of management duties;[5] (3) free transferability of interests, a feature enabling the investors to dispose of their entire interest when they saw fit;[6] and (4) continuity of life.[7] Because these characteristics have a distinctly corporate hue, the regulations provide that any business

---

3.　Reg. § 301.7701–2(a)(1).

4.　Id.

1.　I.R.C. § 701.

2.　See I.R.C. § 469.

3.　Before applying the passive loss limitations, a partner's distributive share of partnership loss is subject to the limitations in Section 704(d) (limiting losses to the partner's basis in his partnership interest) and Section 465 (the at risk limitation).

4.　General partners are jointly liable for all partnership debts and obligations. Uniform Partnership Act § 15.

5.　In a partnership, each general partner is an agent of the partnership and has equal rights in the management and conduct of the partnership's business. Uniform Partnership Act §§ 9, 18(e).

6.　General partners may not unilaterally transfer their right to participate in management to an assignee. Uniform Partnership Act § 27.

7.　A partnership as an entity dissolves, but does not terminate, upon the death, withdrawal or bankruptcy of a general partner and certain other events. Investors typically prefer an enterprise whose

organization with at least three of the four listed attributes will be classified as an association taxable as a corporation for income tax purposes.[8]   In the tax shelter era, corporate classification was enough to poison the atmosphere because of the inability of the enterprise to pass through its losses to the investors.   The challenge was to structure an entity so that it met the investors' tax and nontax objectives.

An alternative vehicle, the limited partnership, became the entity of choice for tax shelters because it allowed the limited partner investors to achieve some corporate characteristics while retaining the tax benefits of a partnership.   Although tax shelters were substantially derailed by the Tax Reform Act of 1986, the limited partnership lives on as an attractive investment vehicle, albeit for different reasons. The strengthening of the corporate regular and alternative minimum taxes, and the recent rate inversion, under which corporate rates exceed individual rates for the first time in our tax history, sharply increases the relative tax costs of conducting business as a Subchapter C corporation.

A limited partnership consists of one or more general partners and one or more limited partners.[9]   Each general partner typically has all the rights and liabilities of a general partner in a general partnership.[10] Limited partners, however, have no right to participate in the management of the organization, cannot bind the partnership and are responsible for partnership liabilities only to the extent of their unpaid contributions.[11]   Consequently, limited partners generally may transfer their partnership interests, and the death or withdrawal of any limited partner does not dissolve the partnership.[12]   As long as there is at least one general partner willing to take on the management of the partnership and remain personally liable for partnership obligations, a limited partnership is a straightforward way to provide investors with limited liability, freedom from management burdens and transferable interests while at the same time permitting them to enjoy the tax advantages available to partnerships.

Because limited partnerships share many corporate characteristics and limited partners are akin to shareholders, a limited partnership strongly resembles a corporation.   The basic difference between the two entities is that the limited partnership has a general partner—someone who bears personal liability, retains management and control over his own investment and the interests of the limited partners, and who, as a result, cannot either transfer his interest or withdraw from the partnership without causing it to dissolve.   As the general partner becomes less substantial, the limited partnership begins to look more like a corporation.

continued existence is not dependent on events relating to their fellow investors. Uniform Partnership Act §§ 29–31.

   8.   Reg. § 301.7701–2(a)(3).

   9.   Revised Uniform Limited Partnership Act (1976) § 101(7).

   10.   Id. § 403.

   11.   Id. § 303.

   12.   §§ 702, 801.

Indeed, many limited partnerships more closely resemble corporations than any other form of doing business. This similarity once prompted the Treasury to propose treating all limited partnerships as corporations for tax purposes if at any time during the taxable year the partnership had more than 35 limited partners.[13] One might have assumed that the existing classification regulations, which require an organization to be treated as an association if its corporate characteristics make it more nearly resemble a corporation than a partnership, would have resolved this issue by treating limited partnerships as corporations. Although this result seems appropriate, it rarely has been reached. The Service's lack of success is best explained by the evolution of the current classification standards. The existing Section 7701 regulations were enacted at a time when professionals (e.g., doctors, lawyers, accountants, etc.), forbidden from incorporating under state law, attempted to form entities that qualified as "associations" taxable as corporations. The taxpayers' goal was to qualify for tax advantages, such as qualified retirement plans and tax-free fringe benefits, that were then available to corporations and their employees but not to partnerships and partners.[14] At the time, the Treasury's mission was to make it more difficult for unincorporated entities to qualify as corporations for federal tax purposes.[15] That goal was undercut by the subsequent willingness of state legislators to permit the formation of professional corporations.[16] The end result, as illustrated by the *Larson* case, which follows, is that the regulations reflect a bias in favor of partnership classification and make it relatively simple for limited partnerships to secure the benefits of partnership status while providing their investors with many of the economic characteristics previously available only to corporate shareholders.

LARSON v. COMMISSIONER *

United States Tax Court, 1976.
66 T.C. 159.

[Somis and Mai-Kai were limited partnerships under the California Limited Partnership Act. The sole general partner in each partnership was GHL. During the years in question, GHL's net worth was roughly

13. U.S. Department of the Treasury, 2 Tax Reform for Fairness, Simplification and Economic Growth—General Explanation of the Treasury Department's Proposals 146–150 (1984). As a result of sharp criticism, this proposal was dropped from President Reagan's 1985 tax reform proposals.

14. United States v. Kintner, 216 F.2d 418 (9th Cir.1954). Cf. Morrissey v. Commissioner, 296 U.S. 344, 56 S.Ct. 289 (1935). Virtually all of the advantages of corporate classification in the retirement plan context were eliminated by the Tax Equity and Fiscal Responsibility Act of 1982 and subsequent legislation.

15. See Scallen, "Federal Income Taxation of Professional Associations and Corporations," 49 Minn.L.Rev. 603 (1965); Fisher, "Classification Under Section 7701—The Past, Present and Prospects for the Future," 30 Tax Lawyer 627 (1977).

16. See, e.g., West's Ann.Cal.Corp.Code §§ 13400–13410; Maryland Code, Corporations and Associations, Title 6, Subtitle 1 (1975); West's Florida Statutes Annotated, ch. 621.

* Some footnotes omitted. For an analysis of this case, see Peel, "Definition of a Partnership: New Suggestions on an Old Issue," 1979 Wis.L.Rev. 989 (1979).

10% of the combined net worth of the partnerships.   No limited partners owned any GHL stock except for one 2% limited partner in Somis who owned 23% of the GHL stock.   GHL was entitled to 20% of the partnership profits after the limited partners had recouped their investment.

The partnership had a life of 33 years unless 60% of the limited partners voted to increase the life.   The limited partners could not transfer or assign their rights without consent of GHL, which consent could not be unreasonably withheld.   Ed.]

TANNENWALD, Judge:

OPINION

Petitioners owned limited partnership interests in Mai-Kai and Somis, two real estate ventures organized under the California Uniform Limited Partnership Act, Cal.Corp.Code secs. 15501 et seq. (West Supp. 1976) (hereinafter referred to as CULPA).   The partnerships incurred losses during the years in issue, and petitioners deducted their distributive shares of such losses on their individual tax returns.   Respondent disallowed those deductions on the ground that the partnerships were associations taxable as corporations as defined in section 7701(a)(3), and not partnerships as defined in section 7701(a)(2).   Petitioners allege that the partnerships fail all of the tests of corporate resemblance established by respondent's regulations (sec. 301.7701–2, Proced. & Admin. Regs.); respondent contends that all those tests are satisfied. Both sides agree that the regulations apply and are controlling, and our opinion and decision are consequently framed in that context; the validity of respondent's regulations is not before us.[8]   In our previous (now withdrawn) opinion dated October 21, 1975, we concluded that respondent should prevail.   Upon reconsideration, we have come to the opposite conclusion and hold for petitioners.

The starting point of the regulations' definition of an "association" is the principle applied in Morrissey v. Commissioner, 296 U.S. 344 (1935), that the term includes entities which resemble corporations although they are not formally organized as such.   *Morrissey* identified several characteristics of the corporate form which the regulations adopt as a test of corporate resemblance.   For the purpose of comparing corporations with partnerships, the significant characteristics are: continuity of life; centralization of management; limited liability; and free transferability of interests.   Other corporate or noncorporate characteristics may also be considered if appropriate in a particular case.

---

8.   In this connection, we note the following passage from the Supreme Court opinion in Morrissey v. Commissioner, 296 U.S. 344, 354–355 (1935):

"As the statute merely provided that the term 'corporation' should include 'associations,' without further definition, the Treasury Department was authorized to supply rules for the enforcement of the Act within the permissible bounds of administrative construction.   Nor can this authority be deemed to be so restricted that the regulations, once issued, could not later be clarified or enlarged so as to meet administrative exigencies or conform to judicial decision."

An organization will be taxed as a corporation if, taking all relevant characteristics into account, it more nearly resembles a corporation than some other entity. Sec. 301.7701–2(a)(1), Proced. & Admin. Regs.; see and compare Bush # 1, 48 T.C. 218, 227–228 (1967), and Giant Auto Parts, Ltd., 13 T.C. 307 (1949). This will be true only if it possesses more corporate than noncorporate characteristics.

The regulations discuss each major corporate characteristic separately, and each apparently bears equal weight in the final balancing. See pp. 185–186 infra. This apparently mechanical approach may perhaps be explained as an attempt to impart a degree of certainty to a subject otherwise fraught with imponderables. In most instances, the regulations also make separate provision for the classification of limited partnerships. Petitioners rely heavily on those provisions, while respondent seeks to distinguish them or to minimize their importance.

1. *Continuity of Life*

Pertinent provisions of the regulation concerning this characteristic are set forth below.[9] A corporation possesses a greater degree of continuity of life than a partnership, since its existence is not dependent upon events personally affecting its separate members. Because of their more intimate legal and financial ties, partners are given a continuing right to choose their associates which is denied to corporate shareholders. A material alteration in the makeup of the partnership, as through the death or incapacity of a partner, either dissolves the partnership relation by operation of law or permits dissolution by order of court. Uniform Partnership Act, secs. 31 and 32 (hereinafter referred to as UPA). Partners are then free to withdraw their shares from the business, though they may agree to form a new partnership to continue it. A partner is also given the right to dissolve the partnership and withdraw his capital (either specific property or the value of his interest) at will at any time (UPA sec. 31(2)), although he may be unable to cause the winding up of the business and may be answerable in damages to other partners if his act breaches an agreement among them (UPA secs. 37 and 38(2)). The significant difference between a corporation and a partnership as regards continuity of life, then, is that a partner can always opt out of continued participation in and exposure to the risks of the enterprise. A corporate shareholder's investment is locked in unless liquidation is voted or he can find a purchaser to buy him out.

In a partnership subject to the Uniform Limited Partnership Act (hereinafter referred to as ULPA), this right of withdrawal is modified. A limited partner can withdraw his interest on dissolution (ULPA sec. 16), but he can neither dissolve the partnership at will (ULPA sec. 10) nor force dissolution at the retirement, death, or insanity of a general partner if the remaining general partners agree to continue the business in accordance with a right granted in the partnership certificate

---

9. [See Reg. § 301.7701–2(b). Ed.]

(ULPA sec. 20).   CULPA section 15520 [10] further provides that a new general partner can be elected to continue the business without causing dissolution, if the certificate permits.

The sole general partner in the limited partnerships involved herein was a corporation, whose business was the promotion and management of real estate ventures.   As a practical matter, it is unlikely that either Mai-Kai or Somis would have been dissolved midstream and the partners afforded an opportunity to withdraw their investments.   Petitioners argue that the partnerships nevertheless lacked continuity of life because they could be dissolved either at will by, or on the bankruptcy of, the general partner.   We turn first to the effect of bankruptcy of GHL.

California Uniform Partnership Act section 15031(5) (West Supp. 1976) (hereinafter referred to as CUPA) provides that a partnership is dissolved on the bankruptcy of a partner.   CUPA section 15006(2) makes that act applicable to limited partnerships unless inconsistent with statutes relating to them.   CULPA nowhere provides for dissolution or nondissolution in the event of bankruptcy.   Section 15520, which merely covers dissolution and countervailing action by the remaining partners under certain circumstances, does not provide for such event.   See n. 10 supra.   CUPA section 15031(5) therefore applies. Since the bankruptcy of GHL would bring about dissolution by operation of law, each limited partner would be entitled to demand the return of his contribution (CULPA sec. 15516).   Somis and Mai-Kai simply do not satisfy the regulations' test of continuity, which requires that the "bankruptcy *   *   * of *any member* will *not* cause a dissolution of the organization."   (Emphasis supplied.) [11]

The fact that under the agreements involved herein a new general partner might be chosen to continue the business does not affect this conclusion.   Respondent seizes upon this aspect of the agreements to argue that the limited partners could anticipate the bankruptcy of GHL [12] and elect a new general partner.   But this element does not detract from the hard fact that if GHL became bankrupt while it was the general partner of Somis and Mai-Kai, there would at best be a

10. That section provided during the years in issue:

The retirement, death, insanity, removal or failure of reelection of a general partner dissolves the partnership, unless the business is continued by the remaining general partners and/or the general partner or general partners elected in place thereof

(a) Under a right so to do stated in the certificate, or

(b) With the consent of all members * * * [Cal.Stats.1963, c. 870, sec. 5 at 2112.]

11. In light of our conclusion, infra at pp. 177–179, that GHL has not been shown to have had a substantial interest in the partnerships, it may be argued that it was not a "member" for the purpose of the regulations. Such an argument, however, we find to be structurally incompatible with the regulations, which consider the substantiality of a partner's interest in the partnership only in connection with centralization of management and transferability of interests. Cf. sec. 301.7701–2(d)(2), Proced. & Admin.Regs., n. 19 infra (fourth sentence).

12. An assumption which, given the startling instances of unexpected bankruptcies in the current business world and the absence of involvement of the limited partners in the operations of GHL, is questionable.

hiatus between the event of bankruptcy and the entry of a new general partner so that, from a legal point of view, the old partnerships would have been dissolved. Moreover, at least in the case of Mai-Kai, a vote of 100 percent of the limited partners was required to elect a new general partner. Glensder Textile Co., 46 B.T.A. 176 (1942), held that such contingent continuity of life did not resemble that of a corporation. Respondent's regulations (see n. 9 supra) incorporate this conclusion.

We hold that the partnerships involved herein do not satisfy the "continuity of life" test as set forth in respondent's regulations. We recognize that our application of respondent's existing regulations to the event of bankruptcy results in a situation where it is unlikely that a limited partnership will ever satisfy the "continuity of life" requirement of those regulations. But the fact that the regulations are so clearly keyed to "dissolution" (a term encompassing the legal relationships between the partners) rather than "termination of the business" (a phrase capable of more pragmatic interpretation encompassing the life of the business enterprise) leaves us with no viable alternative.[13] In this connection, we note that respondent is not without power to alter the impact of our application of his existing regulations. See *Morrissey v. Commissioner,* n. 8 supra.

In view of our conclusion as to the effect of GHL's bankruptcy, we find it unnecessary to deal with the contentions of the parties as to whether, under California law, GHL had the legal power to dissolve both Mai-Kai and Somis so as to counteract the "continuity of life" elements contained in the rights of the limited partners under the partnership agreements and certificates, or whether, in respect of this characteristic, CULPA corresponded to the Uniform Limited Partnership Act. See sec. 301.7701–2(b)(2) and (3), Proced. & Admin.Regs., n. 9, supra. Indeed, since the California law, as we interpret it, does not permit the partners in Mai-Kai and Somis to contract against dissolution in the event of bankruptcy of GHL, the rights and duties created by the agreements and certificates cannot alter our conclusion on the "continuity of life" issue; this is a quite different situation from that which exists when other corporate characteristics such as centralized management * * * and free transferability of interest * * * are considered.

2. *Centralized Management*

In the corporate form, management is centralized in the officers and directors; the involvement of shareholders as such in ordinary operations is limited to choosing these representatives. In a general partnership, authority is decentralized and any partner has the power to make binding decisions in the ordinary course (UPA sec. 9). In a

---

13. It should be noted that under sec. 5(i) of the Bankruptcy Act, 11 U.S.C. sec. 23(i) (1970), bankruptcy of all general partners requires that the partnership itself be adjudicated bankrupt.

limited partnership, however, this authority exists only in the general partners (ULPA secs. 9 and 10), and a limited partner who takes part in the control of the business loses his limited liability status (ULPA sec. 7). From a practical standpoint, it is clear that the management of both Mai-Kai and Somis was centralized in GHL. The sole general partner was empowered by law as well as by the partnership agreements to administer the partnership affairs. However, respondent's regulations specify that—

> In addition, limited partnerships subject to a statute corresponding to the Uniform Limited Partnership Act, generally do not have centralized management, but centralized management ordinarily does exist in such a limited partnership if substantially all the interests in the partnership are owned by the limited partners. [Sec. 301.7701–2(c)(4), Proced. & Admin. Regs.]

In other words, even though there may be centralized administration by a general partner, the "centralization of management" test will not be met if the general partner has a meaningful proprietary interest. See Zuckman v. United States, 524 F.2d 729 (Ct.Cl.1975). In specifying this additional condition, respondent has adopted the theory of *Glensder Textile Co.,* supra, that managing partners with such interests in the business are not "analogous to directors of a corporation" because they act in their own interests "and not *merely* in a representative capacity for a body of persons having a limited investment and a limited liability." (46 B.T.A. at 185; emphasis added.) It is thus necessary to look to the proprietary interest of GHL in order to determine whether the additional condition imposed by respondent's regulations has been met.[14]

Unlike the taxpayers in *Zuckman v. United States,* supra, petitioners herein have failed to show that the limited partners did not own all or substantially all the interests in the partnerships involved herein within the meaning of the regulations. GHL's interests in Mai-Kai and Somis were subordinated to those of the limited partners. Petitioners have not attempted to demonstrate that GHL's capital interests had any present value during the years in issue, and it is clear that, because of the subordination provisions, it had no present right to income during those years. Petitioners would have us look to the anticipated return on the partnership properties in future years to determine that GHL had a substantial proprietary stake in the business independent of its management role. They have not, however, proved by competent evidence that such a return could in fact be expected, relying instead on unsupported projections;[15] nor have they shown that any such future

14. We need not determine what the consequences would be if the respondent's regulations did not contain this additional condition. Cf. John Provence # 1 Well, 37 T.C. 376 (1961), affd. 321 F.2d 840 (3d Cir. 1963).

15. For example, petitioners blithely assume a 3-percent annual increase in the value of the real estate, which they characterize as "conservative," and, in effect, ask us to take judicial notice that their assumption is valid.

profit would be reflected in the present value of GHL's interest. Although there was testimony that GHL expected profits from the subordinated interests when the limited partnerships were liquidated, we are not convinced that the possibility of such income at an indefinite future date had value during the years at issue. GHL reported gross income of $906,930.89 from fiscal 1969 to fiscal 1974, out of which only $118 represented a partnership distribution (from a partnership not involved herein).

Furthermore, the limited partners in Somis and Mai-Kai possessed the right to remove GHL as the general partner. Thus, GHL's right to participate in future growth and profits was wholly contingent on satisfactory performance of its management role,[17] and not at all analogous to the independent proprietary interest of a typical general partner. In *Glensder Textile Co.*, supra, our conclusion that centralization of management was lacking rested not only on the fact that management retained a proprietary interest but also on the fact that the limited partners could not "remove the general partners and control them as agents, as stockholders may control directors." 46 B.T.A. at 185.

Petitioners argue that such power of removal and control could be given to limited partners under ULPA,[18] that CULPA (which makes specific reference to such power) is a statute corresponding to ULPA, and that accordingly respondent's regulation requires a decision in their favor on this issue. In our opinion, the regulation was not intended to provide a blanket exemption from association status for ULPA limited partnerships, regardless of the extent to which the partners by agreement deviate from the statutory scheme. It states only that a limited partnership in an ULPA jurisdiction *generally* will lack centralized management. See p. 176, supra. We have repeatedly held that an organization is to be classified by reference to the rights and duties created by agreement as well as those existing under State law. Bush # 1, 48 T.C. at 228; Western Construction Co., 14 T.C. 453, 467 (1950), affd. per curiam 191 F.2d 401 (9th Cir.1951); Glensder Textile Co., 46 B.T.A. at 183. The effect of such organic laws as ULPA (and CULPA) is to provide a rule which governs in the absence of contrary agreement. Where the theme is obscured by the variations, it is the latter which set the tone of the composition. Neither ULPA nor CULPA requires that the limited partners be given the right to remove the general partner; in fact, ULPA does not even mention such a possibility. By reserving that right, the limited partners in Mai-Kai

17. On removal, GHL would have been entitled to receive the cash value of its interest, both by statute (CUPA sec. 15038(1)) and, in the case of Somis, by agreement. To the extent of that value, GHL would have a vested present proprietary interest to protect. The petitioners had the burden of showing that such value existed and that it was substantial; they have done neither. GHL did not list any partnership interests as assets on its tax returns and apparently did not report any income either on the receipt of a partnership interest or on the lapse of a subordination clause. See secs. 1.61–2(d)(5) and 1.421–6(d)(2), Income Tax Regs.; Sol Diamond, 56 T.C. 530 (1971), affd. 492 F.2d 286 (7th Cir.1974). Cf. sec. 83. * * *

18. Cf. UPA sec. 31.

and Somis took themselves out of the basic framework of ULPA and hence out of the shelter of the regulation, which is based on *Glensder.*

We conclude that Somis and Mai-Kai had centralized management within the meaning of respondent's regulations.

3. *Limited Liability*

Unless some member is personally liable for debts of, and claims against, an entity, section 301.7701–2(d)(1), Proced. & Admin.Regs., states that the entity possesses the corporate characteristic of limited liability. The regulation provides that "in the case of a limited partnership subject to a statute corresponding to the Uniform Limited Partnership Act, personal liability exists with respect to each general partner, except as provided in subparagraph (2) of this paragraph." The first sentence of subparagraph (2) [19] establishes a conjunctive test, under which a general partner is considered not to have personal liability only "when he has no substantial assets (other than his interest in the partnership) which could be reached by a creditor of the organization *and* when he is merely a 'dummy' acting as the agent of the limited partners." (Emphasis added.) In other words, personal liability exists if the general partner *either* has substantial assets *or* is not a dummy for the limited partners. We do not agree with respondent's assertion, made for the first time in connection with the motion for reconsideration, that the regulation should be read disjunctively. Although the purpose of subparagraph (2) was ostensibly to delineate the conditions under which personal liability of a general partner *does not exist,* practically all the remaining material in the subparagraph outlines the conditions under which such personal liability does exist. In several examples, personal liability is said to exist, either because the general partner has substantial assets or because he is not a dummy for the limited partners. See Zuckman v. United States, supra. In no instance is there a suggestion that both conditions established by the first sentence of subparagraph (2) need not be satisfied.

In so concluding, we are mindful that in *Glensder Textile Co.,* supra, the apparent source of the language in the regulations, the term "dummy" was arguably considered applicable to any general partner without substantial assets risked in the business. The opinion in *Glensder* states (46 B.T.A. at 183):

> If, for instance, the general partners were not men with substantial assets risked in the business *but* were mere dummies without real means acting as the agents of the limited partners, whose investments made possible the business, there would be something approaching the corporate form of stockholders and directors. * * * [Emphasis added.]

19. [See Reg. § 301.7701–2(d). Ed.]

Thus, lack of substantial assets seems to be considered the equivalent of being a dummy—an equivalence which respondent apparently sought to avoid by using the word "and" in his existing regulations.[20]

While it may be doubtful that GHL could be considered to have had substantial assets during the years in issue, we find it unnecessary to resolve this question since it is clear that GHL was not a dummy for the limited partners of Somis and Mai-Kai. Respondent contends that GHL fell within the "dummy" concept because it was subject to removal by the limited partners, and thus was subject to their ultimate control. While it is true that a mere "dummy" would be totally under the control of the limited partners, it does not follow that the presence of some control by virtue of the power to remove necessarily makes the general partner a "dummy." It seems clear that the limited partners' rights to remove the general partner were designed to give the limited partners a measure of control over their investment without involving them in the "control of the business"; the rights were not designed to render GHL a mere dummy or to empower the limited partners "to direct the business actively through the general partners." Glensder Textile Co., 46 B.T.A. at 183. Moreover, the record indicates that the limited partners did not use GHL as a screen to conceal their own active involvement in the conduct of the business; far from being a rubber stamp, GHL was the moving force in these enterprises. With a minor exception, the persons controlling GHL were independent of and unrelated to the limited partners.

In view of the foregoing, we conclude that personal liability existed with respect to GHL, and the partnerships lack the corporate characteristic of limited liability.

20. In this connection, it is of interest to note that the proposed regulations were cast solely in economic terms, i.e., relied entirely on substantiality of assets, without any reference whatsoever to a "dummy" situation. See 24 Fed.Reg. 10,450, 10,452 (1959), which reads as follows:

(d) *Limited liability.* (1) An organization has the corporate characteristic of limited liability if there is no member who is personally liable for the debts of or the claims against the organization. Personal liability means that a creditor of an organization may seek personal satisfaction from a member of the organization to the extent that the assets of such organization are insufficient to satisfy the creditor's claim.

(2) For purposes of this paragraph, personal liability does not exist when the only members who are personally liable for the debts of the organization have no substantial assets which could be reached by a creditor of the organization. A member may contribute his services, but no capital, to the organization, but if such member is personally liable for the debts of the organization and has substantial assets, there exists personal liability. Furthermore, if the organization is engaged in financial transactions which involve large sums of money, and if the members who are personally liable have substantial assets, there exists personal liability although the assets of such members would be insufficient to satisfy any substantial portion of the obligations of the organization. However, personal liability does not exist when the members who are personally liable have risked no substantial assets.

4. *Transferability of Interests*

A stockholder's rights and interest in a corporate venture are, absent consensual restrictions, freely transferable by the owner without reference to the wishes of other members. A partner, on the other hand, can unilaterally transfer only his interest in partnership "profits and surplus," and cannot confer on the assignee the other attributes of membership without the consent of all partners (UPA secs. 18(g), 26, and 27). Respondent's regulations recognize and rely upon this distinction.[21]

The regulations state that if substantially all interests are freely transferable, the corporate characteristic of free transferability of interests is present. Since we have concluded, for the purposes of this case, that the limited partners should be considered as owning substantially all the interests in Mai-Kai and Somis * * *, we turn our attention to the question whether their interests were so transferable.

A transferee of a limited partnership interest may become a substituted limited partner with the consent of all members or under a right given in the certificate. CULPA sec. 15519. The partnership certificates of Mai-Kai and Somis are silent in this regard. However, when the provisions of the agreements relating to transferability and the power of an assignee to obtain a judicial amendment of the partnership certificate (see CULPA secs. 15502(1)(a)X and 15525) are taken into account, it would appear that the agreements rather than the certificates should be considered the controlling documents herein. Indeed, petitioners do not seek to draw any solace from the certificates, positing their arguments as to lack of transferability on the agreements themselves.

Both partnership agreements permit the assignment of a limited partner's income interest with the consent of the general partner, which may not unreasonably be withheld. Petitioners have not suggested any ground on which consent could be withheld. The requirement of consent, circumscribed by a standard of reasonableness, is not such a restriction on transfer as is typical of partnership agreements; nor is it the sort referred to by the regulations. In our opinion, the limited partners' income rights were freely transferable. See Outlaw v. United States, 494 F.2d 1376, 1384 (Ct.Cl.1974).

Petitioners also argue that transferability is limited by the requirement that, in the event of a proposed assignment, a limited partner's capital interest first be offered to other members under certain circumstances. While an assignment for less than fair market value could be prevented in this manner, there was no requirement that such an offer be made if an interest was to be sold to a third party at fair market value. Thus, there was no "effort on the part of the parties to select their business associates," as is characteristic of the usual partnership arrangement. J.A. Riggs Tractor Co., 6 T.C. 889, 898 (1946). We think

21. [See Reg. § 301.7701–2(e). Ed.]

that these interests possessed considerably more than the "modified" form of free transferability referred to in subparagraph (2) of the regulation.

In sum, an assignee for fair consideration of a limited partner's interest in Somis or Mai-Kai could acquire all of the rights of a substituted limited partner within the framework of the agreement and governing State law, without discretionary consent of any other member. Any restrictions or conditions on such a transfer were procedural rather than substantive. The right of assignment more closely resembles that attending corporate shares than that typically associated with partnership interests. Mai-Kai and Somis therefore possessed the corporate characteristic of free transferability of interests. See also n. 23 infra.

5. *Other Characteristics*

Both parties have identified other characteristics of Mai-Kai and Somis which they allege are relevant to the determination whether those entities more closely resemble partnerships or corporations. Some of these are within the ambit of the major characteristics already discussed. Petitioners point to the fact that, unlike a corporate board of directors, GHL as manager lacked the discretionary right to retain or distribute profits according to the needs of the business. This argument is in reality directed to the issue of centralized management. The same is true of respondent's analogy between the limited partners' voting rights and those of corporate shareholders. To be sure the partnership interests were not represented by certificates but this factor conceivably is more properly subsumed in the transferability issue. See Morrissey v. Commissioner, 296 U.S. at 360. Moreover, those interests were divided into units or shares and were promoted and marketed in a manner similar to corporate securities—an additional "characteristic" which we have not ignored, (see *Outlaw v. United States,* supra), but which we do not deem of critical significance under the circumstances herein. Similarly, we do not assign any particular additional importance to the facts that the partnerships have not observed corporate formalities and procedures (*Morrissey v. Commissioner,* supra; Giant Auto Parts, Ltd., 13 T.C. 307 (1949)) or that, unlike general partners, limited partners were not required personally to sign the partnership certificates. Finally, respondent argues that the limited partnerships resemble corporations because they provide a means of pooling investments while limiting the liability of the participants. Cf. Helvering v. Combs, 296 U.S. 365 (1935). As it relates to the facts of this case, this point is subsumed in our earlier discussion. To the extent that it presages an attempt to classify *all* limited partnerships as corporations, it is in irreconcilable conflict with respondent's own regulations.

6. *Conclusion*

The regulations provide that an entity will be taxed as a corporation if it more closely resembles a corporation than any other form of organization. They further state that such a resemblance does not exist unless the entity possesses more corporate than noncorporate characteristics. If every characteristic bears equal weight, then Mai-Kai and Somis are partnerships for tax purposes. We have found that they possess only two of the four major corporate characteristics and that none of the other characteristics cited by the parties upsets the balance.[22] On the other hand, if the overall corporate resemblance test, espoused by *Morrissey* and adhered to by the regulations, permits us to weigh each factor according to the degree of corporate similarity it provides, we would be inclined to find that these entities were taxable as corporations. Each possessed a degree of centralized management indistinguishable from that of a pure corporation; the other major factors lie somewhere on the continuum between corporate and partnership resemblance. Were not the regulations' thumb upon the scales, it appears to us that the practical continuity and limited liability of both entities would decisively tip the balance in respondent's favor. However, we can find no warrant for such refined balancing in the regulations or in cases which have considered them. See Zuckman v. United States, 524 F.2d 729 (Ct.Cl.1975); Outlaw v. United States, supra; Kurzner v. United States, 413 F.2d 97, 105 (5th Cir.1969) ("four equally weighted procrustean criteria"); secs. 301.7701–2(a)(3) and 301.7701–3(b)(2), Proced. & Admin.Regs., example (2). Cf. Estate of Smith v. Commissioner, 313 F.2d 724, 736 (8th Cir.1963) ("substantially greater noncorporate characteristics both in number *and in importance"*) (emphasis added). Only in connection with free transferability of interests do the regulations recognize a modified and less significant form of a particular characteristic.[23]

Our task herein is to apply the provisions of respondent's regulations as we find them and not as we think they might or ought to have been written.[24] See and compare David F. Bolger, 59 T.C. 760, 771 (1973). On this basis, petitioners must prevail.

Decisions will be entered under Rule 155.

Reviewed by the Court.

FAY and HALL, JJ., did not participate in the consideration and disposition of this case.

---

22. Indeed, considering the importance of predictability in applying respondent's regulations, we would not be inclined to give such lesser characteristics controlling weight unless their materiality was unmistakable, a situation which does not obtain in this case.

23. Even if we had found that the interests of the limited partners in Somis and Mai-Kai possessed only such modified form of free transferability, petitioners would still prevail, since the balance would be two characteristics favoring partnership status and something less than two characteristics favoring corporate status.

24. As to respondent's future possibilities, see Morrissey v. Commissioner, n. 8 supra.

NOTE

The Internal Revenue Service has agreed to follow the Tax Court's decision in *Larson* in classifying business organizations.[1] In addition, in Revenue Ruling 79–106, the Service announced that it will not consider the factors enumerated as "other characteristics" in the Larson decision in classifying limited partnerships.[2]

PROBLEM

Promoter, an individual, is the sole general partner in a limited partnership. There are 100 limited partners, each of whom has paid $100,000 for a limited partnership interest. The limited partners may transfer their interests without restriction. Promoter has a .05% interest in partnership capital, profits and losses and her net worth (excluding the partnership interest) is $10,000. Promoter will manage the partnership assets (a shopping center) and she is contractually bound to continue managing and to maintain her general partnership interest for fifteen years, but she may be removed as general partner for good cause by a majority vote of the limited partners. How will the business organization, formed under the Uniform Limited Partnership Act, be classified for federal income tax purposes?

b. PUBLICLY TRADED PARTNERSHIPS

Code: § 7704.

The Tax Reform Act of 1986 had a dramatic impact on the choice of entity selected for operating a business enterprise. The double tax on corporate profits was given new vigor and individual tax rates were reduced below corporate rates. These developments generated an increased interest in entities eligible for pass-through taxation. One alternative is an S corporation, which is subject to a partnership-like tax regime in which the corporation's income and loss is taxed currently to its shareholders.[1] The availability of S corporation status is limited, however, because an S corporation may only have one class of stock and no more than 35 shareholders.[2]

Because of the limitations imposed on S corporations, the master limited partnership ("MLP") briefly emerged as a refuge from the costly double tax regime.[3] An MLP may register its limited partnership interests, known as "units," with the Securities and Exchange

---

1. 1979–1 C.B. 1.

2. 1979–1 C.B. 448. Perhaps as a scare tactic or in an effort to quell tax shelter investments, the Internal Revenue Service has imposed very stringent requirements on the issuance of advance rulings as to the classification of a limited partnership as a partnership for tax purposes. See Rev.Proc. 89–12, 1989–1 C.B. 798. As a result, few limited partnerships request advance rulings, and virtually all are now successful in avoiding classification as an association.

1. See generally Chapters 1B4 and 15.

2. I.R.C. § 1361(b)(1)(A), (D).

3. See generally, Limberg, "Master Limited Partnerships Offer Significant Benefits," 65 J.Tax'n 84 (1986).

Commission, and these units are freely tradable on a securities exchange or in the over-the-counter market. A profitable MLP thus avoided the corporate income tax and passed through its income to noncorporate limited partners at the lower individual rates.[4] Consequently, even after the demise of tax shelters, the classification controversy continued—but not for long. Alarmed at the proliferation of master limited partnerships and the potential erosion of the corporate tax base, Congress responded by enacting new Section 7704, which classifies certain "publicly traded partnerships" as corporations for tax purposes. A "publicly traded partnership" is any partnership whose interests are: (1) traded on an established securities market, or (2) readily tradable on a secondary market (or its substantial equivalent).[5] An important exception from reclassification is provided for partnerships if 90 percent or more of their gross income consists of certain passive-type income items (e.g., interest, dividends, real property rents, gains from the sale of real property and income and gains from certain natural resources activities).[6] Transitional relief, in the form of a 10–year delay in reclassification as a corporation, is provided for certain partnerships that were publicly traded (or had an S.E.C. registration pending) on December 17, 1987.[7]

3. CORPORATIONS vs. TRUSTS

Regulations: § 301.7701–4.

Trusts, like corporations, may be tax paying entities, but the income taxation of trusts differs from the taxation of corporations in several important respects. First, a corporation is taxed on its profits as they are earned under the relatively flat rates in Section 11. If it later distributes the remaining after-tax earnings as dividends, the shareholders are subject to a second tax. But there is no double tax on trust income. Under the complex rules of Subchapter J, trust income currently distributed to beneficiaries is generally not taxed to the trust. Rather, the income is taxed to the recipient beneficiaries to the extent of the trust's "distributable net income." If, however, trust income is accumulated, it is taxed to the trust when earned under the rates in Section 1(e) but normally not taxed again when distributed to the beneficiaries. Second, corporate shareholders who receive dividends are taxable at ordinary income rates, regardless of the character of the corporation's earnings. By contrast, trust income retains its tax character in the hands of the beneficiaries.

---

4. In addition, it was believed that income from an MLP might qualify as passive income which could be sheltered by a limited partner's losses from passive activities. See I.R.C. § 469. Congress responded to this opportunity for circumvention of the passive loss rules by enacting Section 469(k), which treats the net income from publicly traded partnerships (not otherwise reclassified as corporations under Section 7704) as "portfolio" rather than "passive" income.

5. I.R.C. § 7704(b). For the Service's guidance on the definition of a publicly traded partnership see I.R.S. Notice 88–75, 1988–2 C.B. 386.

6. I.R.C. § 7704(c).

7. Revenue Act of 1987, P.L. 100–203, § 10211(c).

These tax characteristics have made a trust a useful income-splitting vehicle that is not subject to the double tax. But the trust is not a common choice of entity for conducting a business, and it is virtually impossible to qualify a business entity as a trust for tax purposes. The following ruling discusses some of the criteria applied by the Service in distinguishing trusts from corporations.

REVENUE RULING 79-77
1979-1 Cum.Bull. 448.

ISSUE

What is the classification, for federal income tax purposes, of an arrangement formed under the circumstances described below?

FACTS

Individuals *A*, *B*, and *C*, who owned a commercial building and the land upon which it was situated as tenants in common, established a trust with a bank as trustee. Simultaneously, *A*, *B*, and *C* transferred the land and building to the trust and named themselves as beneficiaries. *A*, *B*, and *C* receive proportionate quarterly distributions of all net income of the trust.

The trust agreement provides that the purpose of the trust is to empower the trustee to act on behalf of the beneficiaries as signatory of leasing agreements and management agreements, to hold title to the land and building and to the proceeds and income of the property, to distribute all trust income and to protect and conserve the property.

The beneficiaries' interests in the trust are evidenced by certificates that are transferable only on the death of a beneficiary or by unanimous written agreement of the beneficiaries. In addition, after the initial contribution no additional contributions may be made to the trust.

The beneficiaries must approve all agreements entered into by the trustee and they are personally liable for all debts of the trust. The trustee may determine whether to allow minor nonstructural alterations to the building and can institute legal or equitable action to enforce any provisions of a lease. The trust will terminate upon the sale of substantially all its assets or upon unanimous agreement of the beneficiaries.

The beneficiaries directed the trustee to sign a lease of the property to *X*, a corporation, for 20 years with options for three six-year extensions. *X* is to pay all taxes, assessments, fees or other charges imposed on the property by federal, state or local authorities. In addition, *X* is to pay for all insurance, maintenance, repairs, and utilities relating to the property.

The trustee as lessor prepared the building for *X*'s use and can approve additional alterations by *X* only if the alterations protect and conserve the building or are required by law. The rent remains fixed for 20 years, but if the lease is renewed the rent will be recomputed based on the fair market value of the property. *X* has an option to purchase the property every tenth year during the term of the initial lease for an amount equal to the greater of the property's cost to the owners or its fair market value.

LAW AND ANALYSIS

Section 301.7701–4(a) of the Procedure and Administration Regulations provides that the term "trust" as used in the Internal Revenue Code of 1954 refers to an arrangement created by will or by an inter vivos declaration whereby trustees take title to property for the purpose of protecting or conserving it for the beneficiaries under the ordinary rules applied in chancery or probate courts. Generally speaking, an arrangement will be treated as a trust under the Code if it can be shown that the purpose of the arrangement is to vest in trustees responsibility for the protection and conservation of property for beneficiaries who cannot share in the discharge of this responsibility and, therefore, are not associates in a joint enterprise for the conduct of business for profit.

Section 301.7701–4(b) of the regulations states that there are other arrangements that are known as trusts because the legal title to property is conveyed to trustees for the benefit of beneficiaries, but which are not classified as trusts for purposes of the Code because they are not simply arrangements to protect or conserve the property for the beneficiaries. These trusts, which are often known as business or commercial trusts, generally are created by the beneficiaries simply as a device to carry on a profit-making business that normally would have been carried on through business organizations that are classified as corporations or partnerships under the Code.

In Wyman Building Trust v. Commissioner, 45 B.T.A. 155 (1941), acq., 1941–2 C.B. 14, the United States Board of Tax Appeals held that a trust created by the heirs of a decedent, who owned a single piece of property under lease, was not a corporation. The Board in *Wyman* found that the trust's purpose was to provide a convenient authority for executing and extending the lease on behalf of the more cumbersome group of beneficial owners, and for receiving and distributing the income of the property. In *Wyman,* the trustees were restricted to dealing with a single piece of property and the lessee of the property was required to pay all expenses, including taxes and repairs. The Board found these factors persuasive in determining that the trust was not carrying on a business and dividing the gains therefrom, but was performing the functions of a trust by protecting and conserving property.

Rev.Rul. 78–371, 1978–2 C.B. 344, concerns a trust that was established by the heirs to a number of contiguous parcels of real estate. Under the trust agreement the trustees have the power to purchase and sell contiguous or adjacent real estate, and to accept and retain contributions of contiguous or adjacent real estate from the beneficiaries or members of their families. The trustees have the power to raze or erect any building or other structure and make any improvements they deem proper on the land originally contributed to the trust or on any adjacent or contiguous land subsequently acquired by the trust. The trustees are also empowered to borrow money and to mortgage and lease the property. Since these powers, when considered in the aggregate, indicate that the trustees are empowered to do more than merely protect and conserve the trust property, Rev.Rul. 78–371 holds that the trust is an association taxable as a corporation.

This case is distinguishable from Rev.Rul. 78–371 in that the trustee is restricted to dealing with a single piece of property subject to a net lease. Further, the trustee has none of the powers described in Rev.Rul. 78–371. Thus, the arrangement is similar to the trust held not to be a corporation in the *Wyman* case.

HOLDING

The arrangement is classified as a trust for federal income tax purposes. Further, *A, B,* and *C* are the owners of the trust and are taxable on the income therefrom under subpart E of subchapter J, chapter 1 of the Code (sections 671–678).

PROBLEM

Elmer owns a dairy farm which generates $100,000 of taxable income per year. Elmer transfers the farm to a trust for 99 years. B, C and D and their heirs, assignees or transferees are the beneficiaries, and Elmer is the trustee. The trust instrument provides that the trustee serves at the discretion of the beneficiaries and directs the trustee to run the farm in the most profitable manner, to sell it and engage in other operations if it becomes unprofitable and to pay out all profits to the beneficiaries.

F, G and H purchase the beneficial interests in the trust. Each year, the farm earns $100,000, and Elmer distributes one-third of the after-tax profits each to F, G and H.

(a) What tax consequences to the parties if the trust is treated as such for tax purposes?

(b) What result if the trust is taxed as an association?

(c) What is the appropriate classification of this entity?

D. RECOGNITION OF THE CORPORATE ENTITY *

The premise underlying Subchapter C is that a corporation is an entity separate and apart from its shareholders. In addition to questions of classification, issues have arisen over the years as to whether an entity organized as a corporation under state law should be

---

* See generally Miller, "The Nominee Conundrum: The Live Dummy is Dead, But the Dead Dummy Should Live," 34 Tax L.Rev. 213 (1979).

respected as such for tax purposes. These cases often involve corporations that are formed to avoid state usury laws or to act as nontaxable agents of a related partnership. The case below is the Supreme Court's latest pronouncement on this issue.

COMMISSIONER v. BOLLINGER

Supreme Court of the United States, 1988.
485 U.S. 340, 108 S.Ct. 1173.

Justice SCALIA delivered the opinion of the Court.

Petitioner the Commissioner of Internal Revenue challenges a decision by the United States Court of Appeals for the Sixth Circuit holding that a corporation which held record title to real property as agent for the corporation's shareholders was not the owner of the property for purposes of federal income taxation. 807 F.2d 65 (1986). We granted certiorari, 482 U.S. 913, 107 S.Ct. 3183, 96 L.Ed.2d 672 (1987), to resolve a conflict in the courts of appeals over the tax treatment of corporations purporting to be agents for their shareholders. * * *

I

Respondent Jesse C. Bollinger, Jr., developed, either individually or in partnership with some or all of the other respondents, eight apartment complexes in Lexington, Kentucky. (For convenience we will refer to all the ventures as "partnerships.") Bollinger initiated development of the first apartment complex, Creekside North Apartments, in 1968. The Massachusetts Mutual Life Insurance Company agreed to provide permanent financing by lending $1,075,000 to "the corporate nominee of Jesse C. Bollinger, Jr." at an annual interest rate of eight percent, secured by a mortgage on the property and a personal guaranty from Bollinger. The loan commitment was structured in this fashion because Kentucky's usury law at the time limited the annual interest rate for noncorporate borrowers to seven percent. Ky.Rev. Stat. §§ 360.010, 360.025 (1972). Lenders willing to provide money only at higher rates required the nominal debtor and record title holder of mortgaged property to be a corporate nominee of the true owner and borrower. On October 14, 1968, Bollinger incorporated Creekside, Inc., under the laws of Kentucky; he was the only stockholder. The next day, Bollinger and Creekside, Inc., entered into a written agreement which provided that the corporation would hold title to the apartment complex as Bollinger's agent for the sole purpose of securing financing, and would convey, assign, or encumber the property and disburse the proceeds thereof only as directed by Bollinger; that Creekside, Inc., had no obligation to maintain the property or assume any liability by reason of the execution of promissory notes or otherwise; and that Bollinger would indemnify and hold the corporation harmless from any liability it might sustain as his agent and nominee.

Having secured the commitment for permanent financing, Bollinger, acting through Creekside, Inc., borrowed the construction funds for the apartment complex from Citizens Fidelity Bank and Trust Company. Creekside, Inc., executed all necessary loan documents including the promissory note and mortgage, and transferred all loan proceeds to Bollinger's individual construction account. Bollinger acted as general contractor for the construction, hired the necessary employees, and paid the expenses out of the construction account. When construction was completed, Bollinger obtained, again through Creekside, Inc., permanent financing from Massachusetts Mutual Life in accordance with the earlier loan commitment. These loan proceeds were used to pay off the Citizens Fidelity construction loan. Bollinger hired a resident manager to rent the apartments, execute leases with tenants, collect and deposit the rents, and maintain operating records. The manager deposited all rental receipts into, and paid all operating expenses from, an operating account, which was first opened in the name of Creekside, Inc., but was later changed to "Creekside Apartments, a partnership." The operation of Creekside North Apartments generated losses for the taxable years 1969, 1971, 1972, 1973, and 1974, and ordinary income for the years 1970, 1975, 1976, and 1977. Throughout, the income and losses were reported by Bollinger on his individual income tax returns.

Following a substantially identical pattern, seven other apartment complexes were developed by respondents through seven separate partnerships. For each venture, a partnership executed a nominee agreement with Creekside, Inc., to obtain financing. (For one of the ventures, a different Kentucky corporation, Cloisters, Inc., in which Bollinger had a 50 percent interest, acted as the borrower and titleholder. For convenience, we will refer to both Creekside and Cloisters as "the corporation.") The corporation transferred the construction loan proceeds to the partnership's construction account, and the partnership hired a construction supervisor who oversaw construction. Upon completion of construction, each partnership actively managed its apartment complex, depositing all rental receipts into, and paying all expenses from, a separate partnership account for each apartment complex. The corporation had no assets, liabilities, employees, or bank accounts. In every case, the lenders regarded the partnership as the owner of the apartments and were aware that the corporation was acting as agent of the partnership in holding record title. The partnerships reported the income and losses generated by the apartment complexes on their partnership tax returns, and respondents reported their distributive share of the partnership income and losses on their individual tax returns.

The Commissioner of Internal Revenue disallowed the losses reported by respondents, on the ground that the standards set out in National Carbide Corp. v. Commissioner, 336 U.S. 422, 69 S.Ct. 726, 93 L.Ed. 779 (1949), were not met. The Commissioner contended that *National Carbide* required a corporation to have an arm's-length relationship with its shareholders before it could be recognized as their agent. Although not all respondents were shareholders of the corporation, the Commissioner took the position that the funds the partnerships disbursed to pay expenses should be deemed contributions to the corporation's capital, thereby making all respondents constructive stockholders. Since, in the Commissioner's view, the corporation rather than its shareholders owned the real estate, any losses sustained by the ventures were attributable to the corporation and not respondents. Respondents sought a redetermination in the United States Tax Court. The Tax Court held that the corporations were the agents of the partnerships and should be disregarded for tax purposes. Bollinger v. Commissioner, 48 TCM 1443 (1984), ¶ 84, 560 P–H Memo TC.   On appeal, the United States Court of Appeals for the Sixth Circuit affirmed. 807 F.2d 65 (1986). We granted the Commissioner's petition for certiorari.

II

For federal income tax purposes, gain or loss from the sale or use of property is attributable to the owner of the property. See Helvering v. Horst, 311 U.S. 112, 116–117, 61 S.Ct. 144, 147, 85 L.Ed. 75 (1940); Blair v. Commissioner, 300 U.S. 5, 12, 57 S.Ct. 330, 333, 81 L.Ed. 465 (1937); see also Commissioner v. Sunnen, 333 U.S. 591, 604, 68 S.Ct. 715, 722, 92 L.Ed. 898 (1948). The problem we face here is that two different taxpayers can plausibly be regarded as the owner. Neither the Internal Revenue Code nor the regulations promulgated by the Secretary of the Treasury provide significant guidance as to which should be selected.   It is common ground between the parties, however, that if a corporation holds title to property as agent for a partnership, then for tax purposes the partnership and not the corporation is the owner. Given agreement on that premise, one would suppose that there would be agreement upon the conclusion as well. For each of respondents' apartment complexes, an agency agreement expressly provided that the corporation would "hold such property as nominee and agent for" the partnership, App. to Pet. for Cert. 21a, n. 4, and that the partnership would have sole control of and responsibility for the apartment complex. The partnership in each instance was identified as the principal and owner of the property during financing, construction, and operation. The lenders, contractors, managers, employees, and tenants—all who had contact with the development—knew that the corporation was merely the agent of the partnership, if they knew of the existence of the corporation at all.   In each instance the relationship between the corporation and the partnership was, in both form and substance, an agency with the partnership as principal.

The Commissioner contends, however, that the normal indicia of agency cannot suffice for tax purposes when, as here, the alleged principals are the controlling shareholders of the alleged agent corporation. That, it asserts, would undermine the principle of Moline Properties v. Commissioner, 319 U.S. 436, 63 S.Ct. 1132, 87 L.Ed. 1499 (1943), which held that a corporation is a separate taxable entity even if it has only one shareholder who exercises total control over its affairs. Obviously, *Moline's* separate-entity principle would be significantly compromised if shareholders of closely held corporations could, by clothing the corporation with some attributes of agency with respect to particular assets, leave themselves free at the end of the tax year to make a claim—perhaps even a good-faith claim—of either agent or owner status, depending upon which choice turns out to minimize their tax liability. The Commissioner does not have the resources to audit and litigate the many cases in which agency status could be thought debatable. Hence, the Commissioner argues, in this shareholder context he can reasonably demand that the taxpayer meet a prophylactically clear test of agency.

We agree with that principle, but the question remains whether the test the Commissioner proposes is appropriate. The parties have debated at length the significance of our opinion in National Carbide Corp. v. Commissioner, supra. In that case, three corporations that were wholly owned subsidiaries of another corporation agreed to operate their production plants as "agents" for the parent, transferring to it all profits except for a nominal sum. The subsidiaries reported as gross income only this sum, but the Commissioner concluded that they should be taxed on the entirety of the profits because they were not really agents. We agreed, reasoning first, that the mere fact of the parent's control over the subsidiaries did not establish the existence of an agency, since such control is typical of all shareholder-corporation relationships, id., 336 U.S. at 429–434, 69 S.Ct., at 730–732; and second, that the agreements to pay the parent all profits above a nominal amount were not determinative since income must be taxed to those who actually earn it without regard to anticipatory assignment, id., at 435–436, 69 S.Ct., at 733–734. We acknowledged, however, that there was such a thing as "a true corporate agent . . . of [an] owner-principal," id., at 437, 69 S.Ct., at 734, and proceeded to set forth four indicia and two requirements of such status, the sum of which has become known in the lore of federal income tax law as the "six *National Carbide* factors":

> "[1] Whether the corporation operates in the name and for the account of the principal, [2] binds the principal by its actions, [3] transmits money received to the principal, and [4] whether receipt of income is attributable to the services of employees of the principal and to assets belonging to the principal are some of the relevant considerations in determining whether a true agency exists. [5] If the corporation is a true agent, its relations with its principal must not be dependent upon the fact that it is owned by the principal, if such is the case. [6] Its business purpose must be the carrying on of the normal duties of an agent." Id., at 437, 69 S.Ct., at 734 (footnotes omitted).

We readily discerned that these factors led to a conclusion of nonagency in *National Carbide* itself. There each subsidiary had represented to its customers that it (not the parent) was the company manufacturing and selling its products; each had sought to shield the parent from service of legal process; and the operations had used thousands of the subsidiaries' employees and nearly $20 million worth of property and equipment listed as assets on the subsidiaries' books. Id., at 425, 434, 438, and n. 21, 69 S.Ct., at 728, 732–733, 734, and n. 21.

The Commissioner contends that the last two *National Carbide* factors are not satisfied in the present case. To take the last first: The Commissioner argues that here the corporation's business purpose with respect to the property at issue was not "the carrying on of the normal duties of an agent," since it was acting not as the agent but rather as the owner of the property for purposes of Kentucky's usury laws. We do not agree. It assuredly was not acting as the owner in fact, since respondents represented themselves as the principals to all parties concerned with the loans. Indeed, it was the lenders themselves who required the use of a corporate nominee. Nor does it make any sense to adopt a contrary-to-fact legal presumption that the corporation was the principal, imposing a federal tax sanction for the apparent evasion of Kentucky's usury law. To begin with, the Commissioner has not established that these transactions were an evasion. Respondents assert without contradiction that use of agency arrangements in order to permit higher interest was common practice, and it is by no means clear that the practice violated the spirit of the Kentucky law, much less its letter. It might well be thought that the borrower does not generally require usury protection in a transaction sophisticated enough to employ a corporate agent—assuredly not the normal *modus operandi* of the loan shark. That the statute positively envisioned corporate nominees is suggested by a provision which forbids charging the higher corporate interest rates "to a corporation, the principal asset of which shall be the ownership of a one (1) or two (2) family dwelling." Ky.Rev.Stat. § 360.025(2) (1987)—which would seem to prevent use of the nominee device for ordinary home-mortgage loans. In any event, even if the transaction did run afoul of the usury law, Kentucky, like most States, regards only the lender as the usurer, and the borrower as the victim. See Ky.Rev.Stat. § 360.020 (1987) (lender liable to borrower for civil penalty), § 360.990 (lender guilty of misdemeanor). Since the Kentucky statute imposed no penalties upon the borrower for allowing himself to be victimized, nor treated him as *in pari delictu*, but to the contrary enabled him to pay back the principal without any interest, and to sue for double the amount of interest already paid (plus attorney's fees), see Ky.Rev.Stat. § 360.020 (1972), the United States would hardly be vindicating Kentucky law by depriving the usury victim of tax advantages he would otherwise enjoy. In sum, we see no basis in either fact or policy for holding that the corporation was the principal because of the nature of its participation in the loans.

Of more general importance is the Commissioner's contention that the arrangements here violate the fifth *National Carbide* factor—that the corporate agent's "relations with its principal must not be dependent upon the fact that it is owned by the principal." The Commissioner asserts that this cannot be satisfied unless the corporate agent and its shareholder principal have an "arm's-length relationship" that includes the payment of a fee for agency services. The meaning of *National Carbide*'s fifth factor is, at the risk of understatement, not entirely clear. Ultimately, the relations between a corporate agent and its owner-principal are *always* dependent upon the fact of ownership, in that the owner can cause the relations to be altered or terminated at any time. Plainly that is not what was meant, since on that interpretation all subsidiary-parent agencies would be invalid for tax purposes, a position which the *National Carbide* opinion specifically disavowed. We think the fifth *National Carbide* factor—so much more abstract than the others—was no more and no less than a generalized statement of the concern, expressed earlier in our own discussion, that the separate-entity doctrine of *Moline* not be subverted.

In any case, we decline to parse the text of *National Carbide* as though that were itself the governing statute. As noted earlier, it is uncontested that the law attributes tax consequences of property held by a genuine agent to the principal; and we agree that it is reasonable for the Commissioner to demand unequivocal evidence of genuineness in the corporation-shareholder context, in order to prevent evasion of *Moline*. We see no basis, however, for holding that unequivocal evidence can only consist of the rigid requirements (arm's-length dealing plus agency fee) that the Commissioner suggests. Neither of those is demanded by the law of agency, which permits agents to be unpaid family members, friends, or associates. See Restatement (Second) of Agency §§ 16, 21, 22 (1958). It seems to us that the genuineness of the agency relationship is adequately assured, and tax-avoiding manipulation adequately avoided, when the fact that the corporation is acting as agent for its shareholders with respect to a particular asset is set forth in a written agreement at the time the asset is acquired, the corporation functions as agent and not principal with respect to the asset for all purposes, and the corporation is held out as the agent and not principal in all dealings with third parties relating to the asset. Since these requirements were met here, the judgment of the Court of Appeals is

Affirmed.

Justice KENNEDY took no part in the consideration or decision of this case.

PART TWO: TAXATION OF C CORPORATIONS

CHAPTER 2. FORMATION OF A CORPORATION

A. INTRODUCTION TO SECTION 351

Code: §§ 351(a), (c), (d)(1)–(2); 358(a), (b)(1); 362(a); 368(c); 1032(a); 1223(1), (2); 1245(b)(3).

Regulations: §§ 1.351–1(a), (b); 1.358–1(a), –2(b)(2); 1.362–1(a); 1.1032–1(a), (d).

In order to commence business operations, a corporation needs assets. It normally acquires these assets—known as the initial "capital" of a corporation—by issuing shares of stock in exchange for cash or other property. If the shares are issued solely for cash, the tax consequences are routine: the shareholder simply has made a cash purchase and takes a cost basis in the shares acquired.[1] If, however, the shares are issued for property other than cash, the exchange would be a taxable event to the shareholder without a special provision of the Code. The shareholder would recognize gain or loss equal to the difference between the fair market value of the stock received and the adjusted basis of the property transferred to the corporation.[2] Without a nonrecognition provision, the exchange also might be taxable to the corporation. Its gain—more theoretical than real—would be the excess of the fair market value of the cash and property received over the corporation's zero basis in the newly issued shares.

A simple example illustrates the possibilities. Assume that A decides to form Venture, Inc. by transferring appreciated property with a value of $100 and a basis of $10 in exchange for Venture stock with a value of $100. A would realize $90 of gain and, in theory, Venture might be said to realize $100 of gain by issuing its stock. If both parties were taxed on this simple transaction, however, the formation of corporations would be severely impeded. Indeed, a newly formed corporation receiving significant assets frequently would find itself subject to tax at the maximum corporate rate on the money or property contributed by its founding investors.

To remove these tax impediments, Congress long ago decided that routine incorporations should be tax-free to the shareholders and the corporation. At the shareholder level, Section 351(a) provides that no gain or loss shall be recognized if property is transferred to a corporation by one or more persons solely in exchange for its stock if the transferor or transferors of property are in "control" of the corporation

---

1. I.R.C. § 1012.   2. I.R.C. § 1001(a).

"immediately after the exchange."[3]   At the corporate level, Section 1032(a) provides that a corporation shall not recognize gain or loss on the receipt of money or other property in exchange for its stock (including treasury stock).[4]   These general rules are accompanied by special basis provisions and are subject to several exceptions, all of which will be discussed as this chapter unfolds.

The policy of Section 351 is one familiar to nonrecognition provisions. The transfer of appreciated or depreciated property to a corporation controlled by the transferor is viewed as a mere change in the form of a shareholder's investment. Consider, for example, the sole proprietor who decides to incorporate an ongoing business. The proprietor clearly *realizes* gain in a theoretical sense when the assets of the business are exchanged for all of the new corporation's stock. But he has neither "cashed in" nor appreciably changed the nature of his investment. He owns and operates the same business with the same assets, only now in corporate solution. Incorporation does not seem to be the appropriate occasion to impose a tax if the transferred assets have appreciated or to allow a deductible loss if the assets have decreased in value.

This policy is more difficult to defend in the case of a minority shareholder. Consider a taxpayer who exchanges appreciated land with a basis of $40 and a fair market value of $100 for a $100 minority stock interest in a newly formed corporation with a total net worth of $1,000. The taxpayer would recognize $60 of gain if he acquired the stock from another shareholder in exchange for the land, and presumably he should recognize the same gain if he acquires the minority interest directly from the corporation, whether it is newly formed or an ongoing business. Similarly, if two or more unrelated taxpayers join together and transfer various assets to a new corporation in exchange for its stock, they arguably have changed the form of their investment; each now owns a part of several assets in corporate solution rather than all of the assets previously owned directly. Despite these arguments, Congress chose not to make such fine distinctions, perhaps because its primary goal in enacting Section 351 was to facilitate a wide variety of corporate formations. Section 351 thus clearly embraces transfers of property by a group of previously unrelated persons— provided, of course, that the specific statutory requirements set forth below have been met.[5]

The three major requirements to qualify for nonrecognition of gain or loss under Section 351 are as follows:

3. Section 351 applies not only to transfers to newly formed corporations but also to preexisting corporations provided that the transferors of property have "control" immediately after the exchange.

4. See Reg. § 1.1032–1(a).

5. But see I.R.C. § 351(e)(1), which disallows nonrecognition in the case of a "transfer of property to an investment company." This anti-abuse provision is designed to preclude a group of taxpayers from achieving a tax-free diversification of their investment portfolio through an exchange with a newly formed investment company. See Reg. § 1.351–1(c) for the details.

(1) One or more persons (including individuals, corporations, partnerships and other entities) must transfer "property" to the corporation;

(2) The transfer must be solely in exchange for stock of the corporation; and

(3) The transferor or transferors, as a group, must be in "control" of the corporation "immediately after the exchange."

"Control" for this purpose is defined by Section 368(c) as "the ownership of stock possessing at least 80 percent of the total combined voting power of all classes of stock entitled to vote and at least 80 percent of the total number of shares of all other classes of stock of the corporation." These requirements are not as simple as they may first appear. Section 351 contains many terms of art, each of which has raised issues over the years. Before studying the requirements in detail, however, it is necessary to complete the basic statutory scheme by turning to the corollary rules on basis and holding period.

If Section 351 applies to a transfer, any gain or loss realized by the shareholder is not currently recognized. The policy of nonrecognition requires the preservation of these tax attributes to prevent total forgiveness of the unrecognized gain or forfeiture of any unrecognized loss. This goal is achieved by Section 358(a)(1), which provides that the basis of the stock ("nonrecognition property") received in a Section 351 exchange shall be the same as the basis of the property transferred by the shareholder to the corporation. Returning to the introductory example, if A transfers property to Venture, Inc. with a basis of $10 and a fair market value of $100 for stock with a value of $100 in a transaction governed by Section 351, A's basis in the stock will be $10. Assuming no decrease in the value of the stock, the $90 of gain that went unrecognized on the exchange will be recognized if and when A sells the stock.[6]

In keeping with this policy, Section 1223(1) provides that where a transferor receives property with an "exchanged basis," [7] such as stock in a Section 351 exchange, the holding period of that property is determined by including the period during which he held the trans-

---

6. If the shareholder dies without selling the stock, however, his basis will be stepped up (or down) to its fair market value on the date of his death (or six months thereafter, if the alternate valuation date is elected for federal estate tax purposes). I.R.C. § 1014(a). This would be the case, of course, if the shareholder had simply continued to hold the transferred assets out of corporate solution and thus is not inconsistent with the policy of Section 358.

7. See I.R.C. § 7701(a)(44), which defines "exchanged basis property" as property having a basis determined in whole or

in part by reference to other property held at any time by the person for whom the basis is to be determined. We formerly called this "substituted basis" but, prodded by a persistent student, we now adopt the terminology added to the Code by the Tax Reform Act of 1984. "Exchanged basis property" is now a subspecies of "substituted basis property," which also includes "transferred" (formerly "carryover") basis property. See I.R.C. § 7701(a)(42)–(44). For more on terminology reform, see K. Rosenberg, "Toward Uniformity in Basis Terminology," 32 Tax Notes 1099 (Sept. 15, 1986.)

ferred property if the transferred property is a capital asset or a Section 1231 asset; if it is not, the transferor's holding period begins on the date of the exchange.

On the corporate side, Section 1032 provides that a corporation does not recognize gain or loss when it issues stock in exchange for money or property. Moreover, a corporation that receives property in exchange for its stock in a Section 351 exchange steps into the shoes of the transferor. Section 362(a) prescribes a transferred basis—i.e., the corporation's basis in any property received in a Section 351 exchange is the same as the transferor's basis, thus preserving the gain or loss inherent in the asset for later recognition by the corporation. And Section 1223(2) provides that if property has a transferred (i.e., carry-over) basis to the corporation, the transferor's holding period likewise will carry over.

Each of these basis rules is subject to modifications to be discussed later in this chapter.[8] In addition, both Sections 358 and 362 apply to a variety of corporate transactions other than Section 351. For the moment, however, ignore these distractions and focus on the policy of continuity of tax characteristics that is an essential corollary to the nonrecognition principle of Section 351.

PROBLEM

A, B, C, D and E, all individuals, form X Corporation to engage in a manufacturing business. X issues 100 shares of common stock. A transfers $25,000 cash for 25 shares; B transfers inventory with a value of $10,000 and a basis of $5,000 for 10 shares; C transfers unimproved land with a value of $20,000 and a basis of $25,000 for 20 shares; D transfers equipment with a basis of $5,000 and a value of $25,000 (prior depreciation taken was $20,000) for 25 shares; and E transfers a $20,000 (face amount and value) installment note for 20 shares. E received the note in exchange for land with a $2,000 basis that he sold last year. The note is payable over a five year period, beginning in two years, at $4,000 per year plus market rate interest.

    (a) What are the tax consequences (gain or loss recognized, basis and holding period in the stock received) to each of the transferors? As to E, see I.R.C. § 453B(a); Reg. 1.453–9(c)(2).

    (b) What are the tax consequences (gain recognized, basis and holding period in each of the assets received) to X Corporation?

    (c) There was $5,000 of gain inherent in the inventory transferred by B. If X Corporation later sells the inventory for $10,000, and B sells his stock for $10,000, how many times will that $5,000 of gain be taxed? Is there any justification for this result?

8. See pp. 71–72, infra.

B. REQUIREMENTS FOR NONRECOGNITION OF GAIN OR LOSS UNDER SECTION 351

The introductory problem illustrates that a tax-free exchange is easily accomplished if a group of individuals forms a corporation by transferring property solely in exchange for common stock. But variations abound in the world of corporate formations, and the desires of the parties for a more complex transaction may conflict with the policy of nonrecognition. This section explores the requirements of Section 351 in more depth and shows that it often is possible, through careful planning, to reconcile these competing objectives.

1. "CONTROL" IMMEDIATELY AFTER THE EXCHANGE

Code: §§ 351(a); 368(c).

Regulations: § 1.351–1(a)(1).

Section 351 applies only if the transferors of property, as a group, "control" the corporation immediately after the exchange. For this purpose, "control" is defined by Section 368(c) as: (1) the ownership of at least 80 percent of the total combined voting power of all classes of stock entitled to vote, and (2) at least 80 percent of the total number of shares of all other classes of stock. The dual standard apparently was designed to ensure that the requisite control would not exist unless the transferors owned more than 80 percent of both the voting power and the total value of the corporation. Both prongs of the "control" test raise potentially thorny definitional questions—e.g., what is "stock entitled to vote?"; how is "voting power" determined? But these questions seldom arise in practice either because the routine corporate formation involves only one class of voting common stock or the transferors of property collectively emerge from the exchange owning 100 percent of all classes of stock.

The requisite control must be obtained by one or more transferors of "property" who act in concert under a single integrated plan. There is no limit on the number of transferors, and some may receive voting stock while others receive nonvoting stock. If the corporation issues more than one class of nonvoting stock, the Service requires that the transferor group must own at least 80 percent of *each* class.[1]

To be part of an integrated plan, the transfers need not be simultaneous. It is sufficient if the rights of the parties are "previously defined" and the agreement proceeds with an "expedition consistent with orderly procedure."[2] More important than timing is whether the transfers are mutually interdependent steps in the formation and carrying on of the business. Thus, it is possible for transfers separated by less than an hour to be considered separately for purposes of the

---

1. Rev.Rul. 59–259, 1959–2 C.B. 115.   2. Reg. § 1.351–1(a)(1).

control requirement or for transfers several years apart to be treated as part of an integrated plan.³

Finally, the transferors of property must be in control "immediately after the exchange." Momentary control will not suffice if the holdings of the transferor group fall below the required 80 percent as a result of dispositions of stock pursuant to a binding agreement or a prearranged plan.⁴ But a voluntary disposition of stock, particularly in a donative setting, should not break control even if the original transferor of property parts with the shares moments after the incorporation exchange.⁵

The courts gradually have taken a practical approach to this much-litigated issue, focusing less on timing and more on the previously defined rights and obligations of the parties. The case below is a leading example of this trend.

INTERMOUNTAIN LUMBER CO. v. COMMISSIONER *

United States Tax Court, 1976.
65 T.C. 1025.

WILES, Judge: * * *

[From 1948 until March, 1964, Mr. Dee Shook owned a sawmill in Montana, where Mr. Milo Wilson had logs processed into rough lumber for a fee. The rough lumber was processed into finished lumber at a separate plant jointly owned by Shook and Wilson. In March, 1964, the sawmill was damaged by fire. Shook and Wilson wanted to replace it with a larger facility, but Shook was financially unable to do so. Shook convinced Wilson to personally coguarantee a $200,000 loan to provide financing and, in return, Wilson insisted on becoming an equal shareholder with Shook in the rebuilt sawmill enterprise.

On May 28, 1964, Shook, Wilson and two other individuals incorporated S & W Sawmill, Inc. ("S & W"). Minutes of the first meeting of shareholders on July 7, 1964, recited in part that "Mr. Shook informed the meeting that a separate agreement was being prepared between he and Mr. Wilson providing for the sale of one-half of his stock to Mr. Wilson." Several days later, Shook transferred his sawmill site to S & W in exchange for 364 shares of S & W common stock. The company also issued one share to each of its four incorporators. No other stock was issued. On the same day, Shook and Wilson entered into "An Agreement for Sale and Purchase of Stock" under which Wilson was to purchase 182 shares of Shook's stock for $500 per share, plus annual interest, to be paid in installments. As each principal payment on the purchase price was made, a proportionate number of shares of stock

---

3. Compare Henricksen v. Braicks, 137 F.2d 632 (9th Cir.1943), with Commissioner v. Ashland Oil & Refining Co., 99 F.2d 588 (6th Cir.1938).

4. See American Bantam Car Co. v. Commissioner, 11 T.C. 397 (1948), affirmed per curiam 177 F.2d 513 (3d Cir.1949), cert. denied 339 U.S. 920, 70 S.Ct. 622 (1950).

5. See D'Angelo Associates, Inc. v. Commissioner, 70 T.C. 121 (1978); Stanton v. United States, 512 F.2d 13 (3d Cir.1975).

* Footnotes omitted.

were to be transferred on the corporate records and delivered to Wilson. A certificate for the 182 shares was placed in escrow. Shook also executed an irrevocable proxy granting Wilson voting rights in the 182 shares.

On August 19, 1964, S & W borrowed $200,000 from an outside lender, in part upon the personal guarantees of Shook and Wilson. On July 1, 1967, the taxpayer in this case, Intermountain Lumber Co. (referred to in the opinion as "petitioner"), acquired all the outstanding S & W stock from Shook and Wilson. S & W became a wholly owned subsidiary of Intermountain, and the companies filed consolidated tax returns for the years involved in this controversy.

The specific question before the Tax Court related to the tax basis of S & W's assets for purposes of depreciation claimed on the Intermountain Lumber group's consolidated return. In a role reversal, the Service contended that the transfer of assets to S & W was tax-free under Section 351, requiring S & W to take a transferred basis in the assets under Section 362. In support of a higher cost basis, the taxpayer argued that the incorporation did not qualify under Section 351 because Mr. Shook did not have control immediately after the exchange. Ed.]

OPINION

Section 351 provides, in part, that no gain shall be recognized if property is transferred to a corporation by one or more persons solely in exchange for stock or securities ["or securities" was deleted from the statute in 1989. Ed.] in such corporation and immediately after the exchange such person or persons are in control of the corporation. "Control" is defined for this purpose in section 368(c) as ownership of stock possessing at least 80 percent of the total combined voting power of all classes of stock entitled to vote and at least 80 percent of the total number of shares of all other classes of stock of the corporation.

In this case, respondent is in the unusual posture of arguing that a transfer to a corporation in return for stock was nontaxable under section 351, and Intermountain is in the equally unusual posture of arguing that the transfer was taxable because section 351 was inapplicable. The explanation is simply that Intermountain purchased all stock of the corporation, S & W, from its incorporators, and that Intermountain and S & W have filed consolidated income tax returns for years in issue. Accordingly, if section 351 was applicable to the incorporators when S & W was formed, S & W and Intermountain must depreciate the assets of S & W on their consolidated returns on the incorporators' basis. Sec. 362(a). If section 351 was inapplicable, and the transfer of assets to S & W was accordingly to be treated as a sale, S & W and Intermountain could base depreciation on those returns on the fair market value of those assets at the time of incorporation, which was higher than the incorporators' cost and which would accordingly provide larger depreciation deductions. Secs. 167(g), 1011, and 1012.

Petitioner thus maintains that the transfer to S & W of all of S & W's property at the time of incorporation by the primary incorporator, one Dee Shook, was a taxable sale. It asserts that section 351 was inapplicable because an agreement for sale required Shook, as part of the incorporation transaction, to sell almost half of the S & W shares outstanding to one Milo Wilson over a period of time, thereby depriving Shook of the requisite percentage of stock necessary for "control" of S & W immediately after the exchange.

Respondent, on the other hand, maintains that the agreement between Shook and Wilson did not deprive Shook of ownership of the shares immediately after the exchange, as the stock purchase agreement merely gave Wilson an option to purchase the shares. Shook accordingly was in "control" of the corporation and the exchange was thus nontaxable under section 351.

Respondent has abandoned on brief his contention that Wilson was a transferor of property and therefore a person to also be counted for purposes of control under section 351. Respondent is correct in doing so, since Wilson did not transfer any property to S & W upon its initial formation in July of 1964. Wilson's agreement to transfer cash for corporate stock in March of 1965 cannot be considered part of the same transaction.

Since Wilson was not a transferor of property and therefore cannot be counted for control under section 351, William A. James, 53 T.C. 63, 69 (1969), we must determine if Shook alone owned the requisite percentage of shares for control. This determination depends upon whether, under all facts and circumstances surrounding the agreement for sale of 182 shares between Shook and Wilson, ownership of those shares was in Shook or Wilson.

A determination of "ownership," as that term is used in section 368(c) and for purposes of control under section 351, depends upon the obligations and freedom of action of the transferee with respect to the stock when he acquired it from the corporation. Such traditional ownership attributes as legal title, voting rights, and possession of stock certificates are not conclusive. If the transferee, as part of the transaction by which the shares were acquired, has irrevocably foregone or relinquished at that time the legal right to determine whether to keep the shares, ownership in such shares is lacking for purposes of section 351. By contrast, if there are no restrictions upon freedom of action at the time he acquired the shares, it is immaterial how soon thereafter the transferee elects to dispose of his stock or whether such disposition is in accord with a preconceived plan not amounting to a binding obligation. * * *

After considering the entire record, we have concluded that Shook and Wilson intended to consummate a sale of the S & W stock, that they never doubted that the sale would be completed, that the sale was an integral part of the incorporation transaction, and that they considered themselves to be coowners of S & W upon execution of the stock purchase agreement in 1964. These conclusions are supported by minutes of the first stockholders meeting on July 7, 1964, at which Shook characterized the agreement for sale as a "sale"; minutes of a special meeting on July 15, 1964, at which Shook stated Wilson was to "purchase" half of Shook's stock; the "Agreement for Sale and Purchase of Stock" itself, dated July 15, 1964, which is drawn as an installment sale and which provides for payment of interest on unpaid principal; Wilson's deduction of interest expenses in connection with the agreement for sale, which would be inconsistent with an option; the S & W loan agreement, in which Shook and Wilson held themselves out as the "principal stockholders" of S & W and in which S & W covenanted to equally insure Shook and Wilson for $100,000; the March 1965 stock purchase agreement with S & W, which indicated that Shook and Wilson "*are* to remain *equal*" (emphasis added) shareholders in S & W; the letter of May 1967 from Shook and Wilson to Intermountain, which indicated that Wilson owed Shook the principal balance due on the shares as an unpaid obligation; and all surrounding facts and circumstances leading to corporate formation and execution of the above documents. Inconsistent and self-serving testimony of Shook and Wilson regarding their intent and understanding of the documents in evidence is unpersuasive in view of the record as a whole to alter interpretation of the transaction as a sale of stock by Shook to Wilson.

We accordingly cannot accept respondent's contention that the substance varied from the form of this transaction, which was, of course, labeled a "sale." The parties executed an "option" agreement on the same day that the "agreement for sale" was executed, and we have no doubt that they could and indeed did correctly distinguish between a sale and an option.

The agreement for sale's forfeiture clause, which provided that Wilson forfeited the right to purchase a proportionate number of shares for which timely principal payments were not made, did not convert it into an option agreement. Furthermore, the agreement for sale made no provision for forgiving interest payments on the remaining principal due should principal payments not be made on earlier dates; indeed, it specifically provided that "Interest payment must always be kept current before any delivery of stock is to be made resulting from a payment of principal."

We thus believe that Shook, as part of the same transaction by which the shares were acquired (indeed, the agreement for sale was executed before the sawmill was deeded to S & W), had relinquished when he acquired those shares the legal right to determine whether to keep them. Shook was under an obligation, upon receipt of the shares, to transfer the stock as he received Wilson's principal payments. * * * We note also that the agreement for sale gave Wilson the right to prepay principal and receive all 182 shares at any time in advance. Shook therefore did not own, within the meaning of section 368(c), the requisite percentage of stock immediately after the exchange to control the corporation as required for nontaxable treatment under section 351.

We note also that the basic premise of section 351 is to avoid recognition of gain or loss resulting from transfer of property to a corporation which works a change of form only. See Bittker & Eustice, Federal Income Taxation of Corporations and Shareholders, par. 3.01, p. 3–4 (3d ed. 1971). Accordingly, if the transferor sells his stock as part of the same transaction, the transaction is taxable because there has been more than a mere change in form. * * * In this case, the transferor agreed to sell and did sell 50 percent of the stock to be received, placed the certificates in the possession of an escrow agent, and granted a binding proxy to the purchaser to vote the stock being sold. Far more than a mere change in form was effected.

We accordingly hold for petitioner.

2.   TRANSFERS OF "PROPERTY" AND SERVICES

Regulations: § 1.351–1(a)(1), (2).

If the transferors of "property" must have control immediately after the exchange, the question then becomes: what is "property?" Although the term is not specifically defined for purposes of Section 351, it has been broadly construed to include cash, capital assets, inventory, accounts receivable, patents, and, in certain circumstances, other intangible assets such as nonexclusive licenses and industrial know-how.[1]

Section 351(d)(1) specifically provides, however, that stock issued for services shall not be considered as issued in return for property.[2] This rule makes good sense in the case of a promoter of the enterprise, or even the company lawyer, who contributes no capital but still receives stock in exchange for services rendered to the corporation. Inasmuch as the stock is compensation for those services, the tax consequences are properly determined under Sections 61 and 83.

Apart from realizing ordinary income, a person who receives stock solely in exchange for services may cause the other parties to the incorporation to recognize gain or loss. The pure service provider is not considered a transferor of property and may not be counted as part of the control group for purposes of qualifying the exchange under Section 351. But if a person receives stock in exchange for both property and services, *all* of his stock is counted toward the 80 percent control requirement.[3]

These rules offer some tempting opportunities for the tax planner. Assume, for example, that Promoter and Investor join forces to form a new corporation. In exchange for his services, Promoter receives 25 percent of the corporation's common stock. In exchange for $500,000 of highly appreciated property, Investor receives the other 75 percent. Investor, as the only transferor of property, does not have control and

---

1.   See, e.g., E.I. Du Pont de Nemours & Co. v. United States, 471 F.2d 1211 (Ct.Cl. 1973); Rev.Rul. 64–56, 1964–1 C.B. 133 (industrial know-how); Rev.Rul. 69–357, 1969–1 C.B. 101 (money is "property").

2.   See also Reg. § 1.351–1(a)(1)(i).

3.   Reg. § 1.351–1(a)(1)(ii), –1(a)(2) Example (3).

thus must recognize gain on the transaction unless Promoter somehow can qualify as a transferor of property—a status easily achieved, perhaps, by the mere transfer of $100 in cash.

Life is not so simple in the world of Subchapter C. To prevent such facile maneuvering around the control requirement, the regulations provide that the stock will not be treated as having been issued for property if the primary purpose of the transfer is to qualify the exchanges of the other property transferors for nonrecognition and if the stock issued to the nominal transferor is "of relatively small value" in comparison to the value of the stock already owned or to be received for services by the transferor.[4] In other words, the accommodation transfer gambit fails if the value of the property transferred is *de minimis* relative to the stock received for services. But this regulation has been interpreted generously by the Service in Revenue Procedure 77–37,[5] which provides that property transferred "will not be considered to be of relatively small value * * * if the fair market value of the property transferred is equal to, or in excess of, 10 percent of the fair market value of the stock already owned (or to be received for services) by * * * [the transferor]."

3. SOLELY FOR "STOCK"

The final requirement for nonrecognition is that the transfers of property be made "solely" in exchange for "stock" of the corporation. "Stock" means a normal equity investment in the company, and in this context the term has presented relatively few definitional problems. It does not include stock rights or warrants.[1] Under prior law, Section 351(a) applied to transfers of property solely in exchange for both stock and corporate debt securities, but the term "securities" was deleted in 1989. A "security" was construed by the courts as a relatively long-term debt obligation (e.g., a bond or debenture) which provided the holder with a continuing degree of participation in corporate affairs, albeit as a creditor.[2] After the 1989 amendment, securities received in a Section 351 transaction, along with all forms of nonsecurity debt (e.g., a short-term note), are treated as boot, leaving only stock to qualify as nonrecognition property. The amendment is generally effective for transfers after October 2, 1989.

PROBLEMS

1. Consider whether the following transactions qualify under Section 351:

> (a) A and B are unrelated individuals. A forms Newco, Inc. on January 2 of the current year by transferring property with

4. Reg. § 1.351–1(a)(1)(ii). See also Estate of Kamborian v. Commissioner, 469 F.2d 219 (1st Cir.1972).

5. 1977–2 C.B. 568, § 3.07.

1. Reg. § 1.351–1(a)(1), last sentence.

2. Camp Wolters Enterprises, Inc. v. Commissioner, 22 T.C. 737 (1954), affirmed 230 F.2d 555 (5th Cir.1956), cert. denied 352 U.S. 826, 77 S.Ct. 39 (1956).

a basis of $10,000 and a value of $50,000 for all 50 shares of Newco common stock. On March 2, in an unrelated transaction, B transfers property with a basis of $1,000 and a value of $10,000 for 10 shares of Newco nonvoting preferred stock.

(b) Same as (a), above, except the transfers by A and B were part of a single integrated plan.

(c) Same as (b), above, except A transferred 25 of her 50 shares to her daughter, D, as a gift on March 5 (three days after B's transfer). Is the result any different if A directs Newco to issue only 25 shares to herself and the other 25 shares directly to D? What if A's gift to D were on January 5?

(d) Same as (b), above, except that two months after the incorporation, A sold 15 shares to E pursuant to a preexisting oral understanding, without which Newco would not have been formed.

2. Mr. Softy ("Softy") has operated a growing frozen yogurt business as a sole proprietorship over the past three years and is now interested in expanding his horizons and limiting his liability. To do so, he wishes to incorporate, raise $150,000 of additional capital and hire an experienced person to manage the business. He has located Venturer, who is willing to invest $150,000 cash and Manager, who has agreed to serve as chief operating officer if the terms are right.

The parties have decided to join forces and form Yummy Yogurt, Inc. ("Yummy"), which will operate a chain of frozen yogurt stores. Softy will transfer assets with an aggregate basis of $50,000 and a fair market value of $200,000 (do not be concerned with the character of the individual assets for this problem); Venturer will contribute $150,000 cash; and Manager will enter into a five year employment contract. Softy would like effective control of the business; Venturer is interested in a guaranteed return on his investment but also wants to share in the growth of the company; and Manager wants to be fairly compensated (she believes her services are worth approximately $80,000 per year) and receive stock in the company, but she can not afford to make a substantial cash investment. All the parties wish to avoid adverse tax consequences.

Consider the following alternative proposals and evaluate whether they meet the tax and non-tax objectives of the parties:

(a) In exchange for their respective contributions, Softy will receive 200 shares and Venturer will receive 150 shares of Yummy stock. Manager will agree to a salary of $40,000 per year for five years and will receive 150 shares of Yummy common stock upon the incorporation. (Assume that the value of the stock is $1,000 per share.)

(b) Same as (a), above, except Manager will receive compensation of $80,000 per year and will pay $150,000 for her Yummy stock. Any difference if Manager, unable to raise the cash, gave Yummy his unsecured $150,000 promissory note, at market rate interest, payable in five equal installments, in exchange for her 150 shares?

(c) Same as (a), above, except Manager will pay $1,000 for her 150 shares and the incorporation documents specify that she is receiving those shares in exchange for her cash contribution rather than for future services.

(d) Same as (c), above, except Manager will pay $20,000 cash rather than $1,000.

(e) Same as (d), above, except Manager will receive only 20 shares of stock without restrictions; the other 130 shares may not be sold by Manager for five years and will revert back to the corporation if Manager should cease to be an employee of the company during the five year period. See I.R.C. § 83. Would you advise Manager to make a § 83(b) election in this situation? What other information would you need?

C. TREATMENT OF BOOT

1. IN GENERAL

Code: §§ 351(b); 358(a), (b)(1); 362(a).

Regulations: §§ 1.351–2(a); 1.358–1, –2; 1.362–1.

In the introductory section of this chapter, a simple example illustrated the need for Section 351. Recall that A decided to form Venture, Inc. by transferring appreciated property with a value of $100 and a basis of $10 in exchange for Venture stock with a value of $100. Without a special provision of the Code, A would have recognized a $90 gain on the exchange. But since A received solely stock and owned 100 percent of Venture, the transaction qualified for nonrecognition under Section 351. To preserve the gain that went unrecognized, A took a $10 exchanged basis in the Venture stock under Section 358, and Venture took a $10 transferred basis in the contributed assets under Section 362. If A had received more than one class of stock, the transaction still would have qualified under Section 351, and A would have been required to allocate his aggregate exchanged basis of $10 among the various classes of stock received in proportion to their relative fair market values.[1]

But suppose that A, perhaps motivated by the tax advantages of corporate debt,[2] capitalizes Venture, Inc. with the same $100 asset by taking back common stock with a value of $80 and a corporate note with a value of $20. The transaction fails to qualify under Section 351(a) because A, although clearly in "control" of Venture, has not

---

1. Reg. § 1.358–2(b)(2).   2. See Chapter 3A, infra.

exchanged his $100 asset "solely" in exchange for stock. A's position is not unlike the real estate investor—desiring a tax-free like-kind exchange—who trades his highly appreciated $500,000 building in exchange for other real estate with a value of $450,000 and $50,000 of cash to even out the deal. The question for both A and the real estate investor becomes: should the presence of this "other property," known in tax parlance as "boot," require full recognition of their realized gain, or should there be a statutory middle ground?

The question is answered in the incorporation setting by Section 351(b). It provides that if an exchange otherwise would have qualified under Section 351(a) but for the fact that the transferor received "other property or money" in addition to stock, then the transferor's realized gain (if any) must be recognized to the extent of the cash plus the fair market value of the other property received. Translated more concisely, Section 351(b) provides that any gain realized by a transferor on an otherwise qualified Section 351(a) exchange must be recognized only to the extent of the boot received. The gain is characterized by reference to the character of the assets transferred, taking into account the impact of the recapture of depreciation provisions.[3] Despite the presence of boot, however, no *loss* may be recognized under Section 351(b).[4]

In the example where A receives $80 of stock and a $20 corporate note in exchange for his $100 asset with a $10 basis, Section 351(b) will require A to recognize $20 of his $90 realized gain.[5] This makes sense, of course, because to the extent that A has transferred his asset in exchange for property other than stock, he has changed not merely the form of his investment but the substance as well. To that extent, nonrecognition treatment is inappropriate.

As noted earlier, if a shareholder transfers property in a tax-free Section 351(a) transaction, the unrecognized gain on the transfer will be preserved through an exchanged basis in the transferor's stock and again through a transferred basis in the corporation's assets. But if a shareholder recognizes some gain as a result of the receipt of boot, not all of his realized gain must be accounted for at a later time. To avoid this potential double recognition of gain, the shareholder may increase his basis in the stock, securities and other property received by an amount equal to the gain recognized on the transfer.[6] This higher basis will result in less gain (or more loss) if and when the shareholder later sells the property received from the corporation.

---

3. See I.R.C. §§ 1245(b)(3), 1250(d)(3). Also relevant is I.R.C. § 1239, which characterizes the recognized gain on the transfer of depreciable property to a corporation as ordinary income if the transferor and certain related parties own more than 50 percent of the value of the transferee corporation's stock.

4. See also I.R.C. § 267(a)(1), disallowing losses on sales or exchanges between related taxpayers, including an individual and a corporation more than 50 percent in value of which is owned by the individual (actually or through attribution rules).

5. This example only addresses the *amount* of A's gain. The *timing* of gain triggered by the receipt of installment boot is considered in Section C2 of the chapter, infra.

6. I.R.C. § 358(a)(1)(B)(ii).

The shareholder's combined basis in the stock, securities and other property received from the corporation thus equals the basis in the property transferred to the corporation increased by the gain recognized on the transfer. This total basis then must be allocated between the nonrecognition property (i.e., the stock) and the boot. Since any gain recognized by the shareholder is attributable to the boot, and since his continuing investment is represented by the nonrecognition property, the unrecognized gain inherent in the property transferred to the corporation should now lurk in the nonrecognition property. These goals are achieved by assigning the boot a fair market value basis and allocating the remaining basis to the nonrecognition property. The basis of the nonrecognition property is thus an exchanged basis, increased by the gain recognized on the transfer, and, finally, decreased by the fair market value of the boot (including cash) received.[7]

Applying these rules to our previous example, if A received $80 of Venture, Inc. stock and a $20 note in exchange for his $100 asset with a basis of $10, his recognized gain would be $20—the fair market value of the boot. A's basis in the note would be $20, its fair market value. A's basis in the stock would be determined as follows:

Basis of Asset Transferred	$ 10
Less: Fair Market Value of Note Received	(20)
Plus: Gain Recognized	20
Basis of Stock	$ 10

The arithmetic makes sense. Remember that the value of the Venture stock was $80. By assigning the stock a $10 basis, Section 358 preserves the $70 of realized gain that went unrecognized on the partially tax-free exchange. There is no more gain to be preserved, so it is logical to give the boot a fair market value basis.[8]

At the corporate level, Section 362(a) provides that the corporation's basis in the property received on a Section 351 exchange is the same as the transferor's basis, increased by any gain recognized on the exchange. This rule ensures that any gain or loss not recognized by the shareholder will be reflected in the corporation's basis in the transferred assets. Returning one last time to the example, since A recognized $20 of gain on the exchange, Venture's basis in the transferred asset would be $30 (a $10 transferred basis in A's hands plus $20 gain recognized).

If a transferor exchanges several assets in exchange for stock and boot, the determination of basis becomes more complex. For purposes of determining the gain recognized (and, if relevant, the character of that gain), it becomes necessary to allocate the boot among the transferred assets. Similar allocations are required to determine the basis of

---

7. I.R.C. § 358(a)(2).

8. As before, this example only addresses the amount of gain recognized un-

der Section 351(b) and the resulting basis consequences.

the assets in the hands of the corporation. Although these questions rarely arise in the routine corporate formation, they have titillated tax commentators and caused unnecessary anguish to students of corporate tax.[9] The ruling below is the Service's attempt at an orderly resolution of this problem.

REVENUE RULING 68–55
1968–1 Cum.Bull. 140.

Advice has been requested as to the correct method of determining the amount and character of the gain to be recognized by Corporation X under section 351(b) of the Internal Revenue Code of 1954 under the circumstances described below.

Corporation Y was organized by X and A, an individual who owned no stock in X. A transferred $20x$ dollars to Y in exchange for stock of Y having a fair market value of $20x$ dollars and X transferred to Y three separate assets and received in exchange stock of Y having a fair market value of $100x$ dollars plus cash of $10x$ dollars.

In accordance with the facts set forth in the table below if X had sold at fair market value each of the three assets it transferred to Y, the result would have been as follows:

	Asset I	Asset II	Asset III
Character of asset	Capital asset held more than 6 months.	Capital asset held not more than 6 months.	Section 1245 property.
Fair market value	$22x$	$33x$	$55x$
Adjusted basis	40x	20x	25x
Gain (loss)	($18x$)	$13x$	$30x$
Character of gain or loss	Long-term capital loss.	Short-term capital gain.	Ordinary income.

The facts in the instant case disclose that with respect to the section 1245 property the depreciation subject to recapture exceeds the amount of gain that would be recognized on a sale at fair market value. Therefore, all of such gain would be treated as ordinary income under section 1245(a)(1) of the Code.

Under section 351(a) of the Code, no gain or loss is recognized if property is transferred to a corporation solely in exchange for its stock and immediately after the exchange the transferor is in control of the corporation. If section 351(a) of the Code would apply to an exchange but for the fact that there is received, in addition to the property permitted to be received without recognition of gain, other property or money, then under section 351(b) of the Code gain (if any) to the recipient will be recognized, but in an amount not in excess of the sum

---

9. For a particularly exhaustive treatment of this issue, see Rabinovitz, "Allocating Boot in Section 351 Exchanges," 24 Tax L.Rev. 337 (1969).

of such money and the fair market value of such other property received, and no loss to the recipient will be recognized.

The first question presented is how to determine the amount of gain to be recognized under section 351(b) of the Code. The general rule is that each asset transferred must be considered to have been separately exchanged. See the authorities cited in Revenue Ruling 67–192, C.B. 1967–2, 140, and in Revenue Ruling 68–23, page 144, this Bulletin, which hold that there is no netting of gains and losses for purposes of applying sections 367 and 356(c) of the Code. Thus, for purposes of making computations under section 351(b) of the Code, it is not proper to total the bases of the various assets transferred and to subtract this total from the fair market value of the total consideration received in the exchange. Moreover, any treatment other than an asset-by-asset approach would have the effect of allowing losses that are specifically disallowed by section 351(b)(2) of the Code.

The second question presented is how, for purposes of making computations under section 351(b) of the Code, to allocate the cash and stock received to the amount realized as to each asset transferred in the exchange. The asset-by-asset approach for computing the amount of gain realized in the exchange requires that for this purpose the fair market value of each category of consideration received must be separately allocated to the transferred assets in proportion to the relative fair market values of the transferred assets. See section 1.1245–4(c)(1) of the Income Tax Regulations which, for the same reasons, requires that for purposes of computing the amount of gain to which section 1245 of the Code applies each category of consideration received must be allocated to the properties transferred in proportion to their relative fair market values.

Accordingly, the amount and character of the gain recognized in the exchange should be computed as follows:

	Total	Asset I	Asset II	Asset III
Fair market value of asset transferred	$110x	$22x	$33x	$55x
Percent of total fair market value		20%	30%	50%
Fair market value of Y stock received in exchange	$100x	$20x	$30x	$50x
Cash received in exchange	10x	2x	3x	5x
Amount realized	$110x	$22x	$33x	$55x
Adjusted basis		40x	20x	25x
Gain (loss) realized		($18x)	$13x	$30x

Under section 351(b)(2) of the Code the loss of 18x dollars realized on the exchange of Asset Number I is not recognized. Such loss may not be used to offset the gains realized on the exchanges of the other assets. Under section 351(b)(1) of the Code, the gain of 13x dollars realized on the exchange of Asset Number II will be recognized as short-term capital gain in the amount of $3x$ dollars, the amount of cash received. Under sections 351(b)(1) and 1245(b)(3) of the Code, the gain of $30x$ dollars realized on the exchange of Asset Number III will be recognized as ordinary income in the amount of $5x$ dollars, the amount of cash received.

NOTE

Overall understanding of Section 351 may be enhanced by an analysis of the additional results to the shareholder ("X") and the corporation ("Y") in the transaction described in Revenue Ruling 68–55. X's basis in the Y stock received will be an exchanged basis ($40 from Asset I, plus $20 from Asset II, plus $25 from Asset III = $85), increased by its total gain recognized on the transfer ($3 on Asset II, plus $5 on Asset III = $8) and decreased by the fair market value of the boot (including cash) received ($10) for a total basis of $83 ($85 + $8 − 10).

The next question is X's holding period for the stock. X received stock worth $100 together with $10 cash for assets with a value of $110 (Asset I $22, Asset II $33, Asset III $55). Thus, it could be said that 22/110 of the stock was received in exchange for Asset I, 33/110 was received in exchange for Asset II, and 55/110 was received in exchange for Asset III. In that event, each share could be considered to have a split holding period allocated in proportion to the fair market value of the transferred assets.[1]

The next step is a determination of Y's basis in the assets received. In the ruling, Y's basis in those assets will be their adjusted bases in X's hands ($40 for Asset I, plus $20 for Asset II, plus $25 for Asset III) increased by the gain recognized to X (zero on Asset I, plus $3 on Asset II, plus $5 on Asset III) for a total of $93 ($40 + $20 + $25 + $3 + $5). Nothing in the Code, regulations or rulings explains how this basis is allocated among the assets. The underlying premise of Section 362, however, is that any gain or loss which is realized but not recognized by the transferor on the Section 351 transfer will be recognized by the corporation on a later sale. This concept is carried out by giving each separate asset its original transferred basis and then increasing the basis by the amount of gain recognized by the transferor on that asset.[2] On the facts in Revenue Ruling 68–55, Y's basis in Asset I would be $40 (transferred basis) since no gain or loss was recognized on that asset. If Y sells Asset I for its $22 fair market value, it then will recognize the $18 loss realized but not recognized by the transferor. Y's basis in Asset II would be $23 (transferred basis of $20 increased by the $3 of

1. This approach was adopted by the Service in Rev.Rul. 85–164, 1985–2 C.B. 117. In so ruling, the Service rejected an alternative approach, under which some shares would take a tacked holding period and other shares a holding period commencing as of the date of the exchange. The latter approach would permit a shareholder selling a portion of his holdings to designate shares with the longer holding period.

2. See, e.g., P.A. Birren & Son v. Commissioner, 116 F.2d 718 (7th Cir.1940).

gain recognized on Asset II). Of the $13 of realized gain on Asset II, $3 already has been recognized, and Y will recognize the $10 additional gain if it sells that asset for its fair market value of $33. Finally, Asset III will take a basis of $30 (transferred basis of $25, increased by $5 gain recognized) so that if Y sold the asset for its fair market value of $55, it will recognize the $25 additional realized gain that was not recognized by X.

2. TIMING OF SECTION 351(b) GAIN

Proposed Regulations: § 1.453–1(f)(1)(iii), –(f)(3)(i), (ii), (iii) Example (1).

The preceding discussion concerned the amount of gain recognized by a transferor who receives boot in a Section 351 transaction. What about the timing of that gain? If the boot is cash or other corporate property, the transferor recognizes any Section 351(b) gain immediately upon receipt of the boot. But newly formed corporations rarely are in a position to transfer cash or other assets to their founding shareholders. Gain is more typically recognized in a corporate formation when a shareholder transfers appreciated property in exchange for a mixture of stock and corporate debt instruments.[1] In that event, the question becomes—*when* must that gain be recognized? And if the gain may be deferred, what is the resulting impact on the shareholder's basis in her stock under Section 358 and the corporation's basis in its assets under Section 362? The answers lie in the relationship between Section 351 and the installment sale rules in Section 453.

For many years, it was not clear whether a shareholder could defer the reporting of Section 351 gain triggered by the receipt of corporate debt obligations. The Installment Sales Revision Act of 1980 resolved the question in an analogous context by permitting deferral of gain for installment boot received in a Section 1031 like-kind exchange and certain other corporate nonrecognition transactions.[2] Although these amendments made no reference to Section 351, the Treasury has since issued proposed regulations allowing a transferor who receives install-ment boot in a Section 351(b) exchange to report gain on the install-ment method provided that the gain otherwise could be deferred under Section 453 on an installment sale.[3] The regulations also permit a transferor to immediately increase the basis in any nonrecognition property received (e.g., stock) by the transferor's total potential recog-nized gain, but they delay the corporation's corresponding Section 362(a) basis increase in its assets until the transferor actually recog-nizes gain on the installment method.[4]

1. For the tax incentives to capitalize a corporation with debt, see Chapter 3, infra.

2. I.R.C. § 453(f)(6).

3. Prop.Reg. § 1.453–1(f)(3)(ii). Gain at-tributable to recapture of depreciation or dispositions of dealer property could not be deferred. I.R.C. § 453(i), (*l*). See generally

Cain, "Taxation of Boot Notes in a 351/453 Transaction," 27 S. Texas L.Rev. 61 (1985); Dentino & Walker, "Impact of the Install-ment Sales Revision Act of 1980 on Evi-dences of Indebtedness in a Section 351 Transaction," 9 J.Corp. Tax'n 330 (1983).

4. Id.

The operation of the proposed regulations is best illustrated by an example. In a conventional installment sale (i.e., a deferred payment sale not made in conjunction with a nonrecognition provision), Section 453 directs the seller to first divide his realized gain (known in Section 453 parlance as the "gross profit") by the total principal payments to be received on the sale ("total contract price").[5] The seller then applies the resulting fraction to each payment received to determine the gain recognized in the year of sale and as installment payments are later received. Adopting the facts of our continuing example, assume A sells his appreciated asset ("Gainacre"), which has an adjusted basis of $10 and a fair market value of $100, for $80 cash and a $20 note with market rate interest and principal payable in equal installments over the next five years. A's realized gain is $90. His total payments received will be $100—$80 in the year of sale and $20 in subsequent years. Under the installment method, $90/100$, or 90 percent, of each payment received must be reported as taxable gain.

Now assume that A transfers Gainacre to Venture, Inc., in exchange for 80 shares of Venture stock (worth $80), and a $20 Venture five-year note. A again realizes $90 of gain but recognizes that gain only to the extent of the $20 boot received. For timing purposes, the regulations divide the exchange into two separate transactions: a Section 351(a) nonrecognition exchange to the extent of the stock received by the transferor and an installment sale to the extent of the boot received. The basis of the transferred property is first allocated to the nonrecognition transaction. The regulations implement this bifurcation approach as follows: [6]

1. A's basis in Gainacre ($10) is first allocated to the Venture stock ("nonrecognition property")[7] received in the exchange in an amount up to the fair market value of that property. The entire $10 of basis is thus allocated to the $80 of Venture stock received by A.

2. If the transferor's basis in the transferred property exceeds the fair market value of the nonrecognition property received, that "excess basis" is then allocated to the installment portion of the transaction. There is no excess basis to allocate in this example because the Gainacre basis ($10) does not exceed the value of the nonrecognition property (stock worth $80).

3. Section 453 is then applied to the installment portion of the transaction. For this purpose, the "selling price" is the sum of the face value of the installment obligation ($20 here) and the fair market value of any other boot (none here). Where, as here, there are no liabilities, the total contract price is the same as the selling price ($20). The gross profit is the selling

5. I.R.C. § 453(c). For purposes of this and subsequent examples, assume that the property sold is unencumbered and is otherwise eligible for installment sale treatment.

6. Prop.Reg. § 1.453–1(f)(1)(iii); –1(f)(3)(ii).

7. The proposed regulations refer to nonrecognition property as "permitted property." Prop.Reg. § 1.453–1(f)(1)(i).

price less any "excess basis" allocated to the installment obligation ($20 – 0 = $20). A's gross profit ratio is thus $^{20}/_{20}$, or 100%. To determine his recognized gain, A applies that percentage to any boot received in the year of sale and to payments as they are received on the installment note. A thus recognizes no gain in the year of the exchange; his entire $20 "boot" gain is recognized as the note is paid off over the next five years. Note that the gross profit ratio is normally 100% if the boot received is less than the realized gain.[8]

For purposes of determining a shareholder's basis in the nonrecognition property received in a Section 351/453 transaction, the regulations treat the shareholder as electing out of the installment method.[9] Returning to the example, A's basis in his Venture stock under Section 358 is $10, determined as follows: $10 (A's basis in Gainacre) decreased by $20 (total boot received by A) and increased by $20 (the entire gain A would have recognized if he reported all his gain in the year of sale).

Determining the corporation's basis in the transferred property is more complicated. Adopting what one commentator has called a "rollercoaster basis" approach,[10] the regulations provide that the corporation's basis in the transferred property is the same as the transferor's basis increased by the gain recognized only if, as and when that gain is actually recognized. In the example, Venture initially takes a transferred basis of $10 in Gainacre, and that basis gradually is increased by $20 as Venture pays off the note and A recognizes his deferred gain on the installment method.[11] Query, whether this rollercoaster basis approach is appropriate, considering that Venture in effect has incurred a liability in connection with its acquisition of Gainacre. If the teachings of the *Crane* case are followed, it would seem that Venture should be permitted to increase its basis by the full $20 liability notwithstanding that A may defer his boot gain over five years. An immediate step-up in basis of the transferred property would be particularly appealing to the corporation when the property is depreciable real estate with no lurking recapture gain.

---

8. If the boot exceeds the transferor's realized gain, then some of the basis of the transferred property must be allocated to the installment portion of the transaction. For example, assume the same transaction, except A's basis in Gainacre is $90 and his realized gain is thus only $10. Although A receives $20 of boot, his recognized gain is limited to $10 under Section 351(b). The proposed regulations again direct A to allocate his basis in Gainacre ($90) to the Venture stock received but only up to the fair market value of that "nonrecognition property" ($80 here). The $10 "excess basis" is allocated to the installment sale, resulting in a gross profit of $10 ($20 selling price less $10 excess basis) and a gross profit ratio of $^{1}/_{2}$. A thus must report $^{1}/_{2}$ of each payment received on the note as taxable gain.

9. Prop.Reg. § 1.453–1(f)(3)(ii).

10. See Bogdanski, "Closely Held Corporations: Section 351 and Installment 'Boot,' " 11 J.Corp.Tax'n 268 (1984).

11. Id. Suppose Venture sells Gainacre prior to the due date of the note. Should Venture recognize a loss when the note is eventually paid off? See Prop. Reg. § 1.453–1(f)(3)(iii) Example (1).

PROBLEM

A, B and C form X Corporation by transferring the following assets, each of which has been held long-term:

Transferor	Asset	Adj. Basis	F.M.V.
A	Equipment (all § 1245 gain)	$15,000	$22,000
B	Inventory $1221 ordinc	7,000	20,000
	Land	25,000	10,000
C	Land	20,000	50,000

In exchange, A receives 15 shares of X common stock (value—$15,000), $2,000 cash and 100 shares of X preferred stock (value—$5,000), B receives 15 shares of X common stock (value—$15,000) and $15,000 cash, and C receives 10 shares of X common stock (value—$10,000), $5,000 cash and X's note for $35,000, payable in two years. None of the transferors is a "dealer."

(a) What are the tax consequences (gain or loss realized and recognized, basis and holding period) of the transfers described above to each shareholder and to X Corporation?

(b) What result to C in (a), above, if instead of land, C transferred depreciable equipment with the same adjusted basis and fair market value as the land and an original cost to C of $50,000? See § 453(i).

D. ASSUMPTION OF LIABILITIES

Code: §§ 357; 358(d).

Regulations: §§ 1.357–1, –2; 1.358–3.

Many corporate formations involve the transfer of encumbered property or the assumption of liabilities by the transferee corporation. In most circumstances, a taxpayer who is relieved of a debt in connection with the disposition of property must include the debt relief in the amount realized even if the debt is nonrecourse. This is the teaching of the celebrated *Crane* case,[1] and the Supreme Court took a similar approach nine years earlier in *United States v. Hendler.*[2] Interpreting the corporate reorganization provisions, the Court held in *Hendler* that the assumption and subsequent payment of the transferor's liabilities by a transferee corporation constituted boot to the transferor. If that rule applied to a corporate formation, however, many incorporations of a going business would become taxable events to the extent of the liabilities assumed, and the policy of Section 351 would be seriously frustrated.

To prevent this result, Congress promptly responded to *Hendler* by enacting the statutory predecessor of Section 357. Section 357(a) now

1. Crane v. Commissioner, 331 U.S. 1, 67 S.Ct. 1047 (1947).   2. 303 U.S. 564, 58 S.Ct. 655 (1938).

provides that the assumption of a liability or the acquisition of property subject to a liability by a transferee corporation in a Section 351 exchange (and several other transactions to be studied later) will neither constitute boot nor prevent the exchange from qualifying under Section 351. Rather than treating the debt relief as boot, the Code postpones the recognition of any gain attributable to the transferred liabilities. This deferral is accomplished by Section 358(d), which reduces the basis in the stock or securities received in the exchange by treating the relieved liabilities as "money received" by the transferor for purposes of determining the shareholder's basis.

Section 357 is subject to two exceptions. The first (Section 357(b)) prevents abuse and the second (Section 357(c)) avoids the tax taboo of a negative basis. Under the Section 357(b) "tax avoidance" exception, the assumption of a liability or the acquisition of property subject to a liability is treated as boot if the taxpayer's "principal purpose" in transferring the liability was the avoidance of federal income taxes or was not a bona fide business purpose. This essentially factual determination is made after "taking into consideration the nature of the liability and the circumstances in the light of which the arrangement for the assumption or acquisition was made." [3] If an improper purpose exists, all the relieved liabilities, not merely the evil debts, are treated as boot. [4] Section 357(b) apparently was designed to prevent taxpayers from transferring personal obligations to a newly formed corporation or from achieving a "bail out without boot" by borrowing against property on the eve of incorporation and then transferring the encumbered asset to the corporation. Perhaps because the rule is more draconian than necessary, it has been sparingly applied. [5]

The origin of the second exception is more technical. Section 357(c) provides that if the liabilities assumed by the corporation or encumbering the transferred property exceed the aggregate adjusted bases of the properties transferred by a particular transferor, [6] the excess shall be considered as gain from the sale or exchange of the property. [7] A simple illustration explains the need for this exception. Assume our friend, A, forms Venture, Inc. by transferring a building with an adjusted basis of $30, a fair market value of $100 and an

3. In evaluating whether the business purpose is bona fide, the regulations require both the transferor and the corporation to demonstrate a "*corporate* business reason" (emphasis added) for the assumption of the liabilities when they report a Section 351 transaction on their income tax returns. Reg. § 1.351–3(a)(6), –3(b)(7).

4. Reg. § 1.357–1(c).

5. Section 357(b) is accompanied by an odd burden of proof rule providing that in "any suit" where the taxpayer has the burden of proving the absence of an improper purpose, that burden shall not be met unless the taxpayer "sustains such burden by the clear preponderance of the

evidence." I.R.C. § 357(b)(2). This standard adds little to the normal burden of proof imposed in tax litigation and has largely been ignored by the courts.

6. Section 357(c) is applied on a transferor-by-transferor basis. Rev.Rul. 66–142, 1966–2 C.B. 66.

7. According to the regulations, the character of the Section 357(c) gain is determined by allocating the gain among the transferred assets in proportion to their respective fair market values. Reg. § 1.357–2(a). As the problems illustrate, this approach is anomalous insofar as it may require an allocation of gain to an asset with no built-in gain.

outstanding mortgage of $55. In exchange, Venture issues common stock with a value of $45 and takes the building subject to the $55 mortgage. If Section 357(a) applied, without more, A would recognize no gain on the exchange, but pause to consider his basis in the stock under Section 358. It would be $30 (the basis of the building), less $55 (the liability, treated as boot for basis purposes under Section 358(d)), or a *minus* $25. Although tax scholars have debated the issue, the Code abhors a negative basis.[8] Section 357(c) conveniently avoids that taboo by requiring A to recognize $25 gain (the excess of the $55 liability over his $30 adjusted basis). A's basis then becomes zero, and the Code is not further complicated by the mysteries of algebra.

Section 357(c) is itself subject to an exception. Under general tax principles, a taxpayer who is relieved of a liability that would be deductible if paid directly by the taxpayer does not recognize gain if the debt is discharged because any potential income would be offset by a corresponding deduction upon payment.[9] For example, a lender's discharge of a borrower's $1,000 interest expense on a home mortgage is economically equivalent to the lender's transfer of $1,000 cash to the borrower (gross income) and a retransfer of $1,000 cash as interest by the borrower to the lender (offsetting deduction). Taken together, these transactions should not result in any net income to the borrower.[10] In keeping with this approach, Section 357(c)(3) excludes from the term "liabilities," for purposes of determining the excess of liabilities over basis, any obligation that would give rise to a deduction if it had been paid by the transferor[11] or which would be described in Section 736(a).[12] The same types of obligations also are not treated as "liabilities" for purposes of determining the basis of the stock or securities received by the transferor under Section 358.[13]

The origin of this exception is best understood by looking back to the difficulties encountered by cash basis proprietors who incorporated

8. For a contrary view on the viability of a negative basis, see Cooper, "Negative Basis," 75 Harv.L.Rev. 1352 (1962).

9. See I.R.C. § 108(e)(2), which provides that no income shall be realized from the discharge of indebtedness to the extent the payment of the liability would have given rise to a deduction.

10. Cf. I.R.C. § 7872. The example assumes that the interest is deductible "qualified residence interest" under Section 163(h).

11. Excepted from this exception are obligations which, when incurred, resulted in the creation of, or an increase in, the basis of any property—e.g., obligations to pay for small tools purchased on credit. I.R.C. § 357(c)(3)(B). To illustrate, assume cash method Proprietor ("P") buys $100 of small tools on credit, promising to pay the seller in two months. Pending payment of the obligation, P has a $100 basis in the obligation (P's cost). One month later, P transfers the tools and the related obligation to a new corporation in a Section 351 transaction. The obligation is appropriately treated as a "liability" for purposes of Section 357(c)—but not to worry because the amount of that liability is offset by P's basis in the transferred tools.

12. Section 736(a) applies to payments made to a retiring partner or to a deceased partner's successor in interest in liquidation of that partner's interest in the partnership. Further details are beyond the scope of our present coverage. Suffice it to note that Section 736(a) payments, like accounts payable of a cash basis taxpayer, have the effect of reducing gross income when paid and thus are appropriately excluded from "liabilities" for purposes of Section 357(c) and 358(d).

13. I.R.C. § 358(d)(2).

a going business prior to the enactment of Section 357(c)(3). Consider the plight of Accountant ("A"), a cash basis taxpayer whose sole proprietorship consisted of the following assets and liabilities:

Assets	Adj. Basis	F.M.V.
Cash	$100	$100
Accounts Receivable	0	200
Equipment	50	250
	$150	$550

Liabilities		
Accounts payable		$400

Assume A incorporates his business by transferring all the assets to Newco in exchange for $150 of Newco stock and Newco's assumption of the $400 accounts payable. If the payables are "liabilities" for purposes of Section 357(c)(1), A recognizes $250 gain—the excess of the $400 liabilities assumed by Newco over the $150 aggregate adjusted basis of the assets transferred to the corporation. A's adjusted basis in the Newco stock would be zero.[14]

The harshness of this result becomes apparent when it is compared to an economically equivalent transaction. Suppose, for example, that A had retained the payables, transferred the $550 in assets to Newco in exchange for $150 of Newco stock and $400 cash and then used the cash to pay his creditors. Although A would recognize $400 gain under Section 351(b), that gain would be cancelled out by the $400 deduction that A would receive on payment of the payables. Alternatively, A could have avoided any gain simply by retaining sufficient assets to pay the deductible accounts payable.

As these examples illustrate, the inclusion of accounts payable as "liabilities" for purposes of Section 357(c) often caused cash basis taxpayers to recognize more gain by having their obligations assumed than they would have recognized if they received equivalent cash boot or withheld sufficient assets to pay the liabilities. Several courts attempted to cure this anomaly by excluding certain deductible liabilities from the scope of Section 357(c), but the cases lacked a uniform rationale.[15] To resolve these ambiguities and halt the litigation, Congress amended Sections 357(c) and 358(d) to provide that deductible obligations no longer would be considered "liabilities" for these limited

14. A's basis is derived as follows: $150 (basis in assets transferred by A) minus $400 (liabilities assumed by Newco, treated as "money received" for basis purposes) plus $250 (gain recognized by A). I.R.C. § 358(a)(1), (d)(1).

15. See Focht v. Commissioner, 68 T.C. 223 (1977) ("liability" under Sections 357(c) and 358(d) limited to obligations which, if transferred, cause gain recognition under *Crane* case); Thatcher v. Commissioner, 61 T.C. 28 (1973), reversed in part and affirmed in part 533 F.2d 1114 (9th Cir.1976) (analyze transaction as "ordinary exchange" and give transferor constructive deduction for accounts payable discharged by corporation in same year as transfer to the extent of the lesser of accounts receivable or Section 357(c) gain); Bongiovanni v. Commissioner, 470 F.2d 921 (2d Cir.1972) (Section 357(c) only applies to "tax liabilities"—i.e., liens, mortgages, etc.).

purposes. Congress also indicated that this exception was not intended to affect either the transferee corporation's tax treatment of the excluded liabilities or the definition of liabilities for any other provision of the Code, including Sections 357(a) and 357(b).[16]

If all else fails, a transferor can avoid recognizing Section 357(c) gain simply by contributing additional cash to the corporation in an amount equal to the excess of assumed liabilities over the aggregate adjusted basis of the other contributed assets. A more intriguing question is whether a cash poor transferor can eliminate the gain by remaining personally liable on the assumed debts or by transferring a personal note to the corporation for the Section 357(c) excess. The courts are confused by these questions, as evidenced by the *Lessinger* case and the Note following.

LESSINGER v. COMMISSIONER
United States Court of Appeals, Second Circuit, 1989.
872 F.2d 519.

OAKES, Chief Judge:

Taxpayers Sol and Edith Lessinger appeal from that portion of a decision of the United States Tax Court, Charles E. Clapp II, Judge, finding them liable for income taxes of $113,242.55 for the tax year 1977 and $608.50 for the tax year 1978. Lessinger v. Commissioner, 85 T.C. 824 (1985). * * *

The Tax Court found, and the parties seem to agree, that section 351 of the Internal Revenue Code governs the transaction at issue here. Section 351 provides for the nonrecognition of income when a controlling shareholder transfers property to a corporation. The taxpayer here transferred the assets and liabilities of a proprietorship he operated to a corporation he owned for reasons entirely unrelated to tax planning. It is clear that he was oblivious to the ramifications of his actions in terms of his tax liability. Prior to the consolidation, the proprietorship had a negative net worth. Nevertheless the Tax Court found that the taxpayer had to recognize a gain because he transferred liabilities to the corporation which exceeded his adjusted basis in the assets of the proprietorship. The Tax Court applied section 357(c) of the Code, which is an exception to the general rule of nonrecognition in section 351 transactions. Under section 357(c), gain is recognized to the extent that a transferor-shareholder disposes of liabilities exceeding the total adjusted basis of the assets transferred. I.R.C. § 357(c) (1982).

The taxpayer attacks the Tax Court's decision from two directions. First, he argues that the Tax Court overstated the amount of liabilities transferred, because, he claims, he did not actually transfer short-term accounts payable to the corporation. His second argument is that the Tax Court understated the amount of assets transferred. The Tax Court decided to ignore a $255,500 accounting entry which, the taxpay-

---

16. Staff of Joint Committee on Taxation, General Explanation of the Revenue Act of 1978, 96th Cong., 1st Sess. 219–220 (1979).

er argues, represented his personal debt to the corporation and should be counted as a transferred asset.

Sol Lessinger operated a proprietorship under the name "Universal Screw and Bolt Co." for over twenty-five years prior to 1977. Since 1962 he was also the sole shareholder and chief executive officer of Universal Screw & Bolt Co., Inc. Both businesses were engaged in the wholesale distribution of metal fasteners, and they were conducted from the same location on Ninth Avenue in New York City.

In 1976, the factor that had provided working capital to the proprietorship refused to continue lending funds to it as a noncorporate entity because under New York law one can charge higher interest rates of a corporation. See N.Y.Gen.Oblig.Law § 5–521 (McKinney 1978) (corporation prohibited from interposing defense of usury). The taxpayer instructed the individual who was his attorney and accountant to do whatever was necessary to make the proprietorship a corporation. The Universal proprietorship was then consolidated into the Universal corporation in 1977. The Tax Court found that the taxpayer was not informed of the details of the transaction.

The proprietorship's unaudited balance sheet dated December 31, 1976, shows that the business had a negative net worth. A summary of the balance sheet, with amounts rounded to thousands, reads as follows:

Assets

Cash, accounts receivable, and inventory		1,314
Marketable securities and mutual funds		267
Fixed assets (net of depreciation)		106
Other (good will, prepaid expenses, etc.)		46
Total assets	approx.	1,733

Liabilities and Capital

Trade accounts payable		416
Notes payable due within one year		991
(Breakdown: Chemical Bank	203	
Trade	464	
Auto loan & ins.	9	
Trefoil (factor)	315)	
Misc. (due to broker, taxes, loans, and exchanges)		12
Accrued expenses		162
Notes payable due after one year		342
(Breakdown: Chemical Bank	338	
Trade	4)	
Sol Lessinger—capital		(190)
Total liabilities and capital	approx.	1,733

The consolidation of the proprietorship into the corporation was conducted in a most casual manner, the transfer transaction being naked in its simplicity. The taxpayer already owned all of the corporation's stock, and no new stock was issued. There were no written agreements documenting the transfer. On January 1, 1977, the proprietorship's bank account was closed, and the corporation took over the proprietorship's operating assets. Only two items of any significance were not transferred: The taxpayer had borrowed funds from Chemical Bank to purchase mutual fund shares, and the shares secured the loan. These items appear on the balance sheet above as the mutual fund shares and the Chemical Bank loan. The taxpayer retained the shares and sold them to pay the loan himself later in January 1977.

The corporation expressly assumed the other proprietorship liabilities except accounts payable. All notes payable were changed to show that the corporation was the maker of the notes, and the debt to the factor was expressly assumed. While the corporation did not expressly assume liability for the proprietorship's accounts payable, it did pay those accounts during the first six months of 1977.

On June 1, 1977, journal entries were made to the corporation's books to reflect the consolidation. Various corporate asset accounts were debited (i.e., increased) to show the addition of the proprietorship's assets, and corporate liability accounts were credited (i.e., increased) by the amount of the proprietorship's liabilities. Total proprietorship liabilities exceeded total proprietorship assets by $255,499.37, and that amount was debited to a corporate asset account in an entry entitled "Loan Receivable—SL." A ledger sheet entitled "Sol Lessinger" showed the debit with the description "[m]erger of company" as well as a $3,500 debit for a personal debt the corporation paid for Sol.

When in January 1977 the taxpayer sold his mutual funds, he used the proceeds not only to pay off the partnership's Chemical Bank loan, but also, with the remaining $62,209.35, to pay the corporation part of his $259,000 debt to it. Thus, at the end of 1977, he owed $196,790 to the corporation. In 1981, Marine Midland Bank, a principal creditor of the corporation, requested that the taxpayer execute a promissory note for the debt, and he did so, the note being used as collateral for the bank's loan to the corporation. No interest was ever paid on the debt, however, and the debt had risen to $237,044 by the end of 1982, by which point the corporation was insolvent. The corporation's retained earnings were $29,638 at the beginning of 1977 and $38,671 at the end of 1977, so the taxpayer's debt to the corporation greatly outweighed his equity in it.

The taxpayer's personal wealth, however, was not limited to that of the corporation (or the mutual fund shares which he sold in 1977). He also owned a realty corporation called "87–89 Chambers Street Corporation" ("Chambers") that, at the time of the consolidation, held about $41,000 in cash equivalents and a long-term leasehold of the premises the corporation occupied. The taxpayer introduced into evidence an appraisal of the property which was conducted in 1980 and which valued the leasehold at $230,000 as of January 1, 1977. The corporation paid Chambers only enough rent to cover Chambers' expense of running the building, while a fair rental might have been $31,000 per year more. Thus, to a certain extent, Sol may be said to have subsidized the manufacturing corporation by that amount each year.

DISCUSSION

The first question is whether section 351 applies when no new shares are issued to the shareholder, having in mind the statutory language that a transfer must be made "solely in exchange for stock or securities." See § 351(a). The Tax Court strained somewhat to analyze this case under, and perhaps to overrule, the case of Abegg v. Commissioner, 50 T.C. 145 (1968), aff'd on other grounds, 429 F.2d 1209 (2d Cir.1970), cert. denied, 400 U.S. 1008, 91 S.Ct. 566, 27 L.Ed.2d 621 (1971), involving transfer under section 367 by a nonresident alien to a wholly-owned corporation. We agree, however, with the Tax Court's ultimate conclusion that the exchange requirements of section 351 are met where a sole stockholder transfers property to a wholly-owned corporation even though no stock or securities are issued therefor. Issuance of new stock in this situation would be a meaningless gesture. * * * Indeed, we do not read the taxpayer's brief as contending the contrary.

The taxpayer's principal argument, broadly stated, is that section 357 is inapplicable to him because in neither an accounting nor an economic sense did he realize a gain. He "merely exchanged creditors" from trade creditors to Universal, and his gain, therefore, was a "phantom" which Congress did not intend to tax.

Narrowly stated, the taxpayer's argument takes two different forms, each of which complements the other:

First, the corporation did not take the affirmative action necessary to assume the trade accounts payable of the taxpayer's proprietorship, in contrast to its affirmative action to assume the notes payable. He argues that New York law did not even permit the "assumption" of the taxpayer's obligations by the corporation because to have done so would have rendered it insolvent, thus making payments by it to his creditors fraudulent transfers. See N.Y. Debt. & Cred.Law § 273 (McKinney 1945).

Second, even if the corporation did "assume" the taxpayer's trade accounts payable, there was no taxable gain since he contributed "property," that is, the account receivable from him in the approximate amount of $250,000, which, contrary to Alderman v. Commissioner, 55 T.C. 662 (1971), should be deemed to have a basis equal to its face value.

The Commissioner responds with the general, unchallenged proposition that discharge of indebtedness may be income. I.R.C. § 61(a)(12) (1982); Diedrich v. Commissioner, 457 U.S. 191, 102 S.Ct. 2414, 72 L.Ed. 2d 777 (1982); United States v. Kirby Lumber Co., 284 U.S. 1, 52 S.Ct. 4, 76 L.Ed. 131 (1931). The Commissioner argues that the taxpayer had a negative net worth with liabilities "tantamount to personal debts" which he was "essentially relieved from meeting" by virtue of the incorporation.[1]

---

1. Nowhere is there the slightest hint or innuendo that the taxpayer had a tax avoidance purpose so as to fall under § 357(b). Rather it can be said—if the

Whether the corporation assumed the proprietorship's accounts payable is a factual question to be determined under state law. * * * The Tax Court found that "[t]he corporation did in fact pay the liabilities [, and the] record is clear that [Lessinger] intended that the corporation should pay the liabilities in the normal course of business." 85 T.C. at 837. The Tax Court rejected Lessinger's argument that the payments were made merely as advances to him. We accept these factual findings. The Commissioner argues that principles of state law that would impose liability on a corporation to protect its alter ego's creditors demonstrate that the corporation here assumed the taxpayer's liabilities. But we do not think that the answer to the assumption question is dispositive, for whether "affirmative" assumption was required or occurred concerns form more than substance. We find it sufficient that the debts were paid, because their payment by the corporation represents the type of relief from liability that section 357(c) was intended to tax.

The taxpayer argues further that New York law precluded assumption of the short-term accounts payable. New York Debtor and Creditor Law § 273 (McKinney 1945) declares that paying or undertaking an obligation that would render one insolvent is fraudulent as to creditors if the payment is made or the obligation is incurred without fair consideration. The Tax Court ignored the taxpayer's purported new debt to the corporation. Under the Tax Court's analysis, then, the corporation would have been insolvent if it assumed the accounts payable. The Commissioner does not respond to this argument. We may safely ignore it, however, because we believe that the taxpayer's debt to the corporation was a real asset for the corporation.

Having determined that the proprietorship's accounts payable should be included in the category of liabilities assumed, we must determine whether the taxpayer's purported debt to his corporation would offset those liabilities and prevent a net excess of liabilities over assets. The obligation which the taxpayer owed to his wholly-owned corporation, it must quickly be conceded, was not as well documented as a debt to a third party would be.

A journal entry of the corporation showed $255,499.37 as a loan receivable from the taxpayer, which in turn was posted on a general ledger sheet as a debit to the taxpayer's account. That account was credited with a $62,209.35 adjustment resulting from the sale of the taxpayer's mutual funds and the paydown of the Chemical Bank loan. No credits on account of subsidized rent, * * * were made, and the debit balance of $196,790 in the taxpayer's account after the adjustment was never paid down; instead it increased to the sum of $237,044 in 1982. Marine Midland Bank required the open account to be formalized in 1981 in a note which collateralized the bank's loan to the corporation.

Commissioner were to prevail—that the factor's demand for higher interest led Lessinger into a § 351 "trap."

The Tax Court refused to count the debt as "property" transferred in the transaction, although its reasoning is not explicit. First, the opinion says that the corporate accounting entry entitled "Loan receivable—[Sol Lessinger]" "merely represents the excess of the liabilities over the adjusted basis," noting that the debt was not at first represented by a promissory note and that Lessinger paid no interest on it. The Tax Court then cites a decision in which it had ignored an entry that the taxpayer had characterized as an "artificial receivable." 85 T.C. at 837 n. 8 (citing Christopher v. Commissioner, 48 Tax Ct.Mem.Dec. (CCH) 663 (1984)). The Tax Court opinion concludes that "[e]ven if [Lessinger] had executed a note, it would have a zero basis in the hands of the corporation." Id. at 837 (citing Alderman v. Commissioner, 55 T.C. 662 (1971)). The Tax Court thus apparently believed there were two independently sufficient reasons to ignore the debt: first, that it was artificial, and, second, that it would have had a zero basis.

We are unpersuaded by the argument that the obligation was artificial. The Commissioner argues:

> This open account was not so much a debt as it was an accommodation by the corporation to its president and sole shareholder, who was having liquidity problems. In effect, he caused the corporation to apply its assets to satisfy his personal obligations, including those owed to trade creditors which were shortly to fall due, intending to pay the money back only as and when he found it convenient to do so.

Brief at 35.[2] The Commissioner points out that the receivable lacked a due date, interest, security, or "other accepted features of true debt," but this analysis begs the question we have before us. The Commissioner's argument is not aided by likening this case to Carolina, Clinchfield and Ohio Railway v. Commissioner, 823 F.2d 33 (2d Cir. 1987) (per curiam), where an existing debt was replaced by a new debt payable ten centuries later, the present value of which was two quadrillionths of a cent. We believe that the receivable was an enforceable demand obligation. The decisions that the Commissioner cites for the definition of "true debt" concern the advance of funds to a close corporation by its shareholders. Gilbert v. Commissioner, 248 F.2d 399, 402 (2d Cir.1957); see also Raymond v. United States, 511 F.2d 185, 190 (6th Cir.1975). A taxpayer in that setting may seek to mischaracterize a capital contribution as debt in order for the corporation to be able to treat the obligation in a way that would disguise nondeductible dividends as deductible interest payments. In that context, the courts have defined "classic debt" narrowly as "an unqualified obligation to pay a sum certain at a reasonably close fixed maturity date along with a fixed percentage in interest," although the essential factor is a "binding obligation." Gilbert, 248 F.2d at 402.

2. We note the "accommodation" and the "[i]n effect," as we previously noted the argument that there were liabilities "tantamount to personal debts" which the taxpayer was "essentially" relieved from meeting. These slippery little phrases do not inspire confidence in the Commissioner's argumentation.

We believe, however, that a due date, interest, and security are not necessary to characterize Lessinger's obligation *to* his corporation as debt, and that his obligation was binding. The promissory note he signed in 1981, which the corporation endorsed to Marine Midland as collateral for a loan, is significant because it shows that Marine Midland depended on his personal responsibility. And, in general, it is obvious that the creditors of the corporation continued to do business with it on the strength of the taxpayer's personal credit (whether as evidenced by the liability on the books or by operation of New York law protecting creditors of a partnership that is succeeded by an alter ego corporation * * *). Lessinger received consideration when he gave his promise to the corporation, and we have no doubt that any court would enforce that promise to protect the corporate creditors if the corporation failed, even in the absence of alter ego liability. We conclude that the taxpayer's obligation to the corporation was real, not artificial.

We now turn to the Tax Court's second reason for ignoring the debt. The Tax Court quoted *Alderman*, supra, which, like our case, involved the incorporation of an accrual basis proprietorship with a negative net worth. In *Alderman*, the Tax Court disregarded the taxpayers' personal promissory note to their corporation because

> [t]he Aldermans incurred no cost in making the note, so its basis to them was zero. The basis to the corporation was the same as in the hands of the transferor, i.e., zero. Consequently, the application of section 357(c) is undisturbed by the creation and transfer of the personal note to the corporation.

55 T.C. at 665; see also Rev.Rul. 68–629, 1968–2 C.B. 154–55 (same). *Alderman* purported to follow the literal language of the Tax Code. Section 357(c) does support the *Alderman* court's reliance on the concept of basis, but the statutory language is not addressed to a transaction such as Lessinger's, where the transferor's obligation has a value to the transferee corporation. The *Alderman* court did not consider the value of the obligation to the transferee.

Section 357(a) provides that generally, the corporation's assumption of the transferor's liabilities should cause no recognition of gain:

> Except as provided in subsection[ ] * * * (c), if—
>
> (1) the taxpayer receives property which would be permitted to be received under section 351, * * * without the recognition of gain if it were the sole consideration, and
>
> (2) as part of the consideration, another party to the exchange assumes a liability of the taxpayer, or acquires from the taxpayer property subject to a liability,
>
> then such assumption or acquisition shall not be treated as money or other property, and shall not prevent the exchange from being within the provisions of section 351. * * *

I.R.C. § 357(a) (1982). Subsection (c)(1) then provides an exception:

(c) Liabilities in excess of basis

   (1) In general

      In the case of an exchange—

      (A) to which section 351 applies,

                   *   *   *

if the sum of the amount of the liabilities assumed, plus the amount of the liabilities to which the property is subject, exceeds the total of the *adjusted basis* of the property transferred pursuant to such exchange, then such excess shall be considered as a gain. * * *

Id. § 357(c) (emphasis added). In general, then, the "adjusted basis" of the property transferred is crucial to the calculation.

"Basis," as used in tax law, refers to assets, not liabilities. Section 1012 provides that "[t]he basis of property shall be the cost of such property, except as otherwise provided." Liabilities by definition have no "basis" in tax law generally or in section 1012 terms specifically.[3] The concept of "basis" prevents double taxation of income by identifying amounts that have already been taxed or are exempt from tax. 3 J. Mertens, Law of Federal Income Taxation § 21.01, at 11 (1988). The taxpayer could, of course, have no "basis" in his own promise to pay the corporation $255,000, because that item is a liability for him. We would add parenthetically that to this extent *Alderman* was correct in describing the taxpayers' note there. But the corporation should have a basis in its obligation from Lessinger, because it incurred a cost in the transaction involving the transfer of the obligation by taking on the liabilities of the proprietorship that exceeded its assets, and because it would have to recognize income upon Lessinger's payment of the debt if it had no basis in the obligation.[4] Assets transferred under section 351

---

3. Basis is "the original cost of property used in computing capital gains or losses for income tax purposes." Webster's Third New International Dictionary 182 (1963). It is a "[t]erm used in accounting, especially in tax accounting, to describe the value of an asset for purpose of determining gain (or loss) on its sale or transfer or in determining value in the hands of a donee of a gift." Black's Law Dictionary 138 (5th ed. 1979). Derived from "[a]cquisition cost, or some substitute therefor," it is the "amount assigned to an asset for income tax purposes." Id.

4. Our approach requires acceptance of the fact that section 362(a), which requires a carryover basis for "property" transferred in nonrecognition transactions under section 351, cannot be applied to the corporation's valuation of its receivable from the taxpayer. The purpose of the predecessor to section 362 was to avoid allowing the corporation a new, stepped-up basis from which to deduct depreciation

expenses. Republic Steel Corp. v. United States, 40 F.Supp. 1017, 1022 (Ct.Cl.1941); see also 3 J. Mertens, Law of Federal Income Taxation § 21.01, at 15 (1988) (the purpose of special basis rules for nonrecognition transactions is, in general, to prevent the transferee from having a stepped-up basis). Another purpose of transferred bases generally is to defer recognition of gain or loss. See, e.g., Steiner, Liabilities in Excess of Basis in Corporate Reorganizations—When Should Gain be Recognized?, 6 J.Corp.Tax'n 39, 40 (1979) (noting that when section 357(a) provides nonrecognition of gain upon the assumption of liabilities, "[a]s in the case of most nonrecognition provisions, this gain potential is preserved in the property received"). In Lessinger's transaction, there simply were no gains or losses to be deferred. The excess of liabilities over assets (which Lessinger's promise to the corporation remedied) was caused by the proprietorship's insolvency—the excess of current payables

are taken by the corporation at the transferor's basis, to which is added any gain recognized in the transfer. § 362(a). Consideration of "adjusted basis" in section 357(c) therefore normally does not require determining whether the section refers to the "adjusted basis" in the hands of the transferor-shareholder or the transferee-corporation, because the basis does not change. But here, the "basis" in the hands of the corporation should be the face amount of the taxpayer's obligation.[5] We now hold that in the situation presented here, where the transferor undertakes genuine personal liability to the transferee, "adjusted basis" in section 357(c) refers to the transferee's basis in the obligation, which is its face amount.[6]

Yet the Commissioner says that to reverse the Tax Court would, as *Alderman,* 55 T.C. at 665, suggested, "effectively eliminate section 357(c) from the Internal Revenue Code." Would it? The question of substance is whether the taxpayer in fact realized a gain from the transaction. He certainly did not do so by a cancellation of his indebtedness. If there was any cancellation, it was illusory: While his trade creditors at the time of the incorporation may have been paid off (or their accounts rolled over as a result of sales and payments by the corporation and further advances of credit by the trade creditors), the taxpayer's indebtedness to the corporation itself continued (except to the extent he paid it off). If Lessinger had a "gain" from the incorporation, it did not show up in his personal balance sheet, let alone by way of economic benefit in his pocket.

The purpose of section 357(c) is to provide a limited exception to section 351's nonrecognition treatment that operates, as the Commissioner reminds us here, "where the transferor realized economic benefit which, if not recognized, would otherwise go untaxed." Brief at 27 (quoting Focht v. Commissioner, 68 T.C. 223, 235 (1977)). Section 351 was intended to allow changes in business form without requiring the recognition of income. Bongiovanni v. Commissioner, 470 F.2d 921, 924 (2d Cir.1972); Raich v. Commissioner, 46 T.C. 604, 608 (1966). The transferor-shareholder recognizes income only to the extent that he receives boot in the form of money or other property. § 351(b). In 1938, the Supreme Court held that under the predecessor of section 351, section 112 of the Revenue Act of 1928, any assumption of liability by the transferee would be considered a payment of money or property to the transferor, causing the transferor to recognize income. United States v. Hendler, 303 U.S. 564, 58 S.Ct. 655, 82 L.Ed. 1018 (1938). Congress reacted immediately by enacting section 112(k) of the Internal

---

over current receivables—rather than by unrecognized gain in any asset's basis.

5. The Commissioner does not suggest that the obligation was so worthless as to warrant reduction of its face amount. We note as well that we do not here address the problem of an obligation whose present value is significantly lower than its face amount.

6. Curiously, the Commissioner does not actually make *Alderman's* zero-basis argument. The taxpayer, on the other hand, attempts to convince us that, as an accrual basis taxpayer, he had a "basis" in his personal obligations to the corporation. We note, however, that the fact that he would have had a liability on his books does not require the conclusion that he had a "basis" in it for tax purposes.

Revenue Code of 1939, the predecessor of section 357(a), which provided that the assumption of a liability should *not* be considered the payment of property or money and should not provoke the recognition of gain. See *Focht*, 68 T.C. at 232 & n. 21 (quoting section 112(k) and its legislative history).

Congress did not add section 357(c), which requires the recognition of gain when liabilities exceed assets, until 1954, when a House committee referred to the section as an "additional safeguard[ ] against tax avoidance not found in existing law." H.R.Rep. No. 1337, 83d Cong., 2d Sess. 40, reprinted in 1954 U.S.Code Cong. & Admin.News 4017, 4066 ("House Report"). Some provision was necessary to ensure that manipulations of credit and depreciation were not used to realize tax-free gains. *Focht*, 68 T.C. at 235. The House and Senate committees that approved section 357(c) both cited a single example of a transaction that the section was intended to govern: If a taxpayer transfers property with an adjusted basis of $20,000 subject to a $50,000 mortgage, he should recognize $30,000 gain. House Report at A129, reprinted in 1954 U.S.Code Cong. & Admin.News at 4267 (describing what was then called § 356); S.Rep. No. 1622, 83d Cong., 2d Sess. 270, reprinted in 1954 U.S.Code Cong. & Admin.News 4621, 4908. While some have argued that section 357(c) was designed to avoid a negative basis,[7] its application in the Congress's example is also quite reasonable. The transferor, who has already benefited by depreciating the property or holding it while its value appreciates, has income because he will never have to pay the mortgage. Forcing the taxpayer in our case to recognize a gain, however, would be contrary to Congress's intent because it would tax a truly phantom gain, because his liability to the corporation, as we have said, was real, continuing, and indirectly, at least, enforceable by the corporation's creditors.

That section 357(c)'s language can be construed to require unjust and economically unfounded results is clear from the continuing debate over other aspects of the section's operation. In Rosen v. Commissioner, 62 T.C. 11 (1974), aff'd mem., 515 F.2d 507 (3d Cir.1975), for example, the Tax Court held that a transferor had to recognize gain from the assumption of liabilities, even though he remained personally liable and, in fact, paid the obligations himself. The Tax Court commented on section 357(c)'s harshness, noting that it "may even result in the realization of a gain for tax purposes where none in fact exists." Id. at 19. After oral argument, counsel for the Commissioner directed us to a case upholding the constitutionality of section 357(c). The court in that case, however, was not confronted with an exception to its optimistic observation that "[i]t is only when some tax benefit occurs, for example depreciation or further indebtedness on the property which yields tax-free cash not included in cost, that the liabilities will exceed the adjusted basis therein." Wiebusch v. Commissioner, 59 T.C. 777, 781,

---

7. E.g., Cooper, Negative Basis, 75 Harv.L.Rev. 1352, 1358–60 (1962) (arguing that Congress created section 357(c) only to prevent the transferor from accumulating a negative basis in his stock in the transferee-corporation).

aff'd per curiam, 487 F.2d 515 (8th Cir.1973). While we do not rest our decision today on constitutional grounds, we note that *Wiebusch's* analysis would not apply here.

Section 357(c) was amended in 1978 to solve a problem that had forced the courts to fashion delicate constructions of the section's language in order to conform with legislative intent. A cash basis transferor has no basis in accounts receivable. The Tax Court originally held that such a transferor would have to recognize gain if, after counting her accounts payable as transferred liabilities, liabilities exceeded assets. See *Raich,* supra. This analysis meant that the owner of almost any ongoing business transferred liabilities exceeding assets when incorporating. The Tax Court later developed an approach that excluded accounts payable from liabilities, see *Focht,* supra, after this court and the Court of Appeals for the Ninth Circuit announced different interpretations that achieved this result. See *Bongiovanni,* supra; Thatcher v. Commissioner, 533 F.2d 1114 (9th Cir.1976). Congress added section 357(c)(3) in 1978, and it now excludes from subsection (c)(1) "a liability the payment of which * * * would give rise to a deduction." This history, while not directly relevant to Lessinger,[8] is instructive. In *Bongiovanni,* "a too literal reading of the words of the statute [would have] produce[d] an inequitable result which cannot be allowed to stand," 470 F.2d at 924, and "Congress certainly could not have intended such an inequitable result especially in light of its expressed purposes in enacting Sections 351 and 357(c)," id. at 925. We find those words equally applicable here.

We conclude that our holding will not "effectively eliminate section 357(c)." Lessinger experienced no enrichment and had no unrecognized gains whose recognition was appropriate at the time of the consolidation. Any logic that would tax him would certainly represent a "trap for the unwary." *Bongiovanni,* 470 F.2d at 924 (quoting the Commissioner's characterization of the Tax Court's early treatment of cash basis taxpayers under section 351). Lessinger could have achieved incorporation without taxation under the Commissioner's theory by borrowing $260,000 cash, transferring the cash to the corporation (or paying some of the trade accounts payable personally), and later causing the corporation to buy his promissory note from the lender (or pay it off in consideration of his new promise to pay the corporation). If taxpayers who transfer liabilities exceeding assets to controlled corporations are willing to undertake genuine personal liability for the excess, we see no reason to require recognition of a gain, and we do not believe that Congress intended for any gain to be recognized.

Our decision under section 357(c) makes it unnecessary to consider Edith Lessinger's claim for relief as an "innocent spouse." Judgment reversed. * * *

8. Section 357(c)(3) is inapplicable because Lessinger's proprietorship was on the accrual basis. None of the liabilities would have produced deductions if paid by the transferor because those expenses had been previously deducted when they were entered in the proprietorship's records. See 3A Stand.Fed.Tax Rep. (CCH) ¶ 2530.04 (1989).

NOTE

Lessinger is the first case to hold that a shareholder can avoid Section 357(c) gain in a Section 351 exchange by transferring his own promissory note to the corporation. The result in *Lessinger* is appealing and may be consistent with general tax principles, but the Second Circuit's reasoning is questionable. Perhaps the court was trying to say that Mr. Lessinger should receive "basis credit" for his own note because of his future obligation to transfer cash to the corporation or its creditors. In other contexts, a taxpayer's acceptance of even a nonrecourse liability on the acquisition of property gives rise to a cost basis that includes the amount of the future obligation.[1] If Mr. Lessinger's liability were genuine and enforceable by the corporation's creditors, as the court concluded, he arguably is as much entitled to basis credit as is the purchaser of property financed with nonrecourse debt.

But that is not exactly what the court said. To rescue an unwary taxpayer and reach an equitable result, the court engaged in backwards reasoning that does not withstand analysis. The Second Circuit's finding that a shareholder's basis in his own note for Section 357(c) purposes equals its face amount because that was the *corporation's* basis is unsupportable under the Code. A recent commentary on *Lessinger* ably illustrates the faulty logic of the court's loose construction: [2]

> Before turning to the court's application of Section 357(c) to the note—a genuinely intriguing question—one should clear the air about the general question of the basis on which Section 357(c) must be focusing. To say that this is the corporation's basis in the transferred assets is preposterous. If nothing else, such a reading will in many cases be circular. Section 362(a) gives the corporation a carryover basis in the assets received from the shareholder, increased by any gain recognized by the shareholder on the exchange. The classic instance of recognized gain on a Section 351 exchange is under Section 357(c); thus, one cannot determine a corporation's basis in its assets without first determining the shareholder's gain under Section 357(c). To declare, as the Second Circuit did, that the amount of the gain generally turns on the corporation's basis in its assets leads to an endless circle.

> To illustrate, assume a shareholder transfers to a corporation, Blackacre, in which the shareholder has a basis of $30,000, subject to a mortgage of $40,000. To determine the gain under Section 357(c) under the appellate decision in *Lessinger,* one would have to first determine the corporation's

1. Parker v. Delaney, 186 F.2d 455 (1st Cir.1950). Cf. Crane v. Commissioner, 331 U.S. 1, 67 S.Ct. 1047 (1947); Commissioner v. Tufts, 461 U.S. 300, 103 S.Ct. 1826 (1983).

2. Bogdanski, "Shareholder Debt, Corporate Debt: Lessons from *Leavitt* and *Lessinger*", 16 J.Corp.Tax'n 348, 352–53 (1990).

basis under Section 362(a). Under the latter section, however, the corporation's basis must reflect the gain under Section 357(c), and thus, one must compute the shareholder's gain in order to determine the corporation's basis. Perhaps the court meant that one should determine the corporation's basis without regard to the debt, or that Section 357(c) looks at different bases depending on whether a shareholder note or hard assets are being transferred, but these are even more thoroughly incredible stretches of the Code language.

The courts also are confused on a closely related question: whether a shareholder's continuing personal liability on debts transferred to a corporation in a Section 351 transaction causes those debts to be excluded for purposes of Section 357(c). The Tax Court has consistently rejected the notion that transferred liabilities are excluded from the Section 357(c) arithmetic if the transferring shareholder remains personally liable for the debt.[3] The Ninth Circuit once appeared to disagree but recently had a change of heart. In *Jackson v. Commissioner*,[4] that court held that Section 357(c) did not apply on an incorporation of a partnership where the taxpayer's share of the partnership's liabilities exceeded his adjusted basis in the transferred partnership interest but the taxpayer remained personally liable on the debts. On these facts, the court reasoned that the corporation had not assumed any liabilities and thus the taxpayer did not have any Section 357(c) gain. This result was criticized by courts and commentators,[5] but it is consistent with the Second Circuit's reasoning in *Lessinger* that taxpayers enjoy no economic benefit (and thus no taxable gain) for the excess of transferred liabilities over basis when they retain genuine personal liability on the debts. More recently, however, the Ninth Circuit upheld the Tax Court's finding of Section 357(c) gain on a transfer of encumbered equipment to a controlled corporation where the liabilities exceeded the taxpayer's basis even though the transferor had guaranteed the liabilities and remained personally liable following the transfer.[6] Although the court purported to distinguish its earlier opinion in *Jackson*, the two decisions are difficult to reconcile.

The uneasy relationship between owner debt, entity debt and basis is raised in many settings. Similar conceptual questions will resurface with varying results in other contexts involving C corporations and S corporations, as well as partnerships.[7]

3. See, e.g., Smith v. Commissioner, 84 T.C. 889 (1985), affirmed 805 F.2d 1073 (D.C.Cir.1986); Rosen v. Commissioner, 62 T.C. 11 (1974), affirmed in unpublished opinion 515 F.2d 507 (3d Cir.1975).

4. 708 F.2d 1402 (9th Cir.1983).

5. See, e.g., Estate of Juden v. Commissioner, 865 F.2d 960, 962 (8th Cir.1989); Bogdanski, "Of Debt, Discharge, and Discord: Jackson v. Com'r, 10 J.Corp.Tax'n 357 (1984).

6. Owen v. Commissioner, 881 F.2d 832 (9th Cir.1989), cert. denied ___ U.S. ___, 110 S.Ct. 1113 (1990).

7. See, e.g., Chapter 3B, infra (treatment of shareholder guaranteed debt for purposes of characterizing debt and equity in C corporation's capital structure); Chapter 15D, infra (treatment of shareholder debt and S corporation debt guaranteed by shareholders in determining basis of S corporation stock under Section 1366; § 752 (allocation of liabilities in determining

PROBLEMS

1. A organized X Corporation by transferring the following: inventory with a basis of $20,000 and a fair market value of $10,000 and unimproved land held for several years with a basis of $20,000, a fair market value of $40,000 and subject to a mortgage of $30,000. In return, A received 20 shares of X stock (fair market value, $20,000) and X took the land subject to the mortgage.

    (a) Assuming no application of Section 357(b), how much gain, if any, does A recognize and what is A's basis and holding period in the stock?

    (b) What result in (a), above, if the basis of the land were only $5,000?

    (c) In (b), above, what is the character of A's recognized gain under Reg. § 1.357–2(b)? Does this result make sense? How else might the character of A's gain be determined?

    (d) In (b), above, what is X Corporation's basis in the properties received from A?

    (e) What might A have done to avoid the recognition of gain in (b), above?

2. B organized Y Corporation and transferred a building with a basis of $100,000 and a fair market value of $400,000. The building was subject to a first mortgage of $80,000 which was incurred two years ago for valid business reasons. Two weeks before the incorporation of Y, B borrowed $10,000 for personal purposes and secured the loan with a second mortgage on the building. In exchange for the building, Y Corporation will issue $310,000 of Y common stock to B and will take the building subject to the mortgages.

    (a) What are the tax consequences to B on the transfer of the building to Y Corporation?

    (b) What result if B did not borrow the additional $10,000 and, instead, Y Corporation borrowed $10,000 from a bank and gave B $310,000 of Y common stock, $10,000 cash and will take the building subject to the $80,000 first mortgage?

    (c) Is the difference in results between (a) and (b), above, justified?

    (d) When might there be legitimate business reasons for a corporation assuming a transferor's debt or taking property subject to debt?

E. INCORPORATION OF A GOING BUSINESS

The preceding sections were designed to illustrate the basic requirements and exceptions for qualifying as a tax-free incorporation. For pedagogical reasons, the problems have involved relatively isolated

partner's basis in partnership interest and
other purposes).

fact patterns, and it has been assumed that the Code and regulations will provide an answer to virtually every question. When a going business is incorporated, however, matters suddenly become more complex. The mix of assets transferred by a sole proprietorship or partnership may include "ordinary income" property, such as accounts receivable and inventory, and the corporation may inherit accounts payable and supplies the cost of which was deducted by the transferor prior to the incorporation. Questions arise as to the proper taxpayer to report the receivables and to deduct the payables. In addition, these items potentially raise a broad issue that will recur throughout our study of Subchapter C: to what extent must a nonrecognition provision yield to judicially created "common law" principles of taxation or to more general provisions of the Code?

This section examines these issues in the context of three broad principles which may override Section 351: the assignment of income doctrine, the tax benefit rule, and the clear reflection of income doctrine.

HEMPT BROTHERS, INC. v. UNITED STATES *

United States Court of Appeals, Third Circuit, 1974.
490 F.2d 1172, cert. denied 419 U.S. 826, 95 S.Ct. 44 (1974).

ALDISERT, Circuit Judge.

[A cash method partnership transferred all its assets, including $662,820 in zero basis accounts receivable, to a newly formed corporation in exchange for all the corporation's stock. Because the exchange qualified under Section 351, the Service contended that the zero basis in the receivables carried over to the corporation under Section 362 and that the corporation thus realized income upon their collection. In an odd reversal of roles, because the statute of limitations had run on earlier years, the corporation contended that the receivables were not "property" within the meaning of Section 351 and that their transfer to the corporation was an assignment of income by the partnership, subjecting the partners to tax when the receivables were transferred or collected and providing the corporation with a cost (i.e., fair market value) basis and no income upon collection. The Court thus was required to address the relationship between Section 351 and the assignment of income doctrine.]

I.

Taxpayer argues here, as it did in the district court, that because the term "property" as used in Section 351 does not embrace accounts receivable, the Commissioner lacked statutory authority to apply principles associated with Section 351. The district court properly rejected the legal interpretation urged by the taxpayer.

* Some footnotes omitted.

The definition of Section 351 "property" has been extensively treated by the Court of Claims in E.I. Du Pont de Nemours and Co. v. United States, 471 F.2d 1211, 1218–1219 (Ct.Cl.1973), describing the transfer of a non-exclusive license to make, use and sell area herbicides under French patents:

> Unless there is some special reason intrinsic to * * * [Section 351] * * * the general word "property" has a broad reach in tax law. * * * For section 351, in particular, courts have advocated a generous definition of "property," * * * and it has been suggested in one capital gains case that nonexclusive licenses can be viewed as property though not as capital assets. * * *

> We see no adequate reason for refusing to follow these leads.

We fail to perceive any special reason why a restrictive meaning should be applied to accounts receivables so as to exclude them from the general meaning of "property." Receivables possess the usual capabilities and attributes associated with jurisprudential concepts of property law. They may be identified, valued, and transferred. Moreover, their role in an ongoing business must be viewed in the context of Section 351 application. The presence of accounts receivable is a normal, rather than an exceptional accoutrement of the type of business included by Congress in the transfer to a corporate form. They are "commonly thought of in the commercial world as a positive business asset." Du Pont v. United States, supra, at 1218. As aptly put by the district court: "There is a compelling reason to construe 'property' to include * * * [accounts receivable]: a new corporation needs working capital, and accounts receivable can be an important source of liquidity." Hempt Bros., Inc. v. United States, supra, at 1176.[3] In any event, this court had no difficulty in characterizing a sale of receivables as "property" within the purview of the "no gain or loss" provision of Section 337 as a "qualified sale of property within a 12-month period." Citizens Acceptance Corp. v. United States, 462 F.2d 751, 756 (3d Cir.1972).

The taxpayer next makes a strenuous argument that "[t]he government is seeking to tax the wrong person."[4] It contends that the assignment of income doctrine as developed by the Supreme Court

---

3. Du Pont v. United States, supra, at 1214, citing P.A. Birren & Son, Inc. v. Commissioner, 116 F.2d 718 (7th Cir.1940), observed that nonrecognition under Section 351 has been granted for accounts receivable. In the recent case of Thatcher v. Commissioner, 61 T.C. 28 (42 U.S.L.W. 2228, October 30, 1973), the Tax Court reaffirmed its decision in Raich v. Commissioner, 46 T.C. 604 (1966), holding that accounts receivable transferred by a cash basis taxpayer to a corporation under Section 351 had a zero basis. By placing a tax basis in that which was transferred, the Tax Court by implication assumed that accounts receivable are "property" within the meaning of Section 351.

4. We put aside the pragmatic consideration that the transferee-corporate taxpayer raises the argument that the partnership should be taxed at a time when the statute of limitations has presumably run against the transferor partners, who ostensibly are the stockholders of the new corporation.

applies to a Section 351 transfer of accounts receivable so that the transferor, not the transferee-corporation, bears the corresponding tax liability. It argues that the assignment of income doctrine dictates that where the right to receive income is transferred to another person in a transaction not giving rise to tax at the time of transfer, the transferor is taxed on the income when it is collected by the transferee; that the only requirement for its application is a transfer of a right to receive ordinary income; and that since the transferred accounts receivable are a present right to future income, the sole requirement for the application of the doctrine is squarely met. In essence, this is a contention that the nonrecognition provision of Section 351 is in conflict with the assignment of income doctrine and that Section 351 should be subordinated thereto. Taxpayer relies on the seminal case of Lucas v. Earl, 281 U.S. 111, 50 S.Ct. 16, 74 L.Ed. 600 (1930), and its progeny for support of its proposition that the application of the doctrine is mandated whenever one transfers a right to receive ordinary income.

On its part, the government concedes that a taxpayer may sell for value a claim to income otherwise his own and he will be taxable upon the proceeds of the sale. Such was the case in Commissioner v. P.G. Lake, Inc., 356 U.S. 260, 78 S.Ct. 691, 2 L.Ed.2d 743 (1958), in which the taxpayer-corporation assigned its oil payment right to its president in consideration for his cancellation of a $600,000 loan. Viewing the oil payment right as a right to receive future income, the Court applied the reasoning of the assignment of income doctrine, normally applicable to a gratuitous assignment, and held that the consideration received by the taxpayer-corporation was taxable as ordinary income since it essentially was a substitute for that which would otherwise be received at a future time as ordinary income.

Turning to the facts of this case, we note that here there was the transfer of accounts receivable from the partnership to the corporation pursuant to Section 351. We view these accounts receivable as a present right to receive future income. In consideration of the transfer of this right, the members of the partnership received stock—a valid consideration. The consideration, therefore, was essentially a substitute for that which would otherwise be received at a future time as ordinary income to the cash basis partnership. Consequently, the holding in *Lake* would normally apply, and income would ordinarily be realized, and thereby taxable, by the cash basis partnership-transferor at the time of receipt of the stock.

But the terms and purpose of Section 351 have to be reckoned with. By its explicit terms Section 351 expresses the Congressional intent that transfers of property for stock or securities will not result in recognition. It therefore becomes apparent that this case vividly illustrates how Section 351 sometimes comes into conflict with another provision of the Internal Revenue Code or a judicial doctrine,[6] and

6. Weiss, Problems in the Tax-Free Incorporation of a Business, 41 Ind.L.J. 666, 676 (1966). See, e.g., Henry McK. Haserot, 41 T.C. 562 (1964), rev'd and rem'd 355 F.2d 200 (6th Cir.1965).

requires a determination of which of two conflicting doctrines will control.

As we must, when we try to reconcile conflicting doctrines in the revenue law, we endeavor to ascertain a controlling Congressional mandate. Section 351 has been described as a deliberate attempt by Congress to facilitate the incorporation of ongoing businesses and to eliminate any technical constructions which are economically unsound.[7]

Appellant-taxpayer seems to recognize this and argues that application of the *Lake* rationale when accounts receivable are transferred would not create any undue hardship to an incorporating taxpayer. "All a taxpayer [transferor] need do is withhold the earned income items and collect them, transferring the net proceeds to the Corporation. Indeed * * * the transferor should retain both accounts receivable and accounts payable to avoid income recognition at the time of transfer and to have sufficient funds with which to pay accounts payable. Where the taxpayer [transferor] is on the cash method of accounting [as here], the deduction of the accounts payable would be applied against the income generated by the accounts receivable." (Appellant's Brief at 32.)

While we cannot fault the general principle "that income be taxed to him who earns it," to adopt taxpayer's argument would be to hamper the incorporation of ongoing businesses; additionally it would impose technical constructions which are economically and practically unsound. None of the cases cited by taxpayer, including *Lake* itself, persuades us otherwise. In *Lake* the Court was required to decide whether the proceeds from the assignment of the oil payment right were taxable as ordinary income or as long term capital gains. Observing that the provision for long term capital gains treatment "has always been narrowly construed so as to protect the revenue against artful devices," 356 U.S. at 265, 78 S.Ct. at 694, the Court predicated its holding upon an emphatic distinction between a conversion of a capital investment—"income-producing property"—and an assignment of income *per se.* "The substance of what was assigned was the right to receive future income. The substance of what was received was the present value of income which the recipient would otherwise obtain in

7. "One of the purposes of this section [Section 202(c)(3) of the Revenue Act of 1921] was to permit changes in form [of business] involving no change in substance to be made without undue restriction from the tax laws." Note, Section 351 of the Internal Revenue Code and "Mid-Stream" Incorporations, 38 U.Cin.L.Rev. 96 (1969). See, S.Rep. No. 275, 67th Cong. 1st Sess. 11 (1921). This intention is also reflected in the report of the House of Representatives accompanying § 351 of the Internal Revenue Code of 1954. H.R.Rep. No. 1337, 83rd Cong. 2d Sess. 34 (1954).

The House Ways and Means Committee recommended that nonrecognition treat-ment be granted for incorporation, reorganization and certain other types of exchanges to "permit business to go forward with the readjustments required by existing conditions" and to prevent "taxpayers from taking colorable losses in wash sales and other fictitious exchanges." See H.R.Rep. 350, 67th Cong., 1st Sess. 10 (1921). The Senate Finance Committee added that such treatment would eliminate "many technical constructions which are economically unsound." See S.Rep. 275, 67th Cong., 1st Sess. 12 (1921).

Weiss, supra, 41 Ind.L.J. 666 n. 4 (1966).

the future." Ibid., at 266, 78 S.Ct. at 695. A Section 351 issue was not presented in *Lake.* Therefore the case does not control in weighing the conflict between the general rule of assignment of income and the Congressional purpose of nonrecognition upon the incorporation of an ongoing business.[8]

We are persuaded that, on balance, the teachings of *Lake* must give way in this case to the broad Congressional interest in facilitating the incorporation of ongoing businesses. As desirable as it is to afford symmetry in revenue law, we do not intend to promulgate a hard and fast rule.[9] We believe that the problems posed by the clash of conflicting internal revenue doctrines are more properly determined by the circumstances of each case. Here we are influenced by the fact that the subject of the assignment was accounts receivable for partnership's goods and services sold in the regular course of business, that the change of business form from partnership to corporation had a basic business purpose and was not designed for the purpose of deliberate tax avoidance, and by the conviction that the totality of circumstances here presented fit the mold of the Congressional intent to give nonrecognition to a transfer of a total business from a non-corporate to a corporate form.

But this too must be said. Even though Section 351(a) immunizes the transferor from immediate tax consequences, Section 358 retains for the transferors a potential income tax liability to be realized and recognized upon a subsequent sale or exchange of the stock certificates received. As to the transferee-corporation, the tax basis of the receivables will be governed by Section 362.

* * *

NOTE

When there is a valid business purpose for the transfer of receivables and payables on the incorporation of a going business, the Service will issue a ruling that the transferee corporation (and not the transferor) must report the receivables in income as they are collected and deduct the payables when they are paid.[1] This position is consistent

---

8. A second issue in *Fleming,* a companion case to *Lake,* raised the question whether an oil payment for real estate was a "like kind" exchange under § 112(b)(1) of the Internal Revenue Code of 1939. The Court held that the exchange was not "like kind" since its effect is a transfer of future income from oil leases in exchange for real estate. There is no "like kind" requirement under Section 351. See note 1, ante.

9. The Commissioner has apparently taken the position that irrespective of the general principle that income is based upon he who earns it, other considerations should normally control Section 351 transfers. "However, the Service's ruling policy apparently is subject to the proviso that

the taxpayer enter into a closing agreement assuring that the corporation will report the income reflected in the receivables upon their collection or other disposition. It would also appear that favorable rulings will not be issued where the timing of the transfer will be such as to result in a distortion of income. For example, such a ruling presumably could not be obtained if a seasonable business were to be incorporated during the portion of the year occurring after sizeable operating expenses had been incurred but before the income attributable thereto was collected." Weiss, supra, 41 Ind.L.J. at 681 (footnote omitted).

1. Rev.Rul. 80–198, 1980–2 C.B. 113.

with the Government's position in *Hempt Brothers* that the assignment of income doctrine normally will not override Section 351. But to prevent abuse in situations where receivables are accumulated or payables prepaid in anticipation of the incorporation, the Service has noted the following limitations: [2]

> Section 351 of the Code does not apply to a transfer of accounts receivable which constitute an assignment of an income right in a case such as Brown v. Commissioner, 40 B.T.A. 565 (1939), aff'd 115 F.2d 337 (2d Cir.1940). In *Brown,* an attorney transferred to a corporation, in which he was the sole owner, a one-half interest in a claim for legal services performed by the attorney and his law partner. In exchange, the attorney received additional stock of the corporation. The claim represented the corporation's only asset. Subsequent to the receipt by the corporation of the proceeds of the claim, the attorney gave all of the stock of the corporation to his wife. The United States Court of Appeals for the Second Circuit found that the transfer of the claim for the fee to the corporation had no purpose other than to avoid taxes and held that in such a case the intervention of the corporation would not prevent the attorney from being liable for the tax on the income which resulted from services under the assignment of income rule of Lucas v. Earl, 281 U.S. 111 (1930). Accordingly, in a case of a transfer to a controlled corporation of an account receivable in respect of services rendered where there is a tax avoidance purpose for the transaction (which might be evidenced by the corporation not conducting an ongoing business), the Internal Revenue Service will continue to apply assignment of income principles and require that the transferor of such a receivable include it in income when received by the transferee corporation.

> Likewise, it may be appropriate in certain situations to allocate income, deductions, credits, or allowances to the transferor or transferee under section 482 of the Code when the timing of the incorporation improperly separates income from related expenses. See Rooney v. United States, 305 F.2d 681 (9th Cir.1962), where a farming operation was incorporated in a transaction described in section 351(a) after the expenses of the crop had been incurred but before the crop had been sold and income realized. The transferor's tax return contained all of the expenses but none of the farming income to which the expenses related. The United States Court of Appeals for the Ninth Circuit held that the expenses could be allocated under section 482 to the corporation, to be matched with the income to which the expenses related. Similar adjustments may be appropriate where some assets, liabilities, or both, are retained

2.   Id.

by the transferor and such retention results in the income of the transferor, transferee, or both, not being clearly reflected.

Now that the maximum 34 percent corporate rate exceeds the 31 percent top individual rate, the stakes have changed on the contribution of accounts receivable to a newly formed corporation. First, the rate differential may be enough to dissuade a sole proprietor from forming a C corporation.[3] Even if a cash basis proprietor does incorporate, he will be motivated to argue, like the taxpayers in *Hempt Brothers*, that accounts receivable contributed to the corporation are not Section 351 property. The goal, of course, is for the receivables to be taxed at the lower individual rates upon collection. Rather than taking on *Hempt Brothers*, a taxpayer could plan around the problem of higher rates by simply holding back the receivables from the incorporation exchange. But if retention of receivables is coupled with the corporation's assumption of accounts payable, in the hope that the payables may be deducted against other income taxed at the higher corporate rates, the Service may invoke the principles of Revenue Ruling 80–198 and allocate the payables back to the transferor.

Even when a transferor clearly contributes "property" to a newly formed corporation, a problem may arise if the transferor deducted the cost of that property prior to the incorporation. Under the tax benefit rule, if an amount has been deducted and a later event occurs that is fundamentally inconsistent with the premise on which the deduction was initially based, the earlier deduction must be effectively "cancelled out" by the recognition of income equal to the amount previously deducted.[4] For example, a taxpayer who pays $1,000 for minor office supplies to be used in his business would deduct that amount when paid on the assumption that those supplies soon would be exhausted. If that taxpayer later incorporates before the supplies are used and receives $1,000 of stock in the exchange, an event has occurred that is inconsistent with the presumption upon which the earlier deduction was based. But recognition of $1,000 of current income on the transfer of the supplies to a controlled corporation in exchange for its stock is also inconsistent with Section 351.

Whether or not the tax benefit rule in fact applies to Section 351 transfers is unsettled. In *Nash v. United States*,[5] an accrual method taxpayer transferred accounts receivable to a newly formed corporation in exchange for stock. The taxpayer already had included the receivables in income and also had deducted a reserve for bad debts. Applying the tax benefit rule, the Service argued that the taxpayer should be taxed on an amount equal to the previously deducted bad debt reserve because the taxpayer's presumption that some of those debts would turn bad while held in his business had proved erroneous. Although the debts still might become worthless, that event would occur only

---

3. See Chapter 1A, supra.

4. See Bittker, Federal Taxation of Income, Estates and Gifts ¶ 5.7.1 (2d ed. 1989).

5. 398 U.S. 1, 90 S.Ct. 1550 (1970). See also Rev.Rul. 78–280, 1978–2 C.B. 139.

when they were held by the new corporation—a separate business. The Supreme Court held that the net amount the taxpayer had included in his income as a result of the receivables (i.e., the excess of all accrued receivables over the deducted reserve for bad debts) equalled the value of the stock received for the receivables, so that the earlier deduction for the reserve for bad debts was not inappropriate and did not generate income under the tax benefit rule.

PROBLEM

Architect, a cash basis taxpayer, has been conducting a business as a sole proprietorship for several years. Architect decides to incorporate, and on July 1 of the current year he forms Design, Inc., to which he transfers the following assets:

Asset	A.B.	F.M.V.
Accounts Receivable	$ 0	$ 60,000
Supplies	0	20,000
Unimproved Land	60,000	120,000
Total	$ 60,000	$200,000

The supplies were acquired nine months ago and their cost was immediately deducted by Architect as an ordinary and necessary business expense.

In exchange, Architect receives 100 shares of Design common stock with a fair market value of $100,000. In addition, Design assumes $70,000 of accounts payable to trade creditors of Architect's sole proprietorship and a $30,000 bank loan incurred by Architect two years ago for valid business reasons.

Design elects to become a cash method, calendar year taxpayer. During the remainder of the current year, it pays $30,000 of the accounts payable and collects $40,000 of the accounts receivable transferred by Architect.

(a) What are the tax consequences (gain or loss recognized, basis and holding period) of the incorporation to Architect and Design, Inc.?

(b) Who will be taxable upon collection of the accounts receivable: Architect, Design or both?

(c) When Design pays the accounts payable assumed from Architect, may it properly deduct the expenses under Section 162?

(d) Assume that Architect was in the 31% marginal tax bracket and that the corporation anticipated significant taxable income for the current year. What result if Architect decides to retain the accounts receivable but causes the corporation to assume and pay the accounts payable?

(e) Would your answers be any different if Architect had been an accrual method taxpayer?

(f) Is Design, Inc. limited in its choice of accounting method (i.e., cash or accrual) or taxable year? See §§ 441; 448.

F. COLLATERAL ISSUES

1. CONTRIBUTIONS TO CAPITAL

Code: §§ 118(a); 362(a)(2), (c).

Regulations: § 1.118–1.

When a shareholder transfers property to a corporation and does not receive stock or other consideration in exchange, the transaction is a contribution to capital. Although Section 351 does not apply to capital contributions, the shareholder does not recognize gain or loss on a contribution of property other than cash. Instead, the shareholder may increase the basis in her stock by the amount of cash and the adjusted basis of any contributed property.[1] Contributions to capital by shareholders also are excludable from the gross income of the transferee corporation.[2] The corporation's basis in property received as a nontaxable shareholder contribution to capital is the same as the transferor's basis.[3]

If a sole shareholder transfers property to a corporation, or if all shareholders transfer property in the same proportion as their holdings, the issuance of new stock has no economic significance. After some waffling on the issue,[4] the courts now agree that issuance of stock in these circumstances would be "a meaningless gesture" and consequently have held that such transfers are constructive Section 351 exchanges.[5]

Majority shareholders of a distressed corporation occasionally may surrender some of their stock back to the company in order to improve its financial condition. The proper tax treatment of a voluntary non-pro rata contribution of stock perplexed the courts for many years, as taxpayers sought to immediately deduct their basis in the surrendered shares as an ordinary loss while the Service contended that the surrender was akin to a contribution to capital. The *Fink* case, below, is the Supreme Court's resolution of this question.

---

1. Reg. § 1.118–1.

2. I.R.C. § 118(a). Contributions to capital by a nonshareholder (e.g., a transfer of property by a municipality to encourage the corporation to build a facility within the city limits) also are excludable. Reg. § 1.118–1.

3. I.R.C. § 362(a)(2). This rule parallels Section 362(a)(1), which provides that the corporation takes a transferred basis in property received in a Section 351 exchange. For the corporation's basis in property contributed by a nonshareholder, see I.R.C. § 362(c).

4. See, e.g., Abegg v. Commissioner, 429 F.2d 1209 (2d Cir.1970), cert. denied 400 U.S. 1008, 91 S.Ct. 566 (1971).

5. See, e.g., Lessinger v. Commissioner, supra page 82. As *Lessinger* illustrates, applying Section 351 to contributions to capital by a sole shareholder may be significant insofar as it triggers the application of other Code sections, such as Section 357, to the transaction.

COMMISSIONER v. FINK

Supreme Court of the United States, 1987.
483 U.S. 89, 107 S.Ct. 2729.

Justice POWELL delivered the opinion of the Court.

The question in this case is whether a dominant shareholder who voluntarily surrenders a portion of his shares to the corporation, but retains control, may immediately deduct from taxable income his basis in the surrendered shares.

I

Respondents Peter and Karla Fink were the principal shareholders of Travco Corporation, a Michigan manufacturer of motor homes. Travco had one class of common stock outstanding and no preferred stock. Mr. Fink owned 52.2 percent, and Mrs. Fink 20.3 percent, of the outstanding shares.[1] Travco urgently needed new capital as a result of financial difficulties it encountered in the mid–1970s. The Finks voluntarily surrendered some of their shares to Travco in an effort to "increase the attractiveness of the corporation to outside investors." * * * Mr. Fink surrendered 116,146 shares in December 1976; Mrs. Fink surrendered 80,000 shares in January 1977. As a result, the Finks' combined percentage ownership of Travco was reduced from 72.5 percent to 68.5 percent. The Finks received no consideration for the surrendered shares, and no other shareholder surrendered any stock. The effort to attract new investors was unsuccessful, and the corporation eventually was liquidated.

On their 1976 and 1977 joint federal income tax returns, the Finks claimed ordinary loss deductions totaling $389,040, the full amount of their adjusted basis in the surrendered shares.[2] The Commissioner of Internal Revenue disallowed the deductions. He concluded that the stock surrendered was a contribution to the corporation's capital. Accordingly, the Commissioner determined that the surrender resulted in no immediate tax consequences, and that the Finks' basis in the surrendered shares should be added to the basis of their remaining shares of Travco stock.

In an unpublished opinion, the Tax Court sustained the Commissioner's determination for the reasons stated in Frantz v. Commissioner, 83 T.C. 162, 174–182 (1984), aff'd, 784 F.2d 119 (CA2 1986), cert. pending, No. 86–11. In *Frantz* the Tax Court held that a stockholder's non pro rata surrender of shares to the corporation does not produce an immediate loss. The court reasoned that "[t]his conclusion * * *

---

1. In addition, Mr. Fink's sister owned 10 percent of the stock, his brother-in-law owned 4.1 percent, and his mother owned 2.2 percent. App. to Pet. for Cert. 30a.

2. The unadjusted basis of shares is their cost. 26 U.S.C. § 1012. Adjustments to basis are made for, among other things, "expenditures, receipts, losses, or other items, properly chargeable to capital account." § 1016(a)(1).

necessarily follows from a recognition of the purpose of the transfer, that is, to bolster the financial position of [the corporation] and, hence, to protect and make more valuable [the stockholder's] retained shares." 83 T.C., at 181. Because the purpose of the shareholder's surrender is "to decrease or avoid a loss on his overall investment," the Tax Court in *Frantz* was "unable to conclude that [he] sustained a loss at the time of the transaction." Ibid. "Whether [the shareholder] would sustain a loss, and if so, the amount thereof, could only be determined when he subsequently disposed of the stock that the surrender was intended to protect and make more valuable." Ibid. The Tax Court recognized that it had sustained the taxpayer's position in a series of prior cases.[3] Id., at 174–175. But it concluded that these decisions were incorrect, in part because they "encourage[d] a conversion of eventual capital losses into immediate ordinary losses." Id., at 182.[4]

In this case, a divided panel of the Court of Appeals for the Sixth Circuit reversed the Tax Court. 789 F.2d 427 (1986). The court concluded that the proper tax treatment of this type of stock surrender turns on the choice between "unitary" and "fragmented" views of stock ownership. Under the "'fragmented view,'" "each share of stock is considered a separate investment," and gain or loss is computed separately on the sale or other disposition of each share. Id., at 429. According to the "'unitary view,'" "the 'stockholder's entire investment is viewed as a single indivisible property unit,'" ibid. (citation omitted), and a sale or disposition of some of the stockholder's shares only produces "as ascertainable gain or loss when the stockholder has disposed of his remaining shares." Id., at 432. The court observed that both it and the Tax Court generally had adhered to the fragmented view, and concluded that "the facts of the instant case [do not] present

---

3. E.g., Tilford v. Commissioner, 75 T.C. 134 (1980), rev'd, 705 F.2d 828 (CA6), cert. denied, 464 U.S. 992, 104 S.Ct. 485, 78 L.Ed.2d 681 (1983); Smith v. Commissioner, 66 T.C. 622, 648 (1976), rev'd sub nom. Schleppy v. Commissioner, 601 F.2d 196 (CA5 1979); Downer v. Commissioner, 48 T.C. 86, 91 (1967); Estate of Foster v. Commissioner, 9 T.C. 930, 934 (1947); Miller v. Commissioner, 45 B.T.A. 292, 299 (1941); Budd International Corp. v. Commissioner, 45 B.T.A. 737, 755–756 (1941). The Commissioner acquiesced in *Miller* and *Budd,* but later withdrew his acquiescence. See 1941–2 C.B. 9, 1942–2 C.B. 3; 1977–1 C.B. 2.

The dissent overstates the extent to which the Commissioner's disallowance of ordinary loss deductions is contrary to the "settled construction of law." Post, at 2738. In fact, the Commissioner's position was uncertain when the Finks surrendered their shares in 1976 and 1977. Although the Commissioner had acquiesced in the Tax Court's holdings that non pro rata surrenders give rise to ordinary losses, "it

often took a contrary position in litigation." Note, Frantz or Fink: Unitary or Fractional View for Non–Prorata Stock Surrenders, 48 U.Pitt.L.Rev. 905, 908 (1987). See, e.g., Smith v. Commissioner, supra, at 647–650; Duell v. Commissioner, 19 T.C.M. (CCH) 1381 (1960). In 1969, moreover, the Commissioner clearly took the position that a non pro rata surrender by a majority shareholder is a contribution to capital that does not result in an immediate loss. Rev.Rul. 69–368, 1969–2 C.B. 27. Thus, the Finks, unlike the taxpayer in Dickman v. Commissioner, 465 U.S. 330, 104 S.Ct. 1086, 79 L.Ed.2d 343 (1984), knew or should have known that their ordinary loss deductions might not be allowed. For this reason, the Commissioner's disallowance of the Finks' deductions was not an abuse of discretion.

4. The Court of Appeals for the Second Circuit affirmed the Tax Court's holding and agreed with its reasoning. Frantz v. Commissioner, 784 F.2d 119, 123–126 (1986), cert. pending. No. 86–11.

sufficient justification for abandoning" it. Id., at 431. It therefore held that the Finks were entitled to deduct their basis in the surrendered shares immediately as an ordinary loss, except to the extent that the surrender had increased the value of their remaining shares. The Court of Appeals remanded the case to the Tax Court for a determination of the increase, if any, in the value of the Finks' remaining shares that was attributable to the surrender.

Judge Joiner dissented. Because the taxpayers' "sole motivation in disposing of certain shares is to benefit the other shares they hold[,] * * * [v]iewing the surrender of each share as the termination of an individual investment ignores the very reason for the surrender." Id., at 435. He concluded: "Particularly in cases such as this, where the diminution in the shareholder's corporate control and equity interest is so minute as to be illusory, the stock surrender should be regarded as a contribution to capital." Ibid.

We granted certiorari to resolve a conflict among the circuits,[5] 479 U.S. 960, 107 S.Ct. 454, 93 L.Ed.2d 401 (1986), and now reverse.

II

A

It is settled that a shareholder's voluntary contribution to the capital of the corporation has no immediate tax consequences. 26 U.S.C. § 263; 26 CFR § 1.263(a)–2(f) (1986). Instead, the shareholder is entitled to increase the basis of his shares by the amount of his basis in the property transferred to the corporation. See 26 U.S.C. § 1016(a)(1). When the shareholder later disposes of his shares, his contribution is reflected as a smaller taxable gain or a larger deductible loss. This rule applies not only to transfers of cash or tangible property, but also to a shareholder's forgiveness of a debt owed to him by the corporation. 26 CFR § 1.61–12(a) (1986). Such transfers are treated as contributions to capital even if the other shareholders make proportionately smaller contributions, or no contribution at all. See, e.g., Sackstein v. Commissioner, 14 T.C. 566, 569 (1950). The rules governing contributions to capital reflect the general principle that a shareholder may not claim an immediate loss for outlays made to benefit the corporation. Deputy v. du Pont, 308 U.S. 488, 60 S.Ct. 363, 84 L.Ed. 416 (1940); Eskimo Pie Corp. v. Commissioner, 4 T.C. 669, 676 (1945), aff'd, 153 F.2d 301 (CA3 1946). We must decide whether this principle also applies to a controlling shareholder's non pro rata surrender of a portion of his shares.[6]

---

5. The Courts of Appeals for the Second and Fifth Circuits have held that a dominant shareholder's non pro rata stock surrender does not give rise to an ordinary loss. Frantz v. Commissioner, supra; Schleppy v. Commissioner, supra.

6. The Finks concede that a pro rata stock surrender, that by definition does not change the percentage ownership of any shareholder, is not a taxable event. Cf. Eisner v. Macomber, 252 U.S. 189, 40 S.Ct. 189, 64 L.Ed. 521 (1920) (pro rata stock dividend does not produce taxable income).

B

The Finks contend that they sustained an immediate loss upon surrendering some of their shares to the corporation. By parting with the shares, they gave up an ownership interest entitling them to future dividends, future capital appreciation, assets in the event of liquidation, and voting rights.[7] Therefore, the Finks contend, they are entitled to an immediate deduction. See 26 U.S.C. §§ 165(a) and (c)(2). In addition, the Finks argue that any non pro rata stock transaction "give[s] rise to immediate tax results." Brief for Respondents 13. For example, a non pro rata stock divident produces income because it increases the recipient's proportionate ownership of the corporation. Koshland v. Helvering, 298 U.S. 441, 445, 56 S.Ct. 767, 769, 80 L.Ed. 1268 (1936).[8] By analogy, the Finks argue that a non pro rata surrender of shares should be recognized as an immediate loss because it reduces the surrendering shareholder's proportionate ownership.

Finally, the Finks contend that their stock surrenders were not contributions to the corporation's capital. They note that a typical contribution to capital, unlike a non pro rata stock surrender, has no effect on the contributing shareholder's proportionate interest in the corporation. Moreover, the Finks argue, a contribution of cash or other property increases the net worth of the corporation. For example, a shareholder's forgiveness of a debt owed to him by the corporation decreases the corporation's liabilities. In contrast, when a shareholder surrenders shares of the corporation's own stock, the corporation's net worth is unchanged. This is because the corporation cannot itself exercise the right to vote, receive dividends, or receive a share of assets in the event of liquidation. G. Johnson & J. Gentry, Finney and Miller's Principles of Accounting 538 (7th ed. 1974).[9]

III

A shareholder who surrenders a portion of his shares to the corporation has parted with an asset, but that alone does not entitle him to an immediate deduction. Indeed, if the shareholder owns less than 100 percent of the corporation's shares, any non pro rata contribution to the corporation's capital will reduce the net worth of the contributing shareholder.[10] A shareholder who surrenders stock thus is

7. As a practical matter, however, the Finks did not give up a great deal. Their percentage interest in the corporation declined by only four percent. Because the Finks retained a majority interest, this reduction in their voting power was inconsequential. Moreover, Travco, like many corporations in financial difficulties, was not paying dividends.

8. In most cases, however, stock dividends are not recognized as income until the shares are sold. See 26 U.S.C. § 305.

9. Treasury stock—that is, stock that has been issued, reacquired by the corporation, and not canceled—generally is shown as an offset to shareholder's equity on the liability side of the balance sheet. G. Johnson & J. Gentry, Finney & Miller's Principles of Accounting 538 (7th ed. 1974).

10. For example, assume that a shareholder holding an 80 percent interest in a corporation with a total liquidation value of $100,000 makes a non pro rata contribution to the corporation's capital of $20,000

similar to one who forgives or surrenders a debt owed to him by the corporation; the latter gives up interest, principal, and also potential voting power in the event of insolvency or bankruptcy. But, as stated above, such forgiveness of corporate debt is treated as a contribution to capital rather than a current deduction. Supra, at 4. The Finks' voluntary surrender of shares, like a shareholder's voluntary forgiveness of debt owed by the corporation, closely resembles an investment or contribution to capital. See B. Bittker & J. Eustice, Federal Income Taxation of Corporations and Shareholders § 3.14, p. 3–59 (4th ed. 1979) ("If the contribution is voluntary, it does not produce gain or loss to the shareholder"). We find the similarity convincing in this case.

The fact that a stock surrender is not recorded as a contribution to capital on the corporation's balance sheet does not compel a different result. Shareholders who forgive a debt owed by the corporation or pay a corporate expense also are denied an immediate deduction, even though neither of these transactions is a contribution to capital in the accounting sense.[11] Nor are we persuaded by the fact that a stock surrender, unlike a typical contribution to capital, reduces the shareholder's proportionate interest in the corporation. This Court has never held that every change in a shareholder's percentage ownership has immediate tax consequences. Of course, a shareholder's receipt of property from the corporation generally is a taxable event. See 26 U.S.C. §§ 301, 316. In contrast, a shareholder's transfer of property to the corporation usually has no immediate tax consequences. § 263.

The Finks concede that the purpose of their stock surrender was to protect or increase the value of their investment in the corporation. Brief for Respondents 3.[12] They hoped to encourage new investors to provide needed capital and in the long run recover the value of the surrendered shares through increased dividends or appreciation in the value of their remaining shares. If the surrender had achieved its purpose, the Finks would not have suffered an economic loss. See Johnson, Tax Models for Nonprorata Shareholder Contributions, 3 Va. Tax.Rev. 81, 104–108 (1983). In this case, as in many cases involving closely-held corporations whose shares are not traded on an open market, there is no reliable method of determining whether the surrender will result in a loss until the shareholder disposes of his remaining shares. Thus, the Finks' stock surrender does not meet the require-

in cash. Assume further that the shareholder has no other assets. Prior to the contribution, the shareholder's net worth was $100,000 ($20,000 plus 80 percent of $100,000). If the corporation were immediately liquidated following the contribution, the shareholder would receive only $96,000 (80 percent of $120,000). Of course such a non pro rata contribution is rare in practice. Typically a shareholder will simply purchase additional shares.

11. It is true that a corporation's stock is not considered an asset of the corpora-

tion. A corporation's own shares nevertheless may be as valuable to the corporation as other property contributed by shareholders, as treasury shares may be resold. This is evidenced by the fact that corporations often purchase their own shares on the open market.

12. Indeed, if the Finks did not make this concession their surrender probably would be treated as a non-deductible gift. See 26 CFR § 25.2511–1(h)(1) (1986).

ment that an immediately deductible loss must be "actually sustained during the taxable year." 26 CFR § 1.165–1(b) (1986).

Finally, treating stock surrenders as ordinary losses might encourage shareholders in failing corporations to convert potential capital losses to ordinary losses by voluntarily surrendering their shares before the corporation fails. In this way shareholders might avoid the consequences of 26 U.S.C. § 165(g)(1), that provides for capital loss treatment of stock that becomes worthless.[13] Similarly, shareholders may be encouraged to transfer corporate stock rather than other property to the corporation in order to realize a current loss.[14]

We therefore hold that a dominant shareholder who voluntarily surrenders a portion of his shares to the corporation, but retains control, does not sustain an immediate loss deductible from taxable income. Rather, the surrendering shareholder must reallocate his basis in the surrendered shares to the shares he retains.[15] The share-

---

13. The Tax Reform Act of 1986, Pub.L. 99–514, §§ 301, 311, 100 Stat. 2216, 2219 (Oct. 22, 1986), eliminated the differential tax rates for capital gains and ordinary income. [A small capital gains rate preference for individuals was restored in the Revenue Reconciliation Act of 1990. Ed.] The difference between a capital loss and an ordinary loss remains important, however, because individuals are permitted to deduct only $3,000 of capital losses against ordinary income each year, and corporations may not deduct any capital losses from ordinary income. 26 U.S.C. § 1211. In contrast, ordinary losses generally are deductible from ordinary income without limitation. §§ 165(a) and (c)(2).

The Court of Appeals in this case did not discuss the possibility of allowing a capital loss rather than an ordinary loss, and the parties raise it only in passing. We note, however that a capital loss is realized only upon the "sal[e] or exchang[e]" of a capital asset. 26 U.S.C. § 1211(b)(3). A voluntary surrender, for no consideration, would not seem to qualify as a sale or exchange. *Frantz v. Commissioner,* 784 F.2d, at 124.

14. Our holding today also draws support from two other sections of the Code. First, § 83 provides that, if a shareholder makes a "bargain sale" of stock to a corporate officer or employee as compensation, the "bargain" element of the sale must be treated as a contribution to the corporation's capital. S.Rep. No. 91–552, pp. 123–124 (1969), 1969 U.S.Code Cong. & Admin. News 1978, pp. 2027, 2155; 26 CFR § 1.83–6(d) (1986). Section 83 reversed the result in *Downer v. Commissioner,* 48 T.C. 86 (1967), a decision predicated on the fragmented view of stock ownership adopted by the Court of Appeals in this case. To be

sure, Congress was concerned in § 83 with transfers of restricted stock to employees as compensation rather than surrenders of stock to improve the corporation's financial condition. In both cases, however, the shareholder's underlying purpose is to increase the value of his investment.

Second, if a shareholder's stock is redeemed—that is, surrendered to the corporation in return for cash or other property—the shareholder is not entitled to an immediate deduction unless the redemption results in a substantial reduction in the shareholder's ownership percentage. §§ 302(a), (b), (d); 26 CFR § 1.302–2(c) (1986). Because the Finks' surrenders resulted in only a slight reduction in their ownership percentage, they would not have been entitled to an immediate loss if they had received consideration for the surrendered shares. 26 U.S.C. § 302(b). Although the Finks did not receive a direct payment of cash or other property, they hoped to be compensated by an increase in the value of their remaining shares.

15. The Finks remained the controlling shareholders after their surrender. We therefore have no occasion to decide in this case whether a surrender that causes the shareholder to lose control of the corporation is immediately deductible. In related contexts, the Code distinguishes between minimal reductions in a shareholder's ownership percentage and loss of corporate control. See § 302(b)(2) (providing "exchange" rather than dividend treatment for a "substantially disproportionate redemption of stock" that brings the shareholder's ownership percentage below 50 percent); § 302(b)(3) (providing similar treatment when the redemption termi-

holder's loss, if any, will be recognized when he disposes of his remaining shares.   A reallocation of basis is consistent with the general principle that "[p]ayments made by a stockholder of a corporation for the purpose of protecting his interest therein must be regarded as [an] additional cost of his stock," and so cannot be deducted immediately. Eskimo Pie Corp. v. Commissioner, 4 T.C. 669, 676 (1945), aff'd, 153 F.2d 301 (CA3 1946).   Our holding today is not inconsistent with the settled rule that the gain or loss on the sale or disposition of shares of stock equals the difference between the amount realized in the sale or disposition and the shareholder's basis in the particular shares sold or exchanged.   See 26 U.S.C. § 1001(a); 26 CFR § 1.1012–1(c)(1) (1986). We conclude only that a controlling shareholder's voluntary surrender of shares, like contributions of other forms of property to the corporation, is not an appropriate occasion for the recognition of gain or loss.

In this case we use the term "control" to mean ownership of more than half of a corporation's voting shares.   We recognize, of course, that in larger corporations—especially those whose shares are listed on a national exchange—a person or entity may exercise control in fact while owning less than a majority of the voting shares.   See Securities Exchange Act of 1934, § 13(d), 48 Stat. 894, 15 U.S.C. § 78m(d) (requiring persons to report acquisition of more than 5 percent of a registered equity security).

IV

For the reasons we have stated, the judgment of the Court of Appeals for the Sixth Circuit is reversed.

It is so ordered.

Justice BLACKMUN concurs in the result.

Justice WHITE, concurring.

Although I join the Court's opinion, I suggest that there is little substance in the reservation in footnote 15 of the question whether a surrender of stock that causes the stockholder to lose control of the corporation is immediately deductible as an ordinary loss.   Of course, this case does not involve a loss of control; but as I understand the rationale of the Court's opinion, it would also apply to a surrender that results in loss of control.   At least I do not find in the opinion any principled ground for distinguishing a loss-of-control case from this one.

Justice SCALIA, concurring in the judgment.

I do not believe that the Finks' surrender of their shares was, or even closely resembles, a shareholder contribution to corporate capital. Since, however, its purpose was to make the corporation a more valuable investment by giving it a more attractive capital structure, I think that it was, no less than a contribution to capital, an "amount paid out *   *   * for *   *   * betterments made to increase the value of

nates the shareholder's interest in the corporation).

* * * property," 26 U.S.C. § 263(a)(1), and thus not entitled to treatment as a current deduction.

Justice STEVENS, dissenting.

The value of certain and predictable rules of law is often underestimated. Particularly in the field of taxation, there is a strong interest in enabling taxpayers to predict the legal consequences of their proposed actions, and there is an even stronger general interest in ensuring that the responsibility for making changes in settled law rests squarely on the shoulders of Congress. In this case, these interests are of decisive importance for me.

The question of tax law presented by this case was definitively answered by the Board of Tax Appeals in 1941. See Miller v. Commissioner, 45 B.T.A. 292, 299; Budd International Corp. v. Commissioner, 45 B.T.A. 737, 755–756.[1] Those decisions were consistently followed for over 40 years, see, e.g., Smith v. Commissioner, 66 T.C. 622, 648 (1976); Downer v. Commissioner, 48 T.C. 86, 91 (1967); Estate of Foster v. Commissioner, 9 T.C. 930, 934 (1947), and the Internal Revenue Service had announced its acquiescence in the decisions. See 1941–2 C.B. 9 (acquiescing in *Miller*); 1942–2 C.B. 3 (acquiescing in *Budd International*). Although Congress dramatically revamped the tax code in 1954, see Internal Revenue Code of 1954, Pub.L. 83–591, 68A Stat. 3, it did not modify the Tax Court's approach to this issue.

It was only in 1977 (after the Finks had transferred their stock to the corporation), that the Commission retracted its acquiescence in the Tax Court's interpretation.[2] But instead of asking Congress to reject the longstanding interpretation, the Commission asked the courts to take another look at the statute. Two Courts of Appeals accepted the Commission's new approach, and reversed the Tax Court without giving much, if any, weight to the Tax Court's nearly half-century old construction.[3] Tilford v. Commissioner, 705 F.2d 828 (CA6 1983); Schleppy v. Commissioner, 601 F.2d 196 (CA5 1979). After these two reversals, the Tax Court itself reversed its position in 1984, believing that "[r]ecent appellate level disapproval of the position renders it inappropriate for us to continue to justify the position solely on the basis of its history." Frantz v. Commissioner, 83 T.C. 162, 174–182 (1984), aff'd, 784 F.2d 119 (CA2 1986), cert. pending, No. 86–11.

I believe that these courts erred in reversing the longstanding interpretation of the Tax Code. The Commissioner of Internal Revenue certainly had a right to advocate a change, but in my opinion he should

---

1. The principle applied in those decisions dates back even further. See Burdick v. Commissioner, 20 B.T.A. 742 (1930), aff'd, 59 F.2d 395 (1932); Wright v. Commissioner, 18 B.T.A. 471 (1929).

2. The Commission appears to have begun reconsidering its position around 1969. See Note, *Frantz or Fink:* Unitary or Fractional View for Non–Prorata Stock Surrenders, 48 U.Pitt.L.Rev. 905, 908–909 (1987) (hereafter Note).

3. Ignoring the import of the long line of Tax Court cases, one court stated: "We find no Court of Appeals decision that determines the correctness of these decisions. We therefore write on a clean sheet." Schleppy v. Commissioner, 601 F.2d 196, 198 (1979).

have requested relief from the body that has the authority to amend the Internal Revenue Code. For I firmly believe that "after a statute has been construed, either by this Court or by a consistent course of decision by other federal judges and agencies, it acquires a meaning that should be as clear as if the judicial gloss had been drafted by the Congress itself." Shearson/American Express v. McMahon, 482 U.S. 220, ——, 107 S.Ct. 2332, 2359, 96 L.Ed.2d 185 (1987) (STEVENS, J., concurring in part and dissenting in part). A rule of statutory construction that "has been consistently recognized for more than 35 years" acquires a clarity that "is simply beyond peradventure." Herman & MacLean v. Huddleston, 459 U.S. 375, 380, 103 S.Ct. 683, 686, 74 L.Ed.2d 548 (1983).

There may, of course, be situations in which a past error is sufficiently blatant "to overcome the strong presumption of continued validity that adheres in the judicial interpretation of a statute." Square D Co. v. Niagara Frontier Tariff Bureau, 476 U.S. 409, 424, 106 S.Ct. 1922, 1930, 90 L.Ed.2d 413 (1986). But this is surely not such a case.[4] The Court makes no serious effort to demonstrate that its result is compelled by—or even consistent with—the language of the statute.[5] The mere fact that the Court's interpretation of the Internal Revenue Code may be preferable to the view that prevailed for years is not, in my opinion, a sufficient reason for changing the law.

If Congress lacked the power to amend statutes to rectify past mistakes, and if the only value to be achieved in construing statutes were accurate interpretation, it would be clear that a court or agency should feel free at any time to reject a past erroneous interpretation and replace it with the one it believes to be correct. But neither of these propositions is true; Congress does have the ability to rectify misinterpretations, and, once a statute has been consistently interpreted in one way, there are institutional and reliance values that are

4. Strong arguments can be made in support of either view, as the split between the Second and Sixth Circuits, and the dissenting opinion of the four Tax Court Judges indicates. See Frantz v. Commissioner, 83 T.C. 162, 187 (1984) (Parker, J., with whom Fay, Goffe, and Wiles, JJ., joined, dissenting). See also Bolding, Non–Pro Rata Stock Surrenders: Capital Contribution, Capital Loss or Ordinary Loss?, 32 Tax Law. 275 (1979); Note, supra. Whether it makes sense to encourage stock surrenders that may enable a sinking corporation to stay afloat in cases like this is at least debatable. But whatever the correct policy choice may be, I would adhere to an interpretation of technical statutory language that has been followed consistently for over 40 years until Congress decides to change the law. Surely that is the wisest course when the language of the statute provides arguable support for the settled rule.

5. Uncharacteristically, the Court does not begin its analysis by quoting any statutory language, cf. Blue Chip Stamps v. Manor Drug Stores, 421 U.S. 723, 756, 95 S.Ct. 1917, 1935, 44 L.Ed.2d 539 (1975) (POWELL, J., concurring), either from § 165 of the Code, which defines "losses," or from § 1016, which deals with adjustments to basis. Rather, it launches into a discussion of voluntary contributions to capital, see ante, at 2732, even though this was clearly not such a contribution because it had no impact on the net worth of the corporation. The opinion includes a discussion of a hypothetical example, ante, at 2733, n. 10, and policy reasons supporting the Court's result, but surprisingly little mention of statutory text. The statutory basis for the taxpayer's position is adequately explained in the opinions cited ante, at 2731, n. 3.

often even more important than the initial goal of accurate interpretation.

The relationship between the courts or agencies, on the one hand, and Congress, on the other, is a dynamic one. In the process of legislating it is inevitable that Congress will leave open spaces in the law that the courts are implicitly authorized to fill. The judicial process of construing statutes must therefore include an exercise of lawmaking power that has been delegated to the courts by the Congress. But after the gap has been filled, regardless of whether it is filled exactly as Congress might have intended or hoped, the purpose of the delegation has been achieved and the responsibility for making any future change should rest on the shoulders of the Congress. Even if it is a consensus of lower federal court decisions, rather than a decision by this Court, that has provided the answer to a question left open or ambiguous in the original text of the statute, there is really no need for this Court to revisit the issue. Moreover, if Congress understands that as long as a statute is interpreted in a consistent manner, it will not be re-examined by the courts except in the most extraordinary circumstances, Congress will be encouraged to give close scrutiny to judicial interpretations of its work product. We should structure our principles of statutory construction to invite continuing congressional oversight of the interpretive process.[6]

Our readiness to reconsider long-settled constructions of statutes takes its toll on the courts as well. Except in the rarest of cases, I believe we should routinely follow Justice Cardozo's admonition:

> "[T]he labor of judges would be increased almost to the breaking point if every past decision could be reopened in every case, and one could not lay one's own course of bricks on the secure foundation of the courses laid by others who had gone before him." B. Cardozo, The Nature of the Judicial Process 149 (1921).

In addition to the institutional ramifications of rejecting settled constructions of law, fairness requires consideration of the effect that changes have on individuals' reasonable reliance on a previous interpretation. This case dramatically illustrates the problem. Mr. Fink surrendered his shares in December 1976. Mrs. Fink surrendered hers in January 1977. At that time the law was well settled: the Tax Court had repeatedly reaffirmed the right to deduct such surrenders as

---

6. "The doctrine of *stare decisis* has a more limited application when the precedent rests on constitutional grounds, because 'correction through legislative action is practically impossible.' Burnet v. Coronado Oil & Gas Co., 285 U.S. 393, 407–408, 52 S.Ct. 443, 447–448, 76 L.Ed. 815 (Brandeis, J., dissenting). See Mitchell v. W.T. Grant Co., 416 U.S. 600, 627, 94 S.Ct. 1895, 1909, 40 L.Ed.2d 406 (POWELL, J., concurring)." Thomas v. Washington Gas Light Co., 448 U.S. 261, 272–273, n. 18, 100 S.Ct. 2647, 2656–2657, n. 18, 65 L.Ed.2d 757 (1980) (plurality opinion).

See also Edelman v. Jordan, 415 U.S. 651, 671, 94 S.Ct. 1347, 1359, 39 L.Ed.2d 662 (1974); Boys Markets v. Retail Clerks, 398 U.S. 235, 259–260, 90 S.Ct. 1583, 1596–1597, 26 L.Ed.2d 199 (1970) (Black, J., dissenting); Swift & Co. v. Wickham, 382 U.S. 111, 133–134, 86 S.Ct. 258, 270–271, 15 L.Ed.2d 194 (1965) (Douglas, J., dissenting).

ordinary losses, and the Commission had acquiesced in this view for 35 years.[7] See supra, p. 2736. It was only on April 11, 1977, that the Commission announced its nonacquiescence. See Internal Revenue Bulletin No. 1977–15, p. 6 (April 11, 1977). "In my view, the retroactive application of the Court's holding in a case like this is unfair to the individual taxpayer as well as unwise judicial administration." Dickman v. Commissioner, 465 U.S. 330, 353, n. 11, 104 S.Ct. 1086, 1094, n. 11, 79 L.Ed.2d 343 (1984) (POWELL, J., dissenting).

I respectfully dissent.

2. INTENTIONAL AVOIDANCE OF SECTION 351

Section 351 is not an elective provision. It applies whenever its requirements are met. Historically taxpayers sometimes attempted to avoid Section 351 in order to recognize a loss [1] or to step-up the basis of an asset after recognizing a gain to increase the transferee corporation's cost recovery deductions.[2] When long-term capital gains enjoyed a significant tax rate preference, taxpayers also found it advantageous to freeze appreciation as capital gain on an asset that was about to be converted into "ordinary income" property—e.g., land held for investment that the taxpayer intended to subdivide. In these cases, the tax savings achieved by converting ordinary income into capital gain outweighed the disadvantage of accelerating part of the gain.

Most of the historical incentives for avoiding Section 351 disappeared under the post–1986 rate structure. For example, with corporate tax rates higher than individual rates, an individual taxpayer holding a loss asset may now prefer to shift the loss and resulting tax benefit to a corporation by transferring the asset in a Section 351 exchange. The modest capital gains rate preference currently in the Code probably is not sufficient to motivate taxpayers to accelerate recognition of a capital gain by avoiding Section 351. Assuming the ultimate sale does not occur for some period of time, the benefits of tax deferral will outweigh any tax savings from the preferential capital gains rate.

7. The Internal Revenue Service's Cumulative Bulletin explains the effect of an announcement of acquiescence:

"In order that taxpayers and the general public may be informed whether the Commissioner has acquiesced in a decision of the Tax Court of the United States, formally known as the United States Board of Tax Appeals, disallowing a deficiency in tax determined by the Commissioner to be due, announcement will be made in the semimonthly Internal Revenue Bulletin at the earliest practicable date. Notice that the Commissioner has acquiesced or nonacquiesced in a decision of the Tax Court relates only to the issue or issues decided adversely to the Government. *Decisions so*

acquiesced in should be relied upon by officers and employees of the Bureau of Internal Revenue as precedents in the disposition of other cases." 1942–2 C.B. IV (emphasis added).

1. Recognition of losses in this manner on a sale between a controlling (more than 50 percent) shareholder and a corporation would be limited by Section 267.

2. But see I.R.C. § 1239, which characterizes gain on sales of property between related taxpayers (e.g., a corporation and a more–than–50–percent shareholder) as ordinary income if the property is depreciable in the hands of the transferee.

On the chance (certainty?) that rates may change again during the shelf life of this edition, a few words about some typical Section 351 avoidance techniques are in order. As illustrated by the *Intermountain Lumber* case earlier in the chapter,[3] one potentially successful avoidance strategy is to break control after the exchange by a prearranged disposition of more than 20 percent of the stock. Another possibility is to structure an incorporation transfer as a taxable "sale" rather than a tax-free Section 351 exchange.[4]

To illustrate the sale technique, assume Investor owns undeveloped land with an adjusted basis of $50,000 and a fair market value of $300,000. Investor intends to subdivide the land and sell home sites at an aggregate sales price of $500,000. If he developed the land as an individual, Investor would recognize $450,000 of ordinary income.[5] But if capital gains are taxed at a significantly lower rate than ordinary income, he might benefit by selling the land to a controlled corporation for $300,000 of corporate installment obligations. He would recognize $250,000 of predevelopment capital gain on the sale, the corporation would take a $300,000 stepped-up basis in the land, and the future ordinary income would be limited to $200,000.

The sale strategy worked in Bradshaw v. United States,[6] where the taxpayer transferred 40 acres of Georgia land in which he had a basis of $8,500 to a new corporation in exchange for $250,000 of unsecured corporate installment notes. The corporation's only other capital was a $4,500 automobile transferred on the same day in exchange for common stock. The court treated the transfer of land as a sale and permitted the taxpayer to report his gain on the installment method.[7] In so doing, the court rejected the Service's claim that the notes were really stock even though it conceded that the corporation was thinly capitalized. A contrary result was reached in Burr Oaks Corp. v. Commissioner,[8] where three taxpayers transferred land to a corporation in exchange for two-year notes with a face amount of $330,000. The corporation's only equity capital was $4,500. The court held that the transfer was a nontaxable Section 351 exchange rather than a sale because the notes, payment of which was dependent on the profitability of an undercapitalized corporation, were really preferred stock.

In the last analysis, resolution of the "Section 351 vs. sale" issue turns on the facts in each case and the court's inclination to reclassify what the taxpayer labels "debt" into what the Service believes to be

---

3. See p. 62, supra.

4. See generally Bittker & Eustice, Federal Income Taxation of Corporations and Shareholders ¶ 3.14 (5th ed. 1987).

5. For convenience, assume no upward adjustments to basis during the subdivision phase.

6. 683 F.2d 365 (Ct.Cl.1982).

7. The deferral achieved by the taxpayer in *Bradshaw* is foreclosed under current law. Because a shareholder and his wholly owned corporation are "related parties," a later sale of the land by the corporation will accelerate recognition of any gain that otherwise would be deferred on the shareholder's installment sale to the corporation. I.R.C. § 453(e), (f)(1).

8. 365 F.2d 24 (7th Cir.1966), cert. denied 385 U.S. 1007, 87 S.Ct. 713 (1967). See also Aqualane Shores, Inc. v. Commissioner, 269 F.2d 116 (5th Cir.1959).

"equity." The debt versus equity classification issue is discussed extensively in Chapter 3.[9]

3. ORGANIZATIONAL EXPENSES

Code: §§ 212(3); 248.

Regulations: § 1.248–1(a), (b).

A corporation incurs a variety of expenses in connection with its incorporation. These organizational expenses traditionally were regarded as capital expenditures that only could be deducted when the corporation was dissolved. Since 1954, however, a corporation may elect under Section 248 to amortize certain qualifying "organizational expenditures" over a period of sixty months or more beginning with the month in which the corporation commences business. "Organizational expenditures" are defined by Section 248(b) as expenditures which are: (1) incident to the creation of the corporation, (2) chargeable to capital account, and (3) of a character which, if expended to create a corporation having a limited life, would be amortizable over that life. Examples include legal fees for drafting the corporate charter and bylaws, fees paid to the state of incorporation, and necessary accounting services.[1] Specifically excluded are the costs of issuing or selling stock and expenditures connected with the transfer of assets to the corporation, presumably because such expenses do not create an asset that is exhausted over the life of the corporation.[2] Expenses incurred by the corporation in connection with the acquisition of a specific asset may be added to the corporation's basis in that asset.

Whether or not they are borne by the corporation, certain items are considered as expenses of the shareholders and, as such, they may neither be deducted nor amortized by the corporation. For example, expenses connected with the acquisition of stock (e.g., appraisal fees) must be capitalized and added to the shareholder's basis in the stock.[3]

PROBLEM

A currently conducts a computer software manufacturing business as a sole proprietorship. With the assistance of B, a wealthy investor, A plans to incorporate and then expand the business. A will contribute the assets and liabilities of her proprietorship and B will invest enough cash to give him a 49 percent interest in the corporation. After numerous appraisals, lengthy negotiations and considerable expense, A and B have agreed that the net worth of A's proprietorship is $510,000. B thus will contribute $490,000 cash for his 49 percent interest.

9. See Chapter 3B, infra.

1. Reg. § 1.248–1(b)(2).

2. Reg. § 1.248–1(b)(3)(i). See S.Rep. No. 1622, 83d Cong.2d Sess. 224.

3. See Woodward v. Commissioner, 397 U.S. 572, 90 S.Ct. 1302 (1970); United States v. Hilton Hotels Corp., 397 U.S. 580, 90 S.Ct. 1307 (1970).

To what extent are the following expenses incurred in connection with the incorporation either currently deductible or amortizable under Section 248:

(a) $3,000 in fees paid by A for appraisals of her proprietorship for purposes of the negotiations with B.

(b) Is there any difference in (a), above, if the appraisal fees are paid by the corporation?

(c) Legal fees paid by the corporation for the following services:

  (i) drafting the articles of incorporation, by laws and minutes of the first meeting of directors and shareholders;

  (ii) preparation of deeds and bills of sale transferring A's assets to the corporation;

  (iii) application for a permit from the state commissioner of corporations to issue the stock and other legal research relating to exempting the stock from registration under federal securities laws;

  (iv) preparation of a request for a Section 351 ruling from the Internal Revenue Service;

  (v) drafting a buy-sell agreement providing for the repurchase of shares by the corporation in the event A or B dies or becomes incapacitated.

(d) Same as (c), above, except the legal fees were all paid by A.

CHAPTER 3. THE CAPITAL STRUCTURE OF A CORPORATION

A. INTRODUCTION

The organizers of a newly formed corporation face a major decision in planning the capital structure of the company. The simplest method of raising corporate capital is by issuing stock in exchange for contributions of money, property or services. Stock—known as "equity" in corporate finance parlance—may be common or preferred, and either type may be issued in various classes with different rights and priorities as to voting, dividends, liquidations and the like. In addition to issuing stock, a corporation may raise capital by borrowing, either from the same insider group that owns the company's stock or from banks and other outside lenders. Corporate loans typically are evidenced by a variety of instruments including bonds, notes and more exotic hybrid securities such as convertible debentures. Although both shareholders and creditors contribute capital, their relationship to the corporation may be markedly different. As one early case put it, a shareholder is "an adventurer in the corporate business," taking risk and profit from success, while a creditor, "in compensation for not sharing the profits, is to be paid independently of the risk of success, and gets a right to dip into capital when the payment date arrives." [1]

To some extent, decisions concerning the proper mix of debt and equity are made apart from tax considerations. Most businesses rely on both short and long-term debt to finance their operations. Quite apart from taxes, traditional corporate finance theorists believed that debt financing contributed to a higher rate of investment return.[2] On the other hand, excessive debt has its pitfalls, and prudent managers of conservatively managed public companies may be reluctant to risk insolvency or a shaky credit rating by loading the corporate balance sheet with liabilities.[3] The simple point is that innumerable factors other than taxes affect corporate financing decisions.

Although tax system may not drive financing behavior, it profoundly influences the capital structure of both publicly traded and closely held C corporations. Consider the decision facing A and B, who each

1. Commissioner v. O.P.P. Holding Corp., 76 F.2d 11, 12 (2d Cir.1935).

2. The traditional view did not go unchallenged. In their well known writings on corporate finance, Professors Miller and Modigiliani take the view that, assuming away taxes and other factors, the value of a corporation is unrelated to the amount of debt used in its capital structure. For general discussions of the debate, see Hamilton, Fundamentals of Modern Business

§ 13.18 (1989); Klein & Coffee, Business Organization and Finance 306–338 (4th ed. 1990).

3. The statement in the text is belied by the surge of debt financing that accompanied the corporate mergers and restructurings of the 1980s. The nontax risks of excessive debt are being well documented by the collapse of the junk bond market and the wave of insolvencies in the early 1990s.

plan to invest $100,000 on the formation of closely held Newco, Inc. At first glance, it might seem that issuing any Newco debt to A and B would be a needless exercise. If the investors agree on their respective contributions and the allocation of ownership and voting power, what difference does it make whether they hold stock, bonds or notes? The answer often lies in the Internal Revenue Code, which distinguishes between debt and equity for tax purposes, tipping the scales in favor of issuing a healthy dose of debt. This tax bias toward debt financing is influential both at the time of formation and on later occasions when an infusion of additional capital is required.

The principal advantage of issuing debt as opposed to equity is avoidance of the "double tax." [4] Dividends are includible in the income of the noncorporate shareholders who receive them but are not deductible by the corporation. The earnings represented by these dividends are thus taxed at both the corporate and shareholder levels.[5] But interest paid on corporate debt, while also includible in the recipient's income, is deductible by the corporation.[6] Assuming the owners of the business desire some ongoing return on their investment, there may be an incentive to distribute earnings with tax-deductible dollars.[7]

Several other features of the tax law reflect a bias in favor of debt over equity. The repayment of principal on a corporate debt is a tax-free return of capital to the lender. If the amount repaid exceeds the lender's basis in the debt, the difference generally is treated as a capital gain under Section 1271. In contrast, when a corporation redeems (i.e., buys back) stock from a shareholder—a transaction quite similar to the repayment of a debt—the entire amount received may be taxed as a dividend if the shareholder or related persons continue to own stock in the corporation.[8]

The issuance of debt at the time of incorporation also may provide a defense against subsequent imposition of the accumulated earnings tax, an "anti-avoidance" penalty to be discussed in a later chapter.[9] The obligation to repay a debt at maturity may qualify as a "reasonable business need," justifying an accumulation of corporate earnings,[10] while the same type of accumulation for a redemption of stock normal-

---

4. See Chapter 1A, supra.

5. The 70 percent dividends received deduction provides relief for corporate shareholders. See I.R.C. § 243 and Chapter 4A, infra.

6. I.R.C. § 163(a).

7. But see Andrews, "Tax Neutrality Between Equity Capital and Debt," 30 Wayne L.Rev. 1057 (1984), suggesting that this traditional "simple view" is inadequate because it fails to recognize the opportunity for corporations to raise equity capital by accumulating earnings—a pro-

cess that redounds to the benefit of shareholders without subjecting them to tax until the earnings are distributed or the shares are sold.

8. I.R.C. § 302. See Chapter 5C, infra.

9. I.R.C. § 531 et seq. See Chapter 9B, infra.

10. Reg. § 1.537–2(b)(3). Repayment of debt owed to shareholders, however, may be subjected to greater scrutiny. See Smoot Sand & Gravel Corp. v. Commissioner, 241 F.2d 197 (4th Cir.), cert. denied 354 U.S. 922, 77 S.Ct. 1383 (1957).

ly is not regarded as reasonable for purposes of the accumulated earnings tax.[11]

The choice between debt and equity has significant tax ramifications in many other contexts. We have seen that the classification of a corporate investment may have an impact on whether a transaction qualifies under Section 351. Complete nonrecognition of gain or loss is available only when the contributing taxpayer receives solely stock.[12] Conversely, taxpayers who wish to recognize gain on the transfer of property to a controlled corporation may attempt to accomplish their objective by taking back boot in the form of installment debt obligations.[13] The goal will be thwarted if the notes are reclassified as stock. Classification of an interest in a corporation also may control the character of a loss if the investment becomes worthless.[14]

The tax distinctions between debt and equity have fueled an ongoing policy debate. The relationship between the favorable tax treatment of debt and the explosive growth in debt-financed corporate acquisitions in the 1980's has captured public attention. But Congress to date has declined to embrace a comprehensive legislative solution to the problems of excessive debt. Instead, it has been content to enact narrowly targeted provisions aimed at isolated abuses that are seen as threats to the integrity of the corporate income tax. The excerpt below from a recent Congressional study on the income tax aspects of corporate financial structures offers some general insights into the debt vs. equity policy debate. Consideration of recent legislation designed to curb leveraged buyouts and other types of debt-financed transactions and the related policy issues is deferred to a later chapter.[15]

EXCERPT FROM JOINT COMMITTEE ON TAXATION, FEDERAL INCOME TAX ASPECTS OF CORPORATE FINANCIAL STRUCTURES *

101st Cong., 1st Sess. pp. 53–58 (Jan. 18, 1989).

A. Tax Advantage of Debt Versus Equity

The total effect of the tax system on the incentives for corporations to use debt or equity depends on the interaction between the tax treatment at the shareholder and corporate levels.

The case of no income taxes.—In a simple world without taxes or additional costs in times of financial distress, economic theory suggests that the value of a corporation, as measured by the total value of the outstanding debt and equity, would be unchanged by the degree of leverage of the firm. This conclusion explicitly recognizes that debt issued by the corporation represents an ownership right to future

---

11. See, e.g., Bittker & Eustice, Federal Income Taxation of Corporations and Shareholders ¶ 8.07 (5th ed. 1987); Chapter 9B2, infra.

12. See Chapter 2B3, supra.

13. See Chapter 2F2, supra.

14. See Section D of this chapter, infra.

15. See Chapter 7C7b, infra.

* Footnotes omitted.

income of the corporation in a fashion similar to that of equity. In this simple world there would be no advantage to debt or to equity and the debt-equity ratio of the firm would not affect the cost of financing investment.

Effect of corporate income tax

Tax advantages

Taxes greatly complicate this analysis. Since the interest expense on debt is deductible for computing the corporate income tax while the return to equity is not, the tax at the corporate level provides a strong incentive for debt rather than equity finance.

The advantages of debt financing can be illustrated by comparing two corporations with $1,000 of assets that are identical except for financial structure: the first is entirely equity financed; while the second is 50–percent debt financed. Both corporations earn $150 of operating income. The all-equity corporation pays $51 in corporate tax and retains or distributes $99 of after-tax income ($150 less $51). Thus, as shown in Table IV–A, the return on equity is 9.9 percent ($99 divided by $1,000).

The leveraged corporation is financed by $500 of debt and $500 of stock. If the interest rate is 10 percent, then interest expense is $50 (10 percent times $500). Taxable income is $100 after deducting interest expense. The leveraged corporation is liable for $34 in corporate tax (34 percent times $100) and distributes or retains $66 of after-tax income ($100 less $34). Consequently, the return on equity is 13.2 percent ($66 divided by $500). Thus, as shown in Table IV–A, increas-

Table IV–A.—Effect of Debt Financing on Returns to Equity Investment

Item	All-equity corporation	50–percent debt-financed corporation
Beginning Balance Sheet:		
Total assets	$1,000	$1,000
Debt	0	500
Shareholders' equity	1,000	500
Income Statement:		
Operating income	150	150
Interest expense.............	0	50
Taxable income	150	100
Income tax..................	51	34
Income after corporate tax ...	99	66
Return on Equity[1] (percent).....	9.9	13.2

1. Return on equity is computed as income after corporate tax divided by beginning shareholders' equity.

ing the debt ratio from zero to 50 percent increases the rate of return on equity from 9.9 to 13.2 percent.

This arithmetic demonstrates that a leveraged corporation can generate a higher return on equity (net of corporate income tax) than an unleveraged company or, equivalently, that an unleveraged company needs to earn a higher profit before corporate tax to provide investors the same return net of corporate tax as could be obtained with an unleveraged company. More generally, the return on equity rises with increasing debt capitalization so long as the interest rate is less than the pre-tax rate of return on corporate assets. This suggests that the Code creates an incentive to raise the debt-equity ratio to the point where the corporate income tax (or outstanding equity) is eliminated.

Costs of financial distress

With higher levels of debt the possibility of financial distress increases, as do the expected costs to the firm which occur with such distress. These additional costs include such items as the increase in the costs of debt funds; constraints on credit, expenditure or operating decisions; and the direct costs of being in bankruptcy. These expected costs of financial distress may, at sufficiently high debt-equity ratios, offset the corporate tax advantage to additional debt finance.

Effect of shareholder income tax

The above analysis focuses solely on the effect of interest deductibility at the corporate level. Shareholder-level income taxation may offset to some degree the corporate tax incentive for corporate debt relative to equity.

Shareholder treatment of debt and equity

The conclusion that debt is tax favored relative to equity remains unchanged if interest on corporate debt and returns on equity are taxed at the same effective rate to investors. In this case, the returns to investors on both debt and equity are reduced proportionately by the income tax; the advantage to debt presented by corporate tax deductibility remains. One noteworthy exception exists if the marginal investments on both debt and equity are effectively tax-exempt. Given the previously documented importance of tax-exempt pension funds in the bond and equity markets, this case may be of some importance.

Shareholder level tax treatment of equity

In general, returns to shareholders and debtholders are not taxed the same. Although dividends, like interest income, are taxed currently, equity income in other forms may reduce the effective investor-level tax on equity below that on debt. First, the firm may retain earnings and not pay dividends currently. In general, the accumulation of earnings by the firm will cause the value of the firm's shares to rise. Rather than being taxed currently on corporate earnings, a shareholder will be able to defer the taxation on the value of the retained earnings reflected in the price of the stock until the shareholder sells the stock. Thus, even though the tax rates on interest, dividends, and capital gains are the same, the ability to defer the tax on returns from equity reduces the effective rate of individual tax on equity investment below that on income from interest on corporate debt.

Other aspects of capital gain taxation serve to reduce further the individual income tax on equity. Since tax on capital gain is normally triggered after a voluntary recognition event (e.g., the sale of stock), the taxpayer can time the realization of capital gain income when the effective rate of tax is low. The rate of tax could be low if the taxpayer is in a low or zero tax bracket because other income is abnormally low, if other capital losses shelter the capital gain, or if changes in the tax law cause the statutory rate on capital gains to be low. Perhaps most important, the step up in the adjusted tax basis of the stock upon the death of the shareholder may permit the shareholder's heirs to avoid tax completely on capital gains. For all these reasons, the effective rate of tax on undistributed earnings may be already quite low.

Corporations can distribute their earnings to owners of equity in forms that generally result in less tax to shareholders than do dividend distributions. Share repurchases have become an important method of distributing corporate earnings to equity holders. When employed by large publicly traded firms, repurchases of the corporation's own shares permit the shareholders to treat the distribution as a sale of stock (i.e., to obtain capital gain treatment, and recover the basis in the stock without tax). The remaining shareholders may benefit because they have rights to a larger fraction of the firm and may see a corresponding increase in the value of their shares. Thus, less individual tax will generally be imposed on a $100 repurchase of stock than on $100 of dividends. In addition, share repurchases allow shareholders to choose whether to receive corporate distributions by choosing whether to sell or retain shares, so as to minimize tax liability.

Acquisitions of the stock of one corporation for cash or property of another corporation provides a similar method for distributing corporate earnings out of corporate solution with less shareholder tax than through a dividend. The target shareholders generally treat the acquisition as a sale and recover their basis free of tax. For purposes of analyzing the individual tax effect of corporate earnings disbursements, this transaction can be thought of as equivalent to a stock merger of the target with the acquiror followed by the repurchase of the target shareholders' shares by the resulting merged firm. The result is similar to the case of a share repurchase in that cash is distributed to shareholders with less than the full dividend tax, except that two firms are involved instead of one.

Since dividends typically are subject to more tax than other methods for providing returns to shareholders, the puzzle of why firms pay dividends remains. Because dividends are paid at the discretion of the firm, it appears that firms cause their shareholders to pay more tax on equity income than is strictly necessary. Until a better understanding of corporate distribution policy exists, the role of dividend taxation on equity financing decisions remain uncertain.

To summarize, although the current taxation of dividends to investors is clearly significant, there are numerous reasons why the overall individual tax on equity investments may be less than that on interest income from debt. Since the effective shareholder tax on returns from equity may be less than that on debt holdings, the shareholder tax may offset some or all of the advantage to debt at the corporate level.

Interaction of corporate and shareholder taxation

With shareholders in different income tax brackets, high tax rate taxpayers will tend to concentrate their wealth in the form of equity and low tax rate taxpayers will tend to concentrate their wealth in the form of debt. The distribution of wealth among investors with different marginal tax rates affects the demand for investments in the form of debt or equity. The interaction between the demand of investors, and the supply provided by corporations, determines the aggregate amount of corporate debt and equity in the economy.

At some aggregate mix between debt and equity, the difference in the investor-level tax on income from equity and debt may be sufficient to offset completely, at the margin, the apparent advantage of debt at the corporate level. Even if the difference in investor tax treatment of debt and equity is not sufficient to offset completely the corporate tax advantage, the advantage to debt may be less than the corporate-level tax treatment alone would provide.

Some believe that, because the top personal tax rate was reduced below the top corporate tax rate in the 1986 Act and because the share of wealth held by tax-exempt entities is substantial, the tax advantage of debt at the corporate level outweighs its disadvantages to investors. They would argue that changes in tax law have provided the motive force in the drive toward higher leverage. However, given that the observed changes in corporate financial behavior began well before 1986, the changes due to the 1986 Act may be of relatively little importance in determining changes in leverage and acquisition behavior. The individual rate reductions in the Economic Recovery Tax Act of 1981, some respond, started the shift toward more debt in corporate structures and the 1986 Act merely provided another push in that direction.

Implications for policy

The analysis above suggests that any policy change designed to reduce the tax incentive for debt must consider the interaction of both corporate and shareholder taxes. For example, proposals to change the income tax rates for individuals or corporations will change the incentive for corporate debt. Likewise, proposals to change the tax treatment of tax-exempt entities may alter the aggregate mix and distribution of debt and equity.

In addition, proposals to reduce the bias toward debt over equity, for example, by reducing the total tax on dividends, must confront the somewhat voluntary nature of the dividend tax. Since the payment of dividends by corporations generally is discretionary and other means exist for providing value to shareholders with less tax, corporations can affect the level of shareholder level tax incurred. Until a better understanding of the determinants of corporate distribution behavior exists, the total impact of policies designed to reduce the bias between debt and equity are uncertain.

* * *

B. DEBT VS. EQUITY

Taxpayers have considerable flexibility to structure corporate instruments as debt or equity. In view of the sharply disparate tax treatment of debt and equity, it is hardly surprising that the Service may be unwilling to accept the taxpayer's label as controlling. Form would be elevated over substance if every piece of paper embossed with a corporate seal and bearing the label "debt" were treated as such for tax purposes. To prevent tax avoidance through the use of excessive debt, the Service frequently pierces the documents and recasts a purported debt obligation as equity. The tax consequences of a recharacterization can be extremely unpleasant. An interest payment becomes a dividend and the corporation loses its deduction. If and when the note is repaid, the "creditor" finds himself in the role of shareholder, and the "loan repayment" may turn into a taxable dividend instead of a tax-free return of capital.

It is one thing to list the advantages of debt and identify the unfortunate ramifications of reclassification. It is quite another to describe with any precision the process employed by the courts and the Service to determine whether a particular instrument is debt or equity. The case law first approaches the issue by describing a spectrum. At one end is equity, a risk investment with the potential to share in corporate profits. At the other end is debt, evidenced by the corporation's unconditional promise to pay back the contributed funds, with market rate interest, at a fixed maturity date. A pure equity investor—the shareholder—has voting rights and upside potential. A pure debt holder—the creditor—is an outsider with no prospect of sharing in the growth of the enterprise. Many classification controversies involve "hybrid securities" which have features common to both debt and equity, and the courts must decide whether these instruments falling in the middle of the spectrum are closer to one end or the other.

Any process that looks at something decidedly gray and tries to determine whether it more closely resembles black or white is bound to be frustrating. And so it is here. The litigated cases are legion and the court decisions have been aptly villified as a "jungle"[1] and a "viper's tangle."[2] The issue is murky because classification of an obligation as debt or equity traditionally is treated as a question of fact to be resolved by applying vague standards that require the weighing of many factors.[3] In a manner reminiscent of the approach to determining whether an asset is "held primarily for sale to customers," the courts have spewed forth laundry lists of "factors," but it is difficult to discern which factors are controlling in a given case. Exhaustive research leaves one with the firm conviction that the courts are applying an amorphous and highly unsatisfactory "smell test."

Synthesizing the decisional morass is a perilous enterprise, but the principal factors enunciated by the courts over the years may be summarized as follows:[4]

Form of the Obligation. Labels are hardly controlling, but the decisions provide some guidance for a corporation that wishes to avoid reclassification of debt as equity. At a minimum, debt instruments should bear the usual indicia of debt—an unconditional promise to pay; a specific term; and a stated, reasonable rate of interest, payable in all events.[5] Equity characteristics should be avoided. For example, the likelihood of reclassification is far greater with a hybrid instrument that makes payment of interest contingent on earnings or provides the holder with voting rights.[6]

The Debt/Equity Ratio. The debt/equity ratio of a corporation is the ratio of the company's liabilities to the shareholders' equity. The ratio has long been used as a tool to determine whether a corporation is thinly capitalized. Thin capitalization, in turn, creates a substantial risk that what purports to be debt will be reclassified as equity on the theory that no rational creditor would lend money to a corporation with such nominal equity.

The trouble with this attempt to quantify the inquiry is that the cases are inconsistent as to what constitutes an excessive debt/equity ratio. For example, depending on all the other factors, a debt/equity ratio of 3-to-1, which most would regard as conservative, has been held to be excessive,[7] while ratios of 50-to-1 and higher have been held to be

1. Commissioner v. Union Mutual Insurance Co. of Providence, 386 F.2d 974, 978 (1st Cir.1967).

2. Bittker & Eustice, Federal Income Taxation of Corporations and Shareholders ¶ 4.04 (4th ed. 1979).

3. For this reason, the Service declines to issue advance rulings on the classification on an instrument as debt or equity. Rev.Proc. 87–3, § 4.02(1), 1987–1 C.B. 523, 527.

4. See generally Plumb, "The Federal Income Tax Significance of Corporate Debt: A Critical Analysis and a Proposal," 26 Tax L.Rev. 369 (1971); Stone, "Debt-Equity Distinctions in the Tax Treatment of the Corporation and Its Shareholders," 42 Tulane L.Rev. 251 (1968).

5. See Wood Preserving Corp. v. United States, 347 F.2d 117, 119 (4th Cir.1965).

6. See Fellinger v. United States, 363 F.2d 826 (6th Cir.1966).

7. See Schnitzer v. Commissioner, 13 T.C. 43 (1949).

acceptable.[8] Some cases apply different norms for different industries,[9] and others ignore the ratio entirely.[10]

And how is the debt/equity ratio to be computed? Consider some of the basic questions on which there is disagreement. Is debt limited to shareholder debt or does it include debts to outsiders? [11] Does outside debt include accounts payable to trade creditors or only long-term liabilities? What about shareholder guaranteed debt? [12] In determining "equity," are assets taken into account at their book value (i.e., adjusted basis) or fair market value? [13] The differences in approach can be considerable.

Intent. Many cases have turned on the "intent" of the parties to create a debtor-creditor relationship.[14] "Intent" presumably is not gleaned by a subjective inquiry; it would be meaningless to place the corporate insiders on the witness stand and ask whether they "intended" to be shareholders or creditors. The more intelligent approach is to measure "intent" by objective criteria such as the lender's reasonable expectation of repayment, evaluated in light of the financial condition of the company, and the corporation's ability to pay principal and interest.[15] Hindsight also plays a role. For example, if the corporation consistently fails to pay interest or repay debts when they are due, its claim to debtor status may be highly questionable.[16]

Proportionality. In a closely held setting, debt held by the shareholders in the same proportion as their stock holdings normally raises

8. See Bradshaw v. United States, 231 Ct.Cl. 144, 683 F.2d 365, 367–68 (1982) (50-to-1 ratio not fatal because corporation was likely to and did in fact pay off debts when due); Baker Commodities Inc. v. Commissioner, 48 T.C. 374, affirmed 415 F.2d 519 (9th Cir.1969), cert. denied 397 U.S. 988, 90 S.Ct. 1117 (1970) (692-to-1 ratio is acceptable because cash flow and earning power of business could cover payments).

9. Compare Tomlinson v. 1661 Corp., 377 F.2d 291 (5th Cir.1967) (improved real estate; debt traditionally high) with John Lizak, Inc. v. Commissioner, 28 T.C.M. 804 (1969) (construction business less able to carry heavy debt burden).

10. See Gooding Amusement Co. v. Commissioner, 23 T.C. 408, 419 (1954), affirmed 236 F.2d 159 (6th Cir.1956), cert. denied 352 U.S. 1031, 77 S.Ct. 595 (1957).

11. Compare Ambassador Apartments, Inc. v. Commissioner, 50 T.C. 236, 245 (1968), affirmed 406 F.2d 288 (2d Cir.1969) (consider outside debt) with P.M. Finance Corp. v. Commissioner, 302 F.2d 786, 788 (3d Cir.1962) (consider only shareholder debt).

12. Compare Murphy Logging Co. v. United States, 378 F.2d 222 (9th Cir.1967)

(disregard shareholder guaranteed debt) with Plantation Patterns, Inc. v. Commissioner, 462 F.2d 712 (5th Cir.1972), cert. denied 409 U.S. 1076, 93 S.Ct. 683 (1972) (shareholder guaranteed debt recharacterized as equity contribution by guarantor.)

13. See Nye v. Commissioner, 50 T.C. 203, 216 (1968). In Bauer v. Commissioner, 748 F.2d 1365 (9th Cir.1984), the court computed stockholders' equity by adding together paid-in capital and retained earnings and arrived at outside debt/equity ratios for different years ranging from approximately 2 to 1 to 8 to 1. The Tax Court had determined a ratio for one year of approximately 92 to 1 by limiting shareholders' equity to initial paid-in capital.

14. See Gooding Amusement Co. v. Commissioner, 236 F.2d 159 (6th Cir.1956), cert. denied 352 U.S. 1031, 77 S.Ct. 595 (1957).

15. Gilbert v. Commissioner, 248 F.2d 399 (2d Cir.1957).

16. See Slappey Drive Industrial Park v. United States, 561 F.2d 572, 582 (5th Cir. 1977); Estate of Mixon v. United States, 464 F.2d 394, 409 (5th Cir.1972).

the eyebrows of the Service.[17]   The rationale is that if debt is held in roughly the same proportion as stock, the "creditors" have no economic incentive to act like creditors by setting or enforcing the terms of the so-called liability. The unanswered question is whether proportionality, without other negative factors, is sufficient in itself to convert the obligation into stock.[18]

Subordination. If a corporation has borrowed from both shareholders and outside sources, the independent creditors frequently will require that the shareholder debt be subordinated to the claims of general creditors. Although subordination of inside debt would appear to be inevitable if significant unsecured outside financing is desired, some courts have regarded it as the smoking pistol.[19] Once again, however, it is difficult to advise a client with any certainty that subordination is fatal per se. The economic realities of closely held corporate life would suggest that it should not be determinative, but it grows in importance when combined with other negative factors such as thin capitalization and proportionality.[20]

This distillation of factors barely scratches the surface. The *Fin Hay Realty* case, which follows, provides an illustration of one court's approach to the problem.[21]

FIN HAY REALTY CO. v. UNITED STATES *

United States Court of Appeals, Third Circuit, 1968.
398 F.2d 694.

OPINION OF THE COURT

FREEDMAN, Circuit Judge.

We are presented in this case with the recurrent problem whether funds paid to a close corporation by its shareholders were additional contributions to capital or loans on which the corporation's payment of interest was deductible under § 163 of the Internal Revenue Code of 1954.

The problem necessarily calls for an evaluation of the facts, which we therefore detail.

Fin Hay Realty Co., the taxpayer was organized on February 14, 1934, by Frank L. Finlaw and J. Louis Hay. Each of them contributed $10,000 for which he received one-half of the corporation's stock and at

---

17. See Charter Wire, Inc. v. United States, 309 F.2d 878, 880 (7th Cir.1962), cert. denied 372 U.S. 965, 83 S.Ct. 1090 (1963).

18. For a negative view, see Harlan v. United States, 409 F.2d 904, 909 (5th Cir. 1969) (proportionality may be considered but has no significant importance).

19. See P.M. Finance Corp. v. Commissioner, 302 F.2d 786, 789–90 (3d Cir.1962); R.C. Owen Co. v. Commissioner, 23 T.C.M.

673, 676 (1964), affirmed 351 F.2d 410 (6th Cir.1965), cert. denied 383 U.S. 967, 86 S.Ct. 1272 (1966).

20. See Tyler v. Tomlinson, 414 F.2d 844 (5th Cir.1969).

21. For a more thorough examination, see Plumb, supra note 4, an article that somehow manages to survey this vexing subject with only 1,591 footnotes.

* Some footnotes omitted.

the same time each advanced an additional $15,000 for which the corporation issued to him its unsecured promissory note payable on demand and bearing interest at the rate of six per cent per annum. The corporation immediately purchased an apartment house in Newark, New Jersey, for $39,000 in cash. About a month later the two shareholders each advanced an additional $35,000 to the corporation in return for six per cent demand promissory notes and next day the corporation purchased two apartment buildings in East Orange, New Jersey, for which it paid $75,000 in cash and gave the seller a six per cent, five year purchase money mortgage for the balance of $100,000.

Three years later, in October, 1937, the corporation created a new mortgage on all three properties and from the proceeds paid off the old mortgage on the East Orange property, which had been partially amortized. The new mortgage was for a five year term in the amount of $82,000 with interest at four and one-half per cent. In the following three years each of the shareholders advanced an additional $3,000 to the corporation, bringing the total advanced by each shareholder to $53,000, in addition to their acknowledged stock subscriptions of $10,000 each.

Finlaw died in 1941 and his stock and notes passed to his two daughters in equal shares. A year later the mortgage, which was about to fall due, was extended for a further period of five years with interest at four per cent. From the record it appears that it was subsequently extended until 1951.[3] In 1949 Hay died and in 1951 his executor requested the retirement of his stock and the payment of his notes. The corporation thereupon refinanced its real estate for $125,000 and sold one of the buildings. With the net proceeds it paid Hay's estate $24,000 in redemption of his stock and $53,000 in retirement of his notes. Finlaw's daughters then became and still remain the sole shareholders of the corporation.

Thereafter the corporation continued to pay and deduct interest on Finlaw's notes, now held by his two daughters. In 1962 the Internal Revenue Service for the first time declared the payments on the notes not allowable as interest deductions and disallowed them for the tax years 1959 and 1960. The corporation thereupon repaid a total of $6,000 on account of the outstanding notes and in the following year after refinancing the mortgage on its real estate repaid the balance of $47,000. A short time later the Internal Revenue Service disallowed the interest deductions for the years 1961 and 1962. When the corporation failed to obtain refunds it brought this refund action in the district court. After a nonjury trial the court denied the claims and entered judgment for the United States. 261 F.Supp. 823 (D.N.J.1967). From this judgment the corporation appeals.

---

3. The corporation's tax returns show a continuing decline in the principal of the debt until that year.

This case arose in a factual setting where it is the corporation which is the party concerned that its obligations be deemed to represent a debt and not a stock interest. In the long run in cases of this kind it is also important to the shareholder that his advance be deemed a loan rather than a capital contribution, for in such a case his receipt of repayment may be treated as the retirement of a loan rather than a taxable dividend.[6] There are other instances in which it is in the shareholder's interest that his advance to the corporation be considered a debt rather than an increase in his equity. A loss resulting from the worthlessness of stock is a capital loss under § 165(g), whereas a bad debt may be treated as an ordinary loss if it qualifies as a business bad debt under § 166. Similarly, it is only if a taxpayer receives debt obligations of a controlled corporation that he can avoid the provision for nonrecognition of gains or losses on transfers of property to such a corporation under § 351.[8] These advantages in having the funds entrusted to a corporation treated as corporate obligations instead of contributions to capital have required the courts to look beyond the literal terms in which the parties have cast the transaction in order to determine its substantive nature.

In attempting to deal with this problem courts and commentators have isolated a number of criteria by which to judge the true nature of an investment which is in form a debt: (1) the intent of the parties; (2) the identity between creditors and shareholders; (3) the extent of participation in management by the holder of the instrument; (4) the ability of the corporation to obtain funds from outside sources; (5) the "thinness" of the capital structure in relation to debt; (6) the risk involved; (7) the formal indicia of the arrangement; (8) the relative position of the obligees as to other creditors regarding the payment of interest and principal; (9) the voting power of the holder of the instrument; (10) the provision of a fixed rate of interest; (11) a contingency on the obligation to repay; (12) the source of the interest payments; (13) the presence or absence of a fixed maturity date; (14) a provision for redemption by the corporation; (15) a provision for redemption at the option of the holder; and (16) the timing of the advance with reference to the organization of the corporation.

While the Internal Revenue Code of 1954 was under consideration, and after its adoption, Congress sought to identify the criteria which would determine whether an investment represents a debt or equity, but these and similar efforts have not found acceptance.[10] It still

---

6. The partial retirement of an equity interest may be considered as essentially equivalent to a dividend under § 302, while the repayment of even a debt whose principal has appreciated is taxed only as a capital gain under [§ 1271(a)(1). Ed.]

8. A taxpayer might wish to avoid § 351 when he transfers depreciated property to the corporation and seeks to recognize the loss immediately and also when the transferred property is to be resold by the corporation but will not qualify for capital gains treatment in the hands of the corporation.

10. The original House version of the 1954 Code, H.R. 8300, 83d Cong., 2d Sess., contained a provision, § 312, which distinguished between "securities", "participating stock", and "nonparticipating stock". Only payments with regard to "securities" were deductible by the corporation as interest. See proposed § 275. "Securities"

remains true that neither any single criterion nor any series of criteria can provide a conclusive answer in the kaleidoscopic circumstances which individual cases present. See John Kelley Co. v. Commissioner of Internal Revenue, 326 U.S. 521, 530, 66 S.Ct. 299, 90 L.Ed. 278 (1946).

The various factors which have been identified in the cases are only aids in answering the ultimate question whether the investment, analyzed in terms of its economic reality, constitutes risk capital entirely subject to the fortunes of the corporate venture or represents a strict debtor-creditor relationship. Since there is often an element of risk in a loan, just as there is an element of risk in an equity interest, the conflicting elements do not end at a clear line in all cases.

In a corporation which has numerous shareholders with varying interests, the arm's-length relationship between the corporation and a shareholder who supplies funds to it inevitably results in a transaction whose form mirrors its substance. Where the corporation is closely held, however, and the same persons occupy both sides of the bargaining table, form does not necessarily correspond to the intrinsic economic nature of the transaction, for the parties may mold it at their will with no countervailing pull. This is particularly so where a shareholder can have the funds he advances to a corporation treated as corporate obligations instead of contributions to capital without affecting his proportionate equity interest. Labels, which are perhaps the best expression of the subjective intention of parties to a transaction, thus lose their meaningfulness.

To seek economic reality in objective terms of course disregards the personal interest which a shareholder may have in the welfare of the corporation in which he is a dominant force. But an objective standard is one imposed by the very fact of his dominant position and is much fairer than one which would presumptively construe all such transactions against the shareholder's interest. Under an objective test of economic reality it is useful to compare the form which a similar transaction would have taken had it been between the corporation and an outside lender, and if the shareholder's advance is far more speculative than what an outsider would make, it is obviously a loan in name only.

In the present case all the formal indicia of an obligation were meticulously made to appear. The corporation, however, was the complete creature of the two shareholders who had the power to create whatever appearance would be of tax benefit to them despite the

were defined as unconditional obligations to pay a sum certain with an unconditional interest requirement not dependent on corporate earnings. The Senate rejected the proposed classification on the ground that it was inflexible. See S.Rep. No. 1622, 83d Cong., 2d Sess., 1954 U.S.C.Cong. & Admin. News, pp. 4621, 4673.

A similar list of determinants was proposed in 1957 by an advisory group to a subcommittee of the House Committee on Ways and Means, but was not acted upon.

In 1954 the American Law Institute embodied such a test in § x500 of its draft income tax statute. See ALI Federal Tax Project, Income Tax Problems of Corporations and Shareholders 396 (1958).

economic reality of the transaction. Each shareholder owned an equal proportion of stock and was making an equal additional contribution, so that whether Finlaw and Hay designated any part of their additional contributions as debt or as stock would not dilute their proportionate equity interests. There was no restriction because of the possible excessive debt structure, for the corporation had been created to acquire real estate and had no outside creditors except mortgagees who, of course, would have no concern for general creditors because they had priority in the security of the real estate. The position of the mortgagees also rendered of no significance the possible subordination of the notes to other debts of the corporation, a matter which in some cases this Court has deemed significant.

The shareholders here, moreover, lacked one of the principal advantages of creditors. Although the corporation issued demand notes for the advances, nevertheless, as the court below found, it could not have repaid them for a number of years. The economic reality was that the corporation used the proceeds of the notes to purchase its original assets, and the advances represented a long term commitment dependent on the future value of the real estate and the ability of the corporation to sell or refinance it. Only because such an entwining of interest existed between the two shareholders and the corporation, so different from the arm's-length relationship between a corporation and an outside creditor, were they willing to invest in the notes and allow them to go unpaid for so many years while the corporation continued to enjoy the advantages of uninterrupted ownership of its real estate.

It is true that real estate values rose steadily with a consequent improvement in the mortgage market, so that looking back the investment now appears to have been a good one. As events unfolded, the corporation reached a point at which it could have repaid the notes through refinancing, but this does not obliterate the uncontradicted testimony that in 1934 it was impossible to obtain any outside mortgage financing for real estate of this kind except through the device of a purchase money mortgage taken back by the seller.

It is argued that the rate of interest at six per cent per annum was far more than the shareholders could have obtained from other investments. This argument, however, is self-defeating, for it implies that the shareholders would damage their own corporation by an overcharge for interest. There was, moreover, enough objective evidence to neutralize this contention. The outside mortgage obtained at the time the corporation purchased the East Orange property bore interest at the rate of six per cent even though the mortgagee was protected by an equity in excess of forty per cent of the value of the property. In any event, to compare the six per cent interest rate of the notes with other 1934 rates ignores the most salient feature of the notes—their risk. It is difficult to escape the inference that a prudent outside businessman would not have risked his capital in six per cent unsecured demand notes in Fin Hay Realty Co. in 1934. The evidence therefore amply justifies the conclusion of the district court that the form which the parties gave to their transaction did not match its economic reality.

It is argued that even if the advances may be deemed to have been contributions to capital when they were originally made in 1934, a decisive change occurred when the original shareholder, Finlaw, died and his heirs continued to hold the notes without demanding payment. This, it is said could be construed as a decision to reinvest, and if by 1941 the notes were sufficiently secure to be considered bona fide debt, they should now be so treated for tax purposes. Such a conclusion, however, does not inevitably follow. Indeed, the weight of the circumstances leads to the opposite conclusion.

First, there is nothing in the record to indicate that the corporation could have readily raised the cash with which to pay off Finlaw's notes on his death in 1941. When Hay, the other shareholder, died in 1949 and his executor two years later requested the retirement of his interest, the corporation in order to carry this out sold one of its properties and refinanced the others. Again, when in 1963 the corporation paid off the notes held by Finlaw's daughters after the Internal Revenue Service had disallowed the interest deductions for 1961 and 1962 it again refinanced its real estate. There is nothing in the record which would sustain a finding that the corporation could have readily undertaken a similar financing in 1941, when Finlaw died even if we assume that the corporation was able to undertake the appropriate refinancing ten years later to liquidate Hay's interest. Moreover, there was no objective evidence to indicate that in 1941 Finlaw's daughters viewed the notes as changed in character or in security, or indeed that they viewed the stock and notes as separate and distinct investments. To indulge in a theoretical conversion of equity contributions into a debt obligation in 1941 when Finlaw died would be to ignore what such a conversion might have entailed. For Finlaw's estate might then have been chargeable with the receipt of dividends at the time the equity was redeemed and converted into a debt. To recognize retrospectively such a change in the character of the obligation would be to assume a conclusion with consequences unfavorable to the parties, which they themselves never acknowledged.

The burden was on the taxpayer to prove that the determination by the Internal Revenue Service that the advances represented capital contributions was incorrect. The district court was justified in holding that the taxpayer had not met this burden.

The judgment of the district court will be affirmed.

[The dissenting opinion of Judge VAN DUSEN has been omitted. Ed.]

C. THE SECTION 385 REGULATIONS SAGA

Code: § 385.

In the course of its deliberations on the Tax Reform Act of 1969, Congress concluded that determined effort was needed to alleviate the uncertainties flowing from the debt/equity case law, especially in light of "the increasing use of debt for corporate acquisition purposes." [1] Frustrated in its attempt to draft precise definitions, Congress delegated the chore to the executive branch by enacting Section 385, which authorizes the Treasury to promulgate such regulations "as may be necessary or appropriate" to determine for all tax purposes whether an interest in a corporation is to be treated as stock or debt. Section 385(b) requires the regulations to set forth "factors" to be taken into account in determining in a particular fact situation whether a debtor-creditor relationship exists and goes on to specify the following factors which may (but need not) be included in the regulations:

1. Form—i.e., whether the instrument is evidenced by a written, unconditional promise to pay a sum certain on demand or on a specific date in return for an adequate consideration and bears a fixed interest rate.

2. Subordination to any indebtedness of the corporation.

3. The debt/equity ratio.

4. Convertibility into stock.

5. Proportionality—i.e., the relationship between holdings of stock in the corporation and holdings of stock in the corporation and holdings of the purported debt interest being scrutinized.

Section 385 was hailed by leading commentators as "perhaps the most important and potentially far-reaching corporate provision added by the Tax Reform Act of 1969," [2] and the literature was replete with predictions as to the content of the regulations. [3] In March, 1980, 11 years after Section 385 was enacted, the Treasury issued a lengthy, detailed and controversial set of proposed regulations. [4] The saga which followed is lamentable. "Final" regulations were promulgated in December, 1980, [5] to be effective for interests in corporations created after April 30, 1981, but the Treasury twice extended their effective date in the face of criticism from the tax bar and special interest groups. [6]

---

1. S.Rep. No. 91–552, 91st Cong., 1st Sess. 511 (1969), reprinted in 1969–3 C.B. 423, 511. See also H.R.Rep. No. 91–413, 91st Cong., 1st Sess. 265 (1969), reprinted in 1969–3 C.B. 200, 265.

2. Bittker & Eustice, Federal Income Taxation of Corporations and Shareholders, ¶ 4.05 (3rd ed. 1971).

3. Id. at 4–16 to 4–19. See also Recommendations as to Federal Tax Distinction between Corporate Stock and Indebtedness,

N.Y. State Bar Association Tax Section Committee on Reorganization Problems, 25 Tax Lawyer 57 (1971).

4. 45 Fed.Reg. 18957 (1980).

5. T.D. 7747 (filed Dec. 29, 1980), 45 Fed.Reg. 86438 (Dec. 31, 1980), known as the "December 29" regulations.

6. See, e.g., T.D. 7774 (filed April 29, 1981), 46 Fed.Reg. 24945 (May 4, 1981),

Extensive amendments were proposed in December, 1981, followed by still further extensions of the effective date.[7] In July, 1983, all versions of the regulations were withdrawn,[8] and it appears that the entire project has been abandoned.

Although detailed examination of the defunct regulations hardly would be productive, some features of the Treasury's monumental effort are noteworthy if only because they represent a concentrated attempt to bring order out of the chaos. In broad outline, the principal themes of the last version of the regulations were as follows: [9]

Distinguishing Straight Debt from Hybrid Instruments. Reacting to decades of ingenuity by corporate lawyers, the regulations appropriately relegated hybrid securities to second class status. A "hybrid" was defined as an instrument convertible into stock or providing for any contingent payment to the holder.[10] In virtually all cases, hybrids would have been treated as preferred stock for tax purposes, at least if they were not held by independent creditors.[11] Straight debt—defined as anything other than a hybrid instrument [12]—still had a fighting chance of avoiding reclassification if certain other requirements were met.

Proportionality as a Super Factor. The concept of proportionality played a central role in the regulatory scheme because, in the words of the preamble to the 1980 version, "it generally makes little economic difference (aside from tax consequences) whether proportionate shareholder advances are made as debt or equity ∗ ∗ ∗." [13] Elaborate definitions of proportionality were provided, and special scrutiny was required for instruments held in substantial proportion to equity investments.[14]

Debt/Equity Ratio. A major contribution of the regulations was their precise definition of two debt/equity ratios—"outside" (which took into account *all* liabilities, including those to independent creditors) and "inside" (considering only shareholder debt).[15] Informative (but controversial) corollary rules provided that assets were to be reflected at adjusted basis rather than fair market value and trade liabilities

---

extending the effective date to interests created after December 31, 1981.

7. T.D. 7801 (filed Dec. 30, 1981), 47 Fed.Reg. 164 (Jan. 5, 1982), known as the "December 30" regulations and intended to apply to interests created after June 30, 1982, a date that was later postponed until April, 1983.

8. T.D. 7920, 48 Fed.Reg. 31054 (July 6, 1983).

9. Unless otherwise indicated, citations which follow are to the December 30, 1981 version of the regulations.

10. Prop.Reg. § 1.385–3(d).

11. Prop.Reg. § 1.385–0(c)(2).

12. Prop.Reg. § 1.385–3(e).

13. T.D. 7747, 45 Fed.Reg. 86438, 86440 (Explanation of Changes), reprinted in 1981–1 C.B. 143.

14. Prop.Reg. § 1.385–6. In general, proportional straight debt instruments were treated as debt only if issued to "independent creditors" or if they were marketable instruments issued by a public company; otherwise they generally were reclassified as equity unless they were: (a) issued for cash or, if issued for property, the stated annual interest rate was "reasonable," and (b) the corporation did not have "excessive debt" at the time of the instrument was issued. Prop.Reg. § 1.385–6(a)(3), (e), (g).

15. Prop.Reg. § 1.385–6(g)(4).

were to be disregarded.[16] The debt/equity ratio was used to determine whether a corporation's debt was "excessive". A debt was excessive if the instrument's terms and conditions, viewed in combination with the corporation's financial structure, would not have been satisfactory to a bank or other financial institution making ordinary commercial loans.[17] It was not excessive, however, if the outside debt/equity ratio did not exceed 10-to-1 and the inside debt/equity ratio did not exceed 3-to-1.[18] Thus, even proportionate straight debt issued for cash would not be reclassified if it fell within this safe harbor from "excessive debt" and bore a "reasonable" (within specified ranges) interest rate. Variations on these themes abounded.

In the last analysis, the unwieldy regulations were controversial because of their negative impact on particular industries and on small businesses generally.[19] Although some of the regulatory themes ultimately may be adopted by the courts, the Treasury is unlikely to initiate the unprecedented peacetime mobilization that would be required to resurrect this project.

Despite the Treasury's notable lack of success in implementing the goals of Section 385, Congress has not given up hope. Section 385 was amended in 1989 to allow (but not require) the Treasury to classify an interest having significant debt and equity characteristics as "in part stock and in part indebtedness." [20] According to the legislative history, bifurcation may be appropriate where a debt instrument provides for payments that are dependent to a significant extent on corporate performance, such as through "equity kickers" (i.e., provisions in a debt instrument that provide the holder with an equity interest in certain circumstances), contingent interests (which are dependent on corporate performance), significant deferral of payment, subordination, or an interest rate high enough to suggest a significant risk of default.[21]

If the Treasury accepts this latest Congressional challenge, several options might be considered. One approach would disallow interest deductions in excess of a specified rate of return to investors on the theory that a higher than normal risk is tantamount to an equity investment. For example, the regulations might specify a reference rate (such as the rate on comparable-term Treasury obligations) that is relatively risk-free and permit interest paid up to that rate to be deductible but deny a deduction for the additional "risk" element because it is more akin to a dividend. Under this type of broad disallowance approach, a corporation that issued a 20–year $100,000 unsecured debt instrument paying 14 percent interest (14,000 per year)

16. Prop.Reg. § 1.385–6(h).

17. Prop.Reg. § 1.385–6(f)(2).

18. Prop.Reg. § 1.385–6(g)(3).

19. See, e.g., Levin & Bowen, "The Section 385 Regulations Regarding Debt Versus Equity: Is the Cure Worse than the Malady?" 35 Tax Lawyer 1 (1981); Stone & McGeehan, "Distinguishing Corporate Debt From Stock Under Section 385," 36 Tax L.Rev. 341 (1981).

20. I.R.C. § 385(a). This regulatory authority may be exercised on a prospective basis only.

21. H.Rep. No. 101–247, 101st Cong., 1st Sess. 1236 (1989).

at a time when comparable Treasury bonds were yielding 10 percent would be permitted to deduct only $10,000 per year as interest and the remaining $4,000 per year would be a nondeductible dividend.[22]

Another option is to limit bifurcation to instruments that provide for a combination of a fixed return and an additional return based on earnings. The regulations might treat the fixed return as interest while classifying the performance-based component as a nondeductible dividend. A closely related alternative, which finds isolated support in the case law, would be to divide one instrument into separate components—i.e., one part as debt and another as equity.[23]

Perhaps in the 21st century, when the Section 385 regulations are reissued, we will know the Treasury's thinking on these questions. In the meantime, the Congressional tax-writing committees have admonished the Treasury to increase the number of published rulings on debt-equity issues to provide guidance to taxpayers in an expeditious manner.[24]

PROBLEMS

1. Aristocrat, Baker and Chef have formed Chez Guevarra, Inc. ("Chez"), which will operate a gourmet restaurant and bakery previously operated by Chef as a sole proprietorship. Aristocrat will contribute $80,000 cash, Baker will contribute a building with a fair market value of $80,000 and an adjusted basis of $20,000, and Chef will contribute $40,000 cash and the goodwill from his proprietorship which the parties agree is worth $40,000 and has a zero basis. In return, each of the parties will receive 100 shares of Chez common stock, the only class outstanding.

Chez requires at least $1,800,000 of additional capital in order to renovate the building, acquire new equipment and provide working capital. It has negotiated a $900,000 loan from Friendly National Bank on the following terms: interest will be payable at two points above the prime rate, determined semi-annually, with principal due in ten years and the loan will be secured by a mortgage on the renovated restaurant building.

Evaluate the following alternative proposals for raising the additional $900,000 needed to commence business, focusing on the possibility that the Service will reclassify corporate debt instruments as equity:

22. In narrowly targeted situations, Congress began moving in this direction with the legislation enacted in 1989. See, e.g., I.R.C. § 163(i), discussed in Chapter 7C7b, infra. Query whether any broader approach would discriminate against start-up companies or firms engaged in high-risk businesses?

23. Two courts have used this approach with respect to so-called hybrid instruments. See Richmond, Fredericksburg and Potomac R.R. v. Commissioner, 528 F.2d 917 (4th Cir.1975); Farley Realty Corp. v. Commissioner, 279 F.2d 701 (2d Cir.1960). In most other cases, the courts have applied an all-or-nothing approach. For a discussion of the possibilities with hybrid instruments, see Rosenberg, "Tax Avoidance and Income Measurement," 87 Mich. L.Rev. 365 (1988).

24. H.R.Rep. No. 101–247, supra note 21, at 1235–36.

(a)   Aristocrat, Baker and Chef each will loan Chez $300,000, and each will take back a $300,000 five-year corporate note with variable interest payable at one point below the prime rate, determined annually.

(b)   Same as (a), above except that each of the parties will take back $300,000 of 10% 20-year subordinated income debentures; interest will be payable only out of the net profits of the business.

(c)   Same as (a), above, except that the $900,000 loan from Friendly National Bank will be unsecured but personally guaranteed by Aristocrat, Baker and Chef, who will be jointly and severally liable.

(d)   Aristocrat will loan the entire $900,000, taking back a $900,000 corporate note with terms identical to those described in (a), above.

(e)   Same as (d), above, except that commencing two years after the incorporation, Chez ceases to pay interest on the notes because of a severe cash flow problem.

2.   In view of the confused state of the law, how can a tax advisor plan the capital structure of a corporation to avoid the risk of reclassification of debt as equity. From the standpoint of the tax advisor, is the vagueness of the law in this area preferable to more detailed "bright line" rules in the Code or regulations? Which approach is preferable as a matter of policy?

D. CHARACTER OF LOSS ON CORPORATE INVESTMENT

Code: §§ 165(g)(1), (2); 166(a), (d), (e); 1244(a)–(c).

Regulations: §§ 1.165–5(a)–(c); 1.166–5; 1.1244(a)–1(a), (b).

UNITED STATES v. GENERES *

Supreme Court of the United States, 1972.
405 U.S. 93, 92 S.Ct. 827.

Mr. Justice BLACKMUN delivered the opinion of the Court.

A debt a closely held corporation owed to an indemnifying shareholder-employee became worthless in 1962. The issue in this federal income tax refund suit is whether, for the shareholder-employee, that worthless obligation was a business or a nonbusiness bad debt within the meaning and reach of §§ 166(a) and (d) of the Internal Revenue Code of 1954, as amended, 26 U.S.C. §§ 166(a) and (d), and of the implementing Regulations § 1.166–5.

The issue's resolution is important for the taxpayer. If the obligation was a business debt, he may use it to offset ordinary income and for carryback purposes under § 172 of the Code, 26 U.S.C. § 172. On

---

* Some footnotes omitted.

the other hand, if the obligation is a nonbusiness debt, it is to be treated as a short-term capital loss subject to the restrictions imposed on such losses by § 166(d)(1)(B) and §§ 1211 and 1212, and its use for carryback purposes is restricted by § 172(d)(4). The debt is one or the other in its entirety, for the Code does not provide for its allocation in part to business and in part to nonbusiness.

In determining whether a bad debt is a business or a nonbusiness obligation, the Regulations focus on the relation the loss bears to the taxpayer's business. If, at the time of worthlessness, that relation is a "proximate" one, the debt qualifies as a business bad debt and the aforementioned desirable tax consequences then ensue.

The present case turns on the proper measure of the required proximate relation. Does this necessitate a "dominant" business motivation on the part of the taxpayer or is a "significant" motivation sufficient?

Tax in an amount somewhat in excess of $40,000 is involved. The taxpayer, Allen H. Generes, prevailed in a jury trial in the District Court. See 67–2 U.S.T.C. ¶ 9754 (ED La.). On the Government's appeal, the Fifth Circuit affirmed by a divided vote. 427 F.2d 279 (CA5 1970). Certiorari was granted, 401 U.S. 972, 91 S.Ct. 1189, 28 L.Ed. 321 (1971), to resolve a conflict among the circuits.

I

The taxpayer as a young man in 1909 began work in the construction business. His son-in-law, William F. Kelly, later engaged independently in similar work. During World War II the two men formed a partnership in which their participation was equal. The enterprise proved successful. In 1954 Kelly-Generes Construction Co., Inc., was organized as the corporate successor to the partnership. It engaged in the heavy-construction business, primarily on public works projects.

The taxpayer and Kelly each owned 44% of the corporation's outstanding capital stock. The taxpayer's original investment in his shares was $38,900. The remaining 12% of the stock was owned by a son of the taxpayer and by another son-in-law. Mr. Generes was president of the corporation and received from it an annual salary of $12,000. Mr. Kelly was executive vice-president and received an annual salary of $15,000.

The taxpayer and Mr. Kelly performed different services for the corporation. Kelly worked full time in the field and was in charge of the day-to-day construction operations. Generes, on the other hand, devoted no more than six to eight hours a week to the enterprise. He reviewed bids and jobs, made cost estimates, sought and obtained bank financing, and assisted in securing the bid and performance bonds that are an essential part of the public-project construction business. Mr. Generes, in addition to being president of the corporation, held a full-time position as president of a savings and loan association he had founded in 1937. He received from the association an annual salary of

$19,000. The taxpayer also had other sources of income. His gross income averaged about $40,000 a year during 1959–1962.

Taxpayer Generes from time to time advanced personal funds to the corporation to enable it to complete construction jobs. He also guaranteed loans made to the corporation by banks for the purchase of construction machinery and other equipment. In addition, his presence with respect to the bid and performance bonds is of particular significance. Most of these were obtained from Maryland Casualty Co. That underwriter required the taxpayer and Kelly to sign an indemnity agreement for each bond it issued for the corporation. In 1958, however, in order to eliminate the need for individual indemnity contracts, taxpayer and Kelly signed a blanket agreement with Maryland whereby they agreed to indemnify it, up to a designated amount, for any loss it suffered as surety for the corporation. Maryland then increased its line of surety credit to $2,000,000. The corporation had over $14,000,000 gross business for the period 1954 through 1962.

In 1962 the corporation seriously underbid two projects and defaulted in its performance of the project contracts. It proved necessary for Maryland to complete the work. Maryland then sought indemnity from Generes and Kelly. The taxpayer indemnified Maryland to the extent of $162,104.57. In the same year he also loaned $158,814.49 to the corporation to assist it in its financial difficulties. The corporation subsequently went into receivership and the taxpayer was unable to obtain reimbursement from it.

In his federal income tax return for 1962 the taxpayer took his loss on his direct loans to the corporation as a nonbusiness bad debt. He claimed the indemnification loss as a business bad debt and deducted it against ordinary income. Later he filed claims for refund for 1959–1961, asserting net operating loss carrybacks under § 172 to those years for the portion, unused in 1962, of the claimed business bad debt deduction.

In due course the claims were made the subject of the jury trial refund suit in the United States District Court for the Eastern District of Louisiana. At the trial Mr. Generes testified that his sole motive in signing the indemnity agreement was to protect his $12,000-a-year employment with the corporation. The jury, by special interrogatory, was asked to determine whether taxpayer's signing of the indemnity agreement with Maryland "was proximately related to his trade or business of being an employee" of the corporation. The District Court charged the jury, over the Government's objection, that *significant* motivation satisfies the Regulations' requirement of proximate relationship.[6] The court refused the Government's request for an instruction

---

6. "A debt is proximately related to the taxpayer's trade or business when its creation was significantly motivated by the taxpayer's trade or business, and it is not rendered a non-business debt merely because there was a non-qualifying motivation as well, even though the non-qualifying motivation was the primary one."

that the applicable standard was that of *dominant* rather than significant motivation.[7]

After twice returning to the court for clarification of the instruction given, the jury found that the taxpayer's signing of the indemnity agreement was proximately related to his trade or business of being an employee of the corporation. Judgment on this verdict was then entered for the taxpayer.

The Fifth Circuit majority approved the significant-motivation standard so specified and agreed with a Second Circuit majority in Weddle v. Commissioner, 325 F.2d 849, 851 (1963), in finding comfort for so doing in the tort law's concept of proximate cause. Judge Simpson dissented. 427 F.2d, at 284. He agreed with the holding of the Seventh Circuit in Niblock v. Commissioner, 417 F.2d 1185 (1969), and with Chief Judge Lumbard, separately concurring in *Weddle,* 325 F.2d, at 852, that dominant and primary motivation is the standard to be applied.

II

A. The fact responsible for the litigation is the taxpayer's dual status relative to the corporation. Generes was both a shareholder and an employee. These interests are not the same, and their differences occasion different tax consequences. In tax jargon, Generes' status as a shareholder was a nonbusiness interest. It was capital in nature and it was composed initially of tax-paid dollars. Its rewards were expectative and would flow, not from personal effort, but from investment earnings and appreciation. On the other hand, Generes' status as an employee was a business interest. Its nature centered in personal effort and labor, and salary for that endeavor would be received. The salary would consist of pre-tax dollars.

Thus, for tax purposes it becomes important and, indeed, necessary to determine the character of the debt that went bad and became uncollectible. Did the debt center on the taxpayer's business interest in the corporation or on his nonbusiness interest? If it was the former, the taxpayer deserves to prevail here. * * *

B. Although arising in somewhat different contexts, two tax cases decided by the Court in recent years merit initial mention. In each of these cases a major shareholder paid out money to or on behalf of his corporation and then was unable to obtain reimbursement from it. In each he claimed a deduction assertable against ordinary income. In each he was unsuccessful in this quest:

7. "You must, in short, determine whether Mr. Generes' dominant motivation in signing the indemnity agreement was to protect his salary and status as an employee or was to protect his investment in the Kelly-Generes Construction Co.

"Mr. Generes is entitled to prevail in this case only if he convinces you that the dominant motivating factor for his signing the indemnity agreement was to insure the receiving of his salary from the company. It is insufficient if the protection or insurance of his salary was only a significant secondary motivation for his signing the indemnity agreement. It must have been his dominant or most important reason for signing the indemnity agreement."

1. In Putnam v. Commissioner, 352 U.S. 82 (1956), the taxpayer was a practicing lawyer who had guaranteed obligations of a labor newspaper corporation in which he owned stock. He claimed his loss as fully deductible in 1948 under § 23(e)(2) of the 1939 Code. The standard prescribed by that statute was incurrence of the loss "in any transaction entered into for profit, though not connected with the trade or business." The Court rejected this approach and held that the loss was a nonbusiness bad debt subject to short-term capital loss treatment under § 23(k)(4). The loss was deductible as a bad debt or not at all. See Rev.Rul. 60–48, 1960–1 Cum.Bull. 112.

2. In Whipple v. Commissioner, 373 U.S. 193 (1963), the taxpayer had provided organizational, promotional, and managerial services to a corporation in which he owned approximately an 80% stock interest. He claimed that this constituted a trade or business and, hence, that debts owing him by the corporation were business bad debts when they became worthless in 1953. The Court also rejected that contention and held that Whipple's investing was not a trade or business, that is, that "[d]evoting one's time and energies to the affairs of a corporation is not of itself, and without more, a trade or business of the person so engaged." 373 U.S., at 202. The rationale was that a contrary conclusion would be inconsistent with the principle that a corporation has a personality separate from its shareholders and that its business is not necessarily their business. The Court indicated its approval of the Regulations' proximate-relation test:

> "Moreover, there is no proof (which might be difficult to furnish where the taxpayer is the sole or dominant stockholder) that the loan was necessary to keep his job or was otherwise proximately related to maintaining his trade or business as an employee. Compare Trent v. Commissioner, [291 F.2d 669 (CA2 1961)]." 373 U.S., at 204.

The Court also carefully noted the distinction between the business and the nonbusiness bad debt for one who is both an employee and a shareholder.[8]

These two cases approach, but do not govern, the present one. They indicate, however, a cautious and not a free-wheeling approach to the business bad debt. Obviously, taxpayer Generes endeavored to frame his case to bring it within the area indicated in the above quotation from *Whipple v. Commissioner.*

III

We conclude that in determining whether a bad debt has a "proximate" relation to the taxpayer's trade or business, as the Regulations specify, and thus qualifies as a business bad debt, the proper measure is

---

8. "Even if the taxpayer demonstrates an independent trade or business of his own, care must be taken to distinguish bad debt losses arising from his own business and those actually arising from activities peculiar to an investor concerned with, and participating in, the conduct of the corporate business." 373 U.S., at 202.

that of dominant motivation, and that only significant motivation is not sufficient. We reach this conclusion for a number of reasons:

A. The Code itself carefully distinguishes between business and nonbusiness items. It does so, for example, in § 165 with respect to losses, in § 166 with respect to bad debts, and in § 162 with respect to expenses. It gives particular tax benefits to business losses, business bad debts, and business expenses, and gives lesser benefits, or none at all, to nonbusiness losses, nonbusiness bad debts, and nonbusiness expenses. It does this despite the fact that the latter are just as adverse in financial consequence to the taxpayer as are the former. But this distinction has been a policy of the income tax structure ever since the Revenue Act of 1916, § 5(a), 39 Stat. 759, provided differently for trade or business losses than it did for losses sustained in another transaction entered into for profit. And it has been the specific policy with respect to bad debts since the Revenue Act of 1942 incorporated into § 23(k) of the 1939 Code the distinction between business and nonbusiness bad debts. 56 Stat. 820.

The point, however, is that the tax statutes have made the distinction, that the Congress therefore intended it to be a meaningful one, and that the distinction is not to be obliterated or blunted by an interpretation that tends to equate the business bad debt with the nonbusiness bad debt. We think that emphasis upon the significant rather than upon the dominant would have a tendency to do just that.

B. Application of the significant-motivation standard would also tend to undermine and circumscribe the Court's holding in *Whipple* and the emphasis there that a shareholder's mere activity in a corporation's affairs is not a trade or business. As Chief Judge Lumbard pointed out in his separate and disagreeing concurrence in *Weddle*, supra, 325 F.2d, at 852–853, both motives—that of protecting the investment and that of protecting the salary—are inevitably involved, and an inquiry whether employee status provides a significant motivation will always produce an affirmative answer and result in a judgment for the taxpayer.

C. The dominant-motivation standard has the attribute of workability. It provides a guideline of certainty for the trier of fact. The trier then may compare the risk against the potential reward and give proper emphasis to the objective rather than to the subjective. As has just been noted, an employee-shareholder, in making or guaranteeing a loan to his corporation, usually acts with two motivations, the one to protect his investment and the other to protect his employment. By making the dominant motivation the measure, the logical tax consequence ensues and prevents the mere presence of a business motive, however small and however insignificant, from controlling the tax result at the taxpayer's convenience. This is of particular importance in a tax system that is so largely dependent on voluntary compliance.

D. The dominant-motivation test strengthens and is consistent with the mandate of § 262 of the Code, 26 U.S.C. § 262, that "no deduction shall be allowed for personal, living, or family expenses" except as otherwise provided. It prevents personal considerations from circumventing this provision.

E. The dominant-motivation approach to § 166(d) is consistent with that given the loss provisions in § 165(c)(1), see, for example, Imbesi v. Commissioner, 361 F.2d 640, 644 (CA3 1966), and in § 165(c)(2), see Austin v. Commissioner, 298 F.2d 583, 584 (CA2 1962). In these related areas, consistency is desirable. See also, Commissioner v. Duberstein, 363 U.S. 278, 286 (1960).

F. We see no inconsistency, such as the taxpayer suggests, between the Government's urging dominant motivation here and its having urged only significant motivation as the appropriate standard for the incurrence of liability for the accumulated-earnings tax under § 531 of the 1954 Code, 26 U.S.C. § 531, and for includability in the gross estate, for federal estate tax purposes, of a transfer made in contemplation of death under § 2035, 26 U.S.C. § 2035. Sections 531 and 2035 are Congress' answer to tax avoidance activity. * * *

G. The Regulations' use of the word "proximate" perhaps is not the most fortunate, for it naturally tempts one to think in tort terms. The temptation, however, is best rejected, and we reject it here. In tort law factors of duty, of foreseeability, of secondary cause, and of plural liability are under consideration, and the concept of proximate cause has been developed as an appropriate application and measure of these factors. It has little place in tax law where plural aspects are not usual, where an item either is or is not a deduction, or either is or is not a business bad debt, and where certainty is desirable.

IV

The conclusion we have reached means that the District Court's instructions, based on a standard of significant rather than dominant motivation, are erroneous and that, at least, a new trial is required. We have examined the record, however, and find nothing that would support a jury verdict in this taxpayer's favor had the dominant-motivation standard been embodied in the instructions. Judgment *n.o.v.* for the United States, therefore, must be ordered. * * *

As Judge Simpson pointed out in his dissent, 427 F.2d, at 284–285, the only real evidence offered by the taxpayer bearing upon motivation was his own testimony that he signed the indemnity agreement "to protect my job," that "I figured in three years' time I would get my money out," and that "I never once gave it [his investment in the corporation] a thought."

The statements obviously are self-serving. In addition, standing alone, they do not bear the light of analysis. What the taxpayer was purporting to say was that his $12,000 annual salary was his sole motivation, and that his $38,900 original investment, the actual value of which prior to the misfortunes of 1962 we do not know, plus his loans to the corporation, plus his personal interest in the integrity of the corporation as a source of living for his son-in-law and as an investment for his son and his other son-in-law, were of no consequence whatever in his thinking. The comparison is strained all the more by the fact that the salary is pre-tax and the investment is taxpaid. With his total annual income about $40,000, Mr. Generes may well have reached a federal income tax bracket of 40% or more for a joint return in 1958–1962. §§ 1 and 2 of the 1954 Code, 68A Stat. 5 and 8. The $12,000 salary thus would produce for him only about $7,000 net after federal tax and before any state income tax. This is the figure, and not $12,000, that has any possible significance for motivation purposes, and it is less than ⅕ of the original stock investment.

We conclude on these facts that the taxpayer's explanation falls of its own weight, and that reasonable minds could not ascribe, on this record, a dominant motivation directed to the preservation of the taxpayer's salary as president of Kelly-Generes Construction Co., Inc.

The judgment is reversed and the case is remanded with direction that judgment be entered for the United States.

It is so ordered.

Mr. Justice POWELL and Mr. Justice REHNQUIST took no part in the consideration or decision of this case.

[The concurring opinion of Mr. Justice MARSHALL and the dissenting opinion of Mr. Justice DOUGLAS have been omitted. Ed.]

NOTE

Even the most optimistic taxpayers who embark on a business venture are well advised to anticipate the tax consequences if their endeavors should result in a loss. Sole proprietors, partners and shareholders in an S corporation usually may deduct the losses from their business operations as they are incurred. But shareholders or creditors of a C corporation normally must be content to recognize a capital loss at the time their investment is sold or becomes worthless. If a loss results from the worthlessness of stock or debt evidenced by a "security" which is a capital asset, the calamity is treated as a hypothetical sale or exchange on the last day of the taxable year in which the loss is incurred.[1]

If a loss is sustained on a debt not evidenced by a "security," its characterization is governed by the bad debt deduction rules in Section 166. Business bad debts are ordinary losses, while nonbusiness bad debts are artifically treated as short-term capital losses.[2] After the *Generes* case, it became almost impossible for shareholders to avoid nonbusiness bad debt treatment if they sustain a loss in their creditor capacity. Whatever their roles, corporate insiders generally are regarded as investors.[3]

1. See I.R.C. § 165(g)(2)(C).

2. I.R.C. § 166(a), (d).

3. See, e.g., Benak v. Commissioner, 77 T.C. 1213 (1981); but see Bowers v. Commissioner, 716 F.2d 1047 (4th Cir.1983).

These rules place corporate investors who suffer losses at a tax disadvantage relative to those who conduct their affairs through other business vehicles. In the case of a small business, this dichotomy makes little sense and may prove to be particularly unfair to those who are forced into the C corporation form for nontax reasons. In 1958, in the same legislation that produced Subchapter S, Congress provided some limited relief by enacting Section 1244 in order to "encourage the flow of new funds into small business" by placing small business shareholders on more of a par with proprietors and partners.[4] If certain detailed statutory requirements are met, an individual shareholder may (within limits) treat a loss from the sale, exchange or worthlessness of "Section 1244 stock" as an ordinary loss even if it might otherwise have been treated as a capital loss.

For the first twenty years of its history, discussions of Section 1244 usually began with a sermonette on the need to comply with the strict technical requirements of the statute, the foremost of which was the need for a formal written "Section 1244 plan." Perhaps because these formalities trapped even wary advisors, Congress simplified Section 1244 by abolishing the plan requirement and removing certain other obstacles. The principal remaining requirements and limitations of Section 1244 may be summarized as follows:

Individual Issuees Only. Because Section 1244 was designed to stimulate investment in small businesses, only individual taxpayers and partnerships (but not trusts and estates) who were original issuees of the stock are eligible for ordinary loss treatment.[5] Donees, heirs and other transferees of the original investor will continue to be limited to capital loss treatment under Section 165.

Common or Preferred Stock. Until 1984, Section 1244 treatment was limited to common stock (either voting or nonvoting) issued by a domestic corporation. The 1984 Act extended Section 1244 eligibility to any class of stock but retained the requirement that the stock must have been issued for money or property.[6] Stock issued for services thus would not qualify.[7]

Small Business Corporation Status. To prevent the benefits of Section 1244 from extending beyond the small business community, its reach is limited to stock of a "small business corporation," a status achieved if the aggregate amount of money and other property received by the corporation for stock, as a contribution to capital and as paid-in surplus does not exceed $1,000,000.[8] This determination is made at the

4. H.R.Rep. No. 2198, 85th Cong., 1st Sess. (1958), reprinted in 1959–2 C.B. 709, 711. See generally Johnson & Cochran, "Looking a Gift-Horse in the Mouth: Some Observations and Suggestions for Improving Internal Revenue Code Section 1244," 39 Sw.L.J. 975 (1986).

5. I.R.C. § 1244(a). A partner qualifies for a Section 1244 ordinary loss only if he was a partner when the partnership ac-

quired the stock. Reg. § 1.1244(a)–1(b)(2). The regulations also provide that ordinary loss treatment is not available to a partner who has received the stock in a distribution from the partnership. Reg. § 1.1244(a)–1(b).

6. I.R.C. § 1244(c)(1).

7. Reg. § 1.1244(c)–1(d).

8. I.R.C. § 1244(c)(3).

time the stock is issued, but the $1,000,000 cap includes both amounts received for the newly issued stock and any stock previously issued by the corporation.[9]

Gross Receipts Test When Loss Sustained. Qualification under Section 1244 when the stock is issued does not automatically guarantee that an ordinary loss will be available when a loss is realized. Section 1244(c)(1)(C) also requires that, for the five taxable years ending before the year in which the loss was sustained, the corporation must have derived more than 50 percent of its aggregate gross receipts from sources other than passive investment income items (royalties, rents, dividends, interest, annuities and sales or exchanges of stock or securities). The requirement is designed to preclude ordinary loss treatment to shareholders of corporations engaged primarily in investment rather than active business activities. If these investment losses had been incurred directly, the taxpayer would have been limited to capital loss treatment and the corporate form should not facilitate an end run around this limitation. If the loss is sustained before the corporation has a five-year measuring period, then the gross receipts test is applied by substituting the taxable years ending before the date of the loss in which the corporation was in existence.[10]

Limit on Amount of Ordinary Loss. The aggregate amount that may be treated by the taxpayer as an ordinary loss for any one taxable year may not exceed $50,000 or, in the case of married couple filing a joint return, $100,000.[11] In the case of partnerships, the limit is determined separately as to each partner.[12]

Section 1244 is a "no lose" provision in the sense that nothing is lost by passing a corporate resolution declaring that an equity interest is being issued as Section 1244 stock even if the stock ultimately fails to qualify. Although there is no longer a requirement for a formal plan, it generally is regarded as good practice to include a reference to Section 1244 in the corporate resolution approving the issuance of stock in a qualifying corporation, if only to remind the shareholders that ordinary loss treatment is available if that unhappy event should later occur.

PROBLEM

High Technologies, Inc. ("Hi-Tech") is a small semiconductor company owned and operated by Thelma High and Allen Woody. Thelma and Allen formed Hi-Tech three years ago by each contributing $400,000 in exchange for 50% of the corporation's common stock. Hi-Tech has been planning a major expansion of its manufacturing facility and has decided to seek outside financing. It recently approached

9. Id. See also Reg. § 1.1244(c)–2(b). If the capital receipts exceed $1,000,000, the corporation may designate certain shares as Section 1244 stock provided that the amounts received for such designated stock do not exceed $1,000,000 less amounts re-

ceived for stock or as capital contributions in prior years.

10. I.R.C. § 1244(c)(2)(A).

11. I.R.C. § 1244(b).

12. Reg. § 1.1244(b)–1(a).

Jennifer Leech, a venture capitalist, about the possibility of her investing $200,000 in Hi-Tech.

After investigating the corporation's financial position, Jennifer has decided to make the investment. Her objectives are to obtain maximum security while at the same time participating in Hi-Tech's potential growth. But Jennifer also is concerned about the rapid change in computer technology and would like to plan for the most favorable tax consequences in the unfortunate event that her investment in Hi-Tech becomes worthless. Consider to what extent Jennifer will realize her goals if, in the alternative, her investment takes the following forms:

(a) A $200,000 unregistered five-year Hi-Tech note bearing market rate interest.

(b) A $200,000 Hi-Tech registered bond bearing market rate interest.

(c) A $190,000 Hi-Tech registered bond bearing market rate interest and warrants to purchase Hi-Tech common stock at a favorable price.

(d) $200,000 of Hi-Tech common stock.

(e) $200,000 of Hi-Tech convertible preferred stock.

(f) Same as (d), above, except that Thelma and Allen originally capitalized Hi-Tech by each contributing $500,000.

(g) Same as (d), above, except that Jennifer plans to give the Hi-Tech common stock to her son, Peter, as a wedding gift.

(h) Same as (d), above, except that Jennifer and her son, Peter, will purchase the Hi-Tech common stock through Leech Associates, a venture capital partnership.

CHAPTER 4. NONLIQUIDATING DISTRIBUTIONS

A. DIVIDENDS: IN GENERAL

Code: §§ 243(a), (b)(1); 301(a), (c); 316(a); 317(a).

Regulations: §§ 1.301–1(c); 1.316–1(a)(1)–(2).

It has been said that a corporation derives no greater pleasure than through making distributions to its shareholders. As one court observed, "like the 'life-rendering pelican,' [a corporation] feeds its shareholders upon dividends."[1] In the case of a close corporation, however, this colorful marine analogy may fail to capture reality. Closely held companies traditionally resist paying dividends and expend considerable energy to avoid the sting of the double tax. Even many public companies choose to retain profits for use in the business. But if an enterprise is successful, the pressure will mount to distribute earnings to the shareholders, and distributions often occur in connection with major changes in a corporation's capital structure, such as liquidations, mergers and recapitalizations. At that point, it becomes necessary to classify the distribution as a taxable dividend or a nontaxable return of capital. Simple as it may seem, drawing this line has been a central issue in the taxation of corporations and shareholders. Not surprisingly, the statutory scheme is complex and sometimes even illogical.

Distributions come in many forms. A corporation may distribute its own stock or debt obligations; redeem (i.e., repurchase) stock from its shareholders by distributing cash or property; or distribute its net assets in liquidation of the entire business. The tax consequences of these and other more complex transactions are considered in later chapters.[2] This chapter lays a foundation by examining the corporate and shareholder level tax treatment of nonliquidating (or "operating") distributions of cash or property—distributions loosely referred to as "dividends" by those unfamiliar with Subchapter C. We are about to learn, however, that not all distributions classified as dividends under state law or designated as such in the corporate minutes are dividends for federal tax purposes.

Determining the tax consequences of a nonliquidating distribution requires an excursion through several sections of the Code. Section 301 governs the amount and classification to corporate and noncorporate shareholders of distributions of "property" made by a C corporation with respect to its stock.[3] Under Section 301(c)(1), distributions that are "dividends" within the meaning of Section 316 must be included in

---

1. Commissioner v. First State Bank of Stratford, 168 F.2d 1004, 1009 (5th Cir. 1948), cert. denied 335 U.S. 867, 69 S.Ct. 137 (1948).

2. See Chapters 5–7, infra.

3. Distributions to shareholders in their other capacities (e.g., employee, creditor, lessor) are thus not embraced by Section 301. "Property" is deemed to include money and other corporate assets but not stock

gross income.[4] In order to prevent multiple taxation, corporate share-holders may deduct 70 percent (or sometimes 80 or 100 percent) of the dividends they receive.[5] Distributions that are not dividends are first treated as a recovery of the shareholder's basis in his stock, and any excess over basis is treated as gain from the sale or exchange of the stock.[6]

Section 316(a) defines a "dividend" as any distribution of property made by a corporation to its shareholders out of (1) earnings and profits accumulated after February 28, 1913 ("accumulated earnings and prof-its") or (2) earnings and profits of the current taxable year ("current earnings and profits"). "Earnings and profits," a term of art to be examined in more detail below, is a concept that attempts to distin-guish distributions of corporate profits from returns of capital. Section 316(a) also includes two irrebuttable presumptions: every distribution is deemed to be made out of earnings and profits to the extent that they exist and is deemed to be made from the most recently accumulated earnings and profits.

In testing for dividend status, the regulations look first to current earnings and profits, determined as of the close of the taxable year in which the distribution is made.[7] A distribution out of current earnings and profits is thus a taxable dividend even if the corporation has an historical deficit.[8] This rule simplifies the inquiry because it is rare for a company to make distributions during a period when it is operating at a loss. Only when distributions exceed current earnings and profits must reference be made to the historical track record of the corpora-tion.

The dual focus in Section 316 on current and accumulated earnings and profits may produce anomalous results because dividend status is determined by reference to the corporation's overall financial success rather than the gain or loss realized by a particular shareholder. To be sure, most dividends represent an increase in the shareholder's wealth

---

in the distributing corporation or rights to acquire stock. I.R.C. § 317(a).

4. See also I.R.C. § 61(a)(7).

5. I.R.C. § 243(a), (b)(1), (c). See Chap-ter 1B1, supra. Potential abuses of the dividends received deduction are policed by an assortment of Code provisions. See Sec-tion F of this chapter, infra.

6. I.R.C. § 301(c)(2), (3). The rules in the text apply to distributions by C corpo-rations that do not file a consolidated re-turn. Distributions received by one mem-ber of a consolidated group from another member generally are tax-free, but the dis-tributee must reduce its basis in the stock of the payor by the amount of the distribu-tion. See Reg. § 1.1502–14(a)(1). See Chapter 14B, infra. Distributions by S cor-porations also are tax-free to the extent of the shareholder's basis, and any excess is treated as gain from a sale of the S corpo-ration stock. § 1368(b). The rules are more complex if an S corporation has accu-mulated earnings and profits from a time when it was a C corporation. § 1368(c). See Chapter 15E, infra.

7. Reg. § 1.316–1(a)(1).

8. This seemingly harsh "nimble divi-dend" rule was enacted in 1937 as a relief measure to permit corporations with defi-cits to pay dividends and thus avoid an undistributed profits tax then in effect. Although the undistributed profits tax was later repealed, the "nimble dividend" rule survived without any Congressional expla-nation of why it was still necessary. See Bittker & Eustice, Federal Income Taxa-tion of Corporations and Shareholders ¶ 7.02 (5th ed. 1987).

rather than a return of capital, but this is not inevitable under the current scheme. For example, the existence of accumulated earnings and profits will cause a distribution to be classified as a dividend even if those profits were earned before the shareholder acquired his stock.

To illustrate, assume that Shareholder forms Corporation with initial paid-in capital of $110. During its first year of operation, Corporation earns $20 and distributes $30 to Shareholder. The distribution consists of a $20 dividend (out of current earnings and profits) and a $10 return of capital, and Shareholder reduces his basis by $10 to $100. In year two, assume Corporation earns $50 and makes no distributions, ending the year with $50 of accumulated earnings and profits. At the beginning of year three, Buyer (an individual) acquires all the stock of Corporation for $150, and Shareholder realizes a $50 long-term capital gain. Assume further that Corporation, now wholly owned by Buyer, suffers a $10 loss in year three, causing its accumulated earnings and profits account to decrease to $40. If Corporation breaks even in year four but distributes $30, Buyer is taxed on the entire distribution because it is made from accumulated earnings and profits. But in substance Buyer has received merely a return of capital. After all, he paid $150 for the stock, and the company has since lost $10 while distributing $30 to Buyer, who is understandably surprised to realize $30 of ordinary income even though the value of his investment has declined.

In an academically tidy world, the curious result illustrated above should not occur. Instead, the tax treatment of distributions should depend on the gain or loss realized by the shareholder rather than the corporation's financial track record over time. Ideally, Shareholder should be taxed at ordinary income rates to the extent that the gain on a sale of his stock is attributable to undistributed corporate earnings while he was a shareholder. It then would be unnecessary to tax those earnings again when they are distributed to Buyer, who logically should be treated as receiving a return of capital rather than a $30 dividend.

In the early days of the income tax, taxpayers in Buyer's position argued that distributions out of preacquisition earnings should not be taxable since they did not represent any real gain to the shareholder. The Supreme Court put this argument to rest, reasoning: [9]

> Dividends are the appropriate fruit of stock ownership, are commonly reckoned as income, and are expended as such by the stockholder without regard to whether they are declared from the most recent earnings, or from a surplus accumulated from the earnings of the past, or are based upon the increased value of the property of the corporation. The stockholder is, in the ordinary case, a different entity from the corporation, and Congress was at liberty to treat the dividends as coming to him

---

9. Lynch v. Hornby, 247 U.S. 339, 334, 38 S.Ct. 543, 545 (1918).

ab extra, and as constituting a part of his income when they came to hand.

Despite its conceptual flaws, the present approach is defensible on practical grounds. Since shares in publicly held corporations are traded daily, it would be difficult to determine precisely the corporation's earnings during the period that any particular shareholder held his stock. The current scheme at least ensures that earnings will be taxed to some shareholder, even if it may not be the theoretically correct one. Indeed, the presumption that distributions are made out of the earnings and profits to the extent they exist often eliminates the chore of tracing the source of a distribution and considerably simplifies the system.[10]

B. EARNINGS AND PROFITS

Code: § 312(a), (c), (f)(1), (k)(1)–(3); 316(a). Skim § 312(n).

Regulations: § 1.312–6(a), (b), (d) (first sentence), 1.312–7(b)(1) (first sentence).

The Code makes it clear that distributions are dividends only to the extent that they come from the corporation's earnings and profits, but it curiously does not take the extra step and actually define earnings and profits. Section 312 describes the effects of certain transactions on earnings and profits, and the accompanying regulations provide ample elaboration, but a precise definition of the term is nowhere to be found in the Code or regulations.[1] The function of earnings and profits, however, is clear: it is a measuring device used to determine the extent to which a distribution is made from a corporation's economic income as opposed to its taxable income or paid-in capital.

The meaning of earnings and profits, which is a concept peculiar to the tax law, has evolved over the years. It is roughly analogous (but not identical) to the accounting concept of earned surplus in that neither amount includes initial paid-in capital or subsequent contributions to capital. The primary difference between the two concepts is that earned surplus is decreased by stock distributions and contingency reserves. If earnings and profits similarly were reduced, a company could avoid ever making a taxable distribution simply by ensuring that

10. In its 1983 preliminary report on the reform and simplification of Subchapter C, the Senate Finance Committee Staff recommended a repeal of the earnings and profits limitation. The proposal would have taxed all ordinary distributions as dividends, with limited relief for distributions made to the original contributing shareholder within three years of his contribution. See Staff of the Senate Finance Committee, Preliminary Report on the Reform and Simplification of the Income Taxation of Corporations, 98th Cong., 1st Sess. 77–78 (Comm.Print 98–85, 1983). The proposal was deleted from the staff's final report. See Staff of the Senate Finance Committee, Subchapter C Revision Act of 1985: A Final Report Prepared by the Staff, 99th Cong., 1st Sess. (S.Prt. 99–47, 1985). For some other alternatives to the present scheme, see Andrews, " 'Out of Its Earnings and Profits': Some Reflections on the Taxation of Dividends," 69 Harv.L.Rev. 1403 (1956); Blum, "The Earnings and Profits Limitation on Dividend Income: A Reappraisal," 53 Taxes 68 (1975).

1. For a history of the earnings and profits concept, see Rudick, " 'Dividends' and 'Earnings or Profits' Under the Income Tax Law: Corporate Non-Liquidating Distributions," 89 U.Pa.L.Rev. 865 (1941).

its distributions were preceded by nontaxable stock dividends or the establishment of reserves for contingencies. Earnings and profits also are not identical to taxable income. The earnings and profits account is intended to measure the economic performance of the corporation. In contrast, taxable income does not provide a true financial picture because that concept is cluttered with a host of policy incentives and relief provisions that bear little or no relationship to the corporation's capacity to pay dividends.

Although earnings and profits can be determined by making adjustments to either earned surplus or taxable income, the traditional approach is to start with a corporation's taxable income and make adjustments that fall into the following four broad categories: [2]

1. *Certain items excluded from taxable income must be added back.* Items that represent true financial gain but are exempt from tax, such as municipal bond interest, life insurance proceeds and federal tax refunds and otherwise excludible discharge of indebtedness income (unless coupled with a basis reduction under Section 1017) are included in earnings and profits.[3] But contributions to capital and gains that are realized but not recognized for tax purposes (e.g., like-kind exchanges, Section 351 transfers, involuntary conversions under Section 1033) are not added back in computing earnings and profits.[4]

2. *Certain items deductible in determining taxable income must be added back.* Certain deductions and benefits allowed in computing taxable income which do not reflect a real decrease in corporate wealth are not permitted or are restricted in determining earnings and profits. For example, a deductible item that involves no actual expenditure, such as the Section 243 dividends received deduction, must be added back to taxable income in determining earnings and profits. Similarly, the depletion allowance must be based on the corporation's cost of a depletable asset even if the corporation deducts percentage depletion in computing taxable income.[5]

3. *Certain nondeductible items must be subtracted.* Some items not allowed as deductions in computing taxable income in fact represent actual expenditures that diminish a corporation's capacity to pay dividends. These items reduce earnings and profits. For example, federal income taxes paid during the year by a cash method corporation will reduce earnings and profits,[6] as will losses and expenses disallowed

---

2. The regulations generally provide that the corporation's accounting method in determining taxable income will be employed in computing earnings and profits. Reg. § 1.312–6(a).

3. Reg. § 1.312–6(b). In the case of life insurance, the Service has ruled that earnings and profits are increased by the proceeds collected less the aggregate premiums paid by the corporation. Rev.Rul. 54–230, 1954–1 C.B. 114. For discharge of indebtedness income, see I.R.C. § 312(*l*)(1).

4. I.R.C. § 312(f)(1).

5. Reg. § 1.312–6(c).

6. Rev.Rul. 70–609, 1970–2 C.B. 78; Webb v. Commissioner, 572 F.2d 135 (5th Cir.1978). A few courts, however, have permitted a cash method corporation to reduce its earnings and profits in the year to which the federal taxes relate even though the taxes have not yet been paid. See e.g., Drybrough v. Commissioner, 238 F.2d 735 (6th Cir.1956).

under provisions such as Sections 265 (expenses allocable to tax-exempt income), 267 (losses between related taxpayers) and 274 (travel and entertainment expenses) and charitable contributions in excess of the ten percent corporate limitation. In addition, net operating losses and capital losses in excess of capital gains reduce earnings and profits in the year they are incurred. In order to avoid a double tax benefit, they may not be carried back or forward in determining earnings and profits.

4. *Certain timing adjustments must be made.* Finally, a variety of adjustments are required to override timing rules that allow corporations to artificially defer income or accelerate deductions in computing taxable income.[7] For example, a corporation may not use the generally applicable accelerated cost recovery system (ACRS) in determining earnings and profits. Instead, the cost of depreciable property may be recovered when computing earnings and profits only under the alternative depreciation system, which employs the straight line method using specially prescribed and generally longer recovery periods than ACRS;[8] the corporation thus must increase its taxable income by the excess ACRS depreciation allowed for tax purposes.[9] Similarly, if the corporation has elected to expense the cost of eligible property under Section 179, it must amortize that expense ratably over five years in determining earnings and profits.[10] Additional timing rules for the calculation of earnings and profits require a corporation to capitalize otherwise amortizable construction period interest and taxes and to amortize normally deductible mineral exploration costs and intangible drilling expenses over extended time periods.[11]

On the income side, gains currently realized but deferred under the installment sale method of Section 453 or by the completed contract method of accounting must be currently included in earnings and profits.[12] Moreover, for earnings and profits purposes, gains on the sale of inventory must be reported under the standard first-in-first-out (FIFO) method rather than the last-in-first-out (LIFO) method.[13]

It should be apparent by now that earnings and profits is simply an accounting concept designed to measure a corporation's true financial results. It is an "account" created by the Code—not an actual bank account or liquid fund set aside by the corporation for the payment of dividends. There is no statute of limitations on earnings and profits issues, and a corporation sometimes will face the onerous task of

---

7. See generally I.R.C. § 312(n). To prevent abuse of the dividends received deduction, the Section 312(n) adjustments do not apply to distributions to any 20 percent or more corporate shareholders. I.R.C. § 301(e). See Section F5 of this chapter, infra.

8. I.R.C. §§ 312(k)(3)(A); 168(g)(2).

9. The adjusted basis of the property determined under this special provision also is used in determining the impact of a

sale or other disposition of property on earnings and profits. I.R.C. § 312(f)(1). In virtually all cases, this rule will cause corporations to have different bases in property for purposes of determining taxable income and earnings and profits.

10. I.R.C. § 312(k)(3)(B).

11. I.R.C. § 312(n)(1), (2).

12. I.R.C. § 312(n)(5), (6).

13. I.R.C. § 312(n)(4).

reconstructing many years of financial history in order to determine the tax consequences of a current distribution.[14]

PROBLEM

X Corporation is a cash method, calendar year taxpayer. During the current year, X has the following income and expenses:

Gross profits from sales	$20,000
Salaries paid to employees	10,250
Tax-exempt interest received	3,000
Dividends received from IBM	5,000
Depreciation (X purchased 5-year property in the current year for $14,000; assume the property has a 7-year class life; no § 179 election was made)	2,800
LTCG on a sale of stock	2,500
LTCL on a sale of stock	5,000
LTCL carryover from prior years	1,000
Estimated federal income taxes paid	800

Determine X's taxable income for the current year and its current earnings and profits.

C. DISTRIBUTIONS OF CASH

Code: §§ 301(a), (b), (c); 312(a); 316(a).

Regulations: §§ 1.301–1(a), (b); 1.316–2(a)–(c).

The taxation of cash distributions by a corporation with respect to its stock is relatively straightforward. The amount of the distribution is simply the amount of money received by the shareholder.[1] That amount is taxable as a dividend to the extent of the distributing corporation's current or accumulated earnings and profits.[2] Amounts distributed in excess of available earnings and profits are first applied against and reduce the basis of the shareholder's stock and, to the extent that they exceed the shareholder's basis, they are treated as gain from the sale or exchange of the stock.[3] The distributing corporation generally is permitted to reduce its earnings and profits by the amount of money distributed, except that earnings and profits may be reduced as a result of a distribution only to the extent they exist.[4] Thus, while a deficit in earnings and profits may result from corporate operations, a deficit may not be created or increased by a distribution.[5]

---

14. Because it usually is an inherently factual question, the Internal Revenue Service will not issue a ruling on a corporation's earnings and profits. Rev.Proc. 87–3, § 3.01(22), 1987–1 C.B. 523, 524.

1. The same rule applies to corporate and noncorporate distributees. I.R.C. § 301(b).

2. I.R.C. §§ 301(c)(1); 316(a).

3. I.R.C. § 301(c)(2), (3).

4. I.R.C. § 312(a).

5. Id.

When there are insufficient current earnings and profits available to cover all cash distributions made during the year, earnings and profits must be allocated to the distributions in order to determine dividend status under the following rules: [6]

(1) First, current earnings and profits, determined as of the end of the year, are prorated among the distributions by using the following formula: [7]

$$\frac{\text{Current E \& P allocated}}{\text{to distribution}} = \frac{\text{Amount of}}{\text{distribution}} \times \frac{\text{Total current E \& P}}{\text{Total distributions}}$$

(2) Next, accumulated earnings and profits are allocated chronologically to distributions (i.e., on a first-come, first-served basis).[8]

(3) If the corporation has a current loss but has accumulated earnings and profits from prior years, it will be necessary to determine the amount of accumulated earnings and profits available on the date of distribution. Unless the loss can be earmarked to a particular period, the current deficit is prorated to the date of the distribution.[9]

Revenue Ruling 74–164, below, and the problem which follows test your ability to understand and apply these principles.

REVENUE RULING 74–164

1974–1 Cum.Bull. 74.

Advice has been requested concerning the taxable status of corporate distributions under the circumstances described below.

X corporation and *Y* corporation each using the calendar year for Federal income tax purposes made distributions of $15,000 to their respective shareholders on July 1, 1971, and made no other distributions to their shareholders during the taxable year. The distributions were taxable as provided by section 301(c) of the Internal Revenue Code of 1954.

Situation 1.

At the beginning of its taxable year 1971, *X* corporation had earnings and profits accumulated after February 28, 1913, of $40,000. It had an operating loss for the period January 1, 1971 through June 30, 1971, of $50,000 but had earnings and profits for the entire year 1971 of $5,000.

Situation 2.

At the beginning of its taxable year 1971, *Y* corporation had a deficit in earnings and profits accumulated after February 28, 1913, of

---

6. This allocation method is significant only if there is a change in shareholder interests during the year or on a non pro rata distribution.

7. Reg. § 1.316–2(b), (c) Example.

8. Id.

9. Reg. § 1.316–2(b).

$60,000. Its net profits for the period January 1, 1971 through June 30, 1971, were $75,000 but its earnings and profits for the entire taxable year 1971 were only $5,000.

Situation 3.

Assume the same facts as in *Situation* 1 except that *X* had a deficit in earnings and profits of $5,000 for the entire taxable year 1971.

Situation 4.

Assume the same facts as in *Situation* 1 except that *X* had a deficit in earnings and profits of $55,000 for the entire taxable year 1971.

Section 301(a) and 301(c) of the Code provides, in part, that: (1) the portion of a distribution of property made by a corporation to a shareholder with respect to its stock which is a dividend (as defined in section 316), shall be included in the shareholder's gross income; (2) the portion of the distribution which is not a dividend shall be applied against and reduce the adjusted basis of the stock; and (3) the portion which is not a dividend to the extent that it exceeds the adjusted basis of the stock and is not out of increase in value accrued before March 1, 1913, shall be treated as gain from the sale or exchange of property.

Section 316(a) of the Code provides that the term "dividend" means any distribution of property made by a corporation to its shareholders out of its earnings and profits accumulated after February 28, 1913, or out of its earnings and profits of the taxable year computed as of the close of the taxable year without diminution by reason of any distribution made during the year, and *without regard to the amount of earnings and profits at the time the distribution was made.*

Section 1.316–2(a) of the Income Tax Regulations provides, in part, that in determining the source of a distribution, consideration should be given first, to the earnings and profits of the taxable year; and second, to the earnings and profits accumulated since February 28, 1913, only in the case where, and to the extent that, the distributions made during the taxable year are not regarded as out of the earnings and profits of that year.

Applying the foregoing principles, in *Situation* 1, the earnings and profits of *X* corporation for the taxable year 1971 of $5,000 and the earnings and profits accumulated since February 28, 1913, and prior to the taxable year 1971, of $40,000 were applicable to the distribution paid by it on July 1, 1971. Thus, $5,000 of the distribution of $15,000 was paid from the earnings and profits of the taxable year 1971 and the balance of $10,000 was paid from the earnings and profits accumulated since February 28, 1913. Therefore, the entire distribution of $15,000 was a dividend within the meaning of section 316 of the Code.

In *Situation* 2 the earnings and profits of *Y* corporation for the taxable year 1971 of $5,000 were applicable to the distribution paid by *Y* corporation on July 1, 1971. *Y* corporation had no earnings and profits accumulated after February 28, 1913, available at the time of the distribution. Thus, only $5,000 of the distribution by *Y* corporation of $15,000 was a dividend within the meaning of section 316 of the Code. The balance of such distribution, $10,000 which was not a dividend, applied against and reduced the adjusted basis of the stock in the hands of the shareholders, and to the extent that it exceeded the adjusted basis of the stock was gain from the sale or exchange of property.

In the case of a deficit in earnings and profits for the taxable year in which distributions are made, the taxable status of distributions is dependent upon the amount of earnings and profits accumulated since February 28, 1913, and available at the dates of distribution. In determining the amount of such earnings and profits, section 1.316–2(b) of the regulations provides, in effect, that the deficit in earnings and profits of the taxable year will be prorated to the dates of distribution.

Applying the foregoing to Situations 3 and 4 the distribution paid by *X* corporation on July 1, 1971, in each situation was a dividend within the meaning of section 316 of the Code to the extent indicated as follows:

Situation #3

Accumulated Earnings and Profits (E & P) 1/1	$ 40,000
E & P deficit for entire taxable year ($5,000) Prorate to date of distribution 7/1 (½ of $5,000)	(2,500)
E & P available 7/1	$ 37,500
Distribution 7/1 ($15,000)	(15,000) taxable as a dividend
E & P deficit from 7/1–12/31	(2,500)
Accumulated E & P balance 12/31	$ 20,000

Situation #4

Accumulated E & P 1/1	$ 40,000
E & P deficit for entire taxable year ($55,000) Prorate to date of distribution 7/1 (½ of $55,000)	(27,500)
E & P available 7/1	$ 12,500
Distribution 7/1 ($15,000)	(12,500) taxable as a dividend
E & P deficit from 7/1–12/31	(27,500)
Accumulated E & P balance 12/31	$ (27,500)

NOTE

Situations 3 and 4 of Revenue Ruling 74–164 do not consider the possibility of earmarking the 1971 deficit to the first half of the year. Under the regulations,[1] if the deficit were sustained in the first half of 1971, the full deficit (not just one-half) would reduce the accumulated earnings and profits available to characterize the July 1 distribution as

1. Reg. § 1.316–2(b).

a dividend. This would not affect the result in Situation 3 but it would change the result in Situation 4, where there would be no dividend.

PROBLEM

Ann owns all of the common stock (the only class outstanding) of Pelican Corporation. Prior to the transactions below and as a result of a § 351 transfer, Ann has a $10,000 basis in her Pelican stock. What results to Ann and Pelican in each of the following alternative situations?

(a) In year one Pelican has $5,000 of current and no accumulated earnings and profits and it distributes $17,500 to Ann?

(b) Pelican has a $15,000 accumulated deficit in its earnings and profits at the beginning of year two. In year two Pelican has $10,000 of current earnings and profits and it distributes $10,000 to Ann.

(c) Pelican has $10,000 of accumulated earnings and profits at the beginning of year two and $4,000 of current earnings and profits in year two. On July 1 of year two, Ann sells half of her Pelican stock to Baker Corporation for $15,000. On April 1 of year two, Pelican distributes $10,000 to Ann, and on October 1 of year 2, Pelican distributes $5,000 to Ann and $5,000 to Baker.

(d) Same as (c), above, except that Pelican has a $10,000 deficit in earnings and profits in year 2 as a result of its business operations.

D. DISTRIBUTIONS OF PROPERTY

1. CONSEQUENCES TO THE DISTRIBUTING CORPORATION

a. BACKGROUND: THE *GENERAL UTILITIES* DOCTRINE

Under the double tax regime of Subchapter C, profits from the sale of appreciated corporate property are taxed twice—first to the corporation when it sells the property and again to the shareholders when the proceeds are distributed as dividends. What if a corporation *distributes* appreciated property to its shareholders? The shareholders, of course, receive a taxable dividend to the extent the distribution is out of current or accumulated earnings and profits. Should the distributing corporation also recognize gain—just as if it had sold the property for its fair market value? Or is the corporation entitled to tax relief because the property was distributed rather than sold? Does the answer depend on the shareholder's basis in the distributed property? If relief is appropriate, should nonliquidating distributions be treated less favorably than liquidating distributions? And what about distributions of loss property? Simple as they may seem, these are among the most controversial questions ever spawned by Subchapter C. The answers will come gradually. The coverage in this chapter is limited to nonliquidating distributions. To set the stage, we begin with a brief history of the rise and fall of what has become known as the *General Utilities* doctrine.

In General Utilities & Operating Co. v. Helvering,[1] the Supreme Court first considered the corporate level tax consequences of a nonliquidating distribution of appreciated property by a corporation to its shareholders. The facts were straightforward. General Utilities Corporation had located a buyer for corporate property with a value of $1,000,000 and an adjusted basis of $2,000. Hoping to escape the large corporate-level tax that would be imposed on a sale by the corporation, General Utilities distributed the property to its shareholders with an "understanding" (but not a legal commitment) that they would sell the targeted property to the prospective buyer. Four days later, the shareholders sold the property to the buyer on the same terms negotiated by the corporation. The Service contended that the distribution was a taxable event at the corporate level.

By the time the controversy reached the Supreme Court, the government's principal argument was based on the premise that General Utilities had created an indebtedness to its shareholders by declaring a dividend. It went on to contend that using appreciated property to discharge that indebtedness was a taxable event. Apparently confining its decision to these narrow grounds, the Court held that General Utilities recognized no gain because the distribution was not a "sale" and the corporation did not discharge indebtedness with appreciated assets.[2] Despite this limited holding, it long was assumed that *General Utilities* stood for the broader proposition that a distributing corporation does not recognize gain or loss when it makes a distribution in kind with respect to its stock.[3]

The result in *General Utilities* raised fundamental policy questions that went to the heart of the double tax regime. The decision created a significant and arguably unwarranted tax distinction between a distribution in kind of appreciated property and a sale of that same property by the corporation followed by a distribution of the proceeds to the shareholders. In the case of a sale at the corporate level, the corpora-

---

1. 296 U.S. 200, 56 S.Ct. 185 (1935).

2. The government also argued that the subsequent sale by the shareholders of the assets could be attributed to the corporation, but the Court declined to consider this question since it had not been raised below. Ten years later, in Commissioner v. Court Holding Co., 324 U.S. 331, 65 S.Ct. 707 (1945), the government successfully advanced the attribution argument in the context of a liquidating distribution. See Chapter 7B2b, infra. In *General Utilities,* the government alternatively contended that a distribution of appreciated property by a corporation in and of itself constitutes

a realization event, but the Court did not address this argument. See Bittker & Eustice, Federal Income Taxation of Corporations and Shareholders ¶ 7.20 n. 143 (5th ed. 1987).

3. See, e.g., Commissioner v. Godley's Estate, 213 F.2d 529, 531 (3d Cir.1954), cert. denied 348 U.S. 862, 75 S.Ct. 86 (1954). Even before the 1954 Code, however, the *General Utilities* nonrecognition rule was subject to judicially-created exceptions, such as the assignment of income doctrine. See S.Rep. No. 1622, 83rd Cong., 2d Sess. 247 (1954).

tion recognizes gain and correspondingly must increase its earnings and profits. On distribution of the sale proceeds, the shareholders also are taxed to the extent of the corporation's earnings and profits. Under *General Utilities,* however, the corporation could distribute the same asset to the shareholders without recognizing gain. The shareholders, of course, were subject to tax on the distribution, but the asset appreciation escaped tax at the corporate level, and a noncorporate shareholder took the asset with a fair market value basis.[4] This simple comparison illustrates that the tax treatment of distributions in kind is critical to the integrity of the double tax regime. Because the *General Utilities* doctrine was incompatible with the double tax, it was criticized by commentators.[5]

Despite these deficiencies, Congress codified *General Utilities* in 1954 by enacting Section 311(a)(2), which provides that a corporation generally does not recognize gain or loss on a nonliquidating distribution of property.[6] This nonrecognition rule was never absolute. Over the years, the courts applied "common law" doctrines, such as assignment of income[7] and the tax benefit rule,[8] to override Section 311(a) and attribute income back to the corporation. The distributing corporation also was taxed when the distributed property was sold by the shareholder but the sale in substance was made by the corporation.[9]

The codification of *General Utilities* also was the subject of considerable legislative attention. When it enacted Section 311(a)(2) in 1954, Congress coupled the general nonrecognition rule with statutory exceptions relating to distributions of installment obligations,[10] LIFO inventory,[11] and property encumbered with liabilities in excess of basis.[12] Congress continued to chip away at the doctrine until 1986, when it completely repealed *General Utilities* in the context of both nonliquidating and liquidating distributions of appreciated property.[13]

b. CORPORATE GAIN OR LOSS

Code: 311.

Although the nonrecognition rule in Section 311(a)(2) remains in the Code, Section 311(b) stands that rule on its head for nonliquidating

---

4. I.R.C. § 301(d).

5. See, e.g., Block, "Liquidations Before and After Repeal of *General Utilities,*" 21 Harv.J.Legis. 307 (1984); Blum, "Taxing Transfers of Incorporated Business: A Proposal for Improvement," 52 Taxes 516 (1974); Raum, "Dividends in Kind: Their Tax Aspects," 63 Harv.L.Rev. 593 (1950).

6. Prior to the Tax Reform Act of 1986, Section 336 provided a similar nonrecognition rule for liquidating distributions. See Chapter 7B2, infra.

7. Reg. § 1.311–1(a). See, e.g., Commissioner v. First State Bank of Stratford, 168 F.2d 1004 (5th Cir. 1948), cert. denied 335 U.S. 867, 69 S.Ct. 137 (1948).

8. Cf. Hillsboro National Bank v. Commissioner, 460 U.S. 370, 103 S.Ct. 1134 (1983).

9. Reg. § 1.311–1(a); Bush Brothers & Co. v. Commissioner, 668 F.2d 252 (6th Cir. 1982); Waltham Netoco Theatres, Inc. v. Commissioner, 401 F.2d 333 (1st Cir. 1968). But see Anderson v. Commissioner, 92 T.C. 138 (1989).

10. I.R.C. § 453B.

11. I.R.C. § 311(b) (pre-1987).

12. I.R.C. § 311(c) (pre-1987).

13. See also Chapter 7B2, infra.

distributions of appreciated property made after 1986. If a corporation distributes appreciated property (other than its own obligations) in a nonliquidating distribution, it must recognize gain in an amount equal to the excess of the fair market value of the property over its adjusted basis.[14] The deceptive "general" rule of Section 311(a)(2) still applies, however, to disallow recognition of loss on a distribution of property that has declined in value. The objective of the piecemeal changes that culminated in the 1986 Act was to strengthen the corporate income tax by ensuring that appreciated property may never leave corporate solution and take a stepped-up basis in the hands of the distributee shareholder without the imposition of a corporate-level tax on the appreciation.[15]

As a result of the 1986 changes, the *General Utilities* doctrine no longer applies to nonliquidating distributions of appreciated property. A later chapter examines the repeal of the doctrine in the area of complete liquidations.[16] Despite what appears to be parallel treatment, some differences between the treatment of liquidating and nonliquidating distributions raise lingering policy issues. For example, a distributing corporation generally may recognize a loss on a liquidating distribution of property with a built-in loss.[17] Should nonliquidating distributions be treated similarly? Is the "general" loss disallowance rule in Section 311(a)(2) an indefensible trap for the uninformed? In considering these questions, one should keep in mind that the double tax regime continues to have its detractors, and some argue that relief through limited *General Utilities* type exceptions is appropriate.[18]

c. EFFECT ON THE DISTRIBUTING CORPORATION'S EARNINGS AND PROFITS

Code: § 312(a)(3), (b), (c), (f)(1).

Regulations: § 1.312–3.

Nonliquidating distributions of property have several effects upon the earnings and profits of the distributing corporation. Gain recognized by the corporation on the distribution naturally increases current earnings and profits.[1] Following a property distribution, the distribut-

---

14. If the liabilities encumbering distributed property exceed its adjusted basis, Section 311(b)(2) provides that rules similar to the rules in Section 336(b) shall apply for purposes of Section 311. See Chapter 7B2b, infra. Thus, if property distributed in a nonliquidating distribution is subject to a liability or if the shareholder assumes a liability of the distributing corporation in connection with the distribution, the fair market value of the distributed property shall be treated as not less than the amount of such liability.

15. Cf. S.Rep.No. 98–169, 98th Cong., 2d Sess. 177 (1984); H.R.Rep.No. 99–426, 99th Cong., 1st Sess. 282 (1985).

16. See Chapter 7B, infra.

17. I.R.C. § 336(a), (d).

18. See Chapter 7C7c, infra. Compare Thompson, "An Analysis of the Proposal to Repeal General Utilities with an Escape Hatch," 31 Tax Notes 1121 (June 16, 1986) with Yin, "General Utilities Repeal: Is Tax Reform Really Going to Pass it By?" 31 Tax Notes 1111 (June 16, 1986).

1. I.R.C. § 312(b)(1), (f)(1). For this purpose and for purposes of determining gain recognized, the adjusted basis of any property is its adjusted basis for purposes of computing earnings and profits. I.R.C. § 312(b), flush language. For example, re-

ing corporation may reduce accumulated earnings and profits (to the extent thereof) under Section 312(a)(3) by the adjusted basis of the distributed property. On a distribution of appreciated property (other than a corporation's own debt obligations), this rule is modified by Section 312(b)(2), which provides that Section 312(a)(3) is applied by substituting the fair market value of the property for its adjusted basis. This special rule logically allows a corporation that distributes appreciated property to make a downward adjustment to accumulated earnings and profits in an amount equal to the full fair market value of the property. The net result of these earnings and profits adjustments— the first relating to the gain recognized on the distribution and the second relating to the effect of the distribution itself—is the same as if the corporation had sold the property (increasing current earnings and profits by the gain recognized) and then distributed cash equal to the fair market value of the property (decreasing accumulated earnings and profits by that amount).[2]

Section 312(c) cryptically adds that "proper adjustment" shall be made for liabilities either assumed by the shareholder or to which the property is subject. Section 1.312–3 of the regulations provides that the "proper adjustment" is a reduction in the Section 312(a)(3) charge to earnings and profits for liabilities assumed or to which the property is subject. This adjustment thus *decreases* the charge to earnings and profits and properly reflects the fact that relief from the liability is an economic benefit to the distributing corporation.

2. CONSEQUENCES TO THE SHAREHOLDERS

Code: §§ 301(a), (b), (c), (d).

The rules governing the shareholder level tax consequences of property distributions are essentially the same as those for cash distributions. The amount of the distribution is the fair market value of the distributed property, reduced by any liabilities assumed by the shareholder or to which the property is subject;[1] that amount is taxed under the now familiar principles in Section 301(c). The shareholder's basis in the distributed property is its fair market value as of the date of the distribution.[2]

PROBLEM

Zane, an individual, owns all of the outstanding common stock in Sturdley Utilities Corporation. Zane purchased his Sturdley stock

covery property depreciated for tax purposes under ACRS must be depreciated for "E & P" purposes under the § 168(g)(2) alternative depreciation system and thus may have a different "E & P" adjusted basis.

2. If the distributing corporation recognizes a gain on the distribution, that gain increases *current* earnings and profits. Any decrease in earnings and profits re-

sulting from the distribution affects only the corporation's *accumulated* earnings and profits account as of the beginning of the year following the distribution.

1. I.R.C. § 301(b). The fair market value of the distributed property is determined as of the date of distribution. I.R.C. § 301(b)(3).

2. I.R.C. § 301(d).

seven years ago and his basis is $8,000. Before the transactions described below, Sturdley had $25,000 of accumulated earnings and profits and no current earnings and profits. Determine the tax consequences to Zane and Sturdley in each of the following alternative situations:

(a) Sturdley distributes inventory ($20,000 fair market value; $11,000 basis) to Zane.

(b) Same as (a), above, except that, before the distribution, Sturdley has no current or accumulated earnings and profits.

(c) Sturdley distributes land ($20,000 fair market value; $11,000 basis) which it has used in its business. Zane takes the land subject to a $16,000 mortgage.

(d) Assume Sturdley has $15,000 of current earnings and profits (in addition to $25,000 of accumulated earnings and profits) and it distributes to Zane land ($20,000 fair market value; $30,000 basis) which it held as an investment. Compare the result if Sturdley first sold the land and then distributed the proceeds.

(e) Sturdley distributes machinery used in its business ($10,000 fair market value, zero adjusted basis for taxable income purposes, and $2,000 adjusted basis for earnings and profits purposes). The machinery is five-year property and has a seven-year class life, was purchased by Sturdley for $14,000 on July 1 of year one (no § 179 election was made), and the distribution is made on January 1 of year seven. See I.R.C. §§ 168(g)(2), 312(k)(3); Reg. § 1.312–15(d).

3. DISTRIBUTIONS OF A CORPORATION'S OWN OBLIGATIONS

Code: §§ 311(a), (b)(1); 312(a)(2). Skim §§ 312(*o*); 1272(a)(1); 1273(a)(1).

Regulations: § 1.301–1(d)(1)(ii).

By virtue of the parenthetical in Section 311(b)(1)(A), "(other than an obligation of such corporation)", the general gain recognition rule does not apply to distributions by a corporation of its own debt obligations. Consequently, the eroded Section 311(a) continues to govern this situation. At the shareholder level, the amount of the distribution is the fair market value of the obligation received,[1] and the shareholder logically takes a fair market value basis in the obligation.[2] The distributing corporation's earnings and profits are reduced by the principal amount of the obligation or, in the case of an obligation having original issue discount, by its issue price.[3]

1.   Reg. § 1.301–1(d)(1)(ii).   3.   I.R.C. § 312(a)(2).

2.   Reg. § 1.301–1(h)(2)(i).

The legislative history which follows describes two Congressional concerns involving distributions of a corporation's own obligations and the solutions developed in the Tax Reform Act of 1984.

EXCERPT FROM THE SENATE FINANCE COMMITTEE EXPLANATION OF THE TAX REFORM ACT OF 1984

S.Rep. No. 98–169, 98th Cong., 2d Sess. 188–89 (1984).

Distributions By a Corporation of Debt Obligations Having a Fair Market Value Less Than Par (sec. 47 of the bill and sec. 312 of the Code)

Present Law

A distribution by a corporation constitutes a dividend only if out of current or accumulated earnings and profits. The fair market value of property distributed as a dividend is includible in the gross income of an individual shareholder.

A corporation can distribute as a dividend its own debt obligations. Those obligations may have a fair market value less than their face amount. That is, they may carry a stated interest rate which is below the prevailing market rate. In such a case, an individual shareholder would have dividend income in an amount equal to the value of the obligations distributed to him. But the corporation may contend that, under present law, it can reduce its earnings and profits by the principal amount of such obligations (sec. 312(a)). The result could be to eliminate earnings and profits at the cost of a relatively small dividend tax. Distributions made by a corporation with no earnings and profits are not dividends but a return of capital.

Furthermore, taxpayers may argue that, under present law, such an obligation is not subject to the original issue discount rules. If that is correct, a shareholder on the cash basis may report no income with respect to the discount until it is paid, and the income may qualify as capital gain. Similarly, an accrual basis obligor may claim interest deductions currently on a straight-line or ratable rather than a constant rate basis, thereby accelerating deduction of the discount.

Reasons for Change

The committee does not believe that a dividend distribution should reduce earnings and profits by more than the amount includible as a dividend in the gross income of an individual recipient of such a distribution. Furthermore, the committee believes that obligations distributed by a corporation that bear economic discount should be subject to the general original issue discount rules.

Explanation of Provisions

In the case of a dividend distribution by a corporation of its own debt securities at a discount, the corporation's earnings and profits are to be reduced by the issue price of the securities at the time of the distribution (determined under the original issue discount rules). Furthermore, any such securities are to be subject to the original issue discount rules. These provisions apply, however, only if the instruments distributed in fact represent indebtedness of the distributing corporation rather than equity. The provisions are not intended to create any inference that purported debt obligations distributed by a corporation should be treated as debt. The characterization of such instruments is governed by generally applicable provisions of present law. Furthermore, no inference is intended as to the proper treatment with respect to discount instruments distributed as dividends under present law.

PROBLEM

Andy owns all of the outstanding stock of Debt Corporation. Andy's stock basis is $100,000. Debt has $100,000 of accumulated earnings and profits and no current earnings and profits. On January 1 of this year, Debt distributed a $100,000 note, payable in 30 years, to Andy. The note bears no interest and because of that fact, the length of the obligation, and the relatively small size of Debt Co., the note currently has a fair market value of $5,000. Assume $5,000 is also the "issue price" of the note for purposes of original issue discount computations. On February 1 of this year, Debt Co. distributed $100,000 cash to Andy. How are the results of these distributions affected by the 1984 statutory changes discussed above?

E. CONSTRUCTIVE DISTRIBUTIONS

Code: Skim § 7872(a), (c)(1)(C).

From a tax standpoint, dividend distributions often combine the worst of all possible worlds: they are fully taxable as ordinary income to a noncorporate shareholder but are not deductible by the distributing corporation. To avoid the double tax, corporations often attempt to distribute earnings in a form that may be deductible at the corporate level. Notable examples include payment of: (1) excessive compensation to shareholders or their relatives;[1] (2) borderline expenses (e.g., travel or entertainment) incurred by shareholders;[2] (3) excessive rent for corporate use of shareholder property;[3] and (4) interest on shareholder debt that in substance represents equity.[4] If these payments are not what they purport to be—i.e., if they are not *really* salary, rent or interest, etc.—they risk being reclassified by the Service as a construc-

---

1. See, e.g., Transport Manufacturing & Equipment Co. v. Commissioner, 434 F.2d 373 (8th Cir.1970). See Rev.Rul. 79–8 at p. 148, infra, and compare Charles McCandless Tile Service v. United States, 191 Ct. Cl. 108, 422 F.2d 1336 (1970) with Elliotts, Inc. v. Commissioner, 716 F.2d 1241 (9th Cir.1983).

2. See, e.g., Ashby v. Commissioner, 50 T.C. 409 (1968).

3. See, e.g., International Artists, Ltd. v. Commissioner, 55 T.C. 94 (1970).

4. See Chapter 3, supra.

tive dividend. In that event, the corporate level deduction will be disallowed. Other disguised dividend strategies include labeling what in reality is a distribution as a loan to the shareholder,[5] bargain sales or rentals of corporate property to shareholders[6] and interest free loans.[7]

The constructive dividend area has produced many entertaining controversies involving blatant attempts by taxpayers to milk their corporations while avoiding the double tax. The prototype transaction involves a direct payment or receipt of an economic benefit by the shareholder, and resolution of the issue requires an evaluation of all the facts and circumstances, applying broad standards such as "reasonable compensation;" "shareholder benefit vs. corporate benefit" and "intent."[8] The case which follows presents the constructive dividend issue in a more subtle context involving a transaction between commonly controlled corporations.

STINNETT'S PONTIAC SERVICE, INC. v. COMMISSIONER *

United States Court of Appeals, Eleventh Circuit, 1984.
730 F.2d 634.

HATCHETT, Circuit Judge: In this case, we review the Tax Court's holding regarding the tax consequences of transactions involving two corporations and their common shareholder, the taxpayer. We affirm.

Facts

Richard W. Stinnett is president of Pontiac, an automobile dealership, and he owns 74% of the stock in the company. * * *

On or about July 2, 1973, Stinnett, Danford L. Sawyer (Sawyer), and Albert L. Bundy (Bundy) purchased the entire stock of Cargo Construction Company, Ltd. (Cargo), a Bahamian corporation. Cargo's principal business activity was commercial fishing, and its only asset was the lobster boat, R/V Victory. Stinnett owned 43%; Sawyer owned 35%; and Bundy owned 22% of Cargo's stock. Stinnett, Sawyer, and Bundy also purchased the R/V Victory for approximately $55,000. The three shareholders realized that Cargo would need additional capital to satisfy certain unforeseen initial costs and, therefore, agreed to contribute additional capital, in proportion to each shareholder's stock ownership in Cargo, to Cargo to meet its needs.

From 1973 to 1975, Sawyer and Bundy contributed funds to Cargo as required by the shareholders' agreement. Stinnett, however, failed to contribute to Cargo pursuant to the shareholders' agreement. Pontiac, the corporation which Stinnett controlled, contributed funds and

5. See, e.g., Williams v. Commissioner, 627 F.2d 1032 (10th Cir.1980).

6. See, e.g., Honigman v. Commissioner, 466 F.2d 69 (6th Cir.1972).

7. Compare Zager v. Commissioner, 72 T.C. 1009 (1979) with I.R.C. § 7872.

8. See generally, Bittker & Eustice, Federal Income Taxation of Corporations (5th ed. 1987).

* Footnotes omitted.

boat parts to Cargo. In 1973, Pontiac transferred $12,969.86 to Cargo, and, in return, Cargo issued interest bearing unsecured demand notes to Pontiac. During this same period, Pontiac also purchased marine parts for Cargo. Although Pontiac usually sold marine parts at 100% markup, it sold the marine parts to Cargo at only a 10% markup. Pontiac also made additional payments of $12,000 to Cargo. Cargo failed to issue any notes to Pontiac for any part of this amount.

From 1974 to 1975, Pontiac transferred an additional $45,000 to Cargo. Pontiac did not obtain any financial statements from Cargo prior to making any of the transfers, nor were the amounts of the transfers secured. After realizing that Cargo's lobster venture was unsuccessful, the shareholders decided to sell the R/V Victory and recoup their investment. On February 23, 1976, therefore, they agreed to sell the boat for $80,000 with Pontiac receiving $20,000 from the sale. That sale never materialized, but the R/V Victory was eventually sold for $42,000, and Cargo paid Richard Stinnett $6,000 for the sale of the boat.

On its 1974 federal income tax return, pursuant to 26 U.S.C.A. § 166(a) (West 1978), Pontiac deducted $56,388.63 as a partially worthless debt for its advances to Cargo. It computed this amount by subtracting $20,000, the anticipated amount Pontiac would have received from the sale of the R/V Victory, from $76,388.63, the total amount Pontiac claimed it had advanced Cargo. The Commissioner disallowed the partially worthless debt deduction, and determined that the contributions from Pontiac to Cargo constituted constructive dividends to Stinnett in 1973 and 1974. Therefore, these dividends were taxable to Stinnett pursuant to 26 U.S.C.A. §§ 301, 316 (West 1978 & Supp.1983). * * * After disallowing the deductions, the Commissioner determined the respective deficiencies. The tax court affirmed the Commissioner's rulings.

Stinnett's Pontiac Service, Stinnett, and Gay P. Stinnett appeal the United States Tax Court's decision determining a $4,047.52 deficiency in Pontiac's corporate income tax for 1972, and determining deficiencies of $16,012.81 and $36,321.46 in Stinnett's personal income taxes for 1973 and 1974.

Pontiac and Stinnett urge us to reverse the tax court's holding, claiming that Pontiac's advances to Cargo were worthless debts and, therefore, were deductible under 26 U.S.C.A. § 166; and, the advances failed to constitute constructive dividends to Stinnett. * * *

[In a portion of the opinion which is omitted the court determined that the advances from Pontiac to Cargo were contributions to capital and not bona fide debts. Ed.]

B. Were Pontiac's Advances to Cargo Constructive Dividends to Stinnett?

A corporate distribution to a shareholder is a dividend which the shareholder must include in his gross income if the distribution comes out of current and accumulated earnings and profits. ＊ ＊ ＊ "[A] transfer of property from one corporation to another corporation may constitute a [constructive] dividend to an individual who has an owner-ship interest in both corporations." Sammons v. Commissioner of Internal Revenue, 472 F.2d 449, 451 (5th Cir.1972).

In *Sammons,* the Fifth Circuit delineated the standard to deter-mine whether a transfer of funds from one corporation to another corporation constitutes a dividend to an individual who owns shares in both corporations:

> In every case, the transfer must be measured by an objective test [the distribution test]: did the transfer cause funds or other property to leave the control of the transferor corpora-tion and did it allow the stockholder to exercise control over such funds or property either directly or indirectly through some instrumentality other than the transferor corporation. If this first assay is satisfied by a transfer of funds from one corporation to another rather than by a transfer to the control-ling shareholder, a second, subjective test of purpose must also be satisfied before dividend characterization results. Though a search for intent or purpose is not ordinarily prerequisite to discovery of a dividend, such a subjective test must necessarily be utilized to differentiate between the normal business trans-actions of related corporations and those transactions designed primarily to benefit the stockowner.

Id. at 451.

The advances from Pontiac to Cargo satisfy the distribution test. Stinnett, the common owner of shares in Cargo and Pontiac, received the funds from Pontiac and transferred them to Cargo as a capital contribution. *Sammons,* 472 F.2d at 453. Such a distribution is effect-ed on the theory "that the funds pass from the transferor to the common stockholder as a dividend and then to the transferee as a capital contribution." Id. The only question, therefore, is whether the purpose test has been met in this case.

In determining whether the primary purpose test has been met, we must determine not only whether a subjective intent to primarily benefit the shareholders exists, but also whether an actual primary economic benefit exists for the shareholders. Kuper v. Commissioner of Internal Revenue, 533 F.2d 152, 160 (5th Cir.1976). The tax court's finding of the primary purposes for the transfers is a question of fact and may not be disturbed unless clearly erroneous. *Kuper,* 533 F.2d at 161; *Sammons,* 472 F.2d at 452. In this case, the tax court concluded that the transfers were motivated to primarily benefit Stinnett and not Pontiac. This finding is not clearly erroneous.

If Pontiac had not made the advances to Cargo on Stinnett's behalf, Stinnett would have forfeited his interest in Cargo. Moreover, when Cargo was liquidated, Stinnett received $6,000 in the distribution. If the advances had not been made, Stinnett would have been unable to recoup any of his investment. Additionally, Stinnett's ownership interest in Cargo increased from 43% to 55% because of these advances. The evidence indicates that the advances from Pontiac to Cargo benefited Stinnett. We, therefore, must affirm the tax court's ruling. Since the contributions from Pontiac to Cargo satisfy the *Sammons* test, they constitute constructive dividends to Stinnett; and therefore, the tax court properly included the amount of the advances in Stinnett's income.

* * *

REVENUE RULING 79–8
1979–1 Cum.Bull. 92.

ISSUE

Will deductions under section 162(a) of the Internal Revenue Code of 1954 be disallowed to a closely held corporation for reasonable compensation paid to its shareholder-employees on the sole ground that the corporation has not paid more than an insubstantial portion of its earnings as dividends on its outstanding stock?

LAW AND ANALYSIS

In Charles McCandless Tile Service v. United States, 422 F.2d 1336 (Ct.Cl.1970), the United States Court of Claims found that the compensation paid by a closely held corporation with a poor dividend history to its two shareholder officers was within the realm of reasonableness, but the court nevertheless concluded, after an examination of the entire record, that a portion of the purported compensation was not in fact paid for services rendered and was therefore in reality a dividend distribution. The court cited among other authorities, Northlich, Stolley, Inc. v. United States, 368 F.2d 272 (Ct.Cl.1966), in which many factors were employed to decide whether certain payments were reasonable compensation or disguised dividends.

As support for its holding that the purported compensation "necessarily" contained a distribution of corporate earnings, the Court of Claims cited among other authorities, Botany Worsted Mills v. United States, 278 U.S. 282 (1929), Ct.D. 39, VIII–I C.B. 279 (1929), aff'g 63 Ct. Cl. 405 (1927), in which the Supreme Court of the United States concluded, after examining several factors including the corporation's dividend history and the compensation practice of other corporations in the same industry as the taxpayer, that certain payments to the stockholders were in fact disguised dividends. The citation to these cases in *McCandless* indicates that the court considered the taxpayer's dividend history as a factor that merited great weight but that was not by itself determinative.

In decisions rendered subsequent to *McCandless,* the United States Tax Court has repudiated any automatic dividend rule based solely on a poor dividend history by stating that "[w]hile the absence of dividends may indicate the presence of disguised dividends, it does not convert compensation determined to be reasonable into dividends." Davis & Sons, Inc. v. Commissioner, T.C. Memo 1975–229. In another opinion the court has held that, although the absence of a dividend history is "significant," other factors may be important. Nor-Cal Adjusters v. Commissioner, T.C. Memo 1971–200, aff'd, 503 F.2d 359 (9th Cir.1974).

Two federal appellate courts that considered this issue declined to adopt an automatic dividend rule. The United States Court of Appeals for the Eighth Circuit has stated that "an absence of profits paid back to the shareholders as dividends justifies an inference that some of the purported compensation really represents a distribution of profits." Charles Schneider & Co. v. Commissioner, 500 F.2d 148, 153 (8th Cir. 1974), cert. denied, 420 U.S. 908 (1975). The court in Schneider attached great weight to the taxpayer's dividend history but did not do so to create a conclusive presumption of a dividend distribution. Instead, the court utilized several factors—including "[a] most significant factor," namely, a comparison of the alleged compensation under consideration and the prevailing rates of compensation paid to those in similar positions in comparable companies within the same industry.

In Edwin's, Inc. v. United States, 501 F.2d 675 (7th Cir.1974), the Seventh Circuit went beyond *Schneider* and repudiated any automatic dividend rule. In a factual situation nearly identical to *McCandless,* the court in *Edwin's* held that while the absence of a dividend history and the fact that workers employed in comparable positions with other companies were paid less than taxpayer were relevant, this evidence did not justify a conclusive presumption of nondeductibility. The court stated that "[w]hile the absence of dividends might be a red flag, it should not deprive compensation demonstrated to be reasonable under all of the circumstances of the status of reasonableness."

HOLDING

The failure of a closely held corporation to pay more than an insubstantial portion of its earnings as dividends on its stock is a very significant factor to be taken into account in determining the deductibility of compensation paid by the corporation to its shareholder-employees. Conversely, where after an examination of all of the facts and circumstances (including the corporation's dividend history) compensation paid to shareholder-employees is found to be reasonable in amount and paid for services rendered, deductions for such compensation under section 162(a) of the Code will not be denied on the sole ground that the corporation has not paid more than an insubstantial portion of its earnings as dividends on its outstanding stock.

F. ANTI–AVOIDANCE LIMITATIONS ON THE DIVIDENDS RECEIVED DEDUCTION

1. IN GENERAL

Code: §§ 243(a)(1), (3), (b)(1); 246(a)(1), (b), (c); 246A; 1059(a), (b), (c), (d), (e)(1). Skim § 1059(e)(2), (3).

Dividends received by corporate shareholders are treated far more generously for tax purposes than dividends received by individuals. If corporate shareholders were taxed in full on the dividends they receive, corporate profits would be subjected to a minimum of three levels of taxation—once when earned, a second time when received as dividends by the corporate shareholder, and again when distributed to the ultimate noncorporate shareholder. To alleviate this multiple taxation, Section 243 generally permits corporate shareholders to deduct 70 percent of dividends received from other corporations. The deduction is increased to 80 percent if the recipient corporation owns 20 percent or more of the distributing corporation [1] and to 100 percent if the payor and recipient corporations are members of an electing affiliated group.[2] As a result, a maximum of only 30 percent of dividends received by corporate shareholders are subject to tax, for an effective rate of only 10.2 percent.[3] The availability of this deduction inspired tax advisors to devise techniques to take advantage of the lower effective rate on dividends received by corporate shareholders. This section examines recent Congressional efforts to curtail some of these abuses.

2. SPECIAL HOLDING PERIOD REQUIREMENTS

Because of the dividends received deduction, corporate shareholders are motivated to convert capital gain (taxable at the 34% maximum corporate rate) to tax sheltered dividend income (taxable at a maximum of 10.2 percent). Assume, for example, that Converter Corporation acquires 100 shares of Distributor, Inc. for $5,250 shortly before the dividend "record date." Converter collects a $250 dividend, includes only 30% ($75) in income, and then sells the stock for its post-dividend value of $5,000, claiming a short-term capital loss of $250 which is available to offset other capital gains normally taxable at 34 percent. Without any patrolling mechanism, this maneuver enables a corporate shareholder to convert short-term gain into 70 percent sheltered income.

Prior to 1984, Section 246(c) purported to close this loophole by denying any dividends received deduction unless the stock was held for more than 15 days (90 days for certain preferred stock). But corporations concocted methods to diminish the risk of loss during this brief 15-day holding period. In response to these inadequacies, Congress increased the holding period in Section 246(c) to 46 days (91 days in the case of certain preferred stock).[4] The 46 or 91 day period is tolled whenever the corporate shareholder diminishes its risk of loss with respect to the stock in any one of several specified manners.[5] As a result, a corporation is not entitled to the dividends received deduction

---

1. I.R.C. § 243(c).

2. I.R.C. § 243(a)(3).

3. The 10.2 percent effective rate is derived by multiplying the 30 percent includible portion of the dividends by the 34 percent maximum corporate rate.

4. I.R.C. § 246(c)(1), (2). For the rules on determination of holding period for purposes of this section, see I.R.C. § 246(c)(3).

5. I.R.C. § 246(c)(4).

unless it is willing to hold the stock and incur a genuine market risk for more than 45 days.

3. EXTRAORDINARY DIVIDENDS: BASIS REDUCTION

If the dividend to be collected is extraordinarily large in relation to the price of the stock, the corporation may incur a minimal risk of loss even if it holds the stock for more than 45 days. This opportunity was illustrated by a dramatic example of a tax-motivated "dividend stripping" transaction in a 1984 Joint Committee on Taxation report: [6]

> Chrysler's cumulative preferred stock sells at $36 per share shortly before Chrysler is scheduled to distribute $11.69 per share of back dividends. Corporation X has a short-term capital gain of $1 million, on which it will owe tax of $460,000 [the example uses pre-1987 rates. Ed.] It buys 85,000 shares of Chrysler preferred for $3,060,000 and holds it for 91 days. When the stock goes ex-dividend, the price drops to $24.31 per share. Assume corporation X eventually sells the stock for $24.31. Corporation X has a capital loss of $11.69 per share, or $993,650, which reduces the tax on its capital gain to $2,921, or by $457,079. It receives a dividend of $993,650, of which 85 percent [now 70 percent. Ed.], or $844,603 is excluded. The tax on the rest of the dividend is $68,562. Thus, the transaction saves $457,079 of capital gain tax at a price of $68,562 of dividend tax, a net gain of $388,517. This gain is likely to exceed, by far, whatever economic consequences result from fluctuations in the market value of Chrysler preferred during the 91-day mandatory holding period.

To deter this opportunity for "tax arbitrage," Congress enacted Section 1059, which provides that a corporate shareholder receiving an "extraordinary dividend" must reduce its basis in the underlying stock (but not below zero) by the amount of the nontaxed portion of the dividend if the corporation has not held the stock for more than two years before the "dividend announcement date"—i.e., the earliest date when the distributing corporation declares, announces or agrees to the amount or payment of the dividend.[7] As originally enacted in 1984, Section 1059 required a basis reduction only when the shareholder sold or otherwise disposed of the stock before it had been held for more than one year. In reconsidering the issue in 1986, Congress concluded that a one-year holding period was an inadequate deterrent to the tax avoid-

---

6. Joint Committee on Taxation, Tax Shelter Proposals and Other Tax-Motivated Transactions, 98th Cong., 2d Sess. 39–40 (1984).

7. I.R.C. § 1059(a)(1), (d)(5). A distribution that otherwise would constitute an extraordinary dividend will not be considered as such if the shareholder has held the stock during the entire existence of the corporation or any predecessor corporation. I.R.C. § 1059(d)(6).

ance transactions at which Section 1059 was directed.[8]   The 1986 Conference Report explained the new holding period test as follows: [9]

> In lieu of the one-year post-acquisition holding period require-
> ment of present law, the conference agreement provides a test
> based on the holding period of the distributee as of the date the
> distribution is declared or publicly announced by the distribut-
> ing corporation's board of directors.   Under this test, a distri-
> bution with respect to stock will constitute an extraordinary
> dividend if the taxpayer has not held the stock for more than
> two years on that date.   If there is a formal or informal
> agreement to pay the particular dividend prior to the declara-
> tion date, the date of such agreement shall be treated as the
> dividend announcement date for purposes of applying the two-
> year holding period requirement.   Whether there is such a
> formal or informal agreement is determined based on all the
> facts and circumstances.   In general, a broad agreement in a
> joint venture arrangement that dividends will be paid as funds
> are available would not be considered an agreement to pay a
> particular dividend in the absence of other facts, such as facts
> showing a particular expectation that a large dividend would
> be paid after the acquisition of an interest in the venture by a
> new party.

To fully understand the workings of Section 1059, some definitions are in order.   An "extraordinary dividend" is defined in terms of the size of the dividend in relation to the shareholder's adjusted basis in the underlying stock.   A dividend is extraordinary if it exceeds certain threshold percentages—five percent of the shareholder's adjusted basis in the case of stock preferred as to dividends and ten percent of the adjusted basis in the case of any other stock.[10]   To prevent easy avoidance of these percentage tests, all dividends received by a share-holder with respect to any shares of stock which have ex-dividend dates within the same period of 85 consecutive days are combined and treated as one dividend.[11]   Under an alternate test, a taxpayer may elect to determine the status of a dividend as extraordinary by reference to the fair market value (rather than the adjusted basis) of the stock as of the day before the ex-dividend date.[12]   This election could be beneficial if the stock had appreciated substantially from the time when it was acquired by the shareholder.

8. S.Rep.No. 99–313, 99th Cong., 2d Sess. 249 (1986).

9. H.R.Rep.No. 99–841, 99th Cong., 2d Sess. II–164 (1986).

10. I.R.C. § 1059(c)(1), (2).

11. I.R.C. § 1059(c)(3)(A).   In addition, all dividends received with respect to a share of stock which have ex-dividend dates during the same period of 365 consec-utive days are treated as extraordinary if

the aggregate of such dividends exceeds 20 percent of the basis in such stock.   I.R.C. § 1059(c)(3)(B).   These rules are extended to include dividends received with respect to shares of stock having a substituted basis.   I.R.C. § 1059(c)(3)(C).

12. I.R.C. § 1059(c)(4).   This option is available only if the taxpayer establishes the fair market value of the stock to the satisfaction of the Commissioner.

The basis reduction required by Section 1059 is only for the "nontaxed portion" of an extraordinary dividend. The "nontaxed portion" is the excess of the total amount of the dividend over the taxable portion—i.e., the portion of the dividend includible in gross income after application of the dividends received deduction.[13] The basis reduction generally occurs immediately before any sale or disposition of the stock.[14] If the nontaxed portion of an extraordinary dividend exceeds the shareholder's adjusted basis in the stock, any excess is treated as gain from the sale or exchange of property when the shareholder subsequently sells or disposes of the stock.[15]

When it reexamined Section 1059 in the 1986 Act, Congress modified the general definition of "extraordinary dividend"—broadening the concept in two special situations and providing relief in two others. Section 1059(e)(1) provides that any amount treated as a Section 301 distribution to a corporate shareholder shall be an extraordinary dividend, irrespective of the shareholder's holding period in the stock or the size of the distribution, if it is a distribution in redemption of stock which is: (1) part of a partial liquidation of the redeeming corporation [16], or (2) is non pro rata as to all shareholders.[17]

Two other special rules carve out liberalizing exceptions. First, certain distributions between an affiliated group of corporations that qualify for the 100 percent dividends received deduction under Section 243(b)(1) are not treated as extraordinary dividends.[18] Second, special relief is provided for "qualified preferred dividends," which are defined as dividends payable with respect to any share of stock which provides for fixed preferred dividends payable not less than annually and was not acquired with dividends in arrears.[19] A "qualified preferred dividend" is not treated as an extraordinary dividend if the dividends received by the shareholder during the period it owned the stock do not exceed an annualized rate of 15 percent of the lower of (a) the shareholder's adjusted basis or (b) the liquidation preference of the stock, and the stock is held by the shareholder for over five years.[20] The theory for this complex exception is that, unlike the typical extraordinary dividend, a qualified preferred dividend offers no potential for effectively purchasing a dividend that accrued prior to the date on which the stock was acquired.[21]

13. I.R.C. § 1059(b).

14. I.R.C. § 1059(d)(1)(A). Section 1059(d)(1)(B) provides that in testing for an extraordinary dividend under Section 1059(c)(1), any reduction in basis required by reason of a prior distribution is treated as occurring at the beginning of the ex-dividend date for such distribution.

15. I.R.C. § 1059(a)(2). This treatment avoids the tax taboo of a negative basis. Cf. I.R.C. § 357(c) and Chapter 2D, supra.

16. "Partial liquidation" is defined for this purpose under the tests in Section 302(e). See Chapter 5D, infra.

17. The tax consequences of stock redemptions are covered in Chapter 5, infra.

18. I.R.C. § 1059(e)(2).

19. I.R.C. § 1059(e)(3)(C)(i).

20. I.R.C. § 1059(e)(3)(A), (B). If all these requirements are met except for the five year holding period, the exclusion from extraordinary dividend treatment is more limited. I.R.C. § 1059(e)(3)(A)(ii).

21. See H.R.Rep.No. 99–841, note 9 supra, II–164–65 (1986), which includes an example of the operation of this rule.

4. DEBT–FINANCED PORTFOLIO STOCK

Corporations also exploited the dividends received deduction by borrowing funds to acquire dividend paying stock. For example, assume Leverage Corporation borrows $10,000 at 12 percent interest to purchase $10,000 of stock that will pay dividends at a 10 percent annual return. Leverage fully deducts the $1,200 interest expense against ordinary income but only $300 of the dividends received would be taxable if the dividends received deduction is available. The deduction thus turns this otherwise uneconomic transaction into a profitable low risk arbitrage maneuver. The interest deduction results in an annual tax savings of $408 ($1,200 × 34%) while the tax owed on the dividends would be $102 if the corporation was in the maximum 34 percent bracket. For an annual outlay of $1,200 in interest and $102 in tax, Leverage receives $1,000 in income and a tax savings of $408, for a $106 after-tax benefit.

Section 246A precludes this strategy by reducing Leverage's Section 243 deduction to the extent the dividends are attributable to "debt-financed portfolio stock." The approach is similar to Section 265(a)(2), which denies a deduction for interest incurred to purchase or carry tax-exempt municipal bonds. Thus, if the "portfolio stock" is entirely debt-financed, Section 246A denies any dividends received deduction. If it is debt-financed in some lesser percentage, then that same percentage of the Section 243 deduction is denied.[22] In all events, however, the reduction in the dividends received deduction may not exceed the amount of any interest deduction allocable to the dividend (i.e., to the borrowed funds directly attributable to the stock).[23]

Stock is "debt-financed" if it is "portfolio stock" that is encumbered by "portfolio indebtedness" during a "base period" prescribed in the statute.[24] "Portfolio stock" is defined as any stock of a corporation unless the corporate shareholder owns either: (1) 50 percent of the total voting power and value of the corporation or (2) at least 20 percent of the total voting power and value and five or fewer corporate shareholders own at least 50 percent of the voting power and value, excluding preferred stock.[25] "Portfolio indebtedness" means any indebtedness directly attributable to the investment in the portfolio stock.[26] This means that the stock must have been purchased with borrowed funds or that the borrowing must be directly traceable to the acquisition, such as where the stock was pledged as security for a subsequently incurred debt in a case where the corporation reasonably could have been expected to sell the stock rather than incur the indebtedness.[27]

To illustrate, assume that Leverage Corporation acquires 100 shares of publicly traded X Corp. stock for $10,000, paying $6,000 cash

22. I.R.C. § 246A(a), (d).

23. I.R.C. § 246A(e).

24. I.R.C. § 246A(c)(1), (d)(4).

25. I.R.C. § 246A(c)(2), (4).

26. I.R.C. § 246A(d)(3)(A).

27. H.R.Rep. No. 98–432, 98th Cong., 2d Sess. 1181 (1984).

from corporate funds and borrowing the $4,000 balance. X Corp. pays Leverage an annual dividend of $1,000. The stock is debt-financed to the extent of $4,000. The percentage of debt-financing is thus 40 percent (the "average portfolio indebtedness," as defined by Section 246A(d)). Under the convoluted formula in Section 246A(a), Leverage subtracts 40 percent from 100 percent and then multiplies the result (60 percent here) by the usual 70 percent dividends received deduction percentage, to reach 42 percent. That lower figure is substituted for 70 percent in determining Leverage's Section 243 deduction. When Leverage receives its $1,000 dividend, it may deduct only $420 (rather than the usual $700).

5. SECTION 301(e)

The adjustments to earnings and profits required by Sections 312(k) and 312(n) for depreciation and other timing items frequently result in an increase to a corporation's earnings and profits [28] and may cause earnings and profits to exceed the corporation's taxable income. For example, a corporation that reports a gain on the installment method may not defer the gain for purposes of determining its earnings and profits.[29] The increase in earnings and profits resulting from these adjustments often ensures that a distribution will be fully taxable as a dividend to noncorporate shareholders. In view of the dividends received deduction, this may prove to be a bonanza to a corporate shareholder. The following example from the legislative history of the Tax Reform Act of 1984 illustrates one type of abuse that concerned Congress: [30]

> For example, assume that P Corporation owns 100 percent of the stock of X Corporation, that P's basis in such stock is $200, that P and X file separate income tax returns, and that X has no current or accumulated earnings and profits. Assume further that X sells an asset for a $1,000 installment note, realizing an $800 gain. Finally, assume that X borrows $500 secured by the installment note and distributes the $500 to P. Under [Section 312(n)], absent a special rule, X Corporation's earnings and profits would be increased by the amount of gain on the installment sale, and P would treat the $500 distribution as a dividend. Thus P would include the $500 in income but would likely qualify for a 100-percent dividends received deduction. If P later sold its X stock for $200 (the value of that stock if it is assumed that X will ultimately have a $300 tax liability, in present value terms, on account of the installment

---

28. The purpose of these adjustments is to ensure that a corporation's earnings and profits more accurately reflect its true economic performance. See Section B of this Chapter, supra.

29. I.R.C. § 312(n)(5).

30. Staff of the Joint Committee on Taxation, General Explanation of the Revenue Provisions of the Deficit Reduction Act of 1984 (hereinafter "General Explanation"), 98th Cong., 2d Sess. 183 (1984).

sale), it would not recognize gain or loss on the sale. As a result, P would have realized an overall profit of $500.

Section 301(e) prevents the result illustrated above by providing that the adjustments required by Sections 312(k) and 312(n) shall not be made for purposes of determining the taxable income of (and the adjusted basis of stock held by) any "20 percent corporate sharehold-er."[31] A 20 percent corporate shareholder is any corporation entitled to a dividends received deduction with respect to a distribution that owns, directly or through the Section 318 attribution rules, either (1) stock in the distributing corporation possessing at least 20 percent of the total combined voting power, or (2) at least 20 percent of the total value of all of the distributing corporation's stock, except nonvoting preferred stock.[32]

The general effect of Section 301(e) is to reduce the distributing corporation's earnings and profits in determining the tax consequences of distributions to 20 percent corporate shareholders. This reduction, in turn, may cause a distribution to be treated as a return of capital coupled with a reduction in the basis of the distributing corporation's stock. Without Section 301(e), the same distribution likely would have been a tax-free dividend with no basis reduction. Thus, applying Section 301(e) to the earlier example, X Corporation will have no earnings and profits for purposes of determining the tax consequences of a distribution to P Corporation. In the absence of earnings and profits, $200 of the distribution by X to P will be a return of capital under Section 301(c)(2), and $300 will be taxed to P as gain from the sale or exchange of its X stock under Section 301(c)(3). P's basis in its X stock will be reduced to zero and it will recognize a $200 gain on the later sale of the stock.[33]

PROBLEM

On June 1, Publicly Held Corporation's common stock is selling for $15 per share. On that date, Publicly Held declares a dividend of $1 per share, payable on June 10 to shareholders of record as of June 5. Investor Corporation purchases 1,000 shares of Publicly Held common stock for $15,000 on June 3, collects a $1,000 dividend on June 10 and sells the stock for $14,000 on June 15.

(a) What are the tax consequences to Investor Corporation?

(b) What result in (a), above, if Investor sold the stock on December 1, instead of June 15?

(c) What result in (b), above, if Publicly Held had paid a second $1 per share dividend on August 15?

(d) What result if Investor receives dividends totalling $3 per share but holds the Publicly Held stock for 25 months before selling it?

31. I.R.C. § 301(e)(1).

32. I.R.C. § 301(e)(2).

33. General Explanation, supra note 30, at 183.

(e)   What result if Investor purchased the Publicly Held stock by borrowing $15,000, secured by the stock, and Investor paid $1,500 interest during the year and received $1,000 of dividends?

(f)   What result in (e), above, if Investor had borrowed only $7,500 of the $15,000 used to buy the stock?

G. USE OF DIVIDENDS IN BOOTSTRAP SALES

TSN LIQUIDATING CORP. v. UNITED STATES

United States Court of Appeals, Fifth Circuit, 1980.
624 F.2d 1328.

RANDALL, Circuit Judge:

This case presents the question whether assets distributed to a corporation by its subsidiary, immediately prior to the sale by such corporation of all the capital stock of such subsidiary, should be treated, for federal income tax purposes, as a dividend or, as the district court held, as part of the consideration received from the sale of such capital stock. We hold that on the facts of this case, the assets so distributed constituted a dividend and we reverse the judgment of the district court.

In 1969, TSN Liquidating Corporation, Inc. ("TSN"), which was then named "Texas State Network, Inc.," owned over 90% of the capital stock of Community Life Insurance Company ("CLIC"), an insurance company chartered under the laws of the State of Maine. In early 1969, negotiations began for the purchase of CLIC by Union Mutual Life Insurance Company ("Union Mutual"). On May 5, 1969, TSN and the other CLIC stockholders entered into an Agreement of Stock Purchase (the "Stock Purchase Agreement") with Union Mutual for the sale of the capital stock of CLIC to Union Mutual. The Stock Purchase Agreement provided that there would be no material adverse change in the business or assets of CLIC prior to the closing "except that as of closing certain shares and capital notes as provided in Section '4.(i).' above will not be a part of the assets of [CLIC]." Since the purchase price of the capital stock of CLIC under the Stock Purchase Agreement was based primarily on the book value (or, in some instances, market value) of those assets owned by CLIC on the closing date, the purchase price would be automatically reduced by the elimination of such shares and notes from the assets of CLIC. On May 14, 1969, as contemplated by the Stock Purchase Agreement, the Board of Directors of CLIC declared a dividend in kind, payable to stockholders of record as of May 19, 1969, consisting primarily of capital stock in small, public companies traded infrequently and in small quantities in the over-the-counter market. On May 20, 1969, the closing was held and Union Mutual purchased substantially all the outstanding capital stock of CLIC, including the shares held by TSN. The final purchase price paid by Union Mutual to the selling stockholders of CLIC was

$823,822, of which TSN's share was $747,436. Union Mutual thereupon contributed to the capital of CLIC $1,120,000 in municipal bonds and purchased from CLIC additional capital stock of CLIC for $824,598 in cash paid to CLIC.

In its income tax return for the fiscal year ended July 31, 1969, TSN reported its receipt of assets from CLIC as a dividend and claimed the 85% dividends received deduction available to corporate stockholders pursuant to § 243(a)(1) of the Internal Revenue Code of 1954. TSN also reported its gain on the sale of the capital stock of CLIC on the installment method pursuant to § 453 of the Code. [Under current law, installment sale treatment would not be allowed if the CLIC stock were publicly traded. I.R.C. § 453(k)(2). Ed.] On audit, the Internal Revenue Service treated the distribution of the assets from CLIC to TSN as having been an integral part of the sale by TSN of capital stock of CLIC to Union Mutual, added its estimate ($1,677,082) of the fair market value of the assets received by TSN to the cash ($747,436) received by TSN on the sale, and disallowed the use by TSN of the installment method for reporting the gain on the sale of the capital stock of CLIC since aggregating the fair market value of the distributed assets and the cash resulted in more than 30% of the proceeds from the sale being received in the year of sale. TSN paid the additional tax due as a result of such treatment by the Internal Revenue Service, filed a claim for a refund and subsequently instituted this action against the Internal Revenue Service.

The district court made the following findings of fact in part II of its opinion:

> With regard to the negotiations between CLIC and Union Mutual in early 1969, the Court finds that Union Mutual was interested in purchasing CLIC and proposed a formula for valuing the assets, liabilities, and insurance in force, which, together with an additional amount, would be the price paid for the CLIC stock.

> The investment portfolio of CLIC was heavily oriented toward equity investments in closely held over-the-counter securities. At least in the mind of CLIC's officers, the makeup of CLIC's investment portfolio was affecting its ability to obtain licenses in various states. As early as the Spring of 1968, the management and principal stockholders of CLIC had begun to seek a solution to the investment portfolio problem. The Court finds, however, that CLIC had never formulated a definite plan on how to solve its investment portfolio problem.

> Union Mutual did not like CLIC's investment portfolio but considered bonds to be more in keeping with insurance industry responsibilities. The management of CLIC regarded the Union Mutual offer as a good one, and tried without success to get Union Mutual to take the entire investment portfolio.

Accordingly, the [Stock Purchase Agreement] required CLIC to dispose some of the investment portfolio assets. Thus, the price that would be paid for the CLIC stock was based upon a formula which valued the assets after excluding certain stocks.

* * *

Plaintiff's disposition of the undesirable over-the-counter stock was necessitated by its sale arrangements with Union Mutual. Plaintiff had no definite plans prior to its negotiations with Union Mutual as to how to get rid of the undesirable stock, when it was to get rid of the undesirable stock, or even that it would definitely get rid of the undesirable stock. Accordingly, the Court finds that the dividend in kind of 14 May 1969 was part and parcel of the purchase agreement with Union Mutual.

TSN Liquidating Corp. v. United States, 77–2 U.S.Tax Cas. ¶ 9741 at 88,523 (N.D.Tex.1977). In part III of its opinion, the district court made the following additional findings:

Union Mutual was interested in purchasing the stock of an approximately $2 million corporation in order that that corporation might be licensed to do business in other states. Tr. 92. As of 30 April 1969, CLIC had assets of $2,115,138. DX 2. On 14 May 1969, CLIC declared a dividend valued at approximately $1.8 million. As a result of this dividend, CLIC was left with assets totaling approximately $300,000. The final purchase price paid by Union Mutual to the selling shareholders of CLIC was $823,822. In addition, Union Mutual contributed $1,120,000 of municipal bonds to the capital of CLIC and purchased additional shares of stock of CLIC for $824,598. DX 3. Thus, subsequent to closing on 20 May 1969, CLIC was worth $2,400,000. DX 3. Thus, CLIC was worth $2 million when the [Stock Purchase Agreement] was signed on 5 May 1969 and worth over $2 million immediately after closing.

There was no business purpose served in this case by the dividend declared by CLIC prior to the sale of all its stock to Union Mutual. It is evident that the dividend benefitted the shareholders of CLIC and not CLIC itself. There was no benefit or business purpose in CLIC's declaration of the dividend separate and apart from the sale. The Court finds that the dividend would not, and could not, have been made without the sale.

* * *

What actually happened in the period 5 through 20 May 1969 was that the stockholders received $1.8 million in virtually tax-free stocks, as well as over $800,000 in cash, for a total of approximately $2.6 million. This was certainly a fair price for a corporation valued at the time of sale at $2,115,138, and reflects a premium paid for good will and policies in force, as well as the fact that CLIC was an existing business with licenses in eight or nine states. Hence, a $2 million corporation was sold for $2.6 million including the dividend and the cash.

Id. at 88,525.

After noting the time-honored principle that the incidence of taxation is to be determined by the substance of the transaction rather than by its form and the related principle that the transaction is generally to be viewed as a whole and not to be separated into its component parts, the district court held:

> The distribution of assets to [TSN] from its subsidiary, CLIC, immediately prior to [TSN's] disposition of its entire stock interest in CLIC should be treated as a part of the gain from the sale of the stock. Thus, the Court concludes that the in-kind distribution of 14 May 1969 to the stockholders of CLIC is taxable to [TSN] as gain from the sale of its stock. The alleged dividend was merely intented [sic] to be part of the purchase price paid by Union Mutual to CLIC for its stock.

Id. at 88,527. The district court relied for its holding primarily on the cases of Waterman Steamship Corp. v. Commissioner, 430 F.2d 1185 (5th Cir.1970), cert. denied, 401 U.S. 939, 91 S.Ct. 936, 28 L.Ed.2d 219 (1971), and Basic, Inc. v. United States, 549 F.2d 740 (Ct.Cl.1977), all discussed infra.

On appeal, TSN argues that the cases relied upon by the district court are exceptions to what TSN characterizes as the established rule, namely, that assets removed from a corporation by a dividend made in contemplation of a sale of the stock of that corporation, when those assets are in good faith to be retained by the selling stockholders and not thereafter transferred to the buyer, are taxable as a dividend and not as a part of the price paid for the stock for the reason that, in economic reality and in substance, the selling stockholders did not sell and the buyer did not purchase or pay for the excluded assets. The principal cases cited by TSN for its position are Gilmore v. Commissioner, 25 T.C. 1321 (1956), Coffey v. Commissioner, 14 T.C. 1410 (1950), and Rosenbloom Finance Corp. v. Commissioner, 24 B.T.A. 763 (1931). According to TSN, the controlling distinction between the *Coffey* line of cases relied upon by TSN and the *Waterman* line of cases relied upon by the district court is whether the buyer negotiated to acquire and pay for the stock, exclusive of the assets distributed out as a dividend, on the one hand, or whether the buyer negotiated to acquire and pay for the stock, including the assets which were then the subject of a sham distribution designed to evade taxes, on the other hand. In the former case, according to TSN, there is a taxable dividend; in the latter case there is not.

We begin by noting that the district court was certainly correct in its position that the substance of the transaction controls over the form and that the transaction should be viewed as a whole, rather than being separated into its parts. Further, having reviewed the record, we are of the view that the operative facts found so carefully by the district court are entirely accurate (except for the valuation of the distributed assets, as to which we express no opinion). We differ with the district court only in the legal characterization of those facts and in the conclusion to be drawn therefrom. We agree with TSN that this case is controlled by the *Coffey, Gilmore* and *Rosenbloom* cases rather than by the *Waterman* and *Basic* cases relied upon by the district court.

In *Coffey,* the principal case relied upon by TSN, the taxpayers owned the stock of Smith Brothers Refinery Co., Inc. and were negotiating for the sale of such stock. Representatives of the purchasers and representatives of the sellers examined and discussed the various assets owned by Smith Brothers Refinery Co., Inc., and the liabilities of the company, with a view to reaching an agreement upon the fair market value of the stock. During these negotiations, the representatives of the purchasers and of the sellers could not agree upon the value of certain assets (including a contingent receivable referred to as the Cabot payment). The representatives of the purchasers informed the representatives of the sellers that the sellers could withdraw those assets from the assets of the company and that they would buy the stock without those assets being a part of the sale, thereby eliminating the necessity for arriving at a valuation of those assets in determining the value of the stock on a net worth basis. The contract of sale provided that the unwanted assets would be distributed by the corporation as a dividend prior to the sale of the stock. The selling stockholders contended before the tax court, as the Internal Revenue Service does in the case before this court, that the Cabot payment distributed to them as a dividend in kind was "part of the consideration for stock sold and that any profit resulting from its receipt by them is taxable as a capital gain." The tax court rejected that contention because it was contrary to the substance of the transaction:

> We do not agree with petitioners that they received the Cabot payment as part of the consideration for the sale of their stock. The purchasers did not agree to buy their stock and then turn over to them $190,000 and the Cabot payment in consideration therefor. From the testimony above set forth it is apparent that they were not interested in the Cabot payment, did not want it included in the assets of the corporation at the time they acquired its stock, and negotiated with petitioners to acquire stock of a corporation whose assets did not include the unwanted Cabot payment. * * * They received $190,000 for their stock. Under the contract of sale, they did not sell or part with their interest in the Cabot contract. It was expressly reserved by them and was a distribution they received as stockholders by virtue of the reservation.

Coffey, 14 T.C. at 1417, 1418. The tax court held the distribution to be a dividend.

In *Gilmore*, the purchasers of corporate stock did not wish to pay for quick assets owned by the corporation, namely cash on hand and United States bonds, and the parties provided for a presale dividend to exclude them from the assets to be transferred to the purchaser by means of the sale of the corporate stock. The tax court held that the assets distributed to the stockholders by means of a dividend were taxable as a dividend and not as a part of the sales proceeds for the corporate stock:

> It may be true the parties could have reached much the same result and have avoided some tax consequences to the stockholders by casting the transaction in the form of a higher purchase offer that would have included all of the quick assets. But this just was not done. * * * The [purchasers] chose to make this offer, one that "waived" the quick assets after payment of indebtedness. * * * The [purchasers] did not agree to pay the stockholders $6.50 or any other sum from the surplus. They "waived any claim" to the surplus and consented that it "may be paid to the present stockholders."
>
> * * *
>
> In *T.J. Coffey, Jr.*, 14 T.C. 1410, a situation similar to the one here was before the Court and we held that the corporate distributions there involved were not a part of the consideration for the sale of stock.

Gilmore, 25 T.C. at 1323, 1324.

In *Rosenbloom*, the sole stockholder of Joseph S. Finch Company was Rosenbloom Finance Corporation. Rosenbloom entered into a contract for the sale of all the capital stock of Joseph S. Finch Company to Shenley Products Company. With respect to the unwanted assets, the contract provided:

> "All other assets of every character whatsoever owned by the Finch Company at the time of the transfer of said shares of stock, as herein provided, shall be transferred to the party of the first part (petitioner) by dividend distribution, prior to the consummation of the sale of said shares of stock herein provided for."

Rosenbloom, 24 B.T.A. at 769. The board of tax appeals held that the assets distributed to Rosenbloom Finance Corporation by Joseph S. Finch Company should be treated as an ordinary dividend and not as an amount distributed in partial liquidation.

The Internal Revenue Service states that it does not disagree with the holdings in *Coffey*, *Gilmore* and *Rosenbloom*, but it takes the position that they do not apply in the circumstances of this case. The Internal Revenue Service focuses on the receipt by the selling stockholders of CLIC of investment assets, followed immediately by an infusion by Union Mutual of a like amount of investment assets into CLIC, and says that the reinfusion of assets brings the case before the court within the "conduit rationale" of *Waterman*. In *Waterman*,

Waterman Steamship Corporation ("Waterman") was the owner of all the outstanding capital stock of Pan-Atlantic Steamship Corporation ("Pan-Atlantic") and Gulf Florida Terminal Company, Incorporated ("Gulf Florida"). Malcolm P. McLean made an offer to Waterman to purchase all the outstanding capital stock of Pan-Atlantic and Gulf Florida for $3,500,000. Since Waterman's tax basis for the stock of the subsidiaries totaled $700,000, a sale of the capital stock of the subsidiaries for $3,500,000 would have produced a taxable gain of approximately $2,800,000. Because the treasury regulations on consolidated returns provided that the dividends received from an affiliated corporation are exempt from tax, a sale of capital stock of the subsidiaries for $700,000, after a dividend payment to Waterman by the subsidiaries of $2,800,000, would, at least in theory, have produced no taxable gain. The Board of Directors of Waterman rejected McLean's offer, but authorized Waterman's president to submit a counter proposal providing for the sale of all the capital stock in the subsidiaries for $700,000, but only after the subsidiaries paid dividends to Waterman in the aggregate amount of $2,800,000. As finally consummated, the dividends and the sale of the capital stock of the subsidiaries took the following form:

(1) Pan-Atlantic gave a promissory note to Waterman for $2,800,000 payable in 30 days as a "dividend."

(2) One hour later, Waterman agreed to sell all of the capital stock of Pan-Atlantic and Gulf Florida for $700,000.

(3) Thirty minutes later, after the closing of the sale of the capital stock of the subsidiaries had occurred, Pan-Atlantic held a special meeting of its new Board of Directors, and the Board authorized Pan-Atlantic to borrow $2,800,000 from McLean and a corporation controlled by McLean. Those funds were used by Pan-Atlantic promptly to pay off the $2,800,000 note to Waterman (which was not yet due).

In its tax return for the fiscal year involved, Waterman eliminated from income the $2,800,000 received as a dividend from Pan-Atlantic and reported $700,000 as the sales price of the capital stock of the two subsidiaries. Since Waterman's tax basis for the stock was the same as the sales price therefor, no taxable gain was realized on the sale. On audit, the Internal Revenue Service took the position that Waterman had realized a long-term capital gain of $2,800,000 on the sale of the capital stock of the subsidiaries and increased its taxable income accordingly. On appeal from a judgment by the tax court in favor of the taxpayer, the Internal Revenue Service contended that the rules applicable to situations where a regular dividend has been declared are not applicable when the parties contemplate that a purported dividend is to be inextricably tied to the purchase price and where, as was the case before the court, the amount of the dividend is not a true distribution of corporate profits. The Internal Revenue Service argued that the funds were supplied by the buyer of the stock, with the corporation acting as a mere conduit for passing the payment through to the seller. This court agreed with the Internal Revenue Service:

> The so-called dividend and sale were one transaction. The note was but one transitory step in a total, pre-arranged plan to sell the stock. We hold that in substance Pan-Atlantic neither declared nor paid a dividend to Waterman, but rather acted as a mere conduit for the payment of the purchase price to Waterman.

Waterman, 430 F.2d at 1192. The opinion of this court began with this sentence:

> This case involves another attempt by a taxpayer to ward off tax blows with paper armor.

Id. at 1185. The opinion stressed the sham, tax motivated aspects of the transaction:

> Here, McLean originally offered Waterman $3,500,000 for the stock of Pan-Atlantic and Gulf Florida. Waterman recognized that since its basis for tax purposes in the stock was $700,180, a taxable gain of approximately $2,800,000 would result from the sale. It declined the original offer and proposed to cast the sale of the stock in a two step transaction. Waterman proposed to McLean that it would sell the stock of the two subsidiaries for $700,180 after it had extracted $2,800,000 of the subsidiaries' earnings and profits. It is undisputed that Waterman intended to sell the two subsidiaries for the original offering price—with $2,800,000 of the amount disguised as a dividend which would be eliminated from income under Section 1502. Waterman also intended that none of the assets owned by the subsidiaries would be removed prior to the sale. Although the distribution was cast in the form of a dividend, the distribution was to be financed by McLean with payment being made to Waterman through Pan-Atlantic. To inject substance into the form of the transaction, Pan-Atlantic issued its note to Waterman before the closing agreement was signed. The creation of a valid indebtedness however, cannot change the true nature of the transaction.   *   *   *
>
> > *   *   *
>
> The form of the transaction used by the parties is relatively unimportant, for the true substance and effect of their agreement was that McLean would pay $3,500,000 for all of the assets, rights and liabilities represented by the stock of Pan-Atlantic and Gulf Florida.

Id. at 1194–95. This court concluded its opinion in *Waterman* by cautioning against "giving force to 'a purported [dividend] which gives off an unmistakeably hollow sound when it is tapped.'" Id. at 1196 (quoting United States v. General Geophysical Co., 296 F.2d 86, 89 (5th Cir.1961), cert. denied, 369 U.S. 849, 82 S.Ct. 1156, 8 L.Ed.2d 8 (1962)).

A final footnote to the opinion stated that the decision should not be interpreted as standing for the proposition that a corporation which is contemplating a sale of its subsidiary's stock could not under any circumstances distribute its subsidiaries' profits prior to the sale without having such distribution deemed part of the purchase price. Id. at 1196 n. 21.

In summary, in *Waterman*, the substance of the transaction, and the way in which it was originally negotiated, was that the purchaser would pay $3,500,000 of its money to the seller in exchange for all the stock of the two subsidiaries and none of the assets of those subsidiaries was to be removed and retained by the sellers. In the case before the court, the district court found that Union Mutual did not want and would not pay for the assets of CLIC which were distributed to TSN and the other stockholders of CLIC. Those assets were retained by the selling stockholders. The fact that bonds and cash were reinfused into CLIC after the closing, in lieu of the unwanted capital stock of small, publicly held corporations, does not convert this case from a *Coffey* situation, in which admittedly unwanted assets were distributed by the corporation to its stockholders and retained by them, into a *Waterman* situation, in which the distribution of assets was clearly a sham, designed solely to achieve a tax free distribution of assets ultimately funded by the purchaser. Indeed, the Internal Revenue Service does not argue, in the case before the court, that the transaction was in any respect a sham. Instead, the Service would have us hold that the mere infusion of assets into the acquired company after the closing, assets which are markedly different in kind from the assets that were distributed prior to the closing, should result in the disallowance of dividend treatment for the distribution of the unwanted assets, and the Service cites *Waterman* as authority for that proposition. We view the sham aspect—the hollow sound—of the transaction described in *Waterman* as one of the critical aspects of that decision, and we decline to extend the *Waterman* rule to a case which admittedly does not involve a sham and which, in other important respects, is factually different from *Waterman*.

The Internal Revenue Service also cites *Basic* as authority for the disallowance of dividend treatment for the distribution of the unwanted assets in this case. Basic Incorporated ("Basic") owned all the capital stock of Falls Industries Incorporated ("Falls"), which in turn owned all the stock of Basic Carbon Corporation ("Carbon"). Carborundum Company ("Carborundum") made an initial offer to acquire all the assets of Falls and Carbon. This offer failed to gel when Basic demanded that Carborundum agree to indemnify Basic for any tax assessments that might become payable on the transaction in excess of those which Basic could anticipate and compute in advance, a proposal that was unacceptable to Carborundum. Carborundum then made a second proposal to acquire directly from Basic the capital stock of Falls and the capital stock of Carbon and requested that Basic transfer the ownership of the capital stock of Carbon from Falls to Basic prior to the transaction. In order to achieve that, Falls distributed the capital stock of Carbon to Basic as a dividend, which put Basic in the position of owning the capital stock of both Falls and Carbon. The sale of such capital stock to Carborundum was then consummated. In its federal income tax return for the year involved, Basic reported dividend income from Falls in the amount of $500,000 as a result of its receipt of the capital stock of Carbon. It thereupon claimed a dividends received deduction in the amount of 85% of the dividend pursuant to § 243(a)(1) of the Code. Finally, it reported a long-term capital gain of $2,300,000 from the sale to Carborundum of the shares of Falls and Carbon. On audit, the Internal Revenue Service determined that the gain from the sale of the shares of capital stock of Falls and Carbon should be increased by the amount of the purported dividend. On those facts, the court of claims held that the distribution of the capital stock of Carbon by Falls to Basic was not a true dividend but was part of the total transaction by which Basic, in substance, sold the capital stock of Falls and Carbon to Carborundum:

> Under the facts and circumstances presented here, plaintiff has not shown that there was a reason for the transfer of the Carbon stock from Falls to Basic aside from the tax consequences attributable to that move. Accordingly, for purposes of taxation, the transfer was not a dividend within the meaning of Section 316(a)(1). Instead, it should be regarded as a transfer that avoided part of the gain to be expected from the sale of the business to Carborundum, and should, therefore, be now taxed accordingly.

Basic, 549 F.2d at 749. Basic was a conduit through which an asset, the capital stock of Carbon, was passed to the buyer. The substance of the transaction was a brief removal of the "dividend" asset (the Carbon stock) on the way to the hands of the waiting buyer. In the case before the court, unlike the situation that obtained in *Basic*, the distributed assets were retained by the stockholders to whom they were distributed, rather than being immediately transferred to the purchaser.

As additional support for its position, the court in *Basic* focused on the absence of a business purpose, viewed from the standpoint of Falls, for the payment of a dividend of a valuable corporate asset, i.e., the capital stock of Carbon, by Falls to Basic. The district court, in the case before this court, applied the same test to the payment of the dividend of the unwanted assets by CLIC to TSN, the controlling stockholder of CLIC, and found that, strictly from the standpoint of CLIC, the dividend was lacking in business purpose and, indeed, could not have taken place apart from the sale and the subsequent infusion of investment assets into CLIC by Union Mutual. However, it seems to us to be inconsistent to take the position that substance must control over form and that a transaction must be viewed as a whole, rather than in parts, and at the same time to state that the business purpose of one participant in a multi-party transaction (particularly where the participant is a corporation controlled by the taxpayer and is not itself a party to the sale transaction) is to be viewed in isolation from the over-all business purpose for the entire transaction. We agree that the transaction must be viewed as a whole and we accept the district court's finding of fact that the dividend of the unwanted assets was "part and parcel of the purchase arrangement with Union Mutual," motivated specifically by Union Mutual's unwillingness to take and pay for such assets. That being the case, we decline to focus on the business purpose of one participant in the transaction—a corporation controlled by the taxpayer—and instead find that the business purpose for the transaction as a whole, viewed from the standpoint of the taxpayer, controls. The facts found by the district court clearly demonstrate a business purpose for the presale dividend of the unwanted assets which fully explains that dividend. We note that there is no suggestion in the district court's opinion of any tax avoidance motivation on the part of the taxpayer TSN. The fact that the dividend may have had incidental tax benefit to the taxpayer, without more, does not necessitate the disallowance of dividend treatment.

Having concluded that the pre-sale distribution by CLIC to its stockholders (including TSN) of assets which Union Mutual did not want, would not pay for and did not ultimately receive is a dividend for tax purposes, and not part of the purchase price of the capital stock of CLIC, we reverse the judgment of the district court and remand for proceedings consistent with this opinion.

Reversed and remanded.

NOTE

Life is not as simple today as it was when the successful tax plan in *TSN Liquidating* was concocted. Several additional provisions of the Code now must be considered in evaluating the continuing viability of a pre-sale distribution of unwanted assets by a corporate shareholder.

As noted earlier,[1] Section 301(e) requires, solely for purposes of computing the amount of any taxable dividend income to a 20 percent or more corporate shareholder and the shareholder's basis in the stock of the distributing corporation, that the distributing corporation's earnings and profits must be determined without regard to the special adjustments in Sections 312(k) and 312(n). Section 301(e), however, will not necessarily impair the technique used in *TSN Liquidating;* it merely limits the utility of pre-acquisition dividend strips to situations where the distributing corporation has substantial earnings and profits before the required earnings and profits timing adjustments.

A more serious impediment is the possibility of a downward adjustment in the basis of the corporate shareholder's stock as a result of the pre-sale dividend. If TSN had been required to reduce the basis in its CLIC stock by the amount of the dividends received deduction that it received on the distribution, the transaction would have lost its allure.

---

1. See Section F5 of this chapter, supra.

A basis reduction would have placed TSN in the position of trading a dollar of dividend income for a dollar of gain on the subsequent sale of its CLIC stock. Since the repeal of the capital gains preference in the Tax Reform Act of 1986, corporations usually are indifferent to the distinction between ordinary income and capital gain.[2] Does current law cause TSN to suffer a basis reduction as a result of the pre-sale dividend? The answer is no unless the distribution is subject to Section 1059. That section requires a basis reduction for the amount of any "extraordinary dividend" which was not taxed to a corporate shareholder because of the dividends received deduction where the stock has not been held for more than two years before the announcement of the dividend.[3] Because of its size (roughly $1.67 million, according to the facts of the case), the dividend to TSN appears to be "extraordinary" under the tests in Section 1059(c). But TSN nonetheless could have avoided any basis reduction if it had held its CLIC stock for more than two years before the dividend was announced.

One final obstacle must be mentioned in the interests of full disclosure. If TSN and CLIC were affiliated corporations and elected to file a consolidated tax return,[4] TSN would have been required to reduce its basis in the CLIC stock as a result of the dividend. The consolidated return regulations, which treat an "affiliated group" as a single taxpaying entity, logically eliminate intracorporate dividends from the consolidated group's joint gross income.[5] The dividend is considered a mere reshuffling of profits within a single taxpayer which should not generate additional income. The regulations also provide that a parent's basis in the stock of a subsidiary is generally reduced by the full amount of any excluded intercompany dividend.[6] It follows that the strategy employed in *TSN Liquidating* has no appeal in the context of a consolidated group.

Despite these technical obstacles, a preacquisition dividend is still viable if the selling parent corporation has held the stock of a subsidiary for more than two years and the corporations do not file a consolidated return. The recent Tax Court decision in Litton Industries, Inc. v. Commissioner [7] illustrates the importance of form and timing to the success of this technique. The issue in *Litton* was whether a $30 million dividend, paid to Litton by a wholly owned subsidiary in the form of a negotiable promissory note five months prior to Litton's sale of the subsidiary's stock to Nestle Corporation, was truly a dividend rather than part of the proceeds received by Litton on the sale of the stock. The promissory note was later satisfied by Nestle at the same time that it purchased the stock. Dividend treatment was preferable to

---

2. Other tax attributes, however, might cause TSN to prefer one or the other type of income. For example, if TSN had unused capital losses, it might prefer capital gains on the sale to fully taxable dividend income.

3. I.R.C. § 1059(a). See Section F2 of this chapter, supra.

4. See Chapter 14, infra.

5. Reg. § 1.1502–14(a).

6. Reg. § 1.1502–32(b)(2).

7. 89 T.C. 1086 (1987).

Litton because of the shelter provided by what was then an 85 percent dividends received deduction.

Distinguishing Waterman Steamship Corp. v. Commissioner [8] (discussed in *TSN Liquidating* at pages 185–188 of the text, supra), the Tax Court held that the payment was a dividend. Favorable (and distinguishing) factors were: (1) unlike *Waterman Steamship,* the dividend and subsequent sale in *Litton* were substantially separated in time (over five months in *Litton* was better than the few hours in *Waterman*); (2) at the time the dividend was declared, no formal action had been taken by the parent to initiate a sale to Nestle and "[t]here was no definite purchaser waiting in the wings with the terms and conditions of sale already agreed upon;" [9] and (3) as in *TSN Liquidating,* the overall transaction was not a sham because a business purpose was served by the dividend. In rejecting the Service's contention that the dividend and subsequent sale of the subsidiary should be treated as one transaction for tax purposes, the court reasoned: [10]

> The term "dividend" is defined in section 316(a) as a distribution by a corporation to its shareholders out of earnings and profits. The parties have stipulated that Stouffer had earnings and profits exceeding $30 million at the time the dividend was declared. This Court has recognized that a dividend may be paid by a note. T.R. Miller Mill Co. v. Commissioner, 37 B.T.A. 43, 49 (1938), affd. 102 F.2d 599 (5th Cir.1939). Based on these criteria, the $30 million distribution by Stouffer would clearly constitute a dividend if the sale of Stouffer had not occurred. We are not persuaded that the subsequent sale of Stouffer to Nestle changes that result merely because it was more advantageous to Litton from a tax perspective.

> It is well established that a taxpayer is entitled to structure his affairs and transactions in order to minimize his taxes. This proposition does not give a taxpayer carte blanche to set up a transaction in any form which will avoid tax consequences, regardless of whether the transaction has substance. Gregory v. Helvering, 293 U.S. 465 (1935). A variety of factors present here preclude a finding of sham or subterfuge. Although the record in this case clearly shows that Litton intended at the time the dividend was declared to sell Stouffer, no formal action had been taken and no announcement had been made. There was no definite purchaser waiting in the wings with the terms and conditions of sale already agreed upon. At that time, Litton had not even decided upon the form of sale of Stouffer. Nothing in the record here suggests that there was any prearranged sale agreement, formal or informal, at the time the dividend was declared.

8. 430 F.2d 1185 (5th Cir.1970).

9. 89 T.C. at 1099.

10. Id. at 1100.

Petitioner further supports its argument that the transaction was not a sham by pointing out Litton's legitimate business purposes in declaring the dividend. Although the code and case law do not require a dividend to have a business purpose, it is a factor to be considered in determining whether the overall transaction was a sham. T.S.N. Liquidating Corp. v. United States, 624 F.2d 1328 (5th Cir.1980). Petitioner argues that the distribution allowed Litton to maximize the gross after-tax amount it could receive from its investment in Stouffer. From the viewpoint of a private purchaser of Stouffer, it is difficult to see how the declaration of a dividend would improve the value of the stock since creating a liability in the form of a promissory note for $30 million would reduce the value of Stouffer by approximately that amount. However, since Litton was considering disposing of all or part of Stouffer through a public or private offering, the payment of a dividend by a promissory note prior to any sale had two advantages. First, Litton hoped to avoid materially diminishing the market value of the Stouffer stock. At that time, one of the factors considered in valuing a stock, and in determining the market value of a stock was the "multiple of earnings" criterion. Payment of the dividend by issuance of a promissory note would not substantially alter Stouffer's earnings. Since many investors were relatively unsophisticated, Litton may have been quite right that it could increase its investment in Stouffer by at least some portion of the $30 million dividend. Second, by declaring a dividend and paying it by a promissory note prior to an anticipated public offering, Litton could avoid sharing the earnings with future additional shareholders while not diminishing to the full extent of the pro rata dividend, the amount received for the stock. Whether Litton could have come out ahead after Stouffer paid the promissory note is at this point merely speculation about a public offering which never occurred. The point, however, is that Litton hoped to achieve some business purpose, and not just tax benefits, in structuring the transaction as it did.

Under these facts, where the dividend was declared 6 months prior to the sale of Stouffer, where the sale was not prearranged, and since Stouffer had earnings and profits exceeding $30 million at the time the dividend was declared, we cannot conclude that the distribution was merely a device designed to give the appearance of a dividend to a part of the sales proceeds. In this case, the form and substance of the transaction coincide; it was not a transaction entered into solely for tax reasons, and it should be recognized as structured by petitioner.

PROBLEM

Strap Corporation is the sole shareholder of X, Inc. Strap and X do not file a consolidated return, and Strap has held its X stock for more than two years. Strap has a $150,000 basis in its X stock. Boot is a prospective buyer and is willing to purchase all of the X stock, but he is unable to pay the $500,000 price demanded by Strap even though he believes it to be fair. X has $100,000 cash on hand and an ample supply of earnings and profits. To solve these problems, the parties have agreed on the following plan: Strap Corporation will cause X, Inc. to distribute $100,000 to it as a dividend. Promptly thereafter, Strap will sell its X stock to Boot for $400,000. What are the tax consequences of this plan? What if Strap were an individual rather than a corporation?

CHAPTER 5. REDEMPTIONS AND PARTIAL LIQUIDATIONS

A. INTRODUCTION

Code: §§ 302; 317(b).

A shareholder generally recognizes a capital gain or loss on the sale of some or all of his stock. Assume, for example, that A purchased 100 shares of X Corporation stock two years ago for $1,000. If A sells 50 of those shares to B, an unrelated outsider, for $750, he will recognize a $250 long-term capital gain. But what if A made the same sale to the corporation? Should that transaction, known as a redemption, also generate a $250 long-term capital gain? We need more facts to answer the question. If A is one of several X shareholders and owns a small percentage of the corporation's stock, a sale of stock to the corporation may be similar (for tax purposes) to a sale to B. But if X has few shareholders and ample earnings and profits and A is a major shareholder, the transaction begins to resemble a dividend.

To illustrate, assume that A's 100 shares constitute all of X Corporation's outstanding stock. In that event, A's "sale" of 50 shares to the corporation in exchange for $750 cash is indistinguishable from a nonliquidating distribution of $750. Although A has surrendered a stock certificate for 50 shares, his proportionate interest in the corporation remains unchanged. When the smoke clears, A continues to control all corporate decisions and he remains the sole shareholder, entitled to 100 percent of X's net assets upon a liquidation. Yet without altering his interest in the business, A has extracted $750 from the corporate coffers. This is the essence of a dividend! But if the "sale" to X were respected, A would be permitted to use a proportionate amount of his stock basis ($500) to offset an equivalent amount of income, and any resulting gain will be taxed at the slightly preferred capital gains rate. If A were permitted to avoid dividend characterization with such ease, proportionate redemption programs by shareholders of closely held corporations quickly would become a national sport whenever the shareholders have a substantial basis in their stock.

These simple examples identify the fundamental problem in determining the shareholder level tax consequences of a redemption. A line must be drawn between redemptions having the effect of a dividend—that is, transactions which enable shareholders to withdraw cash or other property while leaving their proportionate interest intact—and redemptions that resemble sales because they result in a meaningful reduction in the shareholder's proportionate interest. Prior to 1954, there was only one vague standard to resolve this question. A redemption was treated as an operating distribution and taxed as a dividend to the extent of the corporation's current and accumulated earnings and profits unless it was not "essentially equivalent to a taxable dividend." [1] Cases were resolved by looking to all the facts and circumstances, including the corporation's "business purpose" and the "net effect" of the transaction. [2]

The enactment of Section 302 in 1954 introduced a commendable degree of certainty in an area where predictions had been precarious. Section 302(a) provides that a redemption will be treated as an "exchange" if it comes within one of four statutory tests in Section 302(b). "Exchange" status means that the shareholder generally will recognize capital gain or loss to the extent of the difference between the amount of the distribution and the shareholder's basis in his stock. A redemption falling outside of Section 302(b) is treated under Section 302(d) as a "distribution to which Section 301 applies." Under the rules studied in the preceding chapter, the distribution will be a dividend to the extent of the corporation's current and accumulated earnings and profits, then a return of capital to the extent of the shareholder's stock basis and finally gain from the sale or exchange of the stock to the extent of any balance. Consequently, until Congress restores a significant capital gains rate preference, the principal tax stake on a redemption by a C corporation with ample earnings and profits is whether its shareholders may recover their basis in the redeemed stock before reporting income. Whether a redemption is treated as an exchange or a Section 301 distribution, the tax consequences to the distributing corporation of a distribution of property are governed by Section 311. The distributing corporation recognizes gain on a distribution of appreciated property in redemption, but it may not recognize loss on a distribution of property that has declined in value. [3]

Section 302(b) is thus the nerve center for determining the shareholder-level tax consequences of a redemption and the principal focus of this chapter. Three of the four statutory tests (Sections 302(b)(1)–(3)) examine whether there has been a sufficient reduction in the shareholder's ownership interest in the corporation to justify treating the redemption as an exchange. To obtain a more accurate measure, the shareholder's interest before and after the redemption is determined after application of the constructive ownership rules in Section 318. [4] Section 302(b)(4) shifts the focus to the corporate level and provides exchange treatment for any distribution that qualifies as a "partial liquidation" under Section 302(e) because it involves a genuine contraction of the distributing corporation's business.

1. Internal Revenue Code of 1939, § 115(g).

2. See Bittker & Eustice, Federal Income Taxation of Corporations and Shareholders ¶ 9.01 (5th ed. 1987). Another line of authority treated a redemption as not "essentially equivalent to a taxable dividend" if it involved a contraction in the corporation's business activities. This test focused on events at the corporate rather than the shareholder level and gave birth to the tax concept known as a "partial liquidation." The remnants of this concept are considered in Section F of this chapter, infra.

3. I.R.C. § 311(a), (b). For the details and the effect of a redemption on the distributing corporation's earnings and profits, see Section E of this Chapter, infra.

4. I.R.C. § 302(c)(1).

Redemptions are used to accomplish a variety of corporate and shareholder planning objectives, particularly for closely held corporations. A redemption may be the vehicle for a shift of corporate control or for the buyout of a dissatisfied or deceased shareholder. Redemptions also may play a role in a corporate acquisition and facilitate estate planning objectives. Keep these contexts in mind as you study the somewhat mechanical aspects of Section 302. Later sections of the chapter explore some of the planning opportunities provided by Section 302.

B. CONSTRUCTIVE OWNERSHIP OF STOCK

Code: §§ 302(c)(1); 318.

Regulations: § 1.318–1(a), (b), –2, –3(a), (b), –4.

Any system that purports to measure the change in a shareholder's proportionate interest in a corporation would be ineffective if it failed to consider the holdings of closely related shareholders. Returning to our introductory example, assume that A and his daughter, D, each own 50 of the 100 outstanding shares of X Corporation and A sells 30 of his shares to the corporation for $450. A's actual percentage ownership drops from 50 percent (50 out of 100 shares) to 29 percent (20 out of 70 shares). Has he substantially reduced his proportionate interest? Looking only to A's *actual* ownership, the reduction is substantial, but the remaining shares are owned by a close relative. With appropriate skepticism, the drafters of the Code concluded that in determining stock ownership for purposes of the Section 302(b) tests for exchange treatment, an individual taxpayer or entity should be considered as owning stock owned by certain family members and related entities under elaborate attribution rules set forth in Section 318.[1]

Section 318 is one of several sets of constructive ownership rules in the Internal Revenue Code [2] and applies only when it is expressly made applicable by another provision of the Code.[3] Its principal role is in the redemption area, where it treats a taxpayer as "owning" stock that is actually owned by various related parties. The attribution rules in Section 318 fall into the following four categories.

1. *Family Attribution.* An individual is considered as owning stock owned by his spouse, children, grandchildren and parents. Siblings and in-laws are not part of the "family" for this purpose, and there is no attribution from a grandparent to a grandchild.[4]

2. *Entity to Beneficiary Attribution.* Stock owned by or for a partnership or estate is considered as owned by the partners or beneficiaries in proportion to their beneficial interests.[5] Stock owned by a

---

1. I.R.C. § 302(c)(1).

2. Other constructive ownership provisions include Sections 267(c), 341(e)(8), and 544.

3. Section 318(b) contains a partial list of cross references to sections applying Section 318.

4. I.R.C. § 318(a)(1). Cf. I.R.C. § 318(a)(5)(B).

5. I.R.C. § 318(a)(2)(A).

trust (other than a qualified employees' trust) is considered as owned by the beneficiaries in proportion to their actuarial interest in the trust. In the case of grantor trusts, stock is considered owned by the grantor or other person who is taxable on the trust income.[6] Stock owned by a corporation is considered owned proportionately (comparing the value of the shareholder's stock to the value of all stock) by a shareholder who owns, directly or through the attribution rules, 50 percent or more in value of that corporation's stock.[7]

3. *Beneficiary to Entity Attribution.* Stock owned by partners or beneficiaries of an estate is considered as owned by the partnership or estate.[8] Stock owned by trust beneficiaries is attributed to the trust except where the beneficiary's interest is "remote" and "contingent." In the case of a grantor trust, the trust is considered to own stock owned by the grantor or other person taxable on the income of the trust.[9] All the stock owned by a 50 percent or more shareholder of a corporation is attributed to the corporation.[10]

4. *Option Attribution.* A person holding an option to acquire stock is considered as owning that stock.[11]

These general rules are supplemented by a set of "operating rules" in Section 318(a)(5), which generally authorize chain attribution (e.g., parent to child to child's trust) except that there can be no double family attribution (e.g., no attribution from parent to child to child's spouse) or "sidewise" attribution (e.g., stock attributed to an entity from a partner, beneficiary or shareholder may not be reattributed from that entity to another partner, beneficiary or shareholder).[12] In addition, option attribution takes precedence over family attribution where both apply.[13] For Section 318 purposes, an S corporation is treated as a partnership, and S corporation shareholders are treated like partners.[14]

The problems which follow test your ability to apply the attribution rules in some familiar factual contexts.

PROBLEMS

1. Wham Corporation has 100 shares of common stock outstanding. Twenty-five shares are owned by Grandfather, 20 shares are owned by Mother (Grandfather's Daughter), 15 shares are owned by

6. I.R.C. § 318(a)(2)(B).

7. I.R.C. § 318(a)(2)(C).

8. I.R.C. § 318(a)(3)(A).

9. I.R.C. § 318(a)(3)(B). Contingent interests are considered remote if the actuarial value of the interest is 5 percent or less of the value of the trust property, assuming the trustee exercises maximum discretion in favor of the beneficiary.

10. I.R.C. § 318(a)(3)(C).

11. I.R.C. § 318(a)(4). "Options" have been interpreted to include warrants and convertible debentures. Rev.Rul. 68–601,

1968–2 C.B. 124. Even options that are exercisable after the lapse of a fixed period of time are considered as options from the time they are granted. Rev.Rul. 89–64, 1989–1 C.B. 91.

12. I.R.C. § 318(a)(5)(A), (B), (C).

13. I.R.C. § 318(a)(5)(D).

14. I.R.C. § 318(a)(5)(E). This rule applies for purposes of attributing stock to and from the S corporation, but not for determining constructive ownership of stock in the S corporation. Id.

Mother's Daughter, 10 shares are owned by Mother's adopted Son, and the remaining 30 shares are owned by Grandmother's estate, of which Mother is a 50% beneficiary. One of Mother's cousins is the other beneficiary of the estate. Mother also has an option to purchase 5 of Son's shares. How much Wham stock do Grandfather, Daughter and Grandmother's estate own after application of § 318?

2. All the 100 shares of Xerxes Corporation are owned by Partnership, in which A, B, C and D (all unrelated to each other) are equal partners. W, A's wife, owns all of the 100 shares of Yancy Corporation.

(a) How many shares, if any, of Xerxes Corporation are owned by A, W and M (W's mother)?

(b) How many shares, if any, of Xerxes are owned by Yancy? Would Yancy constructively own any shares of Xerxes if W owned only 10 percent of Yancy?

(c) How many shares, if any, of Yancy are owned by Partnership, B, C, D and Xerxes?

C. REDEMPTIONS TESTED AT THE SHAREHOLDER LEVEL *

1. SUBSTANTIALLY DISPROPORTIONATE REDEMPTIONS

Code: § 302(b)(2).

Regulations: § 1.302–3.

The virtue of Section 302(b)(2) is its certainty. If a shareholder's reduction in voting stock as a result of a redemption satisfies three mechanical requirements, the redemption will be treated as an exchange. To qualify as "substantially disproportionate," a redemption must satisfy the following requirements:

1. Immediately after the redemption, the shareholder must own (actually and constructively) less than 50 percent of the total combined voting power of all classes of stock entitled to vote,[1]

2. The percentage of total outstanding voting stock owned by the shareholder immediately after the redemption must be less than 80 percent of the percentage of total voting stock owned by the shareholder immediately before the redemption,[2] and

---

* See generally Kahn, "Stock Redemptions: The Standards for Qualifying as a Purchase Under Section 302(b)," 50 Fordham L.Rev. 1 (1981).

1. I.R.C. § 302(b)(2)(B).

2. I.R.C. § 302(b)(2)(C). This requirement may be expressed by the following formula:

$$\frac{\text{Voting shares owned after redemption}}{\text{Total voting shares outstanding after redemption}} \quad \text{must be less than:} \quad .80 \times \frac{\text{Voting shares owned before redemption}}{\text{Total voting shares outstanding before redemption}}$$

3. The shareholder's percentage ownership of common stock (whether voting or nonvoting) after the redemption also must be less than 80 percent of the percentage of common stock owned before the redemption.[3] If there is more than one class of common stock, the 80 percent test is applied by reference to fair market value.[4]

The attribution rules of Section 318 are applicable in measuring stock ownership for purposes of all these percentage tests.

To illustrate, assume Redeemer owns 60 percent of the common stock of a corporation which has only one class of stock outstanding. A redemption which reduces Redeemer's stock interest to a percentage below 48 percent would satisfy Section 302(b)(2). Below that level, Redeemer would own less than 50 percent of the corporation's total combined voting power, and his percentage of voting stock after the redemption (below 48 percent) would be less than 80 percent of his percentage of voting stock before the redemption (60 percent).

The regulations elaborate on the operation of Section 302(b)(2). Stock with voting rights only upon the happening of a specific event (e.g., a default in a payment of dividends on preferred stock) is not considered voting stock until the event occurs.[5] A redemption of solely nonvoting stock will never satisfy Section 302(b)(2) because there will not be a sufficient reduction in the shareholder's interest in voting stock. But if a redemption qualifies under Section 302(b)(2), a simultaneous redemption of nonvoting preferred stock (which is not Section 306 stock)[6] will be treated as an exchange.[7] The Internal Revenue Service also has ruled that a redemption of voting preferred stock from a shareholder owning no common stock (either directly or by way of attribution) may qualify under Section 302(b)(2), even though the shareholder can not satisfy the 80 percent test relating to common stock.[8]

The substantially disproportionate redemption safe harbor does not apply to any redemption made pursuant to a plan which has the purpose or effect of a series of redemptions that, taken together, result in a distribution that is not substantially disproportionate with respect to the shareholder.[9] This statutory application of the step transaction doctrine is the subject of the ruling that follows.

3. I.R.C. § 302(b)(2)(C).

4. The common stock cutback test is applied on an aggregate rather than a class-by-class basis. Thus, if a shareholder's aggregate reduction in all classes of common stock (measured by value) meets the percentage tests in Section 302(b)(2)(C), the redemption will be treated as an exchange even if the shareholder continues to own 100 percent of one class of outstanding common stock. Rev.Rul. 87–88, 1987–2 C.B. 81.

5. Reg. § 1.302–3(a).

6. See Chapter 6C, infra.

7. Reg. § 1.302–3(a).

8. Rev.Rul. 81–41, 1981–1 C.B. 121.

9. I.R.C. § 302(b)(2)(D).

REVENUE RULING 85–14

1985–1 Cum.Bull. 83.

ISSUE

Should qualification under section 302(b)(2) of the Internal Revenue Code of a redemption of one shareholder be measured immediately after that redemption, or after a second redemption of another shareholder that followed soon after the first redemption, under the following facts?

FACTS

X, a corporation founded by *A*, is engaged in an ongoing business. As of January 1, 1983, *X*'s sole class of stock, voting common stock, was held by *A*, *B*, *C*, and *D*, who are unrelated to each other. *A* owned 1,466 shares, *B* owned 210 shares, *C* owned 200 shares, and *D* owned 155 shares of *X* stock. *A* was president and *B* was vice-president of *X*.

X has a repurchase agreement with all *X* shareholders, except *A*. This agreement provides that if any such shareholder ceases to be actively connected with the business operations of *X*, such shareholder must promptly tender to *X* the then-held *X* shares for an amount equal to the book value of such stock. *X* has a reciprocal obligation to purchase such shares at book value within 6 months of such shareholder's ceasing to be actively connected with *X*'s business operations.

On January 1, 1983, *B* informed *A* of *B*'s intention to resign as of March 22, 1983. Based on this information, *A* caused *X* to adopt a plan of redemption and to redeem 902 shares of *A*'s *X* stock, on March 15, 1983, for which *A* received 700*x* dollars. Thus, *A* then held 564 shares of the 1129 shares (49.96 percent) of the *X* stock still outstanding, temporarily yielding majority control over the affairs of *X* until *B* ceased to be a shareholder. On March 22, 1983, *B* resigned from *X* and, in accordance with the *X* stock purchase agreement, *X* redeemed for cash all of *B*'s shares within the next 6 months, thus leaving 919 shares of *X* stock outstanding, restoring majority control to *A*.

LAW AND ANALYSIS

Section 302(a) of the Code provides that if a corporation redeems its stock and if one of the paragraphs of subsection (b) applies, then such redemption will be treated as a distribution in part or full payment in exchange for the stock.

Section 302(b)(2) of the Code provides that a redemption will be treated as an exchange pursuant to section 302(a) if the redemption is substantially disproportionate with respect to the shareholder, but that this paragraph will not apply unless immediately after the redemption the shareholder owns less than 50 percent of the total combined voting power of all classes of stock entitled to vote.

Under section 302(b)(2)(C) of the Code, one of the requirements for the distribution to be substantially disproportionate is that the ratio that the voting stock of the corporation owned by the shareholder immediately after the redemption bears to all the voting stock of the corporation at such time, is less than 80 percent of the ratio that the voting stock of the corporation owned by the shareholder immediatley before the redemption bears to all the voting stock of the corporation at such time.

Section 302(b)(2)(D) of the Code, in dealing with a series of redemptions, provides that section 302(b)(2) is not applicable to any redemption made pursuant to a plan the purpose or effect of which is a series of redemptions resulting in a distribution which (in the aggregate) is not substantially disproportionate with respect to the shareholder.

The percentage provisions contained in sections 302(b)(2)(B) and 302(b)(2)(C) of the Code provide "safe harbor" exchange treatment. Examined separately, the transaction that occurred on March 15, 1983, would qualify as a substantially disproportionate redemption because (i) A's ownership of X's voting stock immediately after the redemption was less than 50 percent of the total combined voting power of all the X stock and (ii) A's ownership of X's voting stock was reduced from 72.18 percent to 49.96 percent, which meets the 80 percent requirement of section 302(b)(2)(C). However, if A's redemption is considered to be part of a section 302(b)(2)(D) series of redemptions which included X's redemption of B's shares, then A's redemption would not constitute a substantially disproportionate redemption because (i) A's ownership of X's voting stock after the redemptions exceeded 50 percent of the total combined voting power of X and (ii) A's ownership of X's voting stock after the redemptions was reduced from 72.18 percent to 61.37 percent, which does not meet the 80 percent requirement of section 302(b)(2)(C).

Section 1.302–3(a) of the Income Tax Regulations states that whether or not a plan described in section 302(b)(2)(D) of the Code exists will be determined from all the facts and circumstances.

In the present situation, although A and B had no joint plan, arrangement, or agreement for a series of redemptions, the redemption of A's shares was causally related to the redemption of B's shares in that A saw an apparent opportunity to secure exchange treatment under section 302(b)(2) of the Code by temporarily yielding majority control over the affairs of X.

Nothing in section 302(b)(2)(D) of the Code or in the legislative history of this section * * * indicates that the existence of a plan depends upon an agreement between two or more shareholders. Thus, a "plan" for purposes of section 302(b)(2)(D) need be nothing more than a design by a single redeemed shareholder to arrange a redemption as part of a sequence of events that ultimately restores to such shareholder the control that was apparently reduced in the redemption.

Under the facts and circumstances here, section 302(b)(2)(D) of the Code requires that the redemptions of A and B be considered in the aggregate. Accordingly, *A*'s redemption meets neither the 50 percent limitation of section 302(b)(2)(B) nor the 80 percent test of section 302(b)(2)(C). Thus, the redemption of *A*'s shares was not substantially disproportionate within the meaning of section 302(b)(2).

HOLDING

Under the facts of this ruling, qualification under section 302(b)(2) of the Code of *A*'s redemption should not be measured immediately after that redemption, but, instead, should be measured after *B*'s redemption that followed soon after *A*'s redemption.

PROBLEMS

1. Y Corporation has 100 shares of common stock and 200 shares of nonvoting preferred stock outstanding. Alice owns 80 shares of Y common stock and 100 shares of its preferred stock. Cathy owns the remaining 20 shares of Y common and 100 shares of Y preferred stock. Alice and Cathy are not related. In each of the following alternative situations, determine whether the redemption satisfies the requirements of § 302(b)(2):

   (a) On January 15, Y Corporation redeems 75 of Alice's preferred shares.

   (b) Same as (a), above, except that Y also redeems 60 shares of Alice's common stock.

   (c) Same as (a), above, except that Y also redeems 70 shares of Alice's common stock.

   (d) What difference would it make in (c), above, if, on December 1 of the same year, Y redeems 10 shares of Cathy's common stock?

2. Z Corporation has 100 shares of voting common stock and 200 shares of nonvoting common stock outstanding. Every share of Z common stock has a fair market value of $100. Don owns 60 shares of Z voting common stock and 100 shares of Z nonvoting common stock. Jerry owns all of the remaining Z stock. Don and Jerry are not related to one another. If Z redeems 30 of Don's voting common shares, will the redemption qualify for exchange treatment under § 302(b)(2)?

2. COMPLETE TERMINATION OF A SHAREHOLDER'S INTEREST

a. WAIVER OF FAMILY ATTRIBUTION *

Code: § 302(b)(3), (c).

Regulations: § 1.302–4.

---

* See generally, Nuzum, "Waiver of the Family Ownership Rules Under Section 302(c)(2)(A): Retention or Reacquisition of a Prohibited Interest," 11 J.Corp.Tax'n 19 (1984).

The theory of the Section 302(b)(2) safe harbor for substantially disproporticnate redemptions is that exchange rather than dividend treatment is appropriate when a distribution is accompanied by a significant reduction in the shareholder's interest in the corporation's voting stock. This policy applies with even greater force in the case of a complete termination of a shareholder's interest, which not surprisingly qualifies for exchange treatment under Section 302(b)(3). For shareholders of a closely held family corporation, however, the attribution rules present a substantial roadblock to a complete termination. Even if all of the stock of a retiring shareholder is redeemed, she will continue to be treated as a 100 percent owner if her children or other related parties hold the remaining shares.

To provide relief where the redeemed shareholder is willing to cut the corporate cord, Section 302(c)(2) eases the path toward a complete termination by waiving the family attribution rules. This attribution amnesty is a useful planning tool for shareholders of family corporations. If the requirements of Section 302(c)(2) are met, a shareholder can achieve a complete termination even though the remaining shares are held by close relatives. The waiver applies, however, only to *family* attribution; the entity and option attribution rules remain fully applicable.

Waiver of the family attribution rules is available only if immediately after the distribution the redeemed shareholder retains no "interest" in the corporation (other than as a creditor). The ban extends to interests as an officer, director or employee. Section 302(c)(2)(A) also includes a "ten year look forward" rule, under which the shareholder may not retain or acquire (other than by bequest or inheritance) any of the forbidden interests in the corporation "other than an interest as a creditor." [1] To prevent anticipatory bailouts, Section 302(c)(2)(B) provides a "ten year look back" rule, under which the family attribution rules may not be waived if during the ten years preceding the redemption either: (1) the redeemed shareholder acquired any of the redeemed stock from a "Section 318" relative or (2) any such close relative acquired stock from the redeemed shareholder. Neither of these exceptions applies, however, if "tax avoidance" was not one of the principal purposes of the otherwise tainted transfer.[2]

The Internal Revenue Service strictly interprets some of these requirements, but the Tax Court has been much more lenient. The

1. This rule is enforced by requiring the redeemed shareholder to file a form in which the shareholder agrees to notify the Service of any acquisition of a forbidden interest within ten years from the redemption and to retain such records as may be necessary to permit enforcement of this rule by the Service. The normal three year statute of limitations is extended to one year after the shareholder gives notice of acquisition of a forbidden interest in order to permit the Service to make a retroactive assessment of a deficiency. I.R.C. § 302(c)(2)(A).

2. See generally Kuntz, "Stock Redemptions Following Stock Transfers,—An Expanding 'Safe Harbor,' Under Section 302(c)(2)(B)," 58 Taxes 29 (1980).

Lynch case, which follows, is the Service's most recent victory in this often contested area.

LYNCH v. COMMISSIONER *

United States Court of Appeals, Ninth Circuit, 1986.
801 F.2d 1176.

CYNTHIA HOLCOMB HALL, Circuit Judge:

The Commissioner of the Internal Revenue Service (Commissioner) petitions for review of a Tax Court decision holding that a corporate redemption of a taxpayer's stock was a sale or exchange subject to capital gains treatment. The Commissioner argues that the taxpayer held a prohibited interest in the corporation after the redemption and therefore the transaction should be characterized as a dividend distribution taxable as ordinary income. We agree with the Commissioner and reverse the Tax Court.

I

Taxpayers, William and Mima Lynch, formed the W.M. Lynch Co. on April 1, 1960. The corporation issued all of its outstanding stock to William Lynch (taxpayer). The taxpayer specialized in leasing cast-in-place concrete pipe machines. He owned the machines individually but leased them to the corporation which in turn subleased the equipment to independent contractors.

On December 17, 1975 the taxpayer sold 50 shares of the corporation's stock to his son, Gilbert Lynch (Gilbert), for $17,170. Gilbert paid for the stock with a $16,000 check given to him by the taxpayer and $1,170 from his own savings. The taxpayer and his wife also resigned as directors and officers of the corporation on the same day.

On December 31, 1975 the corporation redeemed all 2300 shares of the taxpayer's stock. In exchange for his stock, the taxpayer received $17,900 of property and a promissory note for $771,920. Gilbert, as the sole remaining shareholder, pledged his 50 shares as a guarantee for the note. In the event that the corporation defaulted on any of the note payments, the taxpayer would have the right to vote or sell Gilbert's 50 shares.

In the years immediately preceding the redemption, Gilbert had assumed greater managerial responsibility in the corporation. He wished, however, to retain the taxpayer's technical expertise with cast-in-place concrete pipe machines. On the date of the redemption, the taxpayer also entered into a consulting agreement with the corporation. The consulting agreement provided the taxpayer with payments of $500 per month for five years, plus reimbursement for business related travel, entertainment, and automobile expenses.[2] In February 1977,

---

* Some footnotes omitted.

2. The corporation leased or purchased a pickup truck for the taxpayer's use in 1977. If someone at the corporation needed the truck, the taxpayer would make it available to him.

the corporation and the taxpayer mutually agreed to reduce the monthly payments to $250. The corporation never withheld payroll taxes from payments made to the taxpayer.

After the redemption, the taxpayer shared his former office with Gilbert. The taxpayer came to the office daily for approximately one year; thereafter his appearances dwindled to about once or twice per week. When the corporation moved to a new building in 1979, the taxpayer received a private office.

In addition to the consulting agreement, the taxpayer had other ties to the corporation. He remained covered by the corporation's group medical insurance policy until 1980. When his coverage ended, the taxpayer had received the benefit of $4,487.54 in premiums paid by the corporation. He was also covered by a medical reimbursement plan, created the day of the redemption, which provided a maximum annual payment of $1,000 per member. Payments to the taxpayer under the plan totaled $96.05.

II

We must decide whether the redemption of the taxpayer's stock in this case is taxable as a dividend distribution under 26 U.S.C. § 301 or as long-term capital gain under 26 U.S.C. § 302(a). Section 302(a) provides that a corporate distribution of property in redemption of a shareholder's stock is treated as a sale or exchange of such stock if the redemption falls within one of four categories described in section 302(b). If the redemption falls outside of these categories, then it is treated as a dividend distribution under section 301 to the extent of the corporation's earnings and profits.[4]

Section 302(b)(3) provides that a shareholder is entitled to sale or exchange treatment if the corporation redeems all of the shareholder's stock. In order to determine whether there is a complete redemption for purposes of section 302(b)(3), the family attribution rules of section 318(a) must be applied unless the requirements of section 302(c)(2) are satisfied. Here, if the family attribution rules apply, the taxpayer will be deemed to own constructively the 50 shares held by Gilbert (100% of the corporation's stock) and the transaction would not qualify as a complete redemption within the meaning of section 302(b)(3).

Section 302(c)(2)(A) states in relevant part:

> In the case of a distribution described in subsection (b)(3), [the family attribution rules in] section 318(a)(1) shall not apply if—
>
> (i) immediately after the distribution the distributee has no interest in the corporation (including an interest as officer, director, or employee), other than an interest as a creditor
>
> *　*　*.

---

4. On the date of the redemption, W.M. Lynch Co. had accumulated earnings and profits of $315,863, and had never paid a dividend.

The Commissioner argues that in every case the performance of post-redemption services is a prohibited interest under section 302(c)(2)(A)(i), regardless of whether the taxpayer is an officer, director, employee, or independent contractor.

The Tax Court rejected the Commissioner's argument, finding that the services rendered by the taxpayer did not amount to a prohibited interest in the corporation. In reaching this conclusion, the Tax Court relied on a test derived from Lewis v. Commissioner, 47 T.C. 129, 136 (1966) (Simpson, J., concurring):

> Immediately after the enactment of the 1954 Code, it was recognized that section 302(c)(2)(A)(i) did not prohibit office holding per se, but was concerned with a retained financial stake in the corporation, such as a profit-sharing plan, or in the creation of an ostensible sale that really changed nothing so far as corporate management was concerned. Thus, in determining whether a prohibited interest has been retained under section 302(c)(2)(A)(i), we must look to whether the former stockholder has either retained a financial stake in the corporation or continued to control the corporation and benefit by its operations. In particular, where the interest retained is not that of an officer, director, or employee, we must examine the facts and circumstances to determine whether a prohibited interest has been retained under section 302(c)(2)(A)(i).

Lynch v. Commissioner, 83 T.C. 597, 605 (1984) (citations omitted).

After citing the "control or financial stake" standard, the Tax Court engaged in a two-step analysis. First, the court concluded that the taxpayer was an independent contractor rather than an employee because the corporation had no right under the consulting agreement to control his actions.[5] Id. at 606. Second, the court undertook a "facts and circumstances" analysis to determine whether the taxpayer had a financial stake in the corporation or managerial control after the redemption. Because the consulting agreement was not linked to the future profitability of the corporation, the court found that the taxpayer had no financial stake. *Id.* at 606–07. The court also found no evidence that the taxpayer exerted control over the corporation. Id. at 607. Thus, the Tax Court determined that the taxpayer held no interest prohibited by section 302(c)(2)(A)(i).

III

We review the decisions of the Tax Court on the same basis as decisions in civil bench trials in district courts, * * * The Tax

---

5. Finding that the taxpayer was not an employee obviated the need to decide whether the parenthetical language in section 302(c)(2)(A)(i) prohibited employment relationships per se. See Seda v. Commissioner, 82 T.C. 484, 488 (1984) (court stated that "section 302(c)(2)(A)(i) may not prohibit the retention of all employment relationships").

Court's interpretation of what constitutes a prohibited interest under section 302(c)(2)(A)(i) is a question of law reviewed de novo.

We reject the Tax Court's interpretation of section 302(c)(2)(A)(i). An individualized determination of whether a taxpayer has retained a financial stake or continued to control the corporation after the redemption is inconsistent with Congress' desire to bring a measure of certainty to the tax consequences of a corporate redemption. We hold that a taxpayer who provides post-redemption services, either as an employee or an independent contractor, holds a prohibited interest in the corporation because he is not a creditor.

The legislative history of section 302 states that Congress intended to provide "definite standards in order to provide certainty in specific instances." S.Rep. No. 1622, 83d Cong., 2d Sess. 233, reprinted in 1954 U.S.Code Cong. & Ad.News 4017, 4621, 4870. "In lieu of a factual inquiry in every case, [section 302] is intended to prescribe specific conditions from which the taxpayer may ascertain whether a given redemption" will qualify as a sale or be treated as a dividend distribution. H.R.Rep.No. 1337, 83d Cong.2d Sess. 35, reprinted in 1954 U.S.Cong. & Ad.News 4017, 4210. The facts and circumstances approach created by the Tax Court undermines the ability of taxpayers to execute a redemption and know the tax consequences with certainty.

The taxpayer's claim that the Senate rejected the mechanical operation of the House's version of section 302 is misleading. The Senate did reject the House bill because the "definitive conditions" were "unnecessarily restrictive." S.Rep.No.1622, 83d Cong., 2d Sess. 44, reprinted in 1954 U.S.Code Cong. & Ad.News 4621, 4675. However, the Senate's response was to add paragraph (b)(1) to section 302, which reestablished the flexible, but notoriously vague, "not essentially equivalent to a dividend" test. This test provided that all payments from a corporation that were not essentially equivalent to a dividend should be taxed as capital gains. The confusion that stemmed from a case-by-case inquiry into "dividend equivalence" prompted the Congress to enact definite standards for the safe harbors in section 302(b)(2) and (b)(3). The Tax Court's refusal to recognize that section 302(c)(2)(A)(i) prohibits *all* noncreditor interests in the corporation creates the same uncertainty as the "dividend equivalence" test.

The problem with the Tax Court's approach is apparent when this case is compared with Seda v. Commissioner, 82 T.C. 484 (1984). In *Seda*, a former shareholder, at his son's insistence, continued working for the corporation for two years after the redemption. He received a salary of $1,000 per month. The Tax Court refused to hold that section 302(c)(2)(A)(i) prohibits the retention of employment relations per se, despite the unequivocal language in the statute.[6] Id. at 488. Instead, the court applied the facts and circumstances approach to determine

---

6. Eight of the seventeen Tax Court judges who reviewed *Seda* concurred in the result but would have classified all officer, director, or employee relationships as prohibited interests under section 302(c)(2)(A)(i).

whether the former shareholder retained a financial stake or continued to control the corporation. The Tax Court found that the monthly payments of $1,000 constituted a financial stake in the corporation. Id. This result is at odds with the holding in *Lynch* that payments of $500 per month do *not* constitute a financial stake in the corporation. Compare Lynch, 83 T.C. at 606–07 with Seda, 82 T.C. at 488. The court also found in *Seda* no evidence that the former shareholder had ceased to manage the corporation.   82 T.C. at 488.   Again, this finding is contrary to the holding in *Lynch* that the taxpayer exercised no control over the corporation after the redemption, even though he worked daily for a year and shared his old office with his son. Compare Lynch, 83 T.C. at 607 with Seda, 82 T.C. 488.   *Seda* and *Lynch* thus vividly demonstrate the perils of making an ad hoc determination of "control" or "financial stake."

A recent Tax Court opinion further illustrates the imprecision of the facts and circumstances approach. In Cerone v. Commissioner, 87 T.C. 1 (1986), a father and son owned all the shares of a corporation formed to operate their restaurant. The corporation agreed to redeem all of the father's shares in order to resolve certain diagreements between the father and son concerning the management of the business. However, the father remained an employee of the corporation for at least five years after the redemption, drawing a salary of $14,400 for the first three years and less thereafter. The father claimed that he was entitled to capital gains treatment on the redemption because he had terminated his interest in the corporation within the meaning of section 302(b)(3).

Even on the facts of *Cerone,* the Tax Court refused to find that the father held a prohibited employment interest per se. * * * Instead, the Tax Court engaged in a lengthy analysis, citing both *Seda* and *Lynch*. The court proclaimed that *Lynch* reaffirmed the rationale of *Seda,* even though *Lynch* involved an independent contractor rather than an employee. After comparing the facts of *Seda* and *Cerone,* the Tax Court eventually concluded that the father in *Cerone* held a financial stake in the corporation because he had drawn a salary that was $2,400 per year more than the taxpayer in *Seda* and had been employed by the corporation for a longer period after the redemption. *Cerone,* slip op. at 53. However, the Tax Court was still concerned that prohibited interest in *Seda* might have been based on the finding in that case that the taxpayer had both a financial stake *and* continued control of the corporation. The Tax Court, citing *Lynch,* held that the "test is whether he retained a financial stake *or* continued to control the corporation." * * * Thus, the Tax Court found that the father in *Cerone* held a prohibited interest because he had a financial stake as defined by *Seda.*

Although the Tax Court reached the correct result in *Cerone,* its approach undermines the definite contours of the safe harbor Congress intended to create with sections 302(b)(3) and 302(c)(2)(A)(i). Whether a taxpayer has a financial stake according to the Tax Court seems to depend on two factors, length of employment and the amount of salary. Length of employment after the redemption is irrelevant because Congress wanted taxpayers to know whether they were entitled to capital gains treatment on the date their shares were redeemed. See S.Rep. No. 1622, 83d Cong., 2d Sess., 235–36, reprinted in 1954 U.S.Code Cong. & Ad.News 4621, 4872–73. See also Treas.Reg. § 1.302–4(a)(1) (taxpayer must attach a statement disclaiming any interest in the corporation with the first tax return filed after the distribution). As for the amount of annual salary, the Tax Court's present benchmark appears to be the $12,000 figure in *Seda*. Salary at or above this level will be deemed to be a financial stake in the enterprise, though the $6,000 annual payments in in this case were held not to be a financial stake. There is no support in the legislative history of section 302 for the idea that Congress meant only to prohibit service contracts of a certain worth, and taxpayers should not be left to speculate as to what income level will give rise to a financial stake.

In this case, the taxpayer points to the fact that the taxpayers in *Seda* and *Cerone* were employees, while he was an independent contractor. On appeal, the Commissioner concedes the taxpayer's independent contractor status. We fail to see, however, any meaningful way to distinguish *Seda* and *Cerone* from *Lynch* by differentiating between employees and independent contractors. All of the taxpayers performed services for their corporations following the redemption. To hold that only the employee taxpayers held a prohibited interest would elevate form over substance. The parenthetical language in section 302(c)(2)(A)(i) merely provides a subset of prohibited interests from the universe of such interests, and in no way limits us from finding that an independent contractor retains a prohibited interest. Furthermore, the Tax Court has in effect come to ignore the parenthetical language. If employment relationships are not prohibited interests per se, then the taxpayer's status as an employee or independent contractor is irrelevant. What really matters under the Tax Court's approach is how the taxpayer fares under a facts and circumstances review of whether he has a financial stake in the corporation or managerial control.[7] Tax planners are left to guess where along the continuum of monthly payments from $500 to $1000 capital gains treatment ends and ordinary income tax begins.

7. The Tax Court's focus on managerial control or a financial stake originated with Judge Simpson's concurrence in *Lewis*, 47 T.C. at 136–38. His interpretation of section 302(c)(2)(A) is supported by Bittker, Stock Redemptions and Partial Liquidations Under the Internal Revenue Code of 1954, 9 Stan.L.Rev. 13, 33 n. 72 (1956). Professor Bittker argues that Congress' goal was to ensure that taxpayers who transferred only ostensible control or maintained a financial stake in the corporation did not receive the benefit of capital gains treatment. He is no doubt correct. However, the means selected by Congress to achieve this goal do not allow for an individualized determination of control and financial stakes. Instead, section 302(c)(2)(A)(i) operates mechanically: the taxpayer must sever all but a creditor's interest to avoid the family attribution rules and thereby receive capital gains treatment. Nowhere in the legislative history of section 302(c) does Congress intimate that courts may use a flexible facts and circumstances test to determine the existence of managerial control or a financial stake.

Our holding today that taxpayers who provide post-redemption services have a prohibited interest under section 302(c)(2)(A)(i) is inconsistent with the Tax Court's decision in Estate of Lennard v. Commissioner, 61 T.C. 554 (1974). That case held that a former shareholder who, as an independent contractor, provided post-redemption accounting services for a corporation did not have a prohibited interest. The Tax Court found that "Congress did not intend to include independent contractors possessing no financial stake in the corporation among those who are considered as retaining an interest in the corporation for purposes of the attribution waiver rules." Id. at 561. We disagree. In the context of Lennard, the Tax Court appears to be using financial stake in the sense of having an equity interest or some other claim linked to the future profit of the corporation. Yet, in cases such as Seda and Cerone, the Tax Court has found that fixed salaries of $12,000 and $14,400, respectively, constitute a financial stake. Fees for accounting services could easily exceed these amounts, and it would be irrational to argue that the definition of financial stake varies depending on whether the taxpayer is an employee or an independent contractor. In order to avoid these inconsistencies, we conclude that those who provide post-redemption services, whether as independent contractors or employees, hold an interest prohibited by section 302(c)(2)(A)(i) because they are more than merely creditors.

In addition, both the Tax Court and the Commissioner have agreed that taxpayers who enter into management consulting contracts after the redemption possess prohibited interests. Chertkof v. Commissioner, 72 T.C. 1113, 1124–25 (1979), aff'd, 649 F.2d 264 (4th Cir.1981); Rev.Ruling 70–104, 1970–1 C.B. 66 (1970). Taxpayers who provide such services are, of course, independent contractors. However, unlike the Commissioner's opinion in Rev. Ruling 70–104 that all management consulting agreements are prohibited interests, the Tax Court applies the financial stake or managerial control test. In Chertkof, the court found that because the services provided under the contract "went to the essence" of the corporation's existence, the taxpayer had not effectively ceded control. 72 T.C. at 1124. Here, the Tax Court distinguished Chertkof on the ground that the taxpayer did not retain control of the corporation, but instead provided only limited consulting services. Lynch, 83 T.C. at 608. We believe that any attempt to define prohibited interests based on the level of control leads to the same difficulties inherent in making a case-by-case determination of what constitutes a financial stake.[8]

8. Determining the existence of control is particularly difficult in the context of a family-held corporation. The exercise of control often will not be obvious because a parent may influence a child, and hence corporate decisionmaking, in myriad ways. Our rule that the provision of services is a prohibited interest eliminates the need to make a speculative inquiry into whether the parent still controls the corporation after the redemption. Of course, no rule could or should prohibit post-redemption parent-child communication concerning the management of the corporation.

IV

Our decision today comports with the plain language of section 302 and its legislative history. See Gardner & Randall, Distributions in Redemption of Stock: Changing Definitions for a Termination of Interest, 8 J. Corp. Tax'n 240, 247–48 (1981); Marusic, The Prohibited Interest of I.R.C. Section 302(c)(2)(A)(i) After Seda and Lynch, 65 Neb.L.Rev. 486, 502, 518–19 (1986); Rose, The Prohibited Interest of Section 302(c)(2)(A), 36 Tax L.Rev. 131, 145–49 (1981). Taxpayers who wish to receive capital gains treatment upon the redemption of their shares must completely sever all noncreditor interests in the corporation.[9] We hold that the taxpayer, as an independent contractor, held such a noncreditor interest, and so cannot find shelter in the safe harbor of section 302(c)(2)(A)(i). Accordingly, the family attribution rules of section 318 apply and the taxpayer fails to qualify for a complete redemption under section 302(b)(3). The payments from the corporation in redemption of the taxpayer's shares must be characterized as a dividend distribution taxable as ordinary income under section 301.

Reversed.

REVENUE RULING 59–119

1959–1 Cum.Bull. 68.

A stock redemption agreement between the corporation and the instant shareholder provides that a total of 350x dollars will be paid to such shareholder for all his stock interest in the corporation, 100x dollars to be paid on the closing date and 250x dollars to be paid by the corporation within eight years, payable in quarter-annual installments. The corporation executed an installment judgment note to the shareholder and the judgment note and shares of stock of the corporation to be redeemed are retained by an escrow holder as security for installment payments due. In the event the installment and interest payments are in default, then pursuant to the agreement the escrow holder, upon notice from the taxpayer, may sell the stock of the corporation held by him at public or private sale to satisfy such obligations, however, in no event will the taxpayer become the purchaser of said stock at such sale.

9. Our definition of a prohibited interest still leaves an open question as to the permissible scope of a creditor's interest under section 302(c)(2)(A)(i). See, e.g., Treas.Reg. § 1.302–4(d) (a creditor's claim must not be subordinate to the claims of general creditors or in any other sense proprietary, i.e., principal payments or interest rates must not be contingent on the earnings of the corporation).

The taxpayer argues that some creditor relationships might result in an "opportunity to influence" as great or greater than any officer, director, or employee relationship. He cites Rev.Ruling 77–467, 1977–2 C.B. 92 which concluded that a taxpayer who leased real property to a corporation, after the corporation redeemed his shares, held a creditor's interest under section 302(c)(2)(A)(i). While the taxpayer here may be correct in his assessment of a creditor's "opportunity to influence" a corporation, he overlooks the fact that Congress specifically allowed the right to retain such an interest.

The stock redemption agreement also states that so long as the corporation owes funds to such shareholder it will not, without first receiving the written consent of the shareholder, declare dividends; pay salaries in excess of a certain amount to officers; sell its assets except in the ordinary course of business; or engage in a reorganization, recapitalization, merger, consolidation or liquidation.

Because of the substantial sums due the shareholder, because he plans to reside permanently in another state and will be far removed from the base of operations of the corporation, and pursuant to the advice of persons skilled in creditor protection matters, he considers it advisable to have a member of the law firm representing him serve on the board of directors of the corporation. Therefore, the instant shareholder and the remaining shareholders, all related, entered into a second agreement whereby a nominee of his law firm will serve on the board of directors as long as the corporation is indebted to the shareholder. Such nominee will be paid x dollars by the corporation for each meeting he attends and such additional sums as determined in the sole discretion of the instant shareholder for other services which may be reasonably necessary to determine that his interests as a creditor are being protected in accordance with the agreements.

The sole purpose of this arrangement is to protect the shareholder as a creditor by determining that the aforementioned conditions are being met rather than running the risk of having to engage in extended litigation at some future date if it is then determined that the conditions of the stock redemption agreement were violated.

* * *

According to the agreement in question, the remaining shareholders and the instant shareholder will appoint, indirectly through the law firm representing such shareholder, a member of that law firm to serve on the board of directors of the corporation. Such a nominee director will be acting solely on the taxpayer's behalf and, therefore, will in effect be his agent. The fact that the nominee director will receive remuneration for his service from someone other than the taxpayer does not make him any less the taxpayer's agent, for the source of remuneration to an agent is only one factor to be considered in determining whether an agency exists between two parties. Such an appointment of an agent to the board of directors is contrary to the condition prescribed in section 302(c)(2) of the Code. For the purposes of section 302(c)(2), it is immaterial whether an interest in the corporation is asserted directly or through an agent.

The fact that the director is a "limited" director in that his only duty will be to determine whether the conditions set forth in the stock redemption agreement are being observed is not material, for section 302(c)(2) of the Code does not make any exception for such directors. Furthermore, that section of the Code does not make an exception for a director whose power is limited because he is a minority member of a board.

In view of the foregoing, it is held that the agreement between the instant shareholder and the remaining shareholders of the corporation, under which a nominee is appointed to serve on the board of directors of the corporation, violates the condition prescribed in section 302(c)(2) (A)(i) of the Code. Accordingly, in the event of such an agreement, the redemption of the taxpayer's stock of the corporation shall be treated as a distribution of property to which section 301 of the Code applies.

However, if the taxpayer-shareholder designates a representative of his law firm to attend the board of director's meetings of the corporation solely for the purposes of determining whether the provisions of the agreement described above have been complied with, and not in the capacity of a director, officer or employee, or advisor, such action will not adversely affect section 302(c)(2) of the Code.

REVENUE RULING 77-293
1977-2 Cum.Bull. 91.

Corporation X had 120 shares of common stock outstanding, all of which were owned by A, its president. A's son, B, had been employed by X for many years as its vice-president and general assistant to the president. Realizing that the future successful operation of X required a thorough knowledge of its operation, products lines, and customer needs, A had trained and supervised B in all phases of the business so that upon A's retirement B would be able to assume responsibility for managing the business.

As part of A's plan to retire from the business and to give ownership of the business to B, A gave 60 shares of X stock to B as a gift, and not as consideration for past, present, or future services. Shortly thereafter, A resigned and B assumed the position of chairman of the board and president of X. X redeemed the remaining 60 shares of stock owned by A in exchange for property. Immediately after the redemption, A was not an officer, director, or employee of X and no longer had any interest in X. A's gift of stock to B was for the purpose of giving B complete ownership and control of X. The earnings and profits of X exceeded the amount of the distribution in redemption of the X stock.

* * *

In the instant case, neither section 302(b)(1) of the Code nor section 302(b)(2) applies since A, through the constructive ownership rules of section 318(a), owned 100 percent of the stock of X both before and after the redemption. Therefore, there was no meaningful reduction under section 302(b)(1) or a substantially disproportionate reduction under section 302(b)(2) of A's stock ownership.

Section 302(c)(2)(A) of the Code provides that for purposes of section 302(b)(3), 318(a)(1) will not apply if (i) immediately after the distribution the distributee has no interest in the corporation (including an interest as an officer, director, or employee), other than an interest as a creditor, (ii) the distributee does not acquire any such interest (other than stock acquired by bequest or inheritance) within ten years from the date of such distribution, and (iii) the distributee files an agreement to notify the district director of any acquisition of any such interest in the corporation. However, pursuant to section 302(c)(2)(B)(ii), the provisions of section 302(c)(2)(A) are not applicable if any person owns (at the time of the distribution) stock the ownership of which is attributable to the distributee under section 318(a) and such person acquired any stock in the corporation, directly or indirectly, from the distributee within the ten-year period ending on the date of the distribution, unless such stock so acquired from the distributee is redeemed in the same transaction. However, section 302(c)(2)(B)(ii) will not apply if the disposition by the distributee did not have as one of its principal purposes the avoidance of Federal income tax.

The structure and legislative history of section 302 of the Code make it clear that the purpose of section 302(c)(2)(B) is not to prevent the reduction of capital gains through gifts of appreciated stock prior to the redemption of the remaining stock of the transferor, but to prevent the withdrawal of earnings at capital gains rates by a shareholder of a family controlled corporation who seeks continued control and/or economic interest in the corporation through the stock given to a related person or the stock he retains. Application of this provision thus prevents a taxpayer from bailing out earnings by transferring part of the taxpayer's stock to such a related person and then qualifying the redemption of either the taxpayer's stock or the transferee's stock as a complete termination of interest by virtue of the division of ownership thus created and the availability of the attribution waiver provisions.

Tax avoidance within the meaning of section 302(c)(2)(B) of the Code would occur, for example, if a taxpayer transfers stock of a corporation to a spouse in contemplation of the redemption of the remaining stock of the corporation and terminates all direct interest in the corporation in compliance with section 302(c)(2)(A), but with the intention of retaining effective control of the corporation indirectly through the stock held by the spouse. Another example, which would generally constitute tax avoidance within the meaning of this provision, is the transfer by a taxpayer of part of the stock of a corporation to a spouse in contemplation of the subsequent redemption of the transferred stock from the spouse. * * *

Whether one of the principal purposes of an acquisition or disposition of stock is tax avoidance within the meaning of section 302(c)(2)(B) of the Code can be determined only by an analysis of all of the facts and circumstances of a particular situation. Here, the gift of X stock by A was to B who is active and knowledgeable in the affairs of the business of X and who intends to control and manage the corporation in the future. The gift of stock was intended solely for the purpose of enabling A to retire while leaving the business to B. Therefore, the avoidance of Federal income tax will not be deemed to have been one of the principal purposes of the gift of stock from A to B, notwithstanding the reduction of the capital gains tax payable by A as a result of the gift of appreciated stock prior to the redemption.

Accordingly, if A files the agreement specified in section 302(c)(2)(A)(iii) of the Code, the redemption by X of its stock from A qualifies as a termination of interest under section 302(b)(3).

Rev.Rul. 57–387, 1957–2 C.B. 225, is modified to the extent that it contains implications to the contrary concerning the reduction of the capital gains tax.

NOTE

The prohibition on retaining or acquiring any "interest" (other than as a creditor or by bequest or inheritance) in the corporation is one of the major hurdles to utilizing Section 302(c)(2).[1] Until the Ninth Circuit's decision in *Lynch*, the courts generally had declined to follow the Service's strict view that *any* performances of services, with or without compensation, constitutes a forbidden corporate interest.[2] With the substantially reduced stakes on the dividend vs. exchange issue, it remains to be seen whether this area will continue to generate litigation.

The results are mixed in the many other factual contexts involving the "interest" limitation. The Service has ruled that a prohibited interest is obtained if the redeemed shareholder becomes a custodian under the Uniform Gifts to Minors Act or a voting trustee of corporate stock during the restricted ten year period.[3] But if the shareholder becomes executor of a deceased shareholder's estate and can vote the stock held by the estate, the protection of Section 302(c)(2) is still available by virtue of the exception for stock acquired by bequest or inheritance.[4] In Revenue Ruling 72–380,[5] the Service ruled that since the redeemed shareholder could reacquire a direct stock interest by bequest or inheritance, it was reasonable to permit "acquisition under identical circumstances of the significantly lesser interest embodied in the * * * right of an executor to vote stock in an estate * * *."[6] In Revenue Ruling 79–334[7] the same reasoning was applied to an appointment by will of a previously redeemed shareholder as a trustee of a trust. The ruling concludes that a redeemed shareholder may waive family attribution even though, as trustee, he can vote stock of the corporation in which he once had an interest.

1. See generally Rose, "The Prohibited Interest of Section 302(c)(2)(A)," 36 Tax L.Rev. 131 (1981).

2. Compare Rev.Rul. 56–556, 1956–2 C.B. 177 and Rev.Rul. 59–119, 1959–1 C.B. 68 with Estate of Lennard v. Commissioner, 61 T.C. 554 (1974), nonacq. 1978–2 C.B. 3, and Lewis v. Commissioner, 47 T.C. 129 (1966).

3. Rev.Rul. 81–233, 1981–2 C.B. 83; Rev.Rul. 71–426, 1971–2 C.B. 173.

4. I.R.C. § 302(c)(2)(A)(ii).

5. 1972–2 C.B. 201.

6. An executor who also becomes an officer of the corporation acquires a prohibited interest and loses Section 302(c)(2)'s protection. Rev.Rul. 75–2, 1975–1 C.B. 99.

7. 1979–2 C.B. 127.

In the area of deferred payment redemptions, the Service and the courts have disagreed over what constitutes a forbidden proprietary interest. The regulations provide that to be considered a creditor, the rights of the redeemed shareholder must not be greater than necessary to enforce the claim. An obligation may be treated as proprietary if it is subordinated to claims of general creditors, if payments of principal depend upon corporate earnings, or if the interest rate fluctuates with the corporation's success.[8] Acquisition of corporate property as a result of enforcement of rights as a creditor does not run afoul of Section 302(c)(2) unless the redeemed shareholder acquires stock in the corporation, its parent corporation, or a subsidiary.[9]

The courts, however, have not applied rigid standards to credit redemptions. In Dunn v. Commissioner,[10] a redemption agreement provided for postponement of principal and interest payments on corporate notes given in payment for the shareholder's stock if such payments would violate financial requirements in the corporation's franchise agreement with General Motors. The court concluded that the postponement provision did not require the notes to be classified as equity or give the shareholder an interest in the corporation other than as a creditor. In Estate of Lennard v. Commissioner,[11] the court found that a subordinated demand note, which was paid approximately three months after issuance, did not represent a proprietary interest in the corporation.

The Service has specific guidelines for granting a favorable ruling on an installment redemption. It ordinarily will not rule on the tax consequences of a redemption of stock for notes when the note payment period extends beyond 15 years.[12] Nor will a ruling be issued under Section 302(b) if the shareholder's stock is held in escrow or as security for payments on corporate notes given as consideration for the redeemed stock because of the possibility that the stock may be returned to the shareholder as a result of a default by the corporation.[13]

Once again, however, the courts have been far more lenient. For example, in Lisle v. Commissioner[14] the Tax Court found a Section 302(b)(3) complete termination where the redeemed shareholders were to be paid for their stock over a 20 year period, the shareholders retained their voting rights pursuant to a security agreement, the stock was held in escrow and could be returned to the shareholders and the shareholders continued to serve as corporate directors and officers.

---

8. Reg. § 1.302–4(d). A shareholder's ability to defer gain on a credit redemption under the installment method is a separate issue. Section 453(k)(2)(A), which was added to the Code by the Tax Reform Act of 1986, denies use of the installment method for sales of stock or securities which are traded on an established securities market. This provision thus limits the tax advantage of deferral on a credit redemption to redemptions of stock in closely held corporations.

9. Reg. § 1.302–4(e).

10. 615 F.2d 578 (2d Cir.1980).

11. Note 2, supra.

12. Rev.Proc. 83–22, 1983–1 C.B. 680, 684.

13. Id. at 682.

14. 35 T.C.M. 627 (1976).

The court concluded that the shareholders were directors and officers in name only and that, based upon the facts present in the case, the security provisions were not inconsistent with a finding that the transaction qualified as a complete redemption.

Finally, the Service will permit a redeemed shareholder to lease property to the corporation on an arms length basis provided that the rental payments are not dependent on corporate earnings or subordinated to the claims of the corporation's general creditors.[15]

b. WAIVER OF ATTRIBUTION BY ENTITIES

Section 302(c)(2) only permits waiver of the *family* attribution rules and requires the "distributee" to file an agreement promising to notify the Service of the acquisition of a forbidden interest within the ten year period following the redemption. What if the redeemed shareholder is a trust, estate or other entity that completely terminates its *actual* interest in the corporation but continues to own shares attributed to a beneficiary from a related family member which then are reattributed from the beneficiary to the entity?[1] May the entity waive family attribution or is the waiver opportunity limited to individual shareholders?

Prior to 1982, the Service contended that only individuals could waive family attribution.[2] The Tax Court disagreed, however, holding that an estate or trust that completely terminated its actual interest in a redemption could waive family attribution from a family member to a beneficiary.[3] One appellate court, rejecting what it called a "crabbed reading" of the Code, even held that an entity could waive attribution from a beneficiary to the entity.[4] The problem with these decisions was that they did not prevent the beneficiary from acquiring an interest in the corporation during the ten years after the redemption or require an agreement from the beneficiary to notify the Service if such a forbidden interest were acquired.

Technical as it may seem, this issue was of considerable interest to shareholders of closely held corporations and their estate planners. The Service's rigid position often was an impediment to a redemption of

15. Rev.Rul. 77–467, 1977–2 C.B. 92.

1. For example, assume Mother's Estate, of which Father is the sole beneficiary, owns 50 of the 100 outstanding shares of X Corporation stock. The other 50 shares are owned by Child. If X redeems Estate's 50 shares, Estate continues to constructively own Child's 50 shares, which are attributed from Child to Father via family attribution and then reattributed from Father to Estate. May Estate break the family attribution chain in order to qualify the redemption as a complete termination?

2. Rev.Rul. 59–233, 1959–2 C.B. 106, Rev.Rul. 68–388, 1968–2 C.B. 122.

3. See Crawford v. Commissioner, 59 T.C. 830 (1973); Johnson Trust v. Commissioner, 71 T.C. 941 (1979); but see Metzger Trust v. Commissioner, 76 T.C. 42 (1981), affirmed 693 F.2d 459 (5th Cir.1982).

4. Rickey v. United States, 592 F.2d 1251 (5th Cir.1979). This remarkable example of "flexible" statutory construction was sharply criticized. See Andrews, "Comment: Estate Waiver of the Estate-Beneficiary Attribution Rules in Nonliquidating Redemptions Under Section 302 and Related Matters: The *Rickey* Case in the Fifth Circuit," 35 Tax L.Rev. 147 (1979).

the stock of an estate or trust where family members of the beneficiaries continued to own shares of the company. In the midst of continuing litigation, Congress enacted a special rule for waiver by entities, incorporating appropriate safeguards to preclude the beneficiaries from reacquiring an interest.[5] The Joint Committee on Taxation explained the rule as follows:[6]

> The Act permits an entity to waive the family attribution rules if those through whom ownership is attributed to the entity join in the waiver. Thus, a trust and its beneficiaries may waive family attribution to the beneficiaries if, after the redemption, neither the trust nor the beneficiaries hold an interest in the corporation, do not acquire such an interest within the 10-year period, and join in the agreement to notify the IRS of any acquisition. The entity and beneficiaries are jointly and severally liable in the event of an acquisition by any of them within the 10-year period and the statute of limitations remains open to assess any deficiency. The tax increase is a deficiency in the entity's tax but may be asserted as a deficiency against any beneficiary liable under the rules. Congress intended that the tax will be collected from a beneficiary only when it cannot be assessed against or collected from the entity, such as when the entity no longer exists or has insufficient funds. Further, it was intended that the tax will be assessed and collected from the beneficiary whose acquisition causes the deficiency before it is asserted against any other beneficiary.

> Under the Act, only family attribution under Section 318(a)(1) may be waived by an entity and its beneficiaries. The waiver rules are not extended to waivers of attribution to and from entities and their beneficiaries (secs. 318(a)(2) and 318(a)(3)). The Act thus is intended to overrule Rickey v. United States, 592 F.2d 1251 (5th Cir.1979). Congress intended that the Act should not be construed to provide any inference as to whether the *Rickey* decision adopts a proper construction of prior law. Nor was any inference intended as to whether the other cases extending the waiver rules for family attribution to entities adopt a proper construction of prior law.

> Certain anti-avoidance rules applicable where the redeemed stock was acquired by the distributee from a related party or a related party at the time of the redemption owns stock acquired from the distributee are extended to the entity and affected beneficiaries.

---

5. I.R.C. § 302(c)(2)(C).

6. Staff of Joint Committee on Taxation, General Explanation of the Tax Equi-

ty and Fiscal Responsibility Act of 1982, 98th Cong.2d Sess. 146–47 (1982).

PROBLEMS

1.   Randall Corporation is owned by John, John's daughter Alison and Alison's son Chuck.   John owns 100 shares of Randall stock, Alison owns 50 shares and Chuck owns 25 shares.   Consider whether the following redemptions (in year one) qualify as an exchange under § 302(b)(3):

(a)   Randall redeems Alison's entire 50 shares for cash.

(b)   Same as (a), above, except that Alison fails to file the agreement required in § 302(c)(2)(A)(iii)?   What is the purpose of this requirement?

(c)   Same as (a), above, except the price paid for Alison's shares is contingent upon Randall's future profits?

(d)   Randall redeems 20 of Alison's shares for cash on January 1 of year one and the remaining 30 shares for cash on January 1 of year two.

(e)   Same as (a), above, except Alison remains as a director of Randall?

(f)   Same as (a), above, except that, two years after the redemption, Randall forms a new subsidiary and Alison becomes an employee of the subsidiary?

(g)   Same as (a), above, except that two years after the redemption Chuck dies and leaves his Randall shares to Alison?

2.   The B & B Windshield Wiper Corporation ("B & B") was organized ten years ago by Betty and Billy, who are wife and husband. Betty and Billy formed B & B by transferring cash and other property to the corporation in exchange for 150 shares of the corporation's common stock.   Betty and Billy own B & B's manufacturing plant and lease the plant to the corporation for an annual rental fee.   B & B has been very successful and has a large amount of accumulated earnings and profits.

Five years ago, Betty and Billy's youngest Son, Junior, began working for B & B as a clerk in the domestic subcompact wiper division. Junior's managerial talents were quickly recognized and he has risen rapidly in B & B's corporate structure.   Today, Junior is B & B's Vice President in charge of operations and has overall responsibility for production at B & B's manufacturing plant.

Shortly after Junior came to B & B, his parents agreed that he would eventually take over control and management of the company. Betty and Billy have now decided that the time has come to retire.   To implement this decision, their accountant has suggested the following plan:

(1)   Betty and Billy will give 30 of their 150 B & B shares to Junior to provide him with an ownership interest in the corporation.

(2) B & B will redeem Betty and Billy's remaining 120 shares for $50,000 plus a $400,000 B & B 12% note. The note will be payable monthly over a 20-year term and will be secured by an interest in the corporation's assets. Additionally, B & B will agree to restrict dividend payments, limit new indebtedness, and refrain from taking certain extraordinary corporate action (e.g., merger or liquidation) during the term of the note.

(3) Betty and Billy will continue to lease the manufacturing plant to B & B under a lease which has a rent escalation clause dependent upon the consumer price index. They also will grant B & B a five year option to purchase the plant at its appraised fair market value.

   (a) Will Betty and Billy's redemption be classified as an exchange under Section 302(a)?

   (b) Suppose Betty establishes a management consulting firm after leaving B & B. What would be the tax impact on the redemption if B & B hired Betty's firm to perform an analysis of its proposed entry into the Australian windshield wiper market? ·

3. Cinelab Corporation has 100 shares of common stock outstanding. John owns 50 shares and Mary, John's sister, owns 30 shares. The other 20 shares are owned by the Estate of Sam; Sam was John and Mary's father. Their mother, Bella, is the sole beneficiary of the estate. Consider the tax consequences of the following redemptions of Cinelab stock:

   (a) Cinelab redeems Estate's 20 shares.

   (b) Same as (a), above, except that Bella is the residuary beneficiary of the estate and John and Mary each receive specific legacies.

   (c) Same as (a), above, except that John and Mary are the residuary beneficiaries of the estate.

   (d) Same as (a), above, except the 20 shares were owned and redeemed from a trust established under Sam's will providing income to Bella for her life and the remainder to Nancy, another child of Sam and Bella. The life estate and remainder have equal actuarial values.

   (e) Any change in the result in (d), above, if Nancy acquires stock in Cinelab three years after the redemption by the trust?

3. REDEMPTIONS NOT ESSENTIALLY EQUIVALENT TO A DIVIDEND *

Code: § 302(b)(1).

Regulations: § 1.302–2.

UNITED STATES v. DAVIS **

Supreme Court of the United States, 1970.
397 U.S. 301, 90 S.Ct. 1041, rehearing denied 397 U.S. 1071, 90 S.Ct. 1495
(1970).

Mr. Justice MARSHALL delivered the opinion of the Court.

In 1945, taxpayer and E.B. Bradley organized a corporation. In exchange for property transferred to the new company, Bradley received 500 shares of common stock, and taxpayer and his wife similarly each received 250 such shares. Shortly thereafter, taxpayer made an additional contribution to the corporation, purchasing 1,000 shares of preferred stock at a par value of $25 per share.

The purpose of this latter transaction was to increase the company's working capital and thereby to qualify for a loan previously negotiated through the Reconstruction Finance Corporation. It was understood that the corporation would redeem the preferred stock when the RFC loan had been repaid. Although in the interim taxpayer bought Bradley's 500 shares and divided them between his son and daughter, the total capitalization of the company remained the same until 1963. That year, after the loan was fully repaid and in accordance with the original understanding, the company redeemed taxpayer's preferred stock.

In his 1963 personal income tax return taxpayer did not report the $25,000 received by him upon the redemption of his preferred stock as income. Rather, taxpayer considered the redemption as a sale of his preferred stock to the company—a capital gains transaction under § 302 of the Internal Revenue Code of 1954 resulting in no tax since taxpayer's basis in the stock equaled the amount he received for it. The Commissioner of Internal Revenue, however, did not approve this tax treatment. According to the Commissioner, the redemption of taxpayer's stock was essentially equivalent to a dividend and was thus taxable as ordinary income under §§ 301 and 316 of the Code. Taxpayer paid the resulting deficiency and brought this suit for a refund. The District Court ruled in his favor, 274 F.Supp. 466 (D.C.M.D.Tenn.1967), and on appeal the Court of Appeals affirmed. 408 F.2d 1139 (C.A.6th Cir.1969).

The Court of Appeals held that the $25,000 received by taxpayer was "not essentially equivalent to a dividend" within the meaning of that phrase in § 302(b)(1) of the Code because the redemption was the

---

* See generally, Postlewaite & Finneran, "Section 302(b)(1): The Expanding Minnow", 64 Va.L.Rev. 561 (1978).

** Some footnotes omitted.

final step in a course of action that had a legitimate business (as opposed to a tax avoidance) purpose. That holding represents only one of a variety of treatments accorded similar transactions under § 302(b) (1) in the circuit courts of appeals.[2] We granted certiorari, 396 U.S. 815 (1969), in order to resolve this recurring tax question involving stock redemptions by closely held corporations. We reverse.

I

The Internal Revenue Code of 1954 provides generally in §§ 301 and 316 for the tax treatment of distributions by a corporation to its shareholders; under those provisions, a distribution is includable in a taxpayer's gross income as a dividend out of earnings and profits to the extent such earnings exist. There are exceptions to the application of these general provisions, however, and among them are those found in § 302 involving certain distributions for redeemed stock. The basic question in this case is whether the $25,000 distribution by the corporation to taxpayer falls under that section—more specifically, whether its legitimate business motivation qualifies the distribution under § 302(b) (1) of the Code. Preliminarily, however, we must consider the relationship between § 302(b)(1) and the rules regarding the attribution of stock ownership found in § 318(a) of the Code.

Under subsection (a) of § 302, a distribution is treated as "payment in exchange for the stock," thus qualifying for capital gains rather than ordinary income treatment, if the conditions contained in any one of the four paragraphs of subsection (b) are met. In addition to paragraph (1)'s "not essentially equivalent to a dividend" test, capital gains treatment is available where (2) the taxpayer's voting strength is substantially diminished, [or] (3) his interest in the company is completely terminated. * * * [T]axpayer admits that paragraphs (2) and (3) do not apply. Moreover, taxpayer agrees that for the purposes of §§ 302(b)(2) and (3) the attribution rules of § 318(a) apply and he is considered to own the 750 outstanding shares of common stock held by his wife and children in addition to the 250 shares in his own name.

Taxpayer, however, argues that the attribution rules do not apply in considering whether a distribution is essentially equivalent to a dividend under § 302(b)(1). According to taxpayer, he should thus be considered to own only 25 percent of the corporation's common stock,

---

2. Only the Second Circuit has unequivocally adopted the Commissioner's view and held irrelevant the motivation of the redemption. See Levin v. Commissioner of Internal Revenue, 385 F.2d 521 (1967); Hasbrook v. United States, 343 F.2d 811 (1965). The First Circuit, however, seems almost to have come to that conclusion, too. Compare Wiseman v. United States, 371 F.2d 816 (1967), with Bradbury v. Commissioner, 298 F.2d 111 (1962).

The other courts of appeals that have passed on the question are apparently willing to give at least some weight under § 302(b)(1) to the business motivation of a distribution and redemption. * * * Even among those courts that consider business purpose, however, it is generally required that the business purpose be related, not to the issuance of the stock, but to the redemption of it. See Commissioner v. Berenbaum, supra; Ballenger v. United States, supra.

and the distribution would then qualify under § 302(b)(1) since it was not pro rata or proportionate to his stock interest, the fundamental test of dividend equivalency. See Treas.Reg. 1.302–2(b). However, the plain language of the statute compels rejection of the argument. In subsection (c) of § 302, the attribution rules are made specifically applicable "in determining the ownership of stock for purposes of this section." Applying this language, both courts below held that § 318(a) applies to all of § 302, including § 302(b)(1)—a view in accord with the decisions of the other courts of appeals, a longstanding treasury regulation,[6] and the opinion of the leading commentators.[7]

Against this weight of authority, taxpayer argues that the result under paragraph (1) should be different because there is no explicit reference to stock ownership as there is in paragraphs (2) and (3). Neither that fact, however, nor the purpose and history of § 302(b)(1) support taxpayer's argument. The attribution rules—designed to provide a clear answer to what would otherwise be a difficult tax question—formed part of the tax bill that was subsequently enacted as the 1954 Code. As is discussed further, infra, the bill as passed by the House of Representatives contained no provision comparable to § 302(b) (1). When that provision was added in the Senate, no purpose was evidenced to restrict the applicability of § 318(a). Rather, the attribution rules continued to be made specifically applicable to the entire section, and we believe that Congress intended that they be taken into account wherever ownership of stock was relevant.

Indeed, it was necessary that the attribution rules apply to § 302(b) (1) unless they were to be effectively eliminated from consideration with regard to §§ 302(b)(2) and (3) also. For if a transaction failed to qualify under one of those sections solely because of the attribution rules, it would according to taxpayer's argument nonetheless qualify under § 302(b)(1). We cannot agree that Congress intended so to nullify its explicit directive. We conclude, therefore, that the attribution rules of § 318(a) do apply; and, for the purposes of deciding whether a distribution is "not essentially equivalent to a dividend" under § 302(b)(1), taxpayer must be deemed the owner of all 1,000 shares of the company's common stock.

II

After application of the stock ownership attribution rules, this case viewed most simply involves a sole stockholder who causes part of his shares to be redeemed by the corporation. We conclude that such a redemption is always "essentially equivalent to a dividend" within the meaning of that phrase in § 302(b)(1)[8] and therefore do not reach the

6. See Treas.Reg. 1.302–2(b).

7. See B. Bittker & J. Eustice, Federal Income Taxation of Corporations and Shareholders 292 n. 32 (2d ed. 1966).

8. Of course, this just means that a distribution in redemption to a sole shareholder will be treated under the general provisions of § 301, and it will only be taxed as a dividend under § 316 to the extent that there are earnings and profits.

Government's alternative argument that in any event the distribution should not on the facts of this case qualify for capital gains treatment.[9]

The predecessor of § 302(b)(1) came into the tax law as § 201(d) of the Revenue Act of 1921, 42 Stat. 228:

"A stock dividend shall not be subject to tax but if after the distribution of any such dividend the corporation proceeds to cancel or redeem its stock at such time and in such manner as to make the distribution and cancellation or redemption essentially equivalent to the distribution of a taxable dividend, the amount received in redemption or cancellation of the stock shall be treated as a taxable dividend * * *."

Enacted in response to this Court's decision that pro rata stock dividends do not constitute taxable income, Eisner v. Macomber, 252 U.S. 189 (1920), the provision had the obvious purpose of preventing a corporation from avoiding dividend tax treatment by distributing earnings to its shareholders in two transactions—a pro rata stock dividend followed by a pro rata redemption—that would have the same economic consequences as a simple dividend. Congress, however, soon recognized that even without a prior stock dividend essentially the same result could be effected whereby any corporation, "especially one which has only a few stockholders, might be able to make a distribution to its stockholders which would have the same effect as a taxable dividend." H.R.Rep. No. 1, 69th Cong., 1st Sess., 5. In order to cover this situation, the law was amended to apply "(whether or not such stock was issued as a stock dividend)" whenever a distribution in redemption of stock was made "at such time and in such manner" that it was essentially equivalent to a taxable dividend. Revenue Act of 1926, § 201(g), 44 Stat. 11.

This provision of the 1926 Act was carried forward in each subsequent revenue act and finally became § 115(g)(1) of the Internal Revenue Code of 1939. Unfortunately, however, the policies encompassed within the general language of § 115(g)(1) and its predecessors were not clear, and there resulted much confusion in the tax law. At first, courts assumed that the provision was aimed at tax avoidance schemes and sought only to determine whether such a scheme existed. * * * Although later the emphasis changed and the focus was more on the effect of the distribution, many courts continued to find that distributions otherwise like a dividend were not "essentially equivalent" if, for example, they were motivated by a sufficiently strong nontax business purpose. See cases cited n. 2, supra. There was general disagreement, however, about what would qualify as such a purpose, and the result was a case-by-case determination with each case decided "on the basis

---

9. The Government argues that even if business purpose were relevant under § 302(b)(1), the business purpose present here related only to the original investment and not at all to the necessity for redemption. See cases cited, n. 2, supra. Under either view, taxpayer does not lose his basis in the preferred stock. Under Treas.Reg. 1.302–2(c) that basis is applied to taxpayer's common stock.

of the particular facts of the transaction in question." Bains v. United States, 289 F.2d 644, 646, 153 Ct.Cl. 599, 603 (1961).

By the time of the general revision resulting in the Internal Revenue Code of 1954, the draftsmen were faced with what has aptly been described as "the morass created by the decisions." Ballenger v. United States, 301 F.2d 192, 196 (C.A.4th Cir.1962). In an effort to eliminate "the considerable confusion which exists in this area" and thereby to facilitate tax planning, H.R.Rep. No. 1337, 83d Cong., 2d Sess., 35, the authors of the new Code sought to provide objective tests to govern the tax consequences of stock redemptions. Thus, the tax bill passed by the House of Representatives contained no "essentially equivalent" language. Rather, it provided for "safe harbors" where capital gains treatment would be accorded to corporate redemptions that met the conditions now found in §§ 302(b)(2) and (3) of the Code.

It was in the Senate Finance Committee's consideration of the tax bill that § 302(b)(1) was added, and Congress thereby provided that capital gains treatment should be available "if the redemption is not essentially equivalent to a dividend." Taxpayer argues that the purpose was to continue "existing law," and there is support in the legislative history that § 302(b)(1) reverted "in part" or "in general" to the "essentially equivalent" provision of § 115(g)(1) of the 1939 Code. According to the Government, even under the old law it would have been improper for the Court of Appeals to rely on "a business purpose for the redemption" and "an absence of the proscribed tax avoidance purpose to bail out dividends at favorable tax rates." * * * However, we need not decide that question, for we find from the history of the 1954 revisions and the purpose of § 302(b)(1) that Congress intended more than merely to re-enact the prior law.

In explaining the reason for adding the "essentially equivalent" test, the Senate Committee stated that the House provisions "appeared unnecessarily restrictive, particularly, in the case of redemptions of preferred stock which might be called by the corporation without the shareholder having any control over when the redemption may take place." S.Rep. No. 1622, 83d Cong., 2d Sess., 44. This explanation gives no indication that the purpose behind the redemption should affect the result.[10] Rather, in its more detailed technical evaluation of § 302(b)(1), the Senate Committee reported as follows:

> "The test intended to be incorporated in the interpretation of paragraph (1) is in general that currently employed under section 115(g)(1) of the 1939 Code. Your committee further intends that in applying this test for the future * * * the inquiry will be devoted solely to the question of whether or not the transaction by its nature may properly be characterized as a sale of stock by the redeeming shareholder to the corpora-

---

10. See Bittker & Eustice, supra, n. 7, at 291: "It is not easy to give § 302(b)(1) an expansive construction in view of this indi-cation that its major function was the narrow one of immunizing redemptions of minority holdings of preferred stock."

tion. For this purpose the presence or absence of earnings and profits of the corporation is not material. Example: X, the sole shareholder of a corporation having no earnings or profits causes the corporation to redeem half of its stock. Paragraph (1) does not apply to such redemption notwithstanding the absence of earnings and profits." S.Rep. No. 1622, supra, at 234.

The intended scope of § 302(b)(1) as revealed by this legislative history is certainly not free from doubt. However, we agree with the Government that by making the sole inquiry relevant for the future the narrow one whether the redemption could be characterized as a sale, Congress was apparently rejecting past court decisions that had also considered factors indicating the presence or absence of a tax-avoidance motive.[11] At least that is the implication of the example given. Congress clearly mandated that pro rata distributions be treated under the general rules laid down in §§ 301 and 316 rather than under § 302, and nothing suggests that there should be a different result if there were a "business purpose" for the redemption. Indeed, just the opposite inference must be drawn since there would not likely be a tax-avoidance purpose in a situation where there were no earnings or profits. We conclude that the Court of Appeals was therefore wrong in looking for a business purpose and considering it in deciding whether the redemption was equivalent to a dividend. Rather, we agree with the Court of Appeals for the Second Circuit that "the business purpose of a transaction is irrelevant in determining dividend equivalence" under § 302(b) (1). Hasbrook v. United States, 343 F.2d 811, 814 (1965).

Taxpayer strongly argues that to treat the redemption involved here as essentially equivalent to a dividend is to elevate form over substance. Thus, taxpayer argues, had he not bought Bradley's shares or had he made a subordinated loan to the company instead of buying preferred stock, he could have gotten back his $25,000 with favorable tax treatment. However, the difference between form and substance in the tax law is largely problematical, and taxpayer's complaints have little to do with whether a business purpose is relevant under § 302(b) (1). It was clearly proper for Congress to treat distributions generally as taxable dividends when made out of earnings and profits and then to prevent avoidance of that result without regard to motivation where the distribution is in exchange for redeemed stock.

---

11. This rejection is confirmed by the Committee's acceptance of the House treatment of distributions involving corporate contractions—a factor present in many of the earlier "business purpose" redemptions. In describing its action, the Committee stated as follows:

"Your committee, as did the House bill, separates into their significant elements the kind of transactions now incoherently aggregated in the definition of a partial liquidation. Those distributions which may have capital-gain characteristics *because they are not made pro rata* among the various shareholders would be subjected, at the shareholder level, to the separate tests described in [§§ 301 to 318]. On the other hand, those distributions characterized by what happens solely at the corporate level by reason of the assets distributed would be included as within the concept of a partial liquidation." S.Rep. No. 1622, supra, at 49. (Emphasis added.)

We conclude that that is what Congress did when enacting § 302(b)
(1). If a corporation distributes property as a simple dividend, the
effect is to transfer the property from the company to its shareholders
without a change in the relative economic interests or rights of the
stockholders. Where a redemption has that same effect, it cannot be
said to have satisfied the "not essentially equivalent to a dividend"
requirement of § 302(b)(1). Rather, to qualify for preferred treatment
under that section, a redemption must result in a meaningful reduction
of the shareholder's proportionate interest in the corporation. Clearly,
taxpayer here, who (after application of the attribution rules) was the
sole shareholder of the corporation both before and after the redemption, did not qualify under this test. The decision of the Court of
Appeals must therefore be reversed and the case remanded to the
District Court for dismissal of the complaint.

It is so ordered.

Mr. Justice DOUGLAS, with whom The Chief Justice and Mr.
Justice BRENNAN concur, dissenting.

I agree with the District Court, 274 F.Supp. 466, and with the Court
of Appeals, 408 F.2d 1139, that respondent's contribution of working
capital in the amount of $25,000 in exchange for 1,000 shares of
preferred stock with a par value of $25 was made in order for the
corporation to obtain a loan from the RFC and that the preferred stock
was to be redeemed when the loan was repaid. For the reasons stated
by the two lower courts, this redemption was not "essentially equivalent to a dividend," for the bona fide business purpose of the redemption belies the payment of a dividend. As stated by the Court of
Appeals:

> "Although closely-held corporations call for close scrutiny un-
> der the tax law, we will not, under the facts and circumstances
> of this case, allow mechanical attribution rules to transform a
> legitimate corporate transaction into a tax avoidance scheme."
> 408 F.2d, at 1143–1144.

When the Court holds it was a dividend, it effectively cancels
§ 302(b)(1) from the Code. This result is not a matter of conjecture, for
the Court says that in the case of closely held or one-man corporations
a redemption of stock is "always" equivalent to a dividend. I would
leave such revision to the Congress.

REVENUE RULING 75–502
1975–2 Cum.Bull. 111.

* * *

X corporation had outstanding one class of stock consisting of 1,750
shares of common stock. An estate owned 250 shares of the common
stock and individual *A*, the sole beneficiary of the estate, owned 750
shares of the common stock. Individual *B*, who was not related to
individual *A* within the meaning of section 318(a)(1) of the Code, owned
the remaining 750 shares of *X* common stock. Through the application

of the attribution rules of section 318(a)(3)(A), the estate owned *A*'s common stock. Thus, prior to the redemption described below, the estate owned, actually and constructively, approximately 57 percent of the total voting rights of the outstanding common stock of *X*.

X redeemed for cash all of the common stock held by the estate. After the redemption, the common stock held by *A* represented 50 percent of the total voting rights of the then outstanding stock of *X*. Such stock continued to be owned by the estate through the application of section 318(a)(3)(A). Thus, the redemption reduced the estate's voting rights in *X* from 57 percent to 50 percent.

* * *

In the instant case the redemption of the estate's common stock did not qualify as a substantially disproportionate redemption under section 302(b)(2) of the Code because the estate owned 50 percent of the voting rights of *X* after the redemption. Moreover, the estate's constructive ownership of the *X* stock also prevented the redemption from qualifying as a complete termination of interest under section 302(b)(3). The question, therefore, is whether the redemption was not essentially equivalent to a dividend within the meaning of section 302(b)(1).

Section 1.302–2(b) of the Income Tax Regulations relating to section 302(b)(1) of the Code provides, in part, as follows:

> The question whether a distribution in redemption of stock of a shareholder is not essentially equivalent to a dividend under section 302(b)(1) depends upon the facts and circumstances of each case.

In United States v. Davis, 397 U.S. 301 (1970), rehearing denied, 397 U.S. 1071 (1970), 1970–1 C.B. 62, the Supreme Court of the United States held that a redemption must result in a meaningful reduction of the shareholder's proportionate interest in the corporation in order to qualify as not essentially equivalent to a dividend within the meaning of section 302(b)(1) of the Code and that the business purpose of the redemption is irrelevant to this determination. The Supreme Court further held that section 318(a) applies for the purpose of determining whether a distribution is "not essentially equivalent to a dividend" under section 302(b)(1).

The Supreme Court in *Davis* did not indicate what constitutes an "interest" and what constitutes a "meaningful reduction" in situations different from the factual pattern contained in *Davis* wherein the shareholder owned 100 percent of the redeeming corporation before and after the transaction. The Court of Appeals for the Second Circuit has defined the rights inherent in a shareholder's interest. In Himmel v. Commissioner, 338 F.2d 815 (2d Cir.1964) the court defined a shareholder's interest to include: (1) the right to vote and thereby exercise control; (2) the right to participate in current earnings and accumulated surplus; and (3) the right to share in net assets on liquidation. A redemption which reduces these rights may result in a meaningful reduction in a shareholder's proportionate interest in a corporation within the meaning of *Davis* and, thus, qualify such redemption as not essentially equivalent to a dividend under section 302(b)(1) of the Code. Therefore, *A*'s interest in *X* before and after the redemption must be examined in determining whether the redemption resulted in a meaningful reduction of *A*'s interest under the facts and circumstances of the instant case.

In applying the above principles to the instant case, it is significant that the redemption reduced the estate's voting rights in *X* from 57 percent to 50 percent and also correspondingly reduced the estate's right to participate in current earnings and accumulated surplus and the estate's right to share in net assets on liquidation. Moreover, the reduction of the estate's voting rights from 57 percent to 50 percent produced a situation in which the other 50 percent of the voting rights of *X* were held by a single unrelated shareholder. Thus, under the facts and circumstances of the instant case, the redemption constituted a meaningful reduction of the estate's interest in *X* within the meaning of *Davis*.

Accordingly, the redemption was not essentially equivalent to a dividend within the meaning of section 302(b)(1) of the Code and, therefore, qualified as an exchange under section 302(a).

If in the instant case, the stock of *X* held by the estate was reduced by less than 7 percentage points the redemption would not qualify under section 302(b)(1) because the estate would continue to have dominant voting rights in *X* by virtue of its ownership of more than 50 percent of the *X* stock.

REVENUE RULING 75–512

1975–2 Cum.Bull. 112.

* * *

Corporation *X* had outstanding one class of stock consisting of 1,000 shares of common stock which were held as follows:

Shareholders	Shares
A	625
B	75
C	75
D	75
E	75
Trust	75
Total	1,000

A controls and manages the affairs of *X*. *A* and *B* are the grandparents of *C*, *D*, and *E*. The primary beneficiary of the trust is the father of *C*, *D*, and *E* and the son-in-law of *A* and *B*. *C*, *D*, and *E* are equal remaindermen of the trust and the actuarial interest of each in the trust is more than 5 percent. Therefore, the common stock held by *C*, *D*, and *E* was attributable to the trust under section 318(a)(3)(B) of the Code. Under section 318(a) grandchildren are not considered as owning the stock owned by their grandparents.

X redeemed for cash all 75 of its shares of common stock held by the trust. Prior to the redemption, the trust owned, directly and indirectly, 300 shares or 30 percent of the stock of *X*. After the redemption, the trust's ownership of the common stock decreased to 225 shares or 24.3 percent of the stock of *X*. The percentage of stock owned by the trust after the redemption was 81 percent of the percentage of stock owned by the trust prior to the redemption.

The redemption was not a termination of interest under section 302(b)(3) of the Code because the trust continued to own, through the application of section 318(a)(3)(B), the common stock held by *C, D,* and *E*. Further, the redemption did not qualify as a substantially disproportionate redemption under section 302(b)(2) because the percentage of shares held, directly and indirectly, by the trust after the redemption was more than 80 percent of the percentage of shares held by the trust prior to the redemption.

In the case of United States v. Davis, 397 U.S. 301 (1970), rehearing denied, 397 U.S. 1071 (1970), 1970–1 C.B. 62, the Supreme Court of the United States held that in order to qualify under section 302(b)(1) of the Code a redemption must result in a meaningful reduction of the shareholder's proportionate interest in the corporation, and for purposes of this determination, the attribution rules of section 318(a) apply.

Rev.Rul. 75–502, page 111, this Bulletin, indicates factors to be considered in determining whether a reduction in a shareholder's proportionate interest in a corporation results in a meaningful reduction within the meaning of *Davis*. The factors considered relate to a shareholder's right to vote and exercise control, a shareholder's right to participate in current earnings and accumulated surplus, and a shareholder's right to share in net assets on liquidation.

In the instant case, the trust was a minority shareholder and took no part in the management of *X*. As a result of the redemption, the trust experienced a reduction of its voting rights, its right to participate in current earnings and accumulated surplus, and its right to share in net assets on liquidation. Thus, under the facts and circumstances of the instant case, the redemption constituted a meaningful reduction of the trust's interest in *X* within the meaning of *Davis*.

Accordingly, the redemption was not essentially equivalent to a dividend within the meaning of section 302(b)(1) of the Code, and, therefore, qualified as an exchange under section 302(a).

REVENUE RULING 85–106

1985–2 Cum.Bull. 116.

ISSUE

Is a redemption of nonvoting preferred stock not essentially equivalent to a dividend within the meaning of section 302(b)(1) of the

Internal Revenue Code when there is no reduction in the percentage of voting and nonvoting common stock owned by the redeemed shareholder, and when the redeemed shareholder continues to have an undiminished opportunity to act in concert with other shareholders as a control group, under the circumstances described below?

FACTS

Corporation X had outstanding three classes of stock consisting of 100 shares of voting common stock, 100 shares of nonvoting common stock, and 50 shares of nonvoting 9 percent cumulative preferred stock. The fair market value of each share of common stock was approximately half the fair market value of each share of preferred stock. The voting common stock was held as follows:

Shareholders	Shares
A	19
B	19
C	18
Minority shareholders	44
Total	100

None of the minority shareholders owned more than five shares. None of the holders of the voting common stock were related within the meaning of section 318(a) of the Code. The combined voting power of A, B, and C was sufficient to elect a majority of the board of directors of X.

The nonvoting common stock and the preferred stock were held (directly and indirectly) in approximately the same proportions as the common stock. C held no nonvoting common stock or preferred stock directly, but was the sole remaining beneficiary of a trust, T, which owned 18 percent of both the nonvoting common stock and the preferred stock.

The trustees of T decided that it would be in the best interests of that trust if most of the X preferred stock held by T could be converted into cash. After negotiation, X redeemed six shares of preferred stock for its fair market value of $6x$ dollars. Following this redemption, T continued to hold three shares of preferred stock, and 18 percent of the nonvoting common stock. Under section 318(a)(3)(B) of the Code, T is also considered to own the voting common stock owned by its sole beneficiary, C.

LAW AND ANALYSIS

Section 302(a) of the Code provides, in part, that if a corporation redeems its stock, and if section 302(b)(1), (2), (3), or (4) applies, such redemption will be treated as a distribution in part or full payment in exchange for the stock.

* * *

The lack of any reduction in *T*'s 18 percent vote prevented this redemption from qualifying under section 302(b)(2) of the Code, and the lack of complete termination of interest prevented it from qualifying under section 302(b)(3). The question remains whether the redemption should be considered not essentially equivalent to a dividend so as to qualify under section 302(b)(1). Under section 1.302–2(b) of the Income Tax Regulations, this determination depends upon the facts and circumstances of each case.

In United States v. Davis, 397 U.S. 301 (1970), 1970–1 C.B. 62, the Supreme Court of the United States held that in order to qualify under section 302(b)(1) of the Code, a redemption must result in a meaningful reduction of the shareholder's proportionate interest in the corporation, and that, for this purpose, the attribution rules of section 318 apply.

In determining whether a reduction in interest is "meaningful", the rights inherent in a shareholder's interest must be examined. The three elements of a shareholder's interest that are generally considered most significant are: (1) the right to vote and thereby exercise control; (2) the right to participate in current earnings and accumulated surplus; and (3) the right to share in net assets on liquidation. Rev.Rul. 81–289, 1981–2 C.B. 82.

In applying the above principles, it is significant that (as a result of section 318(a)(3)(B) of the Code) the redemption did not reduce *T*'s percentage of the vote in *X*. It is true that *T* reduced its percentage interest in current earnings, accumulated surplus, and net assets upon liquidation, and reduced the fair market value of its ownership in *X*. However, when the redeemed shareholder has a voting interest (either directly or by attribution), a reduction in voting power is a key factor in determining the applicability of section 302(b)(1) of the Code.

It is also true that *T* was not the largest shareholder. *A* and *B* each held slightly larger voting interests, and larger interests measured by fair market value. *T*, however, was not in the position of a minority shareholder isolated from corporate management and control. Compare Rev.Rul. 75–512, where the majority of the redeeming corporation's voting stock was held by a shareholder unrelated (within the meaning of section 318(a)) to the redeemed trust. Also compare Rev.Rul. 76–385, 1976–2 C.B. 92, where the redeemed shareholder's total interest was *de minimis*.

In the present situation, a significant aspect of *T*'s failure to reduce voting power is the fact that the redemption leaves unchanged *T*'s potential (by attribution from *C*) for participating in a control group by acting in concert with *A* and *B*. Compare Rev.Rul. 76–364, 1976–2 C.B. 91, where a reduction in voting interest was found meaningful in itself when it caused the redeemed shareholder to give up a potential for control by acting in concert with one other shareholder. In addition, the Tax Court has indicated significance for this factor of potential group control (*Johnson Trust*, at 947). See also Bloch v. United States, 261 F.Supp. 597, 611–612 (S.D.Tex.1966), aff'd per curiam, 386 F.2d 839

(5th Cir.1967), where, in finding that "the distributions in question were essentially equivalent to a dividend," the court noted that there was no change in the redeemed shareholder's potential for exercising control "by aligning himself with one or more of the other stockholders."

Although there was a reduction of *T*'s economic interest in *X*, such reduction was not sufficiently large to result in a meaningful reduction of *T*'s interest. The absence of any reduction of *T*'s voting interest in *X* (through *C*) and *T*'s potential (through *C*) for control group participation are compelling factors in this situation.

In Himmel v. Commissioner, 338 F.2d 815 (2d Cir.1964), dealing with a similar question, a decision was reached permitting the applicability of section 302(b)(1) of the Code. That case, however, was decided prior to the decision of the Supreme Court in *Davis*. Thus, *Himmel* fails to reflect the development in the law represented by the *Davis* limitation on section 302(b)(1) applicability where there is no meaningful reduction of the shareholder's proportionate interest in the corporation. Thus, pursuant to *Davis*, it is proper to view *Himmel* as incorrect to the extent it conflicts with the position contained in this revenue ruling.

HOLDING

The redemption of nonvoting preferred stock held by *T* does not qualify as a redemption under section 302(b)(1) of the Code, under the facts of this ruling when there is no reduction in the percentage of voting and nonvoting common stock owned by *T*, and when *T* continues to have an undiminished opportunity to act in concert with other shareholders as a control group. Since the redemption does not otherwise qualify under section 302(b), it is not a distribution in part or full payment for the stock under section 302(a). Consequently, under section 302(d), the redemption will be treated as a distribution of property to which section 301 applies.

NOTE

The Meaningful Reduction Standard. The rulings in the text make it clear that the Service measures dividend equivalency under Section 302(b)(1) primarily by examining the effect of the redemption on the shareholder's control of corporate activities. Suppose that under state law a simple majority of a corporation's outstanding shares can control day-to-day corporate activities through the board of directors but that extraordinary corporate action, such as a merger or liquidation, requires approval by two-thirds of the shares. Should a redemption in which a shareholder loses control of extraordinary corporate action but retains control of routine matters (e.g. a reduction to 60% voting control) qualify for exchange treatment under Section 302(b)(1)? In Wright v. United States,[1] the Eighth Circuit determined that such a

---

1. 482 F.2d 600 (8th Cir.1973).

redemption is not essentially equivalent to a dividend because of the loss of two-thirds control of the corporation. In Revenue Ruling 78–401,[2] the Service takes a more restrictive view of the application of Section 302(b)(1) to these facts. The ruling concludes that if extraordinary corporate action is not "imminent," the retention of day-to-day control of corporate activities is a "predominant factor" and the redemption does not result in a meaningful reduction in the shareholder's interest. It is unclear what position the Service would take if a merger or similar corporate transaction were contemplated or what evidence would substantiate the likelihood of corporate action.

The regulations interpreting Section 302(b)(1) also focus upon the effect of the redemption upon the shareholder's control of corporate affairs. Thus, pro rata redemptions of a corporation's single class of stock do not qualify for exchange treatment, and the redemption of all of one class of stock also fails if all outstanding classes of stock are held proportionately.[3] Any redemption of shares from a shareholder owning only nonvoting preferred stock, however, is not essentially equivalent a dividend since the shareholder does not have control over whether the redemption occurs.[4] The Service also has ruled that a redemption of publicly traded common stock which reduces the shareholder's interest from .0001118 percent to .0001081 percent qualifies for exchange treatment since such a shareholder cannot exercise control over corporate affairs.[5] But a pro rata redemption of stock in a publicly traded corporation will not satisfy the "meaningful reduction" standard in *Davis* even if the shareholder owns only small noncontrolling interest in the corporation.[6] This latter ruling may have a significant chilling effect when a shareholder of a public company wishes to tender some (but not all) of his stock in connection with a desirable repurchase offer by the corporation.

Family Discord. One of the more titillating issues to arise under Section 302(b)(1) involves whether the Section 318(a)(1) family attribution rules should be ignored when there is evidence of family discord between the redeemed shareholder and related continuing shareholders. The typical factual context in which this "family fight" question arises is well illustrated in the following introduction to a recent Tax Court decision:[7]

> Petitioner Michael N. Cerone * * * and his son Michael
> L. Cerone * * * owned and operated the Stockade Cafe

2. 1978–2 C.B. 127.

3. Reg. § 1.302–2(b).

4. Reg. § 1.302–2(a). In Rev.Rul. 77–426, 1977–2 C.B. 87, a redemption of five percent of the outstanding preferred stock from a shareholder owning all of the preferred stock (and only preferred stock) qualified for exchange treatment under Section 302(b)(1).

5. Rev.Rul. 76–385, 1976–2 C.B. 92.

6. Rev.Rul. 81–289, 1981–2 C.B. 82.

7. Cerone v. Commissioner, 87 T.C. 1 (1986). See aso the colorful introduction to the Fifth Circuit's opinion in Metzger Trust v. Commissioner, 693 F.2d 459 (5th Cir.1982) ("We decide today a story driven by tensions as old as Genesis but told in the modern lexicon of the tax law. It is the story of David who built a business and left it in the charge of his eldest son Jacob to be shared with Jacob's two sisters Catherine and Cecilia, of their alienation and resulting quarrel with the tax collectors.")

* * * each owning 50 percent of the stock of the corporation. The father and son had a volatile relationship and frequently disagreed over management decisions. Over the years their disagreements became more serious, and finally they decided one of them should buy the other's interest in the business. Petitioner did not think he could run the business alone, so it was decided that the corporation would redeem all of his stock. After the redemption, petitioner worked at the Stockade Cafe for several years, but he did not exercise any control over the corporation. This case involves the tax treatment of the payments or distributions petitioner received for his stock.

If the family attribution rules applied to the above fact pattern, the redemption of the father's 50 percent stock interest would not qualify under Section 302(b)(1) because the father continued to own 100 percent of the company through attribution from his son. If the attribution chain could be broken, however, the father's reduction of his interest from 50 percent to zero would be "meaningful" and the redemption would qualify for exchange treatment under Section 302(b)(1) even if he failed to meet the specific requirements for waiver of family attribution under Section 302(c).[8]

After its sweeping victory in United States v. Davis,[9] the Service consistently rejected attempts by taxpayers to break the chain of family attribution by proving family hostility.[10] Commentators and the courts are divided on the issue. The authors of a leading treatise once stated that "The *Davis* decision * * * weakens, but does not eliminate the 'family fight' argument in mitigation of § 318 attribution under § 302(b)(1),"[11] and the First Circuit has held that family discord might "negate the presumption" of the attribution rules.[12] The Tax Court and the Fifth Circuit view the matter differently and have refused to allow family discord to nullify the attribution rules in applying Section 302(b)(1).[13] After reviewing the legislative history of Section 302, the Tax Court concluded in Haft Trust v. Commissioner[14] that Congress was seeking to provide definite and specific rules and to avoid the uncertainties of prior law, and went on to elaborate:[15]

---

8. See Section C2 of this chapter, supra. Mr. Cerone was unable to waive family attribution under Section 302(c) because he retained a prohibited employment relationship with the corporation after the redemption. 87 T.C. at 29–33.

9. See p. 222, supra.

10. See, e.g., Rev.Rul. 80–26, 1980–1 C.B. 66.

11. Bittker & Eustice, Federal Income Taxation of Corporations and Shareholders ¶ 9.24 n. 73 (4th ed. 1979). The 1987 edition of this treatise takes no position on the family hostility question.

12. Haft Trust v. Commissioner, 510 F.2d 43 (1st Cir.1975), vacating and remanding 61 T.C. 398 (1973).

13. Cerone v. Commissioner, supra note 1; Metzger Trust v. Commissioner, 76 T.C. 42 (1981), affirmed 693 F.2d 459 (5th Cir.1982), cert. denied 463 U.S. 1207, 103 S.Ct. 3537 (1983); Haft Trust v. Commissioner, 61 T.C. 398 (1973), vacated and remanded 510 F.2d 43 (1st Cir.1975).

14. Supra note 13.

15. 61 T.C. at 403.

If the applicability of the attribution rules depended upon the feelings or attitudes among the members of a family, it would then be necessary to inquire into whether there was hostility or animosity among them, whether such discord was serious, and whether it would actually or likely impair the ability of one member of the family to influence the conduct of other members. By the terms of the statute, the attribution rules are applicable irrespective of the personal relationships which exist among the members of a family, and an interpretation of the statute which made their applicability depend upon whether there was discord among the members of the family— or the extent of any such discord—would frustrate the legislative objective and would be clearly inconsistent with the language and the rationale of *Davis*.

Despite its reversal by the First Circuit in *Haft Trust*, the Tax Court persisted in its position but later conceded that family discord may be relevant in testing for dividend equivalency under Section 302(b)(1) *after* the attribution rules have been applied. In Cerone v. Commissioner,[16] the court summarized its view of the proper role of family hostility:[17]

> Although we [have] rejected the * * * argument that family discord could preclude application of the attribution rules, we nonetheless noted that family discord does have a role, albeit a limited one, in testing for dividend equivalence under section 302(b)(1). We reasoned that under *United States v. Davis*, supra, the proper analysis is as follows: First, the attribution rules are plainly and straightforwardly applied. Second, a determination is made whether there has been a reduction in the stockholder's proportionate interest in the corporation. If not, the inquiry ends because, if there is no change in the stockholder's interest, dividend equivalency results. If there has been a reduction, then all the facts and circumstances must be examined to see if the reduction was meaningful under *United States v. Davis*, supra. It is at this point, *and only then*, that family hostility becomes an appropriate factor for consideration. * * *.

PROBLEMS

1. Z Corporation has 100 shares of common stock outstanding, owned by A (28 shares), B (25 shares), C (23 shares) and D (24 shares.) Unless otherwise indicated, assume the shareholders are not related. In each of the following alternative situations, deter-

---

16. Supra note 7.

17. 87 T.C. at 22. See also Henry T. Patterson Trust v. United States, 729 F.2d 1089 (6th Cir.1984) (percentage reduction from 97 to 93 percent, after applying attribution rules, is meaningful under *Davis* in view of hostility.)

mine whether the redemption is not essentially equivalent to a dividend under § 302(b)(1):

    (a)   Z redeems 7 shares from A.

    (b)   Z redeems 5 shares from A, and A and D are mother and daughter.

    (c)   Z redeems 5 shares from A, and A and B are mother and daughter.

    (d)   Same as (c), above, except that A has not spoken to B since B married "outside her faith."

    2.   Y Corporation has 100 shares of common stock and 100 shares of nonvoting preferred stock outstanding. The preferred stock is not convertible into Y common stock and is not Section 306 stock (i.e., not stock treated specially in § 306 because of its tax avoidance potential). The Y common and preferred stock are owned by the following unrelated shareholders:

Shareholder	Common Shares	Preferred Shares
A	40	0
B	20	55
C	25	10
D	15	15
E	0	20

Will the following alternative redemptions qualify for exchange treatment under § 302(b)?

    (a)   Y redeems 5 preferred shares from E.

    (b)   Y redeems all of its outstanding preferred stock.

    3.   Suppose an individual shareholder owns ten shares of common stock with a basis of $15,000. What happens to the shareholder's basis if five shares are redeemed in a transaction which is <u>properly classified as a dividend?</u> What if all ten shares are redeemed in a transaction which is properly classified as a dividend because a § 302(c)(2) waiver of family attribution is unavailable?

D.   REDEMPTIONS TESTED AT THE CORPORATE LEVEL: PARTIAL LIQUIDATIONS

Code: § 302(b)(4), (e).

    Section 302(b)(4) provides exchange treatment for redemptions of stock held by noncorporate shareholders if the redemption qualifies as a "partial liquidation." Under Section 302(e)(1), a distribution is treated as in partial liquidation if it is pursuant to a plan, occurs within the taxable year in which the plan is adopted or the succeeding taxable year, and is "not essentially equivalent to a dividend." Although the standard for partial liquidations ("not essentially equivalent to a dividend") is identical to the language in Section 302(b)(1), the two provisions have a very different focus. Section 302(e)(1) requires dividend equivalency to be determined at the corporate rather than the share-holder level. Thus, while a pro rata redemption could never escape dividend classification under Section 302(b)(1), Section 302(e)(4) permits exchange treatment for any redemption that results in a genuine contraction of the corporation's business. The legislative history of the predecessor of Section 302(e) explains the corporate contraction standard: [1]

> The general language of the proposed draft would include within the definition of a partial liquidation the type of cases involving the contraction of the corporate business. Such as for example, cases which hold that if the entire floor of a factory is destroyed by fire, the insurance proceeds received may be distributed pro rata to the shareholders without the imposition of a tax at the rates applicable to the distribution of a dividend, if the corporation no longer continues its operations to the same extent maintained by the destroyed facility. Voluntary bona fide contraction of the corporate business may of course also qualify to the same extent as under existing law. In addition to the general definition of what constitutes a partial liquidation, your committee's bill provides a rule to indicate one type of distribution that will in any event constitute a partial liquidation. Under this rule, if a corporation is engaged in two or more active businesses which has [sic] been carried on for at least 5 years, it may distribute the assets of either one of the businesses in kind, or the proceeds of their sale.

The amorphous corporate contraction doctrine is a perilous yard-stick for the tax planner.[2] Recognizing the need for greater certainty, Congress has provided a safe harbor in Section 302(e)(2), which assures partial liquidation status if the distribution is attributable to the termination of a trade or business that has been actively conducted throughout the five-year period ending on the date of the distribution and was not acquired by the corporation in a taxable transaction during that period.[3] After the distribution, the corporation also must continue to conduct another active trade or business with a similar five-year history. The "active" business requirement is designed to patrol against the accumulation of earnings in the form of investment assets, such as real estate or securities, followed by prompt bailout distributions masquerading as corporate contractions.[4]

---

1. S.Rep. No. 1622, 83d Cong., 2d Sess. 49 (1954). See Imler v. Commissioner, 11 T.C. 836 (1948) (the "contraction-by-fire" case referred to in the Senate Report).

2. For the Service's ruling policy on whether a distribution qualifies as a corporate contraction, see Rev.Proc. 82–40, 1982–2 C.B. 761 (no ruling unless distribution results in a 20 percent or greater reduction in gross revenues, net fair market value of assets and employees).

L., S., L. & R. Corp. Tax. 3rd Ed. UCB—11

3. The definition of a "qualified trade or business" is contained in Section 302(e)(3). Prior to 1982, the Section 302(e)(2) safe harbor was contained in Section 346(b), and the tax consequences to the distributee shareholder were determined under Section 331.

4. For the definition of an active trade or business, see Reg. § 1.355–3(b), (c), which govern corporate divisions under Section 355. See Chapter 12B4, infra.

A distribution may qualify as a partial liquidation even if the shareholders do not actually surrender any stock.[5] If the other requirements of either the general contraction doctrine or the statutory safe harbor are met, the transaction will be treated as a constructive redemption of stock.[6]

Congress significantly tightened the rules governing partial liquidations in the Tax Equity and Fiscal Responsibility Act of 1982. Except for some rearrangement of Code sections, the treatment of noncorporate shareholders is essentially unchanged, but distributions to corporate shareholders no longer qualify for partial liquidation treatment.[7] At first glance, it might seem that corporate shareholders would welcome their eviction from the partial liquidation safe harbor because distributions that otherwise would give rise to taxable capital gain would become dividends sheltered by the 70 percent dividends received deduction. But Congress was not acting in a spirit of generosity. Rather, it was attempting to put an end to several widely publicized acquisition techniques that used the partial liquidation as a vehicle for obtaining the best of all tax worlds: a stepped-up basis for selected assets of the acquired corporation along with the preservation of favorable tax attributes (e.g., earnings and profits deficits, loss and credit carryovers, etc.)—all at little or no tax cost.[8]

Congress inflicted further punishment on corporate shareholders in 1986, when it enacted restrictions to prevent abuse of the dividends received deduction.[9] Any amount treated as a dividend to a corporate shareholder under Section 301 is an "extraordinary dividend" under Section 1059 if it is a distribution in redemption of stock which is part of a partial liquidation of the redeeming corporation, regardless of the shareholder's holding period or the size of the distribution.[10] As a result, a corporate shareholder that receives a dividend in a transaction treated as a partial liquidation must reduce its basis in the stock of the redeeming corporation by the portion of the dividend that was not taxed because of the dividends received deduction.[11]

REVENUE RULING 79–184

1979–1 Cum.Bull. 143.

Advice has been requested whether the sale by a parent corporation of all the stock of a wholly owned subsidiary and the distribution of

---

5. Fowler Hosiery Co. v. Commissioner, 301 F.2d 394 (7th Cir.1962); Rev.Rul. 90–13, 1990–1 C.B. 65.

6. See Rev.Rul. 77–245, 1977–2 C.B. 105, for the method of computing the tax consequences of a partial liquidation.

7. For purposes of determining whether a shareholder is corporate or noncorporate, stock held by a partnership, estate or trust is treated as if held proportionately by the partners or beneficiaries. I.R.C. § 302(e) (5).

8. See, e.g., Henderson, "Federal Tax Techniques for Asset Redeployment Transactions," 37 Tax L.Rev. 325 (1982); Ginsburg, "Taxing Corporate Acquisitions," 38 Tax L.Rev. 171 (1983).

9. See Chapter 4F, supra.

10. I.R.C. § 1059(e)(1).

11. I.R.C. § 1059(a), (b).

the sales proceeds by the parent to its shareholders qualifies as a distribution in partial liquidation within the meaning of section 346(a) (2) of the Internal Revenue Code of 1954 [now Section 302(e). Ed.].

Corporation *P* owned all of the single class of outstanding stock of Corporation *S* for many years, during which time each had been engaged in the active conduct of a trade or business.

Pursuant to a plan, *P* sold all of the stock of *S* to an unrelated party for cash and distributed the proceeds of the sale pro rata to its shareholders in redemption of part of their *P* stock.

Section [302(e)(1)] of the Code provides, in part, that a distribution will be treated as a partial liquidation of a corporation if it is not essentially equivalent to a dividend, is in redemption of a part of the stock of the corporation pursuant to a plan, and occurs within the taxable year in which the plan is adopted or within the succeeding taxable year. Section 1.346–1(a)(2) of the Income Tax Regulations provides that a distribution resulting from a genuine contraction of the corporate business is an example of a distribution that will qualify as a partial liquidation under section [302(e)(1)].

Generally, for purposes of section [302(e)] of the Code, the business that is terminated or contracted must be operated directly by the corporation making the distribution. See *H.L. Morgenstern,* 56 T.C. 44 (1971). However, Rev.Rul. 75–223, 1975–1 C.B. 109, provides that when a parent corporation liquidates a wholly owned subsidiary and distributes the subsidiary's assets, or the proceeds from the sale of those assets, to its shareholders, the fact that the distributions were attributable to assets used by the subsidiary rather than directly by the parent will not prevent the distribution from qualifying as a "genuine contraction of the corporate business" to the parent within the meaning of section 1.346–1(a)(2) of the regulations. The basis for this holding is that under section 381 a parent corporation that liquidates a subsidiary under section 332 (when section 334(b)(1) applies) inherits attributes (for example, earnings and profits) of the liquidated subsidiary so that after the liquidation of the subsidiary the parent is viewed as if it had always operated the business of the liquidated subsidiary.

However, when a parent corporation distributes the stock of its subsidiary, as in *Situation 3* of Rev.Rul. 75–223, section 381 of the Code does not apply to integrate the past business results of the subsidiary with those of the parent. Therefore, distribution by the parent of subsidiary's stock does not result in the parent corporation taking into account the past operations of the subsidiary. Thus, there is no analogy between a distribution of stock of the subsidiary and a distribution of the assets of a liquidated subsidiary or the proceeds of a sale of such assets. A distribution of the stock of the subsidiary under such circumstances is a corporate separation, governed by section 355, and not a corporate contraction.

Similarly, as in the present case, where *P* sells all of the stock of its wholly owned subsidiary, *S,* and distributes the proceeds to its shareholders, there is no basis for attributing the business activities of *S* to *P*. It is well established that a corporation is a legal entity separate and distinct from its shareholders. New Colonial Ice Co. v. Helvering, 292 U.S. 435 (1934), XIII–1 C.B. 194 (1934); Moline Properties, Inc. v. Commissioner, 319 U.S. 436 (1943), 1943 C.B. 1011. Although the assets of *P* are reduced by the subsequent distribution of the sale proceeds, the sale by *P* of the *S* stock is not in and of itself sufficient to effect a contraction of the business operations of *P* within the contemplation of section 346(a)(2) of the Code. Rather, the overall transaction has the economic significance of the sale of an investment and distribution of the proceeds.

Accordingly, the distribution by *P* to its shareholders of the proceeds of the sale of the *S* stock does not qualify as a distribution in partial liquidation within the meaning of section [302(e)(1)] of the Code, and the distribution will be treated as a distribution by *P* of property taxable to the *P* shareholders under section 301 by reason of section 302(d). See section 1.302–2(b) of the regulations, which provides that all distributions in pro rata redemption of a part of the stock of a corporation generally will be treated as distributions under section 301 if the corporation has only one class of stock outstanding.

PROBLEM

Alpha Corporation operates a book publishing business ("Books") and a bar exam review course ("Cram") as divisions (i.e., not as separately incorporated entities). Alpha has a single class of common stock outstanding which is owned in equal shares by Michael, Pamela (Michael's wife) and Iris Corporation. Neither Michael nor Pamela owns any stock in Iris. Alpha also owns all of the stock of Beta Corporation, a separately incorporated company which is engaged in the beta processing business. In addition, Alpha owns a diversified securities portfolio.

What are the shareholder level tax consequences of the following alternative transactions:

(a) Alpha has operated Books and Cram for more than five years and it distributes the assets of Books to its three equal shareholders in redemption of 50 shares from each shareholder. Any different result if the redemption is made without an actual surrender of shares?

(b) Is there a different result in (a), above, if Alpha had purchased Books three years ago for cash? If so, why should that matter? What if Alpha acquired Books three years ago in a tax-free reorganization?

(c) What if all the assets of Books were destroyed by fire and Alpha distributes one-half of the insurance proceeds equally to its three shareholders in redemption of an appropriate number of shares of stock and retains the remaining proceeds to carry on Books on a somewhat smaller scale?

(d) Same as (a), above, except that Alpha distributes the assets of Books to Michael in redemption of all of his stock.

(e) Same as (a), above except that Alpha distributes the assets of Books to Iris in redemption of all of its Alpha stock.

(f) Alpha distributes the securities portfolio to its three equal shareholders in redemption of 20 shares from each shareholder.

(g) Alpha sells all of its Beta stock and distributes the proceeds pro rata to the shareholders in redemption of 20 shares from each.

(h) Same as (g), above, except that Alpha liquidates Beta and then distributes the assets of Beta's business, which Beta has operated for more than five years.

E. CONSEQUENCES TO THE DISTRIBUTING CORPORATION

1. DISTRIBUTIONS OF APPRECIATED PROPERTY IN REDEMPTION

Code: § 311.

In the preceding chapter, the story of the decline of the *General Utilities* doctrine began to unfold.[1] That doctrine excused a corporation from recognizing gain on a distribution of appreciated property to shareholders with respect to their stock. Prior to 1969, distributions of appreciated property in redemption were embraced by the general nonrecognition rule in Section 311(a) and, with some exceptions (e.g., recapture, LIFO inventory), the 1954 Code version of Section 336(a) similarly provided for nonrecognition on distributions of property in partial liquidation.

The assault on *General Utilities* in the redemption context gained momentum in the Tax Reform Act of 1969, when Congress discovered that several insurance companies were redeeming large amounts of their own stock by distributing appreciated securities while avoiding recognition of gain at the corporate level.[2] Without pausing to reexamine the broader defects of the nonrecognition rule, Congress curtailed this perceived abuse by enacting Section 311(d), which then provided that a corporation recognized gain on a distribution of appreciated property in a redemption as if the property had been sold for its fair market value. Partial liquidation distributions, however, continued to be protected by the pre-1982 version of Section 336, and seven exceptions demonstrated that Congress was not yet ready to give *General Utilities* a proper burial.[3]

---

1. See Chapter 4D1, *supra*.

2. See S.Rep. No. 91–552, 91st Cong., 1st Sess. 279, reprinted in 1969–3 C.B. 423,600.

3. See I.R.C. § 311(d)(2) (pre-1982).

Corporate takeover specialists were quick to exploit these remaining vestiges of the *General Utilities* doctrine. Through carefully orchestrated transactions, they sought to convert a direct sale of property by a corporation, normally a taxable event to the seller, into a tax-free distribution.[4] After several of these schemes were publicized, Congress responded in the Tax Equity and Fiscal Responsibility Act of 1982 by further narrowing the opportunity for nonrecognition on non-liquidating distributions of appreciated property in redemption.[5] The principal changes were the near repeal of the two major exceptions in former Section 311(d)[6] and the withdrawal of partial liquidation treatment for corporate shareholders.

General Utilities suffered further erosion in the Tax Reform Act of 1984. As a result of these successive revisions, virtually all nonliquidating distributions of appreciated property to *corporate* shareholders were fully taxable events. A corporation distributing appreciated property in redemption to a noncorporate shareholder recognized gain except in the case of distributions in partial liquidation to certain long-term shareholders,[7] certain distributions of stock to controlled corporations,[8] and in a few other specialized situations.[9]

The final demise of *General Utilities* in the redemption context came with the Tax Reform Act of 1986. In adopting Section 311(b), which also applies to nonliquidating distributions,[10] Congress repealed all the remaining exceptions that had provided for nonrecognition to the distributing corporation. As a result, a corporation distributing appreciated property in redemption of stock (including a partial liquidation) always recognizes gain under Section 311(b). Section 311(a) still provides, however, that a distributing corporation may not recognize loss on a distribution of property in redemption.

2. EFFECT ON EARNINGS AND PROFITS

Code: § 312(n)(7).

The effect of a distribution in redemption on the distributing corporation's earnings and profits initially depends upon the treatment of the redemption at the shareholder level. If the redemption is treated as a distribution to which Section 301 applies, earnings and profits are reduced in the same manner as on other nonliquidating distributions—i.e., they are decreased by the amount of cash and by the

4. See Henderson, "Federal Tax Techniques for Asset Redeployment Transactions," 37 Tax L.Rev. 325 (1982). The Service's attack or this strategy was rejected in Esmark, Inc. v. Commissioner, 90 T.C. 171 (1988), affirmed 886 F.2d 1318 (7th Cir. 1989). See Chapter 10B1a, infra.

5. For a description of some of the abuses at which the 1982 changes were directed, see Staff of Joint Committee on Taxation, General Explanation of Tax Equity and Fiscal Responsibility Act of 1982, 97th Cong., 2d Sess. 125 (1982).

6. See note 3, supra.

7. I.R.C. § 311(d)(2)(A)(i) (pre-1987).

8. I.R.C. §§ 311(d)(2)(B), (e)(2) (pre-1987).

9. I.R.C. § 311(d)(2)(C) (pre-1987).

10. See Chapter 4D1, supra.

principal amount of any obligations, and the greater of the adjusted basis or the fair market value of any property distributed.[1]

If a redemption (including a partial liquidation) is treated as an exchange to the redeemed shareholder, the effect on earnings and profits is more complex. Prior to the Tax Reform Act of 1984, earnings and profits were reduced on a redemption distribution by an amount equal to the excess of the amount of the distribution over the amount "properly chargeable" to the corporation's capital account.[2] Stated differently, the portion of a redemption distribution that was *not* properly chargeable to capital account reduced earnings and profits. In applying this rule, profitable corporations were motivated to minimize the charge to capital account and thus maximize the earnings and profits reduction, possibly even sweeping the earnings and profits account clean and paving the way for future nontaxable distributions.

Several cases, and ultimately even the Service, held that a corporation's capital account is limited to the par value of its stock plus the amount, if any, of paid-in surplus, and that this amount is reduced on a redemption in proportion to the amount of the corporation's stock that was redeemed.[3] By narrowing the corporate capital account, this pro-taxpayer approach ignored the redeemed stock's ratable share of unrealized appreciation in the corporation's assets. As a result, earnings and profits often were reduced on a redemption by an amount that exceeded the redeemed stock's proportionate share of earnings and profits. To illustrate, consider the following example from the legislative history of the Tax Reform Act of 1984:[4]

> For example, assume that X corporation has 1,000 shares of $10 par value stock outstanding, and that A and B each acquired 500 of the shares upon their issuance at a price of $20 per share. Assume further that X corporation, which has operated a profitable services business since its inception, holds net assets worth $100,000 consisting of cash ($50,000) and appreciated improved real property ($50,000) and has current and accumulated earnings and profits of $50,000. If X corporation distributes $50,000 in cash to A in complete redemption of A's shares in X corporation, the distribution, under *Jarvis v. Commissioner,* would be charged first against X corporation's capital account, reducing it by $10,000. The remaining $40,000 would reduce earnings and profits. After the transaction, X corporation would have $10,000 of earnings and profits.

1. I.R.C. § 312(a), (b). In addition, the corporation always recognizes gain, and correspondingly increases its earnings and profits, on a distribution of appreciated property. I.R.C. §§ 311(b); 312(b).

2. I.R.C. § 312(e) (pre-1984).

3. See, e.g., Anderson v. Commissioner, 67 T.C. 522 (1976), affirmed per curiam 583 F.2d 953 (7th Cir.1978); Jarvis v. Commissioner, 43 B.T.A. 439 (1941), affirmed 123 F.2d 742 (4th Cir.1941); Rev.Rul. 79–376, 1979–2 C.B. 133.

4. S.Rep. No. 98–169, 98th Cong., 2d Sess. 198 (1984).

A would generally have no dividend income from the redemption.

Congress concluded that the result illustrated above was overly generous to the remaining shareholders. The statutory solution, codified in Section 312(n)(7), provides that if a redemption is treated as an exchange, the part of the distribution which is properly chargeable to earnings and profits shall be an amount which does not exceed the ratable share of earnings and profits of the corporation attributable to the stock that is redeemed. Congress also expressed its intention that earnings and profits never would be reduced by more than the amount of the redemption.[5]

Applying the new approach to the above example from the legislative history, assume once again that X Corporation distributes $50,000 cash to A in redemption of A's 500 shares. Section 312(n)(7) reduces X's earnings and profits by $25,000—the ratable share of X's $50,000 earnings and profits attributable to A's 50 percent stock interest that was redeemed. The remaining $25,000 of the distribution would be charged to capital account and, after the redemption, X would have $25,000 of remaining earnings and profits. The following excerpt from the General Explanation of the Tax Reform Act of 1984 explains the operation of this rule in the case of a corporation with a more complex capital structure:[6]

> If a corporation has more than one class of stock outstanding, its earnings and profits generally should be allocated among the different classes in determining the amount by which a redemption of all or a part of one class of stock reduces earnings and profits. However, earnings and profits generally should not be allocated to preferred stock which is not convertible and which does not participate to any significant extent in corporate growth. Therefore, a redemption of such preferred stock should result in a reduction of the capital account only, unless the distribution includes dividend arrearages, which will reduce earnings and profits.

> Similarly, priorities legally required as between different classes of stock should be taken into account in allocating earnings and profits between classes. For example, assume that corporation X has 1,000 shares of class A common stock and 1,000 shares of class B common stock. Both classes are $10 par value stock and were issued at the same time at a price of $20. The class A common has a preference as to dividends and liquidating distributions in a 2:1 ratio to the class B common, and only the class B common has voting rights. Assume further that Corporation X holds net assets worth $210,000 and has current and accumulated earnings and prof-

---

5. Id. at 202.

6. Staff of Joint Committee on Taxation, General Explanation of the Tax Re-

form Act of 1984, 98th Cong., 2d Sess. 181 (1984).

its of $120,000. If X distributes $140,000 in cash in redemption of all of the class A common, earnings and profits should be reduced by $80,000 and capital account by $60,000.

PROBLEM

X Corporation has 200 shares of common stock outstanding. A and B each acquired 100 shares of X upon their issuance at a price of $1,000 per share. At the beginning of the current year, X has $100,000 of accumulated earnings and profits and it has $50,000 of earnings and profits from operations during the year. Shareholder A owns 100 shares of X stock with an adjusted basis of $100,000. What are the tax consequences to X of the following alternative redemptions, assuming in each case that A qualifies for exchange treatment under § 302(a)?

(a) In redemption of A's 100 shares, X distributes land ($250,000 fair market value; $200,000 adjusted basis) held as an investment.

(b) Same as (a), above, except X's adjusted basis in the land is $300,000.

(c) In redemption of A's 100 shares, X distributes $65,000 cash.

3. STOCK REDEMPTION EXPENSES

Code: § 162(k).

Amounts paid to acquire stock generally must be capitalized as part of the stock's basis.[1] The capitalization requirement applies to the original purchase price of the stock as well as to acquisition expenses, such as brokerage commissions and legal fees.[2] Some authority exists, however, that expenses incurred by a corporation to repurchase its shares, in limited circumstances, may be ordinary and necessary expenses deductible under Section 162.[3] In the midst of the frenzy of hostile corporate takeovers, Congress became concerned that expenditures incurred to purchase shares to fend off unwanted corporate suitors—so-called "greenmail" payments—were being characterized as deductible business expenses.[4] Section 162(k) was enacted as part of the Tax Reform Act of 1986 to make it clear that all expenditures by a corporation incurred in purchasing its own stock, whether representing amounts paid for the stock, a premium paid in excess of the stock's value, or expenses connected with the purchase, are nondeductible, nonamortizable capital expenditures.[5]

1. I.R.C. §§ 263(a), 1012.

2. Reg. § 1.263(a)–2(c), (e). See Woodward v. Commissioner, 397 U.S. 572, 90 S.Ct. 1302 (1970); United States v. Hilton Hotels Corp., 397 U.S. 580, 90 S.Ct. 1307 (1970).

3. Five Star Manufacturing Co. v. Commissioner, 355 F.2d 724 (5th Cir.1966). See generally Note, "Deductibility of Stock Redemption Expenses and the Corporate Survival Doctrine," 58 So.Cal.L.Rev. 895 (1985).

4. S.Rep. No. 99–313, 99th Cong., 2d Sess. 223 (1986).

5. Id.

Section 162(k)(1) sets out the general rule of nondeductibility for amounts paid by a corporation in connection with the redemption of its stock. Section 162(k)(2) contains exceptions for interest payments deductible under Section 163, dividends deductible under Section 561 for purposes of the accumulated earnings tax and personal holding company tax provisions,[6] and a more specialized exception for redemptions by mutual funds.

The difficult interpretive problems under Section 162(k) likely will revolve around the question of whether an amount paid to a shareholder is paid "in connection with" a redemption of stock and therefore disallowed. The legislative history states that while the phrase "in connection with" is to be construed broadly, it is not intended to deny a deduction for "otherwise deductible amounts paid in a transaction which has no nexus with the redemption other than being proximate in time or arising out of the same circumstances."[7] The Conference Report goes on to expand upon this standard:[8]

> For example, if a corporation redeems a departing employee's stock and makes a payment to the employee in discharge of the corporation's obligations under an employment contract, the payment in discharge of the contractual obligation is not subject to disallowance under this provision. Payments in discharge of other types of contractual obligations, in settlement of litigation, or pursuant to other actual or potential legal obligations or rights, may also be outside the intended scope of the provision to the extent it is clearly established that the payment does not represent consideration for the stock or expenses related to its acquisition, and is not a payment that is a fundamental part of a "standstill" or similar agreement.

> The conferees anticipate that, where a transaction is not directly related to a redemption but is proximate in time, the Internal Revenue Service will scrutinize the transaction to determine whether the amount purportedly paid in the transaction is reasonable. Thus, even where the parties have countervailing tax interests, the parties' stated allocation of the total consideration between the redemption and the unrelated transaction will be respected only if it is supported by all the facts and circumstances.

> However, the conferees intend that agreements to refrain from purchasing stock of a corporation or other similar types of "standstill" agreements in all events will be considered related to any redemption of the payee's stock. Accordingly, payments pursuant to such agreements are nondeductible under this provision provided there is an actual purchase of all or part of the payee's stock. The conferees intend no inference

---

6. See Chapter 9, infra.

7. H.R.Rep. No. 99–841, 99th Cong., 2d Sess. II—168 (1986).

8. Id. at II—168–69.

regarding the deductibility of payments under standstill or similar agreements that are unrelated to any redemption of stock owned by the payee.

F. REDEMPTION PLANNING TECHNIQUES

1. BOOTSTRAP SALES *

ZENZ v. QUINLIVAN **

United States Court of Appeals, Sixth Circuit, 1954.
213 F.2d 914.

GOURLEY, District Judge.

The appeal relates to the interpretation of [the 1939 Code predecessor of Section 302(b)(1)] and poses the question—Is a distribution of substantially all of the accumulated earnings and surplus of a corporation, which are not necessary to the conduct of the business of the corporation, in redemption of all outstanding shares of stock of said corporation owned by one person *essentially equivalent to the distribution of a taxable dividend under the Internal Revenue Code?*

The District Court answered in the affirmative and sustained a deficiency assessment by the Commissioner of Internal Revenue.

After consideration of the records, briefs and arguments of counsel for the parties, we believe the judgment should be reversed.

The question stems from the following circumstances:

Appellant is the widow of the person who was the motivating spirit behind the closed corporation which engaged in the business of excavating and laying of sewers. Through death of her husband she became the owner of all shares of stock issued by the corporation. She operated the business until remarriage, when her second husband assumed the management. As a result of a marital rift, separation, and final divorce, taxpayer sought to dispose of her company to a competitor who was anxious to eliminate competition.

Prospective buyer did not want to assume the tax liabilities which it was believed were inherent in the accumulated earnings and profits of the corporation. To avoid said profits and earnings as a source of future taxable dividends, buyer purchased part of taxpayer's stock for cash. Three weeks later, after corporate reorganization and corporate action, the corporation redeemed the balance of taxpayer's stock, purchasing the same as treasury stock which absorbed substantially all of the accumulated earnings and surplus of the corporation.

Taxpayer, in her tax return, invoked Section [302(a)] of the Internal Revenue Code * * * as constituting a cancellation or redemption by a

---

* See generally Lang, "Dividends Essentially Equivalent to Redemptions: The Taxation of Bootstrap Stock Acquisitions," 41 Tax L.Rev. 309 (1986).

** Footnote omitted.

corporation of all the stock of a particular shareholder, and therefore was not subject to being treated as a distribution of a taxable dividend.

The District Court sustained the deficiency assessment of the Commissioner that the amount received from accumulated earnings and profits was ordinary income since the stock redeemed by the corporation was "at such time and in such manner as to make the redemption thereof essentially equivalent to the distribution of a taxable dividend" under Section [302(b)(1)] of the Code.

The District Court's findings were premised upon the view that taxpayer employed a circuitous approach in an attempt to avoid the tax consequences which would have attended the outright distribution of the surplus to the taxpayer by the declaration of a taxable dividend.

The rationale of the District Court is dedicated to piercing the external manifestations of the taxpayer's transactions in order to establish a subterfuge or sham.

Nevertheless, the general principle is well settled that a taxpayer has the legal right to decrease the amount of what otherwise would be his taxes or altogether avoid them, by means which the law permits. * * * The taxpayer's motive to avoid taxation will not establish liability if the transaction does not do so without it. * * *

The question accordingly presented is not whether the overall transaction, admittedly carried out for the purpose of avoiding taxes, actually avoided taxes which would have been incurred if the transaction had taken a different form, but whether the sale constituted a taxable dividend or the sale of a capital asset. Chamberlain v. Commissioner of Internal Revenue, supra.

It is a salutary fact that Section [302(a)] is an exception to Section [316] that all distributions of earnings and profits are taxable as a dividend.

The basic precept underlying the capital gains theory of taxation as distinguished from ordinary income tax is the concept that a person who has developed an enterprise in which earnings have been accumulated over a period of years should not be required to expend the ordinary income tax rate in the one year when he withdraws from his enterprise and realizes his gain.

Common logic dictates that a fair basis of measuring income is not determined upon the profits on hand in the year of liquidation but is properly attributable to each year in which the profits were gained.

We cannot concur with the legal proposition enunciated by the District Court that a corporate distribution can be essentially equivalent to a taxable dividend even though that distribution extinguishes the shareholder's interest in the corporation. To the contrary, we are satisfied that where the taxpayer effects a redemption which completely extinguishes the taxpayer's interest in the corporation, and does not retain any beneficial interest whatever, that such transaction is not the equivalent of the distribution of a taxable dividend as to him. Tiffany v. Commissioner of Internal Revenue, 16 T.C. 1443.

The statutory concept of dividend is a distribution out of earnings and profits, and normally it is proportionate to shares and leaves the shareholder holding his shares as his capital investment. Flinn v. Commissioner of Internal Revenue, 37 B.T.A. 1085.

Complete and partial liquidations are treated for the purpose of the statute, as sales with a consequent measure of gain or loss, even though the proceeds may to some extent be derived from earnings. Hellmich v. Hellman, 276 U.S. 233, 48 S.Ct. 244, 72 L.Ed. 544.

The use of corporate earnings or profits to purchase and make payment for all the shares of a taxpayer's holdings in a corporation is not controlling, and the question as to whether the distribution in connection with the cancellation or the redemption of said stock is essentially equivalent to the distribution of a taxable dividend under the Internal Revenue Code and Treasury Regulation must depend upon the circumstances of each case.

Since the intent of the taxpayer was to bring about a complete liquidation of her holdings and to become separated from all interest in the corporation, the conclusion is inevitable that the distribution of the earnings and profits by the corporation in payment for said stock was not made at such time and in such manner as to make the distribution and cancellation or redemption thereof essentially equivalent to the distribution of a taxable dividend.

In view of the fact that the application of Section [302(b)(1)] of the Internal Revenue Code contemplates that the shareholder receiving the distribution will remain in the corporation, the circumstances of this proceeding militate against treating taxpayer's sale as a distribution of a taxable dividend.

We do not feel that a taxpayer should be penalized for exercising legal means to secure a tax advantage. The conduct of this taxpayer does not appear to contravene the purport or congressional intent of the provisions of the Internal Revenue Act which taxpayer invoked.

We conclude that under the facts and circumstances of the present case the District Court was in error, and the taxpayer is not liable as a distributee of a taxable dividend under Section [302(b)(1)] of the Internal Revenue Code.

The decision and judgment of the District Court is reversed and the case remanded with instructions to enter judgment in accordance with this opinion.

REVENUE RULING 75–447

1975–2 Cum.Bull. 113.

Advice has been requested as to the Federal income tax consequences, in the situations described below, of the redemption by a corporation of part of its stock.

Situation 1

Corporation *X* had outstanding 100 shares of voting common stock of which *A* and *B* each owned 50 shares. In order to bring *C* into the business with an equal stock interest, and pursuant to an integrated plan, *A* and *B* caused *X* to issue, at fair market value, 25 new shares of voting common stock to *C*. Immediately thereafter, as part of the same plan, *A* and *B* caused *X* to redeem 25 shares of *X* voting common stock from each of them. Neither *A*, *B*, nor *C* owned any stock of *X* indirectly under section 318 of the Internal Revenue Code of 1954.

Situation 2

Corporation *X* had outstanding 100 shares of voting common stock of which *A* and *B* each owned 50 shares. In order to bring *C* into the business with an equal stock interest, and pursuant to an integrated plan, *A* and *B* each sold 15 shares of *X* voting common stock to *C* at fair market value and then caused *X* to redeem five shares from both *A* and *B*. Neither *A*, *B*, nor *C* owned any stock of *X* indirectly under section 318 of the Code.

Section 302(b)(2) of the Code states that section 302(a), which provides for treating a redemption of stock as a distribution in part or full payment in exchange for the stock, will apply if the distribution is substantially disproportionate with respect to the shareholder. * * *

In Zenz v. Quinlivan, 213 F.2d 914 (6th Cir.1954), a sole shareholder of a corporation, desiring to dispose of her entire interest therein, sold part of her stock to a competitor and shortly thereafter sold the remainder of her stock to the corporation for an amount of cash and property approximately equal to its earned surplus. The Government contended that the redemption was a dividend on the grounds that the result was the same as if the steps had been reversed, that is, as if the stock had been redeemed first and the sale of stock to the competitor had followed. The United States Court of Appeals rejected the Government's contention and held that the purchase of the stock by the corporation (when coupled with the sale of stock to the competitor) was not a dividend to the selling shareholder and that the proceeds should be treated as payment for the stock surrendered under the provisions of the Internal Revenue Code of 1939.

Rev.Rul. 55–745, 1955–2 C.B. 223, states that in situations similar to that in *Zenz*, the amount received by the shareholder from the corporation will be treated as received in payment for the stock surrendered under section 302(a) of the Code since the transaction when viewed as a whole results in the shareholder terminating his interest in the corporation within the meaning of section 302(b)(3).

In determining whether the "substantially disproportionate" provisions of section 302(b)(2) of the Code have been satisfied in *Situation 1* and in *Situation 2*, it is proper to rely upon the holding in *Zenz* that the sequence in which the events (that is, the redemption and sale) occur is irrelevant as long as both events are clearly part of an overall plan.

Therefore, in situations where the redemption is accompanied by an issuance of new stock (as in *Situation 1*), or a sale of stock (as in *Situation 2*), and both steps (the sale, or issuance, of stock, as the case may be, and the redemption) are clearly part of an integrated plan to reduce a shareholder's interest, effect will be given only to the overall result for purposes of section 302(b)(2) and the sequence in which the events occur will be disregarded.

Since the *Zenz* holding requires that effect be given only to the overall result and proscribes the fragmenting of the whole transaction into its component parts, the computation of the voting stock of the corporation owned by the shareholder *immediately before* the redemption for purposes of section 302(b)(2)(C)(ii) of the Code should be made before any part of the transaction occurs. Likewise, the computation of the voting stock of the corporation owned by the shareholder *immediately after* the redemption for purposes of section 302(b)(2)(C)(i) should be made after the whole transaction is consummated. Making the immediately before and the immediately after computations in this manner properly reflects the extent to which the shareholder involved in each situation actually reduces his stock holdings as a result of the whole transaction.

Therefore, for purposes of the computations required by section 302(b)(2)(C) of the Code, A and B, in *Situation 1*, will each be viewed as having owned 50 percent (50/100 shares) of X before the transaction and 33⅓ percent (25/75 shares) immediately thereafter. In *Situation 2*, A and B will each be viewed as having owned 50 percent (50/100 shares) of X before the transaction and 33⅓ percent (30/90 shares) immediately thereafter. Furthermore, in each situation, the result would be the same if the redemption had preceded the issuance, or sale, of stock.

Accordingly, in both *Situations 1* and *2*, the requirements of section 302(b)(2) of the Code are satisfied. Therefore, the amounts distributed to A and B in both situations are distributions in full payment in exchange for the stock redeemed pursuant to section 302(a).

PROBLEM

Strap is the sole shareholder of Target Corporation. Boot is a prospective buyer and is willing to purchase all of the Target stock, but Boot is unable to pay the $500,000 price demanded by Strap even though he believes it to be fair. Target has $100,000 cash on hand. Should Strap and Boot structure Boot's acquisition of Target along the lines of the *Zenz* case? Is there a better alternative? What additional facts would you like to know? (Compare to *TSN Liquidating* and the problem on page 194, supra.)

2. BUY–SELL AGREEMENTS

Code: §§ 101(a), 264(a)(1).

EXCERPT FROM J. SCHLENGER AND H. NUSSENFELD, "VALUING CLOSELY HELD BUSINESS INTERESTS AND PLANNING THE BUY–SELL AGREEMENT" *

44 N.Y.U.Inst. on Fed. Tax'n 52–1 (1986).

§ 52.05   BUY–SELL AGREEMENTS IN GENERAL

Buy-sell ("stock purchase") agreements are beneficial for both tax and economic reasons in a variety of closely held business contexts. These include:

(1) situations in which all stockholders are members of the same family;

(2) situations in which the business is owned by two or more families; and

(3) situations in which the business is owned by unrelated parties.

The agreements are often entered into for purposes of providing for the orderly administration of an estate and the continuation of a business. The goals of the parties in executing a stock purchase agreement typically include:

(1) To provide a ready market for stock held by a decedent's estate to pay death taxes. This protects survivors from having to effect a forced sale at a distress price. Because of the availability of the unlimited marital deduction,[105] this will be more significant upon the death of the surviving spouse.

(2) To aid in the valuation for estate tax purposes of the stock held by the decedent's estate.

(3) To protect the remaining active stockholders from the passive (and perhaps dissident) stockholders, including retired employees, surviving spouses of deceased employees, personal representatives or despised in-laws.

(4) To protect the inactive stockholders from being "locked in" with no market for their stock.

(5) To extract funds [from corporate solution in a transaction qualifying as an "exchange" Ed.].

(6) To preserve a Subchapter S election by restricting transfers.

(7) To provide for prompt disposition of stock at the death of a stockholder.

A series of basic structuring options confront the practitioner. First, the purchaser must be determined. The choices are entity agreements ("redemption agreements"), cross-purchase agreements or

105. I.R.C. § 2056.

combination agreements. In an entity agreement, upon the happening of the trigger event, the issuing corporation would either be obligated or would have an option to purchase stock from the withdrawing stockholder. The typical cross-purchase agreement provides that upon the happening of the trigger event, the other stockholders would be obligated or would have an option to purchase stock from the stockholder. A combination agreement generally gives the corporation the primary obligation or option to purchase and requires the remaining stockholders to serve as the "backup." Still another possibility is to have the corporation obligated to redeem all stock eligible for favorable treatment under IRC Section 303, and have the remaining stockholders obligated to purchase the balance.[106]

§ 52.06   BASIC OPTIONS IN STRUCTURING
THE AGREEMENT

[1] Purchaser

Under a cross-purchase agreement, the remaining shareholders pay for the stock and receive a stepped-up basis in the shares equal to the amount paid.[107] The seller's tax consequences depend on whether the sale is consummated during the seller's lifetime or at death. If the purchase is effected during life, gain will probably be recognized * * *. For purchases at death, typically no gain will be realized because of the "stepped-up basis" rule.[108]

In a cross-purchase agreement, the shareholders may be tempted to have the corporation purchase the deceased shareholder's stock. If the corporation purchases stock that a continuing shareholder had a "primary and unconditional" obligation to purchase, the purchase will be treated as a constructive dividend to the continuing shareholders who were so obligated.[109] If the continuing shareholders merely had an option, and were not obligated, then no constructive dividend should arise.[110]

In a purchase effected under a redemption agreement, the amounts paid by the corporation in redemption of stock are nondeductible, but decrease corporate earnings and profits. The amount of the decrease is a ratable portion of corporate earnings and profits, in proportion to the outstanding stock redeemed. For example, if 50 percent of the corporation's stock is redeemed, then earnings and profits may be decreased by the lesser of 50 percent or the amount of the redemption.[111]

At the shareholder level, IRC Section 302(d) provides the general rule that a redemption is treated as a distribution of property to which IRC Section 301 applies (i.e., a "dividend"). There are two basic

---

106. I.R.C. § 303.

107. I.R.C. § 1012.

108. I.R.C. § 1015.

109. Rev.Rul. 69–608, 1969–2 C.B. 42; Jacobs v. Comm'r, T.C. Memo. 1981–81, affd. 698 F.2d 800 (6th Cir.1983).

110. Monson v. Comm'r, 79 T.C. 827 (1982); Enoch v. Comm'r, 57 T.C. 781

(1972), acq. 1974–1 C.B. 1. Rev.Rul. 69–608, 1969–2 C.B. 42, provides that the parties may rescind a cross-purchase agreement prior to the trigger event and substitute a redemption (entity) agreement without constructive dividend consequences.

111. I.R.C. § 312(n)(7); S.Rep.No. 159, 98th Cong., 2d Sess. 197 (1984).

exceptions to this rule. First, under IRC Section 303, the redemption proceeds are eligible for [exchange] treatment to the extent that the amount realized does not exceed estate and inheritance taxes, interest and allowable funeral and administration expenses.[112]

Second, IRC Section 302(a) affords [exchange] treatment to gains recognized in a redemption which satisfies one of the four tests codified in IRC Section 302(b). Although variously phrased, the tests are methods of determining whether a true "sale" has taken place, as measured by a reduction in the shareholder's interest in corporate equity, as opposed to a distribution which leaves the stockholder's equity interest essentially unchanged. The Code requires application of the Section 318 attribution rules to the determination of the extent to which the shareholder's equity participation has been reduced.[113] This scrutiny is necessary lest the * * * tax * * * levied on dividend distributions become voluntary.

[2] Trigger Events

Typically, buy-sell agreements provide for a series of different events under which the corporation (or the remaining shareholders) must purchase or have the option to purchase (the "trigger events"). The choice of trigger events is limited only by the needs of the parties and the drafter's imagination.

Nearly every agreement includes death of a shareholder as a trigger event. Depending on whether the primary purpose of the agreement is to protect the estate of the deceased shareholder, or to preserve the ongoing business, typically the estate will have the right to require the corporation to purchase its stock (a "put" option), or the corporation will have the right to purchase the decedent's stock (a "call" option). For situations in which the surviving spouse or heirs are expected to retain stock, the optionees may choose not to sell, and the agreement must be drafted to permit limited rights of transfer.

Retirement, disability or termination of employment are common trigger events. "Retirement" may be defined in any manner, but if an entity agreement is used, a mandatory "call" on retirement can have unexpected consequences. A shareholder who must waive family attribution in order to obtain capital gain tax treatment for redeemed stock may not retain any "prohibited interest" in the corporation.[115] Once retired, the former shareholder may not remain as an officer, director or employee.[116] The parties may try to retain the shareholder as an independent contractor, but the Service may be expected to challenge the arrangement.[117] Other relationships may or may not be permitted,

112. I.R.C. § 303.

113. I.R.C. § 302(c).

115. I.R.C. § 302(c).

116. Seda v. Comm'r, 82 T.C. 484 (1984).

117. See Lynch v. Comm'r, 83 T.C. 597 (1984); Chertkof v. Comm'r, 72 T.C. 1113 (1979), affd. 649 F.2d 264 (4th Cir.1981). [This article was written prior to the Ninth Circuit's decision in Lynch. See supra page 205. Ed.]

depending on how closely the relationship resembles that of a stock-holder.[118]

Termination of employment is an important trigger event which should probably be included in most agreements. It has been observed that there are few things as potentially worthless as a minority interest in a close corporation, and that conversely the potential for discontented minority shareholders to harass management is quite great.[119] The enforceability of an agreement triggered by termination of employment may depend, among other things, on whether the agreement constitutes a device for oppression of minority shareholders by the majority share-holders. Forced sales of stock held by employees who have been discharged without cause may not withstand judicial scrutiny, particularly if the price provided under the agreement is below fair market value.[120]

A disability trigger event is somewhat less common, perhaps due to inherent difficulties in defining "disability." Drafters sometimes default in the definition by defining disability by reference to state law. That is, a shareholder is not disabled within the meaning of the agreement absent an adjudication of incompetence. This is impractical because of the limited scope of the legal definition of disability, and the financial and psychological burdens on all parties that pursuing such a course would entail.

Other possibilities for defining "disability" include using the definition furnished under an applicable disability insurance policy, or using a "certification" process involving one or more physicians. Although disability insurance is a possibility, the cost is frequently beyond the means, desires or goals of a closely held business, and its use is comparatively rare. A certification process could likewise lead to a "battle of physicians," which may also be traumatic to the patient and other shareholders. A possible solution is to follow the technique found in employment agreements, which often define disability in terms of either consecutive or aggregate days of absence within a given period.

Because a buy-sell agreement would be virtually meaningless without lifetime restrictions, typically an offer by a shareholder to transfer his stock to another person is a trigger event. Virtually any business or other contingency imaginable may be used. For example, passage of time, attainment of certain sales or earnings goals, negative business conditions, mergers, acquisitions, or cessation of specific lines of business could all be used singly or in combination, where appropriate.

---

118. E.g., creditor status is permitted, but the debt instrument must not be subordinated to general creditors or proprietary in nature. Reg. § 1.302–4(b); but see Est. of Lennard v. Comm'r, 61 T.C. 554 (1974), nonacq. 1978–2 C.B. 3. Landlord status may be permitted; see Rev.Rul. 77–467, 1977–2 C.B. 92. Coverage under a qualified corporate retirement plan may be permitted; see Rev.Rul. 84–135, 1984–2 C.B. 80; coverage under a corporate health plan may skate on thin ice. Lynch v. Comm'r, 83 T.C. 597 (1984).

119. Zaritsky, "Forgotten Provisions in Buy-Sell Agreements," 19 U.Miami Inst.Est.Plan Ch. 6 (1985).

120. Id. at ¶ 601.3(A).

[3] Should the Purchase be Mandatory or Optional

The choice between mandatory or optional buy-out depends on the circumstances. If a primary concern is to provide liquid assets for the estate, then the estate must be able to compel the purchase. Likewise, if a primary goal is to protect the active stockholders from interference by nonworking stockholders, the corporation must be able to compel the purchase. These goals can be accomplished either through a mandatory purchase agreement or through the use of puts or calls.

In a cross-purchase agreement, no adverse tax consequences should result under a mandatory buy-out agreement. In a typical redemption (entity) agreement, an unconditionally mandatory buy-out is a loaded weapon because of the potential for dividend treatment of the entire redemption proceeds. One possible solution is to structure a mandatory buy-out conditioned on receipt of a favorable letter ruling or opinion of counsel as to tax consequences. The selling shareholders should be given the option to waive this condition.

The buy-out need not be mandatory in all events; agreements sometimes provide for compelled purchase at death, but give one side or both an option under all other trigger events. The key consideration is to anticipate potential deadlock situations and structure an agreement under which the parties can resolve the deadlock. For example, the selling shareholders may be given a put, instead of making the buy-out mandatory. A potential for discontent still exists because the selling shareholder may be faced with the receipt of an unsecured obligation payable over a long term at comparatively low interest rates, in exchange for his equity position. These are negotiating points which must be considered by all of the parties prior to entry into the agreement.

[4] Transfer Restrictions

Structuring transfer restrictions requires consideration of both tax law and state law consequences. For purposes of valuing the stock for estate taxation, the price set by a buy-sell agreement will be disregarded unless the other shareholders of the corporation have an option to purchase the decedent's stock at death, and the decedent is not free to dispose of the securities at any other price during his lifetime.[127] Variations in, and restrictions on, stock transfer rights should also not be deemed to create a "second class of stock" for purposes of Subchapter S.[128] For state law purposes, restrictions on transfer must not violate any prohibition against unreasonable restraints against alienation.[129]

---

127. Reg. § 20.2031–2(h).

128. In Ltr. Rul. 8405077, the Service ruled that differences in stock transfer rights on a shareholder's termination of employment, disability or death, and other agreements regarding voting rights and dividend payments did not create a second class of stock, which would have invalidated the S corporation election. The rights of the shareholders to receive dividends and liquidation proceeds were unaltered by the agreements. See also Ltr. Ruls. 8407082, 8407011.

129. See, e.g., Rafe v. Hindin, 244 N.E.2d 469 (N.Y.1968).

The degree of transfer restrictions vary. Under the most severe, no transfer may take place without the prior written consent of the remaining shareholders. This restriction is needlessly severe, and if absolute, probably constitutes an unenforceable restraint on alienation. More typically, the restriction is couched as a right of first refusal. The shareholder must first obtain a bona fide written offer from an independent party having the means to purchase the stock. The agreement may require the shareholder to furnish the corporation (and perhaps the other shareholders) with a copy of the outside offer. The corporation then is provided a fixed period of time in which to elect to purchase, at either the price and the terms provided in the agreement, or at the price and terms provided in the offer from the third party. If the corporation elects not to purchase, the shareholders may then exercise their option. Any transfers to independent parties should be conditioned on receipt of the transferee's consent to become a party to the buy-sell agreement.

In structuring the restrictions, it may be appropriate to provide for lifetime and post-mortem transfers to certain permitted transferees (i.e., family members). The agreement should also permit transfers to or from trusts, custodial accounts or other nominee arrangements for the benefit of such family members, although the presence of trustees or custodians may involve intrusions by nonfamily members—even by lawyers.

[5] Setting the Price

Setting the price mechanism in the buy-out agreement often involves delicate negotiations. Regardless of whether an entity or cross-purchase agreement is used, if the stockholders are of similar ages, presumably each thinks he will outlast the other. The buying shareholder, or the remaining shareholder of the company that is buying stock, does not wish to pay an extravagant price. On the other hand, the withdrawing shareholder wishes to maximize his return. Regardless of what constitutes a "fair" price, the ability to pay is a limiting factor.

[a] *Agreed Price*

Among the most common price mechanisms is the "agreed value" method under which the parties execute a "certificate of value" setting an initial price at the outset of the agreement. Thereafter, the parties revise the agreed price periodically (e.g., annually) by unanimous consent. If a trigger event occurs more than one year after the date of the most recent agreed price, the agreed price is either adjusted by formula, or becomes inapplicable and an appraised price replaces it. It is important to provide a backup mechanism, lest the agreed price become "stale." The agreed price mechanism requires self-discipline, which parties are frequently reluctant to impose.

[b] *Book Value*

Parties often select "book value" as the price, but book value is generally an unsatisfactory measure. The proper definition of book value is a threshold question. The agreement would ordinarily dictate that book value is determined by the company's regular accountants, and that the determination of book value is binding and conclusive on all parties. The agreement must specify the measuring date for book value, as well as the adjustments which must be made.

The adjustments may be complex. A decision must be made as to the treatment of life insurance policies. If a redemption agreement is intended to be funded with insurance proceeds, and the price is based upon book value, the book value may be inflated by the insurance proceeds, thus frustrating the original intent of the parties. An adjustment may be appropriate for cash surrender value of insurance policies because the policy premiums were paid out of corporate assets. An adjustment may be necessary for investment assets, if book value substantially understates (or overstates) true value. This may be undesirable except in instances where investment assets can readily be "marked to market," lest a dispute arise which can be settled only through appraisal (or litigation).

There are other problems with book value. The value of a cash-basis business with substantial accounts receivable (or payable) may require an additional adjustment. An agreement for a business with substantial investment in inventory should address the valuation issue. Inventory may be maintained on a historical cost, lower-of-cost-or-market basis, LIFO basis and in combination methods. Book value may also be a wholly inappropriate measure for S corporations because the balance sheets of S corporations tend to be unrelated to market value—the shareholders withdraw the earnings. In sum, book value's chief virtue is its simplicity; in general, book value tends to understate true value, and numerous adjustments must be made for "fairness."

[c] *Earnings Formula*

Another common pricing mechanism is to use a formula based upon earnings. For example, the value of the company may be defined as five times the average after-tax income over the three preceding years prior to the trigger event. The drafter must take care to define earnings carefully. It may be necessary to exclude salaries, bonuses, nonrecurring items, and other adjustments. Another way to structure an earnings formula would be to base it on "cash flow" (i.e., earnings adjusted for noncash charges and perhaps for capital investments).

[d] *Combination Formula*

The parties may select a formula based on a combination of book value and earnings factors. This would be particularly appropriate when a business has both an operating and an investment character. Factors may be combined in manners limited only by the imagination of the drafter, and the agreement may call for the lower (or the higher) of two or more methods of valuation to be employed. Even if the agreement does not fix estate tax values as a matter of law, the Service is more likely to be persuaded of the value as set by an agreement in which the *higher* of two formula figures is used. If circumstances suggest that there will be a change in the business condition at some point in time, the agreement may begin with one pricing formula, and switch to another mechanism after the lapse of an interval of several years.

[e] *Appraisal*

Another common pricing mechanism is determination by appraisal. Provisions for selection of an appraiser or panel of appraisers should be stated, and the adjustments and assumptions the appraisers are to use should be spelled out. It must be noted that appraisals are frequently expensive and two or more appraisals of the same business may produce widely differing results.

[f] *Revaluation Subsequent to Buy-Out*

At times, the shareholders may be members of two or more families, and neither interest can predict which side will "buy out" the other side first. In this circumstance, it may be useful to provide for a revaluation mechanism, in the event one group purchases the interest of another group and reaps a "windfall" on a subsequent sale of the business to third parties. The agreement may provide for a revaluation if the business (or substantially all of its assets) is sold (or exchanged, in a reorganization) within a few years of the date of closing under the buy-out. In that case, the former shareholders would receive a share in the proceeds of the sale of the company, as if they had remained shareholders.[131]

[6] Terms of Payment

A cash payment may be difficult for the purchaser to raise unless insurance proceeds are received as a result of the trigger event. The seller may also face severe tax "bunching" and alternative minimum tax problems. Redemption agreements commonly employ deferred payment terms, as preservation of the business is a common goal. A deferred payment plan may assist the buyer by alleviating income bunching through the use of the installment method.[132]

In an installment redemption agreement, the purchasing corporation will issue notes or other contractual obligations. If the seller is not to be faced with the prospect of holding unsecured notes over a long

---

131. The price contingency must not be left open indefinitely, and in redemptions, the Service will look with disfavor on price revaluation clauses. See Rev.Proc. 85–22, 1985–12 I.R.B. 13.

132. I.R.C. § 453. [Note: Section 453(k)(2)(A) now precludes installment re-porting for sales of publicly traded stock or securities. This restriction will not adversely affect buy-sell agreements, however, since they are used almost exclusively by shareholders of closely held corporations. Ed.]

period of time, the seller must obtain security, either in the form of a lien on the corporation's assets, an escrow of the redeemed stock or guarantees from the remaining stockholders and their spouses. Such guarantees could be secured by indemnity mortgages or letters of credit. The selling shareholder may be able to obtain other restrictions, such as salary, dividend and bonus restrictions, restrictions on acquisitions, lines of business, and covenants as to net worth and other balance sheet ratios. Conversely, the greater the security and restrictions, the greater the difficulty experienced by the remaining shareholders in maintaining and expanding the business and in generating funds in payment of the purchase price, which may induce litigation-provoking maneuvers to ease burdens, real or imagined.

The agreement must also address state law restrictions on impairment of stated capital. The cure is to require the corporation and the remaining shareholders to cause surplus to be created, by transfer from capital surplus, reduction in par value or by reappraisal of assets. If the purchase still cannot be completed owing to state law restrictions, the selling shareholder may be able to force a corporate liquidation. As an alternative, the remaining shareholders could be obligated to purchase, if the corporation cannot do so. In a cross-purchase agreement or in a combination agreement in which the remaining shareholders purchase if the corporation elects not to, the selling shareholder faces the risk of the purchasing shareholders' insolvency or bankruptcy. At the minimum, the agreement should require spouses of the purchasing shareholders to guarantee the obligations.

[7] Insurance-Funded Purchases

It is often desirable to plan for the buy-out through the purchase of insurance on the lives of the senior shareholders. The tax treatment of insurance merits consideration. In a cross-purchase arrangement funded by insurance, the policy premiums are nondeductible to the shareholders. In an entity agreement, if the corporation is the owner and beneficiary of the policies, premiums are generally nondeductible if the insured is an officer, employee or a person financially interested in the corporate beneficiary, despite the use of the policy in a fashion otherwise qualifying as a trade or business expense.[133] Premiums may be deductible if the policy is held by a creditor to insure the life of a debtor,[134] or if the corporation is not a beneficiary, directly or indirectly,[135] but these situations generally do not apply to a buy-sell insurance program. Premiums paid by the corporation on the lives of the shareholders are generally excluded from the income of the shareholders,[136] except in situations such as the split-dollar arrangement in which the employee receives an economic benefit.[137]

---

133. I.R.C. § 264(a)(1); Reg. § 1.264–1(a).

134. Rev.Rul. 70–254, 1970–1 C.B. 31.

135. Reg. § 1.264–1(b).

136. Rev.Rul. 59–184, 1957–1 C.B. 65; Sanders v. Fox, 253 F.2d 855 (10th Cir.1958).

137. Johnson v. Comm'r, 74 T.C. 1316 (1980); Rev.Rul. 79–50, 1979–1 C.B. 138.

Normally, receipt of the policy proceeds is not a taxable event.[138] The nontaxable character also passes through to S corporation shareholders.[139] If the policy owner is a "transferee for value," then receipt of the policy proceeds is taxable to the extent of the excess of the proceeds over the cost of the policy plus premiums paid.[140] A purchase of an insurance policy is generally a "transfer for value," but transferees for value do not include the insured, a partner of the insured, a partnership in which the insured is a partner, or a corporation of which the insured is an officer or shareholder.[141] Transfers such as gifts, which result in carryover basis are not transfers for value and do not cause recognition of the policy proceeds as income.[142] In addition, even though the policy proceeds may be excluded from income, the excess of the proceeds over the aggregate insurance premiums paid are included in corporate earnings and profits.[143]

The estate tax consequences of insurance also bear consideration. Life insurance proceeds payable to the corporation should not be included in the decedent's gross estate.[144] Proceeds will be taxable to the estate if the proceeds are payable to the estate of the insured,[145] or if the insured retained any incident of ownership in the policy.[146] Incidents of ownership generally refer to any of the economic benefits of the policy.[147] However, insurance owned by a corporation of which the insured is a sole or a controlling shareholder will not be included in the insured's estate to the extent that the proceeds are payable to, or may be deemed payable to, the corporation.[148]

Insurance may be of some, but likely very little, value in funding lifetime purchases. Life insurance would, of course, be of no benefit in funding lifetime purchases by the corporation. Disability insurance can be obtained with either lump-sum or installment payment features; in either event, the terms of the payout must be structured to meet the policy payments. Disability insurance is relatively expensive. In a cross-purchase agreement, insurance to fund a lifetime purchase would be impractical, if not impossible to obtain at reasonable prices.

Life insurance of different types can be used by the redeeming corporation to fund, in whole or in part, the purchase of stock from a deceased shareholder's estate under a redemption agreement. It will be necessary to monitor the amount of insurance on each shareholder's life. As some shareholders die, and their stock is redeemed, the value of the interest of the remaining shareholders will rise. In structuring the buy-sell agreement, the parties must be made aware of the effect of the insurance proceeds on the value of the corporation. If the proceeds

---

138. I.R.C. § 101(a)(1); Reg. § 1.101–1(a).

139. I.R.C. § 1366(a)(1)(A).

140. I.R.C. § 101(a)(2).

141. I.R.C. § 101(a)(2)(B).

142. I.R.C. § 101(a)(2)(A).

143. Rev.Rul. 54–230, 1954–1 C.B. 114.

144. Rev.Rul. 82–85, 1982–1 C.B. 137; Reg. § 20.2042–1(c)(6).

145. I.R.C. § 2042(1).

146. I.R.C. § 2042(2); Reg. § 20.2042–1(c)(1).

147. Reg. § 20.2042–1(c).

148. Reg. § 20.2042–1(c)(6).

are excluded in determining value, then the last surviving shareholder may enjoy a windfall. If the proceeds are included, the corporation's value will increase for estate tax purposes, and the insurance proceeds will increase the financial burden on the corporation to fund the redemption payments. In structuring a redemption agreement, the shareholders must also be made aware that if the agreement is converted to a cross-purchase agreement, the transfer for value rules may have an impact.[149]

In the cross-purchase context, each stockholder would own life insurance on the others, which could be split-dollar insurance. The corporation cannot pay the policy premiums, lest the shareholder be taxed as having received a constructive dividend. The only solution is to have the corporation pay somewhat increased salaries, thereby making it possible for the taxpayer to purchase the insurance. Unless the shareholders own more or less equivalent holdings, and are insurable at more or less similar rates, problems of economics may arise. In particular, the insurance burden will be substantially unequal among shareholders.

When one stockholder dies, his estate will own policies on the lives of other stockholders. The policies could be surrendered for their cash value, if any, or sold to the remaining stockholders. Sale to a purchaser other than the insured will be a transfer for value. In situations where there are more than two shareholders, insurance-funded cross-purchase arrangements are administratively complex, even with the use of an insurance trust.

§ 52.07 SPECIAL PROBLEMS IN BUY–SELL AGREEMENTS

* * *

[3] Role of the Lawyer

Typically buy-sell agreements are prepared by an attorney representing the corporation and several, if not all, of the stockholders. Under the Code of Professional Responsibility, which still applies in most states, an attorney may represent clients with conflicting interests only if it is obvious that he can adequately represent the interest of each and if each consents after full disclosure.[165] At a minimum, clearly written disclosure to each party may be called for, particularly where minority interests are involved. This would be true even when the conflict appears more theoretical than actual because the restrictions and price formula apply to all shareholders. While fees may be a detriment, separate representation will protect the parties' separate interests, and the professionals.

* * *

---

149. See Ns. 140–143, supra, and accompanying text.

165. Model Code of Professional Responsibility E.C. 5–16.

NOTE

The preceding excerpt noted that one goal of shareholders entering into a buy-sell agreement is to establish the federal estate tax valuation of the stock in a closely held corporation. A decedent's gross estate generally includes all property held by the decedent at the time of death, valued either at the date of death or six months thereafter (the alternate valuation date).[1] In the case of unlisted stock, which cannot be valued by market quotations, fair market value is determined by taking into account a variety of factors, including the corporation's net worth, its earnings history and dividend-paying capacity, and the value of stock of publicly traded companies in the same line of business.[2] In the case of stock subject to an option or contract to purchase, such as a buy-sell agreement, the regulations provide that the option or contract may establish the value if the agreement represents a bona fide business arrangement and is not a device to pass the stock to the natural objects of the decedent's bounty for less than adequate and full consideration.[3] But if the decedent was free to dispose of the stock during his lifetime without price restrictions, "little weight" is given to the price set at death by the option or contract.[4] The courts agree that maintaining control of a closely held business constitutes a bona fide business purpose but they require a separate examination of whether a restriction or option constitutes a "testamentary device."[5]

In 1990, Congress provided statutory guidance for the valuation of property subject to an option or contract to purchase. Section 2703(a) provides that the value of any property for estate, gift and generation-skipping tax purposes, shall be determined without regard to (1) any option, agreement or other right to acquire or use property at a price less than the fair market value of the property, disregarding the option agreement or right, or (2) any restriction on the right to sell or use such property. Thus, under the general rule in Section 2703(a), the effect of a buy-sell agreement on valuation would be disregarded. Section 2703(b), however, provides an exception for any option, agreement, right or restriction which satisfies the standards of the regulations (bona fide business arrangement and not a testamentary device) and has terms "comparable to similar arrangements entered into by persons in an arm's length transaction." In adding this standard, Congress intended the taxpayer to show that the agreement was one that could have been obtained in an arm's length bargain with an unrelated party, considering such factors as the term of the agreement, the present value of the affected property, and its expected value at the time of exercise.[6] In noting that this standard would not be met "by showing

1. I.R.C. §§ 2031; 2032.

2. I.R.C. § 2031(b); Reg. § 20.2031–2(f) (2).

3. Reg. § 20.2031–2(h).

4. Id.

5. See, e.g., St. Louis County Bank v. United States, 674 F.2d 1207 (8th Cir.1982).

6. Senate Finance Committee Explanation of Revenue Provisions, 1991 Budget Reconciliation Bill (Oct. 13, 1990), 101st Cong., 2d Sess. 68 (1990).

isolated comparables but requires a demonstration of the general practice of unrelated parties," the Senate Finance Committee stated that expert testimony—e.g., by an appraiser familiar with the industry—would be evidence of such general practice.[7]

The addition of an "arm's length" standard should satisfy the Treasury's concern about the use of buy-sell agreements as a testamentary device. But the application of the standard remains unsettled, and drafters of buy-sell agreements still appear to have some flexibility in their use of valuation methodologies. The Conference Report accompanying the 1990 Act states that a buy-sell agreement should not be disregarded merely because its terms differ from those used by another similarly situated company.[8] Noting that general business practice may recognize more than one valuation methodology, even within the same industry, the conferees went on to state that "[i]n such situations, one of several generally accepted methodologies may satisfy the standard contained in the conference agreement."[9]

REVENUE RULING 69–608

1969–2 Cum.Bull. 42.

Advice has been requested as to the treatment for Federal income tax purposes of the redemption by a corporation of a retiring shareholder's stock where the remaining shareholder of the corporation has entered into a contract to purchase such stock.

Where the stock of a corporation is held by a small group of people, it is often considered necessary to the continuity of the corporation to have the individuals enter into agreements among themselves to provide for the disposition of the stock of the corporation in the event of the resignation, death, or incapacity of one of them. Such agreements are generally reciprocal among the shareholders and usually provide that on the resignation, death, or incapacity of one of the principal shareholders, the remaining shareholders will purchase his stock. Frequently such agreements are assigned to the corporation by the remaining shareholder and the corporation actually redeems its stock from the retiring shareholder.

Where a corporation redeems stock from a retiring shareholder, the fact that the corporation in purchasing the shares satisfies the continuing shareholder's executory contractual obligation to purchase the redeemed shares does not result in a distribution to the continuing shareholder provided that the continuing shareholder is not subject to an existing primary and unconditional obligation to perform the contract and that the corporation pays no more than fair market value for the stock redeemed.

On the other hand, if the continuing shareholder, at the time of the assignment to the corporation of his contract to purchase the retiring

---

7. Id.

8. H.Rep. No. 101–964, 101st Cong., 2d Sess. 157 (1990).

9. Id.

shareholder's stock, is subject to an unconditional obligation to purchase the retiring shareholder's stock, the satisfaction by the corporation of his obligation results in a constructive distribution to him. The constructive distribution is taxable as a distribution under section 301 of the Internal Revenue Code of 1954.

If the continuing shareholder assigns his stock purchase contract to the redeeming corporation prior to the time when he incurs a primary and unconditional obligation to pay for the shares of stock, no distribution to him will result. If, on the other hand, the assignment takes place after the time when the continuing shareholder is so obligated, a distribution to him will result. While a pre-existing obligation to perform in the future is a necessary element in establishing a distribution in this type of case, it is not until the obligor's duty to perform becomes unconditional that it can be said a primary and unconditional obligation arises.

The application of the above principles may be illustrated by the situations described below.

Situation 1

A and *B* are unrelated individuals who own all of the outstanding stock of corporation *X*. *A* and *B* enter into an agreement that provides in the event *B* leaves the employ of *X*, he will sell his *X* stock to *A* at a price fixed by the agreement. The agreement provides that within a specified number of days of *B*'s offer to sell, *A* will purchase at the price fixed by the agreement all of the *X* stock owned by *B*. *B* terminates his employment and tenders the *X* stock to *A*. Instead of purchasing the stock himself in accordance with the terms of the agreement, *A* causes *X* to assume the contract and to redeem its stock held by *B*. In this case, *A* had a primary and unconditional obligation to perform his contract with *B* at the time the contract was assigned to *X*. Therefore, the redemption by *X* of its stock held by *B* will result in a constructive distribution to *A*. See William J. and Georgia K. Sullivan v. United States of America, 244 F.Supp. 605 (1965), affirmed, 363 F.2d 724 (1966), certiorari denied, 387 U.S. 905 (1967), rehearing denied, 388 U.S. 924 (1967).

Situation 2

A and *B* are unrelated individuals who own all of the outstanding stock of corporation *X*. An agreement between them provides unconditionally that within ninety days of the death of either *A* or *B*, the survivor will purchase the decedent's stock of *X* from his estate. Following the death of *B*, *A* causes *X* to assume the contract and redeem the stock from *B*'s estate.

The assignment of the contract to *X* followed by the redemption by *X* of the stock owned by *B*'s estate will result in a constructive distribution to *A* because immediately on the death of *B*, *A* had a primary and unconditional obligation to perform the contract.

Situation 3

All of the stock of X corporation was owned by a trust that was to terminate in 1968. Individuals A and B were the beneficiaries of the trust. Since B was the trustee of the trust, he had exclusive management authority over X through his control of the board of directors. In 1966, A paid to B the sum of $25x$ dollars and promised to pay an additional $20x$ dollars to B in 1969 for B's interest in the corpus and accumulations of the trust plus B's agreement to resign immediately as supervisor of the trust and release his control over the management of the corporation. The actual transfer of the stock held in trust was to take place on termination of the trust in 1968. In 1969, X reimbursed A for the $25x$ dollars previously paid to B, paid $20x$ dollars to B, and received the X stock held by B.

For all practical purposes, A became the owner of B's shares in 1966. Although naked legal title to the shares could not be transferred until the trust terminated in 1968, B did transfer all of his beneficial and equitable ownership of the X stock to A in exchange for an immediate payment by A of $25x$ dollars and an unconditional promise to pay an additional $20x$ dollars upon termination of the trust. The payment by X of $20x$ dollars to B and $25x$ dollars to A in 1969 constituted a constructive distribution to A in the amount of $45x$ dollars. See Schalk Chemical Company v. Commissioner, 32 T.C. 879 (1959), affirmed 304 F.2d 48 (1962).

Situation 4

A and B owned all of the outstanding stock of X corporation. A and B entered into a contract under which, if B desired to sell his X stock, A agreed to purchase the stock or to cause such stock to be purchased. If B chose to sell his X stock to any person other than A, he could do so at any time. In accordance with the terms of the contract, A caused X to redeem all of B's stock in X.

At the time of the redemption, B was free to sell his stock to A or to any other person, and A had no unconditional obligation to purchase the stock and no fixed liability to pay for the stock. Accordingly, the redemption by X did not result in a constructive distribution to A. See S.K. Ames, Inc. v. Commissioner, 46 B.T.A. 1020 (1942), acquiescence, C.B. 1942–1, 1.

Situation 5

A and B owned all of the outstanding stock of X corporation. An agreement between A and B provided that upon the death of either, X will redeem all of the X stock owned by the decedent at the time of his death. In the event that X does not redeem the shares from the estate, the agreement provided that the surviving shareholder would purchase the unredeemed shares from the decedent's estate. B died and, in accordance with the agreement, X redeemed all of the shares owned by his estate.

In this case *A* was only secondarily liable under the agreement between *A* and *B*. Since *A* was not primarily obligated to purchase the *X* stock from the estate of *B*, he received no constructive distribution when *X* redeemed the stock.

Situation 6

B owned all of the outstanding stock of *X* corporation. *A* and *B* entered into an agreement under which *A* was to purchase all of the *X* stock from *B*. *A* did not contemplate purchasing the *X* stock in his own name. Therefore, the contract between *A* and *B* specifically provided that it could be assigned by *A* to a corporation and that, if the corporation agreed to be bound by the terms, *A* would be released from the contract.

A organized *Y* corporation and assigned the stock purchase contract to it. *Y* borrowed funds and purchased all of the *X* stock from *B* pursuant to the agreement. Subsequently *Y* was merged into *X* and *X* assumed the liabilities that *Y* incurred in connection with the purchase of the *X* stock and subsequently satisfied these liabilities.

The purchase by *Y* of the stock of *X* did not result in a constructive distribution to *A*. Since *A* did not contemplate purchasing the *X* stock in his own name, he provided in the contract that it could be assigned to a corporation prior to the closing date. *A* chose this latter alternative and assigned the contract to *Y*. *A* was not personally subject to an unconditional obligation to purchase the *X* stock from *B*. See Arthur J. Kobacker and Sara Jo Kobacker, et al. v. Commissioner, 37 T.C. 882 (1962), acquiescence, C.B. 1964 2, 6. Compare Ray Edenfield v. Commissioner, 19 T.C. 13 (1952), acquiescence, C.B. 1953–1, 4.

Situation 7

A and *B* owned all of the outstanding stock of *X* corporation. An agreement between the shareholders provided that upon the death of either, the survivor would purchase the decedent's shares from his estate at a price provided in the agreement. Subsequently, the agreement was rescinded and a new agreement entered into which provided that upon the death of either *A* or *B*, *X* would redeem all of the decedent's shares of *X* stock from his estate.

The cancellation of the original contract between the parties in favor of the new contract did not result in a constructive distribution to either *A* or *B*. At the time *X* agreed to purchase the stock pursuant to the terms of the new agreement, neither *A* nor *B* had an unconditional obligation to purchase shares of *X* stock. The subsequent redemption of the stock from the estate of either pursuant to the terms of the new agreement will not constitute a constructive distribution to the surviving shareholder.

PROBLEM

A, B and C, who are unrelated, each own one-third of Y Corporation's outstanding common stock. The shareholders have entered into a cross-purchase agreement under which they agree that the two surviving shareholders will purchase the Y stock owned by the estate of the first shareholder to die. Y purchased a life insurance policy on the life of each shareholder and has continued to pay the annual premiums. Y is the beneficiary under the policies. B died this year, and Y used the proceeds from the policy on B's life to completely redeem the stock held by B's estate. What will be the tax consequences of these events to A, C and Y?

3. CHARITABLE CONTRIBUTION AND REDEMPTION

GROVE v. COMMISSIONER *

United States Court of Appeals, Second Circuit, 1973.
490 F.2d 241.

KAUFMAN, Chief Judge:

We are called upon, once again, to wrestle with the tangled web that is the Internal Revenue Code and decipher the often intricate and ingenious strategies devised by taxpayers to minimize their tax burdens. We undertake this effort mindful that taxpayer ingenuity, although channelled into an effort to reduce or eliminate the incidence of taxation, is ground for neither legal nor moral opprobrium. As Learned Hand so eloquently stated, "any one may so arrange his affairs that his taxes shall be as low as possible: he is not bound to choose that pattern which will best pay the Treasury: there is not even a patriotic duty to increase one's taxes * * *." Helvering v. Gregory, 69 F.2d 809, 810 (2d Cir.1934), aff'd 293 U.S. 465, 55 S.Ct. 266, 79 L.Ed. 596 (1935).

* * *

I.

A full recitation of the undisputed facts underlying this controversy will aid in placing the legal issues raised on appeal in their proper context.

Philip Grove received an engineering degree in 1924 from Rensselaer Polytechnic Institute, a private, tax-exempt educational institution. During the Depression, he founded what is now Grove Shepherd Wilson & Kruge, Inc. and at all times since has controlled a majority of its shares. The balance of the Corporation's shares, with the exception of those held by RPI, are owned by officers and employees of the Corporation or their relatives.

---

* Some footnotes omitted.

The Corporation's business is building airfields, highways, tunnels, canals, and other similar heavy construction projects in both the United States and foreign countries. These projects usually involve the investment of large sums of money over an extended period of time and involve a high degree of risk. Since, in this industry, contract payments normally are made only after specified levels of progress are achieved, a firm must always commit substantial amounts of its own funds, whether borrowed or internally generated, to a project. Moreover, a company can determine an acceptable contract price based only on its best estimate of the cost to complete the project. A bad "guess" or unforeseen contingency may require a firm to complete a project while incurring a loss. Not surprisingly, the mortality rate in this industry is high. To protect against such adverse developments, successful firms seek to maintain liquidity by holding ample cash or other assets easily converted to cash. One method of conserving cash, adopted by the Corporation, is to retain all earnings and refrain from paying dividends.

As we have noted, RPI, like all universities and colleges, pursued its alumni with a wide variety of contribution plans. One plan employed "life income funds," and its terms were simple. An alumnus would make a gift of securities to RPI and retain a life interest in the income from the donated securities. Whatever dividends and interest were paid during the donor's life would belong to the donor, while any capital appreciation would inure to RPI. Upon the death of the donor, RPI would obtain full title to the securities.

In 1954, Dr. Livingston Houston, RPI's president, suggested to Grove that he make a gift under the "life income funds" plan. Grove explained that his only significant holdings were shares of his own corporation, but expressed a willingness to donate some of these shares under the plan, with certain qualifications. The Corporation, he stated, could not agree to any obligation or understanding to redeem shares held by RPI. This condition, of course, stemmed from a fear that RPI might seek redemption at a time when the Corporation was hard pressed for cash, which, as we have noted, was an asset crucial to a company in the heavy construction business. Moreover, since Grove at that time was unsure of RPI's money-management qualifications, he further conditioned his gift on a requirement that if RPI disposed of the shares, any proceeds would be invested and managed by an established professional firm.

RPI found these terms acceptable and on December 30, 1954, Grove made an initial gift of 200 shares, valued at $25,560. A letter accompanying the donation set forth the conditions we have recited. Moreover, in addition to retaining an interest in the income from the gift for his life, Grove specified that in the event he should predecease his wife Harriet, she would receive the income until her death.

On the same day, the Corporation and RPI signed a minority shareholder agreement. RPI agreed not to "sell, transfer, give, pledge

L., S., L. & R. Corp. Tax. 3rd Ed. UCB—12

or hypothecate, or in any way dispose of the whole or any part of the common stock of the Corporation now or hereafter owned * * * until [RPI] shall have first offered the Corporation the opportunity to purchase said shares upon the terms and conditions hereinafter provided." The redemption price was established at book value of the shares as noted on the Corporation's most recent certified financial statement prior to the offer. Pursuant to the contract, the Corporation was "entitled (but not obligated) to purchase all or any part of the shares of stock so offered." If the Corporation did not exercise its option to purchase within sixty days, RPI could transfer the shares to any other party and the Corporation's right of first refusal would not subsequently attach to such transferred shares.[3]

The 1954 gift was the first in a series of annual contributions to RPI by Grove. From 1954 to 1968, Grove donated to RPI between 165 and 250 shares of the Corporation each year, reaching a cumulative total of 2,652 shares, subject to terms substantially similar to those noted earlier.

Generally, RPI offered donated shares to the Corporation for redemption, between one and two years after they were donated by Grove. The transactions followed a similar pattern. On each occasion, the Finance Committee of RPI's Board of Trustees first authorized the sale of specific shares of the Corporation. RPI's treasurer or controller would then write to Sidney Houck, the Corporation's treasurer, informing him of RPI's desire to dispose of the shares. Upon receipt of this letter, Houck would call a special meeting of the Corporation's board of directors to consider whether or not to exercise the Corporation's right of first refusal. The Board would adopt a resolution authorizing redemption and Houck would so inform RPI's financial officer, enclosing a company check for the amount due. By return mail, RPI would forward the appropriate stock certificate to the Corporation for cancellation.

At the time of the first redemption, in December, 1955, RPI opened an investment account at the Albany, New York, office of Merrill Lynch, Pierce, Fenner & Beane ("Merrill Lynch"). The account was captioned "Rensselaer Polytechnic Institute (Philip H. Grove Fund) Account." In accordance with Grove's wishes concerning the management of disposition proceeds, RPI authorized Merrill Lynch to act directly upon investment recommendations made by Scudder, Stevens, & Clark, Grove's personal investment adviser. RPI deposited the proceeds of each redemption transaction into this account which, pursuant to Scudder, Stevens & Clark's instructions, were generally invested in securities of large corporations whose shares traded on organized stock exchanges. Merrill Lynch paid the income from these investments to RPI on a monthly basis. RPI, in turn, made quarterly

3. Other minority shareholders of the Corporation signed similar agreements, which, in effect put in writing the Corporation's practice of redeeming, when financial conditions permitted, any minority-owner shares offered to it, for example, by a departing employee or a deceased employee's widow.

remittances to Grove, accompanied by an analysis of all account transactions.

On his personal income tax return for 1963, Grove reported as taxable income dividends of $4,939.28 and interest of $2,535.73 paid to him by RPI from the Merrill Lynch account. For 1964, Grove reported $6,096.05 in dividends and $3,540.81 in interest. The Commissioner, however, assessed deficiencies in Grove's taxable income for these years, asserting that Grove "realized additional dividends in the amounts of $29,000 and $25,800 in 1963 and 1964, respectively, as the result of the redemption of stock by Grove Shepherd Wilson & Kruge, Inc." Accordingly, the Commissioner increased Grove's taxable income by these amounts and demanded payment of additional taxes—in excess of $13,000—for each year. Grove refused to pay and petitioned the Tax Court for a redetermination of his tax liability. The Court, concluding that Grove had made a bona fide gift to RPI, ruled in favor of the taxpayer and the Commissioner appealed.

II.

The Commissioner's view of this case is relatively simple. In essence, we are urged to disregard the actual form of the Grove-RPI-Corporation donations and redemptions and to rewrite the actual events so that Grove's tax liability is seen in a wholly different light. Support for this position, it is argued, flows from the Supreme Court's decision in Commissioner of Internal Revenue v. Court Holding Co., 324 U.S. 331, 65 S.Ct. 707, 89 L.Ed. 981 (1945), which, in language familiar to law students, cautions that "[t]he incidence of taxation depends upon the substance of a transaction * * *. To permit the true nature of a transaction to be disguised by mere formalisms, which exist solely to alter tax liabilities, would seriously impair the effective administration of the tax policies of Congress." Id. at 334, 65 S.Ct. at 708. In an effort to bring the instant case within this language, the Commissioner insists that whatever the appearance of the transactions here under consideration, their "true nature" is quite different. He maintains that Grove, with the cooperation of RPI, withdrew substantial funds from the Corporation and manipulated them in a manner designed to produce income for his benefit. In the Commissioner's view, the transaction is properly characterized as a redemption by the Corporation of Grove's, not RIP's shares, followed by a cash gift to RPI by Grove. This result, it is said, more accurately reflects "economic reality."

The Commissioner's motives for insisting upon this formulation are easily understood once its tax consequences are examined. Although Grove reported taxable dividends and interest received from the Merrill Lynch account on his 1963 and 1964 tax returns, amounts paid by the Corporation to redeem the donated shares from RPI were not taxed upon distribution. If, however, the transactions are viewed in the manner suggested by the Commissioner, the redemption proceeds would be taxable as income to Grove. Moreover, because the redemptions did

not in substance alter Grove's relationship to the Corporation—he
continued throughout to control a majority of the outstanding shares—
the entire proceeds would be taxed as a dividend payment at high,
progressive ordinary-income rates, rather than as a sale of shares, at
the fixed, and relatively low, capital gains rate. See, 26 U.S.C. § 302;
United States v. Davis, 397 U.S. 301, 90 S.Ct. 1041, 25 L.Ed.2d 323
(1970).

Clearly, then, the stakes involved are high. We do not quarrel
with the maxim that substance must prevail over form, but this
proposition marks the beginning, not the end, of our inquiry. The
court in Sheppard v. United States, 361 F.2d 972, 176 Ct.Cl. 244 (1966)
perceptively remarked that "all such 'maxims' should rather be called
'minims' since they convey a minimum of information with a maximum
of pretense." Id. at 977 n. 9. Each case requires detailed consideration
of its unique facts. Here, our aim is to determine whether Grove's gifts
of the Corporation's shares to RPI prior to redemption should be given
independent significance or whether they should be regarded as meaningless intervening steps in a single, integrated transaction designed to
avoid tax liability by the use of mere formalisms.

The guideposts for our analysis are well marked by earlier judicial
encounters with this problem. "The law with respect to gifts of
appreciated property is well established. A gift of appreciated property
does not result in income to the donor so long as he gives the property
away absolutely and parts with title thereto before the property gives
rise to income by way of sale." Carrington v. Commissioner of Internal
Revenue, 476 F.2d 704, 708 (5th Cir.1973), *quoting* Humacid Co., 42 T.C.
894, 913 (1964). As noted below by the Tax Court, the Commissioner
here "does not contend that the gifts of stock by [Grove] to RPI in 1961
and 1962 were sham transactions, or that they were not completed gifts
when made." If Grove made a valid, binding, and irrevocable gift of
the Corporation's shares to RPI, it would be the purest fiction to treat
the redemption proceeds as having actually been received by Grove.
The Tax Court concluded that the gift was complete and irrevocable
when made. The Commissioner conceded as much and we so find.[9]

It is argued, however, that notwithstanding the conceded validity of
the gifts, other circumstances establish that Grove employed RPI merely as a convenient conduit for withdrawing funds from the Corporation
for his personal use without incurring tax liability. The Commissioner
would have us infer from the systematic nature of the gift-redemption
cycle that Grove and RPI reached a mutually beneficial understanding:
RPI would permit Grove to use its tax-exempt status to drain funds

9. The Commissioner might have argued that at least that portion of the redemption proceeds allocable to Grove's retained life income interest was taxable as a
dividend. He chose not to do so and the
Tax Court "express[ed] no opinion upon the
question, if it were properly presented,
whether petitioner derived taxable income
upon the redemption of stock to the extent
of the life estate which he retained
* * *." Since the Commissioner has by-
passed this aspect, it would be inappropriate in our discussions of the gifts to attach
any special significance to the retained life
interest feature.

from the Corporation in return for a donation of a future interest in such funds.

We are not persuaded by this argument and the totality of the facts and circumstances lead us to a contrary conclusion. Grove testified before the Tax Court concerning the circumstances of these gifts. The court, based on the evidence and the witnesses' credibility, specifically found that "[t]here was no informal agreement between [Grove] and RPI that RPI would offer the stock in question to the corporation for redemption or that, if offered, the corporation would redeem it." Findings of fact by the Tax Court, like those of the district court, are binding upon us unless they are clearly erroneous, 26 U.S.C. § 7482(a); Rule 52, F.R.Civ.P., and "the rule * * * applies also to factual inferences [drawn] from undisputed basic facts." Commissioner of Internal Revenue v. Duberstein, 363 U.S. 278, 291, 80 S.Ct. 1190, 1200, 4 L.Ed.2d 1218 (1960). It cannot seriously be contended that the Tax Court's findings here are "clearly erroneous" and no tax liability can be predicated upon a nonexistent agreement between Grove and RPI or by a fictional one created by the Commissioner.

Grove, of course, owned a substantial majority of the Corporation's shares. His vote alone was sufficient to insure redemption of any shares offered by RPI. But such considerations, without more, are insufficient to permit the Commissioner to ride roughshod over the actual understanding found by the Tax Court to exist between the donor and the donee. Behrend v. United States (4th Cir.1972), 73–1 USTC ¶ 9123, is particularly instructive. There, two brothers donated preferred shares of a corporation jointly controlled by them to a charitable foundation over which they also exercised control. The preferred shares were subsequently redeemed from the foundation by the corporation and the Commissioner sought to tax the redemption as a corporate dividend payment to the brothers. The court, in denying liability, concluded that although "it was understood that the corporation would at intervals take up the preferred according to its financial ability * * *, this factor did not convert into a constructive dividend the proceeds of the redemption * * * [because] the gifts were absolutely perfected before the corporation redeemed the stock." Id.

Nothing in the December, 1954, minority shareholder agreement between the Corporation and RPI serves as a basis for disturbing the conclusion of the Tax Court. Although the Corporation desired a right of first refusal on minority shares—understandably so, in order to reduce the possibility of unrelated, outside ownership interests—it assumed no obligation to redeem any shares so offered. In the absence of such an obligation, the Commissioner's contention that Grove's initial donation was only the first step in a prearranged series of transactions is little more than wishful thinking grounded in a shaky foundation. * * *

We are not so naive as to believe that tax considerations played no role in Grove's planning. But foresight and planning do not transform a non-taxable event into one that is taxable. Were we to adopt the Commissioner's view, we would be required to recast two actual transactions—a gift by Grove to RPI and a redemption from RPI by the Corporation—into two completely fictional transactions—a redemption from Grove by the Corporation and a gift by Grove to RPI. Based upon the facts as found by the Tax Court, we can discover no basis for elevating the Commissioner's "form" over that employed by the taxpayer in good faith. "Useful as the step transaction doctrine may be in the interpretation of equivocal contracts and ambiguous events, it cannot generate events which never took place just so an additional tax liability might be asserted." Sheppard v. United States, supra, at 978. In the absence of any supporting facts in the record we are unable to adopt the Commissioner's view; to do so would be to engage in a process of decision that is arbitrary, capricious and ultimately destructive of traditional notions of judicial review. We decline to embark on such a course.

Accordingly, the judgment of the Tax Court is affirmed.

OAKES, Circuit Judge (dissenting):

Review of the tax consequences of a business transaction requires consideration of the economic realities of the entire transaction. See Gregory v. Helvering, 293 U.S. 465, 55 S.Ct. 266, 79 L.Ed. 596 (1935); South Bay Corp. v. Commissioner of Internal Revenue, 345 F.2d 698, 703, 705 (2d Cir.1965). Whether a transaction should be viewed as two or more steps or as one integrated transaction may result in entirely different tax consequences. * * *

Here, as I see it, the form of the transaction was two-step: a gift of stock followed by a redemption of the stock by the donor controlled corporation. The substance of the transaction, however, was a payment out of corporate earnings and profits to a charity designated by the donor who retained a life interest in the gift.

The factors which distinguish the RPI-Grove transactions from other charitable donations of securities and which persuade me to treat this as an integrated transaction are two: first, the gifts made by the Groves were of stock in a closed corporation that was inevitably redeemed annually; second, by virtue of retaining a life income from the reinvested proceeds and by retaining a measure of control over how those proceeds should be reinvested (by designating the investment adviser who was also the Groves' personal adviser), the Groves were able to achieve a bail-out from their non-dividend-paying closed corporation.

* * *

The majority opinion relies heavily on two cases which I believe are readily distinguishable from the situation here. One is Carrington v. Commissioner of Internal Revenue, 476 F.2d 704 (5th Cir.1973), relied on for the proposition that "[a] gift of appreciated property does not result in income to the donor so long as he gives the property away absolutely and parts with title before the property gives rise to income by way of sale." Here the Groves did *not* part with all interest in the construction company stock. The reservation of a life interest in the stock (or its reinvested proceeds), when coupled with taxpayer's right, however indirect, to direct the manner in which proceeds would be invested, gave the Groves a very great continuing interest and control, a fact of not inconsiderable tax significance. Cf. Corliss v. Bowers, 281 U.S. 376, 378, 50 S.Ct. 336, 74 L.Ed. 916 (1930) (Holmes, J.) ("taxation is not so much concerned with the refinements of title as it is with actual command over the property taxed. * * *"). More importantly, *Carrington* involved only one contribution of stock and one redemption; there was no pattern of redemption of stock as was clearly established here at least by the time of the tax years in question.

In Behrend v. United States, CCH 1973 Stand.Fed.Tax Rep. ¶ 9123 (4th Cir.1972), also relied upon by the majority, the proceeds of the redemption were used wholly for the benefit of the charitable foundation which was the recipient of the stock; there was no life estate reserved for the personal benefit of the donors. See 1973 Stand.Fed. Tax Rep. ¶ 9123 at 80,067 ("[P]redominant force" in *Behrend* decision is "indisputable fact" that the taxpayers therein "did not participate whatsoever in the beneficence of the foundation").

Thus, I believe that when, as here, the nature and conditions of the charitable gift and the pattern of donor-charity behavior are such as to make it for all practical purposes inevitable that the stock given will be offered for redemption and accepted by the closely held corporation, resulting in providing the equivalent of a safe pension fund for the donor stockholders, then the transaction must be treated as a distribution of dividends under §§ 301(a), 301(c) and 316(a) of the Internal Revenue Code of 1954. The majority opinion refers to an "absence of any supporting facts in the record" for the Commissioner's position, but omits to rely upon the one most important fact on which the case should turn: the *pattern of redemption* over years of giving. I accordingly dissent.

NOTE

The *Grove* case is an example of an effective charitable giving technique for the shareholders of a closely held corporation. After losing several similar cases, the Service stopped challenging "charitable bailouts," announcing in Revenue Ruling 78–197 [1] that a charitable contribution of stock followed by a redemption would be treated as a dividend to the donor only if the donee is legally bound or can be compelled by the corporation to surrender the shares for redemption.[2]

1. 1978–1 C.B. 83.

2. See also Palmer v. Commissioner, 62 T.C. 684 (1974), affirmed on another issue 523 F.2d 1308 (8th Cir.1975), where the gift was made to a private foundation controlled by the taxpayer. The Service, however, may continue to challenge transactions where the donated property is later reacquired by the donor, or where the charity uses the redemption proceeds to acquire other property from the donor, pursuant to an informal prearranged understanding. See Blake v. Commissioner, 697 F.2d 473 (2d Cir. 1982).

Although they may not be *bound* to do so, most charities will be highly motivated to offer the shares for redemption in order to convert the stock into a more liquid, and perhaps higher yielding investment.

One desirable aspect of the transaction in *Grove* was Mr. Grove's ability to retain a life income interest in a diversified portfolio managed by his personal investment advisor. This format is no longer available to the philanthropic shareholder unless certain additional requirements are met. In general, a donor who wishes to retain a life income interest in contributed property does not qualify for charitable income and gift tax deductions unless the gift is made to a qualified charitable remainder annuity trust or unitrust or a pooled income fund.[3]

The Tax Reform Act of 1986 did not directly curtailed the effectiveness of "charitable bailouts," but two changes may reduce the tax savings from gifts of appreciated stock. First, the individual rate reductions increase the after-tax cost of charitable giving to most taxpayers and, second, the amount of "untaxed appreciation" in donated property is now treated as a preference item for purposes of the alternative minimum tax.[4]

PROBLEM

Philanthropist ("P") owns 25,000 shares of Family Corporation. The fair market value of P's Family stock is $2,500,000 ($100 per share); P's basis is $25,000 ($1 per share). Family has 100,000 shares of common stock (its only class) outstanding; the remaining shares are owned by P's spouse and children. Family has ample accumulated earnings and profits. The Family bylaws require all shareholders to grant the corporation a right of first refusal to buy their stock at fair market value before the shares are offered for sale to an outsider, but the corporation is not required to redeem the stock.

On the occasion of his 25th college reunion, P wishes to make a $100,000 contribution to State University ("SU"). Consider the tax consequences of the following alternative plans:

   (a) Family Corporation distributes $100,000 to P in redemption of 1,000 shares of stock. P then contributes $100,000 to SU.

   (b) P contributes 1,000 shares of Family stock to SU. Two months later, pursuant to an oral understanding, Family distributes $100,000 to SU in redemption of its 1,000 shares. SU was not legally obligated to surrender the shares for redemption.

   (c) Same as (b), above, except that P contributes 250 shares of Family stock to SU in each of the four years following his reunion. (Assume that the value of the stock was $100 per share throughout this period.) Two months after each contribution, Family distributes $25,000 to SU in redemption of the 250 shares.

3. See I.R.C. §§ 170(f)(2), (3), 664;   4. See I.R.C. §§ 1; 57(a)(6).
2522(c)(2).

G. REDEMPTIONS THROUGH RELATED
CORPORATIONS

Code: § 304 (except § 304(b)(3)(C), (D), (b)(4)).

Regulations: § 1.304–2(a), (c) Examples (1), (3) and (4).

Section 304 is an intricate statutory watchdog designed to prevent an end run around Sections 301 and 302. Despite its complexity, the basic purpose of Section 304—to prevent bailouts of corporate earnings at capital gains rates—can be illustrated by a simple example. Assume that Shareholder A owns all of the common stock (the only class outstanding) of X Corporation and Y Corporation, and both corporations have ample earnings and profits. Having read the *Davis* case, A knows that a redemption of either her X or Y stock will result in a dividend. But what if A sells some of her X shares to Y or vice versa? Because this is a "sale" rather than a redemption or a distribution, A hopes to extract cash while enjoying exchange treatment, but in substance A's "sale" is indistinguishable from a dividend. Section 304 ensures this result by requiring shareholder sales involving "brother-sister" and "parent-subsidiary" corporations to satisfy one of the tests in Section 302 in order to qualify for capital gain status and recovery of basis.

Brother-Sister Acquisitions. Section 304(a)(1) applies when one or more persons who are in "control" of each of two corporations transfer stock of one corporation (the "issuing corporation") to the other (the "acquiring corporation") in exchange for cash or other property.[1] "Control" for this purpose is defined as at least 50 percent ownership of either the corporate voting power or of the total value of all classes of stock.[2]

If Section 304(a)(1) applies, Congress devised an ingenious method to test the "sale" for dividend equivalence. Returning to the example, when A sells X Corporation stock to Y Corporation for cash, she is treated as having received a distribution of cash in redemption of Y stock.[3] The hypothetical redemption is then tested under Section 302(b) standards to determine whether A may treat the transaction as an exchange. Dividend equivalence is tested by reference to A's stock

---

1. For this purpose, "property" does not include stock of the acquiring corporation. I.R.C. § 317(a). See Bhada v. Commissioner, 892 F.2d 39 (6th Cir.1989).

2. I.R.C. § 304(c)(1). In determining control, the Section 318 attribution rules are applicable with certain modifications relating to shareholder-corporation attribution. I.R.C. § 304(c)(3). In the case of a corporation with more than one class of stock, the value prong of the "control" test is applied to the aggregate value of all classes of stock, not class-by-class. Rev.Rul. 89–57, 1989–1 C.B. 90. Thus, a shareholder who owns 50 percent or more of the value of all the corporation's stock has "control" even if that shareholder owns less than 50 percent of a particular class.

3. To the extent that the distribution is treated as a distribution to which Section 301 applies, A will be treated as having made a capital contribution of X stock to Y. I.R.C. § 304(a)(1). If the distribution is treated as an exchange under Section 302(a), Y (the acquiring corporation) will be treated as purchasing the stock of X (the issuing corporation). See S. Rep. No. 99–313, 99th Cong., 2d Sess. 1048 (1986).

ownership of X (the "issuing corporation"—i.e., the company whose stock is sold) before and after the transaction.[4]

In the example, A owned 100 percent of the X stock before the sale to Y. After the sale, A continued to own 100 percent of the stock directly and constructively by virtue of her ownership of Y. Since the sale does not reduce A's interest in X, it fails to satisfy any of the Section 302(b) tests for exchange treatment and thus will be treated as a Section 301 distribution from Y to A. In determining the amount of the distribution that is a dividend, Section 304(b)(2) requires the transaction to be treated as a dividend to A by Y (the "acquiring corporation") to the extent of its earnings and profits and then by X (the "issuing corporation") to the extent of its earnings and profits. Thus, the earnings and profits of both corporations are available to characterize the distribution to A as a dividend.[5]

Parent-Subsidiary Acquisitions. Section 304(a)(2) applies similar principles when a subsidiary acquires stock of its parent from a shareholder of the parent. The parent-subsidiary relationship is defined by the same 50 percent "control" test described above.[6] The transaction is treated as a distribution in redemption of the parent's stock for purposes of testing dividend equivalency under Section 302.[7] If the redemption fails to qualify as an exchange and thus is treated as a Section 301 distribution, the earnings and profits of both the parent and the subsidiary are available to characterize the distribution as a dividend.[8]

If a transaction subject to Section 304 is both a brother-sister and a parent-subsidiary acquisition, the parent-subsidiary rules take precedence.[9] But because the attribution rules transform most actual brother and sister corporations into constructive parents and subsidiaries, the regulations provide that an actual brother-sister acquisition remains subject to Section 304(a)(1).[10]

Collateral Tax Consequences. The regulations prescribe the basis consequences of transactions governed by Section 304. In the basic brother-sister acquisition example, A's sale of X Corporation stock to Y Corporation is treated as a Section 301 distribution from Y to A, and A is treated as having made a capital contribution of X Corporation stock to Y Corporation.[11] The basis in A's Y Corporation stock is thus increased by the basis of the X Corporation stock that A contributed to Y.[12] A's basis in the Y Corporation stock, which was increased by the basis of the transferred X stock, is decreased only if part of the distribution is applied against the Y stock's basis under Section

---

4. I.R.C. § 304(b)(1). Once again, modified Section 318 attribution rules apply in measuring the effect of this hypothetical transaction on A's interest in X.

5. I.R.C. § 304(b)(2).

6. I.R.C. § 304(c)(1).

7. I.R.C. § 304(b)(1).

8. I.R.C. § 304(b)(2).

9. I.R.C. § 304(a)(1).

10. Reg. § 1.304–2(c) Example (1).

11. I.R.C. § 304(a)(1); Reg. § 1.304–2(a).

12. Reg. § 1.304–2(a).

301(c)(2).[13] Finally, in keeping with the capital contribution treatment of the stock acquisition, Y Corporation takes a transferred basis from A under Section 362(a) in the X Corporation stock that it acquires.[14] The reduction in earnings and profits resulting from the dividend logically should follow the ordering rules in Section 304(b)(2)—i.e., first reduce the acquiring corporation's earnings and profits insofar as they are the source of the dividend and then, if necessary, reduce the issuing corporation's earnings and profits.

If A's sale of X Corporation stock to Y Corporation is treated as an exchange under Section 302(a), A is treated as selling Y stock (i.e., stock of the acquiring corporation) with a basis equal to the basis of the transferred X stock. As with any conventional sale or exchange, the basis of the stock that is sold is fully recovered (and thus goes away), and A's basis in her Y stock returns to what it was before the transaction.[15] In this situation, Y Corporation is treated as having purchased the X stock (rather than having received it as a capital contribution) and it thus takes a cost basis under Section 1012.

In the brother-sister exchange scenario, any earnings and profits reduction is limited by Section 312(n)(7) to an amount not in excess of the redeemed stock's ratable share of earnings and profits.[16] The more difficult question is *which* corporation's earnings and profits? The Code and regulations are silent on this technical teaser. Possibilities include the acquiring corporation's (the transaction is treated as a constructive redemption of acquiring corporation stock and the distributed "property" comes from that entity), the issuing corporation's (the redemption is tested by reference to its stock), or neither (the transaction is simply a purchase, not a reduction of either corporation's wealth).[17]

The collateral tax consequences of a parent-subsidiary acquisition are even less settled. If the constructive redemption of the parent's stock is treated as a dividend, the selling shareholder's basis in the parent stock transferred to the subsidiary is added to the basis in the shareholder's remaining parent stock.[18] The subsidiary apparently takes a cost basis in the parent stock that it acquires.[19] Once again tracking Section 304(b)(2), it is logical to first reduce the acquiring subsidiary's earnings and profits to the extent they are the source of

---

13. Id. This would be the case if the distribution were not a dividend because of the absence of earnings and profits. If the shareholder no longer actually owns any shares but is nonetheless taxed under Section 301 (e.g., because of the attribution rules in Section 318), the basis in the surrendered shares is transferred to the stock owned by the related party. See Reg. § 1.304–2(c) Example (2).

14. Reg. § 1.304–2(a).

15. Reg. § 1.302–2(a).

16. See Section E2 of this Chapter, supra.

17. See Bittker & Eustice, Federal Income Taxation of Corporations and Shareholders (1990 Supp. to 5th ed., 1987) ¶ 9.35.

18. Reg. § 1.304–3(a). If the selling shareholder does not directly own any more parent stock after the transfer, his basis apparently disappears. Cf. Rev.Rul. 70–496, 1970–2 C.B. 74.

19. Cf. Rev.Rul. 80–189, 1980–2 C.B. 106; Broadview Lumber Co. v. United States, 561 F.2d 698 (7th Cir.1977).

the dividend and then move on to reduce the parent's earnings and profits. If the redemption is treated as an exchange, the selling shareholder recovers his basis in the transferred parent stock and recognizes capital gain or loss under normal tax principles. The subsidiary most likely takes a cost basis in the acquired parent stock. If the constructive redemption is treated as an exchange, Section 312(n) (7) again may apply, but it is unclear which corporation's earnings and profits are reduced.

Coordination with Section 351. Enactment of an intricate statute such as Section 304 inevitably whets the appetite of tax lawyers. Consider, for example, the sole shareholder of a profitable company with a desire for cash and a distaste for dividends. Assume that the shareholder borrows against his stock for valid business reasons and then contributes the stock to a newly formed holding company in exchange for the holding company's stock plus its assumption of the shareholder's liability. Or assume that the shareholder transferred all the stock of the operating company to a wholly owned holding company in exchange for additional stock of the holding company plus cash. Are the tax consequences of these transactions determined under Section 351? Or should they be governed by Section 304? Prior to 1982, the courts disagreed on which provision should control in these overlap situations.[20]

In a commendable effort to strengthen the anti-bailout objectives of Section 304, Congress settled the overlap issue in the Tax Equity and Responsibility Act of 1982 by providing that Section 304 generally will take precedence.[21] The Joint Committee on Taxation explained the amendment as follows: [22]

> The Act extends the anti-bailout rules of sections 304 * * * to the use of corporations, including holding companies, formed or availed of to avoid such rules. Such rules are made applicable to a transaction that otherwise qualifies as a tax-free incorporation under section 351.
>
> Section 351 generally will not apply to transactions described in section 304. Thus, section 351, if otherwise applicable, will generally apply only to the extent such transaction consists of an exchange of stock for stock in the acquiring corporation. However, section 304 will not apply to debt incurred to acquire the stock of an operating company and assumed by a controlled corporation acquiring the stock since assumption of such debt is an alternative to a debt-financed direct acquisition by the acquiring company. This exception

20. Compare Gunther v. Commissioner, 92 T.C. 39 (1989), affirmed 909 F.2d 291 (7th Cir.1990); Commissioner v. Haserot, 355 F.2d 200 (6th Cir.1965) and Haserot v. Commissioner, 46 T.C. 864 (1966), affirmed sub nom. Commissioner v. Stickney, 399 F.2d 828 (6th Cir.1968) with Coates Trust v. Commissioner, 480 F.2d 468 (9th Cir.1973), cert. denied 414 U.S. 1045, 94 S.Ct. 551 (1973).

21. I.R.C. § 304(b)(3).

22. Staff of Joint Committee on Taxation, General Explanation of Tax Equity and Fiscal Responsibility Act of 1982, 98th Cong., 2d Sess. 142–43 (1982).

for acquisition indebtedness applies to an extension, renewal, or refinancing of such indebtedness. The provisions of section 357 (other than sec. 357(b)) and Section 358 apply to such acquisition indebtedness provided they would be applicable to such transaction without regard to section 304. In applying these rules, indebtedness includes debt to which the stock is subject as well as debt assumed by the acquiring company.

*   *   *

NIEDERMEYER v. COMMISSIONER *

United States Tax Court, 1974.
62 T.C. 280, affirmed per curiam 535 F.2d 500 (9th Cir.1976), cert. denied 429 U.S. 500, 97 S.Ct. 528 (1976).

STERRETT, Judge: *   *   *

[In 1966, the taxpayers, Bernard and Tessie Niedermeyer, owned 22.58% of the common stock of American Timber & Trading Co., Inc. ("AT & T"). They also owned 125 of the 2,136 outstanding shares of AT & T preferred stock. Two of the taxpayers' sons, Bernard, Jr. and Walter, owned 67.91% of the common stock of AT & T.

Lents Industries ("Lents") was another corporation controlled by the Niedermeyer family. In 1966, the taxpayers and their sons, Bernard, Jr. and Walter, did not own any stock of Lents, but three other sons (Ed, Linus and Thomas) each owned 22⅓% of the Lents common stock.

On September 8, 1966, the taxpayers sold their AT & T stock to Lents for $174,975.12, but they retained all their preferred stock until December 28, 1966, when they contributed the preferred to a family foundation. After this contribution, the taxpayers ceased to have any interest in AT & T. Since the time of their sale of AT & T common stock, neither of the taxpayers was an officer, director or employee of the company.

The Niedermeyer family had long been active in the business of manufacturing special wood products in Oregon. During 1963, a family dispute arose between Bernard, Jr. and his brothers, Ed, Linus and Thomas. The brothers had been partners in Niedermeyer-Martin Co., another wood product enterprise, but the dispute caused the partnership to incorporate. During the mid-1960's, Bernard, Jr., as controlling shareholder of AT & T, refused to allow AT & T to do any business with Niedermeyer-Martin Co., which became a competitor. The acquisition by Lents of the taxpayers' common stock in AT & T was part of an effort by Ed, Linus and Thomas Niedermeyer to gain control of AT & T.

On their joint federal income tax return for 1966, the taxpayers reported a long-term capital gain of $168,321.58 on the sale of their AT & T common stock to Lents. The Commissioner determined that the entire proceeds of the sale were taxable as ordinary income because the

* Some footnotes omitted.

transaction was covered by Section 304(a) and was essentially equivalent to a dividend. Ed.]

OPINION

The ultimate question to be decided in this case is whether petitioners realized a capital gain or received a dividend on the sale of their AT & T common stock to Lents in 1966. The resolution of this question depends on whether the sale in question was a redemption through the use of a related corporation under the provisions of section 304(a)(1) and, if so, whether the distribution by Lents to petitioners is to be treated as in exchange for the redeemed stock under the provisions of section 302(a) or as of property to which section 301 applies.

Section 304(a)(1) provides, in pertinent part, that, if one or more persons are in "control" of each of two corporations and if one of those corporations acquires stock in the other corporation from the person or persons in control, then the transaction shall be treated as a distribution in redemption for purposes of section 302. Section 304(c)(1) defines the term "control" as "the ownership of stock possessing at least 50 percent of the total combined voting power of all classes of stock entitled to vote, or at least 50 percent of the total value of shares of all classes of stock." Section 304(c)(2) then states that the constructive ownership of stock rules contained in section 318(a) shall apply for the purpose of determining "control," except that the 50-percent limitations of sections 318(a)(2)(C) and 318(a)(3)(C) shall be disregarded for such purpose.

It is clear that by its terms section 304(a)(1) applies to the factual situation of this case. Prior to the transaction here in question, petitioners, husband and wife, together actually owned 1,083.117 shares out of the 4,803.083 outstanding shares of AT & T common stock, its only class of stock entitled to vote. Two of petitioners' sons owned 3,263.072 shares. Thus a total of 4,346.189 shares, or 90.49 percent, of the outstanding voting stock of AT & T was actually or constructively owned by petitioners. Three of petitioners' other sons owned 48 out of 72 shares, or 67 percent, of the outstanding stock of Lents, the ownership of such stock being constructively attributable to petitioners. Consequently, under section 304(c)(1), either petitioner, or both, are regarded as the person or persons in control of both AT & T and Lents prior to the transaction in question. Accordingly, under section 304(a)(1) the transaction in which Lents acquired petitioners' AT & T common stock must be treated as a redemption. The fact that neither petitioner actually owned stock in the acquiring corporation is of no concern here. * * *

Petitioners object to the applicability of section 304 on the ground that the attribution rules of section 318(a) should not be applied in this case. They base this position upon what they term the "bad blood" exception to the attribution rules as applied in Estate of Arthur H. Squier, 35 T.C. 950 (1961). In *Squier,* a case under section 302 involving the question of whether a distribution was essentially equivalent to a dividend, this Court decided that, based in part on a "sharp cleavage" between the executor of the taxpayer estate and members of the Squier family, and notwithstanding the attribution rules, the redemption in fact resulted in a crucial reduction of the estate's control over the corporation. The Court held that the distribution there was not essentially equivalent to a dividend and implicit in this conclusion was the belief that the attribution rules were not conclusive in all events in determining whether there had been a significant change of control which would allow the conclusion that the distribution was not essentially equivalent to a dividend. We note that in Robin Haft Trust, 61 T.C. 398 (1973), this Court decided that, in light of United States v. Davis, 397 U.S. 301 (1970), the rationale of *Squier* was no longer applicable to section 302(b)(1).

Besides here, as was not the case with *Squier,* no evidence was adduced to show that there were any disputes or cleavage between petitioners and any of their sons. The falling out was apparently between petitioners' sons. Apparently, petitioners would have us infer from the disagreements between Bernard E. Niedermeyer, Jr., majority shareholder of AT & T, and three other of their sons, who together were majority shareholders of Lents, that petitioners did not in fact control either corporation. We are unwilling to make this assumption and consequently petitioners' argument fails on its facts.

Moreover, we are of the opinion that the "control" test of sections 304(a)(1) and 304(c) requires that the attribution rules be applied in every case. Congress expressly indicated that the attribution rules of section 318 are to be applied in determining "control" for section 304 purposes. Section 304(c)(2) states that "Section 318(a) (relating to the constructive ownership of stock) *shall* apply for purposes of determining control under paragraph (1)." (Emphasis supplied.) Under section 304(c)(1) "control" is defined only as the ownership (either actually or constructively) of certain amounts of stock. Through the use of precise rules of attribution Congress intended to remove the uncertainties existing under prior law, which had no specific statutory guidance for constructive ownership of stock in the area of corporate distributions and adjustments, in the administration of the provisions where attribution was deemed appropriate. H.Rept. No. 1337, to accompany H.R. 8300 (Pub.L. No. 591), 83d Cong., 2d Sess., p. A96 (1954). See also *Coyle v. United States,* supra at 490. We think the attribution rules require, through their employment in section 304, that petitioners be treated as in actual control of both AT & T and Lents, notwithstanding any "bad blood" between petitioners' sons. See *Fehrs Finance Co.,* supra at 187–188. Cf. *Robin Haft Trust,* supra at 402–403.

Petitioners assert that even though the sale is to be treated as a distribution in redemption of Lents' stock under section 304(a)(1), they are entitled to treat the distribution as in full payment in exchange for their stock under section 302(a) by meeting one of the tests contained in section 302(b). The determination under section 302(b) is to be made by reference to the issuing corporation's stock, here the AT & T stock, except that the 50-percent limitations of sections 318(a)(2)(C) and 318(a)(3)(C) are to be disregarded in applying the attribution rules of section 318(a). Sec. 304(b)(1).

Section 302(b) sets forth certain conditions under which a redemption of stock shall be treated as an exchange. If none of those conditions are met, section 302(d) provides that the distribution will then be treated as one to which section 301 applies. Petitioners do not contend that section 302(b)(2) or 302(b)(4) is applicable but they argue that the transaction in question meets the test of either section 302(b)(1) or 302(b)(3).

The test of section 302(b)(1) requires that the redemption be "not essentially equivalent to a dividend." To meet the test of nondividend equivalency the redemption must, after application of the attribution rules of section 318(a) to the stock ownership interests as they existed both before and after the redemption, result in "a meaningful reduction of the shareholder's proportionate interest in the corporation." *United States v. Davis,* supra at 313. In resolution of the question of dividend equivalency, the fact that the transaction in issue may have had a bona fide business purpose is no longer relevant. *United States v. Davis,* supra at 312. Furthermore, the applicability of the attribution rules in section 302(b)(1) is not affected by any "bad blood" between petitioners' sons. *Robin Haft Trust,* supra at 402–403.

As stated above, prior to the redemption petitioners owned, either actually or constructively, 90.49 percent of the outstanding common stock of AT & T. After the redemption, petitioners actually owned no AT & T common stock, although they did own 125 shares out of 2,136 outstanding shares of that corporation's preferred stock. However, petitioners constructively owned 82.96 percent of the outstanding common stock of AT & T comprised as follows: 3,055.221 shares actually owned by their son Bernard E. Niedermeyer, Jr., 207.851 shares actually owned by their son Walter E. Niedermeyer, and 67 percent of the 1,083.117 shares, or 725.688 shares, actually owned by Lents and constructively owned by their sons E. C., L. J., and T.J. Niedermeyer. Sec. 318(a)(5)(A). We do not think a reduction in ownership of the AT & T common stock from 90.49 percent to 82.96 percent constitutes a meaningful reduction of petitioners' proportionate interest in AT & T in the instant case. See Friend v. United States, 345 F.2d 761, 764 (C.A.1, 1965); Stanley F. Grabowski Trust, 58 T.C. 650, 659 (1972); *Fehrs Finance Co.,* supra at 185–186. With such a small change in a high percentage interest, petitioners' control and ownership of AT & T is essentially unaltered and cannot be considered to have undergone a meaningful reduction. An 82.96-percent interest clearly is sufficient to dominate and control the policies of the corporation.

Petitioners next assert, under several theories, that they terminated their interest in AT & T as contemplated in section 302(b)(3). The test provided therein allows the redemption to be treated as an exchange "if the redemption is in complete redemption of all of the stock of the corporation owned by the shareholder." Unless the conditions of section 302(c)(2) are satisfied to exempt petitioners from application of the family attribution rules of section 318(a)(1), these rules apply in their entirety in determining whether there has been a redemption of petitioners' complete stock interest in AT & T.

Petitioners sold all their AT & T common stock to Lents on September 8, 1966, and contributed all their AT & T preferred stock to the Niedermeyer Foundation on December 28, 1966. On September 24, 1968, petitioners filed an amended return for the calendar year 1966 to which was attached the agreement called for in section 302(c)(2)(A)(iii).

It is clear that, if they are to meet the requirements of the test of section 302(b)(3), petitioners must show that they completely terminated their stock interest in AT & T and in so doing they must be able to effect a waiver of the family attribution rules of section 318(a)(1) through use of section 302(c)(2).

While section 1.302–4(b), Income Tax Regs., states that the agreement specified in section 302(c)(2)(A)(iii) must be attached to a return timely filed for the year in which the distribution occurs, several cases have held that some delay in filing the agreement does not vitiate it, and we find those cases to be applicable here where petitioners filed the agreement upon discovering their inadvertent failure to do so earlier. United States v. G.W. Van Keppel, 321 F.2d 717 (C.A. 10, 1963); Georgie S. Cary, 41 T.C. 214 (1963).

However, the fact that a proper agreement was filed alone does not effect a waiver of the family attribution rules unless the other requirements of section 302(c)(2) are satisfied. The only other requirement in question here is that petitioners must have had no interest in AT & T, other than an interest as a creditor, immediately after the distribution referred to in section 302(b)(3). In the instant case, however, petitioners retained their 125 shares of AT & T preferred stock, at least until December 28, 1966, after the redemption of all their AT & T common stock on September 8, 1966.

Petitioners contend that ownership of these 125 shares of AT & T preferred stock until December 28, 1966, does not prevent application of the exemption provided in section 302(c)(2) and consequently qualification under section 302(b)(3) as having completely terminated their stock interest in AT & T. Petitioners make the following arguments to show that the AT & T preferred stock retained until December 28, 1966, was not the retention of an interest other than that of a creditor and implicitly was not the retention of a stock interest in AT & T: (1) The preferred stock was actually debt; (2) a de minimis rule should be applied; (3) the relinquishment of their preferred stock interest in AT & T on December 28, 1966, was "immediately after" the sale of their AT & T common stock on September 8, 1966; and (4) at the time of the sale of their AT & T common stock they intended to donate their AT & T preferred stock to charity before the year's end.

While citing no cases in their support, petitioners first argue here that the characteristics of the AT & T preferred stock are those commonly associated with debt instruments. We do not agree. A number of factors have been considered in resolution of this question of fact, see O.H. Kruse Grain & Milling v. Commissioner, 279 F.2d 123, 125–126 (C.A. 9, 1960), affirming a Memorandum Opinion of this Court; Wilbur Security Co., 31 T.C. 938, 948 (1959), affd. 279 F.2d 657 (C.A. 9, 1960); however, we see no useful purpose in reciting all the factors but will confine discussion herein only to those we think relevant.

While it is true that the preferred stockholders had no right to participate in the management of the corporation, such fact is not so uncharacteristic of preferred stock rights as to be conclusive, standing alone, of the question at hand. John Kelley Co. v. Commissioner, 326 U.S. 521, 530 (1946). We think that the following facts are indicative of the equity flavor of the preferred stock: There was no unconditional obligation to pay a principal sum certain on or before a fixed maturity date; the timing of preferred "dividends" was discretionary with the corporate directors; upon liquidation the preferred stockholders would be paid "from the money and/or property available for distribution to shareholders," which indicates to us that the preferred stock was subordinated in priority to the general creditors; AT & T's articles of amendment to the articles of incorporation used the terms "dividends," "preferred stock," and "shareholders" with reference to the instruments in question; and the preferred stock was created during a reorganization by a transfer of earned surplus to AT & T's capital account.

We think petitioners' second argument attempting to interject a de minimis rule allowing the retention of some small stock interest while qualifying under section 302(b)(3) is wholly without merit. Section 302(b)(3) clearly requires no less than a complete termination of all petitioners' stock interest in the corporation.

Petitioners next assert that they had no interest in AT & T "immediately after the distribution," as the phrase is used in section 302(c)(2)(A)(i), because the December 28, 1966, contribution should be considered to have occurred immediately after the September 8, 1966, redemption. We assume petitioners believe that if they satisfy this requirement of having no interest "immediately after" the redemption, they will also satisfy the requirement in section 302(b)(3) of having completely terminated their stock interest in AT & T. While we express no opinion on petitioners' apparent belief, we think the words "immediately after" must be given their ordinary meaning and that consequently December 28 cannot be considered "immediately after" September 8. Cf. Commissioner v. Brown, 380 U.S. 563, 570–571 (1965).

Petitioners' final argument to satisfy the requirements of sections 302(b)(3) and 302(c)(2)(A)(i) is that, at the time of the transfer of their AT & T common stock to Lents, they intended to donate their remaining AT & T preferred stock to charity by the end of 1966. Petitioners did in fact contribute their 125 shares of AT & T preferred stock to the Niedermeyer Foundation on December 28, 1966.

While petitioners' contention in this regard is not entirely clear, their argument appears to be that the September 8, 1966, transfer was but one step in a plan to terminate completely their interest in AT & T, the final step in such plan being their December 28, 1966, contribution of their remaining preferred stock. The only case cited by petitioners, Arthur D. McDonald, 52 T.C. 82 (1969), involved the question of whether a plan, calling for the redemption of that taxpayer's E & M preferred stock which was followed by a reorganization in which the taxpayer exchanged his E & M common stock for Borden stock, resulted in a distribution with respect to the preferred stock, which was essentially equivalent to a dividend under section 302(b)(1). The Court concluded that, after completion of the plan, the taxpayer's direct interest in E & M was terminated and consequently the redemption was not essentially equivalent to a dividend. Petitioners have not urged, and we consider it wise since the attribution rules would frustrate them, that their intention to donate the AT & T preferred stock by year's end shows that the redemption comes within the provisions of section 302(b)(1). Rather, they apparently contend that their intentions to donate the AT & T preferred stock constituted a plan to terminate their interest in AT & T which, with use of section 302(c)(2)(A), satisfies the requirements of section 302(b)(3).

Where redemptions were executed pursuant to a plan to terminate one's interest in a corporation, it has been held that dividend equivalency may be avoided where the individual redemptions are component parts of a single sale or exchange of an entire stock interest. In Re Lukens' Estate, 246 F.2d 403 (C.A. 3, 1957), reversing 26 T.C. 900 (1956); Jackson Howell, 26 T.C. 846 (1956), affd. 247 F.2d 156 (C.A. 9, 1957); Carter Tiffany, 16 T.C. 1443 (1951).[4] Where there is a plan which is comprised of several steps, one involving the redemption of stock that results in a complete termination of the taxpayer's interest in a corporation, section 302(b)(3) may apply. Otis P. Leleux, 54 T.C. 408 (1970); Estate of Oscar L. Mathis, 47 T.C. 248 (1966). However, the redemption must occur as part of a plan which is firm and fixed and in which the steps are clearly integrated. Otis P. Leleux, supra at 418.

We regard the evidence presented on petitioners' behalf as too insubstantial to prove the existence of such a plan. Petitioner Bernard E. Niedermeyer's self-serving statement during the trial that at the time of transfer of the AT & T common stock on September 28, 1966, he intended to donate the AT & T preferred stock to charity by year's end,

---

4. The cited cases were decided under the "essentially equivalent to the distribution of a taxable dividend" standard of sec. 115(g)(1), I.R.C. 1939. Sec. 29.115–9, Regs. 111, provided that "a cancellation or redemption by a corporation of all of the stock of a particular shareholder, so that the shareholder ceases to be interested in the affairs of the corporation, does not effect a distribution of a taxable dividend." Under present law, sec. 302(b)(1) would now appear applicable if completion of the plan results in a meaningful reduction in the taxpayer's proportionate interest in the corporation.

and petitioners' prior history of contributions do not establish to us a firm and fixed plan in which all the steps are clearly integrated.

The plan certainly was not in writing and there was no evidence of communication of petitioners' asserted donative intention to the charity or to anyone. One of petitioners' sons testified that Lents acquired petitioners' AT & T common stock in an attempt to gain control of AT & T. However, no mention at all was made by this son of any desire on petitioners' part to terminate their total interest in AT & T. Petitioners could easily have changed their minds with regard to any intent to donate the preferred stock. Clearly petitioners' decision to donate the preferred stock has not been shown to be in any way fixed or binding. * * * We note that *Arthur D. McDonald,* supra, cited by petitioners, involved a written plan which was fixed as to its terms and apparently binding. By the above discussion we do not mean to indicate that all such plans need to be in writing, absolutely binding, or communicated to others, but we do think that the above-mentioned factors, all of which are lacking here, tend to show a plan which is fixed and firm.

Since petitioners have not established that the redemption is to be treated as an exchange under section 302(a), the proceeds are to be treated as a distribution of property to which section 301 applies and as a dividend as determined by the respondent.

Decision will be entered for the respondent.

PROBLEMS

1. The *Niedermeyer* case is a good example of a tax planning blunder. It illustrates the need for sensitivity to provisions such as § 304. In reading the case, make sure you can answer the following questions:

   (a) Why did § 304 apply to the sale by the taxpayers of their AT & T common stock to Lents?

   (b) Given that § 304 applies, how do you test the "redemption" to determine if the taxpayers have a dividend?

   (c) Why were the taxpayers unable to waive family attribution and qualify for "sale" treatment under § 302(b)(3)?

   (d) How could they have avoided this unfortunate result?

2. Bail Corporation and Out Corporation each have 100 shares of common stock outstanding. Claude owns 80 shares of Bail stock (with a basis of $40,000, or $500 per share) and 60 shares of Out stock (with a basis of $9,000, or $150 per share.) The remaining Bail and Out shares are owned by one individual who is not related to Claude. Bail has no current or accumulated earnings and profits. Out has no current and $5,000 of accumulated earnings and profits. Determine the tax conse-

quences to the various parties in each of the following alternative transactions:

(a) Claude sells 20 of his Out shares, in which he has a $3,000 adjusted basis, to Bail for $4,000.

(b) Same as (a), above, except that Claude receives $3,000 and one share of Bail stock (fair market value—$1,000) for his 20 Out shares.

(c) Same as (a), above, except that Claude receives one share of Bail stock (fair market value—$1,000) and Bail takes the 20 Out shares subject to a $3,000 liability that Claude incurred to buy the 20 shares of Out stock.

(d) Claude sells all of his Out shares to Bail for $12,000.

H. REDEMPTIONS TO PAY DEATH TAXES

Code: § 303(a), (b)(1)–(3), (c). Skim § 6166.

When a shareholder of a closely held corporation dies, it frequently is necessary to liquidate all or part of the decedent's interest in order to raise cash to pay death taxes and other expenses. Since the shares are not readily marketable and the family as a whole may be unwilling to risk loss of control, a redemption may be the centerpiece of the decedent's estate plan. Since the basis of the stock normally will have been stepped-up to its fair market value at the decedent's death,[1] a redemption qualifying for exchange treatment can be accomplished virtually tax-free—a once-in-a-lifetime opportunity for a painless withdrawal of corporate earnings. Section 303, one of several income and estate tax provisions offering relief for owners of closely held business-es,[2] makes it possible to avoid dividend treatment on a redemption even if the transaction does not come within one of the Section 302(b) tests.

The purpose of Section 303 is to remove any income tax impediments to a redemption when an estate faces a liquidity problem. If several detailed requirements are met, distributions in redemption are treated as a sale or exchange rather than a dividend up to the sum of federal and state death taxes and allowable funeral and administrative expenses.[3] Curiously, however, the estate is not required to use (or even need) the redemption proceeds to pay taxes and expenses.

To qualify under Section 303, the value of the redeemed stock must be included in determining the decedent's gross estate for federal estate tax purposes.[4] The other principal requirements relate to the relationship of the decedent's holdings in the corporation to his total gross estate and the timing of the distribution.

1. I.R.C. § 1014(a).

2. E.g., I.R.C. §§ 302(c)(2) (waiver of family attribution when testing redemptions), 2032A (estate tax valuation of certain real property), 6166 (extension of time to pay estate tax). Section 303 contains no "closely held" business requirement, but the vast majority of Section 303 redemptions involve close corporations.

3. I.R.C. § 303(a).

4. Id.

Relationship of Stock to Decedent's Estate. Congress concluded that income tax relief was justified only when a decedent's holdings in the corporation represented a substantial portion of his gross estate. Section 303(b)(2) requires that the value of all the stock of the distributing corporation included in the decedent's gross estate must exceed 35 percent of the total gross estate less certain expenses deductible for federal estate tax purposes. A special rule permits the stock of two or more corporations to be aggregated for purposes of this 35 percent test if 20 percent or more in value of each such corporation's total outstanding stock is included in the gross estate. For purposes of the 20 percent requirement, stock held by the decedent's surviving spouse as community property, or held with the decedent prior to death in joint tenancy, tenancy-by-the-entirety, or tenancy-in-common, is treated as if it were included in determining the value of the decedent's gross estate.[5] If a decedent's holdings are close to the 35 percent mark, it may be desirable to engage in various lifetime and post-mortem maneuvers to ensure that Section 303 will be available.[6]

Timing of the Redemption. Section 303 applies only to amounts distributed within a reasonable time after the decedent's death. The redemption must occur within 90 days after the expiration of the three year assessment period for federal estate taxes.[7] If the estate becomes embroiled in a controversy with the Service and files a petition for redetermination of estate tax with the Tax Court, the period is extended to 60 days after the Tax Court's decision becomes final.[8] A further extension is provided if the estate is eligible and elects to pay estate taxes in installments over the extended period (up to 15 years) provided by Section 6166.[9] But if the redemption occurs more than four years after death, the amount that can qualify for Section 303 treatment is limited to the lesser of unpaid death taxes and administrative expenses immediately before the distribution or death taxes and expenses actually paid during the one year period beginning on the date of distribution.[10]

Eligible Shareholders. Although Section 303 is most commonly used by the decedent's estate, other shareholder-beneficiaries sometimes are eligible for its benefits if their interest "is reduced directly (or through a binding obligation to contribute) by any payment" of death taxes or administrative expenses.[11] In the normal case where the decedent's will provides that taxes and expenses are payable out of the residuary estate, specific legatees of stock (including a spouse receiving a bequest eligible for the unlimited marital deduction) are not eligible to use Section 303.

5. I.R.C. § 303(b)(2)(B).

6. See Kahn, "Closely Held Stocks—Deferral and Financing of Estate Tax Costs through Sections 303 and 6166," 35 Tax Lawyer 639, 676–681 (1982).

7. I.R.C. § 303(b)(1)(A). See I.R.C. § 6501(a).

8. I.R.C. § 303(b)(1)(B).

9. I.R.C. § 303(b)(1)(C).

10. I.R.C. § 303(b)(4).

11. I.R.C. § 303(b)(3).

Distributions of Appreciated Property. The most likely asset for a Section 303 redemption is cash, but a corporation that distributes appreciated property to redeem its shares must recognize gain under the now familiar rule in Section 311(b).

PROBLEM

George died last year and his gross estate for federal estate tax purposes is $1,000,000. George's estate expects to incur a total of $100,000 of death taxes and allowable deductions for expenses and losses under §§ 2053 and 2054. George's gross estate includes stock in X Corporation (fair market value—$100,000) and Y Corporation (fair market value—$200,000). The fair market value of all of the outstanding X and Y stock is $700,000 and $800,000, respectively. George's wife, Adele, also owns $100,000 of X stock. (She and George held a total of $200,000 of X stock as tenants-in-common during his life.)

If Y Corporation redeems shares from George's estate, will the redemption qualify for exchange treatment under § 303?

CHAPTER 6. STOCK DIVIDENDS
AND SECTION 306 STOCK *

A. INTRODUCTION

Code: Skim §§ 305; 306; 317(a).

It should be evident by now that Subchapter C is the backdrop for a continuing cops and robbers saga. The goals of the robbers are clear enough, even if their methods may be a bit obscure. When they run out of ways to avoid the double tax, the robbers shift their focus to bailing out corporate earnings at the least tax cost. As for the cops, they are constantly on the chase and with good cause. But they sometimes lack direction and even have been known to engage in isolated acts of police brutality. Nowhere does this drama have a richer history than in the area of stock dividends and Section 306 stock.[1]

The plot is better appreciated by first putting the underlying transactions into perspective. A stock dividend is simply a distribution of stock (or rights to acquire stock)[2] by a corporation to some or all of its shareholders. If the distributed stock is of the same class as the shareholder's underlying holdings, a stock dividend is similar to what is known as a "stock split." The only difference is that a stock dividend normally requires the corporation to transfer an appropriate amount from earned surplus to paid-in capital while a stock split merely increases the number of outstanding shares without any adjustment to the corporate capital account.[3] A stock dividend, however, need not be of the same class of stock as the shareholder's existing interest in the corporation. Preferred stock may be distributed with respect to common or vice versa, and more complex capital structures present the opportunity for countless variations.

* See generally, Stone, "Back to Fundamentals: Another Version of the Stock Dividend Saga," 79 Colum.L.Rev. 898 (1979); Del Cotto & Wolf, "The Proportionate Interest Test of Section 305 and the Supreme Court," 27 Tax L.Rev. 49 (1971); Lowe, "Bailouts: Their Role in Corporate Planning", 30 Tax L.Rev. 357 (1975).

1. With the elimination of the capital gains preference in 1987, the importance of these issues declined, but a modest capital gains rate differential was restored for some taxpayers in the Revenue Reconciliation Act of 1990. As in the redemption context, the stakes in preferred stock bailout transactions are now principally limited to issues of basis recovery. See text accompanying notes 6–7, infra.

2. I.R.C. § 305(d)(1) defines the term "stock" to include rights to acquire such stock.

3. Apart from the financial accounting distinctions, the line of demarcation between a stock dividend and a stock split usually is drawn by the relationship of the number of shares distributed to the previously outstanding shares. To better inform shareholders, the rules of the New York Stock Exchange provide that a distribution of less than 25 percent of the shares outstanding prior to the distribution will be a stock dividend. Larger distributions (e.g., distributions of one share for each share held) are labelled splits. New York Stock Exchange Company Manual, § 703.02.

Stock dividends are used to accomplish a variety of business objectives. Some public companies periodically pay small "common on common" stock dividends instead of cash ostensibly to provide their shareholders with some tangible evidence of their interest in corporate earnings while allowing the corporation to retain cash for use in the business. Although these distributions may have an incidental impact on the price of the stock, they are more of a shareholder relations gesture than an event of any financial consequence. Stock splits are usually prompted by a desire to increase the number of outstanding shares and thus reduce the price per share in an attempt to increase the marketability (and value) of the stock on a listed exchange. And in the good old days, before the cops got smart, the robbers devised more intricate stock dividend schemes to avoid ordinary income or at least convert it to capital gain.

The business objectives are quite different in the case of a closely held corporation. In that setting, stock distributions frequently are the vehicle for a shift of corporate control.[4] To illustrate, assume that all the outstanding stock of Family Corporation is owned by Mrs. Older and has a fair market value of $1,000 per share. Mr. Younger, Older's son, has been employed by Family for several years and Older expects to gradually shift control of the business to Younger. Older's plan faces several obstacles. Gifts of Family common stock to Younger may not be feasible because Older is unwilling to part with that much wealth or the gift tax liability may be prohibitive. Younger also may not be able to afford a significant purchase of stock from his mother because the current price of Family common stock is too high.

As an alternative, Family might distribute a new class of preferred stock to Older. The preferred stock could be structured with dividend rights and a liquidation preference so that its value absorbs most of the net worth of the company, leaving the common stock with only nominal value. The distribution of preferred stock to Older will be tax-free[5] and, since the value of the common stock will be substantially reduced, Older more easily may shift control to Younger through gifts or even sales of common stock.[6]

The tax consequences of the stock distribution to Older in our example are governed by Section 305. Section 305(a) generally provides that gross income does not include a distribution of stock by a corporation to its shareholders with respect to its stock. This exclusion, however, is subject to various exceptions, the most important of which are found in Section 305(b). Consequently, the applicability of the Section 305(b) exceptions is the critical inquiry in analyzing the tax

---

4. A recapitalization frequently is an alternative method for making adjustments to the corporation's capital structure. In certain situations, a recapitalization may provide more favorable income tax results. See Chapter 11, infra.

5. I.R.C. § 305(a). The preferred stock, however, would be Section 306 stock as-

suming Family has earnings and profits. See Section C of this chapter, infra.

6. But see I.R.C. § 2701 et seq., which may limit the estate planning advantages of this strategy.

consequences of a stock distribution. These exceptions are examined more closely in the next section of this chapter. It is sufficient for now to note that the preferred stock distribution to Older is not a taxable stock dividend. What do you suppose is the rationale for that result?

Lest we forget the cops and robbers saga, there is one other aspect of the previous example to consider. Recall that Older owns 100 percent of the outstanding Family common stock, and Family makes a tax-free distribution of a new class of preferred stock to Older. Assume further that Family has ample earnings and profits. If Older retains her common stock rather than giving it to her son, the preferred stock distribution provides her with an opportunity for tax avoidance. She could sell the preferred stock to Facilitator for cash and, after a short period of time, the corporation could redeem the preferred stock, paying Facilitator an appropriate premium for the shares. When the dust settles, this series of transactions has virtually the same economic effect as a cash distribution by Family to Older: Older has cash in hand, Family's corporate treasury has been depleted and Older still owns 100 percent of the company. But the tax consequences appear to be dramatically different. Rather than being stuck with a taxable dividend, Older may enjoy "sale" treatment on the disposition of the preferred stock to Facilitator. A sale would enable Older to recover her basis in the preferred stock and to recognize a long-term capital gain to the extent the amount realized on the sale exceeded her basis.[7] A closer examination reveals that this potential loophole has been closed. Section 306 is the legislative response to Older's tax avoidance plan— the so-called "preferred stock bailout." In our simple example, the preferred stock will bear the taint of "Section 306 Stock," and Section 306(a)(1) will characterize Older's amount realized on the sale to Facilitator as ordinary income.[8] The last section of this chapter explores the details of Section 306.

B. TAXATION OF STOCK DIVIDENDS UNDER SECTION 305

Code: §§ 305(a), (b), (c), (d); 307; 312(d)(1)(B), (f)(2); 1223(5).

Regulations: §§ 1.305–1; –2; –3(a), (b), (c); (e) Examples (1), (2), (3), (4), (8), (10) and (11); –4; –5(a); –6; –7(a); 1.307–1.

The current scheme for taxing stock distributions is a distant cousin of statutes fashioned during the infancy of the income tax and is the product of a checkered legislative history. The Revenue Act of 1916 provided that a "stock dividend shall be considered income, to the

---

7. This assumes that Older had a long-term holding period in the Family common stock, which could be tacked in determining the holding period of the preferred. I.R.C. § 1223(5).

8. I.R.C. § 306(a)(1)(A), (c)(1)(A). Prior to the enactment of Section 306 as part of the 1954 Code, the Service argued that in substance these transactions were equivalent to a cash distribution. The argument met with sporadic success. Compare Chamberlin v. Commissioner, at p. 305, infra, with Rosenberg v. Commissioner, 36 T.C. 716 (1961).

amount of its cash value."[1] In 1920, the Supreme Court considered the constitutionality of this provision in Eisner v. Macomber.[2] Mrs. Macomber was a common shareholder of a corporation with no other class of stock outstanding who received a proportionate distribution of additional common stock. The Supreme Court held that the distribution was not taxable because it did not constitute "income" within the meaning of the 16th Amendment to the Constitution. Although the Court's constitutional commentary is less firm today,[3] the result in *Macomber* is eminently logical and has been codified in Section 305(a). Whatever reshuffling may occur in the corporation's capital account, a common-on-common stock dividend does little more than crowd the shareholder's safe deposit box with additional stock certificates evidencing the same ownership interest held before the distribution.

An obedient Congress swiftly responded to the Supreme Court's interpretation of the 16th Amendment with a primitive declaration that stock dividends "shall not be subject to tax."[4] The stock dividend terrain remained calm until the Supreme Court generated a minor tremor in 1936 with its decision in Koshland v. Helvering.[5] Corinne Koshland, a shareholder owning cumulative nonvoting preferred stock, received a distribution of voting common stock. She subsequently disposed of her preferred stock and asserted that she was entitled to use the stock's full cost basis in determining her gain. The Service contended that since the prior common stock distribution was received tax-free, a proportionate amount of Mrs. Koshland's basis in her preferred shares should be allocated to the common, thereby increasing the gain on the disposition of her preferred stock. The Supreme Court agreed with the shareholder's contention and in the course of its opinion shed additional light on the meaning of Eisner v. Macomber:[6]

> Although *Eisner v. Macomber* affected only the taxation of dividends declared in the same stock as that presently held by the taxpayer, the Treasury gave the decision a broader interpretation which Congress followed in the Act of 1921. Soon after the passage of that Act, this court pointed out the distinction between a stock dividend which worked no change in the corporate entity, the same interest in the same corporation being represented after the distribution by more shares of precisely the same character, and such a dividend where there had either been changes of corporate identity or a change in the nature of the shares issued as dividends whereby the proportional interest of the stockholder after the distribution

1. Revenue Act of 1916, § 2(a). In Towne v. Eisner, 245 U.S. 418, 38 S.Ct. 158 (1918), the Supreme Court concluded that a stock dividend was not "income" or "dividends" under the Revenue Act of 1913.

2. 252 U.S. 189, 40 S.Ct. 189 (1920).

3. See Bittker & Eustice, Federal Income Taxation of Corporations and Shareholders ¶ 7.41 (5th ed. 1987).

4. Revenue Act of 1921, § 201(d).

5. 298 U.S. 441, 56 S.Ct. 767 (1936).

6. 298 U.S. at 445–46. In Helvering v. Gowran, 302 U.S. 238, 58 S.Ct. 154 (1937), the Court held that a shareholder took a zero basis in preferred shares received as a nontaxable distribution on common stock.

was essentially different from his former interest. Nevertheless the successive statutes and Treasury regulations respecting taxation of stock dividends remained unaltered. We give great weight to an administrative interpretation long and consistently followed, particularly when the Congress, presumably with that construction in mind, has reënacted the statute without change. The question here, however, is not merely of our adopting the administrative construction but whether it should be adopted if in effect it converts an income tax into a capital levy.

We are dealing solely with an income tax act. Under our decisions the payment of a dividend of new common shares, conferring no different rights or interests than did the old,— the new certificates, plus the old, representing the same proportionate interest in the net assets of the corporation as did the old,—does not constitute the receipt of income by the stockholder. On the other hand, where a stock dividend gives the stockholder an interest different from that which his former stock holdings represented he receives income. The latter type of dividend is taxable as income under the Sixteenth Amendment. Whether Congress has taxed it as of the time of its receipt, is immaterial for present purposes.

Koshland at least educated Congress on the subtleties of taxing stock dividends, but the legislators were not yet up to the task of devising a precise statutory solution. Instead, they tossed the ball back into the judiciary's court by providing in the Revenue Act of 1936 that a distribution of stock or rights to acquire stock was not to be treated as a dividend to the extent it did "not constitute income to the shareholder within the meaning of the Sixteenth Amendment to the Constitution." [7] The Supreme Court declined the invitation to reconsider *Eisner v. Macomber,* preferring to develop a "proportionate interest test", under which a stock dividend was taxable if it increased a shareholder's proportionate interest in the corporation.[8]

It was back to the drawing board, however, with the enactment of the Internal Revenue Code of 1954. Seeking a simple approach, Congress enacted the predecessor of current Section 305, largely as an expression of dissatisfaction with the proportionate interest test.[9] A far more elaborate system was adopted in the Tax Reform Act of 1969.

---

7. Revenue Act of 1936, § 115(f)(1). This test was carried over to the 1939 Code.

8. See the legislative history in the text at p. 299, infra. See also Helvering v. Sprouse, 318 U.S. 604, 63 S.Ct. 791 (1943), where the Supreme Court decided that a pro rata distribution of nonvoting common stock to a shareholder owning voting common stock was nontaxable because it did not change the proportionate interests of the shareholders, and Strassburger v. Commissioner, 318 U.S. 604, 63 S.Ct. 791 (1943), where the Court held that a distribution of cumulative nonvoting preferred stock to the corporation's sole shareholder was not taxable because "[b]oth before and after the event he owned exactly the same interest in the net value of the corporation as before." Id. at 607, 63 S.Ct. at 792.

9. See the legislative history in the text at pp. 299–301, infra.

The following excerpt of legislative history describes the 1954 Code provisions and explains the 1969 amendments.

EXCERPT FROM SENATE FINANCE COMMITTEE REPORT ON TAX REFORM ACT OF 1969

S.Rep. No. 91–552, 91st Cong., 1st Sess. 150–54 (1969).

Present law.—In its simplest form, a stock dividend is commonly thought of as a mere readjustment of the stockholder's interest, and not as income. For example, if a corporation with only common stock outstanding issues more common stock as a dividend, no basic change is made in the position of the corporation and its stockholders. No corporate assets are paid out, and the distribution merely gives each stockholder more pieces of paper to represent the same interest in the corporation.

On the other hand, stock dividends may also be used in a way that alters the interests of the stockholders. For example, if a corporation with only common stock outstanding declares a dividend payable at the election of each stockholder, either in additional common stock or in cash, the stockholder who receives a stock dividend is in the same position as if he received a taxable cash dividend and purchased additional stock with the proceeds His interest in the corporation is increased relative to the interests of stockholders who took dividends in cash.

Present law (sec. 305(a)) provides that if a corporation pays a dividend to its shareholders in its own stock (or in rights to acquire its stock), the shareholders are not required to include the value of the dividend in income. There are two exceptions to this general rule. First, stock dividends paid in discharge of preference dividends for the current or immediately preceding taxable year are taxable. Second, a stock dividend is taxable if any shareholder may elect to receive his dividend in cash or other property instead of stock.

These provisions were enacted as part of the Internal Revenue Code of 1954. Before 1954 the taxability of stock dividends was determined under the "proportionate interest test," which developed out of a series of Supreme Court cases, beginning with Eisner v. Macomber, 252 U.S. 189 (1920) [T.D. 3010, C.B. 3, 25]. In these cases the Court held, in general, that a stock dividend was taxable if it increased any shareholder's proportionate interest in the corporation. The lower courts often had difficulty in applying the test as formulated in these cases, particularly where unusual corporate capital structures were involved.

Soon after the proportionate interest test was eliminated in the 1954 Code, corporations began to develop methods by which shareholders could, in effect, be given a choice between receiving cash dividends or increasing their proportionate interests in the corporation in much the same way as if they had received cash dividends and reinvested them in the corporation. The earliest of these methods involves dividing the common stock of the corporation into two classes, A and B. The two classes share equally in earnings and profits and in assets on liquidation. The only difference is that the class A stock pays only stock dividends and class B stock pays only cash dividends. The market value of the stock dividends paid on the class A stock is equated annually to the cash dividends paid on the class B stock. Class A stock may be converted into class B stock at any time. The stockholders can choose, either when the classes are established, when they purchase new stock, or through the convertibility option whether to own class A stock or class B stock.

In 1956, the Treasury Department issued proposed regulations which treated such arrangements as taxable (under sec. 305(b)(2)) as distributions subject to an election by the stockholder to receive cash instead of stock. In recent years, however, increasingly complex and sophisticated variations of this basic arrangement have been created. In some of these arrangements, the proportionate interest of one class of shareholders is increased even though no actual distribution of stock is made. This effect may be achieved, for example, by paying cash dividends on common stock and increasing by a corresponding amount the ratio at which convertible preferred stock or convertible debentures may be converted into common stock. Another method of achieving this result is a systematic periodic redemption plan, under which a small percentage, such as 5 percent, of each shareholder's stock may be redeemed annually at his election. Shareholders who do not choose to have their stock redeemed automatically increase their proportionate interest in the corporation.

On January 10, 1969, the Internal Revenue Service issued final regulations (T.D. 6990) [C.B. 1969–1, 95] under which a number of methods of achieving the effect of a cash dividend to some shareholders and a corresponding increase in the proportionate interest of other shareholders are brought under the exceptions in section 305(b), with the result that shareholders who receive increases in proportionate interest are treated as receiving taxable distributions.

General reasons for change.—The final regulations issued on January 10, 1969, do not cover all of the arrangements by which cash dividends can be paid to some shareholders and other shareholders can be given corresponding increases in proportionate interest. For example, the periodic redemption plan described above is not covered by the regulations, and the committee believes it is not covered by the present statutory language (of sec. 305(b)(2)).

Methods have also been devised to give preferred stockholders the equivalent of dividends on preferred stock which are not taxable as such under present law. For example, a corporation may issue preferred stock for $100 per share which pays no dividends, but which may be redeemed in 20 years for $200. The effect is the same as if the corporation distributed preferred stock equal to 5 percent of the original stock each year during the 20-year period in lieu of cash dividends.

The committee believes that dividends paid on preferred stock should be taxed whether they are received in cash or in another form, such as stock, rights to receive stock, or rights to receive an increased amount on redemption. Moreover, the committee believes that dividends on preferred stock should be taxed to the recipients whether they are attributable to the current or immediately preceding taxable year or to earlier taxable years.

Explanation of provisions.—The bill continues (in sec. 305(b)(1)) the provision of present law that a stock dividend is taxable if it is payable at the election of any shareholder in property instead of stock.

The bill provides (in sec. 305(b)(2)) that if there is a distribution or series of distributions of stock which has the result of the receipt of cash or other property by some shareholders and an increase in the proportionate interests of other shareholders in the assets or earnings and profits of the corporation, the shareholders receiving stock are to be taxable (under sec. 301).

For example, if a corporation has two classes of common stock, one paying regular cash dividends and the other paying corresponding stock dividends (whether in common or preferred stock), the stock dividends are to be taxable.

On the other hand, if a corporation has a single class of common stock and a class of preferred stock which pays cash dividends and is not convertible, and it distributes a pro rata common stock dividend with respect to its common stock, the stock distribution is not taxable because the distribution does not have the result of increasing the proportionate interests of any of the stockholders.

In determining whether there is a disproportionate distribution, any security convertible into stock or any right to acquire stock is to be treated as outstanding stock. For example, if a corporation has common stock and convertible debentures outstanding, and it pays interest on the convertible debentures and stock dividends on the common stock, there is a disproportionate distribution, and the stock dividends are to be taxable (under section 301). In addition, in determining whether there is a disproportionate distribution with respect to a shareholder, each class of stock is to be considered separately.

The committee has added two provisions to the House bill (secs. 305(b)(3) and (4)) which carry out more explicitly the intention of the House with regard to distributions of common and preferred stock on common stock, and stock distributions on preferred stock. The first of these provides that if a distribution or series of distributions has the result of the receipt of preferred stock by some common shareholders and the receipt of common stock by other common shareholders, all of the shareholders are taxable (under sec. 301) on the receipt of the stock.

The second of the provisions added by the committee (sec. 305(b)(4)) provides that distributions of stock with respect to preferred stock are taxable (under sec. 301). This provision applies to all distributions on preferred stock except increases in the conversion ratio of convertible preferred stock made solely to take account of stock dividends or stock splits with respect to the stock into which the convertible stock is convertible.

The bill provides (in section 305(b)(5)) that a distribution of convertible preferred stock is taxable (under sec. 301) unless it is established to the satisfaction of the Secretary or his delegate that it will not have the result of a disproportionate distribution described above. For example, if a corporation makes a pro rata distribution on its common stock of preferred stock convertible into common stock at a price slightly higher than the market price of the common stock on the date of distribution, and the period during which the stock must be converted is 4 months, it is likely that a distribution would have the result of a disproportionate distribution. Those stockholders who wish to increase their interests in the corporation would convert their stock into common stock at the end of the 4-month period, and those stockholders who wish to receive cash would sell their stock or have it redeemed. On the other hand, if the stock were convertible for a period of 20 years from the date of issuance, there would be a likelihood that substantially all of the stock would be converted into common stock, and there would be no change in the proportionate interest of the common shareholders.

The bill provides (in sec. 305(c)) that under regulations prescribed by the Secretary or his delegate, a change in conversion ratio, a change in redemption price, a difference between redemption price and issue price, a redemption treated as a section 301 distribution, or any transaction (including a recapitalization) having a similar effect on the interest of any shareholder is to be treated as a distribution with respect to each shareholder whose proportionate interest is thereby increased. The purpose of this provision is to give the Secretary authority to deal with transactions that have the effect of distributions, but in which stock is not actually distributed.

The proportionate interest of a shareholder can be increased not only by the payment of a stock dividend not paid to other shareholders, but by such methods as increasing the ratio at which his stock, convertible securities, or rights to stock may be converted into other stock, by decreasing the ratio at which other stock, convertible securities, or rights to stock can be converted into stock of the class he owns, or by the periodic redemption of stock owned by other shareholders. It is not clear under present law to what extent increases of this kind would be considered distributions of stock or rights to stock. In order to eliminate uncertainty, the committee has authorized the Secretary or his delegate to prescribe regulations governing the extent to which such transactions shall be treated as taxable distributions.

For example, if a corporation has a single class of common stock which pays no dividends and a class of preferred stock which pays regular cash dividends, and which is convertible into the common stock at a conversion ratio that decreases each year to adjust for the payment of the cash dividends on the preferred stock, it is anticipated that the regulations will provide in appropriate circumstances that the holders of the common stock will be treated as receiving stock in a disproportionate distribution (under sec. 305(b)(2)).

It is anticipated that the regulations will establish rules for determining when and to what extent the automatic increase in proportionate interest accruing to stockholders as a result of redemptions under periodic redemption plan are to be treated as taxable distributions. A periodic redemption plan may exist, for example, where a corporation agrees to redeem a small percentage of each common shareholder's stock annually at the election of the shareholder. The shareholders whose stock is redeemed receive cash, and the shareholders whose stock is not redeemed receive an automatic increase in their proportionate interests. However, the committee does not intend that this regulatory authority is to be used to bring isolated redemptions of stock under the disproportionate distribution rule (of sec. 305(b)(2)). For example, a 30 percent stockholder would not be treated as receiving a constructive dividend because a 70 percent stockholder causes a corporation to redeem 15 percent of its stock from him.

NOTE

The Section 305 amendments in the Tax Reform Act of 1969 are generally applicable to distributions made after January 10, 1969. With respect to stock outstanding or issued pursuant to a contract binding on that date, however, the amendments may not be effective until 1991.[1]

The collateral tax consequences (e.g., basis, holding period, and effect on earnings and profits) of a stock distribution depend upon whether or not the distribution is taxable to the shareholders. Taxable distributions are governed by the rules in Section 301. For this purpose, the amount of the distribution is the fair market value of the stock,[2] the shareholder takes a fair market value basis in the distributed stock and his holding period runs from the date of the distribution.[3] The distributing corporation recognizes no gain or loss under Section 311(a)(1), and it may reduce its earnings and profits by the fair market value of the distributed stock.[4]

If a stock distribution is nontaxable under Section 305(a), the shareholder must allocate the basis in the stock held prior to the distribution between the old and new stock in proportion to the relative fair market values of each on the date of distribution,[5] and the holding period of the old shares may be tacked on in determining the holding period of the distributed stock.[6] The distributing corporation recognizes no gain or loss on the distribution of its stock[7] and, since the

1. Reg. § 1.305–8.

2. Reg. § 1.305–1(b)(1). This rule also applies to corporate shareholders. Reg. § 1.301–1(d)(1)(ii).

3. Reg. § 1.301–1(h).

4. Reg. § 1.312–1(d).

5. I.R.C. § 307(a); Reg. § 1.307–1.

6. I.R.C. § 1223(5).

7. I.R.C. § 311(a)(1).

distribution is nontaxable to the shareholders, it may not reduce its earnings and profits.[8]

Section 305 also governs distributions of stock rights (sometimes know as warrants). Public companies occasionally issue rights to acquire additional stock at a favorable price as a means of raising equity capital.[9] A distribution of rights, like a stock dividend generally, is not taxable unless the distribution comes within one of the Section 305(b) exceptions.[10] In the case of a nontaxable rights distribution, Section 307(a) generally requires an allocation of basis between the underlying stock and the rights in proportion to their relative fair market values on the date of the distribution.[11] In most cases, however, such an allocation is unnecessary because of an administrative convenience exception in Section 307(b), which provides that the rights shall take a zero basis if their fair market value is less than 15 percent of the value of the stock with respect to which they were distributed. Taxpayers with time on their hands (or the incentive to make an allocation) may elect to use the allocation method prescribed in Section 307(a).[12] Taxable rights distributions are treated as Section 301 distributions; as such, their value (if any) is a dividend to the extent of the distributing corporation's earnings and profits.

PROBLEMS

1. Hill Corporation is organized with two classes of voting common stock: Class A and Class B. Shares in each class of stock have an equal right to Hill's assets and earnings and profits. Frank owns 100 shares of Class A stock, and Fay and Joyce each own 50 shares of Class B stock.

Assuming that Hill Corporation has ample earnings and profits, determine whether the following distributions are taxable under § 301 or excludable under § 305(a):

(a) A pro rata distribution of nonconvertible preferred stock to both classes of shareholders.

(b) A pro rata distribution of Class A stock on Class A and Class B on Class B. The Class B shareholders also are given the option to take cash in lieu of additional Class B shares. Joyce exercises this option.

(c) A pro rata distribution of Class A stock on Class A and a cash distribution on Class B.

---

8. I.R.C. § 312(d)(1)(B).

9. See, e.g., Rev.Rul. 72–71, 1972–1 C.B. 99, which is the Service's ruling on a complex 1970 rights offering by American Telephone and Telegraph Co.

10. See I.R.C. § 305(d)(1), which treats rights as "stock" for purposes of Section 305.

11. But the regulations permit this allocation only if the rights are exercised (in which event the basis allocated to the rights is added to the cost of the new stock acquired) or sold. If the rights simply lapse, the shareholder recognizes no loss but the basis returns to the underlying stock. Reg. § 1.307–1(a).

12. I.R.C. § 307(b)(2).

(d) Assume that Class B is a class of nonconvertible preferred stock which pays regular cash dividends and Hill distributes Class B stock to the Class A shareholder.

(e) Same as (d), above, except that Hill distributes a class of nonconvertible preferred stock which has rights to assets and earnings and profits subordinate to those of the existing Class B stock (i.e., "junior" nonconvertible preferred stock) to the Class A shareholder.

(f) Assume that Hill has only one class of common stock outstanding and also has issued a series of 10 percent debentures convertible into common stock at the rate of one share of common stock for each $1,000 debenture. Hill makes an annual interest payment to the debenture holders and one month later distributes a "common on common" stock dividend to the common shareholders without adjusting the conversion ratio on the debentures.

(g) Same as (f), above, except that the debentures are convertible preferred stock. The corporation declares a one-for-one split on the common stock (i.e., each shareholder receives one new share of common stock for each old share) and the conversion ratio of the preferred is doubled.

(h) Assume again that Class A and Class B are both classes of voting common stock. Hill makes a pro rata distribution of Class A on Class A and a distribution of newly issued shares of nonconvertible preferred stock on Class B.

(i) Same as (h), above, except that the preferred stock which is distributed is convertible into Class B stock over 20 years at Class B's market price on the day of the distribution.

2. Z Corporation has one class of common stock outstanding, held by unrelated individuals A (500 shares), B (300 shares) and C (200 shares). Will § 305(c) create any tax problems if Z agrees to redeem annually 50 shares of stock at the election of each shareholder, and A makes such an election for two consecutive years?

C. SECTION 306 STOCK

1. THE PREFERRED STOCK BAILOUT

CHAMBERLIN v. COMMISSIONER

United States Court of Appeals, Sixth Circuit, 1953.
207 F.2d 462, certiorari denied 347 U.S. 918, 74 S.Ct. 516 (1954).

MILLER, Circuit Judge.

[This case involved the tax consequences of a device known as the preferred stock bailout. Metal Moulding Corporation was a prosperous company engaged in manufacturing automobile molding and trim. Since its formation in 1924, the corporation had only common stock outstanding and was substantially controlled by the Chamberlin family. In December, 1946, after a long period during which it paid substantial cash dividends, the corporation declared a stock dividend of 1⅓ newly authorized preferred shares for each share of common stock outstanding. Two days later, as a result of lengthy prior negotiations, virtually all the shareholders agreed to sell their preferred stock to two insurance companies. The investment committees of those companies actually had approved the purchase prior to the issuance of the preferred stock. The terms of the preferred had been discussed with and shaped by the demands of the insurance companies. At all times, it was anticipated that the shares would be redeemed at a negotiated price over a seven year period. The entire plan was designed to enable the shareholders to withdraw corporate earnings at capital gains rates. The insurance companies were willing to act as amiable facilitators because they would receive dividends on the preferred stock and a premium on the redemption.

The shareholders treated the preferred stock dividend as nontaxable and reported the proceeds of sale of the preferred as capital gain. On audit, the Service ruled that the distribution of the preferred stock was a taxable dividend. The Tax Court agreed with the Service, reasoning that the distribution was not made for any bona fide business purpose and was in substance the equivalent of a cash distribution out of earnings and profits.

After reviewing the Supreme Court decisions involving the taxability of stock dividends, the Court of Appeals addressed the tax consequences of Metal Moulding's ingenious bailout device. Ed.]

In our opinion, the declaration and distribution of the preferred stock dividend, considered by itself, falls clearly within the principles established in Towne v. Eisner, supra, and Eisner v. Macomber, supra, and is controlled by the ruling in the Strassburger case. Accordingly, as a preliminary matter, we do not agree with the Tax Court's statement that the stock dividend is taxable because as a result of the dividend and immediate sale thereafter it substantially altered the common stockholders' preexisting proportional interests in the Corporation's net assets. The sale to the insurance companies of course resulted in such a change, but the legal effect of the dividend with respect to rights in the corporate assets is determined at the time of its distribution, not by what the stockholders do with it after its receipt. In Helvering v. Griffiths, supra, 318 U.S. 371, at page 394, 63 S.Ct. at page 648, 87 L.Ed. 843, the Court pointed out: "at the latest the time of receipt of the dividend is the critical one for determining taxability." In none of the Supreme Court cases referred to above is it suggested that events subsequent to the distribution have any bearing on whether the stockholder's proportional interest is changed. The fact that events occur in quick succession does not by itself change their legal effect. * * * It seems clear to us that if taxability exists it is not because of the change in pre-existing proportional interests caused by a later sale, but by reason of the other ground relied upon by the Tax Court, namely, that viewed in all its aspects it was a distribution of cash rather than a distribution of stock. That this is the real basis of the ruling appears from the statement in the opinion that "disregarding the circumstances and terms of the issue, it might be said as a matter of form the stock dividend constituted one which fell within the Sprouse and Strassburger cases. * * * However, * * *, not form but the real substance of the transaction is controlling."

The general principle is well settled that a taxpayer has the legal right to decrease the amount of what otherwise would be his taxes, or altogether avoid them, by means which the law permits; * * * and that the taxpayer's motive to avoid taxation will not establish liability if the transaction does not do so without it. * * *

It is equally well settled that this principle does not prevent the Government from going behind the form which the transaction takes and ascertaining the reality and genuineness of the component parts of the transaction in order to determine whether the transaction is really what it purports to be or is merely a formality without substance which for tax purposes can and should be disregarded. * * *

The question accordingly presented is not whether the overall transaction, admittedly carried out for the purpose of avoiding taxes, actually avoided taxes which would have been incurred if the transaction had taken a different form, but whether the stock dividend was a stock dividend in substance as well as in form.

No question is raised about the legality of the declaration of the dividend. Respondent does not contend that proper corporate procedure was not used in creating the preferred stock and in distributing it to the stockholders in the form of a dividend. If the transaction had stopped there we think it is clear that the dividend would not have been taxable in the hands of the stockholders. Strassburger v. Commissioner, supra. Whether the declaration of the dividend was in furtherance of any corporate business purpose or was the result of correct judgment and proper business policy on the part of the management, we believe is immaterial on this phase of the case. The Supreme Court cases in no way suggest that the taxability of a stock dividend depends on the purpose of its issuance or the good or bad judgment of the directors in capitalizing earnings instead of distributing them. The decisions are based squarely upon the proportional interest doctrine. * * * In Dreyfuss v. Manning, D.C.N.J., 44 F.Supp. 383, a stock dividend of preferred stock, declared solely for the purpose of avoiding taxes on undistributed net income, was held non-taxable, which ruling apparently was not appealed by the Commissioner. The presence or absence of a corporate business purpose may play a part in determining whether a stock dividend is a bona fide one, one in substance as well as in form, but it does not by itself change an otherwise valid dividend into an invalid one. A stock dividend, legally created and distributed, which is a dividend in substance as well as in form, does not change from a non-taxable dividend into a taxable one because of the purpose of its issuance or on account of the good or bad judgment of the directors in declaring it. Eisner v. Macomber, supra, 252 U.S. at page 211, 40 S.Ct. at page 194.

Nor is there any question about the genuineness and unconditional character of the sale of the preferred stock by the stockholders who received it to the two insurance companies. The facts show conclusively that title passed irrevocably from the stockholders to the insurance companies, and that the sellers received in cash without restriction a full consideration, the adequacy of which respondent does not question. But respondent contends that the sale of the stock following immediately upon its receipt resulted in the stockholder acquiring cash instead of stock, thus making it a taxable dividend under Secs. 22(a) and 115(a), Internal Revenue Code. There are two answers to this contention.

A non-taxable stock dividend does not become a taxable cash dividend upon its sale by the recipient. On the contrary, it is a sale of a capital asset. * * * The rulings in those cases make it clear that its character as a capital asset is in no way dependent upon how long it is held by the taxpayer before its sale. In none of the Supreme Court cases referred to above, dealing with the taxability of stock dividends, was the length of the holding period considered as a factor. Obviously, if the non-taxability of a stock dividend rests solely upon the principle that it does not alter the pre-existing proportionate interest of any stockholder or increase the intrinsic value of his holdings, the disposition of the stock dividend by the stockholder thereafter is not a factor in the determination. * * *

The foregoing conclusion is supported by Sec. 117(h)(5), Internal Revenue Code, 26 U.S.C.A. § 117(h)(5), which provides that for the purpose of determining whether a non-taxable stock dividend which has been sold is a long-term capital gain there shall be included in the holding period the period for which the taxpayer held the stock in the distributing corporation prior to the receipt of the stock dividend. This necessarily recognizes that a stock dividend will often be sold before the expiration of six months after its receipt, and makes no distinction between a stock dividend held one day or for any other period less than six months. Likewise, Sec. 29.113(a)(19)–1, Treasury Regulations III, in establishing the cost basis of a non-taxable stock dividend which has been sold for a gain or loss, makes no distinction between a stock dividend sold immediately after receipt and one held a long period of time before sale.

The other answer to the contention is that although the stockholder *acquired* money in the final analysis, he did not *receive* either money or property *from* the corporation. Sec. 115(a), Internal Revenue Code, in dealing with taxable dividends, defines a dividend as "any distribution *made by a corporation* to its shareholders, whether in money or in other property * * * out of its earnings or profits * * *." (Emphasis added.) The money he received was received from the insurance companies. It was not a "distribution" by the corporation declaring the dividend, as required by the statute.

We come then to what in our opinion is the dominant and decisive issue in the case, namely, whether the stock dividend, which, by reason of its redemption feature, enabled the Corporation to ultimately distribute its earnings to its stockholders on a taxable basis materially lower than would have been the case by declaring and paying the usual cash dividend, was a bona fide one, one in substance as well as in form. As pointed out in Chisholm v. Commissioner, supra, 2 Cir., 79 F.2d 14, 15, certiorari denied Helvering v. Chisholm, 296 U.S. 641, 56 S.Ct. 174, 80 L.Ed. 456, the Court cannot ignore the legal effect of a bona fide transaction on the ground that it avoids taxes, and that "The question always is whether the transaction under scrutiny is in fact what it appears to be in form; a marriage may be a joke; a contract may be intended only to deceive others; an agreement may have a collateral defeasance. In such cases the transaction as a whole is different from its appearance." But if the transaction is actually what it purports to be it must be accepted for its legal results. There are numerous cases, some of which are pressed upon us by the respondent, where the Court, in keeping with the above principle, refused to give effect taxwise to transactions on the part of corporations because the facts and circumstances showed that the so-called corporation was one in form only, incorporated for the sole purpose of avoiding taxes and having no legitimate business purpose, masquerading under the corporate form, and accordingly not a bona fide corporation. * * * In other cases a valid conveyance has been disregarded taxwise because the purchaser acquired no real interest in the property conveyed, was a mere conduit in passing title to another, and the conveyance was in fact a sham. * * * In the recent case of Bazley v. Commissioner, supra, 331 U.S. 737, 67 S.Ct. 1489, 91 L.Ed. 1782, the Court disregarded a so-called recapitalization of a corporation which would have resulted in a tax exempt distribution of its securities because the recapitalization was merely a formal paper recapitalization rather than a bona fide one contemplated by the statute. Likewise in Commissioner v. Tower, supra, 327 U.S. 280, 66 S.Ct. 532, 90 L.Ed. 670, the Court disregarded a partnership taxwise because it was a partnership merely in form and not in substance.

In our opinion, the stock dividend in this case does not fall within any of the principles discussed above. It seems clear that it was an issue of stock in substance as well as in form. According to its terms, and in the absence of a finding that it was immediately or shortly thereafter redeemed at a premium, we assume that a large portion of it has remained outstanding over a period of years with some of it still unredeemed after nearly seven years. It has been in the hands of the investing public, free of any control by the corporation over its owners, whose enforceable rights with respect to operations of the corporation would not be waived or neglected. Substantial sums have been paid in dividends. The insurance companies bought it in the regular course of their business and have held it as approved investments. For the Court to now tell them that they have been holding a sham issue of stock would be most startling and disturbing news.

It also seems clear that the insurance companies were not purchasers in form only without acquiring any real interest in the property conveyed. The character of the transaction as a bona fide investment on the part of the insurance companies is not challenged by the respondent. The element of a formal conduit without any business interest is entirely lacking.

If the transaction lacks the good faith necessary to avoid the assessment it must be because of the redemption feature of the stock, which, in the final analysis, is what ultimately permitted the distribution of the corporate earnings and is the key factor in the overall transaction. Redemption features are well known and often used in corporate financing. If the one in question was a reasonable one, not violative of the general principles of bona fide corporate financing, and acceptable to experienced bona fide investors familiar with investment fundamentals and the opportunities afforded by the investment market we fail to see how a court can properly classify the issue, by reason of the redemption feature, as lacking in good faith or as not being what it purports to be. The insurance companies, conservative, experienced investors, analyzed the stock issue very carefully, provisions were required to make it conform to sound investment requirements, and each of the two companies, acting independently of the other, purchased a very substantial amount in the regular course of their investment purchases. If the redemption feature was unreasonable or not in accord with generally accepted investment principles the stock would not have been approved as an investment and purchased by the two insurance companies. In our opinion, the redemption feature, qualified as it was with respect to premiums, amounts subject to redemption in each year, and the length of time the stock would be outstanding, together with the acceptance of the stock as an investment issue, did not destroy the bona fide quality of the issue. We cannot say that the preferred stock was not in fact what it purported to be, namely, an issue of stock in substance as well as in form. * * *

Each case necessarily depends upon its own facts. The facts in this case show tax avoidance, and it is so conceded by petitioner. But they also show a series of legal transactions, no one of which is fictitious or so lacking in substance as to be anything different from what it purports to be. Unless we are to adopt the broad policy of holding taxable any series of transactions, the purpose and result of which is the avoidance of taxes which would otherwise accrue if handled in a different way, regardless of the legality and realities of the component parts, the tax assessed by the Commissioner was successfully avoided in the present case. We do not construe the controlling decisions as having adopted that view. * * *

In deciding this case it must be kept in mind that it does not involve a ruling that the profit derived from the sale of the stock dividend is or is not taxable income. Such profit is conceded to be taxable. The issue is whether it is taxable as income from a cash dividend or as income resulting from a long-term capital gain. Accordingly, it is not the usual case of total tax avoidance. Congress has adopted the policy of taxing long-term capital gains differently from ordinary income. By Sec. 115(g), Internal Revenue Code, it has specifically excluded certain transactions with respect to stock dividends from the classification of a capital gain. The present transaction is not within the exclusion. If the profit from a transaction like the one here involved is to be taxed at the same rate as ordinary income, it should be done by appropriate legislation, not court decision.

The judgment is reversed and the case remanded to the Tax Court for proceedings consistent with the views expressed herein.

NOTE

The *Chamberlin* case was decided under the 1939 Code. Left unchecked, the court's endorsement of the preferred stock bailout would have encouraged other closely held corporations to engage in similar profitable end runs around the distribution rules. Although it is possible that the result in *Chamberlin* would have been overturned in subsequent litigation, the Treasury wisely sought a prompt legislative solution. The central issue facing the drafters of the 1954 Code was whether to attack the bailout by taxing all "preferred on common" stock dividends or defer the punishment until the shareholder disposed of stock with bailout potential.

A common shareholder who receives a proportionate preferred stock dividend has not increased his interest in the corporation. He simply has a tax opportunity which he may choose to forego for nontax reasons. For example, we saw in the introduction to this chapter that there may be valid business reasons (e.g., a shift of control from older to younger generation shareholders) for a preferred stock dividend.[1] Recognizing these and other valid nontax objectives served by preferred stock dividends, Congress concluded that the *receipt* of the dividend was not the appropriate occasion for punitive action.[2] Instead, it chose to label stock with bailout potential as "Section 306 stock" and to require a shareholder to report ordinary income rather than capital gain when Section 306 stock is sold or redeemed. In the case of a sale, the ordinary income amount is generally determined by the amount that would have been a dividend at the time of the stock distribution if cash rather than stock had been distributed.[3] In the case of a redemption, the ordinary income amount is determined at the time of the cash

---

1. See Cohen, Surrey, Tarleau and Warren, "A Technical Revision of the Federal Income Tax Treatment of Corporate Distributions to Shareholders," 52 Colum.L.Rev. 1, 11–14 (1952).

2. S.Rep. No. 1622, 83rd Cong., 2d Sess. 46 (1954).

3. I.R.C. § 306(a)(1).

distribution.[4] Other operational and planning aspects of Section 306 are examined in the remainder of this chapter.

2. THE OPERATION OF SECTION 306

a. SECTION 306 STOCK DEFINED

Code: § 306(c)–(e).

Regulations: §§ 1.306–3(a)–(c), (e).

The definition of Section 306 stock is consistent with the anti-bailout objectives of the statute. The principal category is stock distributed to a shareholder as a tax-free stock dividend under Section 305(a)—other than "common on common." [1] Ordinarily, this is preferred stock distributed to common shareholders by a corporation with earnings and profits. As the *Chamberlin* case illustrates, preferred stock is the primary vehicle for a bailout because it can be sold without diminishing the shareholder's control or right to share in future corporate growth. "Common" stock is excepted because it lacks bailout potential; it may not be sold without diminishing the shareholder's control and interest in corporate growth.[2]

Although the Service has not defined "common stock" in Section 306, it has developed a ruling policy that focuses on whether a sale of the stock would cause a reduction of the shareholder's equity position in the company. The fundamental inquiry is thus whether the stock has a realistic and unrestricted opportunity to participate in the growth of corporate equity.[3] The rulings following this note illustrate the Service's approach to the definition of "common" and "preferred" stock for purposes of Section 306.

Congress also concluded that there is limited bailout potential if the tax-free stock dividend is issued by a corporation having no current or accumulated earnings and profits for the year of the distribution. If cash instead of stock had been distributed, the shareholder would not have realized ordinary income since the corporation had no earnings and profits. Consequently, Section 306(c)(2) provides that Section 306 stock does not include stock which would not have been treated as a dividend at the time of distribution if cash had been distributed in lieu of the stock.

To prevent an easy purge of the taint, Section 306 stock includes stock with a transferred or substituted basis.[4] This category encompasses stock received as a gift which takes a Section 1015 transferred basis, or stock received in exchange for Section 306 stock in a tax-free

---

4. I.R.C. § 306(a)(2). See Section C2b of this chapter, infra.

1. I.R.C. § 306(c)(1)(A).

2. See Walter, " 'Preferred Stock' and 'Common Stock': The Meaning of the Terms and the Importance of the Distinc-

tion for Tax Purposes," 5 J.Corp.Tax'n 211 (1978).

3. See, e.g., Rev.Rul. 75–222, 1975–1 C.B. 105; Rev.Rul. 79–163, 1979–1 C.B. 131.

4. I.R.C. § 306(c)(1)(C).

Section 351 transaction.[5] But the exorcist prevails when stock passes from a decedent and thus qualifies for a date-of-death basis under Section 1014. In that event, the Section 306 taint is buried along with the decedent and her old basis.

An important but more specialized category is stock (which is not common stock) received in a tax-free corporate reorganization or division when the effect of the transaction is substantially the same as the receipt of a stock dividend or when the stock is received in exchange for Section 306 stock. For example, preferred stock received by the shareholders of the target (i.e., acquired) corporation in a tax-free merger may be a prime candidate for Section 306 classification. This aspect of Section 306 is considered in a later chapter.[6]

The final category of Section 306 stock was added by Congress in 1982 to thwart the use of a holding company to bail out earnings. Assume, for example, that Schemer holds only common stock in Profitable Co. Finding that Section 306 presents a substantial roadblock to a bailout, Schemer organizes Holding Co., exchanging her Profitable common stock for newly issued Holding common and preferred stock in a tax-free Section 351 transaction. Until recently, the Holding preferred stock would not be Section 306 stock because Holding had no earnings and profits at the time of its incorporation. This offered shareholders the very bailout opportunity that Section 306 was designed to prevent! Schemer could sell the Holding preferred stock to an institutional investor, recovering her basis and realizing a capital gain, and the stock later could be redeemed by the corporation—all without losing any of her control or share in the growth of Profitable.

Section 306(c)(3) blocks this maneuver by characterizing the preferred stock of Holding Co. (i.e., preferred stock acquired in a Section 351 exchange) as Section 306 stock if the receipt of money instead of the stock would have been treated as a dividend to any extent. Of course, Holding Co. has no earnings and profits so that a distribution of cash would not have been a dividend. To make the statute achieve its objective, Section 306(c)(3)(A) borrows the rules of Section 304 (relating to redemptions through the use of affiliated corporations). In our example, the Holding Co. preferred would be Section 306 stock if Profitable Co. has any current or accumulated earnings and profits. This is because a cash payment by Holding Co. for the Profitable common stock would have resulted in a dividend to Schemer under Section 304(a)(1). In effect, this means that we look to the earnings and profits of the original corporation (Profitable Co.) in determining whether the receipt of cash would have been a dividend.[7]

---

5. In this situation, the old Section 306 stock remains tainted in the hands of the corporation, and the newly issued stock, whatever its class, also is Section 306 stock by virtue of its substituted basis under Section 358. See Rev.Rul. 77–108, 1977–1 C.B. 86.

6. See Chapter 11, infra.

7. In testing for the effect of a dividend, the Section 318 attribution rules apply without regard to the 50 percent limitation in Sections 318(a)(2)(C) and 318(a)(3)(C). I.R.C. § 306(c)(4).

Although Section 306 effectively deters most preferred stock bailouts, some opportunities are still available with careful advance planning.[8] A corporation may issue or distribute the preferred stock at a time when it has no earnings and profits (for example, at the time of incorporation). In that event, the stock will not be Section 306 stock and there is considerable potential for future bailouts. That technique, however, may have a deceptive appeal. By requiring the issuance of preferred stock, the corporation obligates itself to pay cash dividends, probably at a high rate, for at least some period of time prior to the bailout. As we have seen, many closely held corporations are reluctant to distribute earnings in the form of dividends, and it may be unwise to require a new business to drain the corporate treasury because of a substantial dividend obligation. Especially with only a modest capital gains rate preference and a strengthened corporate income tax, it seems preferable to capitalize a corporation with a permissible amount of debt and minimize the double tax—or escape entirely from Subchapter C by electing to be treated as an S corporation.[9]

REVENUE RULING 76–386
1976–2 Cum.Bull. 95.

Advice has been requested whether stock issued under the circumstances described below is "common stock" for purposes of section 306(c)(1)(B) of the Internal Revenue Code of 1954.

Pursuant to a plan of recapitalization under section 368(a)(1)(E) of the Code, corporation X issued shares of new voting common stock and new nonvoting common stocks pro rata to its shareholders in exchange for shares of its outstanding common stock. The exchange was not taxable pursuant to section 354. X's certificate of incorporation granted to the corporation a 90-day right of first refusal to purchase shares of the newly issued voting common stock at their net book value whenever a shareholder (or legal representative in the case of the shareholder's death or incompetency) desired to sell, assign, transfer, or otherwise dispose of any of such stock. The 90-day period starts upon X's receipt of written notice of a stockholder's disposition decision. However, if the shareholder fails to give the required notice, X's option starts on the date the new voting common stock certificates are presented for transfer on the corporation's books. X's right of first refusal also applies to all subsequent holders of such stock.

Section 306(c)(1)(B) of the Code provides, in part, that "section 306 stock" is stock which is not common stock and (1) which was received by the shareholder selling or otherwise disposing of such stock, in pursuance of a plan of reorganization (within the meaning of section 368(a)), and (ii) with respect to the receipt of which gain or loss to the shareholder was to any extent not recognized by reason of Part III, but

8. See generally, Lowe, "Bailouts: Their Role in Corporate Planning," 30 Tax L.Rev. 357 (1975).

9. See Chapter 15, infra.

only to the extent that either the effect of the transaction was substantially the same as the receipt of a stock dividend, or the stock was received in exchange for section 306 stock.

Since the shareholders received the new voting common in pursuance of a plan of reorganization (a recapitalization under section 368(a)(1)(E) of the Code), no gain or loss was recognized (under section 354), and the effect of the transaction was substantially the same as the receipt of a stock dividend (the proportionate interest of each shareholder in the corporation's equity remained the same), the remaining issue is whether the new voting common is "common stock" for the purpose of section 306(c)(1)(B).

In Rev.Rul. 57–132, 1957–1 C.B. 115, a class of new nonvoting common stock, issued in a reorganization (recapitalization) under section 368(a)(1)(E) of the Code, was redeemable by its terms at the discretion of the corporation. Although sale or other disposition of such stock would initially result in a lessening of the disposing shareholder's interest in the equity growth of the corporation, a later redemption of that class of stock would restore the "lost" equitable interest of the disposing shareholder, thereby achieving the bailout abuse to which section 306 is directed. Therefore, such stock although labeled common stock was viewed not to be "common stock" for purposes of section 306(c)(1)(B).

In the instant case, however, the new voting common stock, which is common stock in all other respects, is not redeemable, but is merely subject to the corporation's right of first refusal. That right applies only with respect to individual shareholders. Thus, if a shareholder desired to dispose of some or all of the new voting common stock, thereby giving rise to X's right of first refusal, the shareholder will necessarily part with some or all of the interest in the growth of the corporation. This result obtains because either the corporation will in fact exercise its option or it will not and the disposition will be completed. In either case, the disposing shareholder would have irrevocably and irretrievably parted with some or all interest in the equity growth in X as respects the then existing shareholders. Therefore, the new voting common stock cannot be used to achieve the prohibited bailout.

Accordingly, in the instant case the new voting common stock, although issued subject to the corporation's right of first refusal, is "common stock" for purposes of section 306(c)(1)(B) of the Code.
*   *   *

Rev.Rul. 57–132 is distinguished.

REVENUE RULING 79–163
1979–1 Cum.Bull. 131.

ISSUE

Is the class A common stock received in the two situations described below common stock within the meaning of section 306(c) of the Internal Revenue Code of 1954?

FACTS

Situation (1):

A corporation had outstanding 100x shares of common stock. The corporation effected a reshuffling of its capital structure that qualified as a recapitalization and, therefore, a reorganization within the meaning of section 368(a)(1)(E) of the Code.

Pursuant to the plan of recapitalization, the corporation issued in exchange for each share of its outstanding common stock one share of its newly authorized class A common stock and one share of its newly authorized class B common stock. The class A common stock has a par value of $20 per share and is entitled to voting rights. The class B common stock has a par value of $100 per share and is nonvoting. The class A common stock and the class B common stock are entitled to cash dividends in the ratio of their par values. Upon liquidation the holders of the class A common stock and class B common stock were to be paid the par value of their stock. Any remaining assets were to be distributed to the holders of the class B common stock. Neither class of stock was by its terms redeemable.

LAW AND ANALYSIS

Section 306(a) of the Code provides rules for the tax treatment of the disposition by shareholders of "section 306 stock," which are intended to prevent the "preferred stock bailout" of earnings and profits at capital gain rates. Section 306(c)(1)(A) and (B) defines, in part, the term "section 306 stock" to include certain stock other than common stock.

The term "common stock" as used in section 306 of the Code is not defined in that section or the related regulations. In making the determination as to whether a particular class of stock is common stock for purposes of section 306(c) the determinative factors are whether that class of stock is redeemable by the corporation and whether the stock represents an unrestricted interest in the equity growth of the corporation. See Rev.Rul. 76–386, 1976–2 C.B. 95, and Rev.Rul. 76–387, 1976–2 C.B. 96. A stock represents an unrestricted interest in a corporation's equity growth if it entitles the holder to an unrestricted right to share both in dividends and in liquidation proceeds. If a class of stock is restricted to a maximum amount as to dividends or liquidation proceeds, regardless of the amount available for dividends or distributions in liquidation, such stock is not common stock for purposes of section 306(c). See Rev.Rul. 75–236, 1975–1 C.B. 106.

Although, in the instant case, the extent to which the class A common stock and the class B common stock share in a dividend distribution is based on the par value of the stock of each class, the amount that each class may receive as a dividend distribution is not limited. However, since the amount to which the class A common stock is entitled upon liquidation of the corporation is limited to the par value of the stock, it does not represent an unrestricted right in the equity growth of the corporation.

Situation (2):

The facts are the same as in situation (1), except that the holders of the class A common stock and class B common stock received in the recapitalization are entitled to share equally in cash dividends up to 6 percent of their par value in any taxable year, after which the class B common stock has unlimited rights to such cash dividends. Upon liquidation, the holders of the class A common stock and class B common stock are entitled to share in the distribution of assets in the ratio of the par values of their stock.

Since the dividends on the class A common stock are limited to 6 percent of the par value of the stock in any taxable year, the class A common stock does not represent an unrestricted interest in the equity growth of the corporation.

HOLDING

In each situation, since the class A common stock has either a limited right to dividends or a limited right to assets upon liquidation, it is not common stock within the meaning of section 306(c) of the Code.

b. DISPOSITIONS OF SECTION 306 STOCK

Code: § 306(a).

Regulations: § 1.306–1.

The tax consequences of a disposition of Section 306 stock vary depending on whether the stock is sold or redeemed. If Section 306 stock is sold, the amount realized is treated as ordinary income to the extent of the stock's "ratable share" of the amount that would have been a dividend if the corporation had distributed cash in an amount equal to the fair market value of the stock at the time of the distribution. This rule requires the shareholder to look back to the time of distribution and determine to what extent a cash distribution would have emanated from the corporation's current or accumulated earnings and profits at that time.[1] The balance, if any, of the amount realized is

---

1. I.R.C. § 306(a)(1)(A). This provision also applies to other nonredemption "dispositions" such as certain pledges of Section 306 stock where the pledgee can only look to the stock as security (an unlikely scenario), but it does not apply to charitable contributions of Section 306 stock. Reg. § 1.306–1(b)(1); Rev.Rul. 57–328, 1957–2 C.B. 229.

treated as a reduction of the basis of the Section 306 stock, and any excess is treated as gain from the sale or exchange of the stock.[2] The ordinary income amount is not actually treated as a dividend and thus is not eligible for the Section 243 dividends received deduction, and the corporation is not entitled to reduce its earnings and profits when Section 306 stock is sold.[3] If the shareholder's adjusted basis in the stock exceeds the amount realized, no loss may be recognized, and any unrecovered basis must be allocated back to the stock with respect to which the Section 306 stock was distributed.[4]

A shareholder who receives a nontaxable stock dividend of Section 306 stock that later is redeemed by the corporation has used two steps to achieve what could have been accomplished in a single transaction: the withdrawal of cash from the corporation. To reflect that reality and treat the transactions as a single event, Section 306(a)(2) provides that the amount realized on a redemption of Section 306 stock is treated as a Section 301 distribution, taxable as a dividend to the extent of the current or accumulated earnings and profits in the year of redemption.[5] The balance of the distribution, if any, is treated as a reduction of basis and then capital gain under the rules generally applicable to nonliquidating distributions.[6]

c. DISPOSITIONS EXEMPT FROM SECTION 306

Code: § 306(b).

Regulations: § 1.306–2.

Section 306 is aimed only at bailouts, and not every disposition of Section 306 stock presents that opportunity. For example, a shareholder who sells her entire interest in a corporation (including her Section 306 stock) is not withdrawing corporate earnings while preserving control. She is engaging in a transaction that easily could have qualified for capital gain treatment irrespective of any prior stock dividend. Section 306(b)(1) thus provides that the punitive general rule of Section 306(a) shall not apply to nonredemption dispositions if the shareholder completely terminates her interest in the corporation and does not dispose of the stock to a related person within the Section 318 attribution rules.[1] A similar exception is provided for redemptions of Section 306 stock that result in a complete termination of the shareholder's interest under Section 302(b)(3) or qualify as a partial liquidation under Section 302(b)(4).[2]

Other exempt dispositions include: (1) redemptions of Section 306 stock in a complete liquidation;[3] (2) dispositions that are treated as nonrecognition transactions, such as tax-free Section 351 transfers,

---

2. I.R.C. § 306(a)(1)(B).

3. Reg. § 1.306–1(b)(1).

4. I.R.C. § 306(a)(1)(C); Reg. § 1.306–1(b)(2) Example (3).

5. I.R.C. § 306(a)(2).

6. See I.R.C. § 301(c)(2), (3).

1. For purposes of determining whether there has been a complete termination, the Section 318 attribution rules apply. I.R.C. § 306(b)(1)(A)(iii).

2. I.R.C. § 306(b)(1)(B).

3. I.R.C. § 306(b)(2).

contributions to capital and the like; [4] and (3) distributions and dispositions or redemptions found by the Internal Revenue Service as not made pursuant to a plan having tax avoidance as one of its principal purposes.[5] The "no tax avoidance" exception is explored in the *Fireoved* case, which follows.

FIREOVED v. UNITED STATES *

United States Court of Appeals, Third Circuit, 1972.
462 F.2d 1281.

ADAMS, Circuit Judge.

This appeal calls into question the application of section 306 of the Internal Revenue Code of 1954 and the "first in-first out rule" to a redemption of preferred stock in a corporation by plaintiff, one of its principal shareholders. In particular we are asked to decide whether the transaction here had "as one of its principal purposes the avoidance of Federal income tax," whether a prior sale of a portion of the underlying common stock immunized a like proportion of the section 306 stock from treatment as a noncapital asset, and whether another block of the redeemed stock should be considered to represent stock not subject to section 306.

I. *Factual Background*

On November 24, 1948, Fireoved and Company, Inc. was incorporated for the purpose of printing and selling business forms. At their first meeting, the incorporators elected Eugene Fireoved, his wife, Marie, the plaintiffs, and a nephew, Robert L. Fireoved, as directors of the corporation. Subsequently, the directors elected Eugene Fireoved as President and Treasurer and Marie Fireoved as Secretary. The corporation had authorized capital stock of 500 shares of $100 par value non-voting, non-cumulative preferred stock and 100 shares of $1 par value voting common stock. On December 31, 1948, in consideration for $100 cash, the corporation issued Eugene Fireoved 100 shares of common stock; for $500 cash, it issued him five shares of preferred stock; and in payment for automotive equipment and furniture and fixtures, valued at $6,000, it issued him an additional 60 shares of preferred stock.

In 1954, when Mr. Fireoved learned that his nephew, Robert, was planning to leave the business, he began discussions with Karl Edelmayer and Kenneth Craver concerning the possibility of combining his business with their partnership, Girard Business Forms, that had been printing and selling business forms for some time prior to 1954. Messrs. Fireoved, Edelmayer and Craver agreed that voting control of the new enterprise should be divided equally among the three of them.

---

4. I.R.C. § 306(b)(3).

5. I.R.C. § 306(b)(4). In Rev.Rul. 89–63, 1989–1 C.B. 90, the Service ruled that the mere fact that Section 306 stock is widely held is not an automatic ground for relief under the Section 306(b)(4) no tax avoidance purpose exception.

* Some footnotes omitted.

Because Mr. Fireoved's contribution to capital would be approximately $60,000 whereas the partnership could contribute only $30,000, it was decided that preferred stock should be issued to Mr. Fireoved to compensate for the disparity. In furtherance of this plan, the directors and shareholders of Fireoved and Company, in late 1954 and early 1955, held several meetings at which the following corporate changes were accomplished: The name of the company was changed to Girard Business Forms; the authorized common stock was increased from 100 to 300 shares and the authorized preferred stock was increased to 1000 shares; Mr. Fireoved exchanged his 100 shares of common and 65 shares of preferred stock for equal amounts of the new stock; an agreement of purchase was authorized by which the company would buy all the assets of the Edelmayer-Craver partnership in return for 200 shares of common and 298 shares of preferred stock; and Mr. Fireoved was issued 535 shares of the new preferred stock as a dividend [6] on his 100 shares of common stock, thereby bringing his total holding of preferred stock to 600 shares to indicate his $60,000 capital contribution compared to the $29,800 contributed by the former partnership.

As the business progressed, Mr. Edelmayer demanded more control of the company. In response, Mr. Fireoved and Mr. Craver each sold 24 shares of common stock in the corporation to him on February 28, 1958.

On April 30, 1959, the company redeemed 451 of Mr. Fireoved's 600 shares of preferred stock at $105 per share, resulting in net proceeds to him of $47,355.[7] The gain from this transaction was reported by Mr. and Mrs. Fireoved on their joint return for the year 1959 as a long term capital gain. Subsequently, the Commissioner of Internal Revenue (Commissioner) assessed a deficiency against the Fireoveds of $15,337.13 based on the Commissioner's view that the proceeds from the redemption of the 451 shares of preferred stock should have been reported as ordinary income and the tax paid at that rate based on section 306. Mr. and Mrs. Fireoved paid the assessment on March 14, 1963, but on March 10, 1965, filed a claim for a refund with the Commissioner.

After the Commissioner disallowed the refund claim on March 8, 1966, the Fireoveds instituted the present action against the United States on August 4, 1967 seeking a refund of the $15,337.13 plus interest on the ground that the transaction came within an exception to section 306, and that they were therefore entitled to report the income as a long term capital gain. The case was tried to the court without a jury on stipulated facts. It is from the district court's determination, 318 F.Supp. 133, on October 29, 1970, that $8,885.50 should be refunded to the taxpayers that both parties appeal.

---

6. At the time Mr. Fireoved received his stock dividend, the company had accumulated earnings and profits of $52,993.06.

7. In 1959, the company had accumulated earnings and profits of $48,235.

II. *Background of Section 306*

Because we are the first court of appeals asked to decide questions of law pursuant to section 306, it is appropriate that we first examine the circumstances that led to the inclusion in 1954 of this section in the Code.

Generally, a taxpayer will benefit monetarily if he is able to report income as a long term capital gain rather than as ordinary income. Under normal circumstances a cash dividend from a corporation constitutes ordinary income to the shareholder receiving such money. Therefore, it would be to the advantage of a shareholder if a method could be devised by which the money could be distributed to him, that would otherwise be paid out as cash dividends, in a form that would permit the shareholder to report such income as a long term capital gain.

A temporarily successful plan for converting ordinary income to long term capital gain is described by the facts of Chamberlin v. C.I.R., 207 F.2d 462 (6th Cir.1953). * * *

The legislative reaction to the *Chamberlin* decision was almost immediate, resulting in the addition of section 306 to the 1954 Code, in order to prevent shareholders from obtaining the tax advantage of such bail-outs when such shareholders retain their ownership interests in the company.

* * *

Based on the history of section 306 and its plain meaning evidenced by the provisions, it is not disputed that the 535 shares of preferred stock issued to Mr. Fireoved as a stock dividend in 1954 were section 306 stock. Additionally, it is clear that in 1959, when the company redeemed 451 shares of Mr. Fireoved's preferred stock, the general provisions of section 306—aside from the exceptions—would require that any amount realized by Mr. Fireoved be taxed at ordinary income rates rather than long term capital gain rates, because the company had earnings at that time of $48,235—more than the $47,355 required to redeem the stock at $105 per share.

Thus, the questions to be decided on this appeal are (1) whether certain of the exceptions to section 306 apply to permit the Fireoveds' reporting their gain as a long term capital gain, and (2) whether 65 of the 451 shares redeemed are not section 306 stock because of the first in-first out rule of Treasury Regulation § 1.1012–1(c).

III. *Was the distribution of the stock dividend "in pursuance of a plan having as one of its principal purposes avoidance of Federal income tax?"*

Mr. Fireoved asserts that the entire transaction should fall within the exception established by section 306(b)(4)(A), which provides: "If it is established to the satisfaction of the Secretary or his delegate * * * that the distribution, and the disposition or redemption * * * was not in pursuance of a plan having as one of its principal purposes the avoidance of Federal income tax," then the general rule of section 306(a) will not apply.

As a threshold point on this issue, the Government maintains that because Mr. Fireoved never attempted to obtain a ruling from the "Secretary or his delegate" the redemption should be covered by section 306(a), and the district court should not have reached the question whether the exception applied to Mr. Fireoved. Mr. Fireoved urges that the district court had the power to consider the matter *de novo,* even without a request by the taxpayer to the Secretary or his delegate. Because the ultimate result we reach would not be altered by whichever of these two courses we choose, we do not resolve this potentially complex procedural problem.[10]

The district court, based on the assumption that it had the power to decide the question, found that although one of the purposes involved in the issuance of the preferred stock dividend may have been business related, another principal purpose was the avoidance of Federal income tax.

Mr. Fireoved's analysis of the facts presented in the stipulations would reach the conclusion that the *sole* purpose of the stock dividend was business related. He relies heavily on that portion of the stipulation which describes why the decision was made to combine his business with the Edelmayer-Craver partnership: "The partnership could provide the additional manpower which the expected departure of Robert L. Fireoved from the Corporation would require. Additionally, the partnership needed additional working capital which the Corporation had and could provide." Based primarily on the latter sentence, Mr. Fireoved asserts that the district court had no choice but to find that the transaction was business related and that it therefore had no avoidance incentive.

In making this argument, however, Mr. Fireoved overlooks the plain import of the language of section 306(b)(4). Whether the section requires the decision to be made by the Secretary or the district court, it is clear that "one of [the] principal purposes" of the stock dividend was not for "the avoidance of Federal income tax." The stipulation demonstrates no more than that the reorganized company required more capital than could be supplied by the partnership alone. The stipulation is completely in harmony with the following fact situation: After the partnership was combined with the corporation, the business required the $30,000 contributed by the partnership and all of the $60,000 Mr. Fireoved had in the corporation. Mr. Fireoved decided to take the stock dividend rather than to distribute the cash to himself as a dividend, and then to make a loan to the corporation of the necessary money because if he took the cash, he would subject himself to taxation at ordinary income rates. Therefore "one of the principal purposes" of the stock dividend would be for "the avoidance of Federal income tax."

10. For the same reason, we do not decide this issue in Part II, infra.

In a situation such as the one presented in this case, where the facts necessary to determine the motives for the issuance of a stock dividend are peculiarly within the control of the taxpayer, it is reasonable to require the taxpayer to come forward with the facts that would relieve him of his liability. Here the stipulation was equivocal in determining the purpose of the dividend and is quite compatible with the thought that "one of the principal purposes" was motivated by "tax avoidance." We hold then that the district court did not err in refusing to apply the exception created by section 306(b)(4)(A).[11]

IV. Did the prior sale by Mr. Fireoved of 24% of his underlying common stock immunize such portion of the section 306 stock he redeemed in 1959?

The district court construed section 306(b)(4)(B) to mean that any time a taxpayer in Mr. Fireoved's position sells any portion of his underlying common stock and later sells or redeems his section 306 stock, an equivalent proportion of the section 306 stock redeemed will not be subject to the provisions of section 306(a). The Government has appealed from this portion of the district court's order and urges that we reverse it, based on the history and purpose of section 306 and the particular facts here.

The stipulations indicate that, "On February 28, 1958, Fireoved and Craver each sold 24 shares of common stock in the corporation to Edelmayer," and that appropriate stock certificates were issued. From this fact, Mr. Fireoved reasons that his sale of 24 of his 100 shares of common stock was undertaken solely for the business purpose of satisfying Mr. Edelmayer's desire for more control of the corporation, and therefore he should be given the benefit of section 306(b)(4)(B). In addition, Mr. Fireoved contends that the disposition of his section 306 stock was related to a business purpose because he used part of the proceeds to pay off a $20,000 loan that the company had made to him.

Mr. Fireoved has the same burden here of showing a lack of a tax avoidance purpose that he had in section III supra. It is clear from the limited facts set forth in the stipulations that he has not established that the disposition of 24% of the 535 shares of the section 306 preferred stock he owned "was not in pursuance of a plan having as one of its principal purposes the avoidance of federal income tax."[12] More

---

11. It is important to note that apparently both Mr. Fireoved, in prosecuting this action for a refund, and the Government, in its defense, assumed that if the distribution and redemption of the preferred stock were not controlled by § 306(a), the gain would be subject to taxation as a long term capital gain. This is not necessarily the case at all. Whether or not § 306 governs the transaction, it nonetheless involves a redemption of stock by a corporation to which § 302 could apply. Under the tests set out in § 302(b)—the relevant one of which appears to be

§ 302(b)(1)—Mr. Fireoved, who had the burden of proof, may well have been unable to show that the redemption was not "essentially equivalent to a dividend." United States v. Davis, 397 U.S. 301, 90 S.Ct. 1041, 25 L.Ed.2d 323 (1970). We hold, however, that it is now too late for the Government to raise this issue.

12. Consistent with Mr. Fireoved's sale of 24 shares of common stock in 1958 could have been his knowledge that one year later he would be selling his section 306 stock and a desire on his part to avoid

important, however, is that an examination of the relevant legislative history indicates that Congress did not intend to give capital gains treatment to a portion of the preferred stock redeemed on the facts presented here.

It is apparent from the reaction evinced by Congress to the *Chamberlin* case, supra, that by enacting section 306 Congress was particularly concerned with the tax advantages available to persons who controlled corporations and who could, without sacrificing their control, convert ordinary income to long term capital gains by the device of the preferred stock bail-out. The illustration given in the Senate Report which accompanied section 306(b)(4)(B) is helpful in determining the sort of transactions meant to be exempted by section 306(a):

> Thus if a shareholder received a distribution of 100 shares of section 306 stock on his holdings of 100 shares of voting common stock in a corporation and sells his voting common stock before he disposes of his section 306 stock, the subsequent disposition of his section 306 stock would not ordinarily be considered a tax avoidance disposition *since he has previously parted with the stock which allows him to participate in the ownership of the business.* However, variations of the above example may give rise to tax avoidance possibilities which are not within the exception of subparagraph (B). Thus if a corporation has only one class of common stock outstanding and it issues stock under circumstances that characterize it as section 306 stock, a subsequent issue of a different Class of common having greater voting rights than the original common will not permit a simultaneous disposition of the section 306 stock together with the original common to escape the rules of subsection (a) of section 306.

> S.Rep. No. 1622, 83d Cong., 2d Sess., 1954 U.S.C.C.A. News, pp. 4621, 4881 (emphasis added).

Thus, it is reasonable to assume that Congress realized the general lack of a tax avoidance purpose when a person sells *all* of his control in a corporation and then either simultaneously or subsequently disposes of his section 306 stock. However, when *only a portion* of the underlying common stock is sold, and the taxpayer retains essentially all the control he had previously, it would be unrealistic to conclude that Congress meant to give that taxpayer the advantage of section 306(b)(4)

taxation at ordinary income rates. As noted later in the opinion, the sale of just 24 shares was enough so that he retained effective control—in the form of veto power—over the corporation. Moreover, the fact that Mr. Fireoved needed $20,000 of the proceeds to pay off a loan to the corporation would not meet his burden. The proceeds of the redemption totaled $47,355. Thus, although $20,000 of the redemption may not have been to avoid taxes, we can ascribe no purpose other than tax avoidance to the receipt of the additional $27,355. Therefore, since one of the principal purposes of the redemption of 451 shares of preferred stock was "the avoidance of Federal income tax," Mr. Fireoved may not take advantage of § 306(b)(4)(B) for any part of the redemption.

(B) when he ultimately sells his section 306 stock.[13] Cf. United States v. Davis, 397 U.S. 301, 90 S.Ct. 1041, 25 L.Ed.2d 323 (1970).

Shortly after Mr. Fireoved's corporation had been combined with the Edelmayer-Craver partnership, significant changes to the by-laws were made. The by-laws provided that corporate action could be taken only with the unanimous consent of all the directors. In addition, the by-laws provided that they could be amended either by a vote of 76% of the outstanding common shares or a unanimous vote of the directors. When the businesses were combined in late 1954, each of the directors held ⅓ of the voting stock, thereby necessitating a unanimous vote for amendment to the by-laws. After Messrs. Fireoved and Craver each sold 24 shares of common stock to Mr. Edelmayer, Mr. Fireoved held 25⅓% of the common (voting) stock, Mr. Craver 25⅓% and Mr. Edelmayer 49⅓%. It is crucial to note that the by-laws provided for a unanimous vote for corporate action, and after the common stock transfer, the by-laws were capable of amendment only by a unanimous vote because no two shareholders could vote more than 74⅔% of the common stock and 76% of the common stock was necessary for amendment. Thus, although Mr. Fireoved did sell a portion of his voting stock prior to his disposition of the section 306 stock, he retained as much control in the corporation following the sale of his common stock as he had prior to the sale. Under these circumstances it is not consonant with the history of the legislation to conclude that Congress intended such a sale of underlying common stock to exempt the proceeds of the disposition of section 306 stock from treatment as ordinary income. Accordingly, the district court erred when it held that any of the preferred shares Mr. Fireoved redeemed were not subject to section 306(a) by virtue of section 306(b)(4)(B).[14]

V. *Does the rule of first in-first out mean that 65 of the 451 redeemed shares were those which Mr. Fireoved acquired when he incorporated his business in 1948 and thus should not be treated as section 306 stock?*

The district court held that 65 of 451 shares of preferred stock that Mr. Fireoved redeemed in 1959 represented the original shares issued to him in 1948 and were not, therefore, section 306 stock, and that the

---

13. Although this point was neither briefed nor argued, it might be contended, based on an analogous provision of the Code, § 1239, that § 306 should look strictly to a change in ownership rather than actual control of the corporation. When dealing with questions arising under § 1239, courts have considered only changes in the percentage of ownership without regard to whether control of the corporation has shifted. See, e.g., United States v. Parker, 376 F.2d 402 (5th Cir. 1967); Trotz v. Commissioner, 361 F.2d 927 (10th Cir.1966). However, the legislative intent embodied in § 306 is so different from that of § 1239, that, based on the facts presented here, control is the relevant inquiry under § 306.

14. It is important to note that our decision relates only to the facts of this case. We express no view on the situation in which less than all the voting shares are sold but enough are disposed of to relinquish effective control prior to or simultaneous with the sale of section 306 stock.

proceeds from their sales should be treated as a long term capital gain. The court reached this conclusion by applying Treas.Reg. § 1.1012–1(c). This regulation provides that when an individual acquires shares of the same class of stock in the same corporation on different dates and for different prices, sells a portion of those shares, and cannot adequately identify which lots were sold, for the purpose of determining the basis and the holding period, the first shares acquired are deemed to be the first shares sold.

Both the district court and Mr. Fireoved reason that the 65 preferred shares he received in 1948 were the first such shares owned by him. In 1954, when the corporation was recapitalized, Mr. Fireoved surrendered his certificate for 65 shares, received a 535 share stock dividend and was issued a certificate representing 600 shares of preferred stock. When he disposed of 451 shares in 1959, it was impossible to identify which shares of the 600 share certificate were being sold. By applying the convenient tool of section 1.1012–1(c), one might conclude that the 65 original shares were sold first because they were received first.

Superficially, this analysis appears to be correct. However, it overlooks the existence of Section 1223(5) of the Code and the regulations issued pursuant thereto. This section governs the transaction in question because section 307 required Mr. Fireoved to allocate his investment in the underlying common stock between the stock and the preferred stock issued as a dividend. Section 1223(5) is then clear in that it will apply to all situations in which an allocation of basis has occurred pursuant to section 307. These provisions broadly state that the holding period for stock received as a stock dividend is equal to the period for which the underlying stock was held. Applying this test we discover that the preferred stock dividend of 535 shares was issued with respect to the original 100 shares of common received by Mr. Fireoved. Therefore, the holding period for the 535 shares dividend relates back to the date on which the underlying common was issued. Coincidentally, the original 65 shares of preferred stock were issued on the same date as the common. Because the constructive date of issuance for all of the 600 shares of preferred stock owned by Mr. Fireoved is identical, neither the 65 shares nor the 535 shares are first in, but rather are in at the same time.

Since it is impossible adequately to identify which shares were sold when Mr. Fireoved redeemed 451 shares of preferred stock, we hold that a pro rata portion of the 65 shares were redeemed in 1959. In other words, the percentage of the 600 shares of preferred which were not section 306 stock may be represented by the fraction $65/600$. That percentage of the 451 shares redeemed in 1959, therefore, would not be section 306 stock.[15]

---

15. The number of shares may be determined as follows: $65/600 \times 451 = 48.86$ shares of non-section 306 stock.

VI. Conclusion

Because we affirm in part and reverse in part the judgment of the district court, the cause will be remanded for proceedings consistent with this opinion.

PROBLEMS

1. In year one, Argonaut Corporation distributed nonconvertible nonvoting preferred stock worth $1,000 to each of its two unrelated equal common shareholders, Jason and Vera. The Argonaut common stock owned by each of the shareholders had a basis of $2,000 prior to the distribution and a value of $3,000 immediately after the distribution. At the time of the distribution, Argonaut had $2,000 of earnings and profits. In year three, Argonaut had $3,000 of earnings and profits.

   (a) What are the tax consequences to Jason, Vera and Argonaut of the distribution of preferred stock in year one?

   (b) What results to Vera and Argonaut if Vera sells her preferred stock to Carl, an unrelated party, for $1,000 in year three?

   (c) Same as (b), above, except that Vera sells her preferred stock to Carl for $1,750?

   (d) Same as (b), above, except that Argonaut had no earnings and profits at the time of the distribution of the preferred stock?

   (e) What results if Jason gives his preferred stock to his grandson, Claude, and Claude later sells the stock for $1,000? What if Jason dies and bequeaths his preferred stock to Claude?

   (f) What results to Jason and Argonaut if in year three the corporation redeems half of Jason's common stock for $5,000 and all of his preferred stock for $1,500?

   (g) Same as (f), above, except the corporate bylaws require unanimous shareholder agreement for corporate action, and the bylaws may be amended only with the concurrence of more than 75 percent of the shareholders.

   (h) Same as (f), above, except that Argonaut has no accumulated or current earnings and profits in year three.

2. Zapco Corporation has 100 shares of common stock outstanding all of which are owned by Sam Shifty. Zapco has an ample supply of current and accumulated earnings and profits.

   (a) If Sam forms Holding Co. by transferring 50 Zapco shares in exchange for 100 shares of Holding common stock and 100 shares of Holding preferred stock, will any of the Holding shares be Section 306 stock?

   (b) What result if Zapco were owned equally (50 shares each) by Sam Shifty and Selma Zap, who is unrelated to Sam, and the two shareholders form Holding Co. by transferring all their

Zapco stock with Sam taking back 100 shares of Holding Co. common stock and Selma taking back 50 shares of Holding Co. preferred stock and 50 shares of Holding Co. common stock?

CHAPTER 7. COMPLETE LIQUIDATIONS AND TAXABLE CORPORATE ACQUISITIONS

A. INTRODUCTION

We have been present at the creation of a corporation and nurtured the corporate entity as it engaged in distributions, redemptions, partial liquidations and maneuvers to mitigate the double tax. In this chapter, the focus shifts to the end of a C corporation's life cycle.

A few definitions are in order to set the stage. The Code does not define "complete liquidation," but the regulations provide that liquidation status exists for tax purposes "when the corporation ceases to be a going concern and its activities are merely for the purpose of winding up its affairs, paying its debts, and distributing any remaining balance to its shareholders." [1] Legal dissolution under state law is not required for the liquidation to be complete, and a transaction will be treated as a liquidation even if the corporation retains a nominal amount of assets to pay any remaining debts and preserve its legal existence.[2]

Liquidations often are preceded by a sale of substantially all of a corporation's assets and a distribution of the sales proceeds to the shareholders in exchange for their stock. Alternatively, the buyer of a corporate business may acquire all the stock of the target company and either keep the old corporation alive or cause it to be liquidated. But liquidations do not necessarily involve sales. The corporation simply may distribute its assets in kind to the shareholders, who either may sell the assets or continue to operate the business outside of corporate solution. Or a parent corporation may wish to rearrange its holdings by liquidating or selling the stock of a subsidiary.

All these transactions raise tax issues at the shareholder and corporate levels. Historically, individual shareholders have hoped to emerge from a complete liquidation or sale of a profitable corporate business by realizing a capital gain on their stock and deferring recognition of the gain until cash payments are received. At the corporate level, the goals generally have been to avoid recognition of gain on a distribution or sale of assets while providing the shareholders (in a liquidation) or the purchaser (in an acquisition) with a fair market value basis in the distributed or acquired assets. Prior to 1987, most of these objectives could be met with careful planning, but liquidations and taxable dispositions of a corporate business are far more expensive after the Tax Reform Act of 1986. This chapter surveys the current landscape, examining first the shareholder and corporate level tax

---

1. Reg. § 1.332–2(c). This regulation technically applies only to the liquidation of a subsidiary, but it has long been assumed to apply also to ordinary liquidations.

2. See, e.g., Rev.Rul. 54–518, 1954–2 C.B. 142.

consequences of complete liquidations and then considering a variety of alternative methods to structure a taxable purchase and sale of a corporate business. Later chapters will consider tax-free acquisition techniques known as corporate reorganizations and the carryover of tax attributes following an acquisition.[3]

B. COMPLETE LIQUIDATIONS

1. CONSEQUENCES TO THE SHAREHOLDERS

Code: §§ 331; 334(a); 346(a); 453(h)(1)(A)–(B).

Regulations: § 1.331–1(a), (b), (e).

The complete liquidation of a corporation presents an opportunity to revisit several policy issues that recur throughout the study of Subchapter C. Consider the appropriate tax consequences to Owner, a sole shareholder of X Corporation, who desires to liquidate X and continue to operate its business as a proprietorship. Assume that X has been profitable and has ample earnings and profits at the time of its liquidation. From Owner's standpoint, should the liquidation be treated as: (1) a nonrecognition transaction akin to an incorporation, (2) a dividend distribution, (3) an exchange of the stock for the distributed assets or (4) some combination of the above?

If Owner continues to operate the business as a sole proprietorship, the liquidation results in a mere change in the form of his investment. Since Congress granted nonrecognition treatment to Owner when he transferred the business into corporate solution, is it not also appropriate to treat the transfer of those assets back into Owner's hands as a tax-free event? This analogy has a superficial appeal but Congress has never seriously considered it except in very limited situations.[1] Nonrecognition is inconsistent with the double tax regime of Subchapter C because it would facilitate the tax-free bailout of earnings and profits. Moreover, many complete liquidations involve the sale of a business followed by a distribution of the cash proceeds to the shareholders. Cash distributions do not lend themselves to a nonrecognition regime because it is impossible to assign money the substituted basis that would be necessary to preserve the shareholder's gain for recognition at a later time. Similarly, any attempt to preserve the liquidated corporation's earnings and profits in the hands of its former shareholders would be cumbersome and inconsistent with the termination of the corporation.

A stronger case can be made for treating a liquidating distribution as a dividend to the extent of the corporation's remaining earnings and profits. Because earnings and profits disappear on a complete liquidation, this is the last chance to tax a shareholder's withdrawal of corporate profits as ordinary income. By triggering the distribution

---

3. See Chapters 10 and 13, infra.

1. See, e.g., I.R.C. § 332, discussed in Section B3 of this chapter, infra.

rules of Sections 301 and 316, this approach would focus on the source of the liquidating distribution rather than the shareholder's relationship to his investment. Dividend treatment, however, is inconsistent with Section 302, which treats a distribution in redemption as an exchange if the shareholder completely terminates or substantially reduces his interest in the corporation. Why should a complete termination of the interests of all the shareholders be treated any less favorably? Moreover, if liquidating distributions were treated as dividends to the extent of the corporation's earnings and profits, a shareholder's stock basis might never be recovered.

The redemption analogy leads to a third approach, which would treat a complete liquidation as a sale of stock by the shareholder. This approach is far from perfect, if only because it ignores the disappearance of the earnings and profits account, a clean sweep that does not occur on a sale of stock. But after a period of waffling,[2] Congress opted to treat liquidations as exchanges, an approach that permits shareholders to avoid the dividend sting and be taxed at capital gains rates. Congress concluded that the dividend threat was "preventing liquidation of many corporations" because of the high tax cost it imposed and therefore was generating only minimal revenue.[3] It regarded exchange treatment as "consistent with the entire theory of the [Code]" and as "the only method * * * which can be easily administered."[4] Even without a significant capital gains preference, exchange treatment generally remains preferable to a dividend because shareholders may recover their stock basis.

The Congressional policy is codified in Section 331(a), which provides that amounts received by a shareholder in complete liquidation are treated as full payment in exchange for the shareholder's stock. The vast majority of shareholders hold their stock as a capital asset and will recognize capital gain or loss in an amount equal to the difference between (1) the money and fair market value of the property received and (2) the shareholder's adjusted basis in the stock surrendered. In keeping with the exchange analogy, Section 334(a) provides that the shareholder's basis in property distributed in a complete liquidation that is taxable at the shareholder level shall be the fair market value of the property at the time of the distribution.

Computation of a shareholder's gain or loss on a complete liquidation is ordinarily a straightforward affair. The shareholder's amount realized is the money and the fair market value of all other property received from the liquidating corporation. If a shareholder assumes corporate liabilities or receives property subject to a liability in a liquidating distribution, the amount realized is limited to the value of

---

2. Liquidations were first treated as exchanges in the Revenue Act of 1924. Congress changed its mind briefly from 1934 to 1936 and then reinstated the present system.

3. H.R.Rep. No. 2475, 74th Cong., 2d Sess. (1936), reprinted in 1939–1 (Part 2) C.B. 667, 674.

4. S.Rep. No. 368, 68th Cong., 1st Sess. (1924), reprinted in 1939–1 (Part 2) C.B. 266, 274.

the property received, net of liabilities. In keeping with the principles of the *Crane* case, however, it is assumed that the distributee shareholder will pay the liabilities and he thus obtains a full fair market value basis in the property under Section 334(a).

Shareholders who hold several blocks of stock with different bases and acquisition dates must compute their gain or loss separately for each block rather than on an aggregate basis.[5] This method generally only makes a difference, however, if there is a tax preference for long-term capital gains and some shares are held long-term and others short-term; otherwise, the tax consequences will be identical whether the shareholder uses a share-by-share or an aggregate approach.[6]

The timing of a shareholder's gain or loss on a complete liquidation raises some thornier questions. A liquidating corporation often is unable to distribute all of its property at one time or within the same taxable year. Recognizing these practical constraints, Section 346(a) defines a complete liquidation to include a series of distributions occurring over a period of time if they are all pursuant to a plan of complete liquidation. Shareholders normally prefer to treat these "creeping complete" liquidations as open transactions so they can defer reporting any gain until the amounts received exceed their stock basis.[7] Although this cost recovery approach has been sanctioned by the Service in the liquidation context,[8] it would appear to have been foreclosed by the Installment Sales Revision Act of 1980. In revising Section 453 at that time, Congress sought to limit open transaction reporting even in cases where the selling price could not be readily ascertained.[9] Since liquidating distributions are treated as payments in exchange for the shareholders' stock, Section 453 technically seems to apply and, if so, shareholders wishing to defer their gain should be required to use the installment method, allocating each distribution between recovery of basis and taxable gain.[10]

---

5. Reg. § 1.331–1(e). For example, assume that Shareholder ("S") holds 60 shares of X, Inc. stock long-term with a $30,000 basis and 40 shares short-term with a $50,000 basis. If S receives $100,000 in complete liquidation of X, he must allocate the amount realized ratably between the two blocks as follows:

Long-Term 60 shares		Short-Term 40 shares	
A.R.	$60,000	A.R.	$40,000
A.B.	30,000	A.B.	50,000
LTCG	$30,000	STCL	$10,000

6. For the problems of valuation of the liquidating distribution and handling contingent claims, see Bittker & Eustice, Federal Income Taxation of Corporations & Shareholders ¶ 11.03 (5th ed. 1987).

7. See, e.g., Burnet v. Logan, 283 U.S. 404, 51 S.Ct. 550 (1931). Cf. I.R.C. § 453(d).

8. Rev.Rul. 68–348, 1968–2 C.B. 141, amplified by Rev.Rul. 85–48, 1985–1 C.B. 126.

9. See I.R.C. § 453(j)(2); Reg. § 15A.453-1(c). See also S.Rep. No. 96–1000, 96th Cong., 2d Sess. 24 (1980), reprinted in 1980–2 C.B. 494, 506–507. But see Rev.Rul. 85–48, supra note 8, where in amplifying an earlier ruling, the Service continued to sanction open transaction reporting of gain on a liquidation notwithstanding the enactment of the Installment Sales Revision Act of 1980.

10. Installment sale reporting is not available if the stock of the liquidating corporation is publicly traded. See I.R.C. § 453(k)(2), requiring current inclusion of gain on deferred payment dispositions of stock or securities traded on an established securities market. If open transaction reporting is still generally available to liquidating distributions, this restriction

Shareholders of a liquidating corporation also may defer part of their Section 331(a) gain if the corporation sells certain assets for installment notes and then distributes the notes in complete liquidation. Section 453(h)(1)(A) provides that if a liquidating distribution consists of installment obligations acquired by the corporation in respect of a sale or exchange of property during the 12-month period beginning on the date a plan of complete liquidation is adopted and the liquidation is completed within that 12-month period,[11] the receipt of payments on the obligations (but not the receipt of the obligations) is treated as the receipt of payment for the shareholder's stock. As a result, the shareholder may report a portion of the gain on the liquidation on the installment method as payments are received on the underlying installment obligation.[12]

PROBLEM

A owns 100 shares of Humdrum Corporation which he purchased several years ago for $10,000. Humdrum has $12,000 of accumulated earnings and profits. What are the tax consequences to A on the liquidation of Humdrum Corporation in the following alternative situations:

(a) Humdrum distributes $20,000 to A in exchange for his stock?
　　　　10 K gain

(b) What result in (a), above, if A receives $10,000 in the current year (year one) and $10,000 in year two? Would there be any problem if Humdrum does not adopt a formal plan of complete liquidation in year one?

(c) Humdrum distributes $8,000 cash and an installment obligation with a face and fair market value of $12,000, payable $1,000 per year for 12 years with market rate interest. The installment obligation was received by Humdrum two months ago, after the adoption of the plan of liquidation, on the sale of a capital asset. Would the result be different if Humdrum's stock were publicly traded? See I.R.C. § 453(k).

presumbaly does not apply when a shareholder of a public company receives a series of distributions straddling two or more taxable years. See also I.R.C. § 453(d), which permits a taxpayer to "elect out" of installment sale treatment. In the case of a liquidation, an election out would require the shareholder to report his entire gain in the year of the first distribution except, perhaps, where the value of future distributions is unascertainable. See Reg. § 15A.453–1(d).

11. Installment obligations arising from the sale of inventory or other "dealer property" by the corporation are eligible for installment sale treatment in the hands of the distributee shareholders only if the ob-

ligation resulted from a bulk sale—i.e., the sale was to one person in one transaction and involves substantially all of the property attributable to a trade or business of the corporation. I.R.C. § 453(h)(1)(B).

12. I.R.C. § 453(h)(1)(A). Installment reporting is not available, however, if the stock of the liquidating corporation is publicly traded. I.R.C. § 453(k)(2). If a shareholder receives liquidating distributions that include installment obligations in more than one taxable year, he must recompute his gain, on completion of the liquidation, by allocating his basis in the stock pro rata over all the payments received or to be received. I.R.C. § 453(h)(2).

(d) Same as (c), above, except the installment obligation was received two years ago and no payments have yet been made.

(e) What result in (a), above, if two years later, A is required to pay a $5,000 judgment against Humdrum in his capacity as transferee of the corporation? Compare this with the result if the judgment had been rendered and paid by the corporation prior to the liquidation. See Arrowsmith v. Commissioner, 344 U.S. 6, 73 S.Ct. 71 (1952).

2. CONSEQUENCES TO THE LIQUIDATING CORPORATION *

Code: § 336(a), (b), (c), (d). Skim § 267(a)(1), (b), (c).

It should come as no surprise at this juncture that Subchapter C requires distributions of property by corporations to their shareholders to be analyzed at both the corporate and shareholder levels. Earlier chapters have chronicled the gradual erosion of the *General Utilities* [1] doctrine, under which a corporation generally did not recognize gain on nonliquidating distributions of appreciated property. We have seen that recognition of gain (but not loss) is now the statutory norm in the nonliquidation setting.[2] Should the same rules apply to liquidating distributions and sales of assets by a liquidating corporation? Once again, a brief historical interlude is appropriate before considering the current answers to this much debated question.

a. BACKGROUND

Although the *General Utilities* case involved a distribution of appreciated property by an ongoing business, the doctrine also applied to liquidating distributions. Until the enactment of the 1986 Code, a corporation generally did not recognize gain or loss on the distribution of property in complete liquidation.[3] Prior to 1954, however, sales of assets by a liquidating corporation were fully taxable.

To illustrate the disparate tax treatment of liquidating distributions and sales under the pre–1954 regime, assume that A is the sole shareholder of Target Corporation ("T") and has a $100,000 basis in her T stock. T's only asset is a parcel of undeveloped land ("Gainacre") with a fair market value of $400,000 and a zero adjusted basis. Purchaser ("P") wishes to acquire Gainacre for $400,000 cash. If T distributed Gainacre to A in complete liquidation, it recognized no gain under the General Utilities doctrine, and A took Gainacre with a $400,000 fair

---

* See Yin, "Taxing Corporate Liquidations (and Related Matters) After the Tax Reform Act of 1986," 42 Tax L.Rev. 573 (1987).

1. General Utilities & Operating Co. v. Helvering, 296 U.S. 200, 56 S.Ct. 185 (1935); see Chapters 4D1 and 5E1, supra.

2. I.R.C. § 311(a), (b).

3. I.R.C. § 336(a) (pre–1987). This general nonrecognition rule was subject to various exceptions, such as the statutory recapture of depreciation provisions and the judicially created tax benefit rule and assignment of income doctrine. See, e.g., Hillsboro National Bank v. Commissioner, 460 U.S. 370, 103 S.Ct. 1134 (1983).

market value basis. On a sale of Gainacre to P for $400,000 following the liquidation, A thus would recognize no gain. If, instead, T had sold Gainacre directly to P, it would have recognized $400,000 gain under the pre–1954 regime. In either case, A recognized gain on the liquidation of T, measured by the difference between the amount of the distribution and her $100,000 adjusted basis in the T stock.

The different tax results of these economically equivalent transactions prompted savvy taxpayers to "postpone" sales of corporate assets until after a liquidation in order to avoid a corporate-level tax. The ignorant did what came naturally—and often was a practical necessity for large corporations with many assets and shareholders—by selling assets at the corporate level prior to the liquidation. With such high tax stakes, the courts were called upon to determine who *in substance* made the sale—an inquiry that engendered some anomalous results, as evidenced by the two cases that follow.

COMMISSIONER v. COURT HOLDING CO.*

Supreme Court of the United States, 1945.
324 U.S. 331, 65 S.Ct. 707.

Mr. Justice BLACK delivered the opinion of the Court.

An apartment house, which was the sole asset of the respondent corporation, was transferred in the form of a liquidating dividend to the corporation's two shareholders. They in turn formally conveyed it to a purchaser who had originally negotiated for the purchase from the corporation. The question is whether the Circuit Court of Appeals properly reversed the Tax Court's conclusion that the corporation was taxable under § 22 of the Internal Revenue Code for the gain which accrued from the sale. The answer depends upon whether the findings of the Tax Court that the whole transaction showed a sale by the corporation rather than by the stockholders were final and binding upon the Circuit Court of Appeals.

It is unnecessary to set out in detail the evidence introduced before the Tax Court or its findings. Despite conflicting evidence, the following findings of the Tax Court are supported by the record:

The respondent corporation was organized in 1934 solely to buy and hold the apartment building which was the only property ever owned by it. All of its outstanding stock was owned by Minnie Miller and her husband. Between October 1, 1939 and February, 1940, while the corporation still had legal title to the property, negotiations for its sale took place. These negotiations were between the corporation and the lessees of the property, together with a sister and brother-in-law. An oral agreement was reached as to the terms and conditions of sale, and on February 22, 1940, the parties met to reduce the agreement to writing. The purchaser was then advised by the corporation's attorney that the sale could not be consummated because it would result in the

* Footnotes omitted.

imposition of a large income tax on the corporation. The next day, the corporation declared a "liquidating dividend," which involved complete liquidation of its assets, and surrender of all outstanding stock. Mrs. Miller and her husband surrendered their stock, and the building was deeded to them. A sale contract was then drawn, naming the Millers individually as vendors, and the lessees' sister as vendee, which embodied substantially the same terms and conditions previously agreed upon. One thousand dollars, which a month and a half earlier had been paid to the corporation by the lessees, was applied in part payment of the purchase price. Three days later, the property was conveyed to the lessees' sister.

The Tax Court concluded from these facts that, despite the declaration of a "liquidating dividend" followed by the transfers of legal title, the corporation had not abandoned the sales negotiations; that these were mere formalities designed "to make the transaction appear to be other than what it was" in order to avoid tax liability. The Circuit Court of Appeals drawing different inferences from the record, held that the corporation had "called off" the sale, and treated the stockholders' sale as unrelated to the prior negotiations.

There was evidence to support the findings of the Tax Court, and its findings must therefore be accepted by the courts. Dobson v. Commissioner, 320 U.S. 489; Commissioner v. Heininger, 320 U.S. 467; Commissioner v. Scottish American Investment Co., 323 U.S. 119. On the basis of these findings, the Tax Court was justified in attributing the gain from the sale to respondent corporation. The incidence of taxation depends upon the substance of a transaction. The tax consequences which arise from gains from a sale of property are not finally to be determined solely by the means employed to transfer legal title. Rather, the transaction must be viewed as a whole, and each step, from the commencement of negotiations to the consummation of the sale, is relevant. A sale by one person cannot be transformed for tax purposes into a sale by another by using the latter as a conduit through which to pass title. To permit the true nature of a transaction to be disguised by mere formalisms, which exist solely to alter tax liabilities, would seriously impair the effective administration of the tax policies of Congress.

It is urged that respondent corporation never executed a written agreement, and that an oral agreement to sell land cannot be enforced in Florida because of the Statute of Frauds, Comp.Gen.Laws of Florida, 1927, vol. 3, § 5779. But the fact that respondent corporation itself never executed a written contract is unimportant, since the Tax Court found from the facts of the entire transaction that the executed sale was in substance the sale of the corporation. The decision of the Circuit Court of Appeals is reversed, and that of the Tax Court affirmed.

It is so ordered.

UNITED STATES v. CUMBERLAND PUBLIC SERVICE CO.*

Supreme Court of the United States, 1950.
338 U.S. 451, 70 S.Ct. 280.

Mr. Justice BLACK delivered the opinion of the Court.

A corporation selling its physical properties is taxed on capital gains resulting from the sale. There is no corporate tax, however, on distribution of assets in kind to shareholders as part of a genuine liquidation. The respondent corporation transferred property to its shareholders as a liquidating dividend in kind. The shareholders transferred it to a purchaser. The question is whether, despite contrary findings by the Court of Claims, this record requires a holding that the transaction was in fact a sale by the corporation subjecting the corporation to a capital gains tax.

Details of the transaction are as follows. The respondent, a closely held corporation, was long engaged in the business of generating and distributing electric power in three Kentucky counties. In 1936 a local cooperative began to distribute Tennessee Valley Authority power in the area served by respondent. It soon became obvious that respondent's Diesel-generated power could not compete with TVA power, which respondent had been unable to obtain. Respondent's shareholders, realizing that the corporation must get out of the power business unless it obtained TVA power, accordingly offered to sell all the corporate stock to the cooperative, which was receiving such power. The cooperative refused to buy the stock, but countered with an offer to buy from the corporation its transmission and distribution equipment. The corporation rejected the offer because it would have been compelled to pay a heavy capital gains tax. At the same time the shareholders, desiring to save payment of the corporate capital gains tax, offered to acquire the transmission and distribution equipment and then sell to the cooperative. The cooperative accepted. The corporation transferred the transmission and distribution systems to its shareholders in partial liquidation. The remaining assets were sold and the corporation dissolved. The shareholders then executed the previously contemplated sale to the cooperative.

Upon this sale by the shareholders, the Commissioner assessed and collected a $17,000 tax from the corporation on the theory that the shareholders had been used as a mere conduit for effectuating what was really a corporate sale. Respondent corporation brought this action to recover the amount of the tax. The Court of Claims found that the method by which the stockholders disposed of the properties was avowedly chosen in order to reduce taxes, but that the liquidation and dissolution genuinely ended the corporation's activities and existence. The court also found that at no time did the corporation plan to make the sale itself. Accordingly it found as a fact that the sale was made by

* Some footnotes omitted.

the shareholders rather than the corporation, and entered judgment for respondent.   One judge dissented, believing that our opinion in Commissioner v. Court Holding Co., 324 U.S. 331, required a finding that the sale had been made by the corporation.   Certiorari was granted, 338 U.S. 846, to clear up doubts arising out of the *Court Holding Co.* case.

Our *Court Holding Co.* decision rested on findings of fact by the Tax Court that a sale had been made and gains realized by the taxpayer corporation.   There the corporation had negotiated for sale of its assets and had reached an oral agreement of sale.   When the tax consequences of the corporate sale were belatedly recognized, the corporation purported to "call off" the sale at the last minute and distributed the physical properties in kind to the stockholders.   They promptly conveyed these properties to the same persons who had negotiated with the corporation.   The terms of purchase were substantially those of the previous oral agreement.   One thousand dollars already paid to the corporation was applied as part payment of the purchase price.   The Tax Court found that the corporation never really abandoned its sales negotiations, that it never did dissolve, and that the sole purpose of the so-called liquidation was to disguise a corporate sale through use of mere formalisms in order to avoid tax liability.   The Circuit Court of Appeals took a different view of the evidence.   In this Court the Government contended that whether a liquidation distribution was genuine or merely a sham was traditionally a question of fact.   We agreed with this contention, and reinstated the Tax Court's findings and judgment.   Discussing the evidence which supported the findings of fact, we went on to say that "the incidence of taxation depends upon the substance of a transaction" regardless of "mere formalisms," and that taxes on a corporate sale cannot be avoided by using the shareholders as a "conduit through which to pass title."

This language does not mean that a corporation can be taxed even when the sale has been made by its stockholders following a genuine liquidation and dissolution.[3]   While the distinction between sales by a corporation as compared with distribution in kind followed by shareholder sales may be particularly shadowy and artificial when the corporation is closely held, Congress has chosen to recognize such a distinction for tax purposes.   The corporate tax is thus aimed primarily at the profits of a going concern.   This is true despite the fact that gains realized from corporate sales are taxed, perhaps to prevent tax evasions, even where the cash proceeds are at once distributed in

---

3.   What we said in the *Court Holding Co.* case was an approval of the action of the Tax Court in looking beyond the papers executed by the corporation and shareholders in order to determine whether the sale there had actually been made by the corporation.   We were but emphasizing the established principle that in resolving such questions as who made a sale, fact-finding tribunals in tax cases can consider motives, intent, and conduct in addition to what appears in written instruments used by parties to control rights as among themselves.   See, e.g., Helvering v. Clifford, 309 U.S. 331, 335–337; Commissioner of Internal Revenue v. Tower, 327 U.S. 280.

liquidation.[4] But Congress has imposed no tax on liquidating distributions in kind or on dissolution, whatever may be the motive for such liquidation. Consequently, a corporation may liquidate or dissolve without subjecting itself to the corporate gains tax, even though a primary motive is to avoid the burden of corporate taxation.

Here, on the basis of adequate subsidiary findings, the Court of Claims has found that the sale in question was made by the stockholders rather than the corporation. The Government's argument that the shareholders acted as a mere "conduit" for a sale by respondent corporation must fall before this finding. The subsidiary finding that a major motive of the shareholders was to reduce taxes does not bar this conclusion. Whatever the motive and however relevant it may be in determining whether the transaction was real or a sham, sales of physical properties by shareholders following a genuine liquidation distribution cannot be attributed to the corporation for tax purposes.

The oddities in tax consequences that emerge from the tax provisions here controlling appear to be inherent in the present tax pattern. For a corporation is taxed if it sells all its physical properties and distributes the cash proceeds as liquidating dividends, yet is not taxed if that property is distributed in kind and is then sold by the shareholders. In both instances the interest of the shareholders in the business has been transferred to the purchaser. Again, if these stockholders had succeeded in their original effort to sell all their stock, their interest would have been transferred to the purchasers just as effectively. Yet on such a transaction the corporation would have realized no taxable gain.

Congress having determined that different tax consequences shall flow from different methods by which the shareholders of a closely held corporation may dispose of corporate property, we accept its mandate. It is for the trial court, upon consideration of an entire transaction, to determine the factual category in which a particular transaction belongs. Here as in the *Court Holding Co.* case we accept the ultimate findings of fact of the trial tribunal. Accordingly the judgment of the Court of Claims is

Affirmed.

Mr. Justice DOUGLAS took no part in the consideration or decision of this case.

NOTE

The difficulties faced by the courts in reconciling the results in *Court Holding* and *Cumberland* influenced Congress to extend the *General Utilities* doctrine to liquidating sales. Under the 1954 Code version of Section 337, a corporation generally did not recognize gain or

---

4. It has also been held that where corporate liquidations are effected through trustees or agents, gains from sales are taxable to the corporation as though it were a going concern. See, e.g., First National Bank v. United States, 10 Cir., 86 F.2d 938, 941; Treas.Reg. 103, § 19.22(a)–21.

loss on a sale of property pursuant to a plan of complete liquidation.[1] Aptly named the "anti-*Court Holding*" provision, old Section 337 usually ensured that the tax consequences of liquidating sales and distributions were the same irrespective of the form of the transaction. In either case, the corporation generally did not recognize gain or loss, while the buyer (or distributee shareholder) took a fair market value basis in the acquired or distributed assets. As a result, the principal tax cost of a complete liquidation or taxable disposition of assets by a liquidating corporation was the capital gain recognized at the shareholder level.

Shortly after this extension of the *General Utilities* doctrine, reformers began calling for its repeal.[2] Imposing a tax at the shareholder level, they argued, did not justify exempting a liquidating corporation from tax on the disposition of its appreciated property. Until the 1980's, however, support for repeal was limited to the academic community and a handful of principled practitioners. "The General," it was said, had the loyal backing of the troops—battalions of legislators and their business constituents who looked askance at the double tax.[3] A principal justification for retaining the *General Utilities* doctrine was that it provided relief from the double taxation of corporate earnings by partially integrating the corporate and individual taxes.[4] More specialized pleaders focused on the adverse impact of the double tax on the "largely inflationary gains" on long-held assets of small "Mom and Pop" businesses.[5]

Despite these arguments, the movement for reform gained momentum in 1983, when the Senate Finance Committee Staff, following the lead of an earlier report of the American Law Institute, recommended repeal of *General Utilities* with only limited transitional relief.[6] In its final report issued two years later, the Finance Committee reiterated its call for repeal, but this time with relief for gain recognized on liquidating distributions or sales of certain long-held (over five years)

---

1. As with liquidating distributions, exceptions were provided for recapture income, certain sales of inventory and other dealer property, installment obligations arising from sales of property prior to the adoption of the liquidation plan and tax benefit items. See I.R.C. § 337 (pre–1987).

2. See, e.g., Lewis, "A Proposed New Treatment for Corporate Distributions and Sales in Liquidations," 86th Cong., 1st Sess., House Committee on Ways and Means, 3 Tax Revision Compendium 1643 (1959).

3. We thank Professor Walter Blum for the military analogy. See Blum, "Behind the *General Utilities* Doctrine, or Why Does the General Have So Much Support from the Troops," 62 Taxes 292 (1984).

4. See, e.g., Nolan, "Taxing Corporate Distributions of Appreciated Property: Repeal of the *General Utilities* Doctrine and Relief Measures," 22 San Diego L.Rev. 97 (1985). For an excellent survey and critique of the arguments for retaining *General Utilities*, see Yin, "General Utilities Repeal: Is Tax Reform Really Going to Pass it By?" 31 Tax Notes 1111 (June 11, 1986). See also Section C7c of this Chapter, infra.

5. See, e.g., "Reform of Corporate Taxation," Hearing before the Committee on Finance, United States Senate, 98th Cong., 1st Sess. 148, 151, 153–157, 174–176, 185, 268–270 (Oct. 24, 1983).

6. See Staff of the Senate Finance Committee, Preliminary Report on the Reform and Simplification of the Income Taxation of Corporations, 98th Cong., 1st Sess. 65–66, 76–77 (S.Prt. 98–95, 1983); American Law Institute, Federal Income Tax Project: Subchapter C 102–119 (1982).

assets by small (under $2 million) closely held corporations.[7] The debate then shifted to the House of Representatives, which included *General Utilities* repeal, along with a permanent exception for certain closely held corporations, in its version of the 1986 tax reform legislation.[8] The House Ways and Means Committee report summarized the rationale for repeal in the liquidation setting: [9]

> The committee believes that the *General Utilities* rule, even in the more limited form in which it exists today, produces many incongruities and inequities in the tax system. First, the rule may create significant distortions in business behavior. Economically, a liquidating distribution is indistinguishable from a nonliquidating distribution; yet the Code provides a substantial preference for the former. A corporation acquiring the assets of a liquidating corporation is able to obtain a basis in assets equal to their fair market value, although the transferor recognizes no gain (other than possibly recapture amounts) on the sale. The tax benefits may make the assets more valuable in the hands of the transferee than in the hands of the present owner. The effect may be to induce corporations with substantial appreciated assets to liquidate and transfer their assets to other corporations for tax reasons, when economic considerations might indicate a different course of action. Accordingly, the *General Utilities* rule may be responsible, at least in part, for the dramatic increase in corporate mergers and acquisitions in recent years. The committee believes that the Code should not artificially encourage corporate liquidations and acquisitions, and believes that repeal of the *General Utilities* rule is a major step towards that goal.
>
> Second, the *General Utilities* rule tends to undermine the corporate income tax. Under normally applicable tax principles, nonrecognition of gain is available only if the transferee takes a carryover basis in the transferred property, thus assuring that a tax will eventually be collected on the appreciation. Where the *General Utilities* rule applies, assets generally are permitted to leave corporate solution and to take a stepped-up basis in the hands of the transferee without the imposition of a corporate-level tax. Thus, the effect of the rule is to grant a permanent exemption from the corporate income tax.

The campaign then moved back to the Senate, where *General Utilities* repeal was first included in the Finance Committee's bill and later dropped, reportedly because of concerns over its adverse impact on corporate entrepreneurs.[10] In reconciling the two bills, the Conference Committee adopted the House's approach. To the surprise of even the

---

7. Staff of the Senate Finance Committee, The Subchapter C Revision Act of 1985: A Final Report Prepared by the Staff, 99th Cong., 1st Sess. 6–8, 42–44, 52–54, 59–68 (S.Prt. 99–47, 1985).

8. H.R. 3838, 99th Cong., 1st Sess. (1985), §§ 331–335.

9. H.R.Rep. No. 99–426, 99th Cong., 1st Sess. 281 (1985).

10. See Yin, supra note 4, at 1112–1113.

tax reformers, the conferees went beyond the earlier proposals by eliminating any permanent exceptions for closely held corporations and providing only limited transitional relief. The General, so it seemed, had been deserted by the troops once the battle went behind closed doors. Against that background we turn to the current corporate-level tax treatment of liquidating distributions and sales.

b. LIQUIDATING DISTRIBUTIONS AND SALES

The 1986 Code version of Section 336(a) is the reverse of its 1954 Code predecessor. The general rule requires a liquidating corporation to recognize gain or loss on the distribution of property in complete liquidation as if the property were sold to the distributee at its fair market value. If the distributed property is subject to a liability or the distributee shareholder assumes a liability in connection with the distribution, the fair market value of the property is treated as being not less than the amount of the liability.[11] In strengthening the double tax regime of Subchapter C, Congress greatly increased the tax cost of a complete liquidation. Whenever a corporation makes a liquidating distribution of appreciated property, gain will be recognized at the corporate level and the distribution also will be a taxable event to the shareholders.[12]

Once Congress required a liquidating corporation to recognize gain or loss on liquidating distributions, it took the next logical step by conforming the tax treatment of liquidating sales. With the repeal of former Section 337 in the Tax Reform Act of 1986, a corporation must recognize gain or loss on any sale of its assets pursuant to a complete liquidation plan.[13]

c. LIMITATIONS ON RECOGNITION OF LOSS

The general rule in Section 336(a) differs in one important respect from the rules in Section 311 governing nonliquidating distributions. It allows the distributing corporation to recognize loss as well as gain. Moreover, although Section 267 disallows losses on sales of property by a corporation to a "related" party (e.g., a controlling shareholder), it does not disallow losses on liquidating distributions to related parties.[14]

---

11. I.R.C. § 336(b). Cf. I.R.C. § 7701(g); Commissioner v. Tufts, 461 U.S. 300, 103 S.Ct. 1826 (1983), rehearing denied 463 U.S. 1215, 103 S.Ct. 3555 (1983).

12. A transitional exception for certain small corporations expired at the end of 1989. See Tax Reform Act of 1986, P.L. 99–514, 99th Cong., 2d Sess. § 633(a)(1) (1986). The general rule is subject to two exceptions. Nonrecognition of gain or loss is preserved for: (1) distributions in complete liquidation of a controlled—i.e., 80 percent—subsidiary (I.R.C. § 337, see Section B3b of this chapter, infra), and (2)

distributions in certain tax-free reorganizations (I.R.C. § 336(c), see Chapter 10C2, infra).

13. A corporation that sells or distributes stock in an 80 percent subsidiary may elect under § 336(e), however, to treat the sale as a disposition of the subsidiary's assets and ignore any gain or loss on the sale or distribution of the stock. See also I.R.C. § 338(h)(10) and Section C3c of this chapter, infra.

14. I.R.C. § 267(a)(1).

This new license to recognize losses quickly rattled the Congressional nervous system. To prevent taxpayers from recognizing losses "in inappropriate situations" or inflating the amount of losses actually sustained on a liquidation, the Tax Reform Act of 1986 added Section 336(d), which contains two limitations on the recognition of corporate-level losses.[15]

Distributions to Related Persons. Section 336(d)(1) partially reinstates the policy of Section 267 by providing that no loss shall be recognized by a liquidating corporation on the distribution of property to a Section 267 related person if either: (1) the distribution is not pro rata among the shareholders, or (2) the distributed property was acquired by the liquidating corporation in a Section 351 transaction or as a contribution to capital within the five-year period ending on the date of the distribution. These restrictions thus initially focus on the recipient of the loss property. For this purpose, related persons usually will be shareholders who own directly, or through the Section 267 attribution rules, more than 50 percent in value of the stock of the distributing corporation.[16]

Neither the statute nor the legislative history explains when a distribution is "not pro rata" among the shareholders. Congress presumably intended to single out situations where a majority shareholder receives an interest in loss property that is disproportionate to his stock interest in the corporation.[17] The legislative history provides scant illumination of the rationale for this rule. The conferees merely expressed an intent to restrict the ability of taxpayers to recognize losses in "inappropriate situations." [18] Perhaps Congress believed that it was necessary to apply the loss disallowance policy of Section 267 to liquidating distributions where the parties exercised a measure of control by targeting distributions of loss property to majority shareholders—but at the same time concluded that pro rata liquidating distributions were less likely to be motivated by tax avoidance.[19]

The rationale for limiting losses on distributions of recently contributed property to a related party is easier to discern. As we saw in studying corporate formations, the two-tier tax system not only causes taxpayers to double their gains; it also permits a duplication of losses. To illustrate, assume Sole Shareholder ("Sole") transfers Lossacre (adjusted basis—$1,000; fair market value—$500) to her wholly owned X Corporation ("X") in exchange for $500 of X stock in what clearly

15. See H.R.Rep. No. 99–841, 99th Cong., 2d Sess. II–200 (1986).

16. I.R.C. § 267(b)(2), (c).

17. For example, assume X Corporation has a net worth of $1,000 and is owned 75% by A and 25% by five unrelated shareholders. X distributes Lossacre (value—$750; basis $1,000) to A and $250 cash to the other shareholders. Since Lossacre was not distributed to the shareholders in proportion to their respective stock

interests, the distribution is not pro rata and X may not recognize its $250 loss.

18. H.R.Rep. No. 99–841, supra note 15, at II–200.

19. Even if the distribution is pro rata, however, losses may be disallowed if the asset distributed to a related person is "disqualified property" within the meaning of Section 336(d)(1)(B). See text accompanying notes 24–28, infra.

qualifies as a Section 351 nonrecognition transaction. Sole thus takes a $1,000 exchanged basis in her new X stock,[20] and X takes Lossacre with a $1,000 transferred basis.[21] Assume further that, three years later, when Lossacre has the same basis and value, X liquidates, distributing Lossacre and its other assets to Sole. Without a limitation, Sole would recognize a $500 loss on the liquidation and the corporation also would recognize a $500 loss—two losses for the price of none considering that, when the smoke clears, Sole still owns Lossacre.[22] The same technique would be effective for controlling shareholders who own less than 100 percent of the corporation if on liquidation they receive their pro rata share of each corporate asset.[23]

Section 336(d)(1)(A)(ii) attacks this form of "stuffing" with a rule that extends Section 267 principles to pro rata liquidating distributions of "disqualified property" to a related person. "Disqualified property" is defined as any property acquired by the liquidating corporation during the five-year period preceding the distribution in a Section 351 transaction or as a contribution to capital.[24]

Losses with Tax Avoidance Purpose. Section 336(d)(2) prevents the doubling of precontribution built-in losses even on certain distributions to minority shareholders. This limitation applies only if the distributing corporation acquired property in a Section 351 transaction or as a contribution to capital as part of a plan the principal purpose of which was to recognize loss by the corporation on a liquidating sale, exchange or distribution of the property. In that event, Section 336(d)(2) limits the corporation's deductible loss to losses that accrued after the corporation acquired the property. Precontribution losses are disallowed by a basis step-down rule which requires the corporation to reduce its basis (but not below zero) in the affected property by the amount of built-in loss in the property at the time it was acquired by the corporation.[25] Any contribution of property within the two-year period ending on the date of the adoption of the plan of liquidation is presumed to be part of a forbidden plan to recognize loss, except as the Treasury may provide in regulations.[26]

Congress provided extensive guidance on the operation of the two-year presumption and the escape hatches that it expects to be included in future regulations. Although a contribution made more than two

---

20. I.R.C. § 358(a).

21. I.R.C. § 362(a).

22. Of course, Sole will now hold Lossacre with a stepped-down fair market value basis of $500, but she will have benefited from two losses without ever having disposed of the property.

23. As noted previously, corporate-level losses on non pro rata ("bullet") distributions to controlling shareholders are disallowed under Section 336(d)(1)(A)(i).

24. I.R.C. § 336(d)(1)(B). The term also includes any property the adjusted basis of

which is determined in whole or in part by reference to the adjusted basis of property acquired in a Section 351 transaction or as a contribution to capital—e.g., like-kind property received in a Section 1031 transaction in exchange for property acquired by the corporation in a Section 351 transaction. Id.

25. The built-in loss is the excess of the adjusted basis of the property immediately after its acquisition over its fair market value at that time. I.R.C. § 336(d)(2)(A).

26. I.R.C. § 336(d)(2)(B)(ii).

years prior to the adoption of a liquidation plan might be made with a prohibited purpose, the Conference Report states that the basis step-down rule in Section 336(d)(2) would apply only "in the most rare and unusual cases" in such circumstances.[27] Moreover, the conferees directed the Treasury to issue regulations generally providing that even contributions of property within the two-year presumption window should be disregarded "*unless* there is no clear and substantial relationship between the contributed property and the conduct of the corporation's current or future business enterprises."[28] A "clear and substantial relationship" generally would include a requirement of a corporate business purpose for placing the property in the particular corporation to which it was contributed as compared to retaining the property outside that corporation.[29] If the contributed property has a built-in loss at the time of contribution that is "significant" relative to the built-in corporate gain at that time, "special scrutiny of the business purpose would be appropriate." [30] The following excerpt from the General Explanation of the Tax Reform Act of 1986 elaborates on Congress's expectations: [31]

> As one example, assume that A owns Z Corporation which operates a widget business in New Jersey. That business operates exclusively in the northeastern region of the United States and there are no plans to expand those operations. In his individual capacity, A had acquired unimproved real estate in New Mexico that has declined in value. On March 22, 1988, A contributes such real estate to Z and six months later a plan of complete liquidation is adopted. Thereafter, all of Z's assets are sold to an unrelated party and the liquidation proceeds are distributed. A contributed no other property to Z during the two-year period prior to the adoption of the plan of liquidation. Because A contributed the property to Z less than two years prior to the adoption of the plan of liquidation, it is presumed to have been contributed with a prohibited purpose. Moreover, because there is no clear and substantial relationship between the contributed property and the conduct of Z's business, Congress did not expect that any loss arising from the disposition of the New Mexico real estate would be allowed under the Treasury regulations.

> However, Congress expected that such regulations will permit the allowance of any resulting loss from the disposition of any of the assets of a trade or business (or a line of business) that are contributed to a corporation where prior law would have permitted the allowance of the loss and the clear and

27. H.R.Rep. No. 99–841, supra note 15, at 200. See also Staff of the Joint Committee on Taxation, General Explanation of the Tax Reform Act of 1986, 100th Cong., 1st Sess. 343 (1987).

28. H.R.Rep. No. 99–841, supra note 15, at II–201.

29. 1986 Act General Explanation, supra note 27, at 343.

30. Id.

31. Id. at 343–344.

substantial relationship test is satisfied. In such circumstances, application of the loss disallowance rule is inappropriate assuming there is a meaningful (i.e., clear and substantial) relationship between the contribution and the utilization of the particular corporate form to conduct a business enterprise. If the contributed business is disposed of immediately after the contribution it is expected that it would be particularly difficult to show that the clear and substantial relationship test was satisfied. Congress also anticipated that the basis adjustment rules will generally not apply to a corporation's acquisition of property as part of its ordinary start-up or expansion of operations during its first two years of existence. However, if a corporation has substantial gain assets during its first two years of operation, a contribution of substantial built-in loss property followed by a sale or liquidation of the corporation would be expected to be closely scrutinized.

The loss limitations in Section 336(d)(2) are broad enough to cover dispositions of property in a taxable year that ends prior to the year in which the liquidation plan is adopted. In that event, Section 336(d)(2) (C) permits the Treasury to issue regulations under which a disallowed loss is recaptured in income in the year of the liquidation. If adopted, this approach would provide an alternative to the corporation filing an amended return for the year the loss was reported. The General Explanation of the 1986 Act provides the following example of how the recapture option would work: [32]

Assume that on June 1, 1987, a shareholder who owns 10 percent of the stock of a corporation (which is a calendar year taxpayer) participates with other shareholders in a contribution of property to the corporation that qualifies for nonrecognition under section 351, contributing nondepreciable property with a basis of $1,000 and a value of $100 to the corporation. Also assume that a principal purpose of the acquisition of the property by the corporation was to recognize loss by the corporation and offset corporate-level income or gain in anticipation of the liquidation. On September 30, 1987, the corporation sells the property to an unrelated third party for $200, and includes the resulting $800 loss on its 1987 tax return. Finally, the corporation adopts a plan of liquidation on December 31, 1988.

For purposes of determining the corporation's loss on the sale of the property in 1987, the property's basis is reduced to $100—that is, $1,000 (the transferred basis under section 362) minus $900 (the excess of the property's basis over its value on the date of contribution). No loss would be realized on the sale, since the corporation received $200 for the property. Likewise, the corporation would recognize no gain on the sale,

---

32. Id. at 342.

since its basis for purposes of computing gain is $1,000. Congress expected that regulations might provide for the corporation to file an amended return for 1987 reflecting no gain or loss on the sale of the property. Otherwise, the corporation would be required to reflect the disallowance of the loss by including the amount of the disallowed loss on its 1988 tax return.

Overlap Situations. If both Section 336(d)(1) and Section 336(d)(2) apply to the same transaction, the harsher rule in Section 336(d)(1) (which disallows the entire loss rather than just the precontribution built-in loss) takes precedence.[33]

PROBLEM

All the outstanding stock of X Corporation is owned by Ivan (60 shares) and Flo (40 shares), who are unrelated. X has no liabilities and the following assets:

Asset	Adj. Basis	F.M.V.
Gainacre	$100,000	$400,000
Lossacre	800,000	400,000
Cash	200,000	200,000

Unless otherwise indicated, assume that Gainacre and Lossacre each have been held by X for more than five years.

On January 1 of the current year, X adopted a plan of complete liquidation. What are the tax consequences to X on the distribution of its assets pursuant to the liquidation plan in each of the following alternatives?

(a) X distributes each of its assets to Ivan and Flo as tenants-in-common in proportion to their stock interests (i.e., Ivan takes a 60% interest and Flo a 40% interest in each asset).

(b) Same as (a), above, except X distributes Lossacre and the cash to Ivan and Gainacre to Flo.

(c) Same as (b), above, except X distributes Gainacre and the cash to Ivan and Lossacre to Flo.

(d) Same as (a), above, except X acquired Lossacre as a contribution to capital four years ago. Is the result different if Lossacre had a value of $1,000,000 and a basis of $800,000 at the time it was contributed to the corporation?

(e) What result on the distributions in (c), above (i.e., Gainacre and cash to Ivan, Lossacre to Flo) if Lossacre, which had no relationship to X's business operations, was transferred to X by Ivan and Flo in a § 351 transaction 18 months prior to the adoption of the liquidation plan, when Lossacre had a fair market value of $700,000 and an adjusted basis of $800,000?

---

33. 1986 Act General Explanation, supra note 27, at 342, n. 86.

(f) Same as (e), above except Lossacre was transferred to X in a § 351 transaction 36 months prior to the adoption of the liquidation plan?

(g) Same as (e), above, except, when Lossacre was contributed to X, the corporation planned to develop the property as part of its ongoing real estate business; it later decided to liquidate because of adverse economic conditions.

(h) Could the parties change the result in (e), above, if prior to liquidating, X transferred Lossacre to an unrelated party in a § 1031 like-kind exchange for Newlossacre, and then distributed Gainacre and the cash to Ivan and Newlossacre (also worth $400,000) to Flo?

(i) What result in (e), above, if X sold Lossacre to an unrelated party for its $400,000 fair market value one month after the adoption of the liquidation plan and two months prior to the distributions in liquidation? What if the sale of Lossacre had been for the same price one year prior to the adoption of the liquidation plan?

3. LIQUIDATION OF A SUBSIDIARY

a. CONSEQUENCES TO THE SHAREHOLDERS

Code: §§ 332; 334(b)(1); 1223(1).

Regulations: §§ 1.332–1, –2, –5.

Nonrecognition treatment is inappropriate on an ordinary liquidation because it would permit individual shareholders to achieve a tax-free bailout as they watch the earnings and profits account disappear from the scene. Different policy considerations come into play when a parent corporation liquidates a controlled subsidiary. Since the assets of the subsidiary remain in corporate solution, the liquidation is a mere change in form that should not be impeded by the imposition of a tax. The subsidiary's tax attributes, including its earnings and profits account, can be inherited by the parent without administrative burdens. Moreover, the subsidiary could have paid tax-free dividends to the parent under Section 243. All these factors, together with a desire to encourage the simplification of corporate structures, influenced Congress in 1935 to adopt a nonrecognition scheme by enacting the statutory predecessor of Section 332.

Section 332 provides that a parent corporation recognizes no gain or loss on the receipt of property in complete liquidation of an 80 percent or more subsidiary if certain conditions are met. In that event, the parent takes the distributed assets with a transferred basis under Section 334(b)(1) and inherits the subsidiary's earnings and profits and other tax attributes under Section 381(a)(1).[1]

---

1. The parent's basis in the stock of a subsidiary is not taken into account in determining the tax consequences of a § 332 liquidation and disappears from the scene. This creates the possibility that the parent may be deprived of a loss on its

To qualify under Section 332, the subsidiary must distribute property to its parent in complete cancellation or redemption of its stock pursuant to a plan of liquidation, and the liquidation must meet two formal requirements, one relating to control and the other to timing.

Control. Under Section 332(b)(1), the parent must own at least 80 percent of the total voting power of the stock of the subsidiary and 80 percent of the total value of all outstanding stock of the subsidiary from the date of adoption of the plan of complete liquidation and at all times thereafter until the parent receives the final distribution.[2] This condition normally is not a problem if the subsidiary is wholly owned, but any significant minority ownership creates a risk that the transaction will run afoul of the control requirement. Indeed, a parent corporation sometimes is motivated to intentionally violate the 80 percent tests in order to avoid Section 332 and recognize a loss on its stock in the subsidiary.[3] Conversely, an aspiring parent that does not meet the 80 percent control test may seek to qualify a liquidation under Section 332 by acquiring more stock of the subsidiary or causing the subsidiary to redeem stock held by minority shareholders shortly before the liquidation. As illustrated by the *Riggs* case, below, this strategy may trigger a controversy with the Service over when the liquidation plan was adopted.

Timing. Section 332 includes two timing alternatives. "One-shot" liquidations qualify if the subsidiary distributes all of its assets within one taxable year[4] even if it is not the same year in which the liquidation plan is adopted.[5] Where the distributions span more than one taxable year, the plan must provide that the subsidiary will transfer all of its property within three years after the close of the taxable year in which the plan is adopted.[6] Failure to meet the deadline will cause the liquidation to be retroactively disqualified.[7]

Minority Shareholders. Nonrecognition under Section 332 is only granted to the controlling parent corporation. It is not available to minority shareholders, who must determine their gain or loss in the normal manner under Section 331(a) unless the liquidation also quali-

investment in the subsidiary even though it must inherit a low carryover basis in its assets.

2. The stock ownership requirements are derived from Section 1504(a)(2), which sets forth rules for determining whether a corporation is a member of an "affiliated group." For purposes of the stock ownership requirement, most nonconvertible preferred stock is disregarded. I.R.C. § 1504(a)(4).

3. See Commissioner v. Day & Zimmerman, Inc., 151 F.2d 517 (3d Cir.1945).

4. I.R.C. § 332(b)(2); Reg. § 1.332–3. In this situation, the adoption by the share-

holders of the resolution authorizing the distributions in liquidation is considered an adoption of a "plan" of liquidation even though it may not specify the time for completing the transfers.

5. Rev.Rul. 71–326, 1971–2 C.B. 177.

6. I.R.C. § 332(b)(3); Reg. § 1.332–4.

7. Id. To allow the Service to assert deficiencies for the early distributions in the event of a retroactive disqualification, the parent is required to file a waiver of the normal three year statute of limitations and may be asked to post a bond in order to protect the Commissioner's ability to collect past due taxes.

fies as a tax-free reorganization—a rare situation that will be explored in a later chapter.[8]

GEORGE L. RIGGS, INC. v. COMMISSIONER *

United States Tax Court, 1975.
64 T.C. 474.

DRENNEN, Judge: Respondent determined a deficiency in petitioner's income tax for the taxable year ended March 31, 1969, in the amount of $589,882.28.

The sole issue for determination is whether the plan of liquidation of Riggs–Young Corp., a subsidiary of the petitioner, was adopted subsequent to the time when petitioner owned at least 80 percent of the outstanding stock of Riggs–Young, thereby rendering section 332, I.R.C. 1954, applicable to the liquidation so that the gain to petitioner thereon is not to be recognized.

FINDINGS OF FACT

[George L. Riggs, Inc. (referred to throughout the opinion as "petitioner") was a holding company which as of December, 1967, owned approximately 35.6 percent (2,432 out of 6,840 shares) of the nonvoting preferred stock and 72.13 percent (8,047 out of 11,156 shares) of the common stock of The Standard Electric Time Co. ("Standard"). Standard owned 90 percent of the outstanding stock of a Delaware subsidiary and 99.5 percent of a California subsidiary. The corporations were in the business of manufacturing and marketing electric clocks and signal devices. Standard was the manufacturing arm of the business, and the two subsidiaries handled marketing.

On December 13, 1967, Frances Riggs–Young, the president of Standard and controlling shareholder of petitioner, notified all of Standard's shareholders that the company and its subsidiaries would be seeking approval for a sale of substantially all of the operating assets of the companies. In connection with the sale, Standard changed its name to Riggs–Young Corporation. The sales were consummated on December 29, 1967. In February, 1968, Riggs–Young (formerly Standard) redeemed all of its preferred stock. On April 17, 1968, the directors of Riggs–Young approved the liquidation of the Delaware and California subsidiaries, and authorized Riggs–Young to offer to redeem common stock from all of its shareholders with the exception of petitioner and Frances Riggs–Young. The stated purpose of this tender offer was to eliminate the minority shareholders and provide them with the opportunity to receive cash for their stock. The Tax Court also found that counsel to petitioner and the related subsidiaries "recognized the desirability of petitioner's owning 80 percent of the common stock of Riggs–Young (1) to permit the filing of consolidated returns, and (2) to permit the possible further liquidation of Riggs–Young under

---

8. Reg. § 1.332–5. See Chapter 10B1, infra.   * Some footnotes omitted.

section 332 of the Code to simplify the corporate structure." 64 T.C. at 480. The letter informing shareholders of the redemption offer stated that "If this offer is accepted by substantially all of the stockholders to whom it is directed, the Directors will consider liquidation and final dissolution of the Corporation." 64 T.C. at 479.

At the time of its redemption offer, petitioner owned 72.13 percent of Riggs–Young's common stock. The remaining shares were owned by members of the Riggs family, related trusts and a small group of unrelated minority shareholders.

The tender offer was made on April 26, 1968 and expired on May 28, 1968. During this period, owners of 2,738 shares of common stock tendered their shares for redemption. As a result of these redemptions, petitioner owned at least 80 percent of Riggs–Young's common stock on May 9, 1968, and its ownership increased to 95.6 percent by May 28. On June 20, 1968, the directors and shareholders of Riggs–Young approved a plan of complete liquidation and dissolution of the corporation. Between June and December, 1968, when the liquidation was completed, Riggs–Young made distributions to petitioner in excess of $2.2 million.

Petitioner realized a gain of $2,168,975 from the liquidation of Riggs–Young, representing the difference between the liquidating distributions and petitioner's $42,465 basis in its Riggs–Young stock. The gain was reported on petitioner's tax return but not recognized under the authority of Section 332. Ed.]

OPINION

The only question for decision is whether petitioner owned at least 80 percent of the outstanding stock of its subsidiary, Riggs–Young Corp., at the time Riggs–Young Corp. adopted a plan of liquidation within the meaning of section 332, I.R.C. 1954, so that the gain realized by petitioner on the liquidation of Riggs–Young is not to be recognized by virtue of that section. The vital question is when did Riggs–Young adopt a plan of liquidation within the meaning of section 332.

Respondent argues that the plan of liquidation was adopted on December 27, 1967, when about 90 percent of the stock of Riggs–Young (then Standard) was voted in favor of selling substantially all of the assets of Riggs–Young and its two subsidiaries, Delaware and California, to SET; or not later than about April 17, 1968, when the board of directors of Riggs–Young voted to liquidate Delaware and California and to make an offer to purchase all of the common stock of Riggs–Young then outstanding with the exception of the stock owned by petitioner and Frances Riggs–Young.[2]

---

2. Respondent specifically does not rely on the "end-result" or "step-transaction" theory in this case. See Granite Trust Co. v. United States, 238 F.2d 670 (1st Cir. 1956); Estate of E. Brooks Glass, Jr., 55 T.C. 543, 569, affd. per curiam 453 F.2d 1375 (5th Cir.1972).

On the other hand petitioner contends that the plan of liquidation of Riggs–Young was first adopted when it was formally adopted by vote of the stockholders on June 20, 1968, or at the earliest when counsel for petitioner recommended to petitioner in the early days of June 1968 that it liquidate Riggs–Young. Petitioner also contends that section 332 is an elective section and a taxpayer, by taking appropriate steps, can render that section applicable or inapplicable.

The parties are in agreement that by May 9, 1968, petitioner was the owner of at least 80 percent of the outstanding stock of Riggs–Young.

Section 332(a) of the Code provides as a general rule: "No gain or loss shall be recognized on the receipt by a corporation of property distributed in complete liquidation of another corporation." Subsection (b) of section 332 establishes certain requirements which must be satisfied before subsection (a) becomes applicable. The only requirement of subsection (b) which is in issue in this case is whether petitioner, which received property from Riggs–Young in liquidation, was, on the date of the adoption of the plan of liquidation, the owner of at least 80 percent of the stock of Riggs–Young, the liquidating corporation.

Nowhere in the pertinent statute is the phrase "the date of the adoption of the plan of liquidation" defined. However, in attempting to define this phrase for purposes of the provision of [1954 Code] section 337, the regulations of the Commissioner provide:

> Ordinarily the date of the adoption of a plan of complete liquidation by a corporation is the date of adoption by the shareholders of the resolution authorizing the distribution of all the assets of the corporation (other than those retained to meet claims) in redemption of all of its stock. * * * [Sec. 1.337–2(b), Income Tax Regs; accord, Virginia Ice & Freezing Corp., 30 T.C. 1251 (1958).]

The date of this shareholder resolution should ordinarily be considered the date of the adoption of the plan of liquidation for purposes of section 332. See sec. 332(b)(2).

This Court has noted, in interpreting section 112(b)(6), I.R.C. 1939 (the predecessor of section 332, I.R.C. 1954), that although the adoption of the plan of liquidation "need not be evidenced by formal action of the corporation or the stockholders. * * * even an informal adoption of the plan to liquidate presupposes some kind of definitive determination to achieve dissolution." Distributors Finance Corp., 20 T.C. 768, 784 (1953). The mere general intention to liquidate is not the adoption of a plan of liquidation. City Bank of Washington, 38 T.C. 713 (1962).

Based on the evidence introduced in the case at bar, we must conclude that a plan for the liquidation of Riggs–Young had not been adopted prior to the critical date of May 9, 1968.

Respondent, in an effort to show that the plan of liquidation of Riggs–Young was informally adopted on December 27, 1967, or no later than April 1968, alludes to actions and statements made in connection therewith taken between December 1967 and June 1968. Petitioner offered the testimony of persons involved in those actions to explain what the parties had in mind in taking those actions and making the statements which cast a quite different light on the reasons therefor. This testimony was creditable and not shaken by cross-examination. In light of such evidence, we cannot agree with respondent's inference that these actions constituted an informal adoption of a plan of liquidation of Riggs–Young prior to May 9, 1968.

Respondent argues that the letter dated December 13, 1967, sent to the common shareholders of Standard (Riggs–Young) notifying them of the proposed sale of its assets and that the corporation was contemplating an offer to purchase the common shares held by all shareholders other than petitioner if the sale was approved, clearly indicates that the shareholders at the meeting on December 27, 1967, intended to approve not only the sale of the assets, but also the liquidation of Standard (Riggs–Young).

We believe this infers too much. As petitioner points out, the use of the word "contemplated" shows the acquisition of the common stock of the minority shareholders was merely a possibility about which a final decision had not been made. In any event, from the possibility of a tender offer to the minority shareholders, we cannot conclude, ipso facto, that a plan for the liquidation had been adopted. Petitioner explained that the possibility of this tender offer was made known to the shareholders in order to avoid any possible disclosure problem with the securities law and to apprise the shareholders, from a fairness standpoint, of eventual possibilities resulting from the sale. This explanation is reasonable.

Respondent next points to the fact that on February 23, 1968, all of the 6,840 shares of preferred stock of Riggs–Young were called for redemption as additional evidence that a definite decision to liquidate the corporation had been made. We believe petitioner adequately explained that this redemption was based on sound business reasons. The preferred stock had a par value of $25 per share and a cumulative dividend of 8 percent. This stock was subject to redemption at the option of Riggs–Young upon payment of the par value and any accumulated dividend. The testimony of Norman Vester, a director of Riggs–Young and president of Security National Bank which was cotrustee of Riggs Trust, and Roger Stokey, the attorney for petitioner, Riggs–Young, and Frances Riggs–Young, reveal that the redemption of the preferred stock was motivated by the desire to eliminate the excessive burden of a cumulative dividend of 8 percent and to reduce the number of shareholders with whom Riggs–Young and National Security Bank, as cotrustee of the majority shareholder, would have to deal. Both Vester and Stokey testified that as of January 19, 1968, the date the board of directors of Riggs–Young voted to redeem the preferred stock, no decision had been made to liquidate the corporation, and, therefore, no plan had been adopted.

Respondent next claims that a letter dated April 23, 1968, from Stokey to Scott C. Jordan categorically shows that a plan to liquidate Riggs–Young had been adopted prior to the date of the letter. Stokey's letter was in response to a letter from Jordan on behalf of Frances Riggs–Young inquiring whether she could participate in the tender offer that was about to be made to the minority shareholders of Riggs–Young. In his letter, Stokey said that Frances Riggs–Young might run some tax risks if she accepted a tender offer by Riggs–Young, apparently basing this statement on his belief that the amount she received from a tender offer might be taxed to her at ordinary income rates. As a result of this potential risk, Stokey stated in the letter: "Accordingly, we are arranging for her to receive her money in a liquidation."

Respondent perceives this statement by Stokey as a clear indication that a plan of liquidation of Riggs–Young had been adopted by a definite decision by April 23, 1963. We cannot so conclude. Stokey testified that "we," referred to as arranging the liquidation, meant Stokey and another member of his law firm, William Gorham. This letter merely shows that the attorneys involved in these transactions were contemplating the possibility of a liquidation of Riggs–Young. It in no way proves that the directors or shareholders of the corporation had made a definite decision or informally adopted a plan of liquidation.

Finally, respondent views the letter dated April 26, 1968, drafted by Frances Riggs–Young as president of Riggs–Young, which contained the tender offer to the common shareholders, other than petitioner and Frances Riggs–Young, as an additional indication of a prior adoption of a plan to liquidate. In this letter, Frances Riggs–Young did state that if substantially all of the shareholders accepted the offer, the directors of the corporation would consider liquidation and final dissolution of Riggs–Young.

Stokey testified that Gorham and he inserted, in this April 26 letter, the reference to the possible consideration of liquidating Riggs–Young. He also candidly admitted that he had undoubtedly discussed the possibility of liquidation of Riggs–Young at some prior point with Frances Riggs–Young, but hastened to add that he neither recommended liquidation at this time nor did she direct steps be taken to liquidate. Further, Stokey testified that he would never have recommended liquidation of Riggs–Young if petitioner had failed to achieve the 80–percent ownership.

Petitioner contends that the tender offer to the minority shareholders was made solely for business considerations and not with an eye toward the eventual liquidation of Riggs–Young. Vester and Stokey both testified that since the assets of Riggs–Young had been exchanged for cash, the primary purpose of the tender offer was to eliminate minority shareholders who might have different investment objectives for this cash than the majority shareholder. The bank, as trustee of Riggs, did not want to have to deal with a large group of minority shareholders. Furthermore, Stokey testified that Frances Riggs–Young desired to have the minority shareholders, many of whom were former employees of Standard, receive cash for their stock rather than have them remain locked in as minority shareholders of a personal holding company.

Stokey testified that another objective of the tender offer was to increase petitioner's ownership of Riggs–Young to 80 percent thereby enabling them to file a consolidated return. According to petitioner, the ultimate liquidation of Riggs–Young was not motivated by tax considerations and the sole advantage to be achieved from the liquidation was the simplification of petitioner's corporate structure. Petitioner alleges that Riggs–Young could have been kept in existence without any tax disadvantage. In fact the liquidation of Riggs–Young actually resulted in a tax disadvantage to Frances Riggs–Young personally since she had to pay capital gains tax on her share of the liquidation proceeds. She was a wealthy woman in her seventies and not in need of these funds and could have left this money in corporate solution until her death to enable it to receive a stepped-up basis for the beneficiaries of her estate.

We believe petitioner's explanations of why the actions were taken and the statements were made are true and that the considerations mentioned were taken into account in making the decisions that followed. While the motives enumerated by petitioner do not directly negate the notion that a liquidation may have been contemplated, discussed, or even intended prior to May 9, 1968, they do serve to sufficiently undermine the conclusions drawn by respondent from the actions and statements to offset any presumptions that respondent's inferences are correct. Without more concrete evidence than we have before us, we cannot agree with respondent that a plan of liquidation of Riggs–Young was adopted within the meaning of section 332 prior to May 9, 1968. Lacking such a finding, we believe the date on which the resolution to liquidate was actually adopted by the shareholders should be controlling.

The very most that can be gleaned from the evidence favorable to respondent's contention is that there may have been a general intent on the part of petitioner's advisers somewhere along the line prior to May 9, 1968, to liquidate Riggs–Young when and if petitioner achieved 80–percent ownership of Riggs–Young stock as a result of the tender offer. However, the formation of a conditional general intention to liquidate in the future is not the adoption of a plan of liquidation. *City Bank of Washington,* supra.

A mere intent by a taxpayer-corporation to liquidate a subsidiary prior to meeting the 80–percent requirement of section 332 should not be tantamount to the adoption of a plan of liquidation for the subsidiary at the point in time when that intent is formulated or manifested.

Such a result would thwart the congressional intent of section 332 and prior judicial interpretations of this section and its predecessor.

The predecessor of section 332, I.R.C. 1954, was section 112(b)(6), first enacted in 1935. The purpose of section 112(b)(6) was to encourage the simplification of corporation structures and allow the tax-free liquidation of a subsidiary. * * *

Under section 112(b)(6), the parent corporation not only was required to own at least 80 percent of the stock of the subsidiary from the date of adoption of the plan of liquidation until the property was received (as still required by section 332), but also was forbidden to dispose of any stock between the date of adoption and the time of the receipt of the property. The courts in interpreting section 112(b)(6) determined that a taxpayer could remove itself from the provision of that section by taking the appropriate steps of either intentionally reducing its stock ownership below 80 percent prior to the actual adoption of a liquidation plan or disposing of a small amount of stock between the date of adoption and the time the distributed property was received. * * *

In *Granite Trust Co. v. United States,* supra, the circuit court concluded that section 112(b)(6) was inapplicable and based this decision on the fact that the corporation disposed of stock in violation of the second requirement of section 112(b)(6) (subsequently deleted from section 332, I.R.C. 1954). The court reached this decision even though the corporation had made the dispositions in an attempt to avoid the application of this section. The court then traced this section into the 1954 Code stating at pages 676–677:

> Now, what did the Congress do in 1954 in view of Commissioner of Internal Revenue v. Day & Zimmermann, Inc., holding that a parent corporation contemplating the liquidation of a wholly owned subsidiary might elect, by making a transfer of an appropriate portion of the stock in the subsidiary, to avoid the conditions precedent to the nonrecognition of gain or loss prescribed in § 112(b)(6)? In reenacting that section in 1954, the Congress struck out the second condition, but left in the first condition which the taxpayer had successfully utilized in the Day & Zimmermann case in order to avoid a nonrecognition of a realized loss. This is what the Report of the Senate Finance Committee said at the time:
>
> "Section 332. Complete Liquidations of Subsidiaries.
>
> "Except for subsection (c) section 332 corresponds to and in general restates section 112(b)(6) of the 1939 Code and provides for the liquidation of a subsidiary corporation by its parent without the recognition of gain or loss to the parent corporation. Your committee has, however, deleted a provision which now appears in section 112(b)(6)(A) which removes a liquidation from the application of that section if the parent corporation at some time on or after the time of the adoption of the plan of

liquidation and until the receipt of the property owns more stock than that owned at the time of the receipt of the property. Your committee has removed this provision with the view to limiting the elective features of the section." (Sen. Finance Committee Report, H.R. 8300, 83d Cong., 2d Sess. 255 (1954).)

The above reference to the "elective features" of the subsection seems inescapably to reflect a legislative understanding (admittedly not contemporaneous with enactment, however) that taxpayers can, by taking appropriate steps, render the subsection applicable or inapplicable as they choose, rather than be at the mercy of the Commissioner on an "end-result" theory. Nowhere in the subsection is there any express reference to an "election" or an "option," and the use of the word "elective" in the committee report therefore strongly indicates, as the taxpayer argues, that the committee believed that corporations could avoid the nonrecognition provisions by transfers designed to eliminate the specific conditions contained in the subsection.

Based on legislative history of this section and prior judicial decisions, we conclude that section 332 is elective in the sense that with advance planning and properly structured transactions, a corporation should be able to render section 332 applicable or inapplicable. The Commissioner in his regulations has conceded corporations this power in a seemingly analogous situation. See sec. 1.337–2(b), Income Tax Regs.

Such power of planning presupposes some right to forethought and the accompanying intent to achieve the desired goal. It would be a logical inconsistency equivalent to a "Catch–22" to say that a corporation has the power to control the application of this section, but that once the corporation formulates the intent to do so (assuming that at or subsequent to the time the intent was formed, it owned less than the required 80 percent but enough stock to cause the liquidation of the subsidiary), it has adopted a plan of liquidation and has precluded itself from the section.

A basic tenet of our tax laws is that a taxpayer has the legal right to decrease or altogether avoid his taxes by means which the law permits. Gregory v. Helvering, 293 U.S. 465 (1935); Daniel D. Palmer, 62 T.C. 684 (1974). At most, petitioner did no more than follow this prerogative.

The shareholders of Riggs–Young formally adopted the plan of liquidation of the corporation on June 20, 1968. Stokey testified that based on the records contained in his office diary, he did not discuss definite liquidation of the corporation with the corporate officers prior to June 4, 5, or 6, 1968. He concluded that he recommended liquidation on either the 4th or 5th of June 1968, and that a definite decision to liquidate was probably made on June 6, 1968. The testimony of

Vester corroborates these statements of Stokey. We recognize that the adoption of a plan of liquidation need not be evidenced by formal action of the corporation or shareholders, *Distributors Finance Corp.*, supra. In this case, however, we find on the evidence that the plan of liquidation was adopted when the formal action was taken on June 20, 1968. Furthermore, even if it can be said that a plan of liquidation was adopted when Stokey first recommended it to the management, see *Distributors Finance Corp.*, supra, this occurred in June 1968 and would satisfy the requirements of section 332.

Respondent has cited and relied on Rev.Rul. 70–106, 1970–1 C.B. 70,[4] as supportive of his position. This Court is not bound by a revenue ruling. Andrew A. Sandor, 62 T.C. 469 (1974). In addition, we find the facts of this case are greatly dissimilar to those contained in the ruling. The ruling assumes a prior agreement between the minority and majority shareholders concerning the redemption of the minority stockholders' stock. The ruling concludes that the liquidation plan was adopted when this agreement was reached. In the case at bar, there is no evidence of an agreement between the minority and majority shareholders prior to the tender offer. *Madison Square Garden Corp.*, supra at 624 n. 4. Since this revenue ruling is inapplicable, proper judicial restraint dictates that we do not comment on the validity or invalidity of the ruling as limited to the facts contained therein. Ronald C. Packard, 63 T.C. 621 (1975).

Decision will be entered for the petitioner. Reviewed by the Court.

b. CONSEQUENCES TO THE LIQUIDATING SUBSIDIARY

Code: §§ 332(c); 337(a), (b)(1), (c), (d). Skim §§ 381(a)(1), (c)(2), (3); 453B(d); 1245(b)(3); 1250(d)(3).

Regulations: § 1.332–7.

Distributions of Property. A liquidating corporation generally recognizes gain or loss on distributions of property in a complete liquidation.[1] A major exception to this general rule is contained in Section 337,[2] which provides that a liquidating subsidiary does not recognize

---

4. Rev.Rul. 70–106

Minority shareholders owned twenty-five percent of the capital stock of corporation X. The remaining seventy-five percent of the capital stock of X was owned by Corporation Y. Y desired to liquidate X in a transaction to which section 332 of the Internal Revenue Code of 1954 would apply in order that Y would recognize no gain on the transaction. The minority shareholders agreed to have their stock of X redeemed. Following the distribution to the minority shareholders, Y owned all the stock of X. Y then adopted a formal plan of complete liquidation of X and all of the remaining assets of X were distributed to Y.

Held, all of the shareholders of X received a distribution in liquidation under the provisions of section 331 of the Code, and the gain is recognized to Y and gain or loss is recognized to the minority shareholders under section 331 of the Code. The liquidation fails to meet the eighty percent stock ownership requirements of section 332(b)(1) of the Code since the plan of liquidation was adopted at the time Y reached the agreement with the minority shareholders and at such time, Y owned seventy-five percent of the stock of X.

1. I.R.C. § 336(a).

2. This "new" Section 337 is not to be confused with its 1954 Code counterpart, "old" Section 337, which provided for non-

gain or loss on distributions of property to its parent [3] in a complete liquidation to which Section 332 applies. A nonrecognition rule makes sense in this context because the subsidiary's tax attributes, including the built-in gain or loss in its assets, can be preserved in the hands of the parent. Section 334(b)(1) implements this policy by providing that the parent takes a transferred basis in property received from a subsidiary in a Section 332 liquidation. In keeping with this carryover of tax attributes theme, the depreciation recapture provisions do not override Section 337,[4] and recapture potential continues to lurk in the distributed property through the definition of "recomputed basis" in Section 1245 and "additional depreciation" in Section 1250.[5] A liquidating subsidiary likewise does not recognize gain or loss on the distribution of installment obligations if Section 332 applies,[6] and the parent will take a transferred basis in the obligations under Section 334(b)(1).

Distributions to Minority Shareholders. The nonrecognition rule in Section 337(a) is limited to distributions of property by a liquidating subsidiary to "the 80-percent distributee"—i.e., the parent corporation. Distributions to minority shareholders are treated in the same manner as a distribution in a nonliquidating redemption. Accordingly, the distributing corporation will recognize gain but not loss. Recognition of gain is appropriate because minority shareholders do not inherit any built-in gain in the distributed property through a transferred basis but instead take a fair market value basis under Section 334(a). Distributions of loss property are another matter. In order to prevent a controlled subsidiary from recognizing losses (but not gains) by "bullet" distributions of loss property to minority shareholders, Section 336(d)(3) provides that no loss shall be recognized to a subsidiary on a distribution of property to minority shareholders in a Section 332 liquidation.

Transfer of Property to Satisfy Indebtedness of Subsidiary to Parent. Section 337 applies only to liquidating *distributions.* If a subsidiary is indebted to its parent, a transfer of property to satisfy the debt normally would be a taxable event rather than a nontaxable distribution governed by Section 337(a), causing the subsidiary to recognize gain or loss and the parent to take a fair market value basis in the distributed property. The disparate treatment of distributions in complete liquidation and transfers of property to satisfy intercorporate indebtedness might tempt a subsidiary to distribute appreciated property as part of the liquidation while simultaneously using loss property to

recognition of gain or loss on certain liquidating sales. We wish Congress had avoided confusion by retiring old Section 337's number and placing it on a monument in Yankee Stadium.

3. Section 337(a) refers to the parent as "the 80-percent distributee," which is defined in Section 337(c) as a corporation that meets the 80 percent stock ownership requirements specified in Section 332(b).

4. I.R.C. §§ 1245(b)(3); 1250(d)(3).

5. I.R.C. §§ 1245(a)(2); 1250(b)(1), (3). Issues of depreciation recapture on real estate have waned because virtually all depreciable real property placed in service after 1986 must be depreciated under the straight line method. I.R.C. § 168(b)(3).

6. I.R.C. § 453B(d)(1).

extinguish any indebtedness to the parent. Section 337(b)(1) prevents this ploy by providing that any transfer of property in satisfaction of a subsidiary's debt to its parent shall be treated as a distribution, subjecting the transfer to the general nonrecognition rule of Section 337(a). As a necessary corollary, Section 334(b)(1) provides that the parent takes a transferred basis in the distributed property.

Distributions to Tax-Exempt and Foreign Parents. Ever vigilant, Congress was concerned that taxpayers might turn the deferral provided by Section 337 into a permanent exemption from the corporate-level tax. Consider the following possibility. A and B, the sole shareholders of highly appreciated X Corporation, wish to sell the business and avoid at least one level of tax. They sell all their stock to tax-exempt Charity, Inc. and recognize gain on the sale. Charity now owns 100 percent of the X stock but it does not wish to operate the business. Charity causes X to liquidate in a tax-free transaction at both the corporate and shareholder levels under Sections 332 and 337(a). Although Charity must take a transferred basis in the property distributed by X, no tax ever would be collected on the subsequent sale of those assets because Charity is exempt from tax.

This technique might have been vulnerable under the step transaction and other judicial doctrines, but Congress decided to attack it from within the Code. Section 337(b)(2) thus provides that the general corporate-level nonrecognition rule for liquidations of a subsidiary shall not apply where the parent is a tax-exempt organization. Nonrecognition is restored, however, if the distributed property is used by the tax-exempt parent in an "unrelated trade or business" immediately after the distribution.[7] In that event, there is no loophole to plug because the tax-exempt organization is subject to tax on its unrelated business income.[8] A similar rule requiring recognition of corporate-level gain applies in the case of a liquidating distribution to a parent that is a foreign corporation, except as the Treasury may provide in regulations. The Conference Report indicates that the regulations should permit nonrecognition if the appreciation on the distributed property is not being removed from the U.S. taxing jurisdiction prior to recognition.[9] In both situations where the subsidiary recognizes gain or loss, the parent takes a fair market value basis in the distributed assets.[10]

PROBLEMS

1. P, Inc. ("P") owns 90 percent of the outstanding stock of S, Inc. ("S"). Individual ("I") owns the remaining 10 percent of S. P's basis in

---

7. Exempt organizations may be taxable on income from an "unrelated business"—i.e., a regularly carried on trade or business activity that is not substantially related to the organization's exempt purposes. See I.R.C. § 511 et seq.

8. If the tax-exempt parent later disposes of the distributed property or ceases to use it in an unrelated trade or business, any gain not recognized on the earlier liquidation becomes taxable as unrelated business income. I.R.C. § 337(b)(2)(B)(ii).

9. H.R.Rep. No. 99–841, 99th Cong., 2d Sess. II–202 (1986).

10. I.R.C. § 334(b)(1).

its S stock is $3,000. I's basis in his S stock is $200. S has accumulated earnings and profits of $2,000 and the following assets:

Asset	Adjusted Basis	Fair Market Value
Land	$3,000	$8,000
Equipment	2,500	1,000
Inventory	100	1,000

S wishes to liquidate and distribute all of its assets to its shareholders. What are the tax consequences to P, S and I in the following alternative situations?

(a) S distributes the inventory to I and the other assets to P.

(b) S distributes the equipment to I and the other assets to P. How might S improve this result?

(c) What result in (b), above, if P's basis in its S stock were $30,000 and S had a $30,000 basis in the land?

(d) Is (c), above, a situation where P might wish to avoid the application of § 332? Why? How might this be accomplished? Consider in this regard the § 332 qualification requirements and how a parent might assure that they are not met.

2. Child Corporation has 100 shares of common stock outstanding. Mother Corporation owns 75 shares (basis—$1,000) and Uncle, an individual who recently inherited his stock, owns 25 shares (basis—$3,000). Child has no earnings and profits, a $10,000 net operating loss carryover and the following assets (all held long-term):

Asset	Adjusted Basis	Fair Market Value
Cash	$2,000	$2,000
Installment Note	1,000	4,000
Land	100	1,000
Equipment (all § 1245 gain)	100	1,000
Total	$3,200	$8,000

What are the tax consequences in the following alternative situations, disregarding the impact of any tax paid by Child as a result of its liquidating distributions?

(a) Child adopts a plan of complete liquidation and distributes $2,000 cash to Uncle and all its remaining assets to Mother.

(b) Child distributes $2,000 cash to Uncle in redemption of his 25 shares. One week later, it adopts a plan of complete liquidation and distributes its remaining assets to Mother pursuant to the plan. What are Mother and Child trying to accomplish through this reunion?

3. Parent Corporation ("P") owns all the stock of Subsidiary Corporation ("S"). P has a $1,000 basis in its S stock and also holds S bonds with a basis and face amount of $1,000. S has the following assets:

Asset	Adjusted Basis	Fair Market Value
Inventory	$ 10,000	$1,000
Land	200	10,000
	$ 10,200	$11,000

P intends to liquidate S, but before adopting a formal plan S distributes the inventory in satisfaction of its outstanding $1,000 debt to P. On the next day, S liquidates, distributing the land to P. Why did P and S structure the transactions in this manner? Will they achieve their tax objectives?

C.   TAXABLE CORPORATE ACQUISITIONS

1.   INTRODUCTION

There are many ways to structure a corporate acquisition. In the preceding section, we previewed one method: a sale by the target corporation [1] of all its assets followed by a distribution of the proceeds of sale to the shareholders in complete liquidation of the target.[2] An alternative is a sale by the shareholders of their stock in the target corporation. In either case, the business can be acquired in exchange for cash, notes, stock or bonds of the acquiring corporation, other property, or any combination of consideration. In an asset acquisition, the acquiring corporation may purchase the assets directly, drop them down to a controlled subsidiary or cause a subsidiary to make the acquisition. In a stock acquisition, the target may stay alive as a subsidiary of the acquiring corporation or liquidate. Variations abound on these basic formats.

Although we quickly will turn our attention to the tax consequences of corporate acquisitions, it may be useful at the outset to consider a few nontax factors that may influence the form of a transaction. Stock acquisitions normally are simpler to execute than asset acquisitions. To sell its assets, the target must prepare conveyance documents for many different items of property, give notice to creditors in compliance with local bulk sales laws and incur sales or other local transfer taxes. In a stock acquisition, however, it is unnecessary to transfer any of the target's assets; instead, the acquiring corporation simply buys the target's stock directly from the target shareholders. A stock purchase thus may be desirable (or even essential) if the target holds certain nonassignable assets, such as a favorable lease or employ-

---

1. In discussing acquisitions in this and later chapters, the selling corporation generally will be called the "target," or "T," and the corporate purchaser will be called the "acquiring corporation," or "P." By using the term "target," we do not necessarily mean to suggest that the acquisition is a hostile takeover.

2. A target that sells all or most of its assets usually will liquidate and distribute the proceeds to its shareholders. Alternatively, it could stay alive as an investment company after the sale. If the corporation is closely held, staying alive likely would cause it to be classified as a personal holding company. For the perils of personal holding company status, see Chapter 9C, infra. For the possibility of a sale of assets by a C corporation followed by a conversion to S corporation status, see Chapter 15F, infra.

ment contract, or has valuable rights under state law that might be lost if the corporation were dissolved. On the other hand, a stock acquisition may subject the buyer to liabilities of the target that may be unknown at the time of the transaction. This threat normally can be obviated by warranties and indemnity provisions in the stock purchase agreement. But some buyers still prefer to avoid the risk altogether by buying the assets and not assuming any burdens that might be connected with the corporate entity. The presence of unwanted assets, the unwillingness of minority shareholders of the target to sell their stock, and the requirements of regulatory agencies and local corporate law are additional nontax factors that may influence the choice of form.

The principal tax issues raised on a corporate acquisition are best introduced by revisiting the simple example from earlier in the chapter. Recall that A is the sole shareholder of Target Corporation ("T") and has a $100,000 basis in her T stock. T's only asset is a parcel of undeveloped land ("Gainacre") with a fair market value of $400,000 and a zero adjusted basis. Purchaser, Inc. ("P") wishes to acquire the land for $400,000 cash. Consider three simple methods of structuring the acquisition:

    (1) *Liquidation of T Followed by Shareholder Sale of Assets.* T distributes Gainacre to A in complete liquidation and then A sells Gainacre to P for $400,000.

    (2) *Sale of T Assets Followed by Liquidation.* T sells Gainacre to P for $400,000 and then liquidates, distributing the after-tax proceeds of sale to A.

    (3) *Sale of T Stock.* A sells her T stock to P for $400,000 and P either keeps T alive as a wholly owned subsidiary or causes T to liquidate and distribute Gainacre to P.

Under any of these methods, one would expect A to recognize gain equal to the difference between her amount realized on the liquidation or sale of stock and the $100,000 adjusted basis in her T stock. In addition, T has $400,000 of corporate-level gain inherent in Gainacre. Should that gain also be recognized and, if so, should P (directly or indirectly through its ownership of T stock) take Gainacre with a $400,000 fair market value basis? If T does recognize gain, who bears the economic burden of the corporate-level tax? Alternatively, can the transaction be structured so that T's gain is deferred through a $100,000 transferred basis in the land? Or, perish the thought, might T's gain be permanently forgiven, with P (or T, if it is still alive), taking Gainacre with a $400,000 cost basis? To what extent do the answers to these questions depend on the form of the transaction? And how are they affected if the seller is not an individual but a corporation which owns 100 percent of the T stock.

The after-tax economic outcome of these transactions may differ radically depending on the structure selected by the parties. The remainder of this chapter fills in the details, first considering asset acquisitions and then stock acquisitions.

2. ASSET ACQUISITIONS

A taxable asset acquisition occurs when a purchaser ("P", which may be a corporation or an individual) acquires the assets of a target corporation ("T") in exchange for cash, notes, other property, or a mix of such consideration, and the acquisition does not qualify as a tax-free reorganization under Section 368.[1] T normally liquidates following the sale of its assets and distributes the sales proceeds to its shareholders, but the shareholders may choose to keep T alive and have it reinvest the proceeds. Under the corporate laws of many states, an asset acquisition also may be accomplished by a "forward merger" of T into P (or a subsidiary of P). On the merger, T's shareholders receive cash or notes (or a combination) from P, and T's assets and liabilities automatically transfer to P (or its subsidiary). The Service views such a "cash merger" as if T sold its assets to P and then completely liquidated.[2]

To illustrate the tax consequences of the most basic asset acquisition methods, return again to the example of A, the sole shareholder (stock basis—$100,000) of T, whose only asset is appreciated Gainacre (basis—zero; fair market value—$400,000). Assume that C corporations are taxed at a flat 40 percent rate, and individuals are taxed at a flat 35 percent rate, with a 30 percent preferential rate for capital gains.[3]

Liquidation of T Followed by Shareholder Sale of T Assets. If T distributes Gainacre to A in complete liquidation, it recognizes $400,000 gain under Section 336(a) and incurs a tax liability of $160,000 (40% × $400,000). A bears the economic burden of the tax because T has no assets after it liquidates. A recognizes $140,000 gain on the liquidation ($400,000 distribution less $160,000 corporate-level tax less $100,000 basis in T stock) and incurs a shareholder-level tax of $42,000 (30% × $140,000). A takes Gainacre with a $400,000 basis under Section 334(a) and recognizes no further gain on a sale of Gainacre to P for its fair market value. When the smoke clears, the total corporate and shareholder-level tax on the liquidation and sale is $202,000, leaving A with $198,000.[4] P takes Gainacre with a $400,000 cost basis and, if P is a corporation, it does not succeed to the tax attributes (e.g., earnings and profits, net operating losses, etc.) of T.

Sale of T Assets Followed by Liquidation. The result is identical if T sells Gainacre to P and then liquidates. T recognizes $400,000 gain on the sale, pays a corporate-level tax of $160,000, distributes the

---

1. See Chapter 10, infra.

2. Rev.Rul. 69–6, 1969–1 C.B. 104.

3. We use these rates, which are a rough approximation of the combined federal and state income tax liability in many states as this book goes to press, for computational convenience.

4. Under the actual federal rates in effect as this book goes to press (34 percent corporate rate and 28 percent individual capital gains rate), the combined tax burden on a liquidation of a C corporation can be as high as 52.48 percent (34 percent corporate level plus 18.48 percent shareholder level). The 18.48 percent is derived by multiplying the 28 percent individual capital gains rate times 66 percent, which represents the proceeds remaining after imposition of a 34 percent corporate tax.

$240,000 net proceeds to A in complete liquidation, and A again recognizes $140,000 gain under Section 331(a). P takes Gainacre with a $400,000 cost basis and does not succeed to any of T's tax attributes.

Sale of T Assets Not Followed by Liquidation. If T does not liquidate after selling Gainacre to P, T once again recognizes $400,000 gain and incurs $160,000 in corporate-level tax, but A does not recognize gain if T retains and reinvests the $240,000 net proceeds. Keeping T alive defers and may permanently eliminate any tax at the shareholder level. For example, if A holds the T stock until her death, A's heirs will take a stepped-up basis in the stock under Section 1014 and then may liquidate the corporation without paying a shareholder-level tax. This "no liquidation" strategy may have some appeal if A is elderly and her heirs are on the verge of obtaining a stepped-up basis in the T stock, but it is rarely desirable if the liquidation will be postponed for many years. First, income realized by T is taxed at the somewhat higher corporate rates.[5] Moreover, if T no longer conducts an ongoing business, it likely will be classified as a "personal holding company."[6] As such, it will be required to distribute its net investment income annually to A or face a penalty tax roughly equal to 28 percent[7] of any undistributed income. In view of the increased tax costs of remaining a C corporation, keeping T alive may be more expensive than liquidating.[8]

3. STOCK ACQUISITIONS

a. BACKGROUND

In a taxable stock acquisition, the purchaser ("P") buys the stock of a target corporation ("T") from T's shareholders for cash or a combination of cash, notes and other consideration. If T is closely held, P may negotiate an agreement directly with T's shareholders. In the case of a publicly traded T, a stock acquisition may be structured as a reverse merger, in which P forms a wholly owned transitory subsidiary ("S"), and S merges into T under state law, with T's shareholders receiving

---

5. Dividends, however, would qualify for the 70 percent dividends received deduction under Section 243(a), and corporate-level *regular* tax could be avoided altogether by investing the sales proceeds in tax-exempt municipal bonds. But T still may be subject to the corporate alternative minimum tax even if it is able to shelter its investment income from the regular tax. See, e.g., I.R.C. § 56(g) and Chapter 1B2, supra.

6. See § 541 et seq. and Chapter 9B, infra.

7. When Congress raised the top individual marginal rate to 31 percent in the Revenue Reconciliation Act of 1990, it neglected to make an appropriate increase to the personal holding company rate. A technical correction raising the rate to 31 percent can be expected.

8. T could avoid some of these problems if it becomes an S corporation. For example, T's income would pass through to A and be subject to only one level of tax at the lower individual rates. But as an S corporation, T would face other tax obstacles. To name just two, an S corporation that was once a "C" corporation may lose its S status or be subject to a special corporate-level tax if it has Subchapter C earnings and profits and significant investment income. See I.R.C. §§ 1362(d)(3), 1375 and Chapter 15B and 15F, infra.

cash and debt obligations of P. When the dust settles, P holds T as a wholly owned subsidiary.

Takeovers of public companies are almost always stock acquisitions. They are often launched when P begins acquiring T stock in the open market.[1] Depending on whether the acquisition is friendly or hostile, the next step may be a cash tender offer to T's shareholders or a friendly merger negotiated with T's management. If P succeeds in acquiring control of T, the final step is usually a "back-end" merger where recalcitrant minority shareholders are squeezed out of the picture, sometimes for the same price originally offered to tendering shareholders or perhaps on less attractive terms.[2]

Whether the transaction is structured as a direct stock purchase or a reverse subsidiary cash merger,[3] T's shareholders recognize gain or loss on the sale of their stock, measured by the difference between their amount realized and stock basis, and P takes a cost basis in the T stock it acquires. T shareholders who receive notes generally may report their gain on the installment method if the T stock is not publicly traded.[4] The more difficult conceptual questions relate to the tax consequences to T and the impact of a stock acquisition on the basis of T's assets and T's other tax attributes. Should a stock acquisition be treated as if it were a taxable asset acquisition coupled with a liquidation of T, or should the form of the transaction control? Should the parties be permitted to select which treatment they would prefer?

Not surprisingly, Congress has exhibited considerable hyperactivity in answering these questions. The *Kimbell-Diamond* case, which follows, is the best place to begin describing the evolution of the current tax treatment of stock acquisitions.

KIMBELL–DIAMOND MILLING CO. v. COMMISSIONER

Tax Court of the United States, 1950.
14 T.C. 74.

BLACK, Judge.

[In August, 1942, taxpayer's milling plant was destroyed by fire and two months later the taxpayer collected insurance as a reimburse-

---

1. P may purchase up to five percent of T's stock without any requirement for public disclosure under the federal securities laws. Securities Exchange Act of 1934, § 13(d), 15 U.S.C.A. § 78m(d) (1981).

2. Squeeze outs are facilitated by the modern corporate laws of Delaware and other states where many public companies are incorporated. See, e.g., Del.Corp.Law § 251 (1984). For a good basic description of the mechanics, dynamics and economics of corporate takeovers, see Hamilton, Fundamentals of Modern Business (1989).

3. A reverse subsidiary cash merger is treated for tax purposes as if P purchased

T stock directly from the shareholders. Transitory "S" is disregarded. See Rev. Rul. 73–427, 1973–2 C.B. 301; Rev.Rul. 79–273, 1979–2 C.B. 125; Rev.Rul. 90–95, 1990–46 I.R.B. 5.

4. I.R.C. § 453(k)(2). Installment sales of very large blocks of stock may be affected by Section 453A, enacted in 1988, which imposes what amounts to an annual interest charge on a seller's tax liability that has been deferred by the installment method. In general, this provision applies only if the face amount of the seller's installment receivables during the taxable year exceed $5 million.

ment for its loss. It then purchased for approximately $210,000 cash all the stock of Whaley Mill & Elevator Co. in order to use Whaley's plant and equipment to replace its own destroyed facilities. The purchase price consisted of $120,000 of insurance proceeds and $90,000 of additional funds. The taxpayer's sole intention in purchasing Whaley's stock was to acquire the assets of the company through a prompt liquidation.

Taxpayer liquidated Whaley three days after acquiring the stock. In a prior proceeding, reported at 10 T.C. 7, the Tax Court held that the acquisition of Whaley came within the 1939 Code predecessor of § 1033 so that the taxpayer's gain on the involuntary conversion was not recognized. Since the taxpayer's acquisition of the Whaley stock qualified under § 1033, its basis was $110,000 (the sum of the $20,000 adjusted basis of the destroyed assets and the $90,000 of additional funds that were paid in addition to the insurance proceeds). The assets of Whaley acquired by the taxpayer in the liquidation had an adjusted basis to Whaley of more than $300,000; the depreciable assets represented about $140,000 of this total.

The central dispute in the case was over the taxpayer's basis for depreciation in the assets acquired in the Whaley liquidation. After addressing a procedural issue, the Court proceeded to discuss the merits. Note that this case arose under the 1939 Code, which did not contain former § 334(b)(2) or present § 338. Ed.]

*   *   *

OPINION

Having decided the issue of *res judicata* against petitioner, we must now determine the question of petitioner's basis in Whaley's assets on the merits. Petitioner argues that the acquisition of Whaley's assets and the subsequent liquidation of Whaley brings petitioner within the provisions of [the predecessor of § 332] and, therefore, by reason of [the predecessor of § 334(b)(1)], petitioner's basis in these assets is the same as the basis in Whaley's hands. In so contending, petitioner asks that we treat the acquisition of Whaley's stock and the subsequent liquidation of Whaley as separate transactions. It is well settled that the incidence of taxation depends upon the substance of a transaction. Commissioner v. Court Holding Co., 324 U.S. 331. It is inescapable from petitioner's minutes set out above and from the "Agreement and Program of Complete Liquidation" entered into between petitioner and Whaley, that the only intention petitioner ever had was to acquire Whaley's assets.

We think that this proceeding is governed by the principles of Commissioner v. Ashland Oil & Refining Co., 99 Fed. (2d) 588, certiorari denied, 306 U.S. 661. In that case the stock was retained for almost a year before liquidation. Ruling on the question of whether the stock or the assets of the corporation were purchased, the court stated:

The question remains, however, whether if the entire transaction, whatever its form, was essentially in intent, purpose and result, a purchase by Swiss of property, its several steps may be treated separately and each be given an effect for tax purposes as though each constituted a distinct transaction. * * * And without regard to whether the result is imposition or relief from taxation, the courts have recognized that where the essential nature of a transaction is the acquisition of property, it will be viewed as a whole, and closely related steps will not be separated either at the instance of the taxpayer or the taxing authority. Prairie Oil & Gas Co. v. Motter, 10 Cir., 66 F.2d 309; Tulsa Tribune Co. v. Commissioner, 10 Cir., 58 F.2d 937, 940; Ahles Realty Corp. v. Commissioner, 2 Cir., 71 F.2d 150; Helvering v. Security Savings Bank, 4 Cir., 72 F.2d 874. * * *

See also *Koppers Coal Co.,* 6 T.C. 1209 and cases there cited.

We hold that the purchase of Whaley's stock and its subsequent liquidation must be considered as one transaction, namely, the purchase of Whaley's assets which was petitioner's sole intention. This was not a reorganization within section 112(b)(6), and petitioner's basis in these assets, both depreciable and nondepreciable, is, therefore, its cost, or $110,721.74 ($18,921.90, the basis of petitioner's assets destroyed by fire, plus $91,799.84, the amount expended over the insurance proceeds). Since petitioner does not controvert respondent's allocation of cost to the individual assets acquired from Whaley, both depreciable and nondepreciable, respondent's allocation is sustained.

The determination of the issue of the basis to be used in computing depreciation also determines the issue as to equity invested capital. Petitioner says in its brief: "The invested capital issue involved in this proceeding will be controlled by the decision of this Court as to petitioner's basis for the assets acquired by it upon the complete liquidation of Whaley Mill and Elevator Company." Having decided the depreciation issue in respondent's favor, the issue as to petitioner's equity invested capital is likewise decided in respondent's favor.

The correctness of respondent's other adjustments having been conceded by petitioner,

Decision will be entered for the respondent.

Reviewed by the Court.

NOTE

If the stock purchase and subsequent Section 332 liquidation of the target-subsidiary in *Kimbell-Diamond* had been treated as separate transactions, the buyer would have taken a transferred basis in the target's assets under Section 334(b)(1). Looking to the buyer's intent, however, the court held that the purchase of stock was merely a transitory step in a transaction that was properly characterized as a purchase of assets. Under this application of the step transaction doctrine, the liquidation was disregarded, and the buyer took a cost basis in the assets.

In 1954, Congress enacted a statutory rule to replace the elusive intent standard of *Kimbell-Diamond* with a more objective test.[1] If a corporation purchased a controlling (80 percent or more) stock interest in the target corporation and then liquidated the target within a specific period of time, the acquiring corporation was treated as if it had purchased the target's assets. In general, the acquiring corporation took a cost basis in the assets equal to what it paid for the stock rather than the usual transferred basis that results from the liquidation of a controlled subsidiary. Although more "objective" than *Kimbell-Diamond,* the 1954 Code rules were laden with timetables, control and "purchase" requirements and a host of adjustments for cash distributions, liabilities assumed and transactions occurring after the acquisition but prior to the liquidation. Additional problems were created by the requirement that the buyer liquidate the newly acquired target in order to secure a *Kimbell-Diamond* cost basis in the target's assets.[2]

Congress responded to these deficiencies in 1982 by enacting Section 338, an awesome provision that codifies and expands upon the *Kimbell-Diamond* concept by allowing the acquiring corporation to elect to treat certain stock purchases as asset purchases. Unlike *Kimbell-Diamond* and the prior statutory scheme, which required a buyer of stock to liquidate the target in order to get a cost basis in its assets, Section 338 contains no liquidation requirement—a great convenience in cases where the buyer wishes to keep the target alive as a subsidiary. With the enactment of Section 338, a corporation that acquires control (i.e., at least 80 percent) of a target corporation is presented with four basic choices. It may: (1) not make the Section 338 election, leaving the target's basis in its assets and other tax attributes unaffected;[3] (2) not elect under Section 338, liquidate the target tax-free under Section 332 and inherit its asset bases and other tax attributes;[4] (3) make the Section 338 election and treat the transaction

---

1. I.R.C. § 334(b)(2) (pre-1982). After the enactment of Section 334(b)(2), the courts disagreed over whether the *Kimbell-Diamond* doctrine survived in situations where the requirements of Section 334(b)(2) were not met. Compare American Potash & Chemical Corp. v. United States, 399 F.2d 194 (Ct.Cl.1968) with Chrome Plate, Inc. v. United States, 614 F.2d 990 (5th Cir.1980). See also Dubroff & Daileader, "*Kimbell-Diamond* Revisited: A Critique of Judicial Analysis of the Exclusivity of Section 334(b)(2)," 43 Albany L.Rev. 739 (1979). In 1982, when Congress enacted Section 338, it specifically stated that the new statute was "intended to replace any nonstatutory treatment of a stock purchase as an asset purchase under the *Kimbell-*

Diamond doctrine." S.Rep. No. 97–494, 97th Cong., 2d Sess. 192 (1982).

2. For historians and masochists, see Bittker & Eustice, Federal Income Taxation of Corporations and Shareholders ¶ 11.45 (5th ed. 1987).

3. Under this method, an acquisition of stock is treated for tax purposes in accordance with its form.

4. Note that the tax treatment of this method is contrary to *Kimbell-Diamond,* which would have treated a stock purchase followed by a liquidation of the target as an asset acquisition. See Rev.Rul. 90–95, 1990–46 I.R.B. 5. For Congress's efforts to foreclose use of this method for tax avoidance purposes, see I.R.C. § 269(b).

as an asset acquisition under which "new T" takes a cost basis in its assets and is purged of all of its prior tax attributes; or (4) make the election and then liquidate T.

Before proceeding further, it is important to keep in mind that *Kimbell-Diamond* and Section 338 originated in the *General Utilities* era, when liquidating distributions and sales generally did not trigger a corporate-level tax. The principal question then confronting a corporate buyer of stock was whether to take a cost basis or a transferred basis in the target's assets. If those assets were appreciated, an intelligent corporate buyer would make the Section 338 election in order to step up the basis of the target's assets at little or no corporate-level tax cost. The stakes are vastly different today, where liquidating sales and distributions generally are taxable events. If a stock purchase is treated as an asset acquisition, the target must recognize gain or loss, and one of the parties (buyer or seller, or both) must bear the economic burden of the corporate tax imposed on any gain. Accordingly, the Section 338 election has lost its attractiveness in virtually all cases where the target's assets are appreciated because it makes no economic sense to elect to pay tax currently in order to step up the basis of assets and avoid tax later. Section 338 nonetheless survives in the 1986 Code, along with reams of annoyingly intricate regulations, and it remains a viable option in a few situations to be discussed below. Section 338 also may be triggered inadvertently, with unfortunate ramifications. Consequently, students of Subchapter C are obliged to examine the operation of what may have become one of the Code's younger relics.

b. OPERATION OF SECTION 338

Code: §§ 338(a), (b) (omit (b)(3)), (d), (e)(1), (2)(A) and (D), (g), (h)(1), (2), (3)(A), (4)(A), (5), (9), (11).

Regulations: §§ 1.338–4T(h)(1), (3) Questions and Answers 1, 2(i)–(iii); 1.338(b)–1T(a), (b), (c), (d)(1), (e), (f)(1); 1.338–4T(f)(6)(i)(A).

Overview of Section 338. Section 338 retains the *Kimbell-Diamond* concept (without the liquidation requirement) through a complex statutory mechanism that seeks to equate for tax purposes the purchase of assets and the purchase of an 80 percent or more interest in the stock of the target corporation. In general, the goals are to: (1) ensure that the target and its shareholders bear the same tax burden on a sale of the target's stock that they would have incurred on a sale of its assets followed by a complete liquidation; (2) provide the buyer with a cost basis in the assets of the target; and (3) terminate the tax attributes of the target and start afresh, without regard to whether or not the target is actually liquidated.

To achieve these goals, Section 338 provides that if a purchasing corporation ("P") purchases 80 percent or more of the stock of a target corporation ("T") within 12 months or less, it may elect within a specified time period to treat the target as having sold all of its assets for their fair market value in a single transaction.[1] T thus must recognize gain or loss on the hypothetical asset sale, after which it returns as a virgin corporation ("new T") with a cost basis in its assets and none of its former tax attributes.[2] If T is liquidated, this cost basis simply carries over to the parent under the rules governing liquidations of a subsidiary.[3]

The contours of Section 338 are easier to explain than its details. The section is littered with anti-avoidance provisions, many of which are aimed at sophisticated maneuvers that are beyond the scope of this fundamentals book. The path to understanding the basics may be eased by identifying some of the special problems that the statute seeks to address. To list just a few:

(1) P may not have acquired all the stock of T in one fell swoop. In that event, how much stock must be acquired and in what time period? To what extent should certain acquisitions (e.g., purchases of stock from a related person) not be counted for this purpose?

(2) Since Section 338 is an elective provision, when must the election be made and in what manner? Under what circumstances may it be revoked?

(3) How is the deemed sale price determined? How is the aggregate cost basis of the target stock allocated among T's assets? What is the impact of (and on) minority shareholders?

(4) Can P achieve selective tax benefits by first purchasing T's loss assets and then buying T's stock and deferring any gain by not making a Section 338 election?

Qualification for Section 338. The Section 338 election is available only to a "purchasing corporation," which is defined as "any corporation which makes a qualified purchase of stock of another corporation."[4] A "qualified stock purchase" is a transaction or series of transactions in which one corporation acquires by "purchase" an 80 percent controlling interest in another corporation during a 12-month "acquisition period."[5] "Purchase" is defined to exclude transactions that would not have resulted in the full recognition of gain or loss to the seller (i.e., reorganizations, gifts, bequests, Section 351 transfers) and acquisitions from certain "related persons" within the attribution rules of Section 318.[6] Roughly translated, all of this means that P must buy at least 80 percent of the stock of T within a 12-month period in transactions that are taxable to the sellers.

1. I.R.C. § 338(a).

2. I.R.C. § 338(b).

3. I.R.C. §§ 332; 334(b)(1). See Section B2 of this Chapter, supra.

4. I.R.C. § 338(d)(1).

5. I.R.C. §§ 338(d)(3); 338(h)(1). The requisite stock interest is defined in Section 338(d)(3) by reference to Section 1504(a)(2), which defines "control" as possession of at least 80 percent of the total voting power and 80 percent of the total value of a corporation's stock.

6. I.R.C. § 338(h)(3).

The Election. If a corporation makes a qualified stock purchase and wishes to make the Section 338 election, it must do so no later than the fifteenth day of the ninth month beginning after the month in which the "acquisition date" occurs.[7] The acquisition date is the day within the 12-month acquisition period on which the 80 percent purchase requirement is satisfied.[8] P thus has ample time to evaluate whether or not to make the election. Once P has acquired the requisite 80 percent interest within a 12-month period, it may not create a new acquisition date (and thus extend the deadline for making the election) simply by making additional purchases of T's stock.

Once made, a Section 338 election is irrevocable.[9] There is no turning back, even with the Commissioner's permission, if the results prove to be undesirable.

Effect of Election: Deemed Sale of Target Assets and Termination of Old Target's Existence. If P makes a qualified stock purchase and follows up with a timely Section 338 election, T is treated as having sold all of its assets at the close of the acquisition date for their "fair market value" in a single transaction and is treated as a new corporation which purchased all of its assets as of the beginning of the day after the acquisition date.[10] As a result, T recognizes gain or loss on this hypothetical sale, just as if it had sold its assets.[11] For purposes of this deemed sale, Section 338 provides that T is not treated as a member of an affiliated group if it otherwise might have been.[12] The income realized on the asset sale thus may not be combined with the income of P or its affiliates, but the economic burden of that liability is indirectly borne by P, which presumably will factor it into the price to be paid for the stock. On "the day after" the deemed sale, T is reincarnated. For tax purposes, it returns as a new corporation with no earnings and profits or other tax attributes from its pre-deemed sale era and with a cost basis in the assets that it hypothetically purchased from its former self.[13] If all this talk about deemed transactions seems mysterious, keep in mind that it is simply the mechanism used by the Code to equate purchases of assets and stock.

Determination of Asset Basis After Deemed Purchase. We have described new T's basis in its assets as a *Kimbell-Diamond* type of cost basis, but unfortunately this amount is not always as simple to determine as the cost basis in the *Kimbell-Diamond* case. Essential to a

---

7. I.R.C. § 338(g)(1).

8. I.R.C. § 338(h)(2).

9. I.R.C. § 338(g)(3).

10. For this purpose, the deemed sale price of T's assets (referred to in the regulations as the "aggregate deemed sales price," or "ADSP") may be determined by a proper appraisal or by an intricate elective "ADSP" formula authorized by Section 338(h)(11) which is "to take into account liabilities and other relevant items." See Reg. § 1.338–4T(h).

11. See Section C2 of this chapter, supra.

12. I.R.C. § 338(h)(9). A "consolidated deemed sale return" may be filed, however, by all target corporations acquired by a purchasing corporation on the same acquisition date if the targets were members of the same selling consolidated group. I.R.C. § 338(h)(15). Cf. I.R.C. § 338(h)(10) and Section C3c of this chapter, infra.

13. I.R.C. § 338(a)(2).

determination of the new asset basis is an understanding of the 12-month acquisition period. This period begins on the date of the first acquisition of stock by "purchase" that is part of a "qualified purchase," and it continues for 12 months.[14] The acquisition period thus may extend beyond the acquisition date. For example, assume P Corporation purchases 10 percent of T Corporation's stock on March 1 of year one and purchases another 70 percent of T's stock on May 1. The acquisition date is May 1, but the acquisition period extends from March 1 until the following February 28.

If P purchased all of T's stock within the 12-month acquisition period, the total asset basis is simply the total purchase price of the stock.[15] If P purchased less than 100 percent of the outstanding shares during the 12-month acquisition period and if it owned none of T's stock prior to that period, then the total asset basis is equal to the "grossed-up" basis of the stock acquired during the acquisition period.[16] The grossed-up basis is nothing more than the hypothetical price that P would have paid for T's stock had it purchased all of those shares at the same average price that it paid for the stock actually purchased during the acquisition period. The grossed-up basis is determined by multiplying the basis of the T stock purchased during the acquisition period and held on the acquisition date by the following fraction: [17]

$$\frac{100\%}{\text{\% of stock (by value) of target purchased during acquisition period and held on acquisition date}}$$

The previous explanation assumed that P had not acquired any stock in T prior to the acquisition period—i.e., it held only "recently purchased stock." [18] If P owned T stock prior to the 12-month acquisition period ("nonrecently purchased stock"),[19] the total basis of T's assets after the deemed purchase is equal to the sum of: (1) the grossed-up basis of the recently purchased stock and (2) the actual (or, in some cases, the "stepped-up") basis of the nonrecently purchased stock.[20] This basis can be expressed by the following formula:

$$\begin{array}{ccc} \text{Total} \\ \text{Asset Basis} \end{array} = \begin{array}{c} \text{Basis of Recently} \\ \text{Purchased Stock} \end{array} \times \frac{\begin{array}{c}100\% \text{ less \% of Nonrecently} \\ \text{Purchased Target Stock}\end{array}}{\begin{array}{c}\text{\% of Recently Purchased} \\ \text{Target Stock}\end{array}}$$

$$+ \quad \text{Basis of Nonrecently Purchased Stock}$$

To illustrate, assume that P acquired 10 percent of T's outstanding stock for \$20,000 many years ago. During the 12-month acquisition

---

14. I.R.C. § 338(h)(1).

15. I.R.C. § 338(b)(1), (4). Under the statute, the basis after the deemed purchase is the "grossed-up basis" under Section 338(b)(4). Where all the stock is purchased within the acquisition period, the grossed-up basis fraction is 100/100 and consequently the grossed-up basis equals the purchase price of the stock.

16. I.R.C. § 338(b)(1)(A).

17. I.R.C. § 338(b)(4).

18. I.R.C. § 338(b)(6)(A).

19. I.R.C. § 338(b)(6)(B).

20. I.R.C. § 338(b)(1), (3).

period, P acquired another 80 percent of the T stock for $800,000. If P makes the Section 338 election, its basis in T's assets after the deemed purchase will be $920,000: the sum of $900,000 (the grossed-up basis of the recently purchased stock—i.e., $800,000 $\times$ $\frac{100-10}{80}$) and $20,000 (the actual basis of the nonrecently purchased stock). The purpose of this formula is not to terrorize the tax bar but simply to reduce the basis of T's assets after the deemed purchase by the gain inherent in the nonrecently purchased stock.[21]

Adjustments for Liabilities. The end of determining the basis of the target's assets is not yet in sight. To illustrate why, assume that T has assets worth $1,000 and liabilities of $900. T's net worth is thus $100, which presumably will be the approximate price paid by the buyer ("P") for its stock. But remember that the theory underlying Section 338 is to replicate the tax consequences of an asset acquisition. If P purchased T's assets by paying $100 cash and taking those assets subject to a $900 liability and then transferred the assets to new T, old T's amount realized would be $1,000 and new T's basis in its assets also would be $1,000 under *Crane.* If P purchases the T stock for its net value of $100 and elects Section 338, T is deemed to have sold those assets for their fair market value of $1,000, and new T's asset basis also should be $1,000. Without an adjustment mechanism, however, Section 338(b)(1) would give new T an asset basis of only $100. Section 338(b)(2) addresses this problem by providing that the grossed-up basis may be adjusted for liabilities of the target and other relevant items. The details of these adjustments are the subject of regulations, which in general provide that new T's grossed-up basis shall be increased by the liabilities of old T.[22]

Included among the liabilities that will generate a basis step-up for new T are any income tax liabilities resulting from the deemed sale of T's assets.[23] For example, assume that T has assets with a basis of $150 and a fair market value of $1,150. In an asset sale, T would have a taxable gain of $1,000 and (assuming a flat 34 percent corporate rate) a tax liability of $340 that will be borne by its shareholders. P would pay $1,150 for assets of equivalent value and would take a cost basis in those assets. In a stock purchase followed by a Section 338 election, the selling shareholders will not be burdened by any corporate-level tax

---

21. If P owns nonrecently purchased stock, it may elect to take that stock into account at a special "stepped-up" basis under Section 338(b)(3) rather than at its actual cost basis. The stepped-up basis of each share of nonrecently purchased stock is the average price per share paid for the recently purchased stock, determined by yet another formula in Section 338(b)(3)(B). If P makes the stepped-up basis election, it must currently recognize gain as if it sold the nonrecently purchased stock for an amount equal to its new stepped-up basis. I.R.C. § 338(b)(3)(A). This election was attractive prior to 1987, when the cost of a basis step-up was current taxation at the corporate capital gains rate of 28 percent, and the benefit was a decrease in income otherwise to be taxed at the then 46 percent corporate rate on ordinary income. With no corporate capital gains preference, it would be rare today to elect to pay tax at the 34 percent corporate rate in order to secure a tax benefit, at the same rate, at some later time. Thus, unless the rates change, a Section 338(b)(3) election rarely makes economic sense.

22. Reg. § 1.338(b)–1T(c)(1).

23. Reg. § 1.338(b)–1T(f)(1).

because they have sold only stock and T has not actually sold any assets. Instead, the tax on the $1,000 gain inherent in T's assets will not be payable until after the Section 338 election, when T is owned by P. P thus will acquire assets worth $1,150 but subject to an effective *tax* liability of $340. Since P must pay $340 to the government to acquire T's assets free of their inherent gain, it presumably will pay less than $1,150 to the sellers, who can afford to accept less because of their decreased tax burden. P's real cost for the assets thus includes not only the amount paid for the T stock but also the tax that must be paid by T as a result of its deemed asset sale.[24]

The aggregate adjusted grossed-up basis, as determined under the rules discussed above, then must be allocated among the various T assets. Allocation of the purchase price in actual asset acquisitions and deemed acquisitions under Section 338 is examined later in this chapter.[25]

The Consistency Period. Section 338 allows the purchasing corporation either to take a transferred basis in T's assets (by not making the election) or, at the cost of paying a tax on any gain (or deducting any loss) inherent in the target's assets, to take essentially a fair market value basis in those assets. The consistency requirement was designed to ensure that P is put to a choice: it may select one or the other, but not both (or some of each) of these options. These rules are far less significant now that the *General Utilities* doctrine has been repealed, but they still may act as a trap in some situations.

The consistency period can last up to three years. It begins one year prior to the beginning of the acquisition period, and it lasts until one year following the acquisition date.[26] It can be extended indefinitely if the Secretary determines that there was a plan to avoid its restrictions.[27] For example, if P buys 80 percent of T's stock on July 1, 1991 (which is the first day of the 12–month acquisition period and also the acquisition date) and the remaining 20 percent on September 1, 1991, the consistency period begins on July 1, 1990 and ends on June 30, 1992.

The asset acquisition consistency rules in Section 338(e) are intended to prevent P from acquiring some assets from T or an affiliate of T with a cost basis and other assets with a transferred basis during the consistency period. This goal is achieved by providing that if P acquires an asset of T or a T affiliate at any time within the consistency period, P is deemed to have made a Section 338 election with respect to T. Exceptions are provided where T sold the asset in the ordinary course of its business (e.g., a routine sale of inventory) or P took a transferred basis in the asset.[28]

24. Id. But see I.R.C. § 338(h)(10), discussed in Section C3c of this chapter, infra.

25. See I.R.C. §§ 338(b)(5); 1060; Reg. § 1.338(b)–2T(b); Section C of this chapter, infra.

26. I.R.C. § 338(h)(4)(A). See generally Reg. § 1.338–4T(e), (f), (g).

27. I.R.C. § 338(h)(4)(B).

28. I.R.C. § 338(e)(2)(A) and (B). Another exception is where, under the regula-

The stock acquisition consistency rules in Section 338(f) provide that if P makes a qualified stock purchase with respect to T and one or more affiliates (e.g., a wholly owned subsidiary) of T during any consistency period, then a Section 338 election with respect to the first qualified purchase also applies to all the later qualified stock purchases. Conversely, if P makes no election for the first purchase, none may be made for the subsequent purchases.

The principal lingering significance of the consistency period rules under the post–1986 acquisitions regime is the trap they create for the normal purchaser of stock that does not wish to make the Section 338 election. To illustrate, assume P acquires all the stock of T for cash in a single transaction but does not make a Section 338 election in order to avoid the large corporate level tax that would result on a deemed sale of T's assets. Assume further that at some time during the consistency period, P directly acquires an asset from T or a corporation affiliated with T. Even though these related acquisitions by P may not have been motivated by tax avoidance, the asset acquisition—occurring as it does during the consistency period—would trigger a deemed Section 338 election under Section 338(e), requiring T to fully recognize gain on all of its assets. The regulations allow P to avoid these unpleasant consequences by making what is known as a "protective carryover election." [29] If P makes a timely protective carryover basis election with respect to a qualified stock purchase of T, then a tainted asset acquisition will not cause a deemed election under Section 338(e)(1) for T.[30] The consequences of the election are that P must take a carryover (i.e., transferred) basis in any acquired assets that are subject to the protective carryover basis election.

To illustrate the effect of this election, assume that P acquires all of T's stock from S for $100,000 in a qualified stock purchase. Assume further that T has an aggregate adjusted basis of $10,000 and a fair market value of $100,000 in its assets. Six months earlier, P acquired a machine (adjusted basis—$250; fair market value—$1,000) from a "target affiliate" [31] of T ("T–1") for $1,000 cash. P does not make a Section 338 election because it is unwilling to bear the tax burden on the $90,000 of gain that would result from a deemed sale of T's assets. P's acquisition of the machine from T–1, being within the consistency period, is a tainted asset acquisition and would trigger a deemed Section 338 election under Section 338(e)(1). If, however, P made a protective carryover election, the deemed Section 338 election could be avoided. The trade-off is that P must take a $250 transferred basis in

tions, P makes a "protective carryover basis election." See I.R.C. § 338(e)(2)(D), which is discussed at text accompanying notes 29–32, infra.

29. Reg. § 1.338–4T(f)(6). These regulations are authorized by Section 338(e)(2)(D), which provides that the deemed election rule in Section 338(e)(1) shall not apply with respect to any acquisition by P that is "described in regulations prescribed by the Secretary and meets such conditions as such regulations may provide."

30. For the procedures for making a protective carryover election, see Reg. § 1.338–4T(f)(6)(ii).

31. See I.R.C. § 338(h)(6)(A).

the machine rather than a $1,000 cost basis, even though T–1 recognized $750 gain when it sold the asset to P.

In the new regime, any corporate purchaser of a controlling stock interest in another corporation is well advised to make a protective carryover election to avoid being forced into an undesired Section 338 election resulting from an unintended violation of the consistency period rules. Even if P fails to do so, however, the regulations provide that a tainted asset acquisition will trigger an "affirmative action carryover election" having the same effect unless the Service exercises its authority to override this result and deems P to have made a Section 338 election.[32]

This Congressional obsession with consistency is further exemplified by Section 338(i)(1), which authorizes the Treasury to "prescribe such regulations" as may be necessary to ensure that the consistency requirements are not circumvented "through the use of any provision of law or regulations," including the consolidated return regulations and, no doubt, the United States Constitution and the Geneva Convention.

Subsequent Liquidation of T. If P purchases 80 percent or more of T stock and then immediately liquidates T, the Service has ruled that the stock purchase and subsequent liquidation of T shall be accorded independent significance. P is treated as having made a qualified stock purchase rather than a direct acquisition of assets under the *Kimbell-Diamond* doctrine.[33] On the liquidation, P recognizes no gain or loss under Section 332 and T recognizes no gain or loss on the distribution of its assets to P under Section 337. In any event, neither P nor T would have any significant realized gain or loss because at least 80 percent of the T stock would have been recently purchased, and any built-in gain on T's assets was recognized as a result of the Section 338 deemed asset sale. After the liquidation, P succeeds to T's fair market value basis in its assets.

In short, if P makes a Section 338 election and then liquidates T, the end result is equivalent to a direct purchase of T's assets or a forward cash merger of T into P.

c.   ACQUISITION OF STOCK OF A SUBSIDIARY

Section 338(h)(10) Election. The previous discussion assumed that T was not a subsidiary of another corporation. Consider, however, the situation where T is a wholly owned subsidiary of Seller, Inc. ("S"), and P wishes to acquire T. Assume that the value of T's stock (and also its underlying assets) is $400,000; S has a $100,000 basis in its T stock; and T has a $100,000 aggregate basis in its assets. T could sell its assets directly to P for $400,000 in a taxable transaction and then distribute the sales proceeds to S in a tax-free liquidation under Section 332, with the net result being $300,000 of taxable gain to T on the asset

---

32.   Reg. § 1.338–4T(f)(6)(i)(A).   **33.**   Rev.Rul. 90–95, 1990–46 I.R.B. 5.

sale. Alternatively, T could distribute the assets to S in a tax-free liquidation. S would take the assets with a $100,000 transferred basis under Section 334(b) and recognize $300,000 gain on a sale to P. In either case, S does not recognize gain or loss on its T stock, and P acquires the assets with a $400,000 cost basis. If the disappearance of S's $300,000 gain on its T stock seems inconsistent with the double tax regime, remember that no assets have yet been distributed out of corporate solution to the shareholders of S, the real people who own the enterprise. The policy is to avoid three levels of tax on what may be a single economic gain.

Now assume that for nontax reasons P must acquire T's stock. Under general tax principles, S would recognize gain or loss on the sale of its T stock and P would take the stock with a cost basis. If P makes a Section 338 election, T also is treated as having sold its assets in a taxable transaction. If P does not elect, the bases of T's assets are unchanged and any built-in gain or loss is preserved. Either way, the result is double *corporate* -level gain, with the potential of a third round of taxation when S distributes the sales proceeds to its shareholders.

Section 338(h)(10) offers relief from this potential triple tax by permitting the parties to ignore S's sale of its T stock and treat the transaction as if it were a sale of T's assets.[1] If a Section 338(h)(10) election is made,[2] the transaction is treated as if old T sold its assets to new T while a member of the S consolidated group, and S then liquidated T tax-free under Section 332.[3] The tax consequences of the election are: (1) S recognizes no gain or loss on the sale of its T stock; (2) S inherits T's tax attributes (e.g., net operating losses);[4] (3) T is treated as having sold its assets for their fair market value in a taxable transaction,[5] and any gain or loss is included on the consolidated return filed by S and its affiliates; and (4) "new T," a subsidiary of P, is treated as having acquired old T's assets for an amount equal to their adjusted grossed-up basis.[6] Two levels of corporate-level gain are thus avoided, and the tax burden of the sale remains with the seller.

Returning to the example, if the parties make a Section 338(h)(10) election, S's $300,000 gain on the sale of its T stock is ignored, and the

1. In general, before the transaction T must be a member of "the selling consolidated group." I.R.C. § 338(h)(10)(A). A "selling consolidated group" is any group of corporations which, for the taxable period which includes the transaction, includes T and files a consolidated tax return. I.R.C. § 338(h)(10)(B). Pursuant to regulations, a qualified seller also may be any "affiliated group" of corporations (within the meaning of Section 1504) which includes T, whether or not the group files a consolidated return. Id.

2. The election must be made jointly by the S group and P. See Reg. § 1.338(h)(10)–1T(d)(1).

3. See Reg. § 1.338(h)(10)–1T(e)(3).

4. These inherited tax attributes are reduced in proportion to the percentage of old T stock held by minority shareholders. Reg. §§ 1.381(c)(2)–1(c)(2); 1.338(h)(10)–1T(g) Example (5).

5. The deemed sale price is determined under a formula prescribed by the regulations, which refers to the actual purchase price paid by P for the T stock and is adjusted for liabilities of T and other relevant items. See Reg. § 1.338(h)(10)–1T(f).

6. I.R.C. § 338(b). The adjusted grossed-up basis does not include income tax liabilities resulting from the deemed asset sale because those liabilities were payable by S. Cf. Reg. § 1.338(h)(10)–1T(e) (6)(C).

$300,000 gain on the deemed sale of T's assets [7] is included on the consolidated tax return filed by S and its affiliates. P takes a $400,000 cost basis in the T stock and "new T" takes a $400,000 basis in its assets.

Although the Section 338(h)(10) election is generally desirable because it eliminates two levels of corporate-level gain, it has particular allure when S has a large "outside" gain on its T stock relative to minimal "inside" gain on T's assets. In that scenario, P may purchase T's stock at little or no tax cost to S if the parties make a Section 338(h)(10) election. Of course, the same result could have been achieved if S first liquidated T under Section 332 and sold the assets to P, but this method might not be feasible if P needs to keep T alive as a corporate entity for nontax reasons.

The election also is attractive when S's consolidated group has losses that can be applied to offset any gain recognized by T on the deemed sale of its assets. If Section 338 were elected without an accompanying Section 338(h)(10) election, T must file a separate one day return reporting the income from the deemed sale and it could not offset its gain with any losses from S's other operations. If a Section 338(h)(10) election is made, however, the gain on the deemed sale is reported on S's consolidated return and may be offset by losses of S and its other affiliates.

Section 336(e). Section 336(e) is a close relative of Section 338(h)(10). In some cases, it is an identical twin. Section 336(e) provides that, upon the promulgation of regulations, a corporation that owns at least 80 percent of the voting power and value of the stock of another corporation may elect to treat a sale, exchange or distribution of that subsidiary's stock as if it were a disposition of the subsidiary's assets. If a Section 336(e) election is made, the parent does not recognize gain or loss on the sale, exchange or distribution of the stock. The legislative history of Section 336(e) states that "principles similar to those of Section 338(h)(10)" will be used in determining the operation of the Section 336(e) election. [8]

The overlap between Sections 336(e) and 338(h)(10) is apparent when a parent *sells* the stock of a controlled subsidiary to a corporate purchaser. Section 336(e) is potentially broader, but its scope will remain unclear until regulations are promulgated. Presumably, Section 336(e) could apply even if the buyer were an individual or entity (such as a partnership) that is not qualified to make a Section 338 election. Moreover, Section 336(e) is not confined to sales. It potentially encompasses both liquidating and perhaps even nonliquidating distributions of the stock of a subsidiary. [9]

7. We have assumed for convenience that the deemed sale price equals the $400,000 fair market value of T's assets.

8. H.R.Rep. No. 841, 99th Cong., 2d Sess. II–204.

9. For some of the complexities engendered by Section 336(e) and the many open issues that await regulations, see Ginsburg & Levin, Mergers, Acquisitions and Leveraged Buyouts Vol. F1 ¶ 207; Yin, "Taxing Corporate Liquidations (And Related Matters) After the Tax Reform Act of 1986," 42 Tax L.Rev. 573, 652–664 (1987).

d. STOCK ACQUISITIONS WITH NO SECTION 338 ELECTION

The tax consequences of an acquisition of 80 percent or more of T's stock with no Section 338 election are far less complicated. T's shareholders, as always, recognize gain or loss on the sale of their stock. T becomes a subsidiary of P and retains its tax attributes, including the historic basis in its assets, earnings and profits and the like. If P subsequently liquidates T, neither P nor T recognizes gain or loss, and T's asset bases and other tax attributes transfer to P under Sections 334(b)(1) and 381.[1] The extent to which T (if it stays alive) or P (if it liquidates T) may utilize T's net operating losses after the acquisition is likely to be limited by Section 382, which is examined in a later chapter.[2]

4. COMPARISON OF ACQUISITION METHODS

A typical student's reaction to this chapter (or indeed the entire course up to now) might be something like this: "After considerable effort, I understand the workings of most Code sections as they are studied, but Subchapter C is becoming a conglomeration of random detail." The lament might continue with these questions about corporate acquisitions: "How does it all fit together? Does it matter whether P buys T's assets or stock? What rational buyer ever would make the Section 338 election? Does substance control over form—or form over substance?" In short, the understandable plea is—"Give me some perspective!" This section attempts to respond by comparing taxable acquisition methods in a tax planning context.

The repeal of the *General Utilities* doctrine greatly altered the tax economics of corporate acquisitions. Prior to 1987, the tax consequences of an asset purchase followed by a complete liquidation, or a stock purchase coupled with a Section 338 election, were essentially the same. T's shareholders recognized a capital gain on their investment; T did not recognize gain or loss on the actual or deemed transfer of its assets except for recapture of depreciation and a few other items; and P (or "new T") obtained a fair market value in T's assets. In short, taxable acquisitions involved only a single, shareholder-level tax, which often could be deferred if P used installment notes as partial consideration for the purchase.

---

1. Rev.Rul. 90–95, 1990–46 I.R.B. 5.

2. See Chapter 13, infra. See also I.R.C. § 269(b), which authorizes the Service to disallow deductions and other tax benefits (including, possibly, built-in losses) if: (1) P does not make a Section 338 election after making a qualified stock purchase, (2) T is liquidated pursuant to a plan adopted within two years of the acquisition date, and (3) the principal purpose of the liquidation is tax avoidance. Enacted in 1984 to prevent the result sought by the taxpayer in the *Kimbell–Diamond* case (i.e., a transferred basis that preserved T's built-in losses), Section 269(b) is largely an anachronism in light of the repeal of the *General Utilities* doctrine and the overriding importance of the loss limitations in Section 382.

After *General Utilities* repeal, an asset acquisition requires both T and its shareholders to recognize gain unless T does not liquidate. A stock purchase coupled with a Section 338 election is no better because the deemed asset sale results in full recognition of corporate-level gain. In either case, P obtains a fair market value basis in T's assets—but at the price of an immediate corporate-level tax. Two levels of gain are avoided, however, if P purchases T's stock and does not elect under Section 338. It is perhaps ironic that, after years of effort to equate the tax treatment of different corporate acquisition methods, we are left with an asymmetrical system under which asset acquisitions require two levels of tax with no opportunity for T to defer tax through a transferred basis, while a stock acquisition without a Section 338 election requires only a shareholder-level tax, albeit with the trade-off of a transferred basis in T's assets.[1]

It follows that the preferred alternative for most taxable acquisitions is a stock purchase with no Section 338 election. It is rarely desirable to pay a front-end corporate tax on the gain inherent in T's assets in order to achieve tax savings later from the additional depreciation, amortization and other deductions that would flow from the stepped-up basis in T's assets. The two principal exceptions are: (1) where T has large net operating loss carryovers that would be available to offset the gain recognized on the deemed asset sale;[2] and (2) where T is a subsidiary of another corporation.[3]

The prospect of a two-tier tax also may tilt the method of choice in corporate acquisitions more towards tax-free reorganizations, where neither T nor its shareholders currently recognize gain or loss, but tax attributes at both the corporate and shareholder levels are preserved through transferred and exchanged bases. The acquisitive reorganization alternative will be thoroughly examined in Chapter 10.

PROBLEMS

1. Target Corporation ("T") is a calendar year, accrual basis "C" corporation. T's 1,000 shares of common stock (its only class) are owned by three unrelated shareholders as follows:

Shareholder	No. Shs.	Adj. Basis	F.M.V.
A	500	$ 50,000	$ 500,000
B	400	40,000	400,000
C	100	140,000	100,000
	1,000	$230,000	$1,000,000

1. These lingering discontinuities are discussed in Zolt, "The *General Utilities* Doctrine: Examining the Scope of Repeal," 65 Taxes 819 (1987); Yin, "A Carryover Basis Regime? A Few Words of Caution," 37 Tax Notes 415 (1987); and Lewis, "A Proposal for a Corporate Level Tax on Major Stock Sales," 37 Tax Notes 1041 (1987). See Chapter 10E, infra, for proposed alternatives to the current acquisitions regime.

2. These losses are available without limitation to offset the gain on T's deemed asset sale. If P acquired T and did not elect under Section 338, T's NOLs would not be purged but they likely would be limited in the future under Section 382. See Chapter 13, infra.

3. See I.R.C. § 338(h)(10) and Section C3c of this chapter, supra.

A and B are in their late 60's and have held their T stock since the company was founded many years ago. C recently inherited her stock.

T has $400,000 of accumulated earnings and profits and the following assets (all held long-term) and liabilities:

Assets	Adj. Basis	F.M.V.
Cash	$200,000.	$ 200,000
Inventory	50,000	100,000
Equipment ($100,000 § 1245 recapture)	100,000	200,000
Building (no recapture)	50,000	300,000
Securities	400,000	300,000
Goodwill	0	200,000
	$800,000	$1,300,000

Liabilities		
Bank loan		300,000
		$ 300,000

T and its shareholders are considering a sale of the business. Purchaser Corporation ("P") is interested in acquiring T. Assume (for computational convenience) that C corporations are taxed at a combined federal and state flat corporate rate of 40 percent and all individuals are taxed at a flat 35 percent combined rate with a 30 percent preferential rate for long-term capital gains realized by individuals.

What are the tax consequences of the following alternative acquisition methods to T, T's shareholders, and P?

(a) T adopts a plan of complete liquidation, distributes all of its assets (subject to the liability) to its shareholders in proportion to their stock holdings, and the shareholders then sell the assets to P.

(b) T adopts a plan of complete liquidation, sells all of its assets (subject to the liability) to P for $1,000,000 cash, and distributes the after-tax proceeds to its shareholders in proportion to their stock holdings.

(c) In general, how would the result in (b), above, change if P paid T $400,000 in cash and $600,000 in notes, with market rate interest payable annually and the entire principal payable in five years?

(d) T sells all of its assets to P as in (b), above, except that T does not liquidate but instead invests the after-tax sales proceeds in a portfolio of publicly traded securities.

(e) P purchases all the stock of T for $800 per share and makes a § 338 election. (Why didn't P pay $1,000 per share for the T stock?)

(f) What result to P and T in (e), above, if P purchases the stock of A and B for $800 per share, but C continues to hold her 100 shares?

(g) What result to P and T in (e), above, if P purchased the stock of C five years ago for $50,000 and purchases the stock of A and B for $800 per share in the current year?

(h) P purchases all the stock of T for cash but does not make the § 338 election. (Consider generally what P should pay for the T stock.)

(i) What result in (h), above, if six months prior to purchasing all of T's stock, P purchased a parcel of land from T for $100,000 cash and T had a $20,000 adjusted basis in the land?

(j) Assuming P and T are indifferent to the form of the transaction, would you recommend the acquisition method in (b) (purchase of assets), (e) (purchase of stock with § 338 election) or (h) (purchase of stock without § 338 election), above?

(k) Would your recommendation in (j), above, change if T had $600,000 in net operating loss carryovers?

(*l*) Assume that T is a wholly-owned subsidiary of S, Inc., and S has a $200,000 adjusted basis in its T stock. What result if T distributes all of its assets (subject to the liability) to S in complete liquidation, and S then sells the assets to P?

(m) Same as (*l*), above, except P insists that the transaction must be structured as an acquisition of T stock.

2. Should Congress enact legislation that treats taxable asset and stock acquisitions consistently for tax purposes? If so, what are its options and which would you support?

5. ALLOCATION OF THE PURCHASE PRICE

Code: § 1060.

Regulations: § 1.338(b)–2T(a), (b), (c).

a. BACKGROUND

A sale of assets of a going business for a lump sum is treated for tax purposes as a sale of each individual asset rather than of a single capital asset.[1] This fragmentation approach requires the parties to allocate the purchase price among the various tangible and intangible assets that are sold. The allocation is used to determine the amount and character of the seller's gain or loss, and the buyer's cost basis in each asset for purposes of computing depreciation and amortization deductions and gain or loss on a subsequent sale.

The parties historically had adverse interests when it came to allocating the purchase price among the assets. Buyers wished to allocate as much as possible to inventory, depreciable property and amortizable intangibles and resisted allocations to nondepreciable goodwill. Sellers, by contrast, benefitted by allocating a larger portion of

---

1. Williams v. McGowan, 152 F.2d 570 (2d Cir.1945).

the purchase price to assets yielding a capital gain. Although these historical conflicts diminished with the elimination of a significant capital gains preference, buyers are still motivated to allocate basis to assets that will produce depreciation or amortization deductions.

The parties may include a negotiated purchase price allocation in their written agreement. Because buyers and sellers historically had adverse interests, negotiated allocations generally were respected by the Service. Indeed, the Service and some courts would not permit a party to take a tax reporting position inconsistent with an agreed allocation unless it could be demonstrated that the contract was unenforceable because of mistake, undue influence, fraud or duress.[2] Other courts, using a more lenient standard, permitted a party to override a contractual allocation by a showing of "strong proof" that the agreement should not be respected.[3]

More often than not, however, agreements of sale contained no purchase price allocation, allowing the parties to go their separate ways and possibly "whipsaw" the government in the process by taking inconsistent positions. A typical controversy involved the tension between a covenant not to compete and goodwill. Amounts paid that are attributable to a covenant by the seller not to compete with the buyer for a stated period of time result in ordinary income to the seller and are amortizable by the buyer over the life of the covenant. Payments for goodwill, on the other hand, may not be depreciated or amortized by the buyer, and gain on the sale of goodwill is capital gain to the seller. Thus, when capital gains are taxed at a lower rate than ordinary income, sellers will prefer allocations to goodwill, while buyers, craving deductions, will prefer allocations to a covenant not to compete.

Even without a covenant not to compete, some of the most troublesome allocation controversies have been over the amount properly attributable to goodwill and the going concern value of an acquired business. The allocation is especially critical to a buyer who pays a premium—i.e., an amount that exceeds even the most generous appraised value of the target's identifiable tangible and intangible assets. Prior to the Tax Reform Act of 1986, the Service authorized the "proportionate" method of allocation, under which the value of each acquired asset (including intangibles such as goodwill)[4] was determined, and the aggregate purchase price was allocated in proportion to the relative fair market value of each asset. The proportionate method often had the effect of shifting any premium paid for the business toward depreciable and amortizable assets and away from nondeprecia-

2. Commissioner v. Danielson, 378 F.2d 771 (3d Cir.1967), cert. denied 389 U.S. 858, 88 S.Ct. 94 (1967).

3. See, e.g., Ullman v. Commissioner, 264 F.2d 305 (2d Cir.1959).

4. For this purpose, goodwill was valued by using a complex capitalization of earnings formula, which looked to certain assumed rates of return and historic earnings of the business over time. See generally S.Rep. No. 99–313, 99th Cong., 2d Sess. 251–253 (1986); Staff of the Joint Committee on Taxation, General Explanation of the Tax Reform Act of 1986, 100th Cong., 1st Sess. 356–357 (1987).

ble goodwill. The future tax benefits that resulted from this allocation method were a stimulus to the corporate takeover mania of the 1980's.

Under another valuation approach, known as the residual method, each tangible and intangible asset (excluding goodwill and going concern value) is valued first. If the overall price paid for the business exceeds the aggregate fair market value of these assets, the excess ("residue") is all allocated to goodwill and going concern value. In the case of a "bargain purchase," where the price paid for the business is less than the appraised value of T's assets, nothing is allocated to goodwill and the amount allocated to the identifiable assets (other than cash, cash equivalents and marketable securities) is proportionately reduced.

Congress first moved to regulate purchase price allocations in connection with stock purchases that are treated as asset acquisitions under Section 338. Aware that allocations were a source of controversy and concerned that buyers might improperly manipulate their allocation of the infamous "adjusted grossed-up basis," Congress directed the Treasury to prescribe regulations governing allocation of that basis among the target's assets.[5] Not unexpectedly, the regulations mandated use of the residual method. In 1986, Congress extended this approach to asset acquisitions by enacting Section 1060, which includes reporting requirements to protect the Service from being whipsawed. Since 1986, Congress has enacted legislation to clarify and expand Section 1060.

b. DEEMED ASSET ACQUISITIONS UNDER SECTION 338

The allocation rules that ultimately were incorporated in the Code for asset acquisitions had their genesis in the Section 338 regulations governing stock acquisitions. If the purchaser makes a Section 338 election, the deemed purchase price of the target's assets, known as the adjusted grossed-up basis, generally equals the purchase price of T's stock, adjusted for tax and other liabilities of T.[6] The price paid for T's stock does not necessarily equal the aggregate value of T's assets. For example, P may have paid a premium for T, perhaps in connection with a hostile takeover or leveraged buyout. The regulations promulgated under Section 338(b)(5), which adopt the residual method of allocation, require the adjusted grossed-up basis first to be allocated to specified assets to their extent of their fair market value, and any balance is allocated to goodwill and going concern value.

Specifically, T first must reduce the adjusted grossed-up basis by its cash and cash equivalents, which are referred to as Class I assets.[7] The remaining adjusted grossed-up basis then must be allocated first to liquid assets such as certificates of deposit, U.S. Government securities and other readily marketable stock or securities (Class II assets) to the

---

5. I.R.C. § 338(b)(5).

6. See I.R.C. § 338(b)(1) and (2), and Section C3b of this chapter, supra.

7. Reg. § 1.338(b)–2T(b)(1).

extent of their fair market value,[8] and next to all other tangible and intangible assets (Class III assets), excluding goodwill and going concern value, in proportion to their fair market value.[9] Any remaining adjusted grossed-up basis is allocated to intangible assets in the nature of goodwill and going concern value.[10] If there is insufficient basis for any class of assets, the available basis must be allocated to each asset in the class in proportion to its fair market value.[11]

c. ACTUAL ASSET ACQUISITIONS

The allocation method prescribed by Section 1060, which applies in the case of "any applicable asset acquisition," [12] is identical to the approach adopted by the Section 338 regulations. An "applicable asset acquisition" is any transfer (direct or indirect) of assets which constitute a trade or business and with respect to which the transferee's basis in the purchased assets is determined wholly by reference to the consideration paid for the assets.[13] The legislative history elaborates on this definition: [14]

> Both direct and indirect transfers of a business are intended to be covered by this provision, including, for example, a sale of a business by an individual or a partnership, or a sale of a partnership interest in which the basis of the purchasing partner's proportionate share of the partnership's assets is adjusted to reflect the purchase price. A group of assets will constitute a business for this purpose if their character is such that goodwill or going concern value could under any circumstances attach to such assets. For example, a group of assets that would constitute an active trade or business within the meaning of section 355 [relating to corporate divisions; see Chapter 12, infra. Ed.] will in all events be considered a business for purposes of this provision. Moreover, businesses that are not active businesses under section 355 will also be subject to this rule.

If Section 1060 applies, as it will to any routine sale of the assets of a corporate business, the purchase price must be allocated among the assets in the same manner as prescribed by Section 338(b)(5)—i.e., by the residual method. The effect of this approach is to allocate any premium to nonamortizable goodwill or going concern value. Section 1060 does not necessarily eliminate squabbles between taxpayers and

---

8. Reg. § 1.338(b)–2T(b)(2)(i), (ii).

9. Reg. § 1.338(b)–2T(b)(2)(iii).

10. Reg. § 1.338(b)–2T(b)(2)(iv).

11. Reg. § 1.338(b)–2T(c)(1). These are merely the *general* rules. The regulations contain a maze of other special rules and adjustments for which we provide an obligatory cite but do not particularly recommend for bedtime reading. See Reg. §§ 1.338(b)–2T(c)(3), –3T.

12. I.R.C. § 1060(a). See Reg. § 1.1060–1T

13. I.R.C. § 1060(c). A transfer shall not be treated as failing to be an applicable asset acquisition merely because Section 1031 applies to a *portion* of the assets transferred. Id. See Reg. § 1.1060–1T(b) (4)

14. S.Rep. No. 99–313, supra note 4 at 254–255.

the Service. The buyer still must value all the target's identifiable tangible and intangible assets, and cooperative appraisers can be expected to weight the purchase price to assets that will provide future tax benefits—e.g., depreciable equipment and amortizable intangibles. Recognizing that valuation issues will not disappear under the residual method, the Senate Finance Committee emphasized that it "did not intend to restrict in any way the ability of the Internal Revenue Service to challenge the taxpayer's determination of the fair market value of any asset by any appropriate method." [15] The Committee went on to observe that it would be reasonable for the Service to make an independent showing of the value of goodwill or going concern value as a method of challenging the validity of the taxpayer's valuation of other assets.[16]

As first enacted, Section 1060 did not address the question of whether the parties to a transaction should be bound by any written agreement they reach regarding allocation of the purchase price. Apparently concerned that taxpayers were continuing to take reporting positions that were inconsistent with their agreements, Congress amended Section 1060 to provide that a written agreement governing the allocation of consideration in an applicable asset acquisition shall be binding on both parties unless the Treasury determines that the allocation (or fair market value) is not appropriate. The legislative history indicates that this standard requires a finding that the agreement was unenforceable due to mistake, undue influence, fraud or duress.[17] This is the standard long advanced by the Service and applied by the Third Circuit in the *Danielson* case.[18] In holding the parties to their agreement, however, Congress made it clear that it did not intend to restrict the Service's ability to challenge the taxpayers' allocation to any asset by any appropriate appraisal method, particularly where there is a lack of adverse tax interests between the parties.[19] For example, an allocation that departs from the mandated residual method will not be respected even if it is part of a negotiated agreement.

Section 1060 also includes a reporting requirement. The buyer and seller in an applicable asset acquisition are required to furnish to the Service information regarding the amount of consideration which is allocated to goodwill or going concern value; any modification of that amount; and any other information with respect to other assets transferred in the acquisition as the Service may find necessary to enforce the section.[20]

15. Id. at 255.

16. Id.

17. I.R.C. § 1060(a), last sentence. See H.Rep. No. 101–964, 101st Cong., 2d Sess. 1096 (1990).

18. Commissioner v. Danielson, 378 F.2d 771 (3d Cir.1967), cert. denied 389 U.S. 858, 88 S.Ct. 94 (1967).

19. H.Rep. No. 101–964, supra note 17.

20. I.R.C. § 1060(b). See Reg. § 1.1060–1T(h), which requires that this information be reported on Form 8594 (Asset Acquisition Statement). This form is treated as an information return, and failure to file will trigger a penalty under Section 6724(d). In 1990, Congress extended these

The Section 1060 regulations require the parties to report any collateral agreements related to an acquisition, such as covenants not to compete, employment agreements, licenses, leases and the like.[21] Congress expanded this reporting requirement in 1990 by adding Section 1060(e), which provides that where a person owns at least 10 percent of the value of an entity [22] immediately before a transaction and transfers both an interest in the entity and enters into an employment contract, covenant not to compete, royalty, lease or other agreement with the buyer, the parties must report information concerning the transaction as the Service may require. The legislative history indicates that this reporting requirement applies to both asset and stock acquisitions, whether or not a Section 338 election is made.[23]

6. TAX TREATMENT OF ACQUISITION EXPENSES

The expenses incurred in connection with a corporate acquisition may be substantial. Both the purchaser ("P") and the target ("T") ordinarily must pay fees to lawyers, accountants and investment bankers. P may incur additional expenses to obtain debt and equity financing, and T may be obligated to secure an opinion stating that the proposed acquisition is "fair" to T and its shareholders. In virtually all cases, the central tax question becomes whether the expenses are currently deductible, amortizable, capitalized and added to the basis of a particular tangible or intangible asset, or treated as a permanent nondepreciable capital expenditure.

The tax treatment of P's expenses are relatively settled. Costs of obtaining debt financing (such as fees for negotiating the loan and drafting loan documents, up-front commitment fees and other fees paid to the lender) generally must be amortized over the term of the loan to which the expenses relate.[1] Likewise, expenses of obtaining equity financing (e.g., to register newly issued stock, prepare offering documents, etc.) are treated as permanent capital expenditures that are neither currently deductible nor amortizable.[2] Costs attributable to the acquisition of particular T assets or T stock (e.g., legal expenses for drafting an acquisition agreement, closing costs, finder's fees) also are capital expenditures and must be added to the basis of the acquired property.[3] If P forms a new subsidiary to carry out the acquisition, the organizational expenses should be amortizable over five years under Section 248. In addition, P may attempt to classify certain expenses

---

reporting requirements to stock acquisitions where a Section 338(h)(10) election has been made. See I.R.C. § 338(h)(10)(C).

21. Reg. § 1.1060–1T(h).

22. In determining whether a person is a 10 percent owner, the Section 318 attribution rules shall apply. § 1060(e)(2)(A).

23. House Ways and Means Committee, Explanation of Revenue Provisions of 1991 Budget Reconciliation Bill (Oct. 16, 1990), 101st Cong., 2d Sess. 103 (1990).

1. Rev.Rul. 70–359, 1970–2 C.B. 103; Rev.Rul. 70–360, 1970–2 C.B. 103.

2. Rev.Rul. 69–330, 1969–1 C.B. 51.

3. If P acquires T's stock and makes a Section 338 election, these capital expenditures become part of new T's adjusted grossed-up basis and may be allocated among T's assets in accordance with the rules in Sections 338(b)(5) and 1060. See Section C5 of this chapter, supra.

related to an acquisition as normal business expenses. Examples would include expenses related to employment agreements, executive compensation and retirement planning, tax planning and the annual retainer paid to an investment banker that may have helped arrange the acquisition.

The tax treatment of T's expenses has been more controversial. Assume for example that the target in a friendly corporate takeover incurs legal, investment banking and other fees, including the cost of obtaining an opinion that the terms of the acquisition are fair to T and its shareholders. Are these expenses currently deductible by T as ordinary and necessary businesses expenses under Section 162 or must they be capitalized? Despite the prevalence of takeovers, it was not until recently that this issue reached the courts. In National Starch and Chemical Corp. v. Commissioner,[4] a case of first impression, the Tax Court held that over $2.8 million in fees,[5] though reasonable in amount, were not currently deductible because they were incurred in connection with a shift in ownership "and, accordingly, lead to a benefit 'which could be expected to produce returns for many years in the future.' "[6] Rejecting the taxpayer's argument that the dominant aspect of its expenditures was the fiduciary duty owed by T to its shareholders, the court concluded that the expenditures "were related more to [T's] permanent betterment, and hence capital in nature, than to the carrying on of daily business and production of income."[7] On appeal, the Third Circuit affirmed,[8] rejecting the taxpayer's argument that expenses need not be capitalized unless they result in the creation or enhancement of a separate and distinct asset.[9] The court held that although a payment that creates a separate asset is clearly capital in nature, "it does not necessarily follow that if no asset is created the expenditure is not capital in nature."[10]

National Starch involved a friendly takeover. The Service has waffled on whether expenses incurred to resist a hostile takeover are currently deductible. The contexts in which this issue arises include both defending against a hostile takeover by a corporate raider and arranging for a taxable acquisition by a more friendly "White Knight" buyer. The Service first indicated that these costs were "ordinary" and "necessary" under Section 162(a) because T's directors had a fiduciary responsibility to oppose tender offers which were detrimental to the

---

4. National Starch and Chemical Corp. v. Commissioner, 93 T.C. 67 (1989), affirmed 918 F.2d 426 (3d Cir.1990).

5. The fees included $2.2 million paid to Morgan Stanley, an investment banker, for a fairness opinion; $500,000 in legal fees; and $150,962 in other expenses.

6. 93 T.C. at 75.

7. Id. at 78.

8. National Starch and Chemical Corp. v. Commissioner, 918 F.2d 426 (3d Cir. 1990).

9. See Commissioner v. Lincoln Savings & Loan Ass'n, 403 U.S. 345, 91 S.Ct. 1893 (1971), where the Supreme Court held that certain insurance premium payments by a savings and loan association to the Federal Savings and Loan Insurance Corporation were capital expenditures because they created or enhanced a separate and distinct additional asset. 403 U.S. at 354, 91 S.Ct. at 1899.

10. 918 F.2d at 429.

company or its shareholders.[11]   After the Tax Court's decision in *National Starch*, the Service shifted gears and ruled that expenses incurred in resisting a takeover and arranging for an acquisition by an alternative buyer are nondeductible capital expenditures.[12]   After further study, the Service shifted again, ruling that expenses to resist a hostile takeover are currently deductible but expenses to arrange an acquisition by a White Knight must be capitalized because they create a long-term benefit to the corporation.[13]

If either P or T incurs costs in investigating or attempting to consummate an acquisition that ultimately fails, the transactional costs generally are currently deductible as losses under Section 165.[14]

7.   OTHER ACQUISITION ISSUES: PLANNING AND POLICY

a.   DISPOSITIONS OF UNWANTED ASSETS

A target corporation ("T") may engage in more than one trade or business.   These separate activities may be conducted as unincorporated divisions of T or through wholly owned T subsidiaries.   A purchasing corporation ("P") may wish to acquire some but not all of T's businesses.   Since repeal of the *General Utilities* doctrine in 1986, taxpayers have been embroiled in a fierce battle with Congress and the Service over whether P may acquire all the T stock and then sell off one or more of T's businesses without recognizing corporate-level gain. A familiar context for this controversy is P's acquisition of T in a leveraged buyout followed by "bust up" sales of unwanted T businesses in order to raise funds to service the acquisition debt.   The Service's position on this question has become increasingly clear, but the correct result from a policy perspective is far from intuitive.

The issue is illustrated with a simple fact pattern.   Assume that publicly held T operates two businesses through unincorporated divisions: a restaurant chain ("Eat"—fair market value, $600,000) and a hotel ("Sleep"—fair market value, $400,000).   For convenience, assume that T holds no other properties; the assets of both Eat and Sleep have a zero basis; and T's shareholders have a zero basis in their T stock.   P wishes to acquire and operate Eat but has no interest in owning Sleep. Waiting in the wings, however, is Diversified Properties, Inc. ("DP"), which would like to acquire the hotel.

The most straightforward approach would be for T to sell the assets of its two divisions to the interested buyers and distribute the sales

---

11. Tech.Adv.Mem. 8927005 (Mar. 27, 1989).   Cf. Locke Manufacturing Co. v. United States, 237 F.Supp. 80 (D.Conn. 1964) (expenses incurred in proxy fight with dissident shareholder are currently deductible; costs were incurred for the benefit of all shareholders and proxy contexts had become a part of the corporate way of life).

12. Tech.Adv.Mem. 8945003 (Aug. 1, 1989).

13. Tech.Adv.Memos 9043003, 9043004 (July 9, 1990).

14. Rev.Rul. 73–580, 1973–2 C.B. 86.

proceeds to its shareholders in complete liquidation. The parties usual-ly will resist this method, however, because it triggers taxable gain to T on the asset sales and a second gain to T's shareholders on the complete liquidation.[1] Alternatively, T might first sell Sleep's assets to DP, and recognize $400,000 of gain on the sale. T's shareholders, having rid themselves of the hotel, then could sell their T stock to P and recognize shareholder-level gain.[2] This plan has the virtue of avoiding corporate-level gain on Eat's assets assuming P does not make a Section 338 election. The trade-off is that absent an election T must retain its historic zero basis in the restaurant assets. While this approach is preferable to the alternative in which T sells both divisions and liquidates because the appreciation in Eat's assets is not taxed, the goal was more ambitious—to structure a sale of Eat and Sleep without a corporate-level tax on the built-in gain in either business.

For another variation, assume that P purchases all the T stock for $1,000,000 without making a Section 338 election, and P then causes T to sell the Sleep assets to DP for $400,000. T still has a zero basis in the Sleep assets and thus recognizes $400,000 gain on the sale. If instead P purchased all the T stock, liquidated T under Section 332, and then sold the Sleep assets to DP, P would recognize $400,000 of gain because it takes a transferred zero basis in T's assets under Section 334(b).

In summary, as a result of *General Utilities* repeal, all the conven-tional approaches to structuring the disposition of Eat and Sleep require recognition of corporate-level gain on at least the sale of the unwanted hotel business. Troubled by this prospect, the mergers and acquisitions industry concocted a plan to avoid *all* corporate-level gain. Under what became known as the "mirror subsidiary" technique, P would form two subsidiaries ("Eat, Inc." and "Sleep, Inc."), capitalizing Eat, Inc. with $600,000 and Sleep, Inc. with $400,000 to reflect ("mir-ror") the relative values of the wanted restaurant and unwanted hotel businesses. Eat, Inc. then would acquire 60 percent of the T stock for $600,000 and Sleep, Inc. would acquire the remaining 40 percent for $400,000. On the stock sale, T's shareholders would recognize $1,000,000 gain and P and its two new subsidiaries would become an "affiliated group" of corporations [3] eligible to file a consolidated tax return on which income and deductions are combined.[4]

1. Although it requires more steps, the analysis is essentially the same if T operat-ed the restaurant and hotel businesses through wholly owned subsidiaries. If P and DP purchased the stock of each subsid-iary separately, T would recognize gain on the stock sales, of, if a Section 338(h)(10) election were made, the subsidiaries would recognize gain on their assets.

2. P most likely would use the cash received by T on the sale of Sleep as part of the consideration for the stock of the T shareholders. The stock purchase could be structured as a bootstrap redemption quali-fying under Section 302(b)(3). See Chapter 5F, supra.

3. See I.R.C. § 1504(a)(2) and Chapters 1B4, supra and 14B, infra.

4. See I.R.C. §§ 1501–1504.

The next step required some assistance, which planners believed was supplied by the regulations governing consolidated returns. After the purchase of T stock, Eat, Inc. and Sleep, Inc. caused T to liquidate— a transaction that could be accomplished tax-free under Sections 332 and 337. Even though T was not an 80 percent subsidiary of either Eat or Sleep, Section 332 treatment was available because the consolidated return regulations permitted the stock ownership of members of a consolidated group to be aggregated for purposes of the 80 percent control requirement.[5] After the liquidation, the zero basis in T's assets transferred to Eat and Sleep, respectively, but P retained its *cost* basis in the stock of its two subsidiaries—i.e., $600,000 in Eat and $400,000 in Sleep. P thus would recognize no gain on the sale of its Sleep, Inc. stock to DP for $400,000.[6] To be sure, DP (through Sleep) was stuck with a zero basis in the hotel business assets, but this was taken into account by the parties in negotiating the price of the stock. The appeal of the mirror subsidiary technique was the avoidance of all current corporate-level gain on the sale of a target's unwanted assets.

The legislative history of the Tax Reform Act of 1986 created some doubt as to the viability of the mirror subsidiary technique.[7] Although Section 337(d) grants the Treasury broad authority to ensure that the purpose of *General Utilities* repeal is not circumvented, it was not clear how far this authority would extend. Clarity was not enhanced by "duelling colloquies" on the House and Senate Floors, where Chairman Rostenkowski stated that the technique was foreclosed[8] only to be contradicted several days later by Senators Dole and Packwood.[9] After a period of waffling,[10] the Treasury opted to side with the forces of a comprehensive corporate tax base when it announced that regulations would be forthcoming to curb any exploitation of the consolidated return regulations that would permit P to avoid gain on the sale of a recently purchased but unwanted T business.[11]

It is worth pausing to examine the competing sides in this important policy debate. Chairman Rostenkowski's position was that the mirror subsidiary technique was fundamentally inconsistent with *General Utilities* repeal:[12]

> If the "mirror" transaction were permitted while the [Code, after amendment by the Tax Reform Act of 1986] is in effect,

---

5. Reg. § 1.1502–34.

6. It is assumed that DP did not make a Section 338 election when it acquires 100 percent of Sleep, Inc. If it did elect, Sleep, Inc. would recognize gain on the deemed sale of its assets.

7. In an oblique footnote in the Conference Report, the conferees directed the Treasury to consider, "in a consolidated return context * * * whether aggregation of ownership rules similar to those in Section 1.1502–34 of the regulations should be provided for purposes of determining status as an 80–percent distributee." H.R.

Rep. No. 99–841, 99th Cong., 2d Sess. II–202, fn. 9 (1986).

8. 132 Cong.Rec. H 8358 (daily ed. Sept. 25, 1986).

9. 132 Cong.Rec. S 13958 (daily ed. Sept. 27, 1986).

10. See, e.g., "News: Treasury Punts on Mirror Transactions," 33 Tax Notes 988 (Dec. 15, 1986), describing Treasury's initial unwillingness to take a position.

11. I.R.S. Notice 87–14, 1987–1 C.B. 445.

12. 132 Cong.Rec. E 3389 (daily ed. Oct. 2, 1986).

corporate takeovers would enjoy a significant advantage. New owners of a corporation could sell appreciated corporate property without corporate level tax, placing them in a favored position over the old owners. Old owners who believed it would be desirable for business reasons, and in the best interest of shareholders, to dispose of an appreciated subsidiary, could not do so without corporate level tax. New owners could do so if they could use the "mirror" transaction. This would open a loophole for the sole benefit of those engaged in corporate acquisitions. Such a result would be totally contrary to the fundamental purposes of this legislation.

The competing position—i.e., that mirror transactions and their related offspring do not undermine *General Utilities* repeal—is forcefully argued in the following letter from a prominent corporate tax practitioner to the Joint Committee on Taxation staff.

EXCERPT FROM AUGUST 29, 1986 LETTER OF PETER L. FABER TO STAFF OF JOINT COMMITTEE ON TAXATION
Reproduced in 32 Tax Notes 1022 (Sept. 8, 1986).

Dear Paul:

I have reflected a bit since our telephone conversation about mirror subsidiaries and have come to the conclusion that their use does not involve an abuse of the system and that in any event the abolition of the technique would not come within the staff's mandate to implement *General Utilities* repeal.

The mirror structure permits a step-up of the outside stock basis of corporate subsidiaries, but it does not permit a step-up of inside asset basis. Although the stock of a subsidiary corporation is technically an asset of the parent, a step-up of the basis of the stock of a subsidiary does not result in enhanced depreciation or amortization deductions and therefore does not undermine the integrity of the corporate income tax. It seems to me that the basic objective of *General Utilities* repeal is to ensure that one layer of corporations pays tax on corporate income. The exception for section 332 liquidations in the House Bill and the ease with which consolidated returns can be filed indicate a congressional policy that the income from multiple layers of corporations need only be taxed to one of those layers. The results obtained by the mirror subsidiary structure do not seem to be inconsistent with that policy.

In the typical mirror structure, the target corporation owns several subsidiaries, all of which we will assume have appreciated assets. If the buyer were simply to buy the target's stock, the stock of each subsidiary would keep its old basis and the post-acquisition sale of the stock of one of the subsidiaries by the buyer would result in taxable gain to the extent of the appreciation of that subsidiary's assets. In order to avoid this result, the buyer forms its own group of subsidiaries that it funds with cash so that each buyer subsidiary has an amount of cash equal to the value of one of the target's subsidiaries. The buyer's subsidiaries buy the stock of the target either directly or by forming a jointly owned transitory subsidiary that merges into the target. After the acquisition, the target is liquidated and the assets of each of the target's subsidiaries pass to the buyer's subsidiary that was funded with an amount of cash equal to its value. The liquidation is tax-free under section 332 of the Code because regulations section 1.1502–34 permits aggregation of stock interests. At the end of the transactions, the buyer owns the stock of each of its new subsidiaries that in turn owns the stock or the assets of one of the target's subsidiaries. The buyer's basis in the stock of each of its subsidiaries is equal to the cash that it contributed to its capital which in turn equals the value of the target's subsidiary that it acquired. Thus, the buyer can later sell the stock of any unwanted subsidiary at no gain.

The critical point is that the underlying assets of the target's subsidiaries keep their old bases since no section 338 election is made. On the assumption that the corporate business of the target was conducted by its subsidiaries and will now be conducted by the buyer's subsidiaries, the taxable income earned by that business will not be reduced by these transactions. Depreciation claimed by the buyer's subsidiaries after the transactions will be based on the depreciable basis and depreciation method used by the target's subsidiaries before the transactions. Although the buyer will be able to sell the stock of one of the subsidiaries without paying any tax, the buyer will not realize an economic gain on the sale of the subsidiary's stock and this result does not seem to be inappropriate. If the buyer of a subsidiary's stock from the original buyer makes a section 338 election, it will get a stepped-up basis for the underlying corporate assets, but only if it pays the appropriate toll charge.

I see no abuse in these results nor do I feel that they are inconsistent with *General Utilities* repeal. Indeed, the preservation of the distinction between inside and outside basis is central to the philosophy of *General Utilities* repeal. Many of the opponents of repeal have argued that when a corporation goes out of business there is a liquidation of the shareholders' investment and there is no need to impose the double tax regime that applies to the receipt and distribution of income from normal corporate business operations. Proponents of repeal have argued that the shareholder-level tax and the corporate-level tax should be treated as separate systems, that the integrity of the corporate-level tax will be undermined if the basis of assets that remain in corporate solution can be increased without the imposition of a corporate-level tax on the gain, and that the tax consequences to the corporate parties to the transaction should not be affected by what happens at the shareholder level. Requiring the recognition of gain with respect to the appreciation of corporate assets merely because the shareholders of the corporation get a stepped-up basis for their stock in transactions in which the seller of that stock recognizes gain blurs the distinction between the corporate-level tax and the shareholder-level tax in exactly the same way that the opponents of *General Utilities* repeal do except from the opposite direction. The two approaches are equally indefensible.

* * *

One can argue about whether the stock aggregation rules of regulations section 1.1502–34 are appropriate, but it seems to me that that has nothing to do with *General Utilities* repeal. The proper way to deal with that question is to invite the Treasury Department to re-examine the regulations, as the Ways and Means Committee has done in footnote 32 of its report. The footnote suggests to me that the House Bill, which was the only one of the two bills that addressed *General Utilities* repeal, did *not* contemplate that the mirror subsidiary technique would be addressed by the legislation. The staff's charge at this time is to implement the repeal of *General Utilities*. If it were to attempt to change the current tax treatment of mirror subsidiaries, which neither body of Congress did and which the only body to address the general problem expressly contemplated not doing, it would be exceeding its mandate in a cause that, for the reasons stated above, is dubious at best.

Sincerely,

Peter L. Faber

NOTE

Chairman Rostenkowski's view proved to be more influential than Mr. Faber's. Responding to contentions that the mirror subsidiary technique was incompatible with repeal of the *General Utilities* doctrine, Congress shattered the basic "mirror" strategy in the Revenue Act of 1987 by adding the following new sentence to the definition of an "80–percent distributee" in Section 337(c):

> For purposes of this section, the determination of whether any corporation is an 80–percent distributee shall be made without regard to any consolidated regulation.

After this amendment, it is clear that a corporation will recognize gain on distributions in complete liquidation to a corporate shareholder unless the distributee directly owns 80 percent of the stock of the liquidating corporation. The 1987 Act also curtailed variations of the technique by amendments to Section 304 [13] and Section 355.[14] The Service has continued to respond aggressively to the proliferation of mirror offspring (familiarly known as "Son of Mirror," "Daughter of Mirror," and "Cousin of Mirror," etc.) [15] and Congress rejoined the

---

13. See I.R.C. § 304(b)(4), providing special treatment for certain transactions subject to Section 304(a) between members of an affiliated group of corporations.

14. See I.R.C. § 355(b)(2) and Chapter 13D1, infra.

15. See, e.g., I.R.S. Notice 89–37, 1989–1 C.B. 679, curbing the use of partnerships to avoid corporate-level gain on the sale of assets; Temp.Reg. § 1.1502–20T, disallowing losses on dispositions of stock of a subsidiary in "Son of Mirror" transactions, which exploited certain aspects of the con-

battle with additional amendments in 1990 to curb the use of the corporate division rules in Section 355 to dispose of unwanted businesses without corporate-level gain.[16]

b. CORPORATE ACQUISITIONS AND THE PROBLEM OF EXCESSIVE DEBT

The tax bias in favor of debt financing and the difficulties in distinguishing between debt and equity were discussed in Chapter 3 principally in the context of the capital structure of a closely held C corporation. The wave of corporate restructurings of public companies in the 1980's raised the stakes on this historically vexing issue. From 1984 to 1987, transactions such as corporate takeovers, redemptions of stock, debt-for-equity swaps and extraordinary distributions resulted in a reduction of $313.3 billion in corporate equity while new net corporate borrowing increased by $613.3 billion. The ratio of debt to equity of nonfinancial corporations increased from 30.3 percent in 1981 to 46 percent in 1987.[1] Although these developments undoubtedly were motivated by many factors other than the interest deduction allowed to corporate borrowers, the preferred tax treatment of debt has become a powerful influence on corporate financing behavior. And however difficult it may be to measure precisely the lost revenue resulting from this surge in debt financing,[2] it safely can be assumed that the erosion of the corporate tax base has been substantial.

In early 1989, the Congressional tax-writing committees held hearings to examine the federal income tax aspects of corporate financial structures and to consider the problem of debt-financed acquisitions. In the wake of the $25 billion leveraged buyout of RJR Nabisco, Inc.,[3] a few influential legislators proposed to disallow interest deductions on any debt used to finance a corporate acquisition.[4] The Treasury attempted to change the subject by noting that if the corporate and

---

solidated return regulations to avoid corporate level gain on sales of unwanted assets. The latter regulations were controversial insofar as they disallowed actual economic losses on the sale of a subsidiary even in the absence of a tax avoidance plan and they were replaced by modified rules that allow economic losses. Reg. § 1.1502–20.

16. See I.R.C. § 355(d), discussed in Chapter 13D1, infra.

1. Joint Committee on Taxation, Federal Income Aspects of Corporate Financial Structures, 101st Cong., 1st Sess. 2 (JCS 1–89, 1989).

2. It would not be enough, for example, to measure the revenue loss merely by looking at the increased corporate-level interest deductions. Among the many variables that one also must consider are: the

tax status of the creditor (e.g., individual, domestic or foreign corporation, pension fund or other tax-exempt entity, etc.); the contrasting tax result if earnings were distributed as dividends; the impact of the dividends received deduction available to corporate investors; and the result if corporate earnings were accumulated and reinvested.

3. See generally Burrough and Helyar, Barbarians at the Gate (Harper & Row, 1989.)

4. For a survey of the "Stamp Out LBOs" movement, see Mentz, Carlisle & Nevas, "Leveraged Buyouts: A Washington Perspective of 1989 Legislation and Prospects for 1990," 46 Tax Notes 1047 (Feb. 26, 1990).

individual income taxes were integrated, the problems of excessive debt would disappear.[5]

Some illustrative transactions, the policy issues and possible options for lessening the distinction between the tax treatment of debt and equity are addressed in the excerpts below from a study prepared by the Joint Committee on Taxation in connection with the 1989 hearings. The note following the excerpt discusses the narrowly targeted Congressional response to these concerns.

EXCERPT FROM JOINT COMMITTEE ON TAXATION, FEDERAL INCOME TAX ASPECTS OF CORPORATE FINANCIAL STRUCTURES

101st Cong., 1st Sess. (JCS 1–89, Jan. 18, 1989).

III. EXAMPLES OF TRANSACTIONS THAT INCREASE DEBT OR REDUCE EQUITY, AND TAX CONSEQUENCES

There are various transactions which can increase the debt of a corporation or reduce its equity. The discussion below describes broad categories of these transactions and uses examples to illustrate their tax consequences. The examples assume that no restrictions on interest deductions or other tax benefits stemming from interest expenses apply. In many cases, however, such limitations are applicable.

*   *   *

Although there are significant tax reasons which may lead a corporation to engage in these transactions, such transactions may also be motivated by reasons apart from Federal income tax considerations. For example, such transactions may be undertaken to increase the value of a corporation's stock, to enhance earnings per share calculations, to concentrate common stock holdings, to create treasury stock, as a defensive maneuver to ward off a takeover, or for other reasons.

*   *   *

B.   Stock Repurchases

Description

A stock repurchase refers to a corporation redeeming (or buying back) its own shares from stockholders. A corporation may make a tender offer for a certain percentage of its shares at an announced price or a corporation may simply purchase its shares on the market. A corporation may fund a stock repurchase out of cash the corporation has on hand or it may borrow the funds.[67]

---

5. Id. at 1049, quoting Testimony by Secretary of the Treasury Nicholas F. Brady before the Senate Finance Committee, Jan. 24, 1989. For an overview of the integration issue, see Chapter 1B6, supra.

67. As an alternative to borrowing funds from an outside lender and using the proceeds to repurchase the stock of shareholders, a corporation may repurchase stock by issuing debt directly to redeeming shareholders. This is sometimes called a "debt-for-equity swap."

Tax consequences

A stock repurchase, whether financed out of cash the corporation has on hand or by borrowing, is generally a taxable transaction with respect to the redeeming shareholders.   Taxable shareholders having their stock redeemed recognize any gain (i.e., the excess of the amount received over basis) or loss on the redemption of their shares.[68]   There are no immediate tax consequences of a stock repurchase to the redeeming corporation.

A stock repurchase has further tax consequences to the redeeming corporation and to investors in the redeeming corporation over time.   If a stock repurchase is financed with cash, the primary tax consequence is that the corporate assets of the redeeming corporation have been reduced.   Corporate assets paid out to redeem shareholders' stock no longer produce earnings which are subject to the corporate income tax.[69]   If the stock repurchase is financed through borrowing, the effect of the transaction is to replace the equity of the corporation with debt. Earnings of the corporation once available to be paid to shareholders as non-deductible dividends are instead paid to debtholders as deductible interest.[70]   Thus, a stock redemption using borrowed funds enables the redeeming corporation to reduce its taxable income, or perhaps elimi- nate (or even generate current tax losses which it could carry back to obtain tax refunds).[71]

As indicated by the following example, the resulting reduction in Federal income taxes pays for increased returns to investors.   To the extent increased investor returns are paid to taxable shareholders or debtholders, there may be an increase in investor-level taxes paid.

Example III–B

Consider the same facts as in Example III–A above [The facts were: Corporation M has $1.5 million annual income, 99,000 shares of stock outstanding and no debt.   M's federal income tax is $510,000 ($1.5 million times 34 percent), resulting in after-tax income of $990,000 and earnings per share of $10.   M's stock trades at $80 per share, or 8 times earnings.   Ed.] except that Company M announces it will repurchase up to $11 million of its shares at a redemption price of $120 per share, 50 percent more than the price at which the stock has been trading on the

---

68. Of course, there will be no tax im- posed on those shareholders that are not subject to U.S. income tax on this income, i.e., certain foreign investors and tax-ex- empt investors such as pension funds.

69. This is also the result when the earnings of the distributing corporation are distributed to noncorporate sharehold- ers in circumstances other than in connec- tion with a stock repurchase.

70. A leveraged stock repurchase has exactly the same tax consequences as a leveraged distribution made by a corpora- tion with respect to its stock.

71. A reduction in the redeeming corpo- ration's Federal income tax liability could also increase its cash flow significantly. That increased cash flow might be suffi- cient to enable the redeeming corporation to cover most of its debt service obligations with respect to the borrowed funds and retire much of the debt over a period of years (although the redeeming company might also have to sell some of its assets to raise cash to assist it in paying off the loan).

market. Taxable redeeming shareholders recognize gain or loss on the redemption of their shares.

At $120 per share, $11 million will purchase approximately 93 percent of Company M's outstanding shares. To finance the share repurchase, Company M issues bonds for $11 million paying 12 percent interest. Approximately 93 percent of Company M's outstanding shares are redeemed.

The distribution of the operating income of Company M before and after the stock repurchase is as follows:

	Before	**After**
Redeeming shareholders	$ 920,700	0
Bondholders	0	$1,320,000
Continuing shareholders	69,300	118,800
Corporate income taxes	510,000	61,200
Total operating income	1,500,000	1,500,000
Earnings per share	10	16.20

The leveraged stock redemption has redistributed the income stream of Company M in the same way that the leveraged distribution with respect to stock redistributed the income stream, except that the continuing shareholders of Company M, rather than all the shareholders of Company M, receive the profit of $118,800. The redeeming shareholders of Company M who used to get $920,700 a year in dividends before the redemption receive no part of the income stream after the redemption. New bondholders receive interest of 12 percent a year on $11 million, or $1.32 million. This is one-third more than the entire amount of Company M's after-tax income before the stock repurchases even though the operating income of Company M is unchanged. Continuing shareholders of Company M receive the profit of $118,800 (the remainder of Company M's income after taxes and interest expense).

The taxable income of Company M has been reduced from $1.5 million to $180,000 ($1.5 million minus $1.32 million) because most of the earnings of Company M are now paid out as deductible interest payments. The resulting reduction of corporate Federal income taxes from $510,000 to $61,200 exactly pays for the increased returns to the new bondholders and the continuing shareholders. Depending on whether the increased returns are paid to taxable bondholders and shareholders, there may be an increase in investor-level Federal income taxes paid.

Note also that the earnings per share of Company M have gone up from $10 per share ($990,000 divided by 99,000 shares outstanding) before the leveraged buyout to $16.20 per share ($118,800 divided by 7,333 shares outstanding) after the leveraged buyout. If the stock will still sell for 8 times its earnings on the market after the leveraged buyout, the stock price would rise from $80 to $129.60 ($16.20 times 8).

Taxpayers have also sought similar tax results in connection with so-called "unbundled stock units." On December 5, 1988, four publicly traded companies—American Express Co., Dow Chemical Co., Pfizer Inc. and Sara Lee Corp.—announced offers to their shareholders to exchange a certain portion of their outstanding common stock for unbundled stock units comprised of three separate securities:

(1) a 30–year deep-discount bond which will pay quarterly interest in an amount equal to the current dividend of the common stock exchanged;

(2) a share of preferred stock which will yield dividends equal to any increase in the dividend yield of the company's common stock; and

(3) an "equity appreciation certificate" which entitles the holder to acquire one share of common stock for an amount equal to the redemption value of the 30–year bond plus a share of the preferred stock. The new bond in effect would convert what had been nondeductible ordinary dividends into deductible interest payments, in addition to providing corporate deductions for an element of original issue discount.[72]

Actual transactions

Stock repurchases have become common corporate transactions. A list of the largest stock repurchases during 1988 published by *The Wall Street Journal* indicated that the largest 21 stock buy-back announcements of 1988 were intended to retire almost 500 million shares of stock worth approximately $23.8 billion. Ten transactions were listed with a value in excess of $1 billion. The largest transactions listed were the following: (1) UAL Corporation buying back 35.5 million common shares with a value of $2.84 billion; (2) International Business Machines Corporation buying back 17.8 million common shares with a value of $2 billion; (3) CSX Corp. buying back 60 million shares with a value of $1.86 billion; and (4) Sears Roebuck buying back 40 million common shares with a value of $1.75 billion.

C. Acquisitions Including Leveraged Buyouts

The acquisition of one corporation by another corporation may be structured in many different ways. An acquiring corporation may acquire control of the "target" corporation or it may acquire a small interest in the stock of another corporation as an investment. The acquiring corporation may finance the acquisition with debt (either by a new borrowing of the necessary funds or by keeping an old borrowing

---

72. The four companies currently plan to replace between 6.5 and 20 percent of their outstanding common stock with unbundled stock units. It has been estimated that the four corporations issuing unbundled stock units could save, in the aggregate, up to $5.9 billion in Federal income taxes over the 20–year life of the bonds. Aggregate tax savings in the first year after the exchange may be as much as $85 million, with annual tax savings steadily rising through the 30–year bond term. *New York Times*, December 7, 1988, p. D1. The Internal Revenue Service has not ruled on the tax treatment of unbundled stock units.

outstanding), or with its own retained earnings, or with funds contributed as new equity capital by investors.

An acquisition of the control of a target company may be a hostile or friendly transaction. It may be structured as an acquisition of the stock of the target company or an acquisition of the assets of the target company. The target company may continue to operate as an independent company in the same manner as before it was acquired, or it may be absorbed into the acquiring company or other companies owned by the acquiring company, or it may cease operations entirely and its assets be divided and sold.

1. Stock acquisitions out of retained earnings

A corporation may finance the acquisition of the stock of another corporation with internally generated funds (i.e., its retained earnings). The purchase of the stock has no tax consequences to the shareholders of the purchasing corporation. Likewise, there are no tax consequences to the acquired corporation as a result of the acquisition. The taxable shareholders of the acquired corporation recognize any gain or loss on the sale of their shares.

There are generally no immediate tax consequences to the purchasing corporation as a result of the transaction. However, the total amount of funds in corporate solution, the earnings of which are subject to a corporate-level tax, may be reduced by the amount spent for the acquisition to the extent that shares are acquired by the acquiring corporation from noncorporate shareholders. Moreover, no compensating additional corporate tax may arise when earnings of the acquired corporation are distributed to the acquiring corporation. This is because earnings of the target company which are distributed to the acquiring corporation as dividends will either be nontaxable under the consolidated return rules, or, if the corporations do not file a consolidated return, will be eligible for the dividends received deduction.

2. Debt-financed stock acquisitions including leveraged buyouts

A corporation may finance the acquisition of another corporation's stock by borrowing. The acquiring corporation may borrow using its own assets as security for the loan or it may borrow using the assets of the target company as security for the loan. In either case, debt has been substituted for equity at the corporate level. When the debt is secured by the acquired corporation's assets, the transaction is more likely to be called a "leveraged buyout."

Description

A leveraged buyout refers to a particular type of debt-financed acquisition of a "target" corporation.[74] The purchasers borrow most of the purchase price of the target company, using the assets of the target

---

74. In what is called a "reverse leveraged buyout," public companies which had been converted to private companies in a leveraged buyout become public companies again, with their shares being sold in a public offering to shareholders.

company as security for the loan. After the acquisition, the target corporation may be able to service the debt obligation out of its cash flow from operations or the purchaser may sell the assets of the target company and use the proceeds to retire the debt.

A leveraged buyout may occur in many different contexts and may be used by many different types of purchasers. The leveraged buyout, also sometimes called a bootstrap acquisition, has long been used to acquire private (i.e., closely held) corporations. More recently, leveraged buyouts have been used to acquire large public companies. A public company may be "taken private" through a leveraged buyout if the purchasers of the target public corporation are a relatively small group of investors. If the purchasers of the target corporation in a leveraged buyout include the current management of the target company, the transaction is sometimes called a "management buyout." A division or a subsidiary of a company also may be purchased through a leveraged buyout.

A leveraged buyout of a target company is usually accomplished by a debt-financed tender offer by the existing corporation for its outstanding publicly held stock, or, alternatively, by a tender offer for the target corporation's stock by a largely debt-financed shell corporation established for this purpose. The target corporation will repurchase its stock from its shareholders or the shell corporation will buy all the stock of the target corporation.[76] If a shell corporation is used, the target corporation and the shell corporation will typically merge immediately after the acquisition.

As mentioned above, most of the funds for a leveraged buyout transaction are borrowed, with the purchasers contributing only a small amount of their own funds as equity. Lenders for these transactions have been banks, investment banks, insurance companies, pension funds, and pools of investors. Debt terms reflect the degree of leverage and the loan security involved. Some of the debt incurred frequently is below investment grade, i.e., so-called "junk" bonds.

Tax consequences

A leveraged buyout is generally a taxable transaction with respect to the shareholders of the target corporation.[77] Taxable shareholders selling their stock recognize gain or loss on the sale of their shares.[78] There are no immediate tax consequences of a leveraged buyout at the corporate level since generally neither the repurchase by the target corporation of its own shares nor the purchase of the target corpora-

---

76. Shareholders of the target company typically receive a premium for their stock above the price at which the stock has been trading on the market.

77. Of course, there will be no tax imposed on those shareholders that are not subject to U.S. income tax on their income, i.e., certain foreign investors and tax-exempt investors such as pension funds.

78. Taxable shareholders will generally recognize gain (i.e., the excess of the amount received over their basis in the stock) because acquirors typically pay a substantial premium for stock in a leveraged buyout transaction.

tion's shares by a shell corporation followed by the merger of the target and shell corporation is a taxable transaction.

The primary tax consequences of a leveraged buyout to the target corporation arise from the fact that the equity of the corporation has been replaced by debt. Income of the target corporation once paid to investors as nondeductible dividends on stock is instead paid to creditors as tax-deductible interest on debt.[79] As a result of the interest deductions generated by the borrowing in a leveraged buyout, the target corporation may have little, if any, taxable income in the years following a leveraged buyout and may claim loss carrybacks producing a refund of taxes paid prior to the acquisition.[80] Because the target corporation pays little, if any, of its operating income as Federal income taxes, the portion of the target corporation's income that was once being paid to the Federal government as Federal income taxes may instead be redirected to increase investor returns. However, to the extent increased investor returns are paid to taxable shareholders or holders of debt, there may be an increase in investor-level Federal income taxes paid.

Example III–C

Consider the same facts as in Example III–A [See p. 398, supra. Ed.] Rather than the management of Company M announcing a distribution with respect to its stock, Company M is acquired in a leveraged buyout. The acquirors pay $120 per share of stock, or 50 percent more than the price at which the stock has been trading on the market, for a total price of $11.88 million. Taxable selling shareholders recognize gain or loss on the sale of their shares.

The acquirors put up $880,000 of their own funds and raise the remaining $11 million of the purchase price by issuing notes paying 12 percent interest to be secured by the assets of Company M. The annual income of Company M after the leveraged buyout is unchanged.

The distribution of the operating income of Company M before and after the leveraged buyout is as follows:

	Before	After
Company M shareholders	$ 990,000	0
Bondholders	0	$1,320,000
Acquirors	0	118,800
Corporate income taxes	510,000	61,200
Total operating income	1,500,000	1,500,000

The leveraged buyout has redistributed the income stream of Company M in the same way that the leveraged distribution with

---

79. A leveraged buyout has exactly the same tax effect as a leveraged distribution made by a corporation with respect to its stock and a leveraged stock redemption.

80. Indeed, the target corporation may be able to service its debt obligations out of a cash flow and reduced ＊ ＊ ＊ taxes.

respect to stock, and the leveraged stock redemption, redistributed the income stream of Company M. However, the acquirors of Company M, rather than all the shareholders (in the case of a distribution with respect to stock) or the continuing shareholders of Company M (in the case of a stock redemption) receive the profit of $118,800. Company M shareholders who before the transaction received $990,000 a year in dividends now receive no distributions. New bondholders receive interest of 12 percent on $11 million, or $1.32 million. This is one third more than the entire amount of Company M's after-tax income before the leveraged buyout, even though the operating income of Company M is the same before and after the leveraged buyout.

The taxable income of Company M has, however, been reduced from $1.5 million to $180,000 ($1.5 million minus $1.32 million) because most of the income of the company is paid out to investors as interest rather than dividends. Federal income taxes are thereby reduced from $510,000 to $61,200. Acquirors make an after-tax profit of $118,800 (pre-tax profit of $180,000 reduced by Federal income tax of $61,200), a 13.4 percent return on their $880,000 equity investment. The income tax reduction of $448,800 exactly pays for the increased returns to investors (bondholders and the acquirors) as a result of the leveraged buyout. Depending on whether the increased investor returns are paid to taxable shareholders or holders of debt, there may be an increase in investor-level Federal income taxes paid.

Actual transactions

Leveraged buyouts of public companies have greatly increased in recent years, and the amounts involved in such transactions have risen dramatically. (See the discussion in part I.B. of this pamphlet, supra.) The largest leveraged buyout transaction to date is the proposed acquisition of RJR Nabisco by the investment firm of Kohlberg Kravis Roberts & Co. ("KKR") for nearly $25 billion. It is expected that this acquisition will be completed by February 1989. Other large leveraged buyout transactions include the acquisition of Beatrice Companies by KKR for $6.25 billion in April 1986, and the management buyout of R.H. Macy & Co., Inc. for $3.5 billion in July 1986.

Newspaper reports indicate that out of the approximately $25 billion needed for the RJR Nabisco acquisition, more than $22.5 billion will be borrowed. Secured bank debt will account for approximately $17.5 billion of the borrowing, with most of the remainder being provided by investment banking firms. A pool of investors organized by KKR will put up $1.5 billion as an equity investment. It has been reported that KKR will contribute approximately $15 million of its own funds as equity. RJR Nabisco shareholders will be paid $109 for each share of common stock. This is almost twice the price at which the stock was trading immediately prior to the announcement of the possible sale of the company. It has been reported that due to increased interest deductions, RJR Nabisco could save up to $682 million annually in Federal and state income taxes and be able to seek the refund of additional amounts of taxes paid in prior years due to carryback of net operating losses. Other reports have projected the annual savings at $370 million.

In the Beatrice transaction, each common shareholder received $50 per share ($40 in cash). This price of $50 per share was 45 percent higher than the market value of the stock one month prior to the announcement date of the first offer. Financing for the Beatrice leveraged buyout included $6.5 billion in debt and $1.35 billion in equity capital. Four billion dollars of the debt was lent by banks and $2.5 billion came from a new issue of high yield bonds. The equity came from two sources. Six hundred million came from a buyout fund organized by KKR and subscribed to by institutional investors and $750 million came from converting existing common stock to a new issue of preferred stock.

In the Macy transaction, each common share of stock outstanding received $68 in cash. This price of $68 per share was 55 percent higher than the market value of the stock one month prior to the announcement date of the first offer. On completion of the Macy leveraged buyout, the management group held 20 percent of the new company stock and an additional 20 percent was held by General Electric Co.'s credit union. Financing for the Macy leveraged buyout totalled approximately $3.7 billion. Out of this amount, almost $3.2 billion was debt: $770 million was lent from banks, $1.625 billion came from new issues of high yield bonds, and $800 million came from notes secured by mortgages. The remaining $500 million of the financing consisted of $200 million of excess cash of Macy's and $300 million was equity capital contributed by the acquirors.

* * *

V. POSSIBLE OPTIONS AND RELATED POLICY CONSIDERATIONS

A. Eliminate or Reduce the Distinction Between Debt and Equity by Integrating the Corporate and Individual Income Tax Systems

[Integration of the corporate and individual income taxes is discussed in the excerpts at pages 21–31, supra. Ed.]

* * *

B. Eliminate or Reduce the Distinction Between Debt and Equity by Limiting Interest Deductions

Interest disallowance proposals should be evaluated with reference to various policy issues. These issues include: the potential erosion of the business tax base (including but not necessarily limited to the corporate tax base); the proper measurement of economic income; the non-tax economic impact of business leverage; and whether certain specified types of transactions should be discouraged for various other non-tax economic reasons. In addition, administrability and fairness issues may be raised.

Particular interest disallowance proposals may address one or more of these issues. The proposals may be more or less comprehensive in treatment of the issues they do address. Because the proposals differ widely in the nature of the issues they address, it is necessary to determine which policy issues are considered significant in order to evaluate the desirability of any particular proposal.

The following discussion first describes a number of interest disallowance proposals and discusses the principal issues they address. The discussion then describes certain additional issues common to many of the proposals.

1. Broad interest disallowance proposals not dependent on particular types of corporate transactions

All interest deductions above a specified amount could be disallowed. There are several variations of this approach, each of which computes the amount of the disallowance based on different factors. The factors selected indicate the policy objectives of the proposals.

a. Disallow a flat percentage of all interest deductions

Under this approach, the amount of nondeductible interest would be a percentage of total interest expense. This approach principally addresses concerns about erosion of the revenue base and about the role of debt in facilitating tax arbitrage. It does not address issues of the proper measurement of income (either by trying to distinguish debt from equity, or by trying to limit interest deductions where the debt supports activities that do not produce income taxable to the entity incurring the debt). It also is not limited to any particular types of transactions that might be considered undesirable for non-tax reasons.

While revenue concerns are the main basis for this particular approach, issues arise regarding its effectiveness. For example, if the deduction denial is related only to a percentage of total interest expense, it might be possible for taxpayers in some circumstances to increase the stated interest amount beyond the amount they might have stated absent this provision, thus continuing to reap the benefit of the deduction. Present law provides certain bright-line rules designed to prevent the interest component of an obligation from being understated; but it has no comparable rules designed to prevent the overstatement of interest. Issues related to the design of such rules are addressed below in connection with other proposals.

The impact of this proposal will vary dramatically from industry to industry. For example, financial intermediaries, such as banks, may see enormous increases in taxable income, even though their loans may bear low interest rates. Likewise, this proposal will disproportionately affect activities which support high degrees of leverage, such as real estate, even though the debt involved may not be particularly risky.

b. Disallow interest deductions in excess of a specified rate of return to investors

This approach would disallow interest deductions in excess of a specified rate of return to investors. Deductions not in excess of that rate still would be permitted. The rate could be determined by reference to a rate deemed to represent that of a relatively risk-free investment (for example, the rate on comparable-term Treasury obligations issued at the time of the borrowing, or a few points above that rate). The rate could fluctuate as the reference rate fluctuates.

As with the approach described above, this approach addresses concerns about erosion of the tax base, but to the extent the rate selected reflects a measurement of "risk," this approach also might be described as an attempt to properly measure economic income. If one accepts the premise that all interest on debt is properly deductible without regard to whether the debt supports an asset that produces taxable income, and the further premise that the most fundamental basis for distinguishing debt from equity is the degree of investor risk, this approach seeks to deny a deduction for the "risk" element of stated interest on the theory it more nearly resembles a dividend distribution, while continuing to permit the non-risk portion to be fully deductible.

A primary issue with respect to this type of approach is the selection of the permitted deductible interest rate. To the extent the rate is selected in an attempt to identify excessive risk, questions may be raised regarding the accuracy of a risk analysis based solely on interest rate. On the other hand, to the extent the proposal is viewed as one of administrative convenience designed to address revenue concerns and avoid the need to distinguish between debt and equity, the accuracy of any risk analysis may be considered less important.

Non-tax policy issues also may arise. For example, even though it is arguable that a high degree of risk suggests an equity investment, and that a high interest rate suggests a high degree of risk, the practical result of such an approach may be that certain start-up firms, or firms involved in inherently risky ventures, may be more restricted in their ability to deduct all of the interest demanded by investors than other more established or stable firms. Variations in the permitted rate might be adopted for such situations; however, arguments then may be raised that whichever taxpayers are permitted the higher deductions may obtain a competitive advantage over other ventures also involving risk, which may have implications for neutrality of the tax system in this respect.

c. Disallow interest deductions based on inflation: interest indexing

This approach would disallow a portion of interest deductions based on inflation. A corresponding portion of the recipient's interest income would be treated as nontaxable.

1984 Treasury proposal

The Treasury proposals in 1984 suggested a plan which generally would have rendered the same specified fraction of interest non-deductible and non-includable. Home mortgage interest and a de minimis amount of other individual interest were exempt from these provisions. The Treasury proposal assumed a specified real pre-tax interest rate and would have calculated a percentage each year based on this assumed real rate relative to the sum of inflation and the assumed real interest rate. The allowable interest deduction (and inclusion) each year would have been calculated by multiplying nominal interest payments (and receipts) by this percentage, which would be published periodically by the tax authorities.

As a method for indexing debt, the proposal was relatively simple. Even so, it still had numerous difficulties. Because it applied a single fraction to all interest it did a poor job of coping with debt of differing risk characteristics; in particular, it made too large a percentage of interest on risky debt nondeductible and non-includable. Also, if the fraction were applied to financial intermediaries (e.g., banks), their income could be very lightly taxed. As pointed out by Treasury at the time, even with its problems, the method was likely to provide a more appropriate measure of income than the current method of deducting and including all nominal interest.

Other proposals

Other methods of indexing may better measure real interest deductions but at the cost of increased complexity. One proposal would require the restatement of interest paid by subtracting out the inflationary component of the interest rate. For example, if one paid $100 of interest at a 10 percent nominal rate and the rate of inflation were 7 percent, then one would calculate the inflationary component of the interest paid at a 7 percent rate ($70) and subtract that amount from the interest actually paid. The difference ($30) would be the allowed amount of deductible interest. Similar calculations would be necessary for purposes of income inclusion. This proposal, while having fewer distortions than the Treasury proposal, is significantly more complex and administratively difficult. In general, proposals designed to measure the appropriate amount of interest make a trade-off between simplicity and accuracy.

Issues generally applicable to indexing

A number of issues arise with respect to interest indexing. A principal concern is determining the amount of correction to interest expense or income that accurately reflects inflation. It may be necessary to determine a "real" interest rate prior to risk considerations. Even assuming a correct adjustment is identified, it may be necessary for administrative convenience to apply that adjustment in a relatively rough manner that does not fully account for different real interest rates over different periods of a year. It may be difficult to provide an administrable adjustment that does not involve windfalls to some taxpayers.

Indexing only interest but not other long-term arrangements may put additional pressure on the determination as to whether an instrument is properly characterized as debt. For example, depending on the relative tax situations of the parties, indexing only interest may make it more desirable for a taxpayer with a relatively high effective tax rate to hold an instrument characterized as debt rather than equity. Similarly, it may be more desirable for an arrangment to be characterized as a lending arrangement rather than a lease. To the extent parties in different tax situations recharacterized their arrangements to take advantage of tax arbitrage potential in this additional new disparity between the treatment of debt and other arrangements, there could be a corresponding revenue concern. On the other hand, it can be argued that failure to index may perpetuate a far greater revenue loss if the holders of debt instruments tend to be entities with a low effective tax rate and borrowers tend to be taxpayers with a higher effective rate who are obtaining an excessive interest deduction.

Exempting certain classes of debt, such as home mortgages, from indexing proposals may cause large tax-induced distortions of asset portfolios. Thus, excluding home mortgages would increase further the tax incentives for owner-occupied housing.

Any proposal that reduces interest inclusions and deductions to the same degree will generally reduce nominal interest rates. Because of the fall in nominal interest, the value of tax exemption to pension funds and other tax-exempt institutions will be less than it would be under a system without indexing.

d. Disallow interest deductions in excess of a specified percentage of taxable income (or earnings and profits) as computed before the deductions

This approach would limit the interest deduction by reference to taxable income (or alternatively, earnings and profits) determined prior to the deduction. For example, one version of this approach would limit the deduction to no more than 50 percent (or some other specified percentage) of the taxable income of the corporation computed without regard to the interest deduction. Such an approach was adopted in the 1986 Senate version of H.R. 3838 (the Tax Reform Act of 1986) but was limited to situations where the lender was related to the payor corporation by at least 50–percent ownership and was a tax-exempt or foreign entity that would not pay U.S. tax on interest received from the payor corporation (Senate amendment to H.R. 3838, sec. 984 (1986)). One variation would limit the deduction to no more than 50 percent (or some other specified percentage) of the earnings and profits or the corporation computed without regard to the deduction. Another variation would apply the limitation only for minimum tax purposes.

This approach is principally addressed to revenue concerns and attempts to provide a rough but practical alternative to complex rules for distinguishing equity from debt, which assures that interest alone does not shelter taxable income to an unacceptable degree.

The limitation to a specified percentage of taxable income (or earnings and profits) might arguably be viewed as reflecting concerns about proper measurement of income, on the theory that when interest deductions alone consume a significant proportion of otherwise taxable income, this may suggest excessive risk to the lender implying an equity interest. However, this particular approach is not a targeted method of identifying situations of risk. This is because the ability to pay back indebtedness depends largely on the capacity of the debtor to generate cash flow, either from current operations or from sales of appreciated assets. Neither taxable income nor earnings and profits is an adequate measure of such capacity. For example, an entity with significant cash flow potential may have low taxable income because of other tax deductions that do not reflect economic losses (for example, accelerated depreciation), or because assets are currently held for appreciation and not for current income. The use of earnings and profits as a limitation similarly does not take account of items such as unrealized appreciation, which may be sufficient to avoid undue risk to the debtholder.

This approach also raises an issue whether it is desirable to limit interest deductions, thus increasing the effective tax rate, in times of recession or when taxable income is otherwise small due to real economic losses.

[The report went on to discuss options under which corporate interest deductions would be disallowed in transactions that reduce the corporate equity base or in more specified acquisitions or stock purchase transactions—e.g., proposals introduced in Congress that would limit interest deductions in the case of certain corporate repurchase transactions involving identifiable "risk" or in certain debt-financed acquisitions where appreciation on corporate assets is untaxed, or in certain hostile takeover situations. Ed.]

* * *

C. Combination Interest Disallowance and Dividend Relief Options

1. Provide deductible rate of return for corporate-level equity and limit interest deductions to the same rate

This option would grant a limited corporate-level dividends paid deduction and conform the treatment of debt to that accorded equity by limiting allowable interest deductions to the same rate. The rate of return could be selected to approximate the rate an investor would demand for a relatively risk-free investment (e.g., the rate on comparable-term Treasury obligations, or a rate several points above that).

The major advantage of this proposal is that the treatment of debt and equity would be more closely aligned since the cost of all externally-raised capital generally would be deductible to the same extent. This could remove some of the importance of distinguishing debt from equity.

In addition, the proposal might alleviate pressure for the issuance of debt, and to this extent would address non-tax issues related to concern about the economic consequences of leverage. This proposal, standing alone, is not designed to address any issues related to the potential erosion of the tax base. Although the deduction with respect to debt would be limited, the new deduction for equity might offset that limit in many cases. Depending upon the rate selected and the transitional rules adopted, the total amount of available deductions might be reduced for some corporations, but might increase for others.

Moreover, the proposal does not address issues related to the reduction of the corporate tax base by debt-financed distributions or by other distributions. However, it could be combined with other proposals directed to such issues.

One issue with respect to this approach is the selection of the appropriate deductible rate. The selection of the effective date of the proposal involves additional issues. For example, granting a dividends paid deduction for capital contributed prior to the effective date of the proposal could arguably provide a windfall for such capital. Similarly, cutting back interest deductions for debt incurred prior to that debt could be viewed as undermining existing expectations.

If the deduction for equity is granted only to "new" capital, rules would have to be provided to prevent the retirement of existing capital and its reissuance as "new" capital eligible for the deduction. The minimum distributions tax proposal described below at Part V.D.1. of this pamphlet, infra, might provide a method of enforcing such a limitation.

Providing a deduction only for "new" capital might also raise questions whether new equity (or new corporations) might obtain some advantage over old equity (and old corporations.) Such concerns might be addressed by allowing the deduction for all capital but phasing it in slowly, or by requiring the deduction for each infusion of new capital to be phased out over some period of time.

2. Allow an investor credit for interest and dividends and deny corporate interest deduction

This option would not permit a corporation to deduct any interest. Instead, shareholders and debtholders would be allowed a credit against taxes owed as a result of their receipt of dividends and interest. The credit would be based, in some fashion, on corporate taxes paid with respect to the dividends and interest distributed by a corporation.

One advantage of this option is that the tax treatment of debt and equity would be equalized. One issue raised by this option is the effect it would have on other business entities (e.g., partnerships), depending on whether the option applied only to corporations or to a broader class of business entities. The other issues raised by this option are similar to those discussed in connection with integration proposals generally (see Part V.A. of this pamphlet, supra.

D. Other Options

1. Impose minimum tax on distributions

A minimum tax could be imposed on certain corporate distributions (for example, extraordinary dividends, stock redemption distributions, and amounts distributed in corporate acquisitions) to assure that the corporate revenue base is not reduced without payment of at least a minimum amount of tax.[172]

One approach would impose the tax at a rate equal to the rate on dividends received by individuals (e.g. 28 percent). The tax could be withheld from the dividend distribution by the distributing corporation and a credit provided to the shareholder against any shareholder tax on the distribution.

This approach directly addresses the issue of the erosion of the corporate base by focusing on the cause of the erosion, i.e., distributions out of corporate solution. The approach recognizes that the erosion can occur whether or not debt is incurred and whether or not an acquisition transaction such as a leveraged buyout is involved. Its application to all major corporate distribution transactions would ensure that a minimum tax would in fact be collected, regardless of the nature of the distributee and of the specific tax characterization of the distribution. At the shareholder level, any bias in the tax law in favor of non-dividend distributions (treated as sales) as opposed to dividend distributions would be eliminated.

One issue related to this approach is that certain arguably unfair results may occur from the distributee's standpoint because the same tax is withheld from a distribution regardless of a shareholder's basis in the shares. In addition, the proposal would collect tax with respect to certain distributions to tax-exempt investors that are not currently taxed. This effect would be mitigated to the extent that ordinary distributions (such as ordinary dividends) might be exempted from the proposal.

It is arguable that the proposal might subject corporate income to multiple taxation if the corporation is taxed on earnings, a taxable

---

172. A variation of this approach was suggested by Professor William D. Andrews in a *Reporter's Study on Corporate Distributions,* published as an Appendix to the American Law Institute's *Federal Income Tax Project, Subchapter C, Proposals on Corporate Acquisitions and Dispositions* (1982). The Reporter's Study made three specific proposals relating to the taxation of corporate income. The proposals would (1) provide a deduction for dividends paid on new corporate equity, (2) impose a compensatory tax on nondividend distributions, and (3) modify the tax treatment of intercorporate investment and distributions. The proposals contained in the Reporter's Study have not been adopted by the American Law Institute.

selling shareholder is taxed on gain that is attributable to retained earnings, and the purchasing shareholder is also taxed on the distribution in redemption of his recently-acquired shares. However, such multiple taxation would be mitigated to the extent tax is deferred or eliminated either at the corporate or the shareholder level. For example, the corporation might not pay current tax on corporate earnings or appreciation that may underlie a selling shareholder's gain (because of corporate-level tax deductions that do not reflect economic losses, or because appreciation has not been recognized at the corporate level). Similarly, a selling shareholder may obtain a deferral benefit by not recognizing gain until his stock is sold. Also, such multiple taxation would not occur to the extent that the purchasing shareholder anticipates the new minimum distributions tax (or anticipated a tax on distributions under present law), and accordingly reduced the price paid to the selling shareholder.

2. Require recognition of corporate-level gain to the extent corporate-level debt is incurred in excess of corporate-level underlying asset basis

A portion of corporate-level appreciation could be recognized whenever debt is incurred in excess of underlying corporate-level asset basis. This proposal could be limited to situations where the debt supports a distribution out of corporate solution.

Under this approach, the distributing corporation is viewed as having cashed out a portion of its asset appreciation, since it has removed that value from corporate solution rather than using the funds to pay down corporate-level debt supported in part by appreciation in corporate assets. * * * The approach addresses issues related to the erosion of the corporate revenue base and also issues related to the measurement of economic income.

It is arguable that since the corporation is still liable for its debt, it has not obtained any advantage from the borrowing and distribution and should not be required to accelerate recognition of corporate level gain. On the other hand, to the extent corporate asset appreciation supported the borrowing, the funds have been removed from corporate solution, and the remaining corporate assets are the only source of repayment, it is arguable that the benefits of the corporate appreciation have been realized at this point.

3. Impose excise tax on acquisition indebtedness

A nondeductible excise tax at a rate that would approximate denial of a corporate level interest deduction could be imposed in the case of certain distributions where debt is involved. This tax could be designed to parallel any of the interest disallowance proposals described above that address acquisitions or other types of corporate distributions.

To the extent the tax depends upon identification of an amount of indebtedness that supports a particular type of transaction, it will involve the debt allocation issues discussed above in connection with interest disallowance proposals.

To the extent the tax is imposed only on certain types of indebtedness (for example, where the interest rate or the debt-equity ratio exceeds a certain amount), it raises the further issue whether transactions could be structured to avoid the particular limitations while varying other aspects of the transaction to produce similar economic results.

Finally, to the extent the tax is imposed only on certain types of stock purchases (for example, purchases of 50 percent of the stock of a corporation within a specified time), it will be limited in the extent to which it addresses broader questions relating to erosion of the corporate tax base or the proper matching of corporate-level deductions with income.

The principal issue such an excise tax would attempt to address is the potential concern related to interest disallowance proposals that foreign acquirors able to borrow abroad might be advantaged over U.S. acquirors. However, to the extent the excise tax is dependent upon the identification of some amount of debt supporting the acquisition, it may involve administrative issues since it may be difficult to identify the amount of foreign incurred debt supporting a U.S. acquisition. A presumption might be established that all or a specified percentage of a foreign acquiror's purchase price was debt-financed. Possibly foreign acquirors could be given an opportunity to rebut the presumption. However, it might be difficult for the Internal Revenue Service to audit any such rebuttal statements, which could require obtaining information about the entity's foreign capital structure.

4. Develop objective standards for distinguishing between debt and equity

The possibility of issuing Treasury regulations under section 385 could be revisited. Such an approach could attempt to develop more objective standards for distinguishing between debt and equity. Prior attempts to develop such standards have been unsuccessful. * * *

* * *

NOTE

When Congress first held hearings on the problems of excessive debt, proposals were floated to limit the deductibility of interest used to finance certain "major" and "hostile" acquisitions. Some securities analysts believed that the breadth of these proposals contributed to the stock market crash of October, 1987. A cautious Congress, perhaps squeamish at the prospect of another chilly reception from Wall Street, failed to achieve a consensus on a comprehensive response when it revisited the excessive debt problem in 1989. Instead, the final product is typical of much recent tax legislation: a narrowly targeted set of limitations aimed at particular perceived abuses, accompanied by a delegation to the Treasury to elaborate through regulations. This legislation curbs some of the more egregious uses of "junk bonds," which are high-yield unsecured debt instruments used to finance corporate acquisitions. Other provisions were aimed at the excessive net operating losses generated by debt-financed corporate acquisitions and at corporations paying significant amounts of interest to related tax-exempt entities.

Applicable High–Yield Discount Obligations. The first victim of the recent legislation was a type of high-yield debt instrument that does not currently pay interest in cash to the lender. This type of junk bond is usually structured as a zero-coupon instrument with an issue price that is significantly lower than the stated redemption price at maturity.[1] The "spread" between the issue and redemption price is "original issue discount" ("OID"). In general, the issuer of an OID bond accrues and deducts the "spread" as interest over the life of the bond even though the interest is not actually paid until maturity, and the lender (even if a cash basis taxpayer) includes OID in income over the life of the bond.[2] A related device is the "payment-in-kind" ("PIK") bond, which purports to make interest payments in the form of other debt or stock of the corporate issuer rather than in cash. OID and PIK bonds were attractive financing paper for acquisitions because the issuer received a current interest deduction without a corresponding cash expenditure.

One proposal was to treat high-yield zero coupon and PIK bonds as preferred stock on the theory that their high level of risk and dependence on the profitability of the business causes them to more resemble equity than debt. The legislation ultimately enacted[3] did not go that far. Instead, Congress decided to defer (and in some cases disallow) the issuer's deduction until interest is actually paid in cash but continue to require the lender to recognize interest income as it accrues. This approach represents a new Congressional willingness to bifurcate certain hybrid securities into debt and equity components. The theory is that a portion of the return on certain junk bonds represents a distribution of corporate earnings with respect to an equity interest in the corporation and should be treated as such for tax purposes.

The restrictions in Section 163(e)(5) apply to an "applicable high-yield discount obligation," which is defined in Section 163(i) as an instrument with: (1) a more than five-year maturity, (2) a yield to maturity that is five percentage points or more than the applicable federal rate in effect for the month in which the obligation is issued, and (3) "significant original issue discount."[4] The OID amount on

---

1. A zero coupon bond is a debt instrument that pays no interest and is sold at a significant discount from its face value.

2. See I.R.C. §§ 1272–1273.

3. See I.R.C. § 163(e)(5), (i).

4. A virtually incomprehensible definition of "significant original issue discount" appears in Section 163(i)(2). Oversimplifying considerably, OID is "significant" if the OID income that accrues in periods ending more than five years after the bond is issued exceeds interest actually paid on the bond.

these bonds is divided between an interest element that is deductible but only when interest is actually paid,[5] and a return of equity element ("the disqualified portion") for which no interest deduction is allowed but which may be eligible for the dividends received deduction in the case of a corporate lender.[6] This approach is a compromise between deferral and total disallowance of the issuer's interest deduction. An instrument generally will have a "disqualified portion" of OID and thus face disallowance of part of the interest deduction if it has significant OID and the yield on the instrument is more than six percentage points over the applicable federal rate.[7]

Limitation on Net Operating Losses Created by Debt–Financed Transactions. Congress also was concerned that corporations were financing leveraged buyouts and similar transactions in part through the tax refunds that were generated by net operating loss carrybacks resulting from the payment of interest expense on acquisition debt. In general, a corporation that has a net operating loss ("NOL") may carry the excess deductions back for three taxable years and forward for fifteen years.[8] If a corporation with NOLs had taxable income in the three prior taxable years, the carryback will result in a refund of federal income taxes paid in those years. The interest deductions resulting from debt-financed acquisitions and other corporate restructurings often were large enough to offset not only the corporation's current operating income but also to generate an NOL carryback. Reasoning that NOL carrybacks are intended as an averaging device to smooth out swings in taxable income caused by business cycle variations and unexpected financial losses, Congress concluded that the interest expense triggered by a takeover was not sufficiently related to business operations in prior taxable periods to justify a carryback of NOLs attributable to acquisition interest.[9]

Section 172(h) addresses this concern by limiting the ability of a corporation to carry back NOLs where the losses are created by interest deductions attributable to leveraged buyouts and other debt-financed transactions, such as corporate repurchases of stock (collectively referred to as "corporate equity reduction transactions" or "CERTs").[10] A CERT is either a "major stock acquisition" (a planned acquisition by one corporation of 50 percent or more of the voting power or value of the stock in another corporation [11]) or an "excess distribution" (general-

---

5. "Payments" for this purpose are limited to actual payments of cash or property other than the stock or debt of the issuer. I.R.C. § 163(i)(3)(B).

6. I.R.C. § 163(e)(5)(A), (B).

7. I.R.C. § 163(e)(5)(C).

8. See I.R.C. § 172 and Chapter 13A, infra.

9. See H.R.Rep. No. 101–247, 101st Cong., 1st Sess. (1989).

10. It is important to note that Section 172(h) does not disallow the interest deduc-

tion or limit NOL carryforwards but merely restricts a corporation from carrying back the losses generated by certain debt-financed transactions.

11. I.R.C. § 172(h)(3)(B). A major stock acquisition does not include a qualified stock purchase where the buyer makes a Section 338 election. I.R.C. § 172(h)(3)(B)(ii). As a result of legislation enacted in 1990, a CERT may include the acquisition of a subsidiary of another corporation.

ly, unusually large distributions relative to the corporation's prior distribution history or net worth [12]). Interest attributable to a CERT is generally defined as interest allocable to debt that would not have been incurred but for the CERT.[13] A de minimis rule provides that the limitation applies only if the amount of interest expense at issue exceeds $1 million.[14]

Earnings Stripping. A third practice that was limited in 1989 is known as "earnings stripping"—i.e., the payment of deductible interest by a corporate borrower to an economically related lender that is effectively exempt from United States taxation. Deducting a payment to a tax-exempt entity whose economic interests coincide with the payor is a particularly attractive form of tax arbitrage. Earnings stripping payments, which are not necessarily related to acquisitions, are made primarily in the international setting (e.g., a payment from a U.S. subsidiary to a related foreign parent) or, domestically, where a taxable U.S. corporation is related to one or more tax-exempt charitable organizations.

The particulars of the Congressional response are well beyond the scope of this overview. It is sufficient to note that Section 163(j) defers the deduction for any interest paid or accrued by a corporation to certain related persons who are exempt from U.S. tax.[15] The limitation applies only if: (1) the payor corporation's debt-equity ratio exceeds 1:5 to 1,[16] and (2) the payor has "excess interest expense," which generally is any interest expense for the taxable year in excess of 50 percent of the corporation's taxable income without regard to net interest expense (i.e., interest expense less interest income) or net operating losses.[17] The corporation may carry forward any deduction deferred by Section 163(j) and treat it as interest paid to the related party in future years when it may be deductible if the corporation's debt-equity ratio has improved or if it does not have excess interest expense.[18]

c. RETHINKING *GENERAL UTILITIES* REPEAL

Much of this course has been devoted to the history and current status of the *General Utilities* doctrine—that venerable principle that permitted a corporation to distribute appreciated property to its shareholders and avoid a corporate-level tax.[1] In studying the demise of *General Utilities*, an inquisitive student may have wondered how the principle remained embedded in the Code for so long. Was there

---

12. I.R.C. § 172(h)(3)(C).

13. I.R.C. § 172(h)(2).

14. I.R.C. § 172(h)(2)(D).

15. The definition of "related" for this purpose is borrowed from Sections 267 and 707(b). I.R.C. § 163(j)(4).

16. See I.R.C. § 163(j)(2)(A). Section 163(j)(2)(C) generally defines "ratio of debt to equity" as "the ratio which the total indebtedness of the corporation bears to the sum of its money and all other assets less such total indebtedness." For this purpose, assets are taken into account of their adjusted basis for determining gain. Id.

17. I.R.C. § 163(j)(2)(B).

18. I.R.C. § 163(j)(1)(B).

1. See Chapters 4D1 and 5E1, supra, and Section B2, of this chapter.

opposition to its repeal? What rationale might have supported its retention in the federal tax laws for over 50 years?

To be sure, the *General Utilities* doctrine has its supporters, especially in the liquidation context. These troops may reconnoiter in the near future. The Tax Reform Act of 1986 directed the Treasury to study proposals for further reform of Subchapter C and to report any recommendations by January 1, 1988.[2] That report may result in a proposal for more permanent relief from repeal of *General Utilities* in a liquidation setting.

The two excerpts below address the question of relief from full recognition of corporate gain on a liquidation and the possible form of such relief. The first excerpt is from the testimony of an experienced tax practitioner at hearings before the Senate Finance Committee concerning that committee staff's 1983 preliminary report on Subchapter C reform. By way of clarification, keep in mind that the references to Code sections (e.g., Sections 336 and 337) are to those sections as they existed prior to the Tax Reform Act of 1986, when liquidating distributions and sales could be made without a corporate-level tax. At the time this testimony was presented, the maximum capital gains rate for individuals was 20 percent and the maximum capital gains rate for corporations was 28 percent. The second excerpt is from the Senate Finance Committee staff's final report on reform and simplification of Subchapter C—"The Subchapter C Revision Act of 1985."[3] It surveys various potential relief provisions and could be a model for legislative proposals in the future.

EXCERPT FROM HEARINGS BEFORE THE SENATE FINANCE COMMITTEE, REFORM OF CORPORATE TAXATION *

S.Hrg. 98–556, 98th Cong., 1st Sess. 150–70 (1983).

Statement of John S. Nolan.

Corporate Tax: Asset Appreciation on Complete Liquidation (*General Utilities*)

The result of the Staff proposal as to the *General Utilities* rule would be to impose a double tax on the appreciation in value of corporate assets sold or distributed in the course of a complete liquidation. This would effectively raise the maximum capital gain tax on this increase in asset value from the 20% rate, applicable to all other capital gains, to 42.4%. * * *

2. Tax Reform Act of 1986, P.L. No. 99–514, 99th Cong., 2d Sess. § 634 (1986). At this writing, Congress has extended the due date for the Subchapter C study to January 1, 1992.

3. Staff of the Senate Committee on Finance, The Subchapter C Revision Act of 1985: A Final Report Prepared by the Staff, 99th Cong., 1st Sess. (S.Prt. 99–47, 1985). Although titled an "Act," this entire proposal was not enacted into law, but many of its recommendations (but *not* relief from *General Utilities* repeal) were incorporated in the Tax Reform Act of 1986.

* Some footnotes omitted.

The *additional* gain that would be taxed by the proposed repeal of *General Utilities* would in many cases be largely inflationary gain, not real gain, together in some cases with the value of intangible assets of the business. A tax rate of 42.4% [the combined then effective capital gains rates at the corporate and shareholder levels. Ed.] on these kinds of gain is not justified.

The impact will be almost entirely on closely-held family businesses; large publicly-held companies very seldom undergo complete liquidation. The short-term result will be to bias the decisions of these families in favor of merging their family companies into large publicly-held corporations in a tax-free exchange for stock of those companies, rather than allocating their capital to other uses that could be more efficient. The tax law would thus further interfere with market allocation of capital.

In the longer run, business will tend to avoid incorporation wherever possible. Our capital markets, the largest and most efficient in the world, are based on financial instruments of corporations, not unincorporated businesses. These markets will adjust, to be sure, but at a significant cost to the capital formation process. New instruments subject to new dimensions of risk will be required to replace corporate capital instruments.

As a lawyer experienced in this field, and as a former law teacher of the subject matter, after taking into account the circumstances of my clients and others similarly situated, I strongly oppose this particular element of the Staff's report. While I agree with many of the other major elements of the report, and while I see no strong objection to repeal of the *General Utilities* rule in the case of *ordinary* distributions in kind, I think that its repeal with respect to *complete liquidations* would be a grave error in tax policy.* I have studied the detailed reasons given for its repeal in the Staff report, and I do not find them convincing. They proceed from a fundamentally erroneous premise and are based far too much on unjustified speculation. The reasons given against repeal are understated and require much further development.

---

* I recognize that repeal of *General Utilities* is a key element in the major treatment of acquisitions proposed in the report—that is, the election between cost basis and carryover basis treatment at the corporate level and the separate tax treatment at the shareholder level. If *General Utilities* is not repealed in the corporate liquidation context as I recommend, it will be necessary to retain the basic elements of §§ 337 and 338; it obviously is not desirable to return to the uncertainties of Commissioner v. Court Holding Co., 324 U.S. 331 (1945) versus United States v. Cumberland Public Service Co., 338 U.S. 451 (1950), and Kimbell-Diamond Milling Co. v. Commissioner, 187 F.2d 718 (5th Cir. 1951). If the acquisitions proposals are adopted, but *General Utilities* is not repealed in the complete liquidation context, recapture should be required, but gain or loss should not otherwise be recognized, in transactions generally of the type described in § 337 and § 338 if the acquiring company elects cost basis treatment. The operation of those two provisions could be improved and restricted to their true purpose. It may be that recapture should be required in any such case, whether the acquiring corporation elects cost basis or carryover basis treatment. These are matters which require a great deal more study.

I note that in recent letters to Senator Dole, two prestigious bar associations with great experience in this field, the Association of the Bar of the City of New York and the Tax Section of the New York State Bar Association, have singled out this same matter to urge further careful evaluation. I strongly urge this Committee to exercise great caution in making such a fundamental change in our corporate tax structure.

Impact of the Proposed Change—Family-Held Businesses

As previously stated, by far the greatest impact of the proposed change will be on family-held businesses. These family businesses typically hold a wide range of business assets, including real estate from which the business may be operated, or real estate collected in a family investment company. These assets are likely to have appreciated substantially in value over a long period of years, in large part as a result of inflation. The business will often have developed patents, trademarks, trade secrets, know-how, or other valuable intangible assets. Many family companies have been operated through several generations, thus greatly increasing the inflationary components of these gains. The proposal will tax all of this gain at the corporate level, in addition to the same gain being taxed again at the shareholder level, on complete liquidation of the family company.

Even though the family company may have been operated for many years, the family may have become so large, or the interests of different family members may have become so diverse, that it may make greater economic sense for the family to liquidate the corporation, possibly selling all or part of its assets, or to sell their stock, and undertake other business ventures. It may have become economically more efficient for third parties to acquire the business. There are a wide range of reasons why it may become appropriate for the family to terminate the activities of their corporation by complete liquidation. These families have operated on certain fundamental assumptions as to our taxing system as it has existed at least for the last fifty years, even prior to the time the *General Utilities* case was decided in 1935. These include a clear understanding under our tax system that upon a decision to terminate their business and completely liquidate, they could do so incurring only a single capital gains tax on such a terminal transaction on the appreciation in value of the underlying assets of the business. This has been the case whether they sell the assets of the business to third parties, divide the business among themselves while it remains in corporate solution, or take their respective shares of the assets in kind and operate as sole proprietorships or partnerships.*

In any such case, they seek to put their capital to its most effective uses in our economy. A single capital gains tax on this terminal transaction, just as if the gain had arisen from any other investment asset held by them, is entirely appropriate. As previously stated, much

---

* See United States v. Cumberland Public Service Co., supra, IRC § 337; IRC § 355 and its predecessor in the 1939 Code; IRC § 336.

of the gain is probably inflationary gain, not real gain, and thus deserves only a single capital gain tax. Even the balance of the gain, likely to be largely attributable to real estate or intangible assets, is by nature essentially an investment gain, not income attributable to regular business activity that typically is taxed at higher rates. The gain in question by its nature is *capital* gain. It should attract only a single capital gain tax.

A capital gain tax of 42.4% on this gain is not justified. The result will be that families wishing to terminate their family businesses will effectively have only one option—find a publicly-held corporation and take its stock for their company * * *

[T]he family could no longer sell the assets of the business to a third party, via § 337, or indirectly via § 338, and apply their capital to other uses, except by incurring a 42.4% tax burden.** Nor could they liquidate the corporation and operate the business as a partnership or sole proprietorship, dividing the assets in kind among themselves as they see fit. Much of the healthy flexibility of our existing tax system as it applies to family businesses would be lost. I see no justification for removing this flexibility, which has been an important inducement to the formation of new, privately-held companies with fresh ideas and inventiveness.

The problem could be compounded by the fact that the family company may have been organized originally to incorporate business assets held in a sole proprietorship or partnership. The assets may have appreciated substantially in value, from inflation or otherwise, and specific intangible asset values may have arisen, before any such incorporation. The proposal would tax the pre-incorporation gain on these assets even though it did not arise in corporate solution. The result would be that the family would clearly pay a much greater tax than would have been payable if no corporation had been formed. There can be no tax policy justification for this result.

Staff Report: Questionable Assumptions As To *General Utilities* Rule

The Staff report commendably recognizes that there are substantial questions whether the *General Utilities* rule should be repealed:

> In addition to the preceding recommendations, the Staff has identified a number of options that ought to be considered if the Committee concludes that the outright repeal of the *General Utilities* rule is too harsh. * * *

The American Law Institute, the recommendations of which were a major source of reference for the Staff's report, recognized the severity of a double tax on the long-term appreciation in value of business assets in a complete liquidation. The Institute recommended that the shareholder be allowed a credit for his share of the corporate capital gains

---

** Technically, in a § 338 transaction, the selling shareholders would not directly incur all of the 42.4% tax, but they would bear the burden of it partly through a reduced selling price in a cost basis acquisition.

tax against his individual capital gains tax to eliminate the double taxation. The credit is extremely complex. It also accomplishes little, to the extent the corporate and individual capital gain tax rates are essentially the same (as they should be with respect to the kind of gain in question here). The Staff rejects the ALI credit proposal on grounds of complexity and taxpayer compliance.

The Staff report gives nine arguments favoring repeal of *General Utilities* and three arguments against it. Before reaching them, it is critical to focus upon the basic assumptions of the Report in recommending repeal of *General Utilities*. These assumptions are that: (1) we have an unintegrated corporate tax system, it should be continued, and it should be rigorously applied; (2) the primary consideration should be that the rules should be "simplest and least susceptible to abuse and manipulation"; and (3) tax abuse abounds, despite many Code provisions specifically developed to prevent it, because of the *General Utilities* rule. I respectfully submit that none of these assumptions is valid.

In fact, we have never had a truly unintegrated corporate tax system in which a tax is paid on income at the corporate level and a second tax is paid on corporate income by the shareholders. Over the seventy or more years that our corporate income tax system has developed, we have had a compromise system in which double tax has been imposed on ordinary earnings from regular operations to the extent they are distributed to shareholders as dividends, but only a single tax has been imposed upon extraordinary events, such as a sale or distribution of assets pursuant to a complete liquidation.

In reality, we have to a large extent had only a single ordinary income tax on regular corporate earnings because of the ability to retain earnings. By reason of our provision for step-up in basis of assets at death, earnings taxed at ordinary rates at the corporate level have to a large extent been retained and have not been taxed again at the shareholder level. At most, they have been subjected to a capital gains tax on sale of stock at the shareholder level. A large percentage of corporations in the U.S., both publicly-held and privately-held, retain and reinvest in their business a large percentage of their annual earnings, partly as a result of the tax advantages to their shareholders that flow from this policy.

This is an entirely healthy system. The corporate tax rate and top individual rate are roughly the same. There should be limits on the tax burden on income from capital so that capital formation is not inhibited or misdirected away from business investment. Further, to the extent we provide incentives through tax allowances, such as the investment credit, ACRS, the research and development credit, or the intangible drilling cost deduction, there should be no preference for operating in or out of the corporate structure.

Virtually all major foreign industrialized countries, including the entire European Economic Community and Canada, have moved toward a single integrated tax structure in which only a single income tax is paid on business earnings. Economists tend strongly to favor such a system to avoid undue burdens on capital investment. We have obviously greatly moderated our tax burden on capital by the types of tax incentives previously described. As a practical matter, the effect of our present corporate tax structure is that by a variety of means we have achieved what is a single tax on the returns from capital, and this allows us to remain competitive in the world economy.

There is no important reason at this time to disturb this carefully-developed balance that has resulted from seventy or more years of experience in refining our corporate tax system to accommodate the needs of our economy and our society. It is particularly unwise to do so in a way that would impact harshly on privately-held, smaller companies. The primary consideration affecting our *corporate* tax structure should be economic efficiency, not simplicity or over-reactive concern with abuse and manipulation.*

The preoccupation in this Report with abuse and manipulation is disturbing. Admittedly, the extensive provisions we have developed to prevent abuse of the *General Utilities* rule, such as the recapture rules, the collapsible corporation provisions, new section 338, the recent repeal of the partial liquidation provisions, the ACRS anti-churning rules, and others, are complex. Complexity, however, in a *corporate* tax context is manageable, and we have in fact learned to live with it. Further, despite the impressions suggested by the report, these anti-abuse provisions are effective in practice. In my thirty-plus years as a corporate tax lawyer, I have not seen any *widespread* circumvention of the collapsible corporation rules or these other provisions. When some special forms of abuse have developed, as they did in recent years, the Congressional response was swift and effective, as in TEFRA. We have developed a new legislative capacity to deal with these problems as they arise.

We must not make a fundamental change in our corporate tax structure to meet these relatively narrow concerns if it could substantially affect efficient allocation of capital resources in the United States. The effect of such a change has not yet been studied sufficiently in the context of repeal of the *General Utilities* rule in corporate complete liquidations. In addition, the possible effects of discouraging the use of corporations to operate privately-held businesses, in favor of partnerships the interests in which are not publicly-traded, royalty

---

* Integration of the corporate and individual tax has also been accomplished in other ways in our tax system. The obvious example is Subchapter S, but administrative considerations have forced the imposition of severe limitations on its use. Royalty trusts exist to receive and distribute certain forms of passive income. As recognized in the Staff report, publicly-traded limited partnerships now exist to operate going businesses. The report would treat publicly-traded limited partnerships as corporations. Widely-held limited partnerships, the interests in which are not publicly-traded, also exist, however, and the report would not reach these arrangements.

trusts, or other arrangements have not been fully evaluated. There are critical economic, legal, and social issues to be considered.

Accordingly, I urge this Committee to defer action on this critical matter at least until these kinds of evaluations have been done. Much more analysis is required to make the judgments that are required in changing the tax structure to increase burdens on privately-held companies.

Staff Report: Reasons For and Against Repeal of *General Utilities*

The report * * * argues for taxing gain on corporate assets at the corporate level in complete liquidations first on the ground that taxpayers pay less tax because of the *General Utilities* rule than would be paid in the absence of a corporate tax. This is difficult to understand, since the main thrust of repealing the *General Utilities* rule is to impose a double tax on the appreciation in value of corporate assets, thereby raising the effective rate on such gain from 20% under existing law to 42.4%. No explanation of this argument in the report is given. Contrary to the impression given in the report, taxpayers will generally pay more tax if *General Utilities* is repealed than they would have paid in the absence of a corporate tax.

* * *

In the complete liquidation context, involving privately-held companies, it is useful to recognize that the shareholder's gain on liquidation consists of two elements—retained earnings and appreciation in value of the company's underlying assets. *There is no other source of shareholder gain.* The shareholder may have bought his shares at a time when such elements existed to some degree; if so, his predecessor will have paid tax at the shareholder level on such elements. Retained earnings and appreciation in value of corporate assets ultimately always incur a tax at the shareholder level, except to the extent that stepped-up basis at death occurs or the shareholder is tax-exempt.

Further, the recapture rules insure that the ordinary income portion of asset appreciation ultimately is taxed, and as ordinary income. Retained earnings by definition have been taxed at the corporate level. What remains then is the capital gain portion of appreciation in value of corporate assets, which, as stated above, is ultimately taxed at the shareholder level, except where there has been an intervening death of the shareholder. Repeal of *General Utilities* in complete liquidations would tax this latter portion twice, once at the corporate level, and again immediately at the shareholder level except where there has been an intervening death of the shareholder. If the business had operated in non-corporate form, this double tax would not have been incurred.

The anti-churning rules effectively prevent undue benefit from ACRS. The collapsible corporation rules, despite their complexity, prevent undue benefit from complete liquidations. There is no substantial opportunity to gain greater benefits by operating in corporate form than in non-corporate form.

The other reasons given in the report for this double taxation may be grouped. The second reason relates to complexity and abuse, a matter already discussed. Repeal of the collapsible corporation rules is not necessarily a useful end in and of itself, regardless of what must be done to make it possible. There are important economic and social consequences to be resolved here; the world has lived with the collapsible corporation anti-tax avoidance rules for more than thirty years and can continue to do so. It is said that repeal will block certain tax-motivated acquisitions, but no specifications are given. TEFRA addressed such problems, and if further problems arise, they can be addressed equally promptly and equally specifically. It is said that repeal of *General Utilities* will limit churning under ACRS, but we already have in place an effective set of rules for that purpose. Finally, I submit that the seriousness of the liquidation-reincorporation problem is overstated; in my extensive corporate tax practice, I have seen very few instances of successful liquidation-reincorporations that produce substantial tax benefits. It is a wonderful conversation piece and tax teaching tool; it is not much of a real problem. In point of fact, the report can be read to *endorse* a form of liquidation-reincorporation not presently available. It would tax the corporation at capital gain rates, permit a step-up in basis of the assets (even though continuity of interest clearly exists), and permit depreciation deductions by reference to stepped-up basis to offset subsequent ordinary income from ongoing business operations.

Otherwise, the reasons for double taxation seem to boil down to a preference for greater purity in an unintegrated tax system—

    iv. General recognition of gain provides uniformity. * * *

    v. Recognition broadens the corporate tax base. * * *

    vii. The General Utilities doctrine allows tax on corporate gain to be avoided entirely. * * *

All of these propositions assume there should be a double tax on appreciation in value of corporate assets at the time of a complete liquidation. As previously stated, there is no basis for this assumption, and it would have enormous adverse effects on privately-held companies in the U.S.

* * *

We have a generally efficient, fair, and workable system that presently stimulates capital formation by avoiding interference with allocation of capital to its most efficient uses in the economy. Initiative and productivity are stimulated by the ability to build up capital returns in a privately-held company. For the most part, all income and gain is taxed at least once, except to the extent we provide tax incentives for good reasons, whether economic (for example, business investment or R&D activity) or social (tax-exempt charitable or similar institutions). When abuses develop, they may be quickly corrected, particularly with the recent Congressional ability to move more promptly. We should not disturb the efficient functioning of the present system unless there are reasons of overriding importance. These have not yet been demonstrated.

The reasons given in the Report as against repeal of *General Utilities* are understated. It is not a theoretical argument as to "realization". It is a practical consideration. The repeal as applied in the complete liquidation context would greatly damage privately-held business in the United States.

To answer the question posed in the Report, a corporate liquidation is an event which warrants a single capital gains tax because it represents a liquidation of an investment, just as any other investment. The gain realized is likely to be largely inflationary rather than real. To the extent the gain reflects retained earnings, it represents income already subject to tax at the corporate level. If it has not been fully taxed at the corporate level, it is because some economic or social policy has been regarded by Congress as sufficiently important to call for a tax incentive provision.

Such gain is quite different from the regular earnings of an ongoing business. The comparisons drawn in the report to a 73% tax rate on ordinary income overstate reality. I doubt that any significant amount of income earned through corporations in the U.S. ever bears an effective tax rate even close to 73%.

The argument that liquidation of a corporation is often a highly formal step without economic substance is not valid. Few complete liquidations involve distributions of assets to the shareholders in kind. Most involve sales of assets pursuant to § 337 or sales of stock deemed to be sales of assets under § 338. The liquidation-reincorporation problem, as previously stated, is given far more emphasis in the Report than it deserves. Further, it simply is not the fact that complete liquidations are often tax-driven transactions; they generally result from a business conclusion that someone else can operate the business more efficiently and that the shareholders can direct their capital to more effective uses in the economy.

The Report correctly notes the argument against repeal that 42.4% is too high a tax rate to impose on investment gain at the time of a complete liquidation. The answer, however, is not to tinker with this rate. Instead, we should simply avoid increasing the extent of double taxation. Extraordinary gains arising on complete liquidation of a corporation should be taxed once, at regular capital gains rates, just as is all other investment gain.

* * *

Conclusion

The Committee should not repeal *General Utilities* in the context of complete liquidations and impose a double tax burden on asset appreciation. An effective tax rate of 42.4% on such gain will have severe adverse effects on privately-held companies. It will create a bias, causing owners of family businesses contemplating liquidation to merge their corporations into publicly-held companies in exchange for stock of such companies. Capital will not be directed to its most efficient uses in the United States economy.

EXCERPT FROM THE SUBCHAPTER C REVISION ACT OF 1985: A FINAL REPORT PREPARED BY THE STAFF OF THE SENATE FINANCE COMMITTEE *

S.Prt. 99–47, 99th Cong., 1st Sess. 62–68 (1985).

C. *Relief from repeal of* General Utilities *doctrine*

Many people who testified at the October, 1983 hearing advocated some form of relief from the repeal of *General Utilities*. The original proposal contained in the Staff Report suggested the possibility of transitional relief in the form of a phase-in of the corporate capital gains tax over a 10-year period. Several people testified that such relief would be inadequate, and that some permanent relief was essential.

In deciding what type of permanent relief, if any, might be appropriate, two questions had to be resolved: (1) in what type of transactions should relief be provided; and (2) what form should the relief take?

1. *Eligible transactions*

Almost all who testified in favor of some form of permanent relief confined their remarks to the need for relief in a complete liquidation or liquidating sale. No one testified as to the need for relief in a non-liquidating setting. Indeed, even as to liquidating transactions, most individuals indicated that any permanent relief should be appropriately limited to the potential "double tax" on long-held capital assets.

However, one of the reasons described above in favor of the repeal of *General Utilities* was the concern that current law creates a bias in favor of certain types of transactions over others, providing much complexity and abuse potential. If any *General Utilities* relief were limited as suggested by those who testified, there was the possibility that the same problems as under current law would be revived.

Providing across-the-board relief in all transactions, liquidating and non-liquidating, seemed out of the question because of revenue considerations.[160] It seemed advisable, therefore, that any permanent relief

---

* Some footnotes omitted.

160. *But see* discussion below regarding the possibility of implementing the Treasury Department's dividends paid deduction proposal. The Treasury proposal, which would provide only partial across-the-board relief, is estimated to cost approximately $85 billion during the first four years that it would be implemented. See "Tax Reform for Fairness, Simplicity, and Economic Growth: The Treasury Department Report to the President" (November, 1984) (hereinafter "Treasury Department Tax Reform Proposals") Vol. 1 at 248.

should be targeted as closely as possible to the specific need for the relief.

In the large majority of cases, opposition to the repeal of *General Utilities*, and support for some form of relief, was based upon the concern that a "double tax" on long-held assets of small businesses was too harsh. The view was expressed that a small businessman whose incorporated business holds appreciating capital assets for an extended period of time should not be required to pay both a corporate level and a shareholder level tax upon the liquidation or acquisition of the business. According to this view, this was particularly true because the gains might be largely inflationary. However sympathetic the preceding case might be, the case of a speculator who owns stock of a large publicly-held corporation just prior to the liquidation or acquisition of such corporation appeared clearly less appealing as to the need for "double tax" relief. Thus, it seemed appropriate to consider limiting any relief to long-held gains of small businesses.

Moreover, there was testimony that the impact of the repeal of *General Utilities* (and the consequent need for some form of relief) would fall almost exclusively upon small, closely-held businesses, and that large, publicly-held corporations would rarely be affected. Finally, to the extent the form of the relief (described below) was criticized at the hearing as being too complex, many of those concerns would be eliminated if the relief were limited to a tightly circumscribed number of cases involving smaller corporations.

Accordingly, the bill provides permanent *General Utilities* relief in the case of a small business which incurs gains on long-held assets in a liquidation or liquidating sale. In those circumstances, the "double tax" is effectively eliminated.

Five years was chosen as the appropriate dividing line for "long-held" capital assets because, to the extent the proposal is an attempt to mitigate the effects of inflation, it was believed that some significant holding period should be required.[164] Other proposals have suggested three years as the appropriate test.[165]

The $1 million fair market value test for "small" businesses was chosen because of similar standards used in other sections of the Code.[166] In addition, to avoid a cliff effect, the bill proposes to provide relief, in decreasing amounts, for corporations up to $2 million in value.

---

164. In that regard, should a proposal such as the Treasury Department's recommendaton to index the basis of capital assets for inflation, be enacted, it may be appropriate to rethink the need for the proposed relief. See Treasury Department Tax Reform Proposals, Vol. 11 at 178.

165. ABA Task Force Report, 37 Tax Lawyer 625, 631. The Minority Report did not agree with taxing any capital gains.

166. See, e.g., section 1244 ($1 million paid-in capital test); cf. P.L. 96–223, sec. 403(b), as amended (LIFO recapture amount reduced by $1 million); section 11(b) ($1 million taxable income threshold for graduated rates).

2. Form of the relief

The two principal forms of relief that were considered were a shareholder credit and corporate-level exemption.[167] Testimony was almost evenly divided between the two types of relief. The American Law Institute had recommended a shareholder credit in its proposal.[169] The special ABA Task Force recommended a corporate-level exemption.[170]

The corporate-level exemption was rejected for the same reasons that a complete repeal of *General Utilities* was considered essential. A corporate-level exemption is no more than a partial repeal of *General Utilities*. Thus, a corporate-level exemption was viewed as presenting many of the same problems that an incomplete repeal of *General Utilities* would have presented.

For example, assume that relief were provided in the form of a corporate-level exemption on capital assets with a holding period of 5 years or more. Assume that P corporation acquires all of the assets of T corporation in exchange for P stock. Further, assume that all of the T assets consist of capital assets with a holding period of 5 years or more.

In this example, a cost basis election could be made, resulting in a cost basis to P in the assets acquired. Because of the exemption, no gain or loss would be recognized by T in the transaction. Finally, in the distribution by T of the P stock, the T shareholders would not recognize any gain or loss because of the receipt of qualifying consideration. In short, the acquisition would result in a cost basis being obtained by the acquiring party without any immediate tax being paid by either the target corporation or its shareholders. No one who testified appeared to advocate this result.

Obviously, in most cases, all of T's assets would not consist of capital assets with a holding period of 5 years or more. However, in any transaction, to the extent T's assets did consist of such assets, the potentially inappropriate combination of a cost basis to the acquiring corporation without any immediate tax liability would be available. For many of these reasons, the Treasury Department opposed a corporate-level exemption.

Some consideration was also given to using the S corporation rules as a means to provide the appropriate relief. One individual recommended exploring this option.

The S corporation option was ultimately rejected for two reasons. First, it was clear that many corporations not eligible for S corporation status should, nevertheless, be entitled to relief, so that the S corpora-

---

167. Other relief provided by the bill, including special relief on an in-kind liquidation, is discussed in the next section.

169. American Law Institute, Federal Income Tax Project: Subchapter C, (1982) at 134.

170. ABA Task Force Report, 37 Tax Lawyer 625, 631. The Minority Report did not agree with this recommendation.

tion rules would have to be significantly liberalized. While certain of the restrictions under current law defining an S corporation might appropriately be waived or eliminated, at least in the case of a liquidation or liquidating sale, it was unclear that all of the restrictions could be removed. There was concern that to the extent any S corporation limitations remained, some sympathetic cases would be unfairly excluded from relief.

Second, the S corporation relief was also viewed as too generous in certain cases. The S corporation rules do not limit the size of the eligible corporation in economic terms. To the extent relief would be provided only to a limited number of corporations and their shareholders, it was determined that it would be fairer and closer to the targeted goal to draw a distinction based upon economic size rather than upon some other criterion, such as the number of shareholders of the corporation.

Thus, the bill provides for a shareholder credit type of relief from the repeal of *General Utilities*. Each shareholder of a small corporation is provided a basis adjustment in his stock in the liquidating or acquired corporation to reflect the corporate-level tax on long-held capital assets. The basis adjustment approach rather than a shareholder credit was selected to increase administrative simplicity, in order to harmonize the treatment of shareholders in different tax situations and to reconcile the difference between the corporate and shareholder capital gains rates. The basis adjustment would operate to eliminate the "double tax" on long-held capital assets. Only those shareholders holding the stock for six months or more would be entitled to relief.

D. Other forms of relief

In addition to the basis adjustment relief described above, the bill also provides several other forms of relief, including special relief in an in-kind liquidation. As noted, several witnesses recommended some form of special relief in that situation.

Under the bill, any shareholder of a corporation which liquidates in kind is entitled to defer the shareholder level tax with respect to any property distributed to the shareholder in the liquidation, except for cash, stock, securities, and similar property, received. In that respect, the relief is similar to section 333 of current law, except that several of the limitations of that section have been eliminated.

The relief is available to a shareholder of any corporation that liquidates in kind, not just "small" corporations. Shareholders of small corporations would have the option of selecting either the basis adjustment relief described earlier or the deferral of shareholder tax proposal.

Some consideration was given to a deferral of the corporate level tax rather than the shareholder level tax. Ultimately, this was rejected because of the view that the corporate level tax should not be permitted to be deferred beyond the termination of the corporation.

Many provisions under current law permit the deferral of corporate tax while assets remain within the corporation or in corporate solution. However, if those benefits represent true "deferrals" rather than an exemption, it seemed appropriate to require the deferral to end upon the liquidation of the corporation, when the assets leave corporate solution.

In addition, the deferral of the shareholder level tax is analogous to the deferral permitted under the bill when a shareholder receives qualifying consideration.

Some thought was also given to a relief proposal in an in-kind liquidation that would permit both the shareholder *and* corporate level taxes to be deferred or avoided. It was noted by several witnesses that a shareholder, who organizes a corporation tax-free under section 351 by mistake and then chooses to liquidate the corporation, should be permitted to defer or avoid both the corporate and shareholder level taxes. This was viewed as particularly appealing in the case where the appreciation in the corporate assets occurred prior to the formation of the corporation—i.e., while the assets were held by the individual shareholder. Under this view, the "disincorporation" transaction should be permitted to be tax-free in the same way that an incorporation transaction is tax-free under section 351.

The potential discontinuity with the treatment under section 351 was a matter of some concern. But ultimately, it was determined that to the extent a discontinuity between incorporation and liquidation transactions exists, it is a problem created by section 351 and not by the proposed rules for an in-kind liquidation.

Section 351 arguably serves the policy goal of facilitating the formation of corporations. More importantly, that policy goal is achievable under section 351 with little or no tax avoidance potential. An individual who forms a corporation with appreciated property is moving that property from a potential "one-tax" system to a potential "two-tax" system. Therefore, permitting that individual to defer tax on the gain that would otherwise be recognized in the incorporation transaction will almost assuredly be a true deferral and not an exemption; indeed, the pre-incorporation appreciation may be taxed twice, not once, as a result of the act of incorporation.

The same cannot be said for a liquidation in kind. Arguably, it might be appropriate from a policy standpoint to facilitate certain "disincorporation" transactions by providing tax-free or tax-deferred treatment similar to section 351. But any such relief would be fraught with tax avoidance possibilities. Here, in contrast to section 351, the assets are moving from a potential "two-tax" system to, at most, a potential "one-tax" system. Thus, any "deferrals" permitted at the time of the liquidation may well result in complete exemptions. Possibilities of that sort might well necessitate certain of the complex anti-tax avoidance provisions of current law that are proposed to be eliminated by the bill.

L., S., L. & R. Corp. Tax. 3rd Ed. UCB—17

Finally, a proposal to defer or exempt both the shareholder and corporate level taxes raised a number of unresolved issues with no clear policy direction. For example, should any such relief be limited to a short-term "mistake" case described above, or should it be available only where the shareholders have held the stock for some extended period of time, as was suggested by one witness? Should the relief be limited to built-in gains at the time of the incorporation transaction, or should it be extended to all corporate-level gains, whether they arose before or after the formation of the corporation? Finally, should any such relief be conditioned upon the elimination of a death step-up under section 1014, as was suggested by the Treasury Department? These and other issues raised significant problems of added complexity and potential uncertainty.

Another form of relief provided under the bill is the special election for goodwill and other unamortizable intangibles. Thus, at the election of the taxpayer, the corporate level tax burden of a cost basis election would not include any tax on the appreciation of such intangibles. This relief would not be inconsistent with the repeal of *General Utilities* because the acquiring party would be required to obtain a carryover basis in the intangibles.

A third form of relief is available under Subchapter S. Under current law, a C corporation with appreciated assets may be able to elect S corporation status and thereby avoid the corporate level tax on the appreciation. The bill would limit that possibility by generally not permitting an increase to a shareholder's stock basis in the case of gain (other than gain on long-held capital assets) recognized by the corporation which is attributable to periods when the corporation was a C corporation.[177] (This would have the effect of maintaining a potential "double tax" on gain (other than gain on long-held capital assets) arising when the corporation was a C corporation.) However, the S corporation modifications do not apply to corporations with a fair market value of $1 million or less, and apply only with limited impact to corporations under $2 million in value. This proposal, in combination with the shareholder credit proposal, should permit maximum flexibility in providing shareholder relief to small corporations.

A final form of relief provided is transitional relief. Although it was believed the existence of permanent relief would eliminate much of the need for transitional relief, it seemed appropriate to provide a specific prospective period of time during which businesses and investors could adjust to the new rules. Accordingly, the bill will not be effective any earlier than January 1, 1986.

Two other forms of relief are not specifically included in the bill, but are recommended, contingent upon certain other factors. First, in

---

177. The actual proposal permits an increase in stock basis to reflect the taxable portion of the gain. Thus, a tax-free distribution could be made by the S corporation to its shareholders to enable the shareholders to pay the pass-through tax on the corporate-level gain. Distributions in excess of that, however, would be taxable to the shareholders.

its November, 1984 Report to the President, the Treasury Department recommended an across-the-board 50 percent dividends paid deduction for all corporations. If that proposal, as well as the additional Treasury proposal to eliminate the capital gains preference, is enacted, it is recommended that the same relief should be considered in the case of liquidating distributions. The basis adjustment proposal could then be repealed if this relief were provided.

Second, to the extent necessary to keep this bill revenue-neutral, it is recommended that consideration be given to an across-the-board reduction of the corporate capital gains tax rate.

CHAPTER 8. COLLAPSIBLE CORPORATIONS *

A. INTRODUCTION

Code: § 341(a).

Regulations: § 1.341–1.

A shareholder who holds corporate stock as a capital asset recognizes capital gain or loss on a sale or exchange of the stock or a complete liquidation of the corporation.[1] Prior to the Tax Reform Act of 1986, long-term capital gains were taxed at only 40 percent of the rate imposed on ordinary income. Moreover, during the command of *General Utilities*, a corporation generally recognized no gain or loss on distributions in complete liquidation irrespective of the character of its assets unless one of the statutory or judicial exceptions to the pre-1987 nonrecognition rule applied.[2] As under current law, the shareholders took a fair market value basis under Section 334(a) in any assets distributed in a complete liquidation. This combination of nonrecognition at the corporate level, capital gain at the shareholder level and a stepped-up basis for the shareholders offered a tempting opportunity to convert ordinary income to capital gain through a device historically known as a collapsible corporation.

The essence of this tax avoidance strategy was captured by Judge Wisdom of the Fifth Circuit when he characterized the collapsible corporation as a "brain child of resourceful tax advisers to the motion picture industries" who used "corporate trappings * * * to cloak a single venture or short-term project with the appearance of a long-term investment." [3] A 1983 Congressional study on the reform and simplification of Subchapter C elaborated on the glamorous Hollywood origins of the collapsible corporation by describing the prototype transaction as follows: [4]

> In one form of transaction a corporation would be formed to produce a movie. The principal actors, producer, and director, among others, would receive stock of the corporation rather than any salaries they might earn or any share of the royalties received from the exhibition of the movie. After completion of production, a sale of the shares would be made to the studio

---

* See generally, Ginsburg, "Collapsible Corporations—Revisiting An Old Misfortune," 33 Tax L.Rev. 307 (1978).

1. I.R.C. §§ 331(a); 1001(a).

2. The pre-1987 version of Section 336 permitted nonrecognition on distributions of certain ordinary income assets, such as inventory. See Chapter 7B, supra.

3. Commissioner v. Kelley, 293 F.2d 904, 907–08 (5th Cir.1961), acq. 1972–1 C.B. 2.

4. Staff of the Senate Finance Committee, Preliminary Report on the Reform and Simplification of the Income Taxation of Corporations, 98th Cong., 1st Sess. 17 (Comm. Print S. 98–95, 1983) (footnote omitted).

434

which would cause the corporation to liquidate tax free and then distribute the movie to theaters. The actors and others would recognize capital gain on the sale of the stock, thus converting ordinary income into capital gain. Because the corporation would not recognize gain on the distribution of its assets in liquidation [under pre-1987 law. Ed.] the corporation could be promptly liquidated after the shares had been sold by the actors and others.

The fame of the collapsible corporation quickly spread to the real estate industry. To illustrate another classic abuse transaction, consider the opportunity that was available to Developer, who wished to acquire and subdivide a valuable tract of land and then construct and sell 100 homes. Developer, well aware that he would recognize ordinary income on the sale of the homes, formed Collapse, Inc. to carry out the project. He capitalized the corporation with $1 million cash to finance the acquisition of the land and the construction of the homes. Two years later, when the completed homes were worth $4 million and ready to be sold, Developer caused Collapse to liquidate. The corporation recognized no gain on the distribution of the highly appreciated homes in the complete liquidation, and Developer recognized $3 million of long-term capital gain and took a $4 million basis in the homes, which he could proceed to sell for their fair market value without recognizing any additional gain.

After unsuccessfully attempting to attack this device in the courts,[5] the Treasury turned to Congress for statutory relief.[6] The resulting legislation—now Section 341—blocks this conversion technique by requiring a shareholder of a "collapsible corporation", who otherwise might recognize capital gain, to treat any gain as ordinary income on the sale or exchange of stock, on distributions in complete or partial liquidation, or on nonliquidating distributions in excess of earnings and profits that normally are treated as gain from the sale of the stock under Section 301(c)(3)(A).[7] Applying these rules to the historical

---

5. Prior to the enactment of the 1939 Code predecessor of Section 341, the Service unsuccessfully contended that the collapsible corporation gambit was a sham that also violated the assignment of income and other judicially created doctrines. See Herbert v. Riddell, 103 F.Supp. 369 (S.D. Cal.1952); Jacobs v. Commissioner, 21 T.C. 165 (1953); O'Brien v. Commissioner, 25 T.C. 376 (1955), acq. in part 1957–1 C.B. 4.

6. See H.Rep. No. 2319, 81st Cong., 2d Sess., reprinted in 1950–2 C.B. 380, 423.

7. Congress included sales in addition to liquidations and certain other distributions to preclude a clever shareholder from simply selling his stock to a third party and reporting capital gain, leaving the purchaser with a basis in his stock roughly equal to the net worth of the corporation. In that event, neither the corporation nor

the purchaser would have any significant tax exposure on a subsequent liquidation. A notable exception from the list of transactions encompassed by Section 341 is a redemption (other than a partial liquidation) taxable as an exchange under Section 302(a) or 303. This omission may have been an oversight. In the unlikely event that such a transaction serves as a "collapse" event, a court might be willing to apply Section 341(a) by treating the transaction as a sale or exchange. But see Reg. § 1.341–1, which requires an "actual" sale or exchange. In addition to the "collapse" events listed in Section 341(a), a collapsible corporation did not qualify for nonrecognition of gain on a sale of its assets under former Section 337. I.R.C. §§ 337(c)(1)(A) (pre-1987).

illustration above, Collapse, Inc. still could liquidate tax-free before 1987, but Section 341 would require Developer to report $3 million of ordinary income (the difference between the $4 million value of the homes received in the complete liquidation and Developer's $1 million basis in the Collapse, Inc. stock).[8]

The most aggressive planning strategies for the use of a collapsible corporation, such as those illustrated above, depended on the existence of both a preferential rate on long-term capital gains and a corporation's ability to liquidate or sell property without recognizing gain. In the prior example, if Developer's capital gain had been taxed at even a slightly lower rate than the rate on ordinary income, the conversion of $3 million from ordinary income to capital gain would produce substantial tax savings.[9] But if Collapse had been taxable on its gain on a liquidating sale or distribution (as under current law) the total tax imposed on the transaction even with the help of a capital gains preference would have exceeded the tax imposed if Developer had conducted his business as a sole proprietor.[10]

The necessary ingredients for a useful collapsible corporation strategy are missing from current law. The capital gains preference today is modest and the rules which formerly permitted corporations to avoid recognition of gain on liquidating distributions and sales were repealed by the Tax Reform Act of 1986. But Congress could not bring itself to bid farewell to Section 341. Instead of repealing the section, Congress amended it to conform technically with the other 1986 changes.[11] You may, at this juncture, ask yourself "Why?" Indeed, the authors and other more distinguished commentators have asked the same question. One observer has stated that Section 341 is now "almost a dead letter" [12] and others have suggested that "the continued need for this provision is dubious at best." [13]

And so we ponder the retention of Section 341 in the Code (and the continuing need for this chapter). The continued presence of Section 341 perhaps can best be explained as evidence of Congressional caution over the current instability of the rate structure. Restoration of a significant capital gains preference may be just over the next legislative horizon and advocates of a permanent nonrecognition exception on liquidating distributions and sales may yet prevail. Thus, Congress

---

8. I.R.C. § 341(a)(2)(A).

9. In general, long-term capital gains recognized by individuals receive a three percent rate preference under the current structure. See I.R.C. § 1(h)(1). Disregarding the impact of a corporate-level tax on Collapse, the rate preference saves Developer $90,000. In addition, capital losses are fully deductible against capital gains, but their deductibility is limited against ordinary income. I.R.C. § 1211(b). See Chapter 1A2, supra.

10. Focusing on the generally applicable top rates, the combination of a 34 percent corporate-level tax and 28 percent shareholder-level capital gains tax will greatly exceed the 31 percent tax that Developer would pay as a sole proprietor.

11. See Tax Reform Act of 1986, P.L. 99–514, 99th Cong., 2d Sess. § 631(e)(6)(A).

12. Wolfman, "Subchapter C and the 100th Congress," 33 Tax Notes 669, 670 (Nov. 17, 1986).

13. Eustice et al., The Tax Reform Act of 1986 (1987).

may view Section 341 as a backstop in an unsettled period of tax change.[14] So while the study of Section 341 may appear to be a fruitless exercise at the moment, the restoration of a small capital gains preference in 1991 may have resuscitated the collapsible corporation and future legislative developments may remove it from the endangered species list. Only that perspective will sustain you through the examination of Section 341 that follows in this chapter.

Unfortunately, this simple description of the disease, its intended cure and its minimal relevance does not begin to explain the operation of the collapsible corporation rules. True to its Hollywood origins, Section 341 is a statute of epic proportions that generally is regarded as one of the most complex provisions in the Internal Revenue Code. The definition of a collapsible corporation requires a subjective analysis of the shareholders' purpose, and the statute is laden with highly technical exceptions. One famous sentence in Section 341(e) is nearly twice as long as the Gettysburg Address. This chapter is intended to provide an overview, focusing first on definitional matters and then turning to a general description of the major statutory exceptions.

B. DEFINITION OF A COLLAPSIBLE CORPORATION

Code: § 341(b), (c).

Regulations: §§ 1.341–2, –3, –5.

Collapsible corporations are defined by reference to the purpose for both the formation or utilization of the corporation and the ultimate disposition of the venture. In general, the statute seeks to identify corporations holding a disproportionate amount of appreciated ordinary income property and whose shareholders are using the corporate entity as a vehicle to convert ordinary income to long-term capital gain before the corporation realizes a substantial share of its profits.

More specifically, Section 341(b)(1) generally defines a collapsible corporation as a corporation that is formed or availed of:

(1) principally for the manufacture, construction or production of property, or for the purchase of "Section 341 assets" (defined to include certain ordinary income assets and most types of Section 1231 depreciable business property); and

(2) with a view to (a) a sale of the stock, or a liquidation or distribution before the corporation realizes two-thirds of the taxable income to be derived from the property and (b) a realization by the shareholders of the gain attributable to the property.

This cumbersome definition consists of several elements, each of which requires more detailed explanation.

---

14. It is not as if Congress never considered repeal. The Senate Finance Committee staff's 1985 report on reform of Subchapter C recommended repeal of Section 341 (along with repeal of the *General Utili-* *ties* doctrine). See Staff of the Joint Committee on Taxation, The Subchapter C Revision Act of 1985: A Final Report Prepared by the Staff, 99th Cong., 1st Sess. 53 (S. Prt. 99–47, 1985).

Formed or availed of for the production of property or the purchase of Section 341 assets. The definition of a collapsible corporation begins with the requirement that the corporation must be formed or availed of principally for the manufacture, construction or production of property or the purchase of "Section 341 assets." It is important to note that this requirement is satisfied if the corporation is "availed of" for the proscribed purpose. The fact that a corporation may have been formed long ago will not necessarily immunize it from collapsible status.[1]

If a corporation engages principally in the manufacture or production of property, it normally would realize ordinary income on the sale of the property because its product generally will constitute inventory or property held primarily for sale to customers. It therefore is appropriate for Section 341 to patrol the corporation's activities to prevent the conversion of this ordinary income to shareholder capital gain. But since a corporation need not manufacture or produce property in order to hold ordinary income assets, the definition of a collapsible corporation also includes corporations formed or availed of principally for the purchase of "Section 341 assets."[2] Section 341 assets are defined as property held for less than three years which is stock in trade, inventory, property held primarily for sale to customers, unrealized receivables or fees, or Section 1231(b) property (without regard to holding period) that is not used in connection with the manufacture, construction, production or sale of the previously designated categories of ordinary income assets.[3] The inclusion of Section 1231 property in the definition of Section 341 assets is curious because gain on the sale of these assets normally is capital gain.[4] It has been suggested that Section 1231 property was included to prevent dealers from converting ordinary income on rental real estate to capital gain by separately incorporating each property.[5] Whatever the rationale, this provision may have the surprising effect of converting gain that would have been capital gain if recognized by the shareholder into ordinary income.[6]

Section 341(b)(2) expands the web of Section 341 by providing that a corporation will be deemed to have manufactured, constructed, produced or purchased property if it engaged in those activities "to any extent."[7] A corporation also may be collapsible if it: (1) holds property having a basis determined in whole or part by reference to the cost of the property in the hands of the person who manufactured, constructed,

---

1. But see Rev.Proc. 84–22, 1984–1 C.B. 680, providing that the Service will issue a favorable ruling on collapsible status if the corporation has been in existence for 20 years, not more than 10 percent of its stock has changed hands and it has conducted substantially the same business for the 20 year period. The Service otherwise will not rule on collapsible status. Id.

2. I.R.C. § 341(b)(1).

3. I.R.C. § 341(b)(3).

4. See I.R.C. § 1231(a)(1). This assumes the asset has been held for more than one

year. I.R.C. § 1231(b). Section 1231(c), however, characterizes net Section 1231 gain as ordinary income to the extent such gain does not exceed nonrecaptured net Section 1231 losses.

5. Bittker & Eustice, Federal Income Taxation of Corporations and Shareholders ¶ 12.03 (5th ed. 1987).

6. But see I.R.C. § 341(e), discussed in Section C2 of this chapter, for a complex relief provision for investors.

7. I.R.C. § 341(b)(2)(A).

produced or purchased it, or (2) holds property with a basis determined in whole or part by reference to the cost of property manufactured, constructed, produced or purchased by the corporation.[8] These provisions are designed to prevent avoidance of Section 341 through nonrecognition exchanges under provisions such as Sections 351 and 1031. Section 341(b)(1) also prevents easy avoidance by providing that a holding company is collapsible if it was formed or availed of principally to hold the stock of a collapsible corporation.

With a "view" to a "collapse" event. In order to be collapsible, a corporation also must be formed or availed of with a "view" to a sale, liquidation or distribution before the corporation has a realized two-thirds of the taxable income from its property. It is not necessary for the proscribed view to be clearly present at the outset of the venture. The regulations provide that the requisite view exists if, during the production or purchase of property, persons in a position to determine corporate policies contemplated or recognized the possibility of a collapse event.[9] This is an extremely expansive standard which raises the specter of collapsibility for a large number of corporations. Moreover, if controlling shareholders had the requisite view, the corporation will be collapsible as to all shareholders, including those who were not shareholders when the property was produced or purchased and those who did not share in the view.[10]

Before realization by the corporation of two-thirds of the taxable income to be derived from the property. To avoid collapsibility, a corporation may realize [11] two-thirds of the taxable income to be derived from its produced or purchased assets.[12] Thus, if a corporation's only asset is a constructed real estate development project with a cost basis of $70,000 and a fair market value of $100,000, the venture will lose its collapsible status if the corporation sells off enough of the project to realize $20,000 of the $30,000 of potential income in the property. The Code does not make clear whether the corporation must realize a total of two-thirds of all of the taxable income to be derived from a combination of all property ever produced or purchased, or two-thirds of the taxable income to be derived from each separate property. The regulations, however, explain that a corporation has to recognize a substantial part (now two-thirds) of the taxable income to be derived from each

8. I.R.C. § 341(b)(2)(B), (C).

9. Reg. § 1.341–2(a)(2), (3).

10. Reg. § 1.341–2(a)(2). Section 341 will not apply, however, if a sale or liquidation is caused by unforeseen circumstances such as the illness of a shareholder. See Reg. § 1.341–5(d) Example (3).

11. Although the statute refers to "realization," it has been construed to require recognition. Manassas Airport Industrial Park, Inc. v. Commissioner, 66 T.C. 566 (1976), affirmed per curiam 557 F.2d 1113 (4th Cir.1977).

12. I.R.C. § 341(b)(1)(A). Prior to 1984, a corporation could avoid collapsible status if it realized a "substantial" part of its taxable income from each of its produced or purchased properties. Some courts held that realization of one-third of the potential taxable income was "substantial," and the Service agreed. See Commissioner v. Kelley, 293 F.2d 904 (5th Cir.1961); Rev. Rul. 72–48, 1972–1 C.B. 102. The 1984 Act, by imposing a two-thirds realization requirement, significantly tightens Section 341.

property in order to escape the collapsible taint.[13] In making this determination, the regulations contemplate the possibility of dividing the corporation's properties into separate integrated projects. Unless two-thirds of the taxable income on each separate project has been recognized, the corporation, if it meets the remaining requirements of Section 341(b), is collapsible.

There is one exception to the requirement that income from each project be recognized. If the amount of unrealized income in one property is "not substantial" in relation to the income realized from all properties, the corporation is not collapsible.[14]

Precisely how properties are divided into separate projects is not entirely clear. For example, the regulations determine without analysis that two office buildings built in different years constitute separate properties.[15] They also conclude that individual motion pictures are treated as separate properties.[16] If the corporation's property consists of inventory or of property held primarily for sale to customers in the ordinary course of business, the regulations appear to view the sales business as a single venture, so that past sales as well as current inventory are taken into account in determining whether two-thirds of the potential income from the venture has been realized. Although the regulations are not explicit, they reach the same result by providing that if a corporation dealing with inventory type goods has current inventory which is normal in amount and has a substantial prior business history, it is not collapsible.[17]

Gain Attributable to a Collapsible Project. In order for a corporation to be collapsible, not only must it possess at least one collapsible property, but the shareholders must realize gain attributable to that property on a sale or exchange of their stock or a distribution. If the shareholders recognize *any* gain and if the collapsible property has appreciated in value while the shareholders have held the stock, at least some of the gain will be attributable to the collapsible property. However, if the collapsible projects did not appreciate while the shareholders held their stock, none of their gain is attributable to the collapsible property, and Section 341(a) will not apply.

Section 341(c) Presumption of Collapsibility. Section 341(c) creates a rebuttable presumption of collapsibility if the fair market value of a corporation's Section 341 assets (that is, property held less than three years which is inventory type property, unrealized receivables or certain Section 1231 assets) is at least 50 percent of the fair market value of its total assets and 120 percent of the adjusted basis of the Section 341 assets. Cash, stock, and debt obligations which are capital assets are not counted in determining the corporation's total assets for this purpose.

13.   Reg. §§ 1.341–2(a)(4), –5(b)(5).

14.   Reg. § 1.341–5(c)(2), –5(d) Example (4).

15.   Reg. § 1.341–5(d) Example (2).

16.   Reg. § 1.341–5(d) Example (4).

17.   Reg. § 1.341–5(c)(1).

This presumption apparently is based on the notion that if the appreciation on a corporation's recently constructed or acquired assets is substantial, the corporation should be presumed to be collapsible and bear the burden of proving otherwise. In view of the fact that there is normally a presumption of correctness accompanying the Commissioner's assertion of a tax deficiency, this presumption has limited significance. Section 341(c) also expressly provides that avoidance of the presumption does not give rise to a presumption that the corporation is not collapsible.

PROBLEMS

Developer, who is actively engaged in the real estate development business, organizes Tract Corporation to subdivide and develop real estate. Developer transfers three parcels of undeveloped real estate (basis—$75,000 each) to Tract in exchange for all of Tract's outstanding stock. Tract develops each parcel in separate projects by subdividing and building houses for sale. After completion of the projects, each parcel has a fair market value of $500,000 and has a basis of $100,000.

(a) What result if Developer sells her Tract stock to Entrepreneur for $1,500,000?

(b) What result to Developer and Tract if Tract liquidates by distributing all of its assets to Developer?

(c) Assuming Developer sells her Tract stock, would Tract be collapsible under the following alternatives:

    (i) Tract had not developed the projects but had purchased the already developed properties last year for $300,000 each, intending to sell the 5 houses on each project individually for $100,000 each? The projects are currently worth $500,000 each.

    (ii) What result in (i), above, if Tract had purchased the developed projects four years ago?

    (iii) What result in (i), above, if Tract had already sold four houses in each project for $100,000 each?

C. EXCEPTIONS TO SECTION 341(a)

Sections 341(a) and (b) are so broad in scope and application that, if unchecked, they would convert shareholder capital gain to ordinary income in many circumstances where such a result would be unwarranted. Consequently, Sections 341(d), (e) and (f), provide exceptions that enable a corporation (or some or all of its shareholders) to avoid collapsible treatment if certain intricate requirements are met.

1. SECTION 341(d)

Code: § 341(d).

Regulation: § 1.341–4.

Section 341(d) does not remove a corporation from collapsible status (e.g., as to shareholders who do not qualify for relief under Section

341(d)), but it does permit certain shareholders to recognize capital gain on dispositions of their stock or otherwise tainted distributions. Section 341(d) provides three separate escape hatches, each of which addresses a particular aspect of the definition of a collapsible corporation in Section 341(b).

Five Percent Rule. We have seen that a corporation may be collapsible if the controlling shareholders have the requisite view to collapse. Moreover, if a corporation is collapsible, *all* shareholders, including innocent minority shareholders, suffer the punishment of Section 341(a) regardless of whether they ever intended or foresaw the possibility of collapsing the corporation. To provide relief in this situation, Section 341(d)(1) provides that Section 341(a) will not apply to any shareholder who has not owned, directly or through attribution, more than five percent in value of the corporation's outstanding shares at the commencement of the manufacture, construction or production of the collapsible property, at the time when Section 341 assets are purchased or at any time thereafter.

70:30 Rule. We also have seen that a corporation can be collapsible even if it has just one collapsible property and only a small part of the shareholder's gain is attributable to that property. In response to this possible overreaching of 341(b), Section 341(d)(2) exempts a shareholder of an otherwise collapsible corporation from ordinary income treatment unless more than 70 percent of the shareholder's gain recognized during the year is attributable to collapsible property. To apply Section 341(d)(2), one first must determine the shareholder's total gain recognized and then determine the amount of gain the shareholder would have recognized had the corporation not produced or purchased any of the collapsible property which it had on hand at the time of the collapse event.[1] If the latter figure is at least 30 percent of the total, the shareholder is protected. Thus, if at least 30 percent of the appreciation which has occurred during the shareholder's holding period is attributable to appreciation in projects or ventures which are (a) capital assets, (b) projects purchased more than three years ago, (c) purchased or manufactured projects on which at least two-thirds of the potential taxable income has been recognized,[2] or (d) Section 1231 property used in the manufacturing process, or any combination of the above, the shareholder will not be subject to Section 341(a).

Three-year rule. Section 341(d)(3) exempts from Section 341(a) any gain realized by a shareholder that is attributable to collapsible property held by the corporation for more than three years from the completion of its production or purchase. Thus, if all of the corporation's

---

1. Reg. § 1.341–4(c)(2).

2. Section 341(d) gives the Secretary authority to draft regulations treating all dealer property as a single item for purposes of determining whether projects are rendered noncollapsible by recognition of two-thirds of the potential gain. Thus, if a corporation has two separate but equal housing developments and has recognized 68 percent of its potential gain on one and 50 percent of its potential gain on the other, they would be aggregated and treated as a single, still collapsible, project.

collapsible properties have been held more than three years, none of the shareholder's gain will be tainted by Section 341(a). If some collapsible properties have been held less than three years, only the gain attributed to those properties will be ordinary income.[3]

2.   SECTION 341(e)

Code: § 341(e).

The complexity of this exception is immediately apparent from the infamous Section 341(e)(1), which reputedly is the Code's longest single sentence, if not its most inscrutable. Section 341(e) excuses shareholders from collapsible treatment where the potential amount of income that could be converted from corporate ordinary income to shareholder capital gain is small in comparison to the total net worth of the corporation. Where Section 341(e) applies to an otherwise collapsible corporation, shareholders will receive capital gain treatment on a sale of their stock.

In general, Section 341(e) is applicable as long as the net unrealized ordinary income inherent in the corporation's assets does not exceed 15 percent of the corporation's net worth. If Section 341(e) were that broad, however, an individual still could easily convert ordinary income to capital gain by (1) transferring inventory or dealer property via Section 351 to a corporation which is not a dealer and which holds the property as a capital asset or Section 1231 asset (and therefore has *no* unrealized ordinary income), and then (2) selling the stock to a third party and realizing a capital gain. To prevent this abuse, Section 341(e) looks to the character of assets, ordinary or capital, in the hands of the *shareholders* as well as to the character of those assets to the corporation itself. As a result, the application of Section 341(e) actually depends on the net appreciation in its "subsection (e) assets," not on the net appreciation in the corporation's ordinary income assets. Section 341(e)(5) defines "subsection (e) assets" as:

(1) All property (except Section 1231(b) property) which would produce ordinary income (other than certain recapture income) if sold by the corporation or by any 20 percent shareholder (using attribution rules);[4]

(2) All Section 1231(b) assets (regardless of holding period) if the total bases of all such assets exceeds their total fair market value (i.e., if a sale of all such assets in a single year would result in ordinary gains and losses under the workings of Section 1231);[5]

(3) If category (2), above, is inapplicable, only the Section 1231(b) assets which would produce ordinary income (other than recapture) if sold by any 20 percent shareholder (i.e., Section 1231(b)

3. Reg. § 1.341–4(d).

4. I.R.C. § 341(e)(5)(A)(i), (10), (12). The status of property as "property used in a trade or business" under Section 1231(b) is determined without regard to holding period. I.R.C. § 341(e)(9).

5. I.R.C. § 341(e)(5)(A)(ii); (6)(B), (C); (9).

property which has been held less than six months or which would be dealer property in the hands of any 20 percent shareholder using attribution rules);[6]

(4) Copyrights and other compositions that would not be capital assets under Section 1221(3) in the hands of the corporation or any 5 percent shareholder (using attribution rules).[7]

The definition of subsection (e) assets, however, may be expanded in Section 341(e)(1) for certain shareholders, depending on the shareholder's percentage of stock ownership and on his status as a dealer of property. If the shareholder owns more than 5 percent and not more than 20 percent of the value of outstanding stock, then for purposes of applying Section 341(e)(1) to that shareholder, subsection (e) assets include any assets not already specifically included by Section 341(e)(5) which would be dealer property or inventory in the shareholder's hands. If the shareholder owns more than 20 percent of the value of outstanding stock, then subsection (e)(1) is applied as above, but for purposes of determining whether the 20 percent shareholder is a dealer (so that assets would produce ordinary income if sold by "any 20 percent shareholder", including himself) the shareholder is treated as having made sales made in fact by other corporations in which the shareholder owns more than 20 percent in value of the outstanding stock.[8] This provision precludes the more than 20 percent shareholder who would be a dealer from converting ordinary income into capital gains by putting each asset in a separate corporation so that neither the shareholder nor any corporation reaches dealer status.

3. SECTION 341(f)

Code: § 341(f).

Section 341(f) permits a shareholder to avoid ordinary income treatment on a sale of stock of an otherwise collapsible corporation if the corporation consents to recognize the gain on any disposition (including transactions which would qualify for nonrecognition under provisions such as Sections 1031 and 1033) of a "subsection (f) asset." Subsection (f) assets are defined as assets which, on the date of the shareholder's stock sale, are owned by the consenting corporation (or subject to a purchase option) and are not capital assets.[9] Land or any interest in real property, other than a security interest, also constitutes a subsection (f) asset. A Section 341 consent protects stock sales made within six months of the day on which the consent is filed, and there is no limit to the number of Section 341(f) consents that may be filed. The Section 341(f) consent is binding on the consenting corporation even if the shareholder's stock sale would not have produced ordinary

---

6. I.R.C. § 341(e)(5)(A)(iii), (6)(A), (9), (10).

7. I.R.C. § 341(e)(5)(iv), (10).

8. I.R.C. § 341(e)(1)(C)(i) also treats certain stock sales in such corporations as a

sale of exchange by the shareholder of his proportionate share of the corporation's assets.

9. I.R.C. § 341(f)(4)(A).

income because of Section 341(d), Section 341(e) or because the corporation was not collapsible.

The purpose of Section 341(f) is to permit shareholders of a rapidly growing company with substantially appreciated assets to sell their stock without the threat of ordinary income.[10] Its rationale is (was?) that the shareholders should be entitled to recognize capital gain if the corporation promises to recognize gain (but not loss) on the disposition of its assets, regardless of whether the corporate recognition occurs before or after the shareholder's sale. In keeping with that principle, Section 341(f)(3) provides an exception from the corporate recognition rule for certain intercorporate exchanges of subsection (f) assets which result in a carryover basis (such as Section 351 exchanges, reorganizations and liquidations governed by Section 332) if the corporate-transferee is not a tax-exempt organization and agrees to recognize its gain on a subsequent disposition of the property.

One final point should be made concerning Section 341(f). In the post-1986 tax reform world, a corporation seldom can avoid recognition of its gain when it disposes of property. Thus, a Section 341(f) consent is a relatively painless way of ensuring that a shareholder will recognize capital gain rather than ordinary income. Among the few corporate transactions which might lose their nonrecognition status as a result of a Section 341(f) consent are like-kind exchanges of subsection (f) assets.

PROBLEMS

1. Collapse Corporation has three tracts of developed real estate. Each tract contains 10 homes (basis $70,000, fair market value $100,000 for each home). Collapse also has undeveloped land held as an investment which, in the future, it may decide to trade for other investment real estate. The land has a basis of $700,000 and a value of $1,000,000. Collapse is and always has been owned by A (890 shares), B (100 shares) and C (10 shares). Each shareholder has a $2,800 per share basis in the Collapse stock.

    (a) What result if each shareholder sells ten shares for $40,000? (For convenience, ignore the fact that the buyer likely would pay less than $4,000 per share because of the tax liability Collapse will incur when it disposes of its assets.)

    (b) In (a), above, assume A and B do not wish to recognize ordinary income. Which, if any, of the following alternatives will permit them to recognize capital gain?

        (i) A and B wait four years before selling their stock.

        (ii) Collapse sells three homes from tract one this year for $300,000 and the shareholders sell their stock next year for $4,000 per share.

10. S.Rep. No. 1241, 88th Cong., 2d Sess. 2 (1964), reprinted in 1964–2 C.B. 685–86.

      (iii) Collapse files a Section 341(f) consent. Are there any potential adverse tax consequences from filing a consent?

    2. Hi Rise Corporation's only asset is an apartment building (basis $100,000, fair market value $1,500,000) which it purchased last year and rented out to tenants. You represent some of the owners: A (who owns 50 shares, basis $50,000); B (who owns 20 shares, basis $20,000); and C (who owns 5 shares, basis $5,000). The remaining 25 shares are owned by 25 individuals. A, B and C sell their stock. What result if:

    (a) only A is a dealer in buildings?

    (b) only B is a dealer?

    (c) only C is a dealer?

CHAPTER 9. PREVENTING THE IMPROPER RETENTION OF CORPORATE EARNINGS

A. INTRODUCTION

A maximum corporate income tax rate (34%) that exceeds the top individual rate (31%) is a relatively recent phenomenon.[1] For most of our income tax history, the graduated rates applicable to individuals have greatly exceeded the essentially flat corporate rates. During the 1950's, the top corporate rate was roughly 50 percent while individuals were taxed at rates ranging up to 88 percent. As recently as 1981, there was a considerable spread between the 46 percent top corporate rate and the 70 percent marginal rate applicable to the unearned income of wealthy individuals.[2] This historical rate gap provided an incentive for taxpayers to accumulate business profits or investment income in a corporation. As Professors Bittker and Eustice have said, "use of a corporation as a temporary or permanent refuge from individual income tax rates has been one of the principal landmarks of our tax landscape."[3]

Quite apart from these rate differentials, we have seen in virtually every preceding chapter that the double tax on corporate earnings is at the heart of Subchapter C. A large number of tax advisors have become insomniacs devising strategies to minimize the bite of this double tax regime and, in the process, avoid the impact of the individual rates. The Treasury has responded with an arsenal of weapons to reclassify certain corporate distributions as dividends[4] and, as we are about to see, to encourage corporations to distribute earnings not required for business needs in the form of dividends.

To illustrate a typical accumulation plan that would invite the tax collector's scrutiny, consider the goals of Accumulator ("A"), a sole proprietor with a profitable business in the days of the 70 percent

---

1. Compare I.R.C. § 1 with I.R.C. § 11. An individual taxpayer's marginal rate may exceed 31 percent as a result of the phaseout of personal exemptions and limitation on itemized deductions applicable to high-income individuals. See I.R.C. §§ 151(d)(3); 68.

2. Personal service income, however, was taxed at a maximum rate of 50 percent. I.R.C. § 1348 (pre-1982). The maximum tax on personal service income, which was enacted in 1969, reduced the differential between individual and corporate tax rates and the attractiveness of certain accumulation strategies.

3. Bittker & Eustice, Federal Income Taxation of Corporations and Shareholders ¶ 1.02 (5th ed. 1987).

4. Prime examples are the Treasury's attempts to reclassify purported debt instruments as equity, thereby converting deductible "interest" into nondeductible dividends. See Chapter 3A, supra. Other weapons include Section 304, which applies to redemptions through the use of related corporations and Section 306, which is the Congressional response to the preferred stock bailout. Insofar as these weapons were aimed at preventing bailouts of corporate earnings at capital gains rates, their importance will diminish as long as capital gains and ordinary income are taxed at the same rate.

individual marginal rates. Tempted by the allure of the lower corporate tax, A incorporates his business with a healthy (but permissible) dose of debt and pays himself a hefty (but reasonable) salary. His personal consumption needs are fully satisfied by the salary, the interest payments on the debt and as many nontaxable fringe benefits as the corporation can legally provide. Any additional profits from the business are left to accumulate in the corporation, where they work to increase the value of A's stock. If A needs more funds or later wishes to retire, he can "cash in" on his accumulated profits by selling some stock or liquidating the company. In either case, this historically enabled A to reap the benefits of favorable capital gains rates. Even today, with only a modest capital gains rate preference, a sale or liquidation also benefits A by allowing him to recover his stock basis before reporting any gain. An even more attractive alternative would be to avoid entirely the individual income tax by holding the stock until death, when A's heirs would be entitled to a stepped-up basis under Section 1014. Or A might dispose of the business in a tax-free reorganization, emerging with publicly traded stock, albeit with a low substituted basis, which could be sold or held until A's death.[5]

To curtail these accumulation strategies and the related use of a corporation as a receptacle for investment and personal service income, Congress first enacted the accumulated earnings tax and later the personal holding company tax. Both levies have served as protectors of the graduated individual income tax rates. The accumulated earnings tax is intended to prevent the use of a corporation to escape the individual income tax by an unreasonable accumulation of earnings. Although not part of its original design, it also serves the broader (and still relevant) purpose of inducing corporations to pay dividends and subject their earnings to the double tax when those profits are not required for the reasonable needs of the business.[6] The personal holding company tax is intended to prevent the use of so-called "incorporated pocketbooks" to avoid the graduated individual rates applicable to investment and personal service income. Both taxes are penalties that must be paid by the offending corporations in addition to their regular tax. To avoid overlap, corporations classified as personal holding companies are not subject to the accumulated earnings tax.[7]

Now that the corporate income tax rates exceed the individual rates, the importance of the penalty taxes has diminished to the point where they are possible candidates for repeal or reform in the near future.[8] Some commentators even have suggested that the inverted rate structure will encourage profitable corporations to pay dividends

---

5. See I.R.C. §§ 354; 358; 368. Acquisitive tax-free reorganizations are discussed in Chapter 10, infra.

6. See Staff of Senate Finance Committee, Preliminary Report on the Reform and Simplification of the Income Taxation of Corporations, 98th Cong., 1st Sess. 23 (Comm.Print S. 98–95, 1983).

7. I.R.C. § 532(b)(1).

8. See generally Kwall, "Subchapter G of the Internal Revenue Code: Crusade Without a Cause," 5 Va. Tax Rev. 223 (1985); Wolfman, "Subchapter C and the 100th Congress," 33 Tax Notes 669, 674 (Nov. 17, 1986).

rather than accumulate corporate earnings because the income earned on the accumulated funds invested by individual shareholders will be taxed at a lower rate than the income earned if the same funds were invested by the corporation.[9] The greater availability of S corporation status, which entirely eliminates the double tax in most circumstances, also tends to push the penalty taxes toward the sidelines of Subchapter C.

Although the reduced importance of the penalty taxes is a welcome development, the penalties are by no means defunct, and they occasionally contribute to unintended results. The goal of this chapter is to become literate on the workings of these anti-avoidance provisions by exploring their contours without becoming distracted by unnecessary details.

B. THE ACCUMULATED EARNINGS TAX [*]

1. THE PROSCRIBED TAX AVOIDANCE PURPOSE

Code: §§ 531, 532.

The accumulated earnings tax is a penalty, augmenting the regular corporate tax, that is imposed on a corporation "formed or availed of for the purpose of avoiding the income tax with respect to its shareholders * * * by permitting earnings and profits to accumulate instead of being divided or distributed."[1] The tax is levied on "accumulated taxable income," which is generally defined as taxable income with certain adjustments (e.g., subtracting taxes and dividends paid and adding back the dividends received deduction) to reflect the true dividend paying capacity of the corporation.[2] The tax imposed is 28 percent of a corporation's accumulated taxable income.[3] Most corporations, regardless of motives, are given an accumulated earnings credit that in effect permits an accumulation of up to $250,000.[4] Although

9. See Faber, "Capital Gains v. Dividends in Corporate Transactions: Is the Battle Still Worth Fighting?" 64 Taxes 865, 866 (1986); Eustice et al., The Tax Reform Act of 1986, 2–9 (1987).

* See generally Cunningham, "More Than You Ever Wanted to Know About the Accumulated Earnings Tax," 6 J.Corp. Tax'n 187 (1979).

1. I.R.C. § 532(a). The Sixth Circuit has held that an increase in earnings and profits during the taxable year is not required for imposition of the accumulated earnings tax. In GPD, Inc. v. Commissioner, 508 F.2d 1076 (6th Cir.1974), reversing 60 T.C. 480 (1973), the court held that the accumulated earnings tax was applicable even though the corporation's earnings and profits decreased during the taxable year as a result of a non pro rata redemption. The court reasoned that past accumulations can establish that the corpora-

tion was availed of for the proscribed purposes. For a criticism of this approach, see Doernberg, "The Accumulated Earnings Tax: The Relationship Between Earnings and Profits and Accumulated Taxable Income in a Redemption Transaction," 34 U.Fla.L.Rev. 715 (1982).

2. I.R.C. §§ 531; 535.

3. I.R.C. § 531. When it raised the top individual rate to 31 percent in 1990, Congress neglected to adjust the accumulated earnings tax rate. A technical correction is likely.

4. I.R.C. § 535(a), (c). A corporation is only permitted a $150,000 credit if its principal function is the performance of services in the field of health, law engineering, architecture, accounting, actuarial science, performing arts or consulting. I.R.C. § 535(c)(2)(B).

closely held corporations are the principal target of the tax, Section 532(c) provides that its application is to be determined "without regard to the number of shareholders." [5]   It nonetheless is unlikely that public corporations will be seriously threatened unless they are dominated by a small group of individuals.[6]   In addition, Section 532(b) provides a specific exception from the tax for personal holding companies, foreign personal holding companies, tax-exempt organizations and passive foreign investment companies.

The central issue under the accumulated earnings tax is whether the corporation has been formed or availed of for the proscribed tax avoidance purpose.   The resolution of that elusive question is aided by two statutory presumptions.   First, the fact that corporate earnings and profits are permitted to accumulate "beyond the reasonable needs of the business" is determinative of a tax avoidance purpose unless the corporation proves to the contrary by a "preponderance of the evidence." [7]   In addition, the fact that the corporation is "a mere holding or investment company" is prima facie evidence of a tax avoidance purpose.[8]

The regulations generally provide that the presence of the proscribed tax avoidance purpose is determined by all the circumstances of the particular case, including: [9]

1. Dealings between the corporation and its shareholders, such as shareholder loans or corporate expenditures benefiting the shareholders personally;

2. The presence of corporate investments having no reasonable connection with the corporation's business; and

3. The extent to which the corporation has made dividend distributions.

These factors are not conclusive, but the presence of shareholder loans, unrelated corporate investments and a poor dividend history tend to poison the atmosphere on the question of the proscribed tax avoidance purpose.

Application of the accumulated earnings tax thus ultimately depends on the corporation's purpose.   In United States v. Donruss,[10] a decision that significantly strengthened the tax, the Supreme Court held that the statutory standard was satisfied if tax avoidance is merely

---

5. I.R.C. § 532(c). See Golconda Mining Corp. v. Commissioner, 507 F.2d 594 (9th Cir.1974), where the Ninth Circuit held that the accumulated earnings tax does not apply to publicly held corporations. The Service refused to follow the holding in *Golconda.*   Rev.Rul. 75–305, 1975–2 C.B. 228. Congress resolved the dispute in the Service's favor by enacting Section 532(c).

6. For example, in enacting Section 532(c), the Senate and Conference reports on the Tax Reform Act of 1984 stated that "it may be difficult to establish [a tax avoidance purpose] in the case of a widely-held operating company where no individual or small group of individuals has legal or effective control of the company." S.Rep. No. 98–169, 98th Cong., 2d Sess. 187 (1984); H.R.Rep. No. 98–861, 98th Cong., 2d Sess. 829 (1984).

7. I.R.C. § 533(a).

8. I.R.C. § 533(b).

9. Reg. § 1.533–1(a)(2).

10. 393 U.S. 297, 89 S.Ct. 501 (1969).

one of the purposes for the accumulation even if it is not the corporation's dominant or principal purpose. After reviewing the legislative history, the Court acknowledged the difficulties in applying such a subjective standard and expressed its preference for more objective criteria: [11]

> Two conclusions can be drawn from Congress' efforts. First, Congress recognized the tremendous difficulty of ascertaining the purpose of corporate accumulations. Second, it saw that accumulation was often necessary for legitimate and reasonable business purposes. It appears clear to us that the congressional response to these facts has been to emphasize unreasonable accumulation as the most significant factor in the incidence of the tax. The reasonableness of an accumulation, while subject to honest difference of opinion, is a much more objective inquiry, and is susceptible of more effective scrutiny, than are the vagaries of corporate motive.
>
> Respondent would have us adopt a test that requires that tax avoidance purpose need be dominant, impelling or controlling. It seems to us that such a test would exacerbate the problems that Congress was trying to avoid. Rarely is there one motive, or even one dominant motive, for corporate decisions. Numerous factors contribute to the action ultimately decided upon. Respondent's test would allow taxpayers to escape the tax when it is proved that at least one other motive was equal to tax avoidance. We doubt that such a determination can be made with any accuracy, and it is certainly one which will depend almost exclusively on the interested testimony of corporate management. Respondent's test would thus go a long way toward destroying the presumption that Congress created to meet this very problem. As Judge Learned Hand said of the much weaker presumption contained in the Revenue Act of 1921 * * *, "[a] statute which stands on the footing of the participants' state of mind may need the support of presumption, indeed be practically unenforceable without it * * *." * * * And, "[t]he utility of * * * [that] presumption * * * is well nigh destroyed if * * * [it] is saddled with requirement of proof of 'the primary or dominant purpose' of the accumulation." Barrow Manufacturing Co. v. Commissioner, 294 F.2d 79, 82 (C.A. 5th Cir.1961), cert. denied 369 U.S. 817, 82 S.Ct. 827 (1962).

After *Donruss*, it became clear that the critical inquiry is the reasonableness of the accumulation. As previewed above, Congress came to the aid of the fact finder by creating a statutory presumption under which an accumulation beyond the reasonable needs of the corporation's business is determinative of the proscribed tax avoidance purpose unless the corporation proves to the contrary by a preponder-

---

11. 393 U.S. at 307–08, 89 S.Ct. at 506–07.

ance of the evidence.[12] This procedural device eases the Government's burden of proof and immunizes a growing corporation that accumulates profits for purposes such as bona fide expansion, potential acquisitions, working capital needs and other valid business objectives.

The presumption is rebuttable, and in theory a corporation that accumulates earnings beyond its reasonable needs can avoid the tax by proving that the accumulation was not motivated by a tax avoidance purpose. As the Supreme Court stated in *Donruss*: [13]

> [W]e cannot subscribe to respondent's suggestion that our holding would make purpose totally irrelevant. It still serves to isolate those cases in which tax avoidance motives did not contribute to the decision to accumulate. Obviously in such a case imposition of the tax would be futile. In addition, "purpose" means more than mere knowledge, undoubtedly present in nearly every case. It is still open for the taxpayer to show that even though knowledge of the tax consequences was present, that knowledge did not contribute to the decision to accumulate earnings.

Few corporations, however, are able to make the requisite showing once it is determined that accumulations are unreasonable.[14] Conversely, even if an accumulation is found to be reasonable, the government theoretically might attempt to show the existence of the proscribed purpose.[15] In practice, however, the reasonable business needs standard is almost always the main event, and it therefore will be the focus of our coverage.

2. THE REASONABLE NEEDS OF THE BUSINESS

Code: §§ 533(a); 534(a)–(c); 537(a), (b)(1).

Regulations: §§ 1.537–1(a), (b), (c), –2, –3.

MYRON'S ENTERPRISES v. UNITED STATES *

United States Court of Appeals, Ninth Circuit, 1977.
548 F.2d 331.

SNEED, Circuit Judge:

Taxpayer-corporations sued in district court below for a refund of accumulated earnings taxes imposed by the Commissioner. The Com-

---

12. I.R.C. § 533(a).

13. 393 U.S. at 309.

14. For one isolated example, see T.C. Heyward & Co. v. United States, 66–2 U.S. T.C. ¶ 9667 (W.D.N.C.1966), where a federal district judge held that the corporation's accumulations were so large that it never could have intended to avoid the shareholder tax because no one would be so obvious. Such cases are aberrational. In the future, however, it is still conceivable that a publicly held corporation that is found to have made an unreasonable accumulation might contend that it lacked the proscribed purpose because it is not controlled by any single shareholder or insider group.

15. Such a showing ultimately would be futile, however, in light of Section 535(c)(1), which provides a credit against the accumulated earnings tax in an amount equal to those earnings which have been accumulated for the reasonable needs of the business.

* Some footnotes omitted.

missioner had based the tax on his determination that for taxpayers' fiscal years 1966 through 1968 the reasonable needs of the business stemmed entirely from working capital needs and never exceeded $21,272. The taxpayers contended that their retained earnings for the years in question of $316,000, $374,316, and $415,766 respectively were needed to cover both working capital requirements of $100,000 and the planned purchase and remodeling of the ballroom operated by taxpayers, at an estimated cost of $375,000.

The district court, in Myron's Ballroom v. United States, 382 F.Supp. 582 (C.D.Cal.1974), held that taxpayers had accumulated earnings in excess of the reasonable needs of their business, but not to the extent claimed by the Commissioner. The court also found that the taxpayers had been availed of for the purpose of avoiding income taxes. Thus, the court upheld the surtax, but required a partial refund in light of the Commissioner's underestimation of taxpayers' reasonable business needs.

The taxpayers argue on appeal that they are entitled to a full refund (i) because all of the retained earnings in the years in question were required to meet the reasonable needs of their business, and (ii) because they proved by the preponderance of the evidence that they were not availed of to avoid taxes, despite the contrary finding by the district court. The Government argues, in response, that taxpayers were not even entitled to a partial refund—that the Commissioner's initial determination of the reasonable needs of the business was correct and that taxpayers failed to prove lack of tax-avoidance motivation. We conclude that the taxpayers are entitled to the full refund they seek. Therefore, we reverse and remand for such necessary proceedings as are consistent with this opinion.

I.

Taxpayer-corporations operate a ballroom and adjoining cocktail lounge. At all times since taxpayers were formed, they have leased their operating premises from Miss Pearl Rose, an elderly lady who has owned the property for approximately 30 years. The taxpayers began inquiring into the possibilities of purchasing the property in 1957, in part because they did not wish to make needed improvements unless they owned the building. Taxpayers made offers to Miss Rose of $100,000 and $150,000 for the property in the late 1950s—early 1960s, neither of which was accepted. However, at the time of the second offer, Miss Rose told taxpayers that they would have "first choice" if and when she decided to sell the ballroom.

In 1963, taxpayers learned that Russ Morgan, a former orchestra leader at the ballroom, had offered Miss Rose $300,000 cash for the property, in an attempt apparently to take over the ballroom operation. The price offered by Morgan probably reflected the goodwill that taxpayers had built up in their operations and therefore was considerably higher than the value of the ballroom property by itself. Morgan's actions convinced taxpayers that their business could be involuntarily "acquired" by someone purchasing the ballroom from Miss Rose;[3] taxpayers, therefore, promptly offered Miss Rose the identical sum of $300,000. This offer was renewed in 1964, 1965, 1966, 1967, 1968 and 1970. While Miss Rose never objected to the terms of the offers, she never sold and still owned the ballroom at the time of trial.

As the Government points out, Miss Rose was never particularly clear as to when and if she would sell her building. Nevertheless, the district court found (a) that taxpayers "expected at any time during the years 1966, 1967 and 1968 that [they] would be able to purchase the ballroom property from Pearl Rose for a price of $300,000 cash, no less than that amount, and maybe more," 382 F.Supp. at 587, and moreover (b) that the "expectation that the ballroom property would be acquired at any time during the years in issue was a reasonable expectation," id. at 588. Thus,

> During the years in issue, the acquisition of the ballroom property and the planned improvements and repairs were reasonably anticipated business needs of [taxpayers], and said needs were directly connected with the businesses of the corporations." Id.

The district court further concluded that "[c]onsidering the reasonably anticipated business need of the corporations to purchase the ballroom property * * * the corporations combined required at least $375,000, in addition to their combined working capital needs of $100,000." Id. However, the court went on to hold that in light of taxpayers' sole-shareholder Mrs. Myrna Myron's willingness to loan up to $200,000 to her corporations for purchase of the ballroom "if the corporations did not have sufficient funds to consummate the transactions, * * * a reasonable accumulation [for the purchase] would be $250,000, with Mrs. Myron loaning the balance of funds required," id., thus leading to an excess accumulation in 1967 and 1968.

II.

Section 537 of the Internal Revenue Code provides that the reasonable needs of a business, for purposes of determining whether there has been an excess accumulation of earnings, include "the reasonably anticipated needs of the business." Treas.Reg. § 1.537–1(b)(1) provides that to justify an accumulation of earnings on grounds of reasonably anticipated business needs, a corporation must have "specific, definite,

---

3. While taxpayers had a lease and an option to renew on the ballroom property at the time Morgan made his $300,000 offer to Miss Rose, there was always the possibility that the lease could be broken or evaded. According to Mrs. Myron, Morgan had asked his attorney and Miss Rose's agent "to review [the lease] line by line to see if there was some way or some word—something that could break the lease." R.T. at 73. This possibility of a loophole in the lease left the door open for an involuntary "acquisition."

and feasible plans for the use of such accumulation" and must not postpone execution of the plan "indefinitely." [4]

The Government contends that the district court erred in concluding that the taxpayers had a "specific, definite, and feasible plan" to acquire and remodel the ballroom. The Government notes that Miss Rose never agreed to sell the ballroom and argues that taxpayers could not have reasonably expected Miss Rose to so agree within the taxable years in question after nearly a decade of unsuccessful negotiations.

We agree with other circuits that a determination by the trial court of the reasonably anticipated business needs of a corporation is a finding of fact which must be sustained unless clearly erroneous. * * * A court should be particularly wary of overturning a finding of a trial court *supporting* the taxpayer's determination of its anticipated business needs, since, in the first instance, the "reasonableness of the needs is necessarily for determination by those concerned with the management of the particular enterprise. This determination must prevail unless the facts show clearly the accumulations were for prohibited purposes." * * * We conclude that the district court was not clearly erroneous in finding that taxpayers' expected purchase and remodeling of the ballroom for $375,000 was a "reasonably anticipated need of the business."

The Government argues that if the instant plan to purchase the ballroom is held to be a reasonably anticipated business need,

> "any individual could organize a one-man corporation, lease a building and discuss with the lessor the purchase of the building at some future time, and then assert that in the meantime business needs required accumulation of corporate earnings." I.A. Dress Co. v. Commissioner of Internal Revenue, 273 F.2d 543, 544 (2d Cir.), cert. denied, 362 U.S. 976, 80 S.Ct. 1060, 4 L.Ed.2d 1011 (1960).

Such fears of artificially constructed needs were well-founded in the quoted case of *I.A. Dress Co.;* there, the owner of the building that the taxpayer sought to purchase "was willing to sell but at a price some $300,000 more than the taxpayer was willing to pay." Id. The offer of the taxpayer lacked substance and could easily have been a facade. In the instant case, however, the taxpayers were extremely diligent in their attempts to purchase the ballroom; the taxpayers agreed to all of

---

4. In order for a corporation to justify an accumulation of earnings and profits for reasonably anticipated future needs, there must be an indication that the future needs of the business require such accumulation, and the corporation must have specific, definite, and feasible plans for the use of such accumulation. Such an accumulation need not be used immediately, nor must the plans for its use be consummated within a short period after the close of the taxable year, provided that such accumulation will be used within a reasonable time depending upon all the facts and circumstances relating to the future needs of the business. Where the future needs of the business are uncertain or vague, where the plans for the future use of an accumulation are not specific, definite, and feasible, or where the execution of such a plan is postponed indefinitely, an accumulation cannot be justified on the grounds of reasonably anticipated needs of the business." Treas. Reg. § 1.537–1(b)(1).

Miss Rose's stated terms—including payment in all cash; the price offered, far from being criticized by Miss Rose as too low, was apparently in excess of the property's fair market value.[5]

Neither do we have a situation where taxpayers' planned purchase of the ballroom was clearly infeasible. See *Colonial Amusement Corp.*, 1948 Tax.Ct.Mem.Dec. (P–H) ¶ 48,149 (building restrictions and priorities prevented carrying out of expansion plans). Here, as in *Universal Steel Co.*, 5 T.C. 627 (1945) (war priority restrictions temporarily blocked purchase of pickling plant), the taxpayers "had a right to hope, if not expect," id. at 638, that Miss Rose would sell to them in the near future. Miss Rose never foreclosed the possibility of sale on the terms offered by taxpayers; she merely wanted to "think it over some more." As expressed by Miss Rose's agent at one point during the negotiations, Miss Rose "was an elderly lady and had a very definite mind"; her answers, according to the agent, would differ depending on how she felt on getting up in the morning. Taxpayers were encouraged at several points in the negotiations; in 1965, Miss Rose's agent had told taxpayers, "Be prepared and ready to go." In light of the reasonable possibility that Miss Rose might have decided to accept the offer at any time during the taxable years in issue, calling for quick collection of $375,000 in cash, it would have been unreasonable to force taxpayers to pay out all of their earnings in dividends. Section 537 allows taxpayers to provide for "reasonably anticipated needs," not merely for certainties.

The district court's finding is supported by several tax court cases. In *Magic Mart, Inc.*, 51 T.C. 775 (1969), acq., 1969–2 C.B. xxiv, the Tax Court held that the taxpayer's accumulation of earnings for 1959 through 1962 was reasonable in light of taxpayer's plan to acquire enlarged and expanded facilities, even though it had tried unsuccessfully to buy larger facilities since 1957 and was not able to close a deal until 1967, five years after the taxable years in question. In *Breitfeller Sales, Inc.*, 28 T.C. 1164 (1957), acq., 1958–2 C.B. 4, the Tax Court held that a General Motors dealership's accumulation of earnings was justified, *inter alia*, by "the continuing *possibility* that it might [to avoid harmful competition] be required to finance a new dealership in [a neighboring community]." Id. at 1168 (emphasis added). See also *Universal Steel Co.*, supra.

5. The Government argues that in addition to these steps the taxpayers also should have investigated purchasing other property in the general area, once Miss Rose did not prove totally disposing. Cf. Magic Mart, Inc., 51 T.C. 775 (1969), acq., 1969 2 C.B. xxiv. We agree that the failure of a taxpayer to look into the possibility of purchasing alternative properties generally will be a relevant factor in determining whether the taxpayer actually had a reasonably anticipated business need to purchase the sought-after property. However, other factors also must be considered, including the *uniqueness* of the sought property. Here, as was testified to at trial, a substantial amount of good will was tied up in the ballroom occupied by taxpayers; given that this value would have been lost if taxpayer had moved to another location, we do not believe that taxpayers' failure to pursue other possible properties (if other ballrooms even existed) calls for reversing the finding of the district court.

III.

The Government rests its entire case upon the argued lack of a specific, definite, and feasible plan. No attempt is made to support the trial court's use of Mrs. Myrna Myron's capacity to loan to the taxpayers to reduce the amount of the reasonable accumulation. The Government thus agrees with taxpayers that, assuming a feasible plan, the district court, in determining whether taxpayers unreasonably accumulated earnings, erred in subtracting from the cash needed to purchase the ballroom an amount that Mrs. Myron stated that she would be willing to loan to the taxpayers *if necessary.* We also agree. Having found that the reasonably anticipated business need of the taxpayers to purchase the ballroom property required at least $375,000 in cash, the district court erred in concluding that a reasonable accumulation was any less.[6]

Having determined that the reasonable business needs of taxpayers, within the meaning of section 535, equalled or exceeded the accumulated earnings of taxpayers for the taxable years in question, it is unnecessary for us to consider whether the district court was correct in holding that taxpayers had been availed of to avoid taxes within the meaning of section 531. Taxpayers are entitled to a full refund. The case is remanded to the district court for such necessary proceedings as are consistent with this opinion.

Reversed and remanded.

NOTE

The *Myron's Enterprises* case illustrates the essentially factual nature of the "reasonable business needs" issue. By the time a case reaches the courts, the corporation normally has compiled a laundry

---

6. That the reasonableness of accumulations should be judged without regard to the borrowing capabilities of the corporation-taxpayer is well established by the case law. See, e.g., *General Smelting Co.,* 4 T.C. 313, 323 (1944), acq., 1945 C.B. 3; B. Bittker & J. Eustice, Federal Income Taxation of Corporations and Shareholders 8–20 to 8–21 & n. 42 (3rd ed. 1971). In computing "accumulated taxable income," which forms the base for the accumulated earnings tax, I.R.C. § 535 provides that a credit will be provided for the amount "retained for the reasonable needs of the business." There is no authority for reducing the credit to reflect the lending capacity of taxpayer's shareholders. If the reasonable business needs of taxpayer equal or outstrip the retained earnings, no surtax can be imposed, even though the needs could be financed by borrowing from outside— such financing decisions are for the taxpayer, not the courts to make.

The district court's logic could conceivably be extended to the point of totally nullifying Congress' expressed policy of allowing corporate taxpayers to accumulate earnings necessary for reasonable business needs. A sole shareholder can always loan back any cash distributed by his corporation in dividends if the corporation later needs the money (minus, of course, any income taxes paid). Therefore, to take into account the ability of a shareholder to loan money to the corporation could be construed as virtual authority "for denying all sole stockholder corporations the right ever to maintain accumulations even for reasonable needs. The test expressed by the statute would then be completely abandoned." *Smoot Sand & Gravel Corp. v. Commissioner of Internal Revenue,* 241 F.2d 197, 206 (4th Cir.), cert. denied, 354 U.S. 922, 77 S.Ct. 1383, 1 L.Ed.2d 1437 (1957).

list of reasonable business needs to justify the accumulation, and triers of fact typically are reluctant to second guess the business judgment of corporate management in the absence of a clear pattern of abuse. This note and the materials that follow it survey the principal factors taken into account by the Service and the courts in evaluating the reasonableness of a corporation's accumulation.

Reasonable and Unreasonable Needs: In General. After a general reminder that the reasonableness of a particular accumulation of earnings and profits is dependent "upon the particular circumstances of the case," [1] the regulations provide nonexclusive examples of reasonable and unreasonable accumulations. If supported by the facts, the following grounds "may indicate" that accumulations are being made for the reasonable needs of the business: [2]

1. To provide for bona fide expansion of the business or replacement of plant;

2. To acquire a business enterprise through a stock or asset purchase;

3. To provide for retirement of bona fide indebtedness incurred in the trade or business;

4. To provide necessary working capital for the business; or

5. To provide for investments or loans to suppliers or customers in order to maintain the corporation's business.

The following nonexclusive list of purposes "may indicate" that the accumulations are beyond the reasonable needs of the business: [3]

1. Loans to shareholders or expenditures for the personal benefit of the shareholders;

2. Loans having no reasonable relation to the conduct of the business made to relatives or friends of shareholders or other persons;

3. Loans to another corporation in a different business if the two corporations are controlled, directly or indirectly, by the same shareholders;

4. Investments unrelated to the corporation's business; or

5. Retention of earnings and profits to provide against unrealistic hazards.

Anticipated Needs. Section 537(a) defines the "reasonable needs of the business" as including the reasonably anticipated needs. To justify an accumulation as being for a reasonably anticipated need, a corporation must have a business need for the accumulation and must have plans for the use of the funds which are "specific, definite and feasi-

---

1. Reg. § 1.537–2(a). The Supreme Court has held that in ascertaining the reasonable needs of a business, "readily marketable portfolio securities" are to be taken into account at their "net realizable value" rather than cost. Ivan Allen Co. v. United States, 422 U.S. 617, 95 S.Ct. 2501 (1975).

2. Reg. § 1.537–2(b).

3. Reg. § 1.537–2(c).

ble." [4] The accumulation does not have to be used immediately or even within a short period of time as long as it is used within a "reasonable period," taking into account all the facts and circumstances.[5] The corporation's reasonably anticipated needs are determined based on facts present at the close of the taxable year; subsequent events may not be used to show that the accumulation was unreasonable. Subsequent events, however, can be considered to determine whether the corporation actually intended to consummate its plans for the accumulation.[6] Moreover, if the future plans are not completed, the presence of the accumulation is considered in determining the reasonableness of future accumulations.[7]

The "Business." The regulations expansively define the "business" of a corporation. The "business" includes not only the one in which the corporation has previously engaged but also "any line of business which it may undertake." [8] This definition should provide ample protection for accumulations intended for expansion into activities related to the corporation's business, but it is not clear whether accumulations to move into entirely unrelated activities are similarly protected.[9] If a corporation owns and, in effect, operates a subsidiary, the subsidiary's business may be considered to be the business of the parent for purposes of evaluating the parent's reasonable business needs.[10] The regulations further provide that a subsidiary will be considered a "mere instrumentality" of its parent if the parent owns at least 80 percent of the subsidiary's voting stock.[11] Below the 80 percent figure, the question of attributing the subsidiary's business to the parent is determined by the particular circumstances of the case.[12]

Working Capital. The regulations recognize the need to accumulate earnings to provide "necessary working capital for the business." Working capital needs vary from industry to industry and among enterprises within the same industry, and the courts have struggled to develop standards to ascertain the working capital requirements of any particular business.[13] The judiciary's efforts have evolved into the so-called *Bardahl* formula, named for a 1965 Tax Court case which first employed the approach.[14] The formula, which is a mathematician's delight, attempts to identify a corporation's working capital needs by reference to its "operating cycle"—a concept that remains unsettled.[15] The *Bardahl* formula is viewed as a guidepost rather than a controlling

---

4. Reg. § 1.537–1(b)(1).

5. Id.

6. Reg. § 1.537–1(b)(2).

7. Id.

8. Reg. § 1.537–3(a).

9. See Bittker & Eustice, Federal Income Taxation of Corporations and Shareholders ¶ 8.06 (5th ed. 1987).

10. Reg. § 1.537–3(b).

11. Id.

12. Id.

13. See Cunningham, "More Than You Ever Wanted to Know About the Accumulated Earnings Tax," 6 J.Corp.Tax'n 187, 209 (1979).

14. Bardahl Manufacturing Corp. v. Commissioner, 24 T.C.M. 1030 (1965).

15. See Cunningham, supra note 13, at 212.

legal principle,[16] and the following excerpt provides some insight into its nature and purpose: [17]

> The formula represents a procedure for arriving at working capital needs by calculating the requirements of capital funds for one "operating cycle" of a business entity. One operating cycle is the length of time (usually expressed as a percentage of a year) it takes to purchase raw materials inventory, process those raw materials into finished goods, sell the finished product, and turn any accounts receivable into cash so that the process may be repeated. Hence, the ultimate percentage which represents this cycle must speak to the turnover time of raw materials, accounts receivable, and any credit cycle. The time it takes to turn over inventory can be computed by dividing either the highest or the average inventory for the year by the costs of the goods sold in that year. This results in a percentage of a year. In similar fashion, the time it takes to turn over a receivable account is computed by dividing the highest receivables for the year by the sales for that year. This likewise is expressed as a percentage of a year. Adding inventory cycle to receivables cycle, one arrives at a theoretical time period, again expressed as a percentage of a year, that is required for the total productive process.

> The *Bardahl International* case took the additional step of recognizing that those who supply raw materials and labor are not paid immediately. An appropriate credit period, usually 15 or 30 days, is stated as a percentage of a year (divided by 365 days per year), and this is subtracted from the total of the inventory and receivables percentages. When this ultimate percentage rate is applied to the net operating expenses for the year, the result represents the expenses for one business operating cycle * * *. To this are added reasonably anticipated extraordinary expenses during the tax year in question * * *. The sum represents the total requirements of the firm for liquid assets * * *. This is contrasted against the sum of liquid assets such as cash and equivalents * * * and investments which can be converted into cash readily if necessary * * * in order to ascertain whether there is an excess or shortage of available capital * * *. Cognizance must also be taken of any loans unrelated to the business * * *.

> The result of this whole process is a figure * * * indicating how much the subject firm has accumulated beyond its reasonable needs. This, in conjunction with its findings on the intent of the parties, should permit a factfinder to ascertain

---

16. See generally Thompson Engineering Co. v. Commissioner, 80 T.C. 672 (1983); Atlantic Commerce & Shipping Co. v. Commissioner, 32 T.C.M. 473 (1973), affirmed 500 F.2d 937 (2d Cir.1974).

17. Grob Inc. v. United States, 565 F.Supp. 391, 395 (E.D.Wisc.1983).

whether or not the corporate entity has been availed of for the purpose of avoiding income tax by one or more of the shareholders. * * *

Stock Redemptions. Corporations sometimes contend that an accumulation of earnings was necessary to create a fund for a later redemption of stock. In 1969, in response to conflicting results in the courts, Congress specifically provided that the term "reasonable needs of the business" encompass accumulations in the year of a shareholder's death or in any subsequent year to the extent they are necessary to make a stock redemption to pay death taxes under Section 303.[18]

The cases are inconsistent as to other types of redemptions. Some courts have found the use of accumulations to redeem dissenting minority or 50 percent shareholders to be a reasonable need of the business.[19] But corporations have encountered more difficulty when they have attempted to justify an accumulation on the ground that reasonable business needs include accumulating earnings to redeem either a friendly minority shareholder [20] or a majority shareholder.[21] In each case, the question is whether the redemption satisfies a corporate (e.g., preventing continuous deadlocks in the boardroom) as opposed to a shareholder (e.g., funding a redemption of a retiring shareholder under a buy-sell agreement) purpose.[22] The *Gazette Publishing* case, which follows, illustrates how a redemption can be characterized as a valid response to a threat to the corporation's existence.

GAZETTE PUBLISHING CO. v. SELF

United States District Court, Eastern District of Arkansas, 1952.
103 F.Supp. 779.

TRIMBLE, Chief Judge.

This is an action by the plaintiff, Gazette Publishing Company, a corporation, against the acting collector of Internal Revenue for this district for the recovery of a Section 102, [Now Section 531. Ed.] 26 U.S. C.A. § 102, assessment made for the calendar years, 1946 and 1947.

Plaintiff was incorporated under the laws of Arkansas on June 5, 1889, for the purpose of publishing a newspaper, The Arkansas Gazette, and conducting related business enterprises, and has carried on such business since its incorporation. * * *

* * *

18. I.R.C. § 537(a)(2); 537(b)(1). Similarly, reasonable needs are considered to include amounts necessary to redeem stock held by a private foundation that is required to shed its excess business holdings. I.R.C. § 537(a)(3); 537(b)(2). See I.R.C. § 4943.

19. See, e.g., Wilcox Manufacturing Co. v. Commissioner, 38 T.C.M. 378 (1979); Mountain States Steel Foundries, Inc. v. Commissioner, 284 F.2d 737 (4th Cir.1960).

20. See John B. Lambert & Associates v. United States, 212 Ct.Cl. 71 (1976).

21. See Lamark Shipping Agency, Inc. v. Commissioner, 42 T.C.M. 38 (1981); Pelton Steel Casting Co. v. Commissioner, 251 F.2d 278 (7th Cir.1958).

22. See generally Rudolph, "Stock Redemptions and the Accumulated Earnings Tax—an Update," 4 J.Corp.Tax 101 (1977).

During the years, 1946 and 1947, Mr. J.N. Heiskell was president of the corporation, and Mr. Fred Allsopp was secretary-treasurer and general manager until his death in March, 1946. Upon his death, his son, W.C. Allsopp, who had been assistant business manager, succeeded to the positions held by his father. This situation had existed for many years. The business was run by informal conferences between these men, and no formal meetings of the Board of Directors or stockholders were held in which minutes were kept between March 24, 1944, and November, 1948. Formal meetings were only held when it was necessary to approve or ratify some action of the officers. * * *

* * *

The plaintiff corporation had a long history of paying generous dividends. For the twenty years ending with 1945, the year immediately preceding the questioned years, the corporation had net earnings after taxes of $2,288,000 and paid out $2,167,000 in dividends, retaining in the business for this period no more than $120,000 of the earnings. A study of the record discloses that the dividends paid in 1946 and 1947 were above the Corporation's average dividend in amount over the preceding ten year period. The 1947 dividend of $107,000 was the highest dividend paid since 1936. The record also discloses that more than half of the substantial increase in retained earnings during the period in question over prior years was due to the repeal of World War II excess profits tax. This gave to the officers of the Corporation an opportunity to begin to accumulate funds to meet the reasonable needs of the business, and without the necessity of reducing dividends.

The sale of the Allsopp stock, in 1948, was not the purpose for which the funds were accumulated during 1946 and 1947. The uncontroverted evidence in this case is that the proposed sale of the stock first came up in a flare of temper between Mr. Patterson and W.C. Allsopp in 1948, and that when the sale was proposed in 1948 it was a complete surprise to the president and the board of directors of the corporation. * * *

* * *

Defendant contends that the price of $1,000,000 paid for the Allsopp stock in 1948 was so far in excess of the true market value of that stock, that it is evident that there was in fact no reasonable need for the accumulation of the funds in 1946 and 1947.

It is in evidence that certain special interests have for many years sought to purchase or acquire stock in the corporation, and an interest in the publication of the Arkansas Gazette, the newspaper published by the corporation. The officers testified that the management has always watched the matter closely, fearing that if some group of special interests should acquire stock in the corporation, however minor it might be, such group of special interests would endeavor to break up the harmony existing in the management, and change the editorial and business policy of the corporation, which had conducted the business of the corporation so successfully so many years. When the Allsopp stock was offered for sale at $1,000,000, all the officers and directors of the plaintiff corporation knew this was in excess of its true market value. They were informed by the attorney for the Allsopp stockholders that the stock could be sold to an outsider for that amount of money. They recognized this as a business crisis. Knowing that their failure to acquire this stock for the corporation might in the future affect the interest of the corporation and its stockholders adversely, it was decided to make the acquisition and promote and keep intact the harmony of management and editorial policy of the corporation.

Defendant does not seem to recognize that this business is subject to changes in circumstances and conditions, and that good business judgment upon the part of management requires changes in plans to meet these changes of circumstances. This is true with this plaintiff as with all other business enterprises, and the courts have recognized that this is so. All business needs are relative. The most pressing needs today may not be the most pressing at a later date, because even more pressing needs may arise because of changed circumstances, and courts have frequently refused to sustain Section 102 Assessments where the funds accumulated for reasonable needs and owing to change in circumstances the funds were used only partially or not at all as originally planned.

In Dill Manufacturing Co., 39 B.T.A. 1023, it was the purchase of the minority stock which forced the postponement of plans for a new plant, and the Board of Tax Appeals, in reversing a Section 102 Assessment by the Commissioner, held the purchase of the minority stock was a reasonable business need of the company. The Board of Tax Appeals, said in that case: "The issue of preferred stock with the obligation to retire it within five years evidenced a debt, (cases cited). And this record, at most, does not establish that the liquidation of the syndicate stock by the partial use of that preferred stock, under the circumstances here, was not required as a reasonable business necessity. Cf. Sauk Investment Co., 34 B.T.A. 732; Mellbank Corporation, 38 B.T.A. 1108."

See also National Yarn Corporation, 9 TCM 603; General Smelting Co., 4 T.C. 313; The Wean Engineering Co., Inc., 2 TCM 510; Emeloid Co., Inc., v. Commissioner of Internal Revenue, 3 Cir., 189 F.2d 230. In the case of Fred F. Fisher, 6 TCM 520, the Tax Court held that the promotion of harmony in the conduct of the business is a proper business purpose. There, taxpayer's sister, a minority stockholder, had been constantly complaining about the conduct of the business. To put an end to the dissension, the company purchased the sister's stock at a price considerably in excess of its fair market value. The Commissioner, contending that the stock purchase was prompted by reasons personal to the stockholders and not in furtherance of any corporate purpose, assessed a deficiency on the other stockholders on the theory that the excessive portion of the purchase price constituted a constructive dividend. But the Tax Court held that the Company's purchase of the sister's stock was in furtherance of corporate purposes. The Tax Court pointed out that "there is no foundation for an assumption that a corporation would never, in its own interests, pay more than the fair market value of its stock in order to rid itself of a complaining minority stockholder," and that the excessive price paid for the stock "was not unreasonable for the purpose of promoting harmony in the conduct of the business and securing it from annoying interference and threats of legal proceedings." The Court said, "regardless of whether * * * complaints were justified, they had a nuisance value sufficient to warrant the action of the corporation in purchasing her stock."

The Arkansas Gazette, published by the plaintiff, is said to be the oldest daily paper west of the Mississippi River. It has enjoyed a long, honorable and successful career under able and eminent editors, among them the present President of the Corporation. It has a well established policy, standing firmly and stoutly for all the great moral issues arising from time to time, has had a great part in the development of the whole state, and has at all times supported worthy public causes and men in public life with telling effect. It has consistently over a long term of years refused to accept advertisements for alcoholic liquors of any kind. It also has had and still has strong editorial policies on many issues which special interests might and would oppose. For this Allsopp stock to have fallen into the hands of some special interest antagonistic to the present and the general policy of the paper, could and probably would have been most disruptive of the harmony of the corporation, even though it constituted a minority of all the stock. The purchase of this stock, even at the advanced price paid, was a reasonable need of the corporation, and was a change in circumstances which fully justified a change in the use of funds accumulated for other needs, and justified the borrowing of the $600,000 in addition to using the funds on hand.

* * *

The Court finds from all the evidence in the case, and giving such weight to the statutory presumptions as the law requires, that the earnings and profits were not accumulated in 1946 and 1947 beyond the reasonable needs of the corporation. Nor were such earnings accumulated for the purpose of preventing the imposition of a surtax upon the stockholders.

NOTE

Sections 533 and 534 work together to provide an unusual procedure for regulating the burden of proof if an accumulated earnings tax controversy is litigated in the Tax Court. As we have seen, an accumulation beyond the reasonable needs of the business is determinative of the forbidden purpose unless the corporation proves otherwise by a preponderance of the evidence.[1] The regulations provide that this presumption adds "still more weight" to the usual presumption of correctness that accompanies the Service's determinations of tax liability.[2] The Commissioner nonetheless will bear the burden of proof on

---

1. I.R.C. § 533(a).   2. Reg. § 1.533–1(b).

the question of unreasonable accumulations unless it has informed the taxpayer, prior to sending a formal notice of deficiency, that the proposed notice includes an accumulated earnings tax deficiency.[3] Even in the likely case where the Commissioner provides notice, the taxpayer can shift the burden of proof back to the Commissioner by submitting a statement setting forth the grounds on which it relies to establish that all or part of its earnings and profits have not been permitted to accumulate beyond the reasonable needs of the business.[4] The statement must be filed within 30 days of the Commissioner's notification under Section 534(b).[5] To shift the burden of proof, the taxpayer's statement may not consist merely of vague generalities. It must set forth with specificity and clarity the grounds on which it will rely to prove that its accumulations were reasonable.[6]

3.   CALCULATION OF ACCUMULATED TAXABLE INCOME

Code: §§ 535(a), (b), (c); 561; 562(a), (b), (c); 563(a), (d); 565(a)–(d), (f).

The base for the accumulated earnings tax is accumulated taxable income. Section 535(a) defines accumulated taxable income as taxable income of the corporation, adjusted under Section 535(b), less the sum of the dividends paid deduction and the accumulated earnings credit.

Adjustments to Taxable Income. The base figure for computing accumulated taxable income is the current year's taxable income. The accumulated earnings tax, however, is directed at real retained economic profits because they are a more accurate measure of the corporation's capacity to pay dividends. As a result, taxable income is adjusted in a manner somewhat similar to that used to adjust taxable income to determine earnings and profits. For example, to arrive at accumulated taxable income, taxable income is reduced by certain nondeductible taxes [1] and charitable contributions in excess of the percentage limitations.[2] These items do not affect taxable income but nonetheless result in a decrease in the corporation's wealth. On the other hand, certain deductions allowed for income tax purposes that do not currently reduce the corporation's real wealth are disallowed in computing accumulated taxable income. These include the dividends received deduction [3] and the net operating loss deduction.[4]

Section 535(b) contains special rules governing the treatment of net capital gains and losses for purposes of determining accumulated taxable income.[5] Section 535(b)(6) permits a corporation to reduce taxable income by its net capital gain for the year less attributable taxes. But for purposes of determining net capital gain prior net capital losses are treated as short-term capital losses in succeeding taxable years.[6] Un-

3.   I.R.C. § 534(a), (b).

4.   I.R.C. § 534(c); Reg. § 1.534–2(a), (b).

5.   I.R.C. § 534(c).

6.   Reg. § 1.534–2(d).

1.   I.R.C. § 535(b)(1).

2.   I.R.C. § 535(b)(2).

3.   I.R.C. § 535(b)(3).

4.   I.R.C. § 535(b)(4).

5.   A separate set of rules applies to a "mere holding or investment company." I.R.C. § 535(b)(8).

6.   I.R.C. § 535(b)(6), (7).

der Section 535(b)(5)(A) and (B), a corporation can deduct the amount of a net capital loss reduced by the lesser of its "nonrecaptured capital gains deductions" or its earnings and profits as of the close of the preceding year. "Nonrecaptured capital gains deductions" are generally defined by Section 535(b)(5)(C) as the excess of the aggregate amount allowable as a deduction in prior years for net capital gains over the aggregate reductions to capital losses for prior years.

Dividends Paid Deduction. Section 535(a) logically permits a corporation to reduce accumulated taxable income by dividends paid during the taxable year. Section 561(a) defines the "dividends paid" to include dividends [7] paid during the taxable year and certain "consent dividends." Generally, distributions must be pro rata in order to qualify for the dividends paid deduction.[8] Liquidating distributions and redemptions also may produce a deduction for dividends paid.[9] Because a corporation frequently may not have the facts available to determine its liability for the accumulated earnings tax, Section 563(a) provides that dividends paid on or before the 15th day of the third month following the close of a taxable year are considered paid in the earlier year.

Consent Dividends. Section 565 permits shareholders to file a consent with the corporation's tax return to include in income as dividends amounts which were not in fact distributed. Consent dividends are treated as if they were distributed in cash to the shareholders and then contributed back to the corporation on the last day of the corporation's taxable year.[10]

Accumulated Earnings Credit. To the extent that a corporation's earnings are retained for the reasonable needs of the business, they are not within the ambit of the accumulated earnings tax. To remove these earnings from the grasp of the tax, a corporation is permitted a deduction for the accumulated earnings credit in determining accumulated taxable income. The accumulated earnings credit is equal to the amount of current earnings and profits (less the dividends paid deduction) retained for the reasonable needs of the business minus the deduction permitted for net capital gains.[11] Section 535(c)(2) provides that the credit shall in no case be less than the amount by which $250,000 ($150,000 in the case of certain service corporations) exceeds

---

7. Section 562(a) generally employs the Section 316 definition of "dividend" for purposes of determining the dividends paid deduction. Reg. § 1.562–1(a) provides that if a dividend is paid in property (other than money) the amount of the dividends paid deduction is the corporation's adjusted basis in the property. The regulation was upheld in Fulman v. United States, 434 U.S. 528, 98 S.Ct. 841 (1978).

8. I.R.C. § 562(c). Differences in dividend rights among classes of stock not attributable to shareholder waivers are permitted.

9. I.R.C. § 562(b)(1).

10. I.R.C. § 565(c).

11. I.R.C. § 535(c)(1). Net capital gains are excluded from accumulated taxable income by Section 535(b)(6) but they are part of earnings and profits. If a net capital gain was not excluded from the accumulated earnings credit it would reduce accumulated taxable income twice: once under Section 535(b)(6) and again under Section 535(c).

accumulated earnings and profits at the close of the preceding taxable year.[12] This has the effect of enabling a corporation to accumulate a minimum of $250,000 regardless of its business needs.

PROBLEMS

1.   Which of the following accumulations are likely to be for the reasonable needs of the business?

(a)   A corporation retains $200,000 of earnings and profits per year for five years to finance a $1,000,000 expansion of its manufacturing plant. Should it matter if the corporation could have borrowed 80% of the expansion costs?

(b)   A corporation which manufactures computer chips accumulates $2,000,000 in order to acquire an office building which is rented to an insurance company under a net lease.

(c)   Assume Parent Corporation owns all of the outstanding stock of Brother and Sister Corporations. Can Parent accumulate earnings and profits for Brother? Brother for Parent? Brother for Sister? See Reg. §§ 1.537–2(c)(3), –3(b).

(d)   A corporation accumulates earnings and profits for potential § 531 tax liability.

(e)   A corporation accumulates earnings and profits in order to redeem a class of limited and preferred stock.

2.   T Corporation (a shoe manufacturer) is a calendar year, accrual method corporation which is not a personal holding company and which has accumulated earnings and profits at the end of year one of $200,000. T is a closely held corporation with three shareholders. In year two T has taxable income (all of which is ordinary income) of $60,000. T also has taxable income of $60,000 in both years three and four. There are no distributions to shareholders in any year.

(a)   What tax results to T under §§ 11 and 531, assuming current § 11 rates on all income in years two, three, and four?

(b)   What possible defenses may T have to the application of § 531?

(c)   What effect will § 534 have on these facts?

3.   Should Congress repeal the accumulated earnings tax? Does the tax still serve its original purpose?

C.   THE PERSONAL HOLDING COMPANY TAX

1.   INTRODUCTION

Code: §§ 541, 542(a).

The accumulated earnings tax has not been an entirely effective vehicle to prevent the use of a corporation to avoid the individual tax

---

12. Accumulated earnings and profits at the close of the preceding year are reduced by dividends treated as paid in such year under Section 563(a). I.R.C. § 535(c)(4).

rates. The tax is not imposed unless a corporation has accumulations that are motivated at least in part by tax avoidance. Moreover, the accumulated earnings credit may shelter substantial accumulations from the Section 531 tax. Partially in response to these shortcomings and in order to prevent certain other tax avoidance devices, Congress enacted the personal holding company tax in 1934.[1]

The original purpose of the personal holding company tax was to prevent taxpayers from avoiding the then higher graduated individual tax rates by using devices known as "incorporated pocketbooks," "incorporated talents" and "incorporated properties." These schemes were structured as follows:

1. *Incorporated Pocketbooks.* A high bracket individual would transfer passive investments (e.g., stocks, bonds, rental property) to a corporation in exchange for its stock. The corporation then could take advantage of the lower corporate rates and the dividends received deduction for any dividends that it received. The income could be realized at a later date at capital gain rates through a liquidation of the company or, ideally, the stock could be held until the taxpayer's death when his heirs would take a stepped-up basis.

2. *Incorporated Talents.* A highly compensated individual, such as a movie star, would form a wholly owned corporation and agree to work for the corporation at a small salary. The corporation then would contract out the services of its owner-employee for a substantial sum, and the great bulk of the income would be taxed at the lower corporate rates.[2]

3. *Incorporated Properties.* A taxpayer would transfer both investment property and property which did not generate income, such as a yacht or home, to a corporation. The shareholder then would lease back the property for a nominal amount, and the corporation would attempt to shelter both the rental income and its other income by claiming deductions for depreciation and maintenance on the property.[3]

To combat these plans, Section 541 imposes a 28 percent [4] tax on the "undistributed personal holding company income" of every "personal holding company." The personal holding company tax is imposed in addition to a corporation's Section 11 tax. The remaining sections of this chapter consider the details and operation of the personal holding company tax, first examining the definition of a personal holding company and then turning to the determination of the tax.

1. H.Rep. No. 704, 73rd Cong., 2d Sess. (1934), reprinted in 1939–1 C.B. 554, 562.

2. See Commissioner v. Laughton, 113 F.2d 103 (9th Cir.1940).

3. Bittker & Eustice, Federal Income Taxation of Corporations and Shareholders ¶ 8.20 (5th ed. 1987).

4. After 1990, the top individual rate is 31 percent, and Congress is likely to enact a corresponding increase to the personal holding company rate.

2. DEFINITION OF A PERSONAL HOLDING COMPANY

Code: § 542(a). Skim § 542(c).

Section 542(a) defines a personal holding company as a corporation which satisfies a stock ownership requirement and an adjusted ordinary gross income test. Unlike the accumulated earnings tax, the determination of whether a corporation is a personal holding company is an objective inquiry that does not depend on whether there is a tax avoidance motive.

a. STOCK OWNERSHIP REQUIREMENT

Code: §§ 542(a)(2), 544.

The first leg of the definition of a personal holding company looks to whether the corporation is closely held. The stock ownership requirement in Section 542(a)(2) is satisfied if at any time during the last half of the taxable year more than 50 percent in value of the corporation's outstanding stock is owned, directly or indirectly, by or for not more than five individuals. Not surprisingly, this test is accompanied by special attribution rules in Section 544(a), under which stock owned by a corporation, partnership, estate or trust is considered owned proportionately by its shareholders, partners or beneficiaries.[1] An individual is considered to own stock owned by his family (brothers, sisters, spouse, ancestors and lineal descendants) or partners,[2] as well as stock held under an option to purchase.[3] Section 544(b)(1) provides that securities convertible into stock are considered stock for purposes of Section 542(a)(2) if the effect of their inclusion is to make the corporation a personal holding company.

b. INCOME TEST

Code: §§ 542(a)(1), 543.

The income test seeks to identify corporations with a significant amount of passive investment income or income attributable to the personal services of a major shareholder. Under Section 542(a)(1), at least 60 percent of a corporation's "adjusted ordinary gross income" (AOGI) must be "personal holding company income" before the corporation will be classified as a personal holding company. To apply this test, one must master some special terminology.

Adjusted Ordinary Gross Income. The function of AOGI is to provide an accurate measuring rod against which to compare a corporation's passive investment and personal service income. Its computation begins with the corporation's gross income, which is then reduced by capital and Section 1231 gains to arrive at ordinary gross income (OGI).[4] These gains are excluded from gross income in order to prevent

1. I.R.C. § 544(a)(1).
2. I.R.C. § 544(a)(2).
3. I.R.C. § 544(a)(3).
4. I.R.C. § 543(b)(1)(A), (B).

corporations from timing gains (and inflating their income) to avoid the income test.[5]

Next, a series of adjustments must be made to OGI to determine AOGI. These adjustments also are designed to prevent easy avoidance of the income test by manipulation of the corporation's gross income. For example, gross income includes the full amount of receipts from the rental of property or royalties from mineral exploration. Absent some adjustment mechanism, corporations could generate enough gross income from leveraged investments in these properties to inflate AOGI and escape the personal holding company tax. In order to prevent this technique, AOGI includes not all gross ordinary income but only the corporation's adjusted income from rents and royalties.[6] This amount includes income from rents and mineral, oil and gas royalties only to the extent that the gross income from these activities exceeds the amount deductible for depreciation or depletion, property taxes, interest and rent.[7] Since copyright royalties, royalties from films produced by the corporation and royalties from computer software produced by the corporation generally require more active participation than mineral or oil and gas royalties, the gross amount of royalties from copyrights, produced films or qualifying computer software businesses is included in AOGI.[8] Interest earned by dealers on obligations of the United States and interest on condemnation awards, judgments and tax refunds also is excluded from AOGI.[9]

Personal Holding Company Income. Students of the Internal Revenue Code have come to expect a large degree of complexity when Congress seeks to prevent tax avoidance. Congress must anticipate new efforts to avoid its corrective legislation and simultaneously avoid penalizing taxpayers engaged in legitimate business or investment activities. These dual and often competing goals contribute to a web of special rules and exceptions. And so it is that the definition of personal holding company income in Section 543(a) is one of the Code's most diabolical provisions that may easily exceed your gloomiest expectations. Before turning to the necessary details, a few generalizations are in order. Incorporated pocketbooks and incorporated talents were Congress's prime targets when it enacted and expanded the personal holding company tax in the 1930's. Consistent with that purpose, passive investment income and certain income from personal service contracts are the principal components of personal holding company income. But it is possible for rents, royalties, and other forms of income that appear to be passive to result from a corporation's legitimate active business pursuits. Section 543 attempts to identify the purely passive income and the types of personal service income targeted

5. S.Rep. No. 830, 88th Cong., 2d Sess. (1964), reprinted in 1964–1 (pt. 2) C.B. 505, 611.

6. S.Rep. No. 830, 88th Cong., 2d Sess. (1964), reprinted in 1964–1 (pt. 2) C.B. 505, 610.

7. I.R.C. § 543(b)(2)(A), (B).

8. I.R.C. § 543(b)(1), (3).

9. I.R.C. § 543(b)(2)(C).

by the personal holding company provisions through the use of various mechanical tests, some of which are examined in more detail below.

Passive Investment Income Items: In General.   Passive investment income items are the principal target of the personal holding company tax.   Personal holding company income thus includes dividends, interest, annuities, royalties and rents.[10]   Capital gains and Section 1231 gains presumably are excluded because they historically have enjoyed preferential rates at both the corporate and individual levels.   In any event, when Congress eliminated preferential rates for capital gains in the Tax Reform Act of 1986, it did not include long-term capital gains and Section 1231 gains in the definition of personal holding company income.   Dividends are defined by reference to Section 316 and are not reduced by the dividends received deduction.   Interest includes imputed interest under provisions such as Sections 483 and 7872, but the types of interest excluded from AOGI (e.g., interest on condemnation awards, judgments or tax refunds) do not constitute personal holding company income.   The inclusion of most forms of interest income may create unexpected difficulties for an otherwise active corporation which has sold a substantial portion of its assets on credit in a year when other receipts are minimal.[11]   Royalties include income from licenses to use various types of intangible property (e.g., patents, trademarks, technical know-how) [12]—a broad definition that may threaten a high technology company, such as a computer software manufacturer, that chooses to license its technology rather than market it directly.   Royalties from natural resources, films, copyrights and computer software are treated separately and are discussed below.

Rents.   One of the major sources of complexity in Section 543 results from its attempt to draw objective lines between passive investment income and profits from an active operating business.   Nowhere is this better illustrated than in the area of rents.   The treatment of rents was overhauled as part of substantial revisions to the personal holding company tax enacted in 1964.   The following excerpt from the legislative history describes the Congressional solution: [13]

> *(c)(v) Rental income.*—Under present law rental income is classified as personal holding company income only if it represents less than 50 percent of total gross income.   This is based on the concept that where rental income represents the major activity, the activity involved is more likely to be of an active rather than passive character.   The House bill retains this 50-percent test (applying it, however, to adjusted income from rents and to adjusted ordinary gross income) but adds a second test providing that rental income may be characterized as passive, or personal holding company income even where it

---

10.   I.R.C. § 543(a)(1).

11.   See, e.g., O'Sullivan Rubber Co. v. Commissioner, 120 F.2d 845 (2d Cir.1941).

12.   Reg. § 1.543–1(b)(3).

13.   S.Rep. No. 830, 88th Cong., 2d Sess. (1964), reprinted in 1964–1 (pt. 2) C.B. 505, 611–613.

represents 50 percent or more of the adjusted ordinary gross income if, apart from the rental income, more than 10 percent of the ordinary gross income (gross income excluding capital gains) of the company is personal holding company income. For this purpose, income derived from the use of corporate property by shareholders is not viewed as personal holding company income, but income from copyright royalties and the adjusted income from mineral, oil, and gas royalties is included for this purpose as personal holding company income.

Your committee has accepted the House changes in the 50-percent test with one modification. Your committee has made an amendment to this test with regard to rentals of tangible personal property retained by the lessee for three years or less. Under the amendment, in the case of such property, the income is not to be reduced by depreciation attributable to it for purposes of the 50-percent test and also for purposes of computing ordinary gross income. However, in the case of the provision in the House bill that the personal holding company income (apart from rent) may not exceed 10 percent of the ordinary gross income, your committee's amendments provide that the personal holding company income for this purpose may be reduced by dividends paid during the year, by dividends paid in the next year which are treated as if paid in the year in question, and by consent dividends. Your committee believes that this prevents the 10-percent rule from working harshly where the personal holding company income other than rents may exceed 10 percent of ordinary gross income, perhaps by only a small amount but under the House bill, nevertheless, result in the entire amount of rental income being classified as personal holding company income. Your committee's amendment in effect permits taxpayers to meet the 10-percent test after dividend payments (or amounts treated as paid in dividends). At the same time it gives assurance that the personal holding company income (apart from rent) sheltered in the company may not exceed 10 percent of its ordinary gross income.

The fact that rental income, both in applying the 60-percent test and also in applying the 50-percent provision to the rental income itself, is determined on the basis of reducing rental income by depreciation, amortization, property taxes, interest, and rents paid has already been noted above. However, as previously indicated, tangible personal property rented for three years or less is not reduced by depreciation attributable to it for purposes of these tests, under your committee's amendments.

Mineral, Oil and Gas Royalties. Income from mineral, oil and gas royalties also are singled out for special treatment. The "adjusted income" from these royalties constitutes personal holding company income unless: (1) such adjusted income constitutes 50 percent or more of the corporation's AOGI, (2) certain other forms of the corporation's personal holding company income do not exceed 10 percent of its OGI, and (3) the corporation's trade or business deductions, other than salaries and deductions specifically allowed by sections other than Section 162 (e.g., depreciation, interest, state taxes) exceed 15 percent of AOGI.[14]

Copyright Royalties. Under rules similar to those applicable to mineral royalties, copyright royalties are personal holding company income unless: (1) they constitute 50 percent or more of the corporation's OGI, (2) other personal holding company income after certain adjustments, does not exceed 10 percent of the corporation's OGI, and (3) Section 162 business deductions allocable to the copyright royalties, other than salaries, deductions for royalties paid and deductions specifically allowed by sections other than Section 162, equal or exceed 25 percent of OGI reduced by royalties paid and depreciation deductions attributable to the copyrights.[15]

Produced Film Rents. "Produced film rents" are personal holding company income unless they constitute 50 percent or more of OGI. Active motion picture companies thus have nothing to fear from this provision. The purpose and scope of Section 543(a)(5) are explained in the following excerpt from the 1964 legislative history: [16]

> *(c)(viii) Produced film rents.*—Under present law payments received from the distribution and exhibition of motion picture films are treated as rentals. As a result, under present law, a corporation may be formed by an individual who owns a motion picture negative and have its earnings treated as rents for purposes of the personal holding company tax. Since in such a case more than 50 percent of its gross income would be considered to be from rents, there would be no personal holding company tax payable in this case.
>
> To meet this problem, the bill provides that payments received from the use of, or the right to use, films generally will be characterized as copyright royalty income. Thus, such income will be classified as personal holding company income unless 50 percent or more of the company's ordinary income is from this source, not more than 10 percent of the company's ordinary gross income is personal holding company income, and the deductions properly allocable to this film income represent 25 percent or more of the gross income from this source reduced by royalties paid and depreciation taken.
>
> The bill, however, retains what is essentially the treatment of present law for "produced film rents." Produced film rents are rents arising from an interest in a film acquired

---

14. I.R.C. § 543(a)(3).

15. I.R.C. § 543(a)(4).

16. S.Rep. No. 830, 88th Cong., 2d Sess. (1964), reprinted in 1964–1 (pt. 2) C.B. 505, 612–13.

before the production of the film was substantially complete. It was thought that less severe tests should be applied in such cases because the participation in the production of the film in itself indicates an active business enterprise in this case. For produced film rent to escape characterization as personal holding company income, as under present law, these rents need constitute only 50 percent or more of the ordinary gross income of the company.

Computer Software Royalties. Prior to the Tax Reform Act of 1986, a closely held company which manufactured computer software was confronted with the personal holding company tax if it licensed its technology instead of marketing it directly.[17] Despite the fact that the company was an active operating business, the payments received under the licensing agreements likely constituted personal holding company income under Section 543, which includes both "royalties" and certain "copyright royalties" in the definition of personal holding company income.[18] Congress addressed this problem in the 1986 Act by providing that computer software royalties do not constitute personal holding company income if they are "active business computer software royalties."[19] That term is defined in Section 543(d)(1) as royalties, received by a corporation in connection with the licensing of computer software, which satisfy four requirements.[20] These additional tests are explained in the following excerpt from the legislative history: [21]

> Under the committee bill, personal holding company income does not include certain computer software royalties. To qualify for the exception, four conditions must be met.

> First, computer software royalties must be received by a corporation engaged in the active conduct of the trade or business of developing, manufacturing, or producing computer software; such computer software (a) must be developed, manufactured, or produced by such corporation (or its predecessor) in connection with such trade or business, or (b) must be directly related to such trade or business (the "trade or business test"). For this purpose, predecessor includes a partnership, the partners of which developed software for the partnership and transferred their partnership interests to the corporation in exchange for substantially all of the corporation's stock.

> Second, computer software royalties that meet the first requirement must make up at least 50 percent of the ordinary gross income (as defined in section 543(b)) of the taxpayer for the taxable year (the "50-percent test").

---

17. See generally Morgan, "The Domestic Technology Base Company: The Dilemma of an Operating Company Which Might Be a Personal Holding Company," 33 Tax L.Rev. 233 (1978).

18. I.R.C. § 543(a)(1), (4).

19. I.R.C. § 543(a)(1)(C), (a)(4) (last sentence).

20. I.R.C. § 543(d)(2)–(5).

21. H.R. Rep. No. 99–426, 99th Cong., 1st Sess. 872–73 (1985).

Third, the amount of expenses that are properly allocable to the active business of developing, producing, or manufacturing software and that are allowable to the taxpayer under section 162 (relating to trade or business expenses), section 174 (relating to research and development expenses), or section 195 (relating to amortization of start-up expenses), must equal or exceed 25 percent of the ordinary gross income of the taxpayer for the taxable year (the "25-percent test").[1] Alternatively, the average of such deductions for the period of five taxable years ending with the current taxable year (or such shorter period as the corporation may have been in existence) must equal or exceed 25 percent of the ordinary gross income of the taxpayer for such period.

In computing deductions under section 162, the taxpayer may not take into account payments for personal services rendered by the five shareholders holding the largest percentage (by value) of the outstanding stock of the corporation. In determining the five largest shareholders for this purpose, stock deemed to be owned by a shareholder solely by reason of attribution from a partner (under section 544(a)(2)) is not taken into account, and individuals holding less than five percent of the corporation's stock (by value) are not taken into account.

Fourth, the sum of dividends paid during the taxable year (under section 562), dividends considered paid on the last day of the taxable year (under section 563) and the consent dividends for the taxable year (under section 565) must equal or exceed the amount of the corporation's personal holding company income in excess of 10 percent of the ordinary gross income of the corporation. For purposes of this computation, however, personal holding company income does not include the computer software royalties taken into account for the 50-percent test, and also does not include interest income for the five-year period beginning with the commencement of the active computer software business, provided that the 50-percent test and the 25-percent test also are met in this period.

Personal Service Income. The final major category of personal holding company income is aimed at the incorporated talent. Income from contracts to furnish personal services, including income from the sale or other disposition of such contracts, is tainted if: (1) the individual who is to perform the services is designated by name or description in the contract or can be designated by some person other than the corporation, and (2) the designated individual owns (directly or through

---

1. For purposes of this computation, any deduction specifically allowable under any section of the Code other than section 162 may not be treated as allowable under section 162.

attribution) 25 percent or more of the value of the corporation's stock at any time during the year.[22]

Other Items. Personal holding company income also includes rents for the use of tangible property received from a 25 percent shareholder under certain conditions [23] and income derived by the corporation in its capacity as a beneficiary of an estate or trust.[24]

REVENUE RULING 75–67

1975–1 Cum.Bull. 169.

Advice has been requested whether, under the circumstances described below, a corporation will be considered to have received personal holding company income within the meaning of section 543(a)(7) of the Internal Revenue Code of 1954.

B, a doctor specializing in a certain area of medical services, owns 80 percent of the outstanding stock of *L*, a domestic professional service corporation. *B* is the only officer of *L* who is active in the production of income for *L*, and he is the only medical doctor presently employed by *L*. *B* performs medical services under an employment contract with *L*. *L* furnishes office quarters and equipment, and employs a receptionist to assist *B*. *P*, a patient, solicited the services of and was treated by *B*.

Section 543(a)(7) of the Code provides, in part, that the term personal holding company income includes amounts received under a contract whereby a corporation is to furnish personal services if some person other than the corporation has the right to designate, by name or description, the individual who is to perform the services, or if the individual who is to perform the services is designated, by name or description, in the contract.

In dealing with a professional service corporation providing medical services, an individual will customarily solicit and expect to receive the services of a particular physician, and he will usually be treated by the physician sought.

A physician-patient relationship arises from such a general agreement of treatment. Either party may terminate the relationship at will, although the physician must give the patient reasonable notice of his withdrawal and may not abandon the patient until a replacement, if necessary, can be obtained. C. Morris & A. Mortiz, Doctor and Patient and the Law 135 (5th ed. 1971). Moreover, if a physician who has entered into a general agreement of treatment is unable to treat the patient when his services are needed, he may provide a qualified and competent substitute physician to render the services. *C. Morris & A. Moritz,* supra, at 138, 374–75.

Thus, when an individual solicits, and expects, the services of a particular physician and that physician accepts the individual as a

---

22. I.R.C. § 543(a)(7). For detailed examples of the operation of this provision, see Reg. § 1.543–1(b)(8).

23. I.R.C. § 543(a)(6).

24. I.R.C. § 543(a)(8).

patient and treats him, the relationship of physician-patient established in this manner does not constitute a designation of the individual who is to perform the services under a contract for personal services within the meaning of section 543(a)(7) of the Code.

If, however, the physician or the professional service corporation contracts with the patient that the physician personally will perform particular services for the patient, and he has no right to substitute another physician to perform such services, there is a designation of that physician as the individual to perform services under a contract for personal services within the meaning of section 543(a)(7) of the Code.

The designation of a physician as an individual to perform services can be accomplished by either an oral or written contract. See Rev. Rul. 69–299, 1969–1 C.B. 165.

Moreover, if *L* agreed to perform the type of services that are so unique as to preclude substitution of another physician to perform such services, there is also a designation.

Accordingly, since in the instant case there is no indication that *L* has contracted that *B* will personally perform the services or that the services are so unique as to preclude substitution, it is held that income earned by *L* from providing medical service contracts will not be considered income from personal service contracts within the meaning of section 543(a)(7) of the Code.

REVENUE RULING 84–137
1984–2 Cum.Bull. 116.

ISSUE

Is rental income received by a corporate lessor from a corporate lessee, which [sic] both corporations are owned by the same individual shareholder, compensation for the use of or right to use corporate property by a shareholder under section 543(a)(6) of the Internal Revenue Code for purposes of the personal holding company tax provisions?

FACTS

A, an individual, owns all of the shares of two corporations, *X* and *Y*. *X*'s primary business activity is the leasing of realty and tangible personal property to its sister corporation *Y* for a fair market rental value. *A* makes no personal use of *X*'s leased assets, which are used solely in *Y*'s manufacturing business. In 1983, *X* received 100*x* dollars of rental income from *Y* and 12*x* dollars of interest income from its various bank deposits. The 12*x* dollars of interest income is personal holding company income as defined in section 543(a)(1) of the Code.

LAW AND ANALYSIS

Section 543(a)(6)(A) of the Code provides that amounts received as compensation for the use of, or the right to use, tangible property of the corporation in any case where at any time during the taxable year, 25 percent or more in value of the outstanding stock of the corporation is owned, directly or indirectly, by or for an individual entitled to the use of the property (whether such right is obtained directly from the corporation or by means of a sublease or other arrangement) is personal holding company income.

Section 543(a)(6)(B) of the Code provides that section 543(a)(6)(A) of the Code will apply only to a corporation which has other personal holding company income (as determined under section 543(a)(6)(C)) in excess of 10 percent of its ordinary gross income.

Rev.Rul. 65–259, 1965–2 C.B. 174, states that where rental income is derived from a corporate lessee, any one of whose shareholders also directly or indirectly owns 25 percent or more in value of the outstanding stock of the lessor corporation, the shareholder of the lessee corporation indirectly has the right to use the leased property and such indirect right is obtained by means of an "other arrangement". See *320 East 47th Street Corporation v. Commissioner*, 243 F.2d 894 (2d Cir. 1957), rev'g in part, 26 T.C. 545 (1956). Thus, Rev.Rul. 65–259 holds that the rental income is personal holding company income under section 543(a)(6) of the Code.

The Tax Court in *Allied Industrial Cartage Co. v. Commissioner*, 72 T.C. 515 (1979), aff'd, 647 F.2d 713 (6th Cir.1981), and *Silverman and Sons Realty Trust v. Commissioner*, T.C.M. 1979–404, aff'd, 620 F.2d 314 (1st Cir.1980), disagreed with the holding in *320 East 47th Street Corp.* These cases hold that, as between brother and sister corporations, unless a corporate lessee is shown to be a vehicle for facilitating the individual or personal use of leased property by its shareholders, its separate status should not be disregarded so as to impose the personal holding company tax upon the lessor corporation. See also *New Colonial Ice v. Helvering*, 292 U.S. 435 (1934) XIII–2 C.B. 194; *Minnesota Mortuaries, Inc. v. Commissioner*, 4 T.C. 280 (1944); acq., 1945 C.B. 5, nonacq., 1965–2 C.B. 7, acq. page 5, this Bulletin.

HOLDING

If rental income is received by a corporate lessor from a corporate lessee, when both corporations are wholly owned by the same individual shareholder and the rented property is used solely in the trade or business of the lessee corporation and not for the individual or personal benefit of the shareholder, then such rental income is not compensation for the use of or right to use corporate property by a shareholder under section 543(a)(6) of the Code for purpose of the personal holding company tax provisions.

*   *   *

3.   TAXATION OF PERSONAL HOLDING COMPANIES

Code: §§ 541, 545(a).

Personal holding companies are taxed at the rate of 28 percent of their undistributed personal holding company income.[1] The key to understanding the computation of the personal holding company tax is the concept of undistributed personal holding company income (UPHCI). The definition of UPHCI bears no relationship to the definition of personal holding company income. As defined in Section 545(a), UPHCI is essentially the corporation's after-tax profits less a dividends paid deduction.

a.   ADJUSTMENTS TO TAXABLE INCOME

Code: § 545(b).

The personal holding company tax is imposed on the corporation's real after-tax profits rather than its taxable income. Accordingly, in determining the tax base, certain adjustments are made to the corporation's taxable income so that it more nearly resembles the corporation's true economic income. Deductions are allowed for payments, such as federal taxes [2] and certain excess charitable contributions, which reduce the corporation's real wealth but are not allowable in computing taxable income.[3] Conversely, certain deductions which are allowable in determining taxable income but which do not decrease the corporation's real earnings for the year are not allowed in determining UPHCI. An example is the Section 243 dividends received deduction.[4] Net operating losses also receive special treatment.[5] Finally, in order to exempt long-term capital gains from the personal holding company tax, corporations may eliminate net capital gains less attributable taxes in determining UPHCI.[6]

Another Section 545(b) adjustment relates to a specific tax avoidance scheme mentioned earlier. Individuals cannot depreciate their homes, yachts, vacation homes or other property held for personal use. In order to obtain the benefits of depreciation, individuals would transfer these assets to a corporation with other income and then lease them back in an attempt to convert the assets to income–producing status in the hands of the corporation. We have already seen that the resulting rental income will likely be personal holding company income. Section 545(b)(6) attacks this same scheme from a different angle. For purposes of determining UPHCI, if the corporation leases its property, the allocable business and depreciation deductions are limited to the rental income from the property unless the corporation can establish that: (1) the rent received for the property was the

---

1. I.R.C. § 541.

2. I.R.C. § 545(b)(1).

3. I.R.C. § 545(b)(2). A special mixture of individual and corporate rules apply to determine the amount of the adjustment.

4. I.R.C. § 545(b)(3).

5. I.R.C. § 545(b)(4).

6. I.R.C. § 545(b)(5).

highest obtainable, (2) the property was held by the corporation in the course of a business for profit, and (3) there either was a reasonable expectation of profit from the property or the property was necessary to the conduct of the business.

b. DIVIDENDS PAID DEDUCTION

Code: §§ 561, 316(b), 562(a), (b), (c), 563, 564, 565. Skim § 547.

The purpose of the personal holding company tax is to force personal holding companies to distribute earnings to their individual shareholders. It follows that to the extent a personal holding company distributes its earnings, the Section 541 tax should not apply. To qualify for the dividends paid deduction, distributions generally must be pro rata.[7] Under Section 561(a), the dividends paid deduction equals the sum of the dividends paid during the taxable year, consent dividends, and the dividend carryover under Section 564. The combination of these provisions make it highly unlikely that any well informed personal holding company ever will be subject to the penalty tax.

Dividends Paid During the Year. Dividends paid during the year are determined by reference to the definition of a dividend in Section 316. For purposes of the dividends paid deduction, the regulations provide that a dividend in kind of appreciated property may only be deducted to the extent of the corporation's basis in the distributed property.[8] This rule is at variance with the treatment of such dividends to shareholders, for whom the "amount" of the distribution is the full fair market value of the distributed property under Section 301(b)(1)(A). But the regulation was upheld by the Supreme Court on the general ground that Treasury Regulations should be sustained by the courts whenever they have a "reasonable basis."[9] Query whether the same approach should be used for distributions of property that has declined in value?

Distributions and redemptions treated as Section 301 distributions are, of course, taxable as dividends to the shareholders to the extent of the corporation's available earnings and profits. If a corporation is a personal holding company, however, distributions may be taxed as dividends even if there are no available earnings and profits. Under Section 316(b)(2), if a personal holding company makes distributions in excess of the available earnings and profits, the distributions are nonetheless treated as dividends for all purposes to the extent of the corporation's UPHCI. This rule also applies if a corporation is considered to make a distribution under Section 563(b) (dividends paid after the year) or Section 547 (deficiency dividends) in a year in which it is a personal holding company.

Section 563(b) Election. If a corporation elects under Section 563(b), dividends paid or on before the 15th day of the third month

7. I.R.C. § 562(c).

8. Reg. § 1.562–1(a).

9. Fulman v. United States, 434 U.S. 528, 98 S.Ct. 841 (1978).

following the close of a taxable year will be treated as having been paid during the prior year. The amount allowed as a dividend under Section 563(b) can not exceed either the corporation's UPHCI for the prior taxable year or 20 percent of the actual dividends paid during the prior year.[10]

Consent Dividends. If a corporation does not make actual distributions during the relevant period, then under Section 565 the corporation still can qualify for a dividends paid deduction to the extent that its shareholders consent to be taxed as if they had received pro rata distributions during the year and had immediately made capital contributions of the same amount.[11] Consent dividends are deductible only to the extent that all the shareholders consent to be taxed on a pro rata basis [12] and, of course, only to the extent that actual distributions would be dividends under Section 316(a) or 316(b).

Dividend Carryover. Even if a corporation pays no actual or consent dividends, it is entitled to a current dividend deduction if it has paid sufficient dividends in either or both of the two preceding years. Under Section 564 the amount of this deduction is the greater of the excess of the dividends paid deduction (without carryovers) over taxable income, as adjusted in Section 545, for the preceding year, or the excess of the combined dividends paid deduction (without carryovers) for the preceding two years over the total taxable income (again adjusted under Section 545) for the same two years. Roughly translated, this means that a corporation that over distributes in prior years may distribute less in the current year in determining its exposure to the tax.

Liquidating Distributions. If a corporation is liquidating, it still may be a personal holding company. Indeed, an operating company may become a personal holding company during the process of liquidating if it ceases its operations in a taxable year prior to its final liquidating distribution and has only passive investment income in that terminal year. In order to avoid penalizing liquidating corporations by denying them a dividends paid deduction for actual liquidating distributions, Section 562(b)(2) provides that if the corporation liquidates within 24 months of adopting a plan of liquidation, liquidating distributions to corporate shareholders are treated as dividends for purposes of the dividends paid deduction to the extent of the shareholder's proportionate share of UPHCI for the year of the distribution. At the corporation's election, liquidating distributions to noncorporate shareholders also may be treated as dividends under Section 316(b)(2)(B) to the extent of the shareholders' proportionate share of UPHCI. If they are so treated, the corporation is entitled to take the dividends paid deduction. Unlike corporate shareholders, however, noncorporate shareholders must treat such liquidating distributions as dividend income under Section 316(b) rather than capital gain under Section 331.

---

10. The timing of the shareholder's income is not affected by the Section 563(b) election.

11. I.R.C. § 565(c).

12. I.R.C. § 565(b)(1).

Deficiency Dividends. If a corporation is determined to be a personal holding company for a particular year, Section 547 permits the corporation to reduce its personal holding company tax base (but not interest or penalties) by the amount of its "deficiency dividends." Deficiency dividends are defined as amounts paid within 90 days of the determination of personal holding company tax liability which would have been eligible for the dividends paid deduction if distributed in the year in which Section 541 tax liability exists.[13] A deficiency dividend is allowed as of the date a claim for dividend is filed.[14]

PROBLEMS

1. X Corporation is wholly owned by A. Determine whether X is a personal holding company under each of the following alternatives:

(a) X manufactures umbrellas. In year one, X has $2,000,000 gross receipts from sales, and its cost of goods sold is $800,000. It has no other income or expenses and makes no distributions.

(b) X's business hits a dry spell in year two. Its gross receipts from sales are $900,000, and its cost of goods sold is $890,000. X also receives $30,000 interest on its $200,000 profit from year one, which it deposited in a savings account.

(c) What result in (b), above, if X also had $30,000 of § 1231 gains in year two? What about $10,000 of § 1231 gains and $20,000 of § 1245 gain?

2. Consider whether the following corporations are personal holding companies:

(a) Basketball Corporation is wholly owned by Dr. K, who plays professional basketball. Dr. K contracts to work for the corporation for $150,000 per year. Basketball Corporation then contracts with Team to provide Dr. K's services to Team for $300,000 per year.

(b) What result in (a), above, if Basketball purchases a movie theater by paying $20,000 down and taking the theater subject to a $180,000 mortgage. During the year, the theater has receipts of $300,000 and deductible expenses (depreciation interest, salaries and film rents) of $300,000?

(c) Attorney forms Professional Corporation and incorporates his private practice. During the year the corporation earns fees of $300,000 and pays Attorney a salary of $150,000.

(d) Aside from the personal holding company tax, what other challenges might the Service assert in parts (a)–(c)?

13. I.R.C. § 547(d)(1).

14. I.R.C. § 547(b)(1). A claim must be filed within 120 days after the determina-

tion of personal holding company tax liability. I.R.C. § 547(e).

3.   Iris Securities Company is wholly owned by Investor.   Determine whether Iris is a personal holding company, and if so, the amount of the § 541 tax, under the following circumstances:

(a)   Iris earns a total of $30,000 of interest and dividends in year one.   Iris also owns an apartment complex.   During the past year, it collected rents of $100,000.   Iris's only deductions were depreciation of $35,000, mortgage interest of $30,000, and property taxes of $5,000.   Iris makes no distributions during the year.

(b)   Assume that Investor comes to you for tax advice on December 15 of year one.   If Iris uses the calendar year as its taxable year, can it avoid personal holding company status?   What if Investor comes to you in January of year two?

4.   Operating Company is owned equally by Ms. Active and by X Corporation.   Operating Company has been engaged in the retail sales business.   In June of year one, Operating Company adopts a plan to liquidate.   In December of year one, it sells all its assets for $1,000,000, which it deposits in a short-term savings account.   In June of year two, after having earned $50,000 interest during the year, Operating Company liquidates by distributing $525,000 to each shareholder.

(a)   What are the tax consequences to Operating and its shareholders?

(b)   What alternatives are available?

CHAPTER 10.   ACQUISITIVE REORGANIZATIONS

A.   INTRODUCTION

1.   HISTORICAL BACKGROUND

Some of the major litigation arising under the early federal income tax laws involved a variety of transactions loosely described as corporate reorganizations.   Long before they became distracted by tax considerations, corporate lawyers and investment bankers were busy devising transactions ranging from complicated mergers, acquisitions and recapitalizations to routine changes in the state of incorporation.   With the arrival of the income tax, the courts were required to determine whether and to what extent these fundamental changes in the structure of a corporate entity were taxable events.

Working with a pristine statute and an unsophisticated perspective, the Supreme Court became one of the first protectors of the comprehensive tax base.   In a series of cases, the Court concluded that even minor changes in the form of a corporate business enterprise (e.g., changing the state of incorporation from New Jersey to Delaware) caused the shareholders to realize gain.[1]   While these cases were pending, however, Congress quickly came to the rescue by enacting one of the first nonrecognition provisions.   Preceding even the forerunner of Section 351, Section 202(b) of the Revenue Act of 1918 provided that no gain or loss would be recognized on the "reorganization, merger or consolidation of a corporation" where a person received "in place of stock or securities owned by him new stock or securities of no greater aggregate par face value."[2]

The rationale for the reorganization provisions reflects the broader policies of nonrecognition.   Congress concluded that the tax collector should not impede these diverse transactions because they are mere readjustments of a continuing corporate enterprise, albeit in modified form,[3] and the new property received is "substantially a continuation of the old investment still unliquidated."[4]   But to the extent that a shareholder liquidates a corporate investment, recognition of gain or loss *is* appropriate.   The 1921 predecessor of the present reorganization provisions thus provided that shareholders must recognize their real-

1.   Marr v. United States, 268 U.S. 536, 45 S.Ct. 575 (1925).   See also United States v. Phellis, 257 U.S. 156, 42 S.Ct. 63 (1921); Rockefeller v. United States, 257 U.S. 176, 42 S.Ct. 68 (1921).

2.   Pub.L. No. 254, 40 Stat. 1057 (1919).

3.   Reg. § 1.368–1(b).   See also S.Rep. No. 275, 67th Cong., 1st Sess. (1921), reprinted in 1939–1 (Part 2) C.B. 181, 188–

189, where the Senate Finance Committee justified the principal forerunners of the modern nonrecognition provisions on the ground that they would permit businesses to proceed with necessary adjustments and remove "a source of grave uncertainty" in the law.

4.   Reg. § 1.1002–1(c).

ized gain, if any, to the extent of the "boot" (money and other property) received.[5] Congress soon refined the statutory scheme by making clear what it had suggested in earlier versions: nonrecognition really means deferral rather than total forgiveness of gain or loss. The Revenue Act of 1928 introduced rules for carryover and substituted bases in order to preserve the unrecognized gain or loss for recognition at the time that the shareholder liquidated his investment.[6]

What began as a relatively simple concept has evolved into a vast and challenging body of law that governs some of the most financially significant transactions in the business world. It is important to recognize at the outset that the system you are about to study is not necessarily sensible. Functionally different transactions are lumped together and labelled "reorganizations." At the same time, economically equivalent acquisition methods are tested for reorganization status under sharply different criteria that often place a great premium on the form chosen by the parties. Moreover, determining the tax consequences of a corporate combination or readjustment requires an application of precise statutory provisions and judicially created "common law" principles of uncertain scope. Analysis is further complicated by the possibility of an overlap between the reorganization provisions and other parts of Subchapter C.

In view of these defects in the reorganization scheme, it is not surprising that commentators have called for a complete overhaul of the current system.[7] But it has not happened yet and so we must turn to a more detailed examination of provisions that Professors Bittker and Eustice have described as "extraordinarily complex, even for the [Internal Revenue] Code." [8]

2. OVERVIEW OF REORGANIZATIONS

Code: Skim §§ 336(c); 354; 355; 356; 358; 361; 362(b); 368(a)(1), (b), (c); 381(a); 1032.

The term "reorganization" generally is associated with the rehabilitation of a bankrupt company. Under the Internal Revenue Code, however, "reorganization" is a term of art [1] used to describe corporate combinations or readjustments that fall into the following three broad categories:

> (1) *Acquisitive reorganizations,* which are considered in this chapter, are transactions in which one corporation (the "acquiring corporation") acquires the assets or stock of another corpora-

---

5. Revenue Act of 1921, § 202, Pub.L. No. 98, 42 Stat. 227.

6. Revenue Act of 1928, § 113(a)(6)–(9), Pub.L. No. 562, 45 Stat. 791.

7. See generally Federal Income Tax Project, Subchapter C, American Law Institute (1982); Staff of the Senate Finance Committee, The Subchapter C Revision Act of 1985: A Final Report Prepared by the

Staff, 99th Cong., 1st Sess. 50–58 (S.Prt. 99–47, 1985). See Section E of this chapter, infra.

8. Bittker & Eustice, Federal Income Taxation of Corporations and Shareholders ¶ 14.01 (5th ed. 1987).

1. See I.R.C. § 368(a)(1); Reg. § 1.368–1(c).

tion (the "acquired" or "target" corporation). Included in this category are statutory mergers or consolidations ("A" reorganizations); acquisitions of stock of the target for voting stock of the acquiring corporation ("B" reorganizations); acquisitions of assets of the target for voting stock of the acquiring corporation ("C" reorganizations, sometimes called "practical mergers" because of their similarity to statutory mergers); and several other more complicated acquisition techniques involving the use of a subsidiary.

(2) *Nonacquisitive, nondivisive reorganizations,* which involve adjustments to the corporate structure of a single, continuing corporate enterprise. This category includes recapitalizations ("E" reorganizations); changes in identity, form or place of incorporation ("F" reorganizations); certain transfers of substantially all of the assets from one corporation to another, followed by a liquidation of the first corporation (nondivisive "D" reorganizations); and transfers of a corporation's assets to another corporation pursuant to a bankruptcy reorganization plan ("G" reorganizations). These transactions are considered in Chapter 11.

(3) *Divisive reorganizations,* which result in the division of a single corporation into two or more separate entities and which often are preceded by a "D" reorganization. Corporate divisions are considered in Chapter 12.

A common organizational thread weaves its way through these diverse categories. First, definitional provisions set forth requirements ranging from the general and very flexible test to qualify as a Type A reorganization to the complex criteria imposed by Section 355 for corporate divisions. To qualify as a reorganization, a transaction also must pass muster under "common law" doctrines developed by the courts to reinforce the rationale for nonrecognition. The principal judicial doctrines are continuity of interest, continuity of business enterprise and business purpose. In general, the continuity of interest doctrine requires the shareholders of the target corporation to continue their investment, albeit in another form, by exchanging their target stock for a sufficient amount of stock of the acquiring corporation. In some cases, the continuity of interest doctrine has been incorporated into the statutory definition of "reorganization;" for example, the only permissible consideration in a B reorganization is voting stock of the acquiring corporation.[2] The doctrine assumes far more importance if the statute is imprecise, as with Type A reorganizations, where the Code merely requires a "statutory merger or consolidation" without any elaboration on the permissible consideration.[3] We therefore examine continuity of interest questions in connection with Type A reorganizations—the context in which the doctrine most frequently arises.

---

2. I.R.C. § 368(a)(1)(B).   **3.** I.R.C. § 368(a)(1)(A).

The continuity of business enterprise doctrine, as its name implies, focuses on the continuing business operations of the target. This requirement has been incorporated in the regulations and also is considered with "A" reorganizations. Because the business purpose doctrine was first applied and has the greatest importance in the context of a corporate division, it is discussed in Chapter 12. In general, all these requirements must be satisfied in order for a transaction to qualify as a reorganization.[4] To further complicate matters, the Service sometimes applies the step transaction doctrine to corporate reorganizations to convert what in form may be separate nontaxable steps into what in substance is a taxable transaction, or vice versa.[5]

If these statutory and judicial requirements are met, they unlock the doors to the "operative provisions"—sections of the Code that provide for nonrecognition of gain or loss and that govern collateral matters such as the treatment of liabilities, basis, holding period and carryover of tax attributes.[6] For example, Sections 354 and 356 grant total or partial nonrecognition of gain to the shareholders of the target corporation in an acquisitive reorganization. Section 358, which we encountered earlier in connection with tax-free incorporations, provides a formula for determining the substituted basis of the stock or securities received by these shareholders in a reorganization. At the corporate level, Section 361(a) generally provides for nonrecognition when a corporation transfers its assets in a reorganization and distributes property in a liquidation pursuant to a reorganization plan,[7] and Section 357 generally ensures that the assumption of the target's liabilities is not treated as boot for this purpose. The acquiring corporation is accorded nonrecognition under Section 1032 with respect to stock used to make the acquisition and takes a transferred basis in the target's assets or stock under Section 362(b). In keeping with the continuity of investment principle, the tax attributes of the target corporation (e.g., earnings and profits and net operating losses) generally carry over to the acquiring corporation under Section 381, subject to various limitations to patrol abuse.[8]

If a transaction does not qualify as a reorganization, these operative provisions do not apply and the tax consequences of the transaction must be determined under other parts of Subchapter C. For example, an asset acquisition that fails as a Type A or C reorganization ordinarily would be a taxable transaction to the shareholders under the complete liquidation rules considered in Chapter 7. But it is the rare

---

4. Reg. §§ 1.368–1(b), 1.368–2(g). However, since the "E" reorganization involves only a single corporation, there is neither a continuity of interest nor a continuity of business enterprise requirement. Microdot, Inc. v. United States, 728 F.2d 593 (2d Cir.1984); Golden Nugget, Inc. v. Commissioner, 83 T.C. 28 (1984); Rev.Rul. 82–34, 1982–1 C.B. 59. In addition, the legislative history of the "G" reorganization indicates that both doctrines will be

leniently applied in an insolvency situation. See Chapter 11D, infra.

5. See, e.g., Rev.Rul. 79–250, 1979–2 C.B. 156.

6. See Section C of this chapter, infra.

7. See also I.R.C. § 336(c).

8. See Section D of this chapter and Chapter 13, infra.

reorganization that fails. Because of the high stakes involved, taxpayers are reluctant to proceed with reorganization transactions without first obtaining the Internal Revenue Service's blessing in the form of an advance ruling.[9] Indeed, these transactions normally are conditioned on the receipt of a favorable ruling. The Service's administrative ruling guidelines are tantamount to the law in this area, and taxpayers who disagree with the government's viewpoint must proceed with the transaction at their substantial risk.

B. TYPES OF ACQUISITIVE REORGANIZATIONS

1. TYPE A: STATUTORY MERGERS AND CONSOLIDATIONS

Code: § 368(a)(1)(A). Skim §§ 354(a); 356(a); 357; 358(a); 361; 362(b); 368(a)(2)(C), (b); 381(a)(2); 1032.

Regulations: §§ 1.368–1, –2(a), (b)(1).

The Type A reorganization is defined in the Code as a statutory merger or consolidation. For this purpose, "statutory" refers to a merger or consolidation pursuant to local corporate law.[1] Under a typical state merger statute, the assets and liabilities of the target corporation are transferred to the acquiring corporation without the need for deeds or bills of sale, and the target dissolves by operation of law.[2] The consideration received by the target's shareholders is specified in a formal agreement of merger between the two companies. The shareholders may receive stock or debt instruments of the acquiring corporation, cash or a combination of all three. A consolidation involves a similar transfer of the assets and liabilities of two corporations to a newly created entity followed by the dissolution of the transferor corporations, and the shareholders of the transferors become shareholders of the new entity by operation of law. Either transaction typically requires approval by a simple majority or two-thirds vote of the shareholders of both corporations, and dissenting shareholders often are granted the right to be bought out for cash at a price determined in an appraisal proceeding.[3]

The Code is strangely silent as to the permissible consideration in a Type A reorganization. To fill the gap and preserve the integrity of the nonrecognition scheme, the courts developed the continuity of interest and continuity of business enterprise requirements.[4] Both doctrines are examined in the materials that follow.

9. For the Service's ruling guidelines, see Rev.Proc. 77–37, 1977–2 C.B. 568.

1. Russell v. Commissioner, 40 T.C. 810 (1963), affirmed 345 F.2d 534 (5th Cir. 1965).

2. See, e.g., 8 Del.Code § 251.

3. See generally Cary & Eisenberg, Corporations: Cases and Materials 1088 et seq. (6th ed. unabridged 1988).

4. The earliest continuity of interest cases involved Type C reorganizations but the doctrine now applies primarily to statutory mergers and consolidations.

a. CONTINUITY OF INTEREST

SOUTHWEST NATURAL GAS CO. v. COMMISSIONER *

United States Court of Appeals, Fifth Circuit, 1951.
189 F.2d 332.

RUSSELL, Circuit Judge.

The correctness of asserted deficiencies for corporate income tax for the year 1941 and of declared value excess profits tax and excess profits tax for 1942 due by Southwest Natural Gas Company depends upon whether a merger of Peoples Gas & Fuel Corporation with the taxpayer, effected in accordance with the laws of Delaware, was a sale, as asserted by the Commissioner, or a "reorganization" within the terms of Section 112(g) [the predecessor of Section 368] of the Internal Revenue Code, as contended by the taxpayer. The parties so stipulated the issue in the Tax Court. That Court upheld the Commissioner's determination. Southwest Natural Gas Company has petitioned this Court for review.

The facts found by the Tax Court (which, as facts, are not challenged) and the grounds for its judgment in law thereon are fully set forth in its published opinion. In substance that Court held that literal compliance with the provisions of a state law authorizing a merger would not in itself effect a "reorganization" within the terms applicable under Internal Revenue Statutes; that the test of continuity of interest was nevertheless applicable; and that the transaction in question did not meet this test. This ruling is assigned as error upon grounds which, while variously stated, require for their maintenance establishment of at least one of the propositions that: if the literal language of the statute is complied with, that is if there is a "statutory merger" duly effected in accordance with state law, the statute requires it be treated as a reorganization; or, at least where such merger has been effected the Tax Court must hold the transaction a reorganization in the absence of a finding that it was not in truth and in substance a merger; or, even if this be not correct, that the facts of this case disclose sufficient "continuity of interest." It is insisted in either view the Tax Court was required to hold under the facts found by it that the transaction in question was in truth a "statutory merger" and hence a "reorganization."

Consideration of the underlying purposes of the terms and provisions of Section 112 of the Internal Revenue Code in its entirety and of this Section (g)(1)(A) as involved here, in particular, as being enacted "to free from the imposition of an income tax purely 'paper profits or losses' wherein there is no realization of gain or loss in the business sense but merely the recasting of the same interests in a different form, the tax being postponed to a future date when a more tangible gain or loss is realized." Commissioner of Internal Revenue v. Gilmore's Es-

---

* Footnotes omitted.

tate, 3 Cir., 130 F.2d 791, 794, and thus applicable to transactions which effect only the "readjustment of continuing interest in property under modified corporate forms," clearly discloses, we think, that the accomplishment of a statutory merger does not *ipso facto* constitute a "reorganization" within the terms of the statute here involved. This has been expressly held by the Court of Appeals for the Third Circuit in a well considered opinion, supported by numerous authorities cited. Roebling v. Commissioner, 143 F.2d 810. There is no occasion for elaboration or reiteration of the reasoning and authorities set forth in that opinion. In Bazley v. Commissioner, 331 U.S. 737, 67 S.Ct. 1489, 1491, 91 L.Ed. 1782, the Supreme Court enforced a similar construction with reference to the "re-capitalization" provision of the section. The authorities are clearly to the effect that the terms expressed in the statute are not to be given merely a literal interpretation but are to be considered and applied in accordance with the purpose of Section 112. Thus the benefits of the reorganization provision have been withheld "in situations which might have satisfied provisions of the section treated as inert language, because they were not reorganizations of the kind with which § 112, in its purpose and particulars concerns itself. * * * "

It is thus clear that the test of "continuity of interest" announced and applied by these cited authorities, supra, must be met before a statutory merger may properly be held a reorganization within the terms of Section 112(g)(1)(A), supra. Each case must in its final analysis be controlled by its own peculiar facts. While no precise formula has been expressed for determining whether there has been retention of the requisite interest, it seems clear that the requirement of continuity of interest consistent with the statutory intent is not fulfilled in the absence of a showing: (1) that the transferor corporation or its shareholders retained a substantial proprietary stake in the enterprise represented by a material interest in the affairs of the transferee corporation, and, (2) that such retained interest represents a substantial part of the value of the property transferred.

Among other facts, the Tax Court found that under the merger all of Peoples' assets were acquired by the petitioner in exchange for specified amounts of stock, bonds, cash and the assumption of debts. There was a total of 18,875 shares common stock of Peoples' entitled to participate under the agreement of merger. The stockholders were offered Option A and Option B. The holders of 7,690 of such shares exercised Option B of that agreement and received $30.00 in cash for each share, or a total of $230,700.00. In respect to the stock now involved, the stockholders who exercised Option A, the holders of 59.2 per cent of the common stock received in exchange 16.4 per cent of petitioner's outstanding common stock plus $340,350.00 principal amount of six per cent mortgage bonds (of the market value of 90 per cent of principal), which had been assumed by petitioner in a prior merger and $17,779.59 cash. The 16.4 per cent of the common stock referred to was represented by 111,850 shares having a market value of

$5,592.50, or five cents per share, and represented the continuing proprietary interest of the participating stockholders in the enterprise. This was less than one per cent of the consideration paid by the taxpayers.

We think it clear that these and other facts found by the Tax Court find substantial support in the evidence, and the conclusion of the Tax Court that they failed to evidence sufficient continuity of interest to bring the transaction within the requirements of the applicable statute is correct.

The decision of the Tax Court is affirmed.

[The dissenting opinion of Chief Judge HUTCHESON has been omitted. Ed.]

REVENUE RULING 66–224
1966–2 Cum.Bull. 114.

Corporation *X* was merged under state law into corporation *Y*. Corporation *X* had four stockholders (*A, B, C, D*), each of whom owned 25 percent of its stock. Corporation *Y* paid *A* and *B* each $50,000 in cash for their stock of corporation *X*, and *C* and *D* each received corporation *Y* stock with a value of $50,000 in exchange for their stock of corporation *X*. There are no other facts present that should be taken into account in determining whether the continuity of interest requirement of section 1.368–1(b) of the Income Tax Regulations has been satisfied, such as sales, redemptions or other dispositions of stock prior to or subsequent to the exchange which were part of the plan of reorganization.

Held, the continuity of interest requirement of section 1.368–1(b) of the regulations has been satisfied. It would also be satisfied if the facts were the same except corporation *Y* paid each stockholder $25,000 in cash and each stockholder received corporation *Y* stock with a value of $25,000.

KASS v. COMMISSIONER *
United States Tax Court, 1973.
60 T.C. 218.

DAWSON, Judge: * * *

[The Atlantic City Racing Association ("ACRA") was a corporation formed in 1943 to operate a racetrack. It had 506,000 shares of common stock outstanding and approximately 500 shareholders. Track Associates, Inc. ("TRACK") was a corporation formed in 1965. TRACK originally issued 202,577 shares of common stock, over 50 percent of which was acquired by the Levy family and 8 percent by the Casey family. The remaining TRACK stock was issued to minority shareholders. The Levy and Casey families also were minority shareholders in ACRA. Their purpose in forming TRACK was to gain control over

* Footnotes omitted.

ACRA's racetrack business through a tender offer for at least 80 percent of the ACRA stock which, if successful, would be followed by a merger of ACRA into TRACK.

The Levys acquired 48,300 shares and the Caseys acquired 3,450 of TRACK stock (out of the total original capitalization of 202,577 shares) in exchange for 51,750 of their shares in ACRA. The Levys and Caseys then purchased an additional 70,823 shares of TRACK stock for cash as part of the original capitalization.

The takeover attempt commenced on December 1, 1965, when TRACK offered to purchase ACRA stock at $22 per share subject to the condition that at least 405,000 shares (slightly more than 80 percent of ACRA) be tendered. The offer terminated on February 11, 1966. TRACK, which had received 51,750 shares of ACRA on its formation, acquired 424,764 additional shares, but 29,486 ACRA shares (5.82 percent of the total) were not tendered and remained in the hands of minority shareholders.

As a more than 80 percent shareholder, TRACK was easily able to orchestrate a liquidation of ACRA. This final step was accomplished by a merger of ACRA into TRACK under New Jersey law. The merger agreement provided that each remaining share of ACRA held by minority shareholders would be exchanged for one share of TRACK, and ACRA then would dissolve by operation of law.

Mrs. Kass, the taxpayer in this case (referred to in the opinion as "petitioner"), was one of the minority shareholders of ACRA. She owned 2,000 shares of ACRA stock, with a basis of $1,000 and a fair market value of $440,000. Pursuant to the merger, she exchanged her ACRA stock for 2,000 shares of TRACK stock and did not report any capital gain in connection with the transaction. The issue in the case was whether, on these facts, Mrs. Kass was required to recognize gain on this exchange. Ed.]

Petitioner contends that the merger of ACRA into TRACK, although treated at least in part as a liquidation at the corporate level, is at her level, the shareholder level, (1) a true statutory merger and (2) a section 368(a)(1)(A) reorganization, occasioning no recognition of gain on the ensuing exchange. In support of this she cites Madison Square Garden Corp., 58 T.C. 619 (1972). Respondent, on the other hand, argues that the purchase of stock by TRACK and the liquidation of ACRA into TRACK, which took the form of a merger, must be viewed at all levels as an integrated transaction; that the statutory merger does not qualify as a reorganization because it fails the continuity-of-interest test; and that, as a consequence, petitioner falls outside of section 354(a)(1) and must recognize gain pursuant to section [1001].

The problems presented by these facts are somewhat complex, and the solutions, according to the commentators, are less than clear. Stated one way, the question is whether a statutory merger that follows a [purchase of more than 80 percent of the target's stock and a complete liquidation of the target] can qualify as an "A" reorganization at the shareholder level and, if so, when. Put another way, does the merger of ACRA into TRACK fall under section 368(a)(1)(A), thus placing the exchange of petitioner's ACRA stock for TRACK stock within the applicable nonrecognition provision?

Respondent does not take the position that a statutory merger, such as the one we have here, can never qualify for reorganization-nonrecognition status. He admits that "Theoretically, it is possible for TRACK to get a stepped-up basis in 83.95 percent of the assets of ACRA per section 334(b)(2) [the predecessor of Section 338; see Chapter 7C3, supra] upon a section 332, IRC liquidation of ACRA into TRACK and at the same time allow nonrecognition reorganization treatment to minority shareholders." Rather, his position is simply that the merger in question fails to meet the time-honored continuity-of-interest test. We agree with this and so hold.

*   *   *

Reorganization treatment is appropriate when the parent's stock ownership in the subsidiary was not acquired as a step in a plan to acquire assets of the subsidiary: the parent's stockholding can be counted as contributing to continuity-of-interest, so that since such holding represented more than 80 percent of the stock of the subsidiary, the continuity-of-interest test would be met. Reorganization treatment is inappropriate when the parent's stock ownership in the subsidiary was purchased as the first step in a plan to acquire the subsidiary's assets in conformance with the provisions of [former] section 334(b)(2). The parent's stockholding could not be counted towards continuity-of-interest, so in the last example there would be a continuity-of-interest of less than 20 percent. (Less than 20–percent continuity would be significantly less continuity-of-interest than that allowed in John A. Nelson Co. v. Helvering, 296 U.S. 374 (1935).) In short, where the parent's stock interest is "old and cold," it may contribute to continuity-of-interest. Where the parent's interest is not "old and cold," the sale of shares by the majority of shareholders actually detracts from continuity-of-interest.

In petitioner's case, TRACK's stock in ACRA was acquired as part of an integrated plan to obtain control over ACRA's business. The plan called for, first, the purchase of stock and, second, the subsidiary-into-parent merger. Accordingly, continuity-of-interest must be measured by looking to all the pre-tender offer stockholders rather than to the parent (TRACK) and the nontendering stockholders only; and by that measure the merger fails and petitioner must recognize her gain.

*   *   *

Faced with the general rule as the applicability of the continuity-of-interest test, petitioner makes the following arguments, which we will deal with separately.

One, the continuity-of-interest doctrine should not be applied because TRACK was formed by a few stockholders in ACRA in order to purchase the business and, in the process, to acquire a stepped-up basis for as many of the assets as possible via [former] section 334(b)(2). "In effect, the situation was the same as the sale of stock by some shareholders to other shareholders." The petitioner meets herself coming, so to speak, when making this argument. Confronted with the problem of how to characterize the second event in the present two-event transaction, she contends that the transaction was a true statutory merger in both form and substance, at least insofar as she, a minority shareholder, was concerned. Now, confronted with the continuity-of-interest problem, she would have us treat the transaction in a manner inconsistent with the characterization previously given to the transaction, that of a merger. Furthermore, the parties to these events (the selling shareholders of ACRA, the organizers of TRACK, and the nontendering, nondissenting shareholders such as the petitioner) chose the steps that were followed. To allow one of them in a separate proceeding to characterize the facts as being in substance something else would lay the groundwork for an enormous amount of "whipsawing" by and against both taxpayers and the Government.

Two, in applying the continuity-of-interest test, if it is applied, the purchase of stock by TRACK and the subsequent merger should not be viewed as steps in an integrated transaction because the choice of merger over liquidation as a second step had independent significance to the minority shareholders and either choice would have suited TRACK. By so arguing, the petitioner attempts in effect to avoid the step-transaction doctrine and thus to limit the application of the continuity-of-interest test. If the merger can be separated from the stock purchase, the continuity-of-interest test might be applicable only with regard to ACRA's shareholders at the time of the statutory merger, namely, the parent corporation, TRACK, and the minority shareholders, including petitioner. We note at least one flaw: The choice—liquidation or merger—did make a difference to TRACK. If it had liquidated ACRA, TRACK would not have received all of ACRA's assets. Some of the assets would have gone to the minority shareholders, and it would have had to have purchased them from these shareholders at an additional price. By choosing to merge ACRA into itself, it was able to avoid this and other problems.

Three, if the purchase and merger are to be viewed as parts of a single transaction for continuity and reorganization purposes, then the incorporation of TRACK should also be integrated into the transaction for section 351 purposes; thus the petitioner should be viewed as having participated in a tax-free section 351 transaction along with the Levys and Caseys. Briefly, the answer to this argument is that while the purchase and the merger were interdependent events, petitioner's exchange of ACRA stock for TRACK stock was not "mutually interdependent" with the incorporation transfers made by the Levys, Caseys, and 18 other individuals. American Bantam Car Co., 11 T.C. 397, 405–407 (1948), affirmed per curiam 117 F.2d 513 (C.A.3, 1949). This result merely illustrates the truism that the step-transaction doctrine, even when worded consistently * * * and applied to identical facts, may result in integration in one case and "separateness" in another case simply because the legal question to be answered has changed. See King Enterprises, Inc. v. United States, 418 F.2d 511, 516–519 (Ct.Cl. 1969).

Four, assuming that the continuity-of-interest test is applied, it is met where all 16 percent of the stockholders of ACRA exchanged their stock for a total of 35 percent of the stock of TRACK. The 16–percent figure (really 16.04 percent) is the sum of the percentage of ACRA stock transferred to TRACK at the time of TRACK's formation (10.22 percent) plus the percentage of ACRA stock exchanged for TRACK stock following the statutory merger (5.82 percent). Fortunately, we need not engage in a game of percentages since the continuity figure argued for by petitioner, 16 percent, is not "tantalizingly" high. The plain fact that more than 80 percent of the shareholders of ACRA sold out for cash is sufficient to prevent this merger from meeting the quantitative test expressed in Southwest Natural Gas Co. v. Commissioner, 189 F.2d 332, 334 (C.A.5, 1951), affirming 14 T.C. 81 (1950):

> While no precise formula has been expressed for determining whether there has been retention of the requisite interest, it seems clear that the requirement of continuity of interest consistent with the statutory intent is not fulfilled in the absence of a showing: (1) that the transferor corporation or its shareholders retained a substantial proprietary stake in the enterprise represented by a material interest in the affairs of the transferee corporation, and, (2) *that such retained interest represents a substantial part of the value of the property transferred.* [Emphasis added.]

The two Supreme Court cases on point are John A. Nelson Co. v. Helvering, supra, and Helvering v. Minnesota Tea Co., 296 U.S. 378 (1935).

Finally, we emphasize that the petitioner is not any worse off than her fellow shareholders who sold their stock. She could have also received money instead of stock had she chosen to sell or to dissent from the merger. The nonrecognition of a realized gain is always an important matter. We hold that petitioner is not entitled to such favorable treatment in this case.

Reviewed by the Court.

NOTE

The continuity of interest doctrine requires the shareholders of the target corporation to receive a sufficient proprietary interest in the acquiring corporation to justify treating the transaction as a wholly or partially tax-free reorganization rather than a taxable sale.[1] The early cases focused on both the quality of the consideration received by the

---

1. See Reg. §§ 1.368–1(b); 1.368–2(a). See generally Hutton, "Musings on Continuity of Interest—Recent Developments," 56 Taxes 904 (1978); Wolfman, "Continuity of Interest and the American Law Institute Study," 57 Taxes 840 (1979).

target's shareholders and the percentage of equity consideration received by those shareholders as a group. For example, in one of the first cases to apply the doctrine, the Supreme Court held that a transaction literally satisfying the definition of a reorganization nonetheless was taxable to the shareholders because they received only short-term notes of the acquiring corporation.[2] The Court concluded that the transaction in substance was a taxable sale. In a later case, the Court held that there was sufficient continuity of interest where the shareholders of the target corporation received 38 percent nonvoting preferred stock of the acquiring corporation and 62 percent cash.[3]

In evaluating continuity of interest, it is the overall continuity of the target shareholders that controls, not the continuity of any individual shareholder.[4] All classes of stock, whether voting or nonvoting, provide the requisite continuity while any other consideration (cash, short-term notes, bonds, assumption of liabilities) will fail to meet the test.[5] The lines with respect to the percentage of stock that must be received are not so easily drawn if one refers to the case law,[6] but the Service has provided a practical benchmark by declaring that it will rule favorably on a Type A reorganization if the target shareholders receive at least 50 percent equity consideration.[7] Keep in mind that this "percentage" is the proportion of equity consideration relative to total consideration received by the target shareholders—not their percentage of the acquiring corporation's stock. Moreover, overall qualification as a reorganization under this liberal standard does not mean that all target shareholders may defer recognition of their gain. Those receiving nonequity consideration must recognize gain, if any, perhaps as ordinary income, to the extent they receive boot.[8] But if the entire transaction fails to qualify as a reorganization, all the parties, not merely those receiving nonequity consideration, must recognize gain or loss.

Another aspect of the continuity of interest doctrine relates to the length of time that the target shareholders are required to hold their stock in the acquiring corporation. For example, assume that the shareholders of the target corporation in an otherwise qualifying merger receive only stock of the acquiring corporation but holders of 80 percent of that stock previously made a commitment to sell their shares to a third party. Does the prearranged sale violate the continuity of interest doctrine and convert the transaction into a taxable sale? The selling shareholders, of course, will be taxed in either event, but what

2. Pinellas Ice & Cold Storage Co. v. Commissioner, 287 U.S. 462, 53 S.Ct. 257 (1933). See also Helvering v. Minnesota Tea Co., 296 U.S. 378, 56 S.Ct. 269 (1935).

3. John A. Nelson Co. v. Helvering, 296 U.S. 374, 56 S.Ct. 273 (1935).

4. See Rev.Rul. 66–224 at p. 491 of the text.

5. See, e.g., John A. Nelson Co. v. Helvering, supra note 3.

6. See, e.g., John A. Nelson Co. v. Helvering, supra note 3 (38% redeemable nonvoting preferred sufficient for continuity); Miller v. Commissioner, 84 F.2d 415 (6th Cir.1936) (25% stock sufficient).

7. Rev.Proc. 77–37, 1977–2 C.B. 568.

8. See Section C of this chapter, infra.

about the 20 percent who retained their stock?   Do they lose the
benefits of nonrecognition?   The *McDonald's Restaurants of Illinois*
case, which follows in the text, explores some of these issues and
illustrates the relationship between the continuity of interest requirement and the step transaction doctrine.[9]

McDONALD'S RESTAURANTS OF ILLINOIS
v. COMMISSIONER *

United States Court of Appeals, Seventh Circuit, 1982.
688 F.2d 520.

CUMMINGS, Chief Judge.

This income tax case is an appeal by taxpayers from 27 decisions of
the Tax Court determining deficiencies in their federal income tax
totaling $566,403.   The Tax Court disposed of the various deficiencies in
one opinion reported in 76 T.C. 972 (1981).

The pertinent facts as found by the Tax Court and supplemented
by the record are not in dispute.   In June 1977, when they filed their
petitions in the Tax Court to review the deficiency assessments, taxpayers were 27 wholly-owned subsidiaries of McDonald's Corporation (Mc-
Donald's), the Delaware corporation that franchises and operates fast-
food restaurants.   The taxpayers all had their principal places of
business in Oak Brook, Illinois.   They maintained their books and
records on the accrual method and filed their tax returns on a calendar-
year basis.

On the opposite end of the transaction at issue here were Melvin
Garb, Harold Stern and Lewis Imerman (known collectively as the
Garb-Stern group).   The group had begun with a single McDonald's
franchise in Saginaw, Michigan, in the late 1950's and expanded its
holdings to include McDonald's restaurants elsewhere in Michigan and
in Oklahoma, Wisconsin, Nevada and California.   After 1968 relations
between the Garb-Stern group and McDonald's deteriorated.   In 1971
McDonald's considered buying some of the group's restaurants in Oklahoma, but abandoned the idea when it became clear that the acquisition could not be treated as a "pooling of interests" for accounting
purposes [2] unless all of the Garb-Stern group's restaurants were acquired simultaneously.   In November 1972, however, negotiations re-

---

9.   See also Rev.Rul. 66–23, 1966–1 C.B.
67.

* Some footnotes omitted.

2.   The Tax Court's opinion describes
"pooling of interests" as follows:

The pooling of interests method accounts for a business combination as the
uniting of the ownership interests of two
or more companies by exchange of equity
securities.   No acquisition is recognized
because the combination is accomplished
without disbursing resources of the constituents.   Ownership interests continue

and the former bases of accounting are
retained.   The recorded assets and liabilities of the constituents are carried forward to the combined corporation at
their recorded amounts.   Income of the
combined corporation includes income of
the constituents for the entire fiscal period in which the combination occurs.
The reported income of the constituents
for prior periods is combined and restated as income of the combined corporation.

76 T.C. at 976, n. 4.   See also note 6 infra.

sumed, McDonald's having decided that total acquisition was necessary to eliminate the Garb-Stern group's friction.

The sticking point in the negotiations was that the Garb-Stern group wanted cash for its operations, while McDonald's wanted to acquire the Garb-Stern group's holdings for stock, consistent with its earlier expressed preference for treating the transaction as a "pooling of interests" for accounting purposes. McDonald's proposed a plan to satisfy both sides: it would acquire the Garb-Stern companies for McDonald's common stock, but it would include the common stock in a planned June 1973 registration so that the Garb-Stern group could sell it promptly.[3]

Final agreement was not reached until March 1973. Negotiations then were hectic; for a variety of accounting and securities-law reasons, the acquisition had to be consummated not before and not after April 1, 1973. The final deal was substantially what had been proposed earlier. The Garb-Stern companies would be merged in stages into McDonald's,[4] which would in turn transfer the restaurant assets to the 27 subsidiaries that are the taxpayers here. In return the Garb-Stern group would receive 361,235 shares of unregistered common stock. The agreement provided that the Garb-Stern group could participate in McDonald's planned June 1973 registration and underwriting or in any other registration and underwriting McDonald's might undertake within six years (Art. 7.4); the group also had a one-time right to demand registration in the event that McDonald's did not seek registration within the first year (Art. 7.5). The Garb-Stern group was not obligated by contract to sell its McDonald's stock but fully intended to do so.

After the April 1 closing, both parties proceeded on the assumption that the Garb-Stern group's shares would be included in the June 1973 "piggyback" registration. In mid-June a widely publicized negative report about McDonald's stock caused the price to drop from $60 to $52 a share in two weeks, and McDonald's therefore decided to postpone the registration and sale of additional stock. The Garb-Stern group acquiesced, although it had made no effort to withdraw from the registration before McDonald's decided to cancel it.

Through the rest of the summer, the price of McDonald's stock staged a recovery. In late August McDonald's decided to proceed with the registration, and the Garb-Stern group asked to have its shares included. The registration was announced on September 17 and completed on October 3, 1973. The Garb-Stern group thereupon sold

---

3. The stock the Garb-Stern group received was unregistered. It could not be sold until it was registered or until the Garb-Stern group met the conditions of S.E.C. Rule 144 (2-year holding period and limitation on number of shares sold within a 6-month period thereafter). 76 T.C. at 982 and n. 17. Sale rather than retention was attractive to the Garb-Stern group, because McDonald's stock had paid no cash dividends from 1968 to the time of this transaction. Id. at 985, n. 18.

4. The exact sequence of transactions by which the Garb-Stern group's companies merged into McDonald's is not important for our purposes; the merger was orchestrated so that it would ultimately be a statutory merger under Delaware corporation law.

virtually all of the stock it had acquired in the transaction at a price of more than $71 per share.

In its financial statements McDonald's treated the transaction as a "pooling of interests". In its tax returns for 1973, however, it treated it as a purchase.[6] Consistent with that characterization, McDonald's gave itself a stepped-up basis in the assets acquired from the Garb-Stern group to reflect their cost ($29,029,000, representing the value of the common stock transferred and a $1–2 million "nuisance premium" paid to eliminate the Garb-Stern group from the McDonald's organization). It allocated that basis among various Garb-Stern assets, then dropped the restaurant assets to the 27 taxpayer subsidiaries pursuant to Section 351 of the Internal Revenue Code governing transfers to corporations controlled by the transferor. The subsidiaries used the stepped-up basis allocable to them to compute depreciation and amortization deductions in their own 1973 tax returns.

It is those deductions by the subsidiary taxpayers that the Commissioner reduced. He ruled that the transfer of the Garb-Stern group's assets to McDonald's was not a taxable acquisition but a statutory merger or consolidation under Section 368(a)(1)(A) of the Code, and that under Section 362(b) McDonald's was required to assume the Garb-Stern group's basis in the assets acquired. In turn, the subsidiaries were required to compute depreciation and amortization deductions on this lower, carryover basis. With properly computed deductions, the subsidiary taxpayers owed an additional $566,403 in 1973 income taxes. The Tax Court upheld the Commissioner's deficiency assessments, and this appeal is the result.

The Code distinguishes between taxable acquisitions and nontaxable (or more accurately tax-deferrable) acquisitive reorganizations under Sections 368(a)(1)(A)–(C) and 354(a)(1) for the following common-sense reason: If acquired shareholders exchange stock in the acquired company for stock in the acquiring company, they have simply readjusted the form of their equity holdings. They have continued an investment rather than liquidating one, and the response of the tax system is to adjust their basis to reflect the transaction but postpone tax liability until they have more tangible gain or loss.

To ensure that the tax treatment of acquisitive reorganizations corresponds to the rationale that justifies it, the courts have engrafted a "continuity of interest" requirement onto the Code's provisions. See, e.g., Helvering v. Alabama Asphaltic Limestone Co., 315 U.S. 179, 62 S.Ct. 540, 86 L.Ed. 775; LeTulle v. Scofield, 308 U.S. 415, 60 S.Ct. 313, 84 L.Ed. 355. That test examines the acquired shareholders' proprieta-

---

6. The Commissioner's brief makes much of the differences between the accounting and the tax treatment (Br. 9, 20), characterizing McDonald's strategies as "disingenuous" and "bordering on the duplicitous." The short answer to this argument is found in McDonald's Reply Br. at 9–10: such variations are common and accepted. The service has a special form (Schedule M) for corporations to file in order to reconcile their financial and tax records. McDonald's duly filed such a form.

ry interest before and after the reorganization to see if "the acquired shareholders' investment remains sufficiently 'at risk' after the merger to justify the nonrecognition tax treatment," 76 T.C. at 997.

The taxpayers, the Commissioner, and the Tax Court all agree that the Garb-Stern group holdings were acquired by statutory merger. They also all agree that the "continuity of interest" test is determinative of the tax treatment of the transaction of which the statutory merger was a part. But the taxpayers on the one hand, and the Commissioner and the Tax Court on the other, part company over how the test is to be applied, and what result it should have produced. In affirming the Commissioner, the Tax Court recognized that the Garb-Stern group had a settled and firm determination to sell their McDonald's shares at the first possible opportunity rather than continue as investors, 76 T.C. at 989. It nonetheless concluded that because the Garb-Stern group was not contractually bound to sell, the merger and the sale could be treated as entirely separate transactions and the continuity-of-interest test applied in the narrow time-frame of the April transaction only. Thus tested, the transaction was in Judge Hall's view a nontaxable reorganization, and the taxpayer subsidiaries were therefore saddled with the Garb-Stern group's basis in taking depreciation and amortization deductions. The taxpayers by contrast argue that the step-transaction doctrine should have been applied to treat the April merger and stock transfer and the October sale as one taxable transaction. They also argue that the Tax Court's extremely narrow view of both the step-transaction doctrine and the continuity-of-interest test in this case is not consonant with appellate court case law, the Tax Court's own precedents, or the Service's practices hitherto. We agree with the taxpayers.

The Step-Transaction Doctrine

The step-transaction doctrine is a particular manifestation of the more general tax law principle that purely formal distinctions cannot obscure the substance of a transaction. See e.g., Redding v. Commissioner, 630 F.2d 1169, 1175 (7th Cir.1980), certiorari denied, 450 U.S. 913, 101 S.Ct. 1353, 67 L.Ed.2d 338. As our Court there noted:

> The commentators have attempted to synthesize from judicial decisions several tests to determine whether the step transaction doctrine is applicable to a particular set of circumstances * * *. Unfortunately, these tests are notably abstruse—even for such an abstruse field as tax law.

Nonetheless, under any of the tests devised—including the intermediate one nominally adopted by the Tax Court and the most restrictive one actually applied in its decision—the transactions here would be stepped together. For example, under the "end result test," "purportedly separate transactions will be amalgamated with a single transaction when it appears that they were really component parts of a single transaction intended from the outset to be taken for the purpose of reaching the ultimate result." 76 T.C. at 994, citing King Enterprises, Inc. v. United States, 418 F.2d 511, 516 (Ct.Cl.1969) and referring to *Redding,* supra, 630 F.2d at 1175. Here there can be little doubt that all the steps were taken to cash out the Garb-Stern group, although McDonald's sought to do so in a way that would enable it to use certain accounting procedures. Admittedly, not every transaction would be as pellucid as this one, but here the history of the parties' relationships, the abortive attempt to buy some of the group's holdings, the final comprehensive deal, and the Garb-Stern group's determination to sell out even in the face of falling prices in the stock [12] all are consistent and probative.

A second test is the "interdependence" test, which focuses on whether "the steps are so interdependent that the legal relations created by one transaction would have been fruitless without a comple- tion of the series." *Redding,* supra, at 1177, quoting with approval Paul, Selected Studies in Federal Taxation (2d Series 1938) 200, 254. This is the test the Tax Court purported to apply, 76 T.C. at 997–999, although its version of the test is indistinguishable from yet another formulation, the "binding commitment" test. That is, the Tax Court would have found interdependence only if the Garb-Stern group had itself been legally bound to sell its stock. In fact, the "interdepen- dence" test is more practical and less legalistic than that. It concen- trates on the relationship between the steps, rather than on the "end result" * * *. Here it would ask whether the merger would have taken place without the guarantees of saleability, and the answer is certainly no. The Garb-Stern group's insistence on this point is demon- strated both by its historic stance in these negotiations and by the hammered-out terms of the agreement. Although the Tax Court em- phasized the permissive terms about "piggyback" registration, it glossed over the Garb-Stern group's one-time right to force registration—and hence sale—under the agreement. The very detail of the provisions about how McDonald's would ensure free transferability of the Garb- Stern group's McDonald's stock shows that they were the *quid pro quo* of the merger agreement.

Finally the "binding commitment" test most restricts the applica- tion of the step-transaction doctrine, and is the test the Tax Court actually applied, despite its statements otherwise. The "binding com- mitment" test forbids use of the step-transaction doctrine unless "if one transaction is to be characterized as a 'first step' there [is] a binding commitment to take the later steps." *Redding,* supra, at 1178, quoting Commissioner v. Gordon, 391 U.S. 83, 96, 88 S.Ct. 1517, 1524, 20 L.Ed. 2d 448. The Tax Court found the test unsatisfied because the Garb- Stern group was not legally obliged to sell its McDonald's stock. We think it misconceived the purpose of the test and misapplied it to the facts of this case.

12. As indicated by their participation in the proposed "piggyback" registration scheduled for June 1973. The decision to postpone registration because of adverse publicity and a fall in the price of McDon- ald's shares was entirely McDonald's.

In the first place, the "binding commitment" test is the most rigorous limitation on the step-transaction doctrine because it was formulated to deal with the characterization of a transaction that in fact spanned several tax years and could have remained "not only indeterminable but unfixed for an indefinite and unlimited period in the future, awaiting events that might or might not happen." *Gordon,* supra, 391 U.S. at 96, 88 S.Ct. at 1524. By contrast this transaction was complete in six months and fell entirely within a single tax year. The degree of uncertainty that worried the *Gordon* court is absent here, and a strong antidote for uncertainty is accordingly not needed.

In the second place, the Tax Court underestimated the extent to which the parties were bound to take the later steps. The registration and underwriting provisions in the parties' agreement did not just enhance salability; they were essential to it. Unless and until McDonald's registered the stock, it was essentially untransferable. 76 T.C. at 981–982; see note 3 supra. Second, although McDonald's had the choice of when during the first year after the merger it would seek registration, if it did nothing the Garb-Stern group could make a legally enforceable demand for registration in either year two or year three. On the other hand, if McDonald's did register stock during the first year but the Garb-Stern group chose not to "piggyback," the group's demand registration rights would be lost. These limitations made it extremely likely that the sale would—as it did—take place promptly. They are enough to satisfy the spirit, if not the letter, of the "binding commitment" test.

Under any of the three applicable criteria, then, the merger and subsequent sale should have been stepped together. Substance over form is the key (Kuper v. Commissioner, 533 F.2d 152, 155 (5th Cir. 1976)). Had the Tax Court taken a pragmatic view of the actions of the Garb-Stern group, it would have found that they clearly failed to satisfy the continuity-of-interest requirement that has been engrafted onto the Code provisions governing nonrecognition treatment for acquisitive reorganizations.

Statutory Merger Precedents

Quite apart from the proper application of the step-transaction doctrine, the available precedents dealing with statutory mergers and the effect of post-merger sales by acquired shareholders—though scanty—strongly support the taxpayers. No case supports the myopic position adopted below that although "the crux of the continuity-of-interest test lies in the *continuation* of the acquired shareholders' proprietary interest" (76 T.C. at 997), the test "by itself does not require *any length* of postmerger retention," (id.) (emphasis supplied).

The taxpayers rely on, and the Tax Court was unsuccessful in distinguishing, Heintz v. Commissioner, 25 T.C. 132 (1955). The *Heintz* case differs from this case only in focusing on the tax liability of the acquired shareholders rather than the acquiring corporation. The facts of the case, somewhat simplified, are as follows.

Heintz and Jack (taxpayers) formed a company (Jack & Heintz, Inc.) to manufacture arms and ammunition during World War II. At the war's end, they determined to sell it rather than try to reorganize its production for peacetime. The buyer was the Precision Corporation, which had been formed to acquire Jack & Heintz. On March 5, 1946, Precision acquired almost all the outstanding shares of Jack & Heintz from the taxpayers for $5 million cash and 50,000 preferred shares of Precision, with a par value of $50 each. On March 6 Precision merged its newly acquired subsidiary with itself. At the time the deal was being negotiated, two of the parties representing the buyer assured the taxpayers that the Precision shares they had received as part payment would be sold in a public offering planned for thirty days after the merger (25 T.C. at 135), but this promise was nowhere reflected in the thirty-five page written agreement covering the whole transaction (id. at 137). Owing to unforeseen delays, the contemplated registration and sale did not take place, but the buyers helped arrange a private sale at $30 per share in August 1946. In their 1946 returns, the taxpayers reported long-term capital gain computed on a figure arrived at by deducting from the sale proceeds ($5 million in cash + $2,500,000 worth of Precision stock) their $112,000 basis in the Jack & Heintz stock. They also reported short-term capital losses of $1 million on the August private sale of the Precision stock.

The Commissioner assessed deficiencies, using exactly the reasoning the Tax Court has adopted in McDonald's case. He treated the transaction as a statutory reorganization, which had no immediate tax consequences (except that the cash component of the price was ordinary income). He then gave the taxpayers a carry-over basis of $112,000, rather than a cost basis, in the Precision stock. Finally he treated the August sale as producing sizable capital gains ($1,500,000 less $112,000) rather than capital losses. Although the Commissioner's position is sketchily presented in the Tax Court's opinion, his treatment must have involved a conviction that neither the promise to sell the Precision stock nor the actual sale changed the character of the reorganization.

The Tax Court rejected the Commissioner's position unequivocally.[13] Although a statutory merger had occurred,

> [e]ssential to this arrangement was the promise made to petitioners by members of the purchasing group that the preferred stock * * * would shortly thereafter be sold on their behalf
> * * *.

* * *

13. At oral argument counsel for the Commissioner argued that both the Tax Court and the author of the Commissioner's brief in the *McDonald's* case had misconstrued the *Heintz* case. He advocated treating it as first, last, and always a sale (on March 5, 1946). The March 6, 1946, merger was, he maintained, entirely irrelevant. That was in fact the taxpayers' position in *Heintz*, 25 T.C. at 141, but the Tax Court gives no hint of having accepted it. We suspect that the Tax Court was rightly unwilling to separate transactions that occurred within 24 hours of each other.

The term "reorganization as used in [the predecessor of Section 354(a)(1)], contemplates a readjustment of the corporate structure of an enterprise and requires that those individuals who are owners of the enterprise prior to such readjustment continue to maintain a substantial proprietary interest therein. * * * The terms of the instant plan did not contemplate the petitioners' maintenance of a proprietary interest in the continuing operation. * * * [P]etitioners wished to dispose of their entire interest in Jack & Heintz, Inc. * * * [T]hey settled for cash plus preferred stock * * * only after obtaining the promise of the promoters of [the] purchasing corporation that their preferred stock in that corporation would be sold together with a public offering of that corporation's stock within 30 days." 25 T.C. 142–143.[14]

As in the present case, the taxpayers' wishes to sell were clear and the transaction was designed to accommodate them. As in the present case, the acquiring corporation's promise was to facilitate the sale, not to guarantee it. As in the present case, the acquiring corporation did not require a reciprocal commitment from the acquired shareholders— for all that appears, Heintz and Jack were free to retain their equity interest in Precision. As in the present case, these understandings of the parties were not reflected in the written agreement. There is no principled way to distinguish the two cases, and the Tax Court's efforts to do so here (76 T.C. at 1001) are unsuccessful.

The only other case we have found that involves statutory mergers and the continuity-of-interest requirement is United States v. Adkins-Phelps, Inc., 400 F.2d 737 (8th Cir.1968). The Tax Court here noted the case's existence, 76 T.C. at 996, n. 39, but placed only oblique reliance on it, id. at 996–997 and n. 42. The relevant Government argument there was that a woman who had traded 99% of the stock of a family-owned corporation for a 16% interest in Adkins-Phelps did not exhibit the requisite continuity of interest because Adkins-Phelps had a right of first refusal on all her shares, exercisable (and indeed exercised) for $1 a share. 400 F.2d at 741. The Government did not try to treat the exercise as a sale, but argued that no real equity rights were ever conveyed because of the first-refusal limitation. Id. That argument has no application here. Both the district court and the Court of Appeals rejected the Government's position. Id. at 739, 741.

Given the dearth of precedent and the aptness of the Tax Court's reasoning in Heintz, we think that case dictates a consistent—and favorable—treatment of the taxpayers in this appeal.

Additional Considerations

Part of the reason that there is so little litigation about statutory mergers and the effect of post-merger events on tax treatment is that

14. The Treasury Regulation on which the *Heintz* Court relied (Section 29.112(g) 1 of Regulations 111) is identical to Section 1.368.1(b) of the current regulations (26 C.F.R. § 1.368 1(b)) (quoted in full in note 16 infra.)

people involved in nontaxable reorganizations usually seek advice in the form of private letter rulings beforehand. See McDonald Br. 25–27; cf. also Bittker & Eustice, Federal Income Taxation of Corporations and Shareholders (4th ed. 1979) ¶ 14.01 at 14–7–8 ("Rarely do the participants deliberately invite a test of strength in the courts, even if they feel a good deal of confidence in the outcome. As a result, the Service can make 'law' in this area by a lifted eyebrow.").[15]

The Commissioner's usual position in this context is not the one adopted by the Tax Court, namely, that the intent of the acquired shareholders is irrelevant and no period of post-merger retention is required. 76 T.C. at 990, 992, 997. See, for example, Rev.Proc. 77–37, 1977–2 C.B. 568, 569:

> The "continuity of interest" requirement of section 1.368–1(b) of the Income Tax Regulations is satisfied if there is a *continuing* interest through stock ownership in the acquiring or transferee corporation (or a corporation in "control" thereof within the meaning of section 368(c) of the Code) on the part of the former shareholders of the acquired or transferor corporation which is equal in value, as of the effective date of the reorganization, to at least 50 percent of the value of all of the formerly outstanding stock of the acquired or transferor corporation as of the same date. *   *   * *Sales, redemptions, and other dispositions of stock occurring prior or subsequent to the exchange which are part of the plan of reorganization will be considered in determining whether there is a 50 percent continuing interest through stock ownership as of the effective date of the reorganization.* (Emphasis added.)

Cf. Rev.Proc. 74–26, 1974–2 C.B. 478; Rev.Proc. 66–34, 1966–2 C.B. 1232. Moreover, the Commissioner usually does not limit his scrutiny to explicit, contemporaneous commitments to sell out, Rev.Rul. 77–479, 1977–2 C.B. 119; Rev.Rul. 66–23, 1966–1 C.B. 67. In fact, taxpayers who seek a ruling in advance of a reorganization must represent that there is "no plan *or intention* on the part of the Acquired shareholders to [reduce their new holdings] to a number of shares having, in the aggregate, a value of less than 50 percent of the total value of the Acquired stock outstanding immediately prior to the proposed transaction." McDonald Br. 25; Appendix, Tab B, pp. 3–5 (emphasis added).

Against this background, the Commissioner's treatment of the McDonald's transaction—as affirmed by the Tax Court—seems opportunistic. The agency's practice, described above, suggests that if McDonald's had laid its plan before the Internal Revenue Service ahead of time, it would not have been deemed a nontaxable reorganization. Furthermore the Garb-Stern group has already been fully taxed because of its relatively prompt disposition; the Internal Revenue Service

---

15. This general understanding suggests—although it is far from probative—that the parties here would also have sought the Internal Revenue Service's imprimatur if they had intended to effect a nontaxable reorganization.

has had all the benefits of sale treatment on that end of the transaction. See Prusiecki, "Continuity of Interest in Tax-free Mergers: New Opportunities After McDonald's of Zion," 55 J.Tax. 378, 380 (1981). Now the Service seeks to saddle the taxpayers with the disadvantageously low basis that goes with the "reorganization" label. On the other hand, as the taxpayers note (Reply Br. 14), if the Garb-Stern group's basis had been higher than the fair market price of the McDonald's shares exchanged, the Commissioner could, consistently with his prior positions, have refused reorganization status and forced the taxpayers to accept a lower, cost basis for depreciation and amortization purposes. This is heads-I-win, tails-you-lose law.

If, on the other hand, the treatment here represents a considered change in the Service's treatment of reorganizations, then the Commission's victory in the Tax Court was Pyrrhic and he should welcome reversal. The Tax Court's decision was barely six months old before tax planners were publicizing the possibilities for manipulating it. Prusiecki, *op. cit.,* at 380–381, notes nine new types of tax avoidance that the case opens up, all taking advantage of the new found ability to obtain reorganization status without constraining post-merger sales. The key to all of them is the extraordinary rigidity of the "binding commitment" test and the ephemeral continuity of interest the Tax Court seems to require.

The decisions appealed from are reversed, with instructions to enter fresh decisions in the taxpayers' favor.

NOTE

The issue of post-acquisition continuity of interest also was raised in Penrod v. Commissioner,[1] another case involving an acquisition by McDonald's Corporation of a group of independent franchised McDonald's restaurants. As in *McDonald's Restaurants of Illinois,* the target shareholders received unregistered McDonald's stock in a statutory merger. Because McDonald's was anxious to complete the acquisition quickly, the parties did not request an advance ruling from the Service. The shareholders settled for an opinion letter from their attorney stating that the transaction qualified as a reorganization based on the understanding that the shareholders had no "present intention to sell or otherwise dispose of the McDonald's stock to be received in the reorganizations."[2] Within nine months of the merger but in a subsequent calendar year the shareholders registered the stock and sold 90 percent of it on the open market.

Applying the step transaction doctrine, the Service integrated the merger and subsequent sale of McDonald's stock and contended that the acquisition did not qualify as a Type A reorganization because the shareholders failed to maintain sufficient continuity of interest. This was the reverse of the Service's position in *McDonald's Restaurants of Illinois,* but the taxpayers in *Penrod* were the target shareholders, not

---

1. 88 T.C. 1415 (1987). **2.** Id. at 1421.

the acquiring corporation, and the timing of their gain was at stake. Although the shareholders reported a taxable capital gain in the year that they sold the stock, acceptance of the Service's position would have required them to recognize gain in the earlier year of the merger.

After an obligatory survey of the "binding commitment," "end result" and "interdependence" tests, the Tax Court found that: (1) the shareholders had no binding commitment at the time of the merger to sell their McDonald's stock; (2) the shareholders did not "intend" to sell the stock during the merger negotiations but rather formed their intention to sell subsequent to the acquisition; and (3) the acquisition of the stock and its subsequent sale were neither interdependent transactions nor steps in a plan the end result of which was to cash out the shareholders' interests in McDonald's. Based on these findings, the court held that the continuity of interest requirement was satisfied and the transaction qualified as a Type A reorganization. The Seventh Circuit decision in *McDonald's Restaurants of Illinois* was factually distinguished on the ground that the target shareholders in that case had intended to sell their McDonald's stock from the outset.

Penrod has significance beyond the court's holding on post-acquisition continuity. It suggests an unwillingness on the part of the Tax Court to apply the step transaction doctrine to combine separate transactions structured by the parties to legally avoid taxes into an integrated taxable transaction. Another important example of this trend is Esmark, Inc. v. Commissioner.[3] Although *Esmark* did not involve a reorganization, it is worth pausing to consider its reasoning here because of the significance of the case to tax planning in corporate acquisitions.

The essential facts in *Esmark* are not difficult to grasp. Esmark, Inc. was a diversified, publicly traded holding company. Among its wholly owned subsidiaries was Vickers, itself a holding company with several subsidiaries engaged in the oil business. Faced with liquidity problems and believing that the market price of its stock was undervalued, Esmark devised a plan to sell Vickers to the highest bidder, which turned out to be Mobil Oil. Under the chosen format, Esmark "invited" Mobil, which emerged as the high bidder after negotiations orchestrated by Esmark's investment bankers, to make a tender offer for approximately 54 percent of Esmark's stock—an amount roughly equivalent to the agreed value of the Vickers oil business. Mobil successfully tendered for the requisite 54 percent of the Esmark stock. The next step, which was contemplated from the outset, was the distribution by Esmark of its Vickers stock in redemption of the Esmark stock acquired by Mobil in the tender offer.

The parties conceded that the tender offer/redemption format was chosen in large part for the potential tax savings at the corporate level. Although the tendering Esmark shareholders would recognize a capital

3.   90 T.C. 171 (1988), affirmed 886 F.2d
1318 (7th Cir.1989).

gain or loss on the disposition of the shares, Esmark hoped to avoid corporate-level gain on the appreciation in Vickers. Esmark relied on a since repealed provision of the Code [4] which provided that a parent corporation did not recognize gain on a distribution of stock in a subsidiary (under specified conditions, all formally met in *Esmark*) in redemption of the parent's stock.

The stakes were high, with the Service claiming that Esmark owed over $150 million in taxes on a $452 million long-term capital gain on the distribution of the Vickers stock to Mobil. Relying on all the usual pervasive judicial doctrines, the Service recast the transaction as a sale by Esmark of its Vickers stock to Mobil followed by a redemption of the Esmark stock owned by the tendering shareholders for cash. After rejecting several of these arguments, the court turned to the step transaction doctrine: [5]

> Finally, respondent maintains that Mobil's ownership of the Esmark shares must be disregarded under the step-transaction doctrine. We recently described the step-transaction doctrine as another rule of substance over form that "treats a series of formally separate 'steps' as a single transaction if such steps are in substance integrated, interdependent, and focused toward a particular result." Penrod v. Commissioner, 88 T.C. 1415, 1428 (1987). Respondent contends that Mobil's acquisition and subsequent disposition of petitioner's shares were simply steps in an integrated transaction designed to result in Mobil's acquisition of Vickers and petitioner's redemption of its stock.

> That Mobil's tender offer was but part of an overall plan is not in dispute. The existence of an overall plan does not alone, however, justify application of the step-transaction doctrine. Whether invoked as a result of the "binding commitment," "interdependence," or "end result" tests, the doctrine combines a series of individually meaningless steps into a single transaction. In this case, respondent has pointed to no meaningless or unnecessary steps that should be ignored.

> Petitioner had two objectives: a disposition of its energy business and a redemption of a substantial portion of its stock. Three direct routes to these objectives were available:

> First, petitioner could have distributed the Vickers stock to its shareholders in exchange for their shares. The shareholders could then have sold the Vickers stock for cash to interested buyers. See Commissioner v. Court Holding Co. and Cumberland Public Service Co. v. United States, supra.

4. I.R.C. § 311(d)(2)(B) (pre–1987). This provision was repealed as part of Congress's assault on the *General Utilities* doctrine.

5. 90 T.C. at 195–200.

Second, petitioner could have sold the Vickers stock for cash and then distributed the cash to its shareholders in exchange for their stock. As appears from our findings * * *, however, Mobil might not have been the successful bidder.

Third, the parties could have proceeded as they did, with Mobil purchasing petitioner's stock in a tender offer and exchanging such stock for the Vickers stock. No route was more "direct" than the others. Each route required two steps, and each step involved two of three interested parties. Each route left petitioner, petitioner's shareholders, and the purchaser in the same relative positions. Faced with this choice, petitioner chose the path expected to result in the least tax.

Respondent proposes to recharacterize the tender offer/ redemption as a sale of the Vickers shares to Mobil followed by a self-tender. This recharacterization does not simply combine steps; it invents new ones. Courts have refused to apply the step-transaction doctrine in this manner. In Grove v. Commissioner, 490 F.2d 241 (2d Cir.1973), affg. a Memorandum Opinion of this Court, the Commissioner relied on the step-transaction doctrine to recharacterize a donor's gift of stock followed by a redemption of that stock from the donee as a redemption of the donor's shares followed by a gift of cash to the donee. The Court of Appeals stated:

> We are not so naive as to believe that tax considerations played no role in Grove's planning. But foresight and planning do not transform a non-taxable event into one that is taxable. Were we to adopt the Commissioner's view, we would be required to recast two actual transactions—a gift by Grove to RPI and a redemption from RPI by the Corporation—into two completely fictional transactions—a redemption from Grove by the Corporation and a gift by Grove to RPI. Based upon the facts as found by the Tax Court, we can discover no basis for elevating the Commissioner's "form" over that employed by the taxpayer in good faith. "Useful as the step transaction doctrine may be in the interpretation of equivocal contracts and ambiguous events, it cannot generate events which never took place just so an additional tax liability might be asserted."

* * * On the basis of these precedents, we conclude that the step-transaction doctrine may not appropriately be applied in this case.

* * *

Although much more might be written about each of respondent's attacks on the form of petitioner's transaction, we have refrained from doing so. Stripped to its essentials, this case is a rematch of the principles expressed in Gregory v. Helvering, 293 U.S. 465 (1935), the source of most "substance over form" arguments.

In *Gregory,* the United Mortgage Co. (United) held among its assets 1,000 shares of the stock of Monitor Securities Corp. (Monitor). The taxpayer, United's sole shareholder, planned to sell the shares of Monitor and receive the proceeds of the sale. In order to avoid the double tax that would result if United sold the shares and distributed the proceeds as a dividend, the taxpayer had United contribute the stock of Monitor to a new corporation, which issued its stock to the taxpayer. This transaction was within the literal definition of "reorganiza- tion" under the law as then in effect. Following this "reorgan- ization," the taxpayer dissolved the new corporation and sold the Monitor stock. The Supreme Court disregarded the form of the transaction as having no independent significance.

The Supreme Court framed the issue for decision as fol- lows:

> The legal right of a taxpayer to decrease the amount of what otherwise would be his taxes, or altogether avoid them, by means which the law permits, cannot be doubted. But the question for determination is whether what was done, apart from the tax motive, was the thing which the statute intended.   *   *   * [293 U.S. at 469. Citations omitted.]

In *Gregory,* the taxpayer's transaction was not "the thing that the statute intended" because a reorganization, as that term was defined in the statute, did not in fact take place:

> Putting aside, then, the question of motive in respect of taxation altogether, and fixing the character of the proceeding by what actually occurred, what do we find? Simply an operation having no business or corporate purpose—a mere device which put on the form of a corporate reorganization as a disguise for concealing its real character, and the sole object and accomplishment of which was the consummation of a preconceived plan, not to reorganize a business or any part of a business, but to transfer a parcel of corporate shares to the petitioner. No doubt, a new and valid corporation was created. But that corporation was nothing more than a contrivance to the end last de- scribed. It was brought into existence for no other purpose; it performed, as it was intended from the beginning it should perform, no other function. When that limited function had been exercised, it immedi- ately was put to death. [293 U.S. at 469–470.]

In this case, in contrast, there were no steps without independent function. Each of the steps—the purchase of petitioner's stock by Mobil and the redemption of that stock by petitioner—had permanent economic consequences. Mobil's tender offer was not a "mere device" having no business purpose; the tender offer was an essential element of petitioner's plan to redeem over 50 percent of its stock. Mobil's ownership, however transitory, must thus be respected, and if Mobil's ownership of petitioner's shares is respected, a "distribution with respect to * * * stock" in fact occurred.

But was this transaction truly the "thing that the statute intended?" As discussed above, section 311(a) is said to be the codification of the *General Utilities* doctrine. The rationale behind that doctrine has never been clearly articulated. Presumably, the doctrine represents an attempt to ameliorate the perceived harshness of the two-tier system of corporate taxation. Lewis, "A Proposed New Treatment For Corporate Distributions and Sales in Liquidation," Tax Review Compendium 1643, Staff of House Comm. on Ways and Means, 86th Cong., 1st Sess. (Comm.Print 1959). The doctrine may also rest on the belief that a corporation receives nothing of value for its assets when it makes a dividend distribution or redeems its stock with property. In Houston Bros. Co. v. Commissioner, 21 B.T.A. 804 (1930), the Board of Tax Appeals explained the principle as follows:

> It is quite possible that, by disposing of some of its assets in exchange for or retirement of some of its outstanding shares, a corporation may be in a stronger financial position than before. But this means only that the distributive interests of its shareholders have been potentially improved. The assets of the corporation itself are not more or of greater value. They are actually less, and only the proportionate value of the shares still in the hands of shareholders has been increased. Before it can be said that the corporation has profit, it must be found not only that it has disposed of its property, but that it has received assets of greater value than the cost of those disposed of. But since a corporation's own shares are not assets, but only the convenient machinery for evidencing shareholder interests, it is a fallacy to say it has received anything and *a fortiori* that it has received a gain. * * * [21 B.T.A. at 815.]

In United States v. General Geophysical Co., 296 F.2d 86 (5th Cir.1961), the Court of Appeals for the Fifth Circuit used similar reasoning to explain section 311(a):

The rule may be easily justified by the fact that when a corporation transfers appreciated property to its shareholders, as a dividend or in exchange for their shares, the gain created by the appreciation has not accrued to the corporation and should not be taxed to it. [296 F.2d at 88. Fn. ref. omitted.]

The focus of section 311(a) is on the position of the corporation before and after the transaction rather than on the identity of the shareholder who surrendered stock. Given this explanation of the "policy" behind the *General Utilities* doctrine, we cannot say that petitioner's transaction was not "the thing that the statute intended."

In an economic sense, there is no difference between the form chosen by petitioner and the "substance" alleged by respondent. In this instance, however, tax treatment is dictated by form. That this situation is far from unusual is illustrated by the Supreme Court's decisions in *Court Holding* and *Cumberland Public Service*. As the Court noted in the latter case:

> The oddities in tax consequences that emerge from the tax provisions here controlling appear to be inherent in the present tax pattern. For a corporation is taxed if it sells all its physical properties and distributes the cash proceeds as liquidating dividends, yet is not taxed if that property is distributed in kind and is then sold by the shareholders. In both instances the interest of the shareholders in the business has been transferred to the purchaser. * * *

> Congress having determined that different tax consequences shall flow from different methods by which the shareholders of a closely held corporation may dispose of corporate property, we accept its mandate. * * *

> [338 U.S. at 455–456.]

We, too, must accept the mandate of Congress, particularly where the corporation is publicly and not closely held. Congress resolved the *Court Holding* issue by enacting [pre–1987] section 337. For future years, Congress has resolved the issue presented in this case by abolishing the *General Utilities* doctrine altogether. Tax Reform Act of 1986, Pub.L. 99–514, 100 Stat. 2085. In 1980, however, petitioner was entitled to rely on the literal language of section 311, and the judicially recognized doctrines give us no satisfactory basis for taxing the transaction as if something else had occurred. See Grove v. Commissioner, supra. We have carefully considered the arguments of the parties set forth in their excellent briefs. We believe that ad hoc extension of doctrine to achieve a result on any of the difficult issues in this case is unwarranted and unwise.

b. CONTINUITY OF BUSINESS ENTERPRISE

BENTSEN v. PHINNEY *

United States District Court, Southern District of Texas, 1961.
199 F.Supp. 363.

GARZA, District Judge.

This is a suit for refund of federal income taxes paid by plaintiffs to defendant.

All of the facts have been stipulated, and the case has been submitted to the Court on written briefs and on oral argument.

A brief summary of the stipulated facts is as follows:

Plaintiff taxpayers were shareholders of Rio Development Company, a Texas corporation, which in 1955 was engaged in the land development business in the Rio Grande Valley, along with two other corporations, Bentsen Brothers, Inc., and Bentsen Loan & Investment Company.

The shareholders in such three corporations were all members of the families of Lloyd M. Bentsen, Sr., and Elmer C. Bentsen.

On March 7, 1955, the three corporations transferred all of their respective properties, subject to their liabilities, to the newly formed Consolidated American Life Insurance Company. For the sake of brevity and consistency, the former will be referred to as the "Transfer-or Corporations", and the latter will be referred to as the "Insurance Company".

Immediately thereafter, the stockholders of the three transferor corporations surrendered all of their stock in the three transferor corporations for cancellation. The three transferor corporations were liquidated and dissolved, and the Insurance Company issued all of its voting stock directly to the former stockholders of the three transferor corporations which had been dissolved, to Bentsen Development Company, a partnership, and to Lloyd M. Bentsen, Sr., individually. Bentsen Development Company, a partnership, and Lloyd M. Bentsen, Sr., individually, had also transferred their assets to the Insurance Company.

It is stipulated that prior to the transaction, the transferor corporations were going concerns in the land development business in the Rio Grande Valley of Texas. The Insurance Company was a going concern created to carry on the corporate business of selling life insurance.

It has been stipulated that there were business reasons and purposes for the transaction.

* Footnotes omitted.

It is the exchange by the plaintiff taxpayers of their stock in Rio Development Company for Insurance Company stock that was the specific event out of which this refund suit arose.

It has been stipulated that there was continuity of corporate activity as between the Rio Development Company and the Insurance Company, the only change being that the type of business carried on was changed from the land development business to the insurance business.

The net result of the transactions involved in this case was that all and the same assets which had been owned by the transferor corporations, were, after the transaction, owned by the Insurance Company. The same individuals who had owned stock in the transferor corporations now owned the stock of the Insurance Company.

It has also been stipulated that prior to the consummation of the corporate transaction involved here, the Commissioner of Internal Revenue was requested to rule in advance on the federal income tax consequences of the transaction, and that the said Commissioner on two separate occasions ruled that in his opinion an exchange of stock in the Insurance Company for the land development companies' or transferor corporations' stock, was taxable because the Insurance Company engaged in a different business from the three land development corporations.

Although the plaintiff taxpayers disagreed with the Commissioner's ruling, in their respective 1955 income tax returns they reported the exchange of their Rio Development Company stock for Insurance Company stock as a taxable event and paid a tax thereon.

Thereafter the necessary procedural steps were taken to bring this refund suit before the Court for a decision as to the income tax consequences of such exchange of stock by the taxpayers.

The question for the Court to decide is: Was such corporate transaction a corporate "reorganization", as the term "reorganization" is defined in Section 368(a)(1), Internal Revenue Code of 1954, 26 U.S. C.A. § 368(a)(1), even though Rio Development Company engaged in the land development business and thereafter the new Insurance Company engaged in the insurance business?

The plaintiff taxpayers contend there was a corporate reorganization. The Government, Defendant in this cause, maintains that there was not a corporate reorganization under Section 368(a)(1) of the Internal Revenue Code of 1954, because there was not a continuity of business enterprise before and after the reorganization; and that this is a prerequisite as set out in the Treasury Regulations.

This case is governed by the Internal Revenue Code of 1954, 26 U.S.C., the applicable sections of which provide:

"§ 368. Definitions relating to corporate reorganizations

"(a) Reorganization.—

"(1) In General.—For purposes of parts I and II and this part, the term "reorganization" means—

* * *

"(C) the acquisition by one corporation, in exchange solely for all or a part of its voting stock (or in exchange solely for all or a part of the voting stock of a corporation which is in control of the acquiring corporation), of substantially all of the properties of another corporation, but in determining whether the exchange is solely for stock the assumption by the acquiring corporation of a liability of the other, or the fact that property acquired is subject to a liability, shall be disregarded;

"(D) a transfer by a corporation of all or a part of its assets to another corporation if immediately after the transfer the transferor, or one or more of its shareholders (including persons who were shareholders immediately before the transfer), or any combination thereof, is in control of the corporation to which the assets are transferred; but only if, in pursuance of the plan, stock or securities of the corporation to which the assets are transferred are distributed in a transaction which qualifies under section 354, 355, or 356;"

"Sec. 354. Exchanges of stock and securities in certain reorganizations

"(a) General rule.—

"(1) In General.—No gain or loss shall be recognized if stock or securities in a corporation a party to a reorganization are, in pursuance of the plan of reorganization, exchanged solely for stock or securities in such corporation or in another corporation a party to the reorganization."

It is conceded that the 1939 Internal Revenue Code was the same in this respect as the 1954 Code, and that the corresponding Treasury Regulations issued under the 1939 Code are similar to the corresponding Treasury Regulations issued under the 1954 Code.

The Treasury Regulation states: "Requisite to a reorganization under the Code, are a continuity of business enterprise under the modified corporate form."

The Government contends that since there was a lack of "continuity of the business enterprise", there was not a reorganization as contemplated under the statutes.

The question for this Court to decide is the meaning of "continuity of business enterprise", and whether or not it exists in this case.

The Government takes the position that "continuity of business enterprise" means that the new corporation must engage in the same identical or similar business. Stated in another manner, the Government maintains it is necessary that there must be an identity of type of business before and after the reorganization.

The plaintiff taxpayers have cited to the Court the case of Becher v. Commissioner, 221 F.2d 252 (2d Cir.1955) affirming 22 T.C. 932 (1954), which the Government has tried to distinguish. In this case the taxpayer owned all the stock in a corporation engaged in the sponge rubber and canvass-product manufacturing business. The new corporation engaged in the business of manufacturing upholstered furniture. In that case, the Government took the position that there had been a reorganization and that a cash distribution to the shareholders of the old corporation was taxable as "boot" and was ordinary income to the shareholders. The Government prevailed in that case, and the Court, at 221 F.2d 252, 253, said:

> "* * * but the Tax Court here correctly held that a business purpose does not require an identity of business before and after the reorganization. * * *"

Other cases cited are Pebble Springs Distilling Co. v. Commissioner, 231 F.2d 288 (7th Cir.1956), cert. denied 352 U.S. 836, 77 S.Ct. 56, 1 L.Ed.2d 55 affirming 23 T.C. 196 (1954). There the old corporation had the power to carry on both a whiskey distilling business and a real estate business, but it engaged solely in the real estate business.

Another case cited to the Court is Morley Cypress Trust v. Commissioner, 3 T.C. 84 (1944). In that case the old corporation owned land held for timber and the land was conveyed to a new corporation engaged in the oil business.

The Government tries to distinguish these last two cases by saying that in the Pebble Springs Distilling Co. case the new corporation could engage in the whiskey distilling business if it had wanted to, and that in the Morley Cypress Trust case, after the problem of continuity of business enterprise had been presented, the required continuity could have been found because both the old and the new corporations were actively engaged in exploiting the natural resources of the same land.

The Government also contends that under Texas law an insurance company cannot engage in any business other than that of insurance.

The Morley Cypress Trust case cited above, this Court believes, is the case most like the case before the Court. In the Morley Cypress Trust case the land was held for timber. In this case it was held for development. In the Morley case land was conveyed to a new oil corporation for use in the oil business. In this case, land (plus proceeds from the sale of land) was conveyed to a new corporation to furnish the means to capitalize a new insurance business.

The Government contends that the corresponding Treasury Regulation issued under the 1939 Code was in existence when the 1954 Code was enacted and Congress did not see fit to make any changes; that Treasury Regulations have the force of law when the Code section which they interpret is reenacted after they have once been promulgated, and cites Roberts v. Commissioner, 9 Cir., 176 F.2d 221, 10 A.L.R.2d 186.

The Government has been unable to present the Court with any decision in which the meaning of "continuity of business enterprise" as used in the Treasury Regulations, has been interpreted. Since no Court had upheld the contention made by the Government as to the interpretation to be given said words in the Regulations, it is unfair to say that Congress had an opportunity to make a change in passing the 1954 Code. Congress was not apprised of the meaning that the Government wishes to give to said language in the Regulations, and therefore the rule expressed in Roberts v. Commissioner, supra, is not controlling here.

This Court finds that no court has passed on the question of whether "continuity of business enterprise", as used in the Regulations, means that the new corporation must engage in the identical type of business or a similar business; and it is, therefore, held that this Court is not bound by any Treasury Regulation since it is the province of the Court to decide whether the Treasury Regulation means what the Government contends it means; and whether or not if it means what the Government contends, said Regulation is one that could be promulgated under the appropriate sections of the Internal Revenue Code.

This Court finds that "continuity of business enterprise", as used in the Regulations, does not mean that the new corporation must engage in either the same type of business as the old or a similar business, for if this be the requirement, then said Regulation is without authority.

To qualify as a "reorganization" under the applicable statutes, the new corporation does not have to engage in an identical or similar type of business. All that is required is that there must be continuity of the business activity.

This Court therefore finds that there was a reorganization under the applicable sections of the Internal Revenue Code.

Under the facts stipulated in this case, it is found that there was a continuity of the business activity and all requisites having been complied with, the plaintiff taxpayers have a right to a refund of the income taxes paid on the exchange of stock. The amounts to be refunded by the Government are to be those as stated in the Stipulation.

The Clerk will notify Counsel for the plaintiffs to submit an appropriate order and judgment.

REVENUE RULING 81–25

1981–1 Cum.Bull. 132.

ISSUE

For a transaction to qualify as a reorganization under section 368(a)(1) of the Internal Revenue Code of 1954, does the continuity of business enterprise requirement apply to the business or business assets of the acquiring (transferee) corporation prior to the reorganization?

LAW AND ANALYSIS

Section 1.368–1(b) of the Income Tax Regulations states that in order for a reorganization to qualify under section 368(a)(1) of the Code there must be continuity of the business enterprise under the modified corporate form.

Rev.Rul. 63–29, 1963–1 C.B. 77, holds that the continuity of business enterprise requirement of section 1.368–1(b) of the regulations was satisfied where a transferee corporation sold its assets and discontinued its business, then acquired the assets of another corporation in exchange for its voting stock, and used the sales proceeds realized from the sale of its assets to expand the business formerly conducted by the acquired corporation. The holding of Rev.Rul. 63–29 is now reflected in the recent amendment to section 1.368–1 (1.368–1(d)) of the regulations, which looks only to the transferor's historic business or historic business assets for determining if the continuity of business enterprise requirement is satisfied.

HOLDING

In a section 368(a)(1) reorganization the continuity of business enterprise requirement does not apply to the business or business assets of the transferee corporation prior to the reorganization.

* * *

PROBLEMS

1. Assume that Acquiring Corporation and Target Corporation are incorporated in a state with a merger and consolidation statute that provides in part:

> Any two or more domestic corporations may merge into one of such corporations pursuant to a plan of merger approved in the manner provided in this chapter, and any two or more domestic corporations may consolidate into a new corporation pursuant to a plan of consolidation approved in the manner provided in this chapter.

> A vote of the shareholders shall be taken on the proposed plan of merger or consolidation. The plan of merger or consolidation shall be approved upon receiving the affirmative vote of the holders of a majority of the shares entitled to vote thereon of each such corporation.

Consider whether the following alternative transactions involving Acquiring Corporation ("A") and Target Corporation ("T") qualify as Type A reorganizations:

(a) T merges into A in an "all cash" merger permitted under state law. T transfers all of its assets to A and dissolves. T shareholders receive cash in exchange for their stock.

(b) Same as (a), above, except that the merger agreement provides that all T shareholders shall receive a newly issued class of A nonvoting preferred stock in exchange for their T stock.

(c) The shareholders of A and T agree to form Consolidated Corporation and transfer all the A and T assets to Consolidated in exchange for Consolidated common stock to be issued to the shareholders of both corporations. As a result of the consolidation, A and T both dissolve.

(d) Same as (b), above, except that the T shareholders, all of whom vote to approve the merger, receive nonvoting preferred stock of A worth $200,000 and A notes worth $100,000?

(e) Same as (d), above, except that the T shareholders receive nonvoting preferred stock of A worth $100,000 and A long-term bonds worth $200,000?

(f) Same as (e), above, except that the bonds are convertible at any time into A nonvoting preferred stock?

(g) Same as (d), above, except that 75% of the T shareholders (owning 33⅓% of the T stock) receive the notes worth $100,000 and 25% of the T shareholders (owning 66⅔% of the T stock) receive A stock worth $200,000?

(h) A acquired 70% of the T stock five years ago for cash. In the current year, T merges into A, and the minority shareholders of T receive A stock worth $18,000 and $72,000 cash (i.e., 20% stock and 80% cash).

(i) Same as (h), above, except that A acquired only 20% of the T stock five years ago. On the merger of T into A, the other shareholders of T receive $90,000 of A stock and $150,000 cash.

(j) As part of a takeover plan, A acquired 80% of the T stock six months ago in a tender offer for $240,000 cash. T then merges into A, and the remaining T shareholders receive $60,000 of A stock in exchange for their T stock.

2. Acquiring Corporation ("A") and Target Corporation ("T") agree to a merger of T into A. T shareholders will receive solely A stock. Is there a valid Type A reorganization if:

(a) Shareholders holding 75% of the old T stock make a binding commitment prior to the merger to sell their new A stock to a third party?

(b) The 75% T shareholder group is approached by a third party a week after the transaction and agree to sell their stock at that time?

(c) Which group of shareholders (the 75% or 25% group) is most concerned with the results in (a) and (b), above, and why?

3. Reread Reg. § 1.368–1(d)(5) Example (5).

(a) Is the regulation consistent with the result in Bentsen v. Phinney?

(b) Would the continuity of business enterprise issue arise in the example if P were merged into T and T's farm machinery manufacturing business were sold but P's lumber mill business were continued?

2. TYPE B: ACQUISITIONS OF STOCK SOLELY FOR VOTING STOCK *

Code: §§ 368(a)(1)(B), (c).   Skim §§ 354(a);   358;   362(b);   368(a)(2)(C);   (b); 1032(a).

Regulations: § 1.368–2(c).

CHAPMAN v. COMMISSIONER **
United States Court of Appeals, First Circuit, 1980.
618 F.2d 856.

LEVIN H. CAMPBELL, Circuit Judge.

This appeal by the Internal Revenue Service from a decision of the Tax Court calls for the construction of certain corporate reorganization provisions of the Internal Revenue Code, 26 U.S.C. §§ 354(a)(1) and 368(a)(1). We must decide whether the requirement of Section 368(a)(1) (B) that the acquisition of stock in one corporation by another be solely in exchange for voting stock of the acquiring corporation is met where, in related transactions, the acquiring corporation first acquires 8 percent of the acquiree's stock for cash and then acquires more than 80 percent of the acquiree in an exchange of stock for voting stock. The Tax Court agreed with the taxpayers that the latter exchange constituted a valid tax-free reorganization. Reeves v. Commissioner, 71 T.C. 727 (1979).

The Facts

Appellees were among the more than 17,000 shareholders of the Hartford Fire Insurance Company who exchanged their Hartford stock for shares of the voting stock of International Telephone and Telegraph Corporation pursuant to a formal exchange offer from ITT dated May 26, 1970. On their 1970 tax returns, appellees did not report any gain or loss from these exchanges. Subsequently, the Internal Revenue Service assessed deficiencies in the amounts of $15,452.93 (Chapman), $43,962.66 (Harry), $55,778.45 (Harwood), and $4,851.72 (Ladd). Appellees petitioned the Tax Court for redetermination of these deficiencies, and their cases were consolidated with those of twelve other former Hartford shareholders. The Tax Court, with five judges dissenting,

---

* See generally Steines, "Policy Considerations in the Taxation of B Reorganizations," 31 Hastings L.J. 993 (1980).

** Some footnotes omitted.

granted appellees' motion for summary judgment, and the Commissioner of Internal Revenue filed this appeal.

The events giving rise to this dispute began in 1968, when the management of ITT, a large multinational corporation, became interested in acquiring Hartford as part of a program of diversification. In October 1968, ITT executives approached Hartford about the possibility of merging the two corporations. This proposal was spurned by Hartford, which at the time was considering acquisitions of its own. In November 1968, ITT learned that approximately 1.3 million shares of Hartford, representing some 6 percent of Hartford's voting stock, were available for purchase from a mutual fund. After assuring Hartford's directors that ITT would not attempt to acquire Hartford against its will, ITT consummated the $63.7 million purchase from the mutual fund with Hartford's blessing. From November 13, 1968 to January 10, 1969, ITT also made a series of purchases on the open market totalling 458,000 shares which it acquired for approximately $24.4 million. A further purchase of 400 shares from an ITT subsidiary in March 1969 brought ITT's holdings to about 8 percent of Hartford's outstanding stock, all of which had been bought for cash.

In the midst of this flurry of stock-buying, ITT submitted a written proposal to the Hartford Board of Directors for the merger of Hartford into an ITT subsidiary, based on an exchange of Hartford stock for ITT's $2 cumulative convertible voting preferred stock. Received by Hartford in December of 1968, the proposal was rejected in February of 1969. A counterproposal by Hartford's directors led to further negotiations, and on April 9, 1969 a provisional plan and agreement of merger was executed by the two corporations. While not unlike the proposal Hartford had earlier rejected, this plan was somewhat more favorable to Hartford's stockholders.[4] The merger agreement was conditioned upon approval, as required under state law, by the shareholders of the two corporations and by the Connecticut Insurance Commissioner. In addition, Hartford had an unqualified right to terminate the agreement if it believed there was any likelihood that antitrust litigation would be initiated. Although such litigation in fact materialized, Hartford's board of directors pushed ahead with the merger, and in October 1969 a Justice Department motion to enjoin the merger was denied by the United States District Court for the District of Connecticut.

Meanwhile, on April 15, 1969, attorneys for the parties sought a ruling from the IRS that the proposed transaction would constitute a reorganization under Section 368(a)(1)(B) of the Internal Revenue Code of 1954, so that, among other things, gain realized on the exchange by Hartford shareholders would not be recognized, see 26 U.S.C. § 354(a)(1). By private letter ruling, the Service notified the parties on October 13, 1969 that the proposed merger would constitute a nontaxable reorganization, provided ITT unconditionally sold its 8 percent interest

---

4. In particular, the annual dividend on the preferred shares was to be $2.25 rather than $2.00, and the conversion ratio was set at a rate more favorable to Hartford shareholders.

in Hartford to a third party before Hartford's shareholders voted to approve or disapprove the proposal.   On October 21, the Service ruled that a proposed sale of the stock to Mediobanca, an Italian bank, would satisfy this condition, and such a sale was made on November 9.

On November 10, 1969, the shareholders of Hartford approved the merger, which had already won the support of ITT's shareholders in June.   On December 13, 1969, however, the merger plan ground to a halt, as the Connecticut Insurance Commissioner refused to endorse the arrangement.   ITT then proposed to proceed with a voluntary exchange offer to the shareholders of Hartford on essentially the same terms they would have obtained under the merger plan.[5]   After public hearings and the imposition of certain requirements on the post-acquisition operation of Hartford, the insurance commissioner approved the exchange offer on May 23, 1970, and three days later ITT submitted the exchange offer to all Hartford shareholders.   More than 95 percent of Hartford's outstanding stock was exchanged for shares of ITT's $2.25 cumulative convertible voting preferred stock.   The Italian bank to which ITT had conveyed its original 8 percent interest was among those tendering shares, as were the taxpayers in this case.

In March 1974, the Internal Revenue Service retroactively revoked its ruling approving the sale of Hartford stock to Mediobanca, on the ground that the request on which the ruling was based had misrepresented the nature of the proposed sale.   Concluding that the entire transaction no longer constituted a nontaxable reorganization, the Service assessed tax deficiencies against a number of former Hartford shareholders who had accepted the exchange offer.   Appellees, along with other taxpayers, contested this action in the Tax Court, where the case was decided on appellees' motion for summary judgment.   For purposes of this motion, the taxpayers conceded that questions of the merits of the revocation of the IRS rulings were not to be considered; the facts were to be viewed as though ITT had not sold the shares previously acquired for cash to Mediobanca.   The taxpayers also conceded, solely for purposes of their motion for summary judgment, that the initial cash purchases of Hartford stock had been made for the purpose of furthering ITT's efforts to acquire Hartford.

The Issue

Taxpayers advanced two arguments in support of their motion for summary judgment.   Their first argument related to the severability of the cash purchases from the 1970 exchange offer.   Because 14 months had elapsed between the last of the cash purchases and the effective

---

5. Apparently, the insurance commissioner was concerned, among other things, about the rights of dissenting shareholders, who could have been forced to exchange their Hartford shares under the merger plan.   Minority shareholders under the second proposal were to have the right to withhold some or all of their stock from the exchange if they so chose.   See Pierson v. United States, 472 F.Supp. 957, 959–60 (D.Del.1979).   The second exchange offer provided that ITT would definitely accept the exchange if more than 95 percent of Hartford's shares were tendered, and would have the option to accept if 80 percent or more were tendered.

date of the exchange offer, and because the cash purchases were not part of the formal plan of reorganization entered into by ITT and Hartford, the taxpayers argued that the 1970 exchange offer should be examined in isolation to determine whether it satisfied the terms of Section 368(a)(1)(B) of the 1954 Code. The Service countered that the two sets of transactions—the cash purchases and the exchange offer— were linked by a common acquisitive purpose, and that they should be considered together for the purpose of determining whether the arrangement met the statutory requirement that the stock of the acquired corporation be exchanged "solely for * * * voting stock" of the acquiring corporation. The Tax Court did not reach this argument; in granting summary judgment it relied entirely on the taxpayers' second argument.

For purposes of the second argument, the taxpayers conceded *arguendo* that the 1968 and 1969 cash purchases should be considered "parts of the 1970 exchange offer reorganization." Even so, they insisted upon a right to judgment on the basis that the 1970 exchange of stock for stock satisfied the statutory requirements for a reorganization without regard to the presence of related cash purchases. The Tax Court agreed with the taxpayers, holding that the 1970 exchange in which ITT acquired more than 80 percent of Hartford's single class of stock for ITT voting stock satisfied the requirements of Section 368(a)(1) (B), so that no gain or loss need be recognized on the exchange under Section 354(a)(1). The sole issue on appeal is whether the Tax Court was correct in so holding.

I.

We turn first to the statutory scheme under which this case arose.[7] The basic rule governing exchanges was imported from Section 1002 of the 1954 Code, 26 U.S.C. § 1002. Section 1002 stated that, except as otherwise provided, gain or loss on the exchange of property should be recognized and taken into account in computing a taxpayer's taxable income. One exception to that rule appears in Section 354(a)(1), which provides that gain or loss shall not be recognized if stock or securities in a corporation are, in pursuance of the plan of reorganization, exchanged solely for stock or securities in another corporation which is a party to the reorganization. This exception does not grant a complete tax exemption for reorganizations, but rather defers the recognition of

---

7. The corporate reorganization provisions of the tax code seem at first glance arcane, technical, and all-but-impenetrable. In the words of Justice WHITTAKER, considering a statutory scheme pre-dating the one before us:

"Because of the arbitrary and technical character, and of the somewhat 'hodgepodge' form, of the statutes involved, the interpretation problem presented is highly complicated; and although both parties rely upon the 'plain words' of these statutes, they arrive at diametrically opposed conclusions. That plausible arguments can be and have been made in support of each conclusion must be admitted; and, as might be expected, they have hardly lightened our inescapable burden of decision."

Turnbow v. Commissioner, 368 U.S. 337, 339, 82 S.Ct. 353, 355, 7 L.Ed.2d 326 (1961). See also Daniel 5:7 (King James).

gain or loss until some later event such as a sale of stock acquired in the exchange. Section 354(a)(1) does not apply to an exchange unless the exchange falls within one of the six categories of "reorganization" defined in Section 368(a)(1).[11] The category relevant to the transactions involved in this case is defined in Section 368(a)(1)(B):

"[T]he term 'reorganization' means—

(B) the acquisition by one corporation, in exchange solely for all or a part of its voting stock * * * of stock of another corporation if, immediately after the acquisition, the acquiring corporation has control of such other corporation (whether or not such acquiring corporation had control immediately before the acquisition)."

The concept of "control" is defined in Section 368(c) as "the ownership of stock possessing at least 80 percent of the total combined voting power of all classes of stock entitled to vote and at least 80 percent of the total number of shares of all other classes of stock of the corporation." [13] Subsection (B) thus establishes two basic requirements for a valid, tax-free stock-for-stock reorganization. First, "the acquisition" of another's stock must be "solely for * * * voting stock." Second, the acquiring corporation must have control over the other corporation immediately after the acquisition.

The single issue raised on this appeal is whether "the acquisition" in this case complied with the requirement that it be "solely for * * * voting stock." It is well settled that the "solely" requirement is mandatory; if any part of "the acquisition" includes a form of consideration other than voting stock, the transaction will not qualify as a (B) reorganization. See Helvering v. Southwest Consolidated Corp., 315 U.S. 194, 198, 62 S.Ct. 546, 550, 86 L.Ed. 789 (1942) (" 'Solely' leaves no leeway. Voting stock plus some other consideration does not meet the statutory requirement"). The precise issue before us is thus how

---

11. See footnote 1 for text of Section 368(a)(1). In the tax practice, these six categories are referred to by their alphabetic designations in the 1954 Code: hence, an (A) reorganization is a statutory merger or consolidation, a (B) reorganization is a stock-for-stock acquisition, a (C) reorganization is a stock-for-assets acquisition, a (D) reorganization is a corporate transfer of assets to a controlled corporation, an (E) reorganization is a recapitalization, and an (F) reorganization is a mere change in identity, form, or place of organization.

From the literal language of Section 354(a)(1), it might appear that an exchange is tax-free only where no consideration other than stock or securities is involved. However, it is settled that the presence of "boot"—in the form of money or other property in the exchange—does not lead to full recognition of gain. * * * Thus, where a transaction constitutes a valid reorganization within one of the six categories of Section 368(a)(1), and where it would satisfy Section 354 but for the presence of "boot," gain is recognized in the exchange only to the extent of the value of the "boot." See Turnbow v. Commissioner, 368 U.S. 337, 82 S.Ct. 353, 7 L.Ed.2d 326 (1961). The critical question in a case of this nature is not whether "boot" is a part of the plan of reorganization, but whether the presence of "boot" is consistent with a valid reorganization under some provision of Section 368(a)(1). See id. at 344, 82 S.Ct. at 357.

13. The parties do not contest the fact that ITT had control of Hartford, as defined by Section 368(c), immediately after the 1970 exchange, whether or not the cash purchases were included in ITT's holdings.

broadly to read the term "acquisition." The Internal Revenue Service argues that "the acquisition * * * of stock of another corporation" must be understood to encompass the 1968–69 cash purchases as well as the 1970 exchange offer. If the IRS is correct, "the acquisition" here fails as a (B) reorganization. The taxpayers, on the other hand, would limit "the acquisition" to the part of a sequential transaction of this nature which meets the requirements of subsection (B). They argue that the 1970 exchange of stock for stock was itself an "acquisition" by ITT of stock in Hartford solely in exchange for ITT's voting stock, such that after the exchange took place ITT controlled Hartford. Taxpayers contend that the earlier cash purchases of 8 percent, even if conceded to be part of the same acquisitive plan, are essentially irrelevant to the tax-free reorganization otherwise effected.

The Tax Court accepted the taxpayers' reading of the statute, effectively overruling its own prior decision in Howard v. Commissioner, 24 T.C. 792 (1955), rev'd on other grounds, 238 F.2d 943 (7th Cir. 1956). The plurality opinion stated its "narrow" holding as follows:

> "We hold that where, as is the case herein, 80 percent or more of the stock of a corporation is acquired in one transaction,[18] in exchange for which only voting stock is furnished as consideration, the 'solely for voting stock' requirement of section 368(a) (1)(B) is satisfied.
>
> [18] In determining what constitutes 'one transaction,' we include all the acquisitions from shareholders which were clearly part of the same transaction."

71 T.C. at 741. The plurality treated as "irrelevant" the 8 percent of Hartford's stock purchased for cash, although the opinion left somewhat ambiguous the question whether the 8 percent was irrelevant because of the 14-month time interval separating the transactions or because the statute was not concerned with transactions over and above those mathematically necessary to the acquiring corporation's attainment of control.[15]

II.

For reasons set forth extensively in section III of this opinion, we do not accept the position adopted by the Tax Court. Instead we side with the Commissioner on the narrow issue presented in this appeal, that is, the correctness of taxpayers' so-called "second" argument

---

15. If the holding rested on the former basis, it would be difficult to credit the Tax Court's repeated assertions that it was not reaching or deciding the severability issue. As the taxpayers conceded their cash purchases were "parts of the 1970 exchange offer reorganization," the Tax Court had no reason to consider the actual lapse of time which occurred as a factor in treating the cash purchases as legally irrelevant. We assume, therefore, that any indications in the Tax Court's opinion that the separation in time was necessary to its holding were inadvertent, and that the holding actually rests on the Tax Court's reading of the statute. If the Tax Court wishes explicitly to articulate a rule regarding the time period which will suffice to separate two transactions for purposes of Section 368(a)(1)(B), we think it will have an adequate opportunity to do so in considering on remand the issue of severability raised by taxpayers' first argument.

premised on an assumed relationship between the cash and stock transactions. As explained below, we find a strong implication in the language of the statute, in the legislative history, in the regulations, and in the decisions of other courts that cash purchases which are concededly "parts of" a stock-for-stock exchange must be considered constituent elements of the "acquisition" for purposes of applying the "solely for * * * voting stock" requirement of Section 368(a)(1)(B). We believe the presence of non-stock consideration in such an acquisition, regardless of whether such consideration is necessary to the gaining of control, is inconsistent with treatment of the acquisition as a non-taxable reorganization. It follows for purposes of taxpayers' second argument—which was premised on the assumption that the cash transactions were part of the 1970 exchange offer reorganization—that the stock transfers in question would not qualify for nonrecognition of gain or loss.

Our decision will not, unfortunately, end this case. The Tax Court has yet to rule on taxpayers' "first" argument. To be sure, appellees urge that in the event of our reversing the Tax Court on the single issue it chose to address, we should consider upholding its judgment on the alternative ground that the prior cash purchases in the instant case were, as a matter of law, unrelated to the exchange offer. The taxpayers are correct that an appellee may urge any contention appearing in the record in support of the decree, whether or not the issue was addressed by the lower court. * * * Taxpayers' so-called first argument deserves, however, a more focused and deliberate inquiry than we can give it in the present posture of the case. The Commissioner has briefed the issue in only a cursory fashion, and oral argument was devoted almost entirely to the treatment of cash and stock transactions which, while separate, were conceded to be a part of one another. The question of what factors should determine, for purposes of Section 368(a)(1)(B), whether a given cash purchase is truly "related" to a later exchange of stock requires further consideration by the Tax Court, as does the question of the application of those factors in the present case. We therefore will remand this case to the Tax Court for further proceedings on the question raised by the taxpayers' first argument in support of their motion for summary judgment.

We view the Tax Court's options on remand as threefold. It can hold that the cash and stock transactions here in question are related as a matter of law—the position urged by the Commissioner—in which case, under our present holding, there would not be a valid (B) reorganization. On the other hand, the Tax Court may find that the transactions are as a matter of law unrelated, so that the 1970 exchange offer was simply the final, nontaxable step in a permissible creeping acquisition. Finally, the court may decide that, under the legal standard it adopts, material factual issues remain to be decided, so that a grant of summary judgment would be inappropriate at this time.[17]

17. We do not intend to dictate to the Tax Court what legal standard it should apply in determining whether these transactions are related. We would suggest,

III.

A.

Having summarized in advance our holding, and its intended scope, we shall now revert to the beginning of our analysis, and, in the remainder of this opinion, describe the thinking by which we reached the result just announced. We begin with the words of the statute itself. The reorganization definitions contained in Section 368(a)(1) are precise, technical, and comprehensive. They were intended to define the exclusive means by which nontaxable corporate reorganizations could be effected. See Treas.Reg. § 1.368–1 (1960); 3 J. Mertens, The Law of Federal Income Taxation § 20.86 at 364 (1972). In examining the language of the (B) provision, we discern two possible meanings. On the one hand, the statute could be read to say that a successful reorganization occurs whenever Corporation X exchanges its own voting stock for stock in Corporation Y, and, immediately after the transaction, Corporation X controls more than 80 percent of Y's stock. On this reading, purchases of shares for which any part of the consideration takes the form of "boot" should be ignored, since the definition is only concerned with transactions which meet the statutory requirements as to consideration and control. To take an example, if Corporation X bought 50 percent of the shares of Y, and then almost immediately exchanged part of its voting stock for the remaining 50 percent of

however, that the possibilities should include at least the following; perhaps others may be developed by counsel or by the Tax Court itself.

One possibility—advanced by the taxpayers—is that the only transactions which should be considered related, and so parts of "the acquisition," are those which are included in the formal plan of reorganization adopted by the two corporations. The virtues of this approach—simplicity and clarity—may be outweighed by the considerable scope it would grant the parties to a reorganization to control the tax treatment of their formal plan of reorganization by arbitrarily including or excluding certain transactions. A second possibility—urged by the Commissioner—is that all transactions sharing a single acquisitive purpose should be considered related for purposes of Section 368(a)(1)(B). Relying on an example given in the legislative history, see S.Rep.No.1622, 83d Cong., 2d Sess. 273, reprinted in [1954] U.S.Code Cong. & Admin. News, pp. 4621, 4911 [hereinafter cited as 1954 Senate Report], the Commissioner would require a complete and thoroughgoing separation, both in time and purpose, between cash and stock acquisitions before the latter would qualify for reorganization treatment under subsection (B).

A third possible approach, lying somewhere between the other two, would be to focus on the mutual knowledge and intent of the corporate parties, so that one party could not suffer adverse tax consequences from unilateral activities of the other of which the former had no notice. Cf. Manning, "In Pursuance of the Plan of Reorganization": The Scope of the Reorganization Provisions of the Internal Revenue Code, 72 Harv.L.Rev. 881, 912–13 (1959). Such a rule would prevent, for example, the situation where the acquiree's shareholders expect to receive favorable tax treatment on an exchange offer, only to learn later that an apparently valid (B) reorganization has been nullified by anonymous cash purchases on the part of the acquiring corporation. See Bruce v. Helvering, 64 App.D.C. 192, 76 F.2d 442 (D.C.Cir.1935), rev'g, 30 B.T.A. 80 (1934).

Difficulties suggest themselves with each of these rules, and without benefit of thorough briefing and argument, as well as an informed decision by the lower court, we are reluctant to proceed further in exploring this issue. We leave to the Tax Court the task of breaking ground here.

Y's stock, the question would arise whether the second transaction was a (B) reorganization. Arguably, the statute can be read to support such a finding. In the second transaction, X exchanged only stock for stock (meeting the "solely" requirement), and after the transaction was completed X owned Y (meeting the "control" requirement).

The alternative reading of the statute—the one which we are persuaded to adopt—treats the (B) definition as prescriptive, rather than merely descriptive. We read the statute to mean that the entire transaction which constitutes "the acquisition" must not contain any nonstock consideration if the transaction is to qualify as a (B) reorganization. In the example given above, where X acquired 100 percent of Y's stock, half for cash and half for voting stock, we would interpret "the acquisition" as referring to the entire transaction, so that the "solely for * * * voting stock" requirement would not be met. We believe if Congress had intended the statute to be read as merely descriptive, this intent would have been more clearly spelled out in the statutory language.[18]

We recognize that the Tax Court adopted neither of these two readings. For reasons to be discussed in connection with the legislative history which follows, the Tax Court purported to limit its holding to cases, such as this one, where more than 80 percent of the stock of Corporation Y passes to Corporation X in exchange solely for voting stock. The Tax Court presumably would assert that the 50/50 hypothetical posited above can be distinguished from this case, and that its holding implies no view as to the hypothetical. See 71 T.C. at 742. The plurality opinion recognized that the position it adopted creates no small problem with respect to the proper reading of "the acquisition" in the statutory definition. See 71 T.C. at 739, 741. In order to distinguish the 80 percent case from the 50 percent case, it is necessary to read "the acquisition" as referring to at least the amount of stock constituting "control" (80 percent) where related cash purchases are present. Yet the Tax Court recognized that "the acquisition" cannot always refer to the conveyance of an 80 percent bloc of stock in one transaction, since to do so would frustrate the intent of the 1954 amendments to permit so-called "creeping acquisitions." [19]

---

18. For example, Congress could have used the word "any" rather than the word "the" before "acquisition" in the first line of the (B) definition. This would have tended to negate the implication that this definition prescribes the conditions a transaction *must* meet to qualify, rather than simply describing that part of a transaction which is entitled to the statutory tax deferral.

19. For a more complete discussion of "creeping acquisitions," see Part III B infra. See also Vernava, The Howard and Turnbow Cases and the "Solely" Requirement of B Reorganizations, 20 Tax L.Rev. 387, 409–13 (1965). In the typical creeping acquisition situation, Corporation X acquires a portion of Corporation Y's stock, let us say 40 percent, for cash or other nonstock consideration. If (B) reorganizations were limited to those encompassing 80 percent or more of Y's stock in one transaction, X would thereafter be barred, as a practical matter, from acquiring the remainder of Y's shares in a tax-free (B) reorganization. The 1954 Code, however, clearly permits X to trade voting stock for 40 percent or more of Y's remaining stock so long as the stock acquisition is sufficiently separated from the prior cash purchase. See *1954 Senate Report,* supra note 17 at 273. In these circumstances, there-

The Tax Court's interpretation of the statute suffers from a more fundamental defect, as well. In order to justify the limitation of its holding to transactions involving 80 percent or more of the acquiree's stock, the Tax Court focused on the *passage* of control as the primary requirement of the (B) provision. This focus is misplaced. Under the present version of the statute, the *passage* of control is entirely irrelevant; the only material requirement is that the acquiring corporation *have* control immediately after the acquisition. As the statute explicitly states, it does not matter if the acquiring corporation already has control before the transaction begins, so long as such control exists at the completion of the reorganization. Whatever talismanic quality may have attached to the *acquisition* of control under previous versions of the Code, see Part III B infra, is altogether absent from the version we must apply to this case. In our view, the statute should be read to mean that the related transactions that constitute "the acquisition," whatever percentage of stock they may represent, must meet both the "solely for voting stock" and the "control immediately after" requirements of Section 368(a)(1)(B). Neither the reading given the statute by the Tax Court, nor that proposed as the first alternative above, adequately corresponds to the careful language Congress employed in this section of the Code.

B.

The 1924 Code defined reorganization, in part, as "a merger or consolidation (including the acquisition by one corporation of at least a majority of the voting stock and at least a majority of the total number of shares of all other classes of stock of another corporation, or substantially all the properties of another corporation)." Pub.L. No. 68–176, c. 234, § 203(h)(1), 43 Stat. 257. Although the statute did not specifically limit the consideration that could be given in exchange for stock or assets, courts eventually developed the so-called "continuity of interest" doctrine, which held that exchanges that did not include some quantum of stock as consideration were ineligible for reorganization treatment for lack of a continuing property interest on the part of the acquiree's shareholders. * * *

Despite this judicial development, sentiment was widespread in Congress that the reorganization provisions lent themselves to abuse, particularly in the form of so-called "disguised sales." See, e.g., "Prevention of Tax Avoidance," Report of Subcomm. of House Comm. on Ways and Means, 73d Cong., 2d Sess. (Dec. 4, 1933). In 1934, the House Ways and Means Committee proposed abolition of the stock-acquisition and asset-acquisition reorganizations which had appeared in the parenthetical section of the 1924 Act quoted above. See H.R.Rep. No. 704, 73d Cong., 2d Sess. 12–14 (1939–1 Cum.Bull. (Part 2) 554, 563–65). The Senate Finance Committee countered with a proposal to retain these

fore, "the acquisition" must be interpreted as referring to an amount of stock less than 80 percent. * * *

provisions, but with "restrictions designed to prevent tax avoidance." S.Rep. No. 558, 73d Cong., 2d Sess. 15 (1939–1 Cum.Bull. (Part 2) 586, 598).[20] One of these restrictions was the requirement that the acquiring corporation obtain at least 80 percent, rather than a bare majority, of the stock of the acquiree. The second requirement was stated in the Senate Report as follows: "the acquisition, whether of stock or of substantially all the properties, must be in exchange solely for the voting stock of the acquiring corporation." Id. at 17. The Senate amendments were enacted as Section 112(g)(1) of the Revenue Act of 1934, 48 Stat. 680, which provided in pertinent part:

> "(1) The term 'reorganization' means (A) a statutory merger or consolidation, or (B) the acquisition by one corporation in exchange solely for all or a part of its voting stock: of at least 80 per centum of the voting stock and at least 80 per centum of the total number of shares of all other classes of stock of another corporation; or of substantially all the properties of another corporation * * *."

Congress revised this definition in 1939 in response to the Supreme Court's decision in United States v. Hendler, 303 U.S. 564, 58 S.Ct. 655, 82 L.Ed. 1018 (1938), which held that an acquiring corporation's assumption of the acquiree's liabilities in an asset-acquisition was equivalent to the receipt of "boot" by the acquiree. Since virtually all asset-acquisition reorganizations necessarily involve the assumption of the acquiree's liabilities, a literal application of the "solely for * * * voting stock" requirement would have effectively abolished this form of tax-free reorganization. In the Revenue Act of 1939, Congress separated the stock-acquisition and asset-acquisition provisions in order to exempt the assumption of liabilities in the latter category of cases from the "solely for * * * voting stock" requirement. Section 112(g)(1) of the revised statute then read, in pertinent part, as follows:

> "(1) the term 'reorganization' means (A) a statutory merger or consolidation, or (B) the acquisition by one corporation, in exchange solely for all or a part of its voting stock, of at least 80 per centum of the voting stock and at least 80 per centum of the total number of shares of all other classes of stock of another corporation, or (C) the acquisition by one corporation, in exchange solely for all or a part of its voting stock, of substantially all the properties of another corporation, but in determining whether the exchange is solely for voting stock the assumption by the acquiring corporation of a liability of the other, or the fact that property acquired is subject to liability, shall be disregarded * * *."

The next major change in this provision occurred in 1954. In that year, the House Bill, H.R. 8300, would have drastically altered the

---

20. The Senate's purpose in retaining these provisions was apparently to make available an alternative to statutory merger or consolidation in those states where merger statutes were overly restrictive or nonexistent. See Howard v. Commissioner, 238 F.2d 943, 946 (7th Cir.1956).

corporate reorganization sections of the Tax Code, permitting, for example, both stock and "boot" as consideration in a corporate acquisition, with gain recognized only to the extent of the "boot." See H.R. Rep. No. 1337, 83d Cong., 2d Sess. A118–A119, A132–A134, reprinted in [1954] U.S.Code Cong. & Admin.News, pp. 4017, 4256–4257, 4269–4271. The Senate Finance Committee, in order to preserve the familiar terminology and structure of the 1939 Code, proposed a new version of Section 112(g)(1), which would retain the "solely for * * * voting stock" requirement, but alter the existing control requirement to permit so-called "creeping acquisitions." Under the Senate Bill, it would no longer be necessary for the acquiring corporation to obtain 80 percent or more of the acquiree's stock in one "reorganization." The Senate's proposal permitted an acquisition to occur in stages; a bloc of shares representing less than 80 percent could be added to earlier acquisitions, regardless of the consideration given earlier, to meet the control requirement. The Report of the Senate Finance Committee gave this example of the operation of the creeping acquisition amendment:

> "[C]orporation A purchased 30 percent of the common stock of corporation W (the only class of stock outstanding) for cash in 1939. On March 1, 1955, corporation A offers to exchange its own voting stock, for all the stock of corporation W tendered within 6 months from the date of the offer. Within the 6 months period corporation A acquires an additional 60 percent of the stock of W for its own voting stock. As a result of the 1955 transactions, corporation A will own 90 percent of all of corporation W's stock. No gain or loss is recognized with respect to the exchanges of the A stock for the W stock."

1954 Senate Report, supra note 17, at 273, U.S.Code Cong. & Admin. News 1954, p. 4911. See also Treas.Reg. § 1.368–2(c) (1960).

At the same time the Senate was revising the (B) provision, (while leaving intact the "solely for * * * voting stock" requirement), it was also rewriting the (C) provision to explicitly permit up to 20 percent of the consideration in an asset acquisition to take the form of money or other nonstock property. See 26 U.S.C. § 368(a)(2)(B). The Senate revisions of subsections (B) and (C) were ultimately passed, and have remained largely unchanged since 1954. (See footnote 1 for present text.) Proposals for altering the (B) provision to allow "boot" as consideration have been made, but none has been enacted.

As this history shows, Congress has had conflicting aims in this complex and difficult area. On the one hand, the 1934 Act evidences a strong intention to limit the reorganization provisions to prevent forms of tax avoidance that had proliferated under the earlier revenue acts. This intention arguably has been carried forward in the current versions through retention of the "solely for * * * voting stock" requirement in (B), even while the (C) provision was being loosened. On the other hand, both the 1939 and 1954 revisions represented attempts to make the reorganization procedures more accessible and practical in both the (B) and (C) areas. In light of the conflicting purposes, we can discern no clear Congressional mandate in the present structure of the (B) provision, either in terms of the abuses sought to be remedied or the beneficial transactions sought to be facilitated. At best, we think Congress has drawn somewhat arbitrary lines separating those transactions that resemble mere changes in form of ownership and those that contain elements of a sale or purchase arrangement. In such circumstances we believe it is more appropriate to examine the specific rules and requirements Congress enacted, rather than some questionably delineated "purpose" or "policy," to determine whether a particular transaction qualifies for favorable tax treatment.

To the extent there is any indication in the legislative history of Congress' intent with respect to the meaning of "acquisition" in the (B) provision, we believe the intent plainly was to apply the "solely" requirement to all related transactions. In those statutes where Congress intended to permit cash or other property to be used as consideration, it made explicit provision therefor. See, e.g., 26 U.S.C. § 368(a)(2) (B). It is argued that in a (B) reorganization the statute can be satisfied where only 80 percent of the acquiree's stock is obtained solely for voting stock, so that additional acquisitions are irrelevant and need not be considered. In light of Congress' repeated, and increasingly sophisticated, enactments in this area, we are unpersuaded that such an important question would have been left unaddressed had Congress intended to leave open such a possibility. We are not prepared to believe that Congress intended—either when it enacted the 1934, the 1939, or the 1954 statutes—to permit a corporation to exchange stock tax-free for 80 percent of the stock of another and in a related transaction to purchase the remaining 20 percent for cash. The only question we see clearly left open by the legislative history is the degree of separation required between the two transactions before they can qualify as a creeping acquisition under the 1954 amendments. This is precisely the issue the Tax Court chose not to address, and it is the issue we now remand to the Tax Court for consideration.

C.

Besides finding support for the IRS position both in the design of the statute and in the legislative history, we find support in the regulations adopted by the Treasury Department construing these statutory provisions. We of course give weight to the statutory construction contemporaneously developed by the agency entrusted by Congress with the task of applying these laws. * * * The views of the Treasury on tax matters, while by no means definitive, undoubtedly reflect a familiarity with the intricacies of the tax code that surpasses our own. * * *

D.

Finally, we turn to the body of case law that has developed concerning (B) reorganizations to determine how previous courts have dealt with this question. Of the seven prior cases in this area, all to a greater or lesser degree support the result we have reached, and none supports the result reached by the Tax Court. We recognize that the Tax Court purported to distinguish these precedents from the case before it, and that reasonable persons may differ on the extent to which some of these cases directly control the question raised here. Nevertheless, after carefully reviewing the precedents, we are satisfied that the decision of the Tax Court represents a sharp break with the previous judicial constructions of this statute, and a departure from the usual rule of stare decisis, which applies with special force in the tax field where uncertainty and variety are ordinarily to be avoided.

Of the seven precedents, the most significant would seem to be Howard v. Commissioner, 238 F.2d 943 (7th Cir.1956), rev'g, 24 T.C. 792 (1955), which stands out as the one case prior to *Reeves* that specifically addressed the issue raised herein. In *Howard*, the Truax-Traer Coal Company acquired 80.19 percent of the outstanding stock of Binkley Coal Company solely in exchange for Truax-Traer voting stock. At the same time and as part of the same plan of acquisition, Truax-Traer purchased the other 19.81 percent of Binkley's stock for cash. The taxpayers, former shareholders of Binkley who had exchanged their shares solely for voting stock, sold some of the Truax-Traer stock they had received in August 1950, the same year as the exchange. The Commissioner, treating the exchange as a taxable event and not a reorganization, employed a new holding period, beginning with the effective date of the exchange, and treated the taxpayers' gain on their sale of the Truax-Traer stock as a short-term capital gain. The Tax Court sustained the Commissioner, concluding the exchange had not been made "solely for * * * voting stock," as required by the 1939 Act, even though the cash purchases were not essential to Truax-Traer's acquisition of control. 24 T.C. at 804.[25]

---

25. The Tax Court's decision consisted of two findings. The first concerned the issue of whether the two transactions were related:

"We think it clear that each element and term of the plan and agreement as originated, outlined, and consummated was inseparably interrelated, and designed to accomplish but one purpose, the acquisition by Truax-Traer of * * * Binkley * * * Accordingly, there can be no doubt that petitioners did not take part in an exchange of some Binkley stock for stock of Truax-Traer and a separate and unrelated sale of other shares of Binkley stock * * * to Truax-Traer."

Id. at 802. The second finding specifically addressed the issue before this court:

"Basically the question before us is whether the statute requires all * * * stock acquired * * * to have been acquired only ('solely') for stock, or whether it is sufficient if a minimum of ('at least') 80 per cent * * * was acquired for * * * stock even though the remainder * * * was * * * acquired for a consideration other than stock * * * We recognize that there is force to petitioner's argument that the practical objectives of the statute might well be satisfied if we were to adopt the construction urged. We think, however, that the authorities have clearly estab-

The Seventh Circuit, after reviewing the legislative history of Section 112(g)(1)(B) of the 1939 Code, agreed with the Tax Court's conclusion that the presence of cash purchases prevented the transaction from meeting the "solely" requirement of the statute. Like the Tax Court, the court of appeals relied heavily on two prior decisions arising in slightly different contexts. The principal linchpin of the Seventh Circuit's decision was Helvering v. Southwest Consolidated Corp., 315 U.S. 194, 62 S.Ct. 546, 86 L.Ed. 789 (1942), in which the Supreme Court denied tax-free treatment to an asset acquisition under the 1934 Act because a substantial amount of the consideration was given in the form of stock warrants and cash. The Court first noted that under the law existing before 1934, this transaction would have been a perfectly valid tax-free reorganization. The revised statute, see text at notes 20–21 supra, had made the continuity of interest test much stricter, however:

> "Congress has provided that the assets of the transferor corporation must be acquired in exchange 'solely' for 'voting stock' of the transferee. 'Solely' leaves no leeway. Voting stock plus some other consideration does not meet the statutory requirement."

315 U.S. at 198, 62 S.Ct. at 550. The Seventh Circuit noted that in the 1934 Act the asset and stock acquisition reorganizations were dealt with in the same clause both in the statutory language and in the legislative history. It therefore seemed reasonable to the Seventh Circuit to conclude that the Supreme Court's "no leeway" rule for asset acquisitions applied with equal force to stock acquisitions.

Appellees argue that *Southwest Consolidated* is distinguishable from the present facts, and, implicitly, that it should not have been relied on by the *Howard* court. This argument rests, in our view, on a strained reading of *Southwest Consolidated*. The taxpayers point out that the nonstock consideration in that case amounted to 37 percent of the total consideration, by the Tax Court's reckoning. Further, they say that the stock and nonstock consideration could not be separated where one bundle of assets was exchanged for one bundle of consideration, so that *Southwest Consolidated* was essentially a mixed consideration case. We disagree. Had the Supreme Court chosen to decide the issue of whether "substantially all" the assets of one corporation were obtained solely for voting stock, it could have allocated the consideration on a proportional basis, much as the Tax Court did in making its calculations. The Supreme Court did not consider, however, whether the voting stock consideration was sufficient to cover "substantially all" the assets, so that Section 112(g)(1)(B) would be satisfied. The Court determined rather that the presence of *any* nonstock consideration in the acquisition negated the possibility of a valid tax-free reorganization. While the facts were such that the Court could have reached the same

lished the applicable rule of law to be that the consideration for whatever stock is acquired by the transferee corporation in a transaction such as that before us must be solely the transferee's voting stock, and nothing else." * * *

result on another rationale, this does not detract from the weight of its words. The Seventh Circuit was, in our opinion, justified in resting its holding by analogy on the decision in *Southwest Consolidated.*[27]

* * *

[The court then proceeded to analyze the *Howard* case and other related precedents in exhaustive detail. It concluded that *Howard* was factually indistinguishable and that there was no reason to question its continuing vitality. Ed.]

* * * Even were we doubtful as to the correctness of the result reached in *Howard* (and we are not), we would nonetheless be reluctant to see a rule of tax law which has stood virtually unchallenged by courts for 25 years discarded so unceremoniously. As the dissenting judges of the Tax Court noted, much tax planning must proceed on the basis of settled rules. Avoidance of risk and uncertainty are often the keys to a successful transaction. Transactions may have been structured on the basis of *Howard,* with cash intentionally introduced to prevent reorganization treatment. Where a long standing tax rule of this sort is not clearly contrary to Congressional intent or markedly inconsistent with some generally accepted understanding of correct doctrine, we think the proper body to make changes aimed at improving the law is Congress, and not the courts. The complex and delicate judgments as to proper tax policy, and the balancing of interests between corporations, their shareholders, and the public, required to formulate appropriate rules in this area are not the proper province of courts. Our role is to interpret the mandate of Congress as best we can, and to adhere to the reasonable standards supplied by our predecessors where possible. Our role is emphatically not to read into the tax law our own notions of "a well-ordered universe." Compare Pierson v. United States, 472 F.Supp. 957, 974 (D.Del.1979).

Our reading of the statute is reinforced by another more recent circuit decision as well. In Mills v. Commissioner, 331 F.2d 321 (5th Cir.1964), rev'g, 39 T.C. 393 (1962), the issue was whether cash payments for fractional shares in an exchange prevented a nontaxable reorganization. General Gas Corporation, the acquiror, offered the three taxpayers, sole stockholders in three small gas corporations, shares of General common stock in exchange for all of their stock. The number of General shares to be exchanged—at a value of $14 per share—was to be determined by measuring the net book value of the three small corporations. In the event the purchase price was not evenly divisible by 14, cash was to be paid in lieu of fractional shares. As a result, each taxpayer received 1,595 shares of General stock and $27.36 in cash. The Tax Court held this transaction invalid as a tax-free reorganization, declining to adopt a *de minimis* rule. 39 T.C. at

---

27. Nor is our view of *Southwest Consolidated* undermined in any way by Congress' subsequent actions liberalizing the asset-acquisition rules under Sections 368(a)(1)(C) and (a)(2)(B) of the 1954 Code. As we have earlier pointed out, see Part III B supra, this liberalization actually supports our position, since it indicates that Congress was fully capable of granting leeway where leeway was desired.

400. The Fifth Circuit agreed that cash could not form any part of the consideration in a (B) reorganization, but concluded in reversing the Tax Court that the fractional-share arrangement was merely a book-keeping convenience and not an independent part of the consideration. 331 F.2d at 324–25.

Taxpayers, and the Tax Court, argued that *Mills* was distinguishable, despite its sweeping language, because each shareholder of the acquired corporations received both stock and cash in the exchange. We have discussed earlier our reasons for rejecting any rule premised on the consideration received by the acquiree's shareholders. If *Mills* were distinguishable at all, it would be only because the consideration for some of the *shares* in *Mills* consisted of both stock and cash. But even this distinction evaporates when one notes that the one share in each exchange for which a fractional share would have been necessary never constituted more than 20 percent of the stock of any one of the acquiree corporations (since each shareholder held at least six shares in each corporation). In every exchange it was theoretically possible to identify a bloc of more than 80 percent of the stock of the acquiree which was exchanged solely for the voting stock of the acquiring corporation. Thus, in the only case raising the issue now before us under the 1954 Code, the Tax Court accepted as a premise that no cash was permissible as consideration in a (B) reorganization, even where the facts showed that control had passed solely for voting stock.

IV.

We have stated our ruling, and the reasons that support it. In conclusion, we would like to respond briefly to the arguments raised by the Tax Court, the District Court of Delaware, and the taxpayers in this case against the rule we have reaffirmed today. The principal argument, repeated again and again, concerns the supposed lack of policy behind the rule forbidding cash in a (B) reorganization where the control requirement is met solely for voting stock. It is true that the Service has not pointed to tax loopholes that would be opened were the rule to be relaxed as appellees request. We also recognize, as the Tax Court and others have highlighted, that the rule may produce results which some would view as anomalous. For example, if Corporation X acquires 80 percent of Corporation Y's stock solely for voting stock, and is content to leave the remaining 20 percent outstanding, no one would question that a valid (B) reorganization has taken place. If Corporation X then decides to purchase stock from the remaining shareholders, the *Howard* rule might result in loss of nontaxable treatment for the stock acquisition if the two transactions were found to be related. See 71 T.C. at 740–41. The Tax Court asserted that there is no conceivable Congressional policy that would justify such a result. Further, it argued, Congress could not have felt that prior cash purchases would forever ban a later successful (B) reorganization since the 1954 amendments, as the legislative history makes clear, specifically provided that prior cash purchases would not prevent a creeping acquisition.

While not without force, this line of argument does not in the end persuade us. First of all, as already discussed, the language of the statute, and the longstanding interpretation given it by the courts, are persuasive reasons for our holding even in the absence of any clear policy behind Congress' expression of its will. Furthermore, we perceive statutory anomalies of another sort which the Tax Court's rule would only magnify. It is clear from the regulations, for example, that a corporation which already owned as much as 80 percent of another's stock, acquired solely for cash, could in some circumstances acquire all or a part of the remainder solely for voting stock as a valid (B) reorganization.[38] Why, then, could not as little as 10 percent of an acquisition constitute a (B) reorganization, if made solely for voting stock, even though the remaining transactions—totaling more than 80 percent—were made for nonstock consideration? If it is true that Congress did not view related cash transactions as tainting a stock-acquisition reorganization, why would it enact a "solely for * * * voting stock" requirement at all, except to the extent necessary to prevent mixed consideration of the sort employed in the "disguised sales" of the twenties?

Possibly, Congress' insertion of the "solely for * * * voting stock" requirement into the 1934 Act was, as one commentator has suggested, an overreaction to a problem which could have been dealt with through more precise and discriminating measures.[39] But we do not think it appropriate for a court to tell Congress how to do its job in an area such as this. If a more refined statutory scheme would be appropriate, such changes should be sought from the body empowered to make them. While we adhere to the general practice of construing statutes so as to further their demonstrated policies, we have no license to rework whole statutory schemes in pursuit of policy goals which Congress has nowhere articulated. Appellees have not shown us any reason to believe that reaffirmation of the settled rule in this area will frustrate the Congressional purpose of making the (B) reorganization provision generally available to those who comply with the statutory requirements.[40]

A second major argument, advanced primarily by the district court in *Pierson,* is that the previous cases construing this statute are suspect because they did not give proper weight to the changes wrought by the 1954 amendments. In particular, the court argued the liberalization of the "boot" allowance in (C) reorganizations and the allowance of creeping (B) acquisitions showed that Congress had no intent or desire to forbid "boot" of up to 20 percent in a (B) reorganization. As we have

---

38. See Treas.Reg. § 1.368–2(c).

39. See Dailey, The Voting Stock Requirement of B and C Reorganizations, 26 Tax L.Rev. 725, 731 (1971); Pierson v. United States, 472 F.Supp. 957, 968 n. 37 (D.Del.1979).

40. We do not see how the argument that cash purchases are necessary to buy out the interests of "dissenting shareholders" who decline to take part in the exchange advances taxpayers' cause. One of the purposes of stock-acquisition arrangements, as opposed to statutory mergers, is to provide the option to minority shareholders not to take part. In this case, had such protection not been afforded, the Connecticut Insurance Commissioner evidently would not have approved the acquisition.

discussed earlier, we draw the opposite conclusion from the legislative history. Liberalization of the (C) provision shows only that Congress, when it wished to do so, could grant explicit leeway in the reorganization rules. Nor do the creeping acquisition rules mark such a departure from a strict reading of the "solely" requirement as to persuade us that Congress intended to weaken it with respect to related transactions. One has only to look at the illustration given in the legislative history, with its separation of 16 years between the cash and stock transactions, to see that Congress did not indicate positive approval of the type of acquisition covered by the district court's holding.[41]

A third argument asserts that reliance on the literal language of the 1954 Code, and in particular a focus on the interpretation of "acquisition," is unjustified because the 1954 Code was not intended to alter the status of (B) reorganizations under the 1934 and 1939 Codes. According to this argument, the acquisition of at least 80 percent of the acquiree's stock solely for voting stock was allowed under the pre-1954 version, and must still be allowed even though the present statute refers only to "the acquisition * * * of stock" with no percentage specified. This argument assumes the answer to the question that is asked. As *Howard* and *Southwest Consolidated* illustrate, it has been the undeviating understanding of courts, until now, that the pre-1954 statutes did *not* allow cash or other "boot" in a (B) reorganization. It cannot be inferred that Congress left intact a rule which never existed by enacting language inconsistent with such a rule.

Finally, we see no merit at all in the suggestion that we should permit "boot" in a (B) reorganization simply because "boot" is permitted in some instances in (A) and (C) reorganizations. Congress has never indicated that these three distinct categories of transactions are to be interpreted *in pari materia*. In fact, striking differences in the treatment of the three subsections have been evident in the history of the reorganization statutes. We see no reason to believe a difference in the treatment of "boot" in these transactions is impermissible or irrational.

Accordingly, we vacate the judgment of the Tax Court insofar as it rests on a holding that taxpayers were entitled to summary judgment irrespective of whether the cash purchases in this case were related by purpose or timing to the stock exchange offer of 1970. The case will be remanded to the Tax Court for further proceedings consistent with this opinion.

Vacated and remanded.

[Editor's Note. If the ITT litigation had continued, the Tax Court would have been required to resolve the factual question of whether the

---

41. We also see little merit in the argument that the IRS policy of granting minor deviations from the "solely for * * * voting stock" requirement for such practical purposes as allowing the acquiring corporation to pay transaction costs undermines the strict reading the IRS urges in this case. See *Pierson*, 472 F.Supp. at 972 n. 51. The same is true of revenue rulings permitting purchases of stock indirectly from the acquired corporation itself.

earlier cash purchases of Hartford stock were "old and cold"—i.e., unrelated to the subsequent stock-for-stock exchange—and, if not, whether the sale to Mediobanca was sufficient to cleanse the transaction. In May, 1981, however, the seven year controversy was settled when ITT agreed to pay $18.5 million. The IRS, in turn, agreed not to pursue claims against Hartford shareholders, who were allowed to treat the transaction as a tax-free exchange if they did not claim a stepped-up basis when reporting their gain or loss on a subsequent sale of the ITT stock.

The settlement relieved ITT, which had agreed to reimburse Hartford shareholders for any tax liability resulting from the transaction, of an estimated liability of $100 million. Query, is ITT's $17 million payment on behalf of the former Hartford shareholders deductible by the company and taxable to the shareholders? These thorny questions were resolved as part of the settlement. ITT agreed not to claim any deduction and the IRS agreed that Hartford shareholders would not be deemed to receive additional income as a result of Hartford's payment. I.R. 81–53, (1981), reprinted in P–H Fed.Taxes ¶ 60,299.5 (May 14, 1981).]

REVENUE RULING 67–274

1967–2 Cum.Bull. 141.

Advice has been requested whether the transaction described below qualifies as a reorganization within the meaning of section 368(a)(1)(B) of the Internal Revenue Code of 1954.

Pursuant to a plan of reorganization, corporation Y acquired all of the outstanding stock of corporation X from the X shareholders in exchange solely for voting stock of Y. Thereafter X was completely liquidated as part of the same plan and all of its assets were transferred to Y which assumed all of the liabilities of X. Y continued to conduct the business previously conducted by X. The former shareholders of X continued to hold 16 percent of the fair market value of all the outstanding stock of Y.

Section 368(a)(1)(B) of the Code provides in part that a reorganization is the acquisition by one corporation, in exchange solely for all or a part of its voting stock, of stock of another corporation if, immediately after the acquisition, the acquiring corporation has control (as defined in section 368(c) of the Code) of such other corporation. Section 368(a)(1)(C) of the Code provides in part that a reorganization is the acquisition by one corporation, in exchange solely for all or a part of its voting stock, of substantially all of the properties of another corporation, but in determining whether the exchange is solely for stock the assumption by the acquiring corporation of a liability of the other, or the fact that property acquired is subject to a liability, is disregarded.

Under the circumstances of this case the acquisition of X stock by Y and the liquidation of X by Y are part of the overall plan of reorganization and the two steps may not be considered independently of each other for Federal income tax purposes. See Revenue Ruling 54–96, C.B. 1954–1, 111, as modified by Revenue Ruling 56–100, C.B. 1956–1, 624. The substance of the transaction is an acquisition of assets to which section 368(a)(1)(B) of the Code does not apply.

Accordingly, the acquisition by Y of the outstanding stock of X will not constitute a reorganization within the meaning of section 368(a)(1) (B) of the Code but will be considered an acquisition of the assets of X which in this case is a reorganization described in section 368(a)(1)(C) of the Code. * * *.

REVENUE RULING 55–440
1955–2 Cum.Bull. 226.

Advice has been requested with respect to the tax consequences of a reorganization under the following circumstances.

Pursuant to a plan of reorganization, the X corporation acquired not less than 80 percent of the outstanding common stock of the Y corporation in exchange solely for voting common stock of X. The offer of exchange by X corporation was contingent upon its acceptance by the holders of at least 80 percent of the outstanding common stock of Y corporation.

Y corporation also has voting preferred stock outstanding. The certificate of incorporation provides, in part, that the preferred stock may be called at a specified price per share, plus accrued dividends, on any dividend date upon 30 days' notice to the stockholders of Y's intention to redeem the stock. Prior to the effective date of the exchange, the board of directors of Y resolved to call the preferred stock and the 30 days' notices of the call were mailed to the holders of the preferred stock. The redemption price of all the outstanding preferred stock was deposited with a bank as escrow agent.

After the exchange of common stock was consummated upon the tender of at least 80 percent of the common stock of Y corporation, all of the preferred stock of Y had been previously called, but there were certain shares of the preferred stock which had not been presented for redemption prior to the effective date of the exchange.

Section 368 of the Internal Revenue Code of 1954 provides, in part, as follows:

(a) REORGANIZATION.—

(1) IN GENERAL.—* * * the term "reorganization" means—

* * *

(B) the acquisition by one corporation, in exchange solely for all or a part of its voting stock, of stock of another corporation if, immediately after the acquisition, the acquiring corporation has control of such other corporation (whether or not such acquiring corporation had control immediately before the acquisition);

* * *

(c) CONTROL.—* * * the term "control" means the ownership of stock possessing at least 80 percent of the total combined voting power of all classes of stock entitled to vote and at least 80 percent of the total number of shares of all other classes of stock of the corporation.

The question at issue is whether preferred shares previously called for redemption but not yet surrendered at the effective date of the exchange would be considered to be "stock" within the meaning of section 368(c) of the Code for the purpose of determining whether the X corporation was in control of Y corporation after the exchange of common stock within the meaning of section 368(a)(1)(B) of the Code.

Under the terms of the preferred stock indenture pursuant to the certificate of incorporation, the Y corporation may call for redemption on any dividend date upon 30 days' notice to its stockholders to redeem such stock. Therefore, the rights as preferred stockholders terminated upon the call of the preferred shares. Thereafter, the holders of such shares had only the right to receive the call price upon the surrender of the shares for redemption, there being no issue regarding the rights of creditors. For the purpose of determining control under section 368(c), preferred shares which have been called but not yet presented for redemption will be disregarded.

In view of the foregoing, the acquisition by X corporation in exchange solely for shares of its voting common stock of at least 80 percent of the outstanding common stock of Y corporation constitutes a reorganization within the meaning of section 368(a)(1)(B) of the Code, regardless of the number of shares of preferred stock of Y corporation which, at the time of the consummation of the exchange, had not been presented for redemption. Accordingly, no gain or loss is recognizable to the common stockholders of Y as a result of the exchange of their common stock of Y for common stock of X. The basis in their hands of the common stock of X received upon the exchange is the same as the basis of the common stock of Y exchanged therefor.

NOTE

Solely for Voting Stock Requirement. Before the lower court opinions in the ITT litigation, the courts had uniformly held that "voting stock" was the only permissible consideration in a B reorganization. A divided Tax Court boldly broke with tradition when it held that ITT's acquisition of Hartford qualified as a B reorganization despite ITT's prior cash purchase of 8 percent of the Hartford stock in a "related" transaction. The appellate decisions in *Chapman* and Heverly v. Commissioner [1] restored the status quo: there could be "no boot in a B." But the nagging policy question remains: why should the requirements

---

1. 621 F.2d 1227 (3d Cir.1980).

for a stock-for-stock acquisition be so strict when the acquiring corporation in other types of acquisitive reorganization has the leeway to use from 20 to 50 percent nonequity consideration?

The rigid requirements for a B reorganization have placed considerable pressure on the definition of "voting stock." Although the term is not specifically defined in the Code, "voting stock" has been interpreted to require an unconditional right to vote on regular corporate decisions (election of directors, shareholder proposals, etc.) and not merely extraordinary events such as mergers or liquidations.[2] The class of stock transferred is immaterial provided that it has voting rights. Although the Supreme Court has long held that hybrid equity securities, such as warrants to purchase additional voting stock, do not constitute voting stock, contractual rights to receive additional voting stock may qualify.[3]

The Service has allowed the parties to a B reorganization some flexibility despite the stringency of the voting stock requirement. For example, the "solely" requirement is not violated if the acquiring corporation issues cash in lieu of fractional shares.[4] The acquiring corporation also may pay the target corporation's expenses (e.g., registration fees, legal and accounting fees and other administrative costs) related to the reorganization, but payment of legal, accounting or other expenses of the target's shareholders will constitute forbidden boot.[5]

Buying Out Dissenting Shareholders. A particular challenge in planning a B reorganization involves shareholders of the target who insist on receiving cash. If the acquiring corporation pays cash directly to these dissenters, the transaction will violate the solely for voting stock requirement and all the target's shareholders must recognize gain. But the Service permits the target to redeem the shares of dissenters prior to a valid B reorganization provided that the cash does not emanate from the acquiring corporation and continuity of interest requirements are satisfied.[6] Another possible approach might be for the transaction to proceed as a stock-for-stock exchange, followed by a later redemption of the acquiring corporation stock held by the dissenters.[7] If they were truly dissenters, however, one would assume they would have sought some assurance, albeit informal, that the later redemption would occur. In that event, the redemption surely would be part of the original reorganization plan and, if so, the entire transaction would fail.

Contingent Payments and Escrowed Stock Arrangements. During the negotiations over an acquisitive reorganization, the parties often disagree over the price to be paid for the target corporation. The

2. Cf. Reg. § 1.302–3(a).

3. Helvering v. Southwest Consolidated Corp., 315 U.S. 194, 63 S.Ct. 546 (1942); Rev.Rul. 66–112, 1966–1 C.B. 68.

4. Mills v. Commissioner, 39 T.C. 393 (1962), affirmed on other grounds 331 F.2d 321 (5th Cir.1964); Rev.Rul. 66–365, 1966–2 C.B. 116.

5. Rev.Rul. 73–54, 1973–1 C.B. 187.

6. Rev.Rul. 55–440, p. 540, infra. See also Rev.Rul. 68–285, 1968–1 C.B. 147.

7. See Rev.Rul. 56–345, 1956–2 C.B. 206; Rev.Rul. 57–114, 1957–1 C.B. 122.

acquiring corporation may contend that the target's earnings are unpredictable or that the value of the business is clouded by contingent liabilities. The target may counter by producing optimistic earnings projections. A common method of breaking this type of stalemate is through a contingent consideration agreement. The acquiring corporation may issue a specified amount of stock or securities and agree to issue additional shares under specified contingencies. For example, additional shares may be issued to the former target shareholders if the earnings of the target attain certain levels during a specified time period after the acquisition.

There are a variety of methods to handle the payment of contingent consideration. The parties simply may agree that additional shares will be issued on the happening of specified events. The acquiring corporation may issue negotiable certificates of contingent interest. Or the parties may take the formal step of transferring the additional shares to an escrow agent with instructions to issue the shares if certain future events occur.

At one time, the Service contended that contingent rights to acquire additional stock violated the "solely for voting stock" requirement for a Type B (and Type C) reorganization. This position was not sustained by the courts, however, and the Service now concedes that contingent consideration will not disqualify an acquisitive reorganization if certain conditions are met.[8] For advance ruling purposes, the Service has issued guidelines for approval of contingent and escrowed stock arrangements. The more important requirements for contingent consideration agreements are:[9] (1) to ensure compliance with the continuity of interest doctrine, only additional stock can be received; (2) the acquiring corporation must issue the stock within five years after the reorganization; (3) the arrangement must be based on a valid business reason, such as a valuation dispute; (4) there is a maximum number of contingent shares that can be issued; (5) at least 50 percent of the maximum number of shares of each class of stock must be issued in the initial distribution; (6) the contingent rights may be neither assignable nor readily marketable; and (7) the events triggering the issuance of additional stock are not within the control of the shareholders.[10] Similar requirements are imposed where the acquiring corporation goes beyond merely promising to issue more stock and actually places the shares in escrow with an independent agent. In addition, escrowed stock must be shown as issued and outstanding on the acquiring corporation's financial statements, and the target shareholders must be entitled to any dividends paid on the stock and voting

8. See, e.g., Hamrick v. Commissioner, 43 T.C. 21 (1964), Acq.; Carlberg v. United States, 281 F.2d 507 (8th Cir.1960). The Service now agrees that contingent consideration is not boot but only if the contingent rights to additional shares are not negotiable. See Rev.Rul. 66–112, 1966–1 C.B. 68.

9. See Rev.Proc. 77–37, 1977–2 C.B. 568, amplified by Rev.Proc. 84–42, 1984–1 C.B. 521.

10. Contingent stock arrangements also can trigger issues under the original issue discount rules. See Bittker & Eustice, Federal Income Taxation of Corporations and Shareholders ¶ 14.56 (5th ed. 1987).

rights if, as is required in a Type B reorganization, the escrowed stock has voting rights.[11]

PROBLEMS

1.   Acquiring Corporation ("A") wishes to acquire Target Corporation ("T"). Prior to the proposed acquisition, A has 1,000 shares of voting common stock outstanding with a value of $100 per share. Consider whether the following transactions qualify as Type B reorganizations:

   (a)   In exchange for their T stock, T shareholders receive 100 shares of newly issued A voting preferred stock with a value of $1,000 per share. Each share of the preferred stock has the same voting rights per share as each share of A common stock.

   (b)   Same as (a), above, except that A transfers 85 shares of newly issued A voting common stock worth $85,000 and warrants worth $15,000 to acquire A voting common stock.

   (c)   T shareholders receive A voting common stock with the same terms as the existing shares outstanding except that shareholders entitled to fractional shares receive a cash payment in lieu of those shares.

   (d)   Same as (c), above, except that A also pays T's legal, accounting and SEC registration expenses incurred in connection with the reorganization.

   (e)   Same as (c), above, except that A also pays the attorneys' fees incurred by T's majority shareholders for legal and tax advice relating to the transaction.

2.   Assume the same basic facts as in Problem 1, above, except that Dee Minimis, a 5% minority shareholder, does not wish to participate in the transaction and is unwilling to become a shareholder of Acquiring Corporation.

   (a)   Can A just disregard Dee and simply deal with T's other shareholders?

   (b)   What result if T redeemed Dee's stock prior to the transaction between A and the remaining T shareholders? Would it matter if the cash used by T to redeem Dee's stock was borrowed from A?

   (c)   What result if Dee participates in the transaction and a month later, pursuant to an oral understanding, A redeems Dee's newly acquired A shares?

   (d)   What result if the majority shareholders of T buy out Dee's interest and then proceed to engage in a stock-for-stock exchange with A?

11.   Rev.Proc. 84–42, supra note 9.

3. In the same type of transaction described in the problems above, what are the consequences to the shareholders of Target Corporation in the following alternative situations:

(a) Acquiring Corporation ("A") acquired 30% of the stock of Target Corporation ("T") for cash five years ago. It acquires the remaining 70% from T's shareholders in a single transaction in return for newly issued voting common stock of A.

(b) A acquired 85% of the stock of T in a cash tender offer a year ago, and it acquires the remaining 15% from T shareholders in a single transaction in return for newly issued voting common stock of A.

(c) Same as (a), above (i.e., A already owned 30% of the T stock), except that A acquires the remaining 70% at two different times: 40% in year one and 30% in year two.

(d) Same as (c), above, except that the 40% is acquired for cash.

(e) A, with the hope of ultimately acquiring 100% of T, acquired 10% of the T stock from one shareholder for cash one year ago. Six months ago, A sold the 10% interest to Friendly National Bank, with whom it enjoyed friendly relations. It then acquired 100% of the T stock in a single transaction solely in exchange for newly issued A voting stock.

3. TYPE C: ACQUISITIONS OF ASSETS FOR VOTING STOCK

Code: § 368(a)(1)(C), (a)(2)(B), (a)(2)(G); Skim §§ 336(c); 354(a); 356(a); 357; 358(a); 361; 362(b); 368(a)(2)(C), (b); 381(a)(2); 1032(a).

Regulations: § 1.368–2(d).

Type C reorganizations are known as "practical mergers" because their end result is generally the same as a merger. The difference only may be the form of the transaction under local corporate law. In a statutory merger, all the assets and liabilities of the target are absorbed by the acquiring corporation automatically, while an asset acquisition technically requires a "transfer" of assets and liabilities under a negotiated agreement and does not necessarily require the target to sell all of its assets or to liquidate.[1]

Despite their similarities in form, it is far more difficult to qualify as a Type C stock-for-assets exchange than as a Type A statutory merger because of the more stringent consideration requirements. Section 368(a)(1)(C) requires the target to transfer "substantially all" of its assets *solely* in exchange for voting stock of the acquiring corporation. Although "voting stock" has the same meaning for both B and C reorganizations, the term "solely" in Section 368(a)(1)(C) is subject to two important exceptions. First, the assumption of liabilities by the

---

1. See, e.g., Cal.Corp.Code § 1100; Del. Code Ann. title 8, § 251 (1979): A liquidation of the target is required in a Type C reorganization, however, unless the Commissioner waives the requirement. I.R.C. § 368(a)(2)(G)(ii).

acquiring corporation (or the taking of property subject to liabilities) is not treated as disqualifying boot.[2] Second, a "boot relaxation rule" permits the acquiring corporation to use up to 20 percent boot, but for this purpose the transferred liabilities are considered as cash consideration.[3] A transaction thus can qualify as a Type C reorganization when the consideration consists of a substantial amount of debt relief as long as no other boot is used and sufficient voting stock is transferred to maintain continuity of interest. But a combination of debt relief and other boot likely will spell doom for the transaction.

To illustrate the operation of these rules, assume that Target ("T") has gross assets of $120,000 and liabilities of $30,000. Acquiring Corporation ("A") proposes to acquire all of T's assets in exchange for the assumption of $30,000 of liabilities and $90,000 of A voting stock. The transaction qualifies as a C reorganization because the liabilities are not treated as boot. But if A assumes the $30,000 of liabilities and transfers $80,000 of voting stock and $10,000 of cash, the transaction does not qualify. The liabilities are treated as "money paid" for purposes of the boot relaxation rule, and thus A has acquired only 66⅔ percent of the $120,000 gross assets of T for voting stock. On these facts, A must use at least $96,000 of voting stock (80 percent of $120,000) in order for the transaction to qualify as a Type C reorganization under the boot relaxation rule. This example illustrates that in the normal situation where T's liabilities exceed 20 percent of the value of its gross assets, no boot may be used.

The target also must transfer "substantially all" of its assets. In order to obtain a favorable ruling, the Service requires a transfer of "assets representing at least 90 percent of the fair market value of the net assets and at least 70 percent of the fair market value of the gross assets held by the target corporation immediately preceding the transfer."[4] These guidelines further provide that "all payments to dissenters and all redemptions and distributions (except for regular, normal distributions) made by the corporation immediately preceding the transfer and which are part of the plan of reorganization will be considered as assets held by the corporation immediately prior to the transfer."[5] Other authorities are not as stringent in defining "substantially all," and it is possible that a complete transfer of *operating* assets may qualify even if the Service's percentage tests are not met.[6]

Prior to 1984, the target corporation in a C reorganization was not required to distribute its assets (which ordinarily will consist primarily of voting stock of the acquiring corporation) in complete liquidation. Some targets chose to stay alive as a holding company with a fresh set of tax attributes.[7] Others opted to distribute the voting stock acquired

2. I.R.C. § 368(a)(1)(C).

3. I.R.C. § 368(a)(2)(B).

4. Rev.Proc. 77–37, 1977–2 C.B. 568 at 569.

5. Id.

6. See, e.g., Rev.Rul. 57–518, p. 481, infra; Commissioner v. First National Bank of Altoona, 104 F.2d 865 (3d Cir.1939) (86% of net worth is "substantially all").

7. The tax attributes (e.g., earnings and profits) of the target automatically pass to

in the reorganization while retaining other assets that might trigger adverse tax consequences (e.g., a dividend) if distributed to the shareholders.[8] To prevent these and other perceived abuses, Congress added a new qualification rule that requires the target to distribute all of its assets pursuant to the plan of reorganization unless the Service, pursuant to regulations that it has yet to issue, agrees to waive the distribution requirement.[9] In the event of a waiver, however, the legislative history states that the retained assets must be treated as if they had been distributed to the T shareholders and recontributed to the capital of a new corporation.[10]

A final problem involves "creeping acquisitions," in which the acquiring corporation has previously acquired some stock of the target and now seeks to assume complete control by acquiring all of its assets. We have seen that a creeping acquisition will not necessarily poison the final stock-for-stock exchange in a B reorganization, at least if the stock previously acquired for cash is "old and cold"—i.e., acquired in an unrelated transaction. The *Bausch and Lomb* case at page 551, below, demonstrates the difficulties in accomplishing a creeping C reorganization.

REVENUE RULING 57–518

1957–2 Cum.Bull. 253.

Advice has been requested as to the Federal income tax consequences of a reorganization between two corporations under the circumstances described below.

The *M* and *N* corporations were engaged in the fabrication and sale of various items of steel products. For sound and legitimate business reasons, *N* corporation acquired most of *M* corporation's business and operating assets. Under a plan of reorganization, *M* corporation transferred to *N* corporation (1) all of its fixed assets (plant and equipment) at net book values, (2) 97 percent of all its inventories at book values, and (3) insurance policies and other properties pertaining to the business. In exchange therefor, *N* corporation issued shares of its voting common stock to *M* corporation.

The properties retained by *M* corporation include cash, accounts receivable, notes, and three percent of its total inventory. The fair market value of the assets retained by *M* was roughly equivalent to the amount of its liabilities. *M* corporation proceeded to liquidate its retained properties as expeditiously as possible and applied the proceeds to its outstanding debts. The property remaining after the

the acquiring corporation on a Type C reorganization. I.R.C. § 381(a)(2).

8. See Rev.Rul. 73–552, 1973–2 C.B. 116.

9. I.R.C. § 368(a)(2)(G). See Rev.Proc. 89–50, 1989–2 C.B. 631, for representations

which ordinarily must be included in a request for the Service to waive the liquidation requirement.

10. H.R.Rep. No. 98–861, 98th Cong., 2d Sess. 846 (1984).

discharge of all its liabilities was turned over to *N* corporation, and *M* corporation was liquidated.

Section 368 of the Internal Revenue Code of 1954, in defining corporate reorganizations, provides in part:

> (a) REORGANIZATION.—
>
> > (1) IN GENERAL.—* * * the term "reorganization" means—
>
> > > * * *
>
> > > (C) The acquisition by one corporation, in exchange solely for all or a part of its voting stock (or in exchange solely for all or a part of the voting stock of a corporation which is in control of the acquiring corporation), of substantially all of the properties of another corporation, * * *.

The specific question presented is what constitutes "substantially all of the properties" as defined in the above section of the Code. The answer will depend upon the facts and circumstances in each case rather than upon any particular percentage. Among the elements of importance that are to be considered in arriving at the conclusion are the nature of the properties retained by the transferor, the purpose of the retention, and the amount thereof. In Milton Smith, et al. v. Commissioner, 34 B.T.A. 702, acquiescence, page 7, this Bulletin, withdrawing nonacquiescence, C.B. XV–2, 46 (1936), a corporation transferred 71 percent of its gross assets. It retained assets having a value of $52,000, the major portion of which was in cash and accounts receivable. It was stated that the assets were retained in order to liquidate liabilities of approximately $46,000. Thus, after discharging its liabilities, the outside figure of assets remaining with the petitioner would have been $6,000, which the court stated was not an excessive margin to allow for the collection of receivables with which to meet its liabilities. No assets were retained for the purpose of engaging in any business or for distribution to stockholders. In those circumstances, the court held that there had been a transfer of "substantially all of the assets" of the corporation. The court very definitely indicated that a different conclusion would probably have been reached if the amount retained was clearly in excess of a reasonable amount necessary to liquidate liabilities. Furthermore, the court intimated that transfer of all of the net assets of a corporation would not qualify if the percentage of gross assets transferred was too low. Thus, it stated that, if a corporation having gross assets of $1,000,000 and liabilities of $900,000 transferred only the net assets of $100,000, the result would probably not come within the intent of Congress in its use of the words "substantially all."

The instant case, of the assets not transferred to the corporation [sic], no portion was retained by *M* corporation for its own continued use inasmuch as the plan of reorganization contemplated *M*'s liquidation. Furthermore, the assets retained were for the purpose of meeting liabilities, and these assets at fair market values, approximately equaled the amount of such liabilities. Thus, the facts in this case meet the requirements established in the case of *Milton Smith,* supra.

The instant case is not in conflict with I.T. 2373, C.B. VI–2 19 (1927), which holds that, where one corporation transferred approximately three-fourths of its properties to another corporation for a consideration of bonds and cash, it did not dispose of "substantially all the properties" owned by it at the time and, therefore, no corporate reorganization took place, so that the transaction constituted an exchange of property resulting in a gain or loss to the transferor for income tax purposes. I.T. 2372, supra, is obsolete to the extent that it implies that a corporate reorganization could have occurred where there was no continuity of interest. However, that ruling is still valid with regard to its discussion of the question of what constitutes "substantially all of the properties." From the facts as stated in that case, it appears that a major part of the 25 percent of the assets retained were operating assets, and it does not appear that they were retained for the purpose of liquidating the liabilities of the corporation. On the contrary, it seems likely that the corporation may have contemplated continuation of its business or the sale of the remainder of its operating assets to another purchaser. As a result, I.T. 2373, supra, is clearly distinguishable from the instant case.

Accordingly, since the assets transferred by *M* to *N* constitute "substantially all" of the assets of the transferor corporation within the meaning of that statutory phrase, the acquisition by *N* corporation, in exchange solely for part of its voting common stock, of the properties of *M* corporation pursuant to the plan will constitute a reorganization within the purview of section 368(a)(1)(C) of the Code. No gain or loss is recognized to the transferor as a result of the exchange of its property for common stock of the transferee under section 361 of the Code; and no gain or loss is recognized to the shareholders of *M* corporation, under section 354(a)(1) of such Code, as the result of their receipt of *N* common stock.

REVENUE RULING 88–48
1988–1 Cum.Bull. 117.

ISSUE

If a transferor corporation sold 50 percent of its historic assets to unrelated parties for cash and immediately afterwards transferred to an acquiring corporation all of its assets (including the cash from the sale), did the subsequent transfer meet the "substantially all" requirement of section 368(a)(1)(C) of the Internal Revenue Code?

FACTS

X and Y were unrelated corporations that for many years were engaged in the hardware business. X operated two significant lines of business, a retail hardware business and a wholesale plumbing supply business. Y desired to acquire and continue to operate X's hardware business but did not desire to acquire the other business. Accordingly, pursuant to an overall plan, the following steps were taken. First, in a taxable transaction, X sold its entire interest in the plumbing supply business (constituting 50 percent of its total historic business assets) to purchasers unrelated to either X or Y or their shareholders. Second, X transferred all of its assets, including the cash proceeds from the sale, to Y solely for Y voting stock and the assumption of X's liabilities. Finally, in pursuance of the plan of reorganization, X distributed the Y stock (the sole asset X then held) to the X shareholders in complete liquidation.

Except for the issue relating to the "substantially all" requirement, the transfer of assets from X to Y constituted a corporate reorganization within the meaning of section 368(a)(1)(C) of the Code.

LAW AND ANALYSIS

Section 368(a)(1)(C) of the Code defines a corporate reorganization to include the acquisition by one corporation, in exchange solely for all or part of its voting stock, of substantially all the properties of another corporation.

Section 368(a)(1)(C) of the Code is intended to accommodate transactions that are, in effect, mergers, but which fail to meet the statutory requirements that would bring them within section 368(a)(1)(A). See S.Rep. No. 558, 73d Cong., 2d Sess. 16, 17 (1939), 1939–1 C.B. (Pt. 2) 586, 598.

Congress intended that transactions that are divisive in nature not qualify under section 368(a)(1)(C) of the Code, but, instead, be subject to the tests under section 368(a)(1)(D). See S.Rep. No. 1622, 83d Cong., 2d Sess. 274 (1954). The enactment of section 368(a)(2)(G) indicates the continuing interest in furthering this underlying objective of preventing divisive "C" reorganizations.

Rev.Rul. 57–518, 1957–2 C.B. 253, concerns whether, in a "C" reorganization, assets may be retained to pay liabilities. The ruling states that what constitutes "substantially all" for purposes of section 368(a)(1)(C) of the Code depends on the facts and circumstances in each case. Rev.Rul. 57–518 exemplifies the Service's longstanding position that where some assets are transferred to the acquiring corporation and other assets retained, then the transaction may be divisive and so fail to meet the "substantially all" requirement of section 368(a)(1)(C). See also Rev.Rul. 78–47, 1978–1 C.B. 113.

In the present situation, 50 percent of the X assets acquired by Y consisted of cash from the sale of one of X's significant historic businesses. Although Y acquired substantially all the assets X held at the time of transfer, the prior sale prevented Y from acquiring substantially all of X's historic business assets. The transaction here at issue, however, was not divisive. The sale proceeds were not retained by the transferor corporation or its shareholders, but were transferred to the acquiring corporation. Moreover, the prior sale of the historic business assets was to unrelated purchasers, and the X shareholders retained no interest, direct or indirect, in these assets. Under these circumstances, the "substantially all" requirement of section 368(a)(1)(C) was met because all of the assets of X were transferred to Y.

HOLDING

The transfer of all of its assets by X to Y met the "substantially all" requirement of section 368(a)(1)(C) of the Code, even though immediately prior to the transfer X sold 50 percent of its historic business assets to unrelated parties for cash and transferred that cash to Y instead of the historic assets.

BAUSCH & LOMB OPTICAL COMPANY v. COMMISSIONER

United States Court of Appeals, Second Circuit, 1959.
267 F.2d 75.

MEDINA, Circuit Judge.

Petitioner Bausch & Lomb Optical Company, a New York corporation engaged in the manufacture and sale of ophthalmic products, on March 1, 1950 owned 9923¼ shares of the stock of its subsidiary Riggs Optical Company, or 79.9488% of the 12,412 outstanding shares of Riggs. In order to effectuate certain operating economies, Bausch & Lomb decided to amalgamate Riggs with itself. To this end on April 22, 1950 Bausch & Lomb exchanged 105,508 shares of its unissued voting stock for all of the Riggs assets. An additional 433 shares of Bausch & Lomb stock went to 12 Riggs' employees.

On May 2, 1950, according to a prearranged plan, Riggs dissolved itself, distributing its only asset, Bausch & Lomb stock, pro rata to its shareholders. Bausch & Lomb thus received back 84,347 of its own shares which became treasury stock, while 21,161 shares went to the Riggs minority shareholders.

The Commissioner determined that the substance of these transactions was that Bausch & Lomb received the Riggs assets partly in exchange for its Riggs stock and partly for its own stock, and that the gain which Bausch & Lomb realized upon the Riggs "liquidation" was subject to tax. In other words, that Bausch & Lomb parted with 21,161 shares of its own voting stock, plus 9923¼ shares of its Riggs stock, for the transfer to it of all of the Riggs assets. Bausch & Lomb contends, however, that a "reorganization" was effected under [the 1939 Code predecessor of Section 368(a)(1)(C)] and that it is therefore entitled to tax-free treatment. The Tax Court sustained the Commissioner's position and held that the acquisition of the Riggs assets and the dissolution of Riggs must be viewed together, and that the surrender by Bausch & Lomb of its Riggs stock was additional consideration. The

Tax Court accordingly held that the Riggs assets were not obtained "solely for all or a part of its voting stock." We agree.

Bausch & Lomb concedes that to qualify as a "C" reorganization, it could not furnish any additional consideration over and above its own stock. * * * Moreover, Bausch & Lomb admits, as the correspondence and minutes of pertinent meetings plainly show, that the acquisition of the Riggs assets and the dissolution of Riggs were both part of the same plan. Nevertheless, Bausch & Lomb asserts that the exchange of the Riggs assets for its stock should be treated as separate and distinct from the dissolution. The argument runs to the effect that, if the two steps are viewed apart from one another, a "C" reorganization is effected.

Petitioner contends that, even if a qualification according to the literal terms of Section [368(a)(1)(C)] is not found, the amalgamation was in substance in "reorganization" because it has the attributes of one, including "continuity of interest" and business purpose. This is factually not quite true for, while the amalgamation may have been for genuine business reasons, the division into two steps served only to facilitate the liquidation of Riggs. It was considered easier to distribute Bausch & Lomb stock than distribute the Riggs assets. Hence the "business purpose" of dividing the liquidation into two steps lends no support to Bausch & Lomb's contention that in substance and actuality a reorganization was achieved. Moreover, the Congress has defined in Section [368(a)(1)(C)] how a reorganization thereunder may be effected, and the only question for us to decide, on this phase of the case, is whether the necessary requirements have been truly fulfilled. It is for the Congress and not for us to say whether some other alleged equivalent set of facts should receive the same tax free status.

Nor does the fact that Bausch & Lomb may well have desired to hold the 84,347 shares of its own voting shares as treasury stock change our opinion of the transaction as a whole.

Bausch & Lomb suggests that under our present holding even if it had but a 1% interest in Riggs, the requirement that the acquisition be "solely for * * * its voting stock" could defeat Section [368(a)(1)(C)] reorganization treatment. This hypothesis is a far cry from the facts disclosed in this record, and the lack of controlling interest surrounds it with a mist of unreality. In any event, it will be time to consider such a situation in all its aspects when, as and if it comes before us. We merely hold that the attempt to thwart taxation in this case by carrying out the liquidation process in two steps instead of one fell short of meeting the requirements of a "C" reorganization. * * *

Of course, the fact that Bausch & Lomb "could have" merged with Riggs and hence qualified the transaction as a reorganization under [Section [368(a)(1)(A)]] is beside the point. For reasons of its own it chose not to do so. This is clearly not an "A" reorganization.

Bausch & Lomb also claims that a tax-free liquidation was effected under Section [332] although it plainly lacked the necessary 80% of the voting stock. This belabored effort to claim ownership of the 51 shares of Riggs voting stock for which 12 of Riggs' employees had received credit on Riggs' books, so as to raise Bausch & Lomb's interest slightly above the 80% required by Section [332] has nothing whatever to commend it. As found by the Tax Court, Bausch & Lomb never was the legal or equitable owner of these shares, there was never any agreement on the part of the employees to assign them to Bausch & Lomb, and the original stock purchase agreements of the Riggs employees provided that if Riggs should be reorganized and its business acquired by another corporation, a successor corporation would have the right to assume the contract and substitute its stock in the place of the Riggs' stock originally reserved under the stock purchase agreements. New arrangements were made later, in line with the provision of the original stock purchase agreements just referred to, and the employees received certain cash payments and the 433 shares of Bausch & Lomb stock mentioned in the opening part of this opinion. We find in the facts of this case no foundation whatever for the claim that a liquidation was effected under Section [332].

Affirmed.

PROBLEMS

1. Assuming the judicial requirements are met, determine whether the following transactions qualify as a Type C reorganization:

(a) Target Corporation ("T") has $70,000 of operating assets and $30,000 of cash and securities held as an investment. Acquiring Corporation ("A") issues its voting stock worth $70,000 in exchange for the operating assets and T liquidates, distributing the A stock and its cash and investment securities to its shareholders.

(b) Same as (a), above, except that A acquires $40,000 of operating assets and $30,000 of cash and investment securities in exchange for the A voting stock. T then liquidates, distributing $70,000 of A stock and $30,000 of operating assets to its shareholders.

(c) Same as (a), above, except that T has $100,000 of operating assets and $30,000 of liabilities. A issues $70,000 of its voting stock in exchange for T's assets and liabilities, and T liquidates, distributing the A stock to its shareholders.

(d) Same as (c), above, except that A issues $60,000 of its voting stock and $10,000 cash in exchange for all of T's assets and liabilities, and T liquidates, distributing the A stock and cash to its shareholders.

2. Determine whether the transactions below will qualify as tax-free reorganizations:

(a) Target Corporation ("T") owns $70,000 of operating assets and $30,000 cash and investment securities. T redeems 30% of its stock, distributing the cash and investment securities. Acquiring Corporation ("A") issues $70,000 worth of its voting stock to the remaining T shareholders in exchange for their T stock. A then liquidates T.

(b) Same as (a), above, except that T redeems the 30% shareholders by distributing operating assets rather than cash and investment securities.

(c) A has held 30% of T's stock for several years. A exchanges its voting stock for the remaining 70% of T stock. A then liquidates T.

(d) Same as (c), above, except that A owns 10% of T's stock prior to the transaction and acquires the remaining 90% on its acquisition.

4. TRIANGULAR REORGANIZATIONS *

Code: § 368(a)(1)(B) (first parenthetical) and (C) (first parenthetical), (a)(2)(C), (D) and (E), (b).

Regulations: § 1.368–2(b)(2), (f), (j)(1), (3)–(6).

Background. The three basic types of reorganizations offer rather limited flexibility if the acquiring corporation desires to operate the target as a wholly owned subsidiary. Assume, for example, that Parent Corporation ("P") wishes to acquire Target Corporation ("T") and keep T's business in a separate corporate shell for nontax reasons. Although this objective could be met by a Type B reorganization, the stringent "solely for voting stock" requirement might be an insurmountable obstacle if P desired to use nonvoting stock as consideration or if a large number of T shareholders were unwilling to accept any class of P stock. Even the flexible A reorganization may not be feasible from a nontax standpoint. P may not wish to incur the risk of T's unknown or contingent liabilities which would remain P's responsibility even if T's assets were dropped down to a subsidiary. P also may be reluctant to bear the expense and delay of seeking formal shareholder approval of a merger or unwilling to provide both P and T shareholders with the appraisal rights to which they would be entitled under state law.

To maneuver around these problems, corporate lawyers developed other acquisition methods involving the use of a subsidiary. One approach is for P to acquire T's assets in a qualifying Type A or C reorganization and immediately drop down the acquired assets to a newly created subsidiary. This technique does not solve the hidden liability problem, however, and it may not obviate the need for shareholder approval and appraisal rights.[1] An alternative is for P to transfer its stock to a new subsidiary ("S"), and then cause T to merge

* See generally Ferguson & Ginsburg, "Triangular Reorganizations," 28 Tax L.Rev. 159 (1973).

1. "Drop downs" also are inconvenient because they usually require an inordinate amount of paperwork (e.g., deeds and other documents of transfer, with accompanying recording fees and transfer taxes) as the assets pass from the parent to the subsidiary.

directly into S, with the T shareholders receiving P stock and, perhaps, other consideration in exchange for their T stock. Or P could form S and have S acquire substantially all of the assets of T in exchange for P voting stock.

The tax consequences of these and other triangular acquisition techniques have been one of the major subplots within the reorganization drama. In two early cases, the Supreme Court constructed several large roadblocks by holding that transactions similar to those described above failed to satisfy the continuity of interest doctrine if: (1) T merges into S but T shareholders receive P stock in a triangular reorganization, or (2) P makes the acquisition using P stock but drops T or its assets down to a subsidiary.[2]

Over the years, Congress gradually came to recognize that there was no reason to deny tax-free status to "drop downs" or triangular reorganizations that were economically equivalent to the simpler acquisition methods authorized by Section 368. In 1954, it enacted Section 368(a)(2)(C), which provides that an otherwise qualifying Type A or C reorganization will not lose its tax-free status merely because the acquiring corporation drops down the acquired assets to a subsidiary and in 1964 it added a similar rule for Type B reorganizations. By 1964, Congress also permitted the acquiring corporation in a B or C reorganization to use voting stock of its parent to make the acquisition. For both drop downs and triangular reorganizations, Section 368(b) now makes it clear that the controlling parent will be a "party" to the reorganization. But as late as 1967, the Service persisted in ruling that a merger of the target into a controlled subsidiary of the acquiring corporation was not tax-free when the target shareholders received stock of the parent because the parent was not a "party" to the reorganization and the T shareholder lacked continuity of interest.[3] Once again, Congress responded by adding two new categories of tax-free reorganizations: the Section 368(a)(2)(D) forward triangular merger and the Section 368(a)(2)(E) reverse triangular merger.

Forward Triangular Mergers: Section 368(a)(2)(D). From the time it was authorized as a tax-free reorganization in 1969, the forward triangular merger has become one of the most widely used acquisition techniques. Section 368(a)(2)(D) permits S to acquire T in a statutory merger, using P stock as consideration, provided that: (1) S acquires "substantially all" of the properties of T; (2) no stock of S is used in the transaction; and (3) the transaction would have qualified as a Type A reorganization if T had merged directly into P. In typically perverse fashion, Congress—without expressly articulating its rationale—reached into its bag of requirements and borrowed one from the Type C model ("substantially all of the properties") and another from the Type

2. Groman v. Commissioner, 302 U.S. 654, 58 S.Ct. 108 (1937); Helvering v. Bashford, 302 U.S. 454, 58 S.Ct. 307 (1938). These cases also suggested that in no event could the T shareholders receive stock in both S and P because the receipt of stock in two separate corporations violated continuity of interest requirements.

3. Rev.Rul. 67–448, 1967–2 C.B. 144.

A model (the tests for permissible consideration). Although the legislative history is obscure, it is now clear that the "could have merged with parent" test merely requires the transaction to pass muster under the continuity of interest doctrine.[4] As a result, T shareholders only must receive at least 50 percent P stock (voting or nonvoting) under the Service's continuity guidelines, allowing the parties the freedom to use up to 50 percent cash and other nonequity consideration. Of course, the T shareholders who receive boot must recognize their realized gain to that extent, but those who receive solely stock will enjoy nonrecognition if the overall transaction qualifies under these liberal standards.

Reverse Triangular Mergers: Section 368(a)(2)(E). Before examining the tax consequences of a reverse triangular merger, the transaction itself must be explained. Suppose P desires to acquire the stock of T in a tax-free reorganization and keep T alive as a subsidiary, but P is unable (or unwilling) to structure the deal as a Type B reorganization because of the "solely for voting stock" requirement. Neither a merger nor an asset acquisition is feasible because T, as a corporate entity, has a number of intangible assets (e.g., grandfather rights under state law; franchises or leases; favorable loan agreements) that would be jeopardized if T were dissolved. One ingenious approach to this dilemma is for P to create S, contributing to it P voting stock, and then for S to merge into T under an agreement providing that T shareholders will receive P stock (and, possibly, other consideration) in exchange for their T stock. A variation on the theme would be to use an existing subsidiary with ongoing business activities. In that event, the reverse merger would result in T's business being augmented by S's, all conducted under the same corporate roof. In either case, when the smoke clears P will own all the stock of T and S will disappear as a result of the merger.

Section 368(a)(2)(E) provides that this type of reverse merger will qualify as a tax-free reorganization if: (1) the surviving corporation (T) holds substantially all of the properties formerly held by both corporations (T and S), and (2) the former T shareholders exchange stock constituting "control" (measured by the 80 percent tests in Section 368(c)(1)) for P voting stock.[5] Once again, Congress has borrowed from its bag of requirements and combined tests from Type A (merger), Type B (control) and Type C (substantially all of the properties) reorganizations. The reverse merger is thus far less flexible than the forward triangular merger, perhaps reflecting its Type B origins. But there *can* be boot in an (a)(2)(E) reorganization; only 80 percent of the T stock must be acquired for P voting stock, and the rest may be obtained for cash or other property—or simply not acquired at all if P is willing to put up with minority shareholders.

Although Congress deserves applause for abandoning the formalisms of the old case law, its piecemeal approach to triangular reorgani-

4. Reg. § 1.368–2(b)(2).

5. I.R.C. § 368(a)(2)(E)(ii). See Reg. § 1.368–2(j)(3)(ii).

zations is yet another example of the major flaw in the reorganization scheme. In enacting Sections 368(a)(2)(D) and (E), each with its own distinct requirements, Congress added further embroidery to what already had become a crazy quilt. As the Senate Finance Committee staff lamented in its preliminary report on the reform and simplification of Subchapter C, many of the arcane distinctions in Section 368 "defy rationalization" and "[n]o discernible public policy would so sharply distinguish among the forms of an acquisition that are economically so similar." [6] Congress would be well advised to move toward a system that would impose consistent requirements on economically equivalent acquisition techniques.[7]

PROBLEMS

1. Consider whether the transactions described below qualify as a tax-free reorganization. Assume in all cases that P is the acquiring corporation, T is the target corporation and S is a newly formed 100% subsidiary of P.

(a) T merges into P, with T shareholders receiving P stock, and then P transfers the T assets to S. (Why might this form of transaction be unattractive to the parties for nontax reasons?)

(b) P forms S by transferring P voting common stock to S in exchange for S stock. S then transfers the P stock to T in exchange for all of T's assets, and T liquidates.

(c) P forms S by transferring P voting common stock to S in exchange for S stock. T then merges into S, and T shareholders receive solely P voting stock in exchange for their T stock.

(d) Same as (c), above, except that the T shareholders receive voting stock of both P and S in exchange for their T stock.

(e) Same as (c), above, except that the T shareholders receive 50% P common voting stock and 50% S notes, some of which pass to dissenting shareholders of T.

(f) Same as (c), above, except that the T shareholders receive 30% P nonvoting preferred stock, 20% cash and 50% S notes.

(g) Same as (e), above, except that prior to the merger T redeems all the stock held by T's dissenting shareholders, who hold one-third of T's stock, in exchange for operating assets of T.

2. Consider whether the transactions described below qualify as a tax-free reorganization. Again assume in all cases that P is the acquiring corporation, T is the target and S is a wholly owned subsidiary of P.

---

6. See Staff of the Senate Finance Committee, Preliminary Report on the Reform and Simplification of the Income Taxation of Corporations, 98th Cong., 1st Sess., 26–27, 55–66 (Comm.Print S. 98–95, 1983).

7. See Staff of the Senate Finance Committee: The Subchapter C Revision Act of 1985, A Final Report Prepared by the Staff, 99th Cong., 1st Sess. (S.Prt. 99–47, 1985); Posin, "Taxing Corporate Reorganizations: Purging Penelope's Web," 133 U. Penn.L.Rev. 1335 (1985); Section E of this Chapter, infra.

(a) P forms S by transferring P voting common stock to S in exchange for S stock. S then transfers the P stock to T's shareholders in exchange for all of their T stock.

(b) P forms S by transferring P voting common stock to S in exchange for S stock. S then merges into T, which has only one class of stock. In the merger, T shareholders holding 80% of the stock receive P stock in exchange for their T stock. Holders of the other 20% of T, who dissent from the merger, receive cash from P. After the transaction, T is a wholly owned subsidiary of P.

(c) Same as (b), above, except that P transfers both P stock and P notes (worth 20% of the total consideration) to S; the stock and notes are then transferred to all of T's shareholders in exchange for their T stock. Shareholders holding 80% of the T stock receive P stock and the dissenting T shareholders receive notes.

(d) Same as (c), above, except that shareholders holding 80% of the T stock receive a combination of P stock and notes while the dissenting 20% T shareholders receive cash.

(e) Same as (c), above, except that T's shareholders receive 80% P voting stock and 20% T operating assets.

(f) Same as (e), above, except that P owned 30% of T's stock prior to the transaction and it acquires the remaining 70% of T's stock for P voting stock.

C. TREATMENT OF THE PARTIES TO AN ACQUISITIVE REORGANIZATION

Up to this point, we have been concentrating on the definition of a reorganization in Section 368. Compliance with those statutory requirements and the judicial doctrines unlocks the gate to the operative provisions, which govern the tax treatment of the target shareholders and corporations that are "a party to a reorganization" and provide for transferred and exchanged bases, tacked holding periods and the carryover of corporate tax attributes such as net operating losses. Section 368(b) broadly defines "a party to a reorganization" to include any corporation resulting from a qualifying reorganization (e.g., the surviving corporation in a consolidation), the acquiring and target corporations in a straight acquisitive reorganization and the parent corporation in a "drop down" or triangular reorganization.

This section provides an overview of these operative provisions without becoming immersed in highly specialized minutia. We first focus on the consequences to the shareholders and security holders and then turn to the treatment of the target and acquiring corporations.

1. CONSEQUENCES TO SHAREHOLDERS AND SECURITY HOLDERS

Code: §§ 354(a); 356(a), (c), (d), (e); 358(a), (b), (d), (e); 368(b).

Regulations: §§ 1.354–1(a), (b), (d) Example (3), (e); 1.356–1, –3, –4; 1.358–1, – 2(a)(1)–(4), (b); 1.368–2(f), (g).

Recognition of Gain or Loss. One of the principal benefits of reorganization status is the nonrecognition granted to the shareholders and security holders of the target corporation under Section 354(a). A shareholder is entitled to complete nonrecognition only when he receives solely stock or securities of the acquiring corporation.[1] This invariably occurs in a Type B reorganization, but the target shareholders in a Type A, C or any form of triangular reorganization may receive some boot. In that event, the shareholder must recognize any realized gain to the extent of the money plus the fair market value of any other boot received.[2] For this purpose, boot includes any property other than stock or securities of a party to the reorganization. To prevent a bailout through the use of securities,[3] Section 356(d) provides that if the principal amount of securities received exceeds the principal amount of securities surrendered or if securities are received but none are surrendered, the fair market value of the excess is treated as boot.[4] Consequently, a shareholder holding no securities who receives bonds in connection with a reorganization is treated as having "cashed out" his investment to the extent of the bonds—an appropriate result under the continuity of interest principle. But a security holder who changes his investment to an equity interest or exchanges securities for the same or lesser principal amount has not engaged in a bailout and therefore is entitled to nonrecognition treatment. As might be expected, however, a shareholder or security holder who receives boot may not recognize any realized loss.[5]

Characterization of Gain. Section 356(a)(2) provides that the recognized gain is treated as a dividend to a target shareholder if the exchange "has the effect of the distribution of a dividend." In that event, each distributee must treat as a dividend the amount of his recognized gain that is not in excess of the corporation's accumulated earnings and profits.[6] Any remaining gain is treated as gain from the sale or exchange of the target stock or securities transferred. The "boot dividend" issue has been one of the most difficult questions arising under the operative provisions, but it has diminished in importance with the elimination of any significant capital gains rate prefer-

1. I.R.C. § 354(a)(1).

2. I.R.C. § 356(a)(1).

3. "Securities" are generally defined to encompass relatively long-term corporate debt instruments but not short-term notes, stock rights or warrants.

4. See I.R.C. § 354(a)(2)(A).

5. I.R.C. § 356(c).

6. Note that the gain is not automatically characterized as ordinary income but, if it has the effect of a dividend, it is treated as a Section 301 distribution subject to the Section 243 dividends received deduction. See Rev.Rul. 72–327 at p. 578, infra. In addition, the earnings and profits of the target corporation are reduced under Section 312(a).

ence.   The Service once contended that dividend treatment was automatic if boot was received,[7] but it later conceded that dividend equivalence should be determined by using the tests applicable to stock redemptions in Section 302(b).[8] The *Clark* case, below, is the Supreme Court's resolution of the conflicting views on how Section 302(b) principles should be applied.

Basis and Holding Period. Target shareholders determine the basis of nonrecognition property (i.e., the stock or nonboot securities received in the exchange) under Section 358 by reference to their basis in the stock that they relinquished, increased by any gain recognized and reduced by any boot received and liabilities assumed.   Boot takes a fair market value basis under Section 358(a)(2).   This is the same formula used many chapters ago in determining the basis of stock received in a Section 351 exchange.   If different types of nonrecognition property are received (e.g., two classes of stock or stock and bonds), the aggregate exchanged basis is allocated among those properties in proportion to their relative fair market values under rules provided in the regulations.[9]   The nonrecognition property generally takes a tacked holding period under Section 1223(1) and the holding period of the boot commences on the date of its acquisition.

COMMISSIONER v. CLARK *

Supreme Court of the United States, 1989.
489 U.S. 726, 109 S.Ct. 1455.

Justice STEVENS delivered the opinion of the Court.   This is the third case in which the Government has asked us to decide that a shareholder's receipt of a cash payment in exchange for a portion of his stock was taxable as a dividend.   In the two earlier cases, Commissioner v. Estate of Bedford, 325 U.S. 283 (1945), and United States v. Davis, 397 U.S. 301 (1970), we agreed with the Government largely because the transactions involved redemptions of stock by single corporations that did not "result in a meaningful reduction of the shareholder's proportionate interest in the corporation." Id., at 313.   In the case we decide today, however, the taxpayer in an arm's length transaction exchanged his interest in the acquired corporation for less than one percent of the stock of the acquiring corporation and a substantial cash payment.   The taxpayer held no interest in the acquiring corporation prior to the reorganization.   Viewing the exchange as a whole, we conclude that the cash payment is not appropriately characterized as a dividend.   We accordingly agree with the Tax Court and with the Court of Appeals that the taxpayer is entitled to capital gains treatment of the cash payment.

7. See Commissioner v. Bedford's Estate, 325 U.S. 283, 65 S.Ct. 1157 (1945).

8. In applying Section 302(b) principles, the Section 318 attribution rules are applicable. I.R.C. § 356(a)(2). Rev.Rul. 74–515, 1974–2 C.B. 118; Rev.Rul. 75–83, 1975–1 C.B. 112.   See also Wright v. United States, 482 F.2d 600 (8th Cir.1973).

9. I.R.C. § 358(a)(1); Reg. § 1.358–2.

* Some footnotes omitted.

I

In determining tax liability under the Internal Revenue Code, gain resulting from the sale or exchange of property is generally treated as capital gain, whereas the receipt of cash dividends is treated as ordinary income.[2] The Code, however, imposes no current tax on certain stock-for-stock exchanges. In particular, § 354(a)(1) provides, subject to various limitations, for nonrecognition of gain resulting from the exchange of stock or securities solely for other stock or securities, provided that the exchange is pursuant to a plan of corporate reorganization and that the stock or securities are those of a party to the reorganization. 26 U.S.C. § 354(a)(1).

Under § 356(a)(1) of the Code, if such a stock-for-stock exchange is accompanied by additional consideration in the form of a cash payment or other property—something that tax practitioners refer to as "boot"— "then the gain, if any, to the recipient shall be recognized, but in an amount not in excess of the sum of such money and the fair market value of such other property." 26 U.S.C. § 356(a)(1). That is, if the shareholder receives boot, he or she must recognize the gain on the exchange up to the value of the boot. Boot is accordingly generally treated as a gain from the sale or exchange of property and is recognized in the current tax-year.

Section 356(a)(2), which controls the decision in this case, creates an exception to that general rule. It provides:

> "If an exchange is described in paragraph (1) but has the effect of the distribution of a dividend (determined with the application of section 318(a)), then there shall be treated as a dividend to each distributee such an amount of the gain recognized under paragraph (1) as is not in excess of his ratable share of the undistributed earnings and profits of the corporation accumulated after February 28, 1913. The remainder, if any, of the gain recognized under paragraph (1) shall be treated as gain from the exchange of property."

Thus, if the "exchange * * * has the effect of the distribution of a dividend," the boot must be treated as a dividend and is therefore appropriately taxed as ordinary income to the extent that gain is realized. In contrast, if the exchange does not have "the effect of the distribution of a dividend," the boot must be treated as a payment in exchange for property and, insofar as gain is realized, accorded capital gains treatment. The question in this case is thus whether the ex-

---

2. In 1979, the tax year in question, the distinction between long-term capital gain and ordinary income was of considerable importance. Most significantly, § 1202(a) of the Code allowed individual taxpayers to deduct 60% of their net capital gain from gross income. Although the importance of the distinction declined dramatically in 1986 with the repeal of § 1202(a), see Tax Reform Act of 1986, Pub.L. 99–514, § 301(a), 100 Stat. 2216, the distinction is still significant in a number of respects. For example, § 1211(b) allows individual taxpayers to deduct capital losses to the full extent of their capital gains, but only allows them to offset up to $3000 of ordinary income insofar as their capital losses exceed their capital gains.

change between the taxpayer and the acquiring corporation had "the effect of the distribution of a dividend" within the meaning of § 356(a)(2).

The relevant facts are easily summarized. For approximately 15 years prior to April 1979, the taxpayer was the sole shareholder and president of Basin Surveys, Inc. (Basin), a company in which he had invested approximately $85,000. The corporation operated a successful business providing various technical services to the petroleum industry. In 1978, N.L. Industries, Inc. (NL), a publicly owned corporation engaged in the manufacture and supply of petroleum equipment and services, initiated negotiations with the taxpayer regarding the possible acquisition of Basin. On April 3, 1979, after months of negotiations, the taxpayer and NL entered into a contract.

The agreement provided for a "triangular merger," whereby Basin was merged into a wholly owned subsidiary of NL. In exchange for transferring all of the outstanding shares in Basin to NL's subsidiary, the taxpayer elected to receive 300,000 shares of NL common stock and cash boot of $3,250,000, passing up an alternative offer of 425,000 shares of NL common stock. The 300,000 shares of NL issued to the taxpayer amounted to approximately 0.92% of the outstanding common shares of NL. If the taxpayer had instead accepted the pure stock-for-stock offer, he would have held approximately 1.3% of the outstanding common shares. The Commissioner and the taxpayer agree that the merger at issue qualifies as a reorganization under § 368(a)(1)(A) and (a)(2)(D).

Respondents filed a joint federal income tax return for 1979. As required by § 356(a)(1), they reported the cash boot as taxable gain. In calculating the tax owed, respondents characterized the payment as long-term capital gain. The Commissioner on audit disagreed with this characterization. In his view, the payment had "the effect of the distribution of a dividend" and was thus taxable as ordinary income up to $2,319,611, the amount of Basin's accumulated earnings and profits at the time of the merger. The Commissioner assessed a deficiency of $972,504.74.

Respondents petitioned for review in the Tax Court, which, in a reviewed decision, held in their favor. 86 T.C. 138 (1986). The court started from the premise that the question whether the boot payment had "the effect of the distribution of a dividend" turns on the choice between "two judicially articulated tests." Id., at 140. Under the test advocated by the Commissioner and given voice in Shimberg v. United States, 577 F.2d 283 (CA–5 1978), cert. denied, 439 U.S. 1115 (1979), the boot payment is treated as though it were made in a hypothetical redemption by the acquired corporation (Basin) immediately *prior* to the reorganization. Under this test, the cash payment received by the taxpayer indisputably would have been treated as a dividend.[6] The

6. The parties do not agree as to whether dividend equivalence for the purposes of § 356(a)(2) should be determined with reference to § 302 of the Code, which con-

second test, urged by the taxpayer and finding support in Wright v. United States, 482 F.2d 600 (CA–8 1973), proposes an alternative hypothetical redemption. Rather than concentrating on the taxpayer's pre-reorganization interest in the acquired corporation, this test requires that one imagine a pure stock-for-stock exchange, followed immediately by a *post*-reorganization redemption of a portion of the taxpayer's shares in the acquiring corporation (NL) in return for a payment in an amount equal to the boot. Under § 302 of the Code, which defines when a redemption of stock should be treated as a distribution of dividend, NL's redemption of 125,000 shares of its stock from the taxpayer in exchange for the $3,250,000 boot payment would have been treated as capital gain.[7]

The Tax Court rejected the pre-reorganization test favored by the Commissioner because it considered it improper "to view the cash payment as an isolated event totally separate from the reorganization." 86 T.C., at 151. Indeed, it suggested that this test requires that courts make the "determination of dividend equivalency fantasizing that the reorganization does not exist." Id., at 150 (footnote omitted). The court then acknowledged that a similar criticism could be made of the taxpayer's contention that the cash payment should be viewed as a post-reorganization redemption. It concluded, however, that since it was perfectly clear that the cash payment would not have taken place without the reorganization, it was better to treat the boot "as the equivalent of a redemption *in the course of implementing the reorganization,*" than "as having occurred *prior to and separate from the reorganization.*" Id., at 152 (emphasis in original).[8]

cerns dividend treatment of redemptions of stock by a single corporation outside the context of a reorganization. Compare Brief for the United States 28–30 with Brief for Respondents 18–24. They are in essential agreement, however, about the characteristics of a dividend. Thus, the Government correctly argues that the "basic attribute of a dividend, derived from Sections 301 and 316 of the Code, is a pro rata distribution to shareholders out of corporate earnings and profits. When a distribution is made that is not a formal dividend, 'the fundamental test of dividend equivalency' is whether the distribution is proportionate to the shareholders' stock interests (United States v. Davis, 397 U.S. 301, 306 (1970))." Brief for Petitioner 7. Citing the same authority, but with different emphasis, the taxpayer argues that "the hallmark of a non-dividend distribution is a 'meaningful reduction of the shareholder's proportionate interest in the corporation,' United States v. Davis, 397 U.S. 301, 313 (1970)." Brief for Respondents 5.

Under either test, a pre-reorganization distribution by Basin to the taxpayer would have qualified as a dividend. Because the taxpayer was Basin's sole shareholder, any distribution necessarily would have been pro rata and would not have resulted in a "meaningful reduction of the [taxpayer's] proportionate interest in [Basin]."

7.   *   *   *

As the Tax Court explained, receipt of the cash boot reduced the taxpayer's potential holdings in NL from 1.3% to 0.92%. 86 T.C., at 153. The taxpayer's holdings were thus approximately 71% of what they would have been absent the payment. Ibid. This fact, combined with the fact that the taxpayer held less than 50% of the voting stock of NL after the hypothetical redemption, would have qualified the "distribution" as "substantially disproportionate" under § 302(b)(2).

8. The Tax Court stressed that to adopt the pre-reorganization view "would in effect resurrect the now discredited 'automatic dividend rule' . . ., at least with respect to pro rata distributions made to an acquired corporation's shareholders pursuant to a plan of reorganization." 86

The Court of Appeals for the Fourth Circuit affirmed. 828 F.2d 221 (1987). Like the Tax Court, it concluded that although "[s]ection 302 does not explicitly apply in the reorganization context," id., at 223, and although § 302 differs from § 356 in important respects, id., at 224, it nonetheless provides "the appropriate test for determining whether boot is ordinary income or a capital gain," id., at 223. Thus, as explicated in § 302(b)(2), if the taxpayer relinquished more than 20% of his corporate control and retained less than 50% of the voting shares after the distribution, the boot would be treated as capital gain. However, as the Court of Appeals recognized, "[b]ecause § 302 was designed to deal with a stock redemption by a single corporation, rather than a reorganization involving two companies, the section does not indicate which corporation [the taxpayer] lost interest in." Id., at 224. Thus, like the Tax Court, the Court of Appeals was left to consider whether the hypothetical redemption should be treated as a pre-reorganization distribution coming from the acquired corporation or as a post-reorganization distribution coming from the acquiring corporation. It concluded:

> "Based on the language and legislative history of § 356, the change-in-ownership principle of § 302, and the need to review the reorganization as an integrated transaction, we conclude that the boot should be characterized as a post-reorganization stock redemption by N.L. that affected [the taxpayer's] interest in the new corporation. Because this redemption reduced [the taxpayer's] N.L. holdings by more than 20%, the boot should be taxed as a capital gain." Id., at 224–225.

This decision by the Court of Appeals for the Fourth Circuit is in conflict with the decision of the Fifth Circuit in *Shimberg,* 577 F.2d 283 (1978), in two important respects. In *Shimberg,* the court concluded that it was inappropriate to apply stock redemption principles in reorganization cases "on a wholesale basis." Id., at 287; see also ibid, n. 13. In addition, the court adopted the pre-reorganization test, holding that "§ 356(a)(2) requires a determination of whether the

---

T.C., at 152. On appeal, the Court of Appeals agreed. [87–2 USTC ¶ 9504] 828 F.2d 221, 226–227 (CA–4 1987).

The "automatic dividend rule" developed as a result of some imprecise language in our decision in Commissioner v. Estate of Bedford, 325 U.S. 283 (1945). Although *Estate of Bedford* involved the recapitalization of a single corporation, the opinion employed broad language, asserting that "a distribution, pursuant to a reorganization, of earnings and profits 'has the effect of a distribution of a taxable dividend' within [§ 356(a)(2)]." Id., at 292. The Commissioner read this language as establishing as a matter of law that all payments of boot are to be treated as dividends to the extent of undistributed earnings and profits. See Rev.Rul. 56–220,

1956–1 Cum.Bull. 191. Commentators, see, e.g., Darrel, The Scope of Commissioner v. Bedford Estate, 24 TAXES 266 (1946); Shoulson, Boot Taxation: The Blunt Toe of the Automatic Rule, 20 Tax L.Rev. 573 (1965), and courts, see, e.g., Hawkinson v. Commissioner, 235 F.2d 747 (CA–2 1966), however, soon came to criticize this rule. The courts have long since retreated from the "automatic dividend rule," see, e.g., Idaho Power Co. v. United States, 161 F.Supp. 807 (Ct.Cl.), cert. denied, 368 U.S. 832 (1968), and the Commissioner has followed suit, see Rev.Rul. 74–515, 1974–2 Cum.Bull. 118. As our decision in this case makes plain, we agree that *Estate of Bedford* should not be read to require that all payments of boot be treated as dividends.

distribution would have been taxed as a dividend if made prior to the reorganization or if no reorganization had occurred." Id., at 288.

To resolve this conflict on a question of importance to the administration of the federal tax laws, we granted certiorari. 485 U.S. ―― (1988).

II

We agree with the Tax Court and the Court of Appeals for the Fourth Circuit that the question under § 356(a)(2) of whether an "exchange ＊　＊　＊ has the effect of the distribution of a dividend" should be answered by examining the effect of the exchange as a whole. We think the language and history of the statute, as well as a common-sense understanding of the economic substance of the transaction at issue, support this approach.

The language of § 356(a) strongly supports our understanding that the transaction should be treated as an integrated whole. Section 356(a)(2) asks whether "*an exchange* is described in paragraph (1)" that "has the effect of the distribution of a dividend." (Emphasis supplied.) The statute does not provide that boot shall be treated as a dividend if its payment has the effect of the distribution of a dividend. Rather, the inquiry turns on whether the "exchange" has that effect. Moreover, paragraph (1), in turn, looks to whether "the property received in *the exchange* consists not only of property permitted by section 354 or 355 to be received without the recognition of gain but also of other property or money." (Emphasis supplied.) Again, the statute plainly refers to one integrated transaction and, again, makes clear that we are to look to the character of the exchange as a whole and not simply its component parts. Finally, it is significant that § 356 expressly limits the extent to which boot may be taxed to the amount of gain realized in the reorganization. This limitation suggests that Congress intended that boot not be treated in isolation from the overall reorganization. See Levin, Adess, & McGaffey, Boot Distributions in Corporate Reorganizations—Determination of Dividend Equivalency, 30 Tax Lawyer 287, 303 (1977).

Our reading of the statute as requiring that the transaction be treated as a unified whole is reinforced by the well-established "step-transaction" doctrine, a doctrine that the Government has applied in related contexts, see, e.g., Rev.Rul. 75–447, 1975–2 Cum.Bull. 113, and that we have expressly sanctioned, see Minnesota Tea Co. v. Helvering, 302 U.S. 609, 613 (1938); Commissioner v. Court Holding Co., 324 U.S. 331, 334 (1945). Under this doctrine, interrelated yet formally distinct steps in an integrated transaction may not be considered independently of the overall transaction. By thus "linking together all interdependent steps with legal or business significance, rather than taking them in isolation," federal tax liability may be based "on a realistic view of the entire transaction." 1 B. Bittker, Federal Taxation of Income, Estates and Gifts, ¶ 4.3.5, p. 4–52 (1981).

Viewing the exchange in this case as an integrated whole, we are unable to accept the Commissioner's pre-reorganization analogy. The analogy severs the payment of boot from the context of the reorganization. Indeed, only by straining to abstract the payment of boot from the context of the overall exchange, and thus imagining that Basin made a distribution to the taxpayer independently of NL's planned acquisition, can we reach the rather counterintuitive conclusion urged by the Commissioner—that the taxpayer suffered no meaningful reduction in his ownership interest as a result of the cash payment. We conclude that such a limited view of the transaction is plainly inconsistent with the statute's direction that we look to the effect of the entire exchange.

The pre-reorganization analogy is further flawed in that it adopts an overly expansive reading of § 356(a)(2). As the Court of Appeals recognized, adoption of the pre-reorganization approach would "result in ordinary income treatment in most reorganizations because corporate boot is usually distributed pro rata to the shareholders of the target corporation." 828 F.2d, at 227; see also Golub, "Boot" in Reorganizations—The Dividend Equivalency Test of Section 356(a)(2), 58 Taxes 904, 911 (1980); Note, 20 Boston College L.Rev. 601, 612 (1979). Such a reading of the statute would not simply constitute a return to the widely criticized "automatic dividend rule" (at least as to cases involving a pro rata payment to the shareholders of the acquired corporation), see n. 8, supra, but also would be contrary to our standard approach to construing such provisions. The requirement of § 356(a)(2) that boot be treated as dividend in some circumstances is an exception from the general rule authorizing capital gains treatment for boot. In construing provisions such as § 356, in which a general statement of policy is qualified by an exception, we usually read the exception narrowly in order to preserve the primary operation of the provision. See Phillips, Inc. v. Walling, 324 U.S. 490, 493 (1945) ("To extend an exemption to other than those plainly and unmistakably within its terms and spirit is to abuse the interpretative process and to frustrate the announced will of the people"). Given that Congress has enacted a general rule that treats boot as capital gain, we should not eviscerate that legislative judgment through an expansive reading of a somewhat ambiguous exception.

The post-reorganization approach adopted by the Tax Court and the Court of Appeals is, in our view, preferable to the Commissioner's approach. Most significantly, this approach does a far better job of treating the payment of boot as a component of the overall exchange. Unlike the pre-reorganization view, this approach acknowledges that there would have been no cash payment absent the exchange and also that, by accepting the cash payment, the taxpayer experienced a meaningful reduction in his potential ownership interest.

Once the post-reorganization approach is adopted, the result in this case is pellucidly clear. Section 302(a) of the Code provides that if a redemption fits within any one of the four categories set out in § 302(b), the redemption "shall be treated as a distribution in part or full payment in exchange for the stock," and thus not regarded as a dividend. As the Tax Court and the Court of Appeals correctly determined, the hypothetical post-reorganization redemption by NL of a portion of the taxpayer's shares satisfies at least one of the subsections of § 302(b).[9] In particular, the safe harbor provisions of subsection (b)(2) provide that redemptions in which the taxpayer relinquishes more than 20% of his or her share of the corporation's voting stock and retains less than 50% of the voting stock after the redemption, shall not be treated as distributions of a dividend. See n. 7, supra. Here, we treat the transaction as though NL redeemed 125,000 shares of its common stock (i.e., the number of shares of NL common stock foregone in favor of the boot) in return for a cash payment to the taxpayer of $3,250,000 (i.e., the amount of the boot). As a result of this redemption, the taxpayer's interest in NL was reduced from 1.3% of the outstanding common stock to 0.9%. See 86 T.C., at 153. Thus, the taxpayer relinquished approximately 29% of his interest in NL and retained less than a 1% voting interest in the corporation after the transaction, easily satisfying the "substantially disproportionate" standards of § 302(b)(2). We accordingly conclude that the boot payment did not have the effect of a dividend and that the payment was properly treated as capital gain.

III

The Commissioner objects to this "recasting [of] the merger transaction into a form different from that entered into by the parties," Brief for the United States 11, and argues that the Court of Appeals' formal adherence to the principles embodied in § 302 forced the court to stretch to "find a redemption to which to apply them, since the merger transaction entered into by the parties did not involve a redemption," id., at 28. There are a number of sufficient responses to this argument. We think it first worth emphasizing that the Commissioner overstates the extent to which the redemption is imagined. As the Court of Appeals for the Fifth Circuit noted in *Shimberg,* "[t]he theory behind tax-free corporate reorganizations is that the transaction is merely 'a continuance of the proprietary interests in the continuing enterprise under modified corporate form.' Lewis v. Commissioner of Internal Revenue, 176 F.2d 646, 648 (1 Cir.1949); Treas.Reg. § 1.368–1(b). See generally Cohen, *Conglomerate Mergers and Taxation,* 55 A.B.A.J. 40 (1969)." 577 F.2d at 288. As a result, the boot-for-stock transaction can be viewed as a partial repurchase of stock by the continuing corporate enterprise—i.e., as a redemption. It is of course true that both the pre- and post-reorganization analogies are somewhat artificial

---

9. Because the mechanical requirements of subsection (b)(2) are met, we need not decide whether the hypothetical redemption might also qualify for capital gains treatment under the general "not essentially equivalent to a dividend" language of subsection (b)(1). Subsections (b)(3) and (b)(4), which deal with redemptions of all of the shareholder's stock and with partial liquidations, respectively, are not at issue in this case.

in that they imagine that the redemption occurred outside the confines of the actual reorganization. However, if forced to choose between the two analogies, the post-reorganization view is the less artificial. Although both analogies "recast the merger transaction," the post-reorganization view recognizes that a reorganization has taken place, while the pre-reorganization approach recasts the transaction to the exclusion of the overall exchange.

Moreover, we doubt that abandoning the pre- and post-reorganization analogies and the principles of § 302 in favor of a less artificial understanding of the transaction would lead to a result different from that reached by the Court of Appeals. Although the statute is admittedly ambiguous and the legislative history sparse, we are persuaded— even without relying on § 302—that Congress did not intend to except reorganizations such as that at issue here from the general rule allowing capital gains treatment for cash boot. 26 U.S.C. § 356(a)(1). The legislative history of § 356(a)(2), although perhaps generally "not illuminating," *Estate of Bedford,* 325 U.S., at 290, suggests that Congress was primarily concerned with preventing corporations from "siphon[ing] off" accumulated earnings and profits at a capital gains rate through the ruse of a reorganization. See Golub, 58 Taxes, at 905. This purpose is not served by denying capital gains treatment in a case such as this in which the taxpayer entered into an arm's length transaction with a corporation in which he had no prior interest, exchanging his stock in the acquired corporation for less than a one percent interest in the acquiring corporation and a substantial cash boot.

Section 356(a)(2) finds its genesis in § 203(d)(2) of the Revenue Act of 1924. See 43 Stat. 257. Although modified slightly over the years, the provisions are in relevant substance identical. The accompanying House Report asserts that § 203(d)(2) was designed to "preven[t] evasion." H.R.Rep. No. 179, 68th Cong., 1st Sess., 15 (1924). Without further explication, both the House and Senate Reports simply rely on an example to explain, in the words of both Reports, "[t]he necessity for this provision." Ibid; S.Rep. No. 398, 68th Cong., 1st Sess., 16 (1924). Significantly, the example describes a situation in which there was no change in the stockholders' relative ownership interests, but merely the creation of a wholly owned subsidiary as a mechanism for making a cash distribution to the shareholders:

> "Corporation A has capital stock of $100,000, and earnings and profits accumulated since March 1, 1913, of $50,000. If it distributes the $50,000 as a dividend to its stockholders, the amount distributed will be taxed at the full surtax rates.

> "On the other hand, Corporation A may organize Corporation B, to which it transfers all its assets, the consideration for the transfer being the issuance by B of all its stock and $50,000 in cash to the stockholders of Corporation A in exchange for their stock in Corporation A. Under the existing law, the $50,000

distributed with the stock of Corporation B would be taxed, not as a dividend, but as a capital gain, subject only to the 12½ per cent rate. The effect of such a distribution is obviously the same as if the corporation had declared out as a dividend its $50,000 earnings and profits. If dividends are to be subject to the full surtax rates, then such an amount so distributed should also be subject to the surtax rates and not to the 12½ per cent rate on capital gain." Id., at 16; H.R.Rep. No. 179, at 15.

The "effect" of the transaction in this example is to transfer accumulated earnings and profits to the shareholders without altering their respective ownership interests in the continuing enterprise.

Of course, this example should not be understood as exhaustive of the proper applications of § 356(a)(2). It is nonetheless noteworthy that neither the example, nor any other legislative source, evinces a congressional intent to tax boot accompanying a transaction that involves a bona fide exchange between unrelated parties in the context of a reorganization as though the payment was in fact a dividend. To the contrary, the purpose of avoiding tax evasion suggests that Congress did not intend to impose an ordinary income tax in such cases. Moreover, the legislative history of § 302 supports this reading of § 356(a)(2) as well. In explaining the "essentially equivalent to a dividend" language of § 302(b)(1)—language that is certainly similar to the "has the effect * * * of a dividend" language of § 356(a)(2)—the Senate Finance Committee made clear that the relevant inquiry is "whether or not the transaction by its nature may properly be characterized as a sale of stock * * *." S.Rep. No. 1622, 83d Cong., 2d Sess., 234 (1954); cf. United States v. Davis, 397 U.S., at 311.

Examining the instant transaction in light of the purpose of § 356(a)(2), the boot-for-stock exchange in this case "may properly be characterized as a sale of stock." Significantly, unlike traditional single corporation redemptions and unlike reorganizations involving commonly owned corporations, there is little risk that the reorganization at issue was used as a ruse to distribute dividend. Rather, the transaction appears in all respects relevant to the narrow issue before us to have been comparable to an arm's length sale by the taxpayer to NL. This conclusion, moreover, is supported by the findings of the Tax Court. The court found that "[t]here is not the slightest evidence that the cash payment was a concealed distribution from BASIN." 86 T.C., at 155. As the Tax Court further noted, Basin lacked the funds to make such a distribution:

"Indeed, it is hard to conceive that such a possibility could even have been considered, for a distribution of that amount was not only far in excess of the accumulated earnings and profits ($2,319,611), but also of the total assets of BASIN ($2,758,069). In fact, only if one takes into account unrealized appreciation in the value of BASIN's assets, including good will and/or going concern value, can one possibly arrive at $3,250,000. Such a distribution could only be considered as the equivalent of a complete liquidation of BASIN * * *." Ibid.[10]

In this context, even without relying on § 302 and the post-reorganization analogy, we conclude that the boot is better characterized as a part of the proceeds of a sale of stock than as a proxy for a dividend. As such, the payment qualifies for capital gains treatment.

The judgment of the Court of Appeals is accordingly

Affirmed.

Justice WHITE, dissenting: The question in this case is whether the cash payment of $3,250,000 by N.L. Industries, Inc. (NL) to Donald Clark, which he received in the April 18, 1979, merger of Basin Surveys, Inc. (Basin), into N.L. Acquisition Corporation (NLAC), had the effect of a distribution of a dividend under the Internal Revenue Code, 26 U.S.C. § 356(a)(2), to the extent of Basin's accumulated undistributed earnings and profits. Petitioner, the Commissioner of Internal Revenue (Commissioner) made this determination, taxing the sum as ordinary income, to find a 1979 tax deficiency of $972,504.74. The Court of Appeals disagreed, stating that because the cash payment resembles a hypothetical stock redemption from NL to Clark, the amount is taxable as capital gain. 828 F.2d 221 (CA–4 1987). Because the majority today agrees with that characterization, in spite of Clark's explicit refusal of the stock-for-stock exchange imagined by the Court of Appeals and the majority today, and because the record demonstrates, instead, that the transaction before us involved a boot distribution that had "the effect of the distribution of a dividend" under § 356(a)(2)—hence properly alerted the Commissioner to Clark's tax deficiency—I dissent.

The facts are stipulated. Basin, Clark, NL, and NLAC executed an Agreement and Plan of Merger dated April 3, 1979, which provided that on April 18, 1979, Basin would merge with NLAC. The statutory merger, which occurred pursuant to §§ 368(a)(1)(A) and (a)(2)(D) of the Code, and therefore qualified for tax-free reorganization status under § 354(a)(1), involved the following terms: Each outstanding share of NLAC stock remained outstanding; each outstanding share of Basin common stock was exchanged for $56,034.482 cash and 5,172.4137 shares of NL common stock; and each share of Basin common stock held by Basin was canceled. NLAC's name was amended to Basin Surveys, Inc. The Secretary of State of West Virginia certified that the merger complied with West Virginia law. Clark, the owner of all 58 outstanding shares of Basin, received $3,250,000 in cash and 300,000 shares of NL stock. He expressly refused NL's alternative of 425,000 shares of NL common stock without cash. See App. 56–59.

10. The Commissioner maintains that Basin "could have distributed a dividend in the form of its own obligation (see, e.g., I.R.C. § 312(a)(2)) or it could have borrowed funds to distribute a dividend." Reply Brief for the United States 7. Basin's financial status, however, is nonetheless strong support for the Tax Court's conclusion that the cash payment was not a concealed dividend.

Congress enacted § 354(a)(1) to grant favorable tax treatment to specific corporate transactions (reorganizations) that involve the exchange of stock or securities solely for other stock or securities. See Paulsen v. Commissioner, 469 U.S. 131, 136 (1985) (citing Treas.Reg. § 1.368–1(b), 26 CFR § 1.368–1(b) (1984), and noting the distinctive feature of such reorganizations, namely continuity-of-interests). Clark's "triangular merger" of Basin into NL's subsidiary NLAC qualified as one such tax-free reorganization, pursuant to § 368(a)(2)(D). Because the stock-for-stock exchange was supplemented with a cash payment, however, § 356(a)(1) requires that "the gain, if any, to the recipient shall be recognized, but in an amount not in excess of the sum of such money and the fair market value of such other property." Because this provision permitted taxpayers to withdraw profits during corporate reorganizations without declaring a dividend, Congress enacted the present § 356(a)(2), which states that when an exchange has "the effect of the distribution of a dividend," boot must be treated as a dividend, and taxed as ordinary income, to the extent of the distributee's "ratable share of the undistributed earnings and profits of the corporation * * *." Ibid.; see also H.R.Rep. No. 179, 68th Cong., 1st Sess., 15 (1924) (illustration of § 356(a)(2)'s purpose to frustrate evasion of dividend taxation through corporate reorganization distributions); S.Rep. No. 398, 68th Cong., 1st Sess., 16 (1924) (same).

Thus the question today is whether the cash payment to Clark had the *effect* of a distribution of a dividend. We supplied the straightforward answer in United States v. Davis, 397 U.S. 301, 306, 312 (1970), when we explained that a pro rata redemption of stock by a corporation is "essentially equivalent" to a dividend. A pro rata distribution of stock, with no alteration of basic shareholder relationships, is the hallmark of a dividend. This was precisely Clark's gain. As sole shareholder of Basin, Clark necessarily received a pro rata distribution of monies that exceeded Basin's undistributed earnings and profits of $2,319,611. Because the merger and cash obligation occurred simultaneously on April 18, 1979, and because the statutory merger approved here assumes that Clark's proprietary interests continue in the restructured NLAC, the exact source of the pro rata boot payment is immaterial, which truth Congress acknowledged by requiring only that an exchange have the *effect* of a dividend distribution.

To avoid this conclusion, the Court of Appeals—approved by the majority today—recast the transaction as though the relevant distribution involved a single corporation's (NL's) stock redemption, which dividend equivalency is determined according to § 302 of the Code. Section 302 shields distributions from dividend taxation if the cash redemption is accompanied by sufficient loss of a shareholder's percentage interest in the corporation. The Court of Appeals hypothesized that Clark completed a pure stock-for-stock reorganization, receiving 425,000 NL shares, and thereafter redeemed 125,000 of these shares for his cash earnings of $3,250,000. The sum escapes dividend taxation because Clark's interest in NL theoretically declined from 1.3% to

0.92%, adequate to trigger § 302(b)(2) protection. Transporting § 302 from its purpose to frustrate shareholder sales of equity back to their own corporation, to § 356(a)(2)'s reorganization context, however, is problematic. Neither the majority nor the Court of Appeals explains why § 302 should obscure the core attribute of a dividend as a pro rata distribution to a corporation's shareholders; [1] nor offers insight into the mechanics of valuing hypothetical stock transfers and equity reductions; nor answers the Commissioner's observations that the sole shareholder of an acquired corporation will always have a smaller interest in the continuing enterprise when cash payments combine with a stock exchange. Last, the majority and the Court of Appeals' recharacterization of market happenings describes the exact stock-for-stock exchange, without a cash supplement, that Clark refused when he agreed to the merger.

Because the parties chose to structure the exchange as a tax-free reorganization under § 354(a)(1), and because the pro rata distribution to Clark of $3,250,000 during this reorganization had the *effect* of a dividend under § 356(a)(2), I dissent.[2]

NOTE

Section 356(a)(2) limits the amount of any boot dividend to the shareholder's recognized gain. This approach has been criticized as a "curious mixing of dividend and sale or exchange concepts" which "permits shareholders with a high basis in their stock * * * to withdraw corporate earnings in a reorganization without dividend consequences."[1] When ordinary income and capital gains were taxed at the same rate, the issues raised in the *Clark* case had limited significance.[2] Without a capital gains preference, individual sharehold-

---

1. The Court of Appeals' zeal to excoriate the "automatic dividend rule" leads to an opposite rigidity an automatic non-dividend rule, even for pro rata boot payments. Any significant cash payment in a stock-for-stock exchange distributed to a sole shareholder of an acquired corporation will automatically receive capital gains treatment. Section 356(a)(2)'s exception for such payments that have attributes of a dividend disappears. Congress did not intend to handicap the Commissioner and courts with either absolute; instead, § 356(a)(1) instructs courts to make fact-specific inquiries into whether boot distributions accompanying corporate reorganizations occur on a pro rata basis to shareholders of the acquired corporation, and thus threaten a bailout of the transferor corporation's earnings and profits escaping a proper dividend tax treatment.

2. The majority's alternative holding that no statutory merger occurred at all— rather a taxable sale—is difficult to understand: All parties stipulate to the merger,

which, in turn, was approved under West Virginia law; and Congress endorsed exactly such tax-free corporate transactions pursuant to its § 368(a)(1) reorganization regime. However apt the speculated sale analogy may be, if the April 3 Merger Agreement amounts to a sale of Clark's stock to NL, and not the intended merger, Clark would be subject to taxation on his full gain of over $10 million. The fracas over tax treatment of the cash boot would be irrelevant.

1. Staff of the Senate Committee on Finance, The Subchapter C Revision Act of 1985: A Final Report Prepared by the Staff, 99th Cong., 1st Sess. 45 (S.Prt. 99–47, 1985). See also Wolfman, "Subchapter C and the 100th Congress," 33 Tax Notes 669, 672 (Nov. 17, 1986).

2. See generally Faber, "Capital Gains v. Dividends in Corporate Transactions: Is the Battle Still Worth Fighting?" 64 Taxes 865 (1986).

ers pay the same tax whether or not the distribution has the effect of a dividend. But the reinstatement of a modest capital gains preference has breathed new life into this issue when, as in *Clark,* the amounts at stake are substantial. Corporate shareholders, however, may prefer dividend classification in order to qualify for the dividends received deduction under Section 243.[3] Dividend treatment also might be preferable because it would result in a reduction of earnings and profits of the surviving corporation at no significant cost to individual shareholders. Finally, dividend classification may be quite significant where shareholders receiving notes from the acquiring corporation desire to report their gain on the installment method. Unless the target stock exchanged by the shareholder is publicly traded,[4] installment sale treatment generally would be available if the transaction is treated as a sale but not if the receipt of installment boot is treated as a dividend under Section 356(a)(2).[5]

PROBLEM

Target Corporation ("T") has 10 equal shareholders, $100,000 of accumulated earnings and profits and a net worth of $500,000. Acquiring Corporation ("A") has 500,000 shares of voting common stock outstanding (value—$10 per share) and $500,000 of accumulated earnings and profits. Unless otherwise indicated, assume that each T shareholder owns 100 shares of voting common stock with a basis of $20,000 and a value of $50,000. T merges into A in a qualifying Type A reorganization. Discuss the tax consequences to the T shareholders under the following alternatives:

(a) Each T shareholder receives 4,000 shares of A voting common stock (value—$40,000) and A nonvoting preferred stock worth $10,000.

(b) Same as (a), above, but instead of the preferred stock each shareholder receives 20-year market rate interest bearing A notes with a principal amount and fair market value of $10,000.

(c) Same as (b), above, except that each shareholder has a $45,000 basis in her T stock.

(d) Same as (b), above, except that two of the shareholders receive all the notes (with a principal amount and fair market value of $100,000), and the remaining shareholders receive voting common stock worth $400,000.

(e) Same as (b), above, except that T had $50,000 of accumulated earnings and profits.

3. But see I.R.C. § 1059(e)(1)(B), which treats any amount treated as a dividend on a non pro rata redemption of a corporate shareholder's stock as an "extraordinary dividend." See Chapter 4F3, supra.

4. See I.R.C. § 453(k)(2).

5. See I.R.C. § 453(f)(6); Prop.Reg. § 1.453–1(f)(2).

2. CONSEQUENCES TO THE TARGET CORPORATION

Code: §§ 336(c); 357(a), (b), (c)(1); 358(a), (b)(1), (f); 361.

Regulations: § 1.357–1(a).

Treatment of the Reorganization Exchange. Without a nonrecognition provision, the target corporation in an acquisitive reorganization would recognize gain or loss on the transfer of its assets and the assumption of its liabilities by the acquiring corporation. If the acquisition qualifies as a reorganization, however, Section 361(a) comes to the rescue by providing that the target recognizes no gain or loss if it exchanges property, pursuant to the reorganization plan, solely for stock or securities in a corporation which also is a party to the reorganization. Section 357(a) offers similar protection by providing that the assumption of the target's liabilities in a reorganization exchange will not be treated as boot nor prevent the exchange from being tax-free under Section 361(a).[1] These rules apply primarily to Type A and C reorganizations and forward triangular mergers. In a Type B stock-for-stock exchange or a reverse triangular merger, no assets are transferred because the target corporation remains intact as a controlled subsidiary of the acquiring corporation.

The target in a Type C reorganization may receive a limited amount of boot without disqualifying the transaction under Section 368.[2] In that event, the target must recognize any realized gain (but may not recognize loss) on the reorganization exchange to the extent of the cash and the fair market value of the boot that the target does not distribute pursuant to the plan of reorganization.[3] Any transfer by the target of cash or other boot received in the exchange to creditors in connection with the reorganization is treated as a "distribution" pursuant to the reorganization plan.[4] Since the target in a Type C reorganization is generally required to distribute all of its properties pursuant to the plan,[5] gain or loss rarely will be recognized on the exchange.[6]

Section 361(a) only applies to the *receipt* of boot by the target pursuant to the reorganization plan. An acquiring corporation that transfers appreciated boot property to the target as partial consideration for the target's assets must recognize gain under Section 1001 because, to that extent, the transaction is considered to be a taxable

---

1. As in the Section 351 incorporation area, the general nonrecognition rule in Section 357(a) is subject to an exception in Section 357(b) if the liability assumption is motivated by tax avoidance or lacks a bona fide business purpose. The Section 357(c) exception for liabilities assumed in excess of the basis of the transferred assets only applies to a Type D reorganization. See Chapters 11 and 12, infra.

2. I.R.C. § 368(a)(2)(B). Boot in a Type C reorganization would include any property other than stock or securities of the

acquiring corporation (or its parent). See Section B3 of this Chapter, infra.

3. I.R.C. § 361(b)(1), (2).

4. I.R.C. § 361(b)(3). The Service may prescribe regulations as necessary to prevent tax avoidance through abuse of this rule. Id.

5. I.R.C. § 368(a)(2)(G).

6. A rare situation where gain might be recognized is where liabilities of the target are assumed in a transaction to which Section 357(b) or (c) applies.

exchange.[7] In that event, the target takes the boot property with a fair market value basis.[8]

Treatment of Distributions. Following enactment of the Tax Reform Act of 1986, the tax treatment of distributions by the target in a reorganization raised some nettlesome technical questions thanks to the inept redrafting of Section 361.[9] Congress resolved the confusion by adding new Section 361(c), which generally provides that a corporation does not recognize gain or loss on the distribution of "qualified property" to its shareholders pursuant to a reorganization plan. "Qualified property" is: (1) stock (or rights to acquire stock) in, or obligations (e.g., bonds and notes) of the distributing corporation, or (2) stock (or rights to acquire stock) in, or obligations of, another party to the reorganization which were received by the distributing corporation in the exchange. Thus, any stock, securities or even short-term notes of the acquiring corporation received by the target in the exchange and then distributed to its shareholders would constitute "qualified property." Section 361(c)(3) makes it clear that a transfer of "qualified property" by a target to its creditors in satisfaction of corporate liabilities is treated as a "distribution" pursuant to the reorganization plan.

If the target distributes an asset other than qualified property, it must recognize gain (but may not recognize loss) in the same manner as if the property had been sold to the distributee at its fair market value.[10] For example, the target would recognize gain on the distribution of appreciated retained assets (i.e., assets not acquired in the reorganization) or boot (other than notes of the acquiring corporation) which appreciated between the time it was received and the distribution to shareholders.[11]

Sales Prior to Liquidation. Before liquidating, the target corporation in a Type C reorganization may sell some of the stock or securities received from the acquiring corporation in order to raise money to pay off creditors. Prior to the Tax Reform Act of 1986, the courts were divided over whether these sales were entitled to nonrecognition treatment.[12] The Fifth Circuit, concluding that the liquidation and reorganization provisions could work in tandem, held that sales made pursuant to a plan of complete liquidation were entitled to nonrecognition of gain

---

7. Rev.Rul. 72–327 at p. 578, infra. Section 361(a) does not apply in this situation because it only provides nonrecognition to the *recipient* of distributed boot.

8. I.R.C. § 358(a)(2). See also I.R.C. § 358(f).

9. For those who wish to revisit the muddle, see Eustice, "A Case Study in Technical Tax Reform: Section 361, or How Not to Revise a Statute," 35 Tax Notes 283 (April 20, 1987); Eustice, "Section 361 Redux," 44 Tax Notes 443 (July 24, 1989).

10. I.R.C. § 361(c)(1), (2).

11. Since the target takes a fair market value basis in the boot under Section 358(a)(2) at the time of the exchange, it would recognize only post-acquisition appreciation on a later distribution of the boot.

12. Compare General Housewares Corp. v. United States, 615 F.2d 1056 (5th Cir. 1980) (allowing nonrecognition under former Section 337) with FEC Liquidating Corp. v. United States, 548 F.2d 924 (Ct.Cl. 1977) (taxing such gains on the ground that former Section 337 and the reorganization provisions were conceptually incompatible).

under the 1954 Code version of Section 337.[13] For a time after the 1986 Act, it appeared that Congress may have accepted the result in that case (while rejecting its rationale) when it provided, in a now repealed version of Section 361, that the target would not recognize gain or loss on any "disposition" of stock or securities of the acquiring corporation received pursuant to the reorganization plan.[14] It appeared at the time that the target would not recognize gain or loss if it sold some of the acquiring corporation's stock or securities to pay off creditors, at least if the sale were "pursuant to the reorganization plan," but it would recognize gain or loss if it sold any retained property (i.e., property not acquired in the reorganization) or boot that appreciated after it was received from the acquiring corporation. Under current Section 361, however, only transfers of "qualified property" (i.e., stock or obligations of the acquiring corporation) or boot directly to creditors will qualify for nonrecognition.[15] Sales of property to third parties do not qualify for nonrecognition, even if the sales were necessary to raise money to pay off creditors.

Basis and Holding Period. If the target corporation retains property received from the acquiring corporation, which only could occur in a Type C reorganization where the Commissioner waives the Section 368(a)(2)(G) distribution requirement, it is deemed to have distributed that property to its shareholders, who then are treated as having recontributed the property to a "new" corporation as a contribution to capital.[16] The basis and the holding period of the property in the hands of the "new" corporation depend upon the consequences to the shareholders. If the property is boot to the shareholders, it receives a fair market value basis and no tacked holding period in the hands of either the shareholders or the "new" corporation to which it is constructively recontributed.[17] If the property is nonrecognition property (e.g., stock or securities of the acquiring corporation) to the shareholders, then their exchanged bases and tacked holding periods transfer to the "new" corporation.[18] These rules are irrelevant in the typical Type C reorganization where the target liquidates and distributes the stock, securities and boot received in the transaction, along with any retained assets, to its shareholders. In that event, basis and holding period are determined under the operative provisions governing shareholders and security holders.[19]

13. General Housewares Corp. v. United States, supra note 12. Former Section 337 generally provided that a liquidating corporation did not recognize gain or loss on sales of assets pursuant to a plan of complete liquidation.

14. I.R.C. § 361(b)(3) (pre–1988).

15. I.R.C. § 361(b)(3), (c)(3).

16. See supra note 5.

17. I.R.C. §§ 358(a)(2); 362(a).

18. I.R.C. §§ 358(a)(1); 362(a); 1223(1) and (2).

19. See page 559, supra.

3. CONSEQUENCES TO THE ACQUIRING CORPORATION

Code: §§ 362(b); 368(b); 1032.

Regulations: § 1.1032–1.

Recognition of Gain or Loss. The acquiring corporation does not recognize gain or loss on the issuance of its stock or the stock of its parent in an acquisitive reorganization or, for that matter, in any other transaction.[1] To the extent that it may issue securities as consideration for the acquired property, the acquiring corporation recognizes no gain because the acquisition is a "purchase." If the acquiring corporation transfers any other property to make the acquisition, however, it recognizes any realized gain or loss under general principles governing exchanges of property.[2]

Basis and Holding Period: In General. Under Section 362(b), the target assets acquired in a Type A, Type C or forward triangular reorganization take a transferred basis, increased by any gain recognized by the target on the transfer. Since Section 361(a) generally provides that the target does not recognize gain or loss on any exchange of property pursuant to the plan of reorganization, an upward basis adjustment under Section 362(b) for gain recognized by the target will only be available in the rare Type C reorganization where the target receives boot and does not distribute it to its shareholders or creditors. In the case of a Type B or reverse triangular reorganization, however, the property acquired is corporate stock whose transferred basis is determined by its basis in the hands of the target shareholders.[3] In either case, the property acquired is allowed a tacked holding period under Section 1223(2).

Basis of Target Stock Received in Triangular Reorganization. Determining the acquiring parent corporation's basis in the stock of a subsidiary acquired in a reverse triangular reorganization raises a tantalizing technical question. Under Section 368(a)(2)(E), the acquiring corporation either may form a "phantom" subsidiary or use a preexisting operating subsidiary to merge into the target corporation. It ordinarily will transfer voting stock and possibly some boot to the subsidiary which then transfers that property to the target shareholders as the consideration for the acquisition.

In a straight Type B reorganization, the parent determines its basis in the target stock under Section 362(b) by reference to the stock bases of the former target shareholders. In the case of a reverse subsidiary

---

1. I.R.C. § 1032(a). It was once feared that Section 1032 would not apply where a controlled subsidiary acquired property in exchange for its *parent's* stock. The Service has ruled, however, that the subsidiary does not recognize gain or loss in this situation, presumably because such an acquisition is economically indistinguishable from a direct acquisition by the parent followed by a drop down of the assets to the subsidiary. See Rev.Rul. 57–278, 1957–1 C.B. 124.   Prop.Reg. § 1.1032–2.

2. See Rev.Rul. 72–327, at p. 577, infra.

3. See Rev.Proc. 81–70, 1981–2 C.B. 729, which provides an approach for determining this transferred basis when the large number of target shareholders makes precise determination of their bases impossible.

merger, however, Section 358 would appear to require the acquiring corporation to take an exchanged basis—i.e., its basis in the target stock acquired would be the same as its basis in the stock of the disappearing subsidiary. That basis likely would be zero if a phantom subsidiary were used to effect the merger.

A similar issue arises in the case of forward triangular merger, where the target merges into a subsidiary formed by the acquiring corporation immediately prior to the reorganization. Since the parent normally forms the subsidiary by transferring its own stock, in which it presumably has a zero basis, it would appear that the parent would retain a zero basis in the stock of the subsidiary even after it absorbs the target.

After much procrastination, the Treasury has issued proposed regulations designed to solve the zero basis problem. They provide that the parent's basis in stock of a subsidiary that survives a forward triangular merger or the target corporation acquired in a reverse triangular merger will equal the target's net basis in its assets, adjusted upward by the parent's basis (if any) in the stock of the merged subsidiary before the reorganization and downward by the fair market value of any consideration received by the target shareholders that was not furnished by the parent in connection with the reorganization.[4] The theory of these regulations is that the parent should be treated as if it acquired the assets or stock of the target in a two-party reorganization and then transferred the acquired property to a new subsidiary in a tax-free transaction. Significantly, these rules do not provide for an increase in the parent's basis in the stock of its subsidiary to reflect the transfer of property by the parent to the subsidiary that is subsequently transferred to the target's shareholders. This is appropriate because if the parent had acquired the target's assets or stock in a two-party reorganization in exchange for parent stock and other property and then dropped that property down to a subsidiary, the parent would not have received any upward adjustment in the basis of the subsidiary stock to reflect the transfer of property to the target or its shareholders.

REVENUE RULING 72–327

1972–2 Cum.Bull. 197.

Advice has been requested as to the Federal income tax consequences of the transaction described below:

On July 1, 1969, corporation *X* merged into corporation *Y* in a reorganization qualifying under section 368(a)(1)(A) of the Internal Revenue Code of 1954. Pursuant to the reorganization, *M* corporation,

---

4. Prop.Reg. 1.358–6. "Net basis" is the basis of the target company's assets less liabilities assumed. See generally New York State Bar Association, Tax Section, "Report on Reverse Triangular Mergers and Basis-Nonrecognition Rules in Triangular Reorganizations," 36 Tax L.Rev. 395 (1981). See also Prop.Reg. 1.1032–2, providing for nonrecognition to the acquiring subsidiary in a forward triangular merger or a triangular C reorganization on the receipt of money or property of the target in exchange for stock of the controlling parent corporation.

a stockholder of X, received, in exchange for its X stock, Y stock having a fair market value of $100x$ dollars plus other property having a fair market value of $40x$ dollars but an adjusted basis in the hands of Y of $10x$ dollars. M had a basis of $90x$ dollars in its stock of X. M's ratable share of the undistributed earnings and profits of X accumulated after February 28, 1913, was $30x$ dollars. M realized gain of $50x$ dollars ($140x$ dollars less $90x$ dollars) on the exchange. Of the $50x$ dollar gain, $40x$ dollars was recognized to M pursuant to section 356(a)(1) of the Code. Pursuant to section 356(a)(2) of the Code, $30x$ dollars was treated as a dividend and $10x$ dollars was treated as gain from the exchange of property.

The Federal income tax consequences of the above described transaction are as follows:

(1) The $30x$ dollar gain, treated as a dividend to M under section 356(a)(2) of the Code, is eligible for the corporate dividends received deduction provided by section 243(a) of the Code. M's basis in the stock of Y is $90x$ dollars. Section 358(a)(1) of the Code. M's basis in the other property received is $40x$ dollars, the fair market value thereof. Section 358(a)(2) of the Code.

(2) Pursuant to section * * * 1001 of the Code, gain is recognized by Y in the amount of $30x$ dollars ($40x$ dollars minus $10x$ dollars). See, for example, United States v. Thomas Crawley Davis, 370 U.S. 65 (1962), Ct.D.1873, C.B. 1962–2, 15; E.F. Simms v. Commissioner, 28 B.T.A. 988, at 1029 (1933). Y's basis for the assets acquired from X is the basis of the assets in the hands of X. Section 362(b) of the Code.

(3) No gain or loss is recognized by X on the transaction. Section 361[(a) of the Code. Under Section 358(a)(2), X takes the other property with a basis of $40x$ dollars, and it recognizes no gain on distribution of the other property under Section 361(c). X does not recognize gain on the distribution of the Y stock. I.R.C. §§ 336(c); 361(c)(1). Ed.]

(4) Y's earnings and profits are increased by the $30x$ dollar gain that it recognized on the exchange of the other property. Section 312(f)(1) of the Code.

(5) Y succeeds to, and takes into account, X's earnings and profits, or deficit in earnings and profits, as of the close of the date of the transaction. Section 381(c)(2) of the Code. In computing the earnings and profits of X for purposes of section 381(c)(2) of the Code, account must be taken of the amount of X's earnings and profits properly applicable to the distribution to M. Section 1.381(c)(2)–1(c)(1) of the Income Tax Regulations. X's earnings and profits, for purposes of section 381(c)(2) of the Code, are computed as follows:

(a) X's earnings and profits are not increased by reason of the receipt [or distribution] of the other property. Sections 361[(a)] and 312(f)(1) of the Code.

(b) X's earnings and profits are reduced (but not below zero) by $40x$ dollars as a result of the distribution of the other property to *M*. Section 312(a)(3) of the Code. For purposes of determining earnings and profits, *X* [has] a basis of 40*x* dollars (fair market value) in the other property. Section [358(a)(2)] of the Code.

(6) *M*'s earnings and profits are increased by 40*x* dollars, the amount of gain recognized on the transaction. Sections 356(a)(1) and (2) of the Code and section 312(f)(1) of the Code.

PROBLEMS

1. Acquiring Corporation ("A") has $100,000 of accumulated earnings and profits. Target Corporation ("T") has assets with a basis of $60,000 and a fair market value of $100,000 and $50,000 of accumulated earnings and profits. T's shareholders have a $20,000 aggregate basis in their stock. A acquires all the assets of T in a qualifying Type C reorganization. Discuss the tax consequences to A, T and T's shareholders under each of the following circumstances:

(a) A transfers its voting stock, worth $80,000, in exchange for all of T's assets which are subject to $20,000 of liabilities. T immediately distributes the stock to its shareholders in complete liquidation.

(b) Same as (a), above, except that A transfers $80,000 of voting stock and $20,000 cash to T, which uses the cash to pay off its liabilities and distributes the stock to its shareholders in complete liquidation. Which result in (a) or (b), above, would A prefer?

(c) Same as (a), above, except that A transfers voting stock worth $80,000 and investment securities with a basis of $10,000 and a value of $20,000 in return for all of T's assets which were not subject to any liabilities. T again immediately distributes the consideration it receives pro rata to its shareholders in complete liquidation.

(d) Same as (a), above, except that A transfers $80,000 of its voting stock, $10,000 of A bonds and $10,000 of cash to T in exchange for its assets. Because an immediate distribution would result in substantial hardship to T, T receives the Commissioner's permission not to liquidate and retains the cash, bonds and stock for eventual satisfaction of its liabilities and distribution of the remaining assets to its shareholders.

(e) For this part of the problem, assume T has no liabilities. A transfers $80,000 worth of its voting stock and $20,000 of nonvoting preferred stock to T in exchange for all of T's assets. T liquidates and distributes the voting and nonvoting preferred stock to its shareholders pro rata.

2. Target Corporation ("T") has operating assets with a basis of $18,000 and a value of $90,000, investment land with a basis of $2,000 and a value of $10,000 and liabilities of $40,000.

In a Type C reorganization, Acquiring Corporation ("A") acquires T's operating assets in exchange for A voting stock worth $80,000 and some stock in Bell, Inc. (an unrelated public company) with a basis of $2,000 and a value of $10,000. A does not assume T's liabilities.

Before liquidating, T sells $40,000 of A stock and uses the proceeds to pay off its liabilities. T then distributes the remaining $40,000 of A stock, its investment land and the Bell, Inc. stock (now worth $12,000) in complete liquidation to its shareholders, who have an aggregate basis of $10,000 in their T stock.

Prior to the reorganization, A had $20,000 of earnings and profits and T had $10,000 of earnings and profits.

(a) What are the tax consequences to T, A and T's shareholders?

(b) Would there be a different result in (a), above, if T transferred $40,000 of A stock to its creditors in connection with the liquidation?

3. Parent Corporation ("P") creates Subsidiary Corporation ("S") by transferring P stock as a preliminary step to acquiring the assets of Target Corporation ("T") in a separate subsidiary. T's shareholders own stock worth $200,000 with a basis of $50,000. T has assets worth $200,000 with a basis of $100,000.

(a) Assuming a valid § 368(a)(2)(D) forward triangular merger, what are the tax consequences to P, S, T and T's shareholders?

(b) Assuming a valid § 368(a)(2)(E) reverse triangular merger, what are the tax consequences to P, S, T and T's shareholders?

(c) What results in (a), above, if the transaction fails to qualify as a reorganization?

(d) What results in (b), above, if the transaction fails to qualify as a reorganization?

D. CARRYOVER OF TAX ATTRIBUTES

1. INTRODUCTION

Code: § 381(a). Skim § 381(c).

When one corporation acquires the assets of another corporation in a tax-free reorganization, the acquired properties retain both their bases and holding periods. But what happens to all of the remaining tax attributes of the target—its earnings and profits, depreciation and other accounting methods, unused net operating losses, capital losses and the like?

Prior to 1954, the Code contained few rules regulating the carry-over of corporate tax attributes. The Supreme Court merely followed the lead of lower courts [1] in holding that a corporation's earnings and

---

1. See, e.g., Commissioner v. Sansome, 60 F.2d 931 (2d Cir.1932), cert. denied 287 U.S. 667, 53 S.Ct. 291 (1932).

profits could not be eliminated by means of a reorganization but that instead the acquiring corporation inherited the target's earnings and profits along with its assets.[2] Because any other approach would have allowed a profitable corporation to use a reorganization to sweep its earnings and profits account clean and diminish future dividends, the Court's decision was no more surprising than the reaction of the tax bar to the proposition that corporate attributes could survive a reorganization. They assumed, or at least hoped, that an acquiring corporation could inherit negative as well as positive tax attributes in a tax-free reorganization or liquidation. If that assumption proved true, profitable corporations could acquire the assets of their unprofitable brethren solely to succeed to the target's earnings and profits deficit and net operating losses (NOLs). The acquiring corporation thus could assure itself that future distributions would be sheltered by the newly acquired earnings and profits deficit and that future income would be effectively exempt from tax because of the newly acquired net operating losses.

The Supreme Court responded by holding that earnings and profits deficits did *not* survive a reorganization [3] and that NOLs could be used only by the corporate entity that incurred them.[4] But tax advisors were not to be outdone. Shortly after these decisions, there appeared on the scene several reorganizations which followed a similar pattern. Loss Corp., a corporation with NOLs but no current income to absorb them, would acquire the assets of Profit Corp., a successful company, in a tax-free reorganization. In the process, the Profit Corp. shareholders would receive more than enough Loss Corp. stock to control the continuing and expanded Loss Corp. Since Loss Corp. technically was the surviving entity, it retained its NOLs, which then were used to offset the gains generated by the new business. Once again, the Supreme Court was forced to respond to a device involving trafficking in tax attributes. In Libson Shops, Inc. v. Koehler,[5] the Court decided that even if a loss corporation survives a reorganization, NOLs incurred prior to the transaction only could be used to offset post-acquisition gains if they were generated by substantially the same *business* as well as the same entity which had incurred the losses.

With the arrival of the 1954 Code, the case law regulating the carryover of tax attributes was replaced by a comprehensive statutory scheme.[6] The principal provisions are: (1) Section 381, which generally provides that a target corporation's tax attributes follow its assets in tax-free reorganizations (other than B and E reorganizations) and tax-

2. Commissioner v. Munter, 331 U.S. 210, 67 S.Ct. 1175 (1947).

3. Commissioner v. Phipps, 336 U.S. 410, 69 S.Ct. 616 (1949).

4. New Colonial Ice Co. v. Helvering, 292 U.S. 435, 54 S.Ct. 788 (1934). But see Helvering v. Metropolitan Edison, 306 U.S. 522, 59 S.Ct. 634 (1939), where the Court held that these attributes did follow the target's assets in certain mergers.

5. 353 U.S. 382, 77 S.Ct. 990 (1957).

6. Some commentators and courts have suggested that the *Libson Shops* doctrine survived the 1954 Code, but Congress intended specifically not to incorporate the doctrine into the new statutory scheme governing limitations on net operating loss carryforwards. H.R.Rep. No. 99–841, 99th Cong., 2d Sess. II–194 (1986). See Chapter 13, infra.

free liquidations of a subsidiary; (2) Sections 382 and 383, which restrict the carryforward of net operating losses and certain other losses and credits following a substantial change of ownership; (3) Section 384, which limits the use of loss carryforwards to offset certain gains following a corporate acquisition; and (4) Section 269, which allows the Secretary to disallow deductions, credits or other allowances in certain situations where one corporation's stock or assets were acquired for the principal purpose of obtaining the specific deductions, credits or allowances in question. The limitations on carryforwards of net operating losses and Section 269 are considered in Chapter 13. The remainder of this chapter examines the general rules on carryover of tax attributes in corporate acquisitions.

2. SECTION 381

Code: § 381(a), (b). Skim § 381(c).

Section 381(a) provides that in a tax-free liquidation of a subsidiary or a reorganization (other than a Type B or E reorganization)[1], the acquiring corporation shall "succeed to and take into account" some 26 specified attributes of the target,[2] including earnings and profits, NOLs, accounting and depreciation methods and capital loss, investment credit and charitable contribution carryovers.[3] Section 381 does not apply to a Type B reorganization because it is unnecessary. In a stock-for-stock acquisition, the target corporation remains intact and simply retains all of its previous tax attributes. In a triangular reorganization where substantially all of the target's assets are transferred to a subsidiary of the issuing corporation, the subsidiary is the "acquiring corporation" and succeeds to the target's attributes.[4]

Left unchecked, Section 381 would subject the revenue to some of the same abuses already discussed. As we have seen, one promising tax avoidance strategy is presented where Profit Corp. acquires Loss Corp.'s assets in a reorganization and inherits its earnings and profits deficit and NOL carryovers. To some extent, this abuse is limited by Section 381 itself. Section 381(c)(2) restricts Profit Corp.'s ability to rid itself of its own current or accumulated earnings and profits through a simple acquisition of Loss Corp. by providing that an earnings and profits deficit inherited from Loss Corp. may not be applied against any earnings and profits of Profit Corp. that existed prior to the acquisition. Loss Corp.'s deficit therefore only can be used to offset post-acquisition accumulated earnings and profits.[5]

---

1. In both B and E reorganizations, the acquired or recapitalized corporation remains intact after the transaction and thus no carryover mechanism is necessary.

2. I.R.C. § 381(c)(1)–(26).

3. Cf. I.R.C. § 312(h)(2), which requires a "proper allocation" of earnings and profits between the acquiring corporation and the target if less than 100 percent of the

assets are acquired in a Type C or Type D reorganization.

4. Reg. § 1.381(a)–1(b)(2).

5. I.R.C. § 381(c)(2)(B). Of course, if a distribution is made in a post-acquisition year in which there are current earnings and profits, any offsetting accumulated deficit acquired from Loss Corp. is irrelevant in any event, since the distribution will be

Even though Profit Corp. receives little benefit from Loss Corp.'s earnings and profits deficit, the NOL carryovers still might be used to eliminate Profit's own tax liability. Section 381(c)(1) provides complex rules governing the carryover of NOLs, but it does not prevent them from being misused by Profit Corp. Instead, Section 382—a challenging provision that we will explore later—is the designated policing agent in this situation.

Rather than Profit Corp. acquiring the assets and tax attributes of Loss Corp., we have seen that Loss might acquire Profit's assets in a Type A or C reorganization, maintaining Loss's earnings and profits deficit and NOLs without assistance from Section 381, and use those negative tax attributes to offset Profit's past and future income. If Profit's shareholders receive sufficient Loss Corp. stock to control the combined company, the transaction in substance is identical to the acquisition of Loss Corp. by Profit. The benefits of this transaction also are limited by both Sections 381(b) and 382. The *Bercy Industries* case, which follows, explores the limits of Section 381(b)(3), which in part prevents Loss Corp. from carrying back any NOLs that it incurs subsequent to the acquisition to offset pre-acquisition income of Profit Corp.

BERCY INDUSTRIES, INC. v. COMMISSIONER *

United States Court of Appeals, Ninth Circuit, 1981.
640 F.2d 1058.

TRASK, Circuit Judge:

Appellant Bercy Industries, Inc. (Bercy), appeals from a decision of the Tax Court affirming a deficiency assessment by the Commissioner of Internal Revenue (the Commissioner). This court has jurisdiction pursuant to I.R.C. [26 U.S.C.] § 7482. Bercy contends that the Commissioner improperly denied it a loss carryback under section 381 of the Internal Revenue Code (the Code). Subsection (b)(3) of that section limits post-reorganization loss carry-backs by the surviving corporation of certain tax-free reorganizations. Surviving corporations in other tax-free reorganizations, however, are permitted carryback of post reorganization losses without special limitation. Bercy argues that either Congress intended that corporations that reorganize as Bercy did be permitted to carryback their post-reorganization losses, or Bercy's reorganization qualifies as one of the types entitled to unrestricted carryback treatment. The Commissioner responds that the Code should be strictly construed and that Bercy does not qualify for unrestricted carryback treatment under the terms of section 381. We reverse.

deemed to come from the current earnings and profits of the taxable year and then from Profit Corp.'s own pre-acquisition accumulated earnings and profits. See Chapter 4, supra. Thus, an acquired earnings and profits deficit will do no more than prevent undistributed current earnings and profits from becoming accumulated earnings and profits in a subsequent year.

* Some footnotes omitted.

I

Bercy Industries was incorporated in 1965. In 1968, a corporation named Beverly Enterprises established a subsidiary shell corporation, Beverly Manor. Beverly Manor remained a shell until April 23, 1970, the date of the reorganization here at issue. On that date, Bercy Industries (Old Bercy) was acquired by Beverly Manor by means of a triangular merger. Old Bercy was merged into Beverly Manor, which then changed its name to Bercy Industries (New Bercy). All shareholders of Old Bercy exchanged their stock for shares of stock in Beverly Enterprises, the parent. The Old Bercy stock was then cancelled.

Although it had been anticipated that New Bercy would be as profitable as Old Bercy had been, New Bercy suffered a loss for the post-reorganization period April 23 to December 31, 1970. Relying on the carryover provisions of section 172 of the Code, New Bercy attempted to carry back this loss to offset net operating income of Old Bercy in its two preceding tax years. It is this carryback that the Commissioner disallowed, and that is the subject of this appeal.

Appellant raises two issues: (1) whether Congress, in enacting section 381, intended to prevent the subsidiary corporation in a triangular merger from carrying back post-merger losses to offset pre-merger income of the transferor corporation, where the subsidiary was a mere shell before the merger, and (2) whether the reorganization here at issue should be classified as a type (B) reorganization for purposes of section 381. Both issues are of first impression in this circuit. We address only the first issue.

II

Under I.R.C. § 172, a corporation which incurs a net operating loss in any tax year may carry this loss back three tax years, or forward seven tax years, to offset net operating income earned during those years. Section 172 reflects congressional recognition that business income often fluctuates widely from year to year, and that, consequently, a carryover provision is necessary to mitigate the inequitable and excessive tax liabilities that would result from determination of income on a strictly annual basis. * * *

In 1954, Congress enacted section 381 as part of a substantial revision of the entire Code. The Commissioner argues that Congress intended this provision to preempt and replace prior caselaw with reliable and consistent rules for carrying over pre- and post-reorganization income and loss. Conceding this to be the general purpose of section 381, appellant nevertheless argues that it is an oversimplified characterization of congressional intent with respect to subsection (b) (3). We agree.

Prior to the 1954 revision of the Code, a significant tax avoidance problem for the Internal Revenue Service was the corporate practice of "trafficking in loss corporations." [3] The Commissioner had attempted to combat this practice by ruling that net operating losses could be carried over only to offset income of the particular legal entity that incurred the losses. See, e.g., Libson Shops, Inc. v. Koehler, supra, 353 U.S. at 385–86, 77 S.Ct. at 992 (decided under the 1939 Code). Thus, the acquiring corporation in a triangular merger was effectively prevented from carrying back any post-merger losses to offset pre-merger income of the transferor corporation.

Although approved by the Supreme Court in New Colonial Ice Co. v. Helvering, 292 U.S. 435, 440–41, 54 S.Ct. 788, 790, 78 L.Ed. 1348 (1934), the Commissioner's position was undercut by a succession of adverse court decisions, see, e.g., Helvering v. Metropolitan Edison Co., 306 U.S. 522, 529, 59 S.Ct. 634, 638, 83 L.Ed. 957 (1939); Stanton Brewery v. Commissioner, 176 F.2d 573, 575 (2d Cir.1949), which resulted in substantial confusion among corporations as to when post-reorganization loss carryovers were permitted, see H.R.Rep. No. 1337, 83d Cong., 2d Sess. 41, reprinted in [1954] U.S.Code Cong. & Ad.News 4017, 4066–67; S.Rep. No. 1622, 83d Cong., 2d Sess. 52–53, reprinted in [1954] U.S.Code Cong. & Ad.News 4621, 4683–84. Section 381 and its companion, section 382, rejected the restrictive position taken by the Commissioner and clarified the availability of post-reorganization loss carryovers by prohibiting them only in limited circumstances specified in the two sections. * * *

With respect to the enactment of subsection (b)(3) of section 381, the legislative history shows that Congress was concerned with a complex accounting problem—deciding how a post-reorganization loss should be allocated between the acquiring corporation and the transferor corporations, and, therefore, how much of the loss should be carried back to offset each entity's income in the preceding three tax years. The Senate Finance Committee reported: "Some limitation upon carrybacks in reorganizations and mergers is justifiable on the ground that it is too complex in some cases to determine to which of several component corporations the loss of the surviving corporation is attributable." Senate Finance Committee, supra, at 404. This committee also stated, however, that

> [i]n two important areas * * * *the problem of allocating the loss is not involved,* and it is suggested that *in such cases, at least, there should be no limit on carrybacks.* One is the case of a reincorporation of the same corporation in a different state, or upon expiration of its charter. Another instance is that of the wholly owned subsidiary which is liquidated into its par-

---

3. A profitable corporation would acquire an unprofitable corporation with losses eligible to be carried forward under section 172. After the acquisition, the transferor corporation's pre-reorganization losses were carried forward to offset current and expected income of the acquiring corporation, thereby reducing current tax liability. See generally D. Kahn & P. Gann, Corporate Taxation and the Taxation of Partnerships 848–49 (1979); Note, Section 368(a)(1)(F) and Loss Carrybacks in Corporate Reorganizations, 117 U.Pa.L. Rev. 764, 765 (1969).

ent, which parent suffers a net operating loss in the following year.

Id. (emphasis added). This language strongly suggests that when a reorganization generates no complex problems of post-reorganization loss allocation, Congress intended that the surviving corporate taxpayer be able to carry back such losses without limitation.

Because Congress specifically identified two circumstances in which loss carrybacks should be permitted, the Commissioner argues that if Congress had also intended to permit carrybacks in a triangular merger involving a shell corporation, it would have specifically mentioned this circumstance as well. In 1954, however, the Code did not permit a corporation to use its parent's stock as consideration for the acquisition of another corporation's assets in a tax-free reorganization. This prevented the use of shells in effecting such reorganizations. Congress did not suggest that this type of tax-free reorganization be removed from the carryback restrictions of section 381(b)(3) because such a reorganization was not then tax-free. Such use of parent stock was sanctioned by amendments to the Code in 1968 and 1971. Act of Oct. 22, 1968, Pub.L. No. 90–621, § 1(a), 82 Stat. 1310–11 (triangular mergers); Act of Jan. 12, 1970, Pub.L. No. 91–693, § 1(a), 84 Stat. 2077 (reverse triangular mergers). We find nothing in the text or legislative history of these amendments that would suggest that they were intended to expand the scope of section 381(b)(3) beyond the problem to which it was originally directed, i.e., allocation of post-reorganization loss. * * *

The non-applicability of subsection (b)(3) to type (B), (E), and (F) reorganizations [4] supports our view of congressional intent with respect to this subsection. (B) reorganizations involve exchange of stock at the shareholder level only, (E) reorganizations are a recapitalization of a single corporation, and (F) reorganizations are a mere change in form or identity. A loss carryback after one of these reorganizations generally does not result in the offset of income earned by one corporation by losses incurred by another.[5] Thus, there are no post-reorganization allocation problems.

Both legislative history and statutory structure support the conclusion that Congress was preoccupied with post-reorganization allocation problems when it enacted the loss carryback restriction. We agree with the Second Circuit that the intent of Congress with respect to subsection (b)(3) of section 381 was to prohibit carryback of post-reorganization losses pursuant to section 172 only when such a carryback would entail complex problems of post-reorganization loss allo-

---

4. (F) reorganizations are explicitly exempted by the terms of the statute. See I.R.C. § 381(b). (B) and (E) reorganizations are exempted because they are not described in subsection (a)(2), to which subsection (b)(3) refers. *See* Treas.Reg. 1.381(a)–1(b)(3)(i) (T.D.6500).

5. Such a result occurs in some (F) reorganizations. Such a reorganization, how-

ever, nearly always involves the consolidation of wholly owned subsidiaries into a parent corporation, so that the loss allocation problems are far less significant than would normally be the case. See e.g., Estate of Stauffer v. Commissioner, 403 F.2d 611 (9th Cir.1968). *See also* B. Bittker & J. Eustice, supra, para. 16.12, at 16–22 to –23 & nn. 40–41.

cation. See Aetna Casualty & Surety Co. v. United States, supra, 568 F.2d at 819, 822, 824.

III

The Commissioner states that section 381(b)(3) reflects a policy of not permitting loss carrybacks when the legal and economic identity of the corporation has been substantially altered.[6] The Commissioner argues that Old Bercy was legally transformed by its merger into New Bercy and the subsequent cancellation of its stock. He further argues that the reorganization transformed Old Bercy economically by shifting control of that corporation from its own shareholders to those of Beverly Enterprises.

Even assuming that the Commissioner has correctly articulated the congressional policy underlying subsection (b)(3), we are not persuaded that a material change in identity resulted from the reorganization here at issue. The reorganization involved only one set of operating assets, one set of books, and one tax history. New Bercy is operating the same commercial business that Old Bercy operated. There is no problem of allocating a post-reorganization loss to different pre-reorganization businesses. Regardless of the formal technicalities of the transaction, the indisputable fact is that the same business generated both the income and the loss.[7] The legislative history of section 381 shows that Congress intended that a loss carryback be available in circumstances such as these.

IV

It has long been judicial practice in reviewing tax cases to look through the form of a transaction to its substance when scrutiny of

6. In the Commissioner's view, subsection (b)(3) does not apply to type (B), (E), and (F) reorganizations only because such reorganizations leave the surviving corporation's pre-reorganization legal and economic identity essentially unchanged.

7. The Commissioner makes much of the fact that because of the reorganization, the benefit of the loss carryback will accrue to a different set of shareholders than the one that owned Bercy at the time it earned the income to be offset. We fail to see why this should prevent a carryback. Sections 381 and 382 are grounded on two competing theories: (1) A loss carryover ought to be available only when the shareholders who were the "beneficial sufferers" of such loss retain an interest in its use, as the Commissioner argues; and (2) a loss carryover ought to be available only for use against profits from business activities which gave rise to the loss. Kaufman, Application of a Loss Carryover of One Business Against Profits From Another Business; Lisbon Shops and Sections 381, 382, and 269, 24 N.Y.U.Inst.Fed.Tax. 1199, 1203 (1966). These two theories conflict in large degree, so that any particular subsection of 381 or 382 may favor one theory over the other. See id. As our discussion of congressional intent indicates, see Part II supra, this was the case with section 381(b)(3); theory (2), rather than theory (1), clearly animates subsection (b)(3). Moreover, we note that the former shareholders of Old Bercy are now minority holders of Beverly Enterprises, and have a continuing, albeit diminished, interest in carryback of the post-reorganization loss. Finally, the Commissioner himself concedes that a loss carryback would have been permitted had Bercy reorganized pursuant to a reverse triangular merger, yet such a reorganization would have resulted in the same change in shareholder ownership which the Commissioner now argues should prevent the carryback.

form alone would subvert the purposes of the Code. See, e.g., Gregory v. Helvering, 293 U.S. 465, 469–70, 55 S.Ct. 266, 267, 79 L.Ed. 596 (1935). We have discovered no tax policy, nor does the Commissioner articulate one, that would be promoted by denying a loss carryback in this instance.[8] On the contrary, section 172 manifests a congressional policy preference for loss carryovers which is not to be lightly set aside. Aetna Casualty & Surety Co. v. United States, supra, 568 F.2d at 822, 824. To deny a loss carryback on the facts of this case would exalt form over substance. Accordingly, we hold that subsection (b)(3) of section 381 does not prevent Bercy from using the loss carryback provisions of section 172. The judgment of the Tax Court is Reversed.

PROBLEMS

1. Acquiring Corporation ("A") acquires the assets of Target Corporation ("T") in a valid Type C reorganization. Both corporations are calendar year taxpayers and the transactions are completed on December 31, 1991.

  (a) If A has accumulated earnings and profits of $30,000 and T has an earnings and profits deficit of $50,000, what result to the A shareholders in 1991 if during that year A has $20,000 of current earnings and profits, T breaks even and A distributes $20,000 cash?

  (b) What result in (a), above, if A breaks even in 1991 and makes no distributions during that year but distributes $20,000 in 1992, a year when A also breaks even?

  (c) What result in (b), above, if in 1991, A has a $10,000 current earnings and profits deficit?

  (d) What result in (b), above, if *in addition* in 1993 A has a $10,000 current earnings and profits deficit and makes a $20,000 cash distribution?

  (e) What result in (d), above, if *in addition* in 1994, A has $20,000 of current earnings and profits and makes a $20,000 cash distribution?

  (f) What result in (e), above, if A makes no distribution in 1994, but distributes $40,000 in 1995, a year in which A breaks even.

2. T Corporation merges into A Corporation two-thirds of the way through A's year. What are the results in the following situations:

  (a) A has $30,000 of deficit earnings and profits for the entire year of the acquisition and T has $30,000 of accumulated earnings and profits at the date of the acquisition. The combined corporation makes a distribution of $20,000 in the succeeding year when it breaks even.

8. We are unpersuaded by the Commissioner's argument that chaos and inconsistency will result from permitting loss carrybacks in circumstances such as those in this case.

(b) Same as (a), above, except that A Corporation has $30,000 of current earnings and profits for the year and T has a $30,000 earnings and profits deficit at the time of the acquisition. The combined corporation again makes a distribution of $20,000 in the succeeding year, when it breaks even.

(c) Same as (b), above, except that the combined corporation makes a distribution of $30,000 on the last day of the year of acquisition.

3. T Corporation merges into P Corporation in a tax-free Type A reorganization in which T shareholders receive 51 percent of the outstanding P stock. Both corporations are calendar year, accrual method taxpayers and the merger occurs on December 31, 1991. Both corporations have been in existence for two years, with T sustaining a $20,000 loss in each of those years and P earning a profit of $30,000 in each year.

(a) May the combined corporation carry back T's losses and apply them against P's profits for 1990 and 1991?

(b) Assuming that the loss and income patterns continue, determine the combined corporation's net income for the years 1992 through 1996.

(c) What results in (b), above, if T were a profitable corporation with net income of $20,000 in each of the prior and current years but P sustained a $100,000 loss in 1992 followed by a return to the regular gain pattern in 1993?

(d) What result in (c), above, if T and P consolidated into C Corporation and C sustained the $100,000 loss in 1992 followed by $50,000 in gains in the succeeding years?

4. Consider the following questions concerning the carryover of net operating losses:

(a) May a Type F reorganization be preferable to a Type A reorganization?

(b) Is there ever an overlap between a Type F and a Type A reorganization?

(c) How does the *Bercy Industries* case relate to these questions?

(d) Does *Bercy* apply to all § 368(a)(2)(D) reorganizations?

5. If T Corporation in Problem 3, above, had a § 248 organizational expenditure which had not been entirely amortized, is the carryover of the deduction to P Corporation necessarily precluded by its omission from § 381?

E. POLICY: AN ELECTIVE CARRYOVER BASIS REGIME

Congress has been tinkering with Subchapter C since the enactment of the 1954 Code, but until recently most revisions were aimed at narrow technical problems. Prompted by recommendations from the organized tax bar and the American Law Institute, Congress cautiously began to reexamine a number of fundamental structural issues in 1982, when it enacted Section 338. Shortly thereafter, the Senate Finance Committee began a comprehensive study of Subchapter C. The staff reviewed recommendations of prominent bar and accounting groups and relied heavily on the Subchapter C project of the American Law Institute. In September, 1983, it issued its preliminary report—a controversial document that proposed revisions both large and small. Some of the staff's narrower recommendations were incorporated in the Tax Reform Act of 1984.

The Finance Committee staff followed up in 1985 with its "final report"—The Subchapter C Revision Act of 1985. Some of its aspects, most notably further repeal of the *General Utilities* doctrine and a revised approach to limiting net operating loss carryforwards, were incorporated in the Tax Reform Act of 1986. But even the 1986 Act left for another day the centerpiece of both the ALI and the Senate Finance Committee projects—the adoption of an entirely new scheme governing corporate acquisitions, including the replacement of the tax-free reorganization provisions with an essentially elective system that would permit nonrecognition under consistent standards for any corporate acquisition at the price of a carryover basis in the assets of the target corporation. The following excerpt provides a summary of these acquisition proposals. Keep in mind that it was written prior to the 1986 Act, and thus it assumes that *General Utilities* has not yet been fully repealed and makes references to the former versions of Section 336 and 337. This proposal has considerable support and, if the budget deficit is ever under control, it may be reviewed carefully by the Treasury Department and the Congressional tax-writing committees as they ponder the future of Subchapter C.

EXCERPT FROM THE SUBCHAPTER C REVISION ACT OF 1985: A FINAL REPORT PREPARED BY THE STAFF OF THE SENATE FINANCE COMMITTEE

S. Prt. 99–47, 99th Cong., 1st Sess. 50–53 (1985).

IV. SUMMARY OF PROPOSALS

The principal proposals contained in the bill are described below. A more detailed description of the proposals is set forth in the Technical Explanation accompanying the bill.

A. Definition of qualified acquisition (new section 364 of the Code)

In general, the bill consolidates, simplifies, and makes uniform the rules classifying corporate mergers and acquisitions, whether treated under current law as a "reorganization", a liquidating sale under section 337 of the Code, or a section 338 stock acquisition.

New section 364 defines "qualified acquisition" as meaning any "qualified stock acquisition" or any "qualified asset acquisition." A qualified stock acquisition is defined as any transaction or series of transactions during the 12-month acquisition period in which one corporation acquires stock representing control of another corporation. A qualified asset acquisition means (1) any statutory merger or consolidation, or (2) any other transaction in which one corporation acquires at least 70 percent of the gross fair market value and at least 90 percent of the net fair market value of the assets of another corporation held immediately before the acquisition, and the transferor corporation distributes, within 12 months of the acquisition date, all of its assets (other than assets retained to meet claims) to its shareholders or creditors.

For these purposes, the definition of "control" is conformed to that contained in section 1504(a)(2) of the Code.

Where an acquiring corporation makes a qualified stock acquisition of a target corporation and the target corporation owns stock in a subsidiary, a special rule would treat the acquiring corporation as having also acquired the stock of the subsidiary, for purposes of determining whether the acquiring corporation has made a qualified stock acquisition of the subsidiary.

A special rule is also provided where an acquisition might qualify as both a qualified asset acquisition and a qualified stock acquisition. For example, where an acquiring corporation acquires all of the assets of a target corporation, and certain of those assets consist of all of the stock of a subsidiary, the transaction is treated as a qualified stock acquisition of the subsidiary and a qualified asset acquisition of all of the other assets of the target corporation.

The common-law doctrines of continuity of interest, continuity of business enterprise, and business purpose would have no applicability in determining whether a transaction qualifies as a qualified acquisition.

The bill repeals section 368. Acquisitive reorganizations ("A", "B" and "C" reorganizations and subsidiary mergers) under current law would be replaced by the rules for qualified acquisitions. The "D" reorganization rules would be replaced by special rules (described below) relating to qualified acquisitions between related parties. Transactions qualifying under current law as an "E" reorganization (a recapitalization) and an "F" reorganization (a mere change in identity, form, or place of organization of one corporation) are conformed to the definition of qualified acquisitions. Finally, the "G" reorganization rules (bankruptcy reorganizations), developed largely in response to continuity of interest problems in those types of transactions, are no longer needed and therefore are repealed.

B. Elective tax treatment of qualified acquisitions (new section 365 of the Code)

The corporate level tax consequences of a qualified acquisition are explicitly made elective. Under new section 365, all qualified acquisitions are treated as "carryover basis acquisitions" unless an election to be treated as a "cost basis acquisition" is made.

In general, elections may be made on a corporation-by-corporation basis. Thus, for example, if an acquiring corporation makes a qualified stock acquisition of both a target corporation and a target subsidiary, a cost basis election may be made for the target corporation but, if desired, no such election need be made for the target subsidiary.

Within a single corporation, the same election must generally apply for all of the assets of the corporation. A consistency rule would provide that assets that are acquired which were held by a single corporation during the consistency period must be treated consistently, either as all cost basis or all carryover basis.

Notwithstanding the consistency rule, an inconsistent carryover basis election may be made with respect to goodwill and certain other unamortizable intangibles. For example, a separate carryover basis election may be made with respect to such property even though a cost basis election is made for all of the other assets of the target corporation.

In general, no cost basis election may be made with respect to any qualified acquisition between related parties. These generally refer to transactions where, after application of the attribution rules, there is 50 percent or greater common ownership between the target and acquiring corporations. In addition, no cost basis election may be made with respect to a transaction qualifying as an "E" or "F" reorganization under current law. Finally, a mandatory cost basis election generally applies to a qualified asset acquisition where the acquiring corporation is a non-taxable entity (such as a tax-exempt entity, a regulated investment company, or a foreign corporation).

An election must be made before the later of (1) the 15th day of the 9th month following the month in which the acquisition date occurs, or (2) the date prescribed in regulations. Once made, an election is irrevocable.

C. Corporate level tax consequences of qualified acquisitions (sections 361, 362 and 381 of the Code)

The corporate level tax consequences of a qualified acquisition result directly from the election made at the corporate level. For example, in the case of a carryover basis acquisition, no gain or loss is recognized by the target corporation and the acquiring corporation obtains a carryover basis in any assets acquired. Attributes carry over under section 381.

In the case of a cost basis acquisition, the target corporation recognizes gain or loss and the acquiring corporation obtains a basis in any assets acquired determined under section 1012. Attributes do not carry over. Where the cost basis acquisition is a qualified stock acquisition, the target corporation is deemed to have sold all of its assets for fair market value at the close of the acquisition date in a transaction in which gain or loss is recognized, and then is treated as a new corporation which purchased all of such assets as of the beginning of the day after the acquisition date.

A special rule is provided in the case where a target corporation is a member of an affiliated group and a cost basis election is made. In general, unless the parties elect otherwise, a target corporation in that situation shall not be treated as a member of such group with respect to the gain or loss recognized in the transaction.

The basis of any property received by a target corporation in a qualified asset acquisition is the fair market value of such property on the acquisition date. The basis of stock acquired by an acquiring corporation in a qualified stock acquisition is determined under new section 1020 of the Code (see description below for rules concerning basis of stock of controlled subsidiaries).

Under the bill, sections 337 and 338 of current law are repealed.

D. Shareholder level tax consequences of qualfied acquisitions (sections 354, 356, and 358 of the Code)

In general, shareholder level tax consequences of a qualified acquisition are determined independent of the corporate level tax consequences and independent of the election made at the corporate level. Thus, even if a transaction is treated as a cost basis acquisition at the corporate level, it may be wholly or partly tax free at the shareholder level. In addition, shareholder level consequences are generally determined shareholder-by-shareholder, and the consequences to one shareholder do not affect the tax treatment of other shareholders or investors of the target corporation.

As a general rule, nonrecognition treatment is provided to shareholders or security holders of the target corporation upon receipt of "qualifying consideration," i.e., stock or securities of the acquiring corporation and, where the acquiring corporation is a member of an affiliated group, of the common parent of such group and any other member of such group specified in regulations. The nonrecognition rule applies to the receipt of securities only to the extent the issue price of any securities received does not exceed the adjusted basis of any securities surrendered.

A special rule is provided in the case of investment company stock. In general, stock or securities of an investment company does not qualify as qualifying consideration. An exception applies, however, and such stock or securities will qualify as qualifying consideration, if the target corporation is a diversified investment company. The term "investment company" and "diversified investment company" generally have the same meaning as under current law. In short, the existence of an investment company as the acquiring corporation may affect the tax treatment of the transaction at the shareholder level, but does not affect the corporate level tax consequences.

Receipt of "nonqualifying consideration" (i.e., any consideration other than qualifying consideration) generally results in recognition of gain to the shareholder or security holder. Such gain is treated as gain from the sale or exchange of property unless the receipt of nonqualifying consideration has the effect of a distribution of a dividend. The determination of dividend effect is made by treating the shareholder as having received only qualifying consideration in the exchange, and then as being redeemed of all or a portion of such qualifying consideration (to the extent of the nonqualifying consideration received). For these purposes, earnings and profits of both the target and acquiring corporations are generally taken into account.

Special rules are provided where there is a controlling corporate shareholder of the target corporation. In general, these rules are designed to avoid a second corporate level tax where the target corporation is acquired in a cost basis acquisition. In addition, where the target corporation is acquired in a carryover basis acquisition and all or part of the consideration is nonqualifying consideration, these rules are designed to insure that the controlling corporate shareholder or a distributee of such shareholder will recognize gain on the receipt of the nonqualifying consideration.

In general, shareholders or security holders obtain a substitute basis in any [qualifying] consideration received, and a fair market value basis in any nonqualifying consideration received. Controlling corporate shareholders of the target corporation generally obtain a basis in any qualifying consideration received equal to the lesser of substitute basis or fair market value basis.

CHAPTER 11. NONACQUISITIVE, NONDIVISIVE REORGANIZATIONS

A. TYPE E: RECAPITALIZATIONS

1. INTRODUCTION

Code: §§ 368(a)(1)(E); 354; 356; 358; 1032; 1036; 1223(1). Skim §§ 305, 306.

Regulations: §§ 1.301–1(*l*); 1.305–7(c); 1.368–2(e).

A tax-free reorganization sometimes involves only a single corporation which is undergoing a readjustment to its capital structure. The most common form of nonacquisitive, nondivisive reorganization is the recapitalization, which qualifies as a Type E reorganization if certain requirements are met. Recapitalizations traditionally have been used for a variety of business and tax objectives. A corporation may reshuffle its capital structure by exchanging stock for bonds in order to improve its debt/equity ratio and calm the nerves of creditors or as a condition to borrowing additional funds. Alternatively, it may exchange debt instruments for stock in order to lessen the sting of the double tax by withdrawing earnings in the form of deductible interest rather than nondeductible dividends. For closely held corporations, recapitalizations may be used as a device to shift control among the shareholders.

This overview of recapitalizations begins with an examination of the applicable judicial requirements, many of which have been previously encountered in connection with acquisitive reorganizations. We then consider to the most common type of recapitalization exchanges.

REVENUE RULING 82–34
1982–1 Cum.Bull. 59.

ISSUE

Advice has been requested regarding whether continuity of business enterprise is a requirement for a recapitalization to qualify as a reorganization under section 368(a)(1)(E) of the Internal Revenue Code.

LAW, ANALYSIS AND HOLDING

Section 368(a)(1)(E) of the Code provides that a "recapitalization" is a reorganization. A recapitalization has been defined as a "reshuffling of a capital structure within the framework of an existing corporation." Helvering v. Southwest Consolidated Corp., 315 U.S. 194 (1942), Ct.D. 1544, 1942–1 C.B. 218.

When a shareholder receives stock in a reorganization described in section 368(a)(1) and either before or after the transaction, the principal business assets of the transferor are sold or disposed of, a question arises whether the continuity of business enterprise requirement for a reorganization is satisfied. See sections 1.1002–1(c), 1.368–1(b) and 1.368–1(d) of the Income Tax Regulations.

The purpose of the reorganization provisions is to except from the general rule of recognizing gain or loss certain specifically described exchanges incident to corporate readjustments which effect only a readjustment of continuing interests in property under modified corporate forms. Section 1.368–1(b) of the regulations states that a continuity of the business enterprise under the modified corporate form is required in a reorganization.

Specifically, section 1.368–1(d) of the regulations provides, in general, that the transferee in a corporate reorganization must either (i) continue the transferor's historic business or (ii) use a significant portion of the transferor's historic business assets in a business.

The "continuity of business enterprise" requirement is closely related to the "continuity of shareholder interest" requirement in section 1.368–1(b) of the regulations in that both are concerned with determining whether a transaction involves an otherwise taxable transfer of stock or assets of one corporation to another corporation, as distinguished from a tax-free reorganization, which assumes only a readjustment of continuing interests under modified corporate form. The consideration of whether a transaction involves an otherwise taxable transfer of stock or assets of one corporation to another corporation is not present in a recapitalization because a recapitalization involves only a single corporation. Therefore, Rev.Rul. 77–415, 1977–2 C.B. 311, consistent with several court decisions, concludes that continuity of shareholder interest is not a requirement for a recapitalization to qualify as a reorganization under section 368(a)(1)(E) of the Code. Similarly, continuity of business enterprise is not a requirement for a recapitalization to qualify as a reorganization under section 368(a)(1)(E).

2. TYPES OF RECAPITALIZATIONS

Although immune from the continuity of interest and the continuity of business enterprise requirements, a recapitalization still must serve some business purpose in order to qualify for nonrecognition.[1] The courts have been rather tolerant in this area, and most of the business objectives set forth in the introduction to this chapter are acceptable for purposes of this requirement. In the area of recapitalizations, corporate business purposes frequently overlap or blend with objectives of the shareholders. To obtain an advance ruling, a taxpayer must demonstrate the *corporate* business purpose for the recapitalization.[2] In related situations, however, the courts have recognized that it may be unrealistic and impractical to distinguish corporate purposes from shareholder purposes in a closely held corporation.[3] Thus, share-

---

1. Reg. § 1.368–1(b).

2. Rev.Proc. 81–60, § 4.04, 1981–2 C.B. 680.

3. Lewis v. Commissioner, 176 F.2d 646 (1st Cir.1949); Estate of Parshelsky v. Commissioner, 303 F.2d 14 (2d Cir.1962). But

holder objectives germane to the corporation's business should be sufficient to satisfy the business purpose requirement.[4]

Recapitalizations fall into four broad categories depending upon the consideration exchanged. These categories raise different issues and are best studied separately.

a. BONDS FOR STOCK

The regulations provide that if a corporation discharges outstanding bonds by issuing preferred shares to the bondholders, the transaction qualifies as a Type E reorganization.[5] The result is the same if a corporation used common stock to discharge its obligations to the bondholders. Under Section 354(a), the bondholders generally will recognize no gain or loss on the exchange of their debt instruments solely for stock. Section 354(a)(2)(B) creates an exception to nonrecognition to the extent stock received is attributable to accrued and untaxed interest on the bonds. This interest component will be taxed as ordinary income under Section 61.[6] The basis of the stock received in a bonds-for-stock recapitalization will be determined under the familiar rules of Section 358, and the new shareholder will be entitled to a tacked holding period on the stock under Section 1223(1).

On the corporate side, matters are fairly routine. Since the corporation is issuing its stock, it initially will be excused from recognizing gain or loss by Section 1032. Section 108(e)(10)(A), however, provides that the corporation shall be treated as satisfying its indebtedness with an amount of money equal to the fair market value of its stock. In general, the corporation must recognize income from the cancellation of indebtedness to the extent that the principal plus the accrued but unpaid interest on the debt exceed the value of the stock issued in exchange. Section 108(e)(10)(A) is itself subject to exceptions for Title 11 bankruptcy and insolvency situations.[7] For purposes of this overview, it is sufficient to note that bonds-for-stock recapitalizations are no longer always immune from discharge of indebtedness principles.[8]

b. BONDS FOR BONDS

After initially contesting the issue,[9] the Service now concedes that if a creditor exchanges outstanding bonds for newly issued bonds in the

see Reg. § 1.355–2(b)(2), requiring a corporate business purpose in a tax-free division under Section 355.

4. Rafferty v. Commissioner, 452 F.2d 767 (1st Cir.1971), cert. denied 408 U.S. 922, 92 S.Ct. 2489 (1972).

5. Reg. § 1.368–2(e)(1). A recapitalization should be distinguished from conversion of a bond into stock pursuant to a conversion privilege in the bond. The Service has held that the latter situation does not constitute a taxable event as long as the bond is converted into stock of the

same corporation. Rev.Rul. 72–265, 1972–1 C.B. 222; Rev.Rul. 79–155, 1979–1 C.B. 153.

6. I.R.C. § 354(a)(3)(B).

7. I.R.C. § 108(e)(10)(B).

8. See I.R.C. § 108(e)(8), which generally provided protection prior to the Tax Reform Act of 1984.

9. See I.T. 2035, III–1 C.B. 55 (1924); Commissioner v. Neustadt's Trust, 131 F.2d 528, 530 (2d Cir.1942), affirming 43

same corporation, the transaction qualifies as a Type E reorganization.[10]   The bondholder in a bonds-for-bonds exchange generally will not recognize gain or loss unless the bonds received are attributable to accrued and untaxed interest [11] or the principal amount of the bonds received in the exchange exceeds the principal amount of the bonds surrendered.[12]   Income attributable to interest will be ordinary in character while gain recognized as a result of receipt of excess bonds generally will be either short- or long-term capital gain.[13]   The bondholder's basis in the new bonds will be determined under Section 358 and the new bonds will take a tacked holding period under Section 1223(1).

On the corporate side, the primary concern in a bonds-for-bonds recapitalization will be the discharge of indebtedness rules in Section 108.[14]   In addition, a bonds-for-bonds recapitalization may subject the corporation and bondholders to the intricate original issue discount provisions.[15]

c. STOCK FOR STOCK

The regulations provide three examples of stock-for-stock exchanges which qualify as reorganizations.   Two examples involve exchanges of outstanding preferred stock for common stock and the third involves an exchange of outstanding common for preferred.[16]   Thus, virtually all equity-for-equity exchanges will qualify as Type E reorganizations.[17]   In addition, exchanges of common stock in a corporation for common stock in the same corporation or preferred stock for preferred stock will qualify for nonrecognition under Section 1036.[18]

Sections 354 and 356 govern the shareholder level tax consequences of a stock-for-stock recapitalization.   The shareholders will recognize gain to the extent they receive boot in the exchange, and the gain will be characterized as gain from the exchange of the stock unless the transaction has "the effect of the distribution of a dividend." [19]   The shareholders' basis in the stock received in the exchange will be determined under Section 358 and will take a tacked holding period

B.T.A. 848 (1941), nonacq. 1941–1 C.B. 17, nonacq. withdrawn, acq. 1951–1 C.B. 2.

10. See I.T. 4081, 1952–1 C.B. 65; Rev. Rul. 77–415, 1977–2 C.B. 311.

11. I.R.C. § 354(a)(2)(B).   Cf. I.R.C. § 354(a)(3)(B).

12. I.R.C. §§ 354(a)(2)(A), 356(a)(1), (d).

13. I.R.C. §§ 354(a)(3)(A), 356(a)(1).   See Rev.Rul. 71–427, 1971–2 C.B. 183.

14. See I.R.C. § 108(e)(11).

15. In particular, see I.R.C. §§ 163(e), 1272–1275.

16. Reg. § 1.368–2(e)(2)–(4).

17. It is unlikely that a conversion of preferred stock into common stock in the

same corporation, or vice versa, pursuant to a conversion privilege in the stock would be a taxable event under the theory of Rev. Rul. 72–265, 1972–1 C.B. 222, which deals with convertible debt instruments.   Rev. Rul. 77–238, 1977–2 C.B. 115, however, holds that conversion of stock in furtherance of a corporate business purpose pursuant to a privilege contained in the corporation's certificate of incorporation is a recapitalization under Section 368(a)(1)(E).

18. Section 1036 also applies to exchanges between two individual stockholders.   Reg. § 1.1036–1(a).

19. I.R.C. § 356(a)(2).   See Rev.Rul. 84–114, below.

under Section 1223(1). The corporation will be entitled to nonrecognition under Section 1032 on the exchange of its stock.

Sections 305 and 306 also may come into play in a stock-for-stock recapitalization. The regulations provide that a recapitalization will be deemed to result in a distribution to which Section 305(c) applies if it is (1) pursuant to a plan to periodically increase a shareholder's proportionate interest in the assets or earnings and profits of the corporation or (2) with respect to preferred stock with dividend arrearages and the preferred shareholder increases his proportionate interest in the corporation as a result of the exchange.[20] The second alternative essentially precludes recapitalizations designed to remedy preferred stock dividend arrearages by taxing them under Sections 305(c) and (b)(4).[21]

Stock received in a recapitalization will constitute "Section 306 stock" under Section 306(c)(1)(B) if: (1) it is not common stock, (2) it was received pursuant to a plan of reorganization, (3) on its receipt gain or loss was not recognized to any extent under Sections 354 and 356, and (4) the effect of the transaction was substantially the same as the receipt of a stock dividend or the stock was received in exchange for Section 306 stock. The regulations provide a cash substitute test for determining whether the transaction has the effect of a dividend.[22] If cash received in lieu of the stock obtained in the recapitalization would have been a dividend under Section 356(a)(2), the transaction has substantially the same effect as a dividend. Thus, if the shareholders exchange common stock for common stock and a proportionate amount of preferred stock, the preferred shares will be Section 306 stock.

REVENUE RULING 84–114

1984–2 Cum.Bull. 90.

ISSUE

When nonvoting preferred stock and cash are received in an integrated transaction by a shareholder in exchange for voting common stock in a recapitalization described in section 368(a)(1)(E) of the Internal Revenue Code, does the receipt of cash have the effect of the distribution of a dividend within the meaning of section 356(a)(2)?

FACTS

Corporation *X* had outstanding 420 shares of voting common stock of which *A* owned 120 shares and *B*, *C* and *D* each owned 100 shares.

---

20. Reg. § 1.305–7(c). A preferred shareholder's proportionate interest increases if the greater of the fair market value or liquidation preference of the stock received in the exchange exceeds the issue price of the preferred stock surrendered. In such an exchange, the amount considered distributed to the preferred shareholder under Section 305(c) is the lesser of (1) the greater of the fair market value or liquidation preference of the preferred stock received over the issue price of the preferred stock surrendered or (2) the amount of the dividend arrearages.

21. Reg. § 1.305–5(d) Example (1). See also Reg. § 1.305–3(e) Example (12); Reg. § 1.305–5(d) Examples (2), (3) and (6).

22. Reg. § 1.306–3(d).

A, B, C and *D* were not related within the meaning of section 318(a) of the Code. *X* adopted a plan of recapitalization that permitted a shareholder to exchange each of 30 shares of voting common stock for either one share of nonvoting preferred stock or cash. Pursuant to the plan, *A* first exchanged 15 shares of voting common stock for cash and then exchanged 15 shares of voting common stock for 15 shares of nonvoting preferred stock. The facts and circumstances surrounding these exchanges were such that the exchanges constituted two steps in a single integrated transaction for purposes of sections 368(a)(1)(E) and 356(a)(2). The nonvoting preferred stock had no conversion features. In addition, the dividend and liquidation rights payable to *A* on 15 shares of nonvoting preferred stock were substantially less than the dividend and liquidation rights payable to *A* on 30 shares of voting common stock. *B, C,* and *D* did not participate in the exchange and will retain all their voting common stock in *X*. *X* had a substantial amount of post-1913 earnings and profits.

The exchange by *A* of voting common stock for nonvoting preferred stock and cash qualified as a recapitalization within the meaning of section 368(a)(1)(E) of the Code.

LAW AND ANALYSIS

Section 354(a)(1) of the Code provides that no gain or loss will be recognized if stock or securities in a corporation a party to a reorganization are, in pursuance of the plan of reorganization, exchanged solely for stock or securities in such corporation or in another corporation a party to the reorganization.

Section 356(a)(1) of the Code provides that if section 354 would apply to an exchange but for the fact that the property received in the exchange consists not only of property permitted by section 354 to be received without the recognition of gain but also of other property or money, then the gain, if any, will be recognized, but in an amount not in excess of the sum of the money and fair market value of the other property. Section 356(a)(2) provides that if such exchange has the effect of the distribution of a dividend (determined with the application of section 318(a)), then there will be treated as a dividend to each distributee such an amount of the gain recognized under section 356(a)(1) as is not in excess of each distributee's ratable share of the undistributed earnings and profits of the corporation accumulated after February 28, 1913.

Under section 302(b)(1) and section 302(a) of the Code a redemption will be treated as a distribution in part or full payment in exchange for stock if it is not essentially equivalent to a dividend to the shareholder.

Rev.Rul. 74–515, 1974–2 C.B. 118, and Rev.Rul. 74–516, 1974–2 C.B. 121, state that whether a reorganization distribution to which section 356 of the Code applies has the effect of a dividend must be determined by examining the facts and circumstances surrounding the distribution and looking to the principles for determining dividend equivalency developed under section 356(a)(2) and other provisions of the Code. See Ross v. United States, 173 F.Supp. 793 (Ct.Cl.1959), cert. denied, 361 U.S. 875 (1959). Rev.Rul. 74–516 indicates that in making a dividend equivalency determination under section 356(a)(2), it is proper to analogize to section 302 in appropriate cases. In Shimberg v. United States, 577 F.2d 283 (5th Cir.1978), cert. denied, 439 U.S. 1115 (1979), the courts indicated that in making a dividend equivalency determination under section 356(a)(2), an analogy to section 302 may be appropriate in cases involving single entity reorganizations.

In United States v. Davis, 397 U.S. 301 (1970), rehearing denied, 397 U.S. 1071 (1970), 1970–1 C.B. 62, the Supreme Court of the United States held that a redemption must result in a meaningful reduction of the shareholder's proportionate interest in the corporation in order not to be essentially equivalent to a dividend under section 302(b)(1) of the Code.

Rev.Rul. 75–502, 1975–2 C.B. 111, sets forth factors to be considered in determining whether a reduction in a shareholder's proportionate interest in a corporation is meaningful within the meaning of *Davis*. The factors considered are a shareholder's right to vote and exercise control, to participate in current earnings and accumulated surplus, and to share in net assets on liquidation. The reduction in the right to vote is of particular significance when a redemption causes a redeemed shareholder to lose the potential for controlling the redeeming corporation by acting in concert with only one other shareholder. See Rev.Rul. 76–364, 1976–2 C.B. 91.

The specific issue is whether, in determining dividend equivalency under section 356(a)(2) of the Code, it is proper to look solely at the change in *A*'s proportionate interest in *X* that resulted from *A*'s exchange of voting common stock for cash, or instead, whether consideration should be given to the total change in *A*'s proportionate interest in *X* that resulted from the exchange of voting common stock for both cash and nonvoting preferred stock.

In Rev.Rul. 55–745, 1955–2 C.B. 223, the Internal Revenue Service announced that for purposes of section 302(b)(3) of the Code, it would follow the decision in Zenz v. Quinlivan, 213 F.2d 914 (6th Cir.1954), that a complete termination of shareholder interest may be achieved when a shareholder's entire stock interest in a corporation is disposed of partly through redemption and partly through sale. See also Rev. Rul. 75–447, 1975–2 C.B. 113, in which the *Zenz* rationale was applied to section 302(b)(2).

Since the exchange of voting common stock for cash and the exchange of voting common stock for nonvoting preferred stock constitute an integrated transaction, in this situation involving a single corporation, it is proper to apply the *Zenz* rationale so that both exchanges are taken into consideration in determining whether there has been a meaningful reduction of *A*'s proportionate interest in *X* within the meaning of *Davis*. Compare Rev.Rul. 75–83, 1975–1 C.B.

112, which holds that a distribution in connection with a transaction qualifying under section 368(a)(1)(A) of the Code will be viewed as having been made by the acquired or transferor corporation and not by the acquiring or transferee corporation for purposes of making a dividend equivalency determination under section 356(a)(2).

If the exchange of voting common stock for preferred stock and cash in this situation had been tested under section 302 of the Code as a redemption, it would not have qualified under section 302(b)(2) or (3) because there was neither an adequate reduction in A's voting stock interest nor a complete termination of that interest. In determining whether this situation is analogous to a redemption meeting the requirements of section 302(b)(1), it is significant that A's interest in the voting common stock of X was reduced from 28.57 percent ($^{120}/_{420}$) to 23.08 percent ($^{90}/_{390}$) so that A went from a position of holding a number of shares of voting common stock that afforded A control of X if A acted in concert with only one other shareholder, to a position where such action was not possible. Moreover, it is significant that A no longer holds the largest voting stock interest in X. In addition, although A received dividend and liquidation rights from the 15 shares of nonvoting preferred stock, these were substantially less than the dividend and liquidation rights of the 30 shares of voting common stock A surrendered. Accordingly, the requirements of section 302(b)(1) would have been met if the transaction had been tested under section 302, and, therefore, the cash received by A did not have the effect of the distribution of a dividend within the meaning of section 356(a)(2).

HOLDING

When A received cash and nonvoting preferred stock of X in an integrated transaction in exchange for voting common stock of X in a recapitalization described in section 368(a)(1)(E) of the Code, the receipt of cash did not have the effect of the distribution of a dividend within the meaning of section 356(a)(2).

NOTE

The receipt of boot in a recapitalization is yet another transaction for which the tax stakes were altered by the recent changes in federal tax rates. As the above ruling demonstrates, the treatment of boot received in a recapitalization is governed by Section 356(a)(2), which incorporates the same "dividend within gain" concept studied earlier in connection with acquisitive reorganizations.[1] As a result, even if the receipt of boot has the effect of a dividend, the shareholder's income will be limited to the gain recognized. Since dividends and capital gains are taxed at nearly the same rate, individual shareholders often will be indifferent as to the characterization of their income.

These new economics may prompt the Service to treat the receipt of boot as a separate dividend distribution (without basis recovery)

---

1. See Chapter 10C1, supra.

under the principles of the *Bazley* case, which follows in the next section of this chapter.[2]

d. STOCK FOR BONDS

BAZLEY v. COMMISSIONER

Supreme Court of the United States, 1947.
331 U.S. 737, 67 S.Ct. 1489.

Mr. Justice FRANKFURTER delivered the opinion of the Court.

* * *

In the *Bazley* case, No. 287, the Commissioner of Internal Revenue assessed an income tax deficiency against the taxpayer for the year 1939. Its validity depends on the legal significance of the recapitalization in that year of a family corporation in which the taxpayer and his wife owned all but one of the Company's one thousand shares. These had a par value of $100. Under the plan of reorganization the taxpayer, his wife, and the holder of the additional share were to turn in their old shares and receive in exchange for each old share five new shares of no par value, but of a stated value of $60, and new debenture bonds, having a total face value of $400,000, payable in ten years but callable at any time. Accordingly, the taxpayer received 3,990 shares of the new stock for the 798 shares of his old holding and debentures in the amount of $319,200. At the time of these transactions the earned surplus of the corporation was $855,783.82.

The Commissioner charged to the taxpayer as income the full value of the debentures. The Tax Court affirmed the Commissioner's determination, against the taxpayer's contention that as a "recapitalization" the transaction was a tax-free "reorganization" and that the debentures were "securities in a corporation a party to a reorganization," "exchanged solely for stock or securities in such corporation" "in pursuance of the plan of reorganization," and as such no gain is recognized for income tax purposes. Internal Revenue Code, §§ 112(g)(1)(E) [the predecessor of § 368(a)(1)(E)] and 112(b)(3). The Tax Court found that the recapitalization had "no legitimate corporate business purpose" and was therefore not a "reorganization" within the statute. The distribution of debentures, it concluded, was a disguised dividend, taxable as earned income under §§ [61(a) and 301]. 4 T.C. 897. The Circuit Court of Appeals for the Third Circuit, sitting *en banc*, affirmed, two judges dissenting. 155 F.2d 237.

Unless a transaction is a reorganization contemplated by § [368], any exchange of "stock or securities" in connection with such transaction, cannot be "in pursuance of the plan of reorganization." While § [368(a)] informs us that "reorganization" means, among other things, "a recapitalization," it does not inform us what "recapitalization" means. "Recapitalization" in connection with the income tax has been part of the revenue laws since 1921. 42 Stat. 227, 230, § 202(c)(2).

---

2. See also Reg. § 1.302–1(*l*).

Congress has never defined it and the Treasury Regulations shed only limited light. Treas.Reg. 103, § 19.112(g). One thing is certain. Congress did not incorporate some technical concept, whether that of accountants or of other specialists, into § [368(a)], assuming that there is agreement among specialists as to the meaning of recapitalization. And so, recapitalization as used in § [368(a)] must draw its meaning from its function in that section. It is one of the forms of reorganization which obtains the privileges afforded by § [368(a)]. Therefore, "recapitalization" must be construed with reference to the presuppositions and purpose of § [368(a)]. It was not the purpose of the reorganization provision to exempt from payment of a tax what as a practical matter is realized gain. Normally, a distribution by a corporation, whatever form it takes, is a definite and rather unambiguous event. It furnishes the proper occasion for the determination and taxation of gain. But there are circumstances where a formal distribution, directly or through exchange of securities, represents merely a new form of the previous participation in an enterprise, involving no change of substance in the rights and relations of the interested parties one to another or to the corporate assets. As to these, Congress has said that they are not to be deemed significant occasions for determining taxable gain.

These considerations underlie § [368(a)] and they should dominate the scope to be given to the various sections, all of which converge toward a common purpose. Application of the language of such a revenue provision is not an exercise in framing abstract definitions. In a series of cases this Court has withheld the benefits of the reorganization provision in situations which might have satisfied provisions of the section treated as inert language, because they were not reorganizations of the kind with which § [368], in its purpose and particulars, concerns itself. See Pinellas Ice & Cold Storage Co. v. Commissioner, 287 U.S. 462; Gregory v. Helvering, 293 U.S. 465; LeTulle v. Scofield, 308 U.S. 415.

Congress has not attempted a definition of what is recapitalization and we shall follow its example. The search for relevant meaning is often satisfied not by a futile attempt at abstract definition but by pricking a line through concrete applications. Meaning frequently is built up by assured recognition of what does not come within a concept the content of which is in controversy. Since a recapitalization within the scope of § [368] is an aspect of reorganization, nothing can be a recapitalization for this purpose unless it partakes of those characteristics of a reorganization which underlie the purpose of Congress in postponing the tax liability.

No doubt there was a recapitalization of the Bazley corporation in the sense that the symbols that represented its capital were changed, so that the fiscal basis of its operations would appear very differently on its books. But the form of a transaction as reflected by correct corporate accounting opens questions as to the proper application of a taxing statute; it does not close them. Corporate accounting may represent that correspondence between change in the form of capital structure and essential identity in fact which is of the essence of a transaction relieved from taxation as a reorganization. What is controlling is that a new arrangement intrinsically partake of the elements of reorganization which underlie the Congressional exemption and not merely give the appearance of it to accomplish a distribution of earnings. In the case of a corporation which has undistributed earnings, the creation of new corporate obligations which are transferred to stockholders in relation to their former holdings, so as to produce, for all practical purposes, the same result as a distribution of cash earnings of equivalent value, cannot obtain tax immunity because cast in the form of a recapitalization-reorganization. The governing legal rule can hardly be stated more narrowly. To attempt to do so would only challenge astuteness in evading it. And so it is hard to escape the conclusion that whether in a particular case a paper recapitalization is no more than an admissible attempt to avoid the consequences of an outright distribution of earnings turns on details of corporate affairs, judgment on which must be left to the Tax Court. See Dobson v. Commissioner, 320 U.S. 489.

What have we here? No doubt, if the Bazley corporation had issued the debentures to Bazley and his wife without any recapitalization, it would have made a taxable distribution. Instead, these debentures were issued as part of a family arrangement, the only additional ingredient being an unrelated modification of the capital account. The debentures were found to be worth at least their principal amount, and they were virtually cash because they were callable at the will of the corporation which in this case was the will of the taxpayer. One does not have to pursue the motives behind actions, even in the more ascertainable forms of purpose, to find, as did the Tax Court, that the whole arrangement took this form instead of an outright distribution of cash or debentures, because the latter would undoubtedly have been taxable income whereas what was done could, with a show of reason, claim the shelter of the immunity of a recapitalization-reorganization.

The Commissioner, the Tax Court and the Circuit Court of Appeals agree that nothing was accomplished that would not have been accomplished by an outright debenture dividend. And since we find no misconception of law on the part of the Tax Court and the Circuit Court of Appeals, whatever may have been their choice of phrasing, their application of the law to the facts of this case must stand. A "reorganization" which is merely a vehicle, however elaborate or elegant, for conveying earnings from accumulations to the stockholders is not a reorganization under § [368]. This disposes of the case as a matter of law, since the facts as found by the Tax Court bring them within it. And even if this transaction were deemed a reorganization, the facts would equally sustain the imposition of the tax on the debentures under § [354 and 356]. Commissioner v. Estate of Bedford, 325 U.S. 283.

In the *Adams* case, No. 209, the taxpayer owned all but a few of the 5914 shares of stock outstanding out of an authorized 6000, par value $100. By a plan of reorganization, the authorized capital was reduced by half, to $295,700, divided into 5914 shares of no par value but having a stated value of $50 per share. The 5914 old shares were cancelled and the corporation issued in exchange therefor 5914 shares of the new no-par common stock and 6 per cent 20 year debenture bonds in the principal amount of $295,700. The exchange was made on the basis of one new share of stock and one $50 bond for each old share. The old capital account was debited in the sum of $591,400, a new no-par capital account was credited with $295,700, and the balance of $295,700 was credited to a "Debenture Payable" account. The corporation at this time had accumulated earnings available for distribution in a sum not less than $164,514.82, and this account was left unchanged. At the time of the exchange, the debentures had a value not less than $164,208.82.

The Commissioner determined an income tax deficiency by treating the debenture bonds as a distribution of the corporation's accumulated earnings. The Tax Court sustained the Commissioner's determination, 5 T.C. 351, and the Circuit Court of Appeals affirmed. 155 F.2d 246. The case is governed by our treatment of the *Bazley* case. The finding by the Tax Court that the reorganization had no purpose other than to achieve the distribution of the earnings, is unaffected by the bookkeeping detail of leaving the surplus account unaffected. * * *

Other claims raised have been considered but their rejection does not call for discussion.

Judgments affirmed.

Mr. Justice DOUGLAS and Mr. Justice BURTON dissent in both cases for the reasons stated in the joint dissent of Judges MARIS and GOODRICH in the court below. Bazley v. Commissioner, 3 Cir., 155 F.2d 237, 244.

NOTE

The *Bazley* case involved a pro rata exchange of common stock for common stock and bonds. Later cases have offered some hope for qualifying a stock-for-stock-and-bonds exchange under Section 368(a)(1)(E) if the exchange is not pro rata.[1] Several tax problems remain for an exchanging shareholder even if the transaction constitutes a Type E reorganization. The rules in Section 356(a)(2) and (d) will likely result in characterization of gain as a dividend to the extent of the fair market value of bonds received and the corporation's earnings and profits. Even if the shareholder does not realize a gain on the exchange, the regulations suggest that a stock-for-stock-and-bonds recapitalization may be separately analyzed with the receipt of bonds being

---

1. See Seide v. Commissioner, 18 T.C. 502 (1952).

treated simply as a Section 301 distribution.[2] Stock-for-bonds exchanges also may give rise to original issue discount.[3]

PROBLEMS

1. Recap Corporation has $100,000 of accumulated earnings and profits and makes a pro rata distribution to each of its ten shareholders of new common voting stock worth $20,000 and new callable preferred stock worth $10,000 in exchange for each shareholder's old common voting stock worth $30,000.

(a) What result to the shareholders on the exchange?

(b) What result when Recap calls the preferred stock?

(c) What result if a shareholder sells his preferred stock?

(d) What result if Recap had a deficit in its earnings and profits account at the time of the distribution but it foresaw future potential profits?

2. The ten equal shareholders of Shuffle Corporation each have a $10,000 basis in their Shuffle common voting stock which has a $50,000 fair market value. Shuffle has $250,000 of earnings and profits. What result if the ten shareholders each transfer all their common voting stock in return for common voting stock worth $25,000 and bonds worth $25,000.

3. Leverage Corporation has 8% interest bonds outstanding with a face amount of $1,000,000 and a fair market value of $800,000. It redeems these bonds and issues new 12% interest bonds with a fair market value and a face amount of $800,000.

(a) Will the transaction qualify as a reorganization?

(b) What result in (a), above, if 12% interest bearing bonds with a face amount of $800,000 are redeemed for 8% interest bonds with a face amount of $1,000,000 and both sets of bonds have the same fair market value of $800,000?

4. Does an exchange of bonds for stock qualify as an "E" reorganization? Why would a corporation engage in such an exchange?

B. TYPE D: LIQUIDATION—REINCORPORATION

Code: §§ 368(a)(1)(D), (a)(2)(H); 354(b); 381(a)(2). Skim §§ 331; 336; 354(a); 356(a); 358; 361; 1032.

2. Reg. § 1.301–1(*l*). Reg. § 1.354–1(d) Example (3) provides that if a shareholder surrenders all of his stock solely for bonds, the tax consequences of the exchange are determined under Section 302 whether or not the transaction is a recapitalization under Section 368(a)(1)(E).

3. See I.R.C. §§ 163(e), 1272–1275. See generally Eustice, The Tax Reform Act of 1984 3–35, 36 (1984).

SMOTHERS v. UNITED STATES *

United States Court of Appeals, Fifth Circuit, 1981.
642 F.2d 894.

WISDOM, Circuit Judge:

J.E. and Doris Smothers filed this civil action to obtain a refund of federal income taxes they paid under protest. This dispute arises from the dissolution of one of their wholly-owned business corporations. The taxpayers contend that the assets distributed to them by that corporation should be taxed at the capital gain rate applicable to liquidating distributions. The Internal Revenue Service (IRS) counters by characterizing the dissolution as part of a reorganization, thereby rendering the taxpayers' receipt of the distributed assets taxable at ordinary income rates. The district court viewed the transaction as a reorganization and ruled for the IRS. We affirm.

I.

The facts were stipulated. J.E. and Doris Smothers are married and reside in Corpus Christi, Texas. In 1956, they and an unrelated third party organized Texas Industrial Laundries of San Antonio, Inc. (TIL). The Smothers' owned all of its outstanding stock from 1956 through the tax year in issue, 1969. TIL engaged in the business of renting industrial uniforms and other industrial cleaning equipment, such as wiping cloths, dust control devices, and continuous toweling. It owned its own laundry equipment as well.

Shortly after the incorporation of TIL, the taxpayers organized another corporation, Industrial Uniform Services, Inc. (IUS), specifically to oppose a particular competitor in the San Antonio industrial laundry market. The taxpayers owned all of the stock of IUS from the time of its organization until its dissolution. Unlike TIL, IUS did not own laundry equipment; it had to contract with an unrelated company to launder the uniforms it rented to customers. J.E. Smothers personally managed IUS, as well as TIL, but chose not to pay himself a salary from IUS in any of the years of its existence.[1]

IUS evidently succeeded in drawing business away from competing firms, for TIL purchased its main competitor in 1965. IUS continued in business, however, until 1969. On the advice of their accountant, the taxpayers then decided to dissolve IUS and sell all of its non-liquid assets to TIL. On November 1, 1969, IUS adopted a plan of liquidation in compliance with I.R.C. § 337, and on November 30, it sold the

---

* Some footnotes omitted.

1. Although the record does not specifically so indicate, and although it is unnecessary to our resolution of this case, we think it instructive to note that IUS apparently did not pay any dividends during its existence, either. We deduce that from the following facts of record: (1) the Smothers' cost basis in their IUS stock was $1000.00; (2) IUS had "approximately $148,162.35" in accumulated earnings and profits at the time of its dissolution; (3) IUS's book value at the time of its dissolution was $149,162.35.

following assets to TIL for cash at their fair market value (stipulated to be the same as their book value):

Assets	Amount
Noncompetitive covenant	$ 3,894.60
Fixed assets	491.25
Rental property	18,000.00
Prepaid insurance	240.21
Water deposit	7.50
Total	$22,637.56 [3]

The noncompetitive covenant constituted part of the consideration received by IUS from its purchase of a small competitor. The fixed assets consisted of incidental equipment (baskets, shelves, and a sewing machine), two depreciated delivery vehicles, and IUS's part interest in an airplane. The rental property was an old apartment building in Corpus Christi on land with business potential. These assets collectively represented about 15% of IUS's net value. The parties stipulated that none of these assets were necessary to carry out IUS's business.

After this sale, IUS promptly distributed its remaining assets to its shareholders, the taxpayers, and then dissolved under Texas law:

Assets	Amount
Cash (received from TIL)	$ 22,637.56
Cash (of IUS)	2,003.05
Notes receivable	138,000.00
Accrued interest receivable	35.42
Claim against the State of Texas	889.67
Liabilities assumed	(14,403.35)
Total	$149,162.35

TIL hired all three of IUS's employees immediately after the dissolution, and TIL continued to serve most of IUS's customers.

In computing their federal income tax liability for 1969, the taxpayers treated this distribution by IUS as a distribution in complete liquidation within § 331(a)(1). Accordingly, they reported the difference between the value of the assets they received in that distribution, $149,162.35, and the basis of their IUS stock, $1,000, as long-term capital gain. Upon audit, the IRS recharacterized the transaction between TIL and IUS as a reorganization within § 368(a)(1)(D), and therefore treated the distribution to the taxpayers as equivalent to a dividend under § 356(a)(2). Because IUS had sufficient earnings and profits to cover that distribution, the entire distribution was therefore taxable to the Smothers' at ordinary income rates. The IRS timely assessed a $71,840.84 deficiency against the Smothers'. They paid that amount and filed this suit for a refund.

---

3. The parties stipulated that the purchase price was $22,637.56, and the district court found that as a fact. The items listed add to $22,633.56, however. We ignore the discrepancy and accept the stipulation.

The district court held that the transaction constituted a reorganization and rendered judgment for the IRS. United States v. Smothers, S.D.Tex.1979, 79–1 U.S.Tax.Cas. 86,414, 45 A.F.T.R.2d 80–596.

II.

Subchapter C of the Internal Revenue Code broadly contemplates that the retained earnings of a continuing business carried on in corporate form can be placed in the hands of its shareholders only after they pay a tax on those earnings at ordinary income rates. That general rule is, of course, primarily a consequence of § 301, which taxes dividend distributions as ordinary income. The Code provides for capital gain treatment of corporate distributions in a few limited circumstances, but only when there is either a significant change in relative ownership of the corporation, as in certain redemption transactions, or when the shareholders no longer conduct the business themselves in corporate form, as in true liquidation transactions. The history of Subchapter C in large part has been the story of how Congress, the courts, and the IRS have been called upon to foil attempts by taxpayers to abuse these exceptional provisions. Ingenious taxpayers have repeatedly devised transactions which formally come within these provisions, yet which have the effect of permitting shareholders to withdraw profits at capital gain rates while carrying on a continuing business enterprise in corporate form without substantial change in ownership. This is just such a case.

The transaction in issue here is of the genus known as liquidation-reincorporation, or reincorporation. The common denominator of such transactions is their use of the liquidation provisions of the Code, which permit liquidating distributions to be received at capital gain rates, as a device through which the dividend provisions may be circumvented.[7] Reincorporations come in two basic patterns. In one, the corporation is dissolved and its assets are distributed to its shareholders in liquidation. The shareholders then promptly reincorporate all the assets necessary to the operation of the business, while retaining accumulated cash or other surplus assets. The transaction in this case is of the alternate form. In it, the corporation transfers the assets necessary to its business to another corporation owned by the same shareholders in exchange for securities or, as here, for cash, and then liquidates. If the minimal technical requirements of § [former.] 337 are met, as they indisputably were here, the exchange at the corporate level will not result in the recognition of gain by the transferor corporation. If formal compliance with the liquidation provisions were the only necessity, both patterns would enable shareholders to withdraw profits from

---

7. Other tax benefits may be reaped from reincorporation transactions in appropriate circumstances: e.g., elimination of the earnings and profits account of the old corporation in order to avoid the § 531 tax on unreasonable accumulation; and a step-up in the tax basis of depreciable corporate assets at capital gain rates to the extent permitted by § 1245 and § 1250. In light of IUS's relatively large earnings and profits account, the former benefit is not a trivial one here.

a continuing corporate business enterprise at capital gain rates by paper-shuffling. Unchecked, these reincorporation techniques would eviscerate the dividend provisions of the Code.

That result can be avoided by recharacterizing such transactions, in accordance with their true nature, as reorganizations. A reorganization is, in essence, a transaction between corporations that results merely in "a continuance of the proprietary interests in the continuing enterprise under modified corporate form"—a phrase that precisely describes the effect of a reincorporation. Lewis v. Commissioner, 1 Cir. 1949, 176 F.2d 646, 648. Congress specifically recognized that the throw-off of surplus assets to shareholders in the course of a reorganization can be equivalent to a dividend, and if so, should be taxed as such. §§ 356(a)(1)–(2). The reincorporation transactions described above result in a dividend payment to the shareholders in every meaningful financial sense. The assets retained by the shareholders therefore should be taxed as dividends as long as the transaction can be fitted within the technical requirements of one of the six classes of reorganizations recognized by § 368(a)(1).

In general, reincorporation transactions are most easily assimilated into § 368(a)(1)(D) ("D reorganization"), as the IRS attempted to do in this case.[9] A transaction qualifies as a D reorganization only if it meets six statutory requirements:

(1) There must be a transfer by a corporation (§ 368(a)(1) (D));

(2) of substantially all of its assets (§ 354(b)(1)(A));

(3) to a corporation controlled by the shareholders of the transferor corporation, or by the transferor corporation itself (§ 368(a)(1)(D));

(4) in exchange for stock or securities of the transferee corporation (§ 354(a)(1));

(5) followed by a distribution of the stock or securities of the transferee corporation to the transferor's shareholders (§ 354(b)(1)(B));

(6) pursuant to a plan of reorganization (§ 368(a)(1)(D)).

On this appeal, the taxpayers concede that the transaction in issue meets every technical prerequisite for characterization as a D reorganization, except for one. They argue that since the assets sold by IUS to

---

9. Reincorporations may also fit within § 368(a)(1)(F) ("[a] mere change in identity, form or place of organization, however effected"). * * * The government did not press that theory on appeal. Doubtless that owes to its general reluctance to extend the scope of § 368(a)(1)(F) to acquisitive reorganizations, which derives from the fact that net operating losses may be carried back after an F reorganization. § 381(b)(3). See generally Cohen, The "New F" Reorganization, 36 N.Y.U.Inst. Fed.Tax. 833 (1978). The IRS has in the past occasionally advanced more exotic arguments against reincorporations—e.g., the theory that no real "liquidation" occurs in such transactions, and the theory that even if a liquidation does occur, the distribution of surplus assets is a dividend functionally unrelated to the liquidation— but it did not so argue here. * * *

TIL amounted to only 15% of IUS's net worth, TIL did not acquire "substantially all of the assets" of IUS within the meaning of § 354(b)(1)(A).

We hold to the contrary. The words "substantially all assets" are not self-defining. What proportion of a corporation's assets is "substantially all" in this context, and less obviously, what "assets" are to be counted in making this determination, cannot be answered without reference to the structure of Subchapter C. To maintain the integrity of the dividend provisions of the Code, "substantially all assets" in this context must be interpreted as an inartistic way of expressing the concept of "transfer of a continuing business". As this Court implied in Reef Corp. v. Commissioner, 5 Cir.1966, 368 F.2d 125, 132, cert. denied, 1967, 386 U.S. 1018, 87 S.Ct. 1371, 18 L.Ed.2d 454, it is in a sense simply a limited codification of the general nonstatutory "continuity of business enterprise" requirement applicable to all reorganizations.

This interpretation finds support in the history of § 368(a)(1)(D) and § 354(b)(1)(A). The Internal Revenue Code of 1939 had no provision equivalent to the "substantially all assets" requirement, and courts almost uniformly approved attempts by the IRS to treat reincorporation transactions as reorganizations within the predecessor of § 368(a)(1)(D) in the 1939 Code. The "substantially all assets" requirement of § 354(b)(1)(A) and the amendment of § 368(a)(1)(D) incorporating that requirement were added during the 1954 recodification as part of a package of amendments aimed at plugging a different loophole—the bail-out of corporate earnings and profits at capital gains rates through divisive reorganizations. There is no indication that Congress wished to relax the application of the reorganization provisions to reincorporation transactions. Indeed, the committee reports indicate the contrary. The Senate report accompanying the bill that contained the "substantially all assets" requirement of § 354(b)(1)(A) and the parallel amendment to § 368(a)(1)(D) stated that the purpose of those changes was only "to insure that the tax consequences of the distribution of stocks or securities to shareholders or security holders in connection with divisive reorganizations will be governed by the requirements of section 355". The report expressly noted that except with respect to divisive reorganizations, the reorganization provisions "are the same as under existing law and are stated in substantially the same form". Even more significantly, the original House version of the 1954 Code contained a provision specifically dealing with reincorporation transactions. That provision was dropped in conference because the conferees felt that such transactions "can appropriately be disposed of by judicial decision or by regulation within the framework of the other provisions of the bill". As the court said in Pridemark, Inc. v. Commissioner, 4 Cir.1965, 345 F.2d 35, 40, this response shows that "the committee was aware of the problem and thought the present statutory scheme adequate to deal with it". By implication, this passage approved the IRS's use of the predecessor of § 368(a)(1)(D) to meet the problem, and shows that the "substantially all assets" amendment was not thought to restrict its use.

Courts have almost unanimously so interpreted the "substantially all assets" language. Moreover, they have also interpreted the other technical conditions for a D reorganization in ways that accomplish the congressional intent to reach reincorporation transactions. For example, the literal language of § 368(a)(1)(D) and §§ 354(a), 354(b)(1)(B) requires that the transferee corporation "exchange" some of its "stock or securities" for the assets of the transferor, and that those items be "distributed" to the shareholders of the transferor, before a D reorganization can be found. Yet both of those requirements have uniformly been ignored as "meaningless gestures" in the reincorporation context, in which the same shareholders own all the stock of both corporations.[14] Smothers does not even challenge the applicability of that principle here.

Properly interpreted, therefore, the assets looked to when making the "substantially all assets" determination should be all the assets, and only the assets, necessary to operate the corporate business— whether or not those assets would appear on a corporate balance sheet constructed according to generally accepted accounting principles. Two errors in particular should be avoided. Inclusion of assets unnecessary to the operation of the business in the "substantially all assets" assessment would open the way for the shareholders of any enterprise to turn dividends into capital gain at will. For example, if we assume that "substantially all" means greater than 90%, then a corporation need only cease declaring dividends and accumulate surplus liquid assets until their value exceeds 10% of the total value of all corporate assets. The shareholders could then transfer the assets actively used in the business to a second corporation owned by them and liquidate the old corporation. Such a liquidating distribution would be a dividend in any meaningful sense, but an interpretation of "substantially all assets" that took surplus assets into account would permit the shareholders to treat it as capital gain. Indeed, such an interpretation would perversely treat a merely nominal distribution of retained earnings as a dividend, but would permit substantial distributions to be made at capital gain rates. Courts therefore have invariably ignored all surplus

14. The "meaningless gesture" language is from James Armour, Inc., 1964, 43 T.C. 295, 307. See also, e.g., Atlas Tool Co. v. Commissioner, 3 Cir.1980, 614 F.2d 860, 865, cert. denied, 1980, 449 U.S. 836, 101 S.Ct. 110, 66 L.Ed.2d 43; Davant v. Commissioner, 5 Cir.1966, 366 F.2d 874, 886–87, cert. denied, 1967, 386 U.S. 1022, 87 S.Ct. 1370, 18 L.Ed.2d 460; *Ralph C. Wilson,* 1966, 46 T.C. 334, 344. Other technical requirements have been liberally construed in appropriate situations to foil reincorporations. For instance, § 354(b)(1) (B) technically requires that all properties received from the transferor corporation be distributed before a D reorganization can be found, but a "constructive distribution" was found in *David T. Grubbs,* 1962, 39 T.C. 42. Similarly, § 368(a)(1)(D) requires a "plan of reorganization", but a formal written plan is not necessary and the taxpayer's phraseology is not controlling if the transaction is in substance a reorganization. Atlas Tool Co. v. Commissioner, 614 F.2d at 866; *Ralph C. Wilson,* 46 T.C. at 345.

assets and have focused on the operating assets of the business—the tangible assets actively used in the business—when making the "substantially all assets" assessment.[15]

Second, exclusion of assets not shown on a balance sheet constructed according to generally accepted accounting principles from the "substantially all assets" assessment would offer an unjustified windfall to the owners of service businesses conducted in corporate form. The most important assets of such a business may be its reputation and the availability of skilled management and trained employees, none of which show up on a standard balance sheet. Other courts have correctly recognized that in appropriate cases those intangible assets alone may constitute substantially all of the corporate assets. Otherwise, for example, a sole legal practitioner who owns nothing but a desk and chair could incorporate himself, accumulate earnings, and then set up a new corporation and liquidate the old at capital gain rates—as long as he is careful to buy a new desk and chair for the new corporation, rather than transferring the old.

When these principles are applied to this case, it is plain that "substantially all of the assets" of IUS were transferred to TIL, and that the transaction as a whole constituted a reorganization. TIL and IUS were both managed and wholly owned by Smothers. By the nature of its business, IUS was wholly a service enterprise; indeed, the parties stipulated that none of the tangible assets of IUS were necessary to the operation of its business. The extent to which those tangible assets were transferred to TIL is therefore entirely irrelevant. IUS's most important assets—its reputation, sales staff, and the managerial services of Smothers—were all transferred to TIL. TIL rehired all three of IUS's employees immediately after IUS's liquidation, and continued to serve IUS's old customers. The same business enterprise was conducted by the same people under the same ownership, and the only assets removed from corporate solution were accumulated liquid assets unnecessary to the operation of the business. To treat this transaction as other than a reorganization would deny economic reality; to permit Smothers to extract the retained earnings of IUS at capital gain rates would make a mockery of the dividend provisions of the Internal Revenue Code.

We do not perceive ordinary income treatment here to be particularly harsh, or a "tax trap for the unwary". It places the Smothers' only in the position they would have been in if they had extracted the retained earnings of IUS as the Code contemplates they should have—by periodically declaring dividends.[18]

15. * * * Note that liquid assets are "necessary" to the extent they represent working capital. See Swanson v. United States, 9 Cir.1973, 479 F.2d 539, 545–46; Ross Michel Simon Trust v. United States, Ct.Cl. 1968, 402 F.2d 272, 280.

18. Of course, the progressive structure of the income tax in a sense penalizes the plaintiff, since dividend income that could have been spread over many years is concentrated in one year, but that result was avoidable at the taxpayer's discretion. Similarly, he could have taken out some of the earnings in the form of a salary. Note that in all probability, Smothers did not actually defer enjoyment of the retained

Affirmed.

GARZA, Circuit Judge, dissenting:

After carefully reading the majority's opinion, I find that I must respectfully dissent. Unlike my Brothers, who apparently feel that it is their duty to "plug loopholes", I would remain content in applying the tax law as it reads leaving the United States Congress to deal with the consequences of the tax law as it has been drafted. The only issue before this Court on appeal is whether or not IUS transferred "substantially all of its assets" to TIL. Instead of dealing with this straightforward question, the majority has made a case of evil against liquidation-reincorporation abuses and, in an attempt to remedy every such perceived abuse, they have relieved the Congress of its burden to change the law heretofore requiring that "substantially all" of a corporation's assets be transferred to now read that "only those assets necessary to operate the corporate business" be transferred in order to meet the "D reorganization" requirements. Essentially, the majority has changed the definition of "substantially all assets" to mean only "necessary operating assets." I believe if Congress had meant "necessary operating assets" it would have said so instead of specifically requiring that "substantially all" of the assets be transferred. In my mind "substantially all" plainly means *all* of the assets except for an *insubstantial* amount. Under such a definition, the sale of 15% of IUS's assets to TIL could hardly be defined as "substantially all" of IUS's assets.

However, even after having redefined "substantially all" to mean "necessary operating assets", the IUS liquidation still falls short of the "D reorganization" requirements because the stipulated facts are that absolutely none of the assets sold from IUS to TIL were necessary operating assets for either corporation. Faced with an absence of a proper factual setting, the majority goes on to define necessary operating assets as including a corporation's intangible assets. Now while a sale of intangible assets might be an appropriate consideration in determining whether or not "substantially all" assets of a corporation have been transferred, such a consideration simply has no bearing in this case. All of the assets transferred to TIL were depreciated tangible objects sold at book value after which IUS completely ceased all business operations. There simply was no other transfer of IUS's intangible assets as a continuing business.

The majority has placed great emphasis on the fact that three of IUS's route salesmen were subsequently employed by TIL and that Mr. Smothers' managerial services were available to TIL. Regardless of whether or not these facts enhanced TIL's business, the fact remains that neither the route salesmen or Mr. Smothers' services were *transferred* as assets from one corporation to another. After IUS ceased business its route salesmen were free to seek any employment they

---

earnings of IUS until the reincorporation transaction. IUS's major asset by far was $138,000 in "notes receivable". Although the record does not reveal who issued those notes, the inference could be drawn that Smothers took the earnings out of IUS as they were earned, tax-free, by simply borrowing them from the corporation.

desired. Likewise, Mr. Smothers was never obligated to perform services for TIL. From these facts I cannot agree that there was a transfer of a continuing business. The majority imputes adverse tax consequences to IUS's stockholders simply because TIL offered new employment to the route salesmen who were unemployed upon cessation of IUS's business operations. The majority places future stockholders, in Mr. Smothers' position, of choosing between unfavorable tax consequences and helping secure future employment to loyal and deserving employees whom otherwise would be unemployed.

Although the Internal Revenue Service has never questioned the bona fides of IUS's liquidation, the majority has gone beyond the stipulated facts by characterizing the liquidation as a tax avoidance scam. I simply cannot agree. After starting from scratch, Mr. Smothers worked for over a dozen years refraining from drawing salary in order that IUS could pay its taxes, employees and other operating expenses and in order for IUS to become a successful self-sustaining business enterprise. Mr. Smothers was successful but, now that he no longer could devote his service to IUS, his years of labor are now labeled by the majority as a mere "paper shuffle." I do not share the majority's attitude.

The reasons for my position can be more easily understood by a simple review of the bottom-line facts. After IUS began showing a profit and started accumulating a cash surplus, instead of immediately investing in a building or in other equipment for its operations, it continued its operations as before. Now, if IUS had purchased real property or depreciable personal property for its operations (instead of leasing as it had been) and had sold these properties pursuant to its plan of liquidation, certainly no argument would be made that the money initially invested in those properties should have been declared by IUS as dividends. However, instead of investing its accumulations, IUS simply put them in its bank account as the tax laws allow and presumably faced any tax consequences posed by such an accumulation.

After IUS ceased operations, was liquidated, and its assets distributed to its stockholders in exchange for their stock, the I.R.S. issued a deficiency, not because IUS was reorganized within the meaning of 26 U.S.C. § 368(a)(1)(D), but rather because the I.R.S. felt the accumulated earnings of IUS coupled with long-term capital gains rates applicable to the stock exchange provided an undesirable windfall to IUS's stockholders. In essence, the I.R.S. sought to expand the "D reorganization" provisions, lessen the availability of long-term capital gains treatment to corporate stockholders, and totally ignore the purpose of the tax upon improperly accumulated surplus as provided in 26 U.S.C. § 531. The majority seeks to do equity for the I.R.S. position by "treating" the IUS liquidation as a "D reorganization." I do not believe the taxpayers or the tax laws are served by upholding an I.R.S. deficiency for the sole purpose of "plugging loopholes." The lesson to be learned from the majority's opinion is clear—future corporations faced with similar circumstances need only invest their otherwise accumulated surplus in some method other than savings. In the process of liquidation they need sell whatever assets exist to third parties unrelated to their stockholders and their stockholders should make no effort to find future employment for the corporation's employees.

It seems to me that in its attempt to "plug" a perceived "loophole," the majority is giving this Court's imprimatur to a variation of the same so-called "mockery" of the tax laws sought to be prevented by its opinion.

For these reasons, I respectfully dissent.

NOTE

Type D reorganizations come in two basic forms. The "divisive D" involves a transfer by one corporation of some of its assets to a newly formed controlled subsidiary followed by a distribution of the stock of the subsidiary in a corporate division that qualifies under Section 355. This transaction will be examined in Chapter 12 along with the other aspects of corporate divisions. The second form of Type D reorganization is "nondivisive." It involves the transfer by one corporation of all or part of its assets to a corporation controlled immediately after the transfer by the transferor or its shareholders (or any combination) provided that the stock or securities of the controlled corporation are distributed in a transaction that qualifies under Section 354. Section 354(b) requires that the first corporation must transfer "substantially all" of its assets to the controlled corporation and the stock, securities and other properties that it receives must be distributed, along with its other properties, pursuant to a plan of reorganization.

The "nondivisive" D reorganization has always been an odd character in the reorganization alphabet. As the *Smothers* case illustrates, it historically has been invoked by the Service as a weapon to attack the liquidation-reincorporation transaction, a technique utilized by taxpayers in the days when the *General Utilities* doctrine and a significant capital gains preference worked in tandem to encourage bailouts of corporate earnings at capital gains rates without any corporate-level tax. The narrowing of the tax rates between ordinary income and capital gain may have turned the tables on this transaction. To appreciate why, consider a gambit that might have been used prior to 1987 by Profit Corp., a family company with $800,000 of accumulated earnings and profits and a $2 million net worth, consisting of $1.5 million of operating assets and $500,000 of investment securities. Assume the shareholders wish to extract the securities from corporate solution without the sting of a dividend but to otherwise continue operating their business in a new corporation with fresh tax attributes (e.g., no earnings and profits) and no immediate exposure to the accumulated earnings tax.

One classic plan to accomplish these objectives was for the Profit Corp. shareholders to liquidate the corporation, retain the investment securities and, after an appropriate interval, reincorporate the operating assets under Section 351. Alternatively, Profit Corp. might transfer its operating assets to a new subsidiary in exchange for its stock and then liquidate, distributing the new stock and the investment securities to the shareholders. Whatever the format, the basic objective was to achieve what were then the tax benefits of a liquidation: capital gains at the shareholder level, nonrecognition at the corporate level, a step-up in basis of the assets in the reincorporated enterprise and a fresh start for the earnings and profits account. The Service countered by arguing, with limited success, that the transaction was a reorganization coupled with the receipt of boot that should be taxed as a dividend.[1]

A liquidation-reincorporation rarely makes sense under the current regime if its form is respected for tax purposes. The liquidation will trigger corporate-level gain under Section 336, and the reduction of the capital gains preference eliminates most of the incentive to withdraw corporate earnings at capital gains rates. If the shareholders wish to extract earnings from corporate solution, they might as well simply cause the corporation to pay cash dividends which will be taxed at the relatively low individual rates. Indeed, if the classic liquidation-reincorporation were carried out, it is now *taxpayers* who may prefer to characterize the transactions as a reorganization. In that event, they would recognize ordinary income to the extent of the boot received but would not feel greatly aggrieved because capital gains and ordinary income are taxed at essentially the same rate. More importantly, the ongoing corporation would avoid recognizing gain on its assets because the asset bases would carry over to the transferee. The liquidation-reincorporation strategy may retain its vitality, however, in a few limited situations, such as when the corporation has losses to shelter the gains resulting from the distribution of appreciated assets, where the appreciation in the corporation's assets is negligible, or if the shareholders have relatively high bases in their stock or other capital losses to offset their stock gains.[2]

PROBLEM

Brother and Sister Corporation are owned by the same shareholders in the same proportionate amounts. The shareholders have a $200,000 basis in their Brother stock and Brother Corporation has operating assets with a value of $500,000 and basis of $200,000 as well as $200,000 of cash and $200,000 of earnings and profits. Sister Corporation, which has $300,000 of earnings and profits, purchases the operating assets for $500,000 cash and Brother Corporation immediately liquidates.

   (a) What are the consequences of these transactions to the shareholders and to both corporations?

1. See, e.g., Davant v. Commissioner, 366 F.2d 874 (5th Cir.1966), cert. denied 386 U.S. 1022, 87 S.Ct. 1370 (1967).

2. See generally Faber, "Capital Gains v. Dividends in Corporate Transactions: Is the Battle Still Worth Fighting?" 64 Taxes 865 (1986).

(b) Will the arguments of the taxpayers and the Service concerning the transactions differ from those advanced in the *Smothers* case?

(c) Is there any simpler way for the taxpayers to achieve their objectives?

C. TYPE F: MERE CHANGE IN IDENTITY, FORM, OR PLACE OF ORGANIZATION

Code: §§ 368(a)(1)(F); 381(b). Skim §§ 331; 351; 354(a); 356(a); 358; 361; 1032.

A Type F reorganization is defined by the Code as "a mere change in identity, form, or place of organization of one corporation, however effected." Over forty years ago a noted commentator stated that the Type F reorganization "is so little relied upon by taxpayers that this part of the statute has indeed perished through lack of use." [1] It has survived calls for repeal, however, and experienced a brief renaissance before recently resuming its historical role as a relatively dead letter in the reorganization alphabet.

The resurgence of interest in the Type F reorganization was the result of attempts by taxpayers to carry back the post-acquisition losses of corporations which previously had been operated as an affiliated corporate group to pre-acquisition years of an acquired corporation. Since Section 381(b) only permits such a carryback of net operating losses in an F reorganization, the shareholders argued that the fusion of affiliated corporations qualified as an F reorganization. Although the language of the applicable statute implied that an F reorganization was limited to structural changes in a single corporation, the Commissioner, in his attempt to combat the liquidation-reincorporation bailout device, bolstered the argument that the F reorganization also applied to the merger of two or more active corporations. In the *Davant* case, the Commissioner asserted and the Court accepted the argument that an F reorganization could involve two operating corporations.[2] The Commissioner's argument, together with a ruling in which the Service acknowledged that a reorganization meeting the definition of an F reorganization and some other type of reorganization would be treated as an F reorganization for purposes of Section 381(b),[3] opened the floodgates. The only remaining question was how far shareholders could push combinations of operating corporations into the F reorganization category.[4] In 1975, the Service conceded that a combination of active

---

1. Paul, Studies in Federal Taxation 82 (3d Ed. 1940). But see Pugh, "The F Reorganization: Reveille for a Sleeping Giant?" 24 Tax L.Rev. 437 (1969).

2. Davant v. Commissioner, 366 F.2d 874 (5th Cir. 1966), cert. denied 386 U.S. 1022, 87 S.Ct. 1370 (1967). Actually the Commissioner made the argument at the trial court level, 43 T.C. 540 (1965), and it was adopted by the appellate court in its opinion.

3. Rev.Rul. 57–276, 1957–1 C.B. 126.

4. Compare Movielab, Inc. v. United States, 204 Ct.Cl. 6, 494 F.2d 693 (1974), and Stauffer's Estate v. Commissioner, 403 F.2d 611 (9th Cir.1968), with Berger Machine Products, Inc. v. Commissioner, 68

corporations under common control could qualify as an F reorganization if there was a complete continuity of shareholder and proprietary interests.[5] But Congress slammed the door shut in 1982 by limiting F reorganization status to a single operating corporation through the addition of the words "of one corporation" to Section 368(a)(1)(F). The Type F reorganization thus once again is relegated to its prior role as a minor provision governing reincorporations in another state and other merely formal changes. The following legislative history explains the 1982 amendment: [6]

Present law

A reorganization includes "a mere change in identity, form, or place of organization" (an F reorganization). Generally, present law requires a transferor corporation's taxable year to be closed on the date of a reorganization transfer and precludes a post-reorganization loss from being carried back to a taxable year of the transferor. However, F reorganizations are excluded from these limitations in recognition of the intended scope of such reorganizations as embracing only formal changes in a single operating corporation.

*   *   *

Conference agreement

The conference agreement limits the F reorganization definition to a change in identity, form, or place of organization of a single operating corporation.

This limitation does not preclude the use of more than one entity to consummate the transaction provided only one operating company is involved. The reincorporation of an operating company in a different State, for example, is an F reorganization that requires that more than one corporation be involved.

PROBLEM

Golden State Corporation is incorporated in California. It forms a new corporation in Arizona, Cactus Corporation, transferring all of its assets to Cactus Corporation in exchange for all of the Cactus stock. Golden State Corporation is then liquidated. What tax consequences to the Golden State shareholders?

D.   TYPE G: INSOLVENCY REORGANIZATIONS

Code: §§ 368(a)(1)(G); 354(b). Skim §§ 354; 355; 356.

T.C. 358 (1977), and Romy Hammes, Inc. v. Commissioner, 68 T.C. 900 (1977).

5. See Rev.Rul. 75–561, 1975–2 C.B. 129.

6. H.R.Rep. No. 97–760, 97th Cong., 2d Sess. 540–41 (1982), reprinted in 1982–2 C.B. 634–35.

EXCERPT FROM REPORT OF SENATE FINANCE COMMITTEE ON BANKRUPTCY TAX BILL OF 1980 *

S.Rep. No. 96–1035, 96th Cong., 2d Sess. 34–38,
reprinted in 1980–2 Cum.Bull. 620, 637.

Present Law

Definition of reorganization

A transfer of all or part of a corporation's assets, pursuant to a court order in a proceeding under chapter X of the Bankruptcy Act (or in a receivership, foreclosure, or similar proceeding), to another corporation organized or utilized to effectuate a court-approved plan may qualify for tax-free reorganization treatment under special rules relating to "insolvency reorganizations" (secs. 371–374 of the Internal Revenue Code).

These special rules for insolvency reorganizations generally allow less flexibility in structuring tax-free transactions than the rules applicable to corporate reorganizations as defined in section 368 of the Code. Also, the special rules for insolvency reorganizations do not permit carryover of tax attributes to the transferee corporation, and otherwise differ in important respects from the general reorganization rules.[1] While some reorganizations under chapter X of the Bankruptcy Act may be able to qualify for nonrecognition treatment under Code section 368, other chapter X reorganizations may be able to qualify only under the special rules of sections 371–374 and not under the general reorganization rules of section 368.

Triangular reorganizations

In the case of an insolvency reorganization which can qualify for nonrecognition treatment only under the special rules of Code sections 371–374, the stock or securities used to acquire the assets of the corporation in bankruptcy must be the acquiring corporation's own stock or securities. This limitation generally precludes corporations in bankruptcy from engaging in so-called triangular reorganizations, where the acquired corporation is acquired for stock of the parent of the acquiring corporation. By contrast, tax-free triangular reorganizations generally are permitted under the general rules of Code section 368.

---

* Some footnotes omitted.

1. Under present law, it is not clear to what extent creditors of an insolvent corporation who receive stock in exchange for their claims may be considered to have "stepped into the shoes" of former shareholders for purposes of satisfying the nonstatutory "continuity of interest" rule, under which the owners of the acquired corporation must continue to have a proprietary interest in the acquiring corporation. Generally, the courts have found the "continuity of interest" test satisfied if the creditors' interests were transformed into proprietary interests prior to the reorganization (e.g., Helvering v. Alabama Asphaltic Limestone Co., 315 U.S. 179 (1942); Treas.Reg. § 1.371–1(a)(4)). It is unclear whether affirmative steps by the creditors are required or whether mere receipt of stock is sufficient.

Transfer to controlled subsidiary

In the case of an insolvency reorganization which can qualify for nonrecognition treatment only under the special rules of Code sections 371–374, it is not clear under present law whether and to what extent the acquiring corporation may transfer assets received into a controlled subsidiary. In the case of other corporate reorganizations, the statute expressly defines the situations where transfers to subsidiaries are permitted (Code sec. 368(a)(2)(C)).

Carryover of tax attributes

In the case of an insolvency reorganization which can qualify for nonrecognition treatment only under the special rules of Code sections 371–374, court cases have held that attributes (such as net operating losses) of the corporation in bankruptcy do not carry over to the new corporation. In the case of other corporate reorganizations, however, specific statutory rules permit carryover of tax attributes to the surviving corporation (Code sec. 381).

Reasons for change

The committee believes that the provisions of existing Federal income tax law which are generally applicable to tax-free corporate reorganizations should also apply to reorganizations of corporations in bankruptcy or similar proceedings, in order to facilitate the rehabilitation of financially troubled businesses.

Also, the committee believes that a creditor who exchanges securities in a corporate reorganization (including an insolvency reorganization) should be treated as receiving interest income on the exchange to the extent the creditor receives new securities, stock, or any other property for accrued but unpaid interest on the securities surrendered.

Explanation of provisions

Section 4 of the bill generally conforms the tax rules governing insolvency reorganizations with the existing rules applicable to other corporate reorganizations. These provisions are the same as section 4 of the House bill.

Definition of reorganization

In general

The bill adds a new category—"G" reorganizations—to the general Code definition of tax-free reorganizations (sec. 368(a)(1)). The new category includes certain transfers of assets pursuant to a court-approved reorganization plan in a bankruptcy case under new title 11 of the U.S. Code, or in a receivership, foreclosure, or similar proceeding in a Federal or State court.

* * *

In order to facilitate the rehabilitation of corporate debtors in bankruptcy, etc., these provisions are designed to eliminate many requirements which have effectively precluded financially troubled companies from utilizing the generally applicable tax-free reorganization provisions of present law. To achieve this purpose, the new "G" reorganization provision does not require compliance with State merger laws (as in category "A" reorganizations), does not require that the financially distressed corporation receive solely stock of the acquiring corporation in exchange for its assets (category "C"), and does not require that the former shareholders of the financially distressed corporation control the corporation which receives the assets (category "D").

The "G" reorganization provision added by the bill requires the transfer of assets by a corporation in a bankruptcy or similar case, and the distribution (in pursuance of the court-approved reorganization plan) of stock or securities of the acquiring corporation in a transaction which qualifies under sections 354, 355, or 356 of the Code. This distribution requirement is designed to assure that either substantially all of the assets of the financially troubled corporation, or assets which consist of an active business under the tests of section 355, are transferred to the acquiring corporation.

"Substantially all" test

The "substantially all" test in the "G" reorganization provision is to be interpreted in light of the underlying intent in adding the new "G" category, namely, to facilitate the reorganization of companies in bankruptcy or similar cases for rehabilitative purposes. Accordingly, it is intended that facts and circumstances relevant to this intent, such as the insolvent corporation's need to pay off creditors or to sell assets or divisions to raise cash, are to be taken into account in determining whether a transaction qualifies as a "G" reorganization. For example, a transaction is not precluded from satisfying the "substantially all" test for purposes of the new "G" category merely because, prior to a transfer to the acquiring corporation, payments to creditors and asset sales were made in order to leave the debtor with more manageable operating assets to continue in business.[5]

Relation to other provisions

A transaction which qualifies as a "G" reorganization is not to be treated as also qualifying as a liquidation under section 332, an incorporation under section 351, or a reorganization under another category of section 368(a)(1) of the Code.[6]

---

5. Because the stated intent for adding the new "G" category is not relevant to interpreting the "substantially all" test in the case of other reorganization categories, the comments in the text as to the appropriate interpretation of the "substantially all" test in the context of a "G" reorganization are not intended to apply to, or in any way to affect interpretations under present law of, the "substantially all" test for other reorganization categories.

6. However, if a transfer qualifying as a "G" reorganization also meets the requirements of section 351 or qualifies as a reorganization under section 368(a)(1)(D) of the Code, the "excess liability" rule of section 357(c) applies if any former shareholder of the transferor corporation receives consideration for his stock, but does not apply if no former shareholder of the transferor corporation receives any consideration for his stock (i.e., if the corporation is insol-

A transaction in a bankruptcy or similar case which does not satisfy the requirements of new category "G" is not thereby precluded from qualifying as a tax-free reorganization under one of the other categories of section 368(a)(1). For example, an acquisition of the stock of a company in bankruptcy, or a recapitalization of such a company, which transactions are not covered by the new "G" category, can qualify for nonrecognition treatment under sections 368(a)(1)(B) or (E), respectively.

Continuity of interest rules

The "continuity of interest" requirement which the courts and the Treasury have long imposed as a prerequisite for nonrecognition treatment for a corporate reorganization must be met in order to satisfy the requirements of new category "G". Only reorganizations—as distinguished from liquidations in bankruptcy and sales of property to either new or old interests supplying new capital and discharging the obligations of the debtor corporation—can qualify for tax-free treatment.

It is expected that the courts and the Treasury will apply to "G" reorganizations continuity-of-interest rules which take into account the modification by P.L. 95–598 of the "absolute priority" rule. As a result of that modification, shareholders or junior creditors, who might previously have been excluded, may now retain an interest in the reorganized corporation.

For example, if an insolvent corporation's assets are transferred to a second corporation in a bankruptcy case, the most senior class of creditor to receive stock, together with all equal and junior classes (including shareholders who receive any consideration for their stock), should generally be considered the proprietors of the insolvent corporation for "continuity" purposes. However, if the shareholders receive consideration other than stock of the acquiring corporation, the transaction should be examined to determine if it represents a purchase rather than a reorganization.

Thus, short-term creditors who receive stock for their claims may be counted toward satisfying the continuity of interest rule, although any gain or loss realized by such creditors will be recognized for income tax purposes.

Triangular reorganizations

The bill permits a corporation to acquire a debtor corporation in a "G" reorganization in exchange for stock of the parent of the acquiring corporation rather than for its own stock.

In addition, the bill permits an acquisition in the form of a "reverse merger" of an insolvent corporation (i.e., where no former shareholder of the surviving corporation receives any consideration for his stock) in a bankruptcy or similar case if the former creditors of the surviving

vent). This rule parallels present law, under which insolvency reorganizations under sections 371 or 374 are excluded from the application of section 357(c).

corporation exchange their claims for voting stock of the controlling corporation which has a value equal to at least 80 percent of the value of the debt of the surviving corporation.

Transfer to controlled subsidiary

The bill permits a corporation which acquires substantially all the assets of a debtor corporation in a "G" reorganization to transfer the acquired assets to a controlled subsidiary without endangering the tax-free status of the reorganization. This provision places "G" reorganizations on a similar footing with other categories of reorganizations.

Carryover of tax attributes

Under the bill, the statutory rule generally governing carryover of tax attributes in corporate reorganizations (Code sec. 381) also applies in the case of a "G" reorganization. This eliminates the so-called "clean slate" doctrine.

"Principal amount" rule; "boot" test

Under the bill, "G" reorganizations are subject to the rules governing the tax treatment of exchanging shareholders and security holders which apply to other corporate reorganizations.

Accordingly, an exchanging shareholder or security holder of the debtor company who receives securities with a principal amount exceeding the principal amount of securities surrendered is taxable on the excess, and an exchanging shareholder or security holder who surrenders no securities is taxed on the principal amount of any securities received. Also, any "boot" received is subject to the general dividend-equivalence test of Code section 356.

Treatment of accrued interest

Under the bill, a creditor exchanging securities in any corporate reorganization described in section 368 of the Code (including a "G" reorganization) is treated as receiving interest income on the exchange to the extent the security holder receives new securities, stock, or any other property attributable to accrued but unpaid interest (including accrued original issue discount) on the securities surrendered. This provision, which reverses the so-called *Carman* rule, applies whether or not the exchanging security holder realizes gain on the exchange overall. Under this provision, a security holder which had previously accrued the interest (including original issue discount) as income recognizes a loss to the extent the interest is not paid in the exchange.

Example

The reorganization provisions of the bill are illustrated in part by the following example.

Assume that Corporation A is in a bankruptcy case commenced after December 31, 1980. Immediately prior to a transfer under a plan of reorganization, A's assets have an adjusted basis of $75,000 and a fair market value of $100,000. A has a net operating loss carryover of $200,000. A has outstanding bonds of $100,000 (on which there is no accrued but unpaid interest) and trade debts of $100,000.

Under the plan of reorganization, A is to transfer all its assets to Corporation B in exchange for $100,000 of B stock. Corporation A will distribute the stock, in exchange for their claims against A, one-half to the security holders and one-half to the trade creditors. A's shareholders will receive nothing.

The transaction qualifies as a reorganization under new section 368(a)(1)(G) of the Code, since all the creditors are here treated as proprietors for continuity of interest purposes. Thus, A recognizes no gain or loss on the transfer of its assets to B (Code sec. 361). B's basis in the assets is $75,000 (sec. 362), and B succeeds to A's net operating loss carryover (sec. 381).

Under the bill, the pro-rata distribution of B stock to A's creditors does not result in income from discharge of indebtedness [See I.R.C. § 108(e)(10). For special rules relating to the carryover of A's net operating loss, see Section 382(*l*)(5). Ed.]

Assume the same facts as above except that B also transfers $10,000 in cash, which is distributed by A to its creditors. Although A would otherwise recognize gain on the receipt of boot in an exchange involving appreciated property, the distribution by A of the $10,000 cash to those creditors having a proprietary interest in the corporation's assets for continuity of interest purposes prevents A from recognizing any gain (Code sec. 361(b)(1)(A)).[10]

PROBLEM

Debtor Corporation is in bankruptcy. Debtor's assets have an adjusted basis of $75,000 and a value of $100,000, and the corporation has a net operating loss of $200,000, bonds outstanding (with no accrued unpaid interest) of $100,000 and trade debts of $100,000. Debtor transfers all of its assets to Relief Corporation in return for $100,000 of Relief stock which will pass half to the security holders and half to trade creditors. Debtor's shareholders will receive nothing. What are the tax consequences to the parties?

---

10. See Code sec. 371(a)(2)(A) and Treas. Reg. § 1.371–1(b) for a similar rule relating to distribution of boot to creditors in an insolvency reorganization under present law.

CHAPTER 12. CORPORATE DIVISIONS *

A. INTRODUCTION

Code: Skim §§ 355; 368(a)(1)(D), (c).

The preceding two chapters examined tax-free acquisitive reorganizations and restructurings of a single corporation. We now turn to a variety of transactions in which a single corporate enterprise is divided into two or more separate corporations. Section 355 allows a corporation to make a tax-free distribution to its shareholders of stock and securities in one or more controlled subsidiaries. If an intricate set of statutory and judicial requirements are met, neither the distributing corporation nor the shareholders recognize gain or loss on the distribution. Section 355 also unlocks the gate to other provisions which govern the treatment and characterization of boot, and collateral matters such as basis, holding period and carryover of tax attributes.[1] The rationale for nonrecognition is that the division of a business conducted under one corporate shell into separate corporations is not an appropriate taxable event where no significant assets leave corporate solution and the historic shareholders continue to control all the resulting corporations.

Corporate divisions are motivated by a myriad of nontax considerations, including: (1) resolution of shareholder disputes; (2) insulation of one business from the risks and creditors of another; (3) compliance with regulatory decrees; (4) separation of various functions of a company (e.g., manufacturing from research or sales) to achieve certain management goals; and (5) preparation for a sale of part of the business by removing assets that the buyer does not wish to purchase. And there is the tax motive that once permeated every crevice of Subchapter C and which perhaps has reappeared with the second coming of the capital gains preference: bailing out earnings and profits at capital gains rates. More recently, taxpayers have attempted to use Section 355 to avoid corporate-level gain on the sale of a subsidiary. It should be apparent by now that this chapter represents yet another opportunity to grapple with concepts previously encountered and the uncertainties that have accompanied tax reform.

The three types of corporate divisions are commonly known as spin-offs, split-offs and split-ups. To illustrate the elements of these transactions, assume that Alex and Bertha each own 50 percent of the stock of Diverse Corporation ("D"), which for many years has operated a winery and a chicken ranch as separate divisions. For reasons to be elaborated below, the shareholders wish to divide the business into two

---

* See generally Kaden & Wolfe, "Spin-offs, Split-offs, and Split-ups: A Detailed Analysis of Section 355," 44 Tax Notes 565 (July 31, 1989).

1. See, e.g., I.R.C. §§ 356; 357; 358; 361; 362; 381; 1223(1) and Section C of this chapter, infra.

separate corporations on a tax-free basis. The division method they choose will be influenced by their nontax goals. The possibilities are:

1. *Spin-off.* Assume that to comply with a new state regulation, D is required to operate the chicken ranch and winery as separate corporations. To accomplish the division, D forms a new corporation, Poultry, Inc., contributing the assets of the chicken ranch. It then distributes the stock of Poultry pro rata to Alex and Bertha, who emerge as equal shareholders in each corporation. Because a spin-off involves a distribution of property to shareholders without the surrender of any stock, it resembles a dividend.

2. *Split-off.* Alex and Bertha desire to part company, with Alex operating the winery and Bertha the chicken ranch. To help them go their separate ways, D again forms a new corporation, Poultry, Inc., contributing the assets of the chicken ranch. D then distributes the stock of Poultry to Bertha in complete redemption of her D stock. Alex becomes the sole shareholder of D, which now owns only the winery, and Bertha is the sole owner of the chicken ranch. If Alex and Bertha did not want to part company, D could have made a pro rata distribution of Poultry stock in redemption of an appropriate amount of D stock. In either situation, a split-off resembles a redemption because the shareholders have surrendered stock of D.

3. *Split-up.* To comply with a new state regulation, D is required to terminate its corporate existence and divide up its two businesses. The fission is accomplished by D forming Vineyard, Inc. and Poultry, Inc., contributing the winery assets to Vineyard and the chicken ranch assets to Poultry. D then distributes the stock of the two new corporations pro rata to Alex and Bertha in exchange for all their D stock. Because D has distributed all of its assets and dissolved, this transaction resembles a complete liquidation. If the objectives of the parties had been different (e.g., Alex and Bertha wanted to sever their relationship), the transaction could have been effected by distributing the Vineyard stock to Alex and the Poultry stock to Bertha.

As these examples demonstrate, spin-offs, split-offs and split-ups can be classified for tax purposes in two different ways: as a tax-free corporate division or as the taxable transaction that each method resembles. In order to qualify as tax free to the shareholders, the division must satisfy the requirements of Section 355 and its accompanying judicial doctrines. In general, Section 355 allows a corporation with one or more businesses that have been actively conducted for five years or more to make a tax-free distribution of the stock of a controlled subsidiary (or subsidiaries) provided that the transaction is being carried out for a legitimate business purpose and is not being used principally as a device to bail out earnings and profits. In the absence of Section 355, a spin-off likely would be treated as a dividend under Section 301; a split-off would be tested for dividend equivalency under the redemption rules in Section 302; and a split-up ordinarily would be treated as a complete liquidation under Section 331.

There is one more piece to this introduction to the puzzle. In each of the examples above, Diverse Corporation was required to engage in a preliminary step in order to accomplish its division. Because its two businesses were operated as divisions under one corporate roof rather than as separately incorporated subsidiaries, D had to drop one or more of those businesses into a separate corporate shell before proceeding with the distribution to its shareholders. If that distribution satisfies the tests in Section 355, the initial transfer of assets by D to its new subsidiary (or subsidiaries) will constitute a Type D reorganization.[2] As such, the transfer of assets will be tax free to D under Section 361(a), the assumption of liabilities will be governed by Section 357 and the basis of the transferred assets will carry over to the new subsidiary under Section 362(b).[3] Creation of a new subsidiary, however, is not a condition to qualifying for nonrecognition of gain under Section 355. If its requirements are met, Section 355 applies to distributions of stock of preexisting corporations as well as to new subsidiaries created solely to carry out the division.[4]

B. THE REQUIREMENTS FOR A TAX–FREE CORPORATE DIVISION

1. HISTORICAL BACKGROUND

To better understand the technical requirements for a tax-free corporate division, it is helpful to look back at the historical background of Section 355. The early income tax provisions governing spin-offs were elegantly simple but dangerously naive. Interpreted literally, they permitted a corporation to transfer all or part of its assets to a newly formed subsidiary and then to make a tax-free distribution of the stock of that subsidiary to its shareholders as part of a plan of reorganization.[1] The tax avoidance potential of this blanket exemption from the dividend rules was enormous, and the judiciary swiftly responded by curtailing the use of a spin-off as a bailout device. In Gregory v. Helvering, which follows, the Supreme Court made one of its earliest contributions to the common law of taxation[2] and paved the way toward the enactment of a comprehensive statutory solution to the problem of corporate divisions.

---

2. The initial transaction also would qualify for nonrecognition under Section 351, but Section 368(a)(1)(D) and its accompanying operative provisions take precedence if the transfer of assets is followed by a Section 355 distribution.

3. See Section C of this Chapter, infra.

4. I.R.C. § 355(a)(2)(C).

1. See, e.g., Revenue Act of 1924, P.L. No. 176, § 203(c), 43 Stat. 253, 256.

2. See Blum, "Motive, Intent, and Purpose in Federal Income Taxation," 34 U.Chi.L.Rev. 485 (1967); Chirelstein, "Learned Hand's Contribution to the Law of Tax Avoidance," 77 Yale L.J. 440 (1968).

GREGORY v. HELVERING

Supreme Court of the United States, 1935.
293 U.S. 465, 55 S.Ct. 266.

Mr. Justice SUTHERLAND delivered the opinion of the Court.

Petitioner in 1928 was the owner of all the stock of United Mortgage Corporation. That corporation held among its assets 1,000 shares of the Monitor Securities Corporation. For the sole purpose of procuring a transfer of these shares to herself in order to sell them for her individual profit, and, at the same time, diminish the amount of income tax which would result from a direct transfer by way of dividend, she sought to bring about a "reorganization" under § 112(g) of the Revenue Act of 1928, c. 852, 45 Stat. 791, 818, set forth later in this opinion. To that end, she caused the Averill Corporation to be organized under the laws of Delaware on September 18, 1928. Three days later, the United Mortgage Corporation transferred to the Averill Corporation the 1,000 shares of Monitor stock, for which all the shares of the Averill Corporation were issued to the petitioner. On September 24, the Averill Corporation was dissolved, and liquidated by distributing all its assets, namely, the Monitor shares, to the petitioner. No other business was ever transacted, or intended to be transacted, by that company. Petitioner immediately sold the Monitor shares for $133,333.33. She returned for taxation as capital net gain the sum of $76,007.88, based upon an apportioned cost of $57,325.45. Further details are unnecessary. It is not disputed that if the interposition of the so-called reorganization was ineffective, petitioner became liable for a much larger tax as a result of the transaction.

The Commissioner of Internal Revenue, being of opinion that the reorganization attempted was without substance and must be disregarded, held that petitioner was liable for a tax as though the United corporation had paid her a dividend consisting of the amount realized from the sale of the Monitor shares. In a proceeding before the Board of Tax Appeals, that body rejected the commissioner's view and upheld that of petitioner. 27 B.T.A. 223. Upon a review of the latter decision, the circuit court of appeals sustained the commissioner and reversed the board, holding that there had been no "reorganization" within the meaning of the statute. 69 F. (2d) 809. Petitioner applied to this court for a writ of certiorari, which the government, considering the question one of importance, did not oppose. We granted the writ.

Section 112 of the Revenue Act of 1928 deals with the subject of gain or loss resulting from the sale or exchange of property. Such gain or loss is to be recognized in computing the tax, except as provided in that section. The provisions of the section, so far as they are pertinent to the question here presented, follow:

"Sec. 112. (g) *Distribution of stock on reorganization.*—If there is distributed, in pursuance of a plan of reorganization, to a shareholder in a corporation a party to the reorganization, stock or securities in such corporation or in another corporation a party to the reorganization, without the surrender by such shareholder of stock or securities in such a corporation, no gain to the distributee from the receipt of such stock or securities shall be recognized * * *.

"(i) *Definition of reorganization.*—As used in this section * * *.

"(1) The term 'reorganization' means * * * (B) a transfer by a corporation of all or a part of its assets to another corporation if immediately after the transfer the transferor or its stockholders or both are in control of the corporation to which the assets are transferred, * * *."

It is earnestly contended on behalf of the taxpayer that since every element required by the foregoing subdivision (B) is to be found in what was done, a statutory reorganization was effected; and that the motive of the taxpayer thereby to escape payment of a tax will not alter the result or make unlawful what the statute allows. It is quite true that if a reorganization in reality was effected within the meaning of subdivision (B), the ulterior purpose mentioned will be disregarded. The legal right of a taxpayer to decrease the amount of what otherwise would be his taxes, or altogether avoid them, by means which the law permits, cannot be doubted. * * * But the question for determination is whether what was done, apart from the tax motive, was the thing which the statute intended. The reasoning of the court below in justification of a negative answer leaves little to be said.

When subdivision (B) speaks of a transfer of assets by one corporation to another, it means a transfer made "in pursuance of a plan of reorganization" [§ 112(g)] of corporate business; and not a transfer of assets by one corporation to another in pursuance of a plan having no relation to the business of either, as plainly is the case here. Putting aside, then, the question of motive in respect of taxation altogether, and fixing the character of the proceeding by what actually occurred, what do we find? Simply an operation having no business or corporate purpose—a mere device which put on the form of a corporate reorganization as a disguise for concealing its real character, and the sole object and accomplishment of which was the consummation of a preconceived plan, not to reorganize a business or any part of a business, but to transfer a parcel of corporate shares to the petitioner. No doubt, a new and valid corporation was created. But that corporation was nothing more than a contrivance to the end last described. It was brought into existence for no other purpose; it performed, as it was intended from the beginning it should perform, no other function. When that limited function had been exercised, it immediately was put to death.

In these circumstances, the facts speak for themselves and are susceptible of but one interpretation. The whole undertaking, though conducted according to the terms of subdivision (B), was in fact an elaborate and devious form of conveyance masquerading as a corporate reorganization, and nothing else. The rule which excludes from consideration the motive of tax avoidance is not pertinent to the situation, because the transaction upon its face lies outside the plain intent of the statute. To hold otherwise would be to exalt artifice above reality and to deprive the statutory provision in question of all serious purpose.

Judgment affirmed.

NOTE

The Board of Tax Appeals had been more tolerant in its evaluation of Mrs. Gregory's maneuver. Adopting a strict constructionist approach, the Board reasoned that "[a] statute so meticulously drafted must be interpreted as a literal expression of the taxing policy, and leaves only the small interstices for judicial consideration." [1] On appeal to the Second Circuit, Judge Learned Hand—in one of his most famous pronouncements on tax avoidance—agreed that "[a]ny one may so arrange his affairs that his taxes shall be as low as possible; he is not bound to choose that pattern which will best pay the Treasury; there is not even a patriotic duty to increase one's taxes." [2] But he quickly eschewed literalism in favor of the big picture, reasoning that "the meaning of a sentence may be more than that of the separate words, as a melody is more than the notes, and no degree of particularity can ever obviate recourse to the setting in which all appear, and which all collectively create." [3] The Supreme Court's opinion was a less stylish but equally forceful reaffirmation that the language of the Code must be interpreted in light of its purpose.

Gregory v. Helvering has ramifications that go far beyond corporate divisions. It is one of the earliest articulations of the substance over form and step transaction doctrines. However amorphous they may be, those doctrines serve as a brooding omnipresence in the responsible tax advisor's conscience. They also thwart the schemes of aggressive tax avoiders who might use a literal interpretation of the Code to wreak havoc with its intended purpose. As we will see later in the chapter, the narrower business purpose doctrine emanating from *Gregory* also survives as one of the major judicial requirements for qualification as a tax-free corporate division. [4]

While *Gregory* was pending, Congress saw the light and repealed the tax-free spin off provision involved in that case. Curiously, split-ups (and, for a time, split-offs) continued to qualify for nonrecognition if they did not run afoul of the limitations in *Gregory*. [5] Congress ultimately realized, however, that not every spin-off is a bailout device, and in 1951 it enacted the statutory forerunner of Section 355 to remove any impediment to corporate divisions "undertaken for legitimate busi-

1. Gregory v. Commissioner, 27 B.T.A. 223, 225 (1932).

2. Helvering v. Gregory, 69 F.2d 809, 810 (2d Cir.1934).

3. Id.

4. See Section B4a of this chapter, infra.

5. For the history of corporate divisions before the 1954 Code, see Bittker & Eustice, Federal Income Taxation of Corporations and Shareholders ¶ 13.02 (5th ed. 1987).

ness purposes." [6] In general, the new statute granted nonrecognition to spin-offs that were pursuant to a plan of reorganization unless one of the corporate parties to the reorganization did not intend "to continue the active conduct of a trade or business" or "the corporation whose stock is distributed was used principally as a device for the distribution of earnings and profits * * *." [7] The contours of the present Section 355 thus were being shaped: to qualify as tax free, a spin-off had to be motivated by a genuine business purpose and consist of the separation of one or more active trades or businesses in a transaction that was not being used principally as a bailout device.

With the enactment of Section 355 in the 1954 Code, Congress finally provided a comprehensive statutory scheme governing all three types of corporate divisions.[8] At the same time, the business purpose and continuity of interest doctrines were preserved as independent nonstatutory requirements.

2. OVERVIEW OF REQUIREMENTS

Code: §§ 355; 368(c).

Regulations: § 1.355–1(b).

Before becoming immersed in technical details, it is important to recall the purpose of Section 355. Congress intended to provide tax-free status to corporate divisions serving legitimate business needs. At the same time, it included safeguards to patrol against the bailout of earnings and profits. Most of the statutory and judicial requirements are directed at these broad objectives. But unfortunately their precise meaning and scope are often unclear, and the waters were muddied further by the profound changes made by the Tax Reform Act of 1986.

A corporate division will qualify as tax free to the shareholders and the distributing corporation if it satisfies the following requirements:

1. *Control.* One corporation (the "distributing corporation") must distribute to its shareholders or security holders the stock or securities of a "controlled corporation"—i.e., a corporation that the distributing corporation "controls" immediately before the distribution.[1] For this purpose, "control" is defined by Section 368(c), which requires ownership of 80 percent of the total combined voting power and 80 percent of the total number of shares of all other classes of stock, including nonvoting preferred stock.

2. *Distribution of All Stock or Securities.* The distributing corporation must distribute all the stock or securities of the controlled corporation or, alternatively, an amount of stock sufficient to constitute

---

6. S.Rep. No. 781, 82d Cong., 1st Sess. (1951), reprinted in 1951–2 C.B. 458, 499.

7. Revenue Act of 1951, ch. 521, § 317(a), 65 Stat. 493, amending Internal Revenue Code of 1939, § 112(b)(11).

8. The statute does not explicitly refer to spin-offs, split-offs and split-ups, but Sec-

tion 355(a)(2) makes it clear that Section 355 applies to all three forms of corporate divisions. The different forms continue to be significant if the transaction fails the Section 355 tests.

1. I.R.C. § 355(a)(1)(A).

"control" within the meaning of Section 368(c).[2] If any stock or securities of the controlled corporation are retained, the distributing corporation must establish to the satisfaction of the Service that the retention is not pursuant to a plan having tax avoidance as one of its principal purposes.[3]

    3. *Active Trade or Business Requirement.* Both the distributing corporation and the controlled corporation—or in a split-up, both controlled corporations—must be engaged immediately after the distribution in an actively conducted trade or business which has been so conducted throughout the five-year period ending on the date of the distribution.[4] That business must not have been acquired within the five-year predistribution period in a taxable transaction.[5] Moreover, the distributing corporation must not have purchased a controlling stock interest in a corporation conducting the business in a taxable transaction during the five-year predistribution period.[6]

    4. *Not A "Device."* The division must not be used "principally as a device for the distribution" of the earnings and profits of either the distributing or controlled corporations. The "mere fact" that stock or securities of either corporation are sold after the distribution is not to be considered as evidence of a device unless the sales were pursuant to a prearranged plan.[7]

    5. *Judicial Limitations: Business Purpose and Continuity of Interest.* In addition to the statutory tests, the regulations incorporate two venerable judicially created limitations. Nonrecognition is available only if the distribution is carried out for an independent corporate business purpose [8] and the shareholders of the enterprise prior to the division maintain adequate continuity of interest in the distributing and controlled corporations after the distribution.[9]

    These requirements are applied without regard to the form the parties choose to accomplish the division. Thus, a distribution may qualify as tax-free under Section 355 irrespective of whether it is pro rata and whether or not the distributee shareholder surrenders stock in the distributing corporation or the distribution is preceded by the formation of a new controlled corporation in a Type D reorganization.[10]

    6. *Taxation of the Parties.* Paralleling Section 354, which generally applies to nondivisive reorganizations, Section 355 provides total shareholder-level nonrecognition only where the distributing corporation distributes stock or securities of a controlled corporation.[11] Stock rights or warrants are not treated as "stock or securities" for this

---

2. I.R.C. § 355(a)(1)(D).

3. I.R.C. § 355(a)(1)(D)(ii). See Rev.Rul. 75–469, 1975–2 C.B. 126; Rev.Rul. 75–321, 1975–2 C.B. 123.

4. I.R.C. § 355(a)(1)(C); (b).

5. I.R.C. § 355(b)(2)(C).

6. I.R.C. § 355(b)(2)(D). The active trade or business test also will be violated if the distributee shareholder is a corpora-

tion that acquired control of the distributing corporation within the five-year predistribution period. Id.

7. I.R.C. § 355(a)(1)(B).

8. Reg. § 1.355–2(b).

9. Reg. § 1.355–2(c).

10. I.R.C. § 355(a)(2).

11. I.R.C. § 355(a)(1).

purpose and thus constitute taxable boot under Section 356.[12] In the case of a distribution of securities (e.g., long-term notes, bonds, debentures), if the principal amount of securities of the controlled corporation received by the distributee exceeds the principal amount of the distributing corporation's securities surrendered in connection with the distribution, the value of the excess is treated as boot.[13] If securities of the controlled corporation are received and no securities of the parent are surrendered, the entire value of the securities received is treated as boot.[14] In addition, any stock of a controlled corporation acquired in a taxable transaction within the five years preceding the distribution constitutes boot.[15] The distribution of boot does not necessarily disqualify a transaction under Section 355, but it will cause the distributee shareholder to recognize any realized gain, normally as ordinary income, to the extent of the boot received.[16] At the corporate level, the distributing corporation generally does not recognize gain on the distribution of stock or securities of its subsidiary but may recognize gain on the distribution of appreciated boot or in certain situations where a divisive transaction is used to facilitate the sale of a subsidiary.[17]

The principal hurdles to achieving nonrecognition under Section 355 are the active business test, the business purpose requirement and the "device" limitation. In interpreting these rules, the Treasury has waffled, first emphasizing the active business test and more recently shifting the emphasis to the "device" and business purpose limitations. The current government position is reflected in extensive final regulations issued in 1989. These regulations have largely supplanted the case law and are the principal focus of this chapter.

3. THE ACTIVE TRADE OR BUSINESS REQUIREMENT

Code: § 355(a)(1)(C), (b).

Regulations: § 1.355–3.

12. Reg. § 1.355–1(b). For the beleaguered history of the treatment of stock rights as boot, compare Commissioner v. Gordon, 382 F.2d 499 (2d Cir.1967), reversed on other grounds 391 U.S. 83, 88 S.Ct. 1517 (1968) with Gordon v. Commissioner, 424 F.2d 378 (2d Cir.1970); Commissioner v. Baan, 382 F.2d 485 (9th Cir.1967), rehearing denied with Baan v. Commissioner, 450 F.2d 198 (9th Cir.1971); Redding v. Commissioner, 630 F.2d 1169 (7th Cir.1980), cert. denied 450 U.S. 913, 101 S.Ct. 1353 (1981).

13. I.R.C. §§ 355(a)(3)(A)(i); 356(d)(2)(C).

14. I.R.C. §§ 355(a)(3)(A)(ii); 356(d)(2)(C).

15. I.R.C. § 355(a)(3)(B). See Edna Louise Dunn Trust v. Commissioner, 86 T.C. 745 (1986).

16. I.R.C. §§ 355(a)(4)(A); 356. See Section C of this Chapter, infra, for a more detailed explanation of the treatment of boot and the other operative provisions that accompany Section 355.

17. I.R.C. § 355(c), (d).

LOCKWOOD'S ESTATE v. COMMISSIONER *

United States Court of Appeals, Eighth Circuit, 1965.
350 F.2d 712.

VOGEL, Circuit Judge.

The single question involved in this review of an unreported decision of the Tax Court of the United States, entered August 26, 1964, is whether the "spin-off" of part of the business conducted by the Lockwood Grader Corporation of Gering, Nebraska, (hereinafter Lockwood) through the organization of a new corporation, Lockwood Graders of Maine, Inc. (hereinafter Maine, Inc.) was tax-free to petitioners, recipients of the stock of Maine, Inc., under 26 U.S.C.A. § 355 (Int.Rev. Code).   The government contended that the spin-off was not tax-free since the requirements of § 355(b)(2)(B) relating to the conducting of an active business for five years prior to the date of distribution had not been met.   The government apparently conceded and the Tax Court found that the petitioners had met all other requirements to qualify under § 355 for tax-free treatment.   The Tax Court upheld the government's contention and petitioners appeal.

The now deceased Thorval J. Lockwood, whose interests herein are represented by his duly qualified executor, National Bank of Commerce Trust and Savings Association, and his wife Margaret were the sole stockholders of Lockwood and had been so since its incorporation under Nebraska law in 1946.   Lockwood's predecessor, Lockwood Graders, was a partnership formed in 1935 for the purpose of producing and selling a portable potato sorting machine invented by the decedent. Starting in the early spring of each year Thorval and Margaret drove to Alabama and worked their way north through Missouri to North Dakota for the purpose of selling Lockwood products.   The equipment was sold in "all of the potato growing areas of the United States" but primarily in the biggest growing areas such as North Dakota, Idaho and Colorado.

From 1946 to 1951, inclusive, Lockwood operated its business of manufacturing and selling wash lines, potato machinery, parts and supplies to potato shippers in the potato growing areas.   Though Lockwood continued to have its principal place of business at Gering, Nebraska, branches were opened, as the business expanded, in Grand Forks, North Dakota; Antigo, Wisconsin; Monte Vista, Colorado; and Rupert, Idaho.   These branches performed both manufacturing and sales functions.   In 1952, under a reorganization plan, these branches were separately incorporated to promote greater efficiency and to properly provide for expansion.   Assets of Lockwood were exchanged for all of the stock of each new corporation and the stock so exchanged was passed without consideration to Thorval and Margaret as sole stockholders of Lockwood.   The reorganization plan, among other

* Some footnotes omitted.

things, was specifically designed to make use of the tax-free provisions of what is now § 355.

In the early 1950's Lockwood and the other controlled corporations changed the nature of their business somewhat by selling to individual farmers as well as to potato suppliers. Lockwood had previously dealt primarily in grading equipment but at this time it began to manufacture and sell field equipment such as harvesting pieces, bin holders and vine beaters as well.

Beginning as early as 1947 Lockwood began to make some sporadic and relatively inconsequential sales in the northeastern part of the United States. From 1949 to 1955 the primary sales of products and parts in that part of the country were made to Gould & Smith, Inc., a retailer of farming and industrial equipment, of Presque Isle, Maine (although there are no records of sales made to them in 1952). Such sales were found to be of a relatively small volume by the Tax Court. On November 15, 1954, Lockwood established a branch office in Presque Isle, Maine, from which to handle Lockwood products. On March 1, 1956, pursuant to the 1951 plan for reorganization set out in footnote 2, supra, the Maine branch office was incorporated under the laws of Maine with its principal place of business at Presque Isle, Maine. Maine, Inc., was a wholly owned subsidiary of Lockwood. On incorporating, Lockwood transferred to Maine, Inc., $23,500 in assets consisting of petty cash totalling $150.00, accounts receivable totalling $4,686.67, automobiles and trucks worth $1,100, shop equipment worth $295.00, office furniture and fixtures worth $81.60, and inventory worth $17,186.73. In return for these assets Maine, Inc., issued all of its stock, 235 shares at $100.00 par value, to Lockwood. On March 31, 1956, Lockwood distributed 162 of these shares of Maine, Inc., to Thorval and 73 of them to Margaret. This distribution gave rise to the controversy here involved.

The Tax Court held this distribution to be outside of § 355. According to the Tax Court there was:

> " * * * the absence of evidence that the *Maine business* was actively conducted during the months between March 31, 1951, and August 1953—a span of time totaling over 40 per cent of the requisite five-year period [required by § 355(b)(2) (B).]" (Emphasis supplied.)

The Tax Court found that the Maine business was not actively and continuously conducted until August 1953, at which time a Lockwood salesman traveled to Maine and personally solicited orders from farmers and businessmen other than Gould & Smith. We do not disagree with the factual finding of the Tax Court as to the active conduct of Lockwood's business in Maine prior to the incorporation of Maine, Inc. However, the Tax Court, for reasons set out below, erred in looking only at the business performed by Lockwood in Maine to determine if the five-year active business requirement had been met prior to the incorporation of Maine, Inc. Nothing in the language of § 355 suggests that prior business activity is only to be measured by looking at the business performed in a geographical area where the controlled corporation is eventually formed. In this case, when the entire Lockwood market is viewed, it can be seen that Lockwood was engaged in active business as required by § 355 for the five years prior to the incorporation of Maine, Inc. Since its incorporation Maine, Inc., has carried on the same kind of manufacturing and selling business previously and concurrently performed by Lockwood. Thus all § 355 prerequisites are met and the Tax Court erred in determining this was not a tax-free transfer.

At this point it would be helpful to look at the evolvement of what is now § 355. Prior to 1924 a distribution to stockholders pursuant to a spin-off was taxed as a dividend. From 1924 to 1932, however, the revenue acts changed position and provided spin-offs could be tax-free. From 1934 to 1950 tax-free spin-offs were again abolished since this device was being used as a method for distributing earnings and profits, which would otherwise be taxable dividends, through the issuance of stock in the controlled corporation. Such stock could be disposed of at the more favorable capital gain rates. Because of the usefulness of the spin-off device in the achievement of corporate growth and flexibility, Congress again accorded it tax-free status in 1951. At that time certain conditions were imposed to prevent any abuse from using this device. In 1954 the tax-free spin-off was continued as § 355 of the Code with additional tax avoidance safeguards which included the five-year active business requirement involved in this case.

As stated by the Second Circuit in Bonsall v. Commissioner, 2 Cir., 1963, 317 F.2d 61, at page 65:

> "* * * Only long application may completely clarify the difficult terminology of section 355."

With this we agree. However, certain things have become clear since the enactment of § 355 in 1954. After much controversy it has been determined that tax-free treatment will not be denied to a transaction under § 355 merely because it represents an attempt to divide a single trade or business. See United States v. Marett, 5 Cir., 1963, 325 F.2d 28; Coady v. Commissioner, 33 T.C. 771, affirmed per curiam, 6 Cir., 1962, 289 F.2d 490. The Commissioner has acceded to the holdings of Marett and Coady in Rev.Rule 64–147, 1964–1, Cum.Bull. 136, even though the Commissioner had previously insisted, in § 1.355–1(a) of the Income Tax Regulations, that two or more existing businesses had to be actively operated the five years prior to distribution. The Tax Court in Coady, at pages 777–778 of 33 T.C., states:

> "Respondent maintains that a reading of 355(b)(2)(B) [set out at footnote 1, supra] in conjunction with the requirement of 355(b)(1) [set out at footnote 4, infra] * * * indicates Congress intended the provisions of the statute to apply only where, immediately after the distribution, there exist two separate and distinct businesses, one operated by the distributing corporation and one operated by the controlled corporation, both of

which were actively conducted for the 5-year period immediately preceding the distribution. In our judgment the statute does not support this construction.

"As noted, the only reference to plurality appears in section 355(b)(1), and deals with corporate entities, not businesses. Recognizing the divisive nature of the transaction, subsection (b)(1) contemplates that where there was only one corporate entity prior to the various transfers, immediately subsequent thereto, there will be two or more *corporations*. In order to insure that a tax-free separation will involve the separation only of those assets attributable to the carrying on of an active trade or business, and further to prevent the tax-free division of an active corporation into active and inactive entities, (b)(1) further provides that each of the surviving corporations must be engaged in the active conduct of *a* trade or business. [Emphasis by the court.]

"A careful reading of the definition of the active conduct of a trade or business contained in subsection (b)(2) indicates that its function is also to prevent the tax-free separation of *active* and *inactive* assets into *active* and *inactive* corporate entities. This is apparent from the use of the adjective 'such,' meaning before-mentioned to modify 'trade or business' in subsection (b)(2)(B), thus providing that the trade or business, required by (b)(2)(B) to have had a 5-year active history prior to the distribution, is the same trade or business which (b)(2)(A) requires to be actively conducted immediately after the distribution. Nowhere in (b)(2) do we find, as respondent suggests we should, language denying the benefits of section 355 to the division of a single trade or business. [Emphasis by the court.]

"Nor can respondent derive support for his position by reading subsections (b)(1) and (b)(2) together, inasmuch as the plurality resulting therefrom is occasioned, not by any requirement that there be a multiplicity of businesses, but rather by the divisive nature of the transaction itself: i.e., one corporation becoming two or more corporations. *Moreover, from the fact that the statute requires, immediately after the distribution, that the surviving corporations each be engaged in the conduct of a trade or business with an active 5-year history, we do not think it inevitably follows that each such trade or business necessarily must have been conducted on an individual basis throughout that 5-year period. As long as the trade or business which has been divided has been actively conducted for 5 years preceding the distribution, and the resulting businesses (each of which in this case, happens to be half of the original whole) are actively conducted after the division, we are of the opinion that the active business requirements of the statute have been complied with.*" (Emphasis supplied.)

Respondent in the instant case, although claiming to accept the single business interpretation, points to the language of § 355(b)(1) and argues, as did the government in Coady, that the word *"and"* in that section means that, in determining whether or not the active business requirement was met, one has to look at both the business done by the distributing corporation (Lockwood) *and* the business done as such by the controlled corporation (Maine, Inc.) and its predecessors in Maine. Contrary to the government's position, once it has been ascertained that two or more trades or businesses are not required for § 355 to apply, the crucial question becomes whether or not the two corporations existing after distribution are doing the same type of work and using the same type of assets previously done and used by the prior *single* existing business. § 355(b)(1) has no relevance to respondent's point once it has been determined that only a single business is required.

Here the five years of prior activity we are concerned with involve the prior overall activity of Lockwood. Previous to 1956 Lockwood had carried on *in toto* what Maine, Inc., would later carry on in part in the northeast. We are not concerned with the prior activity of Lockwood in the northeast only, for Congress has never intimated that such a geographical test should be applied and we are not about to apply such a test now. A perusal of the House and Senate Reports indicates conclusively that at no time did the House or the Senate contemplate any kind of geographic test in applying the five-year active business requirement.[5] The facts clearly show that Lockwood, in fact, was actively conducting the trade or business involved five years prior to the distribution period.

One case, Patricia C. Burke v. Commissioner, 1964, 42 T.C. 1021, did discuss the past business of a controlled corporation as performed in a limited geographical area in finding the prequisites of § 355 had been met. That case did not, however, hold that there was in fact a geographical test. Further, at page 1028 that court set out what we believe to be the test:

> " * * * as long as the business which is divided has been actively conducted for 5 years before the distribution and the resulting businesses are actively conducted after the division, the active business requirements of the statute are met. Cf. also H. Grady Lester, 40 T.C. 947 (1963)."

Since there is no Congressional intent evidenced to the contrary, the test, restated, is not whether active business had been carried out in the geographic area later served by the controlled corporation but, simply, whether the distributing corporation, for five years prior to distribu-

---

5. See H.Rep. No. 1337, S.Rep. No. 1622 and Conference Report No. 2543 of the Second Session of the 83rd Congress. (Discussions involving § 355 are set out in 3 U.S.C.Cong. & Adm.News (1954), pp. 4064–4066, 4265–4266, 4681–4683, 4903–4906, 5297–5298.) The Commissioner would seem to be in error in implying such a geographic test exists in Examples 8 and 9 of § 1.355–1(d) of the Income Tax Regulations.

tion, had been actively conducting the type of business now performed by the controlled corporation without reference to the geographic area. In the instant case the facts are abundantly clear that Lockwood had been actively engaged in the type of business later carried on by Maine, Inc., if one refers to a national rather than just the northeastern market.

It was mentioned earlier in this opinion that beginning in 1950 Lockwood began to sell field equipment as well as grading equipment. The respondent apparently does not contend, nor do we find, that Lockwood so changed its business as to be engaged in a new business that had been active for only two years prior to the incorporation of Maine, Inc. Lockwood meets the requirements of an existing five-year active business as set out by the Conference Committee in Conference Report No. 2543 at page 5298 of 3 U.S.C.Cong. & Adm.News, 1954:

> "It is the understanding of the managers on the part of the House, in agreeing to the active business requirements of section 355 and of section 346 (defining partial liquidations), that a trade or business which has been actively conducted throughout the 5-year period described in such sections will meet the requirements of such sections, even though such trade or business underwent change during such 5-year period, for example, *by the addition of new,* or the dropping of old, *products,* changes in production capacity, and the like, provided the changes are not of such a character as to constitute the acquisition of a new or different business." (Emphasis supplied.)

In § 1.355–4(b)(3) of the Income Tax Regulations the Commissioner specifically adopts the above-quoted portion of the Committee Report.

The respondent contends:

> "If the taxpayers' argument prevails, then any corporation with a five-year history could distribute any of its assets regardless of when they were acquired and regardless of what kind of business they are in after the division, as long as the distributing corporation is in an active business. In other words, taxpayer argues that the five-year history rule requires that only the business of the distributing corporation have a five-year history. For instance, suppose a large manufacturing corporation with a ten-year life acquired some data processing machines in order to better control its inventory and work-in-process flow. If taxpayers' argument is correct, a year later this corporation could transfer all the data processing equipment to a new corporation in exchange for its stock, spin off the stock and claim a tax-free distribution under Section 355 since the manufacturing corporation had more than a five-year life and the data processing business, once an integral part of the original business, was being actively conducted after the spin-off. Moreover, the same logic would allow the spin-off of

real estate owned by the manufacturing corporation and used in its business."

The fears of the government are unfounded. The example of the manufacturing company is more closely akin to the Bonsall case, supra, and is factually distinguishable from the instant case. Here Lockwood had not just recently acquired that part or segment of its business that was spun off. Rather, what was spun off was a part of the business Lockwood had always performed in the past and which it has continued to perform since the distribution. If Lockwood had, just before distribution, acquired or opened up a new or entirely different aspect of its business unrelated to prior activities and had spun this off to the controlled corporation, a different result might ensue. In Bonsall the distributing company, a dealer in floor covering materials, attempted to assert a tax-free spin-off occurred when a rental business of *de minimis* proportions was transferred to a subsidiary with the stock of the subsidiary being distributed to the distributor's shareholders. The Second Circuit held at page 64 of 317 F.2d:

> "There is ample support for the factual determination that Albany Linoleum [the distributing company therein] was not actively conducting a real-estate rental business. * * * the portion of its income realized from real estate rentals was minute. * * * No activity appeared beyond a few casual conversations with prospective tenants. Moreover, most of the floor-space of the two buildings combined was occupied by the floor-covering business. Only a very small part was available for rental, and an even smaller part actually leased. The continuing rental to Armstrong Cork Co. which provided most of the rental income appeared to be an accommodation to a large supplier of the floor-covering business and thus an adjunct to it, rather than indicative of an independent business, for the Tax Court found that the premises were let at less than fair rental value over the five-year period. Finally, no separate records of rental income and expenses were kept. Absence of such records is at least probative of the fact that the managers of Albany Linoleum did not regard it as engaged in an independent rental business. The Tax Court was plainly justified in concluding that the small amount of rental activity was merely an incidental part of the sole business of the corporation—wholesale floor-coverings. * * * "

Thus it is clear that in respondent's example and in Bonsall the business sought to be spun off was not actively engaged in for five years prior to distribution, which is not the situation in the instant case. Here, what was spun off was merely an integral part of what had been Lockwood's primary and only business from its inception.

Further, it should be remembered that even if the five-year active business requirement is met, there is further protection in § 355 against spin-offs being used for mere tax avoidance, which would be contrary to Congressional intent. § 355(a)(1)(B) will only allow a tax-free spin-off transaction where " * * * the transaction was not used principally as a device for the distribution of the earnings and profits of the distributing corporation or the controlled corporation or both * * *." Under this section, the government and the courts have great latitude in preventing the abuses which the respondent fears will happen by finding for petitioners in this case. Cf. Gregory v. Helvering, 1935, 293 U.S. 465, 55 S.Ct. 266, 79 L.Ed. 596. Herein the respondent does not contend that the purpose of the spin off was designed primarily for tax avoidance. No earnings and profits were in fact distributed to Thorval and Margaret. The Tax Court stated that:

> " * * * we do not view the distribution as running afoul
> of the congressional purpose behind section 355, * * *."

This being so, and since petitioners otherwise complied with § 355, the decision of the Tax Court will be reversed. The transaction herein involved cannot be treated as a taxable distribution of dividends.

NOTE

Although the anti-bailout objective of the active business requirement is clear enough, this multifaceted test has engendered considerable litigation. The *Lockwood* case is typical of the Commissioner's unsuccessful early efforts to apply the test strictly. The Service retreated on a number of controversial issues and most of these concessions are reflected in the final regulations issued in 1989. This Note surveys some settled and lingering questions.

Trade or Business. Both the distributing corporation and the controlled corporation (or the controlled corporations in the case of a split-up) must be engaged immediately after the distribution in a trade or business with a five-year history. The regulations treat a corporation as being engaged in a trade or business if: [1]

> * * * a specific group of activities are being carried on by
> the corporation for the purpose of earning income or profit,
> and the activities included in such group include every opera-
> tion that forms a part of, or a step in, the process of earning
> income or profit. Such group of activities ordinarily must
> include the collection of income and the payment of expenses.

The regulations go on to create a dichotomy between active business and passive investment activities. Although the determination of whether a trade or business is "actively conducted" is a factual question turning on all the facts and circumstances, active business status generally requires the corporation to itself perform active and substantial management and operational functions. [2] For this purpose, the activities performed by persons outside the corporation, such as inde-

---

1. Reg. § 1.355–3(b)(2)(ii).

2. Reg. § 1.355–3(b)(2)(iii). Some of the corporation's activities, however, can be performed by others. Id.

pendent contractors, generally are not taken into account.[3] To preclude a tax-free separation of passive investment assets, "active conduct" does not include the holding of property for investment (e.g., raw land or portfolio securities) or the ownership and operation (including leasing) of real or personal property used in the owner's trade or business unless the owner performs significant management services with respect to the property.[4]

Vertical Divisions of a Single Integrated Business. Suppose a corporation wishes to divide a single trade or business that has been operated for more than five years? Does Section 355 require two separate predistribution trades or businesses, each with its own five-year history, or may one existing business be divided in two? After several defeats,[5] the Service now acknowledges that Section 355 can apply to the separation of a single business. Thus, assuming the other statutory and judicial requirements are met, a corporation engaged in an integrated business at one location may transfer half of its assets to a new subsidiary and distribute the stock of the subsidiary to a 50 percent shareholder in a tax-free split-off.[6]

Functional Divisions. The treatment of functional divisions—i.e., separations of certain distinct functions of a single business enterprise—is more uncertain. To illustrate the issue, assume that a manufacturer of high technology equipment wishes to spin off its research and development function for valid business reasons. The Service once maintained that such support activities did not constitute a separate trade or business because they did not independently produce income.[7] The regulations now sanction some types of functional divisions, as illustrated in the following example:[8]

> For the past eight years, corporation X has engaged in the manufacture and sale of household products. Throughout this period, X has maintained a research department for use in connection with its manufacturing activities. The research department has 30 employees actively engaged in the development of new products. X transfers the research department to new subsidiary Y and distributes the stock of Y to X's shareholders. After the distribution, Y continues its research operations on a contractual basis with several corporations, including X. X and Y both satisfy the requirements of section 355(b). * * * The result in this example is the same if, after the distribution, Y continues its research operations but furnishes its services only to X. * * *

3. Id.

4. Reg. § 1.355–3(b)(2)(iv).

5. See Coady v. Commissioner, 33 T.C. 771 (1960), affirmed per curiam 289 F.2d 490 (6th Cir.1961) (single construction business divided into two businesses to resolve shareholder dispute); United States v. Marett, 325 F.2d 28 (5th Cir.1963) (food manufacturer operating at three factories spun off one factory opened eight months before the distribution).

6. See, e.g., Reg. § 1.355–3(c) Examples (4) and (5).

7. Reg. § 1.355–1(c)(3) (pre–1989).

8. Reg. § 1.355–3(c) Example (9).

Similarly, if a steel manufacturer spins off a coal mine operated solely to supply its coal requirements, the manufacturing and captive coal mine activities will qualify as separate active businesses after the distribution.[9]

The regulations make it clear that the functional separation in the example above satisfies the active business test whether the research department subsequently provides services only to the business from which it was separated or also to other customers. The coal mine also was treated as an active business even though it did not derive income from outside third parties. These examples reflect the Service's abandonment of any requirement that an active business must "independently" produce income. But tax-free treatment for a functional division is still far from assured. The transaction also must have a corporate business purpose, and it must not run afoul of the "device" limitation. As we will discover shortly, the regulations provide that the same functional separations which pass muster under the active business test may present "evidence" of a prohibited bailout device.[10]

Geographical Divisions. The liberal approach of the *Lockwood* case has been incorporated into the final regulations. Previously, the Service applied a strict geographic test under which, for example, a manufacturer with factories in two locations could not separate one from the other unless they both had a five-year business history. The current regulations dispense with geography and look to the character of the activity and commonality of functions in determining whether geographically dispersed operations constitute a single integrated business. Thus, a new activity in the same line of business as an activity that has been actively conducted by the distributing corporation for more than five years ordinarily will not be considered a separate business. For example, the regulations would permit a nine year old department store to spin off a suburban branch constructed three years ago, where after the distribution each store has its own manager and is operated independently of the other store.[11]

Single or Multiple Businesses: The Five–Year Rule. To satisfy the active business test, a trade or business must have been actively conducted for the five years prior to the distribution, must not have been acquired within that period in a transaction that was taxable to the seller of the business, and must not have been conducted by a corporation the control (i.e., 80 percent) of which was acquired by the distributing corporation in a taxable transaction.[12] The purpose of

---

9. Reg. § 1.355–3(c) Example (11). See also Reg. § 1.355–3(c) Example (10), providing that the separation of the processing and sales functions of a meat products business satisfies the active business test.

10. See Reg. § 1.355–2(d)(2)(iv)(C).

11. Reg. § 1.355–3(c) Example (7). See also Reg. § 1.355–3(c) Example (8), illustrating the same result where the new activity is purchased as a going concern.

12. I.R.C. § 355(b)(2)(B)–(D); Reg. § 1.355–3(b)(1)–(5). For this purpose, a "taxable transaction" is one in which gain or loss was recognized in whole or in part by the seller. If a business is acquired in a tax-free reorganization, its previous history carries over (along with its tax attributes) for purposes of the five-year rule.

these requirements is to prevent a corporation from using Section 355 to avoid the dividend provisions of Subchapter C by temporarily investing its earnings in a business that it plans to spin off to its shareholders.

The five-year rule has spawned numerous controversies over whether a particular activity is a separate business requiring its own five-year history or simply part of an integrated business which has been active for more than five years. We have seen, for example, that a recently opened suburban branch store may be treated as an integral part of an ongoing department store business with a more than five-year history.[13] On the other hand, businesses with clearly distinct products or services (e.g., a chicken ranch and a winery) are considered to be separate.[14] As *Lockwood* illustrates, similar problems arise in the case of a diversification or expansion of a business within the five-year predistribution period. The regulations offer some guidance on this question, suggesting that a newer activity in the same line of business will be treated as an expansion of the original business unless the "purchase, creation, or other acquisition effects a change of such a character as to constitute the acquisition of a new or different business."[15] Revenue Ruling 59–400, which follows this note, addresses yet another aspect of this problem—the situation where the earnings of one business are used to finance the growth of a separate enterprise.

Real Estate. The Service has consistently maintained that investment land or owner-occupied real estate ordinarily do not constitute actively conducted businesses.[16] The regulations provide that the separation of owner-occupied real estate will be subject to "careful scrutiny." Real estate qualifies as an active business only if the owner performs "significant services with respect to the operation and management of the property."[17] Thus, the Service will not approve the spin-off of vacant land or mineral rights on ranch land, even if development activities are imminent.[18] But it will sanction the separation of an office building substantially leased (10 of 11 floors) to outsiders and actively managed by the lessor.[19] Even if the active business hurdle is surmounted, however, separations of real estate may be vulnerable under the "device" and business purpose tests.[20]

Dispositions of Recently Acquired Businesses. In 1987, Congress added a requirement to the active trade or business test as part of its effort to prevent corporations from disposing of a recently acquired

---

13. Reg. § 1.355–3(c) Example (7).

14. See, e.g., Rev.Rul. 56–655, 1956–2 C.B. 214 (retail appliance branch and retail furniture branch considered separate businesses); Rev.Rul. 56–451, 1956–2 C.B. 208 (metal industry magazine separate from magazine to serve electrical industry).

15. Reg. § 1.355–3(b)(3)(ii).

16. Reg. § 1.355–3(b)(2)(iv).

17. Id.

18. Reg. § 1.355–3(c) Examples (2) and (3).

19. Reg. § 1.355–3(c) Example (12). Compare Reg. § 1.355–3(c) Example (13), where the separation of a two-story office building did not qualify where the distributing corporation occupied the ground floor and half of the second floor in the conduct of its banking business and rented the remaining area as storage space.

20. See, e.g., Reg. § 1.355–2(d)(2)(iv)(C).

subsidiary without paying a corporate-level tax.[21] Section 355(b)(2)(D) provides that a distribution will flunk the active trade or business test if a controlling stock interest in the *distributing* corporation was acquired by a corporate distributee within the five-year period preceding the distribution. This precludes a corporation ("P") from purchasing a controlling interest in another corporation ("T") which has a subsidiary ("S") and then causing T to distribute the S stock to P in a tax-free distribution to set the stage for a sale by P of the S stock without recognizing any of the gain inherent in S's assets. Under Section 355(b)(2)(D), as amended, the distribution of S stock would not qualify as tax-free because control of the distributing corporation (T) was acquired by a corporate distributee (P) within the five-year period preceding the distribution. This aspect of Section 355 and related techniques for using a tax-free corporate division to facilitate an acquisition are discussed later in this chapter.[22]

REVENUE RULING 59–400

1959–2 Cum.Bull. 114.

Advice has been requested whether a distribution of stock by a corporation engaged in the hotel and real estate business qualifies under the nontaxable provisions of section 355 of the Internal Revenue Code of 1954.

M corporation was engaged in two businesses, operating a hotel and renting improved real estate (both commercial and residential). The hotel business was started upon organization in 1920 and has been actively conducted up to the present time. In 1934, *M* corporation also entered into the rental real estate business when it purchased property, constructed a garage and automobile agency facilities thereon and rented it to a dealer. In the intervening years, it acquired other rental properties which it has continued to operate. In 1954, the hotel had a fair market value of 550x dollars and a net book value of 350x dollars. The rental properties had a fair market value of 305x dollars and a net book value of 167x dollars.

During the five-year period commencing with 1954, the operation of the hotel business resulted in earnings, after taxes, of 240x dollars, and the operation of the real estate business resulted in earnings of approximately 75x dollars. In 1958, a new rental office building was built for 400x dollars, some 175x dollars thereof being provided by loans from banks. At the beginning of 1959, the hotel business was placed in a new corporation *N*, and the stock thereof distributed to the shareholders of *M* on a pro rata basis. *N* corporation received the hotel, plus certain receivables and other hotel business assets. *M* corporation retained the real estate liabilities and assets, which at that time had a net book value of 372x dollars and a fair market value of 705x dollars.

Section 355 of the Code states, in part, that in order for a distribution of stock to qualify under the nontaxable provisions of such section,

---

21. See Chapter 7C7a, supra.   **22.** See Section D of this chapter, infra.

each of the corporations involved must be engaged in a trade or business which has been actively conducted throughout the five-year period ending on the date of distribution, and that the transaction must not be used principally as a device to distribute the earnings and profits of either corporation.

The purpose behind the five-year limitation of section 355 is to prevent the corporate earnings of one business from being drawn off for such a period and put into a new business and thereby, through the creation of a marketable enterprise, convert what would normally have been dividends into capital assets that are readily saleable by the shareholders.

It is the position of the Internal Revenue Service that where a corporation which is devoted to one type of business also engages in the rental business, and substantial acquisitions of new rental property are made within the five-year period preceding the separation of these businesses, a "spin-off" transaction will not qualify under section 355 unless it can be shown that the property acquisitions were substantially financed out of the earnings of the rental business and not out of the earnings of the other business.

From the facts presented herein, it is readily apparent that there has been a very substantial increase in the rental properties subsequent to 1954, primarily as a result of the addition of the large office building in 1958. Further, it is also apparent that, viewing the transaction most favorably to the taxpayer, earnings properly attributable to the hotel business, in the amount of approximately $150x$ dollars, have been employed in increasing the real estate business. In view of this substantial financing out of the earnings of the hotel business, it is held that the distribution of the stock of N corporation to the shareholders of M corporation will not qualify as a nontaxable distribution under section 355 of the Code.

PROBLEMS

1. Lemon Corporation has been engaged in the manufacture and sale of personal computer equipment for ten years at two plants, one in Boston, Massachusetts and the other in San Jose, California. During this time, Lemon also has operated a separate research and development division at each location. Its common stock, the only class outstanding, is owned equally by Ms. Micro and Mr. Chips. In each of the following alternative transactions, consider whether the division of Lemon Corporation satisfies the active trade or business requirement:

    (a) As a result of a shareholder dispute, Ms. Micro wishes to say goodbye to Mr. Chips. To enable the shareholders to part company but continue in the computer business, Lemon contributes the assets and research division of the Boston facility to a new corporation, Peach, Inc., and distributes all the Peach, Inc. stock to Mr. Chips in redemption of his Lemon stock. Ms. Micro remains as the sole shareholder of Lemon.

(b) Same as (a), above, except that the Boston facility was opened three years ago.

(c) Same as (b), above, except the Boston facility was acquired three years ago in a taxable transaction.

(d) To comply with a divestiture order, Lemon transfers the assets of the research divisions to a new corporation, Research, Inc. and distributes all the Research stock pro rata to the shareholders. After the distribution, Research, Inc. continues to perform services solely for Lemon.

(e) In addition to the operations described above, assume that three years ago Lemon purchased all the stock of Floppy Disk, Inc., a computer software manufacturer, in a taxable transaction. To comply with a regulatory decree, Lemon distributes the stock of Floppy Disk pro rata to its shareholders.

(f) Same as (e), above, except that Floppy Disk merged into Lemon three years ago in a Type A reorganization. The consideration for that acquisition consisted of Lemon nonvoting preferred stock (80%) and Lemon short-term notes (20%).

2. Debit and Credit ("DC") is a large accounting firm which owns the 10 story building in which it conducts its practice. For the past 15 years, it has used six floors for its own operations and rented the other four floors to unrelated tenants. Six years ago, the firm formed a wholly owned subsidiary, Properties, Inc., which leases two other commercial buildings previously owned by DC on a long-term net lease basis, under which the tenants are responsible for property taxes, insurance and maintenance. Consider whether the following alternative transactions satisfy the active trade or business requirement:

(a) On the advice of a management consultant, DC transfers its 10 story office building to a new corporation, Rental, Inc., and distributes the Rental stock pro rata to its shareholders. After the distribution, DC leases from Rental the six floors that it occupies; and Rental continues to rent the other four floors to unrelated tenants. Rental employees actively manage the building and perform repair and maintenance services.

(b) Same as (a), above, except that DC only occupies one floor and the remaining space is leased to unrelated tenants.

(c) Same as (b), above, except the nine floors are rented to outsiders under a long-term net lease.

(d) DC distributes all the stock of Properties, Inc. pro rata to the DC shareholders. After the distribution, Properties continues its rental activities.

4. JUDICIAL AND STATUTORY LIMITATIONS

a. BUSINESS PURPOSE *

Regulations: § 1.355–2(b).

The business purpose doctrine originated in Gregory v. Helvering [1] and rapidly assumed its role as one of the first "common law" principles of federal taxation. The doctrine has become an increasingly important limitation under Section 355 even though it is never mentioned in the Code. As illustrated by the *Rafferty* decision, which follows, the business purpose and device limitations are conceptually linked, both focusing on the taxpayer's motivation for the transaction. It is appropriate to consider the business purpose requirement first because the strength or weakness of a corporate business purpose is evidence in determining whether a transaction was used principally as a device for distributing earnings and profits. [2] Moreover, the regulations provide that the "business purpose requirement is independent of the other requirements under section 355." [3] Thus, a corporate division lacking a business purpose can not be accomplished tax free even if it is not used principally as a device to bail out earnings and profits. [4]

RAFFERTY v. COMMISSIONER **

United States Court of Appeals, First Circuit, 1971.
452 F.2d 767.

McENTEE, Circuit Judge.

Taxpayers, Joseph V. Rafferty and wife, appeal from a decision of the Tax Court, 55 T.C. 491, which held that a distribution to them of all the outstanding stock of a real estate holding corporation did not meet the requirements of § 355 of the Internal Revenue Code of 1954 and therefore was taxable as a dividend. Our opinion requires a construction of § 355 and the regulations thereunder.

The facts, some of which have been stipulated, are relatively simple. The taxpayers own all the outstanding shares of Rafferty Brown Steel Co., Inc. (hereinafter RBS), a Massachusetts corporation engaged in the processing and distribution of cold rolled sheet and strip steel in Longmeadow, Massachusetts. In May 1960, at the suggestion of his accountant, Rafferty organized Teragram Realty Co., Inc., also a Massachusetts corporation. In June of that year RBS transferred its Longmeadow real estate to Teragram in exchange for all of the latter's outstanding stock. Thereupon Teragram leased back this real estate to RBS for ten years at an annual rent of $42,000. In 1962 the taxpayers also organized Rafferty Brown Steel Co., Inc., of Connecticut (RBS

---

* See Faber, "Business Purpose and Section 355," 43 Taxes 855 (1990).

1. See p. 631, supra.

2. Reg. § 1.355–2(b)(4), (d)(3)(ii).

3. Reg. § 1.355–2(b)(1).

4. Reg. § 1.355–2(b)(1).

** Some footnotes omitted.

Conn.), which corporation acquired the assets of Hawkridge Brothers, a general steel products warehouse in Waterbury, Connecticut. Since its inception the taxpayers have owned all of the outstanding stock in RBS Conn. From 1962 to 1965 Hawkridge leased its real estate in Waterbury to RBS Conn. In 1965 Teragram purchased some unimproved real estate in Waterbury and built a plant there. In the same year it leased this plant to RBS Conn. for a term of fourteen years. Teragram has continued to own and lease the Waterbury real estate to RBS Conn. and the Longmeadow realty to RBS, which companies have continued up to the present time to operate their businesses at these locations.[3]

During the period from 1960 through 1965 Teragram derived all of its income from rent paid by RBS and RBS Conn. Its earned surplus increased from $4,119.05 as of March 31, 1961, to $46,743.35 as of March 31, 1965. The earned surplus of RBS increased from $331,117.97 as of June 30, 1959, to $535,395.77 as of June 30, 1965. In August 1965, RBS distributed its Teragram stock to the taxpayers. Other than this distribution, neither RBS nor Teragram has paid any dividends.

Joseph V. Rafferty has been the guiding force behind all three corporations, RBS, RBS Conn., and Teragram. He is the president and treasurer of Teragram which, while it has no office or employees, keeps separate books and records and filed separate tax returns for the years in question.[4]

On various occasions Rafferty consulted his accountant about estate planning, particularly about the orderly disposition of RBS.[5] While he anticipated that his sons would join him at RBS, he wanted to exclude his daughters (and/or his future sons-in-law) from the active management of the steel business. He wished, however, to provide them with property which would produce a steady income. The accountant recommended the formation of Teragram, the distribution of its stock, and the eventual use of this stock as future gifts to the Rafferty daughters. The taxpayers acted on this advice and also on the accountant's opinion that the distribution of Teragram stock would meet the requirements of § 355.

---

3. Both properties are also suitable for use by other companies in other types of business.

4. The tax returns for Teragram for the five fiscal years 1961 through 1965 reveal the following deductions:

Compensation of officers	none
Salaries and wages	none
Rent	none
Travel (all in 1965)	$16.52
Office expenses (all in 1965)	9.25

The total deductions taken by Teragram over the five year period were $171,135.94. The bulk of that amount was as follows:

Taxes	$ 43,980.59
Interest	36,985.57
Depreciation	74,213.21
Insurance	5,565.26
Legal, auditing, and organizational expenses	1,274.25
Repairs (all in 1965)	8,500.00
Fire Loss (all in 1962)	591.29
	$171,110.17

5. Rafferty's concern is understandable in view of the fact that he had nine children.

In their 1965 return the taxpayers treated the distribution of Teragram stock as a nontaxable transaction under § 355. The Commissioner viewed it, however, as a taxable dividend and assessed a deficiency. He claimed (a) that the distribution was used primarily as a device for the distribution of the earnings and profits of RBS or Teragram or both, and (b) that Teragram did not meet the active business requirements of § 355.

We turn first, to the Tax Court's finding that there was no device because there was an adequate business purpose for the separation and distribution of Teragram stock. In examining this finding we are guided by the rule that the taxpayer has the burden of proving that the transaction was not used principally as a device. Wilson v. Commissioner of Internal Revenue, 42 T.C. 914, 922 (1964), rev'd on other grounds, 353 F.2d 184 (9th Cir.1965). Initially, we are disturbed by the somewhat uncritical nature of the Tax Court's finding of a business purpose. Viewing the transaction from the standpoint of RBS, RBS Conn., or Teragram, no immediate business reason existed for the distribution of Teragram's stock to the taxpayers. Over the years the businesses had been profitable, as witnessed by the substantial increase of the earned surplus of every component, yet none had paid dividends. The primary purpose for the distribution found by the Tax Court was to facilitate Rafferty's desire to make bequests to his children in accordance with an estate plan.[6] This was a personal motive. Taxpayers seek to put it in terms relevant to the corporation by speaking of avoidance of possible interference with the operation of the steel business by future sons-in-law, pointing to Coady v. Commissioner of Internal Revenue, 33 T.C. 771 (1960), aff'd per curiam, 289 F.2d 490 (6th Cir.1961).

In *Coady,* however, the separation was in response to a seemingly irreconcilable falling-out between the owners of a business. This falling-out had already occurred and, manifestly, the separation was designed to save the business from a substantial, present problem. See also Olson v. Commissioner of Internal Revenue, 48 T.C. 855, 867 modified, 49 T.C. 84 (1967). In the case at bar there was, at best, only an envisaged possibility of future debilitating nepotism. If avoidance of this danger could be thought a viable business purpose at all, it was so remote and so completely under the taxpayers' control that if, in other respects the transaction was a "device," that purpose could not satisfy the taxpayers' burden of proving that it was not being used "principally as a device" within the meaning of the statute.

Our question, therefore, must be whether taxpayers' desire to put their stockholdings into such form as would facilitate their estate planning, viewed in the circumstances of the case, was a sufficient personal business purpose to prevent the transaction at bar from being

---

6. This plan incorporated two objectives: (1) the exclusion of daughters and sons-in-law from active management of the steel business and (2) providing his daughters with investment assets, safe and independent from the fluctuations of the steel business.

a device for the distribution of earnings and profits. While we remain of the view, which we first expressed in Lewis v. Commissioner of Internal Revenue, 176 F.2d 646 (1st Cir.1949), that a purpose of a shareholder, qua shareholder, may in some cases save a transaction from condemnation as a device, we do not agree with the putative suggestion in Estate of Parshelsky v. Commissioner of Internal Revenue, 303 F.2d 14, 19 (2d Cir.1962), that any investment purpose of the shareholders is sufficient. Indeed, in *Lewis,* although we deprecated the distinction between shareholder and corporate purpose, we were careful to limit that observation to the facts of that case, and to caution that the business purpose formula "must not become a substitute for independent analysis." 176 F.2d at 650. For that reason we based our decision on the Tax Court's finding that the transaction was "undertaken for reasons germane to the continuance of the corporate business." Id. at 647.

This is not to say that a taxpayer's personal motives cannot be considered, but only that a distribution which has considerable potential for use as a device for distributing earnings and profits should not qualify for tax-free treatment on the basis of personal motives unless those motives are germane to the continuance of the corporate business. Cf. Commissioner of Internal Revenue v. Wilson, 353 F.2d 184 (9th Cir., 1965); Treas.Reg. § 1.355–2(c). We prefer this approach over reliance upon formulations such as "business purpose," and "active business." See generally Whitman, Draining the Serbonian Bog: A New Approach to Corporate Separations Under the 1954 Code, 81 Harv. L.Rev. 1194 (1968). The facts of the instant case illustrate the reason for considering substance. Dividends are normally taxable to shareholders upon receipt. Had the taxpayers received cash dividends and made investments to provide for their female descendants, an income tax would, of course, have resulted. Accordingly, once the stock was distributed, if it could potentially be converted into cash without thereby impairing taxpayers' equity interest in RBS, the transaction could easily be used to avoid taxes. The business purpose here alleged, which could be fully satisfied by a bail-out of dividends, is not sufficient to prove that the transaction was not being principally so used.

Given such a purpose, the only question remaining is whether the substance of the transaction is such as to leave the taxpayer in a position to distribute the earnings and profits of the corporation away from, or out of the business. The first factor to be considered is how easily the taxpayer would be able, were he so to choose, to liquidate or sell the spun-off corporation. Even if both corporations are actively engaged in their respective trades, if one of them is a business based principally on highly liquid investment-type, passive assets, the potential for a bail-out is real. The question here is whether the property transferred to the newly organized corporation had a readily realizable value, so that the distributee-shareholders could, if they ever wished, "obtain such cash or property or the cash equivalent thereof, either by selling the distributed stock or liquidating the corporation, thereby converting what would otherwise be dividends taxable as ordinary income into capital gain *   *   *." Wilson v. Commissioner, *supra,* 42 T.C. at 923. In this connection we note that the Tax Court found that a sale of Teragram's real estate properties could be "easily arranged." 55 T.C. at 353. Indeed, taxpayers themselves stressed the fact that the buildings were capable of multiple use.

There must, however, be a further question. If the taxpayers could not effect a bail-out without thereby impairing their control over the on-going business, the fact that a bail-out is theoretically possible should not be enough to demonstrate a device because the likelihood of it ever being so used is slight. "[A] bail-out ordinarily means that earnings and profits have been drawn off without impairing the shareholder's residual equity interest in the corporation's earning power, growth potential, or voting control." B. Bittker & J. Eustice, Federal Income Taxation of Corporations and Shareholders (3d ed. 1971) § 13.06. If sale would adversely affect the shareholders of the on-going company, the assets cannot be said to be sufficiently separated from the corporate solution and the gain sufficiently crystallized as to be taxable. See Lewis v. Commissioner of Internal Revenue, supra, 176 F.2d at 650. In this case, there was no evidence that the land and buildings at which RBS carried on its steel operations were so distinctive that the sale of Teragram stock would impair the continued operation of RBS, or that the sale of those buildings would in any other way impair Rafferty's control and other equity interests in RBS.[7]

In the absence of any direct benefit to the business of the original company, and on a showing that the spin-off put saleable assets in the hands of the taxpayers, the continued retention of which was not needed to continue the business enterprise, or to accomplish taxpayers' purposes, we find no sufficient factor to overcome the Commissioner's determination that the distribution was principally a device to distribute earnings and profits.

*   *   *

[The court went on to hold that the transaction failed to satisfy the active business requirement in Section 355(b). Ed.]

REVENUE RULING 85–122

1985–2 Cum.Bull. 119.

ISSUE

Is the business purpose requirement of section 1.355–2(c) of the Income Tax Regulations met when stock of a controlled corporation is distributed under the circumstances described?

FACTS

P is a closely held corporation that owns and operates a golf and tennis resort in State *A*. *P* has for more than 5 years owned all the

---

7. Our conclusion is reinforced by the fact that RBS and RBS Conn. were guaran- teed occupancy of Teragram property under long term leases at fixed rents.

stock of *S*, a corporation that owns and operates a ski resort in State *B*. The golf and tennis resort operated by *P*, although profitable, is in need of substantial amounts of additional working capital to finance operation adequately. Due to various factors, including poor weather conditions, the ski resort operated by *S* has been experiencing significant losses for several years, and *S* is nearly bankrupt.

It is desired to sell *P* debentures in order to obtain additional working capital for *P*. *P* has approached an underwriter to explore debt financing through a private placement of its debentures. Except for this effort to sell *P* debentures, the underwriter has no relationship with *P* or *P's* shareholders. The underwriter has considerable experience in dealing with debt financing in situations of this type. The underwriter has advised *P* that potential investors could decline to invest in *P* because *P's* balance sheet would divulge its holding of *S*, and raise fears that the funds invested in *P* would be diverted to improve *S's* financial position. The underwriter has stated that, even if sufficient interest could be stimulated among potential investors, the terms and conditions of the debentures would be significantly more burdensome to *P*, if *P* remains associated with *S*. Finally, the underwriter has stated that a holding company structure in which *P* and *S* would both be first tier subsidiaries of a new parent company would not solve *P's* problem, as potential investors would take into account *S's* performance in evaluating the group's financial statements.

The underwriter has engaged in informal preliminary discussions of *P's* situation with persons who frequently purchase the underwriter's offerings. Even though the underwriter has attempted to explain that *P* (as *S's* shareholder) is not liable to *S's* creditors, the underwriter encountered reluctance to invest in *P* as long as *P* and *S* are associated. Based on prior experience with similar situations, and on the result of these informal preliminary discussions, the underwriter has recommended that all the *S* stock be distributed to the *P* shareholders. This would permit *P* to prepare financial statements without reflecting the results and conditions of *S's* operation. The underwriter will then put together a syndicate of investors to purchase the *P* debentures. The amount of capital to be raised is considered adequate to meet the needs of *P's* operations.

In accordance with the underwriter's recommendation that *P* divest itself of *S*, *P* will distribute the *S* stock pro rata to the *P* shareholders. Except for the question here at issue regarding business purposes, distribution of the *S* stock to the *P* shareholders will meet all the requirements of section 355 of the Internal Revenue Code and the regulations thereunder.

LAW AND ANALYSIS

Section 355 of the Code provides that under certain circumstances a corporation may distribute stock or securities in a corporation it controls to its shareholders or its security holders in a transaction that is nontaxable to such shareholders or security holders. Section 1.355–2(c) of the regulations states that a distribution by a corporation of stock or securities of a controlled corporation to its shareholders with respect to its own stock will not qualify under section 355 of the Code when carried out for purposes not germane to the business of the corporations. This requirement is intended to limit the application of section 355 to those readjustments of corporate structure that are required by business exigencies.

The distribution by P of the S stock is for purposes germane to the business of P within the meaning of section 1.355–2(c) of the regulations, since it is the result of a recommendation by an independent and experienced underwriter who, from both prior experience and present contacts, has concluded that any relationship between P and S will have a significant adverse affect on investor perception of P debentures, and since it is reasonable to expect that the distribution of the S stock will be of significant help to P in securing needed additional capital.

HOLDING

The business purpose requirement of section 1.355–2(c) of the regulations is met when the S stock is distributed under the circumstances described.

REVENUE RULING 88–34
1988–1 Cum.Bull. 115.

ISSUE

Is the business purpose requirement of section 355 of the Internal Revenue Code and section 1.355–2(c) of the Income Tax Regulations met where a distribution of the stock of a controlled corporation is made to enable that corporation to hire a new president?

FACTS

X, a large widely held and publicly traded corporation, owned all the stock of Y corporation for more than five years. X and Y were each engaged in the active conduct of a separate and distinct trade or business for over five years. No shareholder of X owns as much as 5 percent of the outstanding stock of X.

The president of Y has recently retired and Y has conducted an extensive search for a new president. Y has interviewed A, an individual with substantial prior experience and an outstanding reputation as the president of a public corporation engaged in the same line of business as Y. Because of A's prior experience and success in managing a similar corporation, A is the person Y wishes to hire as its new president. A is interested in becoming the president of Y but will not accept the position unless permitted to acquire a significant equity interest in Y. A has further advised Y that A is not interested in acquiring X stock or in acquiring an equity interest in Y as a subsidiary of X.

In order to permit Y to obtain the services of A, X has distributed all of the stock of Y pro rata to the shareholders. Thereafter, A will be employed by Y at an annual salary of $250x and, within one year, will purchase newly issued shares of stock from Y having a fair market value of $775x.

Except for the issue of the business purpose for the distribution, the proposed distribution by X of the Y stock meets all the requirements of section 355 of the Code and the pertinent regulations.

LAW AND ANALYSIS

Section 355 of the Code provides that under certain circumstances a corporation may distribute stock or securities in a corporation it controls to its shareholders or security holders in a transaction that is not taxable to those shareholders or security holders. Section 1.355–2(c) of the regulations states that a distribution by a corporation of stock or securities of a controlled corporation will not qualify under section 355 when carried out for purposes not germane to the business of the corporations. This provision is intended to limit the application of section 355 to those readjustments of a corporate structure that are required by business exigencies.

Situation 2 of Rev.Rul. 69–460, 1969–2 C.B. 51, concerns a distribution of the stock of a subsidiary corporation so that key employees of the parent corporation could afford to buy stock in that corporation. That ruling holds that the distribution was undertaken for a valid business purpose. Rev.Rul. 85–127, 1985–2 C.B. 119, holds that the business purpose requirement was also met where a corporation transfers one of its businesses to a new corporation and distributes the stock of the new corporation to its shareholders in order to retain the services of a key employee and permit that employee to obtain a majority of the stock of the new corporation.

In the present situation, the distribution enables the subsidiary corporation to hire the key employee it believes is necessary to the continued success of the business. This is consistent with both Rev.Rul. 69–460 (Situation 2) and Rev.Rul. 85–127.

HOLDING

The pro rata distribution of the stock of Y by X to the X shareholders to enable Y to hire A as its new president is for a valid business purpose within the meaning of section 1.355–2(c) of the regulations. The distribution qualifies under section 355 of the Code because all other requirements of section 355 and the regulations thereunder have been met.

NOTE

The regulations define a corporate business purpose as "a real and substantial non Federal tax purpose germane to the business of the distributing corporation, the controlled corporation or the affiliated group to which the distributing corporation belongs."[1] Valid business purposes include compliance with antitrust and other regulatory decrees, resolution of shareholder disputes, or even amicable partings to permit shareholders to pursue separate business interests.[2] Among other business purposes approved by the courts and the Service are: facilitating a merger of the distributing or controlled corporation;[3] increasing access to credit or new equity investment (such as by enabling either the controlled or distributing corporations to raise capital on more favorable terms through a public offering);[4] resolving labor problems;[5] and warding off a hostile takeover.[6] A pure shareholder purpose, such as personal estate planning, does not suffice under the regulations,[7] but the transaction may pass muster if a shareholder purpose is "so nearly coextensive with a corporate business purpose as to preclude any distinction between them."[8]

The Service has ruled that the reduction of state and local taxes can be a corporate business purpose.[9] But the regulations make it clear that the reduction of "non Federal" taxes is not an independent corporate business purpose if: (1) the transaction will result in a reduction in both Federal and non Federal taxes because of similarities in the respective laws, and (2) the reduction of Federal taxes is greater than or substantially coextensive with the reduction of non Federal taxes.[10] For example, a spin-off of a subsidiary to enable one or both of the resulting corporations to elect S corporation status is not a business purpose[11] even though the transaction may bear little resemblance to the original bailout evil of Gregory v. Helvering.

A business purpose for a distribution also does not exist if the same corporate objectives can be met through a nontaxable transaction that does not require a distribution of stock of a controlled corporation and which is neither impractical nor unduly expensive.[12] For example, assume that a corporation manufactures both toys and candy through divisions which are not separately incorporated, and the shareholders wish to insulate the candy business from the risks of the toy business. If that goal can be achieved by dropping down the assets of one of the businesses to a new subsidiary, a subsequent distribution of the subsidiary stock to the parent's shareholders is not carried out for a corporate business purpose.[13]

---

1. Reg. § 1.355–2(b)(2).

2. Reg. § 1.355–2(b)(5) Examples (1) and (2).

3. Commissioner v. Morris Trust, 367 F.2d 794 (4th Cir.1966). See Section D2 of this chapter, infra.

4. See, e.g., Rev.Rul. 77–22, 1977–1 C.B. 91; Rev.Rul. 85–122, 1985–2 C.B. 119.

5. Olson v. Commissioner, 48 T.C. 855 (1967).

6. See Ltr.Rul. 8819075 (Feb. 17, 1988).

7. Reg. § 1.355–2(b)(2). But see Estate of Parshelsky v. Commissioner, 303 F.2d 14 (2d Cir.1962), where the court held that a shareholder business purpose justified a spin-off even in the absence of a corporate business purpose.

8. Reg. § 1.355–2(b)(2).

9. Rev.Rul. 76–187, 1976–1 C.B. 97.

10. Reg. § 1.355–2(b)(2).

11. Reg. § 1.355–2(d)(5) Example (6).

12. Reg. § 1.355–2(b)(3).

13. Reg. §§ 1.355–2(b)(3), 1.355–2(b)(5) Example (3). See also Reg. § 1.355–2(b)(5) Examples (4) and (5).

b. CONTINUITY OF INTEREST

Regulations: § 1.355–2(c).

The regulations require that those persons who historically owned an interest in the enterprise prior to a corporate division must own, in the aggregate, an amount of stock establishing a continuity of interest in each of the modified corporate forms in which the enterprise is conducted after the distribution.[1] This means that one or more of the shareholders of the distributing corporation must emerge from the transaction (in the aggregate) with at least a 50 percent equity interest in each of the corporations that conduct the enterprise after the division.[2] The continuity of interest test overlaps considerably with the device limitation, which patrols against prearranged postdistribution sales as part of its anti-bailout mission. The regulations nonetheless emphasize that continuity of interest is an independent test that must be met in addition to the other Section 355 requirements.[3]

A common divisive transaction involves the breakup of a corporate enterprise to allow feuding shareholders to part company, with each taking a share of the business in the form of stock in separate corporations. The regulations acknowledge that this type of transaction, whether structured as a split-off or split-up, satisfies the continuity of interest requirement because the prior owners of the integrated enterprise emerge in the aggregate with all the stock of two corporations that survive the separation. Assume, however, that A and B each own 50 percent of the stock of P, Inc., which is engaged in one business, and P owns all the stock of S, Inc., which is engaged in a different business. If new and unrelated shareholder C purchases all of A's stock in P and P then distributes all the stock of S to B in redemption of B's P stock, the transaction fails the continuity of interest test because the owners of P prior to the distribution (A and B) do not, in the aggregate, own an amount of stock establishing continuity of interest in both P and S after the distribution.[4] Only the historic shareholders of P (i.e., A and B) may be counted for continuity of interest purposes, and the smoking pistol here is that none of those shareholders own any stock of P after the distribution. As for who qualifies as an historic shareholder, it appears that a shareholder who acquires P stock prior to the time that P decides to engage in a division should qualify even if the acquisition

---

1. Reg. § 1.355–2(c)(1).

2. Without explicitly saying so, several examples in the regulations indicate that a 50 percent equity interest, the benchmark for Type A reorganizations, is what is needed to "maintain" continuity of interest. See, e.g., Reg. § 1.355–2(c)(2) Example (2); Rev.Proc. 86–41, § 4.06, 1986–2 C.B. 716. Although 50 percent continuity is required to obtain an advance ruling from the Service, the case law supports a lower percentage, and practitioners routinely prepare opinion letters stating that 40 percent equity is sufficient to maintain continuity of interest. See Ginsburg & Levin, Mergers, Acquisitions & Leveraged Buyouts, Vol. II, ¶ 704.021.

3. Reg. § 1.355–2(c)(1). For a rare published ruling on the application of the continuity of interest doctrine to a spin-off, see Rev.Rul. 79–273, 1979–2 C.B. 125.

4. Reg. § 1.355–2(c)(2) Example (3).

occurred shortly before the distribution.[5] Apparently, even a person who acquired P stock in a contemplation of a distribution of S stock will be treated as an historic shareholder if the acquisition was more than two years prior to the distribution.[6]

The shareholders of the distributing corporation also must maintain continuity of interest after the distribution.[7] A post-distribution continuity issue might arise, for example, if shareholders sold more than 50 percent of the stock of either the distributing or controlled corporations shortly after the distribution. Shareholders who committed themselves to sell prior to the distribution or had a fixed intention to do so are not likely to have maintained continuity of interest, but an unanticipated sale should not be a problem.

c. THE "DEVICE" LIMITATION

Code: § 355(a)(1)(B).

Regulations: § 1.355–2(d).

Section 355(a)(1)(B) provides that a corporate division may not be "used principally as a device for the distribution of the earnings and profits" of the distributing corporation or the controlled subsidiary. The historic mission of this requirement apparently was to prevent the conversion of ordinary dividend income into preferentially taxed capital gain through a bailout masquerading as a corporate division.[1] This goal is reaffirmed in the regulations, which provide:[2]

> * * * a tax-free distribution of the stock of a controlled corporation presents a potential for tax avoidance by facilitating the avoidance of the dividend provisions of the Code through the subsequent sale or exchange of stock of one corporation and the retention of the stock of another corporation. A device can include a transaction that effects a recovery of basis.

The repeal of the capital gains preference in the Tax Reform Act of 1986 raised the question of whether the device limitation had waned in significance, perhaps to the vanishing point. If ordinary income and capital gains are taxed at the same rate, a bailout offers minimal potential to avoid tax at the shareholder level. But tax avoidance still might result from a transaction that effects a recovery of basis—for example, a spin-off followed by a subsequent sale of all or part of the controlled corporation's stock. The quoted excerpt from the regulations suggests as much and indicates that the Treasury will enforce the

---

5. See Kaden & Wolfe, "Spin-offs, Split-offs, and Split-ups: A Detailed Analysis of Section 355," 44 Tax Notes 565, 588–589 (July 31, 1989).

6. Id. at 589. Cf. Rev.Rul. 74–5, 1974–1 C.B. 82, declared obsolete on other grounds by Rev.Rul. 89–37, 1989–1 C.B. 107.

7. This is similar to the post-acquisition continuity rule for acquisitive reorganizations. See McDonald's Restaurant of Illinois v. Commissioner, supra p. 497.

1. See, e.g., Rev.Rul. 71–383, 1971–2 C.B. 180.

2. Reg. § 1.355–2(d)(1).

device limitation even in a regime without a capital gains preference or with the modest capital gain rate differential now in the Code.

Even before these recent developments, the meaning and scope of the "device" limitation were mired in obscurity. The regulations initially fail to burn off the fog, declaring that "generally, the determination of whether a transaction was used principally as a device will be made from all of the facts and circumstances." [3] They go on to offer some guidance by identifying certain "device" and "nondevice" factors which are "evidence" of the presence or absence of a device, but the strength of this "evidence" still depends on "the facts and circumstances." [4]

Transactions Ordinarily Not a Device. Notwithstanding the presence or absence of the "device factors" to be discussed below, three transactions "ordinarily" are not considered a tax avoidance device. Distributions are presumed innocent if:

(1) the distributing and controlled corporations have neither accumulated nor current earnings and profits as of the date of the distribution, taking into account the possibility that a distribution by the distributing corporation would create earnings and profits if Section 355 did not apply; [5]

(2) in the absence of Section 355, the distribution would qualify as a redemption to pay death taxes under Section 303; [6] and

(3) in the absence of Section 355, the distribution would qualify, with respect to each distributee shareholder, as an exchange redemption under Section 302(a). [7]

Section 303 and Section 302(a)-type redemptions lose their presumption of innocence, however, if the transaction involves the distribution of the stock of more than one controlled corporation and facilitates the avoidance of the dividend provisions of the Code through the subsequent sale or exchange of stock of one corporation and the retention of the stock of another corporation. [8]

Device and Nondevice Factors: In General. The regulations specify three factors that are "evidence" of a device ("device factors") and three factors that are evidence of a nondevice ("nondevice factors"). The device factors are: (1) a pro rata distribution; (2) a subsequent sale or exchange of stock of either the distributing or controlled corporation; and (3) the nature and use of the assets of the distributing and controlled corporations immediately after the transaction. [9] The three nondevice factors are: (1) the corporate business purpose for the transaction; (2) the fact that the distributing corporation is publicly traded

---

3. Reg. § 1.355–2(d)(1).

4. Reg. § 1.355–2(d)(2)(i), (3)(i).

5. Reg. § 1.355–2(d)(5)(ii).

6. Reg. § 1.355–2(d)(5)(iii). See Chapter 5H, supra.

7. Reg. § 1.355–2(d)(5)(iv). For this purpose, the waiver of family attribution rules apply without regard to the ten year look forward rule and the requirement to file a waiver agreement in Sections 302(c)(2)(A) (ii) and (iii). See Chapter 5C, supra.

8. Reg. § 1.355–2(d)(5)(i). For an example, see Reg. § 1.355–2(d)(5)(v) Example (2).

9. Reg. § 1.355–2(d)(2).

and widely held; and (3) the fact that the stock of the controlled corporation is distributed to one or more domestic corporations which would be entitled to a dividends received deduction under Section 243 if Section 355 does not apply to the transaction.[10] The presence of one or more of these factors is not controlling, however, and the "strength" of the evidence depends on the facts and circumstances.[11]

Pro Rata Distribution. A pro rata distribution—for example, a spin-off—is considered to present the greatest potential for avoidance of the dividend provisions of Subchapter C and thus is more likely to be used principally as a device. As a result, the regulations provide that a pro rata or substantially pro rata distribution is evidence of a device.[12]

Subsequent Sale or Exchange of Stock. A parenthetical clause in Section 355(a)(1)(B) cryptically provides that the "mere fact" that stock or securities of either the distributing or controlled corporations is sold by all or some of the shareholders is not to be construed to mean that the transaction was used principally as a device. But the Service has long contended that a sale of stock of the distributing or controlled corporation shortly after a corporate division is evidence that the transaction was used as a bailout device. The "strength" of the evidence depends upon the percentage of stock disposed of after the distribution, the length of time between the distribution and the subsequent sale and the extent to which the subsequent sale was prearranged.[13]

A subsequent sale or exchange negotiated or agreed upon before the distribution is "substantial evidence" of a device.[14] A sale is always prearranged if it was "pursuant to an arrangement negotiated or agreed upon before the distribution if enforceable rights to buy or sell existed before the distribution." [15] The regulations are more equivocal if a sale was merely discussed by the parties but was "reasonably to be anticipated." In that event, it "ordinarily" will be considered to be previously negotiated or agreed upon.[16] Seemingly ignoring the express language of Section 355(a)(1)(B), the regulations also provide that even in the absence of prior negotiations or agreement, a subsequent sale nonetheless is "evidence of a device." [17] Presumably, the evidence would be fairly weak if the decision to sell was not made until after the distribution.

The perceived bailout abuse of a subsequent sale normally is present only when the selling shareholders cash out their investment. The regulations logically provide that if the shareholders dispose of stock in a subsequent tax-free reorganization in which no more than an "insubstantial" amount of gain is recognized, the transaction will not be treated as a subsequent sale or exchange. Rather, because the shareholders maintain an interest in the continuing enterprise, the

10. Reg. § 1.355–2(d)(3).

11. Reg. § 1.355–2(d)(2)(i); –2(d)(3)(i).

12. Reg. § 1.355–2(d)(2)(ii).

13. Reg. § 1.355–2(d)(2)(iii)(A).

14. Reg. § 1.355–2(d)(2)(iii)(B).

15. Reg. § 1.355–2(d)(2)(iii)(D).

16. Id.

17. Reg. § 1.355–2(d)(2)(iii)(C).

stock received in the exchange is treated as equivalent to the stock surrendered.[18] But any sale of the new stock received will be subject to the "subsequent sale" rules and could be evidence of a device.[19]

The Service's reliance on subsequent stock sales (whether or not prearranged) as substantial evidence of a device has always been questionable. To return to the earlier introductory example, assume that Diverse Corporation has actively conducted profitable winery and chicken ranch businesses for more than five years. If Diverse wished to spin off the chicken ranch as Poultry, Inc., it would have no difficulty satisfying the active business test. But what if the spin-off were the prelude to a prearranged sale of the Poultry, Inc. stock by the controlling shareholders? If gain on that sale were taxable to the shareholders at capital gains rates, or even if it merely effected a recovery of part of the shareholders' basis in their Diverse Corp. stock, should the spin-off be viewed principally as a device to bail out Diverse's earnings and profits?

In considering these questions, keep in mind the alternatives available to Diverse. If the corporation simply had sold the chicken ranch assets and distributed the proceeds to its noncorporate shareholders, the distribution likely would have qualified as a partial liquidation, entitling noncorporate shareholders to exchange treatment.[20] The same result would have occurred if the chicken ranch assets were distributed pro rata to the shareholders and sold shortly thereafter. To be sure, a sale or distribution of the chicken ranch assets by the corporation would have triggered gain at the corporate and shareholder levels.[21] But, historically at least, the principal concern in Section 355 was not with the double taxation of corporate earnings but rather the tax treatment of a distribution to the shareholders. If an economically equivalent transaction (i.e., a partial liquidation) would have qualified for capital gain treatment, it seems anomalous to classify a spin-off followed by a prearranged sale of the same business as a device to convert ordinary dividend income to capital gain. In the last analysis, the answer may be to treat partial liquidation distributions as dividends to noncorporate shareholders. Moreover, even if it is not a device, a distribution followed by a taxable sale is unlikely to satisfy the business purpose test and, if the sale closely follows the distribution but somehow escapes the device limitation, the transaction also may fail the continuity of interest requirement.

Nature and Use of the Assets. The regulations also enforce the device limitation by taking into account the "nature, kind, amount, and use of the assets of the distributing and the controlled corporations (and corporations controlled by them) immediately after the transaction." [22]

18. Reg. § 1.355–2(d)(2)(iii)(E).

19. Id.

20. See I.R.C. § 302(b)(4), (e). But see Rev.Rul. 75–223, 1975–1 C.B. 109, at p. 241, supra, in which the Service ruled that a distribution of stock of a subsidiary may not qualify as a partial liquidation. See also Morgenstern v. Commissioner, 56 T.C. 44 (1971).

21. See Chapter 7, supra.

22. Reg. § 1.355–2(d)(2)(iv).

Thus, the existence of assets that are not used in an active trade or business, such as cash and other liquid assets that are not related to the reasonable needs of the active business, is evidence of a device.[23] To illustrate, assume that Corporation P spins off Corporation S in order to comply with certain regulatory requirements under state law. As part of the separation, P transfers excess cash (not related to the reasonable needs of P or S's business) to S and then distributes the S stock pro rata to P's shareholders. The result of this infusion of cash into S is that the percentage of liquid assets not related to the trade or business is substantially greater for S than for P. The regulations view this as suspect, providing in an example that the transfer of cash by P to S is "relatively strong evidence of device." [24] When coupled with the pro rata nature of the distribution, the transaction is considered to have been used principally as a device notwithstanding the "strong business purpose" because there was no business purpose for the infusion of cash into S.[25]

The regulations also consider the relationship between the distributing and controlled corporations and the effect of a sale of one of the businesses on the overall enterprise. Evidence of a device is presented if the distributing or controlled corporation is a business that principally serves the business of the other corporation (a "secondary business") and it can be sold without adversely affecting the business that it serves.[26] Thus, the spin-off of a captive coal mine from a steel manufacturer, a transaction which satisfied the active business test,[27] nonetheless presents evidence of a device if the principal function of the coal mine is to satisfy the requirements of the steel business and the coal mine could be sold without adversely affecting the steel business.[28] The apparent concern here is not so much with the potential for tax avoidance through non-arm's length intercorporate transactions between the separated corporations. That type of abuse is adequately policed by Section 482, which authorizes the Commissioner to allocate income or deductions between or among commonly controlled trades or businesses. What appears to be bothering the Service is the likelihood for avoidance of the dividend provisions of the Code when the "related function" is not truly integral to the business from which it has been separated.

Nondevice Factors. Acknowledging that the corporate business purposes for a transaction may be sufficiently compelling to outweigh

---

23. Reg. § 1.355–2(d)(2)(iv)(A), (B).

24. Reg. § 1.355–2(d)(4) Example (3).

25. Reg. § 1.355–2(d)(2)(iv)(B); 1.355–2(d)(4) Example (3). Compare Reg. § 1.355–2(d)(4) Example (2), where the transfer of cash and liquid securities from the distributing to the controlled corporation was "relatively weak evidence of device" because after the transfer the two corporations held liquid assets in amounts proportional to the values of their businesses.

26. Reg. § 1.355–2(d)(2)(iv)(C).

27. See Reg. § 1.355–3(c) Example (11).

28. Reg. § 1.355–2(d)(2)(iv)(C). Likewise, the separation of the sales and manufacturing functions will constitute evidence of a device if the principal function of the sales operation after the separation is to sell the output from the manufacturing operation and the sales operation could be sold without adversely affecting the manufacturing operation.

any evidence of a device, the regulations provide that the corporate business purpose for a transaction is evidence of nondevice.[29]   In keeping with the "sliding scale" approach that pervades the device regulations, the stronger the evidence of device, then the stronger is the business purpose required to prevent determination that the transaction was used principally as a device.[30]   The strength of a corporate business purpose, of course, is based on all the facts and circumstances, including but not limited to the importance of achieving the purpose to the success of the business, the extent to which the transaction is prompted by a person not having a proprietary interest in either corporation or by other outside factors beyond the control of the distributing corporation, and the "immediacy of the conditions" prompting the transaction.[31]

The fact that the distributing corporation is publicly traded and widely held, having no shareholder who directly or indirectly owns more than five percent of any class of stock, also is evidence of nondevice.[32]

Finally, the fact that the stock of the controlled corporation is distributed to a domestic corporate distributee which, without Section 355, would be entitled to the Section 243 dividends received deduction, is evidence of a nondevice.[33]

PROBLEM

Assume that Lemon Corporation from Problem 1 at page 649, operates a computer manufacturing business at only one location where it also conducts research and development through a separate division. Lemon also owns all the stock of Floppy Disk, Inc., a computer software manufacturer that Lemon purchased six years ago in a taxable transaction.   The net worths of the computer and software businesses are approximately the same, and both corporations have substantial accumulated earnings and profits.   The common stock of Lemon is owned equally by Ms. Micro and Mr. Chips.   In each of the following alternatives, assume that the active trade or business requirement is met and consider whether the transactions described satisfy the other requirements of Section 355.

   (a)   To resolve a shareholder dispute, Lemon distributes all the stock of Floppy Disk, Inc. to Mr. Chips in complete redemption of his stock in Lemon.

   (b)   Same as (a), above, except that Ms. Micro and Mr. Chips are mother and son.

   (c)   Same as (a), above, except that shortly before the distribution of Floppy Disk stock to Mr. Chips, Ms. Micro sold all of her

---

29. Reg. § 1.355–2(d)(3)(ii).

30. Id.

31. Id.

32. Reg. § 1.355–2(d)(3)(iii).

33. Reg. § 1.355–2(d)(3)(iv).

Lemon stock to Mr. Macro, who wished to acquire the hardware business but not the software company.

(d) To enable the computer manufacturing business to maintain different retirement plans for its manufacturing and research employees, Lemon transfers the assets of the research division to a new corporation, Research, Inc., and distributes all the Research stock pro rata to Ms. Micro and Mr. Chips. After the distribution, Research, Inc. continues to perform services solely for Lemon.

(e) Same as (d), above, except that the purpose of the spin-off is to comply with a regulatory decree. (Compare your answer to Problem 1(e) at page 650).

(f) To comply with a state law providing that computer hardware and software businesses may not be conducted by parent and subsidiary corporations, Lemon must spin off or sell its Floppy Disk, Inc. subsidiary. In anticipation of the new law, Lemon's board of directors informally negotiated a sale of Floppy Disk to Suitor, Inc. Before the agreement is reduced to an enforceable writing, Lemon distributes the Floppy Disk stock to Ms. Micro and Mr. Chips. Two months later, the shareholders sell the Floppy Disk to Suitor on the same terms negotiated by the Lemon board of directors.

(g) Same as (f), above, except that the Lemon board rejects Suitor's offer and instead distributes the Floppy Disk stock pro rata to the shareholders. Four months later, the shareholders sell their Floppy Disk stock to White Knight, Inc.

(h) Same as (f), above, except the sale by the shareholders is made to Suitor, Inc. on essentially the same terms that had been rejected by the Lemon board of directors.

5. THE CHANGING ROLE OF SECTION 355

This chapter has examined the requirements for a tax-free corporate division as they developed in the very different tax regime that existed prior to the 1986 Code. The device limitation and the judicially created business purpose test were born of the same concern—that corporate divisions should be tax free if they are motivated by a legitimate business purpose but not if they are merely a device to convert ordinary income into capital gain. The requirements apparently evolved into separate tests because a corporation might be able to establish some business purpose even for a transaction that was entered into principally as a device for the distribution of earnings and profits. These transactions, in which the device motive and a business purpose coexist, will fail to qualify as tax-free under Section 355. On the other hand, if a transaction is not principally a device for the distribution of earnings and profits and there is no business purpose, the transaction presumably would not have been entered into in the first place.

The changes made by the Tax Reform Act of 1986 raise questions as to the future roles of these two requirements. As for the device limitation, since ordinary income and capital gains are taxed at virtually the same rate, an individual taxpayer without substantial capital losses to offset will not have much of an economic incentive to use a corporate division to convert dividends into capital gain. It follows that the device limitation has waned in importance and one is left to wonder about its current role.

Although the utility of Section 355 as a bailout device and the corresponding significance of the device limitation has declined, the overall appeal of a tax-free corporate division, and the importance of the business purpose requirement, nonetheless increased under the 1986 Code. After repeal of the *General Utilities* doctrine, Section 355 became attractive not as a technique to minimize tax at the shareholder level but rather to avoid a corporate-level tax on the disposition of part of a corporate business.[1] Congress has shifted its attention to these corporate level issues in a piecemeal fashion.[2] A more comprehensive overhaul of Section 355 may be recommended in the Treasury's eagerly awaited study of Subchapter C.

C. TAX TREATMENT OF THE PARTIES TO A CORPORATE DIVISION

Code: §§ 311(a), (b); 312(a), (b), (h); 336(c); 355(a)(1)(A), (3), (c); 356; 358(a)–(c); 361; 362(b); 1032. Skim §§ 301; 302; 355(d); 381(a); 1223(1) and (2).

Regulations: §§ 1.312–10; 1.358–2.

If the requirements of Section 355 and the accompanying judicial doctrines are satisfied, a set of provisions come into play to govern the specific tax consequences (e.g., total or partial nonrecognition of gain, basis, holding period, etc.) to the parties. In this section, we consider the tax consequences if a corporate division is preceded by the formation of one or more new corporations in a Type D reorganization, the consequences of the division itself and the results if the division fails to satisfy the statutory and judicial requirements.

The Relationship of Type D Reorganizations to Corporate Divisions. If one or more corporations are formed as a preparatory step to a qualifying corporate division, the formation of the new subsidiary is a Type D reorganization.[1] The parent corporation does not recognize gain or loss on the transfer of assets to the controlled corporation,[2] and it takes an exchanged basis [3] and may tack the holding period in the new stock or securities that it receives.[4] The newly formed controlled corporation does not recognize gain on the issuance of its stock [5] and it

1. See generally Simon & Simmons, "The Future of Section 355," 40 Tax Notes 291 (July 18, 1988).

2. See Section D1 of this chapter, infra.

1. I.R.C. § 368(a)(1)(D).

2. I.R.C. § 361(a).

3. I.R.C. § 358(a).

4. I.R.C. § 1223(1).

5. I.R.C. § 1032(a).

takes the assets with a transferred basis and a tacked holding period.[6] The earnings and profits of the parent corporation are apportioned between the parent and controlled corporations according to rules provided in the regulations.[7] Section 381, providing for carryover of corporate attributes in certain corporate acquisitions, does not apply to divisive reorganizations and thus the parent corporation retains its tax attributes other than the earnings and profits which are allocated to the controlled corporation.

Consequences to the Shareholders: No Boot Received. If the requirements of Section 355 are met, the shareholders or security holders of the distributing parent corporation will not recognize gain or loss on the distribution of stock or securities of the controlled corporation.[8] The aggregate basis of the stock or securities in the distributing corporation held by the shareholder is allocated among the stock and securities of both the distributing and controlled corporations in proportion to their relative fair market values,[9] and the shareholder's holding period in the stock or securities of the controlled corporation received in the distribution includes the holding period of the stock or securities of the distributing corporation.[10]

Treatment of Boot. As with most other types of reorganizations, the receipt of boot in an otherwise qualifying corporate division does not necessarily spell doom for the transaction but results in the recognition of gain to the shareholder receiving the boot. For this purpose, boot includes cash, any property other than stock or securities of the controlled corporation (e.g., short-term debt obligations, stock rights or warrants), securities of the controlled corporation to the extent that their principal amount exceeds the principal amount of any securities surrendered and any stock of the controlled corporation that was acquired by the distributing corporation in a taxable transaction within the five-year period prior to the distribution.[11]

The treatment of boot depends on the form of the division. In the case of a spin-off, the boot is treated as a distribution to which Section 301 applies (without regard to the shareholder's realized gain) and is thus a dividend to the extent of the distributing corporation's current and accumulated earnings and profits and a return of capital to the extent of any balance.[12] In the case of a split-off or split-up, both of which involve an exchange rather than a distribution, Section 356(a)(1) requires the shareholder to recognize any realized gain to the extent of

6. I.R.C. §§ 362(b); 1223(2).

7. I.R.C. § 312(h); Reg. § 1.312–10(a), (c). In the case of a newly created corporation, this allocation generally is made in proportion to the relative fair market values of the assets retained by the parent corporation and the assets transferred to the controlled corporation. Reg. § 1.312–10(a). In a "proper case," the regulations provide that this allocation should be made in proportion to the "net basis" (after re-duction for liabilities) of the transferred and retained assets. Id.

8. I.R.C. § 355(a)(1).

9. I.R.C. § 358(b), (c).

10. I.R.C. § 1223(1).

11. I.R.C. §§ 355(a)(3), (4); 356(a), (b), (d) (2)(C).

12. I.R.C. § 356(b).

the boot received in the distribution. The characterization of that gain is more problematic. Section 356(a)(2) adopts the same rule used for acquisitive reorganizations by providing that if the exchange has "the effect of the distribution of a dividend," the gain recognized is treated as a dividend to the extent of the shareholder's ratable share of accumulated earnings and profits of the distributing corporation.[13] The balance of any recognized gain is treated as gain from the exchange of property.[14] Dividend equivalence is tested by applying the principles of Section 302 (i.e., meaningful reduction of the shareholder's proportionate interest) using an assumption that the shareholder has surrendered part of his stock in the distributing corporation in a redemption and received boot in exchange.[15] Absent a significant capital gains preference, however, individual shareholders usually will be indifferent to the character of their gain unless the amounts involved are large. Any loss realized by a shareholder in a Section 355 exchange may not be recognized.[16]

Section 358 again governs the basis of the boot and nonrecognition property received in the distribution. The boot takes a fair market value basis and its holding period commences as of the date of the distribution.[17] The aggregate basis of the nonrecognition property (i.e., stock and securities) is the same as the basis of the stock or securities of the distributing corporation plus any gain recognized and less any cash and the fair market value of any boot property received on the exchange.[18] That aggregate basis is then allocated among the old and new stock or securities (or the new stock or securities, in the case of a split-up) in proportion to their relative fair market values.[19] The nonrecognition property ordinarily is eligible for a tacked holding period.[20]

Recognition of Gain or Loss to Distributing Corporation: General Rules. The tax consequences to the distributing corporation in a Section 355 transaction initially are determined by Section 361(c) if the distribution is preceded by a Type D reorganization and by Section 355(c) if it is not. In either case, the results generally are the same. If a Section 355 transaction occurs in conjunction with certain changes in shareholder ownership, the distributing corporation also may be required to recognize gain under Section 355(d).[21]

---

13. In one of the many curiosities in the world of reorganizations, neither Section 356(a)(2) nor the applicable regulations refer to *current* earnings and profits.

14. See Reg. § 1.356–1(b)(2).

15. Rev.Rul. 74–516, 1974–2 C.B. 121.

16. I.R.C. § 356(c).

17. I.R.C. § 358(a)(2).

18. I.R.C. § 358(a)(1).

19. I.R.C. § 358(b)(2), (c); Reg. § 1.358–2. The Service has never provided any guidance as to the precise date to be used

in valuing the corporations for purposes of this allocation. In the case of publicly held companies, the date selected ordinarily is the first day that the stock of the controlled corporation was traded on a listed exchange. For other possibilities, see Bittker & Eustice, Federal Income Taxation of Corporations and Shareholders ¶ 13.12 (5th ed. 1987).

20. I.R.C. § 1223(1).

21. See Section D1 of this chapter, infra.

If a Section 355 distribution is part of a reorganization plan, the distributing corporation does not recognize gain on the distribution to its shareholders of "qualified property"—i.e., stock or debt obligations of the controlled corporation.[22] Thus, in the typical spin-off or split-off, where the distributing corporation's basis in the stock of the controlled corporation is ordinarily less than its fair market value, no corporate-level gain is recognized on the distribution. Section 311(b), which otherwise might have required gain recognition, is not applicable because it only applies to distributions under Subpart A of Subchapter C (Sections 301–307), and Section 355 is not within that portion of the Code.[23] The same result occurs on a split-up. Section 336, which otherwise might have required the recognition of corporate-level gain on a liquidating distribution, does not apply to distributions that are part of a reorganization.[24] Gain is recognized, however, in the rare case where appreciated boot is distributed in a Section 355 transaction that is part of a reorganization.[25]

If the distribution is not preceded by a Type D reorganization—e.g., where the controlled corporation is not a newly formed subsidiary— Section 355(c) takes over for all forms of divisions,[26] providing generally that the distributing corporation recognizes no gain or loss on any distribution to which Section 355 applies.[27] Gain must be recognized, however, on a distribution of appreciated property other than "qualified property,"—i.e., other than stock or securities in the controlled corporation.[28] Thus, no gain will be recognized on a distribution of stock or securities of the controlled corporation in a qualifying corporate division even if the recipient shareholder is taxed,[29] but gain is recognized on a distribution of any other appreciated boot.[30]

In all cases, any stock of the controlled corporation that is acquired by the distributing corporation in a taxable transaction within the five-year period preceding the distribution will constitute boot.[31] For example, assume the distributing corporation had owned 90 percent of the stock of a controlled subsidiary for many years and acquired the remaining 10 percent shortly prior to an otherwise qualifying Section 355 distribution. Because the recently acquired stock is treated as boot, it is taxable to the shareholders and any gain accruing during the period between the acquisition and distribution of the stock will be taxable to the distributing corporation.

---

22. I.R.C. § 361(c)(1), (2).

23. See also I.R.C. § 361(c)(4).

24. I.R.C. § 361(c)(4); see also § 336(c).

25. I.R.C. § 361(c)(2).

26. Section 355(c)(3) makes it clear that Sections 311 (relating to nonliquidating distributions) and 336 (relating to liquidating distributions) do not apply to a distribution governed by Section 355.

27. I.R.C. § 355(c)(1).

28. I.R.C. § 355(c)(2). The definition of "qualified property" in Section 355(c)(2)(B)

is somewhat narrower than the one used to define the same term in Section 361(c)(2)(B), where "qualified property" includes both rights to acquire stock and nonsecurity debt obligations.

29. The recipient would be taxed, for example, if the principal amount of securities received exceeds the principal amount of any securities surrendered. I.R.C. § 355(a)(3)(A).

30. I.R.C. § 355(c)(2)(A).

31. I.R.C. § 355(a)(3)(B).

Recognition of Gain on Certain Disqualified Distributions. The general nonrecognition rule in Section 355(c) does not apply if the distributing corporation makes a "disqualified distribution" of "disqualified stock" within the meaning of Section 355(d). In general, a disqualified distribution is any distribution of stock or securities of a controlled subsidiary ("S") if any person purchased stock or securities in the distributing corporation ("P") and, within five years, 50 percent or more of the S stock is distributed to that person in exchange for the purchased P stock. This rule, which is designed to prevent the use of Section 355 to facilitate the tax-free sale of part of a business following a takeover (and in related transactions), is discussed later in the chapter.[32]

Carryover of Tax Attributes. The method of allocating the earnings and profits of the various parties to a corporate division depends on the form of the transaction. If a division is preceded by a Type D reorganization, the earnings and profits of the distributing corporation are allocated between the distributing and controlled corporations in proportion to the relative fair market values of the assets retained by each corporation.[33] If the division is not preceded by a Type D reorganization—e.g., where the stock of a preexisting subsidiary or subsidiaries is distributed—the regulations provide methods for determining the decrease in the distributing corporation's earnings and profits.[34] In no event may any deficit of the distributing corporation be allocated to the controlled corporation.[35]

Earnings and profits are the only tax attributes affected by a corporate division. The carryover rules of Section 381 relating to other tax attributes are not applicable to divisive reorganizations, and thus the tax history of the distributing corporation will remain intact in a spin-off or a split-off. Since a split-up involves the liquidation of the distributing corporation, its tax attributes will disappear as a result of the transaction.[36]

Consequences of Failed Divisions. If a corporate division fails to qualify under Section 355, the tax consequences depend on the form of the transaction. If the defective division is preceded by the formation of a new corporation, that formation still qualifies for nonrecognition— but under Section 351 rather than Section 368(a)(1)(D).[37]

As for the division itself, the distribution of stock or securities in a nonqualifying spin-off is treated as an ordinary distribution to which Section 301 applies. That means it will be a dividend to the extent of

---

32. See Section D1 of this chapter, infra.

33. I.R.C. § 312(h); Reg. § 1.312–10(a). The regulations also state that in a "proper case" the allocation should be made in proportion to the net bases of the transferred and retained assets.

34. Reg. § 1.312–10(b).

35. Reg. § 1.312–10(c).

36. See Rev.Rul. 56–373, 1956–2 C.B. 217.

37. Although the formation of the new corporation still qualifies for nonrecognition, different operative provisions come into play to govern the transaction. See I.R.C. §§ 351, 358, 362(a), 1032. See Reg. § 1.312–11(a) for the allocation of earnings and profits in these circumstances.

current and accumulated earnings and profits and a return of capital to the extent of any balance. If the distribution takes the form of a split-off, it is tested under the stock redemption rules of Section 302. To avoid being subject to Section 301, the redemption thus must come within one of the Section 302(b) tests for exchange treatment.[38] If the failed division is a split-up, the transaction logically should be governed by the complete liquidation rules, allowing the shareholders to recognize capital gain or loss under Section 331(a).[39]

At the corporate level, the distributing corporation will be required to recognize gain on a distribution of appreciated property in a failed spin-off or split-off under Section 311(b). Section 311(a)(2), however, denies recognition of loss on distributions of property that had declined in value. In a split-up, the distributing corporation will be required to recognize gain or loss under Section 336(a), subject to the limitations on recognition of loss in Section 336(b).

PROBLEM

Father is the sole shareholder of an incorporated department store which he has owned for 15 years. He has a basis of $200,000 in his Store Corporation stock, which is currently worth $2 million. Store has $400,000 of accumulated earnings and profits. Three years ago, Store acquired land in Suburb, where it constructed and then opened a new branch store. The branch has been quite successful and represents $500,000 of the $2 million net worth of Store Corporation. The assets of the branch have a $100,000 basis.

Father recently celebrated his 65th birthday and is exploring some estate planning alternatives. His attorney has suggested that he should have Store Corporation transfer the Suburb store to newly created Branch Corporation in exchange for Branch stock worth $400,000 and Branch securities worth $100,000. Store Corporation, which would be worth $1.5 million after this transaction, then would distribute the Branch stock and securities to Father who in turn would give the Branch stock to his children.

Discuss all the income tax consequences of the above transactions to Father, Store Corporation and Branch Corporation, assuming first that the corporate division totally or partially qualifies under Section 355 and then that it fails to qualify.

---

38. If the distribution is pro rata, dividend treatment is thus assured. The distribution of stock in a failed split-off would not qualify for partial liquidation treatment under Section 302(b)(4). See Morgenstern v. Commissioner, 56 T.C. 44 (1971); Rev.Rul. 75–223, 1975–1 C.B. 109.

tion coupled with a dividend. This might occur on a split-up involving a failed division of an operating business from liquid assets in preparation for a sale of the liquid assets. See Bittker & Eustice, Federal Income Taxation of Corporations and Shareholders ¶ 13.15 (5th ed. 1987).

39. It is possible, however, that certain split-ups may be treated as a reorganiza-

D. USE OF SECTION 355 IN CORPORATE ACQUISITIONS

1. LIMITATIONS ON USE OF SECTION 355 IN TAXABLE ACQUISITIONS *

a. INTRODUCTION

The repeal of the *General Utilities* doctrine required tax advisors to search for new techniques to avoid corporate-level gain on the sale of all or part of a business. The problem frequently arises when one corporation acquires a controlling stock interest in a target corporation and then wishes to dispose of unwanted pieces of the target, perhaps to help finance the acquisition or maximize overall shareholder value. The tax goal is to consummate those sales without recognizing gain. Ill fated attempts to achieve this objective through ingenious uses of the consolidated return regulations—the "mirror subsidiary" technique and its progeny—were discussed in Chapter 7.[1] When it became clear that Congress would shatter the mirror technique, taxpayers turned to Section 355 to facilitate tax-free sales of unwanted assets in corporate solution. Congress once again reacted by curtailing the benefits of nonrecognition for certain transactions that previously would have qualified as tax-free divisions. These new anti-avoidance limitations, which were previewed earlier in this chapter, are best explained in the context of the transactions at which they were directed.

b. DISPOSITIONS OF RECENTLY ACQUIRED BUSINESSES

Code: § 355(a)(2)(D).

Congress's first line of attack was to amend the active trade or business requirement in Section 355(b)(2)(D) in order to prevent a purchasing corporation ("P") that had recently acquired a controlling stock interest in a target corporation ("T") from disposing of a target subsidiary ("S") without paying a corporate-level tax. To illustrate the prototype transaction at which this rule is aimed, assume that P purchases all the stock of T, which has engaged directly in the active conduct of a trade or business for more than five years. T owns the stock of S, which also has engaged in the active conduct of a trade or business for the requisite five-year period. Both T and S have highly appreciated assets. P does not make a Section 338 election when it purchases T's stock and, as a result, T and S retain their historic asset bases. P intends to dispose of S shortly after the takeover of T.

Prior to 1987, the parties could have used a two-step transaction to sell S without recognizing gain. T first distributed the S stock to P in a

---

* See generally Stephan, "Disaggregation and Subchapter C: Rethinking Corporate Tax Reform," 76 Va.L.Rev. 655 (1990).

1. See Chapter 7C7a, supra.

tax-free distribution under Section 355.[2] The Service had ruled that such a distribution qualified as tax-free and did not violate the active trade or business requirement unless P attempted a bailout by distributing the S stock to its shareholders.[3] P would allocate the cost basis in its T stock under Section 358 between the T stock and the S stock it received in the distribution, obtaining essentially a fair market value basis in the stock of both corporations.[4] After a respectable interval, P then would sell the S stock without recognition of any corporate-level gain. Although the new buyer would take a cost basis in the S stock, S would retain its historic lower asset bases. This is noteworthy because the gain inherent in S's assets was not avoided by this technique; it merely was deferred. Moreover, that gain did not accrue while P owned T (and thus indirectly S), and any economic gain that did accrue during P's ownership would be taxed on P's sale of the S stock.[5]

Section 355(b)(2)(D) nonetheless forecloses this strategy by providing that the active trade or business requirement is not met if control of the distributing corporation (T) was acquired by a corporate distributee (P) within the five-year period preceding the distribution of stock in the controlled corporation (S).[6] Distributee corporations that are members of the same affiliated group (as defined in Section 1504(a)) are treated as a single corporate distributee for this purpose.[7]

The principal sanction that results from denying Section 355 treatment to the fact pattern in the example is that T must recognize gain on the distribution of its S stock to P. In addition, assuming that T has ample earnings and profits, P has a dividend on receipt of the S stock, but as a corporate parent of T, P likely would be entitled to a 100 percent dividends received deduction.[8] P would obtain a fair market

---

2. To avoid problems under the continuity of interest doctrine, P needed to hold the T stock for a respectable period of time (two years was considered safest) to become a "historic" shareholder of T. See Section B4b of this Chapter, supra.

3. Rev.Rul. 74–5, 1974–1 C.B. 82. The key to the ruling was that T (the distributing corporation) and S (the controlled corporation) both had been engaged in the active conduct of a trade or business for five years. It did not matter that P (the distributee shareholder of T) had acquired a controlling interest in P in a taxable transaction within the five-year period preceding the distribution.

4. P thus obtained a basis in the S stock that was significantly higher than T's basis in the S stock. T's basis would disappear if the spin-off qualified under Section 355. Cf. I.R.C. §§ 332; 336(e); 338(h)(10).

5. Of course, T could not have sold its S stock without recognizing at least one level of gain. Query whether P should be able to avoid gain on a sale of a piece of T's business when T could not have done so.

On the other hand, no corporate-level gain was recognized when T's shareholders sold all their T stock to P and no Section 338 election was made. Query why T or P should not be able to sell S without corporate-level gain provided that gain is preserved through transferred asset bases.

6. The limitation does not apply, however, if P acquired T in a wholly tax-free transaction (such as an acquisitive reorganization). I.R.C. § 355(b)(2)(D)(ii).

7. Thus, if in the example P had two existing wholly owned subsidiaries (X and Y) and each acquired 50 percent of the T stock for cash, a distribution by T of its S stock within five years after the acquisition would not qualify under Section 355 because X and Y, as members of the same affiliated group, are treated as a single corporation that acquired a controlling stock interest in T within five years preceding the distribution.

8. I.R.C. § 243(a)(3), (b). If P, T and S were members of a consolidated group, the dividend would be deferred and P's basis in its T stock would be reduced by the

value basis in the distributed S stock[9] and thus recognize no further gain on the subsequent sale. But in the likely event that the buyer of the S stock does not make a Section 338 election, the gain inherent in S's assets is preserved through their transferred bases, raising the spectre of yet another corporate-level tax.[10]

PROBLEM

T Corporation ("T") and its wholly owned subsidiary, S Corporation ("S") each have actively conducted a trade or business for more than five years. P Corporation ("P") wishes to acquire T but is not interested in owning the business conducted by S. The assets of T (including its S stock) and S are highly appreciated, and the businesses operated by T and S are equal in value. Consider generally the tax consequences of the following alternative transactions:

(a) T sells its S stock to Buyer Corporation. T's shareholders then sell their T stock to P.

(b) In 1991, P purchases all of T's stock from T's shareholders for cash and does not make a Section 338 election. In 1993, for a valid business purpose, T distributes its S stock to P and nine months later P sells the S stock to Buyer Corporation.

(c) Same as (b), above, except that P is an individual.

(d) Same as (b), above, except that P acquired all the stock of T in a tax-free Type B reorganization.

(e) In 1991, P purchases 50% of the T stock from T's shareholders and Buyer Corporation ("B") purchases the remaining 50%. In 1993, T distributes all of its S stock to B in exchange for all the T stock held by B.

c. CORPORATE–LEVEL TAX ON DIVISIVE TRANSACTIONS IN CONNECTION WITH CERTAIN CHANGES OF OWNERSHIP

Code: § 355(c), (d).

The active business limitation in Section 355(b)(2)(D) only applies if P acquires a controlling stock interest in T within the five years preceding the distribution of S stock. It does not apply in many other situations that offered promising avenues of escape from corporate-level tax in ostensibly divisive transactions that were really sales. For example, if P did not acquire a controlling stock interest in T, the active business limitation in Section 355(b)(2)(D) would not preclude essential-

---

amount of the distribution. Reg. §§ 1.1502–14(a)(1), 1.1502–32(b)(2). See Chapter 14B, infra.

9. I.R.C. § 301(d).

10. This double *corporate*-level tax could be avoided if T sold its S stock directly to the new buyer, and the parties jointly made an election under Section 338(h)(10).

In that event, T could ignore the gain on the sale of its S stock but S would recognize gain on a deemed sale of its assets, and "new S" would obtain a stepped-up basis in those assets. See Chapter 7C3c, supra. Query why the result is worse in a comparable transaction caught by the Section 355(b)(2)(D) trap.

ly the same transaction described in the example above. This opportunity may be illustrated through a simple fact pattern in which four unrelated corporations (A, B, C and D) each purchase a portion of the stock of T with the ultimate objective of winding up with different pieces of T's business that are conducted through separate T subsidiaries. After waiting two years to establish their status as historic shareholders for continuity of interest purposes, A, B and C could exchange their T stock for stock of the desired T subsidiary in a split-off that would qualify under Section 355.[11] All of this could be accomplished without waiting five years after the acquisition of T because no single corporate distributee acquired a controlling stock interest in T. The five-year holding period requirement also does not apply to acquisitions of a controlling interest in T through a partnership or by any other noncorporate purchaser. A variety of other avoidance techniques quickly revealed that Congress had not successfully curtailed the use of Section 355 to avoid corporate-level gain on essentially acquisitive transactions.[12]

The Treasury might have attacked a Section 355 transaction that was inconsistent with *General Utilities* repeal by exercising its authority to issue regulations under Section 337(d).[13] Instead, it returned to Congress in 1990 for a more comprehensive solution. The result is Section 355(d), which imposes a corporate-level tax on divisive transactions in connection with certain changes of ownership. The House Ways and Means Committee explained the reasons for the change: [14]

> Some corporate taxpayers may attempt, under present-law rules governing divisive transactions, to dispose of subsidiaries in transactions that resemble sales, or to obtain a fair market value stepped-up basis for any future dispositions, without incurring corporate-level tax. The avoidance of corporate-level

---

11. For this purpose, it is assumed that all relevant business of T have a five-year history; the business purpose requirement can be satisfied; and the parties could structure the transaction to avoid the step transaction doctrine. On the last point, compare Esmark, Inc. v. Commissioner, 90 T.C. 171 (1988), affirmed per curiam 886 F.2d 1318 (7th Cir.1989) and Standard Linen Service, Inc. v. Commissioner, 33 T.C. 1 (1959) (holding that separate steps will not be combined) with Idol v. Commissioner, 38 T.C. 444 (1962), affirmed 319 F.2d 647 (8th Cir.1963) (applying step transaction doctrine to prevent bailout transaction).

12. See generally Kaden & Wolfe, "Spin-offs, Split-offs, and Split-ups: A Detailed Analysis of Section 355," 44 Tax Notes 565, 577–579 (July 31, 1989); Walter, "Spin–Offs, Split–Offs and Split–Ups in Two–Step Acquisitions and Dispositions," 66 Taxes 970, 980–986 (1988); Schler,

"Avoiding the Technical Requirements of New Section 355," 38 Tax Notes 417 (Jan. 25, 1988).

13. Section 337(d) grants the Service authority to promulgate regulations to prevent circumvention of the purposes of certain amendments made by The Tax Reform Act of 1986 (i.e., repeal of the *General Utilities* doctrine) through the use of any provision of the Code or regulations. The Treasury chose to exercise its authority in connection with perceived misuse of the consolidated return regulations (see Chapter 7C6a, supra) but has not yet addressed the use of Section 355 to avoid *General Utilities* repeal.

14. House Ways and Means Committee, Explanation of Revenue Provisions to 1991 Budget Reconciliation Bill (Oct. 16, 1990), 101st Cong., 2d Sess. 90–92 (1990).

tax is inconsistent with the repeal of the *General Utilities* doctrine as part of the Tax Reform Act of 1986.

Under the present-law rules, individual purchasers, or corporate purchasers of less than 80 percent, of the stock of a parent corporation may attempt to utilize section 355 to acquire a subsidiary (or a division incorporated for this purpose) from the parent without the parent incurring any corporate-level tax. The purchaser may acquire stock of the parent equal in value to the value of the desired subsidiary or division, and later surrender that stock for stock of the subsidiary, in a transaction intended to qualify as a non-pro-rata tax-free divisive transaction. Alternatively, the transaction might be structured as a surrender of the parent stock by all shareholders other than the acquiror, in exchange for a distribution (intended to be tax-free) of all subsidiaries or activities other than those the acquiror desires.

In addition, a non-corporate purchaser, or a corporate purchaser of less than 80 percent of the stock of another corporation, may attempt to utilize section 355 to obtain a stepped up fair market value basis in a subsidiary of an acquired corporation, enabling a subsequent disposition of that subsidiary without a corporate-level tax.

The provisions for tax-free divisive transactions under section 355 were a limited exception to the repeal of the *General Utilities* doctrine, intended to permit historic shareholders to continue to carry on their historic corporate businesses in separate corporations. It is believed that the benefit of tax-free treatment should not apply where the divisive transaction, combined with a stock purchase resulting in a change of ownership, in effect results in the disposition of a significant part of the historic shareholders' interests in one or more of the divided corporations.

The present-law provisions granting tax-free treatment at the corporate level are particularly troublesome because they may offer taxpayers an opportunity to avoid the general rule that corporate-level gain is recognized when an asset (including the stock of a subsidiary) is disposed of. There is special concern about the possibility for the distributing corporation to avoid corporate-level tax on the transfer of a subsidiary. Therefore, although the provision does not affect shareholder treatment if section 355 is otherwise available, it does impose tax at the corporate level, in light of the potential avoidance of corporate tax on what is in effect a sale of a subsidiary.

The bill is not intended to limit in any way the continuing Treasury Department authority to issue regulations to prevent the avoidance of the repeal of the *General Utilities* doctrine through any provision of law or regulations, including Section 355.

Because Section 355(d) attempts to reach such a wide range of transactions, its operation is complex. This summary is intended as an overview and will not address many of the statutory details. In general, Section 355(d) requires recognition of gain by the distributing corporation (but not the distributee shareholders) on a "disqualified distribution" of stock or securities of a controlled corporation regardless of whether the distribution is part of a reorganization.[15] A "disqualified distribution" is any Section 355 distribution if, immediately after the distribution, any person holds "disqualified stock" in either the distributing corporation or any distributed controlled corporation constituting a 50 percent or greater interest (measured by total combined voting power or value) in such corporation.[16] "Disqualified stock" is any stock in either the distributing corporation or any controlled corporation acquired by purchase during the five-year period before the distribution.[17]

In effect, Section 355(d) creates a five-year predistribution continuity of interest test. If violated, the test requires the distributing corporation to recognize gain on the distribution of stock or securities of a subsidiary to a person who ends up with 50 percent or more of the stock of the subsidiary. Some typical situations where Section 355(d) applies are illustrated by the following excerpt from the legislative history: [18]

> Example 1. Assume that after the effective date, individual A acquires by purchase a 20–percent interest in the stock of corporation P and a 10–percent interest in the stock of its subsidiary, S, and 40 percent or more of the stock of S is distributed to A within 5 years in exchange for his 20–percent interest in P. (The remainder of the S stock distributed in the section 355 distribution is distributed to other shareholders). Under the provision P must recognize gain with respect to the distributed stock of the S because all 50 percent of the stock of S held by A is disqualified stock.

> Example 2. Assume that after the effective date individual A acquires by purchase a 20–percent interest in corporation P and P redeems stock of other shareholders so that A's

---

15. This is technically accomplished by removing the stock or securities of the controlled corporation from the category of "qualified property" under Sections 361(c)(2) and 355(c)(2) in the case of a disqualified distribution. I.R.C. § 355(d)(1). This forces the distributing corporation to recognize gain as if the stock and securities were appreciated boot.

16. I.R.C. § 355(d)(2).

17. I.R.C. § 355(d)(3). The stock must have been acquired after October 9, 1990.

Disqualified stock also includes stock in any controlled corporation received in a distribution to the extent attributable to distributions of stock or securities in the distributing corporation acquired by purchase after October 9, 1990 and during the five-year period before the distribution. I.R.C. § 355(d)(2)–(4).

18. H.Rep. No. 101–964, 101st Cong., 2d Sess. 85 (1990).

interest in P increases to a 30 percent interest. Within 5 years of A's purchase, P distributes 50 percent of the stock of its subsidiary, S, to A in exchange for his 30 percent interest in P (the remainder of the stock of S distributed in the section 355 transaction is distributed to the other shareholders). P recognizes gain on the distribution of the stock of S because all 50 percent of the stock of S held by A is disqualified stock.

For purposes of the definition of disqualified stock, stock or securities generally are considered acquired by "purchase" if they do not have either a transferred basis or a Section 1014 date-of-death basis, and were not acquired in an exchange to which Section 351 or the corporate reorganization provision applies.[19] An acquisition of property in a Section 351 exchange, however, is considered a purchase to the extent such property is acquired for cash or a cash item, marketable stock or securities, or any debt of the transferor.[20] In the case of transferred basis property which was purchased by the transferor, the acquirer of the property is treated as having purchased the property on the date it was purchased by the transferor.[21]

To prevent easy avoidance of the 50 percent or more ownership test, an array of aggregation and attribution rules are applied to test shareholder ownership after a distribution. First, a shareholder and all persons related to the shareholder under Sections 267(b) or 707(b) are treated as one person.[22] If two or more otherwise unrelated persons act pursuant to a plan or arrangement with respect to acquisitions of distributing corporation or controlled corporation stock or securities, they are treated as a single person for purposes of Section 355(d).[23] Special rules also apply to attribution of stock from a corporation to its shareholders. The Section 318(a)(2) attribution rules apply to both stock and securities with the threshold for attribution from a corporation reduced to 10 percent.[24] In addition, if a person acquires by purchase an interest in an entity through which stock or securities are attributed, such stock or securities are deemed purchased on the later of the date of the purchase of the interest in the entity or the date the stock or securities are acquired by purchase by the entity.[25]

In yet another anti-avoidance provision, the running of the five-year predistribution period for holding stock or securities is suspended during any period in which the holder's risk of loss with respect to the stock or securities or any portion of the corporation's activities is

---

19. I.R.C. § 355(d)(5)(A). The legislative history states that there will be an exception for reorganization exchanges in which gain is recognized on receipt of boot. H.Rep. No. 101–964, supra note 18, at 90.

20. I.R.C. § 355(d)(5)(B). The legislative history states that it is expected that regulations will provide an exception for Section 351 exchanges in which such items are transferred as part of an active trade or business (including debts incurred in the ordinary course of the trade or business) and do not exceed the reasonable needs of the business. H.Rep. No. 101–964, supra note 19, at 91.

21. I.R.C. § 355(d)(5)(C).

22. I.R.C. § 355(d)(7)(A).

23. I.R.C. § 355(d)(7)(B).

24. I.R.C. § 355(d)(8)(A).

25. I.R.C. § 355(d)(8)(B).

substantially diminished. Such a reduction in risk can be accomplished by an option in favor of the holder, a short sale, a special class of stock or any other device or transaction.[26] The Service also is granted broad power to prescribe regulations which modify the definition of "purchase" and prevent avoidance of Section 355(d) through the use of related persons, intermediaries, pass-thru entities, options or other arrangements.

PROBLEM

In 1991, individual A purchases 30% of the stock of P Corp. ("P"), which owns 100% of the stock of S, Inc. ("S"). In each of the following situations, determine whether Section 355(d) requires P to recognize gain on its distribution of S stock. Assume that each distribution satisfies all the requirements of Section 355 and, unless otherwise indicated, A and the other P shareholders are unrelated.

(a) In 1993, P distributes all of the S stock pro rata to the P shareholders.

(b) Same as (a), above, except that A's sister, B, also owns 25% of P. B purchased the 25% interest in 1989. What if B had purchased the 25% interest in 1992?

(c) In 1993, P distributes 50% of the S stock to A in exchange for A's P stock and the remainder of the S stock is distributed to the other P shareholders.

(d) Same as (c), above, except the distribution takes place in 1997.

(e) In 1993, P distributes all of the S stock to the P shareholders other than A in exchange for their P stock and after the distribution A is the sole shareholder of P.

(f) Assume it is 1999 and A has owned 30% of P's stock for more than five years. In 1999, A purchases an additional 25% of the stock of P and P later that year distributes all of the S stock pro rata to the P shareholders.

2. DISPOSITIONS OF UNWANTED ASSETS IN CONJUNCTION WITH TAX–FREE REORGANIZATIONS

A corporate division is sometimes the vehicle for a spin-off of unwanted assets in preparation for an acquisition of the rest of the target corporation's business. There are many permutations to this common transactional model. The shareholders of the target may continue to operate the unwanted business or sell it to another buyer. The original purchaser may acquire the wanted business in a taxable transaction or a tax-free Type A, B or C reorganization. All these scenarios present a challenge to the target corporation's tax advisor and provide the student of Subchapter C with an opportunity to relate

26. I.R.C. § 355(d)(6).

the requirements for a tax-free corporate division to the acquisitive reorganization concepts encountered in previous chapters.

COMMISSIONER v. MORRIS TRUST **

United States Court of Appeals, Fourth Circuit, 1966.
367 F.2d 794.

HAYNSWORTH, Chief Judge.

Its nubility impaired by the existence of an insurance department it had operated for many years, a state bank divested itself of that business before merging with a national bank. The divestiture was in the form of a traditional "spin-off," but, because it was a preliminary step to the merger of the banks, the Commissioner treated their receipt of stock of the insurance company as ordinary income to the stockholders of the state bank. We agree with the Tax Court, that gain to the stockholders of the state bank was not recognizable under § 355 of the 1954 Code.

In 1960, a merger agreement was negotiated by the directors of American Commercial Bank, a North Carolina corporation with its principal office in Charlotte, and Security National Bank of Greensboro, a national bank. American was the product of an earlier merger of American Trust Company and a national bank, the Commercial National Bank of Charlotte. This time, however, though American was slightly larger than Security, it was found desirable to operate the merged institutions under Security's national charter, after changing the name to North Carolina National Bank. It was contemplated that the merged institution would open branches in other cities.

For many years, American had operated an insurance department. This was a substantial impediment to the accomplishment of the merger, for a national bank is prohibited from operating an insurance department except in towns having a population of not more than 5000 inhabitants. To avoid a violation of the national banking laws, therefore, and to accomplish the merger under Security's national charter, it was prerequisite that American rid itself of its insurance business.

The required step to make it nubile was accomplished by American's organization of a new corporation, American Commercial Agency, Inc., to which American transferred its insurance business assets in exchange for Agency's stock which was immediately distributed to American's stockholders. At the same time, American paid a cash dividend fully taxable to its stockholders. The merger of the two banks was then accomplished.

Though American's spin-off of its insurance business was a "D" reorganization, as defined in § 368(a)(1), provided the distribution of Agency's stock qualified for non-recognition of gain under § 355, the Commissioner contended that the active business requirements of § 355(b)(1)(A) were not met, since American's banking business was not

** Footnotes omitted.

continued in unaltered corporate form. He also finds an inherent incompatibility in substantially simultaneous divisive and amalgamating reorganizations.

Section 355(b)(1)(A) requires that both the distributing corporation and the controlled corporation be "engaged immediately after the distribution in the active conduct of a trade or business." There was literal compliance with that requirement, for the spin-off, including the distribution of Agency's stock to American's stockholders, preceded the merger. The Commissioner asks that we look at both steps together, contending that North Carolina National Bank was not the distributing corporation and that its subsequent conduct of American's banking business does not satisfy the requirement.

A brief look at an earlier history may clarify the problem.

Initially, the active business requirement was one of several judicial innovations designed to limit nonrecognition of gain to the implicit, but unelucidated, intention of earlier Congresses.

Nonrecognition of gain in "spin-offs" was introduced by the Revenue Act of 1924. Its § 203(b)(3), as earlier Revenue Acts, provided for nonrecognition of gain at the corporate level when one corporate party to a reorganization exchanged property solely for stock or securities of another, but it added a provision in subsection (c) extending the nonrecognition of gain to a stockholder of a corporate party to a reorganization who received stock of another party without surrendering any of his old stock. Thus, with respect to the nonrecognition of gain, treatment previously extended to "split-offs" was extended to the economically indistinguishable "spin-off."

The only limitation upon those provisions extending nonrecognition to spin-offs was contained in § 203(h) and (i) defining reorganizations. The definition required that immediately after the transfer, the transferor or its stockholders or both be in control of the corporation to which the assets had been transferred, and "control" was defined as being the ownership of not less than eighty per cent of the voting stock and eighty per cent of the total number of shares of all other classes of stock.

With no restriction other than the requirement of control of the transferee, these provisions were a fertile source of tax avoidance schemes. By spinning-off liquid assets or all productive assets, they provided the means by which ordinary distributions of earnings could be cast in the form of a reorganization within their literal language.

The renowned case of Gregory v. Helvering, 293 U.S. 465, 55 S.Ct. 266, 79 L.Ed. 596, brought the problem to the Supreme Court. The taxpayer there owned all of the stock of United Mortgage Corporation which, in turn, owned 1000 shares of Monitor Securities Corporation. She wished to sell the Monitor stock and possess herself of the proceeds. If the sale were effected by United Mortgage, gain would be recognized to it, and its subsequent distribution of the net proceeds of the sale would have been a dividend to the taxpayer, taxable as ordinary income. If the Monitor stock were distributed to the taxpayer before sale, its full value would have been taxable to her as ordinary income. In order materially to reduce that tax cost, United Mortgage spun-off the Monitor stock to a new corporation, Averill, the stock of which was distributed to the taxpayer. Averill was then liquidated, and the taxpayer sold the Monitor stock. She contended that she was taxable only on the proceeds of the sale, reduced by an allocated part of her cost basis of United Mortgage, and at capital gain rates.

The Supreme Court found the transaction quite foreign to the congressional purpose. It limited the statute's definition of a reorganization to a reorganization of a corporate business or businesses motivated by a business purpose. It was never intended that Averill engage in any business, and it had not. Its creation, the distribution of its stock and its liquidation, the court concluded, was only a masquerade for the distribution of an ordinary dividend, as, of course, it was.

In similar vein, it was held that the interposition of new corporations of fleeting duration, though the transactions were literally within the congressional definition of a reorganization and the language of a nonrecognition section, would not avail in the achievement of the tax avoidance purpose when it was only a mask for a transaction which was essentially and substantively the payment of a liquidating dividend, a sale for cash, or a taxable exchange.

Such cases exposed a number of fundamental principles which limited the application of the nonrecognition of gain sections of the reorganization provisions of the Code. Mertens defines them in terms of permanence, which encompasses the concepts of business purpose and a purpose to continue an active business in altered corporate form. As concomitants to the primary principle and supplements of it, there were other requirements that the transferor, or its stockholders, retain a common stock interest and that a substantial part of the value of the properties transferred be represented by equity securities.

Underlying such judicially developed rules limiting the scope of the nonrecognition provisions of the Code, was an acceptance of a general congressional purpose to facilitate the reorganization of businesses, not to exalt economically meaningless formalisms and diversions through corporate structures hastily created and as hastily demolished. Continuation of a business in altered corporate form was to be encouraged, but immunization of taxable transactions through the interposition of short-lived, empty, corporate entities was never intended and ought not to be allowed.

While these judicial principles were evolving and before the Supreme Court declared itself in Gregory v. Helvering, an alarmed Congress withdrew nonrecognition of gain to a stockholder receiving securities in a spin-off. It did so by omitting from the Revenue Act of 1934, a provision comparable to § 203(c) of the Revenue Act of 1924.

Nonrecognition of gain to the stockholder in spin-off situations, however, was again extended by § 317(a) of the Revenue Act of 1951, amending the 1939 Code by adding § 112(b)(11). This time, the judicially developed restrictions upon the application of the earlier statutes were partially codified. Nonrecognition of gain was extended "unless it appears that (A) any corporation which is a party to such reorganization was not intended to continue the active conduct of a trade or business after such reorganization, or (B) the corporation whose stock is distributed was used principally as a device for the distribution of earnings and profits to the shareholders of any corporation a party to the reorganization."

If this transaction were governed by the 1939 Code, as amended in 1951, the Commissioner would have had the support of a literal reading of the A limitation, for it was not intended that American, in its then corporate form, should continue the active conduct of the banking business. From the prior history, however, it would appear that the intention of the A limitation was to withhold the statute's benefits from schemes of the Gregory v. Helvering type. It effectively reached those situations in which one of the parties to the reorganization was left only with liquid assets not intended for use in the acquisition of an active business or in which the early demise of one of the parties was contemplated, particularly, if its only office was a conduit for the transmission of title. The B limitation was an additional precaution intended to encompass any other possible use of the device for the masquerading of a dividend distribution.

The 1954 Code was the product of a careful attempt to codify the judicial limiting principles in a more particularized form. The congressional particularization extended the principles in some areas, as in the requirement that a business, to be considered an active one, must have been conducted for a period of at least five years ending on the distribution date and must not have been acquired in a taxable transaction during the five-year period. In other areas, it relaxed and ameliorated them, as in its express sanction of non-prorata distributions. While there are such particularized variations, the 1954 Code is a legislative re-expression of generally established principles developed in response to definite classes of abuses which had manifested themselves many years earlier. The perversions of the general congressional purpose and the principles the courts had developed to thwart them, as revealed in the earlier cases, are still an enlightening history with which an interpretation of the reorganization sections of the 1954 Code should be approached.

Section 355(b) requires that the distributing corporation be engaged in the active conduct of a trade or business "immediately after the distribution." This is in contrast to the provisions of the 1951 Act, which, as we have noted, required an intention that the parent, as well as the other corporate parties to the reorganization, continue the conduct of an active business. It is in marked contrast to § 355(b)'s highly particularized requirements respecting the duration of the active business prior to the reorganization and the methods by which it was acquired. These contrasts suggest a literal reading of the post-reorganization requirement and a holding that the Congress intended to restrict it to the situation existing "immediately after the distribution."

Such a reading is quite consistent with the prior history. It quite adequately meets the problem posed by the Gregory v. Helvering situation in which, immediately after the distribution, one of the corporations held only liquid or investment assets. It sufficiently serves the requirements of permanence and of continuity, for as long as an active business is being conducted immediately after the distribution, there is no substantial opportunity for the stockholders to sever their interest in the business except through a separable, taxable transaction. If the corporation proceeds to withdraw assets from the conduct of the active business and to abandon it, the Commissioner has recourse to the back-up provisions of § 355(a)(1)(B) and to the limitations of the underlying principles. At the same time, the limitation, so construed, will not inhibit continued stockholder conduct of the active business through altered corporate form and with further changes in corporate structure, the very thing the reorganization sections were intended to facilitate.

Applied, to this case, there is no violation of any of the underlying limiting principles. There was no empty formalism, no utilization of empty corporate structures, no attempt to recast a taxable transaction in nontaxable form and no withdrawal of liquid assets. There is no question but that American's insurance and banking businesses met all of the active business requirements of § 355(b)(2). It was intended that both businesses be continued indefinitely, and each has been. American's merger with Security, in no sense, was a discontinuance of American's banking business, which opened the day after the merger with the same employees, the same depositors and customers. There was clearly the requisite continuity of stockholder interest, for American's former stockholders remained in 100% control of the insurance company, while, in the merger, they received 54.385% of the common stock of North Carolina National Bank, the remainder going to Security's former stockholders. There was a strong business purpose for both the spin-off and the merger, and tax avoidance by American's stockholders was neither a predominant nor a subordinate purpose. In short, though both of the transactions be viewed together, there were none of the evils or misuses which the limiting principles and the statutory limitations were designed to exclude.

We are thus led to the conclusion that this carefully drawn statute should not be read more broadly than it was written to deny nonrecognition of gain to reorganizations of real businesses of the type which Congress clearly intended to facilitate by according to them nonrecognition of present gain.

The Commissioner, indeed, concedes that American's stockholders would have realized no gain had American not been merged into Security after, but substantially contemporaneously with, Agency's spin-off. Insofar as it is contended that § 355(b)(A) requires the distributing corporation to continue the conduct of an active business, recognition of gain to American's stockholders on their receipt of Agency's stock would depend upon the economically irrelevant technicality of the identity of the surviving corporation in the merger. Had American been the survivor, it would in every literal and substantive sense have continued the conduct of its banking business.

Surely, the Congress which drafted these comprehensive provisions did not intend the incidence of taxation to turn upon so insubstantial a technicality. Its differentiation on the basis of the economic substance of transactions is too evident to permit such a conclusion.

This, too, the Commissioner seems to recognize, at least conditionally, for he says that gain to the stockholders would have been recognized even if American had been the surviving corporation. This would necessitate our reading into § 355(b)(1)(A) an implicit requirement that the distributing corporation, without undergoing any reorganization whatever, whether or not it resulted in a change in its corporate identity, continue the conduct of its active business.

We cannot read this broader limitation into the statute for the same reasons we cannot read into it the narrower one of maintenance of the same corporate identity. The congressional limitation of the post-distribution active business requirement to the situation existing "immediately after the distribution" was deliberate. Consistent with the general statutory scheme, it is quite inconsistent with the Commissioner's contention.

The requirement of § 368(a)(1)(D) that the transferor or its stockholders be in control of the spun-off corporation immediately after the transfer is of no assistance to the Commissioner. It is directed solely to control of the transferee, and was fully met here. It contains no requirement of continuing control of the transferor. Though a subsequent sale of the transferor's stock, under some circumstances, might form the basis of a contention that the transaction was the equivalent of a dividend within the meaning of § 355(a)(1)(B) and the underlying principles, the control requirements imply no limitation upon subsequent reorganizations of the transferor.

There is no distinction in the statute between subsequent amalgamating reorganizations in which the stockholders of the spin-off transferor would own 80% or more of the relevant classes of stock of the reorganized transferor, and those in which they would not. The statute draws no line between major and minor amalgamations in prospect at the time of the spin-off. Nothing of the sort is suggested by the detailed control-active business requirements in the five-year predistribution period, for there the distinction is between taxable and nontaxable acquisitions, and a tax free exchange within the five-year period does not violate the active business-control requirement whether it was a major or a minor acquisition. Reorganizations in which no gain or loss is recognized, sanctioned by the statute's control provision when occurring in the five years preceding the spin-off, are not prohibited in the post-distribution period.

As we have noticed above, the merger cannot by any stretch of imagination be said to have affected the continuity of interest of American's stockholders or to have constituted a violation of the principle underlying the statutory control requirement. The view is the same whether it be directed to each of the successive steps severally or to the whole.

Nor can we find elsewhere in the Code any support for the Commissioner's suggestion of incompatibility between substantially contemporaneous divisive and amalgamating reorganizations. The 1954 Code contains no inkling of it; nor does its immediate legislative history. The difficulties encountered under the 1924 Code and its successors, in dealing with formalistic distortions of taxable transactions into the spin-off shape, contain no implication of any such incompatibility. Section 317 of the Revenue Act of 1951 and the Senate Committee Report, to which we have referred, did require an intention that the distributing corporation continue the conduct of its active business, but that transitory requirement is of slight relevance to an interpretation of the very different provisions of the 1954 Code and is devoid of any implication of incompatibility. If that provision, during the years it was in effect, would have resulted in recognition of gain in a spin-off if the distributing corporation later, but substantially simultaneously, was a party to a merger in which it lost its identity, a question we do not decide, it would not inhibit successive reorganizations if the merger preceded the spin-off.

The Congress intended to encourage six types of reorganizations. They are defined in § 368 and designated by the letters "A" through "F." The "A" merger, the "B" exchange of stock for stock and the "C" exchange of stock for substantially all of the properties of another are all amalgamating reorganizations. The "D" reorganization is the divisive spin-off, while the "E" and "F" reorganizations, recapitalizations and reincorporations, are neither amalgamating nor divisive. All are sanctioned equally, however. Recognition of gain is withheld from each and successively so. Merger may follow merger, and an "A" reorganization by which Y is merged into X corporation may proceed substantially simultaneously with a "C" reorganization by which X acquires substantially all of the properties of Z and with an "F" reorganization by which X is reincorporated in another state. The "D" reorganization has no lesser standing. It is on the same plane as the others and, provided all of the "D" requirements are met, is as available as the others in successive reorganizations.

We have not placed our reliance upon that provision of the National Banking Act which continues the identity of each merging bank in the consolidated banking association which is deemed the same bank as each of the merging constituents. We have not done so, for, at best, it would supply an answer only to the Commissioner's most limited contention. Moreover, we have had previous occasion to point out the narrow purpose of that statute. It was enacted to secure the continuing efficacy of previous fiduciary appointments of each of the constituent banks. It was not intended, as we held in *Fidelity-Baltimore,* to exempt merging banks from stamp taxes to which all other merging corporations are subject. Nor do we think it was intended, when enacted in 1959, to amend the reorganization sections of the 1954 Code or to accord to the stockholders of reorganizing banks more favorable tax treatment than that accorded the stockholders of other corporations undergoing comparable reorganizations. The comprehensive scheme of the 1954 Code was intended to have a uniform application. The courts should not import artificial distinctions into it.

Our conclusion that gain was not recognizable to American's stockholders as a result of the spin-off, therefore, is uninfluenced by the fact that the subsequent merger was under the National Banking Act. It would have been the same if the merger had been accomplished under state laws.

In a substantive sense, however, in every merger there is a continuation of each constituent. Each makes its contribution to the continuing combination, and the substantiality of that contribution is unaffected by such technicalities as a choice to operate under the charter of one constitutent rather than that of another. After the merger, North Carolina National Bank was as much American as Security. It was not one or the other, except in the sense of the most technical of legalisms; it was both, and with respect to the Charlotte operation, old American's business, it was almost entirely American. North Carolina National Bank's business in the Charlotte area after the merger was American's business conducted by American's employees in American's banking houses for the service of American's customers. Probably the only change immediately noticeable was the new name.

While we reject the technical provision of the National Banking Act as a basis for decision, therefore, it is important to the result that, as in every merger, there was substantive continuity of each constituent and its business. In framing the 1954 Code, the Congress was concerned with substance, not formalisms. Its approach was that of the courts in the Gregory v. Helvering series of cases. Ours must be the same. The technicalities of corporate structure cannot obscure the continuity of American's business, its employees, its customers, its locations or the substantive fact that North Carolina National Bank was both American and Security.

A decision of the Sixth Circuit appears to be at odds with our conclusion. In *Curtis,* it appears that one corporation was merged into another after spinning-off a warehouse building which was an unwanted asset because the negotiators could not agree upon its value. The Court of Appeals for the Sixth Circuit affirmed a District Court judgment holding that the value of the warehouse company shares was taxable as ordinary income to the stockholders of the first corporation.

A possible distinction may lie between the spin-off of an asset unwanted by the acquiring corporation in an "A" reorganization solely because of disagreement as to its value and the preliminary spin-off of an active business which the acquiring corporation is prohibited by law from operating. We cannot stand upon so nebulous a distinction, however. We simply take a different view. The reliance in *Curtis* upon the Report of the Senate Committee explaining § 317 of the Revenue Act of 1951, quite dissimilar to the 1954 Code, reinforces our appraisal of the relevant materials.

To the extent that our own decision in *Elkhorn* is relevant, it tends to support our conclusion, not to militate against it.

Elkhorn was one of the interesting cases which contributed to the development of the judicial principles which served, as best they could, to confine pretensive arrangements in the early days long before adoption of the 1954 Code. Mill Creek Coal Company wanted to acquire for Mill Creek stock one of the mining properties of Elkhorn. Had the bargain been effectuated, directly, it would have been clearly a taxable transaction, for Elkhorn had other mining properties. In an attempt to avoid the tax, Elkhorn's other properties were spun-off to a new Elkhorn; old Elkhorn conveyed its remaining properties to Mill Creek for stock and by successive transactions, Elkhorn stockholders wound up owning stock in new Elkhorn which owned all of old Elkhorn's mining properties, except the ones transferred to Mill Creek, and the Mill Creek stock received by old Elkhorn. They were in precisely the same position as they would have been in if old Elkhorn had transferred the Mill Creek properties to Mill Creek for stock. It was an obviously transparent attempt to circumvent the requirement that substantially all of the properties must be transferred to qualify for nonrecognition in what would now be classified as a "C" reorganization.

The contention in *Elkhorn* was not that its stockholders realized gain on the spin-off. The opinion denying a rehearing, particularly, suggests the absence of recognizable gain as a result of the spin-off. It approved the recognition of gain as a result of the subsequent "C" reorganization.

It is difficult now to envision any other result in *Elkhorn,* since the stockholders' purpose of formalistic transformation of a clearly taxable transaction into the form of a series of untaxable transactions was so blatant. Nothing of the sort is present here. Interestingly, however, *Elkhorn* would question the recognition of gain in the merger exchange here, as to which the Commissioner wisely makes no contention under the 1954 Code, not recognition of gain at the earlier spin-off step. As to the first step, the *Elkhorn* opinion appears to oppose the Commissioner's present position.

For the reasons which we have canvassed, we think the Tax Court, which had before it the opinion of the District Court in *Curtis,* though not that of the affirming Court of Appeals, correctly decided that

American's stockholders realized no recognizable taxable gain upon their receipt in the "D" reorganization of the stock of Agency.

Affirmed.

REVENUE RULING 70–225
1970–1 Cum.Bull. 80.

Advice has been requested whether the transactions described below qualify as (1) a reorganization under section 368(a)(1)(D) of the Internal Revenue Code of 1954, (2) a distribution of stock of a controlled corporation under section 355 of the Code, and (3) a reorganization under section 368(a)(1)(B) of the Code.

R, a corporation with one shareholder, A, for many years has operated a taxicab business and a car rental business. T, an unrelated widely held corporation, desired to acquire R's car rental business. Pursuant to a plan, R transferred the assets of its car rental business to a newly formed corporation, S, in exchange for all the stock of S and distributed the stock of S to its sole shareholder (A) in a transaction intended to qualify under sections 368(a)(1)(D) and 355 of the Code. As part of the prearranged plan, A immediately exchanged all his S stock for some of the outstanding voting stock of T in an exchange intended to meet the requirements of section 368(a)(1)(B) of the Code.

Section 368(a)(1)(D) of the Code defines a "reorganization" to include a transfer by a corporation of all or a part of its assets to another corporation if immediately after the transfer the transferor, or one or more of its shareholders (including persons who were shareholders immediately before the transfer), or any combination thereof is in control of the corporation to which the assets are transferred; but only if, in pursuance of the plan, stock or securities of the corporation to which the assets are transferred are distributed in a transaction which qualifies under section 354, 355, or 356 of the Code.

Section 368(c) of the Code defines the term "control" as ownership of stock possessing at least 80 percent of the total combined voting power of all classes of stock entitled to vote and at least 80 percent of the total number of shares of each other class of stock of the corporation.

Section 355 of the Code provides rules for the distribution, without recognition of gain or loss to the shareholders, of stock of a corporation controlled by the distributing corporation.

Section 368(a)(1)(B) of the Code provides that the term "reorganization" includes the acquisition by one corporation, in exchange solely for all or a part of its voting stock, of stock of another corporation if, immediately after the acquisition, the acquiring corporation has control of such corporation.

Revenue Ruling 54–96, C.B. 1954–1, 111, as modified by Revenue Ruling 56–100, C.B. 1956–1, 624, discusses a situation where X corporation organized a new corporation, Y, to which X transferred one of two separate businesses X had operated in exchange for all the stock of Y. As part of a prearranged plan X transferred all the stock of Y to an unrelated corporation, Z, in exchange for 20 percent of the outstanding voting stock of Z. That Revenue Ruling holds that since the two steps were part of a prearranged, integrated, plan they may not be considered independently of each other. Consequently, since X was not in control of Y after transferring a part of its assets to that corporation, the transfer did not constitute a reorganization as defined in the predecessor of section 368(a)(1)(D) of the Code nor did it constitute a tax-free transfer under the predecessor of section 351 of the Code. That Revenue Ruling also holds that the predecessor of section 368(a)(1)(B) of the Code was not applicable, for in net effect X transferred part of its assets to Z in exchange for a part of the Z stock, rather than all the stock of a previously existing corporation.

Similarly, in the instant case, the transfer by R of part of its assets to S in exchange for all the stock of S followed by the distribution of the S stock to A and by the transfer of the S stock to T by A in exchange for T stock is a series of integrated steps which likewise may not be considered independently of each other. Accordingly, neither R nor its sole shareholder A is in control of S after the transfer and the transaction does not constitute a reorganization under section 368(a)(1)(D) of the Code nor a transfer under section 351 of the Code. Section 368(a)(1)(B) of the Code is not applicable to the transaction, since in effect R transferred part of its assets to T in exchange for a part of the T stock, rather than T having acquired all the stock of a previously existing corporation solely in exchange for its own voting stock.

Accordingly, the receipt by A of the stock of T is not a distribution to which section 355 of the Code applies. The fair market value of the stock of T is taxable to A as a distribution by R under section 301 of the Code. In addition, gain or loss is recognized to R on the transaction.

REVENUE RULING 75–406
1975–2 Cum.Bull. 125.

Advice has been requested as to the Federal income tax consequences of the transaction described below.

X corporation, whose stock is widely held and actively traded, is engaged in the manufacture and sale of machinery. Y corporation, engaged in the production and distribution of chemicals, has been a wholly owned subsidiary of X since X purchased the Y stock eight years ago. Both X and Y have actively conducted their respective businesses for more than five years.

In order to comply with an order of a governmental agency requiring X to divest itself of any interest in Y, X adopted a plan whereby it distributed pro rata to its shareholders all of the Y stock. No stock of X was surrendered.

Soon after the distribution, a plan of reorganization was submitted to the then Y shareholders by the management of Y in which Y was to be merged into Z, an unrelated corporation. The X shareholders were free to vote their Y stock for or against the merger. The Y shareholders approved the merger at a shareholder meeting, subsequent to the distribution, specifically called for such purpose. Y then merged into Z and as a result the Y stock was converted into Z stock. The Z stock so received represented 25 percent of the outstanding stock of Z.

Section 355(a) of the Internal Revenue Code of 1954 provides, in part, that where (1) a corporation distributes to its shareholders, with respect to its stock, all of the stock of a corporation which it controls immediately before the distribution, (2) the active-trade-or-business requirements of section 355(b) are met, and (3) the transaction is not used principally as a device to distribute earnings and profits, no gain or loss will be recognized to (and no amount will be includible in the income of) such shareholders on the receipt of such stock.

Section 368(a)(1)(A) of the Code defines the term "reorganization" to include a statutory merger.

Section 355(a) of the Code specifies that the distributing corporation must distribute to its shareholders an amount of stock in the controlled corporation constituting control within the meaning of section 368(c), but it does not require that the shareholders thereafter retain stock of the controlled corporation for an indefinite period. Nevertheless, any disposition of stock of either the distributing corporation or the controlled corporation by the shareholders pursuant to an arrangement negotiated or agreed upon by the shareholders prior to such distribution must be examined to determine whether the transaction was used principally as a device for the distribution of the earnings and profits of the distributing corporation or the controlled corporation or both. See section 1.355–2(b)(1) of the [pre-1989 version of the] Income Tax Regulations.

In addition, any disposition of such stock by the shareholders in a subsequent reorganization negotiated or agreed upon by them prior to such distribution must be examined to determine whether the continuity-of-interest requirement set forth in section 1.355–2(c) of the regulations has been satisfied.

The subsequent disposition of the Y stock by the X shareholders in exchange for Z stock, pursuant to the statutory merger of Y into Z, resulted in a continuing stock interest in the business enterprise of Y by the X shareholders who, through their ownership of Z stock, were indirect owners of the enterprise subsequent to the exchange. Thus, the exchange soon after the distribution of Y stock did not violate the continuity-of-interest requirement of section 1.355–2(c) and section 1.368–1(b) of the regulations. Furthermore, the distribution of the Y stock to the X shareholders was not a transaction used principally as a device to distribute the earnings and profits of either corporation because afterwards the shareholders maintained a continuing stock interest in the business enterprise of X through their stock ownership in X and a continuing stock interest in the business enterprise of Y through their stock ownership in Z, which acquired the Y enterprise in a statutory merger. See Rev.Rul. 70–434, 1970–2 C.B. 83, and Commissioner v. Morris, 367 F.2d 794 (4th Cir.1966).

After the distribution of the Y stock to the X shareholders, the ownership of the Y stock by the X shareholders was real and meaningful since the X shareholders were free to vote their Y stock for or against the merger of Y into Z.

Accordingly, the distribution of Y stock to the X shareholders qualifies as a distribution under section 355 of the Code, and the merger of Y into Z qualifies as a reorganization under section 368(a)(1)(A).

PROBLEM

Leisure, Inc. is a publicly held corporation that operates a chain of motels and manufactures leisure apparel. Each business has roughly the same net worth and has been operated by Leisure for over five years. Denim Corporation wishes to acquire the apparel business but is not interested in the motels. Leisure would like to dispose of the apparel business, preferably in a tax-free reorganization. It is willing to continue in the motel business unless it can find an interested buyer at the right price. Consider the tax consequences of the following alternative plans for carrying out the objectives of the parties:

(a) Leisure will transfer the motel assets to a newly formed corporation, Motel, Inc., and distribute the Motel stock pro rata to the Leisure shareholders. Leisure then will transfer the assets and liabilities of the apparel business to Denim in exchange for Denim voting stock, and then Leisure will liquidate, distributing the Denim stock pro rata to its shareholders.

(b) Same as (a), above, except that after the spin-off, Leisure merges into Denim. Under the terms of the merger, Leisure shareholders receive Denim nonvoting preferred stock.

(c) Same as (a), above, except that after the spin-off Denim acquires all the Leisure stock solely in exchange for Denim voting stock.

(d) What result if Leisure transfers the apparel business to a new corporation, Cords, Inc., and then distributes the Cords stock pro rata to the Leisure shareholders. Leisure continues to operate the motel business, but Cords, Inc. merges into Denim, Inc., and the Cords shareholders receive Denim voting stock.

(e) Same as (d), above, except that Denim acquires the stock of Cords, Inc. from all the Cords shareholders solely in exchange for Denim voting stock.

(f) As in (a), above, Leisure transfers the motel assets to Motel, Inc. and distributes the Motel stock pro rata to its shareholders. Leisure then sells its apparel business to Denim for cash and distributes the proceeds to its shareholders in complete liquidation.

(g) What is the best method to dispose of unwanted assets in preparation for a tax-free reorganization?

CHAPTER 13. LIMITATIONS ON CARRYOVERS OF CORPORATE ATTRIBUTES *

A. INTRODUCTION

In traveling through Subchapter C, we have encountered a myriad of corporate acquisitions—some fully taxable, others partially taxable and still others tax-free. We have seen that tax considerations often influence the format of a particular acquisition but have yet to consider the possibility that not only the method but also the very *fact* of a corporate acquisition may be tax motivated. C corporations sometimes have been attractive takeover candidates not because of the inherent value of their assets or their future earning power but solely because of tax attributes. Indeed, the economics of an acquisition may be driven by the acquiring corporation's ability to utilize the target's net operating loss carryforwards as a shelter against profits from other business operations.[1] If the stock of the target is acquired, those carryforwards remain in the target and may benefit the acquiring corporation if the two companies are eligible to file consolidated tax returns.[2] If its assets are acquired in a reorganization (or in a tax-free Section 332 liquidation, if the target is already a controlled subsidiary), those loss carryforwards, along with the target's other tax attributes, are inherited by the acquiring corporation under Section 381.[3]

This chapter focuses primarily on the limitations imposed by the Code on the carryover of net operating losses after a corporate acquisition or other substantial change of ownership. The most significant limitations are in Section 382, which limits the use of net operating loss ("NOL") carryforwards and certain built-in losses following a change of corporate ownership. Section 383 limits the carryforward of certain other tax attributes, such as excess credits and capital losses. Other rules preclude a loss corporation from sheltering built-in gains of a previously unrelated gain corporation[4] and patrol against acquisitions motivated by a tax avoidance purpose.[5] In examining these intricate loss carryover limitations, this chapter makes a special effort to go beyond the sometimes overwhelming statutory mechanics by explaining the policies underlying these provisions.

Before proceeding to the limitations, the concept of a net operating loss should be reviewed. In general, a net operating loss, often identi-

---

* See generally Simmons, "Net Operating Losses and Section 382: Searching for a Limitation on Loss Carryovers," 63 Tul.L.Rev. 1045 (1989).

1. Section 172 generally allows such losses to be carried forward and used as deductions for up to fifteen years.

2. See Chapter 13D3, infra.

3. See Chapter 10D, supra.

4. I.R.C. § 384.

5. I.R.C. § 269.

fied by its initials "NOL," is the excess of business deductions allowed by the Code over the taxpayer's gross income in a single taxable period.[6] A net operating loss ordinarily may be carried back to the three taxable years preceding the loss year and may be carried forward to the fifteen following years. An NOL carryback reduces the taxpayer's taxable income in the earlier year and typically results in a refund. Carryforwards serve as deductions in the subsequent years to which they are carried and reduce the tax due for those periods. NOLs must first be carried to the earliest available year and, to the extent not used, are then carried forward to the next available taxable periods.[7] Net operating losses thus stand as an exception to the annual taxable year concept. The purpose of the carryover scheme is to serve as an averaging device that ameliorates the harsh consequences that would result for a business taxpayer with a fluctuating economic track record. As the Supreme Court has described NOL carryovers, "[t]hey were designed to permit a taxpayer to set off its lean years against its lush years, and to strike something like an average taxable income computed over a period longer than one year."[8] All of this works smoothly in the corporate setting if the owners of the entity are unchanged during the 19-year carryover period. This chapter addresses the problems that arise if the ownership of a loss corporation changes at a time that the company has unexpired net operating losses.

B. LIMITATIONS ON NET OPERATING LOSS CARRYFORWARDS: SECTION 382

1. INTRODUCTION

Code: Skim § 382(a), (b)(1), (g)(1), (i)(1).

A profitable company seeking tax savings may be tempted to acquire a corporation with net operating loss carryovers in order to use those deductions to shelter its taxable income. To illustrate, assume that Mr. Loser forms Loss Co. to engage in the manufacture and sale of passing fads. The company is initially capitalized with $1,000,000, all represented by Mr. Loser's equity investment. Despite Loser's high hopes, Loss Co. incurs $999,999 in deductible expenses in the first two years of its operation and never earns a cent. At the end of two years, the company has nothing left except $1 in its checking account and a $999,999 NOL deduction that is useless because Loss Co. has no income to offset. The company's value at that point is $1 plus the value, if any, of its deductions. If Loss Co. is liquidated, the sad story ends. If Loser infuses new property or cash into the corporation to keep the business afloat, then Loss Co. may deduct its loss carryforwards against any future income as long as Loser continues to own a controlling interest in the company.

---

6. See generally I.R.C. § 172.

7. I.R.C. § 172(b).

8. United States v. Foster Lumber Co., 429 U.S. 32, 97 S.Ct. 204 (1976). See gener-

ally Bittker, Federal Taxation of Income, Estates and Gifts ¶ 25.11 (2d ed. 1989).

But what if Profit Co., shopping around for tax deductions, learns of Loss Co.'s difficulties? If Profit wishes to acquire Loss, it has many options. It could: (1) acquire all of Loss Co.'s assets (i.e., $1) in exchange for Profit Co. stock in an acquisitive Type A or C tax-free reorganization, as a result of which Profit Co. would inherit all of Loss Co.'s tax attributes (i.e., its $999,999 NOL deduction); [1] (2) acquire the stock of Loss Co. in either a taxable purchase, a tax-free Type B reorganization, or reverse triangular merger, and later liquidate Loss Co. under Section 332, thereby inheriting its NOL carryforwards; [2] (3) acquire Loss Co.'s stock and then transfer its own assets into Loss Co. in a Section 351 exchange; in that case Loss Co., now a wholly owned subsidiary of Profit Co., can operate the Profit business while retaining its own NOLs; or (4) Loss Co. can acquire the assets of Profit Co. in an acquisitive tax-free reorganization by exchanging enough Loss Co. stock to give the Profit Co. shareholders virtually 100 percent ownership of Loss Co. The Profit Co. shareholders then will own Loss Co., which will own all of old Profit Co.'s assets plus a $999,999 NOL carryforward.

Is something wrong here? If Loss Co. lost money, should its NOLs be available to offset Profit's future income or should the use of those NOLs be limited to offsetting later income earned by Loss? Should Profit be able to avoid tax on $1,000,000 of its future income by acquiring (or being acquired by) the corporate shell of an unsuccessful business?

After pondering these questions for many years, Congress enacted ineffective legislation in 1954 aimed at limiting the use of NOL carryforwards in the corporate acquisitions setting. Amendments followed in 1976, but they were so unappealing that their effective date was delayed four times until 1986, when they were discarded completely in favor of a new Section 382.[3] The new statutory scheme is the outgrowth of decades of study, most notably the Subchapter C Project of the American Law Institute and the Senate Finance Committee staff's Subchapter C study.[4]

When applicable, Section 382 limits the use of a loss corporation's NOL carryforwards when there is a change of ownership of more than 50 percent of the stock of that company over a period of three years or less.[5] Stating this general rule in the language of the Code, the loss

---

1. I.R.C. § 381(a)(2).

2. I.R.C. § 381(a)(1). If the liquidation occurs immediately after a Type B reorganization, it would be treated as a Type C reorganization. See Rev.Rul. 67–274, Chapter 10B3, supra. In addition, if Profit Co. acquires the Loss Co. stock and files a consolidated return, the availability of Loss Co.'s losses will be limited by the consolidated return regulations. See, Section D3 of this chapter, infra.

3. See generally Jacobs, "Tax Treatment of Corporate Net Operating Losses

and Other Tax Attribute Carryovers," 5 Va. Tax Rev. 701 (1986).

4. See American Law Institute, Federal Income Tax Project, Subchapter C (1986); Staff of the Senate Finance Committee, The Subchapter C Revision Act of 1985: A Final Report Prepared by the Staff, 99th Cong., 1st Sess. 32–35, 55–56, 68–71 (S.Prt. 99–47, 1985); Eustice, "Alternatives for Limiting Loss Carryovers," 22 San Diego L.Rev. 149 (1985).

5. I.R.C. § 382(g)(1), (i).

limitations are triggered only after an "ownership change,"[6] which is either an "owner shift involving a 5-percent shareholder", or an "equity structure shift,"[7] coupled with a more than 50 percent increase in the stock ownership of "5-percent shareholders" which occurs during a three-year "testing period".[8] If Section 382 is triggered, it limits the use by a "new loss corporation" of any NOLs of an "old loss corporation" for any "post-change year" (i.e., any year after the ownership change).[9] In general, the taxable income of a new loss corporation that may be offset by preacquisition NOLs is limited to the value of the old loss corporation's stock on the date of the ownership change multiplied by a prescribed "long-term tax-exempt rate."[10] These and many other statutory terms will be explained in detail later in the chapter.

The rationale of Section 382 is to allow the use of a loss company's NOLs to offset only the future income generated by that company's business. If the section is triggered by an ownership change, its limitations apply in two different ways. First, if the Loss Co. business is not continued (or substantially all of its assets are not used) for at least two years after the change of ownership, all of its NOLs are disallowed.[11] Second, if the Loss Co. business is continued or if its assets are used for at least two years, the losses are allowable only to the extent of the income generated from the old Loss Co.'s assets. Because the transactions that trigger Section 382 involve the combining of a loss company with a profitable company, it is impossible to determine exactly what part of the combined company's income is generated by the Loss Co.'s business or assets. Section 382 solves this problem by adopting a method to approximate Loss Co.'s income. It irrebuttably assumes that the return on Loss Co.'s equity will be the rate of return payable on long-term tax-exempt bonds. Thus, in any year, Loss Co.'s NOLs can be used by the combined company only to the extent of the value of old Loss Co. multiplied by an assumed return on equity known as the long-term tax-exempt rate.[12] These basic rules are augmented by attribution rules, technical adjustments and a swarm of anti-avoidance provisions that give new dimension to Congress's increasing paranoia.

Our study of Section 382 begins with an examination of the ownership change requirement and then turns to the effect of such a change on the ability to use Loss Co.'s NOL carryforwards.

6. I.R.C. § 382(a), (g), (k)(3).

7. I.R.C. § 382(g), (k)(7).

8. I.R.C. § 382(g), (i), (k)(7).

9. I.R.C. § 382(a), (d)(2). The "new loss corporation" is the successor to Loss Co. in a merger or asset acquisition; it is Loss Co. itself in a stock acquisition. See I.R.C.

§ 382(k)(3). The "old loss corporation" is Loss Co. prior to the ownership change. I.R.C. § 382(k)(2).

10. I.R.C. § 382(b).

11. I.R.C. § 382(c).

12. I.R.C. § 382(b)(1).

2. THE OWNERSHIP CHANGE REQUIREMENTS

Code: § 382(g), (i), (k), (*l*)(3) and (4).   See § 318.

In General.   Since the economic burden of corporate losses falls on the individuals who were shareholders when the corporation was losing money, the Section 382 limitations do not intercede as long as those individuals continue as shareholders. After all, they suffered through the losses, so it is only fair to give them the benefit of the accompanying tax deductions. Consequently, Section 382 applies only if there is an "ownership change," which occurs if the percentage of Loss Co. stock owned by one or more "5-percent shareholders" increases by more than 50 percentage points [1] during the three-year "testing period." [2] Thus, if Profit Co. purchases 51 percent or more of Loss Co.'s stock within a three-year period, or if Loss Co. is acquired in a corporate reorganization and its ownership changes by more than 50 percent, the loss limitations will apply. Similarly, if ten unrelated individuals each purchase six percent of the Loss Co. stock, Section 382 applies.

These various types of ownership changes are divided by the statute into two categories: an "owner shift involving a 5-percent shareholder" and an "equity structure shift." [3] An "owner shift" generally occurs upon any change in the stock ownership (either an increase or a decrease) of any 5-percent or more shareholder (e.g., the taxable purchases illustrated above). [4] An "equity structure shift" includes tax-free reorganizations, certain public offerings and reorganization-type transactions such as cash mergers. [5]

Owner Shift Involving 5-Percent Shareholder.   An owner shift involving a 5-percent shareholder is any change in stock ownership (increase or decrease) that affects the percentage of stock owned by any person who is a 5-percent shareholder before or after the change. [6] Most owner shifts are purchases. Thus, if Profit Co. purchases 10 percent of Loss Co. stock from one shareholder, an owner shift has occurred. Apart from purchases, owner shifts can occur as a result of

---

1. I.R.C. § 382(g)(1).

2. Id. I.R.C. § 382(i)(1). If there is a more than 50 percent ownership change, a new testing period begins on the first day following the ownership change. I.R.C. § 382(i)(2). Since the object of Section 382 is to limit the acquisition of loss carryforwards, the testing period does not include any year before the year that the Section 172 net operating loss occurs. I.R.C. § 382(i)(3).

3. I.R.C. § 382(g)(2), (3).

4. I.R.C. § 382(g)(2).

5. I.R.C. § 382(g)(3). Section 382 also applies if there is a combination of both an owner shift and equity structure shift which occurs within the testing period and results in a more than 50 percent change in the ownership of Loss Co. Cf. I.R.C. § 382(g)(1). See H.R.Rep. No. 99–841, 99th Cong., 2d Sess. II–178 (1986). Moreover, a single transaction may constitute both an owner shift and an equity structure shift. H.R.Rep. No. 99–841, supra, at II–177 Example 9. Indeed, it appears that there can be no equity structure shift that is not also an owner shift.

6. I.R.C. § 382(g)(2). A 5-percent shareholder is defined as any person holding 5 percent or more of the stock of the loss corporation at any time during the three year testing period. I.R.C. § 382(k)(7).

Section 351 transfers, redemptions, debt-to-stock conversions or recapitalizations.[7]

Keep in mind that a single "owner shift" is not enough to trigger Section 382; there also must be a more than 50 percent change in ownership of Loss Co.[8] And while a more than 50 percentage point change in ownership is an essential ingredient in the Section 382 recipe, it is not the only one. Here is where the "5-percent shareholder" concept enters the scene. Consider, for example, the consequences of a simple 50 percent change in ownership rule to a publicly traded company that has loss carryforwards. Those NOLs might be limited as a result of random public trading if more than 50 percent of the company's shares happened to change hands during a three-year period. To preclude such a result, the type of "owner shift" required to trigger Section 382 occurs only if the percentage of stock of Loss Co. owned by one or more "5-percent shareholders" increases by the requisite 50 percent.[9]

A rule that only counted the increased ownership of 5-percent shareholders might be easily circumvented. For example, a shareholder who held Loss Co. stock while the losses were incurred might sell four percent interests to 25 equal purchasers rather than to a single individual. In so doing, the owner would avoid selling any of his stock to a 5-percent shareholder despite an obvious sale and purchase of tax benefits. To assure that the loss limitations apply in these circumstances, Section 382 generally treats all less than 5-percent shareholders as a single 5-percent shareholder.[10] Thus, the sales to 25 four percent shareholders in the example are treated as sales to a single 5-percent shareholder, and the Section 382 limits apply because that 5-percent shareholder's ownership shifts from zero percent to 100 percent. But in the earlier publicly traded example, the group of less than 5-percent shareholders always would have held 100 percent both before and after the transfers, and thus Section 382 would not apply. Unfortunately, not all "owner shifts" are the result of such simple purchases. The problems at the end of this section explore some of these additional complications.

Equity Structure Shifts. Recall that Section 382 first must be triggered by either an "owner shift involving a 5-percent shareholder" or an "equity structure shift," [11] either of which must result in an "ownership change." An "equity structure shift" is defined to include tax-free reorganizations [12] and certain taxable "reorganization-type"

---

7. H.R.Rep. No. 99–841, supra note 5 at II–174–176. The statute specifically excludes owner shifts as a result of a gift, death or divorce transfer. Changes in proportionate ownership attributable solely to fluctuations in the market values of different classes of stock also are disregarded, except to the extent provided in regulations. I.R.C. § 382(*l*)(3)(B), (C).

8. I.R.C. § 382(g)(1).

9. I.R.C. § 382(g)(1)(A). See H.R.Rep. No. 99–841, supra note 5, at II–176.

10. I.R.C. § 382(g)(4)(A).

11. I.R.C. § 382(g)(1).

12. I.R.C. § 382(g)(3)(A). Some reorganizations are excluded from the definition of "equity structure shift." Section 382(g)(3)(A) excludes a Type D or G reorganization, unless the requirements of Sec-

transactions, public offerings and similar transactions.[13] Consequently, if there is a shift in the ownership of Loss Co. stock in a reorganization, which when combined with any other stock transfers within the three-year period results in a more than 50 percent change of ownership, such an equity structure shift will bring the Section 382 limitations into play.[14]

Special Rules for Determining Change in Ownership. In determining whether a change in ownership has occurred, reorganizations involve some special complications. In a Type A or C reorganization, the acquiring company that inherits the loss is probably an entirely different company from Loss Co. In that event, what ownership is tested under Section 382? This question is answered indirectly by Section 382(k), which defines the "loss corporation" affected by Section 382. Thus, in a Type A statutory merger or a Type C stock-for-assets reorganization involving a loss corporation and another corporation, the limits apply to the survivor. In order to determine the extent of ownership change that has occurred, the ownership of the surviving corporation must be compared to the pre-reorganization ownership of the old Loss Co. In effect, the statute looks at the pre- and post-reorganization ownership of whatever company possesses the losses— whether this is the acquiring corporation or the target. For example, if Loss Co. is merged into Profit Co., Section 382 requires a comparison of the ownership of pre-merger Loss Co. and post-merger Profit Co. If the pre-merger Loss Co. shareholders own at least 50 percent of the post-merger Profit Co. (defined as "new loss corporation") [15] an ownership change within the meaning of Section 382(g) will not have occurred. On the other hand, if Loss Co. acquires the stock (in a Type B reorganization or reverse triangular merger) or assets (in a Type A or C reorganization, or a forward triangular merger) of Profit Co. in exchange for Loss Co. stock, Section 382 will apply unless at least 50 percent of the post-reorganization Loss Co. stock continues to be owned by the pre-reorganization Loss Co. shareholders.

In order to assure proper results in the context of the fusion of two corporations, one more special rule is required. We have seen that all shareholders who own less than five percent of a company's stock are treated as a single 5-percent shareholder. In a reorganization, there may be at least two groups of less than 5-percent shareholders—in our examples, the shareholders of Loss Co. and those of Profit Co. If these two groups were treated as a single shareholder, virtually all reorganizations of publicly held companies would escape Section 382. For example, assume that Loss Co. and Profit Co. are both public compa-

---

tion 354(b)(1) are met, and a Type F reorganization.

13. I.R.C. § 382(g)(3)(B).

14. Since an ownership change can occur after either an "owner shift" involving a 5-percent shareholder or an equity structure shift, and since the ownership change can be the result of two or more sales or reorganizations or other combinations, it may be inconsequential whether a transaction is defined as an owner shift or an equity structure shift.

15. I.R.C. § 382(k)(3).

nies, with no shareholder owning stock of both and no individual owning (directly or indirectly) five percent of either company. If Profit Co. acquires the Loss Co. assets in a merger pursuant to which the old Loss Co. shareholders receive enough Profit Co. stock to become, as a group, 15 percent shareholders of Profit Co., it would appear that Section 382 should apply because the Profit Co. shareholders went from zero to 85 percent ownership of the "new loss corporation." But if all less-than-5-percent shareholders of Loss Co. and Profit Co. are treated as a single shareholder, 100 percent ownership of Loss Co. has remained within the exclusive ownership of that "single" shareholder— i.e., the group of less than 5-percent shareholders owned all of Loss Co. and all of Profit Co. and still owns all of Profit Co. In order to assure that Section 382 will apply in this and similar situations, the statute segregates public shareholders by providing that the group of less than 5-percent shareholders of Profit Co. and the group of less than 5-percent shareholders of Loss Co. are treated as separate shareholders.[16] In the example, ownership of Loss Co. by the Profit Co. shareholders will have increased from zero to 85 percent and Section 382 therefore will apply.

Attribution Rules. The rules outlined above are generally sensible, but they still have some deficiencies that are best illustrated by a few examples. Assume that Loser owns all the stock of Profit Co. and Loss Co. As long as Loser continues to own at least 51 percent of Loss Co. or any other company that inherits its loss carryforwards, Section 382 will not limit Loss Co.'s use of those losses. Loser can transfer the Profit Co. stock to Loss Co. and then liquidate Profit Co., or he could have Loss Co. merge into Profit Co., bringing along its NOLs under Section 381. In either case, Section 382 does not and should not apply because Loser bore the brunt of Loss Co.'s economic misfortunes and will continue to be the ultimate beneficiary of Loss Co.'s deductions. But what if Loser transfers the Loss Co. stock to Profit Co.? Logically, the result should be the same as if Loser transferred the Profit Co. stock to Loss Co.—i.e., Section 382 should not apply. But under the rules studied up to now, this last transfer would result in a transfer of 100 percent of the Loss Co. stock from Loser to Profit Co. and would therefore be classified as an ownership change requiring the application of Section 382's limitations.

On the other hand, assume that Big Brother owns all the stock of Holding Co., which in turn owns all the stock of Loss Co. If Holding Co. sells the stock of Loss Co. to Janis, there will, of course, be an ownership change that will trigger Section 382. But what if Big Brother simply sells Holding Co. to Janis? Because Holding Co. still owns all the stock of Loss Co., no ownership change within the meaning of Section 382(g) has occurred. Since the ultimate beneficiary of Loss Co.'s deductions will now be Janis rather than Big Brother, Section 382 should apply. But the direct ownership of Loss Co. has not changed, and it thus appears that the grasp of the section has been avoided.

16. I.R.C. § 382(g)(4)(B)(i).

The cure for this problem is the use of attribution rules. The taxpayers who ultimately bear the burden of a corporation's losses, and who reap the ultimate benefit of its deductions, arguably are *individual* shareholders. They are the only true consumers of profit and they must consume less if the company loses money. The corporation serves only to earn a profit for ultimate distribution to the shareholders. Section 382 implicitly acknowledges these realities by borrowing and expanding upon the familiar attribution rules of Section 318, and by disregarding any attribution rules that are inconsistent with this conceptual framework. Specifically, Section 382(*l*)(3) provides for attribution from entities (i.e., corporations, partnerships, trusts, etc.) to their shareholders or beneficiaries in proportion to their interest in the entity, but it dispenses with the 50 percent minimum ownership for corporate-shareholder attribution.[17] In addition, so that determinations of ownership changes are made only by viewing the actual individual beneficiaries of stock ownership, the statute provides that once ownership is attributed from an entity to a beneficiary, the entity's actual ownership is disregarded.[18]

The upshot of these attribution rules is that all stock is deemed owned by individuals, and only actual or constructive ownership by individuals is relevant for purposes of Section 382. Applying the attribution rules to our earlier examples yields appropriate results. If Loser owns all of the stock of both Profit Co. and Loss Co. and then transfers the stock of Loss Co. to Profit Co., the only "owner" of either company whose ownership is relevant for purposes of Section 382 is Loser, who is the 100 percent owner of both companies both before and after the transfer. This is the case because after the transfer of the Loss Co. stock to Profit Co., the Loss Co. stock is attributed to Loser [19] and is treated as no longer owned by Profit Co.[20]

On the other hand, if Big Brother, who owns Holding Co., which in turn owns all the stock of Loss Co., sells the Holding Co. stock to Janis, actual ownership of Loss Co. will not have changed. But for purposes of Section 382, exclusive 100 percent ownership of Loss Co. will be treated as transferred from Big Brother to Janis so that the Section 382 limits will be triggered.[21]

Section 382 contains another significant departure from the Section 318 attribution rules that avoids application of the loss limitations in inappropriate situations. Section 382 is designed to prevent the sale of tax deductions but it is not intended to limit losses because of transfers that occur out of personal, nontax motives. Unless the attribution rules were altered, however, the unintended would become

17. I.R.C. § 382(*l*)(3)(A)(ii). See I.R.C. § 318(a)(2)(C).

18. I.R.C. § 382(*l*)(3)(A)(ii)(II). As a corollary, there is no need under this scheme for attribution *to* an entity and such attribution is thus disregarded. I.R.C. § 382(*l*)(3)(A)(iii).

19. I.R.C. § 382(*l*)(3)(A)(ii)(I).

20. I.R.C. § 382(*l*)(3)(A)(ii)(II).

21. I.R.C. § 382(*l*)(3)(A)(ii).

the norm. To illustrate, assume that Mr. Loser and Ms. Winner each own 100 percent of the stock of Loss Co. and Win Co., respectively. Loss Co. has loss carryforwards and Win Co. is profitable. Under the normal Section 318 attribution rules, if Ms. Winner and Mr. Loser join forces and marry, her ownership of Loss Co. will increase from zero to 100 percent, as would his ownership of Win Co. So both companies then would be subject to Section 382! To avoid this result, the statute treats all family members as a single individual.[22] Thus, since the "family's" stock ownership in each corporation is always 100 percent, Section 382 does not apply.

Finally, in order to avoid triggering the loss limitations as a result of bequests, gifts or transfers between spouses or incident to a divorce, Section 382(*l*)(3)(B) treats transferees in such cases as having owned the stock during the period it was actually owned by the transferor.

PROBLEMS

1. Loss Co. has 100 shares of common stock outstanding and is owned equally by Shareholders 1 through 25, who are not related to one another. Loss Co. has assets worth $1,000,000 and net operating loss carryovers of $8,000,000. Will the Section 382 loss limitations apply in the following situations?

(a) All shareholders sell their stock to Ms. Julie ("J")?

(b) Shareholders 1 through 13 sell their stock to J?

(c) Shareholders 1 through 12 sell their stock to J?

(d) What result in (c), above, if Loss Co. redeems the stock of Shareholders 13 and 14 two years later?

(e) What result in (c), above, if Shareholder 13 sells his stock to New Shareholder 26?

(f) What result in (e), above, if Shareholder 14 also sells her stock to New Shareholder 26?

(g) What result if Shareholders 1 through 25 sell their stock to New Shareholders 26 through 50?

2. Loss Co. is owned 40 percent by Bill and 60 percent by the general public. Loss Co.'s stock is worth $10,000,000. Loss Co. acquires all the assets of Gain Co. (net worth—$10,500,000) in a Type C reorganization in exchange for $10,500,000 worth of Loss Co. voting stock. If no shareholders of Gain Co. owned any Loss Co. stock prior to the transaction, has there been an ownership change?

3. Whale Co. and Minnow Co. (which has loss carryovers) are both publicly held companies, neither of which has any 5-percent shareholder. Whale Co. purchases all the stock of Minnow Co. for cash. Does § 382 apply?

---

22. I.R.C. § 382(*l*)(3)(A)(i).

3. RESULTS OF AN OWNERSHIP CHANGE

Code: § 382(a)–(f), (h), (*l*)(1) and (4).

In General. If an ownership change occurs, the Section 382 loss limitations then must be applied. Before considering any further details, the function of the limitations should be disclosed. We have seen that Congress designed Section 382 to prevent taxpayers from selling and purchasing tax deductions. If that were the only relevant consideration, the rest would be easy—whenever there is an ownership change, simply eliminate all loss carryforwards. But our study of Subchapter C has revealed one other salient factor—a corporation is treated as a separate entity for tax purposes. Although the individual shareholder may bear the ultimate burden or reap the ultimate benefit of a corporation's losses or profits, it is the corporation itself that is the focus of the corporate income tax.

In Section 382, Congress has adopted a principle of "neutrality" toward a loss company. While the Section 382 limitations restrict trafficking in deductions, they permit the purchaser of a loss corporation to use that corporation's net operating losses to offset the old loss corporation's own subsequent income. What Section 382 seeks to prevent is the use of a corporation's losses to offset another taxpayer's income after an ownership change.[1] It is from this policy that the two limitations in Section 382 directly flow.

Continuity of Business Enterprise Limit. The first limit is found in Section 382(c),[2] which incorporates the continuity of business enterprise doctrine [3] by disallowing all net operating loss carryovers if the old loss corporation business is not continued for at least two years after the ownership change.[4] As described in the regulations governing reorganizations, continuity of business enterprise requires either that the historic business of the loss corporation be continued for at least two years or that a significant portion of its assets are used in some other business carried on by the new loss corporation.[5] As a result, a

---

1. For example, assume that Loss Co. is capitalized with $1,000,000 and has operating losses of $500,000 in year one and $300,000 in year two. At the end of the two years, Loss Co. will have a net worth of $200,000 and loss carryforwards of $800,000. Loss Co. can use those carryforwards to offset any subsequent income it may realize. But what if the owner of Loss Co. transfers a new business (which has a value of $1,000,000) to Loss Co. and the new business generates $400,000 of income? While it may be true that Loss Co. suffered the losses and Loss Co. is now generating income, the profitable company is a significantly different entity from the Loss Co. that accumulated the loss carryforwards. Losses from one business are being used to offset what is essentially unrelated income from a different busi-ness. In that event, Section 172 is operating not as an income averaging device but as a means of allowing one business to make use of a different taxpayer's deductions. Of course, Section 172 can be used in this manner, unless there has been an ownership change that triggers Section 382.

2. This limitation is inapplicable to the extent of any built-in gains or gains resulting from a Section 338 election as well as any Section 382(b)(2) carryovers related to such gains. See I.R.C. § 382(c)(2) and page 711, infra.

3. See Chapter 10B1b, supra.

4. I.R.C. § 382(c)(1).

5. Reg. § 1.368–1(d).

corporation that runs afoul of this first limit in the second year following an ownership change may be required to amend its tax return for the earlier year and remove any inherited NOL deductions that had been applied against taxable income.

The Section 382 Limitation. A second, more complex, and likely more prevalent limitation is "the Section 382 limitation," under which losses can be used in any "post-change year" only to the extent of the value of the old loss corporation multiplied by the "long-term tax-exempt rate."[6] To illustrate, assume Loss Co. has a value of $200,000 and has losses of $800,000 at a time when the long-term tax-exempt rate is 6 percent. After an ownership change, New Loss Co. may use its loss carryforwards only to the extent of $200,000 multiplied by 6 percent, or $12,000 per year.

The theory of this limit is to allow the loss carryforwards to offset any income earned by the old loss business. But since most of the acquisitions that will trigger the limit involve combining a loss business with some other more profitable enterprise, it is impossible to determine exactly how much income will be generated by the old company. To solve this problem, Section 382 irrebuttably presumes that the old loss business will generate income on its assets at a predetermined rate—the long-term tax-exempt rate. Because the amount of available loss carryforwards depends on the value of the old loss company, the greater the value (and cost) of that company, the more loss carryforwards may be used each year.[7] Although the object of this limit is to defer the use of loss carryforwards by limiting the amount that can be used in any one year, the deferral will turn into a complete disallowance if the losses cannot be used before their expiration under Section 172.[8] Any attempt by Loss Co.'s new ownership to increase the use of those carryforwards by transferring additional assets and thereby increasing the company's value will be futile.[9]

Carryforwards of Unused Limitation. The Section 382 limitation results in some further complexity if it exceeds a corporation's taxable income in a given post-change year. To illustrate, if Loss Co. in the example above, with a value of $200,000, had at least $12,000 of taxable income (disregarding its NOL carryover), the full $12,000 of NOLs that were available in each year after the change of ownership would be used. But if the combined taxable income of the new loss company were only $4,000, the full amount available under the Section 382(b)(1)

6. I.R.C. § 382(b)(1), (f). "Post-change year" is any taxable year ending after the "change date"—i.e., in the case of an owner shift, the date on which the shift occurs and, in the case of an equity structure shift, the date of the reorganization. I.R.C. § 382(d)(2), (j).

7. Thus, if we reverse the figures in the example, and Loss Co. is worth $800,000 with a $200,000 loss carryforward, and the long-term tax-exempt rate is six percent, the company could use $48,000 per year in

loss carryforwards and should have no difficulty using up the losses.

8. For example, if Loss Co. has a value of $100,000, losses of $400,000 and the tax-exempt rate is 6 percent, only $6,000 of losses could be deducted annually. Since all losses expire after a maximum of 15 years, at least $310,000 of losses would go unused.

9. See text accompanying notes 18–22, infra.

limitation would not be utilized. In that situation, the $8,000 of available but unused NOLs may be carried forward [10] and the limitation in the following year would be $20,000 (the sum of the regular $12,000 limitation plus the $8,000 carryover).[11]

Mid-Year Ownership Change. Another special rule applies if the "change date" [12] occurs on a date other than the last day of a year. In that event, the Section 382 limitation for the portion of the year after the change is a prorated amount derived by applying a ratio of the remaining days in the year to the total days in the year.[13] Thus, if the change occurs two-thirds of the way through the year, the limitation for that year is one-third of what otherwise would be available—i.e., $12,000 × ⅓, or $4,000 in the example above.[14]

The Long-Term Tax-Exempt Rate. Returning to the basic Section 382 limitation, recall that it is the value of the old loss corporation multiplied by the long-term tax-exempt rate. The use of this measure to predict the expected return on Loss Co.'s assets is the product of substantial Congressional debate.[15] Loss Co. presumably can generate earnings on its assets at a rate at least equal to the higher federal long-term taxable rate. Indeed, if it could not do so some other way, Loss Co. simply could sell its assets and invest the proceeds in long-term federal obligations. Use of the lower tax-exempt rate to predict Loss Co.'s earnings is intended to offset the fact that the amount against which this rate is applied will exceed the real value of Loss Co.'s income-generating assets. How so? Because under Section 382(e)(1), the value of Loss Co. is the value of its stock immediately before the ownership change. Since Loss Co. has loss carryforwards to offset any income it earns in the near future, that income will be essentially tax-free. Loss Co.'s after-tax return will equal its before-tax profit, and the value of its stock will reflect not only the value of its income-generating assets but also the fact that the income which is generated will be tax free.[16]

The Value of the Company. The second component of the Section 382 limitation is the value of the old loss corporation immediately

---

10. I.R.C. § 382(b)(2).

11. Id.

12. I.R.C. § 382(j).

13. I.R.C. § 382(b)(3)(B).

14. In addition, the limitation is inapplicable to the days of the year prior to the change date. I.R.C. § 382(b)(3)(A).

15. The long-term tax-exempt rate is defined by Section 382(f) as the highest federal long-term rate determined under Section 1274(d) in effect for the three-month period ending with the month of the ownership change, adjusted to reflect differences between returns on long-term taxable and tax-exempt obligations. It is expected that the long-term tax-exempt rate will be approximately between 66 and 100

percent of the long-term applicable federal rate. H.R.Rep. No. 99–841, 99th Cong., 2d Sess. II–188 (1986).

16. Indeed, logic would dictate that application of the tax-exempt rate to what will be essentially tax-free income should exactly equal the yield generated by applying the higher taxable federal rate to the lower price that would be paid for the assets if they were not generating tax-free income. This is because the tax-exempt status of Loss Co.'s earnings should increase the company's value by exactly the same proportion that the rate of interest payable on taxable bonds exceeds the rate payable on tax-free obligations. In short, the results will mirror the effect of the tax status of municipal bonds.

preceding the ownership change.[17]   Congress included several special rules to guard against predictable efforts to abuse this rule by inflating the value of the loss company.

One obvious technique to increase the available NOLs after an ownership change would be for the shareholders to increase the value of the loss company just prior to the change by contributing cash or other property to the corporation.   Congress attacked this maneuver with an "anti-stuffing" rule, under which the value of any pre-change capital contribution received by the loss company as part of a plan to increase the Section 382 limitation is disregarded.[18]   Any contribution received within two years before an ownership change is generally treated as part of such a plan.[19]

Even without "stuffing" in anticipation of a planned ownership change, shareholders of a loss company may be tempted to transfer cash or income-producing investments to the company.   If there is a later ownership change, the allowable losses then would be greater; and if there is not a change, the investment income could be accumulated tax-free at the corporate level because it would be offset by the loss carryforwards.   If the shareholders do not wish to transfer portfolio investments to the loss company, they at least might be tempted to prevent the company's profits (assuming it later becomes profitable) from being taken out of the company in order to reinvest these profits in portfolio investments which can accumulate tax-free at the corporate level and be available to increase the Section 382 limit in the event of a subsequent ownership change.

These possibilities did not go unnoticed by an ever suspicious Congress.   If at least one-third of a loss corporation's assets consist of nonbusiness (i.e., investment) assets, the value of the corporation for purposes of Section 382 includes only the percentage of its actual net value that represents the percentage of its gross assets which are business assets.[20]   To illustrate, if Loss Co. has $2,000,000 of investment assets, $3,000,000 of business assets and $1,000,000 of debt, it has a net value of $4,000,000, but only 60 percent of that value is taken into account for purposes of the Section 382 limitation because only 60 percent of its gross assets are business assets.[21]

---

17. I.R.C. § 382(b)(1), (e)(1). For purposes of determining the value of the loss corporation, all stock is counted, even preferred stock that would be ignored in determining whether an ownership change has occurred.   I.R.C. §§ 382(e)(1), (k)(6)(A); 1504(a)(4).

18. I.R.C. § 382(*l*)(1).

19. I.R.C. § 382(*l*)(1)(B). Exempted from this presumption are any contributions to be specified in regulations. The Conference Report instructs the Treasury that the regulations should generally exempt contributions only if they occurred prior to the accrual of the losses or if they

were contributions of necessary operating capital.   H.R.Rep. No. 99–841, supra note 15, at II–182.

20. I.R.C. § 382(*l*)(4).

21. When it applies, Section 382(*l*)(4) specifically requires that the value of the loss corporation shall be reduced by the excess of the value of its nonbusiness assets over an amount of the corporation's debt which bears the same ratio to all the company's debt which the nonbusiness assets bear to all the company's assets.   I.R.C. § 382(*l*)(4)(A). See § 382(*l*)(4)(D). The net result is as described in the text above.

If taxpayers are unable to increase useable NOLs by inflating the value of the loss corporation prior to an ownership change, they might be tempted to at least enable a profitable corporation to more easily avail itself of these losses by decreasing the value of the loss corporation after an ownership change. To illustrate, assume Loss Co. has a value of $1,000,000 and loss carryforwards of $1,000,000 and the tax-exempt rate is 6 percent. Profit Co. could acquire Loss Co. for $1,000,000 and use loss carryforwards at the rate of $60,000 per year, which probably would be enough only to offset Loss Co.'s own income. But what if Profit Co. pays $510,000 for 51 percent of Loss Co., and then Loss Co. redeems the remaining 49 percent of its outstanding shares? Loss Co.'s value has decreased by 49 percent (the amount paid to redeem its stock), and its revenues presumably will decrease by the same 49 percent. Profit Co. will have paid only $510,000, but the smaller New Loss Co. may deduct its loss carryovers to the extent of 6 percent times $1,000,000, or $60,000 per year. Once again, Congress cuts off a promising strategy at the pass. Section 382(e)(2) provides that if a redemption or other corporate contraction occurs in connection with an ownership change, the value of the loss corporation is determined only after taking the redemption or contraction into account.[22]

Limit on Built-in Losses. Finally, a corporation generally is subject to the Section 382 limitations only if it has loss carryforwards. A prospective buyer of deductions might be tempted to avoid the section by simply acquiring an asset that did not have the carryforwards themselves but rather the ability to produce them. Specifically, instead of acquiring a corporation that had loss carryforwards, a taxpayer could acquire a corporation that had substantial unrealized losses and other deductions built into its assets. Assuming a buyer is in the market for deductions, a company with assets having an aggregate basis of $1,000,000 and a value of $100,000 may be as attractive as a company with a $900,000 loss carryforward. Once the company is acquired, the profitable company could sell those assets and use the losses against its own profits.

In its eternal race to stay one step ahead of the taxpayer, Congress has extended the limitations in Section 382 to certain built-in unrealized losses and deductions that economically accrue prior to an ownership change but are not recognized until after the change.[23] If a corporation has assets whose aggregate bases exceed their total value— i.e., a "net unrealized built-in loss" [24]—then any built-in losses which are recognized within five years [25] of an ownership change are treated as loss carryforwards of the old loss corporation and are subject to the Section 382 deduction limits.[26] Depreciation, amortization or depletion deductions during the five-year recognition period are treated as recog-

---

22. The legislative history suggests that the "in connection with" standard should be broadly construed to include any redemption that is contemplated at the time of the ownership change. See H.R.Rep. No. 99–841, supra note 15, at II–187.

23. I.R.C. § 382(h)(1)(B).

24. I.R.C. § 382(h)(3)(A).

25. This is known as the "recognition period." I.R.C. § 382(h)(7).

26. I.R.C. § 382(h)(1)(B).

nized built-in losses for purposes of this rule unless the corporation establishes that such amounts are not attributable to the excess of the adjusted basis over the fair market value of the asset on the change date.[27] To the extent that the new loss corporation establishes that a loss recognized during the five-year period accrued after the ownership change, the loss may be deducted without limitation.[28] Even if the new loss company is unable to establish when any particular loss was accrued, the total amount of loss subject to this rule may not exceed the net unrealized loss built into the old loss corporation's assets.[29] A special de minimis rule provides that a corporation's net unrealized built-in loss is considered to be zero if it does not exceed the lesser of (1) 15 percent of the fair market value of the assets of the corporation, or (2) $10 million.[30]

Special Rules for Built-in Gains. On occasion, Congress is as eager to be fair as it is to be vigilant. In that spirit, the Section 382 limitation is increased to reflect built-in gains and other income items that accrued prior to the ownership change but are recognized within five years after the change. If on the change date the aggregate fair market value of a loss corporation's assets exceeds the aggregate adjusted basis of those assets—i.e., the corporation has a "net unrealized built-in gain"[31]—the Section 382 limitation is increased by any built-in gain (up to total net unrealized built-in gain) which is recognized during the five-year "recognition period" following an ownership change.[32] As a result, the new loss company can use its loss carryforwards (in addition to otherwise allowable post-change losses) to offset any built-in gains which it recognizes either on a disposition of an asset of the old loss corporation[33] or because of a Section 338 election made with respect to the loss corporation.[34] The corporation must be able to prove that the built-in gains accrued prior to the change date;[35] and the total increase in the Section 382 limitation may not exceed the net

---

27. I.R.C. § 382(h)(2)(B). For example, depreciation deductions attributable to capital improvements made with respect to an asset after the change date would not be subject to the limitation.

28. I.R.C. § 382(h)(2)(B)(i).

29. I.R.C. § 382(h)(1)(B)(ii).

30. I.R.C. § 382(h)(3)(B)(i). For purposes of this test, cash, cash equivalents and marketable securities with a value not substantially different from their bases generally are disregarded. § 382(h)(3)(B)(ii).

31. I.R.C. § 382(h)(3)(A).

32. I.R.C. § 382(h)(1).

33. Id. The Service has announced that if a taxpayer sells a built-in gain asset prior to or during the recognition period in an installment sale under Section 453, the provisions of Section 382(h) continue to apply to gain recognized from the sale (in-cluding a disposition of the installment obligations) after the recognition period. I.R.S. Notice 90–27, 1990–1 C.B. 336.

34. I.R.C. § 382(h)(1)(C). If an ownership change and Section 338 qualified stock purchase occur simultaneously, the target is treated as selling its assets to itself ("new T") at the close of the acquisition date. I.R.C. § 338(a). In that situation, the Section 382 limit does not apply to the Section 338 deemed sale gain because the losses do not carry over to a "post-change year." I.R.C. § 382(a), (d)(2). When an ownership change takes place prior to a qualified stock purchase (i.e., a creeping qualified stock purchase), Section 382(h)(1) (C) provides special rules when the Section 382(h)(3)(B) de minimis threshold is not satisfied and the corporation's built-in gains are considered to be zero.

35. I.R.C. § 382(h)(2)(A).

unrealized built-in gain as of the change date.[36]   Once again, a de minimis rule provides that net unrealized built-in gains do not increase the Section 382 limitation if they do not exceed the lesser of (1) 15 percent of the fair market value of the corporation's assets, or (2) $10 million.[37]

PROBLEMS

1.   Loss Co. has net operating loss carryforwards of $10,000,000.   It has assets worth $10,000,000 and liabilities of $2,000,000.   Profit Co. is a publicly held company worth $100,000,000.

(a)   On January 1, 1990, Profit Co. acquires all of the Loss Co. assets in a merger of Loss Co. into Profit Co. where Loss Co. shareholders receive Profit Co. stock worth $8,500,000.   The long-term tax-exempt rate at that time is 5 percent.   Assuming the Loss Co. business is continued, to what extent can Profit Co. deduct Loss Co.'s loss carryforwards in 1990?

(b)   What result in (a), above, if Profit Co. instead purchases all of the Loss Co. stock for $8,500,000?

(c)   What result in (a), above, if Profit Co.'s taxable income, disregarding any loss carryforward, is $300,000 in 1990?

(d)   What result in (a), above, if Profit Co. discontinues the Loss Co. business and disposes of its assets in 1990?

(e)   What result in (a), above, if the merger occurs on June 30, 1990?   Assume the date is halfway through each corporation's taxable year.

2.   Loss Co. has loss carryforwards of $10,000,000.   It has the following assets, all of which have been held for more than two years unless otherwise indicated:

Asset	Adj. Basis	F.M.V.
Equipment	$2,000,000	$4,500,000
Land	6,000,000	3,000,000
IBM stock	2,000,000	2,000,000
Cash	500,000	500,000

Loss Co. has liabilities of $2,000,000.   Profit Co. is a publicly held company worth $100,000,000.   On January 1, 1990, Profit Co. acquires all of the Loss Co. assets in exchange for Profit Co. stock worth $8,500,000.   The long-term tax-exempt rate is 5 percent.

(a)   Assuming that the business conducted by Loss Co. is continued, to what extent can Profit Co. deduct Loss Co.'s loss carryforwards in 1990?

(b)   What result in (a), above, if the stock and cash had been contributed to the capital of Loss Co. in November, 1989?

36.   I.R.C. § 382(h)(1)(A)(ii).   **37.**   I.R.C. § 382(h)(3)(B).

(c)   What result in (a), above, if the IBM stock had a value and basis of $5,000,000?

(d)   What result in (c), above, if IBM were a wholly owned subsidiary of Loss Co.?

(e)   What result in (a), above, if Profit Co. acquires 70 percent of the Loss Co. stock for Profit Co. stock on January 1 and the IBM stock and the cash are distributed to Joe, a 30 percent shareholder of Loss Co., on March 1 in redemption of all of his stock?

(f)   Will the result in (a), above, change if Profit Co. sells the equipment in February? Would the answer be different if the land had a basis of zero?

(g)   Assume in (a), above, that the land had a basis of $8,000,000 and that Profit Co. sells the land for $3,000,000 two years later. Is the loss deductible? What if Profit Co. sells the land for $2,700,000?

C. LIMITATIONS ON OTHER TAX ATTRIBUTES: SECTION 383

Code: § 383.

Section 383 is a short section which is easily mastered if one understands the operation of Section 382. The section essentially calls for the Treasury to issue regulations that will adopt the principles of Section 382 (i.e., the continuity of business enterprise requirement and ownership change rules coupled with limitations) to limit corporate attributes other than loss carryforwards. Section 383 applies to the Section 39 carryforward of the general business credit,[1] the Section 53 carryforward of the alternative minimum tax credit,[2] and the Section 904(c) carryforward of the foreign tax credit.[3] Section 383 also calls for regulations to employ Section 382 principles to limit capital loss carryforwards of a loss company.[4] In addition, the regulations must provide that any permitted use of a capital loss carryforward in any year will reduce the Section 382 limitation on loss carryforwards for that year.[5]

D. OTHER LOSS LIMITATIONS

1. ACQUISITIONS MADE TO EVADE TAX: SECTION 269

Code: § 269.

If a corporation surmounts the hurdles of Section 382, it still may find its losses limited by Section 269. The subjective approach of Section 269 is fundamentally different from the objective tests of

---

1.   I.R.C. § 383(a)(2)(A).

2.   I.R.C. § 383(a)(2)(B).

3   I.R.C. § 383(c).

4.   I.R.C. § 383(b).

5.   I.R.C. § 383(b). For temporary regulations implementing Section 383, see Reg. § 1.383–IT.

Section 382.   Section 269 applies to a transaction only if the principal purpose of the acquisition was "evasion or avoidance of Federal income tax by acquiring the benefit of a deduction, credit, or other allowance" which the taxpayer otherwise might not enjoy.   Section 269(a) potentially applies to Type A and C reorganizations and forward triangular mergers and to Type B reorganizations or stock purchases where the acquiring corporation previously owned less than 50 percent of the target.[1] Section 269(b) applies to liquidations which occur within two years after a corporation makes a stock purchase which would have qualified for a Section 338 election but only if no such election was made.[2]

If Section 269 applies, the Commissioner has the power to deny any "deduction, credit or allowance."   In theory, Section 269 thus has a potentially broader reach than Section 382.   Although Congress has indicated that Section 269 should not be applied to a transaction where carryovers were limited by the prior versions of Section 382,[3] the proposed regulations make it clear that current Sections 382 and 383 do not limit the Service's ability to invoke Section 269.[4] Thus, if a tax avoidance device or scheme is detected, Section 269 can deny even those NOLs that otherwise slip by the limits of Section 382.   It is expected, however, that Section 269 will be applied more sparingly now that the objective limits on loss carryovers have been strengthened.

To illustrate how Section 269 has been invoked in the past, consider the case of D'Arcy-Macmanus & Masius, Inc. v. Commissioner,[5] where the Tax Court was faced with the following fact pattern: WWB-Cal Corporation had acquired the assets of HSI Corporation in a Type C reorganization.   HSI had assets worth less than $25,000 and an unused net operating loss of over $125,000.   Within a year of the acquisition, all the old HSI employees were gone and all that was left for WWB-Cal was a substantial net operating loss.   In deciding that Section 269 did not apply, the court made the following observations: [6]

> In order for section 269(a) to be applicable, the tax-evasion or -avoidance motive must be the principal purpose for the acquisition and to be so the evasion or avoidance purpose must outrank, or exceed in importance, any other one purpose. S.Rep. No. 627, 78th Cong., 1st Sess. (1943), 1944 C.B. 1017. *Commodores Point Terminal Corporation,* 11 T.C. 411, 416 (1948).   The determination of the purpose of the acquisition presents a question of fact which must be resolved by consider-

1.   I.R.C. § 269(a)(2).

2.   See Chapter 7C3d, supra.

3.   See, e.g., S.Rep. No. 94–938, 94th Cong., 2d Sess. 206 (1976), reprinted in 1976–3 C.B. (Part 1) 244; S.Rep. No. 1622, 83d Cong., 2d Sess. 284 (1954).

4.   Prop.Reg. § 1.269–7 provides that Section 269 may be applied to disallow a deduction, credit or other allowance when the item is limited or reduced under Section 382 or 383.   The fact that an item is limited under Section 382(a) or 383 is relevant to the determination of whether the principal purpose of the acquisition is evasion or avoidance of federal tax.

5.   63 T.C. 440 (1975).

6.   Id. at 449–50.

ing all the facts and circumstances of the entire transaction with the burden of proof on petitioner. *Industrial Suppliers, Inc.,* 50 T.C. 635, 645–646 (1968).

* * *

In a case such as this which necessarily requires delving into intent, we think the testimony of the acquiring corporation's top management is of particular importance. * * *

* * *

Respondent emphasizes the fact that within 1 year after the acquisition only a small percentage of HSI's accounts and billings remained with WWB-Cal. Undoubtedly hindsight is better than foresight but it is certainly not controlling in determination of the question herein. Zanesville Investment Co. v. Commissioner, 335 F.2d at 514.

* * *

In order to show a predominant tax-avoidance purpose, respondent next stresses the facts that as of March 15, 1967, Getz knew of and had received an accountant's estimate of the potential tax benefits to be derived from HSI's net operating loss carryover, that the method of acquisition was changed from a B reorganization to a C reorganization in May 1967, and that the tax aspects of the net operating loss carry-forward were discussed in an attorney's internal memorandum dated July 10, 1967 (several days prior to the closing). It is clear, however, that consideration of the tax aspects of a transaction does not mandatorily require application of section 269 and that such consideration is only prudent business planning. * * * While consideration of the tax factors in a transaction may create an unfavorable atmosphere in a taxpayer's attempt to avoid the consequences of section 269, it does not automatically follow that tax avoidance was the principal purpose of an acquisition.

* * *

Of more difficulty in our conclusion in the instant case is the fact that the acquisition, as originally contemplated, apparently envisioned the continuation of HSI as a subsidiary of WWB-Cal through a B reorganization. The method of acquisition ultimately arrived at was an asset acquisition via a C reorganization. Respondent argues, on the basis of Canaveral International Corp., 61 T.C. 520 (1974), that the change in form of acquisition, which technically allows WWB-Cal the use of HSI's net operating loss carryover, requires application of section 269. In that case the taxpayer desired to acquire a yacht, Norango, Inc.'s principal tangible asset, but, after discovering the potential tax benefits involved, the taxpayer therein acquired the stock of Norango, Inc., instead. In that case we stated (at p. 541):

But when section 269 is placed in issue, it does require a showing that the most favorable tax route, *when that route involves the acquisition of a corporation,* was principally motivated by non-tax-related business reasons. [Emphasis supplied.]

It is clear that the above-quoted statement does not apply to the instant case because here we have the acquisition of assets, not the acquisition of a corporation. While there is a great deal of difference between acquiring one asset, the yacht in *Canaveral International Corp.,* supra, or the inventory in *Industrial Suppliers, Inc.,* supra, and acquiring a corporation, we do not see so great a difference between acquiring a corporation's entire operation (i.e., acquisition of assets) as here, and acquiring the corporation itself. We do not think a change in form of acquisition from the acquisition of a corporation to the acquisition of a corporation's entire operation is so drastic to warrant a mandatory denial of the carryover of tax attributes.

In order to buttress his determination that the principal purpose of the acquisition of HSI's assets and personnel was tax avoidance respondent points to section 269(c). We have previously stated that the relationship between the test provided in section 269(c) and tax-avoidance purposes is far from clear. That provision is merely a "procedural device" which accords further weight to the presumption of correctness already existing in respondent's determination by creating a rebuttable presumption of tax avoidance. Glen Raven Mills, Inc., 59 T.C. 1, 16 (1972); Baton Rouge Supply Co., 36 T.C. 1, 13 (1961). We do not think it necessary to consider whether the consideration paid in the instant case is "substantially disproportionate" since we are convinced that petitioner's proof meets any burden placed upon it by section 269(c).

2. LIMITATIONS ON USE OF PREACQUISITION LOSSES TO OFFSET BUILT–IN GAINS: SECTION 384

Code § 384.

Section 384 restricts an acquiring corporation from using its preacquisition losses to offset built-in gains of an acquired corporation. The policy and operation of Section 384 can best be illustrated by an example. Assume that Loss Corporation ("L") has $100,000 of net operating loss carryforwards. At the beginning of the current year, profitable Target Corporation ("T") merges into L in a tax-free Type A reorganization. L and T are owned by unrelated individual shareholders, and the merger does not result in a Section 382 ownership change to L. T's only asset, Gainacre, has a value of $200,000 and an adjusted basis of $125,000 which will transfer to L under Section 362(b). Assume that L sells Gainacre for $200,000 shortly after the merger, realizing a $75,000 gain.

Unless Section 269 or 382 applied, L could apply its preacquisition losses to shelter any gains recognized on the disposition of the assets acquired from T. Thus, L could use its net operating loss carryforwards to offset the $75,000 gain on the sale of Gainacre. Because it was not clear that Section 269 would effectively deter this strategy, Congress became concerned that loss corporations would become vehicles for "laundering" the built-in gains of profitable target companies. Section 384—yet another attack on the real and perceived abuses flowing from corporate acquisitions—is the legislative response. Its purpose is to preclude a corporation from using its preacquisition losses to shelter built-in gains of another (usually, a target) corporation which are recognized within five years of an acquisition of the gain corporation's assets or stock. In the example above, L would be prevented from using its preacquisition net operating loss as a deduction against the $75,000 "recognized built-in gain" on the disposition of Gainacre.

Section 384 is triggered in two situations: (1) stock acquisitions, where one corporation acquires "control" (defined by reference to the 80 percent benchmark in Section 1504(a)(2)) of another corporation, and (2) asset acquisitions in an acquisitive Type A, C or D reorganization, if either corporation is a "gain corporation"—i.e., a corporation having built-in gains.[1] As originally enacted, Section 384 applied only when a loss corporation acquired the stock or assets of a gain corporation, but Congress later expanded the provision to apply regardless of which corporation acquired the other. If applicable, Section 384(a) provides that the corporation's income, to the extent attributable to "recognized built-in gains," shall not be offset by any "preacquisition loss" other than a preacquisition loss of the gain corporation. This punishment occurs during any "recognition period taxable year," which is any taxable year within the five-year period beginning on the "acquisition date."[2] Significantly, these rules apply whether or not there is a change in ownership in the stock of either corporation.

1. I.R.C. § 384(a), (c)(4) and (5). Section 384 does not displace any of the other Code provisions limiting loss carryovers—e.g., Sections 269, 382, and certain provisions in the consolidated return regulations. Congress has indicated that the limitations of Section 384 apply independently of and in addition to the limitations of Section 382. Staff of the Joint Committee on Taxation, Description of the Technical Corrections Bill of 1988, 100th Cong., 2d Sess. 421 (1988). In contrast to Section 269, the application of Section 384 is not dependent on the subjective intent of the acquiring corporation.

2. See I.R.C. §§ 384(c)(8); 382(h)(7). The Section 384 limitation applies to any "successor" corporation to the same extent it applied to its predecessor. I.R.C.

§ 384(c)(7). For example, assume that Loss Corporation ("L") acquires control of Gain Corporation ("G"), and the two corporations subsequently file a consolidated return. Income attributable to G's recognized built-in gains may not be offset by L's preacquisition losses during the subsequent five-year recognition period. If G is liquidated into L under Section 332 within five years of the acquisition, income attributable to G's recognized built-in gains may not be offset by L's preacquisition losses during the remainder of the five-year period. The same result would occur if L merged into G. See Staff of Joint Committee on Taxation, Description of the Technical Corrections Bill of 1988, 100th Cong., 2d Sess. 421 (1988).

Understanding the operation of Section 384 requires a mastery of its glossary, much of which is borrowed from Section 382. The essential terms are as follows:

(1) The "acquisition date" is the date on which control is acquired, in the case of a stock acquisition, or the date of the transfer, in the case of an asset acquisition.[3]

(2) A "preacquisition loss" is any net operating loss carryforward to the taxable year in which the acquisition date occurs and the portion of any net operating loss for the taxable year of the acquisition to the extent the loss is allocable to the period before the acquisition date.[4]

(3) A "recognized built-in gain" is any gain recognized on the disposition of any asset during the five-year recognition period except to the extent that the gain corporation (in the case of an acquisition of control) or the acquiring corporation (in the case of an asset acquisition) establishes that the asset was not held by the gain corporation on the acquisition date, or that the gain accrued after the acquisition date.[5] Income items recognized after the acquisition date but attributable to prior periods are also treated as recognized built-in gain.[6] This definition should be familiar; it is similar to the definition of the same term in Section 382(h)(2)(A) except that the burden of proof is different. Under Section 382, the burden is on the taxpayer to establish that the asset was held by the old loss corporation before the change date and the recognized gain does not exceed the appreciation in the asset on that date. Under Section 384, it is presumed that a gain recognized during the recognition period is a built-in gain unless the corporation establishes that the asset was not held on the acquisition date or that the recognized gain exceeds the built-in gain at the time of the acquisition.

(4) The amount of recognized built-in gain for any taxable year is limited to the "net unrealized built-in gain" reduced by recognized built-in gains for prior years in the recognition period which, but for Section 384, would have been offset by preacquisition losses.[7] For this purpose, the definition of "net unrealized built-in gain" is borrowed from Section 382(h)(3), substituting the acquisition date for the ownership "change date."[8] Thus, it is the excess of the aggregate fair market value of the assets of the "gain corporation" over the aggregate

---

3. I.R.C. § 384(c)(2).

4. I.R.C. § 384(c)(3)(A). In the case of a corporation with a net unrealized built-in loss, as defined by Section 382(h)(1)(B), the term "preacquisition loss" also includes any built-in loss recognized during the five-year recognition period. I.R.C. § 384(c)(3)(B).

5. I.R.C. § 384(c)(1)(A).

6. I.R.C. § 384(c)(1)(B).

7. I.R.C. § 384(c)(1)(C).

8. I.R.C. § 384(c)(8).

adjusted bases of those assets, except that the net unrealized built-in gain will be deemed to be zero unless it is greater than the lesser of (1) 15 percent of the fair market value of the corporation's assets other than cash and certain marketable securities or (2) $10 million.[9]

The limitations in Section 384(a) do not apply to the preacquisition loss of any corporation that was a member of the same "controlled group" that included the gain corporation at all times during the five-year period ending on the acquisition date. For this purpose, the definition of controlled group is borrowed from Section 1563 (as modified to generally require more than 50 percent common ownership of both voting power and value).[10]

As if the foregoing rules were not enough, Section 384(f) authorizes the Treasury to promulgate regulations as may be necessary to carry out the anti-abuse mission of the section.

PROBLEM

Gain Corp., which is wholly owned by individual A, has the following assets and no liabilities:

Asset	Adj. Basis	F.M.V.
Inventory	$150,000	$300,000
Machinery	300,000	200,000
Gainacre	100,000	350,000

Loss Corp., which is wholly owned by unrelated individual B, has $500,000 in net operating loss carryforwards.

Unless otherwise indicated below, assume that Loss Corp. acquired all the assets of Gain Corp. in a tax-free Type A reorganization on January 1, 1989. After the acquisition, B owned 80% and A owned 20% of the Loss Corp. stock. To what extent, if any, may Loss Corp. use its preacquisition net operating loss carryforwards against the gains recognized in the following alternative transactions?:

(a) Loss Corp. sells Gainacre for $500,000 in 1990.

(b) Same as (a), above, except that Loss Corp. acquired all of Gain Corp.'s stock from A for cash (not making a § 338 election) on January 1, 1989, after which it liquidated Gain Corp. under § 332.

(c) Same as (a), above, except Loss Corp. also sells the inventory for $400,000 in 1990.

(d) Instead of (a)–(c), above, Loss Corp. sells Gainacre for $900,000 in 1995.

---

9. I.R.C. §§ 384(c)(8); 382(h)(3)(B).

10. I.R.C. § 384(b). The common control testing period would be shortened if the gain corporation was not in existence for the full five-year preacquisition date period by substituting its period of existence. I.R.C. § 384(b)(3).

(e) Same as (a), above, except that Loss Corp. has no net operating loss carryforwards at the time of the acquisition but its only asset is Lossacre, which had a fair market value of $300,000 and an adjusted basis of $500,000. In 1990, Loss Corp. sells Lossacre for $200,000 at the same time that it sells Gainacre for $500,000.

3. CONSOLIDATED RETURN RULES

a. INTRODUCTION

C corporations generally determine their taxable income and tax liability without regard to the income and losses of other affiliated entities. The consolidated return rules are an exception to this separate entity principle. Section 1501 permits an "affiliated group of corporations" to elect to file a consolidated tax return in which their separate taxable income and losses are aggregated.[1] An "affiliated group" is defined as a chain of corporations linked by specific levels of stock ownership. The common parent of the group must own at least 80 percent of the total voting power and value of at least one corporation in the chain, and every corporation in the chain must be 80 percent owned (based on voting power and value) by other members of the group.[2]

When computing the consolidated taxable income or loss of an affiliated group of corporations, each member of the group first determines its separate taxable income or loss.[3] The separate taxable income or loss figures of the members of the group are then combined, and the Section 11 tax rates are applied to the aggregate figure to arrive at the group's tax liability.

Because the consolidated return rules permit aggregation of the separate taxable income and loss of the members, the potential exists for one member of the group to offset its taxable income with the losses of another member. For example, without a specific limitation, a profitable corporation could acquire the requisite ownership of a corporation with a large net operating loss, the two corporations could elect to file a consolidated return, and the joint tax liability of the corporate family would be reduced as the net operating losses of one member are deducted against the income of the other. A multi-layer of statutes and regulations limit the use of net operating losses by corporations filing a consolidated return. First, all of the statutory limitations on the use of NOLs studied earlier in this chapter (i.e., Sections 382, 383, 384 and 269) potentially apply to a consolidated group.[4] If any loss somehow

1. See generally, Chapter 1B4, supra and Chapter 14, infra.

2. I.R.C. § 1504(a)(1), (2). In general, preferred stock is not counted for purposes of the ownership tests and certain corporations subject to special tax regimes, such as tax-exempt and foreign corporations, are not permitted to be part of an affiliated group. I.R.C. § 1504(a)(4), (b).

3. Reg. §§ 1.1502-2, 1.1502-11(a)(1), 1.1502-12.

4. Reg. § 1.1502-21(e) (referring to the pre-1986 version of Section 382) provides that Section 382 applies prior to the loss

should survive these statutory gatekeepers, the consolidated return regulations contain two additional rules to patrol abuse: the "separate return limitation year" ("SRLY") and the consolidated return change of ownership ("CRCO") limitations.[5] The operation of these rules should be familiar because they reflect many of the same policies embodied in the generally applicable statutory limitations.

b. THE "SRLY" LIMITATION

The SRLY limitation is designed to prevent the use by an affiliated group of net operating losses arising in a separate return limitation year of a member of the group. A separate return limitation year is a taxable year in which the member filed either its own separate tax return or filed as part of another affiliated group.[6] In general, the net operating losses of a member of an affiliated group arising in a SRLY only may be carried over and used to offset consolidated income attributable to that member.[7] Thus, if a profitable corporation ("P") acquires a target corporation ("T") with large net operating losses, and the two corporations file a consolidated tax return, preacquisition losses and built-in deductions of T may not be used to reduce the post-acquisition tax liability on consolidated taxable income attributable to P.

c. THE "CRCO" LIMITATION

The CRCO limitation focuses on changes in ownership of the parent of an affiliated group. In general, a consolidated return change of ownership occurs if at the end of the taxable year certain persons have increased their percentage of ownership of the common parent by more than 50 percentage points through purchases or redemptions over their percentage ownership at the beginning of either the taxable year or the preceding taxable year.[8] Following a CRCO, net operating losses of the pre-CRCO group may be used only to offset consolidated taxable income produced by the pre-CRCO members.[9] The purpose and operation of the CRCO limitation are illustrated in the following example taken from the regulations: [10]

(i) Corporation P is formed on January 1, 1967 and on the same day it forms corporation S. P and S file a consolidated return for the calendar year 1967, reflecting a consolidated net operating loss of $500,000. On January 1, 1968, individual X purchases all of the outstanding stock of P. X subsequently contributes $1,000,000 to P and P purchases the stock of

limitations in the consolidated return regulations.

5. The regulations also include limitations on the use of built-in deductions (i.e., deductions which economically accrued in a separate return limitation year) and capital loss carryovers and carrybacks. See Reg. §§ 1.1502–15; 1.1502–22(c), (d).

6. Reg. § 1.1502–1(e), (f).

7. Reg. § 1.1502–21(c).

8. Reg. § 1.1502–1(g)(1).

9. Reg. § 1.1502–21(d).

10. Reg. § 1.1502–21(d)(3).

corporation T. P, S, and T file a consolidated return for 1968 reflecting consolidated taxable income of $600,000 (computed without regard to the consolidated net operating loss deduction). Such consolidated taxable income recomputed by including only the items of income and deduction of P and S is $350,000.

(ii) Since a consolidated return change of ownership took place in 1968 (there was more than a 50 percent change of ownership of P), the amount of the consolidated net operating loss from 1967 which can be carried over to 1968 is limited to $350,000, the excess of $350,000 (consolidated taxable income recomputed by including only the items of income and deduction of the old members of the group, P and S) over zero (the amount of the consolidated net operating loss carryovers attributable to the old members of the group arising in taxable years ending before 1967).

The consolidated return regulations also guard against abuse through "reverse" acquisitions of a profitable corporation by an affiliated group with net operating losses. For example, assume Loss Affiliated Group ("LAG") acquires the stock of Profit Co., which joins the group. Without more, the LAG net operating losses can be carried over and deducted against Profit's future taxable income since LAG's losses did not arise in a SRLY. But if the Profit shareholders end up owning more than 50 percent of the fair market value of the acquiring corporation, a "reverse acquisition" has taken place.[11] As a result, LAG ceases to exist and a new affiliated group with Profit as the common parent comes into existence.[12] The transaction, as restructured, subjects LAG's net operating losses to the SRLY limitation, which permits the losses to be deducted only against future consolidated taxable income generated by LAG.

11. Reg. § 1.1502–75(d)(3)(i).   12. Id.

CHAPTER 14. AFFILIATED CORPORATIONS

A. RESTRICTIONS ON AFFILIATED CORPORATIONS

1. LIMITATIONS ON MULTIPLE TAX BENEFITS

Code: § 1561(a). Skim §§ 11(b)(1); 535(c); 1551; 1563.

UNITED STATES v. VOGEL FERTILIZER CO.*
Supreme Court of the United States, 1982.
455 U.S. 16, 102 S.Ct. 821.

Justice BRENNAN delivered the opinion of the Court.

Section 1561(a) of the Internal Revenue Code of 1954, 26 U.S.C. § 1561(a), limits a "controlled group of corporations" to a single corporate surtax exemption. Section 1563(a)(2) provides that a "controlled group of corporations" includes a "brother-sister controlled group," defined as "[t]wo or more corporations if 5 or fewer persons * * * own * * * stock possessing (A) at least 80 percent of the total combined voting power * * * or at least 80 percent of the total value * * * of each corporation, and (B) more than 50 percent of the total combined voting power * * * or more than 50 percent of the total value * * * of each corporation, taking into account the stock ownership of each such person only to the extent such stock ownership is identical with respect to each such corporation." The interpretation of the statutory provision by Treas.Reg. § 1.1563–1(a)(3), 26 CFR § 1.1563–1(a)(3) (1981), is that the "term of 'brother-sister controlled group' means two or more corporations if the same five or fewer persons * * * own * * * *singly or in combination*" the two prescribed percentages of voting power or total value. The question presented is whether the regulatory interpretation—that the statutory definition is met by the ownership of the prescribed stock by five or fewer persons "singly or in combination"—is a reasonable implementation of the statute or whether Congress intended the statute to apply only where each person whose stock is taken into account owns stock in each corporation of the group.

I

Respondent, Vogel Fertilizer Co. (Vogel Fertilizer), an Iowa corporation, sells farm fertilizer products. During the tax years in question—1973, 1974 and 1975—Vogel Fertilizer had only common stock issued and outstanding and Arthur Vogel (Vogel) owned 77.49 percent of that stock. Richard Crain (Crain), who is unrelated to Arthur Vogel, owned the remaining 22.51 percent. Vogel Popcorn Co. (Vogel Popcorn), another Iowa corporation, sells popcorn in both the wholesale and retail markets. For the tax years in question Crain owned no stock in

* Some footnotes omitted.

Vogel Popcorn. Vogel, however, held 87.5 percent of the voting power, and between 90.66 percent and 93.42 percent of the value of Vogel Popcorn's stock.

Vogel Fertilizer did not claim a full surtax exemption on its tax returns for the years in question, believing that Treas.Reg. § 1.1563–1(a)(3) barred such a claim. But when the United States Tax Court, in 1976, held that Treas.Reg. 1.1563–1(a)(3) was invalid because the statute did not permit the Commissioner to take a person's stock ownership into account for purposes of the 80-percent requirement unless that person owned stock in each corporation within the brother-sister controlled group, Fairfax Auto Parts of Northern Virginia, Inc. v. Commissioner, 65 T.C. 798 (1976), rev'd, 548 F.2d 501 (CA4 1977), Vogel Fertilizer filed timely claims for refunds, asserting that Vogel Fertilizer and Vogel Popcorn were not members of a controlled group and that Vogel Fertilizer was therefore entitled to a full surtax exemption for each taxable year. The Internal Revenue Service disallowed the claims and respondent brought this suit for a refund in the United States Court of Claims. The Court of Claims held that Vogel Fertilizer and Vogel Popcorn did not constitute a brother-sister controlled group within the meaning of § 1563(a)(2)(A); that Treas.Reg. § 1.1563–1(a)(3) is invalid to the extent that it takes into account, with respect to the 80-percent requirement, stock held by a shareholder who owns stock in only one corporation of the controlled group; and that respondent was, accordingly, entitled to a refund. 225 Ct.Cl. 15, 634 F.2d 497 (1980). We granted certiorari to resolve a conflict among the Circuits on this issue, 450 U.S. 994, 101 S.Ct. 1693, 68 L.Ed.2d 192 (1981), and now affirm.

II

Arthur Vogel's ownership of more than 50 percent of both Vogel Fertilizer and Vogel Popcorn satisfies Part (B) of the statutory test—the 50-percent identical-ownership requirement. The controversy centers on Part (A) of the test—the 80-percent requirement.

Respondent argues that the statute must be construed as including a common-ownership requirement—Congress was attempting to identify interrelated corporations that are in reality subdivided portions of a larger entity. In the taxpayer's view, Congress thus did not intend that a person's stock ownership be taken into account for purposes of the 80-percent requirement unless that shareholder owned stock in *all* of the corporations within the controlled group. The same "5 or fewer" individuals cannot be said to control 80 percent of both Vogel Fertilizer and Vogel Popcorn because Crain owns no stock in Vogel Popcorn and therefore his 22.51 percent of Vogel Fertilizer cannot be added to Vogel's 77.49 percent of that corporation to satisfy § 1563(a)(2)(A). The Commissioner takes the position, however, reflected in his addition of the words "singly or in combination" in Treas.Reg. § 1.1563–1(a)(3) to the statutory language, that there is no common-ownership requirement—various subgroups of "5 or fewer persons" can own the requisite 80 percent of the different corporations within the controlled group. The Commissioner acknowledges that under this interpretation, Part (A)'s 80-percent requirement in no respect measures the interrelationship between two corporations. The Commissioner's view is that only the 50-percent requirement measures this interrelationship. He contends the 80-percent requirement "continues to have independent significance" in that it "insures that all the members of the corporate group will be closely held," so that "the more-than-50-percent shareholder control group can obtain additional control in those instances where a greater interest is needed without the necessity of dealing with a large number of other shareholders." Brief for United States 35.[7]

A

Our role is limited to determining the validity of Treas.Reg. § 1.1563–1(a)(3). Deference is ordinarily owing to the agency construction if we can conclude that the regulation "implement[s] the congressional mandate in some reasonable manner." United States v. Correll, 389 U.S. 299, 307 (1967). But this general principle of deference, while fundamental, only sets "the framework for judicial analysis; it does not displace it." United States v. Cartwright, 411 U.S. 546, 550 (1973).

The framework for analysis is refined by consideration of the source of the authority to promulgate the regulation at issue. The Commissioner has promulgated Treas.Reg. § 1.1563–1(a)(3) interpreting this statute only under his general authority to "prescribe all needful rules and regulations." 26 U.S.C. § 7805(a). Accordingly, "we owe the interpretation less deference than a regulation issued under a specific grant of authority to define a statutory term or prescribe a method of executing a statutory provision." Rowan Cos. v. United States, 452 U.S. 247, 253 (1981). In addition, Treas.Reg. § 1.1563–1(a)(3) purports to do no more than add a clarifying gloss on a term—"brother-sister controlled group"—that has already been defined with considerable specificity by Congress. The Commissioner's authority is consequently more circumscribed than would be the case if Congress had used a term

---

7. The difference between the Commissioner's and the taxpayer's positions is illustrated by the following example:

| Indi- | Corporations | | | | | Identical |
viduals	U	V	W	X	Y	Ownership
A	55%	51%	55%	55%	55%	51%
B......	45%	49%	—	—	—	—(45% in U & V)
C......	—	—	45%	—	—	
D	—	—	—	45%	—	
E......	—	—	—	—	45%	

The parties would agree that the 50-percent identical-ownership requirement

in Part (B) is met for all corporations by shareholder A's identical ownership of 51 percent of all of the corporations. The Commissioner would find the 80-percent requirement met as well, and would therefore define all five corporations as part of a controlled group, because various subgroups of the five or fewer shareholders can account for 80 percent of each corporation. The taxpayer's position is that only corporations U and V are part of a brother-sister controlled group, because they are the only two corporations in which precisely the same five or fewer persons account for 80 percent of the stock of the putative "brother-sister controlled" corporations.

" 'so general * * * as to render an interpretive regulation appropriate.' " * * *

B

We consider first whether the Regulation harmonizes with the statutory language. National Muffler Dealers Assn., Inc. v. United States, supra, at 477. That language, * * * while not completely unambiguous, is in closer harmony with the taxpayer's interpretation than with the Commissioner's Regulation. The term that the statute defines—"brother-sister controlled group"—connotes a close horizontal relationship *between* two or more corporations, suggesting that the same indivisible group of five or fewer persons must represent 80 percent of the ownership of each corporation.

This interpretation is strengthened by the structure of the statute. Section 1563(a)(2) defines the controlling group of shareholders ("5 or fewer"), and then sets forth the two ownership requirements (80-percent and 50-percent). This structure suggests that precisely the same shareholders must satisfy both the 80-percent and 50-percent requirements. As the Tax Court stated it, "5 or fewer persons" is the "conjunctive subject" of *both* requirements. Fairfax Auto Parts of Northern Virginia, Inc. v. Commissioner, 65 T.C., at 803. Since under Part (B)'s 50-percent requirement, stock ownership is taken into account only to the extent it is "identical," that part of the statutory test clearly includes a common-ownership requirement. If, as the statutory structure suggests, the shareholders whose holdings are considered for purposes of Part (A) must be precisely the same shareholders as those whose holdings are considered for purposes of Part (B), the former also requires common ownership.[8]

Of course, a Treasury Regulation is not invalid simply because the statutory language will support a contrary interpretation. But the mere fact that there are no words in Part (A) explicitly requiring that each shareholder own stock in each corporation does not mean that the Regulation's interpretation "singly or in combination," must be accept-

---

8. This interpretation of the statutory language is also strengthened by the presence of the phrase "each such person" in Part (B). The Tax Court pointed out:

"The words 'each such person' appearing therein refer to the 'five or fewer persons' constituting the ownership group for purposes of both the 80-percent and 50-percent tests. The import of such usage is that each person—and not just some of the persons—counted for purposes of the 80-percent test must be also counted for purposes of the 50-percent test." Fairfax Auto Parts of Northern Virginia, Inc. v. Commissioner, 65 T.C., at 803.

The Government argues that there is no justification for singling out the phrase "each such person" in Part (B) of the test and transporting it for application in the context of Part (A). This argument, however, mischaracterizes the reasoning of the Tax Court. The court merely intended to show that the term "each such person" refers back to the antecedent "5 or fewer persons," which precedes the 80-percent requirement, thereby strengthening the suggestion that there is one fixed, indivisible group of shareholders whose holdings are to be considered throughout application of both the 80-percent requirement in Part (A) and the 50-percent requirement in Part (B).

ed as reasonable. This Court has firmly rejected the suggestion that a regulation is to be sustained simply because it is not "technically inconsistent" with the statutory language, when that regulation is fundamentally at odds with the manifest congressional design. United States v. Cartwright, 411 U.S. at 557. The challenged Regulation is not a reasonable statutory interpretation unless it harmonizes with the statute's "origin and purpose." National Muffler Dealers Assn., Inc. v. United States, supra, at 477.

C

The legislative history of § 1563(a)(2) resolves any ambiguity in the statutory language and makes it plain that Treas.Reg. § 1.1563–1(a)(3) is not a reasonable statutory interpretation. Through the controlled-group test, Congress intended to curb the abuse of multiple incorporation—large organizations subdividing into smaller corporations and receiving unintended tax benefits from the multiple use of surtax exemptions, accumulated earnings credits, and various other tax provisions designed to aid small businesses. S.Rep. No. 91–552, p. 134 (1969). The House Ways and Means Committee Report noted that "large organizations have been able to obtain substantial benefits ∗ ∗ ∗ by dividing the organization's income among a number of related corporations. Your committee does not believe that large organizations which operate through multiple corporations should be allowed to receive the substantial and unintended tax benefits resulting from the multiple use of the surtax exemption and the other provisions of present law." H.R.Rep. No. 91–413, pt. 1, p. 98 (1969). The intended targets of § 1563(a)(2) were groups of *interrelated* corporations—corporations characterized by *common* control and ownership. Although the 50-percent requirement measures, to a lesser degree, the overlap between two corporations, the history of the enactment of § 1563(a)(2) illustrates that Congress intended that the *80-percent* requirement be the primary requirement for defining the interrelationship between two or more corporations.

Until 1964, the method prescribed by the Code to curb the abuse of multiple incorporation was subjective: Multiple exemptions or benefits were allowed or disallowed depending on the reasons for the taxpayer's actions.[9] The Revenue Act of 1964 changed this approach, adding

9. Before 1964, the Code provisions designed to prevent taxpayers from using the multiple form of corporate organization in order to avoid taxes were §§ 269, 482, and 1551. H.R.Rep. No. 749, 88th Cong., 1st Sess., 117 (1963). Section 269 gives the Secretary the authority to disallow a tax deduction, credit, or other allowance when an acquisition was made to avoid income tax. Section 482 gives the Secretary the authority to allocate income, deductions, credits, or allowances between or among taxpayers if he determines that such an allocation is necessary in order to prevent evasion of taxes or clearly to reflect the income of the taxpayers. Section 1551 permits the Secretary to disallow a surtax exemption or accumulated earnings credit when a transfer of property between two "controlled" corporations occurs, unless the taxpayer can show that the "major purpose" of the transfer was not the securing of such benefits. All of these sections are still in effect, but they are no longer the primary weapons employed against the abuse of multiple incorporation. Rather,

§§ 1561–1563 to the Code. Pub.L. 88–272, § 235(a), 78 Stat. 116–125. These sections prescribed the application of mechanical, objective tests for determining whether two corporations were a "controlled group" and thereby restricted to one surtax exemption. The original, 1964, definition of a "brother-sister controlled group" was:

> "Two or more corporations if stock possessing at least 80 percent of the total combined voting power of all classes of stock entitled to vote or at least 80 percent of the total value of shares of all classes of stock of each of the corporations is owned * * * by one person who is an individual, estate, or trust." 26 U.S.C. § 1563(a)(2) (1964 ed.).

Because corporations were not part of a controlled group unless the same person owned 80 percent of all corporations within the group, the 1964 provision clearly included a common-ownership requirement.

In 1969 Congress adopted the present two-part percentage test codified in § 1563(a)(2). Pub.L. 91–172, § 401(c), 83 Stat. 602. This change was proposed by the Treasury Department as part of an extensive package of tax reform proposals. * * * The Treasury Department proposed, *inter alia*, that the definition of a brother-sister controlled group "be broadened to include groups of corporations owned and controlled by five or fewer persons, rather than only those owned and controlled by one person," as was the case under then existing law. Id., at 5166. In setting forth the "Technical Explanation" for this new definition of brother-sister controlled groups, the Treasury Department was most explicit that the 80-percent requirement, like the 50-percent requirement, included common ownership: "[T]he *same five* or fewer persons [must] own at least 80 percent of the voting stock or value of shares of *each* corporation and * * * *these* five or fewer individuals" must satisfy the 50-percent requirement in Part (B). Id., at 5168 (emphasis added except for "*five*").

The Treasury Department's "General Explanation" of the amendment to § 1563(a)(2) defined a brother-sister controlled group as one "in which five or fewer persons own, to a large extent in identical proportions, at least 80 percent of the stock of each of the corporations." * * * The General Explanation then set forth the respective roles of the expanded 80-percent requirement and the new 50-percent requirement:

> "This provision expands present law by considering the combined stock ownership of five individuals, rather than one individual, in applying the 80-percent test. * * *
>
> "However, in order to insure that this expanded definition of brother-sister controlled group applies only to those cases where the five or fewer individuals hold their 80 percent in a way which allows them to operate the corporations as one

the purely objective tests of §§ 1561–1563 have proved to be more effective. See Thomas, Brother-Sister Multiple Corporations—The Tax Reform Act of 1969 Reformed by Regulation, 28 Tax.L.Rev. 65, 66–67 (1972).

economic entity, the proposal would add an additional rule that the ownership of the five or fewer individuals must constitute more than 50 percent of the stock of each corporation considering, in this test of ownership, stock of a particular person only to the extent that it is owned identically with respect to each corporation." Ibid.

The General Explanation made it clear that, under the 1969 amendment to § 1563(a)(2), the 80-percent requirement would remain the primary basis for determining whether two or more corporations represent the *same* financial interests. Part (A) of the 1969 test was simply an expansion of the 1964 test, which considered the two or more corporations to be a brother-sister controlled group only when one person owned 80 percent of all of the corporations. This "expansion" was necessary to "close the present opportunity for easy avoidance" of the 80-percent test. * * * Because five persons now played the role previously played by one, this expanded version of the test required a new safeguard—the 50-percent requirement—to "insure that the new expanded definition is limited to cases where the brother-sister corporations are, in fact, *controlled* by the group of stockholders as one economic enterprise." Ibid. (emphasis added).

The "singly or in combination" provision of Treas.Reg. § 1.1563–1(a)(3) is clearly incompatible with the explanation offered by the Treasury Department when it proposed the statute. In addition to the explicit statement that the members of the controlling group must own stock in "each" corporation, the Treasury Department presented a test in which the 80-percent requirement remained the primary indicia of interrelationship. But under the challenged Regulation, the 80-percent requirement measures *only* whether or not the brother-sister corporations are closely held. The fact that a corporation is closely held, absent common ownership, is irrelevant to the congressional purpose of identifying interrelationship: "It is not the *smallness* of the number of persons in each company that triggers § 1563; it is the *sameness* of that small number." T.L. Hunt, Inc. v. Commissioner, 562 F.2d 532, 537 (CA8 1977) (Webster, J. dissenting).

The Treasury Department's explanations of the proposed statute are not, as the dissent in the Court of Claims suggested, a mere "admission against interest" by the Commissioner. 225 Ct.Cl., at 44, 634 F.2d, at 514. The expanded definition of "brother-sister controlled group" was proposed by the Treasury Department and adopted in the same form in which it was presented. Of course, it is Congress' understanding of what it was enacting that ultimately controls. But we necessarily attach "great weight" to agency representations to Congress when the administrators "participated in drafting and directly made known their views to Congress in committee hearings." Zuber v. Allen, 396 U.S. 168, 192 (1969). The subsequent legislative history of § 1563(a)(2) confirms that Congress adopted not only the proposal of the Treasury Department, but also the Department's explanation and interpretation which are wholly incompatible with the "singly or in combination" interpretation of the Regulation. The Ways and Means Committee Report stated:

> "This bill expands the definition [of a brother-sister controlled group] to include two or more corporations which are owned 80 percent or more (by voting power or value) by five or fewer persons (individuals, estates, or trusts) provided that these five or fewer persons own more than 50 percent of each corporation when the stock of each person is considered only to the extent it is owned identically with respect to each corporation."
> H.R.Rep. No. 91–413, pt. 1, p. 99 (1969).

The House Committee Report thus reflects the Treasury Department's explanations—the 80-percent requirement is an expanded version of the 1964 statute and measures overlapping interests, while the 50-percent requirement is an additional proviso necessary in light of the expanded number of shareholders whose overlapping interests were to be considered.

D

The Commissioner's further reasons for sustaining his interpretation are unpersuasive.

The Commissioner relies on the fact that, in expanding the coverage of § 1563(a)(2), Congress expressly adopted part of the language used in § 1551(b)(2) of the Code to describe a transfer from one corporation to another "controlled" by the same "five or fewer" individuals. The Commissioner contends that Congress thereby approved the interpretation the Commissioner had placed on § 1551(b)(2). Even if we could assume that Congress was aware of Treasury Regulations interpreting § 1551, promulgated only two years before § 1563 was enacted, see 32 Fed.Reg. 3214–3216 (1967), the promulgated regulations do not support the Commissioner's present interpretation of the statutory language in § 1563(a)(2). The Regulations defining control under § 1551 contain no language similar to the words "singly or in combination" found in Treas.Reg. § 1.1563–1(a)(3) and they contain no suggestion that the Treasury Department had interpreted § 1551(b)(2) as *not* having a common-ownership requirement. See Treas.Reg. § 1.1551–1(e), 26 CFR § 1.1551–1(e) (1981).

Also unpersuasive is the Commissioner's reliance on the fact that § 1563(a)(2) is referred to in § 1015 of the Employee Retirement Income Security Act of 1974, 26 U.S.C. § 414. From this the Commissioner infers congressional approval of all the Regulations promulgated under § 1563(a)(2), including the Regulation at issue in this case. But it is the intent of the Congress that amended § 1563(a), not the views of the subsequent Congress that enacted § 414, that are controlling. See Teamsters v. United States, 431 U.S. 324, 354, n. 39 (1977). In any event, this passing reference in 26 U.S.C. § 414(b), enacted only two years after Treas.Reg. § 1.1563–1(a)(3) was promulgated, 37 Fed.Reg. 8068–8070 (1972), hardly constitutes legislative approval of a longstanding administrative interpretation, from which we could infer any congressional acceptance. Cf. United States v. Correll, 389 U.S., at 305–306.

Finally, the Commissioner seeks to uphold the Regulation on the ground that a common-ownership requirement leads to the assertedly nonsensical result that ownership of only one share could be determinative. For example, if Richard Crain owned but one share of Vogel Popcorn, then the 80-percent requirement would be met and the taxpayer corporation would be part of a controlled group even under the taxpayer's interpretation of the statute. This argument is without merit, for several reasons. First, Congress purposefully substituted the mechanical formula of § 1563(a)(2) for the subjective, case-by-case analysis that had previously prevailed. Inherent in such an objective test is a sharp dividing line that is crossed by incremental changes in ownership. Moreover, it is obvious that a shareholder would not buy a small amount of stock in order to *create* a controlled group, since it is to the taxpayer's advantage not to be part of such a group. Finally, a person's "mere" ownership of one share of stock plays an important role in the operation of the test. It insures that each of the "5 or fewer" shareholders representing the bulk of the financial interest of the corporations actually knows of the other corporations within the putative brother-sister controlled group. Under this construction of the statute, controlled-group membership cannot catch such a shareholder by surprise, as it could under the Commissioner's construction.

Affirmed.

[The dissenting opinion of Mr. Justice BLACKMUN, which was joined by Mr. Justice WHITE, is omitted.]

PROBLEMS

1. What is the purpose of § 1561? Why is it needed?

2. A, B, and C, all individuals, own the following percentages of the common stock of the following corporations:

Shareholder	X, Inc.	Y, Inc.	Z, Inc.
A	50	30	50
B	25	35	49
C	25	35	1

In addition, B owns 20% of Y, Inc.'s nonvoting preferred stock, and C owns 10% of Z, Inc.'s nonvoting preferred.

(a) Does this constitute a "controlled group?"

(b) Same as (a), above, except that B owns 50% of Z, Inc. common and C owns no Z, Inc. common.

2. SECTION 482

Code: § 482.

Regulations: §§ 1.482–1(a), (b), (c); –2(a)(1)–(2).

B. FORMAN COMPANY v. COMMISSIONER *

United States Court of Appeals, Second Circuit, 1972.
453 F.2d 1144.

ZAVATT, District Judge.

[The taxpayers in this case, B. Forman Company, Inc. and McCurdy and Company, Inc. operated competing department stores on adjacent sides of the same block in downtown Rochester, New York. They were owned by the Forman and McCurdy families, respectively, and had no common shareholders, directors or officers. In 1958, the two stores organized Midtown Holdings Corporation for the purpose of constructing and operating an enclosed mall shopping center and office building complex adjoining their stores. Upon incorporation, each received 50 percent of Midtown's stock. They subsequently executed a written agreement providing that additional stock purchases from Midtown would be made equally by each corporation and that each would have equal representation on the Midtown board of directors. If either party requested, an additional director could be appointed, either by mutual consent or, if there was a dispute, by an independent third party.

Forman and McCurdy also agreed to loan funds to Midtown from time to time. These loans were to be made in equal amounts and were to be evidenced by notes or other evidences of indebtedness bearing interest at five percent per annum, with principal due and payable in 30 years. To help finance construction of the mall, the taxpayers made several loans to Midtown, which were consolidated into 30 year notes totalling $662,500 to each taxpayer and bearing interest at five percent. Midtown paid off these notes in July, 1959, with proceeds of a line of credit established with a local bank. Shortly thereafter, each taxpayer loaned Midtown an additional $1 million and took back three year notes, which initially bore interest but later were cancelled and replaced by backdated non-interest bearing notes. These notes subsequently were renewed for new three year terms in 1963 and 1966.

During the period when the interest-free loans remained outstanding, the taxpayers each borrowed in excess of $1 million from various commercial banks at interest rates averaging at least five percent. Midtown also borrowed from commercial lenders during this period at interest rates ranging from four and one half to six percent per annum.

Pursuant to Section 482, the Commissioner allocated $50,000 in interest income to each taxpayer during their fiscal years 1965 through 1967 and determined deficiencies accordingly. The allocation was based on an arm's length interest rate of five percent per annum on the $1 million loans to Midtown. The Tax Court held that the Commissioner had no authority to make the allocation because the taxpayers and Midtown were not owned or controlled by the same interests. Having held that the requisite statutory control was lacking, the Tax Court had no occasion to address the propriety of the allocation. Ed.]

* Footnotes omitted.

Legislative History

26 U.S.C. § 482 derives from section 45 of the Internal Revenue Code of 1928. The House report with reference to section 45 of the 1928 Code explained that its purpose was to allow the Commissioner to

"distribute the income or deductions between or among [commonly controlled taxpayers] * * *, as may be necessary in order to prevent evasion (by the shifting of profits, the making of fictitious sales, and other methods frequently adopted for the purpose of 'milking'), and in order clearly to reflect their true tax liability." H.Rep. No. 2, 70th Cong., 1st Sess., pp. 16–17 (1939–1 Cum.Bull. Part 2 384, 395).

Provisions somewhat similar to those in section 45 were contained in prior Revenue Acts. * * * The Revenue Act of 1928 eliminated the right of affiliated corporations to file consolidated returns and the right of the Commissioner to consolidate the accounts of two or more related trades or businesses controlled by the same interests. In lieu thereof section 45 was inserted which "broadened considerably" former section 240(f) of the 1926 Act "in order to afford adequate protection to the Government made necessary by the elimination of the consolidated return provisions of the 1926 Act." * * *

Lake Erie

The decision of the Tax Court in Lake Erie & Pittsburg Railway Co. v. Commissioner, 5 T.C. 558 (1945), is the only judicial determination based on facts substantially similar to those in the instant case. The Tax Court reaffirmed that decision in the instant case. In *Lake Erie,* the New York Central Railroad and the Pennsylvania Railroad (two independent competing corporations, having no common stockholders, officers or directors), formed a third corporation, the Lake Erie & Pittsburg Railway Co. (Lake Erie), for the purpose of acquiring, building, maintaining, leasing and operating a railroad between Lorain and Youngstown, Ohio. New York Central and Pennsylvania railroads were the sole, equal stockholders of Lake Erie. They used the facilities of Lake Erie for which use they originally paid rent pursuant to a 1908 agreement and Lake Erie paid dividends to these two stockholders. This agreement was modified in 1939 so as to release the two railroads from their obligation to pay rent to Lake Erie and release Lake Erie of its obligation to pay them (as stockholders) dividends. The Commissioner allocated to Lake Erie as income to it, during 1937, 1938, 1939 and 1940, from the gross income of the railroads an amount equal to the rent which the railroads were originally obligated to pay to Lake Erie. Lake Erie had reported no taxable net income for each of these years. The Tax Court reversed the determination of the Commissioner on the ground that he was without authority to make the questioned allocation pursuant to section 45 of the Internal Revenue Code of 1939:

"The stockholders of the New York Central are not the 'same interests' as the stockholders of Pennsylvania and neither the New York Central nor the Pennsylvania has control of the petitioner. Together they do have. But that amounts to saying nothing more than that the stockholders of a corporation control it. We do not think that it can be said that where two or more corporations owned by different sets of stockholders control another corporation such other corporation is controlled by the same interests." 5 T.C. at 564–565.

The Commissioner acquiesced in the decision of the Tax Court in Lake Erie. 1945 Cum.Bull. 5. In 1965, however, the Commissioner withdrew the prior acquiescence and substituted nonacquiescence. Rev.Rul. 65–142, 1965–1 Cum.Bull. 223.

The declared purpose of section 482 is "to prevent evasion of taxes or clearly to reflect the income of ∗ ∗ ∗ organizations ∗ ∗ ∗ owned or controlled directly or indirectly by the same interests." This legislative purpose is reflected in the Treasury Regulations where it is stated that:

"The purpose of section 482 is to place a controlled taxpayer on a tax parity with an uncontrolled taxpayer, by determining, according to the standard of an uncontrolled taxpayer, the true taxable income from the property and business of a controlled taxpayer. ∗ ∗ ∗ The standard to be applied in every case is that of an uncontrolled taxpayer dealing at arm's length with another uncontrolled taxpayer. ∗ ∗ ∗ Transactions between one controlled taxpayer and another will be subjected to special scrutiny to ascertain whether the common control is being used to reduce, avoid, or escape taxes." Treas.Reg. § 1.482–1(b)(c).

The courts recognize the congressional purpose of section 482 to prevent evasion or avoidance of otherwise payable taxes by means of shifting profits or by other financial devices and have given broad scope to the Commissioner's discretion in making reallocations of income, where the exercise of this power is not unreasonable or arbitrary. ∗ ∗ ∗ The courts have also construed this statute liberally in order to achieve the declared purpose of Congress. In Asiatic Petroleum Co. v. Commissioner of Internal Revenue, 79 F.2d 234 (2d Cir.), cert. denied, 296 U.S. 645, 56 S.Ct. 248, 80 L.Ed. 459 (1935), it was held that the phrase "evasion of taxes" in section 45 of the Revenue Act of 1928 "is broad enough to include the avoidance of the realization for taxation of such a profit through its transfer to another branch of the same business enterprise in a way which only changes its place in the business set up." 79 F.2d at 236. The court also gave a broad meaning to the term "gross income" in section 45. It referred to the progress of section 45 of the Revenue Act of 1928 in support of its liberal interpretation of that statute. ∗ ∗ ∗

Whether the Commissioner was correct in allocating to McCurdy and Forman interest on their respective loans of $1,000,000.00 each is essentially one of fact, and his decision must be affirmed if supported by substantial evidence. *Advance Machinery Exchange,* supra, at 1007. Where, as here however, the Tax Court has reversed the Commissioner, the decision of the Tax Court must be affirmed unless clearly erroneous. * * * In order to justify an allocating of income pursuant to section 482, the Commissioner must find that (1) there are two or more trades, businesses or organizations (2) owned or controlled by the same interests and (3) that it is necessary to allocate gross income, deductions, credits, or allowances among them in order to prevent evasion of taxes or in order to clearly reflect their income.

Treasury Regulations

Treasury regulations must be sustained unless unreasonable and plainly inconsistent with the revenue statutes. * * *

Organization

The terms "organization," "trade," "business" are broadly defined in Treas.Reg. § 1.482–1(a)(1) and (2). In Borge v. Commissioner of Internal Revenue, 405 F.2d 673 (2d Cir.1968), cert. denied, sub nom., Danica Enterprises, Inc. v. Commissioner of Internal Revenue, 395 U.S. 933, 89 S.Ct. 1994, 23 L.Ed.2d 448 (1969), this court found that an individual stockholder and his wholly owned corporation satisfied the two or more business prerequisites of section 482. Certainly, Midtown, McCurdy and Forman satisfy this prerequisite.

Control

No definition of "control" is contained in section 482. It has been opined that this omission was intentional in order to allow for flexibility of administration. Plumb and Kapp, Reallocation of Income and Deductions Under Section 482, 41 Taxes 808, 811 (1963).

Guidelines for determining control are contained in Treas.Reg. 1.482–1(a)(3):

> "The term 'controlled' includes any kind of control, direct or indirect, whether legally enforceable, and however exercisable or exercised. It is the reality of the control which is decisive, not its form or the mode of its exercise. A presumption of control arises if income or deductions have been arbitrarily shifted."

To the same effect see Treas.Reg. 39.45–1(a)(3) and annual Treasury regulations thereafter.

As to "same interests," there is no statutory definition and no Treasury regulations guidelines.

In order to find control, no percentage requirements are specified nor are any precise requirements necessary. The trend in the recent case law is to apply the realistic approach. * * * Despite the fact that these cases are all distinguishable on their facts, they lend support to the view that the Commissioner urges here.

In Borge v. Commissioner of Internal Revenue, supra, this Court held that an individual (the entertainer Victor Borge) and his wholly owned corporation, conducting a poultry business, were commonly controlled within the purview of § 482 and that the Commissioner was justified in allocating income from the corporation to Victor Borge, because the contract between him and his wholly owned corporation would never have been made between two unrelated parties dealing at arm's length.

In Hall v. Commissioner, supra, the taxpayer (Hall) conducted a business individually. Thereafter he formed a corporation and transferred nearly all of his shares of stock of that corporation to his son. The court upheld the allocation of income between Hall and the corporation under § 45 of the 1939 Code. It disregarded the issue of who actually owned the stock, holding that Hall, in fact, actively controlled the corporation, despite his contention that he had transferred ownership of the stock. The Tax Court, in Ach v. Commissioner, 42 T.C. 114 (1964), aff'd, 358 F.2d 342 (6th Cir.), cert. denied, 385 U.S. 899, 87 S.Ct. 205, 17 L.Ed.2d 131 (1966), restated its view that it is not the record ownership of stock which determines control; that control is to be determined by ascertaining who, in fact, has control.

In Grenada Industries, Inc. v. Commissioner, supra, two corporations and two partnerships were owned by four families in identical 35%–35%–20%–10% proportions. In upholding an allocation of income among the four organizations, the court noted that it was immaterial that the record ownership of the stock and the partnership interests may not have been in the identical persons at the same time. Control was inferred from the actions of the parties.

If Midtown was the creature of only one of the taxpayers, and all of its stock were owned by that single parent, i.e., if Midtown were a strange creature having a father but no mother, the most rigid, literal wooden interpretation of section 482 would bring Midtown within the ambit of that section. It is the contention of the taxpayers, however, that section 482 is not applicable because Midtown is the normal child of a father and a mother, the product of an earthy relationship between McCurdy and Forman, twentieth century parents exercising no control over their progeny.

Midtown is the creation of a union of McCurdy and Forman—not in holy matrimony but in a legitimate business enterprise. Their interests in the existence and career of Midtown and the interests of Midtown are identical.

To contend that these parents do not control their child is to fly in the face of reality. They have had complete control of Midtown from the day of conception (its incorporation) throughout the years relevant to this case. Every act of Midtown has been dictated by papa and mamma who, directly or indirectly, have financed its career and controlled its every move.

In apparent disregard of the reality of the circumstances, the Tax Court below looked only to the record ownership of Midtown. Ignored was reality of the control of Midtown. In withdrawing his acquiescence in *Lake Erie,* the Commissioner concluded that *Lake Erie* was inconsistent with the broad language of § 482 and the trend of cases discussed supra, and noted that *Lake Erie* ignored the reality of the control in that case.

The Commission is supported by the views of commentators.

The loans by taxpayers to Midtown, without interest, affected the incomes of taxpayers and of Midtown. By not reporting interest on these loans, taxpayers reported lower earnings and, in turn, lower taxes. Midtown, in not paying interest, eliminated a business expense which would have further increased its yearly losses. Because of Midtown's unfavorable financial condition, it was encountering difficulty in the rental of stores, a matter of concern to McCurdy and Forman, the actual owners of Midtown. Midtown, McCurdy and Forman were loathe to show as further losses annual interest payments on $2,000,000.00 of loans at 5% i.e., $100,000.00 per year, and the elimination of annual payments of $150,000.00 by McCurdy and Forman. Reference to these payments will be made infra. Mr. Chiarella, general manager of Midtown, testifying before the Tax Court as to these annual payments of $150,000.00, said that they definitely helped to narrow Midtown's deficit; that without these payments Midtown would have had to get that money from some place. * * * This explanation is equally applicable to the waiver of interest on the loans aggregating $2,000,000.00.

Whether McCurdy and Forman are regarded as a partnership or joint venture, *de facto*, in forming Midtown, the conclusion is inescapable that they acted in concert in making loans without interest to a corporation, all of whose stock they owned and all of whose directors and officers were their alter egos. They were not competitors in their dealings with one another or with Midtown as to Midtown. Their interests in Midtown were identical. When the Commissioner withdrew his acquiescence in *Lake Erie,* he gave reality of control as one of the reasons for doing so. "[T]he reality of control by the same interests is present no less than if they [the two parent railroads] had formed a partnership * * * to deal with the petitioner [Lake Erie Railway Company] or had formed another corporation to deal with petitioner." Rev.Rul. 64–142. We agree.

We find clearly erroneous the holding of the Tax Court that the requisite control of Midtown by the taxpayers was not present and find further that McCurdy and Forman had the same interests in Midtown.

Having found two businesses under common control, we reach the question as to whether the Commissioner properly allocated interest on the two loans of $1,000,000.00 each as income to the taxpayers.

"Transactions between one controlled taxpayer and another will be subjected to special scrutiny to ascertain whether the common control is being used to reduce, avoid, or escape taxes." Treas.Reg. 1.482–1(c). To same effect, see Local Finance Corp. v. Commissioner of Internal Revenue, 407 F.2d 629, 632 (7th Cir.), cert. denied, 396 U.S. 956, 90 S.Ct. 428, 24 L.Ed.2d 420 (1969). To justify the allocation as income to McCurdy and Forman of interest on their loans, it must be found that their waiver of interest "is other than it would have been had the taxpayer in the conduct of his affairs been an uncontrolled taxpayer dealing at arm's length with another controlled taxpayer." Treas.Reg. 1.482–1(c). * * * "In determining the true taxable income of a controlled taxpayer, the district director is not restricted to the case of improper accounting, to the case of a fraudulent, colorable, or sham transaction, or to the case of a device designed to reduce or avoid tax by shifting or distorting income, deductions, credits, or allowances." Treas.Reg. 1.482–1(c).

Reallocation is necessary here in order to properly reflect the income of taxpayers and Midtown. Taxpayers have advanced an argument, supported by case law, that the Commissioner may not create income where none actually existed. In Tennessee-Arkansas Gravel Co. v. Commissioner of Internal Revenue, 112 F.2d 508 (6th Cir.1940), the court held that the Commissioner could not increase the income of a taxpayer whose property had been used by a related corporation without the payment of rent. The court concluded that, since no rent was called for, none could be created. In Smith-Bridgman & Co. v. Commissioner, 16 T.C. 287 (1951), the Commissioner had added interest to the taxable income of Smith-Bridgman & Co., as allegedly constituting interest which should have been charged by it on noninterest bearing loans to its parent corporation, Continental Department Stores (Continental). Taxpayer did not report as income any interest on these loans. The Tax Court, in overruling the Commissioner, who had allocated interest to Smith-Bridgman, refused to authorize the creation of income where no income was realized. This decision was thought to rest on the fact that the Commissioner had added interest to taxpayer, but had failed to make an adjustment to the income of Continental. However, the rationale of *Smith-Bridgman* was clarified in Huber Homes, Inc. v. Commissioner, 55 T.C. 598 (1971), where it was held that the failure to make the adjustment was only a possible supporting factor, not a controlling factor. *Smith* was reaffirmed in PPG Industries, Inc. v. Commissioner, 55 T.C. 928 (1970), where the Tax Court held that § 482 did not authorize the Commissioner to impute interest on non-interest bearing loans where in fact no interest was created.

Several cases have held that one related party is not required to charge another related party interest on a loan; that the lender is not to be taxed on interest, with respect to a loan, where it was not intended that interest be collected. In Combs Lumber Co. v. Commissioner, 41 B.T.A. 339 (1940), it was the practice of the corporation to lend money to its stockholders without interest. The Board of Tax

Appeals ruled that, under the circumstances, no liability for interest was created and, thus, the Commissioner could not impute interest to the lender. In Society Brand Clothes, Inc. v. Commissioner, 18 T.C. 304 (1952), a corporation held a ten year note of its wholly owned subsidiary. The note provided for the payment of interest, but it was executed with the understanding that no interest would be charged until some date in the future. The Tax Court held that the corporation was not required to report any interest not received by it. A similar result was reached in Atchison, Topeka & Santa Fe Railway Co. v. Commissioner, 36 T.C. 584 (1961).

To the extent that the above cases cited by taxpayers may be read as holding that no interest can be allocated under § 482 under the facts of this case, they are not in accord with either economic reality, or with the declared purpose of section 482. They seriously impair the usefulness of § 482. Those cases may be correct from a pure accounting standpoint. Nevertheless, interest income may be added to taxpayers' incomes, as long as a correlative adjustment is made to Midtown, for then the true taxable income of all involved will be properly reflected. Treas.Reg. § 1.482–1(a)(6) provides:

> "The term 'true taxable income' means * * * the taxable income * * * which would have resulted to the controlled taxpayer, had it in the conduct of its affairs * * * dealt with the other member * * * at arm's length. It does not mean the income * * * or allowances, resulting to the controlled taxpayer by reason of the particular * * * transaction * * * the controlled taxpayer * * * chose to make (even though such * * * transaction * * * may be legally binding upon the parties thereto)."

Treas.Reg. § 1.482–2(a) provides:

> "Where one member of a group of controlled entities makes a loan or advance directly or indirectly to, or otherwise becomes a creditor of, another member of such group, and charges no interest * * * the district director may make appropriate allocations to reflect an arm's length interest rate for the use of such loan * * *"

These regulations must prevail, for they are entirely consistent with the scope and purpose of § 482. The instant loans without interest are obviously not at arm's length, since no unrelated parties would loan such large sums without interest. The allocation of the interest income to taxpayers was necessary in order to properly reflect their taxable incomes.

Taxpayers contend that the $1,000,000.00 loans were not in fact loans; that they were contributions to capital. This argument is completely without merit. The terms of the loans plus the terms of the 1959 Agreement, specifying the creation of $1,000,000.00 loans, leave no doubt that the parties intended to and did treat these transactions as loans. Further, there is no evidence in the record that the taxpayers received additional stock of Midtown for these alleged capital contributions.

Our remaining concern is with whether the allocation of interest at 5 percent was proper. The Tax Court in its decision did not reach this issue. A remand is not necessary because, under both the regulations and the circumstances of this case, the 5% interest charge was eminently reasonable. Treas.Reg. 1.482–2(a)(2) provides the standard for determining the appropriate interest to be charged:

> "For the purposes of this paragraph, the arm's length interest rate shall be the rate of interest which * * * would have been charged at the time the indebtedness arose, in independent transactions with or between unrelated parties under similar circumstances.
>
> * * * If the creditor was not regularly engaged in the business of making loans or advances of the same general type as the loan or advance in question to unrelated parties, the arm's length rate for purposes of this paragraph shall be—
>
> > (i) The rate of interest actually charged of at least 4 but not in excess of 6 percent per annum simple interest,
> >
> > (ii) 5 percent per annum simple interest if no interest was charged or if the rate of interest charged was less than 4, or in excess of 6 per cent per annum simple interest,
>
> unless the taxpayer establishes a more appropriate rate * * *"

Midtown's balance sheets reveal that it paid interest on various loans, ranging from 4 and ½% to 6% per annum. (See for example pp. 97, 106, 109, 112, 133 and 166 of the Exhibit file.) Midtown had outstanding loans from Lincoln Rochester Trust Co. payable at 5 and ½% interest; from Central Trust Co. payable at 5 and ½% per annum and from D. Raffelson payable at 5% per annum. Considering the rate of interest Midtown paid on its arm's length loans and the Treasury Regulations, 5% is an appropriate rate of interest.

This Court finds that the reversal by the Tax Court of the determination of the Commissioner allocating to the taxpayers interest income at 5% on their respective loans of $1,000,000.00 to Midtown is clearly erroneous.

NOTE

The use of a commonly controlled business structure often has enabled the owners of multiple trades or businesses to manipulate intercompany transactions in an effort to reduce the overall tax liability of the corporate family. Even in the absence of tax avoidance motives, common control may foster arbitrary shifting of income and deductions between related taxpayers. Section 482 was originally enacted to limit this type of manipulation in a domestic context, but today it is principally applied to multinational enterprises to prevent deflection of income from a domestic corporation to a more lightly taxed foreign affiliate. The most common devices, all of which are patrolled by the detailed Section 482 regulations, are intercompany loans, excessive charges for services, leases, manipulative pricing and other milking techniques. As *Forman* illustrates, however, the Service has applied Section 482 in a purely domestic setting when an intercompany transaction has the effect of reducing the overall tax liability of commonly controlled taxpayers.[1]

In scrutinizing intercompany transactions under Section 482, the accepted standard is "that of an uncontrolled taxpayer dealing at arm's length with another uncontrolled taxpayer."[2] In other words, the arrangements contrived by the controlling taxpayer among its related business entities must be tested by what those arrangements would have been if the businesses were not commonly controlled. If the related parties have not acted as they would have in identical but controlled arm's length dealings, the Commissioner has broad authority to make a Section 482 allocation. Because the Commissioner has been given wide discretion to appraise a particular fact situation, the courts normally are reluctant to set aside an allocation unless it is clearly shown to be unreasonable, arbitrary and capricious.[3]

These standards are fairly simple to apply in the interest-free loan situation exemplified by the *Forman* case. After surmounting the control issue, which also arises in the international setting (e.g., two American oil companies form a joint venture in a lightly taxed foreign jurisdiction), the Commissioner's principal hurdle in *Forman* was to convince the court that he was not "creating" income where none before existed but merely allocating income that the parties were attempting to deflect. In this regard, keep in mind that the Section 482 regulations require the Commissioner to make a "correlative adjustment" to the income of the controlled entity from which an allocation has been made.[4] Thus, the allocation in *Forman* resulted not merely in an increase in the taxpayers' income but also a reduction in their joint subsidiary's income that would be reflected by increased net operating loss carryovers.

Far more difficult factual questions are raised in Section 482 "pricing" cases, where the Service normally contends that a domestic corporation has overcharged a foreign affiliate in order to shift income

---

1. The safe haven rates used in *Forman* are periodically adjusted. If no interest is charged or if the interest charged is below the safe haven range, (100 percent to 130 percent of the "applicable federal rate" under Section 1274(d)) interest is imputed at 100 percent of the applicable federal rate. If interest is charged at a rate above the top safe haven rate, interest is imputed at 130 percent of the applicable federal rate. Reg. § 1.482–2(a)(2)(iii). The imputed interest rules of Section 7872 now large-

ly supersede Section 482 in the context of an intercompany loan. See Prop.Reg. § 1.7872–2(a)(2)(iii).

2. Reg. § 1.482–1(b)(1).

3. See, e.g., G.U.R. Co. v. Commissioner, 117 F.2d 187 (7th Cir.1941); Rooney v. United States, 305 F.2d 681 (9th Cir.1962). But see Commissioner v. First Security Bank of Utah, 405 U.S. 394, 92 S.Ct. 1085 (1972).

4. Reg. § 1.482–1(d)(2).

beyond the borders of the United States. These cases go on for years and often are settled at the administrative level.

B. CONSOLIDATED RETURNS

Code: §§ 1501; 1502; 1503(a); 1504(a) and (b); 1552. Skim § 243(a)(3).

EXCERPT FROM "CONSOLIDATED TAX RETURNS: POST ACQUISITION LOSSES" *

Patrick G. Jones, 27 Emory Law Journal 79 (1978).

I. INTRODUCTION

Since the early 1960s there has been a vast increase in the number of corporations filing consolidated tax returns. While this increase has had a more direct impact on the accounting profession, its effect has also been felt by the legal profession in that more attorneys are now dealing with corporate clients who file consolidated returns. Consequently, the corporate attorney has a greater need for a working knowledge of the consolidated return area. The purpose of this article is to give the reader a general overview of consolidated returns, to survey some of the relevant provisions in the Internal Revenue Code (Code) and Treasury Regulations (Regulations), to outline some of the important advantages and disadvantages which need to be considered in deciding whether to file a consolidated return, and to discuss in detail a very important problem area which is unsettled at the present time—whether postacquisition losses of a subsidiary can be utilized in a consolidated return.

II. GENERAL OVERVIEW

The principal concept underlying consolidated returns is that, for tax purposes, certain groups of corporations closely related through common ownership should be treated as a single entity. This does not mean, however, that the consolidated group is converted into a single corporation for tax purposes, as is evidenced by the various provisions which retain the separate identity concept of individual members.[2] More properly, the group is deemed to be a single federal income tax computing and reporting unit.[3] The lack of a uniform theory underlying the consolidated return provisions is one of the primary reasons for the complexity of the Regulations. Recognizing which provisions fall under the single entity concept and which fall under the separate entity concept will not only help in understanding the consolidated

---

* Reprinted by permission of Emory Law Journal, Emory University School of Law, Atlanta, Ga. 30322. Copyright ©, 1978, Emory Law Journal. Some footnotes omitted.

2. Included among the provisions designed to preserve the separate identities of the individual members of the group are

Treas.Reg. § 1.1502–17 (1966), which allows the use of different accounting methods by individual members, and id. § 1.1502–31(a) (1973), which provides that the basis of property acquired in a deferred intercompany transaction is determined as if separate returns were filed.

3. See id. §§ 1.1502–2 (1971), –11 (1973).

return Regulations, but will also be important in reaching sound decisions with respect to problem areas unanswered by the Regulations.

The statutory provisions relating to consolidated returns are surprisingly brief.[4] The consolidated return Regulations, however, are very extensive,[5] and can be divided into major categories as follows: (1) consolidated tax liability;[6] (2) computation of consolidated taxable income;[7] (3) computation of separate taxable income;[8] (4) computation of consolidated items;[9] (5) basis, stock ownership, and earnings and profits rules;[10] (6) special taxes and taxpayers;[11] and (7) administrative provisions and other rules.[12] It should be noted that Regulation section 1.1502–0 provides that Regulation sections 1.1502–1 through 1.1502–80 are applicable to years beginning after December 31, 1965. These are commonly referred to as the "new" Regulations.[13] Aside from their application to any years which remain open to Internal Revenue Service examination, certain of the old Regulations continue to have effect on later years where a pre-1966 affiliated group continues to file on a consolidated basis.

III. THE DECISION TO FILE A CONSOLIDATED RETURN

A. *Eligibility*

The threshold inquiry in deciding to file a consolidated return is whether the group is eligible, with the principal requirement being that only an "affiliated group" may file such a return.[15] An affiliated group consists of one or more chains of "includible corporations" connected through stock ownership with a common parent corporation, which is itself an includible corporation.[16] Basically, an includible corporation

---

4. I.R.C. §§ 1501–1505, 1552. Section 1501 grants affiliated groups the privilege of filing a consolidated return, while § 1502 provides authority to the Secretary of the Treasury to prescribe regulations governing consolidated returns. Section 1503 provides basically for the determination, computation, assessment, collection, and adjustment of tax in accordance with regulations under § 1502. Section 1504 is a definition section, and § 1505 sets forth cross references. Section 1552 relates to methods of allocating consolidated federal income tax liability for purposes of determining earnings and profits of members of a group.

5. The consolidated return Regulations cover approximately 125 pages in the Treasury Regulations.

6. Treas.Reg. §§ 1.1502–2 (1971), –3 (1973), –4 (1966), –5 (1970), –6 (1966), –7 (1971), .1503–1 (1972).

7. Id. § 1.1502–11 (1972).

8. Id. §§ 1.1502–12 to –15 (1973), –16 (1972), –17 (1966), –18 to –19 (1973).

9. Id. §§ 1.1502–21 to –22 (1966), –23 (1973), –24 to –25 (1966), –26 (1973), –27 (1966).

10. Id. §§ 1.1502–31 to –33 (1973), –34 (1966), .1552–1 (1968).

11. Id. §§ 1.1502–41 (1966), –42 (1973).

12. Id. §§ 1.1501–1 (1960), .1502–0 (1966), –1 (1973), –75 to –76 (1973), –77 (1974), –78 (1973), –79 to –80 (1966), –100 (1972), .1504–1 (1960).

13. When these Regulations were adopted, the old Regulations, instead of being withdrawn, were amended and renumbered by placing an "A" after the old numbers.

15. I.R.C. § 1501.

16. Id. § 1504(a). An affiliated group is a subset of the parent-subsidiary controlled group of corporations defined in id. § 1563(a)(1). A parent-subsidiary controlled group exists if the parent corporation owns at least 80% of the combined voting power or value of all classes of stock. Id. This definition, in which value prevails over voting power, Treas.Reg. § 1.1563–1(c)(1) (1973), is broader than the

is any corporation, except corporations exempt from taxation under Code section 501,[17] which relates primarily to nonprofit organizations; insurance companies subject to taxation under section 802 * * * of the Code; foreign corporations * * *; corporations with respect to which an election under Code section 936 is in effect for the taxable year; corporations organized under the China Trade Act of 1922; regulated investment companies and real estate investment trusts subject to tax under subchapter M of chapter 1 of the Code; and a DISC [or any other corporation which has accumulated DISC income which is derived after 1984. Ed.] The common parent corporation must directly own at least eighty percent of the voting power of all classes of stock and [at least eighty percent of the total value of the stock of at least one other includible corporation.[29] Ed.] These ownership tests must also be met for each includible corporation directly owned by one or more of the other includible corporations.[30] The language of the statute[31] indicates that the sole test for affiliation is compliance with the stock ownership requirements; however, as discussed below, there are some very significant qualifications to this interpretation of the test.

If an election to file a consolidated return is made by the affiliated group, all includible corporations in the group must join in the filing of the consolidated return. In addition, all corporations that have been members of the affiliated group at any time during the taxable year are required to consent to all the consolidated return Regulations.[34] The common parent presumably consents to the Regulations by exercising the privilege of filing the first consolidated return. Each subsidiary consents to the Regulations by executing a Form 1122, which is attached to the first consolidated return. Form 1122 is not required for a taxable year if a consolidated return was filed, or was required to be filed, by the group for the immediately preceding taxable year. If a member of a group fails to file Form 1122, the Commissioner of Internal Revenue (Commissioner) may nevertheless determine that such member has joined in the making of a consolidated return by such group. New members joining the group after the first consolidated return year are deemed to have consented to the continued filing requirement contained in the Regulations.

As a general rule, a consolidated return must be filed on the basis of the common parent's taxable year, and each subsidiary must adopt

definition of an affiliated group for consolidated return purposes. A brother-sister controlled group exists if five or fewer persons (individuals, estates, or trusts) own (1) at least 80% of the voting power or value of the stock of two or more corporations and (2) own more than 50% of the voting power or value of such stock taking into account only identical common ownership. I.R.C. § 1563(a)(2). In summary, a brother-sister controlled group may not file a consolidated return, and only certain parent-subsidiary groups are eligible to do so.

17. I.R.C. § 1504(b)(1).

29. Id. § 1504(a) [(1) and] (2).

30. Id. § 1504(a)(1). * * *

31. I.R.C. § 1504(a).

34. I.R.C. § 1501; Treas.Reg. § 1.1502–75(a)(1) (1973). A corporation which has been a member of a consolidated group for 30 days or less, however, can be excepted from this requirement. Id. § 1.1502–76(b)(5).

the parent's annual accounting period when the group first files a consolidated return or when the subsidiary becomes a member of a group filing a consolidated return. Finally, the parent corporation is, with certain exceptions, the sole agent for each subsidiary in the group with regard to all matters relating to the tax liability for consolidated years.

B. Advantages and Disadvantages

Once it is determined that the corporate group is eligible to file a consolidated return, the various advantages and disadvantages require serious consideration. An incorrect decision can be costly, since the current provisions[43] permitting the discontinuance of the filing of a consolidated return are very restrictive, and thus may bind the group to file consolidated returns in subsequent years when a change in circumstances may make a consolidated return undesirable. The most obvious advantage of filing a consolidated return, and probably the most important, is that the ordinary, capital, and Code section 1231 losses of one or more members of the group may be used to offset the income and gains of other members. This has to be balanced, however, against the possibility that such losses could be better utilized on a separate return basis. For example, a section 1231 loss, which would be deducted against ordinary income in a separate return, may be required in a consolidated return to offset section 1231 gains of other members which would otherwise be taxable at capital gain rates. [Beginning in 1988, corporate capital gains no longer are taxed at a preferential rate. Ed.]

Another advantage is that intercompany dividends received by members of the consolidated group are completely eliminated from consolidated income and are not subject to income tax, which will result in a maximum 7.2% tax savings. [With a top marginal corporate rate of 34 percent, the maximum tax savings is now 6.8 percent. Ed.] A 100% dividends received deduction may also be obtained under Code section 243 by a corporation which is not a member of a consolidated group; however, this deduction is limited to certain qualifying dividends distributed out of earnings and profits of a taxable year ending after December 31, 1963.

The deferral of gains on deferred intercompany transactions is another advantage of filing a consolidated return. The gain on such a transaction is not recognized until the occurrence of an event which would result in the realization of the profit by the group as a single entity, such as disposition outside the group. The converse disadvantage is that losses on deferred intercompany transactions will also be deferred. Additionally, since the clerical difficulties of accounting for deferred gains and losses can outweigh the advantages of deferring relatively small gains, the Regulations provide for an election not to defer intercompany gains and losses.

---

43. [Also, under § 1504(a)(3) a corporation which ceases to be a member of a consolidated group may generally not reconsolidate with the group for five years. Ed.]

In many cases the filing of a consolidated return will result in larger deductions or credits due to the application of limitations based upon consolidated, rather than separate taxable income. For example, charitable contributions that are not deductible on a separate return basis due to the [ten] percent limitation may be deductible using consolidated return limitations. Where the income of a member is reduced by losses of other members of the consolidated group, however, a current and sometimes permanent loss of deductions or credits can occur by applying limitations based upon consolidated income.

Before the final decision to file a consolidated return is reached, complete computations should be made comparing consolidated tax liability against the aggregate tax liabilities of the members on a separate return basis. If the net result, based on these computations and taking into consideration the various advantages and disadvantages, is only a slight tax advantage in favor of filing on a consolidated basis, it may be preferable to refrain from filing a consolidated return in order to preserve flexibility in future years.

NOTE

The theory of the consolidated return rules is easy to grasp. A family of commonly controlled corporations—the affiliated group—is treated as a single economic unit for tax purposes. Just like a husband and wife may opt to be taxed as an economic unit by filing a joint income tax return, so may an affiliated group elect to be treated as a single taxable entity and report the results of its transactions outside the group on one consolidated return.[1] Dealings within the group, like interspousal transfers,[2] are generally not considered currently taxable events.

Although the theory is simple, the operation of the consolidated regulations can become extremely complex. In general, when computing the consolidated taxable income or loss of the group, the first step is for each member to compute its separate taxable income or loss using its own accounting method and the taxable year of the parent of the group.[3] These results are then aggregated into a consolidated taxable income or loss figure that serves as the base for computing the group's corporate income tax. The earnings and profits of a member of the group also are reflected in upward or downward basis adjustments in the stock of that member held by other members of the affiliated group.[4] For example, if the only two corporations in an affiliated group are a parent ("P") and its wholly owned subsidiary ("S"), and S has only

---

1. Reg. § 1.1502–2.

2. See, e.g., I.R.C. § 1041.

3. Reg. § 1.1502–17(a). In this respect, the consolidated return rules differ significantly from the joint return filed by a married couple.

4. Reg. § 1.1502–32. Section 1503(e) contains special rules regarding these adjustments for purposes of determining gain or loss on the sale by a member of the group of stock in another member. In general, Section 1503(e) requires computation of earnings and profits without regard to the adjustments in Section 312(k) or (n). See Chapter 4B, *supra*.

one class of common stock outstanding, P would make a year-end upward adjustment to the basis in its S stock to the extent of S's undistributed earnings and profits for the year. P would reduce its stock basis by current earnings and profits deficits.[5] This rolling basis mechanism, which notably is linked to earnings and profits rather than taxable income, prevents P from incurring a second round of corporate level tax (or enjoying a double deduction) with respect to its investment in S when S's income or loss has already been reflected in the P–S group's consolidated return. The consolidated return regulations even permit P to have a negative basis (called an "excess loss account") in its S stock.[6]

This basic taxing pattern is subject to a number of modifications and special rules, the most important of which deal with intercompany distributions and transactions.[7] In keeping with the single-entity theory, intercompany dividends are eliminated from the computation of the separate taxable incomes of the members and are reflected in a downward basis adjustment in the stock held by the distributee member of the group.[8]

The tax consequences of an intercompany transaction differ depending on whether or not it is a "deferred intercompany transaction." Deferred intercompany transactions are sales or exchanges of property, performances of services or other expenditures, such as prepaid items, where the outlay must be capitalized.[9] In a deferred intercompany transaction, the payor-member may capitalize the cost of the property or the expenditure as if a separate return were filed.[10] On the other side of the transaction, the payee-member (e.g., the seller of the property or provider of capitalized services) is allowed to delay recognition of any income or loss until an event takes place that is inconsistent with such deferral.[11] For example, if one member of an affiliated group sells property to another member, the seller generally is permitted to defer recognition of any gain or loss. But if the buyer takes cost recovery deductions with respect to the property, the selling member must recognize a corresponding amount of gain or loss as those deductions are taken.[12] A disposition of the property outside the group by the purchasing member also will trigger recognition of deferred gain or loss by the selling member.[13] Similarly, where one member of an affiliated group provides capitalized services to another member, the service

5. This description of the investment basis adjustment rules is vastly oversimplified. See Reg. § 1.1502–32, among other places, for the details.

6. See Reg. § 1.1502–32(e)(1). Certain trigger events, such as a sale or worthlessness of the S stock, may cause P to recognize gain in an amount equal to the excess loss account. Reg. § 1.1502–19(b).

7. See generally Reg. § 1.1502–2 for a list of modifications in determining the separate taxable income of a member of the group.

8. Reg. §§ 1.1502–14(a)(1); 1.1502–32(b)(2)(iii). For the tax treatment of various nondividend intercompany distributions (e.g., return of capital distributions), see generally Reg. § 1.1502–14(a)(2), (b), (c).

9. Reg. § 1.1502–13(a)(2).

10. Reg. § 1.1502–13(a).

11. Reg. § 1.1502–13(c).

12. Reg. § 1.1502–13(d).

13. Reg. § 1.1502–13(f). Additional gain or loss also may be recognized on a sale outside the group by the member actu-

provider recognizes income as the payor amortizes the expenditure for the services.[14]

In the case of other intercompany transactions (e.g., payments for noncapitalized services, rent or interest), the payor and payee both take the transaction into account in calculating their separate taxable income.[15] For example, an interest payment from a subsidiary to its parent will produce an interest deduction for the payor and result in interest income for the payee. The principal limitation is that if in any "nondeferred" intercompany transaction the accounting methods of the payor and payee cause a mismatching of income and the corresponding deduction, the income and deduction from the transaction are taken into account in the later of the relevant years.[16]

The consolidated return regulations also include rules which guard against improper use of another member's net operating losses. These provisions are best considered in the context of the Code's general limitations on net operating loss carryovers.[17]

PROBLEMS

1. The management of Gain, Inc. has recently been considering the acquisition of Loss, Inc. Loss currently has one class of voting common stock outstanding. The parties have developed a plan whereby Gain will acquire a new class of Loss common stock which will entitle Gain to 80% voting control of Loss and 30% of all Loss dividends. If the plan is consummated, will Gain and Loss be eligible to file a consolidated tax return?

2. Corporation P owns 90% of Corporations A and B. Corporations A and B each own 40% of Corporation C. Corporation C owns 80% of Corporation D. Corporation D owns 100% of Corporation E, a tax-exempt organization. Corporation E owns 100% of Corporation F which owns 100% of Corporation G. All of the indicated percentages reflect total voting power and total value owned by the shareholder.

   (a) To what extent do the above corporations constitute an "affiliated group?"

   (b) What result in (a), above, if Corporation B sells 10% of its stock in Corporation C?

3. Without becoming involved with mechanics, consider the advantages and disadvantages of filing consolidated returns.

ally making the sale if the property has appreciated after the intercompany transaction.

14. Reg. § 1.1502–13(d).

15. Reg. § 1.1502–13(b)(1).

16. Reg. § 1.1502–13(b)(2).

17. See Chapter 13B4, infra.

PART THREE: TAXATION OF S CORPORATIONS

CHAPTER 15.   THE S CORPORATION *

A.   INTRODUCTION

We have seen in the preceding chapters that a C corporation has a tax existence separate and apart from its shareholders and is subject to tax on its net income at rates ranging from 15 to 34 percent.[1] Because dividends generally are taxable to the shareholders but not deductible by the corporation, earnings withdrawn from a corporate enterprise are taxed at both the corporate and shareholder levels before finally coming to rest in the shareholders' pockets.[2] Although many techniques have been devised to avoid the double tax, it nonetheless remains the principal feature distinguishing the taxation of incorporated and unincorporated businesses. A partnership, on the other hand, is treated for tax purposes as a conduit whose income and deductions pass through to the partners as they are realized, with the various items retaining their original character in the hands of the partners.[3] Because income is taxed at the partner level, partnership distributions of cash and property generally do not produce any additional tax liability.[4]

It is not surprising that taxpayers have sought to obtain the state law benefits of the corporate form (limited liability, centralized management, etc.) without the sting of the double tax. Congress attempted to accommodate this desire in 1958 by enacting Subchapter S, which then permitted the shareholders of a "small business corporation" to elect to avoid a corporate level tax in most situations.[5] Subchapter S was enacted with the stated purpose of permitting a business to select its

---

* See generally Eustice and Kuntz, Federal Income Taxation of Subchapter S Corporations (rev. ed. 1985); Schenk, Federal Taxation of S Corporations (1985); Bravenec, Federal Taxation of S Corporations and Shareholders (1988).

1. I.R.C. § 11.

2. I.R.C. §§ 61(a)(7), 301. Because an S corporation may not have a corporate shareholder (I.R.C. § 1361(b)(1)(B)), this discussion is confined to noncorporate shareholders.

3. I.R.C. § 702(a), (b). See generally Lind, Schwarz, Lathrope & Rosenberg, Fundamentals of Partnership Taxation (2d ed. 1988).

4. I.R.C. § 731(a).

5. The enactment of Subchapter S came four years after President Eisenhower had proposed that certain "small corporations" should be allowed an election to be taxed as partnerships and that unincorporated businesses should be allowed an election to be taxed as corporations. The Senate was receptive to both concepts, but the House balked and only the election for partnerships and proprietorships to be treated as corporations was included, as Subchapter R, in the 1954 Code. Subchapter R, however, was little used and short lived; it was later repealed, effective in 1969. See S.Rep. No. 1622, 83rd Cong., 2d Sess. 119 (1954), reprinted in [1954 U.S. Code Cong. & Ad.News 4629, 4752.

legal form "without the necessity of taking into account major differences in tax consequence." [6]

The pre-1983 version of Subchapter S, however, actually increased the tax choices available to a business enterprise. As originally adopted, Subchapter S was a modified corporate scheme of taxation rather than a partnership-like conduit. Each person who was a shareholder of an "electing small business corporation" on the last day of the corporation's taxable year was required to include in income as a dividend his pro rata share of the corporation's "undistributed taxable income," an amount which roughly approximated the corporation's taxable income less cash dividends paid during the year.[7] If the corporation had a net operating loss for the year, each person who was a shareholder during the year reported his share of the loss computed on a pro rata, per day basis.[8] With the exception of long-term capital gains, income and deduction items did not retain their character in the hands of the shareholders.[9] Elaborate mechanical rules were included to prevent a second round of taxation on the distribution of previously taxed income.[10] In short, far from simplifying the choices faced by a small business, Subchapter S was a strange hybrid of corporate and partnership concepts, laden with complexity. An electing small business necessarily depended on skilled lawyers and accountants to avoid its many technical traps.

Calls for reform of Subchapter S began with a 1969 Treasury Department study, which in general proposed a liberalization of the eligibility requirements and the adoption of a conduit approach more closely conforming to the tax treatment of partnerships.[11] Congress gradually relaxed the eligibility requirements through piecemeal legislation, but it was not until the Subchapter S Revision Act of 1982 [12] that true reform was achieved. The 1982 Act greatly reduced the tax disparities between Subchapter S corporations and partnerships by replacing the modified corporate structure of Subchapter S with a statutory scheme which is similar to the tax treatment of partnerships and partners under Subchapter K. The Act also introduced the terminology now used in the Code. Electing small business corporations are called "S corporations" while other corporations are known as "C corporations." [13]

The reforms to Subchapter S were long overdue. Since the 1982 Act, the tax differences between partnerships and S corporations have narrowed, making operation as an S corporation an attractive alternative to conducting business in the partnership form. But the Act did

6. S.Rep. No. 1983, 85th Cong., 2d Sess. § 68 (1958), reprinted in 1958–3 C.B. 922.

7. I.R.C. § 1373, prior to Subchapter S Revision Act of 1982 (hereinafter "pre-1983").

8. I.R.C. § 1374 (pre-1983).

9. I.R.C. § 1375(a) (pre-1983).

10. I.R.C. § 1375(d), (f) (pre-1983).

11. See U.S. Treasury Department, Technical Explanation of Treasury Tax Reform Proposals: Hearings Before the House Comm. on Ways and Means, 91st Cong., 1st Sess. 5228–5275 (April 22, 1969).

12. Pub.L. No. 97–354 (1982), reprinted in 1982–2 C.B. 702.

13. I.R.C. § 1361(a).

not eliminate the need for careful planning when selecting the proper form for a business enterprise. Subchapter S is available only for corporations that satisfy the statutory definition of "small business corporation" contained in Section 1361(b). More importantly, significant differences remain between S corporations and partnerships subject to Subchapter K. For example, a partnership is treated as an aggregate of its partners with respect to partnership borrowings. A partner's basis in his partnership interest is increased by his share of partnership liabilities.[14] However, debts incurred by an S corporation have no effect on the bases of the corporation's shareholders in their stock. This difference may have an impact upon the ability of investors to utilize losses generated by the enterprise and the treatment of distributions.[15] Subchapter K also offers partners more flexibility in determining their individual tax results from partnership operations. Partnership allocations of specific items of income or deduction to a particular partner will be respected as long as the allocation has substantial economic effect, while shareholders of an S corporation are required to report a pro rata share of each corporate item.[16]

The individual and corporate rate structure introduced by the Tax Reform Act of 1986 greatly expanded the role of S corporations. By reducing the highest overall rate for individuals from 50 to 28 percent and capping the top rate for C corporations at 34 percent while broadening the corporate tax base, Congress rewrote the tax planning agenda for the closely held business enterprise.[17] Although rates for high-income individuals are creeping back up,[18] S corporations continue to be more attractive than their Subchapter C counterparts. Under current law, for example, $1 of S corporation income is generally taxed at a maximum overall rate of 31 percent, leaving 69 cents for the shareholders. If a C corporation earns the same $1 of income, the tax bite may be more than 54 cents if corporate after-tax profits are distributed as dividends and the corporation and shareholders are taxed at the top 34 percent corporate and 31 percent individual rates. It follows that under this revised rate structure, Subchapter S often will be the entity of choice for individuals seeking the nontax benefits of the corporate form.

B. ELIGIBILITY FOR S CORPORATION STATUS *

Code: § 1361.

Proposed Regulations: § 1.1361–1A(e).

---

14. I.R.C. § 752(a), Reg. § 1.752–1T.

15. See also I.R.C. § 469, limiting the current deductibility of losses from certain passive activities.

16. Compare I.R.C. § 704(b)(2) with I.R.C. §§ 1366(a) and 1377(a).

17. See Chapter 1A, supra.

18. Beginning in 1991, the maximum rate on high-income individuals is 31 per-

cent. I.R.C. § 1(a). Marginal rates between certain income ranges may be higher than 31 percent because of the phase-out of personal exemptions and the limitation on itemized deductions. See I.R.C. §§ 151(d)(3); 68.

 * See generally, Meale, "Eligibility, Election and Termination Under the Subchapter S Revision Act of 1982," 11 Fla.St. U.L.Rev. 93 (1983).

A corporation that wishes to elect S corporation status under Section 1362 must be a "small business corporation," which is defined in Section 1361(b) as a domestic corporation [1] that meets the following additional requirements.

Ineligible Corporations. Only a domestic corporation which is not an "ineligible corporation" may qualify as a small business corporation.[2] Ineligible corporations are defined to include any corporation which is a member of an "affiliated group." [3] This restriction generally prevents an S corporation from owning 80 percent or more of the stock of another corporation.[4] Certain other specialized categories of corporations are "ineligible" because they qualify for tax benefits generally not available to individuals or are subject to other tax regimes.[5]

Number of Shareholders. A small business corporation may not have more than 35 shareholders.[6] For purposes of this limit, a husband and wife (and their estates) are counted as one shareholder regardless of the form in which they own the stock.[7] If stock is jointly owned (e.g., as tenants in common or joint tenants) by other than a husband and wife, each joint owner is considered a separate shareholder.[8] In the case of a nominee, guardian, custodian or agent holding stock in a representative capacity, the beneficial owners of the stock are counted toward the 35 shareholder limit.[9]

Qualifying Shareholders. An S corporation may not have as a shareholder a person (other than an estate[10] or certain trusts) who is not an individual.[11] Thus, a corporation will not qualify as a "small business corporation" if any of its shareholders are corporations, partnerships or ineligible trusts. Nonresident alien individuals also are not permissible shareholders.[12]

When Subchapter S was first enacted, trusts were not eligible shareholders. In a series of reforms culminating in the Subchapter S

---

1. I.R.C. § 1361(b)(1). A domestic corporation is defined as a corporation created or organized in the United States or under the laws of the United States or of any state or territory. Prop.Reg. § 1.1361–1A(c).

2. I.R.C. § 1361(b)(1).

3. I.R.C. § 1361(b)(2)(A). An "affiliated group" generally includes a corporate parent and its controlled (i.e., 80% owned) subsidiaries. I.R.C. § 1504(a). The definition of affiliated group for Subchapter S purposes is modified to exclude certain highly specialized exceptions in Section 1504(b).

4. A subsidiary is excepted from this restriction, however, for any period during which it has not begun business and has no gross income. I.R.C. § 1361(c)(6). This permits an S corporation to control an inactive subsidiary which it may wish to keep alive to preserve a valuable corporate name. See Prop.Reg. § 1.1361–1A(d)(2).

5. Examples include financial institutions which are eligible for certain specialized deductions, insurance companies subject to special tax rules in Subchapter L and domestic international sales corporations. I.R.C. § 1361(b)(2).

6. I.R.C. § 1361(b)(1)(A). The legislative history indicates that this number was chosen because it corresponds to the private placement exception under the federal securities laws. S.Rep. No. 97–640, 97th Cong.2d Sess. 7 (1982).

7. I.R.C. § 1361(c)(1); Prop.Reg. § 1.1361–1A(e)(2).

8. Prop.Reg. § 1.1361–1A(e)(1).

9. Id.

10. The estate of an individual in bankruptcy is an eligible shareholder. I.R.C. § 1361(c)(3).

11. I.R.C. § 1361(b)(1)(B).

12. I.R.C. § 1361(b)(1)(C).

Revision Act of 1982, Congress has liberalized the eligibility requirements by permitting certain types of trusts with clearly identifiable beneficiaries to be shareholders of an S corporation. A trust may be a shareholder if it is: (1) treated as owned under the grantor trust rules [13] by an individual who is a United States citizen or resident;[14] (2) a former grantor trust which continues in existence after the grantor's death, but only for the 60-day period beginning on the day of the decedent's death;[15] (3) a trust that receives S corporation stock under the terms of a will, but only for the 60-day period beginning on the day on which the stock is transferred to the trust;[16] and (4) a voting trust, in which case each beneficiary is treated as a separate shareholder.[17]

Section 1361(d) opens the door a bit further by permitting a "qualified subchapter S trust" to be a shareholder if the beneficiary of the trust so elects. In that event, the beneficiary is treated as the owner for tax purposes of the portion of the trust consisting of the S corporation stock with respect to which the election is made.[18] A qualified subchapter S trust is a trust, all of the income of which is distributed (or required to be distributed) currently to one individual who is a United States citizen or resident and the terms of which require that:[19]

(1) During the life of the current income beneficiary, there shall be only one income beneficiary;

(2) Any corpus distributed during the life of the current income beneficiary may be distributed only to such beneficiary;

(3) The income interest of the current income beneficiary shall terminate on the earlier of the beneficiary's death or termination of the trust; and

(4) Upon termination of the trust during the life of the current income beneficiary, the trust shall distribute all of its assets to such beneficiary.

The qualified subchapter S trust is a useful estate planning vehicle if the owners of an enterprise wish to conduct the business as an S corporation. The definition embraces the two most widely used types of marital trusts that qualify for the federal estate tax marital deduction: the qualified terminable interest trust ("QTIP")[20] and a marital

---

13. See I.R.C. § 671 et seq.

14. I.R.C. § 1361(c)(2)(A)(i). In this case, the deemed owner of the trust is treated as the shareholder. I.R.C. § 1361(c)(2)(B)(i). No foreign trust is eligible to be an S corporation shareholder. I.R.C. § 1361(c)(2)(A).

15. I.R.C. § 1361(c)(2)(A)(ii). The estate of the deemed owner will be treated as the shareholder. I.R.C. § 1361(c)(2)(B)(i). If the entire corpus of the trust is includible in the gross estate of the deemed owner for federal estate tax purposes, the time period is extended to two years.

16. I.R.C. § 1361(c)(2)(A)(iii). The estate of the testator is treated as the shareholder. I.R.C. § 1361(c)(2)(B)(iii).

17. I.R.C. § 1361(c)(2)(A)(iv), (B)(iv). A voting trust is the only type of eligible trust that may have multiple "deemed owners."

18. I.R.C. § 1361(d)(1). For the rules governing the election, see I.R.C. § 1361(d)(2); Prop.Reg. § 1.1361–1A(i)(3)–(6).

19. I.R.C. § 1361(d)(3).

20. I.R.C. § 2056(b)(7).

trust providing income to the surviving spouse for life coupled with a general power of appointment over the remainder.[21] It also includes certain trusts for minor children that qualify for the annual gift tax exclusion.[22] But the definition does not encompass more flexible trust vehicles with more than one income beneficiary, such as a "family pot" trust under which the trustee has discretion to distribute income among a group of children. As a result, the shareholders of a family business operating as an S corporation may have more limited estate planning options than if the business were conducted as a partnership or a C corporation.

One Class of Stock Requirement. A small business corporation may not have more than one class of stock.[23] For purposes of determining whether a corporation has more than one class of stock, differences in voting rights among classes of common stock are disregarded,[24] as are buy-sell agreements among shareholders and stock transfer restrictions.[25] Both voting and nonvoting common stock must continue to be identical, however, with respect to the rights of the shareholders to distributions and liquidation proceeds, and any differences in rights among the outstanding shares under the corporate charter, articles of incorporation or bylaws, or by operation of state law, administrative action,[26] or agreement creates a second class of stock.[27] The existence of various corporate instruments giving the holder the right to acquire stock (e.g., call options or warrants) also may create a second class of stock depending upon whether the right is substantially certain to be exercised by the holder.[28]

Straight Debt Safe Harbor. The potentially knotty problems raised by the interaction of the one-class-of-stock rule and debt vs. equity classification issues[29] are reduced by a safe harbor provision in Section 1361(c)(5) under which "straight debt" instruments are not treated as a disqualifying second class of stock. "Straight debt" is defined as any written unconditional promise to pay on demand or on a specified date a sum certain in money if (1) the interest rate and payment dates are not contingent on profits, the borrower's discretion or similar factors; (2) the instrument is not convertible (directly or indirectly) into stock; and (3) the creditor is an individual, estate or a trust which would be a qualifying shareholder in a small business corporation. The proposed regulations provide that an obligation must bear a "reasonable rate of

21. I.R.C. § 2056(b)(5).

22. See I.R.C. § 2503(b), (c).

23. I.R.C. § 1361(b)(1)(D).

24. I.R.C. § 1361(c)(4).

25. Prop.Reg. § 1.1361–1(*l*)(2)(i).

26. See also Paige v. United States, 580 F.2d 960 (9th Cir.1978), where differences in rights imposed by the California Commissioner of Corporations to protect investors created a second class of stock.

27. Prop.Reg. 1.1361–1(*l*)(2)(i). Stock which is substantially nonvested under

Section 83 is not treated as outstanding unless the holder has made a Section 83(b) election. Prop.Reg. § 1.1361–1(b)(3).

28. Prop.Reg. § 1.1361–1(*l*)(3)(iii)(A). Exceptions are provided for certain call options in connection with loans or to employees. If the strike price of a call option is at least 90 percent of its fair market value at its issuance, it is not substantially certain to be exercised. Prop.Reg. § 1.1361–1(*l*)(3)(iii)(B)–(C).

29. See Chapter 3B, infra.

interest" in order to qualify as "straight debt." Whether an interest rate is "reasonable" is based upon all the facts and circumstances, including the amount borrowed and the timing and amount of payments due under the obligation.[30] Variable interest rates based on a published interest index (such as the applicable Federal rate under Section 1274) are permissible.[31] To provide additional certainty, the proposed regulations also set forth two safe harbors for satisfaction of the reasonable interest rate requirement.[32] Finally, the fact that an obligation is subordinated to other debt of the corporation will not prevent it from qualifying as straight debt.[33]

An obligation that satisfies the straight debt definition is not classified as a second class of stock, and the tax principles generally applicable to debt will apply to the obligation unless the Service determines that a principal purpose for its issuance is tax avoidance. Thus, interest paid or accrued on straight debt is treated as interest by the corporation and the recipient and is not considered as a distribution governed by Section 1368.[34] If a C corporation has outstanding debt obligations that satisfy the straight debt definition but may be classified as equity under general tax principles, the safe harbor ensures that the obligation will not be treated as a second class of stock if the C corporation elects to convert to S status. The conversion and change of status also is not treated as an exchange of the debt instrument for stock.[35]

PROBLEM

Unless otherwise indicated, Z Corporation ("Z") is a domestic corporation which has 50 shares of voting common stock outstanding. In each of the following alternative situations, determine whether Z is eligible to elect S corporation status:

(a) Z has 34 individual shareholders, each of whom owns one share of Z stock. The remaining 16 shares are owned by A and his brother, B, as joint tenants with right of survivorship.

(b) Same as (a), above, except that A and B are married and own 10 of the 16 shares as community property. The remaining 6 shares are owned 3 by A as her separate property and 3 by B as his separate property.

(c) In (b), above, assume that the shareholders of Z elected S corporation status. What will be the effect on Z's election if one year later A dies and bequeaths her interest in Z stock to her son, S?

30. Prop.Reg. § 1.1361–1(*l*)(4)(i)(B), (ii) (A).

31. Prop.Reg. § 1.1361–1(*l*)(4)(ii)(B).

32. Prop.Reg. § 1.1361–1(*l*)(4)(ii)(C).

33. Prop.Reg. § 1.1361–1(*l*)(4)(iii).

34. Prop.Reg. § 1.1361–1(*l*)(4)(v). See Section E of this Chapter, infra.

35. Prop.Reg. § 1.1361–1(*l*)(4)(ii).

(d) Same as (a), above, except that the remaining 16 shares are held by a trust which has three beneficiaries. Does the result change if the trust is only a voting trust?

(e) Same as (a), above, except that the remaining 16 shares are owned by a revocable trust created by an individual, the income of which is taxed to the grantor under § 671.

(f) Same as (a), above, except that the remaining 16 shares are owned by a testamentary trust under which the surviving spouse has the right to income for her life, with the remainder passing to her children. The trust is a "qualified terminable interest trust" (see § 2056(b)(7)).

(g) Z has 100 shares of Class A voting common stock and 50 shares of Class B nonvoting common stock outstanding. Apart from the differences in voting rights, the two classes of common stock have equal rights with regard to dividends and liquidation distributions. Z also has an authorized but unissued class of nonvoting stock which would be limited and preferred as to dividends. The Class A common stock is owned by four individuals and the Class B common stock is owned by E and F (a married couple) as tenants-in-common.

(h) Z has four individual shareholders each of whom own 100 shares of Z common stock for which each paid $10 per share. Each shareholder also owns $25,000 of 15-year Z bonds. The bonds bear interest at 3% above the prime lending rate established by the Chase Manhattan Bank, adjusted quarterly, and are subordinated to general creditors of Z.

C. ELECTION, REVOCATION AND TERMINATION

Code: §§ 444(a), (b), (c)(1), (e); 1362 (omit (e)(5)–(6)); 1378. Skim § 7519(a), (b), (d)(1), (e)(4).

Proposed Regulations: §§ 1.1362–1(c)(1), (3); 1.1362–2(b)(1); 1.1362–3(b)(1), (c); 1.1362–5(b).

Electing S Corporation Status. An otherwise eligible corporation may elect S corporation status under Section 1362 if all the shareholders consent.[1] Once made, an election remains effective until it is terminated under Section 1362(d).[2] An election is effective as of the beginning of a taxable year if it is made either during the preceding taxable year or on or before the fifteenth day of the third month of the current taxable year.[3] If the election is made during the first 2½ months of the year, the S corporation eligibility requirements must

---

1. I.R.C. § 1362(a). For rules and procedures on shareholders' consent to an S election, see Prop.Reg. §§ 1.1362–1, –2.

2. I.R.C. § 1362(c). See generally Prop.Reg. § 1.1362–3.

3. I.R.C. § 1362(b)(1). Elections made not later than 2 months and 15 days after the first day of the taxable year are deemed made during the year even if the year is shorter than 2 months and 15 days. I.R.C. § 1362(b)(4). For rules on how to count months and days for this purpose, see Prop.Reg. § 1.1362–1(c), (e).

have been met for the portion of the taxable year prior to the election, and all shareholders at any time during the pre-election portion of the year must consent to the election.[4] If the eligibility requirements are not met during the pre-election period or if any shareholder who held stock during that period does not consent, the election does not become effective until the following taxable year.[5]

Revocation of Election. An S corporation election may be revoked if shareholders holding more than one-half of the corporation's shares (including nonvoting shares) consent to the revocation.[6] The revocation may specify a prospective effective date.[7] If a prospective effective date is not specified, a revocation made on or before the fifteenth day of the third month of the taxable year is effective on the first day of the taxable year and a revocation made after that date is effective on the first day of the following taxable year.[8]

Termination of Election. Apart from revocation, an S corporation election may be terminated if the corporation ceases to be a small business corporation or, in certain circumstances, if the corporation earns an excessive amount of passive investment income.[9] The first ground for termination is easily illustrated. Terminating events include: (1) exceeding 35 shareholders; (2) issuance of a second class of stock; (3) transfer of stock to an ineligible shareholder; or (4) acquisition of an operating subsidiary. In all those cases, the corporation will cease to be a small business corporation and its S corporation election will terminate on the day after the disqualifying event.[10] To prevent or cure transfers that may jeopardize a corporation's S corporation status, the shareholders will be well advised at the outset to enter into an agreement restricting stock transfers.[11]

The limitation on passive investment income is more complex. Under Section 1362(d)(3), an election to be an S corporation will terminate if for three consecutive taxable years the corporation's "passive investment income" exceeds 25 percent of its gross receipts and the corporation has Subchapter C earnings and profits.[12] A termination triggered by excess passive investment income is effective beginning on the first day of the taxable year following the three year testing period.[13] It is important to note that the Subchapter C earnings and

---

4. I.R.C. § 1362(b)(2).

5. I.R.C. § 1362(b)(2)(B).

6. I.R.C. § 1362(d)(1)(B). See Prop.Reg. § 1.1362–3(b).

7. I.R.C. § 1362(d)(1)(D).

8. I.R.C. § 1362(d)(1)(C). If the revocation is effective on a day other than the first day of a taxable year (e.g., because a prospective date is selected in the middle of the year), the taxable year will be an "S termination year," and the corporation will be taxed pursuant to rules in Section 1362(e). See text accompanying notes 17–19, infra.

9. I.R.C. § 1362(d)(2), (3).

10. I.R.C. §§ 1361(b)(1)(A)–(D); 1362(d)(2)(B). See Prop.Reg. § 1.1362–3(c).

11. See generally Bravenec & Gray, "Shareholder Agreements Can Preserve the S Election and Remedy Its Termination," 63 J. Tax'n 130 (1985).

12. See Prop.Reg. § 1.1362–3(d). Prior years in which the corporation was not an S corporation are not considered for purposes of the passive investment income component of this test. I.R.C. § 1362(c)(3)(A)(iii)(II).

13. I.R.C. § 1362(c)(3)(A)(ii).

profits requirement has the effect of rendering this limitation inapplicable to a corporation that has always been an S corporation or which has been purged of its earnings and profits.[14] Passive investment income generally is defined as gross receipts from royalties, rents, dividends, interest, annuities and gains from sales or exchanges of stock or securities.[15] For purposes of this definition, gross receipts from sales or exchanges of stock or securities are considered only to the extent of gains [16], and for purposes of the overall gross receipts definition, gross receipts on the disposition of capital assets other than stock or securities are taken into account only to the extent of the excess of capital gains over capital losses from such dispositions.[17]

When an S corporation election terminates during the S corporation's taxable year, the corporation experiences an "S termination year," which is divided into two short years: an S short year and a C short year.[18] Income, gains, losses, deductions and credits for an S termination year generally may be allocated between the two short years on a pro rata basis or the corporation may elect to make the allocation under its normal accounting rules.[19] The corporation's tax liability for the short taxable year as a C corporation is then computed on an annualized basis.[20]

Inadvertent Terminations. If an S corporation election is terminated, the corporation generally is not eligible to make another election for five taxable years unless the Treasury consents to an earlier election.[21] Section 1362(f) provides relief if a termination is caused by the corporation ceasing to be a small business corporation or by excessive passive investment income. If (1) the Service determines that the termination was inadvertent, (2) the corporation takes steps within a reasonable time to rectify the problem, and (3) the corporation and its shareholders agree to make whatever adjustments are required by the Service, then the corporation will be treated as continuing as an S corporation and the terminating event will be disregarded.[22] The proposed regulations state that the fact that the terminating event was not reasonably within the control of the corporation and not part of a plan to terminate the election, or the fact that the terminating event took place

---

14. An S corporation, however, may acquire earnings and profits under Section 381 in a corporate acquisition.

15. I.R.C. § 1362(d)(3)(D)(i). Losses from sales or exchanges of stock or securities do not offset gains for purposes of determining passive investment income. Id. The statute also contains rules for certain specialized items. See I.R.C. § 1362(d)(3)(D)(ii)–(v).

16. I.R.C. § 1362(d)(3)(D)(i).

17. I.R.C. § 1362(d)(3)(C).

18. I.R.C. § 1362(e)(1). The C short year begins on the first day the termination is effective. I.R.C. § 1362(e)(1)(B).

19. To use normal accounting rules, an election must be filed by all persons who are shareholders during the S short year and all persons who are shareholders on the first day of the C short year. I.R.C. § 1362(e)(3). The pro rata allocation method may not be used in an S termination year if there is a sale or exchange of 50 percent or more of the stock in the corporation during the year. I.R.C. § 1362(e)(6)(D). For more rules on taxing an S termination year, see I.R.C. § 1362(e)(6).

20. I.R.C. § 1362(e)(5)(A).

21. I.R.C. § 1362(g).

22. I.R.C. § 1362(f).

without the knowledge of the corporation notwithstanding its due diligence to prevent the event, tends to establish that the termination was inadvertent. For example, if a corporation in good faith determines that it had no Subchapter C earnings and profits and its S election later terminates because it violates the passive income limitation for three years and in fact had earnings and profits, the regulations provide that it may be appropriate for the Service to determine that the termination was inadvertent.[23]

Taxable Year of an S Corporation. To preclude S corporations from using fiscal years to achieve a deferral of the shareholders' tax liability, S corporations must use a "permitted year," which is defined as either a calendar year or an accounting period for which the taxpayer establishes a business purpose.[24] The Service has ruled that the business purpose requirement may be satisfied if the desired tax accounting period coincides with a "natural business year" [25] and has quantified the concept with the following mathematical standard: [26]

> [T]he natural business year of a * * * corporation electing to be an S corporation, * * * is determined by the following "25-percent test":
>
> (a) Gross receipts from sales and services for the most recent 12-month period that ends before the filing of the request and that ends with the last month of the requested fiscal year are computed. This amount is divided into the amount of gross receipts from sales and services for the last two months of this 12-month period.
>
> (b) The same computation as in (a) above is made for the two 12-month periods immediately preceding the 12-month period described in (a).
>
> (c) If each of the three results described in (a) and (b) equals or exceeds 25 percent, then the requested fiscal year is the taxpayer's natural business year.
>
> (d) Notwithstanding (c), if the taxpayer qualifies under (c) for more than one natural business year, the fiscal year producing the highest average of the three percentages (rounded to 1/100 of a percent) described in (a) and (b) is the taxpayer's natural business year.

Section 1378 makes it clear that tax deferral for shareholders does not constitute a business purpose. The legislative history also identi-

---

23. Prop.Reg. § 1.1362–5(b).

24. I.R.C. § 1378(b).

25. Rev.Proc. 74–33, 1974–2 C.B. 489.

26. Rev.Proc. 87–32, 1987–2 C.B. 396, 399. If a corporation has a predecessor organization and is continuing the same business as its predecessor, it must use the gross receipts of its predecessor for purposes of satisfying the 25 percent test. If the taxpayer does not have the required period of gross receipts, it cannot establish a natural business year under the revenue procedure.

fies several factors which generally do not support a claim of business purpose: [27]

> The conferees intend that (1) the use of a particular year for regulatory or financial accounting purposes; (2) the hiring patterns of a particular business, e.g., the fact that a firm typically hires staff during certain times of the year; (3) the use of a particular year for administrative purposes, such as the admission or retirement of partners or shareholders, promotion of staff, and compensation or retirement arrangements with staff, partners, or shareholders; and (4) the fact that a particular business involves the use of price lists, model year, or other items that change on an annual basis ordinarily will not be sufficient to establish that the business purpose requirement for a particular taxable year has been met.

Fiscal Year Election. Soon after Congress limited the ability of S corporations (and partnerships) [28] to use a fiscal year, it heard howls of protest from the tax return preparation industry. Quite apart from the tax savings offered by a fiscal year, tax preparers historically enjoyed some relief from the crush of individual returns due on April 15 by using fiscal years for entities that were not required to file on a calendar year basis. Congress responded to these concerns by enacting Section 444, which relaxes the permitted year requirements in Section 1378 without reopening the door to tax deferral. Section 444 permits an S corporation to elect to use a taxable year other than the calendar year required by Section 1378 provided that the year elected results in no more than a three-month deferral of income to the shareholders.[29]

The trade-off for a Section 444 fiscal year election is that the corporation must make a "required payment" under Section 7519 for any taxable year for which the election is in effect. The mechanics of the required payment are annoyingly complex, but the concept is clear. An electing S corporation must pay and keep "on deposit" an amount roughly approximating the value of the tax deferral that the shareholders would have achieved from the use of a fiscal year. Thus, if an S corporation whose shareholders all used calendar years elected a fiscal year ending September 30, the corporation would be required to pay a tax that supposedly equalled the tax benefit from the three months deferral received by the shareholders.[30] Under a de minimis rule, no payment is required if the amount due is less than $500,[31] and a payment made in one year generates a balance "on deposit" that may be used in subsequent years.[32]

27. H.R.Rep. No. 99–841, 99th Cong., 2d Sess. II–319 (1986).

28. See I.R.C. § 706(b).

29. I.R.C. § 444(a), (b)(1). S corporations formed or electing prior to 1987 also were permitted to retain a taxable year that was the same as the entity's last taxable year beginning in 1986. I.R.C. § 444(b)(3).

30. We say "supposedly" because the Section 7519 "required payment" is determined mechanically, without regard to amounts actually deferred by the shareholders. See I.R.C. §§ 7519(b), (c) and (d) for the details.

31. I.R.C. § 7519(a)(2).

32. I.R.C. § 7519(b)(2), (e)(4).

Significantly, a Section 444 election and Section 7519 required payment are not required for any S corporation that has established a business purpose for a fiscal year under Section 1378(b)(2).[33]

PROBLEM

Snowshoe, Inc. ("Snowshoe"), a ski resort located in Colorado, was organized by its four individual shareholders (A, B, C and D) and began operations on October 3 of the current year. A owns 300 shares of Snowshoe voting common stock and B, C and D each own 100 shares of Snowshoe nonvoting common stock. Each share of common stock has equal rights with respect to dividends and liquidation distributions. Consider the following questions in connection with the election and termination of Snowshoe's S corporation status:

(a) If the shareholders wish to elect S corporation status for Snowshoe's first taxable year, who must consent to the election? What difference would it make if, prior to the election, B sold her stock to her brother, G? What difference would it make if B is a partnership which, prior to the election, sold its stock to H, an individual?

(b) What is the last day an effective Subchapter S election for Snowshoe's first taxable year is permitted?

(c) If the shareholders elect S corporation status, what taxable year will Snowshoe be allowed to select?

In the following parts of the problem, assume that Snowshoe elected S corporation status during its first taxable year.

(d) Can A revoke Snowshoe's Subchapter S election without the consent of B, C or D?

(e) If C sold all of his stock to Olga, a citizen of Sweden living in Stockholm, what effect would the sale have on Snowshoe's status as an S corporation?

(f) Same as (e), above, except that C only sold five shares to Olga and had no idea that the sale might adversely affect Snowshoe's S corporation status.

(g) Would it matter if Snowshoe's business is diversified and 45% of its gross receipts come from real estate rentals, dividends and interest?

D. TREATMENT OF THE SHAREHOLDERS

Code: §§ 1363(b), (c); 1366(a)–(e); 1367. Skim §§ 1366(f); 1371(b); 1377.

Except in a few limited situations to be discussed later in this chapter,[1] an S corporation is not subject to the corporate income tax. Rather, its income, deductions and other tax attributes pass through to the shareholders. Unlike the pre-1983 era, when an S corporation was an odd hybrid of corporation and partnership for tax purposes, these

---

33. I.R.S. Notice 88–10, 1988–1 C.B. 478.   **1.** See Section F of this chapter, infra.

items now retain their distinct tax characteristics in the hands of the shareholders.

Although an S corporation is generally exempt from tax, it nonetheless must determine its gross income,[2] deductions and other tax items in order to establish the amounts which pass through to the shareholders. For this purpose, Section 1363(b) provides that an S corporation computes its "taxable income" in the same manner as an individual except that certain deductions peculiar to individuals (e.g., personal exemptions, alimony, medical and moving expenses) are not allowed.[3] In addition, deductions which normally are available only to corporations, such as the 70 percent dividends received deduction, are not allowed,[4] but an S corporation may elect to amortize its organizational expenses over 60 months or more under Section 248.[5] Finally a wide variety of items, ranging from charitable contributions and capital gains to depletion, must be separately stated in order to preserve their special tax character for purposes of the pass-through to the shareholders.[6] Thus, an S corporation is not entitled to any charitable deduction, but corporate charitable gifts may pass through to the shareholders without regard to the normal 10 percent limit on corporate contributions.

Although an S corporation is not a taxable entity, it is treated as an entity for various purposes. For example, tax elections affecting the computation of items derived from an S corporation (e.g., to defer recognition of gain on an involuntary conversion under Section 1033) generally are made at the corporate level.[7] Likewise, limitations on deductions (e.g., the dollar limitation under Section 179 on expensing the cost of certain recovery property) apply at the corporate level and often at the shareholder level as well.[8] And like a partnership, an S corporation is treated as an entity for filing tax returns and other procedural purposes.[9]

Once the corporate items have been identified, the next step is to determine the manner in which they pass through to the shareholders. The pass-through scheme applicable to S corporations will have a familiar ring to students of partnership taxation. First, income and deductions are characterized at the corporate level.[10] Section 1366(a)(1)(A) provides that items which may have potentially varying tax consequences to the individual shareholders must be separately reported. The most common separately stated items are capital and Section 1231 gains and losses, dividends, interest and other types of "portfolio income" under the Section 469 passive loss limitations, tax-exempt

2. Section 1366(c) provides that a shareholder's pro rata share of the S corporation's gross income is used to determine the shareholder's gross income.

3. I.R.C. § 1363(b)(2).

4. S.Rep. No. 97–640, 97th Cong., 2d Sess. 15 (1982), reprinted in 1982–2 C.B. 718, 724.

5. I.R.C. § 1363(b)(3).

6. I.R.C. §§ 1363(b)(1), 1366(a)(1)(A).

7. I.R.C. § 1363(c)(1).

8. See, e.g., I.R.C. § 179(d)(8).

9. I.R.C. §§ 6241–6245. Cf. I.R.C. §§ 6221–6233.

10. I.R.C. § 1366(b).

interest, charitable contributions, investment interest, foreign taxes, intangible drilling expenses and depletion on oil and gas properties.[11] Thus, Section 1231 gains and losses do not fall into any corporate hotchpot; rather, they pass through and are aggregated with each shareholder's other Section 1231 gains and losses in order to determine their ultimate character. All the nonseparately stated items are aggregated and the resulting lump sum passes through as ordinary income or loss.

The timing of the shareholders' income and the allocation of pass-through items also is virtually a mirror image of the partnership rules. The shareholders of an S corporation take into account their respective pro rata shares of income, deductions and other separately stated items on a pro rata, per share daily basis.[12] These items are reported in the shareholder's taxable year in which the corporation's taxable year ends.[13] For example, if an S corporation with a natural business year uses a fiscal year ending January 31, 1992, the shareholders will report the respective pass-through items on their 1992 calendar year tax returns, thus achieving a healthy deferral of any gains or an unfortunate delay in recognizing any losses. A deceased shareholder's Subchapter S items are allocated on a daily basis between the shareholder's final income tax return and the initial return of the decedent's estate.[14]

Section 1366(d) limits the amount of losses or deductions that may pass through to a shareholder to the sum of the shareholder's adjusted basis in the stock plus his adjusted basis in any indebtedness of the corporation to the shareholder. Losses disallowed because of an inadequate basis may be carried forward indefinitely and treated as a loss in any subsequent year in which the shareholder has a basis in either stock or debt.[15]

Section 1367 requires the basis of each shareholder's S corporation stock to be increased by his share of income items (including tax-exempt income) and decreased (but not below zero) by losses, deductions, and non-deductible expenses which do not constitute capital expenditures. Any additional losses must be applied to reduce the shareholder's basis (again, not below zero) in any corporate indebtedness to the shareholder.[16] If the basis of both stock and debt is reduced, any subsequent upward adjustments must first be applied to restore the basis in the indebtedness to the extent that it was previously reduced before the basis of the stock may be increased.[17]

Losses that pass through to a shareholder of an S corporation also may be restricted by the at-risk limitations in Section 465 and the

11. S.Rep. No. 97–640, supra note 4, at 16–17, reprinted in 1982–2 C.B. 718, 725. See Rev.Rul. 84–131, 1984–2 C.B. 37, where the Service ruled that a shareholder's share of an S corporation's investment interest is a separately stated item.

12. I.R.C. § 1366(a)(1). See § 1377(a)(1) for the method of determining each shareholder's "pro rata share."

13. I.R.C. § 1366(a)(1).

14. Id.

15. I.R.C. §§ 1366(d)(2), 1366(a)(1).

16. I.R.C. § 1367(b)(2)(A).

17. I.R.C. § 1367(b)(2)(B).

passive activity loss limitations in Section 469.[18] In the case of an S corporation, the at-risk rules are applied on an activity-by-activity basis, except that activities which constitute a trade or business are aggregated if the taxpayer actively participates in the management of the trade or business and at least 65 percent of the losses are allocable to persons actively engaged in the management of the trade or business.[19]

The passive activity loss limitations cast a wider net, however, and often will limit an investor in a new business operating as an S corporation from deducting the legitimate economic losses that pass through during the start-up years of the enterprise. Section 469 generally provides that losses from passive activities may only be deducted against income from passive activities; consequently, excess passive losses may not be used to shelter compensation or other income from an active trade or business.[20] An activity is "passive" if it involves the conduct of a trade or business in which the taxpayer does not "materially participate."[21] A taxpayer generally is treated as materially participating in an activity only if the taxpayer is involved in the activity on a basis which is regular, continuous and substantial.[22] Thus, the level of activity by each shareholder in an S corporation will become the critical inquiry in applying Section 469.

Section 469 also separately identifies "portfolio income," which generally consists of interest, dividends, annuities and royalties, together with directly related expenses, and gains and losses from property producing such income or held for investment.[23] To prevent avoidance of the passive activity loss limitations, passive losses may not be deducted against portfolio income.[24] Thus, a taxpayer with an otherwise nondeductible passive loss may not shift assets from an active business to income-producing stocks or bonds and deduct the passive loss against the investment income. Income from an S corporation is not classified as portfolio income except to the extent that the corporation itself holds assets producing portfolio income.[25] This rule appar-

---

18. Both these limitations apply on a shareholder-by-shareholder basis rather than at the corporate level. I.R.C. §§ 465(a)(1)(A); 469(a)(2)(A).

19. I.R.C. § 465(c)(3)(B). However, activities involving filming or taping, equipment leasing, farming, oil and gas and geothermal property are not aggregated under this rule. I.R.C. § 465(c)(2)(A), (B). All activities with respect to equipment leasing are generally treated as a single activity. I.R.C. § 465(c)(2)(B).

20. Section 469 operates to defer the deduction of the losses; it does not forever disallow them. Disallowed losses may be carried forward and treated as a deduction in the following taxable years. I.R.C. § 469(b). Any remaining deferred losses may be used as a deduction against passive income from the same passive activity (including gain recognized on the disposition, then against other passive income and, finally, against any other income or gain). I.R.C. § 469(g).

21. I.R.C. § 469(c)(1).

22. I.R.C. § 469(h)(1). This standard is met, for example, if the shareholder participates in the activity for more than 500 hours during the year. See Temp.Reg. § 1.469–5T for the rules for determining material participation.

23. I.R.C. § 469(e)(1).

24. Id.

25. S.Rep. No. 99–313, 99th Cong., 2d Sess. 728–29 (1986). See Temp. Reg. § 1.469–2T(c)(3)(i)(B).

ently will permit S corporations and general partnerships to be used as vehicles to conduct active businesses that will pass through to their investors passive income that may be offset by losses from other passive investments.

To illustrate the impact of these rules, assume Manager and Investor are each 50 percent shareholders in an S corporation that owns and operates a small flower shop. Manager materially participates in the business but Investor has no active management role. Prior to the enactment of Section 469, if the flower shop suffered losses both Manager and Investor could deduct the losses passing through from the corporation against their income from other sources. Under current law, however, Investor's ability to currently deduct the losses is sharply curtailed and, in fact, may even discourage her from making the investment in the first place.

HARRIS v. UNITED STATES *

United States Court of Appeals, Fifth Circuit, 1990.
902 F.2d 439.

GARWOOD, Circuit Judge:

Facts and Proceedings Below

In June 1982, Taxpayers contracted with Trans–Lux New Orleans Corporation to purchase for $665,585 cash a New Orleans pornographic theater that they intended to convert into a wedding hall. The Taxpayers' obligations under the contract were conditioned on their being able to secure from a third party a loan for not less than $600,000 repayable in fifteen to twenty years.[1] Shortly before this time, Taxpayers had contacted John Smith (Smith), a real estate loan officer with Hibernia National Bank (Hibernia), to discuss the possibility of obtaining financing for the impending acquisition. Smith orally committed to lend Taxpayers $700,000.[2]

Subsequently, to shield themselves from the potential adverse publicity that could follow from the purchase of the pornographic theater, as well as to limit their personal liability and enhance their chances of qualifying for industrial revenue bonds to finance the theater's renovation, in July 1982 Taxpayers formed Harmar (Harmar), a Louisiana corporation, which elected to be taxed pursuant to Subchapter S of the Internal Revenue Code, to purchase and operate the subject property. Harris and Martin each initially contributed $1,000 to the corporation, receiving its stock in return, and each also loaned

---

* Some footnotes omitted.

1. As part of the contract, Taxpayers deposited with the seller $32,500, all of which was to be applied to the purchase price. In the event Taxpayers were unable to procure the loan, the purchase contract called for their deposit to be refunded.

2. Smith asserted in his deposition that he did not know the purpose of the borrowed funds in excess of the purchase price, but he surmised that the money was intended for improvements to the theater. No written loan commitment was ever issued.

Harmar $47,500 to satisfy operating expenses. Harris and Martin were the sole shareholders of Harmar, each owning half of its stock.

The purchase of the theater closed on November 1, 1982, and the theater was conveyed to Harmar on that date. Hibernia furnished the $700,000 necessary to close the transaction.[3] In borrowing the funds necessary to acquire the subject property, Harmar executed two promissory notes payable to Hibernia for $350,000 each, each dated November 1, 1982. One of these notes was secured by a $50,322.09 Hibernia certificate of deposit in Harris' name and another $304,972.49 certificate of deposit in the name of his wholly-owned corporation, Harris Mortgage Corporation. Harmar secured the other note, in accordance with its collateral pledge agreement, by its $3,000,000 note (which was unfunded apart from the $700,000) and its collateral mortgage on the theater, each executed by Harmar in favor of Hibernia and dated November 1, 1982. Under the terms of the collateral pledge agreement executed by Harmar in reference to the $3,000,000 note and mortgage, the mortgage secured "not only" Harmar's $350,000 note to Hibernia, "but also any and every other debts, liabilities and obligations" (other than consumer credit debt) of Harmar to Hibernia whether "due or to become due, or whether such debts, liabilities and obligations" of Harmar "are now existing or will arise in the future." Thus, the collateral mortgage secured the full $700,000 loan from Hibernia. Additionally, Taxpayers each executed personal continuing guarantees of Harmar indebtedness in the amount of $700,000 in favor of Hibernia. Smith testified in his deposition that the transaction was structured so that half the loan, as represented by one of the $350,000 notes, would be primarily secured by the certificates of deposit and the other half, represented by the other $350,000 note, primarily by the mortgage on the property purchased, with the entire amount also secured by Taxpayers' individual guarantees.

On its income tax return for the year ending December 31, 1982, Harmar reported a net operating loss of $104,013. Pursuant to [the predecessor of Section 1366], Taxpayers each claimed half of the loss as a deduction on their 1982 individual returns,[5] concluding that their bases in Harmar were in fact greater than Harmar's net operating loss for that year and that they therefore were entitled to deduct the entire loss on their personal returns. On audit, the Internal Revenue Service (IRS) found to the contrary and determined that Harris and Martin each had a basis of $1,000 in his Harmar stock and an adjusted basis in Harmar's indebtedness to each of them as shareholders of $47,500.

3. As noted, the purchase price was $665,585. Harris testified in his deposition that at closing there was also paid some $10,000 in miscellaneous closing costs and a $35,000 real estate commission, so "the entire $700,000 was accounted for at the closing." It is unclear whether the $32,500 escrow previously deposited by the Taxpayers with the seller was wholly or partially refunded to them or was credited to Harmar. Harmar's 1982 income tax return shows that as of December 31, 1982, it had land and buildings with an original cost of $674,367.

5. Harris and Martin claimed deductions for Harmar's loss of $52,006 and $52,007, respectively.

Pursuant to I.R.C. [§ 1366(d)], the IRS limited Taxpayers' deductions of the net operating loss to what it considered to be their bases in Harmar, $48,500 each.   The IRS's disallowance of a portion of the deductions claimed by Taxpayers [6] resulted in additional tax liability, including interest, for Martin of $3,150.58 and for Harris of $1,280.   Taxpayers paid the tax in dispute and now appeal the district court's summary judgment dismissing their suit for refund.

Discussion

Taxpayers contend on appeal that in determining the deduction allowable for Harmar's net operating loss, the IRS should have included in Taxpayers' bases in their Harmar stock the full value of the $700,000 Hibernia loan they guaranteed.   I.R.C. [§ 1366] permits a Subchapter S shareholder to deduct from his personal return a proportionate share of his corporation's net operating loss to the extent that the loss does not exceed the sum of the adjusted basis of his Subchapter S corporation stock and any corporate indebtedness to him.   See section [1366(d)(1)]. To arrive at their basis figure, Taxpayers seek to recast the transaction in question.   They in essence urge that we disregard the form of the Hibernia loan—one from Hibernia to Harmar—in favor of what Taxpayers consider as the substance of the transaction—a $700,000 loan from Hibernia to them, the $700,000 proceeds of which they then equally contributed to Harmar's capital account.   As evidence of their view of the substance of the transaction, Taxpayers point to the deposition testimony of Smith indicating that Hibernia looked primarily to Taxpayers, rather than to Harmar, for repayment of the loan, and they call attention to the $700,000 guarantees they each provided Hibernia as well as the $355,294.58 in certificates of deposit that Harris pledged to Hibernia as part of the November 1, 1982 loan transaction.

In its summary judgment memorandum, the district court declared that *Brown v. Commissioner,* 706 F.2d 755 (6th Cir.1983), was "on all fours" with the instant case and therefore resolved it.   In *Brown,* the Sixth Circuit rejected shareholders' substance over form argument in ruling that the shareholders' guarantees of loans to their Subchapter S corporation could not increase their bases in their stock in the corporation unless the shareholders made an economic outlay by satisfying at least a portion of the guaranteed debt.   Id. at 757.   Without such an outlay, the *Brown* court concluded that " 'the substance matched the form' " of the transaction before it.   Id. at 756.   The reasoning of *Brown* was followed by the Fourth Circuit in Estate of *Leavitt v. Commissioner,* 875 F.2d 420 (4th Cir.1989), *aff'g,* 90 T.C. 206 (1988). There, the court, affirming the en banc Tax Court, held that shareholder guarantees of a loan to a Subchapter S corporation did not increase shareholders' stock basis because such guarantees had not "cost" shareholders anything and thus did not constitute an economic outlay.

---

6.   The IRS disallowed $4,506 of Harris' deduction and $4,507 of Martin's.

Leavitt, 875 F.2d at 422 & n. 9.[7]　In reaching this conclusion, the Fourth Circuit affirmed as not clearly erroneous a finding of the Tax Court that the loan, in form as well as in substance, was made to the corporation rather than to the shareholders.[8]　Id. at 424.　The court rejected appellants' suggestion that it employ the debt/equity principles espoused in Plantation Patterns, Inc. v. Commissioner, 462 F.2d 712 (5th Cir.1972), in determining whether the shareholders had actually made an economic outlay,[9] instead choosing to employ a debt/equity analysis only after making a finding that an economic outlay had occurred.[10]　*Leavitt,* 875 F.2d at 427.　The *Leavitt* court reasoned that the legislative history of section [1366] limiting the basis of a Subchapter S shareholder to his corporate investment or outlay could not be circumvented through the use of debt/equity principles.[11]　Id. at 426

7. In reasoning that the shareholders had not increased their stock bases as a result of their guarantees, the court turned to I.R.C. § 1012, which defines basis of property as its cost. Id. at 422 n. 9. Cost of property, in turn, is defined in the Treasury Regulations as the "amount paid for such property in cash or other property." 26 C.F.R. § 1.1012–1(a).

8. The court noted that the loan in question had been made by the bank directly to the corporation, the loan payments were made by the corporation directly to the bank, and neither the corporation nor the shareholders reported the payments as constructive dividends. Id.

Under *Leavitt,* the presumption is that the form will control and that presumption will not be surmounted absent the shareholder's satisfying the higher standard applicable to a taxpayer's seeking to disavow the form he selected and recast a transaction. See Bowers, Building Up an S Shareholder's Basis through Loans and Acquisitions, J. Tax'n S Corp., Fall 1989, at 22, 29.

9. In *Plantation Patterns,* this Court considered whether a Subchapter C corporation could deduct interest payments made on its debt and whether its shareholders had resulting dividend income. The Court, using a debt/equity analysis, affirmed a Tax Court finding that a corporation's interest payments on debentures were constructive dividends and could not be deducted as interest payments. Id. at 723–24.

Subsequent decisions have elaborated on *Plantation Patterns* and identified thirteen factors used to establish whether shareholder advances to a corporation are debt or equity. They are:

"(1) the names given to the certificates evidencing the indebtedness;

"(2) the presence or absence of a fixed maturity date;

"(3) the source of payments;

"(4) the right to enforce payment of principal and interest;

"(5) participation in management flowing as a result;

"(6) the status of the contribution in relation to regular corporate creditors;

"(7) the intent of the parties;

"(8) 'thin' or adequate capitalization;

"(9) identity of interest between creditor and stockholder;

"(10) source of interest payments;

"(11) the ability of the corporation to obtain loans from outside lending institutions;

"(12) the extent to which the advance was used to acquire capital assets; and

"(13) the failure of the debtor to repay on the due date or to seek a postponement." In re Lane, 742 F.2d 1311, 1314–15 (11th Cir.1984) (quoting Estate of Mixon v. United States, 464 F.2d 394, 402 (5th Cir.1972)).

10. The Fourth Circuit embraced the Tax Court's interpretation of its earlier opinion in Blum v. Commissioner, 59 T.C. 436 (1972). In *Blum,* the court rejected the taxpayer's substance over form argument. The *Leavitt* Tax Court asserted that the *Blum* court never reached the debt/equity issue "because the taxpayer had failed his burden of proving that the bank in substance had loaned the funds to the taxpayer and not to the corporation." *Leavitt,* 90 T.C. at 215. Thus construed, *Blum* in no way undermines the Fourth Circuit's § 1374 analysis.

11. See S.Rep. No. 1983, 85th Cong., 2d Sess. at 220, U.S.Code Cong. & Admin. News 1958, p. 4791, (1958–3 Cum.Bull. at

& n. 16. See generally Bogdanski, Shareholder Guarantees, Interest Deductions, and S Corporation Stock Basis: The Problems with Putnam, 13 J.Corp.Tax'n 264, 268–89 (1986).

Taxpayers press this Court to follow the contrary holding of Selfe v. United States, 778 F.2d 769 (11th Cir.1985). There, the Eleventh Circuit ruled that a shareholder's guaranty of a Subchapter S corporation loan could result in an increase in equity or debt basis even though the shareholder had not satisfied any portion of the obligation. *Selfe,* 778 F.2d at 775. The court remanded the case to the district court for it to employ debt/equity principles in determining if the loan in question was in substance one to the shareholder rather than to the corporation. Id.

The courts have uniformly ruled that a shareholder must make an economic outlay to increase his Subchapter S corporation stock basis. See *Leavitt,* 875 F.2d at 422; *Selfe,* 778 F.2d at 772; *Brown,* 706 F.2d at 756; Underwood v. Commissioner, 535 F.2d 309, 311–12 (5th Cir.1976). Taxpayers assert that if we look beyond the form of the transaction at what they contend is its substance—a loan from Hibernia to them, which in turn they contributed to Harmar as capital—we must find that a $700,000 outlay occurred and that their stock bases therefore correspondingly increased. They contend that use of debt/equity principles will lead us to such a conclusion.

Ordinarily, taxpayers are bound by the form of the transaction they have chosen; taxpayers may not in hindsight recast the transaction as one that they might have made in order to obtain tax advantages. * * * The IRS, however, often may disregard form and recharacterize a transaction by looking to its substance. Higgins v. Smith, 308 U.S. 473, 60 S.Ct. 355, 357, 84 L.Ed. 406 (1940). The Tax Court has recognized an exception to the rule that a taxpayer may not question a transaction's form in cases such as this one in which the shareholder argues that guaranteed corporate debt should be recast as an equity investment on the shareholder's part. Blum v. Commissioner, 59 T.C. 436, 440 (1972).

In this case we find that the transaction as structured did not lack adequate substance or reality and that an economic outlay justifying the basis claimed by Taxpayers never occurred.

The summary judgment evidence reflects that the parties to this transaction intended that the Hibernia loan be one to the corporation. Each of the two $350,000 promissory notes was executed by and only in the name of Harmar. The notes have been renewed and remain in the same form, namely notes payable to Hibernia in which the sole maker is Harmar.[12] Hibernia, an independent party, in substance earmarked

1141); see also Comment, Subchapter S Loss Limitation: The Effect of Shareholder Loan Guarantees on Basis, 40 Sw.L.J. 1241, 1263 (1987).

12. In his deposition, when discussing the documentation required to make the loan, Smith stated that items such as the corporate certificate of good standing, corporate charter, and articles of incorporation were prerequisites to closing the loan because Hibernia needed to know that it was "dealing with a valid entity." Harris'

the loan proceeds for use in purchasing the subject property to which Harmar took title, Harmar contemporaneously giving Hibernia a mortgage to secure Harmar's debt to Hibernia. The bank sent interest due notices to Harmar, and all note payments were made by checks to Hibernia drawn on Harmar's corporate account.[13] Harmar's books and records for all years through the year ended December 31, 1985, prepared by its certified public accountant, reflect the $700,000 loan simply as an indebtedness of Harmar to Hibernia. They do not in any way account for or reflect any of the $700,000 as a capital contribution or loan by Taxpayers to Harmar, although they do reflect the $1,000 capital contribution each Taxpayer made and Harmar's indebtedness to Taxpayers for the various cash advances Taxpayers made to it. The Harmar financial statements for the year ended December 31, 1986, are the first to show any contributed capital attributable to the Hibernia loan. Further, Hibernia's records showed Harmar as the "borrower" in respect to the $700,000 loan and the renewals of it. Harmar's 1982 tax return, which covered August 15 through December 31, 1982, indicates that Harmar deducted $12,506 in interest expenses. Because only the Hibernia loan generated such expenses for that period, it is reasonably inferable that the deduction corresponded to that loan. The 1982 Harmar return showed no distribution to Taxpayers, as it should have if the $700,000 Hibernia loan on which Harmar paid interest was a loan to the Taxpayers. Further, the return shows the only capital contributed as $2,000 and the only loan from stockholders as $68,000, but shows other indebtedness of $675,000. In short, Harmar's 1982 income tax return is flatly inconsistent with Taxpayers' present position. Moreover, there is no indication that Taxpayers treated the loan as a personal one on their individual returns by reporting Harmar's interest payments to Hibernia as constructive dividend income. In sum, the parties' treatment of the transaction, from the time it was entered into and for years thereafter, has been wholly consistent with its unambiguous documentation and inconsistent with the way in which Taxpayers now seek to recast it. Hibernia was clearly an independent third party, and the real and bona fide, separate existence of Harmar is not challenged. The parties did what they intended to do, and the transaction as structured did not lack adequate reality or substance.[14]

---

deposition demonstrates that he intended the loan to be one to Harmar. He acknowledged there that his legal and tax consultants had advised him that it was to his advantage to have a corporation borrow the funds from Hibernia. Martin stated that he was aware that in signing the promissory notes on November 1, 1982, he was executing them on behalf of Harmar.

13. To the extent Harmar did not have funds available, Taxpayers would deposit personal funds into Harmar's account, but the checks were always drawn on Harmar's checking account. These and other amounts advanced by Taxpayers to Harmar were carried on its books as part of its interest-bearing indebtedness *to Taxpayers.*

14. This is unlike the situation in *Underwood,* 535 F.2d at 312 & n. 2, where we allowed the IRS to disregard a note of the shareholders of the Subchapter S corporation to another of their wholly-owned corporations that was substituted for the Subchapter S corporation's note, because it was not shown that the shareholders there intended to or would ever "make a demand upon themselves * * * for payment of their note." Here, Hibernia was clearly an independent third party (and it is those

Moreover, if the transaction is to be "recast," it is by no means clear that it should be recast in the form sought by Taxpayers, namely as a cash loan to them from Hibernia followed by their payment of the cash to Harmar as a contribution to its capital, and Harmar's then using the cash to purchase the building. Such recasting does not account for Hibernia's mortgage on the building. In any event, if the transaction is to be recast, why should it not be recast as a loan by Hibernia to Taxpayers, with the Taxpayers using the funds to themselves purchase the building, giving Hibernia a mortgage on the building to secure their debt to it, and then transferring the building, subject to the mortgage, to Harmar as a contribution to capital? Presumably in that situation Taxpayers' bases in their Harmar stock would be reduced by the amount of the debt secured by the mortgage under I.R.C. § 358(d). See Wiebusch v. Commissioner, 59 T.C. 777, aff'd per curiam "on the basis of the opinion of the Tax Court," Wiebusch v. Commissioner, 487 F.2d 515 (8th Cir.1973).[15] While section 358(d) likely does not affect stockholder basis in the debt of the Subchapter S corporation to the stockholder, Taxpayers have not sought to recast the transaction as a loan by Hibernia to them followed by their loan of the proceeds to Harmar; indeed even after Harmar's books were rearranged starting with the year ending December 31, 1986, the books do not show any indebtedness in this respect of Harmar to Taxpayers and do continue to show Harmar as owing the money in question to Hibernia. There is simply no evidence of Harmar indebtedness to Taxpayers in respect to these funds.

Taxpayers' guarantees and Harris' pledge of certificates of deposit do not undermine the intent of the parties that Harmar be the borrower in this transaction. It certainly is not difficult to fathom that a careful lender to a new, small, closely held corporation such as Harmar would seek personal guarantees from all of its shareholders.

who structured the transaction, not the IRS, who seek to recast it).

We also observe that this case stands in contrast to those involving nominees or dummy corporations. In such instances, courts may look beyond the form of a transaction if it is clear that the corporation served no significant business activity and that the shareholders intended that the corporation serve only as a dummy for them. See, e.g., Paymer v. Commissioner, 150 F.2d 334, 337 (2d Cir.1945); B. Bittker & J. Eustice, Federal Income Taxation of Corporations and Shareholders ¶ 2.10 (1979). In this case, Taxpayers intended that Harmar conduct significant business activity, and they do not contend that Harmar's separate, corporate identity should be disregarded or that it was a mere sham.

We do not suggest that had the transaction been structured in a different manner it would have lacked adequate substance or reality, or that there was no way the transaction could have been structured to afford Taxpayers a further $700,000 basis in Harmar under section 1374(c)(2) (now section 1366(d)(1)).

15. See also Megaard, No Stock Basis for Shareholder Guarantee of S Corporation Debt, 15 J.Corp.Tax'n 340 (1989). Megaard explains that "[u]nder Section 358(d), the assumption by a corporation of its shareholder's debt is treated as money received which reduces the shareholder's basis in the stock." Id. at 349. Cf. id. at 350 ("Having the corporation's assets encumbered by the shareholder's personal debt runs the risk of a basis reduction under Section 358 should the Service argue that the transaction was a purchase by the shareholder of the * * * assets followed by a contribution of the assets to the corporation subject to the debt.").

See Bogdanski, supra, at 269. Moreover, the wholly unperformed guarantees do not satisfy the requirement that an economic outlay be made before a corresponding increase in basis can occur. See generally *Underwood*, 535 F.2d at 312. In the same light, Harris' pledge to Hibernia of some $355,000 in certificates of deposit of his (and Harris Mortgage Corporation) does not provide such an outlay.[16]

We conclude that the transaction must be treated as it purports to be and as the parties treated it—namely as a loan by Hibernia to Harmar, all payments on which through the relevant time have been made by Harmar to Hibernia. For any funds or other assets Taxpayers have actually provided to Harmar as loans or contributions, Taxpayers are, of course, entitled to basis additions as of the time such contributions or loans were furnished by them to Harmar, but they are not entitled to a 1982 basis addition for Hibernia's 1982 $700,000 loan to Harmar, notwithstanding that it was also secured by Taxpayers' execution of guarantees and Harris' pledge to Hibernia of his and Harris Mortgage Corporation's certificates of deposit in the total face amount of some $355,000.

Conclusion

There was no genuine dispute as to any material fact necessary to sustain the Government's summary judgment motion. The district court's judgment is correct and it is therefore

AFFIRMED.

NOTE

In *Harris*, the Fifth Circuit joins the Sixth and Fourth Circuits[1] and the Tax Court[2] in holding that the guarantee of an S corporation's loan by its shareholders may not be treated as an additional investment in the corporation which will increase the shareholders' bases for purposes of the loss limitation rule in Section 1366(d). In conflict with this line of authority is the Eleventh Circuit's decision in Selfe v. United States.[3] In *Selfe*, the court reasoned that debt-equity principles under Subchapter C were applicable in determining whether a shareholder-guaranteed debt should be characterized as a capital contribution. In remanding the case for a determination of whether the shareholder's guarantee amounted to either an equity investment or a shareholder loan to the corporation, the court directed the district court to apply the principles of *Plantation Patterns*, a Subchapter C case discussed in *Harris*.

---

16. Taxpayers would have us, in effect, convert this pledge to Hibernia into a $700,000 cash contribution made to Harmar by Taxpayers equally. But that did not happen. Taxpayers do not contend that the certificates of deposit were contributed to Harmar's capital.

1. Brown v. Commissioner, 706 F.2d 755 (6th Cir.1983); Estate of Leavitt v. Commissioner, 875 F.2d 420 (4th Cir.1989), cert. denied ___ U.S. ___, 110 S.Ct. 376 (1989).

2. Estate of Leavitt v. Commissioner, 90 T.C. 206 (1988).

3. 778 F.2d 769 (11th Cir.1985).

Despite the seeming conflict among the circuits, the Supreme Court has declined to add this fascinating tax issue to its docket.[4]

PROBLEMS

1. S Corporation is a calendar year taxpayer which elected S corporation status in its first year of operation. S's common stock is owned by A (200 shares with a $12,000 basis) and B (100 shares with a $6,000 basis). During the current year, S will have the following income and expenses:

Business income *NS*	$ 92,000
Tax-exempt interest *S*	1,000
Salary expense *NS*	44,000
Depreciation *NS*	8,000
Property taxes *NS*	7,000
Supplies *NS*	4,000
Interest expense paid on a margin account maintained with S Corp.'s stock broker *S*	6,000
Gain from the sale of a building:	
§ 1250 gain *NS — recapture*	7,000
§ 1231 gain *S*	12,000
STCG from the sale of AT & T stock *S*	7,500
LTCG from the sale of Chrysler stock *S Net*	15,000
LTCL from the sale of investment real estate	9,000
~~Bribe of government official~~ *NS* *except reduce each basis*	6,000
Recovery of a bad debt previously deducted *S*	4,500

(a) How will S Corporation, A and B report these events? Compare § 704(b)(2) and (c).

(b) What is A's basis in his S stock at the end of the current year? *increase by % income; decrease deduct §1367*

(c) Whose accounting method will control the timing of income and deductions? *Corporate level   §1363(d)(i)*

(d) If S realizes a gain upon an involuntary conversion, who makes the election under § 1033 to limit recognition of gain? *Corp. §1363(d)(i)*

(e) Would it matter if the building would have been property described in § 1221(1) if held by A? *watch out for conversion, C inv. to S inv.*

2. D, E and F each own one-third of the outstanding stock of R Corporation (an S corporation). During the current year, R will have $120,000 of net income from business operations. The net income is realized at a rate of $10,000 per month. Additionally, in January of this year R sold § 1231 property and recognized a $60,000 loss. *Collapse corp.*

(a) Assume D's basis in her R stock at the beginning of the year is $10,000. If D sells one-half of her stock to G midway through the year for $25,000, what will be the tax results to D and G?

---

4. The Court denied the taxpayer's petition for certiorari in the *Estate of Leavitt* case, supra note 1.

(b) What difference would it make in (a), above, if D sold all of her stock to G for $50,000?

3. The Ace Sporting Goods Store (an S corporation) is owned by Dick and Harry. Dick and Harry each own one-half of Ace's stock and have a $2,000 basis in their respective shares. At incorporation, Dick loaned $4,000 to Ace and received a five year, 12% note from the corporation.

(a) If Ace has an $8,000 loss from business operations this year, what will be the results to Dick and Harry? Do you have any suggestions for Harry? Would it matter if on December 15 Ace borrowed $4,000 from its bank on a full recourse basis? What if Dick and Harry personally guaranteed the loan? Compare §§ 752(a) and 722.

(b) If Ace has $6,000 of net income from business operations next year, what will be the results to Dick and Harry?

(c) What difference would it make in (a), above, if the $8,000 loss was made up of $2,000 of losses from business operation and a $6,000 long-term capital loss? See Reg. § 1.704–1(d)(2).

(d) What would be the effect in (a), above, if Ace's S corporation status was terminated at the end of the current year?

4. Allied Technologies, an S corporation, is owned by Betty (25%), Chuck (35%) and Diana (40%). Betty and Chuck also each own one-half of the stock of the Portland Exporting Corporation, also an S corporation.

(a) If Allied sells investment real estate which it purchased two years ago for $40,000 to Portland for $20,000, what will be the result to Allied? See § 267.

(b) What difference would it make in (a), above, if Portland were a C corporation?

(c) Assume Allied is an accrual method taxpayer and owes $1,500 to Betty (a cash method taxpayer) for her December salary. If Allied pays the salary on January 15 of the following year, what will be the tax results to Allied and Betty, assuming both are calendar year taxpayers? See § 267(e).

E. DISTRIBUTIONS TO SHAREHOLDERS

Code: §§ 311(b); 1368; 1371(a)(1), (c), (e); Skim § 301(a), (b) and (d).

One of the more unpleasant technical issues under the pre-1983 version of Subchapter S was the treatment of distributions by an S corporation to its shareholders. The 1982 Act greatly simplified the area, particularly in the case of an S corporation with no accumulated earnings and profits. In that event, a distribution is treated as a tax-free return of capital which is first applied to reduce the shareholder's basis in his stock.[1] Any distribution in excess of basis is treated as gain

---

1. I.R.C. § 1368(b)(1).

from the sale or exchange of property—capital gain if the stock is a capital asset.[2] Virtually all S corporations formed after 1982 do not generate earnings and profits [3] and are governed by this simple regime. This basic taxing pattern for distributions by S corporations also governs any distribution of property to which Section 301(c) would apply.[4] Thus, the tax consequences of transactions characterized as Section 301 distributions by other Code provisions, such as Sections 302 (redemptions) and 305 (stock dividends), are determined under Section 1368.

S corporations with earnings and profits present more challenging problems because of the need to harmonize the Subchapter S rules with the corporation's prior C history. Distributions by a C corporation to its shareholders are taxable as dividends to the extent of the corporation's current and accumulated earnings and profits.[5] Some S corporations may have accumulated earnings and profits attributable to prior years when they were governed by Subchapter C. In addition, an S corporation might have accumulated earnings and profits from pre-1983 taxable years when a Subchapter S election was in effect or it may have inherited the earnings and profits of another company in a corporate acquisition subject to Section 381. In all these cases, the undistributed earnings have not been taxed at the shareholder level and represent an irresistible temptation for a tax-free bailout. There is no free lunch, however, and it thus becomes necessary to identify those distributions which should be taxed at the shareholder level because they are made out of accumulated earnings and profits.

The drafters of the 1982 Act devised a new tax concept—the "accumulated adjustments account" ("AAA")—to serve as the reference point for determining the source of distributions by an S corporation with accumulated earnings and profits. The AAA represents the post-1982 undistributed net income of the corporation. It begins at zero and is increased and decreased annually in a manner similar to the adjustment of the basis in a shareholder's stock.[6]xxxxx Any distribution by an S corporation with accumulated earnings and profits is treated as a tax-free return of capital to the extent it does not exceed the AAA.[7] A distribution in excess of the AAA is treated as a dividend to the extent

---

2. I.R.C. § 1368(b)(2).

3. I.R.C. § 1371(c)(1). An S corporation formed after 1982 may generate earnings and profits for any year in which it is not an S corporation and may acquire earnings and profits under Section 381 in a corporate acquisition.

4. I.R.C. § 1368(c). See Section G of this Chapter, infra.

5. I.R.C. §§ 301(c)(1), 316.

6. I.R.C. § 1368(e)(1)(A). Unlike a shareholder's basis, however, the AAA is not increased by tax-exempt income items and is not decreased for expenses related to

tax-exempt income. The adjustments also may result in a negative AAA. In addition, no adjustment is made for federal taxes attributable to any taxable year in which the corporation was a C corporation. Id. For a critical analysis of the AAA, see Bravenec & Orbach, "Accumulated Adjustments Account of S Corporation Should Not Strictly Mirror Shareholders' Basis Adjustments," 39 Tax Notes 111 (April 4, 1988).

7. I.R.C. § 1368(c)(1). Except to the extent provided in regulations, the AAA is allocated proportionately among distributions if the distributions exceed the AAA.

of accumulated earnings and profits,[8] and any portion of the distribution still remaining after both the AAA and accumulated earnings and profits are exhausted is treated first as a recovery of basis and then as gain from the sale of property.[9]

One might reasonably ask at this point: what is the purpose of this statutory scheme? The answer is more straightforward than it first appears. The function of the AAA is to identify the source of distributions by those few S corporations with accumulated earnings and profits. It permits the corporation to make a tax-free distribution of the net income recognized during its S corporation era which already was taxed at the shareholder level. Only after these previously taxed earnings are exhausted will a distribution be considered as emanating from accumulated earnings and profits.[10]

At the shareholder level, the Section 1368 makes no distinction between distributions of cash and of property other than cash. At the corporate level, however, an S corporation that distributes appreciated property (other than its own obligations) will recognize gain in the same manner as if the property had been sold to the shareholder at its fair market value.[11] This familiar rule, which is borrowed from Subchapter C, applies to liquidating and nonliquidating distributions of property by an S corporation.[12] Like other corporate level income, this gain will not be taxed to the corporation but will pass through to the shareholders. The shareholder will take a fair market value basis in the distributed property,[13] and the shareholder's basis in his S corporation stock will be reduced by the fair market value (not the adjusted basis) of the distributed property.[14] These rules are required to prevent the appreciation from escaping tax through a distribution which is tax-free at both the corporate and shareholder levels followed by a tax-free sale by the shareholder, who would take the property with a fair market value basis.

---

8. I.R.C. § 1368(c)(2).

9. I.R.C. § 1368(c)(2), (3).

10. In lieu of these rules, an S corporation may elect, with the consent of all shareholders who have received distributions during the year, to treat distributions as a dividend to the extent of accumulated earnings and profits. I.R.C. § 1368(e)(3). There normally is little incentive to make this election. One possible motivation would be to enable the corporation to sweep its Subchapter C earnings and profits account clean and thus avoid the corporate level tax and possible termination of S corporation status that would result from the co-existence of Subchapter C earnings and profits and excessive passive investment income. See I.R.C. § 1375. A simi-

lar election is provided during a post-termination transition period. I.R.C. § 1371(e)(2).

11. I.R.C. § 311(b). An S corporation may not recognize loss, however, on a distribution of property that has declined in value. I.R.C. § 311(a).

12. See I.R.C. § 1371(a), which provides that, except as otherwise provided in Subchapter S, the provisions of Subchapter C apply to S corporations and their shareholders. For more on the coordination of Subchapters S and C, see Section G of this chapter, infra.

13. I.R.C. § 301(d)(1).

14. I.R.C. §§ 1367(a)(2)(A), 1368.

PROBLEMS

1.   Ajax Corporation is a calendar year taxpayer which was organized in 1983 and elected S corporation status for its first taxable year. Ajax's stock is owned one-third by Dewey and two-thirds by Milt. At the beginning of the current year, Dewey's basis in his Ajax shares was $3,000 and Milt's basis in his shares was $5,000. During the year, Ajax will earn $9,000 of net income from operations and have a $3,000 long-term capital gain on the sale of 100 shares of Exxon stock. What results to Dewey, Milt and Ajax in the following alternative situations?

   (a)   On October 15, Ajax distributes $5,000 to Dewey and $10,000 to Milt.

   (b)   On October 15, Ajax distributes $8,000 to Dewey and $16,000 to Milt.

   (c)   Ajax redeems all of Dewey's stock on the last day of the year for $20,000. What result to Dewey?

   (d)   On October 15, Ajax redeems one-fourth of Dewey's stock for $5,000 and one-fourth of Milt's stock for $10,000.

   (e)   Ajax distributes a parcel of land with a basis of $9,000 and a fair market value of $8,000 to Dewey and a different parcel with a basis of $13,000 and fair market value of $16,000 to Milt.

   (f)   On October 15, Ajax distributes its own notes to Dewey and Milt. Dewey receives an Ajax five year, 12% note with a face amount and fair market value of $8,000 and Milt receives an Ajax five year, 12% note with a face amount and fair market value of $16,000.

2.   P Corporation was formed in 1981 by its two equal shareholders, Nancy and Opal, and elected S corporation status at the beginning of the current year. On January 1, Nancy had a $1,000 basis in her P stock and Opal had a $5,000 basis in her stock. P has $6,000 of accumulated earnings and profits from its prior C corporation operations and has the following results from operations this year:

Gross Income	$32,000
Long-term capital gain	4,000
Salary Expense	18,000
Depreciation	8,000

What are the tax consequences to Nancy, Opal and P Corporation in the following alternative situations.

   (a)   On November 1, P distributes $5,000 to Nancy and $5,000 to Opal.

   (b)   Same as (a), above, except that P distributes $10,000 to Nancy and $10,000 to Opal.

(c) What difference would it make in (a), above, if P also received $4,000 of tax-exempt interest during the year and distributed $2,000 of the interest to Nancy and $2,000 to Opal?

(d) During the current year P makes no distributions. On January 1 of next year Nancy sells her P stock to Rose for $6,000. If P breaks even on its operations next year, what will be the result to Rose if P distributes $6,000 to each of its shareholders next February 15?

(e) During the current year P makes no distributions. Nancy and Opal revoke P's Subchapter S election effective January 1 of next year. Assume P Co. has $5,000 of earnings and profits next year. What results to Nancy and Opal if P distributes $7,000 to each of them on August 1 of next year?

F. TAXATION OF THE S CORPORATION

Code: §§ 1363; 1374; 1375.

The major benefit of a Subchapter S election is the elimination of tax at the corporate level. But this immunity from tax is not absolute. As part of its continuing mission to patrol abuse, Congress has provided that in certain limited situations an S corporation may be subject to tax under Section 1374 on certain built-in gains inherent in corporate property and under Section 1375 on a portion of its passive investment income.

Tax on Certain Built-in Gains: Section 1374. When Congress repealed the *General Utilities* doctrine, it recognized that the shareholders of a C corporation might elect S corporation status in order to avoid the corporate-level tax imposed under the new statutory scheme.[1] For example, assume Liquidating Co. is a C corporation, holds highly appreciated assets, and is owned by shareholders A and B, who also would realize large taxable gains if they sell their stock or liquidate the company. If A and B cause Liquidating Co. to sell its assets and liquidate, or to distribute its assets in complete liquidation, Liquidating Co. will be taxed on its gains and A and B also will be taxed on their stock gains.[2] If Liquidating Co. qualified as a small business corporation, A and B could elect S corporation status in order to avoid the double-tax burden on the sale or liquidation. Liquidating Co. then could sell its assets and the gains would pass through to A and B, whose stock bases would receive a corresponding increase. The effect of the S corporation/liquidation strategy would be to erode the full impact of the double tax.[3]

1. See Chapters 4D, 5E and 7B2, supra.

2. See I.R.C. §§ 331, 336, 1001(a).

3. Under this strategy, it is possible that Liquidating Co. would have to pay some tax under the pre-1987 version of Section 1374. This additional cost, however, would not substantially reduce the potential benefits of electing S corporation status prior to liquidation. The pre–1987 version of Section 1374 was aimed at "one-shot" S elections by C corporations expecting a large long-term capital gain and generally applies only in very limited situations involving corporations electing S status prior to 1987.

Section 1374 deters this avoidance strategy by taxing an S corporation that has a "net recognized built-in gain" at any time within ten years of the effective date of its S corporation election.[4] At the outset, two important limitations on this tax should be noted. First, Section 1374 applies only if the corporation's S election was made after December 31, 1986.[5] Second, it does not apply to a corporation that always has been subject to Subchapter S.[6]

In general, Section 1374 is designed to tax an S corporation on the net gain that accrued while it was subject to Subchapter C if that gain is subsequently recognized on sales, distributions and other dispositions of property within a ten-year "recognition period" beginning with the first taxable year in which the corporation is an S corporation. For this purpose, any gain recognized during the recognition period is a "recognized built-in gain" unless the corporation establishes either that it did not hold the asset at the beginning of its first S taxable year or the recognized gain exceeds the gain inherent in the asset at that time.[7] Conversely, any loss recognized during the recognition period is a "recognized built-in loss" to the extent that the S corporation establishes that it held the asset at the beginning of its first S year and the loss does not exceed the loss inherent in the asset at that time.[8] Since the taxpayer has the burden of proof under these definitions, a corporation making an S election after 1986 is well advised to obtain an independent appraisal of its assets to establish their value on the relevant date in order to avoid being taxed on gain arising under the S regime and to benefit from the losses that accrued during the corporation's C years.

The Section 1374 tax is computed by applying the highest rate applicable to C corporations (currently 34 percent) to the S corporation's "net recognized built-in gain," which is defined as the corporation's taxable income computed by taking into account only recognized built-in gains and losses but limited to the corporation's taxable income computed generally as if it were a C corporation.[9] The purpose of the taxable income limitation is to ensure that Section 1374 does not tax the corporation on more income than it actually realizes during the taxable year. To prevent taxpayers from avoiding the tax by manipulating the timing of post-conversion losses, Section 1374(d)(2)(B) provides that any net recognized built-in gains not taxed because of the

---

4.　I.R.C. § 1374(a), (d)(7).

5.　Tax Reform Act of 1986, P.L. No. 99–514, 99th Cong., 2d Sess. § 633(b) (1986).

6.　I.R.C. § 1374(c)(1). This exemption may not apply, however, if the S corporation had a "predecessor" that was a C corporation. Id. This could occur, for example, where a C corporation was acquired by the S corporation in a tax-free reorganization.

7.　I.R.C. § 1374(d)(3).

8.　I.R.C. § 1374(d)(4).

9.　I.R.C. § 1374(b)(1), (d)(2). Taxable income, as defined in Section 63(a), is modified by disregarding certain deductions (e.g., the dividends received deduction) and net operating losses. I.R.C. §§ 1374(d)(2) (A)(ii); 1375(b)(1)(B). Net operating loss and capital loss carryforwards from prior years as a C corporation are taken into account in computing the amount subject to tax under Section 1374. I.R.C. § 1374(b) (2).

taxable income limitation are carried forward and treated as recognized built-in gain in succeeding years in the recognition period.[10] Finally, the amount of net recognized built-in gain taken into account for any taxable year may not exceed the net unrealized built-in gain at the time the corporation became an S corporation reduced by any net recognized built-in gains which were subject to Section 1374 in prior taxable years.[11]

The Section 1374 tax easily could be avoided if it applied only to built-in gains recognized on the disposition of assets that were held by the S corporation at the beginning of its first S taxable year. For example, assume that a C corporation converting to S status holds an asset (Oldacre) with a built-in gain which it subsequently exchanges for property of like kind (Newacre) in a Section 1031 nonrecognition transaction. The gain inherent in Oldacre is preserved in Newacre's exchanged basis under Section 1031(d). If the corporation disposes of Newacre within ten years after switching to S status, the Section 1374 tax should apply to the built-in "C gain" even though Newacre was not held on the first day that the corporation was subject to Subchapter S. Section 1374(d)(6) ensures this result by providing that an asset taking an exchanged basis from another asset held by the corporation at the time it converted to S status shall be treated as having been held as of the beginning of the corporation's first S year. In the above example, the built-in gain inherent in Oldacre on the conversion from C to S status is recognized under Section 1374 if the corporation disposes of Newacre at a gain during the recognition period.

Section 1374(d)(8) is another testament to Congress's protective attitude toward the double tax. It ensures that built-in gain in assets acquired by an S corporation from a C corporation in a tax-free reorganization does not escape a corporate level tax. For this purpose, the recognition period commences as of the date the asset is acquired rather than on the beginning of the first taxable year for which the corporation was an S corporation.[12]

Tax advisors began to plot strategies to reduce the impact of Section 1374 soon after it was enacted. Some suggested that the tax might be avoided if an S corporation sold an asset with built-in gain during the 10–year recognition period on the installment method but delayed receipt of any payments (and thus any recognized gain) until after the recognition period had expired.[13] Not surprisingly, the Service has expressed its displeasure with this gambit. In a preview to forthcoming regulations, the Service announced that the built-in gain rules will continue to apply to income recognized under the installment

---

10. The carryover rule applies only to corporations that elected S status on or after March 31, 1988. I.R.C. § 1374(d)(2) (B).

11. I.R.C. § 1374(c)(2), (d)(1).

12. I.R.C. § 1374(d)(8). See Section G of this Chapter, infra, for an overview of the tax consequences when an S corporation is the acquiring or target corporation in a tax-free reorganization.

13. See, e.g., Taggart, "Emerging Tax Issues in Corporate Acquisitions," 44 Tax L.Rev. 459, 481 (1989).

method during taxable years ending after the expiration of the recognition period. When recognized, the gain will be taxed to the extent that it would have been taxed under Section 1374 if the corporation had elected out of the installment method.[14] The Service's announcement includes the following example:

> In year 1 of the recognition period under section 1374, a corporation realizes a gain of $100,000 on the sale of an asset with built-in gain. The corporation is to receive full payment for the asset in year 11. Because the corporation does not make an election under section 453(d), all $100,000 of the gain from the sale is reported under the installment method in year 11. If the corporation had made an election under section 453(d) with respect to the sale, the gain would have been recognized in year 1 and, taking into account the corporation's income and gains from other sources, application of the taxable income limitation of section 1374(d)(2)(A)(ii) and the built-in gain carryover rule of section 1374(d)(2)(B) would have resulted in $40,000 of the gain being subject to tax during the recognition period under section 1374. Therefore, the regulations will subject $40,000 of the gain recognized in year 11 to tax under section 1374.

Tax on Passive Investment Income. When it widened the gates to Subchapter S, Congress became concerned that a C corporation with earnings and profits might make an S election and redeploy substantial amounts in liquid assets yielding passive investment income such as dividends and interest. Left unchecked, this strategy would enable a profitable C corporation to move to the single-tax regime of Subchapter S and pass through the investment income to its shareholders, who might delay, perhaps forever, paying any shareholder-level tax on the Subchapter C earnings and profits. This plan had particular allure when a C corporation sold all of its operating assets and was seeking an alternative to the shareholder-level tax that would be imposed under Section 331 on a distribution of the proceeds in complete liquidation.[15]

The Code includes two weapons to foil the Subchapter S/passive income ploy. As discussed earlier, an S corporation with accumulated earnings and profits from its prior life as a C corporation will lose its S status if it has passive investment income that exceeds 25 percent of its gross receipts for three consecutive taxable years.[16] In addition, even before its S status is terminated, the corporation will be subject to a corporate-level tax under Section 1375. The tax, which equals 34 percent of the corporation's "excess net passive income," is imposed if an S corporation has earnings and profits from a taxable year prior to its S election and more than 25 percent of the corporation's gross receipts for the taxable year consist of "passive investment income."

---

14. I.R.S. Notice 90–27, 1990–1 C.B. 336. This policy is effective for installment sales occurring on or after March 26, 1990.

15. See Chapter 7C2, supra.

16. I.R.C. § 1362(d)(3). See Section C of this chapter, supra.

For purposes of the Section 1375 tax, "passive investment income" is defined as gross receipts from royalties, rents, dividends, interest, and annuities, together with gains from sales or exchanges of stock or securities.[17] Interest earned on obligations acquired from the sale of inventory, the gross receipts of certain lending and finance institutions, and gains received as a result of the liquidation of a more than 50% controlled corporation are not passive investment income.[18] To prevent manipulation of the gross receipts test, only the excess of gains over losses from dispositions of capital assets (other than stock and securities) is included in gross receipts, and gross receipts from the sales or exchanges of stock or securities are taken into account only to the extent of gains.[19]

The term "stock or securities" is interpreted expansively and includes stock rights, warrants, debentures, partnership interests, and "certificates of interest" in profit-sharing arrangements.[20] It also has been held that the specified income items are tainted even if the taxpayer's activity is not "passive". A securities dealer's gains from trades thus constitute passive investment income even though they are derived in a trade or business.[21]

The computation of the Section 1375 tax is a technician's dream (and a student's nightmare?). The base for the Section 1375 tax, "excess net passive income," is a percentage of the corporation's "net passive income," which is generally equal to passive investment income less deductions directly connected with the production of such income.[22] To arrive at excess net passive income, net passive income is multiplied by a ratio, which has a numerator equal to the excess of passive investment income over 25 percent of gross receipts for the year, and a denominator equal to passive investment income for the year.[23] There is one final caveat: excess net passive income cannot exceed the corporation's taxable income for the year computed with the special changes described in Section 1374(d)(4).[24]

An example may help control the pollution. Assume that X Corporation made a Subchapter S election last year and will have accumulated earnings and profits from prior C corporation operations at the end of its current taxable year, in which X has $50,000 of income from its regular business operations and $35,000 of business deductions. X also receives $15,000 of interest income and $10,000 of dividends and incurs $5,000 of expenses directly related to the production of the investment income.

17. I.R.C. §§ 1375(b)(3), 1362(d)(3)(D)(i).

18. I.R.C. § 1362(d)(3)(D)(ii)–(iv).

19. I.R.C. §§ 1375(b)(3), 1362(d)(3)(C), 1222(9).

20. See Reg. § 1.1362–3(d)(4)(ii)(B).

21. Reg. § 1.1362–3(d)(4)(ii)(B); Zychinski v. Commissioner, 506 F.2d 637 (8th Cir. 1974), cert. denied 421 U.S. 999, 95 S.Ct. 2397 (1975).

22. I.R.C. § 1375(b)(2).

23. I.R.C. § 1375(b)(1)(A).

24. I.R.C. § 1375(b)(1)(B).

Is X subject to the Section 1375 tax? The corporation will have Subchapter C earnings and profits at the close of its taxable year and more than 25 percent of its gross receipts are passive investment income ($25,000 out of $75,000 of gross receipts), so the tax is potentially applicable. X's net passive income is $20,000 ($25,000 of passive investment income less directly connected expenses), and it will have $5,000 of excess net passive income ($20,000 of net passive income multiplied by a ratio having $6,250 as the numerator ($25,000 of passive investment income reduced by 25 percent of gross receipts) and $25,000 as the denominator (passive investment income)). Since excess net passive income does not exceed X's taxable income as determined under Section 1374(d)(4), the corporation's tax liability will be $1,700 ($5,000 $\times$ 34 percent).

Section 1375(d) offers one avenue for relief from the Section 1375 tax. The tax may be waived if the S corporation establishes to the satisfaction of the Service that it determined, in good faith, that it had no earnings and profits at the close of a taxable year and, within a reasonable period after discovering earnings and profits, they were distributed. The addition of an "anti-blunder" provision to this complex area is a welcome sign and one hopes the Service will be merciful in its administration of Section 1375(d).

Because the definition of passive investment income includes gross receipts from sales or exchanges of stock or securities, the same gain might be taxed under both Sections 1374 and 1375. To prevent this possibility, Congress provided in Section 1375(b)(4) that the amount of passive investment income taken into account under Section 1375 is reduced by any recognized built-in gain or loss of the S corporation for any taxable year in the recognition period. Congress also considered the interaction of Sections 1374 and 1375 with the provisions taxing the shareholders of an S corporation. Any Section 1374 tax is treated as a loss (characterized according to the built-in gain subject to tax) sustained by the S corporation which will pass through to the shareholders, and each item of passive investment income is reduced by its proportionate share of the Section 1375 tax.[25]

It is important to keep the application of Sections 1374 and 1375 in perspective. A new corporation making a Subchapter S election generally does not have to be concerned with either provision. Section 1374(c)(1) will protect the corporation from the Section 1374 tax and, since the corporation's activities will not generate earnings and profits,[26] Section 1375 cannot apply to the corporation. Therefore, Sections 1374 and 1375 normally will not play a role in deciding whether to utilize a partnership or an S corporation for a new venture.

Additional considerations come into play if a C corporation is considering a move to a single tax regime. An operating C corporation must consider the impact of Sections 1374 and 1375 on a possible Subchapter S election. Weighed against these penalty provisions is the

---

25. I.R.C. § 1366(f)(2), (3).   **26.** I.R.C. § 1371(c)(1).

fact that a shift from C corporation status to partnership status requires a liquidation of the corporation, which may result in significant current corporate and shareholder tax liability.[27] The immediate tax cost of moving to a partnership format may be significant enough to tip the balance in favor of a Subchapter S election and force an accommodation with Sections 1374 and 1375, if planning cannot successfully eliminate their impact.

REVENUE RULING 65–91

1965–1 Cum.Bull. 431.

Advice has been requested whether payments received by corporations for the storage of personal property, under the circumstances described below, are rents within the meaning of section 1372(e)(5) [pre-1983. Ed.] of the Internal Revenue Code of 1954.

Several corporations are in the business of providing storage space for personal property. Each corporation is a small business corporation which has elected pursuant to section 1372(a) [now section 1362] of the Code, not to be subject to a corporate income tax, but to have all its income taxed directly to its shareholders.

Under section 1372(e)(5) of the Code, such an election is terminated in any year in which more than 20 percent of the gross receipts of an electing corporation is derived from rents and certain other types of income.

Section 1.1372–4(b)(5)(vi) of the Income Tax Regulations provides, in part, that the term "rents," as used in section 1372(e)(5) of the Code, means amounts received for the use of, or right to use, property (whether real or personal) of the corporation. [Current Prop.Reg. § 1.1362–3(d)(5)(iv) corresponds to this provision. Ed.] However, the term does not include payments for the use or occupancy of rooms or other space where significant services are also rendered to the occupant. Generally, services are considered rendered to the occupant if they are primarily for his convenience and are other than those usually or customarily rendered in connection with the rental of rooms or other space for occupancy only. Thus, payments for the parking of automobiles ordinarily do not constitute rents. Payments for the warehousing of goods or for the use of personal property do not constitute rents if significant services are rendered in connection with such payments.

The question for each corporation involved in this Revenue Ruling is whether payments received by it for the storage of property are rents within the meaning of section 1372(e)(5) of the Code.

(1) *M* corporation owns two buildings and related equipment used for the storage of grain. Separate fees are charged for receiving the grain and for taking the grain out of storage and loading it on carriers for shipment. While in storage, services must be performed to prevent spoilage and infestation of the grain. These services include periodic

---

27. See I.R.C. §§ 331, 336, 1001.

inspection and turning of the grain. If the grain were to be improperly handled during storage, the corporation would be liable without the possibility of insurance protection for the full value of the spoiled grain.

Under these circumstances, it is held that fees received for the storage of grain are not rents within the meaning of section 1372(e)(5) of the Code because of the significant services performed in connection with the storage.

(2) *O* corporation operates a cotton warehouse. Because the cotton available for storage in the area where *O*'s warehouse is located has declined in recent years, the corporation has endeavored to store other commodities in its warehouse. At the present time, three of the eight rooms in the warehouse are used for the storage of manufactured goods under a specific contract between *O* and a manufacturer of cotton cloth. Under this contract, denominated a lease, the manufacturer has the right to use for a term of 1 year specific rooms in the warehouse for storage. The manufacturer uses his own employees for transporting the cloth in and out of storage and assumes all liability for the hazards of handling and storage in the leased areas. The manufacturer is also responsible for the locks and fastenings on the doors of the rented compartments.

Since, under the terms of the contract, the owner of the stored goods is entitled to specific space for a fixed term and provides for its own storing, loading, unloading, and other handling and protecting services required for its goods, the payments received under the contract are rents within the meaning of section 1372(e)(5) of the Code.

(3) The gross receipts of *P* corporation are derived from payments received for the handling and storage of goods in its refrigerated warehouse. Most owners of goods pay on a per pound or per container basis. These charges include refrigeration service, maintenance of proper humidities, housekeeping, handling in and out of the warehouse, and record keeping in connection with the preservation of and accounting for the commodities in storage. An arrangement is occasionally made whereby a customer has exclusive use for a fixed term of specified space. Charges for this type of arrangement are usually on a square foot or flat-rate basis and vary depending on whether *P* or the customer supplies the necessary labor for moving the goods in and out of the warehouse and for providing housekeeping services. In any event, *P* supplies the refrigeration and other necessary services, and is responsible for maintenance.

Under these circumstances, it is held that none of the payments received by *P* corporation are rents within the meaning of section 1372(e)(5) of the Code.

(4) *Q* corporation owns and operates an automobile parking lot. The cars are left with an attendant at the entrance to the lot who parks them in any available space.

The payments received by Q from the customers under these circumstances are not rents within the meaning of section 1372(e)(5) of the Code.

PROBLEMS

1. Built-in Corporation ("B") was formed in 1985 as a C corporation. The shareholders of B elected S corporation status effective as of January 1, 1990, when it had no Subchapter C earnings and profits and the following assets:

Asset	Adj. Basis	F.M.V.
Land	$30,000	$20,000
Building	10,000	35,000
Machinery	15,000	30,000

For purposes of this problem, disregard any cost recovery deductions that may be available to B. Consider the shareholder and corporate level tax consequences of the following alternative transactions:

(a) B sells the building for $50,000 in 1991; its taxable income for 1991 if it were not an S corporation would be $75,000.

(b) Same as (a), above, except that B's taxable income for 1991 if it were not an S corporation would be $20,000.

(c) Same as (a), above, except that B also sells the machinery for $40,000 in 1992, when it would have substantial taxable income if it were not an S corporation.

(d) B trades the building for an apartment building in a tax-free § 1031 exchange and then sells the apartment for $50,000 in 1991, when it would have substantial taxable income if it were not an S corporation.

(e) B sells the building for $90,000 in 2000.

2. S Corporation elected S corporation status beginning in 1986 and will have Subchapter C earnings and profits at the close of the current taxable year. This year, S expects that its business operations and investments will produce the following tax results:

Gross income from operations	$75,000
Business deductions	60,000
Tax-exempt interest	5,000
Dividends	12,000
Long-term capital gain from the sale of investment real property	35,000
Long-term capital gain from the sale of IBM stock	18,000
Long-term capital loss from the sale of General Motors stock	8,000

(a) Is S Corporation subject to the § 1375 tax on passive investment income? If so, compute the amount of tax.

(b) Same as (a), above, except that S receives an additional $5,000 of tax-exempt interest.

3. The San Diego Bay Boat Storage and Marina Corporation ("Bay") was formed in 1983 as a C corporation and has substantial accumulated earnings and profits. Bay's business consists of three primary activities. About one-third of Bay's gross receipts are derived from marine service and repair work conducted by its two mechanics. Another one-third of Bay's total receipts come from the rental of berths to boat owners. Berthing fees vary depending upon the size of the particular boat. A boat owner renting a berth from Bay must pay a separate charge to have Bay's employees launch or haul out his boat. However, if given advance notice, Bay employees will fuel an owner's boat, charging only for the fuel. The remainder of Bay's receipts come from dry storage of boats. Owners pay $50 per month for dry storage in Bay's warehouse where a Bay employee is on duty 24 hours a day. For this fee, Bay employees will launch, fuel (with a charge for fuel) and haul out the boat whenever requested by the owner. Bay's mechanics also will perform a free engine analysis every other year for owners of power boats in dry storage.

Bay is considering the possibility of making a Subchapter S election and has requested your advice concerning any problems which it may have. What difference would it make if Bay were a newly formed corporation?

G. COORDINATION WITH SUBCHAPTER C

Code: §§ 1371; 1372.

It is important to remember that an S corporation is still a corporation for many tax purposes. It is organized in the same manner as other corporations and may engage in the transactions and experience the corporate adjustments encountered throughout the course.

After incorporating or escaping from Subchapter C, S corporations may make nonliquidating distributions of property or stock, engage in redemptions, or acquire other businesses in either taxable or tax-free transactions. They may sell their assets and liquidate, be acquired by another corporation, or divide up into two or more separate corporations. The tax consequences of these and other events in an S corporation's life cycle are determined by a patchwork quilt of Code sections pieced together from Subchapters C and S. The resulting product, though a bit frayed at the edges, provides a challenging opportunity to study the uneasy relationship between a double tax regime and a pass-through scheme.

Section 1371(a)(1) begins the statutory snake dance with the deceptively simple general rule that the provisions of Subchapter C apply to an S corporation and its shareholders. This broad admonition is subject to two related exceptions. First, any provision in the Code specifically applicable to S corporations naturally will apply. Second, if the provisions of Subchapter C are "inconsistent with Subchapter S," the S rules are controlling. Reliable authority is sparse on precisely how Congress intended to harmonize the rules, but the Service gradually is offering guidance as S corporations become more widely used. The details and some lurking questions are best raised in the context of specific transactions.

Formation of a Corporation. All the basic rules studied in connection with the formation of a C corporation apply with equal force to newly formed S corporations.[1] Founding shareholders do not recognize gain or loss on the transfer of property if the requirements of Section 351(a) are met, but realized gain is recognized to the extent the shareholder receives boot[2] or if the transferred liabilities exceed the shareholder's basis for the transferred property.[3] Shareholders determine their basis in stock, debt obligations and other boot received under Section 358. The corporation takes a transferred basis in any contributed assets under Section 362(a). Organizational expenditures may be amortized over 60 months if the corporation elects to do so under Section 248, and the benefit of the deduction passes through to the shareholders.

Several other formation issues, most relating to the "small business corporation requirements," are unique to S corporations. To qualify for the S election, the corporation must be mindful of the 35–shareholder limit, the prohibition against certain types of shareholders (e.g., nonresident aliens, other corporations, partnerships and complex trusts), the one class of stock requirement and the prohibition against being a member of an affiliated group.

As for capital structure, an S corporation may not issue preferred stock but it is free to issue debt, preferably in a form that qualifies for the straight debt safe harbor.[4] Unlike a corporation facing the double tax, an S corporation has no particular incentive to issue pro rata debt to its shareholders.[5]

S Corporations as Shareholders. Section 1371(a)(2) provides that for purposes of Subchapter C, an S corporation in its capacity as a shareholder of another corporation shall be treated as an individual. When first enacted this rule was intended to apply principally to the receipt of dividends.[6] By treating an S corporation as an individual in this context, the rule ensures that an S corporation does not qualify for the Section 243 dividends received deduction, which is designed to prevent double taxation at the corporate level and thus should not be available to a pass-through entity. As drafted, Section 1371(a)(2) is broad enough to have a ripple effect on other transactions, such as

---

1. See generally Chapter 2, supra.

2. I.R.C. § 351(b).

3. I.R.C. § 357(c).

4. I.R.C. § 1361(c)(5).

5. For the advantages and disadvantages of issuing debt in the S corporation setting, see Eustice & Kuntz, Federal Income Taxation of S Corporations ¶ 6.03 (2d ed. 1985).

6. See, e.g., S.Rep. No. 640, 97th Cong., 2d Sess. 15, reprinted in 1982–2 C.B. 718, 724–725.

liquidations, stock purchases and reorganizations, where Subchapters C and S may intersect. Some of these thorny issues are explored below.

Distributions and Liquidating Sales. As discussed earlier,[7] Subchapter S generally preempts Subchapter C in determining the tax consequences of nonliquidating distributions. Section 1368 specifically provides that it shall apply to any distribution to which Section 301(c) otherwise would apply. This means that Section 1368 is the reference point not only for routine nonliquidating distributions but also other transactions, such as dividend-equivalent redemptions and taxable stock distributions, which are classified under Subchapter C as distributions to which Section 301 applies.[8] We have seen that an S corporation recognizes gain under Section 311(b) on a distribution of appreciated property, but unless Section 1374 applies the gain is not taxed at the corporate level. Instead, the gain passes through to the shareholders, who may increase their stock basis by their respective shares of the gain.

In the case of liquidating distributions and sales, Subchapter C reassumes center stage. Liquidating distributions generally trigger recognition of gain or loss to an S corporation under Section 336 in the same manner as if the corporation were subject to Subchapter C. Sales of assets pursuant to a plan of complete liquidation also are taxable. In either case, however, these gains will pass through to the shareholders and be subject to a single shareholder-level tax unless Section 1374 intercedes. An S corporation also may make a liquidating sale on the installment method. Under certain conditions, these installment obligations may be distributed without triggering corporate-level gain (unless Section 1374 applies), and the shareholders may use the installment method to report the gain.[9] The *character* of the shareholder's gain in this situation is not determined by reference to their stock, which ordinarily would be a capital asset, but rather "in accordance with the principles of Section 1366(d)"[10]—i.e., as if the corporate-level gain on the sale of the asset had been passed through to the shareholders.[11]

Subchapter C also governs the shareholder-level consequences of a complete liquidation. An S corporation shareholder treats distributions in complete liquidation as in full payment in exchange for the stock under Section 331. Although liquidating distributions and sales

---

7. See Section E of this chapter, supra.

8. See, e.g., I.R.C. §§ 302(d); 305(b). Section 306 is unlikely to apply in the S setting, however, because an S corporation may not issue preferred stock.

9. See I.R.C. § 453B(h). To qualify for corporate-level nonrecognition, the S corporation must distribute the obligation in complete liquidation. In addition, the obligations must result from sales of assets (other than nonbulk sales of inventory) during the 12–month period following the adoption of the liquidation plan. See I.R.C. § 453(h).

10. I.R.C. § 453B(h).

11. Thus, if the installment sale would have given rise to ordinary income, that character will pass through to the shareholders when they collect the installment obligations.

result in only one level of tax to an S corporation and its shareholders,[12] variations between the shareholder's stock basis and the corporation's basis in its assets may have an impact on the character of the shareholder's gain or loss. For example, assume A owns all of the stock of S, Inc. (an S corporation with no prior C history) and has a $2,000 basis in her S stock. Assume S owns one ordinary income asset which has a $10,000 fair market value and a $1,000 adjusted basis. If S sells the asset, it will recognize $9,000 of ordinary income. The gain passes through to A, and her stock basis is increased by $9,000, to $11,000, under Section 1367. When S liquidates and distributes $10,000 cash to A, she recognizes a $1,000 long-term capital loss. Alternatively, if the ordinary income asset had a $2,000 basis, S would recognize $8,000 of ordinary income on its sale which would pass through to A, increasing her stock basis to $10,000. When S liquidates and distributes $10,000 cash to A, she would recognize no additional gain or loss.

Taxable Acquisitions of S Corporations. An acquisition of an S corporation may be structured as either a purchase of stock from the shareholders or a purchase of assets from the corporation. The method chosen affects not only the amount, character and timing of gain but also may have an impact on the tax status of the S corporation and perhaps even the acquiring party if it also is an S corporation.

An asset acquisition usually is preferable because the purchaser will obtain a cost basis in the S corporation's assets at the cost of only a shareholder-level tax.[13] For example, assume P, Inc. wishes to acquire T, Inc. (an S corporation with no prior C history). If P purchases T's assets, any gain or loss recognized by T on the sale will pass through to its shareholders, and P will obtain a cost basis in the assets. T's shareholders will increase their stock basis by any gain recognized on the sale under Section 1367, thus avoiding a second tax on the same economic gain when T liquidates.

If P instead purchases the T stock, the T shareholders recognize gain or loss on the sale, and P takes a cost basis in the stock it acquires. T's S election will terminate, however, because an S corporation may not have any corporate shareholders.[14] If P does not make a Section 338 election, T will retain its historic bases in its assets, and as a new C corporation it will face the prospect of a corporate-level tax on any built-in gain. If P makes a Section 338 election to obtain a cost basis in T's assets, T—which loses its S status on the acquisition—must pay a corporate-level tax as a result of the deemed asset sale.[15]

12. This is because the corporate-level gain on a liquidating distribution or sale results in upward basis adjustments to the shareholder's stock under Section 1367. A double tax would be imposed, however, if Section 1374 applies.

13. In contrast, an acquisition of assets from a C corporation generates tax at both the corporate and shareholder levels if the target liquidates. See Chapter 7C, *supra.*

Once again, this assumes that the corporation has no built-in gains that would be taxed under Section 1374.

14. I.R.C. §§ 1362(d)(2); 1361(b)(1)(B).

15. T's S election terminates when P acquires T's stock, and its short C year includes the day of the terminating event. Thus, the gain on the deemed asset sale must be reported on a one-day return for

Taxable Acquisitions by S Corporations. When the purchasing corporation ("P") is an S corporation, the primary concern usually will be the preservation of P's S status. If P purchases the assets of T, the mix of consideration used in the transaction must be tailored to the S corporation eligibility requirements. P thus should avoid using its own stock or hybrid debt in order to avoid running afoul of the 35–shareholder limit or the prohibition against having more than one class of stock.[16]

When an S corporation acquires the stock of T, it must be mindful of the prohibition against an S corporation having an 80 percent or more subsidiary.[17] The Service has ruled that if an S corporation acquires all the stock of T as the initial step in a plan to acquire T's assets, P's transitory ownership of the T stock prior to the liquidation will not terminate its S election.[18] But since Section 1371(a)(2) provides that an S corporation is treated as an individual in its capacity as a shareholder of another corporation, the Service also has ruled that an S corporation may not liquidate a target corporation under Section 332 and avoid gain recognition under Section 337.[19] As a result, a liquidation of T to preserve P's S status will trigger immediate recognition of gain or loss under Section 336 on the distribution of T's assets. For the same reason, the Service takes the position that an S corporation may not make a Section 338 election.[20]

Tax–Free Reorganizations. An S corporation may be either the target or the acquiring corporation in a tax-free acquisitive reorganization.[21] Looking first to situations where the S corporation is the target, it will lose its S status if it remains in existence as an 80 percent or more subsidiary following a tax-free acquisition of its stock in a Type B reorganization or reverse triangular merger. If an S corporation-target's assets are acquired in a merger or Type C reorganization, the transaction may proceed on a tax-free basis, and the target will terminate its existence as a result of the merger or the liquidation that necessarily must follow a Type C reorganization.[22]

old T's "short C year." See I.R.C. §§ 1362(e)(1)(B); 338(a)(1). The economic burden of the corporate-level tax is borne by P unless it is reflected in the price paid for the stock.

16. See generally I.R.C. § 1361(b).

17. I.R.C. §§ 1361(b)(2)(A); 1504(a).

18. Rev.Rul. 73–496, 1973–2 C.B. 313. In the ruling, the liquidation of T took place within 30 days of the stock purchase.

19. Ltr.Rul. 8818049 (Feb. 10, 1988). See Bonovitz, "S Corporations and Section 332," Tax Notes 1545 (Sept. 17, 1990), where the author argues that this ruling is incorrect.

20. Ltr.Rul. 8818049, supra note 19. For a more detailed discussion of the

thorny issues raised by an S corporation's taxable purchase of stock and methods to avoid termination of the acquiring corporation's S status, see Ginsburg & Levin, Mergers, Acquisitions and Leveraged Buyouts (Vol. F2) ¶ 1105.

21. Rev.Rul. 69–566, 1969–2 C.B. 165; G.C.M. 39768 (Dec. 9, 1988).

22. The Service has ruled that an S corporation may be the target in a tax-free reorganization despite the rule in Section 1371(a)(2) that treats an S corporation as an individual in its capacity as a shareholder of another corporation. G.C.M. 39768 (Dec. 9, 1988).

If an S corporation is the acquiring corporation in a tax-free reorganization, it necessarily must issue new stock to the target shareholders. In that situation, care must be exercised to avoid termination of the election by exceeding the 35 shareholder limit or inheriting an ineligible shareholder. An S corporation's acquisition of a subsidiary in a Type B reorganization also will terminate its S election.[23] An S corporation that is the acquiring corporation in a Type A or C reorganization or a forward triangular merger will inherit the target's tax attributes, including its earnings and profits, under Section 381, and presumably its accumulated adjustments account if the target is an S corporation with a prior C history. Although an asset acquisition should not adversely affect a corporation's S election, the earnings and profits from the target's C years could jeopardize the acquiring corporation's S status or subject it to the Section 1375 tax if it has substantial passive investment income.[24] Moreover, assets acquired from a C corporation in a tax-free reorganization trigger a new ten-year recognition period for purposes of the Section 1374 tax on built-in gains.[25]

Corporate Divisions. If it meets all the requirements of Section 355, an S corporation may divide itself into separate corporations in a transaction that is tax-free at both the corporate and shareholder levels. To prepare for such a division (e.g., a spin off), the corporation must first create a new subsidiary—a momentary event that potentially could terminate the S status of both corporations.[26] The Service has been tolerant in this area, however, ignoring the transitory nature of the subsidiary and also disregarding the rule in Section 1371(a)(2) that treats S corporations as individuals in their capacity as shareholders of other corporations.[27] When the smoke clears, both the distributing and controlled corporations—if otherwise eligible—each may elect S status.[28]

PROBLEMS

1. Hi-Flying Co. is an aggressive growth company which was formed as a C corporation prior to the Tax Reform Act of 1986 to develop new innovative technology. Hi-Flying has been successful and expects to receive inquiries concerning possible taxable and tax-free takeovers in the next few years. Can Hi-Flying's shareholders improve

23. This assumes that an S corporation is even capable of being the acquiring corporation in an acquisitive stock reorganization. The Service's position that Section 1371(a)(2) precludes an S corporation from liquidating a subsidiary under Section 332 or making a Section 338 election may extend to Type B reorganizations. See notes 19–20, supra and accompanying text.

24. I.R.C. §§ 1362(b)(3); 1375.

25. I.R.C. § 1374(d)(8).

26. The parent would be disqualified because it would be a member of an affili-

ated group. I.R.C. § 1361(b)(2). The subsidiary would have an ineligible corporate shareholder. I.R.C. § 1361(b)(1)(B).

27. See Rev.Rul. 72–320, 1972–1 C.B. 270.

28. For all the other details, such as the momentous question of how the accumulated adjustments account (if any) might be allocated between the newly separated corporations, see Eustice & Kuntz, supra note 5, at ¶ 12.10.

their tax situation in a future takeover by making an S election? In general, if Hi-Flying makes an S election, would you advise a potential corporate purchaser desiring a cost basis in Hi-Flying's assets to structure its acquisition as a purchase of stock or assets?

2. Target Corporation ("T") is a C corporation which has substantially appreciated assets and is a takeover candidate being pursued by several suitors. Purchasing Corporation ("P") has a Subchapter S election in effect and is considering making a bid for T. Consider the tax consequences of the following acquisition offers by P:

(a) P will offer to purchase T's stock for cash or a combination of cash and P notes.

(b) P will acquire T in a Type C reorganization.

H. TAX PLANNING WITH THE S CORPORATION

1. COMPENSATION ISSUES

It is not uncommon for S corporation shareholders also to serve as officers, directors and employees. Individuals with this multiple status may have a choice as to whether to withdraw cash as compensation or as a shareholder distribution. Payments of salary are deductible by the corporation as a business expense (with the benefit of the deduction passing through to the shareholders), and are includible to the employee. In addition, employee wages are subject to various federal and state employment taxes that often are imposed on both the employer and the employee (e.g., federal social security and medicare taxes).[1] Distributions, by contrast, generally may be received tax-free by shareholders to the extent of their stock basis, but they do not give rise to a deduction at the corporate level.

Because the payment of salaries to shareholders usually results in a tax "wash" in the case of a profitable corporation (the compensation deduction reduces the operating income that passes through to the shareholders), the *income* tax consequences of salaries and distributions may be identical.[2] The escalating employment tax base has influenced some S corporation shareholders to avoid this additional federal levy by foregoing salaries in lieu of larger shareholder distributions. The *Radtke* case, below, is one court's reaction to this maneuver.

1. In 1991, for example, both the employer and employee must pay social security and medicare hospital insurance taxes (often collectively known as "FICA") of 7.65% of the first $53,400 of an employee's taxable wages. I.R.C. §§ 3201; 3221. An additional medicare tax of 1.45%, again payable by both the employer and employ-

ee, is imposed on wages between $53,400 and $125,000. I.R.C. § 3121(x).

2. The tax results are more complex, however, if the S corporation has losses for the taxable year. See Eustice & Kuntz, Federal Income Taxation of S Corporations ¶ 11.02[2] (2d ed. 1985).

JOSEPH RADTKE, S.C. v. UNITED STATES *

United States District Court, Eastern District of Wisconsin, 1989.
712 F.Supp. 143, affirmed 895 F.2d 1196 (7th Cir.1990).

ORDER

TERENCE T. EVANS, District Judge.

* * *

FACTS

None of the facts are disputed.

Joseph Radtke received his law degree from Marquette University in 1978. The Radtke corporation was incorporated in 1979 to provide legal services in Milwaukee. Mr. Radtke is the firm's sole incorporator, director, and shareholder. In 1982, he also served as the unpaid president and treasurer of the corporation, while his wife Joyce was the unpaid and nominal vice-president and secretary. The corporation is an electing small business corporation, otherwise known as a subchapter S corporation. This means that it is not taxed at the corporate level. All corporate income is taxed to the shareholder, whether or not the income is distributed.

In 1982, Mr. Radtke was the only full-time employee of the corporation, though it employed a few other persons on a piece-meal and part-time basis. Under an employment contract executed between Mr. Radtke and his corporation in 1980, he received "an annual base salary, to be determined by its board of directors, but in no event shall such annual salary be less than $0 per year * * *. Employee's original annual base salary shall be $0." This base salary of $0 continued through 1982, a year in which Mr. Radtke devoted all of his working time to representing the corporation's clients.

Mr. Radtke received $18,225 in dividends from the corporation in 1982. Whenever he needed money, and whenever the corporation was showing a profit—that is, when there was money in its bank account—he would do what was necessary under Wisconsin corporate law to have the board declare a dividend, and he would write a corporate check to himself.

Mr. Radtke paid personal income tax on the dividends in 1982. The Radtke corporation also declared the $18,225 on its form 1120S, the small business corporation income tax return. But the corporation did not file a federal employment tax form (Form 941) or a federal unemployment tax form (Form 940). In other words, it did not deduct a portion of the $18,225 for Social Security (FICA) and unemployment compensation (FUTA). The IRS subsequently assessed deficiencies as well as interest and penalties. The Radtke corporation paid the full amount that IRS demanded under FUTA—$366.44—and it also paid

* Footnotes omitted.

$593.75 toward the assessed FICA taxes, interest, and penalties. Then the corporation sued here after a fruitless claim for refunds.

DISCUSSION

* * *

The Radtke corporation acknowledges that wages are subject to FICA and FUTA taxes, but it argues that the Internal Revenue Code nowhere treats a shareholder-employee's dividends as wages for the purpose of employment taxes. The government, on the other hand, contends that "since Joseph Radtke performed substantial services for Joseph Radtke, S.C., and did not receive reasonable compensation for such services other than 'dividends', the 'dividends' constitute 'wages' subject to federal employment taxes." The government does not allege that the Radtke corporation is a fiction that somehow failed to comply with Wisconsin statutes governing corporations.

The Federal Insurance Contributions Act defines "wages" as "all remuneration for employment," with various exceptions that are not relevant to this dispute. 26 U.S.C. § 3121(a). Similarly, the Federal Unemployment Tax Act defines "wages" as "all remuneration for employment," with certain exceptions that are not relevant. 26 U.S.C. § 3306(b). (Dividends are not specifically excepted in either act, and "remuneration" is not defined.) Mr. Radtke was clearly an "employee" of the Radtke corporation, as the plaintiff concedes. *See* 26 U.S.C. §§ 3121(d) and 3306(i). Likewise, his work for the enterprise was obviously "employment." *See* 26 U.S.C. §§ 3121(b) and 3306(c).

According to the Radtke corporation, not all "income" can be characterized as "wages." I agree. See Royster Company v. United States, 479 F.2d 387, 390 (4th Cir.1973) (free lunches did not constitute "wages" subject to FICA and FUTA); Central Illinois Public Service Co. v. United States, 435 U.S. 21, 25, 98 S.Ct. 917, 919, 55 L.Ed.2d 82 (1978) (reimbursement for lunches not "wages" subject to withholding tax; Court says in dicta that dividends are not wages).

At the same time, however, I am not moved by the Radtke corporation's connected argument that "dividends" cannot be "wages." Courts reviewing tax questions are obligated to look at the substance, not the form, of the transactions at issue. Frank Lyon Co. v. United States, 435 U.S. 561, 573, 98 S.Ct. 1291, 1298, 55 L.Ed.2d 550 (1978). Transactions between a closely held corporation and its principals, who may have multiple relationships with the corporation, are subject to particularly careful scrutiny. Tulia Feedlot, Inc. v. United States, 513 F.2d 800, 805 (5th Cir.1975). Whether dividends represent a distribution of profits or instead are compensation for employment is a matter to be determined in view of all the evidence. Cf. Logan Lumber Co. v. Commissioner, 365 F.2d 846, 851 (5th Cir.1966) (examining whether dividends were paid in guise of salaries).

In the circumstances of this case—where the corporation's only director had the corporation pay himself, the only significant employee, *no* salary for substantial services—I believe that Mr. Radtke's "dividends" were in fact "wages" subject to FICA and FUTA taxation. His "dividends" functioned as remuneration for employment.

It seems only logical that a corporation is required to pay employment taxes when it employs an employee. See Automated Typesetting, Inc. v. United States, 527 F.Supp. 515, 519 (E.D.Wis.1981) (corporation liable for employment taxes on payments to officers who performed more than nominal services for corporation); C.D. Ulrich, Ltd. v. United States, 692 F.Supp. 1053, 1055 (D.Minn.1988) (discussing case law defining who is an "employee"; court refuses to enjoin IRS from collecting employment taxes from S corporation that paid dividends but no salary to sole shareholder and director, a certified public accountant who worked for the firm). See also Rev.Rul. 73–361, 1973–2 C.B. 331 (stockholder-officer who performed substantial services for S corporation is "employee," and his salary is subject to FICA and FUTA tax); Rev.Rul. 71–86, 1971–1 C.B. 285 (president and sole stockholder of corporation is "employee" whose salary is subject to employment taxes, even though he alone fixes his salary and determines his duties).

An employer should not be permitted to evade FICA and FUTA by characterizing *all* of an employee's remuneration as something other than "wages." Cf. Greenlee v. United States, 87–1 U.S.T.C. Para. 9306 (corporation's interest-free loans to sole shareholder constituted "wages" for FICA and FUTA where loans were made at shareholder's discretion and he performed substantial services for corporation). This is simply the flip side of those instances in which corporations attempt to disguise profit distributions as salaries for whatever tax benefits that may produce. See, e.g., Miles–Conley Co. v. Commissioner, 173 F.2d 958, 960–61 (4th Cir.1949) (corporation could not deduct from its gross income excessive salary paid to president and sole stockholder).

Accordingly, the plaintiff's motion for summary judgment is DENIED, and the defendant's motion for summary judgment is GRANTED. The plaintiff is ORDERED to pay the remaining deficiency on its 1982 FICA taxes along with the assessed interest, penalties, and fees.

NOTE

Fringe benefits paid by an S corporation to its shareholder-employees also are subject to special treatment. Prior to the Subchapter S Revision Act of 1982, an S corporation could provide tax-deductible benefits in the same manner as C corporations. Section 1372 now provides that for purposes of employee fringe benefits, an S corporation shall be treated as a partnership and any shareholder owning either more than two percent of the corporation's outstanding stock or more than two percent of the total voting power of all stock will be treated as a partner in that partnership. As a result, unless a transitional rule applies, an S corporation seldom is able to provide tax deductible benefits, such as a medical reimbursement plan or group-term life insurance, to its shareholder-employees.[1]

2. FAMILY INCOME SPLITTING

Code: Section 1366(e).

A Subchapter S election may result in substantial tax savings while preserving the investors' ability to operate in the corporate form. Corporate earnings may reach the shareholders with only one tax being imposed and, subject to the passive loss limitations in Section 469, the Subchapter S taxing mechanism may be an attractive alternative for enterprises expecting losses in the initial years of operation.

Operation as an S corporation also eliminates the need for much of the defensive tax planning required for closely held C corporations and may be one way of coping with potential tax problems. For example, there is no need to utilize debt in the corporation's capital structure as a means of generating tax deductible interest payments to avoid corporate-level tax. Unreasonable compensation issues will be less important since no additional tax will be generated by disallowance of the corporate-level deduction for salary payments to shareholders. An election also insulates a corporation from the punitive provisions of the accumulated earnings tax and personal holding company tax.[1]

The *Davis* case, which follows, demonstrates that with careful planning an S corporation may be successfully employed as an income splitting device.

DAVIS v. COMMISSIONER *
United States Tax Court, 1975.
64 T.C. 1034.

GOFFE, Judge:

* * *

OPINION

The petitioner, Dr. Davis, is an orthopedic surgeon who was engaged in a complete medical practice in that specialty. In his diagnostic work he relied upon X-rays made in his office and in cases where treatment was administered, the physical therapy was performed in his office. He organized two corporations, one of which performed the X-ray function and the other carried out physical therapy treatment which he prescribed. He made gifts of 90 percent of the stock of each of the corporations to his three minor children and they and the corporations elected to be taxed as small business corporations under the provisions of subchapter S.

---

1. For special rules relating to health insurance, see I.R.C. § 162*l*(1), (5).

* Some footnotes omitted.

1. I.R.C. § 1363(a).

The Commissioner determined that the income of the corporations should be taxed to Dr. Davis under three distinct principles: (1) That under section 61 Dr. Davis attempted to assign the income or "fruit of the tree" when, in reality, Dr. Davis earned the income reported by the corporations; (2) section 482 required allocation of the income from the corporations to Dr. Davis in order to prevent avoidance of tax; and (3) Dr. Davis performed services for the corporations and [the predecessor of Section 1366(e)] therefore, required allocation back to him of the income reported by the corporations.

Respondent has limited the scope of his challenge to the reporting of the income by apparently conceding that X-Ray and Therapy were not " 'shams' or 'fictions' in the purest sense." Likewise, respondent concedes that Dr. Davis' transfer of the stock to his children had substance and should, therefore, be recognized. Compare *Henry D. Duarte,* 44 T.C. 193 (1965), *Michael F. Beirne,* 52 T.C. 210 (1969), and sec. 1.1373–1(a)(2), Income Tax Regs., with Brooke v. United States, 468 F.2d 1155 (9th Cir.1972). We are urged, on the authority of Gregory v. Helvering, 293 U.S. 465, 470 (1935), Commissioner v. Court Holding Co., 324 U.S. 331, 334 (1945), and Kimbrell v. Commissioner, 371 F.2d 897, 902 (5th Cir.1967), to find that the economic practicalities and substance of the arrangement requires taxation of the income to Dr. Davis rather than to the corporations.

Respondent further submits that the transfer of the X-ray and therapy facilities by Dr. Davis to the corporations followed by his transfer of the stock to his children constituted an anticipatory assignment of a portion of his future income. See, e.g., Lucas v. Earl, 281 U.S. 111 (1930); Helvering v. Clifford, 309 U.S. 331, 335 (1940); Commissioner v. Sunnen, 333 U.S. 591 (1948). Alternatively, respondent advocates an allocation of the entire net taxable income of the corporations to Dr. Davis on the theory that the corporate contributions to the earning of the net taxable income were de minimis as compared to the services rendered by Dr. Davis. In this regard, he relies on the presumption accorded his determination under section 482, *Grenada Industries, Inc.,* 17 T.C. 231 (1951), affd. 202 F.2d 873 (5th Cir.1953), cert.denied 346 U.S. 819 (1953), and, in the main, upon the inferences that may be drawn from all the circumstances where income is generated by a controlled business activity dependent upon the direction of patients, clients, or consumers from a controlling business activity which is closely related. Respondent also contends that the net taxable income of the corporations should be allocated to Dr. Davis pursuant to section [1366(e)] to reflect the value of his services to the corporations.

Respondent does not contend that X-Ray and Therapy were not viable business entities. Instead, respondent relies upon Gregory v. Helvering, 293 U.S. 465 (1935), and challenges taxation of the income to the corporations rather than to Dr. Davis on the grounds that his purpose in organizing the corporations was solely tax motivated. The primary reasons given by Dr. Davis for the transfers of the X-ray and physical therapy functions to the corporations and gifts of the stock to his children were as follows:

(1) To provide security for his children in view of his marital difficulties and his personal health problems;

(2) To insulate him personally from damage suits arising from negligent use of the potentially dangerous X-ray and physical therapy equipment; and

(3) To separate the personnel problems into the X-ray and physical therapy functions and away from the personnel problems of his medical practice. Respondent counters with alternative remedies to the concerns of Dr. Davis. He could have made cash gifts to his children; he could have purchased liability insurance to insulate him from liability arising from the negligent use of the X-ray and physical therapy equipment; and he could have issued mandates to resolve the personnel problems.

We do not agree with respondent that Dr. Davis' purposes were tenuous. The transfer of valuable property rights with a known potential to produce income seems a logical reason to establish the corporations and give the stock to his children instead of giving cash which would have to be invested. Using the corporate form to insulate the taxpayer from liability has long been recognized as a valid reason for incorporating. *Sam Siegel,* 45 T.C. 566 (1966). It is especially applicable here because Dr. Davis had recently experienced the possibility of liability caused by serious burns received by a patient who was receiving heat therapy. We find Dr. Davis' explanation of resolving personnel differences by separation of the operations a plausible and satisfactory reason.

Respondent's reliance upon Kimbrell v. Commissioner, supra, is unavailing. In that case the corporations merely executed contracts, hired employees, negotiated loans, and collected interest thereon, and filed income tax returns. In the instant case the corporations X-rayed patients and administered physical therapy to patients.

Moreover, a taxpayer is not required to continue one form of business organization which results in the maximum tax on business income. *Polak's Frutal Works, Inc.,* 21 T.C. 953, 974–975 (1954).

Respondent contends that the earnings of the corporations should be taxed to Dr. Davis because he had control over the earning of the profits by performing the services. The facts are otherwise. Dr. Davis prescribed the type of X-ray or X-rays to be made for each patient and he prescribed the physical therapy to be administered. The X-ray prescriptions to the corporation were no different than were those to a radiologist he referred patients to before he owned X-ray equipment or those given to the hospital when he would prescribe X-rays for a patient who was admitted to the emergency room. We see little difference in prescribing X-rays or physical therapy and prescribing drugs to be compounded by a pharmacist. Dr. Davis' division of his endeavors is not particularly unusual. It is common knowledge that an orthopedic surgeon does not himself normally take X-rays nor does he administer physical therapy. If, on the other hand, Dr. Davis attempted to separate his diagnostic work from his surgery, this would be unusual because a doctor personally performs both of these services for a patient. The income of the corporations was generated by the services of persons employed by the corporations not by the services performed by Dr. Davis. Dr. Davis' direct services to the corporations were minimal. Under section 61, we conclude that the corporations controlled the capacity to produce the income through their employees and they, not Dr. Davis, are taxable on that income. *Ronan State Bank*, 62 T.C. 27 (1974).

Section 482 authorizes the Commissioner to allocate income and other items among related taxpayers in order to clearly reflect income or to prevent evasion of taxes.[4]

In his notices of deficiency the Commissioner allocated the net taxable income of the corporations to Dr. Davis. In his brief the Commissioner contends that the corporate employees were adequately compensated for the services they performed and that he advocates allocation only of the net taxable income of the corporations to Dr. Davis because the corporations' contributions of earning that portion of the income were minimal. This line of reasoning is fallacious. The corporations were paid fees comparable to those charged by other X-ray laboratories and physical therapists in the community and those fees were received by the corporations for the services performed by their employees, not Dr. Davis. Again, the analogy to the pharmacist is appropriate. The X-ray technician, the physical therapist, and the pharmacist all carry out prescriptions made by the doctor. Respondent's blanket characterization of the tasks of the employees of the corporations which include the X-ray technician and the physical therapist as "routine" is not warranted. Both are specialists trained to carry out a doctor's order just as a pharmacist fills a prescription. As pointed out above in our discussion of section 61, the division of Dr. Davis' practice into medical practice, X-ray, and physical therapy is not unusual in that the different endeavors are frequently engaged in by separate persons or entities. It is also not unusual in the respect that X-ray laboratories and physical therapists rely on referrals for their business. Again, we see a close analogy to the better-known relationship of doctor and pharmacist. The entire arrangement was comparable to others in the community except that Dr. Davis was in a position to forward business to the corporations. For example, before he owned X-ray equipment, he referred his patients to a radiologist which did not give him a referral fee in return. The radiologist performed no service for the patient different from what the X-Ray corporation now per-

---

4. Petitioner seeks to distinguish management and control by directing our attention to a series of decisions which are concerned with the assignment-of-income question under Lucas v. Earl, 281 U.S. 111 (1930). Accordingly, we find those decisions distinguishable. We find the reality of control obvious. Sec. 1.482–1(a)(3) and (4), Income Tax Regs.

forms; i.e., in both instances the X-rays were interpreted and acted upon by Dr. Davis. Based on all the evidence we conclude that petitioners have made an adequate showing that the Commissioner abused the discretion granted to him by section 482 in allocating the net taxable income of the corporations to Dr. Davis.

Respondent relies upon *Pauline W. Ach,* 42 T.C. 114 (1964), affd. 358 F.2d 342 (6th Cir.1966). That case is factually distinguishable. *Ach* involved the transfer of a lucrative dress shop business from one member of a family to a related family-owned corporation which had operated a losing dairy business. The transfer was for a promissory note equal to the book value of the assets of the dress shop business. The income of the dress shop business was absorbed by net operating loss carryovers of the dairy business. We sustained disallowance of the net operating loss carryovers under the provisions of section 269 and we approved allocation under section 482 of 70 percent of the dress business profits to Pauline Ach because that portion was attributable to her services. In the instant case we have found as a fact that the gross income of the corporations was not generated by Dr. Davis but, instead, by the employees of the corporations. The referrals, because they are not unusual as explained above, do not constitute services rendered by Dr. Davis to the corporations.

Respondent points to the failure of Dr. Davis to charge rent for the first 6 months of 1966, the failure to charge Dr. Davis for use of the X-ray machine, and the failure to share common overhead expenses as indicative that his reallocation was proper. As explained above, we have held the reallocation of the Commissioner to be unreasonable. Respondent has not pleaded in the alternative that the specific items described above should be allocated nor did he request amendment of his pleadings following the trial to conform them to the proof. It is obvious that there is some basis for reallocation of the three items, minimal as they are. We will not voluntarily attempt to make such an allocation at this point because the pleadings never apprised petitioners of that issue in order that they could offer proof of the proper allocation of those specific items. The issue presented at trial was allocation of net taxable income upon the broad concept that Dr. Davis generated the income. The size of these three items in relation to the gross income and other expenses cannot justify allocation of the entire net taxable income to Dr. Davis.

As a final "string to his bow" the Commissioner relies upon section [1366(e)] [5] which permits him to allocate from one shareholder in a

---

5. SEC. 1375. SPECIAL RULES APPLICABLE TO DISTRIBUTIONS OF ELECTING SMALL BUSINESS CORPORATIONS.

(c) TREATMENT OF FAMILY GROUPS.—Any dividend received by a shareholder from an electing small business corporation (including any amount treated as a dividend under section 1373(b)) may be apportioned or allocated by the Secretary or his delegate between or among shareholders of such corporation who are members of such shareholder's family (as defined in section 704(e)(3)), if he determines that such apportionment or allocation is necessary in order to reflect the value of services rendered to the corporation by such shareholders.

"Small Business Corporation" (subchapter S corporation) amounts treated as dividends which should be allocated to other shareholders who are members of the shareholder's family to reflect the value of services rendered to the corporation by such shareholders. The purpose of section [1366(e)] is to tax each shareholder of a subchapter S corporation on the full value of the income he earns. No deflection of that income is to be permitted through artificial salary or dividend payments. S.Rept. No. 1983, 85th Cong., 2d Sess. (1958), 1958–3 C.B. 1143–1144; *Charles Rocco,* 57 T.C. 826, 831 (1972).

> In determining the value of services rendered by a shareholder, consideration shall be given to all the facts and circumstances of the business, including the managerial responsibilities of the shareholder, and the amount that would ordinarily be paid in order to obtain comparable services from a person not having an interest in the corporation. * * * [This regulation is under the predecessor of Section 1366(e)].

The determination is factual and tests applied to ascertain the value of the shareholder's services include "the nature of the services performed, the responsibilities involved, the time spent, the size and complexity of the business, prevailing economic conditions, compensation paid by comparable firms for comparable services, and salary paid to company officers in prior years." *Walter J. Roob,* 50 T.C. 891, 898, 899 (1968).

As in *Charles Rocco,* supra at 832, we need not decide whether section [1366(e)] requires petitioner to merely overcome the presumptive correctness of the Commissioner's determination or requires him to prove that the Commissioner abused his discretion (if section [1366(e)] provides the Commissioner with the same authority he possesses under section 482) because here we find that petitioners have satisfied both tests.

The Commissioner allocated 100 percent of the net taxable income of the subchapter S corporations to Dr. Davis. The undisputed testimony is that he did not actually spend more than 20 hours per year in direct duties to the corporations, which is minimal.

Respondent would have us consider the referral activities of Dr. Davis as being personal services rendered by him to the corporations. This we will not do. As stated above, one of the tests we enumerated above from *Roob* is compensation paid by comparable firms for comparable services. When Dr. Davis referred X-ray patients to a radiologist before he acquired X-ray equipment, the radiologist did not pay him a fee. The same is true as to referrals to a physical therapist. The fees earned by the corporations were the result of the use of the equipment which they owned and the services of their employees, not as a result of services performed by Dr. Davis for the corporations. Respondent's theory, therefore, fails under the comparability test and our holding under section [1366(e)] is consistent with our holdings under section 61 and 482. The Commissioner erred in allocating the net taxable income of the corporations to Dr. Davis under section [1366(e)].

Accordingly, we find that none of the net taxable income of X-Ray and Therapy was taxable to petitioners Edwin D. Davis and Sandra W. Davis for the taxable years 1966 and 1967.

Decisions will be entered under Rule 155.

NOTE

To be successful today, Dr. Davis's plan also would have to surmount the so-called "kiddie tax" in Section 1(i). Under Section 1(i), the net unearned income exceeding $1,000 of a child under age 14 will be taxed at the parents' marginal tax rate.[1] Thus, if Dr. Davis's children were under age 14, the income splitting potential of his plan would be substantially reduced. Even if they were age 14 or over, the compressed rate schedule for individuals reduces the tax savings from income splitting strategies.

PROBLEM

S and T each own one-half of the outstanding stock of U Corporation (an S corporation). If F (S and T's father) provides services to U Corporation and is not fully compensated, may the Treasury utilize § 1366(e) to attribute additional income to F?

---

1. Assuming the child is claimed by a parent as a dependent under Section 151, the child can offset $500 of unearned income with the standard deduction but will not be entitled to a personal exemption deduction. I.R.C. §§ 63(c)(5), 151(d)(2). Section 1(i) then applies to earned income over $500, thus limiting the impact of the "kiddie tax" to unearned income over $1,000. I.R.C. § 1(i)(4)(A)(i). These offset amounts will be adjusted in the future for inflation. I.R.C. § 63(c)(4).

*

INDEX

References are to Pages

ACCUMULATED EARNINGS TAX
Generally, 5, 447–449
Accumulated earnings credit, 466–467
Accumulated taxable income, 465–467
Burden of proof, 464–465
Reasonable needs of the business, 452–465
Stock redemptions, 461
Working capital, 459–461
Tax avoidance purpose, 449–452

ACQUISITIONS
See Acquisitive Reorganizations; Taxable Acquisitions

ACQUISITIVE REORGANIZATIONS
See also, Carryover of Corporate Tax Attributes
Generally, 484–488
Acquiring corporation, consequences to, 577–580
Basis and holding period, 577
Nonrecognition of gain or loss, 577
Triangular reorganizations, 577–578
Assets-for-stock acquisitions (Type C), 545–554
Boot relaxation rule, 546
Creeping acquisitions, 547, 551–553
Distribution requirement, 546–547
Liabilities, impact of, 545–546
Substantially all of the assets, 546–551
Business purpose doctrine, 487
Carryover of corporate tax attributes, 581–590
Continuity of business enterprise doctrine, 487, 513–518
Continuity of interest doctrine, 489–513
History, 484–485
Mergers and consolidations (Type A), 488–520
Reform proposals, 590–595
Rulings, 488
Shareholders and security holders, consequences to, 559–573
Basis and holding period, 560
Boot dividend rule, 559–573
Nonrecognition of gain or loss, 559
Step transaction doctrine, 497–513
Stock-for-stock acquisitions (Type B), 520–544
Contingent consideration, 542–544
Dissenting shareholders, 542
Solely for voting stock requirement, 520–542

ACQUISITIVE REORGANIZATIONS— Cont'd
Target corporation, consequences to, 574–576
Basis and holding period, 576
Distributions to creditors, 575
Nonrecognition of gain or loss, 574–575
Triangular reorganizations, 554–557
Forward triangular mergers, 555–556
History, 554–555
Reverse triangular mergers, 556–557

AFFILIATED CORPORATIONS
See also, Allocation of Income and Deductions
Generally, 18–19
Consolidated returns, 742–748
Limits on multiple tax benefits, 723–731
Redemptions through, 279–290

ALLOCATION OF INCOME AND DEDUCTIONS
Section 482, 731–742

ALTERNATIVE MINIMUM TAX
See Corporate Income Tax

ASSIGNMENT OF INCOME
Formation of a corporation, 95–100

BASIS
Acquisitive reorganizations, 576–577
Complete liquidations, 332
Corporate divisions, 669–670
Formation of a corporation, 59–60, 70–72, 80–81
Liquidation of a subsidiary, 348
Nonliquidating distributions, 164
S corporation stock, 763
Stock dividends, to shareholders, 303–304

BOOT
Acquisitive reorganizations, 559–573
Corporate divisions, 669–670
Formation of a corporation, 69–77
Installment reporting, 75–77
Recapitalizations, 603–604

BOOTSTRAP SALES
Dividends, use of, 180–193
Redemptions, with, 249–253

BUSINESS PURPOSE
See Judicial Doctrines

BUY–SELL AGREEMENTS
See Redemptions

CAPITAL STRUCTURE
See also, Formation of a Corporation
Advantages of debt, 119–121
Debt vs. equity, 126–134
    Debt/equity ratio, 127–128
    Form of obligation, 127
    Intent, 128
    Proportionality, 128–129
    Subordination, 129
Loss on corporate investment, 139–148
    Business vs. nonbusiness bad debts, 139–146
    Non pro rata surrender of stock, 105–115
    Section 1244 stock, 147–148
    Worthless securities, 146–147
Policy, 121–126
Section 385 regulations, 135–138

CARRYOVER OF CORPORATE TAX ATTRIBUTES
Generally, 581–590
Acquisitions to evade or avoid tax, 713–716
Consolidated return rules, 720–722
Corporate divisions, 672
Net operating losses, limitations, 697–720
    Attribution rules, 703–705
    Built-in gains, 711–712
    Built-in losses, limits, 710–711
    Continuity of business enterprise limit, 706–707
    Equity structure shifts, 701–702
    Long-term tax-exempt rate, 708
    Owner shift, 700–701
    Ownership change, 700–705
    Section 382 limitation, 707–708
    Value of the company, 708–710
Other tax attributes, limitations, 713
Preacquisition losses, limitations, 716–719

CLASSIFICATION AS A CORPORATION
Generally, 31–32
Partnerships, compared, 32–46
Publicly traded partnerships, 46–47
Trusts, compared, 47–50

COLLAPSIBLE CORPORATIONS
Generally, 434–437
Definition, 437–441
Five percent rule, 442
Section 341(e) exceptions, 443–444
Section 341(f) exceptions, 444–445
Seventy thirty rule, 441–442

COMPLETE LIQUIDATIONS
See also, Taxable Acquisitions
Generally, 329–330
Basis of distributed assets, 332
Complete liquidation, defined, 329
Distributions of property, consequences to corporation, 334–348
    Court Holding doctrine, 335–340

COMPLETE LIQUIDATIONS—Cont'd
    General Utilities doctrine, 334, 340–342
    Limitations on recognition of loss, 342–347
Liquidation of a subsidiary, 348–360
    Basis of distributed assets, 348
    Control requirement, 349, 350–358
    Distributing corporation, consequences to, 358–360
    Indebtedness of subsidiary, transfers to satisfy, 359–360
    Minority shareholders, 349–350, 359
    Parent shareholder, consequences to, 348–349
    Tax-exempt and foreign parents, 360
Shareholders, consequences to, 333–339
    Installment obligations, 333
    Timing of gain, 332–333

CONSOLIDATED TAX RETURNS
See Affiliated Corporations

CONSTRUCTIVE OWNERSHIP OF STOCK
Family discord, 235–237
Personal holding companies, 469
Limitation on carryover of net operating losses, 703–705
Redemptions, relationship to, 197–198
Waiver of attribution by entities, 218–219
Waiver of family attribution, 203–218

CORPORATE DIVISIONS
Generally, 628–630, 634–636
Active trade or business requirement, 636–650
    Five-Year rule, 637–644, 646–649
    Functional divisions, 645–646
    Geographical divisions, 646
    Real estate, 647
    Recently acquired businesses, 647–648, 674–676
    Trade or business, 644–645
    Vertical divisions, 645
Basis and holding period, 669–670
Boot, 669–670
Business purpose doctrine, 651–659
Carryover of tax attributes, 672
Changing role of § 355, pp. 667–668
Continuity of interest doctrine, 660–661
D reorganizations, relationship to, 630, 668–669
Device limitation, 661–667
Disqualified distributions, 672, 676–681
Distributing corporation, consequences to, 670–671
Failed divisions, 672–673
History, 630–634
Shareholders, consequences to, 669
Unwanted assets, disposition of prior to reorganization, 681–695

CORPORATE ENTITY, RECOGNITION OF,
50–56

CORPORATE INCOME TAX
See also, Double Tax; Integration
Generally, 11–12
Accounting methods, 14
Alternative minimum tax, 15–18
Capital gains and losses, 13
Credits, 15
Rate structure, 11
Taxable income, 12–13
Taxable year, 13

DEBT vs. EQUITY
See Capital Structure

DISTRIBUTIONS
See Complete Liquidations; Dividends; General Utilities Doctrine; Nonliquidating Distributions; Partial Liquidations; Redemptions; Stock Dividends

DIVIDENDS
See also, Dividends Received Deduction; Earnings and Profits; Nonliquidating Distributions; Redemptions; Stock Dividends
Bootstrap sales, 180–193
Cash distributions, 156–160
Constructive dividends, 167–172
Definition, 151–153
Reorganizations, 559–573

DIVIDENDS RECEIVED DEDUCTION
Generally, 12–13, 173
Anti-avoidance limitations, 172–180
Debt-financed portfolio stock, 177–178
Extraordinary dividends, 174–176
Holding period requirements, 173–174
Section 301(e), pp. 178–179

DIVISIVE REORGANIZATIONS
See Corporate Divisions

DOUBLE TAX
See also, Integration
Generally, 2–4
Capital structure, influence on, 119–126
Reform proposals, 21–31

EARNINGS AND PROFITS
Generally, 153–154
Carryovers, 583–584
Corporate divisions, 672
Determination of, 153–156
Nonliquidating distributions, effect of, 163–164
Redemptions and partial liquidations, effect of, 244–247
Section 301(e), adjustments, 178–179
Stock dividends, effect of, 303–304

FORMATION OF A CORPORATION
Generally, 57–60
Accounts payable, 80–82, 100–102
Accounts receivable, 100–102

FORMATION OF A CORPORATION— Cont'd
Assignment of income, 95–100
Avoidance of § 351, pp. 115–117
Basis, 59–60, 70–72, 80–81
Boot, treatment of, 69–77
Capital contribution vs. sale, 104–115
Control, 61–62
Going business, incorporation of, 95–103
Holding period, 59–60
Immediately after the exchange, 61–66
Interaction with § 304, pp. 282–283
Liabilities, 78–94
Organizational expenses, 117
Solely for stock, 67
Tax benefit rule, 102–103
Timing of gain, 75–77
Transfers of "property" and services, 66–67

GENERAL UTILITIES DOCTRINE
See also, Complete Liquidations; Nonliquidating Distributions; Partial Liquidations; Redemptions
Generally, 160–162
Corporate divisions, 667–668, 674–681
Liquidating distributions, 340–342
Policy aspects, 417–433
Redemptions, 243–244
Relief from repeal, 427–433
S corporations, 778–781

HOLDING PERIOD
Acquisitive reorganizations, 560, 576–577
Corporate divisions, 670
Formation of a corporation, 59–60
Stock dividends, 304

INCORPORATIONS
See Formation of a Corporation

INTEGRATION, 21–31

JUDICIAL DOCTRINES
Generally, 8
Business purpose, 10, 651–659
Sham transactions, 8–9
Step transactions, 10, 500–513
Substance over form, 9–10

LIABILITIES
Formation of a corporation, 78–94

LIQUIDATION–REINCORPORATION
See Nonacquisitive, Nondivisive Reorganizations

LIQUIDATIONS
See Complete Liquidations; Partial Liquidations; Taxable Acquisitions

MERGERS
See Acquisitive Reorganizations

MULTIPLE CORPORATIONS
See Affiliated Corporations

NONACQUISITIVE, NONDIVISIVE REORGANIZATIONS
Bankruptcy or insolvency (Type G), 622–627
Change in form, etc. (Type F), 620–626
Liquidation-reincorporation, 608–619
Nondivisive Type D reorganizations, 618–619
Recapitalizations (Type E), 596–608
    Bonds for bonds, 598–599
    Bonds for stock, 598
    Boot, 603–604
    Continuity of business enterprise doctrine, 596–597
    Dividend treatment, 599–600, 603–608
    Section 306 stock, 600
    Stock for bonds, 604–608
    Stock for stock, 595–604

NONLIQUIDATING DISTRIBUTIONS
    See also, Dividends; Earnings and Profits; Redemptions
    Generally, 150–153
Cash distributions, 156–160
Earnings and profits, effect on, 163–164
General Utilities doctrine, 160–162
Obligations of corporation, 165–167
Property distributions, 160–165
    Corporations, consequences to, 162–164
    Shareholders, consequences to, 164

ORGANIZATION OF A CORPORATION
See Formation of a Corporation

PARTIAL LIQUIDATIONS
    See also, Redemptions
    Generally, 238–240
Corporate contraction doctrine, 238–240
Definition, 238–239
Distributing corporation, consequences to, 243–244
Earnings and profits, effect on, 244–247
Shareholders, consequences to, 238–239

PARTNERSHIPS
C corporations, compared, 1–3
S corporations, compared, 750–751

PERSONAL HOLDING COMPANIES
    Generally, 5, 447–449, 467–468
Adjusted ordinary gross income, 469–470
Computer software royalties, 474–475
Consent dividends, 481
Deficiency dividends, 482
Dividends carryover, 481
Dividends paid deduction, 480–482
Income test, 469–478
Liquidating distributions, 481
Personal holding company income, 470–471
Personal service income, 475–478
Produced film rents, 473–474
Rents, 471–472, 477–478
Stock ownership requirement, 469
Taxation of, 479–483

PERSONAL SERVICE CORPORATIONS
Rates, 11–12
Taxable year, 13–14

PREFERRED STOCK BAILOUT
See Section 306 Stock

PUBLICLY TRADED PARTNERSHIPS, 46–47

RECAPITALIZATIONS
See Nonacquisitive, Nondivisive Reorganizations

REDEMPTIONS
    See also, Partial Liquidations
    Generally, 195–197
Accumulated earnings tax, 461
Constructive ownership of stock, 197–198
Death taxes, redemptions to pay, 291–293
Distributing corporation, consequences to, 243–247
Earnings and profits, effect on, 244–247
General Utilities doctrine, 243–244
Not essentially equivalent to a dividend, 222–237
    Family discord, 235–237
    Meaningful reduction of shareholder's interest, 222–238
Planning techniques, 249–278
    Bootstrap sales, 249–253
    Buy-sell agreements, 254–269
    Charitable contribution and redemption, 270–278
Redemption expenses, deduction of, 247–249
Related corporations, through use of, 279–290
    Interaction with § 351, pp. 282–283
Substantially disproportionate redemptions, 199–203
Termination of shareholder's entire interest, 203–219
    Waiver of attribution by entities, 218–219
    Waiver of family attribution, 203–218

REORGANIZATIONS
See Acquisitive Reorganizations; Carryover of Corporate Tax Attributes; Corporate Divisions; Nonacquisitive, Nondivisive Reorganizations

S CORPORATIONS
    Generally, 19–20, 749–751
Accumulated adjustments account, 775–776
Acquisitions, 790–792
At-risk limitation, 763–764
Basis, 763
Built-in gains, tax on, 774–778
Distributions to shareholders, 774–778
Election of S corporation status, 756–759
Eligibility, 752–755

S CORPORATIONS—Cont'd
Loss limitations, basis, 763–773
Partnerships, compared, 750–751
Passive activity loss limitations, 763–765
Passive investment income, 781–786
Planning, 793–803
　Compensation, 793–797
　Income splitting, 797–803
Revocation of election, 757
Shareholders, treatment of, 761–774
Straight debt safe harbor, 784–785
Subchapter C, coordination with, 787–793
Taxable year, 759–761
Taxation of, 778–787
Termination of election, 757–758

SECTION 306 STOCK
　Generally, 294–296
Defined, 312–314
Exempt dispositions, 318–327
Ordinary income treatment, on disposition, 317–318
Preferred stock bailout, background, 305–312
Recapitalizations, 600

SECTION 1244 STOCK
See Capital Structure

SHAM TRANSACTIONS
See Judicial Doctrines

STEP TRANSACTIONS
See Judicial Doctrines

STOCK DIVIDENDS
　Generally, 294–296
Basis, 303–304
Earnings and profits, effect on, 303–304
History, 296–299
Recapitalizations, 600
Shareholders, consequences to, 296–304
Stock rights, 304

SUBCHAPTER C
Double tax concept, 2–4
History, 1
Reform proposals, corporate acquisitions, 590–595

SUBCHAPTER S
See S Corporations

SUBSTANCE OVER FORM DOCTRINE
See Judicial Doctrines

TAXABLE ACQUISITIONS
　See also, Complete Liquidations
　Generally, 362–363
Acquisition expenses, 388–390
Allocation of purchase price, 383–390
　Asset acquisitions, 386–388
　Stock acquisitions, 385–386
Asset acquisitions, 364–365
Comparison of methods, 380–381
Debt-financed acquisitions, 396–417
　Earnings stripping, 417
　Junk bonds, 415–416
　Leveraged buyouts, 400–405
　Policy options, 405–414
　Stock repurchases, 396–400
　Net operating losses, 416–417
Mirror subsidiaries, 390–396
Stock acquisitions, 365–381
　Consistency period, 375–377
　Deemed sale of assets, 372–374
　Election under § 338, p. 372
　Grossed-up basis, 372–374
　Kimbell-Diamond doctrine, 365–369
　Section 338 election, 370–377
　Section 338(h)(10) election, 377–380
Unwanted assets, 390–396

TAX BENEFIT RULE
Formation of a corporation, 102–103

†